ELSEVIER'S
DICTIONARY OF
PSYCHOLOGICAL
THEORIES

ELSEVIER'S DICTIONARY OF PSYCHOLOGICAL THEORIES

compiled by

J.E. ROECKELEIN
Fountain Hills, USA

ELSEVIER

Amsterdam – Boston – Heidelberg – London – New York – Oxford
Paris – San Diego – San Francisco – Singapore – Sydney – Tokyo

ELSEVIER B.V.
Radarweg 29
P.O. Box 211
1000 AE Amsterdam
The Netherlands

ELSEVIER Inc.
525 B Street, Suite 1900
San Diego, CA 92101-4495
USA

ELSEVIER Ltd
The Boulevard, Langford Lane
Kidlington, Oxford OX5 1GB
UK

ELSEVIER Ltd
84 Theobalds Road
London WC1X 8RR
UK

3 2280 00909 6272

First edition 2006

Library of Congress Cataloging in Publication Data
A catalog record is available from the Library of Congress.

British Library Cataloguing in Publication Data
A catalogue record is available from the British Library.

ISBN-13:   978-0-444-51750-0
ISBN-10:   0-444-51750-2

∞ The paper used in this publication meets the requirements of ANSI/NISO Z39.48-1992 (Permanence of Paper).
Printed in The Netherlands.

Contents

Preface   VII

Introduction   VIII

Dictionary of Psychological Theories   1

Appendix A: Auditory, Cognitive, Tactile, and Visual Illusions/Effects   647

Appendix B: Theories of Humor   658

Appendix C: Imagery Theories   660

Selected Bibliography   662

(Dedication)

To my better half - my wife Renee Marie; and to the Ettores (John, Hope, Elliott, Isabella, Lily, and Samuel); the Rupps (Jim, Laurie, Stephen, Christine, David, Evie, Gloria, and Grace); the Weirs (Joshua, Natalie, Taylor, Jonathan, and Caleb); and to Margie Harris, Brad Ettore, and Gary Kiefer.

Preface

When the famous German-born American social psychologist Kurt Lewin suggested that nothing is as important as a good theory, he most likely was emphasizing the word "theory" and the significant role of *theory* in scientific psychology. However, another important word (along with "theory") in Lewin's epigram - in my opinion - is the word "good." That is, there are both "good" and "not-so-good" theories, especially in the discipline of psychology.

How *does* one distinguish, precisely, between a "good" and a "not-so-good" theory? Psychologists have provided various standards for examining this issue, including use of the criteria of *parsimony* (all other things being equal, the most "economical" theory - the one with the fewest statements - is the "best" theory), *testability* (theories that permit their propositions to be tested empirically, or are open to experimental manipulation, are the "better" theories), and *generalizability* (the theory that extends its boundaries beyond a small group or number of cases to a larger group or number of cases is a "better" theory), among other factors.

This dictionary of psychological theories includes in its contents *both* types of theories - the "good" and the "not-so-good." The astute reader - whether he or she is a layperson or a professional - is invited to discern the "good" from the "not-so-good" theories and, along the way, is encouraged to maintain a healthy sense of humor when examining psychologists' many attempts to identify, define, describe, and understand phenomena in their field. For example, it is suggested that the reader look up the *Dodo hypothesis* and *Maier's law*, and then decide for oneself the formal scientific status of these pronouncements. As one may see immediately, some theoretical propositions in psychology are just downright humorous. However, on the other hand, readers will find in this dictionary some of psychology's most important, celebrated, and critical theoretical notions - the very stuff and substance which contributes to psychology's stature as a science. For instance, consider *reinforcement theory* and the *law of effect* for two of the most substantive and enduring ideas in the history of scientific psychology.

In response to the question "Where do you get the entries for your dictionary?" my answer is simple: If any of the various descriptors - such as *theory, law, principle, effect, doctrine, model, paradigm,* or *hypothesis* - have been applied *explicitly* to a phenomenon reported in the psychological and social/behavioral sciences literature, then that phenomenon, consequently, is an acceptable candidate for inclusion in this dictionary. Accordingly, by virtue of this standard, entries contained in this dictionary are considered to have achieved a somewhat "formal" level of acceptance as *theoretical* concepts as judged by the psychological community and as reflected by the frequent usage of those concepts, as such, in scientific journals and publications.

I hope the reader will find the material in this book to be both entertaining and academically sound, and will discover a happy balance between the humorous and the serious in this dictionary of psychological theories.

Introduction

In attempting to understand and explain various behaviors, events, and phenomena in their field, psychologists have developed and enunciated an enormous number of "best guesses" or *theories* concerning the phenomenon in question. Such theories - it may be argued - involve speculations and statements that range on a potency continuum from "strong" to "weak." The term *theory*, itself, has been conceived of in various ways in the psychological literature. For instance, the following chronologically-ordered sample of approaches indicates the diverse concerns of psychologists vis-à-vis the notion of *theory*. Warren (1934) refers to *theory* as a general principle or formula propounded for the purpose of explaining some given group of phenomena, and distinguishes it from the term *hypothesis* in that theory relates to a body of evidence that is more substantial than that of a hypothesis. Tolman (1938) states that a *theory* essentially consists of a set of "intervening variables" (i.e., constructs that mediate between observable-cause and observable-effect events).

Lewin (1943) analyzed both the basic structure of science (involving the three evolutionary stages/levels of speculative, descriptive, and constructive aspects), and the history of acceptance of new theories in science (involving the three phases of initial outright rejection, then the raising of contradictory objections, and finally general acceptance by scientists). In his theoretical developments concerning a "psychological field," Lewin stressed the notion that a "situation-at-a-given-time" actually does not refer to a moment without time extension, but only to a certain time-period - a fact that is of great theoretical and methodological significance for scientific psychology in general.

Skinner (1950) acknowledges that certain non-factual statements and basic assumptions - essential to any scientific activity - are sometimes called *theories*, but he then makes an interesting argument *against* the need for developing psychological theories, in particular, theories of learning. Although Skinner suggests that theories are "fun," he recommends that the most rapid progress toward an understanding of learning may be made by research that is *not* designed to test theories. Rather, according to Skinner, an adequate scientific program is demonstrated by the collection of experimental data showing orderly changes that are characteristic of the learning process - *without* the use of extra-dimensional systems and theories.

English and English (1958) view *theory* as a general principle, supported by considerable data, proposed as an explanation of a group of phenomena; and is a statement of the relations believed to prevail in a comprehensive body of facts. *Theory* is considered to be more solidly supported by evidence than is *hypothesis*; it is less firmly established than *law*; and it generally covers a wider range than a single law, which is usually limited to a single kind of relationship.

Maier (1960) tweaks our self-assurance somewhat, and humorously nudges us, when he suggests that a "good" theory can be expressed as a formula, and any theory that cannot be so quantified is inadequate - even if it works (!)

Marx (1963) asserts that there are various different meanings of *theory*, and these must be kept separate; for instance, he describes the following four aspects of *theory*: it may refer in a very broad sense to any characteristic of the formal, or conceptual, processes of science as contrasted with the strictly empirical, or observational, aspects; it may refer to any generalized explanatory principle (e.g., statements of functional relationship among variables); it may refer to a group of logically organized (deductively related) laws; and it may refer to summary statements which give order (in an essentially descriptive manner) to the cluster of laws which have been empirically developed in some subject matter.

Harriman (1966) considers *theory* to be a coherent explanation (of an array of logically interrelated propositions about a set of phenomena) which has undergone some validation and which may be applied to many data, but which does not have the status of a law.

Neel (1969) discusses the formal organization of psychological theory, as well as the logical, philosophical, and scientific conventions of theory construction.

Wolman (1973) characterizes *theory* as any scientific system that is comprised of empirical data derived from observation and/or experimentation, and of their interpretation. The set of statements of propositions explaining factual data is called *theory*. Wolman notes that some scientists start with empirical data whereas others pose several theoretical statements and deduce from them the empirical laws. Whichever way scientists proceed, however, a *theory* is a system of hypothetical statements concerning a certain area of scientific inquiry.

Marx and Goodson (1976) prefer to categorize scientific *theories* into three major types: *deductive* (i.e., derivation of empirically-testable propositions on the basis of logically-related prior premises), *inductive* (i.e., accumulation of disparate pieces of data that are turned into theoretical propositions without any explicit prior premises), and *functional* (i.e., use of small and modified hypotheses to study specific behavioral problems) *theories*. Marx and Hillix (1979) emphasize that *no* theory, whatever its qualities, is ever final, and always remains tentative - even though all the predictive statements made from it have been verified perfectly; that is, there always remains the possibility that any given theory will be replaced by another theory that is simpler, more general, or more consistent with other relevant theories.

Hillner (1984) views *theory* as a set of higher-order interpretive statements that is used to explain already verified empirical relationships, or to generate hypotheses subject to experimental test; further, a *theory* is a hypothetical device that resolves the nature of a given psychological fact or helps explain the particular behavior or experience generated in a given psychological experiment.

Reber (1995) suggests that the term *theory* has three distinct uses that range from the highly formal and precise of the philosophy of science to the informal and loose usage of popular language; essentially, and foremost, *theory* is a coherent set of formal expressions that provides a complete and consistent characterization of a well-articulated domain of investigation with explanations for all attendant facts and empirical data (*theory*, in this sense, is conceptualized ideally as beginning with the induction of a set of primitive terms or "axioms" which are used, in turn, to deduce "theorems" which are tested, subsequently, for their truth value, their factual-explanatory ability, and their ability to predict new phenomena not yet enunciated completely). According to Reber, a *theory*, pragmatically speaking, is also a general principle or a collection of interrelated general principles that is put forward as an explanation of a set of known facts and empirical findings, as well as, informally, a kind of catch-word for any reasonable set of ideas or principles. Reber observes that in psychology the pragmatic sense of *theory* applies widely to proposed explanations that fall well short of the formal criteria for meaning; for instance, Freud's *theory of personality development* fails the test of "unambiguous deduction of theorems," which is perhaps why many researchers argue that it cannot be rigorously tested. Nevertheless, notes Reber, many people still refer to Freud's propositions in this case as a "theory."

Church (1997) asserts that many *theories* in psychology are not fully specified. They provide basic concepts, and a general approach to an explanation, but they typically are not stated with sufficient precision that different investigators would obtain the same predictions and results using the same *theory*. Such a lack of clarity is represented, often, as a scientific virtue regarding one's unwillingness to make premature conclusions. At the early stages of the development of a *theory* this may be justifiable because it provides the flexibility that may encourage others to be creative with those theoretical concepts and approaches. However, this is a view of *theory* as a toy (with which to interact), rather than as a game containing rules.

Colman (2001) notes that *theory* in the fields of mathematics and logic is a coherent system of primitive concepts, axioms, and rules of inference from which theorems may be derived. Further, Colman defines *theory* (derived from the Greek *theoria* meaning "view" or "theory," and from *theoreein* meaning "to view" or "to observe") as a proposition, or set of propositions, used as a conjectured explanation for an observed phenomenon, state of affairs, or event; he also defines *grounded theory*, often used in qualitative research, as a theory constructed from naturalistic observations of a phenomenon, and generally reflects the observer's/participant's own interpretations rather than those of the investigator or experimenter. Colman invites comparisons of the terms *hypothesis* and *model* with that of *theory* (where *hypothesis* is a tentative explanation for a phenomenon that is subject to criticism by rational argument and may be refuted by empirical evidence, and *model* is a deliberately simplified, idealized, or imaginary representation of a phenomenon containing basic properties that are explicitly defined, or sometimes even physically constructed, and from which other properties may be deduced via logical reasoning and/or empirical observation). Colman suggests that inferences from a model apply only to the model and not necessarily to the reality that it attempts to represent; however, if the model captures the important features of the phenomenon, then such inferences may apply equally well to the phenomenon itself [cf., Harre & Lamb (1983, pp. 397-398) for the role of "models" in theories, and Rosenblueth & Wiener (1945) for the role of "models" in science].

Corsini (2002) states simply that *theory* is a body of interrelated principles and hypotheses that purport to explain or predict a group of phenomena that have been verified largely by facts or data; *hypothesis* is defined as a testable proposition based on theory, stating an expected empirical outcome that results from specific observable conditions; an *ad hoc hypothesis* is an explanation for a phenomenon when no theoretical explanation existed prior to the event, that is, a theory of explanation advanced after a fact; and *metatheory* is the science of theories, a set of rules regulating the construction of a theory, or a "theory about a theory." Furthermore, Corsini notes that a *theory* - in common usage and parlance - has been viewed as a guess, an opinion, a conjecture, or a supposition.

In my previous dictionary (Roeckelein, 1998), I review the tradition and practice in the psychological literature wherein psychologists' "best guesses" about certain psychological phenomena have been assigned to general descriptive categories involving labels such as "principle," "law," "theory," "model," "paradigm," "effect," "hypothesis," and "doctrine," and all of which involve theoretical statements (i.e., propositions indicating the relationships between cause-and-effect variables) to some greater, or lesser, degree.

In the present dictionary, I have adopted the strategy of lumping together all the various traditional descriptive labels regarding psychologists' "best guesses" under the single descriptive term *theory*. That is, whereas a "principle" or "law" is viewed traditionally, in science (including psychology), as the *strongest* formal statement of a cause-effect relationship, it may - at its foundation - still be considered to be a form of a *theory* (cf., Cummins, 2000; Foley, 1936; Johnson & Wilson, 1947; Simonton, 1995; Teigen, 2002). Likewise, whereas an "effect" or "hypothesis" is viewed, traditionally, as a relatively *weak* proposition of cause-and-effect regarding a certain phenomenon, it may - at its core - be considered, also, to be a type of *theory*. Additionally, because one of the characteristics of the science of psychology is the occasional tendency to "borrow" various theories from other sciences (cf., Roeckelein, 1997a,b), this dictionary includes a few theories that originated in sciences *other* than psychology but which, nevertheless, appear in the psychological literature (e.g., from biology - *Darwin's evolution theory*; from sociology - *Comte's theory of a hierarchy of the sciences*; from physics - *Newton's law/principles of color mixture*). Again, in the present dictionary, the descriptive labels of *principle, law, theory, model, paradigm, effect, hypothesis*, and *doctrine* are attached to many of the entries, and all such descriptive labels are subsumed here under the umbrella term *theory*. Accordingly, the title of this dictionary emphasizes the term *theory* (implying *both* strong and weak "best guesses") and is a way of indicating, overall, the contents of this comprehensive dictionary in a parsimonious and felicitous fashion.

It is my impression that although there are a number of excellent dictionaries of psychology available in the marketplace today that cover the popular and significant terms employed in the field of psychology, the present dictionary is unique in that it covers a very specialized area in the scientific discipline of psychology, viz., *theories* (both classical and contemporary) in psychology. To the best of my knowledge and awareness, there is *no* other dictionary of psychology, to date (with the exception of my previous work, Roeckelein, 1998), that is dedicated *solely* to the compilation of *psychological theories* [cf., Bothamley's (1993) multidisciplinary dictionary]. Furthermore, due to the proliferation of the "best guesses" and theories in the last half-century that have appeared in the psychological literature, especially, it seems to be appropriate now to provide both academic and non-academic readers with a useful one-volume   book, as represented by this dictionary, that discusses *psychological theories* exclusively. The dramatic growth in the number of theories in psychology in the last few decades is probably due to the creative, imaginative, and personalistic nature of psychologists themselves. As one of my popular psychology teachers used to say, "One psychologist would rather use another psychologist's *toothbrush* than to use his/her theory!"

The seeds for this dictionary were planted firmly in my previous dictionary of psychological terms (Roeckelein, 1998) in which I attempted to provide theoretical concepts in psychology that are founded on empirical grounds. That is, I provide terms that have been identified or described *explicitly* as "theoretical" terms and concepts in the psychological literature. My choice of terms for my dictionaries is *not* based implicitly on a random, informal, or *Alice in Wonderland* type of approach where "a theory is anything that *I* say is a theory." Rather, my rule for the selection of terms to be included in my dictionaries is based on the *usage* of the terms in psychology as *formal theoretical* terms. The only exceptions to this rule are a very few "quasi-theoretical" terms that I include for reasons of novelty or creativity (e.g., *Skinner's destructured learning theory*), humor or frivolity (e.g., *Murphy's laws*; *Parkinson's law*; *Putt's laws*; *Reber's law*), and self-enhancement or self-indulgence (e.g., *Roeckelein's law*). Generally, I adopt a "consensual agreement" or "consensual validation" rationale in my work (i.e., a "theory" is any proposition *explicitly* so identified in the psychological and social/behavioral sciences literature). Moreover, the many "theories" contained in this dictionary may be located conjointly - and identified on a consensual or corroborative basis - via the references section provided at the end of each entry.

My overall goals in the present dictionary are to provide information on several levels wherever possible, including the origination, development, and evolution of various psychological terms, as well as the historical definition, analysis, and occasional criticism of psychological concepts. The references section at the end of each entry contains several important references - usually including the source article or book in which the particular term or theory was first introduced into psychology. Also, regarding the references sections - especially in several cases where there are more than just a few citations for the entry - I adopt the practice of arranging the references according to a "chronological rule" (i.e., earlier publication dates are listed first, followed by later publication dates) rather than employing an "alphabetical rule" (i.e., references are listed/ordered according to alphabetization of researcher/writer's last name). My purpose in this practice is to indicate and emphasize the evolution and development of ideas across a temporal dimension which seems to me to be more significant for the historical appreciation (e.g., concerning "intellectual proprietary rights" or origination of ideas) of theoretical notions than would be immediately apparent in an alphabetic arrangement of references. Thus, I argue - as indicated by this strategy - that a good dictionary should supply the key reference(s) or essential source(s) for the terms that are presented so that interested readers may have easy access to more detailed accounts of particular theories (cf., the similar approach used in so-called "encyclopedic dictionaries," such as that of Harre & Lamb, 1983). In the present dictionary, I provide a reasonable amount of cross-referencing for ease of identification and location of terms; and several appendixes are provided that contain additional information on the topics of illusions, humor, and imagery; also, for the interested reader and researcher, I provide a "Selected Bibliography - Psychological Theories" section that contains numerous citations and sources concerning basic, new, supplemental, and/or follow-up information on theoretical issues in psychology. I've categorized these sources as to content areas (e.g., abnormal, developmental, learning, social, etc.) and, generally, I've tried here not to duplicate the references appearing in the main entries section of the dictionary (however, in cases where duplications do occur it is to emphasize the importance, in my opinion, of those sources).

As regards the style in the present dictionary, there is some variation in length of entries due to the following reasons: the entry refers to a broad or general area (e.g., *decision-making theories*; *learning theories*; *personality theories*; *audition/hearing theories*; *vision/sight theories*; *perception theories*) and requires, necessarily, greater length in exposition; or the entry refers to a specific, narrow, or technical phenomenon (e.g., *Maier's law*; *Mozart effect*; *Ribot's law*; *Lotka-Price law*) that requires only a brief description. Moreover, when *informal* theories (e.g., some humor theories are given in epigrammatic or slogan-like phrases) are cited, the description/definition is likely to be shorter than when more *formal* theories (e.g., *Freud's theory of personality*, which contains numerous sub-concepts and terms) are described. When synonymous terms and related theories are used in the psychological literature, they are indicated here under each entry, as appropriate, with an = sign; for instance, *Hering-Hurvich-Jameson color vision theory = Hering's color theory = Hurvich-Jameson color vision theory = opponent-process color vision theory = tetrachromatic theory.*

Finally, the result of my present approach is that many theoretical propositions, conjectures, speculations, and "best guesses" that are not identified and described in any previous dictionary of psychological terms are provided here. In this effort, I try not to sacrifice quality for the sake of quantity. I hope the reader - whether he or she is a layperson or a professional psychologist - will discover a satisfactory balance between these factors of quality and quantity in the present dictionary that is intended to be a comprehensive account of both classical ("historical") and contemporary ("current cutting-edge") psychological theories.

About the Author

JON E. ROECKELEIN is a professor of psychology at Mesa College in Arizona. He has taught and conducted psychological research for more than thirty years, including research on intelligence systems for the U.S. Army/Department of Defense at the Human Resources Research Office and Army Research Institute. His earlier books include *Imagery in Psychology* (Praeger, 2004), *The Psychology of Humor* (Greenwood Press, 2002), *The Concept of Time in Psychology* (Greenwood Press, 2000), and *Dictionary of Theories, Laws, and Concepts in Psychology* (Greenwood Press, 1998).

A

ABC THEORY/MODEL. A psychological theory/model that is used in several ways: (1) As a short-hand description and mnemonic of the series of events that take place during the operant conditioning paradigm developed by the American psychologist Burrhus Frederic Skinner (1904-1990) where behavior may be altered by manipulating either the antecedent (A) of the behavior (B) and/or the consequent (C) conditions that follow the behavior; moreover, consequences that are reinforcing/ rewarding to the individual tend to increase the frequency of the target behavior in future situations, while consequences that are punishing tend to decrease the frequency of the target behavior in future situations; in more technical terms in the psychological literature, according to this first usage, the antecedent conditions have been called "discriminative stimuli" (that is, stimuli which "set the occasion" for reinforcing or punishing a target behavior when it occurs) and the consequent conditions have been called either "reinforcing" or "punishing" stimuli (depending on whether the target behavior - in the future - increases or decreases). (2) As an account of the sequence of events occurring during rational-emotive therapy (RET), or rational-emotive behavior therapy (REBT), as developed by the American psychologist Albert Ellis (1913-) where *A* refers to the *activating* condition, *B* is the person's *belief* about the condition, and *C* is the emotional *consequence* that follows; in this approach - which is a directive, confrontational psychotherapy designed to challenge and modify clients' irrational beliefs that are thought to cause personal distress - theoretically it is not the event that causes the emotional consequence but rather the client's belief about the event (that is, *A* does not cause *C*, but *B* causes *C*); if the person's belief is irrational, then the emotional consequence can be extreme distress; moreover, because reality does not conform to irrational beliefs such as "Everyone should love me" or "I must be perfect in all ways," patients who hold such beliefs are open to frustrations and unhappiness; irrational beliefs cause people to view an undesirable event as a catastrophe rather than merely as a disappointment, anxiety, or inconvenience (additionally, in clinically-circular terms, persons may go on to feel anxious about their anxiety and depressed about their depression). The promise of *RET* and *ABC theory*, in this context, is to help clients to see rationally and logically that their false beliefs and unrealistic expectations are the real causes of their problems (as clients begin to replace irrational beliefs with rational beliefs, their emotional reactions become less distressing, more appropriate, and more likely to lead to constructive behaviors). The *RET/ABC theory* has been reformulated into *ABCDE therapy* which includes disputing or debating (*D*) the client's irrational beliefs, resulting in three types of effects (*E*): rational cognitions, appropriate feelings and emotions, and more desirable behaviors. (3) As the *ABC theory of personality* (Enfield, 1984) which embodies the RET procedures and tenets and emphasizes the role of unrealistic expectations and irrational beliefs in the human personality where emotions follow largely from internal cognitions and not from external events. (4) As the corpus of the *ABC-X theory of family crisis* (Hill, 1949) dealing with the effects of stress related to family separation and reunion resulting from the events of World War II; this usage involves the potential stressor event called *A*, interacting with the resources of the family as regards the event called *B*, both of which interact with the family's definition or interpretation of the event called *C*, and all of which combined together produce *X*, the crisis for the family; the course of adjustment or recovery from the crisis by the family involves an initial period of disorganization followed by activation of the family's crisis-meeting resources, and finally to a new level of organization in the family's structure. (5) As a descriptor in the *ABC technique/theory of group therapy* (Klapman, 1959) that is employed often with schizophrenic patients and involves, initially, the printing of the letters ABC of the alphabet on a chalkboard by the therapist, and subsequently requiring the patients one at a time to work through printing the rest of the letters of the alphabet successively on the chalkboard, thus promoting contact, communication, cooperation, and conversation among the members of the therapy group. (6) As a descriptor in *ABC relaxation theory* (Smith, 1999) that provides word-for-word scripts and teaches clinicians/therapists how to implement a number of techniques employing Attentional (*A*), Behavioral (*B*), and Cognitive (*C*) elements in the relaxation and centering therapeutic strategy. See also COGNITIVE THERAPY, THEORIES OF.

REFERENCES

Ellis, A. (1977). The basic clinical theory of rational-emotive therapy. In A. Ellis & R. & Grieger (Eds.), *Handbook of rational-emotive therapy.* New York: Springer.

Enfield, R. E. (1984). Rational-emotive therapy. In R. J. Corsini (Ed.), *Encyclopedia of psychology.* Vol. 3 (pp. 207-208). New York: Wiley.

Hill, R. (1949). *Families under stress: Adjustment to the crisis of way, separation, and reunion.* New York: Harper.

Klapman, J. W. (1959). *Group psychotherapy: Theory and practice.* New York: Grune & Stratton.

Skinner, B. F. (1938). *The behavior of organisms: An experimental analysis.* New York: Appleton-Century-Crofts.

Smith, J. C. (1999). *ABC relaxation theory: An evidence-based approach.* New York: Springer.

ABNEY'S EFFECT. See ABNEY'S LAW.

ABNEY'S LAW. The English chemist and physiologist William de Wiveleslie Abney (1844-1920) developed this principle concerning the additivity of heterochromatic luminances (brightness) which states that the luminance of a mixture of differently colored lights is equal to the sum of the luminances of the components. *Abney's law* has not generally been fully supported by later research and, interestingly, questions about the law lie at the root of a theoretical debate in the area of colrimetry. The deficiencies of *Abney's law* have been known for a long time, but the weaknesses have been evaded or tolerated by scientists only until recently. A phenomenon of perception called *Abney's effect* refers to visual conditions involving the sudden illumination of a large surface area [cf., *Lambert's law/cosine law* - named after the German physicist and mathematician Johann H. Lambert (1728-1777) which states that the illumination on a surface varies directly as the cosine of the angle between the incident ray and the perpendicular to the surface]. The perception of light in *Abney's effect* is that it seems to come on first in the center of the patch of area and then spread to the edges instead of appearing on the total area equally all at the same time. Subsequently, when the light is extinguished, the outer edges disappear first, followed by the center area disappearing last. In addition to these phenomena, Abney is prominent for his contributions to the science of photography, including stellar photography, and for his discovery of how to make photographic plates that are sensitive to red and infrared light. See also COLOR MIXTURE LAWS/THEORY OF; GRASSMANN'S LAWS; NEWTON'S LAW/PRINCIPLE(S) OF COLOR MIXTURE.

REFERENCES

Abney, W., & Festing, E. (1886). Colour photometry. *Philosophical Transactions of the Royal Society of London, 177,* 423-456.

Abney, W. (1897). The sensitiveness of the retina to light and colour. *Philosophical Transactions of the Royal Society of London, 190A,* 155-193.

ABNORMALITY, THEORIES OF. See PSYCHOPATHOLOGY, THEORIES OF.

ABRAHAM LINCOLN EFFECT. A visual and perceptual effect developed and studied by the American biomedical engineer Leon D. Harmon (1922-) and his colleagues, and named after president Abraham Lincoln (1809-1865) whose facial image was used to construct the first published "block portrait" (i.e., a degraded image that is divided into large rectangles/blocks whereby the lightness of each block is set to the average light-value of the image in that region) in 1971. The *Abraham Lincoln effect* refers to the difficulty in a human perceiver of recognizing a meaningful image in a block-constructed picture or portrait when viewed close up, but is easily recognizable when seen from a distance or by half-closing one's eyes during viewing. The effect is interesting in that - in perceptual or information-processing terms - a loss of sensory/stimulus information (that is, viewing stimulus blocks at a distance) paradoxically increases the recognizability and meaningfulness of the block-formed image. Harmon and Julesz (1973) conducted experiments showing that - in *signal-detection theory* terms - noise bands that are spectrally adjacent to the picture or portrait's spectrum are effective in suppressing visual recognition. See also PATTERN/OBJECT RECOGNITION THEORY; SIGNAL DETECTION, THEORY OF.

REFERENCES

Harmon, L. D. (1971). Some aspects of recognition of human faces. In O. –J. Crusser & R. Klinke (Eds.), *Pattern recognition in biological and technical systems: Proceedings of the Fourth Congress of the Deutsche Gesellschaft fur Kybernetic.* New York: Springer-Verlag.

Goldstein, A. J., Harmon, L. D., & Lesk, A. B. (1971). Identification of human faces. *Proceedings of the IEEE, 59,* 748-760.

Harmon, L. D. (1973). The recognition of faces. *Scientific American, 229,* 70-82.

Harmon, L. D., & Julesz, B. (1973). Masking in visual recognition: Effects of two-dimensional filtered noise. Science, *180,* 1194-1196.

ABSOLUTE STIMULUS THEORY. See SPENCE'S THEORY.

ABSTRACTION, LAWS AND PRINCIPLES OF. See COGNITIVE STYLE MODELS.

ABSTRACTION/PROTOTYPE THEORY. See TRANSFER OF TRAINING, THORNDIKE'S THEORY OF.

ABX MODEL/PARADIGM. An experimental method used in the area of psychophysics for determining an organism's sensory *difference threshold* (i.e, the smallest detectable change in a stimulus or difference between two stimuli that can be detected reliably; also, called *discrimination threshold, difference limen,* or *just noticeable difference, jnd*) by presenting two stimuli, A and B, and a third stimulus, X, that is identical to one of the others. The individual's task is to decide whether stimulus X matches stimulus A or B. Another sensory threshold method employed in psychophysics, called the *absolute threshold* (also called the *absolute limen* or *reiz limen*) refers to the smallest intensity of a stimulus that can be detected or that reliably produces a sensation in the organism. See also BUNSEN-ROSCOE LAW; FECHNER'S LAW; FULLERTON-CATTELL LAW; NEURAL QUANTUM THEORY; PSYCHOPHYSICAL LAWS AND THEORIES; RICCO'S/PIPER'S LAWS; SIGNAL DETECTION, THEORY OF; THRESHOLD, LAW OF; WEBER'S LAW; WEBER-FECHNER LAW.

REFERENCE

Gescheider, G. A. (1997). *Psychophysics: The fundamentals.* 3rd ed. Mahwah, NJ: Erlbaum.

ACCELERATION, LAW OF. See DEVELOPMENTAL THEORY.

ACCIDENTALISM, THEORY OF. See PROBABILITY THEORY/LAWS.

ACCOMMODATION, LAW/PRINCIPLE OF. The concept of *accommodation* in psychology has a variety of meanings depending on the context in which it is used. In general terms, it refers to any movement or adjustment (physical or psychological) that is made to prepare the organism for some stimulus input. In the context of vision, it refers to the automatic adjustment process wherein the shape of the lens of the eye changes to focus on objects situated at different distances from the observer. The suspensory ligaments hold the lens in a relatively flattened position when the normal eye is at rest and can focus clearly on objects that are about 20 feet away (distant vision). When objects are closer than 20 feet (near vision), the ciliary muscles contract, which causes relaxation of the suspensory ligaments and which, in turn, allows the flattened lens to thicken or bulge in shape, causing a sharper focus of light rays on the retina. The term *accommodation sensation* refers to a sensation that accompanies changes of visual adjustment that is attributable to changes in tension of the ciliary muscles that control the shape of the lens, and the term *accommodation time* refers to temporal duration from the moment a visual stimulus is presented in the line of vision until the lenses of the eyes have adjusted for clear vision of an object. S. Bartley reports that level of illumination has an influence on visual accommodation and that the most likely theory of the physiological mechanism for accommodation is that of a basic tonal background caused by vascular innervation of the sympathetic nervous system that affects the oculomotor nerve to make specific focusing adjustments. In the context of infant and childhood development, the Swiss psychologist Jean Piaget (1896-1980) uses the term *accommodation* to refer to the child's modification of ideas or concepts of the world in response to new experiences in the environment or in response to experiences that are inconsistent with previously known concepts or ideas. When *accommodation* is used in the context of nerve activity, it describes the increased excitability of the nerve that occurs when a constant stimulus (such as an electric current) is applied to the nerve, and the subsequent slow decrease ("accommodation") in nerve excitability with continued stimulation. When the stimulus is terminated, a sudden drop in nerve excitability occurs. After such a sequence of events and following termination of the stimulating event, the nerve is less sensitive briefly to stimulation than it was before initiation of the original stimulus. *Accommodation* is used in social psychological and sociological contexts to refer to a process of social adjustment that is designed to create or maintain group harmony. The notion of *accommodation* in the case of social behavior may take the form of bargaining, conciliation, conflict resolution, compromise, arbitration, negotiation, or truce-making among the concerned or antagonistic individuals, groups, or nations. In a historical context, in the area of attention, the term *accommodation* is archaic and once referred to the person's adjustment or readjustment that was essential to the maximal clearness (E. B. Titchener referred to "sensory clearness" or "attensity") of

an impression when the normal mean *accommodation time* was measured to be about one and one-half second with a range between 0.2 and 3.0 seconds. See also ATTENTION, LAWS/PRINCIPLES OF; BALANCE, PRINCIPLES AND THEORIES OF; FESTINGER'S COGNITIVE DISSONANCE THEORY; PIAGET'S THEORY OF DEVELOPMENTAL STAGES.

REFERENCES

Titchener, E. R. (1908). *Lectures on the experimental psychology of feeling and attention.* New York: Macmillan.

Bartley, S. (1951). The psychophysiology of vision. In S. S. Stevens (Ed.), *Handbook of experimental psychology.* New York: Wiley.

Piaget, J. (1954). *The construction of reality in the child.* New York: Basic Books.

Alpern, M. (1962). Accommodation. In H. Darson (Ed.), *The eye.* Vol. 3. New York: Academic Press.

ACHIEVEMENT MOTIVATION, THEORY OF. = need achievement = achievement need. The American psychologist Henry A. Murray (1893-1988) first defined an individual's need for achievement (*achievement motivation* or *nAch*) as a desire for significant accomplishments, for mastering skills, for overcoming obstacles in the way of one's success, or for rapidly attaining high standards. Murray and other researchers, such as the American psychologists David C. McClelland (1917-1998) and John W. Atkinson (1923-), developed various ways to measure *achievement motivation*, prominent among which is the use of personality "projective" tests (such as the Thematic Apperception Test, or TAT, where the person's task is to invent stories about the content of ambiguous pictures or photos). McClelland extended the concept of *nAch* from the level of analysis of the individual to that of entire societies and cultures. The theoretical underpinnings of *achievement motivation*, including both "intrinsic" and "extrinsic" motives, have two essential components: an assumed energizing or motivating mechanism that directs a person toward goals, and a set of internalized conditions or standards (whether created by oneself or by others) that represent personal fulfillment or achievement. A number of criticisms have been leveled against the *theory of nAch.* For example, low reliability and questionable validity assessments have been found for the TAT measures; and the *nAch* researchers place a narrow emphasis on personality as a crucial determinant of behavior and demonstrate an inability to find adequate results concerning *nAch* in women. On the other hand, it's been suggested that the unsatisfactory validity and reliability assessments of *nAch* measures may be due to the attempt to measure a spectrum of personality traits that is too broad, and forced-choice types of questions, rather than projective-types of tests, be used where individuals being tested would choose between "achievement-related" and "affiliation-related" personal styles. The *nAch* viewpoint was augmented in the 1970s when the field of *cognitive psychology* first appeared and emphasized a person's "cognitions" about the nature and purpose of achievement in a cultural context. Then, by the 1980s, the unresolved question was raised as to whether *nAch* should be studied as a personality trait, as suggested by personality psychologists, or as a cognitive behavior, as suggested by cognitive psychologists. Perhaps future research on the concept of *nAch* will show greater reconciliation of the areas of personality psychology and cognitive psychology. See also MOTIVATION, THEORIES OF.

REFERENCES

Murray, H. A. (1938). *Explorations in personality.* New York: Oxford University Press.

Atkinson, J. W. (1958). *Motives in fantasy, action, and society.* New York: Van Nostrand.

McClelland, D. C. (1961). *The achieving society.* New York: Van Nostrand.

Atkinson, J. W., & Feather, N. (Eds.) (1966). *A theory of achievement motivation.* New York: Wiley.

Heckhausen, H. (1968). Achievement motivation: Current problems and some contributions toward a general theory of motivation. In W. Arnold (Ed.), *Nebraska Symposium on Motivation.* Lincoln: University of Nebraska Press.

Horner, M. (1972). Toward an understanding of achievement-related conflicts in women. *Journal of Social Issues, 28,* 147-172.

McClelland, D. C. (1973). Testing for competence rather than for "intelligence." *American Psychologist, 28,* 1-14.

Weiner, B. (Ed.) (1974). *Achievement motivation and attribution theory.* Morristown, NJ: General Learning Press.

McClelland, D. C., Atkinson, J. W., Clark, R., & Lowell, E. (1976). *The achievement motive.* New York: Irvington.

Heckhausen, H. (1977). Achievement motivation and its constructs: A cognitive model. *Motivation & Emotion, 1,* 283-329.

ACHIEVEMENT MOTIVATION THEORY OF WORK. See WORK/CAREER/OCCUPATION, THEORIES OF.

ACHIEVEMENT NEED, THEORY OF. See ACHIEVEMENT MOTIVATION, THEORY OF.

ACH'S LAWS/PRINCIPLES/THEORY. The German psychologist Narziss Ach (1871-1946) was one member of the group of researchers (others included O. Kulpe, H. Watt, K. Marbe, and K. Buhler) at the famous Wurzburg "new" experimental school in Germany during the early 1900s. The Wurzburg group studied thought processes via verbalized introspection and complex cognitive events (as opposed to studying sensations, which was the primary emphasis at the University of Leipzig under Wilhelm Wundt's leadership). Ach's work on systematic experimental introspection, awareness, and *determining tendency* was germinal to the exodus of experimental psychologists away from the exclusive use of introspection as a research method. Ach's method was systematic in that it clearly delineated the limits of a participant's introspection (i.e., "looking into one's own experience and reporting on it") to the "fore," "mid," and "after" periods for making introspective reports during the conduct of an experiment. Ach also achieved relatively high levels of precision in his studies by using devices such as the "Hipp chronoscope" [an apparatus for measuring time intervals, first constructed by the German inventor/watchmaker Mathias Hipp (1813-1893) in

1843] in his experiments. Ach's principles concerning *determining tendencies* in experiments contain what are, perhaps, the most important aspects of his work for present-day experimentalists. Ach showed that there were *unconscious influences* operating on participants' behavior during experiments, including factors such as the instructions given by the experimenter to the participants. The *determining tendencies* were thought to be known by some means other than the participants' introspections. An example of *determining tendency* is given by Boring, Langfeld, and Weld (1939, p. 389), who describe an experiment on hypnosis. After the "subject" (the word "participant" seems to be the favored term to use today in experimental contexts) was hypnotized, the suggestion was made that after waking, two cards with two digits on each would be shown. For the first card, the person was to give the sum of the digits, and for the second card, to give the difference between the two digits. Upon waking from the hypnotic state, a card was shown on which the digits 6 and 2 were written; the person immediately said "8." When the second card was shown, containing the digits 4 and 2, the same person said "2." The individual had no memory of the prior suggestion and could give no explanation of what he had said about the cards, nor did it occur to the person that 8 was the sum of 2 and 6 or that 2 was the difference between 4 and 2. According to *Ach's principle*, the determining tendencies "fix" the course of thought by favoring certain "associations" that spring from the immediate situation and inhibit other associations. In this way, the tendencies give directive order in a situation containing a number of competing possibilities and enable an answer to be given to the question of why a particular possibility is materialized rather than any other one. Other experiments have indicated that *determining tendencies* function to give completion to already established patterns of thought (cf., *Zeigarnik effect; mind/mental set*) and may reinforce old associations that the person may have established partially. According to *Ach's principle*, the directive or *determining tendency* makes the action of a person more than a rigid mechanical sequence of events such as is found in the movements of a machine. The term determining tendencies is somewhat archaic today and is being replaced by validity- and control-sensitive terms in experimental psychology such as "preparatory set," "demand characteristics of the situation," "ecological validity of the experiment," and "experimenter effect." Such contemporary terms seek to sensitize and motivate the experimenter to control various potentially confounding variables that may exist in the psychological experiment where there is a dynamic interplay between the participant, the experimenter, and the experimental setting or context. See also ASSOCIATION, LAWS AND PRINCIPLES OF; MIND/MENTAL SET, LAW OF; PERCEPTION (I. GENERAL), THEORIES OF; ZEIGNARIK EFFECT/PHENOMENON.

REFERENCES

Ach, N. (1905). *Uber die willenstatigkeit und das denken, eine experimentalle untersuchung mit einem anhange: Uber das Hippsche chronoskop*. Gottingen, West Germany: Vandenhoech & Ruprecht.

Boring, E. G., Langfeld, H., & Weld, H. (1939). *Introduction to psychology*. New York: Wiley.

Ach, N. (1944). *Lehrbuch der psychologie*. Vol. 3. *Praktische psychologie*. Bamberg: Buchner.

ACOUSTIC SIMILARITY EFFECT. See SKAGGS-ROBINSON HYPOTHESIS.

ACROSS-FIBER PATTERN THEORY. See GUSTATION/TASTE, THEORIES OF.

ACT THEORY. See ADAPTIVE CONTROL OF THOUGHT THEORY/MODEL.

ACT THEORY/THERAPY. See BEHAVIOR THERAPY/COGNITIVE THERAPY, THEORIES OF.

ACTION THEORY. See MOTIVATION, THEORIES OF.

ACTIVATION/AROUSAL THEORY. The term *activation theory* was most prominently used by the American physiological psychologist Donald B. Lindsley (1907-2003) as a working theory for emotion. The concept *activate* means not only "to make active" but also "to render capable of reacting." At one end of a continuum of activation is a strong reaction to stimulation, and at the other end is the condition of quiescence, sleep, or death, with little or no reaction to stimulation. The *activation/arousal theory* developed from work in the area of physiology, specifically on the electrical activity of the brain where the cerebral cortex was seen to be aroused by discharge of a lower center of the brain in the hypothalamic region. The general form of the *activation theory* is a form of the older "energy-mobilization" concept of emotion (e.g., Cannon, 1915) where early studies showed how the body prepares for emergency action during states of rage and fear. The use of the term *activation* is restricted generally to the energizing influence of one internal system, such as the reticular activating system, on another one and is not an exact synonym for either "arousal" (a general term) or "stimulation" (activation produced by specific external sources). Historically, the concept of *activation* was central to the study and development of drives, motives, and emotions in psychology (cf., *affective arousal theory* - the speculation that individuals learn to seek out anticipated pleasure and to avoid anticipated pain, and where motives originate in changes in affective states; McClelland, 1951). It has been relatively easy to identify behavioral states as levels of arousal (cf., D. Berlyne's "aesthetic arousal," which may be raised via properties of stimulus patterns such as novelty), but parallel physiological processes are more difficult to discover. The electroencephalograph (EEG) has been a somewhat successful indicator of arousal level where the lower frequency EEG is observed when behavioral arousal declines but, given certain exceptions to this simple relationship, the EEG is only an approximate indicator of arousal. Associated also with the *arousal theory* is the sleep-wakefulness cycle of organisms where an individual goes to sleep when input falls below a certain level. This hypothesis is tenable when considering the general nocturnal sleeping habits of humans, but it has difficulty when explaining the behavior of certain animal species that sleep during the day and are most active at night. The sensory input interpretation of *arousal* was predominant until the studies by G. Moruzzi and H. Magoun at the University of Pisa in Italy, and D. B. Lindsley, J. Bowden, and H. Magoun at the University of California at Los Angeles, showed that severing all the sensory nerves in cats (without damaging the reticular formation) was accompanied by normal wakefulness-sleep patterns in the EEG. The view today has changed somewhat from the simple picture of the reticular formation as the major activator for arousal patterns and includes the recognition that EEG arousal signs are not always consistent with changes in behavioral arousal. See also CANNON/CANNON-BARD THEORY; DRIVE, THEORIES OF; EMOTION, THEORIES/LAWS OF; LINDSLEY'S ACTIVATION THEORY; MOTIVATION, THEORIES OF; SPREADING-ACTIVATION MODEL OF MEMORY.

REFERENCES

Cannon, W. (1915). *Bodily changes in pain, hunger, fear, and rage*. New York: Appleton.

Lindsley, D. B., Bowden, J., & Magoun, H. (1949). Effect upon EEG of acute injury to the brain stem activating system. *EEG & Clinical Neurophysiology*, *1*, 475-486.

Moruzzi, G., & Magoun, H. (1949). Brain stem reticular formation and activation of the EEG. *EEG & Clinical Neurophysiology*, *1*, 455-473.

Duffy, E. (1951). The concept of energy mobilization. *Psychological Review*, *58*, 30-40.

Lindsley, D. B. (1951). Emotion. In S. S. Stevens (Ed.), *Handbook of experimental psychology*, pp. 473-516. New York: Wiley.

McClelland, D. C. (1951). *Personality*. New York: Holt, Rinehart & Winston.

Duffy, E. (1957). The psychological significance of the concept of "arousal" or "activation." *Psychological Review*, *64*, 265-275.

Malmo, R. (1959). Activation: A neuropsychological dimension. *Psychological Review*, *66*, 367-386.

Berlyne, D. (1960). *Conflict, arousal, and curiosity*. New York: McGraw-Hill.

ACTIVATION MODEL OF MEMORY ORGANIZATION. See FORGETTING AND MEMORY, THEORIES OF.

ACTIVATION-SYNTHESIS THEORY. See DREAM THEORY.

ACTIVITY THEORY OF AGING. See AGING, THEORIES OF.

ACTOR-OBSERVER DISCREPANCY EFFECT. See ATTRIBUTION THEORY.

ACUPUNCTURE THEORY OF PAIN. See GATE-CONTROL THEORY.

ADAM/EVE PLAN/PRINCIPLE. See DEVELOPMENTAL THEORY.

ADAMS' ZONE THEORY. See COLOR VISION, THEORIES/LAWS OF.

ADAPTATION, PRINCIPLES/LAWS OF. The term *adaptation* derives from the Latin word *adaptare*, meaning "to fit," and has a variety of meanings in science. In biology, *adaptation* refers to structural or behavioral changes of an organism, or part of an organism, that fit it more perfectly for the environmental conditions in which it lives where the changes have evolutionary survival value. In physiology, *adaptation* is the change or adjustment of a sense organ to some incoming stimulation, and the term *sensory adaptation* (also called *negative adaptation*) involves a decreased sensitivity to stimuli due to prolonged stimulation. In psychology, *adaptation* is the change in quality, clarity, or intensity of a sensory experience that occurs with continuous and unchanged stimulation. In psychology, in particular, *adaptation* may be discussed in a multitude of contexts, among which are auditory adaptation, visual adaptation, olfactory adaptation, pain adaptation, cutaneous adaptation, and gustatory adaptation. In *auditory adaptation* there is a transient loss of hearing sensitivity to tones of certain frequencies after prolonged exposure to an unchanging sound wave frequency; *auditory fatigue* occurs when the sound causing the effect is loud and the hearing loss is more than transient. In *visual adaptation*, a set of processes takes place after change of exposure from dark to light (or light to dark) whereby the eye is more capable of receiving stimuli under the new conditions; included here are dark, light, and chromatic adaptation. *Dark* ("scotopic") *adaptation* is the process of adjustment of the eyes to low intensities of illumination that takes about four hours to complete, even though effective dark adaptation takes only about 30 minutes (where the retinal cones take only about seven minutes to adapt, and the rods take the full four hours to adapt). It is estimated that the totally dark-adapted eye is about one million times as sensitive as the normally illuminated eye. *Light* ("photopic") *adaptation* is the process of adjustment of the eye to a high level of light intensity where the pupil of the eye is constricted, and the retinal cones are activated, making the eye relatively insensitive to light of lower intensities. *Dark adaptation* is the shift in retinal receptors from the photopic (cones) system to the scotopic (rods) system, whereas *light adaptation* is the shift from the scotopic to the photopic system. The term *brightness adaptation* refers to a decrease in the brilliance of a stimulus that is caused by an increase in the general illumination of the surrounding visual field. *Color* ("chromatic" or "spectral") *adaptation* (also called *color fatigue*) is alteration of hue or saturation or both, due to a previous exposure to light of some other wavelength; during *color adaptation*, a person's absolute threshold of sensitivity to hue is raised. *Cross adaptation* is adjustment to all stimuli of a group of stimuli after exposure to only one of the stimuli from that group. In *olfactory adaptation*, for instance, a person may become adapted to one odor that subsequently produces a diminution in sensitivity to a large number and variety of other odors. *Social* (or "cultural") *adaptation* is the modification or adjustment of personal behavior that is necessary to maintain harmonious interaction with other individuals in the group ("social accommodation"), such as exhibiting conformity behavior to the customs (or taboos) of a particular social group. When used in a learning context, *adaptation* refers to a change in an organism's mode of behavior that results in more effective and satisfactory adjustment to the prevailing situation, as well as the elimination of irrelevant behavior as learning pro-

9

gresses. As used in the area of personality psychology, *adaptation* has been used to denote a process of upward adjustment and compensation for one's innate deficiencies, as a modification in drives, emotions, and attitudes in adjusting to the environment, and as a critical concept in a *theory of the ego* [cf., *adaptive act hypothesis* - advanced by the American behaviorist Harvey Carr (1873-1954), suggests that organisms adapt to their environment by three steps: a motivating stimulus that arouses the individual; a sensory stimulus to which the activity is directed; and a reaction that leads eventually to satisfaction; and the *adaptive hypothesis* - postulated by the German physician Heinz Hartmann (1894-1970), suggesting that the primary function of the autonomous *ego* is to cope with an "average expectable environment" via memory, perception, and motility]. The term *adaptation time* is defined as the time that elapses from the onset of a continuous stimulus up to the point where any further stimulation causes no further change in the responsiveness of the sensory organ or system. As used in more informal terms, *adaptation time* is the time needed in adjustment for efficient performance of a task. Also, there is *genetic adaptation* (species-specific characteristics, such as long necks in giraffes, that are distillations of evolutionary processes over many generations that help the organism to survive in a changing environment), *phenotypic adaptation* (temporary adjustments of the individual, such as the return of one's ability to see clearly after a period in a darkened room following exposure to bright lights), and *perceptual adaptation* (the ability to adjust to an artificially displaced, or even inverted, visual field). The related concept of *habituation* - whose older definition involved the process of becoming adapted to a given stimulus, situation, or general environment - has been redefined today in more modern terms involving the gradual elimination of an unconditioned response, especially an orienting response, by the repeated presentation of the unconditioned stimulus, and does not occur to highly noxious stimuli. Thus, the *principle/law of adaptation* has been a valuable omnibus concept in the history of psychology and other disciplines, where it has helped to advance the scientific understanding of organisms' functional, physi-

cal, and social adjustments to an ever-changing environment. See also DARWIN'S EVOLUTION THEORY; HABIT/HABIT FORMATION, LAWS AND PRINCIPLES OF; HABITUATION, PRINCIPLE/LAW OF; HELSON'S ADAPTATION-LEVEL THEORY; PIAGET'S THEORY; PURKINJE EFFECT; SELYE'S THEORY/MODEL OF STRESS.

REFERENCES

Stratton, G. (1897). Vision without inversion of the retinal image. *Psychological Review, 4*, 341-360.

Crozier, W. (1940). The theory of the visual threshold. II. On the kinetics of adaptation. *Proceedings of the National Academy of Sciences, 26*, 334-339.

Cohen, J. (1946). Color adaptation of the human eye. *American Journal of Psychology, 59*, 84-110.

Hess, E. (1956). Space perception in the chick. *Scientific American, 195*, 71-80.

Hartmann, H. (1964). *Ego psychology and the problem of adaptation.* New York: International Universities Press.

Rock, I. (1966). *The nature of perceptual adaptation.* New York: Basic Books.

ADAPTATION-LEVEL THEORY. See HELSON'S ADAPTATION-LEVEL THEORY.

ADAPTIVE ACT HYPOTHESIS. See ADAPTATION, PRINCIPLES/LAWS OF.

ADAPTIVE CONTROL OF THOUGHT THEORY/MODEL. This advanced computer simulation version of a "network" model of information processing, called *Adaptive Control of Thought (ACT)*, or *Adaptive Character of Thought-Rational (ACT-R)*, theory/model, was proposed by the Canadian-born American psychologist John Robert Anderson (1947-). The *ACT model* consists of two separate long-term memory stores: *declarative memory* (a semantic network of interconnected concepts represented by "nodes") that contains "declarative knowledge" or the active part of the *declarative memory* system that essentially defines "working memory;" and *procedural memory* (consisting of a "production system") that contains "procedural knowledge" or information about how to carry out a series of operations in some task. *Declarative memory* refers to *knowing that* (e.g., as regards some factual information about the world), whereas *procedural memory* refers to *knowing how* (e.g., as regards the correct sequence of movements to accomplish a particular job). The *ACT theory/model* is referred to, also, as the *ACT-super(*) theory* which states that all cognitive behavior is controlled by "production rules" which specify the steps of cognition. The *ACT theory* is an "elaborated theory" of the earlier framework by A. Newell and H.A. Simon (1972) dealing with problem solving skills and behavior. In another of Anderson's computer simulation programs - developed in collaboration with the American psychologist Gordon Bower (1932-) - called *human associative memory* (*HAM*), and based on their "free recall in an associative net" (called *FRAN*), there is an account of a complete model of the structures and processes of human memory, having as its central construct a propositional network representation. Where *HAM* concentrates on a theory of the declarative system in knowledge, *ACT* employs a production system in order to interpret a propositional network ("production systems" are an analogy for condition-action pairs that theoretically underlie human cognition). See also EPAM THEORY/MODEL/PROGRAM; FAN EFFECT; INFORMATION AND INFORMATION-PROCESSING THEORY; NETWORK MODELS OF INFORMATION PROCESSING; SHORT-TERM AND LONG TERM MEMORY, THEORIES OF; WORKING MEMORY, THEORY OF.

REFERENCES

Anderson, J. R., & Bower, G. H. (1972). Recognition and retrieval processes in free recall. *Psychological Review, 79*, 97-123.

Newell, A., & Simon, H. A. (1972). *Human problem solving.* Englewood Cliffs, NJ: Prentice-Hall.

Anderson, J. R., & Bower, G. H. (1973). *Human associative memory.* Washington, D.C.: Winston.

Anderson, J. R. (1983). A spreading activation theory of memory. *Journal of Verbal Learning & Verbal Behavior, 22,* 261-295.

Anderson, J. R. (1990). *The adaptive character of thought.* Hillsdale, NJ: Erlbaum.

Anderson, J. R. (1992). Automaticity and the ACT-super(*) theory. *American Journal of Psychology, 105,* 165-180.

Anderson, J. R. (1996). ACT: A simple theory of complex cognition. *American Psychologist, 51,* 355-365.

ADAPTIVE HYPOTHESIS. See ADAPTATION, PRINCIPLES/LAWS OF.

ADAPTIVE NONRESPONDING THEORY. See SLEEP, THEORIES OF.

ADDICTION, THEORIES OF. In general, *addiction* relates to almost any substance or activity where individuals uncontrollably may be "compelled/drawn" to things such as food, gambling, play, sex, smoking, buying, and work. In particular, *addiction* in our society originally was related to a state of periodic or chronic intoxication and cognitive-function disruption produced by the repeated consumption of a natural or synthetic drug for which one has an overwhelming need or desire/compulsion, and involves the tendency to increase the dosage level, to show higher tolerances with increased usage, and to demonstrate difficulties when attempting to withdraw from the substance where there is always psychic and physical "dependence" on the effects of the drug or substance. There appears to be no single "addictive personality" type, and specific ethnic, familial, peer, inter- and intra-personal, environmental, constitutional, and genetic factors contribute collectively to one's vulnerability to addiction. However, the addict is typically an individual who experienced early in life one, or several, polarized excesses, inconsistencies, or deprivation in areas such as: discipline, intimacy, parental role models, passivity-aggressivity, frustration tolerance, play-work functions, and ability to delay gratification or to live in moderation. Deterioration and/or destruction of one's control and self-esteem predictably occurs in varying degrees when there is impairment in these areas of personal and social adjustment. It has been observed, also, that the development of addiction involves the transition from casual to compulsive patterns of drug and substance use. The *addiction theories*, based upon how drug-induced alterations in psychological function cause such a transition to addiction, include the following: the traditional *hedonic theory* - drug-related pleasure, and subsequent unpleasant withdrawal symptoms, are the chief causes of addiction; *aberrant-learning theory* - addiction is due to faulty learning patterns, especially the development of strong stimulus-response connections and habits; *incentive-sensitization theory* - suggests that sensitization of a neural system that attributes incentive salience causes compulsive motivation or "desiring" to take addictive drugs; and *frontal cortical dysfunction theory* - proposes that malfunctioning of the frontal cortical systems, which normally regulate decision-making and inhibitory control over behavior, leads to faulty judgment and impulsivity in addicted individuals. In attempting to understand and treat addictions, it is suggested that the researcher or therapist go beyond the specific addictive agent and evaluate the multivariant etiologies, dynamics, and interpersonal interactions in an examination of the "addictive process." Additionally, it is recommended that one look for the "addictive complement" (that is, the person, group, or environment that keeps the addictive process alive) and various "trigger mechanisms" (that is, factors and features in the environment that initiate the addictive process). It seems, also, that the addictive process has a life history of its own in which there may be shifts from one addiction to another, or multiple addictions at different stages. See also DECISION-MAKING THEORIES; DELAY OF GRATIFICATION HYPOTHESIS; HEDONISM, THEORY OF; INCENTIVE THEORY; LEARNING THEO-RIES AND LAWS; PSYCHOPATHOLOGY, THEORIES OF; SCHIZOPHRENIA, THEORIES OF; SENSITIZATION, PRINCIPLE OF.

REFERENCES

Savitt, R. A. (1968). The psychopathology of the addiction process. *Journal of Hillside Hospital, 17*, 277-286.

Tamerin, J. S., & Neuman, C. P. (1971). Prognostic factors in the evaluation of addicted individuals. *International Pharmacopsychology, 6*, 69-76.

Wise, R., & Bozarth, M. (1987). A psychomotor stimulant theory of addiction. *Psychological Review, 94*, 469-492.

Leonard, K. E., & Blane, H. T. (1999). *Psychological theories of drinking and alcoholism*. New York: Guilford Press.

Robinson, T. E., & Berridge, K. C. (2003). Addiction. *Annual Review of Psychology, 54*, 25-53.

ADDITIVE COLOR MIXTURE, PRINCIPLE OF. See COLOR MIXTURE, LAWS AND THEORY OF.

ADDITIVE LAW OF PROBABILITY. See PROBABILITY THEORY/LAWS.

ADJACENCY EFFECT. See SHORT-TERM AND LONG-TERM MEMORY, THEORIES OF.

ADLER'S THEORY OF PERSONALITY. The Austrian psychoanalyst Alfred Adler (1870-1937) received his medical degree in 1895 from the University of Vienna with a specialty in ophthalmology but then changed to psychiatry after practicing in general medicine. Adler was one of the charter members of the Vienna Psychoanalytic Society, serving as its president in 1910, but resigned from the society in 1911 because of theoretical differences with Sigmund Freud. Adler went on to establish his own school, called the Society for Free Psychoanalytic Research (later called the Society of Individual Psychology) which attracted followers throughout the world and inspired, also, the establishment of an experimental school in Vienna that employed his theories of education. Adler's theoretical approach to personality generally emphasized the concepts of goal striving, unity, and active participation of the individual and stressed the cognitive rather than the unconscious processes of personality. Adler's *theory of personality* is an extremely "economical" one where a few basic assumptions sustain the whole theoretical structure: (1) fictional finalism - humans are motivated more by their subjective expectations of the future than by their objective experiences of the past; (2) striving for superiority (formerly called the "will to power" by Adler) - humans' final goal is to be aggressive, powerful, and superior where one strives for perfect completion and is driven upwardly toward higher goals; (3) inferiority feelings and compensation (Adler accepted being called the "father of the inferiority complex") - humans are motivated by the need to overcome any perceived or felt level of inferiority that arises from a sense of incompletion or imperfection in any area of their lives (cf., Adler's term *masculine protest* which denotes a cluster of personality traits in either gender arising as overcompensation for feelings of inferiority and rejection of the feminine role); (4) innate social interest - humans' striving for superiority becomes socialized where working for the common good permits individuals to compensate for their weaknesses; (5) style of life - the system principle, or self-created life plan, by which the unique individual personality achieves a higher level of functioning in life and where all the person's drives, feelings, memories, emotions, and cognitive processes are subordinate to that individual's lifestyle; (6) the creative self - this doctrine asserts that humans construct their own personalities out of the raw material of heredity and experience and that one's creative self gives meaning to life by creating the goals themselves, as well as the means to get to the goals in life; the creative self is the "active" principle of human life and is not unlike the older concept of the *soul*. Adler's *theory of therapy* emphasizes the goals of the therapist to be the establishment of a relationship of trust, to discover and understand the patient's "assumptive universe," to reveal these assumptions to the person is such as way that they become subject to self-correction and facilitate change, to convey a sense of worth and faith in the person's inner strength, and to offer the patient a model for good behavior and effective coping strategies. *Adler's personality theory* exemplifies a humanistic orientation toward individual development that is contrary to Freud's more materialistic conception of the person and gives humans the characteristics of altruism, cooperation, humanitarianism, awareness, uniqueness, dignity, and creativity. Adler's work and concepts (while yet unrecognized by some psychologists) have been validated generally, have influenced most current personality theories (including psychoanalytic approaches), and have led to a continuation of the Adlerian tradition in this country. See also ALLPORT'S THEORY OF PERSONALITY; BIRTH ORDER THEORY; FREUD'S THEORY OF PERSONALITY; MASLOW'S THEORY OF PERSONALITY; ROGERS' THEORY OF PERSONALITY.

REFERENCES

Adler, A. (1912). *The neurotic constitution.* New York: Arno Press.

Adler, A. (1929). *Problems of neurosis.* London: Kegan Paul.

Adler, A. (1930). Individual psychology. In C. Murchison (Ed.), *Psychologies of 1930.* Worcester, MA: Clark University Press.

Adler, A. (1939). *Social interest: A challenge to mankind.* New York: Putnam.

Adler, A. (1957). *The education of children.* London: Allen & Unwin.

ADVANTAGE, LAW OF. See VIGILANCE, THEORIES OF.

AESTHETICS, PRINCIPLE OF. See ZEISING'S PRINCIPLE.

AFFECTIVE AROUSAL THEORY. See ACTIVATION/AROUSAL THEORY.

AFFORDANCE THEORY. This theory in perception psychology, formulated by the American psychologist James Jerome Gibson (1904-1979), states that organisms are given, furnished, provided, or "afforded" support and resources by the environment so that the individual has an opportunity to behave in a particular manner. For example, the *affordances* of an edible substance, a smiling face, and a solid surface provide, respectively, the individual with the opportunities to eat, to engage in conversation, and to walk securely across an unfamiliar expanse (cf., B. F. Skinner's notion of *discriminative stimuli* - environmental stimuli which serve to "set the occasion" for reinforced responding). See also DIRECT PERCEPTION THEORY; SKINNER'S OPERANT CONDITIONING THEORY.

REFERENCE

Gibson, J. J. (1977). The theory of affordances. In R. Shaw & J. Bransford (Eds.), *Perceiving, acting, and knowing:*

Toward an ecological psychology. Hillsdale, NJ: Erlbaum.

AFTERDISCHARGE, LAW OF. See SKINNER'S DESCRIPTIVE BEHAVIOR/OPERANT CONDITIONING THEORY.

AFTEREFFECTS HYPOTHESIS. See APPARENT MOVEMENT, PRINCIPLES AND THEORIES OF; CAPALDI'S THEORY.

AFTERIMAGE LAW. See EMMERT'S LAW.

AFTERIMAGES, POSITIVE/NEGATIVE, THEORY OF. See PURKINJE EFFECT/PHENOMENON/SHIFT.

AGEISM, THEORY OF. The American gerontologist Robert N. Butler (1927-) proposed that people have a strong belief in the intrinsic superiority of those individuals who occupy a certain age range (typically the younger age brackets before age 60) that is accompanied, also, by discrimination, stereotyping, and prejudice on the part of the believer. The *theory of ageism* indicates a potential societal bias - usually against old people - on the basis of age that is equivalent to traditional societal biases that are based on an individual's race, sex, or ethnicity. See also PREJUDICE, THEORIES OF; AGING, THEORIES OF.
REFERENCE
Butler, R. N. (1975). *Why survive? Being old in America.* New York: Harper & Row.

AGGREGATION THEORY. See INTELLIGENCE, THEORIES/LAWS OF.

AGGRESSION, THEORIES OF. The concept of *aggression* is a very general and complex phenomenon that refers to a wide variety of acts, has many causes, and is hard to predict and control. Commonly, the term is used for behaviors that may be motivated by frustration or fear, by a desire to cause fear in others, or by a desire to promote one's won interests and ideas. Patterns of usage of *aggression* usually indicate some theoretical orientation bias on the writer's part. For instance, ethologists consider aggression to be an evolutionary or genetically determined instinctual pattern of behaviors involving specific environmental stimuli (e.g., territorial invasion); classical psychoanalysts (i.e., Freudians) consider aggression to be a conscious correlate of Thanatos (e.g., "death wish" behaviors); learning theorists may regard aggression as a displaced response to any frustrating situation (e.g., *frustration-aggression hypothesis* - where one person may attack an innocent bystander out of an inability to achieve some unrelated goal); and social-learning theorists may consider aggression to be a form of learned and reinforced behavior gained by imitating or observing some other person who engages in aggressive acts (e.g., a young boy imitates his father's aggression toward an ethnic-minority person). The concept of *aggression*, much like the concept of *personality*, seems to play a central role in many theoretical orientations where usage follows theory, and it is difficult to discover mutually agreed-upon definitions of the term. The *theories of aggression* may be categorized as to their theoretical contexts and as to their association with concepts such as instincts, drives, and learning/social-learning factors. There is a persistent popular belief that aggression is *instinctual*, where acts of aggression are merely the manifestation of an innate tendency to fight. According to this view, aggressive energy stemming from this uncontrollable urge is generated spontaneously, continuously, and at a constant rate in the individual. Such aggressive energy builds up over time (e.g., K. Lorenz's *hydraulic model of aggression*), and the more that accumulates, the weaker the stimulus that is needed to set it off into overt aggressive acts. Also, if too much time elapses since the last aggressive act, it may occur spontaneously for no apparent reason. Thus, according to this orientation, aggressive energy inevitably accumulates, and inevitably it must be expressed. Perhaps this is the reason that competitive sports events (particularly bodily-contact sports) have been so popular throughout history. Even though empirical studies do not verify the "draining off" or "cathartic-expression" rationale for aggression, *instinct theory* is attractive to many people as a basis for aggression because it is a comprehensive and easy blend of anecdote, analogical leaps, unsystematic journalism, self-serving rationalization, irresponsibility, and undefined or ill-defined concepts. According to the *drive theory* of aggression, aggressive acts stem from a heightened state of arousal or drive that is reduced through overt expression of aggressive behavior. Consistent with this approach is the classical frustration-aggression hypothesis, which states in its modified form that frustration produces instigations to a number of different types of responses, one of which is an instigation to aggression. Variations of this hypothesis are the *frustration-regression hypothesis* (i.e., when under frustration, the individual may show regressive, child-like behaviors such as crying and extreme dependency) and the *frustration-fixation hypothesis* (e.g., the performance of the same strongly established reaction pattern to different frustration conditions). Certain other aspects of the *drive theory* toward understanding aggression emphasize the strength of the instigating events, the importance of the frustrated goal response to the individual, the number of frustrated response sequences, the degree of frustration, the amount of potential punishment for aggression, and the dynamics of displacement and catharsis in dealing with aggression. The research on the *frustration-aggression hypothesis* and its related ideas was eventually tempered by the fact that it essentially involves a logical circularity of reasoning (cf., *law of effect*), and the *drive theory* approach gave way somewhat to the *social learning theory* of aggression, which emphasizes that the causes of aggressive behavior are not found exclusively in the organism but in environmental forces as well. *Social learning theory* focuses on the processes that are responsible for the individual's *acquisition* (physiological as well as psychological) of aggressive behaviors, the *instigation* of overt aggressive acts at particular times, and the *maintenance* of aggressive behavior. Research in this area has been concerned, also, with the *prediction* and *control* of aggression [cf., Anderson & Bushman (2002) who cite the following *"domain-specific" theories of aggression*: cognitive neoassociation theory; social learning theory; script theory; excitation transfer theory; and social interaction theory; as well as outlining a *general aggression model*]. In a practical context, research on ag-

gression has indicated that aggressive *criminal behavior* correlates with the factors of past criminal behavior, sex/gender, age, race, socio-economic status, and alcohol or opiate abuse. However, such actuarial probabilities concerning criminal aggression most likely contain, at best, only modest value for the prediction of overt aggressive acts in any given person at any given time. See also BANDURA'S THEORY; EFFECT, LAW OF; HYDRAULIC THEORY; INSTINCT THEORY; PERSONALITY THEORIES.

REFERENCES

Dollard, J., Doob, L., Miller, N., Mowrer, O. H., & Sears, R. (1939). *Frustration and aggression.* New Haven, CT: Yale University Press.

Miller, N. (1941). The frustration-aggression hypothesis. *Psychological Review, 48,* 337-342.

Maier, N. R. F. (1949). *Frustration: The study of behavior without a goal.* New York: McGraw-Hill.

Buss, A. (1961*). The psychology of aggression.* New York: Wiley.

Berkowitz, L. (1962). *Aggression: A social psychological analysis.* New York: McGraw-Hill.

Lorenz, K. (1966). *On aggression.* New York: Harcourt Brace Jovanovich.

Bandura, A. (1973). *Aggression: A social learning analysis.* Englewood Cliffs, NJ: Prentice-Hall.

Kornadt, H.-J. (1974). Toward a motivation theory of aggression and aggression inhibition. In J. deWit & W. Hartup (Eds.), *Determinants and origins of aggressive behavior.* The Hague: Mouton.

Maccoby, E., & Jacklin, C. (1980). Sex differences in aggression: A rejoinder and reprise. *Child Development, 51,* 964-980.

Freedman, J. (1984). Effect of television violence on aggressiveness. *Psychological Bulletin, 96,* 227-246.

Berkowitz, L. (1989). Frustration-aggression hypothesis: Examination and reformulation. *Psychological Bulletin, 106,* 59-73.

Anderson, C. A., & Bushman, B. J. (2002). Human aggression. *Annual Review of Psychology, 53,* 27-51.

AGING, THEORIES OF. Studies of aging and behavior-changes over the entire life span leads to the conclusion that cognitive and other functions increase and improve through the first 20 years or so of life, hold that level for the next 40-60 years, and then narrow and close down in a final deterioration phase. Research at the Gesell Institute of Child Development suggests the principle that children should be promoted in school on the basis of their *behavioral age* rather than on their *chronological age* and, by extension, that this same principle should guide one's expectations of an individual's functioning. Differences in persons as a result of age have been studied by *cross-sectional-* (groups of persons at different ages are observed at the same time), *longitudinal-* (the same group of persons is observed at different ages), and *sequential-methods* (combination of cross-sectional with longitudinal methods to study *cohort/generation effects* or influences that occur in the experiences of groups of people who are studied repeatedly over an extended period). The relatively new field called geriatric psychology (the science of the behavior and diseases of the aged) has emerged in the last 50 years where experimental studies of the aging process have been conducted (cf., the broader science of aging called *gerontology*). A number of generalizations, some fairly obvious and predictable, concerning behavior changes in later life have been documented. For example, about 40 percent of one's cortical cells may be lost by age 80-90; fats increase, and water content decreases, over the life span; visual abilities start to decline in middle age, where accommodation and acuity lessen due to elasticity loss in the eyes' lens and where changes in the retina in older age increase sensitivity to glare and affect color vision; auditory abilities begin to decline in middle age, where perception of the higher frequencies may disappear and where hearing loss later in life may lead to stress, depression, and emotional disturbances; and long-term memory deficits in the aged are usually retrieval problems, and short-term memory difficulties occur when the learning task requires divided attention, but span of memory remains intact until extreme old age (cf., *anchorage*

effect - a behavior especially apparent in older persons where there is a tendency to resist changes, usually in regard to their attitudes). Alzheimer's disease [named after the German neurologist Alois Alzheimer (1864-1915), who first described it in 1907] - involving progressive mental impairment that usually begins with a deficit in recent memory and is caused by consistent cellular changes in the aging brain - may be observed beginning in middle age (45-60 years of age). In problem-solving situations, older people tend to ask uninformative questions, to be distracted by redundant and irrelevant information, and to treat both negative and positive instances of a concept as positive; the apparent rigidity in old persons may be due to their inability to profit from negative information. *Theories of aging* are basically models of *balance* or "trade off": in old age, a person may lose energy reserve but gain an ability to control emotional reactions and, thereby, conserve energy. According to this view, two general kinds of changes (i.e., *losses* or *gains*) may be expected with old age. The German-born developmental psychologist and gerontologist Paul B. Baltes (1939-), a pioneer of *life-span developmental psychology*, stresses that persons continue to maintain a capacity for change across the entire life span. Baltes and his colleagues argue for the plasticity of intelligence in aging persons and, also, advance the notion of interdisciplinary collaboration in order to more fully understand the role of social change in psychological development. Various perspectives on the causes of aging have been proposed, and many fall under the main headings of *genetic programming theories* (which suggest that aging is the result of built-in, or genetically-determined, biological clocks) and *wear-and-tear theories* (including the *eversion theory of aging* or *cross-linkage theory*; which suggest that aging results from the gradual wearing-out of organ systems in the body and, in particular, changes in the structure of the body's collagen molecules). Two principal theories concerning one's successful adjustment to the social and physical changes of aging are the *disengagement theory* and the *activity theory*. According to the *disengagement theory*, it is assumed to be normal and desirable for individuals to withdraw from society as they age because it relieves them of roles and responsibilities they become less able to fulfill. The *disengagement theory* of social aging, however, has been discredited largely for a number of reasons. For instance, not all social contact is limited or eliminated in older people, and emotional detachment does not always necessarily occur in older people as *disengagement theory* falsely implies. The *activity theory* of aging, a "use-it-or-lose-it" approach, assumes that activity is the essence of life for people of all ages and predicts that people who remain active physically, mentally, and socially will adjust better to aging (cf., *cybernetic theory* of aging - holds that aging is related to a loss of ability to handle information-processing and transfer functions from environmental inputs, and suggests that the loss is related to the rate at which neurons and neural activity decrease gradually with advancing age). Another theoretical approach, the *selective social interaction* viewpoint, suggests that as people age, they become more selective in choosing their social partners. This perspective indicates a practical way for older persons to regulate emotional experiences and conserve physical energy. The discrimination or prejudice against individuals on the basis of age is called *ageism* and may be countered by dispelling some of the myths that have developed over time concerning the aged. For example, the myth that older workers perform less effectively on jobs requiring both speed and skill may be disputed, and the myths that older persons become isolated and neglected by their families or that the majority of elderly persons show signs of senility, mental decay, or mental illness may be refuted. On the positive side, several prescriptions for well-being in old age emphasize that older persons should establish patterns for self-acceptance, positive relations with others, autonomy or personal freedom, mastery over the environment, a purpose in life, and continued personal growth. See also AGEISM, THEORY OF; DEVELOPMENTAL THEORY; INTELLIGENCE, THEORIES/LAWS OF.

REFERENCES

Gesell, A. (1928). *Infancy and human growth.* New York: Macmillan.

Cumming, E., & Henry, W. (1961). *Growing old: The process of disengagement.* New York: Basic Books.

Schaie, K. (1965). A genetic model for the study of developmental problems. *Psychological Bulletin, 64,* 92-107.

Goulet, L., & Baltes, P. (Eds.) (1970). *Life-span developmental psychology: Research and theory.* New York: Academic Press.

Sheehy, C. (1976). *Passages: Predictable crises of adult life.* New York: Dutton.

Craik, F. (1977). Age differences in human memory. In J. Birren & K. Schaie (Eds.), *Handbook of the psychology of aging.* New York: Van Nostrand Reinhold.

Barrow, G., & Smith, P. (1979). *Aging, ageism, and society.* St. Paul, MN: West.

Baltes, P. (1987). Theoretical propositions on life-span developmental psychology: On the dynamics between growth and decline. *Developmental Psychology, 23,* 611-626.

Palmore, E. (1990). *Ageism: Negative and positive.* New York: Springer.

Carstensen, L. (1991). Selectivity theory: Social activity in life-span context. In K. Schaie (Ed.), *Annual review of geriatrics and gerontology.* New York: Springer.

AGREEMENT, LAW OF. See PARSIMONY, LAW/PRINCIPLE OF.

AHA EXPERIENCE/EFFECT. See EMOTIONS, THEORIES AND LAWS OF.

AHSEN'S TRIPLE CODE MODEL. See NEW STRUCTURALISM THEORY OR PARADIGM; MOTOR LEARNING THEORIES.

AIM-INHIBITION THEORY. This psychoanalytic proposition states that one's natural and instinctual aims and behaviors are not directly and completely satisfied but are only partially fulfilled via remote approximations to the target behavior/activity. The notion of *aim-inhibition* attempts to explain the origin of sociable feelings of affection between individuals where the assumption is that if friendships and/or affection - say between relatives - were not governed by *aim-inhibition*, then they would be expressed in overtly sexual behaviors. The *aim-inhibition theory* is the epitome of Sigmund Freud's instinctual/sexual drive theoretical orientation. Whereas Freud used the German word *Trieb* for his identification of the powerful dynamic force of biological origin (represented mentally by images and ideas that have an emotional charge called "cathexis," and which generate psychic pressure directing and governing one's behavior), the terms *instinct* and *drive*, instead, have come to be used by scholars, interpreters, and translators of Freud's writings. See also FREUD'S INSTINCT THEORY; FREUD'S THEORY OF PERSONALITY.

REFERENCE

Freud, S. (1921/1960). *Group psychology and the analysis of the ego.* New York: Bantam Books.

AIR THEORY. The American psychologist James Jerome Gibson (1904-1979) asserted that any theory of perception that explains perceptual phenomena (e.g., space and object perception) without making reference to the surrounding context in which the perceptions are experienced may be called an *air theory*. Thus, such an approach refers to psychic or perceptual events that are "suspended," theoretically, in mid-air without having any ancillary or "anchoring" support. See also DIRECT PERCEPTION THEORY; PERCEPTION (I. GENERAL), THEORIES OF.

REFERENCES

Gibson, J. J. (1950). *The perception of the visual world.* Boston: Houghton Mifflin.

Gibson, J. J. (1979). *The ecological approach to visual perception.* Boston: Houghton Mifflin.

ALEATORY THEORY. See PROBABILITY THEORY/LAWS.

ALEXANDERISM. A theoretical term in psychopathology that refers to an overwhelming desire to conquer or to destroy nations, and derives from the reign and conquests of the Macedonian king Alexander III, also known as Alexander the Great (356-323 B.C.); *Alexanderism* is also called *agriothymia ambitiosa*

("wild spirit with desire for power"). See also PSYCHOPATHOLOGY, THEORIES OF.

REFERENCE

Zusne, L. (1987). *Eponyms in psychology: A dictionary and biographical sourcebook.* New York: Greenwood Press.

ALEXANDER MODEL OR TECHNIQUE. The Australian actor/physiotherapist Frederick Mathias Alexander (1869-1955) developed this technique for improving one's posture, breathing, and bodily movements. This *physical model* attempts to reduce stress, promotes mental well-being, and increases confidence in individuals who practice the method, and is especially popular among performing artists such as actors and musicians. Alexander developed his technique initially to deal with a voice difficulty he had as a young Shakespearean actor; he observed how his bodily movements/tension around his head and neck affected his voice. Following the correction of his own problem, Alexander applied his approach to a wide range of problems, as well as training teachers in the technique. *Alexander's technique* involves the following steps: allow your neck to be free of tension before beginning any movement of the body; let your head move up rather than pulling it down or back, as movement begins; and allow your entire torso to lengthen, and follow the head upward, rather than slouching down to arch or twist the spine. In advocating the wholeness and integration of one's body and mind, Alexander maintained that one's emotional and mental problems may be mitigated, also, by use of his technique. See also MIND-BODY THEORIES; PERSONALITY THEORIES; STRESS THEORY.

REFERENCES

Alexander, F. M. (1923). *Constructive conscious control of the individual.* New York: Dutton.

Barlow, W. (1973). *The Alexander technique.* New York: Knopf.

Barker, S. (1978). *The Alexander technique.* New York: Bantam Books.

ALEXANDER'S LAW. See VISION AND SIGHT, THEORIES OF.

ALEXANDER'S PRINCIPLE OF SURPLUS ENERGY. The German-born American psychoanalyst Franz Gabriel Alexander (1891-1964) formulated the *principle of surplus energy* (derived from the work of the Hungarian psychoanalyst Sandor Ferenczi) which states that the concept of *sexuality* is a specific discharge of unused excitation in the person where, in the psychoanalytic therapeutic context, an emphasis is placed on "corrective emotional experience" to release such surplus energy. Thus, the notion of *surplus energy* is viewed as a form of "abreaction" (release/discharge of emotional energy following the recall of a painful repressed memory) and involves a procedure that was central to Alexander's therapeutic approach in the neo-Freudian Chicago Institute of Psychoanalysis. See also FERENCZI'S CATASTROPHE THEORY; HYDRAULIC THEORY; PLAY, THEORIES OF; SPENCER'S THEORY OF LAUGHTER/HUMOR.

REFERENCE

Alexander, F. G., & French, T. M. (1946). *Psychoanalytic therapy.* New York: Ronald Press.

ALGEBRAIC SUMMATION, LAW OF. See SKINNER'S OPERANT CONDITIONING THEORY.

ALGORITHMIC-HEURISTIC THEORY. The term *algorithm* refers to a precise and unambiguous direction ("prescription") for carrying out a defined sequence of relatively elementary operations in order to solve a certain class or type of problem. An example of an algorithm is the use of a flowchart (a technique that first poses a question and then, depending on the answer, directs the person to go to another question, etc., until a final answer is achieved) for finding the greatest common denominator of two natural numbers. The execution of the cognitive operations according to the directions of an algorithm is called the *algorithmic process* and, because each algorithm is applicable to a wide set of problems that belong to a certain class, it represents a general and guaranteed method for problem solving. The related term *heuristic*, however, denotes only a "rule of thumb" approach that may direct a problem-solving process but does not guarantee a solution to the problem [the concept of *heuristic* is traceable to the work of

the American economist Herbert A. Simon (1916-), and was introduced into psychology in the early 1970s by the Israeli psychologists Amos Tversky (1937-1996) and Daniel Kahneman (1934-)]. An example of a *heuristic rule* is: try to solve a related problem if the proposed problem cannot immediately be solved. In this case, the set of directions is called a *heuristic prescription* which, when compared to *algorithmic prescriptions*, contain a certain amount of ambiguity and uncertainty. Classes of problems, according to this approach, may be viewed as "algorithmically solvable," "algorithmically unsolvable," or "unknown as to algorithmical solvability." Thus, in the case of some problems, an appropriate algorithm may not exist (e.g., algorithms for proving most mathematical theorems), or an algorithm may be inefficient (e.g., an algorithm for finding the optimum move in a chess game). The practical significance of using algorithms for problem-solving tasks is that it allows children and average adult learners to solve certain problems that, otherwise, might seem to be beyond their cognitive, intellectual, or sensorimotor capabilities. The *algorithmic-heuristic theory* (AHT), formulated by the Russian educational specialist Lev N. Landa is able to deal with a wide variety of learning, instructional, and performance problems, which include the development of general methods of thinking in students (*Landamatics theory*); the psychological and logical structure of different methods of thinking; classification of particular methods by different functional and logical characteristics; differences between algorithmic prescriptions and processes and their interactions; and methods of designing individualized adaptive instruction in *algo-heuristics*, including usage of computers. The area of research involving *instructional theory* (e.g., Bruner, 1966) prescribes the steps used to design effective instructional strategies, such as the identification of the educational goals and the prototypic cognitive processes and cognitive "rules" of the learner. Historically, the *theory/doctrine of formal discipline/training* was an approach to education that advocated that some courses of study (e.g., Latin) ought to be taken, independently of any content that they might have, because they acquainted the student with basic principles (or "forms") that may ultimately prove of value in other ways, and generally serve to "train the mind." However, the enthusiasm for this theory has waxed and waned several times over the years. Contemporary *instructional theory* provides a generalized basis for instructional prescriptions that, in principle, may be used with any particular subject matter - no matter how complex that subject matter. See also COGNITIVE STYLE MODELS; DECISION-MAKING THEORIES.

REFERENCES

Bruner, J. (1966). *Toward a theory of instruction.* Cambridge, MA: Harvard University Press.

Scandura, J. (1973). *Structural learning. I. Theory and research.* London: Gordon & Breach.

Reigeluth, C. M. (Ed.) (1981). *Prescriptive theories of instruction.* New York: Academic Press.

Landa, L. N. (1983). The algo-heuristic theory of instruction. In C. M. Reigeluth (Ed.), *Instructional-design theories and models: A new paradigm of instructional theory.* Vol. 1. Mahwah, NJ: Erlbaum.

Glaser, R. (1990). The reemergence of learning theory within instructional research. *American Psychologist, 45,* 29-39.

Landa, L. N. (1999). Landamatics instructional design theory and methodology for teaching general methods of thinking. In C. M. Reigeluth (Ed.), *Instructional-design theories and models: A new paradigm of instructional theory.* Vol. II. Mahwah, NJ: Erlbaum.

ALIASING/STROBOSCOPIC PHENOMENON. The American statistician John Wilder Tukey (1915-2000) described this distortion in an oscillating visual or auditory signal that results from inadequate high resolution when the signal is sampled at a frequency that is too low relative to the signal's frequency. The *eliasing* or *stroboscopic phenomenon* is commonly seen in the "wagon wheel illusion" in movies where the wheels of a stagecoach, for example, appear to turn slowly in one direction, then slowly turn in the opposite direction as it picks up speed. If the movie picture/stroboscopic frequency is synchronized exactly to a multiple of the rotation frequency, then the rotating object or wheel appears to be stationary. See also APPARENT MOVEMENT, PRINCIPLES AND THEORIES OF; KINETIC DEPTH EFFECT; PERCEPTION (I. GENERAL), THEORIES OF; PERCEPTION (II. COMPARATIVE APPRAISAL), THEORIES OF.

REFERENCES

Tukey, J. W. (1940). *Convergence and uniformity in topology.* Princeton: Princeton University Press.

Tukey, J. W. (1998). *Collected works of John W. Tukey.* Boca Raton, FL: Chapman & Hall.

ALICE IN WONDERLAND EFFECT. See VISION/SIGHT, THEORIES OF.

ALIENATION THEORIES. See HORNEY'S THEORY OF PERSONALITY; PSYCHOPATHOLOGY, THEORIES OF.

ALLAIS PARADOX/EFFECT. The French economist Maurice Allais (1911-) described this paradox/effect of decision-making that typically yields results that are inconsistent with *expected utility theory.* In choosing between sets of alternative probability statements, people usually prefer the total certainty or *high* probability of winning a *large* amount of money, for example, to the *small* probability of winning an even *larger* amount that is associated with a risk of winning nothing at all. However, in subsequent alternative choice situations, the same people prefer a condition in which the payoff is much larger in one than in the other condition - even though the probabilities of winning are nearly the same in both of the two conditions. Such a contradiction in people's choice behavior indicates that *expected utility theory* does not completely or accurately describe humans' decision-making behaviors. Other related paradoxes/effects in choice decision-making situations include: the *common ratio effect* - situations where people prefer a guaranteed substantial payoff *without* an associative risk, but also prefer a high payoff in a condition having only a *slightly greater* associative risk; the *Ellsberg paradox,* also called the *Ellsberg-Fellner paradox* and the *modified Ellsberg paradox* - named after the American political analyst Daniel Ellsberg (1931-) and the American economist William Fellner (1905-1983) - situations where people tend to maximize expected utility or subjective expected utility in judgments involving risk, to use "maximin strategies" to maximize minimum utility in judgments involving uncertainty, and to use "compromise strategies" when the degree of confidence in their probability estimates is intermediate between risk (high confidence) and uncertainty (low confidence); according to the *Ellsberg paradox*, when personal confidence is derived from the type, amount, reliability, and unanimity of information, it is suggested that *expected utility theory* and *subjective utility theory* apply to situations of risk but not necessarily to situations involving uncertainty; and the *St. Petersburg paradox/game* - named after the St. Petersburg Academy where the Swiss mathematician/physicist Daniel Bernoulli (1700-1782) first presented it in 1738 - hypothetical gambling situations where payoffs increase with each trial but where, also, there is a trade-off in which one must make choices as to how much to pay to play the game; in such cases, according to *probability theory*, it becomes absurd to pay a large amount for the opportunity to play the game because there is a high probability of losing everything, and such gaming conditions destroy the principle of maximizing expected utility; Bernoulli's notion of "mental worth" - which later was called *utility* (i.e., a measure of the subjective desirability of an event or outcome that corresponds to the person's preference for it) - followed directly from the enunciation of the *St. Petersburg paradox/game*. All of these paradoxical effects in choice decision-making situations point out instances in which people's choice responses either violate, or are inconsistent with, classical *expected utility theory*. See also DECISION-MAKING THEORIES; EXPECTED UTILITY THEORY; PROBABILITY THEORY/LAWS; PROSPECT THEORY.

REFERENCES

Bernoulli, D. (1738). *Hydrodynamica*. Argentorati: Dulseckeri.

Ellsberg, D. (1961). Risk, ambiguity, and the Savage axioms. *Quarterly Journal of Economics, 75*, 643-669.

Fellner, W. (1961). Distortion of subjective probabilities as a reaction to uncertainty. *Quarterly Journal of Economics, 75*, 670-689.

Allais, M., & Hagen, O. (Eds.) (1979). *Expected utility hypotheses and the Allais paradox: Contemporary discussions of decisions under uncertainty*. Boston: D. Reidel.

Kadane, J. B. (1992). Healthy skepticism as an expected utility explanation of the phenomenon of Allais and Ellsberg. *Theory & Decision, 32*, 57-64.

ALLEGIANCE EFFECT. See DODO HYPOTHESIS.

ALL-OR-NONE LAW/PRINCIPLE. = Bowditch's law. This principle, discovered by the American physiologist Henry Pickering Bowditch (1840-1911) while he was studying cardiac muscle, states that in any single nerve or muscle fiber the response to a stimulus above threshold level is maximal, independent of the intensity of the stimulus, and dependent only on the condition of the cell at the moment of stimulation. The *all-or-none* property of the nerve impulse is contained in the fact that its amplitude is always the same where the neural code is determined by frequency rather than size of the nerve response. Stronger stimuli result in more impulses being generated per second, but each stimulus has the same amplitude. The process of nerve conduction has been likened to the burning of a fuse because both processes involve the progressive release of energy by local action. However, it is true that not all fuses or all nerve fibers have the same amount of energy available; thick fuses and thick nerve fibers transmit a larger disturbance and transmit it faster. It is true, also, that the available energy in any nerve fiber varies from time to time with corresponding changes in the magnitude and speed of the impulse. The *all-or-none law*, however, is still valid because the nerve fiber either reacts with all of its available energy, or else (if the stimulus is too weak), it does not react at all. The top speed of the nerve impulse is estimated to be 100 meters per second and is attained only in the larger fibers of the body. Thin fibers conduct impulses at much slower rates, down to about one meter per second in some animal species. The major difference between the fuse and the nerve fiber in this analogy is that the nerve fiber restores itself after each impulse occurs, whereas the fuse does not. Only a small amount of the stored energy is available momentarily at the surface of the nerve fiber where the local activity takes place. The energy is replaced promptly as soon as this portion is consumed by the single nerve impulse. However, the replacement process takes a short amount of time, and a second impulse cannot follow immediately. At this stage in the process, the fiber is said to be in its *absolute refractory phase* (these events taken collectively are known as the *refractory law*). Then, within a millisecond or so, the fiber recovers enough to allow a very strong stimulus to create a very weak impulse. Following this *relative refractory phase* of firing, there is a gradual buildup of available energy where the stimulus threshold is decreased and the magnitude and speed of the impulse are increased. The American psychologist Charles Osgood (1916-1991) coined the term *essential identity law*, which is related to the physiological *all-or-none law* and refers to the fact that nerve impulses are all the same in kind. For example, impulses traveling in optic nerve fibers differ qualitatively in no way from impulses in cutaneous fibers, and activity in the visual areas of the cortex does not appear to differ qualitatively from activity in the somesthetic, or even in the motor, areas. The *all-or-none principle* from physiology has been expanded conceptually, also, to the area of the psychology of learning where it refers to associations of learned materials that are either formed completely on a single trial or not formed at all (e.g., one-trial learning). The valid *all-or-none law/principle* has been consistently well-referenced in psychology textbooks from 1885 through 1996 (cf., Roeckelein, 1996). See also CONTINUITY THEORY; GUTHRIE'S THEORY OF BEHAVIOR; SKINNER'S DESCRIPTIVE BEHAVIOR/OPERANT CONDITIONING THEORY.

REFERENCES

Bowditch, H. P. (1871). [All-or-none law of nerve impulse transmission in heart fiber muscles]. *Berichte uber die Verhandlungen der koniglichen sa-*chsischen Gesellschaft der Wissenschaften zu Leipzig, mathematischphysische Classe, 23*, 652-689.

Adrian, E. (1914). The all-or-none principle in nerves. *Journal of Physiology, 47*, 450-474.

Osgood, C. (1953). *Method and theory in experimental psychology*. New York: Oxford University Press.

Roeckelein J. E. (1996). Citation of laws and theories in textbooks across 112 years of psychology. *Psychological Reports, 79*, 979-998.

ALLPORT'S CONFORMITY HYPOTHESIS. The American social psychologist Floyd Henry Allport (1890-1978) proposed that *conforming* behavior may be recognized by its distinctive distribution, which takes the shape of an inverted J curve. A few people overconform (are to the left of the curve's peak), the overwhelming majority are positioned exactly at the peak, which accounts for the spike of the J, and a minority deviate from the norm, which accounts for an elongated, but low-level, tail. Allport validated his *conformity hypothesis* mainly by observations in field situations involving activities such as reporting to work, using holy water in a Catholic church, and stopping at a stop sign. The *friction-conformity model* states that a pedestrian's rate of walking is affected by the number of obstacles met and by conformity to the pace set by other nearby pedestrians. Allport's data refer primarily to situations where adherence to standards is enforced ("compliant behavior"). Conformity is viewed as an intermediate stage between superficial compliance and permanent internalization, and as a conflict between what a person basically is and what group membership requires from the individual (cf., *group-relations theory* - states that behavior is determined not only by a person's unique pattern of traits, but also by the individual's need to conform to social demands and expectations). See also ASCH CONFORMITY EFFECT; ATTITUDE AND ATTITUDE CHANGE, THEORIES OF; BYSTANDER INTERVENTION EFFECT; COMPLIANCE EFFECTS AND TECHNIQUES; CONFLICT, THEORIES OF; GROUPTHINK PHENOMENON.

REFERENCES

Allport, F. (1934). The J-curve hypothesis of conforming behavior. *Journal of Social Psychology, 5*, 141-183.

Allen, V. (1965). Situational factors in conformity. In L. Berkowitz (Ed.), *Advances in experimental social psychology*. Vol. 2. New York: Academic Press.

Hollander, E., & Willis, R. (1967). Some current issues in the psychology of conformity and nonconformity. *Psychological Bulletin, 68*, 62-76.

ALLPORT'S FUNCTIONAL AUTONOMY PRINCIPLE. The American psychologist Gordon Willard Allport (1897-1967) studied, researched, and taught in the area of personality, which he regarded as the natural subject matter of psychology. In his exploration and development of personality theory, Allport formulated the concept of *functional autonomy of motives*, which emphasizes the emergence of new motivational systems in a person's life. The *principle of functional autonomy* describes the case where well-established habits (such as a person's going to work for 12 hours a day for many years and earning a great deal of money) may become ends or motives in themselves (such as continuing to go to work for 12 hours a day, even though the person has become wealthy, could retire easily, and actually does not need to work at all). According to the *principle of functional autonomy of motives*, the means to a goal become ends in themselves where the original activities have now become motives and function independently of the purposes or needs that they served initially. When it was first introduced, the notion of *functional autonomy* was both controversial and radical because it ran counter to the prevailing theories of motivation, which stressed mechanisms directly linked to basic physiological needs. Allport's idea raised the possibility that simple and complex motives can function quite separately from any direct physiological drive or need. The concept of *functional autonomy* liberalized the area of motivation inasmuch as it allowed the individual to be an active (rather than a passive) entity whose behavior could be present-oriented, as well as future-oriented, and not merely past-oriented. Judging by its absence in most current introductory psychology textbooks, the *principle of functional autonomy of motives* seems to be less referenced, generally, today than it was years ago, even though the term seems, from casual observation, to have become part of psychologists' informal vocabulary. Thus the notion of *functionally autonomous motives* (though controversial at one time) no longer seems particularly strange, but has been accepted and absorbed into the mainstream of psychology. Indeed, recent theories of motivation have proposed and described "supra-" or "extra-physiologically based" needs in shaping individuals' personality such as motives for exploration, curiosity, mastery, manipulation, self-actualization, sensation-seeking, and competence. See also ALLPORT'S THEORY OF PERSONALITY; MOTIVATION, THEORIES OF.

REFERENCE

Allport, G. W. (1937). The functional autonomy of motives. *American Journal of Psychology, 50*, 141-156.

ALLPORT'S THEORY OF ENESTRUENCE. = event-structure theory. This theory of perception, developed by Floyd Henry Allport (1890-1978), whom many consider to be the father of experimental social psychology, consists of a kinetic geometry ("kinematics") of the self-closedness of ongoing-events series and associative probability concepts of the energies (i.e., events) involved in the self-closed structures and their interrelationships. As one may sense here, the programmatic nature of this rather intriguing theory is stated in somewhat abstract terms. This is because the model is intended to be applied to many different phenomena at various levels of analysis. Allport's theoretical model of *event-structure* attempts to cast the laws of nature under two headings: a formal principle of nature in terms *other* than "quantitative" and a principle of "corporation" of many perceptual and social phenomena. If the theory is true, said Allport (1955, p. 666), "nature is not a machine, nor are organisms controlled by quantitative or mechanical laws [T]he theory is advanced merely as one way of looking at the problem of structure, one attempt to fathom the mystery of the form and unity of nature which have thus

far been left largely untouched by science."
Allport's *theory of enestruence* holds that social structure has no physical or anatomical
basis but consists of cycles of events that
"hoop" and return upon themselves to complete and sustain the cycle. To many psychologists, the *event-structure theory* formulated by
Allport seems to be a rather ambitious prescription for the synthesis and consolidation of
other theories of perception and social behavior
into a unifying and cohesive system. See also
PERCEPTION (I. GENERAL), THEORIES
OF; PERCEPTION (II. COMPARATIVE
APPRAISAL), THEORIES OF.

REFERENCES

Allport, F. (1940). An event-system of collective action. *Journal of Social Psychology, 11,* 417-445.

Allport, F. (1954). The structuring of events:
Outline of a general theory with applications to psychology. *Psychological Review, 61,* 281-303.

Allport, F. (1955). *Theories of perception and
the concept of structure.* New York:
Wiley.

Allport, F. (1967). A theory of enestruence
(event-structure). *American Psychologist, 22,* 1-14.

ALLPORT'S THEORY OF PERSONAL-
ITY.

In taking an eclectic and humanistic approach to the study of personality, Gordon
Willard Allport (1897-1967) drew on a wide
variety of sources, from William McDougall's
theory of motives to the experimental-social
psychological analysis of behavior. Whereas
Allport also drew some of his ideas from the
psychodynamic theories of personality, he was
opposed strongly to the Freudian views of the
unconscious, and he rejected any *reductionist
theory* (i.e., attempts to understand complex
processes through the study of their simpler
units and their interrelations with other simple
units) that attributed human behavior to innate
instincts, childhood conditioning, or repressed
complexes. In examining the other sciences
and scientific methods, Allport opposed extensive borrowing from the natural sciences and
asserted that the methods and theoretical models that have been useful in the physical sciences may only mislead one when attempting
to study complex human behavior. Allport

conceived of personality as an organized entity
that is future-oriented and not merely a bundle
of habits and fixations. He argued that one's
self (or *proprium*) is able to make choices
where it can influence the development of its
own personality along with adjusting to the
emergence of new motivational systems
("functional autonomy of motives"). Allport
emphasized a multifaceted methodological
approach toward personality study that combined the *idiographic* (study and analysis of
single cases) and the *nomothetic* (discovery of
general or universal laws that apply to all humans) viewpoints. Even though Allport developed various tests of personality traits, values,
and attitudes, he saw little merit in conducting
factorial-type studies of personality. Allport's
theory of personality is often called a *trait
theory* where traits (i.e., enduring predispositions to respond in certain ways) occupy the
position of a major motivational construct (cf.,
H. Murray's *need*; S. Freud's *instinct*; and W.
McDougall's *sentiment* theories). One of Allport's early studies found almost 18,000 words
in the dictionary that could be used as *trait*
names to describe personality. Using an idiographic approach of analysis where an individual's unique personality traits are arranged into
a hierarchy from "most important" at the top to
"least important" at the bottom, Allport then
divided the hierarchy into three separate groups
of traits: *cardinal* (the uncommon, but pervasive and all-encompassing characteristics that
influence most areas of only a few people's
lives, such as humanitarianism and honesty),
central (specific behavioral tendencies that are
highly characteristic of an individual, such as
outgoing and ambitious), and *secondary* (the
less-enduring and transitory characteristics
such as liking to cycle or hike). Allport emphasized that no two people have exactly the same
traits, and his *trait theory* of personality
stressed the uniqueness of the individual. Although few psychologists have embraced Allport's personality theory in its total form, it has
nevertheless been influential and useful, especially in its restoration and purification of the
ego concept, and Allport himself was one of
the few theorists who provided an effective
bridge between academic psychology and
clinical-personality psychology. Whereas Allport's main work was on the development of a

comprehensive personality theory, his interests were wide-ranging, including studies on rumor, social attitudes, religion, graphology, eidetic imagery, radio voices, and prejudice. Critics of Allport's theoretical orientation and work (cf., Allport, 1966) include: P. Bertocci, J. Seward, and N. Sanford. Perhaps the most remarkable aspect of Allport's work has been its ability to exert a broad influence and sense of novelty in psychology in spite of its pluralism and eclecticism. See also ALLPORT'S FUNCTIONAL AUTONOMY PRINCIPLE; FREUD'S THEORY OF PERSONALITY; IDIOGRAPHIC AND NOMOTHETIC LAWS; MCDOUGALL'S HORMIC AND INSTINCT THEORY/DOCTRINE; MURRAY'S THEORY OF PERSONALITY.

REFERENCES

Allport, F., & Allport, G. W. (1921). Personality traits: Their classification and measurement. *Journal of Abnormal and Social Psychology, 16,* 6-40.

Allport, G. W., & Odbert, H. (1936). Trait names: A psycho-lexical study. *Psychological Monographs, 47,* No. 211.

Allport, G. W. (1937). *Personality: A psychological interpretation.* New York: Holt, Rinehart & Winston.

Bertocci, P. (1940). A critique of G. W. Allport's theory of motivation. *Psychological Review, 47,* 501-532; 533-554.

Allport, G. W. (1947). Scientific models and human morals. *Psychological Review, 54,* 182-192.

Seward, J. (1948). The sign of a symbol: A reply to Professor Allport, *Psychological Review, 55,* 277-296.

Allport, G. W. (1955). *Becoming: Basic considerations for a psychology of personality.* New Haven, CT: Yale University Press.

Allport, G. W. (1960). *Personality and social encounter.* Boston: Beacon Press.

Allport, G. W. (1961). *Pattern and growth in personality.* New York: Holt, Rinehart & Winston.

Sanford, N. (1963). Personality: Its place in psychology. In S. Koch (Ed.), *Psychology: A study of a science.* Vol. 5. New York: McGraw-Hill.

Allport, G. W. (1966). Traits revisited. *American Psychologist, 21,* 1-10.

ALPHA-, BETA-, AND GAMMA-HYPO-THESES. See LEARNING THEORIES AND LAWS.

ALPHA-FUNCTION HYPOTHESIS. The Indian-born British psychoanalyst Wilfred R. Bion (1897-1979) proposed that a psychodynamic *alpha function process* operates in analytic psychology whereby the raw materials of emotions and sensory experience (called *beta elements*) are transformed into psychic elements (called *alpha elements*) that are suitable, in turn, for the individual's "mental digestion." See also FREUD'S THEORY OF PERSONALITY.

REFERENCES

Bion, W. R. (1952). Group dynamics: A review. *International Journal of Psychoanalysis, 33,* 235-247.

Bion, W. R. (1961). *Experiences in groups.* New York: Basic Books.

ALPHA MOVEMENT EFFECT. See APPARENT MOVEMENT, PRINCIPLES AND THEORIES OF.

ALRUTZ'S THEORY. The Swedish psychologist Sydney Alrutz (1868-1925) made the suggestion at the turn of the 20th century that the simultaneous arousal of both warm and cold receptors in the skin give the resultant sensation of heat. A clear demonstration of a hot sensation that results from the simultaneous stimulation of neighboring warmth and cold receptors is the so-called *synthetic heat experiment*, where no genuine heat is applied, but warm spots are subjected to moderate warmth and cold spots to cold. Under these conditions, the first sensation is usually cold, which is followed by heat, which disappears after a few seconds and then gives the sensation of cold again. This theory is related to the phenomenon of *paradoxical cold*, where the sensation of cold results from a warm stimulus (von Frey, 1895). The case for *paradoxical cold* and *synthetic heat* is not completely conclusive, and there is some evidence against *Alrutz's theory*. Related theories in this area of the stimulation of cutaneous senses are the *concentration the-*

ory of cutaneous cold and the *spot theory of temperature senses* (Jenkins, 1941). See also NAFE'S THEORY OF CUTANEOUS SENSITIVITY.

REFERENCES

Von Frey, M. (1895). Beitrage zur sinnesphysiologie des haut. *Berichte sachsischen Gesellschaft der Wissenschaft, Leipzig, Math./Physiks, 47,* 166-184.

Alrutz, S. (1897). Omfornimmelsen "hett." *Uppsala Lakforen, 2,* 340-359.

Alrutz, S. (1908). Untersuchungen uber die temperatursinne. *Zeitschrift fur Psychologie, 47,* 161-202; 241-286.

Burnett, N., & Dallenbach, K. (1927). The experience of heat. *American Journal of Psychology, 38,* 418-431.

Jenkins, W. (1938). Studies in thermal sensitivity. Further evidence against the Alrutz theory. *Journal of Experimental Psychology, 23,* 411-422.

Jenkins, W. (1941). Studies in thermal sensitivity. Further evidence on the effects of stimulus temperature. *Journal of Experimental Psychology, 29,* 413-419.

ALTERNATION-OF-RESPONSE THEORY. See SHORT-TERM AND LONG-TERM MEMORY, THEORIES OF.

ALTERNATIVE BRAIN PROCESS THEORY. See LASHLEY'S THEORY.

ALTERNATIVE HYPOTHESIS. See NULL HYPOTHESIS.

ALVEOLAR THEORY. See LIFE, THEORIES OF.

ALZHEIMER'S DISEASE THEORY. In 1907, the German physician/neurologist Alois Alzheimer (1864-1915) first described the brain lesions associated with the degenerative brain disease, now called *Alzheimer's disease,* which is characterized by loss of memory and emotional/psychological instability, and is accompanied by postmortem evidence of amyloid "plaques" and neurofibrillary "tangles" (insoluble nerve fibers). Some theorists speculate that the amyloid plaques (insoluble beta-amyloid proteins) are responsible for the symp-toms where the neurofibrillary tangles are primary and the amyloid plaques are secondary. Related to the disorder is a deficit of the neurotransmitter acetylcholine and, perhaps, is caused by mutations/defects in mitochondrial DNA, prion (an infectious, rogue particle of protein), or "chromosome-21" (a chromosome implicated in genetic defects). See also FORGETTING/MEMORY, THEORIES OF.

REFERENCE

Aronson, M. K. (1988). *Understanding Alzheimer's disease.* New York: Scribner's.

AMBIVALENCE THEORIES OF HUMOR. The *ambivalence theories of humor* generally are characterized by oscillation, conflict-mixture, and simultaneously experienced incompatible emotions and feelings. The concepts of *ambivalence* and *incongruity* overlap, often, in *humor theories* and possess common features. However, the *incongruity theories* tend to emphasize cognitive, ideas, and perceptions whereas the *ambivalence theories* emphasize feelings and emotions as central to the humor experience. See also DESCARTES' THEORY OF HUMOR AND LAUGHTER; HUMOR, THEORIES OF; INCONGRUITY AND INCONSISTENCY THEORIES OF HUMOR.

REFERENCE

Roeckelein, J. E. (2002). *The psychology of humor.* Westport, CT: Greenwood Press.

AMBIVALENCE THEORY. This proposition by the Swiss psychiatrist Eugen Bleuler (1857-1939) and the Austrian neurologist and psychoanalyst Sigmund Freud (1856-1939) asserts that two opposing ("ambivalent") beliefs, desires, behavioral tendencies, or emotions (e.g., love and hate) may coexist concurrently in one person, and are directed toward the same instinctual object or individual. At one time, the presence of ambivalence in a person was thought to be a major sign of schizoid (i.e., emotional coldness, withdrawal, and a general inability to form intimate attachments to others) tendencies, but today the notion of *ambivalence* carries less pejorative connotations, and is a commonly accepted aspect of one's personal and social development. The concept of *ambivalence* is traceable, also, to the early work of the German-born American psychologist Kurt Lewin (1890-1947), especially in his *field theory* dealing with conflict, and denotes a decisional state in which one is pulled simultaneously in two mutually exclusive directions or toward two opposite goals. See also FREUD'S THEORY OF PERSONALITY; GOOD BREAST- BAD BREAST THEORY; LEWIN'S FIELD THEORY.

REFERENCES

Freud, S. (1912). The dynamics of transference. In *The standard edition of the complete psychological works of Sigmund Freud*. Vol. 12. London: Hogarth Press.

Bleuler, E. (1916). *Texbook of psychiatry*. New York: Macmillan.

Lewin, K. (1948). *Resolving social conflicts: Selected theoretical papers*. New York: Harper & Row.

AMSEL'S HYPOTHESIS/THEORY. The Canadian-born American psychologist Abram Amsel (1922-) formulated the *frustration hypothesis* concerning nonreward and extinction of instrumental behavior where the occurrence of nonreward at a moment when the organism is expecting a reward causes the elicitation of a primary "frustration reaction." The feedback stimulation from this reaction is aversive and has short-term, persisting motivational effects upon subsequent instrumental behavior. Amsel states that fractional parts of the frustration reaction become classically conditioned to stimuli preceding its elicitation; cues from "anticipatory" frustration are connected to avoidance responses where the connections are modifiable through training. Earlier treatments and interpretations of the nonreward situation viewed it in a *passive* role (e.g., E. C. Tolman assumed that nonreward served simply to weaken an organism's expectancy of reward; and C. L. Hull conceived of nonreward trials as allowing the buildup of inhibitory factors without being offset by corresponding increases in habit or incentive motivation). On the other hand, Amsel's *frustration hypothesis* considers the condition of nonreward as an *actively* punishing and aversive event, rather than as a *passive* condition. The consequence of Amsel's position is that many of the effects of nonreward upon responding are viewed today as analogous to the effects produced upon that same behavior by the application of *punishment*. Although Amsel's *frustration theory* is one of the dominant conceptions of extinction, it does require critical analysis in light of a few failings. For example, studies indicate that no frustration effect occurs if the organism is expecting different incentives in two different goal locations. Amsel's *extinction theory* seems to apply only to instrumental, appetitive responses and not to extinction in classical conditioning or instrumental escape conditioning situations. Different resistance levels to extinction may be produced by variations in the sequential pattern of reward and nonreward trials during acquisition of responses; and some studies suggest that extinction is a multiple-deter-minant process whereas Amsel's *frustration hypothesis* is only one component of the total phenomenon. See also CAPALDI'S THEORY; EXTINCTION THEORY; HULL'S LEARNING THEORY; INSTRUMENTAL CONDITIONING, PRINCIPLE OF; PAVLOVIAN CONDITIONING PRINCIPLES; PUNISHMENT, THEORIES OF; TOLMAN'S THEORY.

REFERENCES

Tolman, E. C. (1932). *Purposive behavior in animals and men*. New York: Appleton-Century-Crofts.

Hull, C. L. (1943). *Principles of behavior*. New York: Appleton-Century-Cro-fts.

Amsel, A. (1958). The role of frustrative nonreward in noncontinuous reward situations. *Psychological Bulletin, 55*, 102-119.

Amsel, A. (1962). Frustrative nonreward in partial reinforcement and discrimination learning. *Psychological Bulletin, 69*, 306-328.

Amsel, A. (1992). Frustration theory - many years later. *Psychological Bulletin, 112*, 396-399.

ANACLITIC THEORY. = anaclitic object-choice theory. A supposition in Freudian psychoanalysis that certain individuals have a strong emotional attachment or dependence on another individual (e.g., the behavior of the infant at its mother's breast). *Anaclitic object-*

choice refers to a form of object-choice in which the person chooses a "love-object" (instinctual object that helps to attain an instinctual aim) to resemble a parental figure, and is attracted to other people who have the potential for protecting, caring, and feeding him or her. The dynamics in *anaclitic theory* usually revolve around the notion that the sexual instinct develops initially in individuals regarding the instinct of self-preservation. In the clinical condition known as *anaclitic depression*, a type of depression (accompanied by crying, apprehension, anorexia, sleep disorders, and withdrawal) is exhibited by infants that is precipitated, typically, by sudden separation ("separation anxiety") from a parent after having had a normal-contact relationship or attachment to the parent for about six months. See also CUPBOARD THEORY; FREUD'S THEORY OF PERSONALITY; GOOD BREAST/OBJECT-BAD BREAST/ OBJECT THEORY; INFANT ATTACH-MENT THEORIES.

REFERENCES

Freud, S. (1905). Three essays on the theory of sexuality. In *The standard edition of the complete psychological works of Sigmund Freud*. Vol. 7. London: Hogarth Press.

Freud, S. (1914). On narcissism: An introduction. In *The standard edition of the complete psychological works of Sigmund Freud*. Vol. 14. London: Hogarth Press.

Spitz, R. A. (1947). Anaclitic depression. In R. A. Spitz (Ed.), *Psychoanalytic studies of the child*. Vol. 2. New York: International Universities Press.

ANAGOGIC THEORY. The *anagogic* (literally, "lifting up") viewpoint is a psychoanalytic proposition exemplified in the analytical approach of the Swiss psychiatrist and psychoanalyst Carl Gustav Jung (1875-1961), whereby dreams, myths, and other symbolic representations are interpreted on the basis of their elevated or higher allegorical meaning and spiritual significance for the individual. *Anagogic* theoretical interpretations are considered by many psychologists to be the opposite of ordinary psychoanalytical interpretations where the latter reduce and translate such protocols as dreams and myths into a basic, often sexual, form or content. Sigmund Freud rejected the *anagogic* interpretations given by Jung and his *analytic psychology* approach, and considered such interpretations to be merely reversions to "pre-analytic" theoretical modes of content analysis and interpretation. See also FREUD'S THEORY OF PERSONALITY; JUNG'S THEORY OF PERSONALITY.

REFERENCES

Jung, C. G. (1913). The theory of psychoanalysis. In *The collected works of C. G. Jung*. Vol. 4. Princeton, NJ: Princeton University Press.

Freud, S. (1922). Dreams and telepathy. In *The standard edition of the complete psychological works of Sigmund Freud*. Vol. 18. London: Hogarth Press.

ANAL-EXPULSIVE THEORY. The German psychoanalyst Karl Abraham (1877-1925) expanded on the Freudian *anal stage* of the *theory of psychosexual stages of development* by suggesting two phases of the anal stage. In the first phase, "anal erotism" or "eroticism" (i.e., sensuous pleasure derived from stimulation of the anus) is associated with evacuation of the bowels (and the "sadist instinct," or the drive toward cruelty, is satisfied via "feces destruction"); in the second phase (the "anal-retentive" phase), anal erotism/eroticism is linked with retention of the feces (and the "sadist instinct" is associated with "possessive control"). According to the tenets of Abraham's *anal-expulsive theory*, the successful progression from the first to the second anal phase of the anal stage is critical for the future development of the person's ability to form loving relationships with others. See also FREUD'S THEORY OF PERSONALITY; LIBIDO THEORY.

REFERENCES

Freud, S. (1917). On transformations of instinct as exemplified in anal erotism. In *The standard edition of the complete psychological works of Sigmund Freud*. Vol. 17. London: Hogarth Press.

Abraham, K. (1921/1927). Contributions to the theory of the anal character. In *Se-*

lected papers on psychoanalysis. London: Hogarth Press.

Abraham, K. (1966). *On character and libido development: Six essays by Karl Abraham.* New York: Norton.

ANALOGUE THEORY OF MEMORY. See FORGETTING/MEMORY, THEORIES OF.

ANALYSIS-BY-SYNTHESIS THEORY. See TOP-DOWN PROCESSING THEORIES.

ANCESTRAL INHERITANCE, LAW OF. See GALTON'S LAWS.

ANCHORAGE EFFECT. See AGING, THEORIES OF.

ANCHORING EFFECT. See PSYCHOPATHOLOGY, THEORIES OF.

ANCIENT MARINER EFFECT. See RECIPROCITY OF LIKING EFFECT.

AND-SUMMATION HYPOTHESIS. See GESTALT THEORY/LAWS.

ANGYAL'S PERSONALITY THEORY. The Hungarian-American personality psychologist Andras Angyal (1902-1960) developed a theory of personality in which he describes two basic types of motivational processes in humans: striving toward love ("homonomy") and striving toward mastery ("autonomy"). Angyal conceived of personality as an interdependent system where tensions arise between the person and the environment and is controlled by both homonomy and autonomy processes. In Angyal's formulation, the connection between the parts of the system are subordinate to the overall whole where, for example, neurosis is one system, and overall health is another system. Also, when the systems (through "system analysis") become disturbed or disrupted, the process of therapy is indicated and refers to the restoration of the health system to its normally dominant role. In its dynamics, *Angyal's personality theory* may be characterized as *organismic* or *holistic* (cf., C. Bernard; M. Wertheimer; J. R. Kantor; J. Smuts; G. Coghill; K. Goldstein; and G. Murphy). In the genesis of his theory, Angyal em-

phasized the need for a new science that is not primarily psychological, physiological, or sociological in character but that viewed the person as an integrated whole entity. Angyal (unlike K. Goldstein) insisted that it is impossible to differentiate the organism from the environment because they interpenetrate one another in such a complex fashion that any attempt to distinguish them would be artificial and tend to destroy the natural unity of the whole (Angyal coined the term *biospheric* to indicate the holistic relationship between one individual and the environment). *Angyal's personality theory* has not had a significant impact on academic psychology, perhaps because it was developed predominantly within a clinical, or nonacademic, context. See also GOLDSTEIN'S ORGANISMIC THEORY; MURPHY'S BIOSOCIAL THEORY.

REFERENCES

Bernard, C. (1866/1957). *An introduction to the study of experimental medicine.* New York: Dover.

Wertheimer, M. (1923). Untersuchungen zur lehre von der gestalt. *Psychologische Forschung, 4,* 301-350.

Smuts, J. (1926). *Holism and evolution.* New York: Macmillan.

Coghill, G. (1929). *Anatomy and the problem of behavior.* London: Cambridge University Press.

Kantor, J. R. (1933). *A survey of the science of psychology.* Bloomington, IN: Principia Press.

Angyal, A. (1941). *Foundations for a science of personality.* New York: Commonwealth Foundation.

Angyal, A. (1951). A theoretical model for personality studies. *Journal of Personality, 20,* 131-142.

Angyal, A. (1965). *Neurosis and treatment: A holistic theory.* New York: Wiley.

ANIMAL-CRY/BOW-WOW THEORY. See LANGUAGE ORIGINS, THEORIES OF.

ANIMAL MAGNETISM THEORY. See HYPNOSIS/HYPNOTISM, THEORIES OF.

ANIMISM THEORY. This speculation has several connotations and contexts. In one case, it is the doctrine propounded by the Greek philosophers Pythagoras (c. 560 – c. 480 B.C.) and Plato (c. 427 – c. 347 B.C.) that "anima" (i.e., air, breath, life principle, soul) is an immaterial force that organizes and moves the material world. In another case, *animism theory* is the doctrine advanced by the German physician Georg Ernest Stahl (1660-1734) that the soul is the essential or vital principle ("anima mundi") on which all organic development and progression depends; cf., the notion of *élan vital*, or "vital force," proposed by the French philosopher Henri Bergson (1859-1941), referring to the original vital/life impulse comprising the basic substance of all consciousness and nature. In a psychological context, *animism theory* is embedded in the Swiss psychologist Jean Piaget's (1896-1980) *cognitive/developmental theory* (cf., *Jung's theory of personality*), especially as it relates to the thinking of children who have not yet learned to distinguish animate or living objects from inanimate objects. In Piaget's usage, the notion of *animism* [borrowed from the British social anthropologist Sir Edward Burnett Tylor (1832-1917), who suggested that psychological traits and aspects such as intentions and desires are ascribed by individuals in some primitive cultures to inanimate objects, plants, and other natural phenomena] - as reflected in children's cognitive processes - undergoes four developmental stages: the child's belief that everything in the environment is alive (ages 4-6 years); the belief that everything that moves is alive (ages 6-7 years); the belief that everything that moves by itself is alive (ages 8-10 years); and the correct or proper distinction between animate and inanimate objects (after age 10 years). In the related animistic concept of *anthropomorphism*, the individual gives specific human characteristics (such as humor, love, or reflective feelings) to non-human animals and objects. See also JUNG'S THEORY OF PERSONALITY; PIAGET'S THEORY OF DEVELOPMENTAL STAGES.

REFERENCES

Stahl, G. E. (1707). *Theori medica vera*. Halae: Orphanotrophei.

Tylor, E. B. (1871). *Primitive culture: Researches into the development of mythology, philosophy, religion, art, and custom*. London: Murray.

Piaget, J. (1929/1963). *The child's conception of the world*. New York: Littlefield, Adams.

ANIMISTIC THINKING. See PIAGET'S THEORY OF DEVELOPMENTAL STAGES.

ANOMIE THEORY. The major proposition made by the French sociologist Emile Durkheim (1858-1917) in *anomie theory* is that there is a connection or correlation between certain personal behaviors (such as suicide) and *anomie* (a general state of society where rules, conduct, and standards of belief have broken down or become weakened; also, *anomie* refers to the analogous psychological condition in a person that is characterized by hopelessness, despair, social isolation, depression, and loss of sense of purpose in life). Upon reflection, *anomie theory* appears to contain an element of circular reasoning to many observers regarding cause-effect relationships, especially as it relates to suicide: does anomie cause suicide, or do increasing rates of suicide lead to anomie? See also SCHIZOPHRENIA, THEORIES OF; SOCIAL DRIFT THEORY; SUICIDE, THEORIES OF.

REFERENCE

Durkheim, E. (1897/1966). *Suicide: A study in sociology*. Glencoe, IL: Free Press.

ANOMIE THEORY OF CRIME. See LOMBROSIAN THEORY.

ANSBACHER EFFECT. See PERCEPTION (I. GENERAL), THEORIES OF.

ANTAGONISTIC/OPPONENT-PROCESS THEORY. See VISION/SIGHT, THEORIES OF; HERING'S COLOR THEORY.

ANTHROPOMETRIC/STEROID THEORY. See SEXUAL ORIENTATION THEORIES.

ANTHROPOSOPHY, DOCTRINE OF. The Austrian philosopher Rudolf Steiner (1861-1925) developed this spiritualistic or mystical doctrine that emphasized the psychological and educational values derived from including creative activities in educational curricula -

such as exposing the individual to mythology and the types of myth-making that were popular in earlier eras of human existence. The *doctrine of anthroposophy* contains elements that are similar to the tenets of *theosophy* (literally, "knowledge of divine things;" a religious, or semi-religious, set of occult beliefs rejecting Judeo-Christian revelation and theology, often incorporating aspects of Buddhism and Brahmanism, and held to be based on a special mystical insight or on superior speculation), also founded by Steiner in the early 1900s. See also JUNG'S THEORY OF PERSONALITY.

REFERENCE

Steiner, R. (1947). *Knowledge of the higher worlds and its attainment.* 3rd ed. New York: Anthroposophic Press.

ANTICIPATION, LAW OF. See CONDUCT, LAWS OF.

ANTI-CONFIRMATIONISM. See NULL HYPOTHESIS.

ANXIETY, THEORIES OF. Anxiety is a subjective emotional state that is characterized by pervasive feelings such as dread and apprehension, and is often accompanied by physical symptoms such as tremors, muscle tension, chest pain, palpitations, dizziness, headache, and gastrointestinal distress (cf., *anxiety-matching hypothesis* - the common-sense conjecture that cognitive treatment will be most effective for persons with problems of cognitive anxiety, whereas somatic intervention approaches are more effective with those persons showing critical levels of somatic anxiety). Anxiety may or may not be associated with fearful or stressful stimuli; it is an emotional attitude or sentiment concerning the future, characterized by an unpleasant alternation or mingling of dread and hope. *Anxiety neurosis* is a functional disorder of the nervous system for which no actual lesion is found and whose most prominent symptom is a marked degree of morbid and objectively unfounded dread. Anxiety is distinguished often from fear in that an anxiety state is often objectless, whereas fear assumes a specific feared object, person, or event; and anxiety disorder is a cover term for a variety of maladaptive syndromes that have severe anxiety as the dominant disturbance. *Theories of anxiety* may be classified generally as *psychoanalytic/psychodynamic theories* or as *learning/behavioral theories*. The concept of *anxiety neurosis* was first formulated in a psychoanalytic context in 1894 by Sigmund Freud who thought it to be a result of the discharge of repressed *libido* (accumulated somatic sexual tension). Freud theorized that when libidinal excitation produces threatening sexual wishes, fantasies, or experiences, such mental constructions are repressed, and the blocked libidinal energy subsequently develops into anxiety or somatic symptoms. Freud later reformulated his notion of *anxiety* to relate it to the conflict between the *ego* (reality principle) and the *id* (pleasure principle). The emotion that is experienced during the traumatic state created by the tension between the *ego* and the *id* is called *anxiety*. Freud's development of his *anxiety theory* included a chronological sequence of early sources of anxiety that emphasized the absence of mother, punishments leading to fear of losing parental love, castration fear during the oedipal stage, and disapproval by the *superego* (conscience). In such instances of anxiety, a child may come to fear her or his own instinctual wishes, and the means by which the ego opposes the id's wishes are revealed by the various defense systems that are sent into action by the anxiety. The *defense mechanisms* or systems include: identification, denial, intellectualization, projection, and repression, among others. Other *psychoanalytic/psychodynamic theories of anxiety* are those of Melanie Klein, Rollo May, Harry Stack Sullivan, and Irwin L. Kutash. Klein's theory focuses on the child's fear of death as the basic cause of anxiety. May's theory emphasizes the creation of anxiety as a result of one's value system being threatened. Sullivan's theory examines the unpleasant state of tension that is caused by disapproval involved in interpersonal relationships. Kutash's *anxiety-stress theory* points to the disequilibrium (anxiety) that occurs when one is not experiencing optimal stress levels for one's constitution either in a healthy balance (equilibrium) or in an unhealthy balance (malequilibrium), and where anxiety may be adaptive (when a need to change is indicated by an optimal stress level) or maladaptive (when stress is either too high or too low). *Learning/behavioral theories of anxiety* have been distinguished from the psychodynamic and psychoanalytic theories on the basis of the type of stimuli (proximal versus distal) involved, where proximal cues/stimuli (such as reinforcement in a stimulus-response sequence) are associated with learning and behavioral theory, and the distal cues/stimuli (such as some intrapsychic conflict) are associated with the analytic or dynamic theories. The *learning and behavioral anxiety theories* have been advanced by researchers such as J. B. Watson and R. Rayner, I. Pavlov, A. Wagner and R. Rescorla, O. H. Mowrer, R. Herrnstein, and A. Bandura. This approach is characterized by empirical conditioning studies (rather than personality and clinical studies), and attempts to understand, explain, and treat anxiety by invoking concepts such as reinforcement, punishment, information processing, expectancy, efficacy expectations, fear reduction, discriminative or signaling value of stimuli, predictive value of stimuli, avoidance behavior, successive approximations of desired behavior, incompatible behaviors, cognitive processes, modeling behavior, observational learning, and biofeedback. Various *anti-anxiety* drugs (such as the "sedative-hyp-notics" named Valium and Librium) have been prescribed by physicians for individuals who experience the often overwhelming effects of anxiety. See also FREUD'S THEORY OF PERSONALITY; KLEIN'S THEORY; LEARNING THEORIES/LAWS; LIBIDO THEORY; PUNISHMENT, THEORIES OF; REINFORCEMENT THEORY.

REFERENCES

Freud, S. (1894). On the grounds for detaching a particular syndrome from neurasthenia under the description "anxiety neurosis." In *The standard edition of the complete psychological works of Sigmund Freud*. London: Hogarth Press.

Watson, J. B., & Rayner, R. (1920). Conditioned emotional reactions. *Journal of Experimental Psychology, 3*, 1-14.

Pavlov, I. (1927). *Conditioned reflexes*. New York: Dover.

Freud, S. (1936). *The problem of anxiety*. New York: Norton.

May, R. (1950). *The meaning of anxiety*. New York: Ronald Press.

Klein, M. (1952). On the theory of anxiety and guilt. In J. Riviere (Ed.), *Developments in psychoanalysis*. London: Hogarth Press.

Sullivan, H. S. (1953). *The interpersonal theory of psychiatry*. New York: Norton.

Mowrer, O. H. (1960). *Learning theory and behavior*; and *Learning theory and symbolic processes*. New York: Wiley.

Herrnstein, R. (1969). Method and theory in the study of avoidance. *Psychological Review, 76*, 49-69.

Wagner, A., & Rescorla, R. (1972). Inhibition in Pavlovian conditioning: Applications of a theory. In R. Bokes & M. Halliday (Eds.), *Inhibition and learning*. New York: Academic Press.

Bandura, A. (1977). *Social learning theory*. Englewood Cliffs, NJ: Prentice-Hall.

Kutash, I. L. (1980). Prevention and equilibrium-disequilibrium theory. In I. L. Kutash & L. Schlesinger (Eds.), *Handbook on stress and anxiety*. San Francisco: Jossey-Bass.

ANXIETY-MATCHING HYPOTHESIS. See ANXIETY, THEORIES OF.

ANXIETY-STRESS THEORY. See ANXIETY, THEORIES OF.

APERTURAL HYPOTHESIS. See MCDOUGALL'S HORMIC OR INSTINCT THEORY/DOCTRINE.

APOLLONIAN/DIONYSIAN DISTINCTION. The German philosopher Friedrich Wilhelm Nietzsche (1844-1900) made a theoretical distinction - often employed in psychological discussions of personality and temperament - between the terms *Apollonian* and *Dionysian* in his philosophy where the former term (named after Apollo, the Greek god of light, music, poetry, prophesy and healing) refers to rational, controlled, and serene behavior and relates to static qualities of reason, form, sobriety, and harmony; and the latter term (named after Dionysus, the Greek god of wine and revelry) refers to uncontrolled, wild, sensuous, and spontaneous behavior and relates to dynamic/creative qualities of irrationality, spontaneity, and rejection of discipline. See also PERSONALITY THEORIES.

REFERENCE

Nietzsche, F. W. (1887/1935). *Beyond good and evil*. Chicago: Regency.

A POSTERIORI AND A PRIORI DISTINCTION. Use of the theoretically-related terms *a posteriori* and *a priori* originated with the medieval scholastic philosophers of the 14th and 15th centuries, and were popularized later by the 17th century philosophers Gott-fried Wilhelm von Leibniz (1646-1716) and Rene Descartes (1596-1650). *A posteriori* (Latin for "what comes *after*") refers to propositions, concepts, or arguments that originate in, and progress from, observation or experience ("empiricism"), whereas *a priori* (Latin for "what comes *before*") refers to propositions, concepts, or arguments that originate in, and progress from, theoretical inference or deduction ("rationalism"). Some philosophers (e.g., the British Empiricists John Locke, Bishop George Berkeley, and David Hume) reflect the *a posteriori* orientation, whereas other philosophers (e.g., Plato, and Leibniz) indicate the *a priori* viewpoint in their philosophical systems. Still other philosophers (e.g., the German "idealist" Immanuel Kant) argued that experience and observation (the *a posteriori* approach), in themselves, presuppose an inferential (deductive) type of knowledge base (the *a priori* perspective) Such philosophical distinctions, such as that between the terms *a posteriori* and *a priori*, are reflected in modern theoretical and methodological orientations in psychology. For example, the *a posteriori* orientation is indicated in the experimental psychology of learning where the researcher (e.g., B. F. Skinner) initially collects empirical facts and data that may be used at a later time to describe (inductively developed) hypotheses, whereas the *a priori* orientation is indicated in cases where the researcher (e.g., C. L. Hull) initially forms rational hypotheses as the basis of definitions and principles that have already been set up or assumed. Also, the two terms are reflected in the area of psychological statistics where an *a priori test* is a "planned" statistical procedure used to test for significance of individual comparisons, whereas an *a posteriori test* is an "after-the-fact" statistical procedure ("post hoc test") that is introduced after the data have already been collected and scrutinized. The *a posteriori fallacy* (Reber, 1995) refers to the fallacious conclusion that some event Y was *caused* by some other event X on the grounds that an "after-the-fact" analysis of one's data showed that Y did, indeed, *occur* after X (also called "data snooping" or "fishing expeditions"). However, in fact, such a logical reasoning process only *suggests* that X *actually* may have *caused* Y, and such a retrospective analysis, in itself, is insufficient to make a "cause-effect" conclusion. See also EMPIRICIST VERSUS NATIVIST THEORIES.

REFERENCE

Reber, A. S. (1995). *The Penguin dictionary of psychology*. New York: Penguin Books.

APPARENT MOVEMENT, PRINCIPLES AND THEORIES OF. The phenomenon of *apparent movement* refers to the subjective visual perception of movement in the absence of any real or objective physical motion. Common types of apparent movement include the *phi phenomenon/movement*, the autokinetic effect, and the *aftereffects of seen movement*. Other kinds of apparent movement are *alpha-, beta-, delta-, epsilon-, gamma-, induced-,* and *stroboscopic* movement. The *phi phenomenon/movement* of stroboscopic movement may be observed when two adjacent stimulus lights are flashed in rapid succession. If the interstimulus period is too long, the lights appear to go on and off separately. If the interstimulus period is too short, the lights appear to flash at the same time. When the interstimulus period is about 30-200 milliseconds, however, one gets the sensation of a light moving from one location to another location (stroboscopic movement is the basis for the effect of motion seen on television and motion pictures). The *autokinetic effect* [first described by the German physiologist and psychologist Hermann Aubert (1826-1892)] refers to movement that seems to occur when a stationary object is viewed against a dark or ill-defined background, and where the stationary object appears to move after looking at it for a few minutes. *Aftereffects of seen movement* may occur when an individual stares for a few minutes at some continuous motion of an object in one direction and then shifts the gaze to a different surface (such as looking at a waterfall for a few minutes and then looking away to a textured surface where the surface now appears to be going in the opposite, or upward, direction). *Induced movement* refers to the illusion of movement where a visual frame of reference is actually moving in one direction (such as clouds moving across the moon), and a stationary object (such as the moon) subsequently seems to move in the opposite direction. *Alpha movement* occurs when there appears to be a change of size in parts of a figure that are exposed in succession. *Beta movement* refers to the illusion of movement when differently sized, or positioned, objects are exposed in succession. *Delta movement* is the apparent movement of a light stimulus to a darker stimulus after successive exposure when the variables of stimulus size, distance, and interstimulus interval are controlled. *Epsilon movement* is the visual perception of movement when a white line viewed against a black background is changed so that one now views a black line against a white background. *Gamma movement* refers to the apparent contraction and expansion of a figure that is shown suddenly (or is withdrawn) or a figure that is exposed to sudden illumination changes. Various *theories of apparent movement* have been developed and described, and include the *inference theory* (where one actually sees only the initial and terminal positions and infers that the object must have moved); the *eye-movement theory* (which emphasizes that the eyes objectively move across from the initial stimulus position to the final position, and where eye movement itself contributes to the sensation of motion); and the *brain-field theory* (which suggests that the retina, or the visual cortex, is actually stimulated in the region lying between the initial and the terminal positions of the stimuli). There appears to be no generally accepted *theory of apparent movement* except, perhaps, for the potential development of some future novel theory that would regard perception as a type of response to the incoming sensory stimulation and that subsequently applies the *principle of stimulus generalization* to the ul-timate explanation of movement. Thus, if the stimuli that are received are sufficiently similar to those that were received from real movement, then the perceptual response would likely be the same. C. Graham (1965) suggests that new analyses and investigations in the field of perceptual/apparent movement would lead to needed theoretical improvements. See also ALIASING AND STROBOSCOPIC PHENOM-ENON; GENERALIZATION, PRINCIPLES OF; KORTE'S LAWS; THREE-SYSTEMS THEORY OF MOTION PERCEPTION; VISION/SIGHT, THEORIES OF.

REFERENCES

Vierordt, K. (1876). Die bewegungsempfindung. *Zeitschrift fur Biologisch, 12*, 226-240.

Aubert, H. (1886). Die bewegungsempfindung. *Archiv fur die Gesamte Physiologie, 39*, 347-370.

Wertheimer, M. (1912). Experimentelle studien uber das sehen von bewegung. *Zeitschrift fur Psychologie, 61*, 161-265.

Higginson, G. (1926). The visual apprehension of movement under successive retinal excitations. *American Journal of Psychology, 37*, 63-115.

Guilford, J., & Helson, H. (1929). Eye-movements and the phi phenomenon. *American Journal of Psychology, 41*, 595-606.

Neff, W. (1936). A critical investigation of the visual apprehension of movement. *American Journal of Psychology, 48*, 1-42.

Kolers, P. (1963). Some differences between real and apparent visual movement. *Vision Research, 3*, 191-206.

Graham, C. (1965). Perception of movement. In C. Graham (Ed.), *Vision and visual perception*. New York: Wiley.

APPERCEPTION, DOCTRINE OF. See HERBART'S DOCTRINE OF APPERCEPTION; WUNDT'S THEORIES.

APPRAISAL THEORIES OF EMOTION. See COGNITIVE THEORIES OF EMOTION.

A PRIORI THEORY OF PROBABILITY. See PROBABILITY THEORY/LAWS.

A PRIORISM, DOCTRINE OF. See UN-CONSCIOUS INFERENCE, DOCTRINE OF.

APTE'S THEORY OF HUMOR AND LAUGHTER. In his humor theory, the Asian Indian anthropologist Mahadev L. Apte (1985) examines the influences of social structure, cultural expressions, and behavioral responses on humor. According to Apte, whereas *laughter* and *smiling* are the most overt and direct indicators of the covert humor experience, they differ from *humor* itself in being physiologically and anatomically observable events. In Apte's approach, laughter, besides being linked to humor, appears to express the primordial human emotion of sheer joy. In Apte's terminology, *humor* refers, first, to a cognitive, often unconscious, experience involving *internal* redefinition of "sociocultural reality" and results in a mirthful state of mind; second, to the external sociocultural factors that trigger the cognitive experience; and third, to the pleasure derived from the cognitive experience labeled "humor;" and fourth, to the *external* manifestation of the cognitive experience and the resultant pleasure. *Apte's theory of humor/laughter* explores - by cross-cultural comparisons - the interdependence of humor and sociocultural factors in societies around the world; it also attempts to provide generalizations concerning such cross-cultural studies, and to formulate theoretical propositions regarding the similar and dissimilar ways in which humor is linked to sociocultural variables. See also COMMUNICATION THEORY OF LAUGHTER; HUMOR, THEORIES OF.

REFERENCE

Apte, M. L. (1985). *Humor and laughter: An anthropological approach.* Ithaca, NY: Cornell University Press.

APTER'S REVERSAL THEORY OF HUMOR. The *reversal theory of humor* of the English psychologist Michael J. Apter (1939-) makes the assumption that to experience humor, the person needs to be in a particular "state of mind" (or "metamotivational state") and, if the individual is not already in such a mind-state, then the "comedy" stimulus or material will need to induce it for humor to be manifested. When a person is in the metamotivational state, the greater the arousal in response to humorous material, the more intense is the pleasure or humor that is experienced. *Reversal theory* is an inclusive overarching approach that attempts to show, in this case, where humor fits into a more general structure of emotions and cognitions. One of the basic notions in *reversal theory* (M. J. Apter & K. C. Smith) is that there are a number of pairs of metamotivational or synergistic states that operate whereby one or the other of each pair is always activated during waking life and a switch, or reversal, from one to the other may be manifested under a variety of conditions with the result that individuals tend to switch back and forth between these states during their daily experiences. For example, one of the metamotivational pairs may consist of the "telic" and "paratelic" states where the former refers to a serious, goal-oriented state of mind, and the latter to a more playful state in which the person is involved with the immediate enjoyment of an experience where goals are "excuses" for the current behavior rather than the genuine reason for the behavior. Theoretically, when a person is in the "telic" state, *high* arousal is experienced as *unpleasant* and the accompanying anxiety is avoided, whereas *low* arousal is felt to be *pleasant* and relaxing. In contrast, for a person in the "paratelic" state, *high* arousal is experienced as *pleasant* and exciting, whereas *low* arousal or boredom is *unpleasant*. Typical results of studies employing the "telic-paratelic" dimension indicate that humorous material tends to induce the "paratelic" state - even in "telic state dominant" persons; and frequency of laughter in the "paratelic" state is correlated positively with the variables of degree of perceived arousal and arousal preference - which confirms a linear, rather than a ditonic, relation of hedonic tone to perceived arousal in the "paratelic" state. See also AROUSAL THEORY; HEDONISM, THEORY/LAW OF; HUMOR, THEORIES OF; PLEASURE-PAIN, DOCTRINE OF.

REFERENCES

Apter, M. J., & Smith, K. C. (1979). Psychological reversals: Some new perspectives on the family and family communication. *Family Therapy*, *6*, 89-100.

Apter, M. J. (1982). *The experience of motivation: The theory of psychological reversals*. London: Academic Press.

Svebak, S., & Apter, M. J. (1987). Laughter: An empirical test of some reversal theory hypotheses. *Scandinavian Journal of Psychology*, *28*, 189-198.

Apter, M. J. (Ed.) (2001). *Motivational styles in everyday life: A guide to reversal theory*. Washington, D.C.: American Psychological Association.

ARAGO PHENOMENON. See VISION AND SIGHT, THEORIES OF.

ARCHITECTURAL DETERMINISM. See DETERMINISM, DOCTRINE/THEORY OF.

ARISTOCRACY THEORY. See CONSTRUCTIVISM, THEORIES OF.

ARISTOTLE'S DOCTRINES/THEORIES. The Greek philosopher Aristotle (384-322 B.C.) was a student in Plato's Academy in Athens, where he was schooled in the *theory of ideas* (cf., Ackermann, 1965). Aristotle argued that man is a rational animal endowed with an innate capacity for attaining knowledge from sense perception and "memory-associations," and that knowledge is the result of deduction of universals and principles from perceptual information and not the recovering of innate ideas, as Plato taught. Aristotle's *empirical* methodology parallels his psychological theory when he advocated the use of close observation and accurate classification of natural phenomena; he also formalized a system of deductive propositional logic. The term *Aristotelian* is used to indicate the principle of careful deduction of scientific or personal knowledge from systematic observation of natural events. Aristotle's work exerted a powerful influence on medieval philosophy (especially through St. Thomas Aquinas), on Islamic philosophy, and on the whole Western intellectual and scientific tradition. In the Middle Ages, Aristotle was referred to simply as "the Philosopher," and the uncritical and almost religious acceptance of his doctrines was to hamper the progress of science until the scientific revolution of the 16th and 17th centuries. Aristotle's writings represent an enormous encyclopedic output over virtually every field of knowledge: logic, metaphysics, ethics, politics, rhetoric, poetry, biology, zoology, physics, and psychology. See also ASSOCIATION, LAWS/PRINCIPLES OF; HEDONISM, THEORY/LAW OF; LEARNING THEORIES/LAWS; PLEASURE-PAIN, DOCTRINE/THEORY/LAW OF.

REFERENCES

Aristotle. (1941). De anima (On the soul); De memoria et reminiscentia (On memory and reminiscence). In R. McKeon (Ed.), *The basic works of Aristotle*. New York: Random House.

Ackermann, R. (1965). *Theories of knowledge*. New York: McGraw-Hill.

ARISTOTLE'S ILLUSION AND EXPERIMENT. See APPENDIX A.

ARISTOTLE'S THEORY OF HUMOR. The Greek philosopher Aristotle advanced a theory of humor and laughter (which may be called the *"not-too-tragic-defect" theory*) that is consistent with Plato's earlier proposition that laughter basically involves malice, derisiveness, and ridicule, and that when we are amused by someone we essentially see that person as "inferior" to us in some way. Such *derisive theories* as enunciated by Plato and Aristotle have been categorized as *superiority theories of humor* where humor depends, theoretically, on a comparative sense of one's own superiority, or at least on a sense of the inferiority of other people. Thus, our personal amusement and elation is increased when we implicitly compare ourselves favorably to others, and where we appear to be less ugly, less weak, less stupid, or less unfortunate than someone else. The concepts and behaviors of ridicule, mockery, and laughter over the foolish actions of others are central to the *superiority theories of humor*. In his *Poetics*, Aristotle suggests that the "ludicrous" is merely a subdivision of the ugly where such a defect is not too painful or destructive - much like a comic mask that is ugly and distorted but does not cause pain. Aristotle makes a literary distinction between the *ludicrous* (e.g., when characters of a lower moral order are depicted) and *tragedy* (e.g., when characters are depicted as better than they are in real life and their imperfections are explored). Although Aristotle essentially subscribed to Plato's assumption that malice is basic to laughter, he also enlarged the scope of the issue by differentiating between comedy and irony directed at individuals. Aristotle also introduced the phenomenon of "aesthetics" in laughter where he maintained that the malicious element, though indispensable to laughter, is undesirable from an aesthetic viewpoint. Aristotle did not agree completely with Plato's recommendation that one should generally suppress laughter, but he did suggest that most people overdo joking and laughing. Consistent with Aristotle's general philosophical position, the moral ideal ("golden mean") is to avoid the extremes: that of the humorless boor on one end and the overzealous buffoon on the other end. According to Aristotle, the ideal demeanor is to be ready-witted but tactful. In addition to his theory of laughter as derision, Aristotle anticipated the later *incongruity theories of humor* that state that laughter is a reaction to many kinds of incongruity or inconsistency and not just to human shortcomings. For instance, in his *Rhetorica*, Aristotle asserts that a speaker may get a laugh by setting up a certain expectation in the audience, and then jolting them suddenly ("surprise") with something they did not expect. As John Cleese of *Monty Python's Flying Circus* puts it, "And now for something completely different." See also HUMOR, THEORIES OF; MORREALL'S THEORY OF HUMOR; PLATO'S THEORY OF HUMOR.

REFERENCES

Aristotle. (1895). The Poetics. In S. H. Butcher (Ed./Translator), *Aristotle's theory of poetry and fine art*. New York: Macmillan.

Cooper, L. (1922). *An Aristotelian theory of comedy*. New York: Harcourt.

Ross, W. D. (ed.) (1931) *The works of Aristotle translated into English*. Oxford, UK: Clarendon Press.

ARISTOTLE'S TIME THEORY AND PARADOX. The Greek philosopher Aristotle was the first to ask in a formal manner *how* we perceive *time*. In discussing time, Aristotle asserted that motion can be uniform or nonuniform and such concepts, themselves, are defined by time, whereas time cannot be defined by itself. Although time is not identical to motion, it seemed to Aristotle to be dependent on motion. Aristotle argued that time is a kind of "number" where time becomes a numbering process that is founded on one's perception of "before" and "after" in motion. In psychological terms, according to Aristotle, time is an immediate (central) sense-percep-tion of the "number of motion" (and where *time-perception* is a direct *sense-perception*); he regarded time and motion as reciprocal entities, but he recognized, also, that motion can cease (aside from the unceasing continuity and motion of the heavens) but time cannot cease. The factors of motion, time, and magnitude all go together in Aristotle's view and he refers to time as the number of the local movement in which the "now" is carried along (like a moving point in space) as the fundamental generating unit. Thus, Aristotle held that the "now" is, in one sense, always the same, whereas in another sense (as it occupies different positions in the series) it is always different. In the identity of the "now," Aristotle finds the ground of the self-identity of time taken as a whole and, although relative to motion, time is always changing. *Aristotle's time paradox*, then, may be stated as follows: we apprehend time only when we have marked motion, and not only do we measure the movement by the time, but also the time by the movement, because they define each other. When Aristotle attempts to explain the nature and cause of motion, however, his approach runs into difficulty. He accepted the idea that any moving body has a natural tendency to come to a resting position, and nothing moves of itself, but something must be causing it to move. Only later did philosophers and scholars take the theoretical step of adding the motion-related idea of "velocity" into the discussion and, thereby, invoke the concept of *time*. Thus, a moving object simply changes its position in space, and *velocity* is defined as how much an object's position changes in a given amount of *time* (e.g., "feet per second;" "miles per hour"). See also EARLY GREEK AND LATER PHILOSOPHICAL THEORIES OF TIME; FRAISSE'S THEORY OF TIME; GUYAU'S THEORY OF TIME; PLOTINUS' THEORY OF TIME;

ST. AUGUSTINE'S PARADOX OF TIME; TIME, THEORIES OF.

REFERENCES

Nichols, H. (1891). The psychology of time. *American Journal of Psychology*, 3, 453-529.

Goudsmit, S., & Claiborne, R. (1980). *Time*. Alexandria, VA: Time-Life Books.

Inwood, M. (1991). Aristotle on the reality of time. In L. Judson (Ed.), *Aristotle's Physics*. Oxford, UK: Clarendon.

ARNOLD'S THEORY OF EMOTIONS. The American psychologist Magda B. Arnold's (1903-2002) *theory of emotions* emphasizes the cognitive factors associated with emotional behavior that involves a continuous sequence of reaction and appraisal where a series of information-processing steps takes place. In the first phase of processing, the person typically *perceives* some event, object, or person and is prepared to evaluate it in a particular way: as "good," which leads to approach behavior, as "bad," which leads to avoidance behavior, or as "indifferent," which leads to ignoring the event. The next phase is *appraisal*, where the person decides whether what is happening will hurt, help, or have no effect on her or him. The third and fourth phases are *bodily change* and *emotion*, both of which typically occur at almost the same time. Phase five is *action*; some individuals in certain situations skip from the bodily changes in stage three and go directly to stage five. For example, if a strange dog comes running toward you with its teeth bared, you take rapid action and run away without thinking (as epinephrine rushes into your system). When you reach safety, you become aware of your heart pounding and, at that time, you experience the emotion of *fear*. Arnold's theory assumes that the entire appraisal sequence takes place in an instant. Arnold distinguishes among a few basic emotions that are simple reactions to the appraisal of basic situations: dislike, love (liking), aversion, despair, desire, anger, fear, hope, daring, sorrow, and joy. *Arnold's theory* stresses that the intuitive, spontaneous appraisal in an emotional episode is supplemented by a deliberate value judgment, especially in adults, and it functions in the same way that one's sensory knowledge is complemented by cognitions. According to *Arnold's cognitive theory*, emotions can be socialized where social attitudes and customs influence one's intuitive appraisal of events, and where *affective memory* preserves one's previous encounters with intense emotion-arousing stimuli. *Affective memory* may account for many of the "instinctive" feelings one experiences, such as immediate dislikes or likes for something or someone, reactions to fearful stimuli that later become phobias, prejudice connected with unresolved and unpleasant situations from the past, and even "love at first sight." See also COGNITIVE THEORIES OF EMOTIONS; EMOTIONS, THEORIES AND LAWS OF; LAZARUS' THEORY OF EMOTIONS; SCHACHTER-SINGER'S THEORY OF EMOTIONS.

REFERENCES

Arnold, M. B. (1960). *Emotion and personality*. New York: Columbia University Press.

Arnold, M. B. (1970). *Feelings and emotions: The Loyola Symposium*. New York: Academic Press.

Arnold, M. B. (1984). *Memory and the brain*. Hillsdale, NJ: Erlbaum.

AROUSAL-CHANGE HYPOTHESIS OF HUMOR. See BEHAVIORAL THEORIES OF HUMOR/LAUGHTER.

AROUSAL-COGNITIVE THEORIES OF EMOTION. See COGNITIVE THEORIES OF EMOTIONS.

AROUSAL THEORY. See ACTIVATION/AROUSAL THEORY.

ARPEGGIO PARADOX. See AUDITION/HEARING, THEORIES OF.

ARROW'S PARADOX/IMPOSSIBILITY THEOREM. The American economist Kenneth J. Arrow (1921-) formulated this theorem showing that no social-choice (e.g., a voting system) function can guarantee to aggregate the individual preferences of a social group into a collective preference ranking so as to satisfy the following four "criteria of fairness": an ordering is always produced; universally-shared preferences are reflected; the outcome does not depend on preferences for irrelevant options; and each individual can influence the outcome (i.e., "non-dictator-ship"). Thus, *Arrow's impossibility theorem* refers to the modeling of any democratic process where one would like a fixed procedure for "aggregating" the preferences of a group of individuals into an overall ordering; and Arrow's result shows that this is not possible, in general, for a group larger than two individuals if the procedure is required to fulfill these four "criteria of fairness." The proof of *Arrow's paradox* rests on the profile of individual preferences invoking "Condorcet's paradox of intransitive preferences" - named after the French philosopher and mathematician Marie Antoine Condorcet (1743-1794) who enunciated it in 1785 - which deals with the complexity of voting and choices, by which a final choice is made by the rejection of all other alternatives in a series of paired contests; Condorcet noted that majority voting is the best voting rule/system when only two people can vote. *Arrow's paradox* shows that any social-choice function that satisfies the first three "criteria of fairness" necessarily violates the fourth criterion and, as a consequence, results in a "dictatorial" situation or outcome. See also DECISION-MAKING THEORIES; EXCHANGE AND SOCIAL EXCHANGE THEORY.

REFERENCE

Arrow, K. J. (1951). Alternative approaches to the theory of choice in risk-taking situations. *Econometrica, 19,* 417-426.

ARTIFICIAL INTELLIGENCE. See CELLULAR AUTOMATON MODEL.

ASCH CONFORMITY EFFECT. The American social psychologist Solomon E. Asch (1907-1996) conducted a series of experiments where American college students were asked to make judgments about the length of vertical lines. Seven male students made these simple judgments out loud, one by one, in a group setting, but the sixth student in the sequence was the only true participant or subject. The other students were Asch's accomplices (called *confederates*) and, without the true subject's knowledge, on many trials they all deliberately made the same incorrect guess. Asch's results showed that even in this simple judgment task, only about one-fourth of the subjects completely resisted the confederates' answers and made no errors. Other subjects followed the unanimous, but incorrect, opinion on every trial, showing complete acquiescence to the group's pressure (cf., the *bandwagon effect/technique* - the tendency for people, in political and social situations, to align themselves or their opinions with the perceived majority's opinions). In later debriefing sessions, the subjects greatly under-estimated their degree of *conformity*. Similar experiments with French, Norwegian, Arabian, and British students supported Asch's findings with American subjects. The *Asch effect*, then, refers to the powerful influence of a unanimous group and its decisions on the behavior of an individual that results in *conformity* to that group. *Conformity*, for better or worse, is defined as the tendency for people to adopt the behaviors, attitudes, and values of other members of a reference group. In subsequent studies, group size and group unanimity turned out to be key determinants of *conformity*. The factor of gender, however, does not seem to be a distinguishing factor in *conformity*. Some mixed results have appeared in recent years concerning Asch's paradigm and make the *Asch effect* a topic of continued interest in current psychology. See also BYSTANDER INTERVENTION EFFECT; DECISION-MAKING THEORIES; DEINDIVIDUATION THEORY; GROUPTHINK PHENOMENON.

REFERENCES

Asch, S. (1940). Studies in the principles of judgments and attitudes. II. Determination of judgments by group and by ego standards. *Journal of Social Psychology, 12,* 433-465.

Asch, S. (1951). Effects of group pressure upon the modification and distortion of judgment. In H. Guetzkow (Ed.), *Groups, leadership, and men.* Pittsburgh: Carnegie.

Asch, S. (1956). Studies of independence and conformity. I. A minority of one against a unanimous majority. *Psychological Monographs, 70,* No. 416.

ASHBY'S LAW OF REQUISITE VARIETY. See INFORMATION AND INFORMATION-PROCESSING THEORY.

AS-IF HYPOTHESIS. See PERSONALITY THEORIES.

ASSIMILATION EFFECT. See ASSIMILATION, LAW OF.

ASSIMILATION, LAW OF. The once versatile term *assimilation* appears largely to be obsolete, as judged by its infrequent use by writers of psychology textbooks today, although it does find modern resuscitation in terms such as *generalization* and *analogy*. The *law of assimilation* states that when an individual is in a new situation, he will behave in a way that is similar to the way he did in similar circumstances in the past (cf., *assimilation effect* - as shift in judgment toward an anchor, or reference standard, after it is introduced in a study). R. Woodworth and H. Schlosberg consider the term *assimilation* to be under the rubric of *theory* rather than of *law*. C. Hovland, however, refers to the *law* of assimilation. J. Piaget employs the term *assimilation* as a working descriptive term in his study of the development of intellectual competence in children, where *assimilation* is a functional mechanism that preserves cognitive structure and promotes integration and similarity between the elements/content of the structure. The term *assimilation* itself was introduced into psychology by O. Lauenstein in 1933, who was a student of the German-born American psychologist Wolfgang Kohler. In psychophysical experiments on hearing, where standard stimuli were studied against interpolated stimuli, Lauenstein obtained results on loudness showing that participants "assimilated" or integrated standard stimulus "traces" toward an interpolated stimulus in such a way that assimilation occurred *upward* toward a *loud* interpolated stimulus but *downward* toward a *soft* one. In human learning/memory contexts, the term *assimilation* has been characterized as a "law." The *law of assimilation*, according to H. Carr, states that each new stimulating condition tends to elicit the response that has been connected with similar stimulating conditions in the past. Terms related to *assimilation* in a learning/retention context are *associative interference* (occurs when learning of a new association is made more *difficult* because of a prior association) and *associative facilitation*

(occurs when learning of a new association is made *easier* due to a prior association). More modern substitutes for these latter two terms in the current vocabulary of psychologists are *negative transfer of training* and *positive transfer of training*, respectively. See also ASSOCIATION, LAWS/PRINCIPLES OF; GENERALIZATION, PRINCIPLE OF; PIAGET'S THEORY OF DEVELOPMENTAL STAGES; TRANSFER OF TRAINING, THORNDIKE'S THEORY OF.

REFERENCES

Carr, H. (1925). *Psychology: A study of mental activity*. New York: Longmans, Green.

Yum, L. (1931). An experimental test of the law of assimilation. *Journal of Experimental Psychology, 14*, 68-82.

Lauenstein, O. (1933). Ansatz zu einer physiologischen theorie des vergleichs und der zeitfehler. *Psychologische Forschung, 17*, 130-177.

Hovland, C. (1951). Human learning and retention. In S. S. Stevens (Ed.), *Handbook of Experimental Psychology*. New York: Wiley.

Piaget, J. (1963). *The origins of intelligence in children*. New York: Norton.

Woodworth, R., & Schlosberg, H. (1965). *Experimental psychology*. New York: Holt, Rinehart, & Winston.

ASSIMILATION-CONTRAST THEORY AND EFFECT. This theory of attitude change and judgment was developed by the Turkish psychologist Muzafer Sherif (1906-1988) and the American psychologist Carl Hovland (1912-1961), and posits that one's initial attitude/judgment acts as an anchor in a manner where items of information (e.g., new persuasive communications) that are not very discrepant from the anchor - and that fall within the individual's "latitude of acceptance" - are assimilated. In such a case, the person's attitude/judgment changes in the direction of the new communication. However, in cases where there are highly discrepant items of information, either minimal change is produced (if they fall within the person's "latitude of neutrality") or contrast effects are produced (if they fall within the person's "latitude of rejection"), and the person's attitude/judgment changes in the opposite direction (called the *boomerang effect*). The variable of "ego involvement" operates in these situations such that attitudes associated with *high* ego involvement tend to have narrow "latitudes of acceptance" and wide "latitudes of rejection," whereas the opposite is true concerning attitudes having *low* ego involvement. This theory of "discrepancy effects" predicts that an extreme and ego-involving attitude/judgment will be polarized and become even more extreme in response to most types of information and/or persuasive communications. See also ATTITUDE AND ATTITUDE CHANGE, THEORIES OF; BOOMERANG EFFECT; FALSE-CONSENSUS EFFECT; INGROUP BIAS THEORIES; ORGANIZATIONAL, INDUSTRIAL, AND SYSTEMS THEORY; PERSUASION AND INFLUENCE THEORIES.

REFERENCE

Sherif, M., & Hovland, C. I. (1961). *Social judgment: Assimilation and contrast effects in communication and attitude change.* New Haven, CT: Yale University Press.

ASSIMILATIVE ILLUSION. See APPENDIX A.

ASSOCIATED SPECIFICITY THEORY. See PSYCHOSOMATICS THEORY.

ASSOCIATION, LAWS/PRINCIPLES OF. = association, doctrine of = associationism = connectionism. The term *association* referred originally to an association of ideas and was used by the early Greeks in their philosophies. For example, Empedocles (495-435 B.C.) taught that the process of thinking is the creation and destruction of percepts that takes place in the churning of blood in the heart after being carried from the sense organs by the bloodstream; Plato (427-347 B.C.) posited a *learning theory* based on association where recollection of similar ideas was emphasized; Aristotle (384-322 B.C.) observed that when a person thinks of something, it reminds that person of something else, where one idea leads to another idea in a manner that the two ideas have some kind of relation, connection, or association. Aristotle proposed in his essays on memory that three "relations" exist between ele-

ments that lead to associations: *contiguity, similarity,* and *contrast.* Thomas Hobbes (1588-1679) was the first to suggest that Aristotle's "relations" could serve as an associationistic model of human cognition. Later, John Locke (1632-1704) coined the phrase *association of ideas,* and regarded associations as interruptions to rational ways of thinking. Other 18th and 19th century philosophers transformed the notion of the association of ideas into the systematic viewpoint called *associationism.* Chief among the British empiricists or "associationistic" philosophers were George Berkeley (1685-1753), David Hume (1711-1776), David Hartley (1705-1757), James Mill (1773-1836), John Stuart Mill (1806-1873), Alexander Bain (1818-1903), and Thomas Brown (1778-1820). Hume reduced the mind to the association of ideas and maintained that the mind contains either perceptions or their copies ("ideas"), and ideas are glued together by two *laws of association: similarity* and *contiguity.* Hartley is usually recognized as the founder of *psychological associationism,* and he speculated, also, on *physiological laws of association* between nerve vibrations to explain the *mental laws of association.* The *principle of associative learning* was refined further by the Mills and Bain, who developed a type of psychological associationism that made the association of ideas the central process of acting and thinking. For this initial philosophical context, the *principle of association* moved toward an empirically researchable form as developed by Thomas Brown in his *secondary laws of association: duration, liveliness, frequency,* and *recency.* These first four of Brown's secondary laws, perhaps, have the most vital significance for associationism. The other secondary laws include the concepts of "fewer alternative associates," "constitutional differences," "variations in the same individual," "diversities of state," and "habits of life." Brown's terminological approach permitted casting the general laws of "suggestion" into a form that contained the concepts of the relative recency, frequency, and liveliness of particular experiences. Brown's emphasis on emotional and constitutional factors was significant, also, and contrasted with the associationists' usual neglect of individual differences. Of the three primary *principles/laws of association* (contiguity, similarity, and contrast), the *principle of contiguity* was the most popular among the early writers, including Aristotle, Hobbes, Locke, Berkeley, Hume, Hartley, J. Mill, J. S. Mill, Bain, and Spencer. At one time the notion of *association* was characterized as "mental mechanics" (James Mill) and "mental chemistry" (J. S. Mill), in which simple ideas could be linked to form more complex ideas. The decomposition of mental life into elements (simple ideas) and the compounding of these elements to form complex ideas subsequently formed the core of the new scientific psychology. Historically, it is noteworthy also, in the advancement of *associationism*, to take account of the systematic research based on associationistic principles that was conducted by Hermann von Ebbinghaus (1850-1909), Ivan Pavlov (1849-1936), and Edward L. Thorndike (1874-1949). Ebbinghaus constructed lists of "nonsense syllables" as learning material and used himself over many years as participant/subject ("n=1") in his memory studies. He found that the more times he repeated a list of syllables, the better his memory of it, thus supporting Brown's *law of frequency*. Ebbinghaus was able to show, also, that memory is influenced by such factors as the number of syllables on the list, and the time between learning the list and having to recall the syllables (*law of recency*). Such factors are still studied today in memory research. Ivan Pavlov, the Russian physiologist, is credited - along with Vladimir Bekhterev (1857-1927) - for shifting the kind of association studied from philosophical "ideas" to laboratory-based "stimulus-response connections." Pavlov's (and Bekhterev's) prior research on the *conditioned reflex* helped to objectify psychology as well as strengthen the concept of *association*. E. L. Thorndike had developed the most complete account, up to that time, of psychological phenomena along associationistic lines (his approach is called *connectionism*), and his system was considered to be the most appropriate representative of *associationism* in psychology. More recently, in the 20th century, and under the influence of the *behavioristic* viewpoint, the *laws of association* became the *laws of learning*, the *law of frequency* became the gradually rising "learning curve," the *law of similarity* became the "generalization gradi-

ent," and the *law of contiguity* became the temporal relationship between "unconditioned" and "conditioned" stimuli. Currently, the 18th century association concepts have been revived somewhat with the advent and development of the field of *cognitive psychology*, which considers memory to be an associative network of ideas that are embedded in a complex information-processing system. In its historical evolution, the *principle of association* was challenged by various psychologists, in particular by the Gestalt psychologists who renounced it completely. However, many *associative laws* were developed during the history of the *doctrine of associationism*, and these principles have been used often as hypotheses or as explanatory concepts in psychology. Perhaps the most popular principle has been *temporal contiguity* (where things that occur close together in time tend to become associated with each other). The other surviving *associative laws* deriving mainly from Aristotle's "relations" and Brown's "secondary laws" are *vividness*, *clearness*, or *intensity* (the more vivid, lively, or intense the experience, the stronger the associative bond); *frequency*, or *repetition* [things that occur repeatedly together tend to become associated with each other; cf., *Marbe's law* - named after the German psychologist Karl Marbe (1869-1953), and also called the *Marbe-Thumb law* - which is the generalization that in word association tasks the more *frequently* a response occurs, the more *rapidly* it tends to occur, and where *latency* is inversely related to *frequency*]; *recency* (associations that are formed recently are easiest to recall); *similarity* or *resemblance* (aspects of ideas, sensations, or movements that are similar tend to become associated with each other); and *contrast* (when two contrary or opposing sensations or other mental data are juxtaposed, the contrary characteristics are intensified, where given the idea of one, the idea of its opposite tends to be recalled). William James (1890) refers to a *law of dissociation by varying concomitants* as something that is associated now with one thing and now with another and tends to become dissociated from either, and to grow into an object of abstract contemplation of the mind. The difficulty with the *associative laws*, even though they may be quite valid generally, is that all too often they have been expected to assume an explanatory role far beyond their capacities. For instance, the *principle of contiguity* has been valuable in the area of *learning theory*, but it cannot account for all mental experiences and events, many of which have emotional or motivational aspects. Also, in recent years, the concept of *associationism* may have lost some of its explanatory power in the fields of cognition, perception, psycholinguistics, and developmental psychology because of the feeling that most mental or cognitive processes are too complex to submit to an analysis based simply on associative connections. Nevertheless, the *doctrine of the association of ideas* and the concept of *association*, along with their various laws and principles, have shown themselves to be some of the most durable of psychological concepts, having maintained an unbroken record of influence for over 2,000 years from Plato to the present (cf., consistent citation of the *association* concept in psychology for more than 112 years; Roeckelein, 1996). See also GESTALT THEORY/LAWS; GUTHRIE'S THEORY OF BEHAVIOR; HULL'S LEARNING THEORY; LEARNING THEORIES AND LAWS; THORN-DIKE'S LAW OF EFFECT; TOLMAN'S THEORY.

REFERENCES

Locke, J. (1700). *Essay concerning human understanding*. London: Dent.

Ebbinghaus, H. von (1885). *Uber das gedachtnis*. Liepzig: Duncker.

James, W. (1890). *The principles of psychology*. New York: Holt.

Thorndike, E. L. (1898). *Animal intelligence*. New York: Macmillan.

Bekhterev, V. (1913). *Objektive psychologie: Oder psychoreflexologie, die lehre von den assoziationsreflexen*. Leipzig: Teubner.

Watson, J. B. (1919). *Psychology from the standpoint of a behaviorist*. Philadelphia: Lippincott.

Warren, H. (1921). *A history of the association psychology*. New York: Scribners.

Pavlov, I. (1927). *Conditioned reflexes*. New York: Dover.

Carr, H. A. (1931). The laws of association. *Psychological Review, 38*, 212-228.

Robinson, E. (1932). *Association theory today*. New York: Appleton-Century-Crofts.

McKeon, R. (Ed.) (1941). *The basic works of Aristotle: De anima; De memoria et reminiscentia*. New York: Random House.

Anderson, J., & Bower, G. (1973). *Human associative memory*. Washington, D. C.: Winston.

Rapaport, D. (1974). *The history of the concept of association of ideas*. New York: International Universities Press.

Roeckelein, J. E. (1996). Citation of *laws* and *theories* in textbooks across 112 years of psychology. *Psychological Reports, 79*, 979-998.

ASSOCIATION/SENSATION (A/S) RATIO. See EMOTIONAL INTELLIGENCE, THEORY OF.

ASSOCIATIVE CHAIN THEORY. See SKINNER'S OPERANT CONDITIONING THEORY.

ASSOCIATIVE/CONTIGUITY THEORY. See GUTHRIE'S THEORY OF BEHAVIOR; REINFORCEMENT THEORY.

ASSOCIATIVE FACILITATION AND INTERFERENCE EFFECTS. See ASSIMILATION, LAW OF.

ASSOCIATIVE/GEOMETRIC ILLUSION. See APPENDIX A.

ASSOCIATIVE LEARNING, PRINCIPLE OF. See ASSOCIATION, LAWS AND PRINCIPLES OF.

ASSOCIATIVE LEARNING IN ANIMALS, THEORIES OF. In general, *associative learning theories* are concerned with the factors that determine association formation when two stimuli are presented together in an experimental or conditioning setting. In *classical conditioning*, the focus is on the associations formed between "conditioned stimuli" (CS) and "unconditioned stimuli" (US), whereas in *operant conditioning*, the emphasis is on the associations formed between "responses" and "reinforcers." Among the *theories of associative learning*, some accentuate the role of attention in association formation, but differ in the rules proposed for determining whether or not attention is paid to a stimulus. Other theories examine the nature of the association that is formed, but differ as to whether the association is regarded as configural, elemental, or hierarchical. The *first* theory of associative learning in animals was formulated in 1898 by E. L. Thorndike who argued that learning consists of the formation of connections between stimuli and responses, and such connections are created whenever a response is followed by a "satisfier/reward." Thorndike's *connectionism theory* refers to his interpretation of "trial-and-error" learning regarding the formation of associations between stimuli or situations (*not* "ideas") and responses; and this formed the basis of several subsequent *associative learning theories* (e.g., C. L. Hull's learning theory) - all of which shared the assumption that learning is based on the growth of stimulus-response connections. While stimulus-response connections are still thought to play an important role in learning and behavior, *theories of associative learning* since about 1970 have focused more on "stimulus-stimulus" (e.g., I. Pavlov's conditioning theory) than on "stimulus-response" connections. In emphasizing the importance of the "stimulus-stimulus" connections in learning, recent experiments show that the CS is able to activate a representation/memory of the US with which it has been paired. The most *influential* theory of associative learning was proposed by R. A. Rescorla and A. R. Wagner in 1972 and there appears to be no sign of decline in interest in this theory - even though the *Rescorla-Wagner model/theory* has not gone unchallenged. The most important feature of this theory is the assumption that the change in associative strength of a stimulus on any trial is determined by the discrepancy between the magnitude of the US and the sum of the associative strengths of all the stimuli present on the trial in question. In previous theories (cf., Bush & Mosteller, 1955), the degree of learning about a stimulus was determined by the discrepancy between the asymptote for conditioning and the associative strength of the stimulus by itself. Much of the attraction of the Rescorla-Wagner theory for experimental psychologists may be attributed to the successful predictions it makes regarding such stimulus-selection effects as "blocking" and to the account it offers of "inhibitory conditioning." Still lacking, however, are theoretical analyses concerning "absent stimuli" (such as "biological significance" of the stimulus) presumed to be involved in the experimental paradigms and procedures. In generalizing results from animal-learning experiments to human-learning contexts, there are two relatively recent research areas in which *theories of associative learning in animals* are relevant to human learning: *causality judgment* (persons making judgments about "cause-effect" relationships; according to *contingency-based theories*, individuals make such judgments on the basis of a mental "statistical computation;" according to principles in *theories of associative learning*, such causal judgments are made on a "trial-by-trial" basis where causes are believed to be associated with effects in the same way as a CS becomes associated with an US); and *categorization* (persons assessing whether a given stimulus belongs to a particular class from among several possible classes; according to the *Rescorla-Wagner theory*, individuals may take features of "exemplars" and associate them with categories in the same way that a CS is associated with an US). Two weaknesses of the current *theories of associative learning* (especially the *Rescorla-Wagner theory*), however, are that they say relatively little about how associations, once formed, are manifested in the *behaving* organism; and how the important variable of *time/timing* (e.g., if, when, and how, the organism responds during acquisition and extinction processes) relates to associative-learning analyses and principles. See also BEHAVIORAL THEORY OF TIMING; BLOCKING, PHENOMENON OF; HULL'S LEARNING THEORY; PAVLOV-IAN CONDITIONING PRINCIPLES, RESCORLA-WAGNER THEORY; SKINNER'S OPERANT CONDITIONING THEORY; EFFECT, LAW OF; REINFORCEMENT, THORNDIKE'S THEORY OF.

REFERENCES

Bush, R. R., & Mosteller, E. (1955). *Stochastic models for learning*. New York: Wiley.

Pearce, J. M., & Bouton, M. E. (2001). Theories of associative learning in animals. *Annual Review of Psychology, 52*, 111-139.

ASSOCIATIVE SHIFTING, LAW OF. This is one of E. L. Thorndike's (1874-1949) minor subsidiary laws to his *law of effect* that is similar to Ivan Pavlov's *principle of stimulus association* and also bears some resemblance to the conditioning *principle of generalization*. The *law of associative shifting* states that when two stimuli are present and one elicits a response, the other takes on the ability to elicit the same response. This law became a central axiom to E. R. Guthrie's *contiguity learning theory*. Thorndike considered the general aspects of conditioning to be akin to *associative shifting* where the occurrence of a "trial-and-error" process may not be necessary. An example of *associative shifting* is the learning by a child to come to you when you call her name using different variations (e.g., differences in tone, pronunciation, intensity, inflection, etc.) of the name (and you subsequently hug the child). According to Thorn-dike, the ancillary concepts of *belongingness* and *satisfaction* operate in *associative shifting*, but other scientists (e.g., Pavlov, 1927) regarded the *time* relations between the stimulus-response event to be solely adequate for establishing conditioned responses. See also ASSOCIATIVE LEARNING IN ANIMALS, THEORIES OF; BELONGINGNESS, LAW OF; EFFECT, LAW OF; GENERALIZATION, PRINCIPLE OF; GUTHRIE'S THEORY OF BEHAVIOR; PAVLOVIAN CONDITIONING PRINCIPLES/LAWS; TRANSFER OF TRAINING, THORNDIKE'S THE-ORY OF.

REFERENCES
Pavlov, I. (1927). *Conditioned reflexes.* New York: Oxford University Press.
Thorndike, E. L. (1932). *The fundamentals of learning.* New York: Teachers College, Columbia University.

ASSUMED SIMILARITY BIAS EFFECT. See LOVE, THEORIES OF.

ASTONISHING HYPOTHESIS. This speculation made in 1994 by the English molecular biologist Francis Harry Compton Crick (1916-) - who earlier in 1953, along with the work of the American biologist James Watson (1928-), the English biophysicist Rosalind E. Franklin (1920-1958), and the New Zealand-born biophysicist Maurice H. F. Wilkins (1916-), is credited (via a Nobel Prize in 1962) with the discovery of the molecular structure of DNA (two spirals of helixes, the "double helix," coiled around a single axis with complementary base pairings between the strands) - refers to the *reductionistic* notion (i.e., the viewpoint that neurological and biochemical factors ultimately underlie all behavior and experience) that an individual's mental experiences may be entirely explained by the behavior of neurons, glial cells, and the microstructures such as atoms, ions, and molecules that comprise and govern them. See also CELL ASSEMBLY THEORY; HEBB'S THEORY OF PERCEPTUAL LEARNING; MIND-BODY THEORIES.

REFERENCE
Crick, F. H. C. (1994). *Astonishing hypothesis: The scientific search for the soul.* New York: Scribners.

ASTROLOGY, THEORY OF. This tenacious, and unsubstantiated, theory is based on the belief that celestial bodies, in particular, the stars, have an influence on human behavior and personality (cf., *Barnum effect*). Historically, *astrology* is primitive *astronomy* but, whereas the latter is now a legitimate scientific endeavor, the former is considered as a "pseudoscience" founded in the notion that the positions of the moon, sun, and stars affect human affairs, and that one can foretell the future by studying the stars. The name "Chaldeans" (late Babylonians, c. 1000 B.C.) came to mean "astrologer" among the early biblical writers (cf., Daniel 2: 2, 10) and the early Romans. The earliest astronomers were priests, and no attempt was made in those days to separate *astronomy* from the pseudoscience of *astrology*. Today, of course, the situation has changed and there is a great gulf separating *astronomy* from *astrology*. The American psychologist/lexicographer Arthur S. Reber (1940-) probably put the proper perspective on *astrology* when he wrote that contemporary scientific interest in *astrology* is mainly for insight into human gullibility, and that most psychologists today are led to the conclusion that the stars have about as much influence on our behavior as we have on theirs! See also BARNUM EFFECT; BIORHYTHM THEORY; GRAPHOLOGY, THEORY OF; PERSONALITY THEORIES; PSEUDOSCIENTIFIC AND UNCONVENTIONAL THEORIES.

REFERENCES

French, C., Fowler, M., McCarthy, K., & Peers, D. (1991). Belief in astrology: A test of the Barnum effect. *Skeptical Inquirer, 15*, 166-172.

Reber, A. S. (1995). *The Penguin dictionary of psychology.* 2nd ed. New York: Penguin Books.

ATAVISTIC THEORY. See LOMBROSIAN THEORY.

ATMOSPHERE/CONTEXT EFFECTS. See PERCEPTION (II. COMPARATIVE APPRAISAL), THEORIES OF.

ATMOSPHERE HYPOTHESIS. See CONVERSION HYPOTHESIS.

ATTACHMENT, PRINCIPLE OF. See CUPBOARD THEORY; INFANT ATTACHMENT THEORIES.

ATTENTION, LAWS/PRINCIPLES AND THEORIES OF. The term *attention* is defined differently depending on the context in which it is used. In a functional sense, for instance, attention refers to the process of focusing on certain portions of an experience so that the parts become relatively more distinctive (cf., readiness potential - a large negative difference in voltage across the cerebral cortex, hypothesized to be indicative of attention, and developing about eight-tenths of a second before an individual makes a preplanned bodily movement). In a *behavioral* context (cf., *behaviorist school* context, where attention was rejected as a more traditional mentalistic concept), *attention* is defined more precisely as an adjustment of the sensory apparatus that facilitates optimal excitation by a specific stimulus (or a complex of stimuli) and inhibits the action of all other details. Attention may be conscious, in that some stimulus elements are actively selected out of the total input, even though there is no explicit awareness of the factors that cause the person to perceive only some small part of the total stimulus complex. Historically, the English psychologist George F. Stout (1860-1944) considered attention to be "conation" (i.e., craving, desire, or will) insofar as it required for its satisfaction fuller cognizance of its object; and others (e.g., M. Maher, 1900) distinguished between sensation and attention where sensation involves a *passive* faculty, and attention is the exercise of an *activity* or the application of intellectual energy. For the English-born American psychologist E. B. Titchener (1867-1927), the concept of *attention* was given attributive status where it was nothing more nor less than that which changes in experience and where attentional shifts are due to the clarity or vividness ("attensity") of the sensory processes. Many early psychology textbook authors (who seem, generally, to use the term *law* quite liberally and effusively in "nonpositivistic" ways) refer to the *laws* or *theories* of attention. For example, C. Buell (1900) lists *six laws of attention*: intensity of the stimulus, curiosity, size, adaptation, motive, and change. C. Seashore (1923) lists *14 laws of attention*: tension, novelty, intensity, action change, periodicity, timing, rest, grouping, division of energy, purpose, interest, effort, form, and skill. H. von Ebbinghaus (1908) refers to the *laws of practice, memory*, and *attention*. R. Halleck (1895), J. M. Baldwin (1894), and E. B. Titchener (1928) describe *laws of attention*. M. Calkins (1916) describes *eight theories of attention*: activity theory, motor theory, negative theories, element theory, Bradley's theory, inhibition theory, Ribot's theory, and Wundt's theory. J. M. Baldwin (1894), in addition to referring to the *general law of attention*, describes *Horwicz's theory of attention* and the *spiritual theories of reflex attention*. H. Hoffding (1908) describes *Condillac's theory of attention*; and R. Woodworth (1921) refers to a *theory of attention*, as well as to the *laws of attention*. In the late 19th and early 20th centuries, the *Structuralist* and *Functionalist* schools of psychology considered the topic of attention to be a core problem in the field and emphasized different aspects of it. For instance, the *Structuralists* viewed attention as a state of consciousness that consisted of increased concentration and sensory clearness; they studied the conditions that maximized the clearness of a sensation. On the other hand, the *Functionalists* focused on the selective and volitional nature of attention; they studied the motivational state and active functioning of the individual. Recent experimental work on attention focuses on variables (or "problems" of attention) such as stimulus intensity, distraction, shifts and fluctuations, stimulus duration, attention span, attentional value of stimuli in different sensory modalities, locations, levels of novelty, temporal relations of stimuli as determiners of attention and selectivity, and the neurophysiological basis of attention. Attention may be controlled automatically (e.g., a loud sound captures one's attention), by instructions (e.g., "pay attention to the red one over there"), or by the demands of a particular task (e.g., when driving a car, the driver looks out for other cars, pedestrians, and road signs). A person's attentional mechanisms serve to enhance responsiveness to certain stimuli and to tune out irrelevant information. An interesting aspect of attention, called the *cocktail-party phenomenon* (Cherry, 1953; Wood & Cowan, 1995), refers to the ability to attend selectively to a single person's speech across a room and in the midst of the competing speech of many other people (such as at a noisy cocktail party). Three possible *functions of attention* have been identified: as a sensory filter, as response selection, and as a gateway to consciousness. Recent formalized *theories of attention* include the English psychologist Donald Eric Broadbent's (1926-1993) *filter theory/model* (where all sensory input is processed in a parallel manner, initially occurring in an automatic "preattentive compartment," and then some of it is selected to enter the "attentive compartment" for further processing; this theory, also known as *bottleneck theory*, can account for a person's ability to selectively hear or see things based on physical distinctions and for a person's failure to register the meanings of unattended stimuli); *late selection theories* (e.g., R. Shiffrin & W. Schneider, 1977) - in this type of attention theory, the preattentive stage can process very familiar stimuli for meaning, and based on such processing, the selection can pass such stimuli onto the attentive stage, where they become conscious to the person; this theory can account

for one's ability to hear one's own name in an unattended message or the ability to be influenced by the meaning of a stimulus that is not consciously perceived; and *early-selection theories* [e.g., A. M. Treisman's (1969) *attenuation theory* - these theories suggest that a great quantity of information passes into the attentive stage and is analyzed for meaning at any of various levels of consciousness, but only some of the information is analyzed at a level that permits the individual to describe it]. Currently, research on the psychological, as well as the neurological, aspects of attention continues unabated (cf., Logan, 2004), and there are promising connections between the experimental work on attention and the eventual explanation and understanding of various psychopathological disorders such hyperactivity, schizophrenia, and mental retardation. See also BLOCKING, PHENOMENON/EFFECT OF; CONDILLAC'S THEORY OF ATTENTION; ELICITED OBSERVING RATE HYPOTHESIS; PSYCHOPATHOLOGY, THEORIES OF; VIGILANCE, THEORIES OF.

REFERENCES

Baldwin, J. M. (1894). *Handbook of psychology*. New York: Holt.

Halleck, R. (1895). *Psychology and psychic culture*. New York: American Book.

Stout, G. (1896). *Analytic psychology*. London: Sonnenschein.

Buell, C. (1900). *Essentials of psychology*. Boston: Ginn.

Maher, M. (1900). *Psychology: Empirical and rational*. London: Longmans and Green.

Ebbinghaus, H. von (1908). *Psychology: An elementary textbook*. Boston: Heath Co.

Hoffding, H. (1908). *Outlines of psychology*. London: Macmillan.

Titchener, E. B. (1908). *Lectures on the experimental psychology of feeling and attention*. New York: Macmillan.

Calkins, M. (1916). *An introduction to psychology*. New York: Macmillan.

Woodworth, R. (1921). *Psychology: A study of mental life*. New York: Holt.

Seashore, C. (1923). *Introduction to psychology*. New York: Macmillan.

Titchener, E. B. (1928). *A textbook of psychology*. New York: Macmillan.

Cherry, E. (1953). Some experiments on the recognition of speech, with one and with two ears. *Journal of the Acoustical Society of America, 25*, 975-979.

Broadbent, D. E. (1957). A mechanical model for human attention and immediate memory. *Psychological Review, 64*, 205-215.

Deutsch, J., & Deutsch, D. (1963). Attention: Some theoretical considerations. *Psychological Review, 70*, 80-90.

Trabasso, T., & Bower, G. H. (1968). *Attention in learning: Theory and research*. New York: Wiley.

Treisman, A. M. (1969). Strategies and models of selective attention. *Psychological Review, 76*, 282-299.

McKay, D. (1973). Aspects of the theory of comprehension, memory, and attention. *Quarterly Journal of Psychology, 25*, 22-40.

Shiffrin, R., & Schneider, W. (1977). Controlled and automatic information processing. II. Perceptual learning, automatic attending, and a general theory. *Psychological Review, 84*, 127-190.

Carver, C., & Scheier, M. (1981). *Attention and self-regulation: A control theory approach to human behavior*. New York: Springer.

Posner, M. (1982). Cumulative development of attentional theory. *American Psychologist, 37*, 168-179.

Kahneman, D., & Treisman, A. M. (1984). Changing views of attention and automaticity. In R. Parasuraman & D. Davies (Eds.), *Varieties of attention*. New York: Academic Press.

Wood, N., & Cowan, N. (1995). The cocktail party phenomenon revisited: Attention and memory in the classic selective listening procedure of Cherry (1953). *Journal of Experimental Psychology: General, 124*, 243-262.

Logan, G. D. (2004). Cumulative progress in formal theories of attention. *Annual Review of Psychology, 55*, 207-234.

ATTENTIONAL-GATE MODEL OF TIME. See PSYCHOLOGICAL TIME, MODELS OF.

ATTENUATION THEORY OF ATTENTION. See ATTENTION, LAWS, PRINCIPLES, THEORIES OF.

ATTITUDE AND ATTITUDE CHANGE, THEORIES OF. The term *attitude* may be defined as a learned predisposition ("set") to evaluate or react consistently in a particular manner, either positively or negatively, to certain persons, places, concept, things, or events. The concept of *attitude* was first introduced formally in the field of sociology by W. I. Thomas and F. Znaniecki in 1918 and has come to be a core concept in the field of social psychology. The *tricomponent model of attitude* states that attitudes contain three elements: affective/evaluative, cognitive/belief, and behavioral/action/conative. This model assumes both that there is a tendency within persons to maintain consistency among the three components and that, once formed, attitudes and the components become functional by preparing the individual for "inconflicted" action. Of the three components, the most prominent is the affective/evaluative (feeling) dimension, where most attempts at changing attitudes by persuasion are aimed at changing the evaluative component. Psychologists in this field assert that a comprehensive *attitude theory* should be able to explain data in the five areas of the communication process: the *source* (i.e., who initiates the communication, and how credible is the person or institution?), the *message* (i.e., what is the nature of the communication, and does it involve fear tactics?), the *channel* (i.e., how is the communication transmitted: face-to-face, television, newspaper, etc.?), the *receiver* (i.e., who is the target audience, and what is the level of receiver intelligence, emotion, and motivation?), and the *destination* (i.e., are the time frame, goal, and purpose for change of the communication?). Unfortunately, no single or unifying theory of attitudes is accepted by all scientists working in the field. There are over 30 distinct theoretical formulations described in textbooks on *attitude theory*. There are, however, common views among researchers concerning the notion that attitudes can be represented as an evaluative disposition on a continuum ranging from agreement to disagreement. Within these parameters, four separate classes of *attitude theory* may generally be identified: *evaluative disposition/undifferentiated* viewpoint (e.g., theories that employ principles of reinforcement and classical conditioning); *set of beliefs* (e.g., theories that suggest an averaging process across a person's cognitions or beliefs to get an overall evaluative disposition); *set of motivational forces* (e.g., theories that emphasize the more functional and enduring dispositions based on the person's values, needs, drives, and motives); and *attitude nonexistence* (e.g., theories that approach the concept of *attitude* as being a "social fiction" and advocate the examination of the processes of "self-perception"). The ideal *attitude theory* should contain, also, accounts of both the antecedents and the consequences of attitude formation, but most theoretical efforts are limited and have concentrated only on the antecedent conditions. The following sample of four systematic *theories of attitude change*, or *persuasion theories*, indicates the range of attitude theories acknowledged by most social psychologists today: *cognitive-consistency theories*, *information-processing models/theories*, *functional theories*, and *perceptual theories*. The *cognitive-consistency theories* encompass the "balance," "congruity," "dissonance," and "probabilistic" theories because they all assume that the person has an acquired or learned drive to maintain the optimal consistency among beliefs, and when inconsistency among beliefs (or between attitudes and overt behavior) occurs, the person will take action to avoid or reduce the resultant state of tension (cf., Osgood & Tannenbaum, 1955). Various concepts of the *dissonance theory* approach include "post-decisional dissonance" (when a person must choose between two attractive alternatives, and after the choice is made, the individual rationalizes the decision by upgrading the features of the chosen alternative and downgrading the rejected alternative), "selective exposure to information" (persons may search out information that supports their beliefs and avoid information that challenges them in order to reduce dissonance), and "forced compliance" (the seemingly paradoxical notion of

dissonance theory that the less a person is paid to engage in a distasteful task, the more the task will be enjoyed). The *information-processing models/theories* suggest that successful attitude change through *persuasion* involves five sequential processes: attention (get the target audience's attention), comprehension (make clear the arguments and expected behaviors of the audience), yielding (assess target audience's consent), retention (ensure that the audience maintains its decision until action is required), and action (ensure that the audience is motivated to act in accordance with the new attitude). According to this approach, if this sequence of processes is interrupted at any point, the expected attitude change will not occur [cf., *sleeper effect* - first reported by the American psychologists Carl Hovland (1912-1961) and Walter Weiss (1925-), refers to the tendency for the recipient of a persuasive message from a source of low credibility to show increased attitude change a short while after exposure to the message, either relative to recipients of the same message attributed to a source of high credibility, called the *relative sleeper effect*, or relative to the amount of attitude change occurring immediately after exposure to the message, called the *absolute sleeper effect*]. The *functional theories* assume that persons maintain a particular attitude because it has adaptive value and serves some personal basic need. The *functional theories* have examined the "authoritarian personality" and have been favored by the psychoanalytically oriented theorists, who attempt to explain negative attitudes and prejudices in terms of past patterns of childhood socialization. The *perceptual theories* argue that attitudes change in conjunction with persons' self-perceptions, their perceptions of the environment, and their own needs. This approach emphasizes the categories, frames of reference, and labels that individuals use to organize their social environment. Another current cognitive theoretical approach concerns the use of *persuasion* to change attitudes and is called the *elaboration likelihood model*, which states that persuasion may occur in either of two distinct ways (depending on how important or relevant the issues are to the persons who are the target of persuasion): via a "central" route (where an "important" message is carefully processed, and degree of attitude change depends on the quality of the arguments advanced), and via a "perceptual" route (where an "unimportant" message is only casually processed, and degree of attitude change depends on the presence of persuasion cues such as the expertise or status of the persuader; cf., *heuristic*, or *rough-and-ready, theory of persuasion*). The formulation of attitude theories in psychology is an active area involving practical applications and consequences. However, various unresolved issues remain that are not yet well understood by attitude theorists. Among these are the lack of knowledge concerning the sudden and intense emotional arousal that attitudes may produce, the manner in which attitudes can lead individuals to make great personal sacrifices for their ideals and loved ones, and the dynamics underlying the dramatic attitude reversals that may occur in a person's life (such as love at first sight, religious conversion, etc.). In psychology, the study of attitudes and the theories of attitude change reflect an overwhelming diversity of viewpoints and attitudes on the part of psychologists themselves about the relevant processes involved. See also ATTRIBUTION THEORY; BRAINWASHING TECHNIQUES AND THEORY; COMMUNICATION THEORY; CONFLICT, THEORIES OF; FESTINGER'S COGNITIVE DISSONANCE THEORY; INGROUP BIAS THEORIES; MEANING, THEORY/ASSESSMENT OF; PERSUASION/INFLUENCE THEORIES; PREJUDICE, THEORIES OF; REASONED ACTION AND PLANNED BEHAVIOR THEORIES; REINFORCEMENT THEORY.

REFERENCES

Thomas, W., & Znaniecki, F. (1927). *The Polish peasant in Europe and America*. New York: Knopf.

Hovland, C., & Weiss, W. (1951). The influence of source credibility on communication effectiveness. *Public Opinion Quarterly, 15*, 635-650.

Christie, R., & Jahoda, M. (Eds.) (1954). *Studies in the scope and method of the "authoritarian personality."* New York: Free Press.

Osgood, C. E., & Tannenbaum, P. (1955). The principle of congruity in the prediction of attitude change. *Psychological Review, 62*, 42-55.

Katz, D. (1960). The functional approach to the study of attitudes. *Public Opinion Quarterly, 24*, 163-204.

Kelman, H. C. (1961). Processes of opinion change. *Public Opinion Quarterly, 25*, 57-78.

Fleming, D. (1967). Attitude: The history of a concept. *Perspectives in American History, 1*, 287-365.

Abelson, R., Aronson, E., McGuire, W., Newcomb, T., Rosenberg, M., & Tannenbaum, P. (Eds.) (1968). *Theories of cognitive consistency: A sourcebook*. Chicago: Rand-McNally.

Ajzen, I., & Fishbein, M. (1980). *Understanding attitudes and predicting social behavior*. Englewood Cliffs, NJ: Prentice-Hall.

Cialdini, R., Petty, R., & Cacioppo, J. (1981). Attitude and attitude change. *Annual Review of Psychology, 32*, 357-404.

Cooper, J., & Croyle, R. (1984). Attitudes and attitude change. *Annual Review of Psychology, 35*, 395-426.

McGuire, W. (1985). The nature of attitudes and attitude change. In G. Lindzey & E. Aronson (Eds.), *Handbook of social psychology*. Vol. 2. New York: Random House.

Herek, G. (1986). The instrumentality of attitudes: Toward a neofunctional theory. *Journal of Social Issues, 42*, 99-114.

Petty, R., & Cacioppo, J. (1986). The elaboration likelihood model of persuasion. In L. Berkowitz (Ed.), *Advances in experimental social psychology*. New York: Academic Press.

Chaiken, S., & Strangor, C. (1987). Attitudes and attitude change. *Annual Review of Psychology, 38*, 575-630.

Tessor, A., & Shaffer, D. (1990). Attitude and attitude change. *Annual Review of Psychology, 41*, 479-523.

Eagly, A., & Chaiken, S. (1993). *The psychology of attitudes*. Orlando, FL: Harcourt Brace Jovanovich.

Olson, J., & Zanna, M. (1993). Attitudes and attitude change. *Annual Review of Psychology, 44*, 117-154.

ATTITUDE SIMILARITY HYPOTHESIS.
See LOVE, THEORIES OF.

**ATTRIBUTION/ATTITUDE BOOMER-
ANG EFFECT.** See ATTRIBUTION THE-
ORY.

ATTRIBUTION THEORY. The Austrian-
American psychologist Fritz Heider (1896-
1988) was preeminent in the formulation of
balance theory in the study of attitudes (i.e.,
people are motivated to maintain balance, harmony, or "cognitive consonance" among their
attitudes, perceptions, and beliefs; cf., state of
imbalance, disharmony, or "cognitive dissonance") and of *attribution theory* in the study
of social perception that originated in social
psychology and is a general approach for describing the ways individuals use information
to generate causal explanations for behavior
and events; Heider's term *causal schema* denotes a conceptual organization of a sequence
of events in which some are identified as
"causes" and others as "effects." Heider argued
the people continually make causal analyses
about others' behavior where the behavior is
attributed either to *dispositions* (internal factors
or causes, such as one's personality) or to
situations (external factors or causes, such as
one's environment). For example, is the other
person's overt hostility due to his aggressive
personality (*dispositional attribution*) or due to
abuse and stress in that person's environment
(*situational attribution*)? Heider suggested that
instead of developing theories of how people
are supposed to act or think, psychologists
should examine the personal theories (belief
systems) that ordinary people themselves use
as "intuitive psychologists" to assess the causes
and effects of behavior (cf., *positivity
bias/effect* - a pervasive tendency for people,
especially those with high self-esteem, to rate
positive traits as being more applicable to
themselves than negative traits, and where, in
balance theory, there is a general preference
demonstrated by most people for positive relations). A prolific number of subtheories, hypotheses, effects, and principles relating to
attribution theory have followed Heider's initial formulations (cf., *attribution/attitude boomerang effect*, which refers to a shift in atti-
tude/attributions that not only goes against

what was intended but actually is in the opposite direction). Although it is possible that an
individual may choose to make a *situational
attribution* of another's behavior, most people
tend to be biased toward making *dispositional
attributions*. Thus, there seems to be a tendency to view persons as *origins* of events, and
this leads many individuals to regard the needs,
wishes, dispositions, skills, and motives of
others as responsible for both natural and social phenomena. This tendency of people to
ignore the *external* circumstantial causes of
behavior and to emphasize the *internal* per-
sonal-character causes is referred to as the
fundamental attribution error, or the *overattribution effect*. According to the *automaticity
hypothesis*, such attributions to internal characteristics are automatic, whereas attributions to
external causes are, by comparison, more controlled. Another hypothesis concerning *attribution theory*, the *cultural-norm hypothesis*,
states that the fundamental attribution error
(underestimating situational influences) is at
least partly learned from one's larger culture.
For example, persons in a Western culture -
which emphasizes the idea that people are in
charge of their own destinies - will learn to
attribute behavior more to *internal* character
than to *external* environment. The *actor-
observer discrepancy* is a concept of *attribution theory* that suggests that the fundamental
attribution error is less likely to occur when
people make attributions about their own behavior than when they make attributions about
others' behaviors. Various hypotheses have
been offered to explain the *actor-observer
discrepancy*: the *knowledge-across-situations
hypothesis* states that people become more
sensitized to the variations in their own behavior because they have seen themselves in many
more situations than they have seen others; and
the *visual-orientation hypothesis* stems from
the basic characteristic of visual perception that
our eyes point outward and, when we watch
someone else's behavior, our eyes are fixed on
that person and, thereby, attribute internal
causes to the person. On the other hand, when
we ourselves engage in behaviors, we see the
surrounding, external environment (not ourselves) and attribute external causes for our
own behavior. The *correspondent inference
theory* (cf., Jones & Davis, 1965) is a system-

atic analysis of the processes described by Heider and describes the situational factors that influence the appearance of external and internal attributions. This theory states, among other things, that individuals observe actions and effects produced by actions where such action-effect connections become the basis for inferences about others' behaviors and intentions. When "knowledge" and "ability" intentions are attributed, an internal disposition is assumed to be the cause of the other person's behavior. In another case, the *just-world hypothesis* (first described by the Canadian American-based psychologist Melvin J. Lerner) in *attribution theory* argues for the notion that people need to believe that the world is fair and that justice is served consistently, where bad people are punished and good people are rewarded. The *illusion of control theory*, described by the American psychologist Ellen J. Langer (1947-), refers to the belief that one has control over events that are actually determined by chance, and is found most frequently in situations involving apparent skill, containing apparent familiarity, involving competition with seemingly incompetent opponents, and stressing the importance of success. A theory related to the idea that people attribute and infer internal dispositions concerning others' behavior is the *self-perception theory*. This *attribution theory* proposes that individuals use the same information to make inferences about their own dispositional makeup as they use to make inferences about others'. Thus, according to this approach, we observe our own actions and subsequently attribute those actions to external or internal causes, and in the absence of a reasonable external cause for our own behavior, we attribute it to an internal cause. In this way, for example, a person develops attitudes about issues and events by self-observation of the opinions she expresses. Another integrative theory of attribution processes has been formulated by the American psychologist Harold H. Kelley (1921-) who emphasizes the idea that people often make causal attributions for events under conditions of uncertainty, and he developed a model of the logic that people might use to judge whether a specific behavior should be attributed to internal (personality-character) causes or to external (environ-

mental) causes. According to Kelley's model (also called *Kelley's cube*), before making an attribution (either internal or external), one would ideally ask three questions about another's behavior: (1) Is it consistent? (2) Is it consensual/normative? (3) Is it distinctive? If the answer to (1) is no, the attribution will probably be external. If the answer to (1) is yes, *either* an external or internal attribution will be made, depending on the answers to (2) and (3). If the answer to both (1) and (2) is yes, the attribution will probably be external. If the answers to both (1), (2), and (3) are yes, no, ye, respectively, the attribution will probably be internal. If the answers to (1), (2), and (3) are yes, no, no, respectively, the attribution will probably be a combination of both external and internal factors. Also, according to Kelley, a *covariation/correlation principle* is employed when people infer the causes of events, including the behavior of other people, by observing whether two events vary together or simply occur together (such as lightning and thunder). In this way, an effect is attributed to that condition that is present when the effect is present and that condition that is absent when the effect is absent. Kelley also refers to the concepts of *discounting principle* (also called the *discounting effect*) and *augmentation principle* (also called the *augmentation effect*) to describe the plausibility of internal versus external causes in the assessment of another's behavior. *Discounting* is the tendency to reject dispositional (internal) factors as causes of a behavior when the behavior is apparently one that most people would perform under the existing circumstances. *Augmenting* is the tendency for one to increase acceptance of an internal dispositional cause when a potential external cause is also present. Occasionally, the attributional process may be biased in a way where one's own personal goals, attitudes, and motives disrupt a rational and systematic analysis of the causes of behavior. One example of this type of attributional bias is called the *self-serving bias*, which occurs when one tends to take credit for one's successes but deny responsibility for one's failures. Numerous studies have been conducted to extend and refine *attribution theory*, but they all attempt generally to examine the dynamics and conditions under which causal explanations about others' (and one's own) behaviors are made. In addition to social psychological issues, *attribution theory* has been used as an explanatory system or model for many other psychological issues and areas, including the study of marriage, spousal abuse, cultural influence, achievement motivation, emotions, and clinical depression. See also ACHIEVEMENT MOTIVATION, THEORY OF; ATTITUDE/ATTITUDE CHANGE, THEORIES OF; BOOMERANG EFFECT; CORRESPONDENCE BIAS HYPOTHESIS; FALSE-CONSENSUS EFFECT; FESTINGER'S COGNITIVE DISSONANCE THEORY; IMPRESSION FORMATION, THEORIES OF; KELLEY'S COVARIATION THEORY.

REFERENCES

Cartwright, D. & Haray, F. (1956). Structural balance: A generalization of Heider's theory. *Psychological Review, 63*, 277-293.

Festinger, L. (1957). *A theory of cognitive dissonance.* Evanston, IL: Row, Peterson.

Heider, F. (1958). *The psychology of interpersonal relationships.* New York: Wiley.

Jones, E. E., & Davis, K. (1965). From acts to dispositions: The attribution process in person perception. In L. Berkowitz (Ed.), *Advances in experimental social psychology.* New York: Academic Press.

Kelley, H. (1971). *Attribution in social interaction.* Morristown, NJ: General Learning Press.

Bem, D. (1972). Self-perception theory. In L. Berkowitz (Ed.), *Advances in experimental social psychology.* New York: Academic Press.

Kelley, H. (1973). The process of causal attribution. *American Psychologist, 28*, 107-128.

Nisbett, R., Caputo, C., Legant, P., & Marecek, J. (1973). Behavior as seen by the actor and as seen by the observer. *Journal of Personality and Social Psychology, 27*, 154-164.

Langer, E. (1975). The illusion of control. *Journal of Personality and Social Psycology, 32*, 311-328.

Ross, L. D. (1977). The intuitive psychologist and his shortcomings: Distortions in the attribution process. In L. Berkowitz (Ed.), *Advances in experimental social psychology.* New York: Academic Press.

Arkin, R., Cooper, H., & Kolditz, T. (1980). A statistical review of the literature concerning the self-serving attribution bias in interpersonal influence situations. *Journal of Personality, 48*, 435-448.

Heider, F. (1980). On balance and attribution. In D. Gorlitz (Ed.), *Perspectives on attribution research and theory.* Cambridge, MA: Ballinger.

Lerner, M. J. (1980). *The belief in a just world: A fundamental delusion.* New York: Plenum.

Jellison, J., & Green, J. (1981). A self-presentation approach to the fundamental attribution error: The norm of internality. *Journal of Personality and Social Psychology, 40*, 643-649.

Weiner, B. (1986). *An attributional theory of motivation and emotion.* New York: Springer.

Lee, F., Hallahan, M., & Herzog, T. (1996). Explaining real life events: How culture and domain shape attributions. *Personality and Social Psychology Bulletin, 22*, 732-741.

ATTRIBUTION THEORY OF LEADERSHIP. See LEADERSHIP, THEORIES OF.

AUBERT-FLEISCHL PARADOX OR PHENOMENON. See VISION/SIGHT, THEORIES OF.

AUBERT-FORSTER PHENOMENON OR LAW. See VISION/SIGHT, THEORIES OF.

AUBERT PHENOMENON. See VISION AND SIGHT, THEORIES OF.

AUDIENCE EFFECT. See ZAJONC'S AROUSAL AND CONFLUENCE THEORIES.

AUDIOGRAVIC/AUDIOGYRAL ILLUSIONS/EFFECTS. See APPENDIX A.

AUDITION/HEARING, THEORIES OF. In general, the *audition theories* attempt to explain how physical sound vibrations are transformed into the neural impulses that are the basis of hearing. Historically, there have been five major audition theories: *resonance* or *place theories*, *frequency theories*, *volley* or *periodicity theories*, *hydraulic theories*, and *sound-pattern theories*. The *resonance theory* of hearing - often called the *Helmholtz theory*, named after the German physiologist and psychologist Hermann L. F. Helmholtz (1821-1894) - asserts that pitch is determined by the place on the basilar membrane (i.e., a delicate membrane in the cochlea of the inner ear) that is stimulated, where the short fibers are sensitive to high-pitched sounds, the long fibers are sensitive to low-pitched sounds, and the fibers in the middle of the membrane are attuned to sounds of medium pitch. Loudness and tonal discriminability are assumed to be determined by the number of neurons activated by the incoming stimulus. The *resonance theory* is known, also, as the *harp theory*, the *place theory* [cf., the Hungarian-American engineering/sensory psychologist George von Bekesy's (1899-1972) *traveling-wave theory* which states that sounds of different frequencies set up different wave patterns in the cochlear fluids], and the *piano theory* (cf., Bekesy's argument that this theory is incorrect because the basilar membrane fibers are not free to resonate like the strings of a piano with sustaining pedal depressed; rather, the fibers are connected as if a sheet of light cloth were laid across the piano strings). The *frequency theory* of hearing - developed by the American physiologist William Rutherford (1839-1899) - holds that the basilar membrane in the ear responds as a whole entity to aural stimuli and then transmits the stimuli to the brain for further analysis. Rutherford's *frequency theory*, often called the *telephone theory*, assumes that the basilar membrane responds much like a telephone diaphragm mechanism; the *frequency theory*, however, does not explain adequately the perception of higher-pitched sounds within the range of audition. The *volley* or *periodicity* (or *platoon-volley*) *theory* of audition of the American psychologists Ernest Glen Wever (1902-1991) and Charles William Bray (1904-1982), called the *Wever-Bray theory* [cf., Wever's (1949) combined *resonance-volley theory*] maintains that nerve fibers of the basilar membrane respond in groups or "volleys," not in unison, which results in more transmission of aural impulses. Thus, *periodicity theory* emphasizes the synchronized firing of neurons and depends largely on the *volley principle*, which proposes that groups of basilar membrane fibers work as squads and fire in synchronized volleys. The *volley principle* is necessary to this theory because the auditory nerve follows signals only with frequencies up to 3,000-4,000 Hz [i.e., cycles per second or hertz - named after the German physicist Heinrich Rudolph Hertz (1857-1894) who discovered radio waves in 1887]; cf., the *arpeggio paradox* - a tendency for a person who is conditioned to respond to a particular tone, to not respond when that tone is one of a series of tones. The *Wever-Bray effect* refers to an aural potential that can be recorded using gross electrodes placed near the auditory nerve of an animal; it is made up of two separate potentials: one is the whole nerve-action potential, and the other is the "cochlear microphonic." It is interesting to note that if the changes in the electrical potentials are amplified and fed through an ordinary telephone receiver, one may actually understand words spoken through it into the animal's ear. The *hydraulic theory* of hearing of the German-American psychologist Max F. Meyer (1873-1967) asserts that hearing is dependent on the amount of basilar membrane involved in the sensation of different tones. The *sound-pattern theory* (or the *pressure-pattern theory*) of the German physiologist Julius Richard Ewald (1855-1921) states that the sense of hearing is dependent on the pattern of vibration on the basilar membrane where different vibration patterns are imposed on the membrane by stimuli of different complexities or pitches. The current view of audition seems to favor a form of amalgamation of the *place* and *periodicity theories*: for stimuli below about 3,000 Hz, both *place* and *periodicity* combine, and for those frequencies above this level, the *place* on the basilar membrane is probably the critical factor. The variable of loudness seems to be mediated by the overall number of impulses arriving at the brain [cf., the *Egan effect* - named after the American psychologist James Pendleton Egan

(1917-) - refers to the finding that the loudness of speech in one ear is increased if noise is applied to the opposite ear]. Thus, in general, no one theory of audition/hearing seems adequate today, perhaps because the human sense of hearing is a relatively complex phenomenon. Appendix A provides a listing of various *auditory illusions* and *effects*. See also DOPPLER EFFECT, PRINCIPLE/SHIFT; HYDRAULIC THEORY; STUMPF'S THEORY OF MUSICAL CONSONANCE AND DISSONANCE.

REFERENCES

Helmholtz, H. von (1863). *Die lehre von den tonempfindungen als physiologische grundlage fur die theorie der musik.* Braunschweig: Wieweg.

Rutherford, W. (1886). A new theory of hearing. *Journal of Anatomy and Physiology, London, 21*, 166-168.

Ewald, J. (1899). Zur physiologie des labyrinths. VI. Eine neue hortheorie. *Archiv fur die Gesamte Physiologie, 76*, 147-188.

Meyer, M. (1928). The hydraulic principles governing the function of the cochlea. *Journal of General Psychology, 1*, 239-265.

Wever, E., & Bray, C. (1930a). Present possibilities for auditory theory. *Psychological Review, 37*, 365-380.

Wever, E., & Bray, C. (1930b). The nature of the acoustic response: The relation between sound frequency and frequency of impulses in the auditory nerve. *Journal of Experimental Psychology, 13*, 373-387.

Bekesy, G. von, & Rosenblith, W. (1948). The early history of hearing: Observations and theories. *Journal of the Acoustical Society of America, 20*, 727-748.

Egan, J. P. (1948). The effect of noise in one ear upon the loudness of speech in the other ear. *Journal of the Acoustical Society of America, 20*, 58-62.

Wever, E. (1949). *Theories of hearing.* New York: Wiley.

Bekesy, G. von (1960). *Experiments in hearing.* New York: McGraw-Hill.

Tobias, J. (Ed.) (1972). *Foundations of modern auditory theory.* New York: Academic Press.

AUDITORY FLUTTER-FUSION AND FLICKER-FUSION EFFECTS. See APPENDIX A.

AUDITORY FUSION AND BINAURAL FUSION EFFECTS. See APPENDIX A.

AUDITORY MASKING EFFECT. See APPENDIX A.

AUDITORY STAIRCASE ILLUSION AND CIRCULAR PITCH ILLUSION. See APPENDIX A.

AUDITORY SUFFIX EFFECT. See APPENDIX A.

AUFGABE, LAW OF THE. See MIND OR MENTAL SET, LAW OF.

AUGMENTATION PRINCIPLE. See ATTRIBUTION THEORY.

AUTISM THEORY OF LANGUAGE LEARNING. See LANGUAGE ORIGINS, THEORIES OF.

AUTOCHTHONOUS LAWS. See GESTALT THEORY/LAWS.

AUTOCORRELATION THEORY. See NEURON/NEURAL/NERVE THEORY.

AUTOKINETIC EFFECT. See APPARENT MOVEMENT, PRINCIPLES AND THEORIES OF; APPENDIX A, SIZE AND WEIGHT ILLUSION

AUTOMATICITY HYPOTHESIS. See ATTRIBUTION THEORY; STROOP EFFECT.

AUTONOMY, PRINCIPLE OF. See ALLPORT'S FUNCTIONAL AUTONOMY PRINCIPLE; CONDUCT, LAWS OF.

AUTOREGRESSIVE INTEGRATED MOVING AVERAGE (ARIMA) MODEL. The

English-born American-based statistician George E. P. Box (1919-) and the English statistician Gwilym M. Jenkins (1933-1982) developed the *autoregressive integrated moving average model*, or *ARIMA* (also called *Box-Jenkins models*), a class of statistical models used frequently in time-series analyses (i.e., a procedure in which any series of values of a variable are taken or sampled in a fixed order or at successive times), and where the acronym *ARIMA* refers to the three coefficient components of the model: *autoregression* (a time-series property in which each score is a linear function of the preceding score, and where each score is correlated with all preceding scores); *integration* (differencing), and *moving average* (a sequence of numbers consisting of the averages of successive sub-sequences of a sequence of numbers calculated in order to smooth out short-term fluctuations and to clarify underlying or hidden trends in the data). See also STIMULUS SAMPLING THEORY.

REFERENCE

Box, G. E. P. , & Jenkins, G. M. (1970/1976). *Time-series analysis: Forecasting and control.* San Francisco: Holden-Day. [Also published in 1994 with a third author: G. C. Reinsell].

AUTOTELIC THEORY. See PLAY, THEORIES OF.

AVALANCHE LAW. See NEURON/NEURAL, AND NERVE THEORY.

AVERAGES, LAW OF. See PROBABILITY THEORY/LAWS.

AVOIDANCE HYPOTHESIS. See PUNISHMENT, THEORIES OF.

AWARENESS, LAW OF. See CONDUCT, LAWS OF.

AXIOMATIC/ABSTRACT MEASUREMENT THEORY. See CONJOINT MEASUREMENT THEORY.

AXIOMATIC CONJOINT MEASUREMENT THEORY. See CONJOINT MEASUREMENT THEORY.

B

BACK-PROPAGATION ALGORITHM MODEL. See PARALLEL DISTRIBUTED PROCESSING MODEL.

BACONIAN METHOD. See SKINNER'S DESCRIPTIVE BEHAVIOR AND OPERANT CONDITIONING THEORY.

BAER'S/VON BAER'S LAW. See RECAPITULATION, THEORY/LAW OF.

BAIN'S THEORY OF HUMOR AND LAUGHTER. The Scottish philosopher and psychologist Alexander Bain (1818-1903) elaborates on Thomas Hobbes' "sudden glory" humor theory in which one of the causes of laughter is the "triumph" over an enemy or a challenging or fatiguing task (e.g., after a period of intense activity and upon completing one's work, the person needs to "let off steam" via the spasmodic outburst of laughter; cf., Herbert Spencer's "overflow of nervous energy" humor theory). According to Bain, laughter becomes so intimately related to the pleasure aroused by "victory" that it has become a sign of pleasure in general and, for the same reason, a person may feel intense pain whenever he is made the target of ridicule. Bain maintained that the first causes of laughter are *physical* (such as acute pain, coldness, hysteria, or tickling), and among the *mental* causes of laughter are "animal spirits" or "hilarity" (such as an outburst of "liberty" after a period of restraint or restriction). As well as critiquing the humor theories of Aristotle and Hobbes, Bain provides criticism of humor theories that regard "incongruity" as the essential or sole element of the ludicrous (e.g., many situations exhibit incongruity, but do not provoke laughter). According to *Bain's theory of humor/laughter*, there are two elements in laughter: a feeling of "superiority" and a "sudden release" from constraint. Bain suggested, also, that the truly comic nature arises from a natural *inability* for expression of the serious, the solemn, or the dignified. See also ARISTOTLE'S THEORY OF HUMOR; HOBBES' THEORY OF HUMOR AND LAUGHTER; HUMOR, THEORIES OF; SPENCER'S THEORY OF LAUGHTER AND HUMOR.

REFERENCE

Bain, A. (1859). *The emotions and the will.* London: Longman.

BAIT-SHYNESS EFFECT. See GARCIA EFFECT.

BALANCE, PRINCIPLES AND THEORY OF. See ATTRIBUTION THEORY; FESTINGER'S COGNITIVE DISSONANCE THEORY.

BALDWIN EFFECT. The American developmental psychologist James Mark Baldwin (1861-1934) formulated a refined Darwinian genetic psychology. Baldwin's chief goal was to explain the adaptive correspondence of mental life and thoughts to material things, which he argued evolves through the formation and transformation of habits via the interacting processes of assimilation and imitation. Baldwin held a functional view of mind as sensorimotor process and emphasized the importance of intentional action as the mechanism of selection in the development of mental faculties. In his approach, Baldwin combined Darwinian and Lamarckian ideas of evolution to formulate his own sophisticated hypothesis of organic selection, which accounts for the course and direction of growth. Baldwin's notion of organic selection came to be known as the *Baldwin effect*. Baldwin also applied his model of intentional action to the moral, religious, and social aspects of human behavior where cycles of suggestion and imitation are mechanisms by which individuals develop socially, and where social progress is viewed as *social selection* along with the transmission and conservation of adaptive values. In some of his writings, Baldwin refers to numerous *laws* that occur in psychology. For example, he describes *laws* of: nervous accommodation, habit, inheritance, evolution, motives, contradictory representation, reversion to type, mental dynamogenesis, attention, voluntary interest, imagination, association, associative reproduction, correlation, preference in associations, identity in judgment, contiguity, contradiction, partial effect, sensation, passive imagination, sufficient reason, habit, and thought. Thus, Baldwin, like many other early psychologists who were schooled and grounded in *mental philosophy*, seems to demonstrate a penchant for a rather generous, liberal, and nonrigorous or noncritical use of the term *law* in describing various psychological phenomena. See also ATTENTION, LAWS, PRINCIPLES, AND THEORIES OF; DARWIN'S EVOLUTION THEORY; DYNAMOGENESIS, LAW OF.

REFERENCES

Baldwin, J. M. (1894). *Mental development in the child and in the race.* New York: Macmillan.

Baldwin, J. M. (Ed.) (1901-1905). *Dictionary of philosophy and psychology.* 4 vols. New York: Macmillan.

Baldwin, J. M. (1902). *Development and evolution.* New York: A.M.S. Press.

BALDWIN'S TIME-THEORY TYPES. At the turn of the 20th century, the American philosopher/psychologist James Mark Baldwin (1861-1934) described the general *types of theories* of the apprehension, cognition, and awareness of *time: intuitive and a priori theories* - hold that in some form time (whether succession or duration) is a part of the person's "mental furniture" (a moment or temporal character is contributed by the mind to the structure of its experience as such); these theories are called "nativistic" and may be "nativism of product," "nativism of process" (or "genetic nativism"), or "nativism of temporal datum" (which is analogous to the "extensity theory" of the cognition of space); and *empirical theories* - hold that time cognition is a gradual growth under the conditions of actual experiences of time (bits of time are perceived, cognized, or experienced simply as such or as a property of events); time is "built up" by abstraction and generalization as an independent mental object; in this approach, the mind get time out of its experience instead of contributing time to its experience (cf., Nichols, 1891). See also EMPIRICIST VERSUS NATIVIST THEORIES; TIME, THEORIES OF.

REFERENCES

Nichols, H. (1891). The psychology of time. *American Journal of Psychology, 3,* 453-529; *4,* 60-112.

Baldwin, J. M. (Ed.) (1901-1905). *Dictionary of philosophy and psychology.* New York: Macmillan.

BANDURA'S THEORY. = social cognition theory. The Canadian-American psychologist Albert Bandura (1925-) is a proponent of *social/cognitive learning theory*, which attempts to explain human behavior in terms of a reciprocal interaction between the three aspects of behavior, cognitions, and environmental events. Whereas *social learning theory* had its origins in the behaviorally oriented writings of Ivan Pavlov, J. B. Watson, and B. F. Skinner (and in the work of J. Dollard and N. Miller, K. Lewin, E. Tolman, G. H. Mead, and H. S. Sullivan), Bandura is preeminent (along with Julian Rotter, Walter Mischel, and Arthur Staats) in the formulation and application of *social learning theory*. According to *Bandura's theory*, humans learn to satisfy their needs, wishes, and desires by observing the *outcomes* of behaviors and events, where the observations lead to *expectations* about what will happen in the future and about one's ability to perform behaviors and to express emotions. Individuals compare their behaviors with those of others and make value judgments about their own and others' behaviors. In this way, according to *social-cognitive theory*, it is not simply the external conditions alone that determine behavior (as extreme behaviorists might claim), but it is also the decisions one makes based on one's cognitions ("knowledge") about the conditions. *Bandura's theory* includes several key concepts concerning the development of personal and social behaviors, among which are *reciprocal determination* - the idea that the person's behavior and the social learning environment continually influence each other in reciprocal ways; one learns behavior from interactions with other persons, and our behavior influences how other persons interact with us; *self-efficacy* - the perception that one is capable of achieving one's goals; *self-regulation* - the process of cognitively punishing and reinforcing one's own behavior depending on whether or not it meets one's personal standards; *modeling/observational learning* - a procedure in which an individual observes another person perform some behavior, notes the consequences of that behavior, and then attempts to imitate that behavior; *vicarious punishment* - the observation of the punishment of a model's behavior that results in the decrease of the probability of that same behavior in the observer; and *vicarious reinforcement* - the observation of the reinforcement of a model's behavior that results in the increase of the probability of that same behavior in the observer. Bandura's essential research and theoretical formulations have focused on observational learning, the role of thought in establishing and maintaining behavior, the application of behavior principles and social learning to therapeutic contexts, and the ways in which children learn to be aggressive. See also AGGRESSION, THEORIES OF; BEHAVIOR THERAPY AND COGNITIVE THERAPY, THEORIES OF; ROTTER'S SOCIAL LEARNING THEORY.

REFERENCES

Bandura, A., & Walters, R. (1963). *Social learning and personality development*. New York: Holt, Rinehart, & Winston.

Bandura, A. (1969). *Principles of behavior modification*. New York: Holt, Rinehart, & Winston.

Bandura, A. (Ed.) (1971). *Psychological modeling: Conflicting theories*. Chicago: Aldine-Atherton.

Bandura, A. (1973). *Aggression: A social learning analysis*. Englewood Cliffs, NJ: Prentice-Hall.

Bandura, A. (1977a). Self-efficacy: Toward a unifying theory of behavioral change. *Psychological Review, 84*, 191-215.

Bandura, A. (1977b). *Social learning theory*. Englewood Cliffs, NJ: Prentice-Hall.

Bandura, A. (1986). *Social foundations of thought and action: A social cognitive theory*. Englewood Cliffs, NJ: Prentice-Hall.

BANDWAGON EFFECT. See ASCH CONFORMITY EFFECT; BYSTANDER INTERVENTION EFFECT.

BARANY METHOD/EFFECT. The Austrian-Swedish physiologist Robert Barany (1876-1936) designed the *Barany method/test* to reveal whether the semicircular canals and the labyrinth system of the inner ears are functioning properly by rotating the person in a specially-constructed chair (called the *Barany chair*) which allows for rotation of the individual's head/body in three planes. Thus, the *Barany effect* is the participant's response as she is seated in a revolving chair that rotates in each of the three planes in which the semicircular canals are positioned. See also APPARENT MOVEMENT, PRINCIPLES, AND THEORIES OF.

REFERENCE

Barany, R. (1906). [Barany chair]. *Archiv fur Ohren-, Nasen- und Kehlkopfheilkunde, 68*, 1-30.

BARBER'S POLE EFFECT. See PERCEPTION (I. GENERAL), THEORIES OF.

BARGAINING THEORY OF COALITION FORMATION. A widespread phenomenon of social interaction is the formation of *coalitions* (two or more persons acting jointly to influence the outcomes of one or more other persons; or situations where a subset of a group agrees to cooperate in the joint use of resources in order to maximize rewards). A salient feature of current *theories of coalition formation* is their parsimony where each theory proposes one guiding principle for predicting coalition formation. However, in the *bargaining theory of coalition formation* (a descriptive theory), there is an emphasis on the bargaining process leading to a given coalition and focuses on how negotiations might change as a result of the nature and outcome of prior events (cf., *game theory* which is a normative/prescriptive approach dealing with how individuals *ought* to behave whereas *bargaining theory* deals with how individuals *do* behave). Among the several assumptions and hypotheses of the *bargaining theory of coalition formation* are the following: given a competitive orientation, persons are motivated to form a coalition which maximizes expected reward; persons either implicitly or explicitly evaluate the most favorable outcome they can expect (Emax); the least favorable outcome they can expect (Emin), and the most probable expected outcome (E-hat) in each of the possible winning coalitions; an individual *strong* in resources is more likely to expect and advocate the "parity norm" as a basis for reward division, whereas an individual *weak* in resources is more likely to expect and advocate the "equality norm;" a person's most probable expected outcome (E-hat) is that value which is halfway between Emax and Emin; a person who has been *excluded* as a member of the winning coalition is more likely to concede more than a person who was *included* (also, the larger the number of excluded trials, the greater the concession rate); the extent to which a member of the winning coalition will be tempted to defect - or actively seek a counter-coalition - is a function of the deviation of his share in the present coalition from his maximum expectation (maxEmax) in alternative coalitions; the larger the offer to defect, the greater the probability that it will be accepted; and the stability of a coalition is an inverse function of the temptation values of the coalition members. Essentially, the *bargaining theory of coalition formation* draws heavily from several theoretical contributions, in particular, the *exchange theory* proposed by the American social psychologists John Thibaut (1917-1986) and Harold H. Kelley (1921-2003); for example, the concept of "expected outcome (E-hat)" in *bargaining theory* is equivalent to the concept of "comparison level" in *exchange theory*, and the concept of "maxEmax" in the former theory is equivalent to the concept of "comparison level for alternatives" in the latter theory. Various sources for the *bargaining theory of coalition formation* include F. C. Ikle and N. Leites regarding the concepts of "maximum and minimum expectations" and "most probable expected outcome;" T. C. Schelling regarding the concept of "split-the-difference;" G. C. Homans concerning "two norms for the division of rewards;" J. S. Adams regarding the concept of "equity;" and W. A. Gamson concerning the concept of "parity norm." Other theories of coalition formation (cf., Kahan &

Rapoport, 1984) include T. Caplow's "triad theory;" J. M. Chertkoff's "modification of reciprocated choices theory;" W. A. Gamson's "minimum resources" or "minimum winning coalition theory;" W. H. Riker's "political coalitions theory;" and L. S. Shapley and M. Shubik's "pivotal power index/theory." See also DECISION-MAKING THEORIES; EXCHANGE AND SOCIAL EXCHANGE THEORY.

REFERENCES

Shapley, L. S., & Shubik, M. (1954). A method of evaluating the distribution of power in a committee system. *American Political Science Review, 48*, 787-792.

Caplow, T. (1956). A theory of coalitions in the triad. *American Sociological Review, 21*, 489-493.

Thibaut, J., & Kelley, H. H. (1959). *The social psychology of groups*. New York: Wiley.

Schelling, T. C. (1960). *The strategy of conflict*. Cambridge, MA: Harvard University Press.

Gamson, W. A. (1961). A theory of coalition formation. *American Sociological Review, 26*, 373-382.

Homans, G. C. (1961). *Social behavior: Its elementary forms*. New York: Harcourt, Brace & World.

Ikle, F. C., & Leites, N. (1962). Political negotiation as a process of modifying utilities. *Journal of Conflict Resolution, 6*, 19-28.

Riker, W. H. (1962). *The theory of political coalitions*. New Haven, CT: Yale University Press.

Adams, J. S. (1965). Inequity in social exchange. In L. Berkowitz (Ed.), *Advances in experimental social psychology*. New York: Academic Press.

Chertkoff, J. M. (1967). A revision of Caplow's coalition theory. *Journal of Experimental Social Psychology, 3*, 172-177.

Chertkoff, J. M. (1970). Sociopsychological theories and research on coalition formation. In S. Groennings, E. W. Kelley, & M. Leiserson (Eds.), *The*

60

study of coalition behavior. New York: Holt, Rinehart, & Winston.

Rapoport, A. (1970). *N-person game theory: Concepts and applications.* Ann Arbor: University of Michigan Press.

Komorita, S. S., & Chertkoff, J. M. (1973). A bargaining theory of coalition formation. *Psychological Review, 80,* 149-162.

Kahan, J., & Rapoport, A. (1984). *Theories of coalition formation.* Hillsdale, NJ: Erlbaum.

BARNUM EFFECT/PHENOMENON. The *Barnum effect*, named after the American showman, charlatan, and entrepreneur Phineas T. Barnum (1810-1891), refers to the fact that a cleverly worded "personal" description based on general, stereotyped statements will be accepted readily as an accurate self-description by most people. The *Barnum phenomenon* is behind the fakery of fortune-tellers, astrologers, and mind readers and often has contaminated legitimate study of personality assessment. The effect is consistent with Barnum's often-quoted aphorism "There's a sucker born every minute." Barnum, a circus showman, knew that the formula for success was to "have a little something for everybody." An early study of the *Barnum effect* (Forer, 1949) had a group of college students take a projective test on which they were given bogus feedback. In fact, each student was given the *same* interpretation. In general, the students felt that these interpretations were accurate and fitted them well. Thus, the tendency to accept standard feedback of a vague, universalist nature is the *Barnum effect*. Other studies, also, report that when the same vague, positive, and flattering statements are given to individuals as a personalized horoscope, personality profile, or handwriting analysis, they believe them to be accurate descriptions of them personally. Some researchers report that people are more willing to believe flattering statements about themselves than statements that are scientifically accurate. Various suggestions have been offered by researchers to avoid falling prey to the *Barnum effect*, such as beware of all-purpose descriptions that could apply to anyone, beware of one's own selective perceptions, and resist undue flattery. See also ASTROLOGY, THEORY OF; GRAPHOLOGY, THEORY OF; PERSONALITY THEORIES; PSEUDOSCIENTIFIC AND UNCONVENTIONAL THEORIES.

REFERENCES

Forer, B. (1949). The fallacy of personal validation: A classroom demonstration of gullibility. *Journal of Abnormal and Social Psychology, 44,* 118-123.

Halperin, K., & Snyder, C. (1979). Effects of enhanced psychological test feedback on treatment outcome: Therapeutic implications of the Barnum effect. *Journal of Consulting and Clinical Psychology, 47,* 140-146.

Johnson, J., Cain, L., Falke, T., Hayman, J., & Perillo, E. (1985). The "Barnum effect" revisited: Cognitive and motivational factors in the acceptance of personality descriptions. *Journal of Personality and Social Psychology, 49,* 1378-1391.

BARTLETT'S SCHEMATA THEORY. = schema theory. The English psychologist Sir Frederic Charles Bartlett (1886-1969) proposed an admittedly vague theory - the *schemata theory of memory* - as a way of invalidating and repudiating the classical *trace theory of memory* (i.e., the hypothesized modification of neural tissue resulting from any form of stimulation such as learning new material). Bartlett stressed the constructive, over the reproductive, aspects of recall and adapted his *schemata theory* (based on the assumption that *schemata* are cognitive, mental plans that are abstract guides for action, structures for interpreting and retrieving information, and organized frameworks for solving problems) from the English neurologist Sir Henry Head's (1861-1940) work on sensation, neurology, and the cerebral cortex. Unfortunately, *Bartlett's theory* apparently was too speculative to gain wide acceptance in the psychological community, even though it led many people to think somewhat differently about the dynamics and nature of memory. Other forms of *schema theory* - the mental representation of some aspect of experience based on prior experience or memory, structured to facilitate perception and cognition - are Sir Henry Head's approach that emphasized a person's internal body image; and the concept of a "frame" described by the American cognitive scientist Marvin L. Minsky (1927-), which is a schema formalized in terms of artificial intelligence, along with his concept of "knowledge-line," or "K-line," that is a hypothesized connection that reactivates a memory in an associative network model. See also ARTIFICIAL INTELLIGENCE; CONSTRUCTIVIST THEORY OF PERCEPTION; MEMORY, THEORIES OF; TRACE THEORY.

REFERENCES

Head, H. (1920). *Studies in neurology II*. London: Oxford University Press.

Bartlett, F. C. (1932). *Remembering: A study in experimental and social psychology*. Cambridge, UK: Cambridge University Press.

Oldfield, R., & Zangwill, O. (1943). Head's concept of the schema and its application in contemporary British psychology: Part III. Bartlett's theory of memory. *British Journal of Psychology, 33*, 113-129.

Minsky, M. L. (1967). *Computation: Finite and infinite machines*. Englewood Cliffs, NJ: Prentice-Hall.

Zangwill, O. (1972). "Remembering" revisited. *Quarterly Journal of Experimental Psychology, 24*, 124-138.

Minsky, M. L. (1980). K-lines: A theory of memory. *Cognitive Science, 4*, 117-133.

BASEMENT/FLOOR EFFECT. See MEASUREMENT THEORY.

BASE-RATE FALLACY. See PROBABILITY THEORY/LAWS.

BASIC RULE. See FREUD'S THEORY OF PERSONALITY.

BATESON'S VIBRATORY THEORY. See MENDEL'S LAWS/PRINCIPLES.

BAYES' THEOREM. This theoretical speculation, often employed in psychological statistics (e.g., Hays, 1963/1994), indicates the relation among various conditional probabilities. *Bayes' theorem* is named in honor of Thomas Bayes (1702-1761), an 18th century English clergyman and mathematician who did early work in probability and decision theory. Although Bayes wrote on theology, he is best known for his two mathematical works, "Introduction to the Doctrine of Fluxions" (1736) - a defense of the logical foundations of Newton's calculus against the attack of Bishop Berkeley; and "Essay Towards Solving a Problem in the Doctrine of Chances" (1763) - a posthumously published work that attempts to establish that the rule for determining the probability of an event is the same whether or not anything is known beforehand on any trials or observations concerning the event in question. In its simplest version, *Bayes' theorem* may be expressed in the following way: For two events, A and B, in which none of the probabilities p(A), p(B), and p(A and B) is either 1.00 or 0, the following relation holds: $p(A|B) = p(B|A)p(A)/p(B|A)p(A) + p(B|\sim A)p(\sim A)$. *Bayes' theorem* gives a way to determine the conditional probability of event A given event B, provided that one knows the probability of A, the conditional probability of B given A, and the conditional probability of B given ~A [Note: Once the probability of A is known, then the probability of ~A is simply 1-p(A)]. In psychology, *Bayes' theorem* has been used frequently as a model of choice behavior and attitude formation because it gives a mathematical rule for deciding how prior information (e.g., one's past choices or opinions) may be modified maximally in the light of new information. Moreover, in various practical situations - such as educational and clinical settings - good selection or diagnostic procedures are those that permit an increase in the probability of being correct about an individual given some prior information or evidence, and such conditional probabilities often may be calculated via *Bayes' theorem*. As a mathematical device, this theorem is necessarily true for conditional probabilities that satisfy the basic axioms of probability theory and *Bayes' theorem*, in itself, is not controversial. However, the question of its appropriate use has been an issue in the controversy between those who favor a strict "relative-frequency" interpretation of probability and those who allow a "subjective" interpretation of probability as well. This issue emerges clearly when some of the probabilities used in figuring *Bayes' theorem* in a given situation are associated with "states of nature" or with "non-repetitive" events in which it is usually difficult to give meaningful "relative-frequency" interpretations to probabilities for such states or "one-time" events. A term in probability reasoning related to *Bayes' theorem*, and advanced by the French mathematician Pierre Simon La Place (1749-1827), is called *insufficient reason* (or the *principle of indifference*) which states that a person is entitled to consider two events as equally probable if the individual has no reason to consider one more probable than the other. The criterion of *insufficient reason* enables the notion of "uncertainty" to be transformed into "risk" statements and provides a justification for the employment of "prior probabilities" in Bayesian inference in the absence of other bases for estimating them. Critics of this approach suggest that it leads to contradictions eventually and assert, consequently, that nothing useful may be inferred from such a result. See also ATTITUDE/ATTITUDE CHANGE, THEORIES OF; CHOICE AND PREFERENCE, THEORY OF; DECISION-MAKING THEORIES; PROBABILITY THEORY/LAWS.

REFERENCES

Bayes, T. (1958). Essay towards solving a problem in the doctrine of chances (1763). *Biometrika, 45,* 293-315.

Hays, W. L. (1963/1994). *Statistics for psychologists.* New York: Holt, Rinehart, and Winston/Harcourt Brace.

BEAUTY AND PHYSICAL APPEARANCE PRINCIPLE. See INTERPERSONAL ATTRACTION THEORIES; LIPPS' EMPATHY THEORY.

BECK'S COGNITIVE THERAPY THEORY. See BEHAVIOR THERAPY AND COGNITIVE THERAPY, THEORIES OF.

BEHAVIOR-EXCHANGE MODEL AND THEORY. See EXCHANGE AND SOCIAL EXCHANGE THEORY.

BEHAVIOR THEORY OF PERCEPTION. See PERCEPTION (II. COMPARATIVE APPRAISAL), THEORIES OF.

BEHAVIOR THERAPY AND COGNITIVE THERAPY, THEORIES OF. The term *behavior therapy* originated in a 1953 report by O. Lindsley, B. F. Skinner, and H. Solomon that described their use of operant conditioning principles with psychotic patients. Later, A. Lazarus (1958) used the term in referring to J. Wolpe's application of the technique of *reciprocal inhibition* to neurotic patients, and H. Eysenck (1959) used *behavior therapy* to refer to the application of *modern learning theory* to neurotic patients' behavior. The early usage of the term *behavior therapy* was linked consistently to *learning theory*; it was called *conditioning therapy*, also, which had as its goal the elimination of nonadaptive behavior and the initiation and strengthening of adaptive habits. L. Krasner (1971) asserts that 15 factors within psychology coalesced during the 1950s and 1960s to create and form the *behavior therapy* theoretical approach: the concept of *behaviorism* in experimental psychology; instrumental/operant conditioning research; the treatment procedure of *reciprocal inhibition*; studies at Maudsley Hospital in London; the application of conditioning and learning concepts to human behavior problems in the United States from the 1920s through the 1950s; *learning theory* interpretations of psychoanalysis; use of Pavlovian classical conditioning to explain and change both normal and deviant behaviors; impact of concepts and research from social role learning and interactionism in social psychology and sociology; research in developmental and child psychology emphasizing modeling and vicarious learning; formulation of social influence variables and concepts such as demand characteristics, experimenter bias, placebo, and hypnosis; development of the *social learning model* as an alternative to the *disease model* of behavior; dissatisfaction with, and critiques of, traditional psychotherapy and the *psychoanalytic model* (cf., Gross, 1979); advancement of the idea of the clinical psychologist as "scientist-practitioner;" development in psychiatry of human and social interaction and environmental influences; and resurgence of utopian views of social-environmental planning. The unifying theme in *behavior therapy* is its derivation from empirically based principles and procedures.

Four general types of *behavior therapy* have been advanced by psychologists: interactive, instigation, replication, and intervention therapies; and five different approaches in contemporary *behavior therapy* are recognized: applied behavior analysis, neobehavioristic mediational S-R model, social learning theory, multimodal behavior therapy, and cognitive-behavior modification. A number of specific behavior and cognitive therapies based on these principles and theories have been developed since the 1960s, such as *rational-emotive therapy/ABC theory*; *cognitive therapy* [the American psychiatrist Aaron Temkin Beck (1921-) is often called the "father of cognitive therapy"]; *self-instructional/stress inoculation*; and *covert modeling therapy* [cf., *ACT theory and therapy* - formulation of the basic concepts of "acceptance and commitment therapy," or "ACT," that is grounded in radical behaviorism; corollary terms are "ACT-R," or behavioral analysis of a client seeking therapy; and "ACT-HC," or acceptance of limitations and commitment to healthy behavior and care]. It has been suggested that the various challenges facing *behavior* and *cognitive therapy theories* today concerning their procedures and effectiveness may best be met by the use of a "technical eclecticism" (cf., Lazarus, 1981), where there is a willingness to employ appropriate techniques across the various theoretical perspectives. However, the specific methods used in the diverse *behavior therapy theories* all have the common attributes of scientific examination of behavior grounded in *learning theory*, including the control of appropriate variables, the appreciation of data-based concepts, and the high regard for operational definitions of terms and replicability of results. The development of *behavior therapy* was not monolithic in concept, theory, or practice, and its roots are wide and varied. Thus, essentially, *behavior therapy theory* (cf., O'Donohue & Krasner, 1995) may best be characterized, generally, as the application of the laws of *modern learning theory* to all types of disorder, including individual, situational, and environmental aspects. See also ABC THEORY/MODEL; BANDURA'S THEORY; BEHAVIORIST THEORY; DEPRESSION, THEORIES OF; LEARNING THEORIES AND LAWS; SKINNER'S DESCRIPTIVE BEHAVIOR AND OPERANT CONDITIONING THEORY; WOLPE'S THEORY AND TECHNIQUE OF RECIPROCAL INHIBITION.

REFERENCES

Lindsley, O., Skinner, B. F., & Solomon, H. (1953). *Studies in behavior therapy.* Waltham, MA: Metropolitan State Hospital.

Lazarus, A. (1958). New methods in psychotherapy: A case study. *South African Medical Journal, 33,* 660-664.

Wolpe, J. (1958). *Psychotherapy by reciprocal inhibition.* Stanford, CA: Stanford University Press.

Eysenck, H. (1959). Learning theory and behaviour therapy. *Journal of Mental Science, 195,* 61-75.

Eysenck, H. (Ed.) (1964). *Experiments in behavior therapy: Readings in modern methods of mental disorders derived from learning theory.* Oxford, UK: Pergamon Press.

Beck, A. T. (1967). *Depression: Clinical, experimental, and theoretical aspects.* New York: Hoeber.

Kanfer, F., & Phillips, J. (1970). *Learning foundations of behavior therapy.* New York: Wiley.

Cautela, J. (1971). Covert conditioning. In A. Jacobs & L. Sachs (Eds.), *The psychology of private events: Perspectives on covert response systems.* New York: Academic Press.

Krasner, L. (1971). Behavior therapy. *Annual Review of Psychology, 22,* 483-532.

Beck, A. T. (1974). *Cognitive therapy and the emotional disorders.* New York: International Universities Press.

Meichenbaum, D. (1977). *Cognitive-behavior modification: An integrative approach.* New York: Plenum.

Kazdin, A, & Wilson, G. (1978). *Evaluation of behavior therapy.* Cambridge, MA: Ballinger.

Gross, M. (1979). *The psychological society.* New York: Simon & Schuster.

Kendall, P., & Hollon, S. (Eds.) (1979). *Cognitive behavioral interventions: Theory, research, and procedures.* New York: Academic Press.

Lazarus, A. (1981). *Multimodal theory*. New York: Guilford Press.

O'Donohue, W., & Krasner, L. (1995). *Theories of behavior therapy*. Washington, D. C.: A.P.A.

BEHAVIORAL CONTRAST EFFECT OR PHENOMENON. See GENERALIZATION, PRINCIPLE OF.

BEHAVIORAL DECISION-MAKING THEORY. See DECISION-MAKING THEORIES.

BEHAVIORAL MECHANICS, THEORY OF. The *theory of behavioral mechanics* is the behavioral and psychological counterpart of Sir Isaac Newton's laws of motion in physics where the rate of responding in the psychologist's operant conditioning paradigm is analogous to the phenomenon of velocity in the field of physics. The three major propositions or principles of the *theory of behavioral mechanics* - which are considered to hold for groups as well as for individual organisms - may be stated as follows: once a course of action or behavior has been initiated, that particular behavior or course of action will continue until such time as a force may be imposed upon it; the strength of a course of action or behavior is characterized by its "behavioral momentum" whose two components are its "behavioral mass" and "behavioral velocity;" and when a force is imposed upon a course of action or behavior, that force produces a change in the behavioral momentum and that change evokes a "behavioral counterforce" that acts in opposition to the imposed force. In various empirical studies, the basic relation between the organisms' rate of responding and experimental sessions involving both fixed-interval and variable-interval schedules of reinforcement has yielded a power function which, in turn, yields functions for the specific behavioral variables of acceleration, mass, and momentum. In practical terms, this overall numerical approach allows behavioral force values to be assigned to diverse experimental conditions or scenarios, such as the clinical assessment of the behavioral influence/force of a medication dosage. See also OPERANT CONDITIONING PARADIGM; OPERANT CONDITIONING/BEHAVIOR, LAWS/THEORY OF.

REFERENCES

Dzendolet, E. (1999). On the theory of behavioral mechanics. *Psychological Reports, 85,* 707-742.

Killeen, P. R. (1992). Mechanics of the animate. *Journal of the Experimental Analysis of Behavior, 57,* 429-463.

BEHAVIORAL POTENTIAL THEORY. See ROTTER'S SOCIAL LEARNING THEORY; TOLMAN'S THEORY.

BEHAVIORAL THEORIES OF HUMOR AND LAUGHTER. Within the context of humor and laughter theory analyses, the phenomenon of *play* may be considered as a behavior consisting of the following elements: an emotional aspect of pleasure; a demonstration more often in the immature, than in the adult, individual; a lack of immediate biological effect concerning the continued existence of the individual or the species; embodiment of species-specific features and forms; a relationship of the duration, amount, and diversity of play to the position of the species on the phylogenetic scale; a demonstration of freedom from conflicts; and a behavior that is relatively unorganized, spontaneous, and appears to be an end in itself. *Behavioral theories of humor and laughter*, also, may contain instinctive, exploratory, aesthetic, and learned actions without subsuming their basic functions. Contemporary approaches that employ the behavioral paradigm to humor analysis may be found in studies that examine the "drive-reduction/stimulus-response learning" aspects, and the *arousal-change* or *experimental arousal* aspects of humor responses. For example, concerning the latter, it has been suggested that humor springs from an "arousal jag" that stems from an experience of threat, discomfort, uncertainty, unfamiliarity, or surprise that is followed by some event that signifies safety, readjustment, release, or clarification; in this sense, the humor experience may be more or a behavioral or neurophysiological event than a psychological state. Regarding the *drive-reduction model* and humor, the basic experimental premise is that the humor response takes on the function of a "secondary reinforcer" because humor reduces the person's sexual and/or aggressive drives. The tenets of classical *behavioral theory* are indicated, also, in the famous "nature versus nurture" theoretical controversy that permeates the history of psychology. In the present context, at issue is whether humor-related behaviors are learned ("nurture") or are innate ("nature"). Many psychologists assume that laughter and humor are maturational processes demonstrating individual differences in expressive frequency and time of onset. However, some psychologists label laughter as an "instinct," an "orienting response," an "unconditioned mechanism," or a "reflex," while others accept the inborn nature of the laughter response, but maintain that what is laughed at is extended or elaborated via learning, repetitive behavior, habit, and experience. See also DARWIN-HECKER HYPOTHESIS OF LAUGHTER/HUMOR; FREUD'S THEORY OF WIT/HUMOR; HUMOR, THEORIES OF; INSTINCT THEORY OF LAUGHTER AND HUMOR; NATURE VERSUS NURTURE THEORIES; SULLY'S THEORY OF LAUGHTER/HUMOR.

REFERENCE

Roeckelein, J. E. (2002). *The psychology of humor*. Westport, CT: Greenwood Press.

BEHAVIORAL THEORY OF TIMING. The *behavioral theory of timing* (Killeen & Fetterman, 1988) is based on the observation that signals of reinforcement elicit "adjunctive" (elicited or emitted, interim or terminal) behaviors where transitions between such behaviors are caused by pulses from an "internal clock." The interbehavioral transitions are described as a Poisson process, with a rate constant proportional to the rate of reinforcement in the experimental context. Additionally, these adjunctive behaviors may come to serve as the basis for conditional discriminations of the passage of time. This *behavioral theory of timing* constitutes a formalization of the notion that behavior is the mediator of temporal control, and relies on a classical model of timing, the *clock-counter model*, or *pacemaker-accumulator system*, in which an oscillator of some type generates pulses that are summed by a hypothetical "accumulator."

P. Killeen and N. Weiss (1982) have generalized the behavioral timing system to one in which variability may arise not only from inaccuracy in the "pacemaker," but also from errors in the "clock-counter;" such a generalized model is consistent with many of the data on relative accuracy in human time perception. The "accumulator," "pacemaker," "clock," and "counter" are key hypothetical constructs in the *behavioral theory of timing*. See also SCALAR TIMING THEORY; TIME, THEORIES OF.

REFERENCES

Killeen, P., & Weiss, N. (1987). Optimal timing and the Weber function. *Psychological Review*, *94*, 455-468.

Killeen, P., & Fetterman, J. G. (1988). A behavioral theory of timing. *Psychological Review*, *95*, 274-295.

Church, R., Broadbent, H., & Gibbon, J. (1992). Biological and psychological descriptions of an internal clock. In I. Gormezano & E. Wasserman (Eds.), *Learning and memory: The behavioral and biological substrates*. Hillsdale, NJ: Erlbaum.

Fetterman, J. G., & Killeen, P. (1995). Categorical scaling of time: Implications for clock-counter models. *Journal of Experimental Psychology: Animal Behavior Processes*, *21*, 43-63.

Church, R. (1997). Timing and temporal events. In C. Bradshaw & E. Szabadi (Eds.), *Time and behavior: Psychological and neurobehavioral analyses*. Amsterdam, Netherlands: North-Holland.

BEHAVIORIST, BEHAVIORISTIC, AND BEHAVIORISM THEORY. *Behaviorist theory* ("behaviorism") was the most significant movement in experimental psychology from 1900 to about 1975. It was launched formally in 1913 by the American psychologist John Broadus Watson (1878-1958) but had its origins in the writings and work of the French philosophers Rene Descartes (1596-1650) and Julien Offray de LaMettrie (1709-1751), as well as the later experimentalists Ivan Pavlov, Jacques Loeb, and E. L. Thorndike. *Behaviorist theory* remains influential today in spite of much criticism leveled against it after about 1960. In general, *behaviorist theory* developed as an alternative orientation toward studying and explaining one's conscious experience, and it originally rejected both the methods and tenets of *mentalism* (where the proper subject matter of psychology was purported to be the study of mind, favoring the method of *introspection*, or "looking into one's own experience"). In Watson's classical approach, *behaviorist theory* was formulated as a purely objective experimental branch of natural science whose goal was the prediction and control of behavior, whose boundaries recognized no dividing line between humans and "lower" animals, and which rejected concepts such as *mind, consciousness*, and *introspection*. Various reformulations and versions of Watson's classical behaviorist approach, called *neobehaviorist theory* (or "neobehaviorism"), appeared in the 20th century under the labels of *formal behaviorism* (including *logical behaviorism* and *purposive/cognitive behaviorism*), *informal behaviorism*, and *radical behaviorism. Formal behaviorist theory*, under the influence of *logical positivism* (where propositions in science need to be verified by empirical and observable means), attempted to explain behavior in terms of a theory that consisted of operational definitions of concepts, processes, and events both directly observed and unobserved. The *logical behaviorism* of the American psychologist Clark Leonard Hull (1884-1952), formulated in terms of a *hypothetico-deductive learning theory*, was the most systematized theory of the *formal behaviorists*. Another variation of the *formal behaviorist theories* was the American psychologist Edward Chace Tolman's (1886-1959) *purposive/cognitive behaviorist theory*, which rejected the highly mechanistic approach of Watson and Hull, and espoused the notion that organisms are always acting to move toward or away from some goal where their purpose is to learn about their environments, not simply to respond to stimuli. *Tolman's theory* developed the "internal" concepts of *purpose, cognition, cognitive maps*, and *expectancies* as a way of explaining behavior. *Informal behaviorist theory*, or *liberalized stimulus-response theory*, formulated "covert mediating events" (called "fractional, unobservable responses")

between the initial stimulus and the final response in a learned behavior. In this way, the covert behaviors of memory, thinking, language, and problem solving could be cast into *behavior theory* terms where the notion of the "central mediating response" was a core concept. *Radical behaviorist theory* is closest of all the neobehaviorist variations to Watson's classical theory. This approach proposes that whatever cannot be observed and measured does not exist; it also rejects the "fuzzy" and ill-defined concepts in psychology such as *mind, free will, personality, self*, and *feelings*, even though it allows an organism's "private world" to be studied scientifically (Skinner, 1938, 1953, 1963, 1974). The theoretical approach of the *radical behaviorists* is the only type of *behaviorist theory* that is exerting a serious influence on mainstream psychology today, while the other behaviorist variations have passed into history. It is possible that present-day cognitive psychology is a new form of *behaviorist theory* with historical roots in Tolman's *purposive/cognitive psychology* and Hull's *logical behaviorism*, and a new term (such as *behavioralism*; cf., Ions, 1977) may be needed to combine the *behaviorist* position with the *cognitivist* position, both of which commonly reject traditional *mentalism* (i.e., the doctrine that an adequate account of human behavior is not possible without invoking mental events as explanatory devices, and which also posits that mental phenomena cannot be reduced to physiological or physical events). See also HULL'S LEARNING THEORY; LASHLEY'S THEORY; LOEB'S TROPISTIC THEORY; SKINNER'S BEHAVIOR THEORY/OPERANT CONDITIONING THEORY; SPENCE'S THEORY; TOLMAN'S THEORY.

REFERENCES

LaMettrie, J. (1748/1961). *Man as machine*. LaSalle, IL: Open Court.

Watson, J. B. (1913). Psychology as the behaviorist views it. *Psychological Review, 20*, 158-177.

Watson, J. B. (1919). *Psychology from the standpoint of a behaviorist*. Philadelphia: Lippincott.

Watson, J. B. (1925). *Behaviorism*. New York: Norton.

Watson, J. B. (1928). *The ways of behaviorism*. New York: Norton.

Watson, J. B., & McDougall, W. (1929). *The battle of behaviorism*. New York: Norton.

Tolman, E. C. (1932). *Purposive behavior*. New York: Appleton-Century.

Skinner, B. F. (1938). *The behavior of organisms: An experimental analysis*. New York: Appleton-Century.

Hull, C. L. (1943). *Principles of behavior*. New York: Appleton-Century-Crofts.

Hull, C. L. (1952). *A behavior system: An introduction to behavior theory concerning the individual organism*. New Haven, CT: Yale University Press.

Skinner, B. F. (1953). *Science and human behavior*. New York: Macmillan.

Miller, N. E. (1959). Liberalization of basic S-R concepts: Extensions to conflict behavior, motivation, and social learning. In S. Koch (Ed.), *Psychology: A study of a science*. Vol. 2. New York: McGraw-Hill.

Skinner, B. F. (1963). Behaviorism at fifty. *Science, 140*, 951-958.

Skinner, B. F. (1974). *About behaviorism*. New York: Knopf.

Ions, E. (1977). *Against behavioralism*. Oxford, UK: Blackwell.

BEKESY'S THEORY. See AUDITION AND HEARING, THEORIES OF.

BELL-MAGENDIE LAW. This generalized principle, initially described by the Scottish anatomist, surgeon, and neurophysiological pioneer Sir Charles Bell (1774-1842) in 1811, was restated independently in 1818 by the French physiologist Francois Magendie (1783-1855). The *Bell-Magendie law* states that the *ventral* roots of the spinal nerves ("efferents") have *motor* functions, whereas the *dorsal* roots of the spinal nerves ("afferents") have *sensory* functions. Bell's work in physiology was considered in his own time as the most important since the English physician William Harvey's (1578-1657) discovery of the circulation of the blood in 1628. The differentiation of the sensory and motor nerve functions had been known by the early Greek physician Galen (c. 130-200), but this knowledge was lost by later physiologists who believed that the nerves functioned nondifferentially in transmitting both sensory and motor impulses. Bell's explorations of the sensorimotor functions of the spinal nerves triggered a bitter and prolonged priority dispute (i.e., who discovered the principle first?) with Magendie. Apparently, Magendie did not know of Bell's discovery, which was published privately in 1811 as a monograph of only 100 copies. Today, both scientists are given credit for the discovery known as the *Bell-Magendie law*. The discovery of the distinction between sensory and motor nerves in the *Bell-Magendie law* provided the basis for the English physician/physiologist Marshall Hall's (1790-1857) work on the reflex arc and reflex functions. Bell's experimental work led to the discovery of the long thoracic nerve in the body named *Bell's nerve*. Additionally, the term *Bell's palsy* refers to Bell's demonstration that lesions of the seventh cranial nerve creates facial paralysis. Magendie's work, on the other hand, was concerned with wide-ranging and comprehensive studies in experimental physiology extending from the relationships between sensations and the nervous system to the relationships between intellect and the number of convolutions in the brains of animals on different levels of the phylogenetic scale. The *Bell-Magendie law* - stating that afferent neurons enter the spinal cord dorsally (from the back), and efferent neurons exit the spinal cord ventrally (from the front) - was elaborated by later workers in physiology into the principle that conduction from cell to cell within the central nervous system occurs only in the direction from receptor to effector. See also NEURON, NEURAL, AND NERVE THEORY.

REFERENCES

Bell, C. (1811). *Idea of a new anatomy of the brain*. London: Strahan & Preston.

Hall, M. (1833). On the reflex action of the medulla oblongata and medulla spinalis. *Philosophical Transactions of the Royal Society of London, 123*, 635-665.

BELONGINGNESS, LAW OR PRINCI-PLE OF. This is one of E. L. Thorndike's accessory/secondary laws to his main *law of effect*, whereby the properties of one item, when closely related to the properties of another item, cause a bond to be formed easily between the two items. This principle implicitly acknowledges the contributions made by *Gestalt theory* and the Gestalt school in psychology, especially when considering the Gestaltists' *laws of perceptual organization*, whereby some kinds of stimuli seem to go together more naturally than others. For example, first and last names presented together may be grouped perceptually or learned better than a set of first names only or a set of last names only. The *principle of belongingness* has been reactivated in recent work on learning, where the basic principles of classical and operant conditioning are incomplete without some recognition of the relationship that exists between the items to be associated and the specific properties of the organism undergoing the learning experience. See also ASSOCIATIVE SHIFTING, LAW OF; EFFECT, LAW OF; GESTALT THEORY/LAWS; PERCEPTUAL ORGANIZATION, LAWS OF; REINFORCEMENT, THORNDIKE'S THEORY OF.
REFERENCE
Thorndike, E. L. (1932). *The fundamentals of learning*. New York: Teachers College, Columbia University.

BEM'S SELF-PERCEPTION THEORY. See ATTRIBUTION THEORY.

BENEKE'S DOCTRINE OF TRACES. See GESTALT THEORY/LAWS.

BERGLER'S THEORY OF HUMOR AND LAUGHTER. The American psychiatrist and psychoanalyst Edmund Bergler (1899-1991) asserted that laughter is not an inborn instinct and, therefore, the term "sense of humor" is a misnomer. In his theoretical approach to humor and laughter, Bergler adopted a psychoanalytic perspective and advanced the notion that laughter has a highly complex and individual "case history" that is connected intimately with infantile fears which are perpetuated in the "fantastic severity" of the inner conscience of the *superego*. *Bergler's theory of humor and laughter* attempts to understand those phenomena within the framework of the *superego* and the all-important *defense mechanism* of "psychic masochism" that is based on oral regression created by the unconscious *ego's* attempt to escape the *superego's* tyranny or oppression. Bergler suggested that the irony of all studies on laughter lies in an apparent contradiction: on the one hand, laughter is concentrated, split-second *euphoria*, and, on the other hand, laughter consists of concentrated, interminable *dysphoria*. See also FREUD'S THEORY OF WIT/HUMOR; HUMOR, THEORIES OF.
REFERENCE
Bergler, E. (1956). *Laughter and the sense of humor*. New York: Intercontinental Medical Book Corporation.

BERGSON'S THEORY OF HUMOR AND LAUGHTER. The French philosopher Henri Bergson (1859-1941) developed a humor theory that has survived over many years, and is often characterized as the "mechanization theory of laughter" (i.e., the ludicrous is something mechanical that is "encrusted on the living"). According to *Bergson's theory of humor/laughter*, a necessary condition of laughter is the absence of feeling, because the "greatest foe" of laughter is emotion. In Bergson's approach, the essence of the comic involves a kind of "momentary anesthesia" of the heart - its appeal is to one's intelligence, pure and simple. Also, according to Bergson, in order to understand the "why" of humor, one must determine the *social* function of laughter. Bergson's logical sequence of reasoning concerning the social basis of humor is as follows: life and society demand from the individual both elasticity and tension, adaptability and alertness; life sets a lower standard than does society; a moderate degree of adaptability enables one to live; to live well - which is the aim of society - requires much greater flexibility; society is compelled to be suspicious of all tendencies towards the inelastic, and for this reason, has devised the "social gesture" of laughter to serve as a "corrective" of all unsocial deviations. Bergson suggests that the comic is always something rigid, inelastic, and inflexible (i.e., "something mechanical encrusted on the living"), and usurps the place in human activities of the fine adjustment that society requires. In Bergson's view, laughter is corrective in purpose, whether consciously or unconsciously applied; in laughter and humor, one always finds an intention to humiliate and, consequently, to "correct" one's neighbor - if not in his will, at least in his deed. Thus, laughter is the "revenge of society on the unsocial." In dealing with the simplest form of the comic (i.e., physical deformities which are ludicrous rather than ugly), Bergson formulates the following "law": A deformity that may become comic is a deformity that a normally-built person could successfully imitate. The reasoning behind this principle is that the deformity suggests a certain rigidity that is required as a habitual feature of a normal person (e.g., the figure of a hunchback suggests a "person who holds himself badly"); this is always, in such cases, the suggestion of a certain "rigidity" or "automatism" that produces the effect. Thus, as Bergson observed, the attitudes, gestures, and movements of the human body are laughable in exact proportion as that body reminds us of a "mere machine." The purpose of laughter, in Bergson's account, is to remove the "mechanical encrustation on the living" through humiliation and, thereby, promote free, healthy, and well-adapted social behaviors. As a supplement to *superiority humor theories*, Bergson adds a perspective about the object of the mockery (i.e., "mechanical inelasticity") as well as developing the social function/aspect of laughter. See also HUMOR, THEORIES OF; SUPERIORITY THEORIES OF HUMOR.

REFERENCE

Bergson, H. (1911). *Le rire*. (*Laughter: An essay on the meaning of the comic*). New York: Macmillan.

BERGSON'S THEORY OF TIME. The French philosopher Henri Bergson (1859-1941) made the experience of *time* central to his overall philosophy. He developed a "relational subjective" basis in his approach to explaining time and, thereby, reacted against the scientific and mechanistic thought that was present in the late 19th and early 20th centuries. Bergson distinguishes between *chronological*

time (which symbolizes space) and *duration* (which is apprehended through intuition and is identical with the "essence of life"). Whereas *chronological time* is to Bergson a mere social convenience, *duration* to him is an immeasurable flow or continuous progression of time where past, present, and future are dynamically fused and dissolve into an unbroken flux. See also FRAISSE'S THEORY OF TIME; TIME, THEORIES OF.

REFERENCES

Bergson, H. (1910). *Time and free will*. London: Allen & Unwin.

Bergson, H. (1912). Time and free will. *Psychological Bulletin, 9*, 176-180.

Bergson, H. (1922/1965). *Duration and simultaneity*. Indianapolis: Bobbs-Merrill.

BERKELEY'S THEORY OF VISUAL SPACE PERCEPTION. In 1709, the Irish philosopher and theologian Bishop George Berkeley (1685-1753) argued for an *empiricist* (experience) position of vision and against a *nativist* (inborn) ability of persons to judge distance. Berkeley's account of perceptual distance is that various cues (such as the size of objects encountered in one's experience) were learned previously and that people make the association between particular distances and the sensations that arise from their eye muscle movements and positions. N. Smith (1905) suggests that the French philosopher Nicolas de Malebranche (1638-1715) formulated a theory of the perception of distance and magnitude that anticipated *Berkeley's theory of visual space perception*. Berkeley's theory posits that the perception of distance is an act of judgment that is grounded in experience, and he described the equivalents of what today are called the "secondary criteria" for appreciating visual space perception (such as aerial perspective, interposition, and relative size). Berkeley also listed three "primary criteria" for the appraisal of distance: the physical space between the pupils, which is changed by turning one's eyes as an object approaches or recedes (today, this is called the cue of *convergence*); the "blurring" of objects when they are too close to the eye (this factor is probably not valid today as a distance cue); and the "straining" of the eye (the cue that today may be called *accommodation*, involving the adjustment of the shape of the lens of the eye to compensate for the distance of the object of focus from the retina). E. G. Boring suggests that one must not be deceived about the extent of Berkeley's knowledge of visual space perception because he only vaguely understood the mechanism of the perception of distance. Berkeley was correct, essentially, in two of his three primary criteria, but he was a long way off from knowing about the physiology of convergence, corresponding points (including the *horopter theory* - the effect that when both eyes are fixated on a certain point in the visual field, there is a collection of points, called the *horopter*, in the field whose images fall on corresponding retinal points), and *Helmholtz's theory* of the physiology of accommodation. Apparently, Berkeley made the question of the perception of distance a matter of sensation or idea when he exemplified the introspectionist's *context theory* of the visual perception of distance and, in so doing, Berkeley generally anticipated the ideas of modern associationism. Berkeley's "subjective idealism" was influential in the historical development of the role of association in psychology as well as in advancing arguments for experiential factors in perception and against innate factors as the basis for vision (cf., *Hamilton's hypothesis of space* in H. Spencer, 1892). See also ASSOCIATION, LAWS AND PRINCIPLES OF; EMMERT'S LAW; EMPIRICIST VERSUS NATIVIST THEORIES; LOTZE'S THEORY OF LOCAL SIGNS; NATURE VERSUS NURTURE THEORIES; PANUM PHEN-OMENON; PERCEPTION (II. COMPARATIVE APPRAISAL), THEORIES OF; WITKINS' PERCEPTION THEORY.

REFERENCES

Berkeley, G. (1709/1948). Essay toward a new theory of vision. In A. Luce & T. Jessop (Eds.), *The works of George Berkeley, bishop of Cloyne*. Toronto: Nelson.

Berkeley, G. (1710/1950). *A treatise concerning the principles of human knowledge*. LaSalle, IL: Open Court.

Spencer, H. (1892). *The principles of psychology*. New York: Appleton.

Smith, N. (1905). Malebranche's theory of the perception of distance and magnitude. *British Journal of Psychology*, *1*, 191-204.

Boring, E. G. (1957). *A history of experimental psychology*. New York: Appleton-Century-Crofts.

Graham, C. (1965). Visual space perception. In C. Graham (Ed.), *Vision and visual perception*. New York: Wiley.

BERNE'S SCRIPT THEORY. = transactional analysis theory. The Canadian-born American psychologist/psychiatrist Eric L. Berne (1910-1970) formulated his *script theory* concerning personality (ego) development and relationships between individuals (cf., A. Adler's concept of *lifestyle*), which states that each person creates a *life script* early in life as a way of meeting one's needs, and it is usually carried out unknowingly. *Berne's theory* assumes that individuals develop one of four life positions: "I'm OK, you're OK," "I'm OK, you're not OK," "I'm not OK, you're OK," and "I'm not OK, you're not OK," and persons engage in games to play out their life scripts in order to obtain "stroking" (i.e., the attention and time of other people). The life position of "I'm not OK, you're OK" (or the "kick me" life script) indicates a maladaptive person who most likely suffers from depression. Treating maladjusted individuals involves explanation of the roles ("games") people play and how they treat other people in those roles, and where interpersonal transactions (*transactional analysis*) are analyzed concerning parent (*P*), adult (*A*), and child (*C*) roles. According to this once-popular approach, when a person's *PAC* roles are positioned opposite another person's *PAC* roles, and the lines of communication or interaction between them are *crossed*, the transaction is considered to be *unhealthy*. On the other hand, when the lines of communication between two sets of aligned *PAC* roles are *parallel*, the interpersonal transaction is considered to be *healthy*. An example of an *unhealthy* transaction is a patient's *A* personality (or "ego state") saying to a nurse's *A* personality: "I think working in a hospital would be challenging," but having the nurse's *P* personality reply to the patient's *C* personality by saying, "You're sick because you can't cope with your problems" (a *crossed* interchange from *P* to *C*, crossing the *A* to *A* communication line). *Berne's theory* and the *PAC* concepts contain obvious similarities to Sigmund Freud's *tripartite personality theory* concepts of *id*, *ego*, and *superego*, an accusation that Berne denied. See also ADLER'S THEORY OF PERSONALITY; FREUD'S THEORY OF PERSONALITY.

REFERENCES

Freud, S. (1920). *A general introduction to psychoanalysis*. New York: Pocket Books.

Adler, A. (1927). *Practice and theory of individual psychology*. New York: Humanities Press.

Berne, E. (1961). *Transactional analysis in psychotherapy: A systematic individual and social psychiatry*. New York: Grove Press.

Berne, E. (1964). *Games people play: The psychology of human relationships*. New York: Grove Press.

BERNOULLI DISTRIBUTION. See BERNOULLI'S THEOREM.

BERNOULLI'S THEOREM. In psychological statistics, the theoretical proposition named in honor of the 17th century Swiss mathematician Jakob (Jacques or James) Bernoulli (1654-1705) who - as well as being one of the chief developers both of the ordinary calculus and of the calculus of variations - wrote an important treatise on the *theory of probability* (posthumously published in 1713), and discovered the series of number that now carry his name (cf., *Daniel Bernoulli's theorem* of 1738 in physics - which anticipated the principle of the "conservation of energy"). *Jakob Bernoulli's theorem* may be stated as follows: If the probability of occurrence of the event *X* is *p(X)* and if *N* trials are made, independently and under exactly the same conditions, the probability that the relative frequency of occurrence of *X* differs from *p(X)* by any amount, however small, approaches zero as the number of trials grows indefinitely large. In common terms, *Bernoulli's theorem* says that even if one has only a limited number of trials, it may be expected that the probability of any event is reflected in the relative frequency one actually observes for that event; in the long run, such an observed relative frequency should approach the "true" probability. Essentially, *Bernoulli's theorem* holds because departures from what one expects to occur are simply "swamped out" as the number of observations or trials becomes very large. However, statisticians warn, in this context, that one should not fall into the error of thinking that an event is ever *due* to occur on any given trial. Rather, one's best guess about the probability of an event is the actual relative frequency one has observed from some *N* trials, and the larger the *N*, the better is one's guess. An example typically used to demonstrate *Bernoulli's theorem* is that of tossing a "fair" coin and counting the number of heads versus the number of tails that come up over a number of trials; in this case, .50 is the relative frequency of heads one should expect to observe in any given number (*N*) of tosses, and that it is increasingly probable that one observes close to 50 percent heads as the number of tosses increases (i.e., as *N* grows larger). The terms *Bernoulli trial* (i.e., any case or trial containing two mutually-exclusive and exhaustive possible outcomes, such as heads versus tails in coin-tossing) and *Bernoulli distribution* (i.e., a series of *Bernoulli trials* yields this special distribution, also called a "binomial distribution;" this theoretically-expected probability distribution occurs when random samples of size *N* are taken from a "Bernoulli-like" population containing exactly two classes or categories, such as flipping a coin; as the sample size increases, the binomial distribution approximates the "normal distribution curve") are used, often, in this area of *probability theory*. See also NORMAL DISTRIBUTION THEORY; PROBABILITY THEORY/LAWS.

REFERENCES

Bernoulli, J. (1713/1968). *Ars conjectandi*. Bruxelles: C. et C.

Feller, W. (1968/1971). *An introduction to probability theory and its applications*. New York: Wiley.

BERNOULLI TRIAL(S). See BERNOULLI'S THEOREM.

BERTRAND'S BOX PARADOX. See THREE-DOOR GAME SHOW PROBLEM.

BETA MOVEMENT EFFECT. See AP-
PARENT MOVEMENT, PRINCIPLES AND
THEORIES OF.

**BEZOLD-BRUCKE EFFECT, PHENOM-
ENON, OR HUE SHIFT.** This phenomenon,
first described between 1873 and 1878, is
credited to the German meteorologist Wilhelm
von Bezold (1837-1907) and the German
physiologist Ernst Wilhelm von Brucke
(1819-1892), who found that the hue of spectral colors of objects changes with the level of
illumination. The effect applies to bluish reds
and bluish greens, where the reds and greens
are perceived as bluer with increased illumination, and to yellowish reds and yellowish
greens, where the reds and greens are perceived as yellower with increased illumination. However, the *Bezold-Brucke effect* does
not occur with the "purer" reds, greens, blues,
and yellows. The phenomenon is usually obtained as an aspect of the negative afterimage
produced by retinal adaptation. See also AD-
APTATION, PRINCIPLES/LAWS OF; AF-
TERIMAGE LAW; COLOR VISION, THE-
ORIES/LAWS OF; PURKINJE EFFECT
AND PHENOMENON/SHIFT.
REFERENCES
Brucke, E. (1851). Untersuchungen uber sub-
jektive farben. *Poggendorf Annales
der Physiologie und Chemie, 84,*
418-452.
Brucke, E. (1884). *Vorlesungen uber physiologie.* Vol. 2. Vienna: Braumueller.

BICHAT, LAW OF. The French physician,
pathologist, and histologist/anatomist Marie
Francois Xavier Bichat (1771-1802) proposed
the principle that there are two main body
systems, which are in inverse relationship
regarding the development of ontogenetic
evolution, called the *vegetative* and the *animal*, with the *vegetative* system providing for
assimilation and augmentation of mass
(anabolism) and the *animal* system providing
for the transformation and expenditure of
energy (catabolism). Bichat's main contribution to medicine and physiology was his perception that the diverse organs of the body
contain particular tissues or *membranes*, and
he described 21 such membranes, including
connective, muscle, and nerve tissues. Bichat

maintained that in the case of disease in an
organ, generally not the whole organ but only
certain tissues are affected. Bichat did not use
the microscope, which he distrusted, so his
tissue analyses did not include any acknowledgement of their cellular structure. Bichat
established the significance and centrality of
the study of tissues ("histology"), and his
lasting importance lay in simplifying anatomy
and physiology by showing how the complex
structures of organs may be examined in terms
of their elementary tissues. Bichat's work,
done with great intensity during the last years
of his short life (he performed over 600 post-
mortems), had much influence in medical
science, and he formed a bridge between the
earlier *organ pathology* of Giovanni Battista
Morgagni (1682-1771) and the later *cell pathology* of Rudolf Ludwig Carl Virchow
(1821-1902). See also GENERAL SYSTEMS
THEORY.
REFERENCE
Bichat, M. F. X. (1812). *Anatomie generale
appliquee a la physiologie et a la
medecine.* 2nd ed. Paris: Brosson.

BIDWELL'S GHOST. See PURKINJE EF-
FECT/PHENOMENON/SHIFT.

BIEDERMAN'S THEORY. See PATTERN,
OBJECT RECOGNITION THEORY.

**BIFACTORIAL THEORY OF CONDI-
TIONING.** See PAVLOVIAN CONDITION-
ING PRINCIPLES, LAWS, AND THEO-
RIES.

BIG BANG HYPOTHESIS/THEORY. See
TIME, THEORIES OF.

**BIG FIVE MODEL/THEORY OF PER-
SONALITY.** See PERSONALITY THEO-
RIES.

BIG LIE THEORY. See PERSUASION/
INFLUENCE THEORIES.
BILLIARD BALL THEORY. See CON-
TEMPORANEITY, PRINCIPLE OF.

BINAURAL SHIFT EFFECT. See APPEN-
DIX A.

BIOBEHAVIORAL INTERACTION HYPOTHESIS. See GENERAL SYSTEMS THEORY.

BIOCHEMICAL THEORIES OF DEPRESSION. See DEPRESSION, THEORIES OF.

BIOCHEMICAL THEORIES OF PERSONALITY AND ABNORMALITY. See PSYCHOPATHOLOGY, THEORIES OF; SCHIZOPHRENIA, THEORIES OF.

BIOCHEMICAL/NEUROLOGICAL THEORIES OF SCHIZOPHRENIA. See SCHIZOPHRENIA, THEORIES OF.

BIOFEEDBACK, PRINCIPLES OF. See CONTROL/SYSTEMS THEORY.

BIOGENETIC LAW. See RECAPITULATION, THEORY/LAW OF.

BIOGENETIC RECAPITULATION THEORY. See RECAPITULATION, THEORY/LAW OF.

BIOGENIC AMINE THEORIES. See DEPRESSION, THEORIES OF.

BIOLOGICAL EVOLUTION, DOCTRINE OF. See DARWIN'S EVOLUTION THEORY.

BIOLOGICAL THEORIES OF DEPRESSION. See DEPRESSION, THEORIES OF.

BIORHYTHM THEORY. This speculation states - in its modern version - that there are three different biorhythm cycles that influence three different general aspects of human behavior: a 23-day cycle that affects *physical* aspects of behavior, a 28-day cycle that influences *emotions*, and a 33-day cycle that affects *intellectual* functions. Moreover, according to the *biorhythm theory*, the three cycles purportedly start at birth and progress in a sinusoidal fashion throughout one's life and do not vary with either physiological or environmental factors. Thus, theoretically, the three rhythms/cycles interact to determine "critical days" on which personal difficulties

and problems are likely to occur throughout one's life. The history of the biorhythm theory is traceable back to the late 19th century in Europe. Initially (in 1897), a Berlin surgeon, Wilhelm Fliess (1848-1928), proposed that a 23-day "male period" and a 28-day "female period" occurs in humans (it is interesting that Sigmund Freud seems to have been an admirer of Fliess's *biorhythm theory*, as noted in their mutual letters and correspondence; in one case, Freud referred to Fliess as the "Kepler of biology"). There are several features in "modern" *biorhythm theory* (beginning in the 1970s) that are not present in Fliess's original version of the theory (e.g., three cycles instead of two; the beginning of the cycles at the moment of birth; no variations in the durations of 23-, 28-, or 33-day periods). It was the three-cycle sinusoidal version of *biorhythm theory* that became a huge fad with the general public in the United States in the 1970s. For a comprehensive review of *biorhythm theory*, see Hines (1998) who examined over 11 dozen studies of the theory, both published and unpublished (less than 30 percent of these studies reported some support for the theory). According to Hines, one of the reasons that the *biorhythm theory* had fallen from scientific favor so rapidly is that the predictions made by the theory were tested and found to be inadequate; it is suggested that had the proponents of *biorhythm theory* adopted a host of ancillary hypotheses about variables that modified the influences of the major variables in the theory (e.g., as was the case with astrology), the theory may have been much more difficult to test and may have survived longer. See also ASTROLOGY, THEORY OF.

REFERENCES
Fliess, W. (1897). *Die beziehungen zwischen nas und weiblichen geschlechtsorganen: In ihrer biologischen bedeutung dargestellt.* Leipzig: Deuticke.

Hines, T. M. (1998). Comprehensive review of biorhythm theory. *Psychological Reports, 83,* 19-64.

BIOSOCIAL EFFECT. See EXPERIMENTER EFFECTS.

BIOSOCIAL THEORY. See MURPHY'S BIOSOCIAL THEORY.

BIRTH ORDER EFFECT. See ZAJONC'S AROUSAL/ CONFLUENCE THEORIES.

BIRTH ORDER THEORY. Even though there is a wealth of empirical research on *birth order* and its purported influence on personality, most of the results are restricted to isolated phenomena and incomplete explanations due to the absence of an underlying and comprehensive *theory of birth order*. However, one of Alfred Adler's most significant contributions to psychology is his formulation of the relationship between birth order and personality development. Adler hypothesized that the child's position in the family creates specific problems that are handled by families generally in the same way, and such birth order experiences may reveal a characteristic personality pattern for each ordinal birth position. According to Adler, as the family group develops, different demands arise, and need-fulfillment is assigned to each child in order of birth. The style of coping is never the same for any two children as the situation changes. Adler asserted that the needs that influence a specific lifestyle correspond to the child's *perceived* birth order, where it isn't the child's number in order of successive births that affects her character, but the *situation* into which she is born and the way in which it is *interpreted*. Thus, according to Adler and others, "psychological positioning" is the most important factor, where an individual's own *subjective psychological birth order perception* is superordinate to mere *biological birth order*. Research indicates that personality differences emerge in children, within a specific birth order group, relative to factors of absence/presence of a sibling, gender of the sibling, aspects of the parents' relationship, age, family size, exceptional status, available roles, and relationships with the extended family. In distinguishing between *idiographic* and *nomothetic laws*, as related to Adler's *theory of birth order*, one may make general guesses about an individual's personality based upon ordinal position, where the guesses are based on *nomothetic laws* (such as "youngest children tend to be" "oldest children tend to be" etc.), but the actual, specific case may be different depending on how the person perceives the situation and what that person does about it (which are called *idiographic laws*). Thus, *nomothetic laws* concerning the family constellation help in understanding the person's *idiographic laws* or "lifestyle." The major reviews of the literature concerning the influence of *birth order* on personality show the rubrics "Firstborn," "Middle-born," "Youngest," and "Only Child" to be the most frequently used and common divisions. The assumption of *birth order theory* that birth order *causes* the different personality traits is considered to be false, and it would be erroneous to overgeneralize or typecast a person on that basis. Adler's approach, which emphasizes the social determinants of personality and the predisposition of early influences to a "faulty lifestyle," seems to have merit for some psychologists who assert that no two people develop in exactly the same way. Some persons strive for "superiority," some attempt to cope with "basic inferiority," and one's family constellation may intensify or modify the child's feelings in either case. Recent research on *birth order theory* suggests that the *attitudes* of the *parents* may have a far greater affect than birth order on the child's psychological development and, also, that such *parents' attitudes* may have no relation to the child's ordinal birth position in the family. The problems of *birth order theory* are numerous and psychologists, generally, may be either pessimistic or optimistic concerning its long-range development and importance in explaining personality. See also ADLER'S THEORY OF PERSONALITY; IDIOGRAPHIC/NOMOTHETIC LAWS; SEXUAL ORIENTATION THEORIES.

REFERENCES

Adler, A. (1927). *Practice and theory of individual psychology.* New York: Humanities Press.

Adler, A. (1937). Position in family constellation influences life style. International *Journal of Individual Psychology, 3,* 211-227.

Schooler, C. (1972). Birth order effects: Not here not now! *Psychological Bulletin, 78,* 161-175.

Driscoll, R., & Eckstein, D. (1982). Empirical studies of the relationship between birth order and personality. In D.

Eckstein (Ed.), *Life style: What it is and how to do it*. Dubuque, IA: Kendall/Hunt.

BLAU'S EXCHANGE THEORY. See EXCHANGE/SOCIAL EXCHANGE THEORY.

BLENDING, LAW OF. See SKINNER'S DESCRIPTIVE BEHAVIOR AND OPERANT CONDITIONING THEORY.

BLEULER'S THEORIES. The Swiss physician/psychiatrist Eugen Bleuler (1857-1939) formulated theories of *schizophrenia* and *mania-depression* that include the following conjectures: there are four fundamental *symptoms* (the "four As") of schizophrenia: autism, ambivalence, inappropriate affect, and loosening of associations; there is a "fragmentation of thinking," i. e., a psychological disturbance in which thoughts and actions that are normally integrated are split apart, and thinking processes become confused where actions and ideas are impossible to complete; there is a total incapacity to feel sympathy for, or to be concerned with, the welfare of others (Bleuler used the obsolete terms "moral idiocy" and "imbecility"); there are inconsistencies in the explanations and reasons that some patients create to justify their previous behaviors ("pseudomotivations"); there may be episodes of elation or mental disturbance that tend to occur on the anniversary ("anniversary excitement") of a significant date in the person's life; there may be "blunted affect" or dulled feeling tone; there may be high "affectivity," or susceptibility to emotional stimuli to the extent that they disturb bodily states and functions; there may be episodes of "dereism," that is, mental activity that is not in accord with logic or reality, such as "delusional daydreams" or irrational beliefs, for example, believing that someone can cure diseases merely with a glance; there may be a "deterioration of attention" where there is a constant shifting of attention and the person cannot concentrate on external reality; and there are interruptions of thought associations that lead to confused, random, and/or bizarre thinking and speech. See also PSYCHOPATHOLOGY, THEORIES OF; SCHIZOPHRENIA, THEORIES OF.

REFERENCE

Bleuler, E. (1911/1950). *Dementia praecox: Or the group of schizophrenias*. New York: International Universities Press.

BLOCH'S LAW. See BUNSEN-ROSCOE LAW.

BLOCKING, PHENOMENON OR EFFECT OF. The phenomenon of *blocking* is an example in the psychology of learning and conditioning that the temporal contiguity alone between events is not sufficient for an association to be formed between them. Although the *blocking effect* was at one time claimed by *selective attention theories*, the American experimental psychologist Leon J. Kamin (1924-) first described the *blocking experiment* where two groups of participants are used. One group is presented with a compound stimulus (called "AX") that is paired with an unconditioned stimulus (US), such as a noxious puff of air to the eye. A second group, before receiving an identical treatment, is given pretraining during which the "A" component of the compound stimulus is paired with the US (air puff). Following the "AX-US" pairing, the portion "X" of the compound stimulus is tested alone. It is found that "X" is more likely to elicit a conditioned response (CR), such as the eye blink, when the participants do *not* have prior training with the "A" component alone. The stimulus portion "X" of the compound stimulus is paired with the US (and, therefore, with the unconditioned response, UR) the same number of times in both groups. Contiguity between stimulus and response is established equally in both groups, and yet learning is not equal. The *blocking phenomenon/effect* indicates that there must be something more to conditioning and learning than mere stimulus-response contiguity. That is, if stimulus-response contiguity is a sufficient condition for learning to occur, then "X" should become an equally effective conditioned stimulus, or CS, in both groups, which it does not. Thus, *blocking* occurs when conditioning to a stimulus is attenuated, or "blocked," because that stimulus signals an outcome that was previously predicted by another stimulus or cue. Kamin's interpretation of the *blocking effect* is that conditioning depends on the predictability of reinforcement such that stimuli support learning only to the extent that the outcomes (that they signal) are "surprising." The first formal model to use Kamin's idea of "surprise" was developed by the American experimental psychologists Robert A. Rescorla (1940-) and Allan R. Wagner. Their model differs from previous theories by assuming that the associative strength of a CS decreases over trials because the US becomes less effective when it is signaled by a stimulus with increasingly greater associative strength; thus, the US is reinforcing only to the extent that it is "surprising." Theories that have followed the *Rescorla-Wagner model* have been distinguished on the basis of whether they focus attention on the processing of the US or on the processing of the CS. The *information-processing theory* of A. Wagner (1978) focuses on the processing of the US; the *attentional theory* of N. Mackintosh (1975) and research by J. Pearce and G. Hall (1980) focus on the processing of the CS. However, none of the theories as yet developed can accommodate all of the observations made from the *blocking experiments*, even though they have stimulated much research in the field of learning/conditioning. See also ASSOCIATION, LAWS/PRINCIPLES OF; ATTENTION, LAWS, PRINCIPLES, AND THEORIES OF; INFORMATION AND IN-FORMATION-PROCESSING THEORIES; LEARNING THEORIES/LAWS; PAVLOV-IAN CONDITIONING PRINCIPLES/LAWS, AND THEORIES.

REFERENCES

Kamin, L. J. (1968). "Attention-like" processes in classical conditioning. In M. Jones (Ed.), *Miami symposium on the prediction of behavior*. Miami, FL: University of Miami Press.

Kamin, L. J. (1969). Predictability, surprise, attention, and conditioning. In B. Campbell & R. Church (Eds.), *Punishment and aversive behavior*. New York: Appleton-Century-Crofts.

Rescorla, R. A., & Wagner, A. R. (1972). A theory of Pavlovian conditioning. Variations in the effectiveness of reinforcement and nonreinforcement. In A. Black & W. Prokasy (Eds.),
Classical conditioning. II. Current research and theory. New York: Appleton-Century-Crofts.

Mackintosh, N. (1975). A theory of attention: Variations in the associability of stimuli with reinforcement. *Psychological Review, 82*, 276-298.

Wagner, A. R. (1978). Expectancies and the priming of STM. In S. Hulse, H. Fowler, & W. Honig (Eds.), *Cognitive processes in animal behavior*. Hillsdale, NJ: Erlbaum.

Pearce, J., & Hall, G. (1980). A model for Pavlovian learning: Variations in the effectiveness of conditioned but not of unconditioned stimuli. *Psychological Review, 87*, 532-552.

BLOCK'S CONTEXTUALISTIC MODEL OF TIME. The American cognitive and experimental psychologist Richard A. Block (1946-) proposed a general *contextualistic model of time* which summarizes the interactions of four kinds of factors influencing psychological time and temporal experience: *characteristics* of the time *experiencer*; *contents* of the time period; the individual's *activities* during the time period; and the individual's *time-related behaviors and judgments*. Block acknowledges that although his approach clarifies many experimental findings and process-models of temporal experience, it does not yet provide the precise ways in which the four factors interact. See also FRASER'S INTERDISCIPLINARY TIME THEORY; ORNSTEIN'S THEORY OF TIME; PSYCHOLOGICAL TIME, MODELS OF; TIME, THEORIES OF.

REFERENCES

Block, R. A., & Reed, M. (1978). Remembered duration: Evidence for a contextual change hypothesis. *Journal of Experimental Psychology: Human Learning and Memory, 4*, 656-665.

Block, R. A. (1982). Temporal judgments and contextual change. *Journal of Experimental Psychology: Learning, Memory, and Cognition, 8*, 530-544.

Block, R. A. (1989). A contextualistic view of time and mind. In J. T. Fraser (Ed.), *Time and mind: Interdisciplinary is-*

sues. Madison, CT: International Universities Press.

BLOOD-GLUCOSE THEORY. See HUNGER, THEORIES OF.

BLUE-ARC PHENOMENON. See VISION AND SIGHT, THEORIES OF.

BODILY HUMORS, DOCTRINE OF. See GALEN'S DOCTRINE OF THE FOUR TEMPERAMENTS.

BODILY ROTATION, THEORY OF. See WITKIN'S PERCEPTION, PERSONALITY, AND COGNITIVE STYLE THEORY.

BODY BUFFER ZONE THEORY. See INTERPERSONAL ATTRACTION THEORIES.

BOHR'S COMPLEMENTARITY PRINCIPLE. See VISION/SIGHT, THEORIES OF.

BONDING THEORY OF CRIMINOLOGY. See LOMBROSIAN THEORY.

BOOLEAN SET THEORY. Between 1847 and 1854 the English mathematician George Boole (1815-1864) formulated a system of algebra and symbolic logic in which propositions are represented by the binary digits 0 (referring to "false") and 1 (referring to "true"). In *Boolean set theory*, in particular, the "Boolean sum" is known as "set union," the "Boolean product" as "set intersection," 0 as the "null set," and 1 as the "universal set." In *Boolean logic*, however, the "Boolean sum" is known as "or," the "Boolean product" as "and," 0 as "false," and 1 as "true." The formulations of *Boolean set theory* and *Boolean logic* (calculus of finite differences) are considered to be isomorphic; that is, they demonstrate a one-to-one correspondence between the elements of two or more sets or classes, and between the sums or products of the elements of one set and the sums or products of the equivalent elements of the other set. Boole's ideas have been used extensively in the areas of electronics and the computer sciences, and in psychology, specifically, in research on "artificial intelligence." Such applications are noteworthy because Boole originally considered his work to be representative of the basic processes and principles involved in human thought. See also ARTIFICIAL INTELLIGENCE; FUZZY SET THEORY; KOLMOGOROV'S AXIOMS AND THEORY; PROBABILITY THEORY/LAWS; SET THEORY.

REFERENCES

Boole, G. (1847/1948). *The mathematical analysis of logic, being an essay towards a calculus of deductive reasoning*. Oxford, UK: B. Blackwell.

Boole, G. (1854/1940). *An investigation of the laws of thought*. London: Walton & Maberly/Open Court.

BOOMERANG EFFECT. See ASSIMILATION-CONTRAST THEORY/EFFECT; ATTRIBUTION THEORY.

BOOSTING EFFECT OF SOCIAL SUPPORT. See BUFFERING MODEL/HYPOTHESIS OF SOCIAL SUPPORT.

BOSS-CONSCIOUSNESS THEORY OF COGNITION. This general model of cognition, called the *boss-consciousness theory* (e.g., Morris & Hampson, 1983; Hampson & Morris, 1990), postulates that some central control system is required to explain the many-faceted phenomena of consciousness, introspection, automaticity, and the interrelationships of cognitive processes. In this theory, a basic distinction is made between the central (*boss*) control function/process and the subordinate (*employee*) systems. Among the assumed characteristics of *boss-processing* are its "intentionality" and its suitability for performing novel tasks, where the concept of *consciousness* is equivalent to the reception of information made available to *boss*, and where introspection is involved in the reporting on this information. The role of *boss-consciousness* in imaging depends on its specific links with *top-down perceptual processing*; also, for a majority of the time, the perceptual *employee* systems may run without *boss* involvement even when they are involved in *top-down* operations. Occasionally, however, when the incoming stimulus information is

78

poor or inadequate, or when perceptual decisions are difficult, *boss-consciousness* may take more direct control of *top-down processing*. According to the model, *imagery* is the limiting case of perception without any stimulus information (i.e., *imagery* is equivalent to the perceptual system working in a purely *top-down* mode, normally under the direct control of a *boss program*; in this way, some organisms/individuals may learn the trick of "perceiving" without any actual stimulus data). The *boss-consciousness model* and *theory* incorporates differences between mental models and propositions where the perceivable aspects of models are representations that are expressed in the high-level language that *boss* deals in, and that allow it to plan subsequent processing. See also BOTTOM-UP PROCESSING THEORIES; IMAGERY AND MENTAL IMAGERY, THEORIES OF; TOP-DOWN PROCESSING THEORIES.

REFERENCES

Morris, P. E., & Hampson, P. J. (1983). *Imagery and consciousness.* New York: Academic Press.
Hampson, P. J., & Morris, P. E. (1990). Imagery, consciousness, and cognitive control: The BOSS model reviewed. In P. J. Hampson, D. F. Marks, & J. T. E. Richardson (Eds.), *Imagery: Current developments*. London: Routledge.

BOTTLENECK THEORY. See ATTENTION, LAWS/PRINCIPLES/THEORIES OF.

BOTTOM-UP PROCESSING THEORIES. *Bottom-up theories* is a general term referring to the direction of information processing in any given aspect of *perceptual* or *cognitive* theory. The term *bottom-up*, also called *data-driven processing*, was introduced by the American psychologists Donald A. Norman (1935-) and David E. Rumelhart (1942-), and refers to any form of information processing that is initiated, guided, and controlled by input that occurs in sequential stages, with each stage coming closer to a final interpretation than the last one. For example, in *object perception theory*, the analysis of objects into parts is called *bottom-up processing* because processing starts with basic units, and one's

perception is then built on the foundation laid by these units. Object perception is influenced not only by the nature of the units that make up objects but, also, by the observer's knowledge of the world (cf., *top-down processing*). In *cognitive theory*, similarly, *bottom-up processing* refers to the determination of a process primarily by the physical stimulus. The notion is that observers deal with the information in a given situation by beginning with the "raw" stimulus and then "work their way up" to the more abstract, cognitive operations. Thus, taking sensory data into the perceptual system first by the receptors and then sending it upward to the cortex for extraction and analysis of relevant information is called *bottom-up processing* or *data-driven processing*. Sensations of visual features and perceptions of organized objects are largely the result of *bottom-up processes*. See also INFORMATION AND INFORMATION-PROCESSING THEORY; PATTERN AND OBJECT RECOGNITION THEORY; PERCEPTION (I. GENERAL), THEORIES OF; PERCEPTION (II. COMPARATIVE APPRAISAL), THEORIES OF; TOP-DOWN PROCESSING/THEORIES.

REFERENCES

Norman, D. A., & Rumelhart, D. E. (1975). *Explorations in cognition.* San Francisco: Freeman.
Goldstein, E. (1996). *Sensation and perception.* Pacific Grove, CA: Books, Cole.

BOUGUER-WEBER LAW. See WEBER-FECHNER LAW.

BOUNDED RATIONALITY PRINCIPLE. See DECISION-MAKING THEORIES.

BOURDON EFFECT/ILLUSION. See APPENDIX A; PERCEPTION (I. GENERAL), THEORIES OF.

BOWDITCH'S LAW. See ALL-OR-NONE LAW/PRINCIPLE; MULLER'S DOCTRINE OF SPECIFIC NERVE ENERGIES.

BOW-WOW AND ANIMAL CRY THEORY. See LANGUAGE ORIGINS, THEORIES OF.

BRAIN-FIELD THEORY. See APPARENT MOVEMENT, PRINCIPLES OF.

BRAIN-LOCALIZATION THEORY. See GALEN'S DOCTRINE; LEARNING THEORIES AND LAWS.

BRAIN-SPOT HYPOTHESIS. See SCHIZOPHRENIA, THEORIES OF.

BRAIN-WASHING TECHNIQUES AND THEORY. The goal of the so-called "brain-washing" process/procedure is the production of extreme changes in a person's beliefs and attitudes through the application of methods such as sleep deprivation, induced hunger, pain, social isolation, physical discomfort, use of "good-cop versus bad-cop" interrogations by alternating kind and cruel inquisitors, and use of *sensory deprivation*. Under conditions of *sensory deprivation* (*SD*), for example, the individual is cut off from almost all sensory stimulation from the external environment. The early *SD* experiments reported in the 1950s indicate that volunteer participants who remained in *SD* for two to four days exhibited undirected thinking accompanied by hallucinations and fantasies, as well as an inability to distinguish sleep from waking states. The concept of *activation* or *arousal* is central to most *physiological theories of SD*. *Brain-washing* as a mind-control or programming technique gained widespread attention during, and after, the Korean War (1950-1953) in which the Chinese used a combination of coersive propaganda techniques presented to political prisoners or prisoners of war under conditions of physical and emotional intimidation (cf., the *Stockholm syndrome* or *effect* - the formation of an emotional bond between captors and hostages when the two parties are in close relationships and under stressful conditions for a relatively long period of time; this effect was identified originally in a bank robbery situation that lasted for five days in 1973 in Stockholm, Sweden; theoretically, the meaning of this effect extends beyond a simple identification of the hostage with the aggressor: it includes the captive's deep gratitude to the captor for being spared extreme physical harm and for being allowed to live). Even though some psychological researchers contend that the essential effects of suboptimal and superoptimal stimulation are similar in nature, it may be suggested that there are significant differences between *brain-washing* and *SD*. For example, the method of *brain-washing* most frequently employed by the Communists in China was dependent on "over-" rather than "under-stimulation" of the prisoner where the lack of sleep, lack of privacy, hard labor, and constant arguing and heckling are the opposite of what the participant-volunteer experiences in a typical *SD* experiment. See also ACTIVATION AND AROUSAL THEORY; ATTITUDE AND ATTITUDE-CHANGE, THEORIES OF; PERSUASION AND INFLUENCE THEORIES.

REFERENCES

Lifton, R. J. (1961). *Thought reform and the psychology of totalism*. New York: Norton.

Schein, E. H. (1961). *Coercive persuasion*. New York: Norton.

Zubek, J. P. (Ed.) (1969). *Sensory deprivation: Fifteen years of research*. New York: Appleton-Century-Crofts.

BRETON'S LAW. See WEBER'S LAW.

BREWSTER EFFECT. See BUNSEN-ROSCOE LAW.

BRIGGS' LAW. This is a civil-court (*not* scientific) law - named after the American psychiatrist Lloyd Vernon Briggs (1863-1941) and enacted in the state of Massachusetts - which requires in a criminal case that a psychiatric examination be completed for a defendant who has been indicted or convicted previously for an offense. The purpose of the *Brigg's law* is to determine if the defendant suffers from a mental disorder that affected his/her sense of responsibility; its intended significance is to provide for the prompt identification of defendants who should be in hospitals, thus preventing or pre-empting the trial of mentally ill persons. See also PSYCHOPATHOLOGY, THEORIES OF.

REFERENCES

Briggs, L. V. (1921). *The manner of man that kills*. Boston: Gorham Press.

Briggs, L. V. (1923). *A history of the passage of two bills through the Massachusetts legislature*. Boston: Wright & Potter.

Hagopian, P. B. (1953). Mental abnormalities in criminals based on Briggs' law cases. *American Journal of Psychiatry, 109*, 486-490.

BROADBENT'S FILTER THEORY, MODEL, AND EFFECT. See ATTENTION, LAWS/THEORIES OF.

BROCA-SULZER EFFECT. See BUNSEN-ROSCOE LAW.

BROWN-PETERSON PARADIGM AND TECHNIQUE. See SHORT-TERM AND LONG-TERM MEMORY, THEORIES OF.

BROWN SHRINKAGE EFFECT. See PERCEPTION (I. GENERAL), THEORIES OF.

BROWN'S THEORY OF TIME AWARENESS. This philosophical/neurological *theory of time awareness* by the American neurologist/physician Jason W. Brown proposes that mind transforms the physical space-time continuity into *moments* (the "microstructure of the present moment") called the "absolute Now" and mixes these *moments* into an apparent continuity via an overlap of "unfolding capsules" in which the flow of psychological time is an illusion based on the rapid replacement of the capsules. Brown suggests, also, that each mind computes measures of duration from the decay of the surface present in relation to a core of past events. Brown's speculations about time stem from *microgenetic theory* which examines how behavior unfolds simultaneously in various dimensions and scales of time and space; included in this philosophical approach are analyses of evolutionary brain processes that run from the oldest and deepest layers of the central nervous system in a general upward and outward direction. According to *microgenetic theory*, in a fraction of a second the brain reproduces the whole history of its evolution and development to produce a behavior that emerges on the surface as the visible end of a process

lying buried within. The assumption here is the theoretical notion that that which is buried under the surface always remains a part of that which emerges. It is suggested that living, perceiving, thinking, feeling, and acting are determined and guided *not* by *states* of being (which, in reality, last only for micro-seconds, then give way to the next), but by the *process* itself of passing from state to state. See also MIND/MENTAL STATES, THEORIES OF; RECAPITULATION THEORY/LAW OF; TIME, THEORIES OF.

REFERENCE

Brown, J. W. (1990). Psychology of time awareness. *Brain and Cognition, 14*, 144-164.

BRUCE EFFECT. = pregnancy blockage effect. This phenomenon describes the influence of *social odor communication* from one organism to another where, for example, a female mouse that has mated with one male will display a blockage of pregnancy (called the *Bruce effect*) if she is exposed to a strange male, or the odor of a strange male, a few days later. The *Bruce effect* was first observed in mice by the English reproductive biologist Hilda M. Bruce (1903-1974), where the termination of a pregnancy was brought about by substances in the urine of a virile male mouse other than the one that impregnated the female. Having thus eliminated the offspring of the other male, the animal was now able to impregnate the female himself and, thus, increase the likelihood of passing his own genes on to future generations. Other related chemical signals that facilitate communication among members of a species are *pheromones* and *allomones* (chemical substances that signal within, and among, a species messages of sexual receptivity, alarm, or territoriality). Female rats emit a "maternal pheromone" that helps the offspring find them. Also, female rats that are housed near each other tend to have estrous cycles that become synchronized over time; a similar menstrual synchrony has been found between human females who live together. See also COMMUNICATION THEORY; OLFACTION AND SMELL THEORIES OF.

REFERENCES

Bruce, H. M. (1959). An exteroreceptive block to pregnancy in the mouse. *Nature, 184*, 105.

Bruce, H. M. (1960). A block to pregnancy in the mouse caused by proximity to strange males. *Journal of Reproduction & Fertility, 1*, 96-103.

Wilson, E. (1963). Pheromones. *Scientific American, 208*, 100-115.

Leon, M. (1974). Maternal pheromone. *Physiology and Behavior, 13*, 441-453.

Brown, R. (1979). Mammalian social odors: A critical review. *Advances in the Study of Behavior, 10*, 103-162.

Graham, C., & McGrew, W. (1980). Menstrual synchrony in female undergraduates living on a coeducational campus. *Psychoneuroendocrinology, 5*, 245-252.

BRUCE-YOUNG FUNCTIONAL MODEL OF FACE RECOGNITION. See FACE RECOGNITION AND FACIAL IDENTITY THEORY.

BRUCKE EFFECT. See BUNSEN-ROSCOE LAW.

BRUNER'S CONCEPT FORMATION THEORY. The American developmental psychologist Jerome Seymour Bruner (1915-) and his colleagues outline four strategies in their *concept formation theory* that people typically use in formulating concepts: simultaneous scanning (e.g., testing different hypotheses); successive scanning (e.g., testing one hypothesis at a time); conservative focusing (e.g., testing hypotheses by elimination of the incorrect guesses, one at a time); and focus gambling (e.g., elimination of combinations of guesses). In his *constructivist theory* and *concept-attainment model* of teaching and education, Bruner emphasizes the attainment and development of concepts through the process/method of *inductive reasoning* (i.e., a form of reasoning, also called "empirical induction," in which a general law or principle is inferred from particular instances that have been observed previously). See also ALGORITHMIC-HEURISTIC THEORY; CONCEPT LEARNING/ CONCEPT FORMA-TION, THEORIES OF; INDUCTIVE METHOD.

REFERENCES

Bruner, J. S., Goodnow, J., & Austin, G. (1956). *A study of thinking*. New York: Wiley.

Bruner, J. S. (1960). *The process of education*. Cambridge, MA: Harvard University Press.

Bruner, J. S. (1966/1974). *Toward a theory of instruction*. Cambrigde, MA: Belknap Press.

Bruner, J. S. (1968). *Processes of cognitive growth*. Worcester, MA: Clark University Press.

BRUNER'S THEORY OF COGNITIVE DEVELOPMENT. See PIAGET'S THEORY OF DEVELOPMENTAL STAGES.

BRUNER'S THEORY OF INSTRUCTION. See ALGORITHMIC-HEURISTIC THEORY.

BRUNSWIK RATIO. See CONSTANCY HYPOTHESIS.

BRUNSWIK'S PROBABILISTIC FUNCTIONALISM THEORY. See PERCEPTION (II. COMPARATIVE APPRAISAL), THEORIES OF.

BUCK FEVER EFFECT. See REASONED ACTION AND PLANNED BEHAVIOR THEORIES.

BUDDHISM AND ZEN BUDDHISM, DOCTRINE OF. The *Buddhist doctrine*, or religious approach, developed around the life and teachings of the Indian religious leader "Buddha" or Siddhartha Gautama (c. 566-480 B.C.); the doctrine advances the notion that life's suffering is caused by desire where the transcendence of suffering and desire leads, eventually, to enlightenment or "nirvana" (i.e., the extinction of consciousness and desire). *Buddhism* teaches, also, that any sort of concept regarding an "eternal self" is basically an illusion. *Zen Buddhism* is a Japanese version of *Buddhism* in which illumination, spiritual unity, and "satori" are achieved via direct and intuitive experience as compared to the scientific, rational, and intellectual approaches. One Zen master asserted that to study Buddhism is to study the self, and to study the self is to forget the self, and to forget the self is to be one with others. The *doctrine of Buddhism and Zen Buddhism*, including, also, the approaches of Hinduism, Taoism, and Sufism, is pervasive among the major Asian psychologies. Generally, the Asian psychologies attempt to cultivate exceptional levels of well-being and transcendent states of consciousness. Over 2,500 years ago, the Buddha employed concepts similar to those of: altered states of consciousness, state dependent learning, cognitive behavior modification, social constructionist models of reality, and meditative and reciprocal-inhibition conditioning processes that are now studied by Western psychology. Although the Asian psychologies lack a high level of scientific rigor and methodology, they do place primary emphasis on phenomenology, existential meaning, and personal experience. Recently, a rapidly growing number of Western psychologists and other mental health professionals have begun personal exploration and applications of these religious doctrines into their methodologies, techniques, and treatment regimens. See also CONDUCT, LAWS OF; MASLOW'S THEORY OF PERSONALITY; MORITA THERAPY THEORY; NIRVANA PRINCIPLE.

REFERENCES

Kapleau, P. (1965). *The three pillars of Zen: Teaching, practice, and enlightenment*. Boston: Beacon Press.

Shapiro, D. H., & Zifferblatt, S. (1976). Zen meditation and behavioral self-control: Similarities, differences, clinical applications. *American Psychologist, 31*, 519-532.

Ram Dass. (1978). *Journey of awakening: A meditator's guidebook*. New York: Doubleday.

Walsh, R. N. (1982). The ten paramis (perfections) of Buddhism. In R. N. Walsh & D. H. Shapiro (Eds.), *Beyond health and normality: Toward a vision of exceptional psychological health*. New York: Van Nostrand.

Walsh, R. N. (1983). *The universe within us: Contemporary perspectives on Buddhist psychology*. New York: Morrow.

BUFFERING MODEL/HYPOTHESIS OF SOCIAL SUPPORT.

In distinguishing between "structural" and "functional" components of the construct *social support*, S. Cohen and T. A. Wills suggest that the structural component refers to the degree to which a person is integrated into his/her social environment, and the functional component refers to the person's perceptions of the availability of network members to provide supportive resources when needed. Structural measures are associated with a *main effect model* (in which *social support* has a direct and beneficial impact on psychological and physical health). In contrast, functional measures are associated with an *interaction effect model* (the *buffering model of social support*). According to the *buffering model/hypothesis*, *social support* moderates the negative life events-symptomatology relation by mitigating the adverse effects of negative life events on psychological and physical well-being. By extension, and based on the results of other studies in this area, it has been found that *social support* not only buffers the adverse effects of *negative* life events, but it may boost or enhance (the *boosting effect of social support*) also, the beneficial impact of *positive* life events on one's psychological and physical health. See also FIT THEORY OF COLLEGE SATISFACTION; SELF-CONSISTENCY AND SELF-ENHANCEMENT THEORIES; STUDENT RETENTION AND ATTRITION MODEL.

REFERENCES

Cohen, S., & Wills, T. A. (1985). Stress, social support, and the buffering hypothesis. *Psychological Bulletin, 98*, 310-357.

Barrera, M., Jr. (1988). Models of social support and life stress: Beyond the buffering hypothesis. In L. H. Cohen (Ed.), *Life events and psychological functioning: Theoretical and methodological issues*. Thousand Oaks, CA: Sage.

Weir, R. M., & Okun, M. A. (1989). Social support, positive college events, and college satisfaction: Evidence for boosting effects. *Journal of Applied Social Psychology*, 19, 758-771.

BUNDLE HYPOTHESIS. See GESTALT THEORY/LAWS.

BUNSEN-ROSCOE LAW. = Bloch's law = reciprocity law. This generalized principle, developed by the German chemist/physicist Robert Wilhelm Bunsen (1811-1899) and the English chemist Sir Henry Enfield Roscoe (1833-1915), states that the absolute threshold for vision is a reciprocity relation and multiplicative function of the intensity and duration of the stimulus. For example, a flash of light of short duration, presented to the eye under adaptation, provides a given effect that can be achieved by the reciprocal manipulation of duration and luminance of the flash. This means that the given effect may be produced by an intense flash that acts for a short time or by a dim light that acts for a relatively long time. This relationship, when applied to many photochemical systems, is known as the *Bunsen-Roscoe law* (also called the *photographic law* when used in the context of the effect of light on photographic emulsion). For instance, when chlorine and hydrogen are combined in the presence of light, the extent of the photochemical action varies inversely with the distance from the light source and is directly proportional to its intensity. However, when this relationship is applied to studies of human vision, it is sometimes known as *Bloch's law* - named after the French biologist A. M. Bloch. Considerable confirming evidence has accrued over the years that verifies the applicability of *Bloch's law* for threshold determination with durations of one millisecond or longer and, as long as the area of stimulation is small and the duration is not excessive, a further critical factor in the law is the total energy involved in the stimulation for very short durations. Another synonym for the *Bunsen-Roscoe law* is the *reciprocity law*, which states that response is determined by the product of the intensity and duration of the stimulus, independently of the magnitude of either one alone, and holds within rather narrow limits for various visual and other biological phenomena [cf., *Broca-Sulzer effect*, named after the French physicist and physician Andre Broca (1863-1925) and

the French ophthalmologist David E. Sulzer (1858-1918); also called the *Brucke effect*, named after the German physiologist Ernst W. Brucke (1819-1892) and the *Brewster effect*, named after the Scottish physicist David Brewster (1781-1868) -   refers to the phenomenon that a *flash* of light appears to be brighter than a *steady* light of the same intensity]. See also RICCO'S/PIPER'S LAWS.

REFERENCES

Bloch, A. M. (1885). Experiences sur la vision. *Societe Biologique Memoirs, Paris, 37*, 493-495.

Broca, A., & Sulzer, D. E. (1902) [no title]. *Journal de Physiologie et de Pathologie Generale, 4*, 632-640.

Brindley, G. (1952). The Bunsen-Roscoe law for the human eye at very short durations. *Journal of Physiology, 118*, 135-139.

BURIDAN'S DONKEY/ASS. See CONFLICT, THEORIES OF.

BUTTERFLY EFFECT. See ORGANIZATIONAL, INDUSTRIAL, AND SYSTEMS THEORY.

BYSTANDER APATHY EFFECT. See BYSTANDER INTERVENTION EFFECT.

BYSTANDER INTERVENTION EFFECT. = bystander apathy effect. This phenomenon was described by the American social psychologists Bibb Latane (1937-) and John Darley (1938-), and suggests that bystanders are engaged in a series of decisions, rather than a single decision, as whether to intervene or not in situations when help is needed by another person; for example, the bystander must notice that something is happening; the bystander must interpret the happening as an emergency event; the bystander must decide that she or he has a responsibility to become involved; the bystander must decide on the form of assistance to give the "victim;" and the bystander must make a decision as to how to implement the previous decision. Research findings from the laboratory and field settings indicate the importance that social factors play in the *bystander effect* (also called *group inhibition of helping*) where the actions of others in the situation (such as passivity versus activity on the part of other onlookers) may serve as cues to the bystander's involvement. The *bystander effect* concerning "altruism," "prosocial behavior," or "helping behavior" refers to the finding that the more people who are present when help is needed, the less likely any one of them is to provide assistance. Even when a bystander interprets the event to be an emergency, the presence of other people may help to "diffuse responsibility" for taking any action [cf., *bandwagon effect* - accelerated diffusion of a pattern of behavior through a group of people, the probability of any individual adopting it increasing with the proportion of those who have already demonstrated the target behavior; *social loafing effect* - coined by B. Latane in 1979; also called the *Ringelmann effect*, named after the French agricultural engineer Maximilien Ringelmann (1861-1931) - refers to the tendency for one to exert less effort on a task when working as part of a team or cooperative group than when working on one's own; and *cost-reward model* of helping - suggests that individuals consider the costs versus the rewards of helping and not helping others in emergency/danger situations; in more general terms, *cost-reward models* aid individuals and organizations in the calculation of the highest "reward-to-cost ratios" which serve as indicators and directives for personal and/or corporate action]. Factors that relate to the bystander's personality (cf., *negative state relief model* - an approach that states that individuals who are in a bad mood themselves help others for the purpose of improving their own bad mood; also, helping behavior may be used by some people in conditions of stress, boredom, or inactivity for the purpose of avoiding or escaping dysphoric moods) and to demographic characteristics have been found to provide a poorer prediction of bystander intervention behavior than do the particular features of the "emergency" situation. See also ALLPORT'S CONFORMITY HYPOTHESIS; DECISION-MAKING THEORIES; DEINDIVIDUATION THEORY; EMPATHY-ALTRUISM HYPOTHESIS; SOCIAL IMPACT, LAW OF.

REFERENCES

Latane, B., & Darley, J. (1968). Group inhibition of bystander intervention in emergencies. *Journal of Personality and Social Psychology, 10*, 215-221.

Latane, B., & Darley, J. (1970). *The unresponsive bystander: Why doesn't he help?* New York: Appleton-Century-Crofts.

Latane, B., Williams, K., & Harkins, S. (1979). Many hands make light the work: Cases and consequences of social loafing. *Journal of Personality and Social Psychology, 37*, 822-832.

Bar-Tal, D. (1976). *Prosocial behavior: Theory and research.* New York: Halsted.

Eisenberg-Berg, N. (1982). *Development of prosocial behavior.* New York: Academic Press.

Dovidio, J. (1984). Helping behavior and altruism: An empirical and conceptual overview. In L. Berkowitz (Ed.), *Advances in experimental social psychology.* Vol. 17. New York: Academic Press.

C

CAFÉ-WALL ILLUSION. See APPENDIX A, MUNSTERBERG ILLUSION.

CAMEL-IN-THE-TENT TECHNIQUE. See COMPLIANCE EFFECTS AND TECHNIQUES.

CANALIZATION HYPOTHESIS. See MURPHY'S BIOSOCIAL THEORY.

CANNON/CANNON-BARD THEORY. = thalamic theory of Cannon = hypothalamic theory of Cannon. The American physiologist Walter B. Cannon (1871-1945) is given the major initial credit for this theory, and the American psychologist Philip Bard (1898-1977) is given partial recognition for his research support in its development and refinement. Another name for this theory is the *thalamic theory of emotion.* The *Cannon-Bard theory* proposes that the integration of emotional expressiveness is controlled and directed by the thalamus, which sends relevant excitation patterns to the cortex at the same time that the hypothalamus controls the behavior, and emphasizes the simultaneous arousal of both the central and autonomic nervous systems. Cannon argued that the function of the autonomic nervous system arousal was to prepare the organism to deal with the immediate event - to fight or to flee, for example. An event that might cause harm generates arousal (an "emergency" response), which prepares the individual to cope with the event. Other alternative names for the *Cannon-Bard theory*, therefore, are the *fight or flight theory* and the *emergency theory.* The *Cannon-Bard theory* is based on evolutionary-survival value for the organism where increase in heart rate, respiration, and so on permit it to respond more quickly and strongly and, thereby, increase its chances of survival. The *Cannon-Bard theory* was a predominant opponent to the earlier *James-Lange theory* and argued that emotionality results from a removal of the inhibition that is normally exerted by the neocortex upon the thalamus. The neocortex, according to the Cannon-Bard approach, ordinarily suppresses the activity of the thalamus, but if emotion-eliciting stimuli reach the cortex, impulses are sent downward and act to release the inhibitory influences. Subsequently, the thalamus signals the neo-cortex to initiate the emotional experience while it also signals the rest of the body to begin the pattern of behavior associated with the specific emotion. The *Cannon-Bard theory* predicts that the removal of an animal's thalamus in a laboratory procedure called "decortication" reduces its emotional hyperreactivity, but research shows this not to be the case. Thus, the research findings do not confirm a key feature of the theory. However, the *Cannon-Bard theory* is important historically for two reasons: it focused attention on possible central nervous system structures that may handle emotionality; and it focused attention on the possible ways the neocortex may interact with structures in the lower brain regions. Today, the Cannon-Bard idea of cortical-subcortical interaction and involvement in emotionality is reflected in modern *emotion theories.* The difficulty with the *Cannon-Bard theory* is that it concentrates too heavily on the thalamus rather than the hypothalamus, and other physiological-behavioral research shows that the hypothalamus seems to dominate emotional behavior. See also AROUSAL THEORY; EMOTION THEORIES/LAWS OF; JAMES-LANGE/LANGE-JAMES THEORY OF EMOTIONS.

REFERENCES

Cannon, W. (1915). *Bodily changes in pain, hunger, fear, and rage: An account of recent researches into the function of emotional excitement.* New York: Appleton-Century-Crofts.

Cannon, W. (1931). Again the James-Lange and the thalamic theories of emotion. *Psychological Review, 38,* 281-295.

Cannon, W. (1932). *The wisdom of the body*. New York: Norton.

Bard, P. (1934). On emotional expression after decortication with some remarks on certain theoretical views. *Psychological Review, 41,* 309-329, 424-449.

Cannon, W. (1936). Gray's objective theory of emotion. *Psychological Review, 43,* 100-106.

Leeper, R. (1948). A motivational theory of emotion to replace "emotion as disorganized response." *Psychological Review, 55,* 5-21.

Webb, W. (1948). A motivational theory of emotion. *Psychological Review, 55,* 329-335.

Cannon, W., & Rosenblueth, A. (1949). *The supersensitivity of denervated struc-tures: A law of denervation.* New York: Macmillan.

Bard, P. (1950). Central nervous mechanisms for the expression of anger. In M. Reymert (Ed.), *The second international symposium on feelings and emotions.* New York: McGraw-Hill.

CAPALDI'S THEORY. With the development in the contemporary conception of *reinforcement* and the *law of effect* in the last few decades, there have been changes, also, in the interpretation of the concepts of *extinction* and *nonreward* where a number of new hypotheses have been proposed. For example, E. J. Capaldi's *sequential patterning theory* of nonreward and the *partial reinforcement extinction effect* (i.e., the observation that responses established by partial reinforcement are more resistant to extinction than responses established by continuous reinforcement) are refinements of two earlier hypotheses: the *discrimination/generalization hypothesis*, which supposes that organisms will persist in responding as long as they cannot discriminate the extinction series from a run of nonreinforcements embedded within the training series, and the *stimulus aftereffects hypothesis*, which supposes that reward and nonreward events on one trial set up distinctive stimulus traces that persist over the intertrial interval and are part of the stimulus complex at the time the next response occurs. Thus, the *stimulus aftereffects hypothesis* assumes that during partial reinforcement training, persisting stimulus traces from nonreinforced trials become conditioned to the next response because of frequent reinforced trials following a nonreinforced trial, and lead to stimuli arising during extinction which maintains responding [cf., the *response-unit hypothesis*, proposed by the American psychologist Orval Hobart Mowrer (1907-1982), which attempts to account for conflicting evidence relating to the extinction of behavior when it is no longer reinforced; the hypothesis focuses on the difficulty of defining a behavioral response in terms of a single act rather than of a larger behavioral sequence). *Capaldi's theory* deviates from the older *aftereffects hypothesis* concerning the time decay of information about the reinforcing event of the prior trial. The *aftereffects hypothesis* suggests that reward and nonreward events set up relatively short-term stimulus traces that decay after a few minutes, but this approach has no way to explain the *partial reinforcement effects* that have been obtained with widely spaced trials (such as one trial every 24 hours). *Capaldi's theory*, on the other hand, assumes that a trace of the prior reward or nonreward event persists indefinitely until it is modified or replaced by the next event to happen in the goal box of this situation. For Capaldi, the prior reward or nonreward stimuli are now available in something like a "memory," which is reactivated when the organism is placed back in the stimulus/testing situation. This "memory" interpretation is somewhat more heuristic than the older stimulus trace interpretation. Capaldi uses his hypothesis to explain a wide range of different scheduling phenomena such as the accelerated extinction and relearning that occur in multiple blocks of extinction and acquisition trials, the effects of patterned schedules and their discrimination, the effects of reward delay, the contrast effects in shifts of reward magnitude, the effects of different intertrial intervals, human probability learning, and application to *statistical learning theory*. There is current consensus among researchers that *Capaldi's sequential theory* is the best one available for predicting extinction resistance produced by most reinforcement schedules. However, a theoretical problem that remains to be solved is the combination of the *sequential hypothesis* with the concepts of frustrative reward and inhibition in order to produce a more general theory of extinction and nonreinforcement. See also AMSEL'S HYPOTHESIS/THEORY; ESTES' STIMULUS SAMPLING THEORY; PREMACK'S PRINCIPLE/LAW; TOLMAN'S THEORY; TRACE DECAY THEORY.

REFERENCES

Mowrer, O. H., & Jones, H. M. (1945). Habit strength as a function of the pattern of reinforcement. *Journal of Experimental Psychology, 35,* 293-311.

Capaldi, E. J. (1966). Partial reinforcement: An hypothesis of sequential effects. *Psychological Review, 73,* 459-477.

Capaldi, E. J., & Capaldi, E. D. (1970). Magnitude of partial reward, irregular reward schedules, and a 24-hour ITI: A test of several hypotheses. *Journal of Comparative and Phy-siological Psychology, 72,* 203-209.

Robbins, D. (1971). Partial reinforcement: A selective review of the alleyway literature since 1960. *Psychological Bulletin, 76,* 415-431.

Koteskey, R. (1972). A stimulus sampling model of the partial reinforcement effect. *Psychological Review, 79,* 161-171.

Capaldi, E. J., & Proctor, R. W. (1999). *Contextualism in psychological research: A critical review.* Thousand Oaks, CA: Sage.

CAPGRAS ILLUSION/SYNDROME. See APPENDIX A.

CAREER DEVELOPMENT THEORIES. See WORK/CAREER/OCCUPATION, THEORIES OF.

CARPENTERED-WORLD HYPOTHESIS. This proposition recognizes and develops the idea that people living in urban, industrialized, and "built" environments (cf. the term *carpentered environment* - a "minimalist" environment consisting of straight lines, such as buildings of the "Bauhaus" era, based on the notion that "less is more") have a great deal of perceptual experience in judging various aspects of rectangular/manufactured objects (such as the lines, corners, edges, etc. of those objects) that influence their perceptions of the world. People in such modern, developed, or "carpentered" cultures, according to the *carpentered-world hypothesis*, are *more* susceptible to (i.e., are "fooled by") particular geometric illusions (e.g., such as the Muller-Lyer illusion which involves a straight line with arrow-heads on the ends either jutting toward or away from the perceiver and results in a misperception of the actual length of the line). On the other hand, people who live in primitive, undeveloped and unbuilt, or "non-carpentered" cultures and environments are *less* susceptible to (i.e., they are *not* "fooled by") such illusions. The rationale for such a "cultural-relativity" response is that those persons who live in "non-carpentered" cultures more frequently encounter natural, rounded, and non-angled objects where right angles and straight lines are relatively rare in their perceptual experiences. Such a phenomenon as the *carpentered-world hypothesis* underscores the importance of one's environment, culture, and cultural experiences in shaping one's perception of the world. Historically, in the early 1910s, psychologists in the school of Gestalt psychology proposed that perceptual processes are inborn - a viewpoint called the "nativist" position - and suggested that people everywhere, no matter what their background, perceive the world in the same way because they share in common the same "perceptual rules." Opposing the "nativist" position is the "empiricist" position, advocated by other psychologists, suggesting that people actively "construct" their perceptions of the world by relying on their previous learning and cultural experiences. Thus, the *carpentered-world hypothesis* supports the "empiricist" position in the psychology of perception; that is, one's perception is the result of an interaction between a stimulus and a perceiver shaped by previous experience, and people from very different cultural backgrounds may well perceive features of the world in different ways. See also CONSTRUCTIVIST THEORY OF PERCEPTION; GESTALT THEORY/LAWS; NATIVIST VERSUS EMPIRICIST THEORIES; UNCONSCIOUS INFERENCE, DOCTRINE OF.

REFERENCES

Hudson, W. (1960). Pictorial depth perception in sub-cultural groups in Africa. *Journal of Social Psychology, 52,* 183-208.

Segall, M. H., Campbell, D. T., & Herskovits, M. J. (1963). Cultural differences in the perception of geometric illusions. *Science, 193,* 769-771.

Deregowski, J. B. (1989). Real space and represented space: Cross-cultural perspectives. *Behavioral and Brain Sciences, 12,* 51-119.

CARTESIAN DUALISM. See LEARNING THEORIES/LAWS.

CASCADE PROCESSING MODEL. The *cascade processing model* was described by the American cognitive psychologist James Lloyd McClelland (1948-) in 1979, and accounts for the implementation of later stages of information processing before the earlier stages are actually completed. According to previous "discrete processing models," of information processing, items are not passed on to the next stage until processing at the current stage is complete, but in a *cascade processing model* an item may be matched against items in the lexicon-base by use of guesses or hypotheses - before all of the elements of the item (such as the letters of a word) have been identified. In this approach, for example, conjectures about the "meaning" of an item may

be made before an actual or complete lexical match has been provided. In an associative computational processing method, called "parallel processing," an information process is split into subunits that are carried out simultaneously by independent processing units, whereas in the method called "serial processing," information processing involves steps that are carried out one at a time in a fixed sequence (this latter method is the manner in which computers normally execute steps, but the human brain is assumed to be capable of processing information and computations in a "parallel processing" fashion). The *cascade processing model* has been shown to be compatible with the general form of the relation between the variables of time and accuracy in "speed-accuracy trade-off" experiments. See also INFORMATION AND INFORMATION-PROCESSING THEORY; NEURAL NETWORK MODELS OF INFORMATION-PROCESSING; PARALLEL DISTRIBUTED PROCESSING MODEL.

REFERENCE

McClelland, J. L. (1979). On the time relations of mental processes: An examination of systems of processes in cascade. *Psychological Review, 86,* 287-330.

CATASTROPHE THEORY/MODEL. This notion, as developed in psychology by the Hungarian psychoanalyst Sandor Ferenczi (1873-1933), states that the act of sexual intercourse is destructive - in a psychodynamic sense - to the male's penis; that is, the neurotically anxious patient may hold a belief that sexual intercourse is damaging to his penis. In his ontogenetic and phylogenetic *catastrophe theory* of coitus, Ferenczi notes that in the normal coitus of non-neurotic men, the inner tension-seeking for discharge overcomes any extant anxiety even though small traces of anxiety may still be present. In his early "active therapy" approach to the treatment of neurosis, Ferenczi advanced Sigmund Freud's *theory of privation*. For example, when patients resisted the psychoanalyst's techniques and procedures, such as the requirement to engage in the verbal activity of free association, Ferenczi had those patients abstain from behaviors such as eating, sex, or defecation with the expected result that the patients' consequent pent-up libido provided the energy or force necessary for therapy to continue (cf. *relaxation principle* in therapy - a psychotherapeutic technique based on the idea that a permissive and loving approach to patients is more effective - than a strict application of privation theory - in releasing repressed impulses and making patients more amenable to analysis). Additionally, in psychology, the *catastrophe model* refers to conditions in which anxiety influences one's performance in an inverted-U relationship under low cognitive anxiety levels; however, when high levels of bodily anxiety are accompanied by high levels of cognitive anxiety, the result is a catastrophic or extreme decrease in one's performance level. The versatile notion of *catastrophe theory* has been developed in non-psychological disciplines as well as in the psychological and psychoanalytical contexts. For instance, in the field of economics, *catastrophe theory* refers to the transition from one state of equilibrium to another and the resultant instability; in mathematics, the theory distinguishes among the classes of surfaces that may be transformed into one another by functions that have regular tangents at each point, and where sections of the surfaces may be predicted regarding the occurrence of sudden changes and involves suggested methods to use for avoiding such changes; in political science, the theory refers to the development of political or other system up to a point where internal contradictions result in a disruption or catastrophe, and the point beyond which other theories that formerly explained the historical order of events no longer hold; in physics and astronomy, the theory deals with the issue of the formation of the planets during a catastrophic encounter in the solar system between the Sun and other objects or masses; and in biology and geology, the theory attempts to describe Earth's history in terms of a succession of worlds, each separated by epochs when sudden catastrophic and unexplainable

events (such as earthquakes and floods) were dominant. Thus, as an omnibus appellation across many scientific disciplines, the notion of *catastrophe theory* has enjoyed a considerable degree of widespread success. See also INVERTED-U HYPOTHESIS; ORGANIZTIONAL/ INDUSTRIAL/ SYSTEMS THEORY; PSYCHOANALYTICAL THEORY.

REFERENCES

Ferenczi, S. (1924/1968). *Versuch einer genitaltheorie (Thalassa: A theory of genitality).* Translated by H. A. Bunker. Wien: Internationalere Psychoanalytischer Verlag/New York: W. W. Norton.

Ferenczi, S. (1926). *Further contributions to the theory and technique of psychoanalysis.* London: Institute of Psychoanalysis.

Saunders, P. T. (1980). *An introduction to catastrophe theory.* New York: Cambridge University Press.

CATASTROPHISM. See DARWIN'S EVOLUTION THEORY.

CATECHOLAMINE HYPOTHESIS/THE-ORY OF DEPRESSION. See DEPRESSION, THEORIES OF.

CATEGORICAL JUDGMENT, LAW OF. See THURSTONE'S LAW OF COMPARATIVE JUDGMENT.

CATEGORIZATION THEORY. See INGROUP BIAS THEORIES.

CATHARSIS THEORY. See FREUD'S INSTINCT THEORY.

CATTELL'S THEORY OF PERSONALITY. The British-born American psychologist Raymond Bernard Cattell (1905-1998) developed a comprehensive theory of personality based on the statistical procedure of *factor analysis* introduced by the English statistician and psychologist Charles Edward Spearman (1863-1945) and expanded by the American psychometrician Louis Leon Thurstone (1887-1955) in the formulation of *multiple factor analysis.* The factor analytic approach typically begins with a large number of scores derived from tests, then applies a statistical technique to such "surface" scores to determine the underlying "basic" factors whose operation theoretically accounts for the variation in the large number of initial scores. Once the "basic" factors are identified, the theorist can then develop ways of measuring the factors in a more efficient manner. Thus, *factor analysis* is a procedure in which variables may be formulated to account for the diverse complexity of "surface" behaviors. Personality is defined by Cattell as "that which permits a prediction of what a person will do in a given situation" (Cattell, 1950, p. 2), and is considered to be a complex and differentiated structure of *traits* ("mental structures" inferred from observed behavior). Cattell distinguishes between the concepts of *surface traits* - clusters of overt variables that have common aspects, such as a syndrome of behaviors, and *source traits* - underlying variables that determine surface variables, such as physiological and temperamental factors; between *environmental-mold traits* - traits resulting from external environmental conditions, and *constitutional traits* - traits resulting from internal or hereditary conditions; and between *dynamic traits* - traits which set the person into action toward some goal, *ability traits* - effectiveness of the person in reaching a goal, and *temperament traits* - constitutional response aspects such as energy, speed, and emotional reactivity. Cattell identified 16 bipolar personality factors (i.e., *source traits* of the "core personality") that are derived from testing protocols such as a person's life record and self-rating questionnaires: outgoing-reserved, more intelligent-less intelligent, stable-emotional, assertive-humble, happy-go-lucky vs. sober, conscientious-expedient, venturesome-shy, tender-minded vs. tough-minded, suspicious-trusting, imaginative- practical, shrewd -forthright, apprehensive-placid, conservative-experimenting, group-depen dent vs. self-sufficient, uncontrolled-controlled, and relaxed-tense. Based on the premise that personality may be described in terms of ability, temperament, and other types of traits, Cattell developed a *specification equation* that implies a multidimensional representation of the individual within a given psychological situation to yield a predicted response. Such *specification equations* have practical applications in settings such as employment screening situations and in academic achievement contexts. The important *dynamic traits* in *Cattell's theory* are "attitudes" (observable or measurable expression of one's dynamic structure), "ergs" (biologically-based drives), and "sentiments" (environmental-mold, acquired attitude structures). A *dynamic lattice* is Cattell's (pictorial) representation of the interrelationships among the *dynamic traits*, and forms a pattern of "subsidiation" where, generally, "attitudes" are subsidiary to "sentiments," "sentiments" are subsidiary to "ergs," and "ergs" are the basic driving forces in the personality. One of the most important of Cattell's "sentiments" is the "master sentiment" of *self-sentiment*, which is similar to Sigmund Freud's concepts of *ego* and *superego*, and Gordon Allport's concept of *ego*, and has the crucial role of integrating the different aspects of the personality. Cattell proposed that a useful way of assessing the degree of conflict that a person may have in a specific situation is to state the *specification equation* that expresses the involvement of the person's "ergs" and "sentiments" in a given course of action. Various other concepts in *Cattell's theory* (e.g., "states," "roles," "sets") have been described and investigated, also, by the factor analytic technique. Cattell developed a novel method for assessing the relative weight of genetic and environmental factors in traits called *multiple abstract variance analyses* (*MAVA*) where initial results showed negative correlations between heredity and environmental factors. Cattell interpreted this result as evidence for a *law of coercion to the biosocial mean*, which refers to the tendency for environmental influences to oppose the systematic expression of genetic variation (e.g., when parents require that their two different children behave in the same way, even though one child is outgoing and the other one is bashful). Cattell extended his concepts of traits from his *personality theory* to descriptions of group behavior (called *syntality*), including the behavior of nations. Evaluations and reviews of Cattell's work indicate a mixture of both admiration and uneasiness. *Cattell's personality theory* may not be popular in the sense that S. Freud's, C. Rogers', H. S. Sullivan's, G. Allport's, or H. Murray's theories have been popular, but it has attracted an active band of adherents, many of whom appreciate the widespread empirical grounding and economy of factor analytic formulations that his theory possesses. See also ALLPORT'S THEORY OF PERSONALITY; FREUD'S THEORY OF PERSONALITY; INTELLIGENCE, THEORIES/LAWS OF; NATURE VERSUS NURTURE THEORIES; PESONALITY THEORIES.

REFERENCES

Spearman, C. E. (1927). *Abilities of man.* New York: Macmillan.

Thurstone, L. L. (1931). Multiple factor analysis. *Psychological Review, 38,* 406-427.

Cattell, R. B. (1948). Concepts and methods in the measurement of group syntality. *Psychological Review, 55,* 48-63.

Cattell, R. B. (1950). *Personality: A systematic, theoretical, and factual study.* New York: McGraw-Hill.

Sells, S. (1959). Structured measurement of personality and motivation: A review of contributions of Raymond B. Cattell. *Journal of Clinical Psychology, 15,* 3-21.

Cattell, R. B. (1960). The multiple abstract variance analysis equations and solutions: For nature-nurture research on continuous variables. *Psychological Review, 67,* 353-372.

Cattell, R. B. (1963a). Personality, role, mood, and situation-perception: A unifying theory of modulators. *Psychological Review, 70,* 1-18.

Cattell, R. B. (1963b). Theory of fluid and crystallized intelligence: A critical experiment. *Journal of Educational Psychology, 54,* 1-22.

Cattell, R. B., & Gorsuch, R. (1965). The definition and measurement of national morale and morality. *Journal of Social Psychology, 67,* 77-96.

Cattell, R. B. (1966). *The scientific analysis of personality.* Chicago: Aldine.

Cattell, R. B. (1979-1980). *Personality and learning theory.* New York: Sprin-ger.

Cattell, R. B. (1990). Advances in Cattellian personality theory. In L. Pervin (Ed.), *Handbook of personality: Theory and research.* New York: Guilford Press.

CEILING EFFECT. See MEASUREMENT THEORY; NORMAL DISTRIBUTION THEORY.

CELESTIAL ILLUSION EFFECT. See EMMERT'S LAW.

CELL ASSEMBLY THEORY. See PERCEPTION (II. COMPARATIVE APRAISAL), THEORIES OF.

CELLULAR AUTOMATON MODEL. The Hungarian-born American mathematician John von Neumann (1903-1957) described the *cellular automaton model*, a mathematical model of self-replication and destruction that is represented, typically, by a checkerboard of either fixed or infinite dimensions - each cell of which has a finite number of states (including, usually, a "quiescent/empty" state), and a finite set of neighboring cells that may influence its state. In the model, the pattern of changes are determined by transition rules that apply simultaneously to all cells in each discrete time unit. The cellular automata also incorporate certain universal features, such as "Turing machines" - named after the English mathematician Alan Mathison Turing (1912-1954) - which are hypothetical computing machines consisting of a movable head that reads, writes, or erases discrete symbols drawn from a finite set (usually, just "1" or "0"); a "Turing machine" deals with the symbols, one at a time, in separate frames marked on a limitless length of tape, and that always assumes one of a finite number of states; in principle, a "universal Turing machine" can compute anything that is computable, given sufficient time. Other related terms are *Turing's test* - a hypothetical test, also called the "imitation game," that attempts to determine whether or not computers can "think" (involving an actual person and an actual interrogator in different rooms who engage in a dialogue over an electronic link; at some point the first person is replaced by an "intelligent software" program that simulates human responses; Turing argued that if the remaining interrogator is free to ask probing questions, but is unable to determine whether the replies are generated by a human being or by a computer, then the computer passes the test and it is declared that the computer can "think"); and *artificial intelligence (AI)* - first described by the American computer engineer John McCarthy (1927-) - refers to the design of hypothetical, or actual, computer programs or machines to accomplish things normally done by human minds, such as writing poetry, playing chess, thinking logically, or composing music; the most demanding situations for *AI* (also called "machine intelligence") are problems simulating functions of intelligence that are mainly unconscious (e.g., vision and language functions); *strong AI* refers to the viewpoint that all thinking is computation where conscious thought may be explained according to computational principles, and where feelings of "conscious awareness" are elicited merely by particular computations performed by the brain or by a computer; and *weak AI* refers to the viewpoint that "conscious awareness" is a property of certain brain processes, and advances the notion that - whereas any physical behavior may be simulated by a computer using purely computational processes - computational simulation does not, in itself, elicit "conscious awareness" (cf. *adaptive production system* - in *AI*, a production system that is able to learn by building new productions which it then adds to its memory). One of the first major events in the history of *AI* was the appearance of the "General Problem Solver" - a computer program designed to simulate human problem solving, developed in 1958, and improved in 1972, by the American cognitive scientist Allen Newell (1927-1992) and the American economists/decision theorists John Clark Shaw (1933-) and Herbert Alexander Simon (1916-2001). See also FUZZY SET THEORY; GODEL'S THEOREM.

REFERENCES

Turing, A. M. (1936-37). On computable numbers. *Proceedings of the London Mathematical Society, 42*, pt. 3-4 (Nov.-Dec.).

Turing, A. M. (1950). Computing machinery and intelligence. *Mind, 59*, 433-453.

Newell, A., Shaw, J. C., & Simon, H. A. (1958). Elements on a theory of human problem solving. *Psychological Review, 65*, 151-166.

von Neumann, J. (1958). *Computer and the brain.* New Haven: Yale University Press.

von Neumann, J. (1966). *Theory of self-reproducing automata.* Edited and completed by Arthur W. Burks. Urbana: University of Illinois Press.

Minsky, M. L., & Papert, S. (1969). *Perceptrons.* Oxford, UK: M. I. T. Press.

McCarthy, J., & Lifschitz, V. (1991). *Artificial intelligence and mathematical theory of computation.* Boston: Academic Press.

CENTRAL DOGMA PRINCIPLE. See WEISMANN'S THEORY.

CENTRAL-LIMIT THEOREM. This theoretical proposition - the earliest version of which was proved in 1818 by the French mathematician and astronomer Pierre Simon, Marquis de Laplace (1749-1827) who also founded the modern form of *probability theory* - states the following: if a population has a finite variance (σ^2) and a finite mean (μ), the distribution of sample means from samples of N independent observations approaches the form of a normal distribution with variance σ^2/N and mean μ

as the sample size N increases. When N is very large, the sampling distribution of the sample mean is approximately normal. Thus, at the heart of the *central limit theorem* is the notion that - regardless of the form of the population distribution - if sample size N is large enough, the normal distribution is a good approximation to the sampling distribution of the mean. In a great many cases, especially in psychology and the social sciences, a sample size of 30 or more cases, items, or individuals is considered large enough to permit a satisfactory use of normal probabilities to approximate the unknown exact probabilities associated with the sampling distribution of sample means. Therefore, even though the *central limit theorem* is actually a statement about what happens *in the limit* as N approaches an infinite value, the principle at work is so powerful that, in most instances, the theorem is practically useful even for only moderately large samples. See also NORMAL DISTRIBUTION THEORY; PROBABILITY THEORY/LAWS.
REFERENCE
Laplace, P. S. (1818). *Essai philosophique sur les probabilities*. Paris: Courcier.

CENTRAL THEORY OF THINKING. See WHORF-SAPIR HYPOTHESIS/THEORY.

CEREBRAL DOMINANCE THEORY. See LATERALITY THEORIES.

CERTAINTY EFFECT. See ORGANIZATIONAL/INDUSTRIAL/SYSTEMS THEORY.

CHAINING, LAW OF. See SKINNER'S DESCRIPTIVE BEHAVIOR THEORY.

CHANCE, LAWS OF. See PROBABILITY THEORY/LAWS.

CHANCE/ABSOLUTE CHANCE, THEORY OF. See ACCIDENTALISM, THEORY OF.

CHANGE, LAW OF. See HEDONISM, THEORY/LAW OF.

CHANGE EFFECT. See PARANORMAL PHENOMENA/THEORIES.

CHANGED-TRACE HYPOTHESIS. See EYEWITNESS MISINFORMATION EFFECT.

CHAOS THEORY. See ORGANIZATIONAL, INDUSTRIAL, AND SYSTEMS THEORY.

CHARACTER ANALYSIS THEORY. See REICH'S ORGONE/ORGONOMY THE-ORY.

CHARPENTIER'S ILLUSION. See APPENDIX A, SIZE-WEIGHT ILLUSION.

CHARPENTIER'S LAW. See VISION AND SIGHT, THEORIES OF.

CHATTERBOX EFFECT. See GESTALT THEORY/LAWS.

CHEMICAL PROFILE THEORY. See HUNGER, THEORIES OF.

CHEMOAFFINITY HYPOTHESIS. See NEURON/NEURAL/NERVE THEORY.

CHESHIRE CAT EFFECT. See VISION AND SIGHT, THEORIES OF.

CHOICE THEORIES. See DECISION-MAKING THEORIES; DELAY OF GRATI-FICATION HYPOTHESIS; DELAYED-REACTION PARADIGM/MODEL; DEMBER-EARL THEORY OF CHOICE AND PREFERENCE; ELIMINATION BY ASPECTS THEORY; EXEMPLAR THEORY OF BEHAVIORAL CHOICE; GLASSER'S CHOICE THEORY.

CHOMSKY'S PSYCHOLINGUISTIC THEORY. The American psychologist/linguist/philosopher Noam Avram Chomsky (1928-) formulated a *theory of psycholinguistics* that views language as genetically determined where it develops in ways similar to other bodily organs. According to Chomsky's prominent theory, the human brain is preprogrammed by a cognitive mechanism called the *language acquisition device (LAD)*, which allows individuals to generate grammatically correct sentences in a universal or culture-free manner. Chomsky suggests that humans have an innate capacity for understanding and emitting language behaviors. Only humans have language acquisition abilities (a "species-specific" feature), and all human languages share a common logical structure (a "species-uniform" feature). Chomsky's conceptualization of a *transformational generative grammar (TGG)* is an important advancement over the older viewpoint of language acquisition known as *phase-structure grammars* (i.e., a formal system for analyzing the structure of a sentence by assigning labels, such as noun, noun phrase, verb, etc. to parts of the sentence). Transformational grammar is grounded in the hypothesization of several necessary components: *semantics* - the rules for "meaning;" *deep structure* - the representation of underlying "meaning" (cf., *markedness hypothesis* - states that oppositional terms, or antonym pairs, are learned by children in a piecemeal fashion, where they concentrate first on the more obvious features; thus, a child will learn to use the word "big" before learning to use "little" and will initially use "big" to designate small as well as large objects); *transformational deviation* - the rules for mapping deep structures on a *surface structure* (i.e., consistency of the sequence of elements, such as phonemes, syllables, words, phrases, and sentences that constitute a written or spoken message); and *phonology* - the rules for providing the appropriate sound patterns, or phonetic sounds, of the language [cf., *pivot grammar* - this grammar, suggested by the Singaporean-born American psycholinguist Martin D. S. Braine (1926-1996), describes the two-word utterances of very young children at an early stage of language development (about 18 months to 2 years of age); an example is the child's "sentence" of: "Allgone ball;" this grammar

is more advanced than the child's earlier use of the *holophrase*, a grammatically unstructured speech segment, usually a single word such as "Allgone" to stand for "It is all gone," and may be interpreted or analyzable as one-word sentences in the young child's, and even in adult's, utterances; the *semantic-feature hypothesis* - the proposition that the order of the appearance of words in the development/acquisition of a child's language are governed by the complexity and type of the semantic features or components that they contain (such as the elements of a word's denotative meaning); the *verbal deprivation hypothesis* - holds that the form of language learned by a child may possibly confuse or hinder the child when he/she comes to learn abstract forms of material; and the *verbal loop hypothesis* - states that remembering and understanding verbal language is based on the brain's translation into words what is deposited there by the senses]. Thus, based on his introduction of the important distinction between *deep* and *surface* structure in psycholinguistics, Chomsky's *TGG* is a system that integrates both the deep (logical) and surface (phonetics) structures of language (cf., *linguistic performance* - Chomsky's term for the specific utterances of a native speaker of a language, including factors such as hesitations, speech errors, and false starts, and as distinguished from the underlying "linguistic competence" of the utterances or the person's unconscious knowledge of the grammatical rules of a language). *Chomsky's theory of language acquisition* has been challenged, most notably by proponents of *behaviorism* (e.g., Skinner, 1957) and the *behavioristic* viewpoint concerning verbal learning. According to the *behavioristic* approach, children learn to talk via the processes of classical and operant conditioning, which helps to explain why one child may be more skilled in the use of language than another child. Chomsky's *cognitivist* approach, on the other hand, helps to explain why children all over the world follow similar or invariant sequences of language development. Although both the *behaviorist* and the *cognitivist* viewpoints may account for some of the data of language acquisition, a third perspective emphasizes the personal *interaction* between infant and caregiver, between one person and another, and between the person and the environment as the heart of language learning (cf., *neurolinguistic theory* - study of language via analyses of deficits and impairments of language function resulting from neurological damage; and *semiotic theory* - study of patterned human communication in all its forms, including spoken and written signs and symbols, touch, gestures, and facial expression). Chomsky's notions concerning transformational grammar, although they revolutionized the field of linguistics, do not provide all the answers to the many problems of language acquisition. Psychologists, while retaining many of Chomsky's ideas, have moved on to new research regarding language behavior. See also GREEN-SPOON EFFECT; LAN-GUAGE ORIGINS, THEORIES OF; NATURE VERSUS NURTURE THEORIES; SKINNER'S DESCRIPTIVE BEHAVIOR AND OPERANT CONDITIONING THE-ORY; SPEECH THEORIES; WHORF-SAPIR HYPOTHESIS/THEORY; WORK-ING MEMORY, THEORY OF.

REFERENCES

Skinner, B. F. (1957). *Verbal behavior*. New York: Appleton-Century-Crofts.

Chomsky, N. A. (1959). A review of Skinner's "Verbal Behavior." *Language, 35,* 26-58.

Chomsky, N. A. (1964). *Current issues in linguistic theory*. The Hague: Mouton.

Chomsky, N. A. (1965). *Aspects of the theory of syntax*. Cambridge, MA: M.I.T. Press.

Chomsky, N. A. (1966). *Topics in the theory of generative grammar*. The Hague: Mouton.

Smith, F., & Miller, G. (Eds.) (1966). *The genesis of language: A psycholinguistic approach*. Cambridge, MA: M.I.T. Press.

Chomsky, N. A. (1968). *Language and the mind*. New York: Harcourt, Brace, & World.

McNeill, D. (1970). *The acquisition of language: The study of developmental psycholinguistics*. New York: Harper & Row.

Brown, R. (1973). Development of the first language in the human species. *American Psychologist, 28,* 97-106.

Braine, M. D. S. (1976). *Children's first word combinations*. Chicago: University of Chicago Press.

DeVilliers, J., & DeVilliers, P. (1978). *Language acquisition*. Cambridge, MA: Harvard University Press.

Chomsky, N. A. (1980). *Rules and representations*. New York: Columbia University Press.

CICERO'S THEORY OF HUMOR. The Roman statesman, orator, and philosopher Cicero (106-43 B.C.) echoes the Aristotelian elements and themes of the "deformity" and "baseness" in humor. *Cicero's theory of humor* emphasizes the notion that the "defeat or deceit of expectation" causes laughter where it is by satirizing the character of others, by talking seeming nonsense, or by reproving follies that laughter is stimulated. Thus, Cicero calls attention to the laughs that arise from surprise, from expectation defeated, and from the turning of another person's words to express a meaning not intended by him. As well as following Aristotle's lead in speculating about humor and laughter, Cicero adds at least one new rhetoric idea of some theoretical significance: he makes a distinction between humor regarding *what* is being talked about (the subject matter) and humor arising from the *language* used (the linguistic styling); such a distinction is similar to the more modern semantic differentiation between the "comedian" (i.e., one who says *funny* things) and the "comic" (i.e., one who says *things* funny). Also, Cicero divides *wit* into the same two main types: the cases in which the humor arises from the *subject matter* (e.g., caricature, anecdotes) and those cases involving *verbal form* (e.g., ambiguity, surprise, puns, allegory, metaphor, irony). See also ARISTOTLE'S

THEORY OF HUMOR; HUMOR, THEORIES OF; MORREALL'S THEORY OF HUMOR/LAUGHTER.

REFERENCES

Greig, J. Y. T. (1923/1969). *The psychology of laughter and comedy*. New York: Dodd, Mead/Cooper Square.

Morreall, J. (Ed.) (1987). *The philosophy of laughter and humor*. Albany: State University of New York Press.

CLASSICAL CONDITIONING, LAWS OF. See PAVLOVIAN CONDITIONING PRINCIPLES/LAWS/THEORIES.

CLASSICAL STRENGTH THEORY. See DECISION-MAKING THEORIES.

CLASSICAL TEST and MEASUREMENT THEORY. In the speculative domain within psychological testing, *classical test theory* (also called *classical measurement theory*) is a statistical approach according to which a person's measured score is assumed to be equal to the true score plus random measurement error, where this error is assumed usually to have a mean of zero and is considered to be uncorrelated with the true score. This theoretical approach defines the "reliability" (internal consistency or stability) of a test item as the proportion of the total variance in scores that is due to variance in the true scores. The major alternative to *classical test theory* is the *item response theory* (also called *latent trait theory*) which is based on the assumption that the probability of a particular response to a test item is a joint function of one or more aspects of the respondent and one or more aspects of the test item itself. The concept of "item response function" defines the relationship of these parameters to the probability of a particular response, where values are estimated from the measurable responses of respondents to the test item. The *Rasch Scale* - named after the Danish psychometrician Georg Rasch (1901-1980) - is a psychometric application of *item response theory* and assumes, similarly, that the probability of a particular response to a

test item depends on two independently estimated parameters: the extent to which the item elicits a "latent trait," and the status of the respondent on that trait which is constant across test items. See also MEASUREMENT THEORY; PROBABILITY THEORY AND LAWS.

REFERENCES

Dunlap, J. W. (1938/1941). Recent advances in statistical theory and applications. *American Journal of Psychology, 51*, 558-571; *54*, 583-601.

Rasch, G. (1960). *Studies in mathematical psychology: I. Probabilistic models for some intelligence and attainment tests*. Oxford, UK: Nielsen & Lyd-ische.

Magnusson, D. (1966). *Test theory*. Reading, MA: Addison-Wesley.

Nunnally, J. (1978). *Psychometric theory*. New York: McGraw-Hill.

Lord, F. M. (1980). *Applications of item response theory to practical testing problems*. Hillsdale, NJ: Erlbaum.

Aiken, L. R. (1982). *Psychological testing and assessment*. Boston: Allyn & Bacon.

CLASSICAL THEORIES OF INTELLIGENCE. See INTELLIGENCE, THEORY/ LAWS OF.

CLASSICAL THEORY OF SENSORY DISCRIMINATION. See NEURAL QUAN-TUM THEORY.

CLEVER HANS EFFECT/ PHENOMENON. Hans was the name of a "talented" horse, among the world-famous Elberfeld horses of Germany, which was trained by Wilhelm von Osten of Berlin. Hans' talent was his ability to perform some rather remarkable abstract/mental tasks such as addition, subtraction, division, multiplication, obtaining square roots, and spelling various words. After many people were thoroughly mystified by Hans' abilities, the German psychologist Oskar Pfungst (1874-1932) tested Hans and ultimately discovered that the horse was actually performing and solving his mathematical and mental problems by responding to subtle and totally unintentional, very tiny visual cues that were provided by von Osten (such as the questioner's bending forward slightly after presenting the horse with a problem and bending backward and upward slightly when the correct tap of Hans' hoof was reached). That is, the horse's method was to "count up" to the answer of a problem by stamping his hoof the required number of times. Hans "knew" when to stop stamping by taking his cues from the humans around him who unconsciously responded with changes in breathing patterns and bodily positions. Thus, Hans was simply responding to visual cues that were, to him, the "start" and "stop" signals of hoof-tapping. The term *Clever Hans effect/phenomenon* has come to denote communication that is transmitted through slight, unintentional, nonverbal cues. Prior to Pfungst's work, such cues had not been reported in the scientific/research literature, yet today they are recognized as unconscious signals in posture, gesture, and vocal tone emitted by individuals even as they speak their language. The *Clever Hans effect* may be an important concern in psychological experiments where the experimenter's expectations, hopes, habits, and personal characteristics can influence, unwittingly, the outcome of a research investigation. Such conditions of unintentional cuing are called, also, *experimenter effects*, *experimenter bias*, *Rosenthal effect*, or *Der Kluge Hans*. See also EXPERIMENTER EFFECTS.

REFERENCES

Pfungst, O. (1907/1911). *The horse of Mr. von Osten*. C. Rahn (Trans.). New York: Holt.

Rosenthal, R. (Ed.) (1965). *Clever Hans: The horse of Mr. von Osten*. New York: Holt, Rinehart, & Winston.

CLOACA/CLOACAL THEORY. See FREUD'S THEORY OF PERSONALITY.

CLOAK THEORY OF LANGUAGE. See WHORF-SAPIR HYPOTHESIS/THEORY.

CLOCK-COUNTER MODEL OF TEMPORAL DURATION. See BEHAVIORAL THEORY OF TIMING; PSYCHOLOGICAL TIME, MODELS OF.

CLOSED-LOOP MODEL OF STRESS. See SELYE'S THEORY AND MODEL OF STRESS.

CLOSED-LOOP THEORY. See MOTOR LEARNING/PROCESS THEORIES.

CLOSURE, PRINCIPLE OF. See GESTALT THEORY/LAWS.

CLOUDING EFFECT. See JUNG'S THE-ORY OF PERSONALITY.

CLUSTER HYPOTHESIS OF CONE FUNCTION . See HARTRIDGE'S POLYCHROMATIC VISION THEORY.

COACTION EFFECT. See ZAJONC'S AROUSAL AND CONFLUENCE THEORIES.

COALITION FORMATION THEORIES. See BARGAINING THEORY OF CO-ALITION FORMATION.

COCKTAIL PARTY EFFECT/PHENOM-ENON. See ATTENTION, LAWS/PRIN-CIPLES/THEORIES OF; GESTALT THEORY/LAWS.

CODING THEORIES. In general, a *code* is a system of symbols or signals representing information. Examples of codes are semaphore signals, magnetic fields on a recording tape, spoken English, written German, and the electrical zeroes and ones in a computer's memory chip. As long as one knows the rules of a code, a message can be converted from one medium to another without losing any information. Although the precise rules that sensory systems use to transmit information to the brain are not known, it is recognizes that they take two forms: *anatomical coding* (activity of particular neurons) and *temporal coding* (time or rate of neuron firing). The term *coding* is used in many content areas of psychology when examining and

98

describing various aspects of stimuli and responses. In sensation, the sensory organs collect environmental physical energies as input and prepare the stimuli for the next process, called *transduction* of the stimulus energy into neural impulse form, after which coding occurs at higher neural centers. In this way, stimulus information is translated or coded into the different aspects of sensation that are experienced. Some of the coded information concerns the factors of stimulus intensity (e.g., a loud versus a quiet sound) and stimulus quality (e.g., a high pitch versus a low pitch sound). Coding occurs in the processing of certain kinds of visual information, but individuals, also, have a verbal "channel" for processing information contained in words and ideas. A. Paivio refers to the process of coding information by both visual and verbal means as a dual-coding system/theory. Coding is used, also, in the area of cognitive psychology to describe the mechanisms of memory where concepts such as "encoding," "recoding," "decoding," "chunks," "subjective units," "functional stimuli," and "coding responses" are described, and where coding processes and responses need not be conscious or reportable. In one case, the *encoding specificity hypothesis/principle* (also called the *procedural reinstatement hypothesis*) refers to the generalization that the initial encoding (i.e., the process of choosing the information to be retained and transforming that information into a form than can be saved) of learned material reflects the influence of the *context* in which the learning took place. The notion of *encoding specificity* (also known as *encoding-retrieval interaction* and *transfer-appropriate processing*) is traceable to the American psychologist Harry Levi Hollingworth (1880-1956) in 1928 where it was called the *principle of reinstatement of stimulating conditions* (cf., *encoding variability principle* - refers to the degree of variability in the environment and mood in which one learns material; the larger the encoding variability, the more likely one has of performing well in an examination of that material; the effect is due to the increased likelihood that the

examining situation resembles one of those in which the material originally was acquired, and is similar to the *state-dependent learning/memory effects*). In terms of terminological analysis and experimental methodology, the phenomenon of *coding* is a construct that is defined by *converging operations* (e.g., Garner, Hake, & Eriksen, 1956) where it is viewed as a system for representing thoughts of any type, including schemata, propositions, concepts, percepts, ideas, images, segments, features, and "knowing" responses. Thus, there are many attributes to stimuli, and not all of them are involved in every memory, action, or thought, but cortical regions provide the *neural coding* processes necessary to register one's experiences. See also INFORMATION/INFORMATION-PROCESSING THEORY; MEMORY, THEORIES OF; NEURON, NEURAL, AND NERVE THEORY; REDINTEGRATION, PRINCIPLE/LAWS OF; STATE DEPENDENT MEMORY AND LEARNING EFFECTS.

REFERENCES

Hollingworth, H. L. (1928). *Psychology: Its facts and principles*. New York: D. Appleton.

Garner, W., Hake, H., & Eriksen, C. (1956). Operationism and the concept of perception. *Psychological Review*, *63*, 149-159.

Melton, A., & Martin, E. (Eds.) (1972). *Coding processes in human memory*. Washington, D.C.: Winston.

Tulving, E., & Thomson, D. (1973). Encoding specificity and retrieval processes in episodic memory. *Psychological Review*, *80*, 352-373.

Uttal, W. (1973). *The psychobiology of sensory coding*. New York: Harper.

DeValois, R., & DeValois, K. (1975). Neural coding of color. In E. Carterette & M. Friedman (Eds.), *Handbook of perception*. Vol. 5. New York: Academic Press.

Wiseman, S., & Tulving, E. (1975). A test of the confusion theory of encoding specificity. *Journal of Verbal*

Learning and Verbal Behavior,
14, 370-381.
Paivio, A. (1991). Dual coding theory: Retrospect and current status. *Cana-*
dian Journal of Psychology, 45,
255-287.

COEFFICIENT LAW. See FECHNER'S
LAW.

**COERCION TO THE BIOSOCIAL
MEAN, LAW OF.** See CATTELL'S THE-
ORY OF PERSONALITY.

COEXISTENCE, LAW OF. See PAV-
LOVIAN CONDITIONING PRINCIPLES,
LAWS, AND THEORIES.

COGNITION, UNIFIED THEORY OF.
See PROBLEM-SOLVING AND CREA-
TIVITY STAGE THEORIES.

COGNITIVE ALGEBRA THEORY. See
IMPRESSION FORMATION, THEORIES
OF; INFORMATION INTEGRATION
THE-ORY.

COGNITIVE APPRAISAL THEORY.
See COGNITIVE THEORIES OF EMO-
TION.

**COGNITIVE ARMS RACE HY-
POTHESIS.** See MACHIAVELLIAN
THEORY.

**COGNITIVE CONSISTENCY THEO-
RIES OF ATTITUDE CHANGE.** See
ATTITUDE/ATTITUDE CHANGE, THE-
ORIES OF.

**COGNITIVE CONSISTENCY THE-
ORY.** See FESTINGER'S COGNITIVE
DISSO-NANCE THEORY.

**COGNITIVE DEVELOPMENTAL
THE-ORIES.** See DEVELOPMENTAL
THEORY; ERIKSON'S THEORY OF
PERSONALITY; LEARNING THEO-
RIES/LAWS; PIAGET'S THEORY OF
DEVELOPMENTAL STA-GES; WHORF-
SAPIR HYPOTHESIS/THE-ORY.

**COGNITIVE DISSONANCE, THEORY
OF.** See FESTINGER'S COGNITIVE
DISSONANCE THEORY.

**COGNITIVE EVALUATION THE-
ORY.** See FESTINGER'S COGNITIVE
DISSONANCE THEORY.

COGNITIVE ILLUSIONS. See APPEN-
DIX A.

COGNITIVE MAPS. See COGNITIVE
STYLE MODELS; TOLMAN'S THE-
ORY.

COGNITIVE MODEL OF SUICIDE.
This *model of suicide* suggests that suicide
is linked on a continuum with other escape
and noncoping behaviors or strategies, and
emphasizes the suicidal individual's distortions of temporal/time perspective and personal views regarding his/her psychological
future and psychological past existing at a
given period of time. See also SUICIDE,
THEORIES OF; TIME, THEORIES OF.
REFERENCE
Lennings, C. (1994). A cognitive understanding of adolescent suicide.
Genetic, Social, and General
Psychology Monographs, 120,
287-307.

**COGNITIVE MODELS OF DURA-
TION JUDGMENT.** See PSYCHO-
LOGICAL TIME, MODELS OF.

**COGNITIVE-PERCEPTUAL THEO-
RIES OF HUMOR.** The *cognitive-*
perceptual theories of humor subsume the
concepts of superiority, incongruity, surprise, ambivalence, configurations, and
motives as the basis for systematizing and
classifying humor theories in the psychological literature. Thus, as a generic label
for humor theories, the *cognitive-*
perceptual theories include the following
notions: self versus others comparisons, and
the resultant feelings of triumph or elation
("superiority" theories); cognitions involving divergency from expected or habitual
customs ("incongruity" theories); perceptions and cognitions involving suddenness,

surprise, or shock ("surprise" theories); perceptions and cognitions consisting of conflict-mixture or oscillations ("ambivalence" theories); perceptions of unrelated elements that suddenly fall into their proper place ("configurational" theories); and drive for closure involving the successful and surprising resolution of an incongruity, paradox, or double-meaning ("motivational" theories). Theorists who favor the *cognitive-perceptual theories of humor* suggest that "getting the joke" is the real source of pleasure in humor; in comprehending the "point" of a joke, one is able to master the symbolic properties of the event with its multiple meanings and its allegorical or figurative allusions. In a sense, the process is similar to solving a complex problem or puzzle where the sudden discrepancy gained by the reshuffling of the meanings and symbols into a surprisingly novel relationship is the main source of personal gratification. See also AMBIVALENCE THEORIES OF HUMOR; COGNITIVE THEORIES OF HUMOR; CONFIGURATIONAL THEORIES OF HUMOR; HUMOR, THEORIES OF; INCONGRUITY/INCONSISTENCY THEORIES OF HUMOR; MOTIVATIONAL THEORIES OF HUMOR; SUPERIORITY THEORIES OF HUMOR; SURPRISE THEORIES OF HUMOR.

REFERENCE

Roeckelein, J. E. (2002). *The psychology of humor*. Westport, CT: Greenwood.

COGNITIVE RESOURCE THEORY. See LEADERSHIP, THEORIES OF.

COGNITIVE-SALIENCE MODEL OF HUMOR. The *cognitive-salience model of humor* assumes that - in the experimental manipulations of materials in humor studies - a *cognitive* set for processing sexual and aggressive stimuli occurs more easily than that assumed by *motivational theories* in which a drive/motive state is modified. In one test of this model (Kuhlman, 1985), participants gave humor ratings to three sets of jokes containing "salient," "taboo," and "neutral" themes; the salience category

required participants to rate jokes under one of three conditions: control; before taking an exam; and 20 minutes after beginning an exam. Results did not confirm the hypotheses derived solely from the *cognitive-salience model*; on the other hand, *motivational* factors were observed to be associated with high humor ratings. It may be suggested, based upon such experimental studies, that a conceptual integration of *both* cognitive and psychoanalytic/motivational mechanisms of humor may be the most fruitful approach to take for analyzing the humor experience. See also COGNITIVE THEORIES OF HUMOR; HUMOR, THEORIES OF; MOTIVATIONAL THEORIES OF HUMOR.

REFERENCES

Goldstein, J. H., Suls, J. M., & Anthony, S. (1972). Enjoyment of specific types of humor content: Motivation or salience? In J. H. Goldstein & P. E. McGhee (Eds.), *The psychology of humor: Theoretical perspectives and empirical issues*. New York: Academic Press.

Kuhlman, T. L. (1985). A study of salience and motivational theories of humor. *Journal of Personality and Social Psychology, 49*, 281-286.

COGNITIVE-SHIFT THEORY. See LATTA'S COGNITIVE-SHIFT THEORY OF HUMOR.

COGNITIVE SIGN PRINCIPLE. See LEARNING THEORIES/LAWS.

COGNITIVE STRUCTURE ACTIVATION, LAW OF. This cognitive and social psychological law is an empirical generalization that specifies the conditions under which an activated structure will be used to process new stimulus input. The law may be stated, formally, as: when a stimulus is ambiguous enough to be encodable as an instance of multiple cognitive structures, the stimulus most likely will be encoded as an instance of that cognitive structure that is the most activated in memory and is the most semantically similar to the stimulus. This encoding will, in turn, affect structure-relevant judgmental and behavioral processes. The *law of cognitive structure activation* suggests that the influence of activated cognitive structures extends into every stage of information-processing, including attention, stimulus encoding, organization and storage of stimuli in memory, retrieval and reconstruction of stimuli, and judgments made after information retrieval. See also FORGETTING/MEMORY, THEORIES OF; INFORMATION AND INFORMATION-PROCESSING THEORY.

REFERENCES

Solso, R. L. (1974). *Theories in cognitive psychology.* Potomac, MD: Erlbaum.

Pratto, F. (1991). Control, emotions, and laws of human behavior. *Psychological Inquiry, 2*, 202-204.

Sedikides, C., & Skowronski, J. J. (1991). The law of cognitive structure activation. *Psychological Inquiry, 2*, 169-184, 211-219.

COGNITIVE STYLE MODELS. The construct of *cognitive learning style* may be defined as the relatively stable individual preferences for perceptual and conceptual organization and categorization of the external environment (cf., the early *laws/principles of abstraction*; Moore, 1910). The terms *cognitive style* and *cognition* have been introduced and reintroduced into the psychological literature over a period of time extending back to the German psychologists at the turn of the 20th century. Also, the Swiss psychologist Carl Gustav Jung (1875-1961) suggested one of the earliest classifications of *cognitive styles* and *cognitive types* in the early 1920s. Because *cognitive style* deals with qualitative, rather than quantitative, differences and dimensions, and is concerned with behavior and preference, it is largely value-free and resists pronouncements of moral judgment. A number of *cognitive style models* (or *learning styles*) formulated on a dimensional or continuum basis have been proposed, including the following factors: field independence versus field dependence; scanning versus focusing; broad versus narrow categorizing; leveling versus sharpening; constricted versus flexible control; tolerance versus intolerance for ambiguity/incongruity; impulsive versus reflective responding; analytic versus nonanalytic conceptualizing styles; risk-taking versus cautious; perceptive versus receptive; systematic versus intuitive; convergence versus divergence; internal versus external locus of control; and cognitive complexity versus simplicity (cf., *accentuation theory* - one's tendency to exaggerate the extent of similarities between items located in the same category and to exaggerate dissimilarities of items located in different categories). In general, a person's *cognitive style* may be determined by the way she assesses her surroundings, seeks out meanings, and becomes informed (cf., *synthetic effect/approach* - a cognitive/perceptual effect or style in which the individual tends to make judgments based on an integrated whole, as distinguished from making judgments based on an analysis of the parts). In particular, a battery of tests concerning preferences for different ways of learning may be given to persons, and results can be interpreted to produce a "map" of the many ways each person seeks meaning, such as preferences for theoretical symbolic input, qualitative code input, modalities of inference, and cultural determinants. Thus, a *cognitive map* describes each person's *cognitive style* by relating score results on about two dozen aspects where the resultant map indicates a preferred or optimal learning environment. *Cognitive style mapping* is a diagnostic testing program useful for educational planning and may be used to identify and maximize an individual's strengths in a learning setting. *Cognitive style* is represented, theoretically, in observable behaviors where inconsistencies may occur in the choice of particular behaviors to be examined. Various measuring instruments have been developed to elicit specific behaviors for analyzing a person's cognitive style (e.g., "Myers-Briggs Type Indicator"), but it has been found that some measures of *cognitive style* do not correlate highly with other cognitive measures. The philosophy behind *cognitive style models* and *cognitive style mapping* in educational contexts is that individuals learn in diverse and unique ways, and no single educational method can serve everyone in an equal or optimal fashion. See also JUNG'S THEORY OF PERSONALITY; KELLY'S PERSONAL CONSTRUCT THEORY; LEARNING STYLE THEORY; PIAGET'S THEORY OF DEVELOPMENTAL STAGES; TOLMAN'S THEORY; WITKIN'S PERCEPTION/PERSONALITY/COGNITIVE STYLE THEORY.

REFERENCES

Beare, J. I. (1906/1992). *Greek theories of elementary cognition from Alcmae-on to Aristotle.* Bristol, UK: Thoem-mes Press.

Moore, T. (1910). The process of abstraction. *University of California Publications in Psychology, 1,* 73-197.

Jung, C. G. (1921/1976). *Psychological types.* Princeton, NJ: Princeton University Press.

Bieri, J. (1955). Cognitive complexity-simpli-city and predictive behaviors. *Journal of Abnormal and Social Psychology, 51,* 263-268.

Kagan, J., Moss, H., & Sigel, I. (1963). The psychological significance of styles of conceptualization. In J. Wright & J. Kagan (Eds.), *Basic cognitive processes in children. Monograph of the Society for Research in Child Development.* No. 28, 73-112.

Bruner, J. (1964). The course of cognitive thought. *American Psychologist, 19,* 1-15.

Coop, R., & Sigel, I. (1971). Cognitive style: Implications for learning and instruction. *Psychology in the Schools, 8,* 152-161.

Kreitler, H., & Kreitler, S. (1976). *Cognitive orientation and behavior.* New York: Springer.

Entwistle, N. (1981). *Styles of learning and teaching.* New York: Wiley.

COGNITIVE THEORIES OF EMOTIONS. *Cognitive theory of emotions* is a general term for a relatively recent class of theories of emotion that view the cognitive interpretation and appraisal of emotional stimuli from both inside and outside the body to be the major event in emotions. *Cognitive theories* have a long history, however, going back to the early Greek philosophers. Aristotle (384-322 B.C.) suggested that humans and animals can make sensory evaluations of things as being "good" or "bad" for them where the evaluation involves the arousal of emotions. Thomas Aquinas (1225-1274) agreed with Aristotle in his explanation of the arousal of emotions. Rene Descartes (1596-1650) asserted that all emotions are aroused directly through excitation of "animal spirits" or by arousal of innate reflex actions in combination with physiological changes that are necessary for the organism's survival. Charles Darwin (1809-1882) essentially shared Descartes' notion of emotions. Later, William James (1842-1910) and Carl Lange (1834-1900) reversed the classical, intuitive, or commonsense view that emotion produces bodily changes by arguing that bodily changes occur after the perception of the arousing event where one's sensation of the bodily changes is the emotion. Sigmund Freud (1856-1939) conceived of emotions as an "affect change" of the twin drives of love and aggression, and fear as the reliving of the birth trauma. Alfred Adler (1870-1937) rejected Freud's concept of libido as the source of all motivation and accounted for human motivation and emotion in terms of a desire for power. Carl Jung (1875-1961) proposed that feelings are a kind of psychological function different from intellectual judgment that is somewhat similar in nature to the ideas of Aristotle and Aquinas. Jung's insistence on feeling as a rational judgment function makes him the first modern *cognitive theorist* of feeling; however, Jung did not connect the "feeling function" with emotion, which he viewed as an irrational phenomenon arising from the unconscious. With the appearance of the school of *behaviorism,* where internal concepts such as feeling and emotion were considered to be too mentalistic, the topic of emotion was either subordinated to motivation or almost completely lost in the stimulus-response paradigm of the behaviorists (cf., however, the current *COPE model* - a behavioral-cognitive strategy, standing for "control-organize-plan-execute," often used in sports psychology, for dealing with a performer's anxiety, which focuses on controlling emotions, organizing input, planning for the next action/response, and execution of the action/response). Between the 1920s and the 1950s, the topic of emotion seems to have been abandoned in psychology. By the 1950s and 1960s, however, theorists began to return to the intuitive idea that a situation must be interpreted in some way before it can instigate an emotion. Magda Arnold (1954) introduced the concept of *appraisal* into academic psychology where emotion was defined as a felt action tendency toward things that are intuitively appraised as good for oneself or away from things that are appraised as bad, and where a pattern of physiological changes is organized around particular types of approach or withdrawal. It is interesting to note how some of the early writers in psychology anticipated the modern notion of *cognitive theory* in emotions. For instance, Walter Pillsbury asserted that all emotions have an instinctive basis, and emotion may be defined as the *conscious* side of instinct. As used today, the *cognitive theory of emotions* is regarded, often, as a single theory (e.g., Leventhal & Tomarken, 1986; Frijda, 1988), even though a number of different investigators over many years have contributed various aspects and refinements to the theory. For example, M. Arnold, A. Ellis, R. Lazarus, S. Schachter, and J. Singer have been prominent in the development of the *cognitive theory of emotions* and collectively propose, in general, that there are two steps in the process of cognitive interpretation of an emotional episode: the interpretation and appraisal of stimuli from the *external* environment; and the interpretation and appraisal of stimuli from the *internal* autonomic arousal system. See also ABC THEORY; ACTIVATION/AROUSAL THE-ORY; ADLER'S THEORY OF PERSONALITY; ARNOLD'S THEORY OF EMOTIONS; EMOTIONS, THEORIES/LAWS OF; FREUD'S THEORY OF PERSONALITY; JAMES-LANGE OR LANGE-JAMES THEORY OF EMOTIONS; JUNGS'S THEORY OF PERSONALITY; KELLY'S PERSONAL CONSTRUCT THEORY; LAZARUS' THEORY OF EMOTIONS; SCHACHTER-SINGER'S THEORY OF EMOTIONS; ZAJONC'S AROUSAL AND CONFLUENCE THEORIES.

REFERENCES

Descartes, R. (1650). *Les passions de l'ame*. Paris: Loyson.

Darwin, C. (1872). *The expression of the emotions in man and animals*. Chicago: University of Chicago Press.

James, W. (1890). *The principles of psychology*. New York: Holt.

Pillsbury, W. (1918). *The essentials of psychology*. New York: Macmillan.

Jung, C. G. (1921). *Psychological types*. Princeton, NJ: Princeton University Press.

Adler, A. (1927). *Practice and theory of individual psychology*. New York: Humanities Press.

Freud, S. (1933). New introductory lectures on psychoanalysis. In *The standard edition of the complete psychological works of Sigmund Freud*. Vol. 22. London: Hogarth Press.

Aristotle. (1941). De anima (On the soul). In R. McKeon (Ed.), *The basic works of Aristotle*. New York: Random House.

Thomas Aquinas. (1951). *Commentary of St. Thomas Aquinas*. New Haven, CT: Yale University Press.

Arnold, M. (1954). Feelings and emotions as dynamic factors in personality integration. In M. Arnold & J. Gasson (Eds.), *The human person*. New York: Ronald Press.

Ellis, A. (1962). *Reason and emotion in psychotherapy*. New York: Lyle Stuart.

Leventhal, H., & Tomarken, A. (1986). Emotion: Today's problem. *Annual Review of Psychology, 37,* 565-610.

Frijda, N. (1988). The laws of emotion. *American Pychologist, 43,* 349-357.

Lazarus, R. (1991). *Emotion and adaptation.* New York: Oxford University Press.

COGNITIVE THEORIES OF HUMOR. = incongruity-resolution theories. The *cognitive theories of humor* are characterized, generally, by a two-stage process: the perception of some complexity, incongruity, discrepancy, ambiguity, or novelty in the humor stimulus; and the resolution of the discrepancy in the stimulus via cognitive integration or understanding. According to such a cognitive approach to humor analysis and theorizing, humor implicitly is a process that involves the interaction between the recipient and some structural aspect of the stimulus, and that a joke, cartoon, or riddle, for example, may be understood and appreciated by assimilation of the humor stimulus into the individual's existing cognitive structures or framework. Thus, the pleasure one derives from joke-humor comes from the unexpected cognitive resolution of a series of paradoxes climaxed by the "punch line" of the joke. Also, an important ingredient in humor appreciation, according to the *cognitive theories,* is the degree to which the humor stimulus makes a *cognitive demand* on the individual. See also HUMOR, THEORIES OF; INCONGRUITY AND INCONSISTENCY THEORIES OF HUMOR; LATTA'S COGNITIVE-SHIFT THEORY OF HUMOR.

REFERENCE

Roeckelein, J. E. (2002). *The psychology of humor.* Westport, CT: Greenwood Press.

COGNITIVE THEORY. See BOTTOM-UP PROCESSING THEORIES; CHOMSKY'S PSYCHOLINGUISTIC THEORY; COGNITIVE THEORIES OF EMOTIONS; CONCEPT LEARNING/CONCEPT FORMA-TION, THEORIES OF; CONSTRUCTIVIST THEORY OF PERCEPTION; DECISION-MAKING THEORIES; DEPRESSION, THE-ORIES OF; FESTINGER'S COGNITIVE DISSO-NANCE THEORY; IMAGERY AND MENTAL IMAGERY, THEORIES OF; LEADERSHIP, THEORIES OF; MO-TIVA-TION, THEORIES OF; TOLMAN'S THEORY; TOP-DOWN PROCESSING THEORIES; WUNDT'S THEORIES, DOCTRINES, AND PRINCIPLES.

COGNITIVE THERAPY, THEORIES OF. See BEHAVIOR THER-APY/COGNITIVE THERAPY, THEO-RIES OF.

COGNITIVE VULNERABILITY HYPO-THESIS. See DEPRESSION, THEORIES OF.

COHESION, LAW OF. See PAV-LOVIAN CONDITIONING PRINCIPLES, LAWS, AND THEORIES.

COHESION PRINCIPLE/LAW. = law of association = law of combination. The Greek philosopher Aristotle (384-322 B.C.) early advanced the *cohesion principle/law* which is the notion that ideas or acts (or, in modern times: stimuli and responses) that occur simultaneously, or in close succession, tend to become combined or unified and, thus, form an integrated idea or act of a more complex character (or, in modern times: a stimulus-response connection). The *law of combination* suggests that two stimuli or two responses both occurring either simultaneously or in close proximity may act as either one stimulus or one response. Much later, in the early 1900s, the *law of cohesion* may be recognized in the theoretical position of the Gestalt psychologists who suggested, in particular, that parts of a visual perception tend to generate a sense of wholeness of an object. The American psychologist Edward Chace Tolman (1886-1959) proposed a *law of cohesion* which states that behavioral acts that are temporally and spatially proximate tend to become integrated into more complex acts. The *law of cohesion* has been employed, also, in the area of group dynamics to refer to the forces that hold a group together, where cohesion is dependent upon the extent to which a group's activities are rewarding for its members, the extent to which interaction within a group has positive qualities for the group's members, and the utility of group membership for achieving a person's objectives. See also ASSOCIATION, LAWS/PRINCIPLES OF; GESTALT THEORY/LAWS; PAVLOVIAN CONDITIONING PRINCIPLES, LAWS, AND THEORIES; TOLMAN'S THEORY.

REFERENCES

McKeon, R. (Ed.) (1941). *The basic works of Aristotle*. New York: Random House.

Tolman, E. C. (1959). Principles of purposive behavior. In S. Koch (Ed.), *Psychology: A study of a science*, Vol. 2. New York: McGraw-Hill.

COHORT EFFECTS. See AGING, THEORIES OF.

COLD EFFECTS. See LOMBROSIAN THEORY.

COLLECTIVE UNCONSCIOUS, THEORY OF. See JUNG'S THEORY OF PERSONALITY.

COLOR-CONTINGENT AFTEREFFECT. See McCOLLOUGH EFFECT.

COLOR CONTRAST PHENOMENON. See HERING-HURVICH-JAMESON COL-OR VISION THEORY.

COLOR MIXING, PRINCIPLES OF. See COLOR MIXTURE, LAWS/THEORIES OF.

COLOR MIXTURE, LAWS/THEORY OF. = additive color mixture, principles of. = subtractive color mixture, principles of. = color mixing, principles of. The color of objects in the environment are determined by pigments hat are chemicals on the objects' surface that absorb some wavelengths of light and, consequently, prevent those wavelengths of light from being reflected. Also, different pigments permit different wavelengths to be reflected. For example, a pigment that absorbs short and medium wavelengths of light appears to be "red" because only long ("red") wavelengths are reflected; a pigment that permits only short wavelengths to be reflected appears to be "blue;" and a pigment that permits only medium wavelengths to be reflected appears to be "yellow" or "green." When all wavelengths are reflected equally by a pigment, one gets the experience of "white," "gray," or "black," depending on whether the relative amount of light reflected is high ("white"), medium ("gray"), or low ("black"). The term *additive color mixing* refers to the mixture of colored *lights*, whereas the term *subtractive color mixing* refers to the mixture of *pigments* (such as paints). *Subtractive color mixing* occurs when *pigments* create the perception of color by "subtracting" (i.e., absorbing) some of the light waves that would otherwise be reflected to the eye. For instance, if a blue pigment (which absorbs long wavelengths of light) is mixed with a yellow pigment (which absorbs short wavelengths of light), only the medium-length waves will be reflected, and the resultant mixture will be perceived as "green." Amateur painters, working with pigments, experience *subtractive color mixing* when they mix all of the paints on the palette together, with the result of a muddy "brown" or "black" color. In this case, the painter "subtracts out" *all* of the wavelengths by mixing all of the pigments together. *Additive color mixing*, on the other hand, describes the results of mixing colored *lights* together. For example, shining a blue light together with red and green-yellow lights on the same spot on a white screen reflects the mixed lights back and gives the perception of a "white" light. Two general *laws of additive color mixing*, known to scientists as early as the 18th century (e.g., Newton, 1704), are called the *three-primaries law* and the *law of complementarity*. The *three-primaries law* states that three different wavelengths of light (the "primaries") may be used to match any color that the eye can see, if they are mixed in the proper proportions. The "primaries" can be any three wavelengths as long as each one is taken from the three types of wavelengths: one from the long-wave ("red") end of the spectrum, one from the medium-wave ("green," "green-yellow") region, and one from the short-wave ("blue," "violet") end of the visible spectrum. The *law of complementarity* states that pairs "complements") of wavelengths of light can be reflected so that, when they are added together, they give the visual sensation of a "white" light. An important subfield in the area of color vision and color mixture is called *colorimetry*, which is the science that aims at specifying and reproducing colors as a result of measurement. Colorimeters may be of three types: color filter samples for empirical comparison; monochromatic colorimeters that match colors with a mixture of monochromatic and white lights; and trichromatic colorimeters in which a match is achieved by a mixture of three colors. See also ABNEY'S LAW; COLOR VISION, THEORIES/LAWS OF; GRASSMAN'S LAWS; NEWTON'S LAW/PRINCIPLES OF COLOR MIXTURE; VISION/SIGHT, THEORIES/LAWS OF.

REFERENCES

Newton, I. (1704). *Opticks*. London: Smith.

Grassman, H. (1853). Sur theorie der far-benmischung. *Poggendorf Annales der Physik , 89*, 69.

OSA Committee on Colorimetry. (1943). The concept of color. *Journal of the Optical Society of America, 33*, 544.

OSA Committee on Colorimetry. (1944). The psychophysics of color. *Journal of the Optical Society of America, 246*, 254-255.

COLOR VISION, THEORIES/LAWS OF. The concept of *color* is a psychological (subjective) experience or sensation that is associated with the presence of a physical light source and depends on three aspects of the actual physical energy: intensity ("brightness"), wavelength ("hue"), and purity ("saturation"). Most humans see the shorter visible wavelengths of the electromagnetic radiation spectrum as "bluish" (about 480 nanometers, or *nm*); the medium wavelengths as "greenish" (about 510 *nm*) and "yellowish" (about 580 *nm*); and the longer wavelengths as "reddish" (about 700 *nm*). The term *chromatic* refers to stimuli that have all three of these aspects (and have *color*), whereas the term *achromatic* refers to stimuli that have only the "brightness" aspect (and are "white-gray-black"). Typically, the better *theories of color vision* can account for several phenomena: the *primary colors* ("unique hues") of blue, green, yellow, and red; the *complementary colors* (i.e., any of the colors that are opposite to each other on the color wheel and when additively mixed produce an achromatic gray) and their influence in afterimages and contrast effects; the *laws of color mixture*; and the different symptoms of various types of *color blindness* [e.g., protanopes, deuteranopes, tritanopes; cf., *Horner's law* - named after the Swiss ophthalmologist Johann Friedrich Horner (1831-1886), which is the genetic principle that the most common form of color blindness, red-green, is transmitted from male to male through female unaffected carriers; cf., *Konig's theory* - named after the German physicist Arthur Konig (1856-1901), which accounts for changes in the *Weber fraction* for colors as a function of light intensity). R. Wheeler (1929) describes a number of minor *theories of color vision*, such as those by Venable, Schanz, and Forbes. Another early writer (A. Reid, 1938) lists the *laws of color vision* as: adapting, color mixture, contrast, and induction. *Kirschmann's law of contrast* - named after the German researcher August Kirschmann (1860-1932), is the principle that contrast is proportional to the logarithm of the saturation of the contrast-inducing color. D. Judd (1951) summarizes a few of the better known visual theories, citing their fun-damental colors and their chief limitations: *Young-Helmholtz three components theory* (red, green, violet) - fails to explain dichromatic vision and color perceptions of protanopes (red-color deficiency) and deuteranopes (green-color deficiency); *dominator-modu-lator theory* ("late-Konig theory;" red, green, violet) - fails to explain color perception of protanopes and deuteranopes; *Ladd-Franklin three components* *theory* ("early Konig theory;" red, green, blue) - implies that the blue function has a negative luminosity for normals and deuteranopes and a positive luminosity for protanopes; *Hering opponent colors theory* (red-green, yellow-blue, white-black) - fails to give an account of protanopia and tritanopia (blue-light deficiency); *von Kries-Schrodinger zone theory* (red, green, blue; and green-red, blue-yellow, white-black) - implies that the blue function has a negative luminosity for normals and deuteranopes, and a positive luminosity for protanopes, and fails to account for tritanopia; *Adams' zone theory* (red, green, violet; red, green, blue; red-green, blue-yellow, white-black) - explanations of protanopia and tritanopia are based on other "extra" or "subsidiary" assumptions; *Muller's zone theory* (red, green, violet; red-green, yellow-blue, white-black) - implausible explanation of protanopic luminosity; cf., the German psychologist Georg Elias *Muller's* (1850-1934) *color theory*, similar to *Hering's color theory*, which proposes that all colors are reducible to two pairs of opposed or antagonistic colors with a chemical substance of reversible action in the retina for each pair). It is a well-accepted fact that the cones and rods of the retina are the immediate organs of vision and that they contain substances, or mixtures of substances, that absorb radiant energy falling on these receptors. In turn, the receptors respond by initiating nerve impulses that go to the fibers of the optic nerve. It is well-established, also, that the response of the rods is due to a photochemical substance called *rhodopsin*, but the substances giving the cones their precise spectral characteristics are still being researched, as well as the combinations of cone responses that produce impulses in the optic nerve. Recent theories of the underlying mechanisms mediating color vision feature a merger of two accounts that were initially considered to be in conflict. One approach, the *trichromatic theory* of Thomas Young and Hermann von Helmholtz, stresses the relative activity of cones that are maximally sensitive to red, blue, or green. The other approach, the *opponent-process theory* of

Ewald Hering, Leo Hurvich, and Dorothea Jameson, considers red-green as well as blue-yellow to be antagonistic processes. These two accounts have been reconciled now so that *the trichromatic theory* describes activity at the "lower" receptor level, and the *opponent-process theory* describes integration events at the "higher" level of neural organization. A current *theory of color vision*, the *retinex theory*, formulated by the American physicist/sensory psychologist Edwin Herbert Land (1909-1991), maintains the existence of three separate visual systems ("retinexes") where one is responsive primarily to long-wavelength light, one to moderate-wavelength light, and the third to short-wavelength light. Each system is represented as an analog to a black-and-white picture taken through a particular filter with each one producing maximum activity in response to red, green, and blue light for the long-, moderate-, and short-wavelength retinexes, respectively (cf., the *Land effect* - a vivid impression of a full range of colors produced by monochromatic light; in its simplest form, two black and white photographs are taken of a scene, one through a red filter and one through a blue-green filter; the two are then projected together onto a screen, the former through a red filter and the latter through a green one; the resulting scene is perceived as one composed of a wide range of colors, including blues that are not typically produced by a mixture of red and green). See also COLOR MIXTURE, LAWS/THEORY OF; GRANIT'S COLOR VISION THEORY; HECHT'S COLOR VISION THEORY; HERING-HURVICH-JAMESON COLOR VISION THEORY; LADD-FRANKLIN AND FRANKLIN COLOR VISION THEORY; VISION/SIGHT, THEORIES OF; WEBER'S LAW; WILLMER'S COLOR THEORY; YOUNG-HELMHOLTZ COLOR VISION THEORY.

REFERENCES

Kirschmann, A. (1891). Uber die quantitativen verhaltnisse des simultanen helligkeits- und farben-contrastes. *Philosophische Studien*, *6*, 417-491.

Konig, A (1897). Uber blaublindheit. *Sitzungsberichte Akademie der Wissenschaffen, Berlin.*

Adams, E. Q. (1923). A theory of color vision. *Psychological Review, 30,* 56-76.

Ladd-Franklin, C. (1929). *Colour and colour theories.* London: Kegan Paul, Trench & Trubner.

Wheeler, R. (1929). *The science of psychology.* New York: Crowell.

Reid, A. (1938). *Elements of psychology.* New York: Prentice-Hall.

Judd, D. (1951). Basic correlates of the visual system. In S. S. Stevens (Ed.), *Handbook of Experimental Psychology.* New York: Wiley.

Land, E. (1959). Color vision and the natural image. *Proceedings of the National Academy of Sciences, 45,* 115-129, 636-644.

MacNichol, E. (1964). Retinal mechanisms of color vision. *Vision Research, 4,* 119-133.

Graham, C. (1965). Color: Data and theories. In C. Graham (Ed.), *Vision and visual perception.* New York: Wiley.

Symposium on New Developments in the Study of Color Vision (1969). *Proceedings of the National Academy of Sciences, 55,* 89-115.

Riley, C. A. (1995). *Color codes: Modern theories of color in philosophy, painting, architecture, literature, music, and psychology.* Hanover, NH: University Press of New Eng-land.

COMBINATION, LAW OF. See COHESION PRINCIPLE/LAW; VIGILANCE, THEORIES OF.

COMBINATION/RESULTANT TONES, PHENOMENON/THEORY OF. See STUMPF'S THEORY OF MUSICAL CON-SONANCE AND DISSONANCE.

COMMODITY THEORY. See FESTINGER'S COGNITIVE DISSONANCE THEORY.

COMMON DIRECTION, COMMON FATE, GOOD CONTINUATION, LAW OF. See GESTALT THEORY/LAWS.

COMMON RATIO EFFECT. See ALLAIS PARADOX/EFFECT.

COMMONS DILEMMA. See RESOURCE DILEMMA MODEL/PARADIGM.

COMMONSENSE THEORY OF EMOTIONS. See JAMES-LANGE/LANGE-JAMES THEORY OF EMOTIONS.

COMMUNICATION THEORY. In broad terms, *communication* refers to the transmission of something from one location to another where the "thing" that is transmitted may be a message, a signal, a meaning, and so on, where both the transmitter and the receiver must share a common code so that the meaning of the information contained in the message may be interpreted without error (cf., *interpreter effect* - refers to the misunderstanding that may occur between people due to each of them employing a different definition of terms discussed; in a research context, this effect may be viewed as a potential *experimenter bias effect* that results from a misunderstanding of the language used between participant and experimenter and which may, ultimately, lead to invalid conclusions regarding the research findings in question; in an interview context, the *interview contrast effect* refers to the tendency for an interviewer's judgment of the person being interviewed to be influenced by a previous interview of another person; and the *interviewer bias/effect* refers to the influence of the interviewer's own expectations, attributes, training, theoretical assumptions, and behavior on the interview process). *Communication theory* is the process whereby one system influences another system by regulation of the transmitted signals. In psychology, *communication theory* has proven useful in developing models of interpersonal attraction, memory processes, language, and physiological functions (cf., *dyadic effect* - refers to the tendency in a situation where two people are interacting that the more one person "self-discloses," the more the other person will do likewise). The general *communication process* consists of five elements: the source; the transmitter; the channel; the source of potential noise; and the receiver (cf., the social psychological analysis of *persuasion* involving the basis elements of source, message, and audience). The channel may alter a certain amount and type of data where the translation of data into a form acceptable to the channel (coding) and the reverse process for use by the receiver (decoding) are critical issues in the analysis and design of *communication systems*. The concept of *noise* is defined as the origin of errors in transmission where the signal reaching the receiver is a function of the original signal plus extraneous data or "noise" (cf., the concept of *noise* in *signal detection theory*). The *communication model* proposed by C. Shannon and W. Weaver (1949) invites mathematical analysis and quantitative measurements of the concepts of information, channel capacity, error reduction, redundancy, and efficiency of coding systems. This approach allows analyses to be made of communication processes in different areas of study from molecular genetics to literary criticism. Communication in the social sciences may be divided into interpersonal versus mass communication categories. In interpersonal communication, the receiver may respond immediately and create a network of several communication chains, whereas in mass communication each transmission link is separated, largely. The theoretical approaches in the study of interpersonal communication are dependent on particular methods of research, experiments, observation, or field study. Two models or theories that emphasize the *type* of message in the communication process are those of R. Bales and E. Chapple. Bales developed 12 formal categories for describing the interaction/communication process occurring among members in small groups; by combining some of the categories in certain ways, Bales was able to define and elaborate various subsets of "communication

climates," as well as to identify problems of communication, evaluation, control, decision making, tension reduction, and reintegration. Chapple's model is more abstract than Bales' system and measures only the *amount* of talking, overlap, and lengths of contradiction. Both Bales' and Chapple's approaches avoid any mention of communication *content* per se. In other theoretical approaches, however, such as the experimental method in measuring communication, the actual communication processes are inferred from measurement of the conditions and the effect of the process. Some experimental approaches may control informal social communication processes by instruction and inputs from the experimenter with outcomes measured via questionnaires or joint actions by the group members (cf., "actual" communication sequences in methodologies such as *simulations* and *role-playing* scenarios). Theories and studies of interpersonal communication have focused, also, on the *practical* aspects of communication, such as intimacy/marital problems, and effective communication issues and strategies [cf., *Janis-Feyerabend hypothesis* - named after the American psychologist Irving Lester Janis (1918-1990) and the Austrian-born American philosopher Paul K. Feyerabend (1924-1994), which posits that it is better to rebut positive arguments before defending negative ones]. It is recognized that the method of field observation (usually devoid of a good theory to guide data collection and analysis) of interpersonal communication is a relatively weak approach due to the paucity of results relative to the large technical apparatus necessary to collect data. On the other hand, the theoretical work of some researchers has succeeded in bridging the gap between the interpersonal and the mass communication approaches (e.g., Katz & Lazarsfeld's *two–step theory of communications*; Lerner's *societal progress theory*; McLuan's *communication theory*; Klapp's *sociological theory of communication*). For example, in the *two-step flow/two-step communication theory*, it is suggested that most members of a population are not directly influenced by messages sent via the mass media, but are affected by face-to-face, interpersonal contact with a relatively small number of recipients, called "opinion leaders," who do respond to mass media appeals. Thus, *communication theory* includes a number of disciplines where each focuses on a number of different factors. Three approaches to the study of both verbal and nonverbal communication have been identified: the *dimensional* approach (delineates specific components of communication, including a source, a message, a channel, and a receiver where typically there is a two-way exchange of communication); the *process* approach (focuses on the internal and external dynamics of the sender and receiver of a message); and the *functional* approach (studies the functions and purposes of communication, including "syntactics" or structural elements, "semantics" or meanings, and "pragmatics" or practical consequences of communication) (cf., *verbal context effect* - refers to the probability of a particular word following another word, such as the word "you" following the greeting/query "Hello, how are - ?"). Also, four main "perspectives" on the study of communication have been identified: *mechanistic* (physical elements of communication, including the transmission and reception of messages along a linear model); *psychological* (a behavioristic conceptualization of communication, including concepts such as stimulus field, sensory inputs, emitted response, reinforcement, and processing of cognitive-behavioral events); *interactional* (a humanistic orientation where communication focuses on the development of one's potential via social interaction, including concepts such as self, social roles, cultural symbols, self-understanding, and self-dis-closure) [cf., *symbolic interactionism theory* - described by the American social philosopher George Herbert Mead (1863-1931), is a conjecture in which people are observed to respond to aspects of their environment in terms of the meanings they attach to those aspects, where such meanings are created and modified via social interaction involving symbolic communication with other members of the social unit]; and *pragmatic* (focuses

on outcomes and consequences of communication, especially as developed in the area of psychotherapy). Apparently, no matter what particular theoretical perspective, approach, or direction one takes, most investigators of communication subscribe to the principle that an individual cannot *not* communicate. Even *without* verbal communicative signals, people would emit an infinite variety and number of nonverbal behaviors, the purpose of which is to communicate meaning. See also ATTITUDE/ATTITUDE CHANGE, THEORIES OF; CODING THEORIES; EXPERIMENTER EFFECTS; INFORMATION AND INFORMATION-PROCESSING THEORY; IN-TERACTION PROCESS ANALYSIS TECH-NIQUE; INTERPERSONAL ATTRACTION THEORIES; PERSUASION AND INFLUENCE THEORIES; SIGNAL DETECTION THEORY.

REFERENCES

Mead, G. H. (1934). *Mind, self, and society: From the standpoint of a social behaviorist.* Chicago: University of Chicago Press.

Chapple, E. (1949). The interaction chronograph: Its evolution and present applications. *Personnel, 25*, 295-307.

Shannon, C., & Weaver, W. (1949). *The mathematical theory of communica-tion.* Urbana: University of Illinois Press.

Bales, R. (1950). *Interaction process analysis: A method for the study of small groups.* Reading, MA: Addison-Wesley.

Katz, E., & Lazarsfeld, P. (1955). *Personal influence: The part played by people in the flow of mass communications.* Glencoe, IL: Free Press.

Lerner, D. (1958). *The passing of traditional society.* Glencoe, IL: Free Press.

McLuan, M. (1962). *The Gutenberg galaxy.* Toronto: University of Toronto Press.

Green, D., & Swets, J. (1966). *Signal detection theory and psychophysics.* New York: Wiley.

Borden, G. (1971). *An introduction to human communication theory.* Dubuque, IA: Brown.

Klapp, O. (1978). *Opening and closing.* Cambridge, UK: Cambridge University Press.

Littlejohn, S. W. (1999). *Theories of human communication.* Belmont, CA: Wadsworth.

Bazerman, M., Curhan, J., Moore, D., & Valley, K. (2000). Negotiation. *Annual Review of Psychology, 51,* 279-314.

Griffin, E. (2000). *A first look at communication theory.* Boston, MA: McGraw-Hill.

COMMUNION PRINCIPLE. See DODO HYPOTHESIS.

COMMUNITARIANISM THEORY. See LABELING/DEVIANCE THEORY.

COMPARATIVE JUDGMENT, LAW OF. See THURSTONE'S LAW OF COMPARATIVE JUDGMENT.

COMPATIBILITY, LAW OF. See SKINNER'S DESCRIPTIVE BEHAVIOR AND OPERANT CONDITIONING THEORY.

COMPENSATORY THEORY OF DREAMING. See DREAM THEORY.

COMPETENCE THEORY. See PLAY, THEORIES OF.

COMPETITIVE EXCLUSION PRINCIPLE. See DARWIN'S EVOLUTION THEORY.

COMPLEMENTARITY, LAW OF. See COLOR MIXTURE, LAWS/THEORIES OF.

COMPLEMENTARITY PRINCIPLE. See VISION/SIGHT, THEORIES OF.

COMPLEMENTARY NEEDS, THEORY OF. See LOVE, THEORIES OF.

COMPLEMENTARY ODORS, LAW OF. See OLFACTION/SMELL, THEORIES OF.

COMPLEX MAN THEORY. See ORGANIZATIONAL/ INDUSTRIAL / SYSTEMS THEORY.

COMPLEXES, THEORY OF. The Austrian physician Josef Breuer (1842-1925) first introduced the theoretical notion of *complex* (i.e., a presumed organized structure or collection of ideas, impulses, and memories sharing a common emotional tone that is excluded wholly or partly from consciousness, but continues to affect a person's thoughts and behaviors) into psychology and psychoanalysis in 1895, and was adapted later by the psychoanalysts Sigmund Freud (1856-1939), Alfred Adler (1870-1937), and Carl Jung (1875-1961). In 1910, Jung introduced the term *complex indicator* into psychology which, in the context of an association test, refers to any behavior - such as blushing or responding slowly - that is caused by a repressed complex (cf., Jung, 1918). Among the classical psychic *complexes* are the following: *Diana complex* - the repressed wish of a woman to be a man (named after Diana, the virginal Roman goddess of the moon); *Electra complex* - the female counterpart to the male Oedipus complex, refers to the female child's sexual feelings/love for her father and hatred/jealousy toward her mother (named after Electra in Greek mythology who arranged for the murder of her mother Clytemnestra who, in turn, had murdered Electra's father Agamemnon); *Father complex* - a male child's feelings of ambivalence towards his father, and is one of the aspects of the Oedipus complex; *Inferiority complex* - a combination of emotionally-toned ideas deriving from repressed fear or resentment, related to real or imagined inferiority, and resulting in pugnacity towards others or in withdrawal into oneself; *Inverted Oedipus complex* - the child's sexual desire/love for the same-sex parent and hatred/jealousy of the opposite-sex parent; *Jocasta complex* - the sexual desire of a mother for her son (named after the Greek mythological figure Jocasta, the Queen of Thebes, who married Oedipus without knowing that he was her son); *Mother complex* - a female child's feelings of ambivalence towards her mother, and is one of the aspects of the Oedipus complex; *Oedipus complex* - an organized collection of loving and hostile feelings of a child towards its parents where, in its positive form, it is a sexual desire for the opposite-sex parent and a jealous hatred of the same-sex parent; and, in its negative/inverted form, it is a sexual desire for the same-sex parent and hatred of the opposite-sex parent (named after the Greek mythological character Oedipus, who killed his father Laius, married his mother Jocasta, and then blinded himself when the truth about his parentage emerged); *Orestes complex* - the desire of a son to kill his mother (named after the Greek mythological figure Orestes, the son of Agamemnon and Clytemnestra, who killed his mother and her lover as revenge for the murder of his father); *Phaedra complex* - the sexual desire/love of a mother for her son (named after the Greek mythological character Phaedra, the wife of Theseus, who accused her stepson Hippolytus of raping her after he declined her sexual advances). Although the term *complex* was intended originally as a descriptive/metaphorical device, it has come to have pathological connotations, perhaps because of the pervasive theme in *complexes* that they are often unconscious and repressed and are, theoretically, in conflict with other behaviors. See also ADLER'S THEORY OF PERSONALITY; FREUD'S THEORY OF PERSONALITY; JUNG'S THEORY OF PERSONALITY.

REFERENCES

Breuer, J., & Freud, S. (1895/1957). *Studies on hysteria.* New York: Basic Books.

Freud, S. (1905). Three essays on the theory of sexuality. In *The standard edition of the complete psychological works of Sigmund Freud.* Vol. 7. London: Hogarth Press.

Freud, S. (1910). A special type of choice of object made by men. In *Collected papers.* Vol. 4. London: Hogarth Press.

Jung, C. G. (1918). *Studies in word association.* London: Heinemann.

Freud, S. (1931). Female sexuality. In *The standard edition of the complete psychological works of Sigmund Freud.* Vol. 21. London: Hogarth Press.

Jung, C. G. (1960). A review of the complex theory. In *The collected works of C. G. Jung.* Vol. 8. Princeton, NJ: Princeton University Press.

Adler, A. (1964). Advantages and disadvantages of the inferiority feeling. In H. L. Ansbacher & R. R. Ansbacher (Eds.), *Superiority and social interest.* New York: Viking Press.

COMPLEXITY DISCREPANCY THEORY. See DEMBER-EARL THEORY OF CHOICE/PREFERENCE.

COMPLIANCE EFFECTS AND TECHNIQUES. In their study of the phenomena of *persuasion* and *social compliance* (i.e., a form of social influence where one person yields to the explicit requests from another person or persons; cf., *forced compliance* - yielding to social pressure to behave in a manner conflicting with one's attitudes; and *law of the first night* or "right of the lord" - a medieval concept that permitted feudal lords, as a symbol of their authority, to take to bed the bride of a serf and to "deflower" her; such a practice of compliance indicated the attitude that regarded women as sexual property), social psychologists have described a number of *compliance effects/techniques* based upon empirical findings. For example, the *door-in-the-face technique* (also called the *rejection-then-retreat technique*) elicits compliance by making a very large initial request - which the target recipient is sure to turn down - follow-ed by a smaller request with which the recipient invariably complies; the *foot-in-the-door technique* (also called the *camel-in-the-tent technique*) elicits compliance from a recipient by preceding a request for a large commitment with a request for a small one, the initial small request serving the function of "softening up" the target person; the *lowball technique* elicits compliance, often in commercial transactions (such as buying a new or used car), where the customer is first induced to agree to purchase an item by being quoted an unrealistically low price; however, before the deal is completed, the salesperson says he has discovered a mistake and tells the customer that the sale may still proceed only at a much higher price; thus, already having made a commitment, the customer is more likely to agree to purchase the item than if the real/true price had been revealed at the beginning of the negotiation. See also ATTRIBUTION THEORY; FESTINGER'S COGNITIVE DISSONANCE THEORY; PERSUASION AND INFLUENCE THEORIES; SOCIAL IMPACT, LAW OF.

REFERENCES

Freedman, J. L., & Fraser, S. C. (1966). Compliance without pressure: The foot-in-the-door technique. *Journal of Personality and Social Psychology, 4*, 195-202.

Cialdini, R. R. (1975). Reciprocal concessions procedure for inducing compliance: The door-in-the-face technique. *Journal of Personality and Social Psychology, 31*, 206-215.

Cialdini, R. B. (1978). The lowball procedure for inducing compliance: Commitment then cost. *Journal of Personality and Social Psychology, 36*, 463-476.

Cialdini, R. B., & Goldstein, N. J. (2004). Social influence: Compliance and conformity. *Annual Review of Psychology, 55*, 591-621.

COMPONENTIAL RECOVERY, PRINCIPLE OF. See PATTERN/OBJECT RECOGNITION THEORY.

COMPONENTIAL THEORY. See CONCEPT LEARNING AND CONCEPT FORMATION, THEORIES OF; PROTOTYPE THEORY.

COMPREHENSION-ELABORATION THEORY. See MOTIVATIONAL THEORIES OF HUMOR; WYER AND COLLINS' THEORY OF HUMOR ELICITATION.

COMPRESENCE EFFECT. See ZAJONC'S AROUSAL AND CONFLUENCE THEORIES.

COMPUTATIONAL THEORY OF MIND. See MIND/MENTAL STATES, THEORIES OF.

COMPUTATIONAL THEORY OF VISION. See VISION/SIGHT, THEORIES OF.

COMTE'S LAW/THEORY. The French philosopher and sociologist Auguste Comte (1798-1857) initially belonged to the French philosophical movement called *materialism* (which viewed humans as machines) but subsequently founded another movement called *positivism* [this movement, however, may be traced back to the French socialist Claude-Henri de Rouvroy Comte de Saint-Simon (1760-1825) and the English philosopher Francis Bacon (1561-1626)]. According to Comte's *positivistic doctrine*, the only knowledge that is valid is observable and objective knowledge. Introspection, which focuses on the inner analysis of conscious experience, is rejected completely. Concerning the evolution of thought, Comte asserted that individuals pass through three stages (called *Comte's law of three stages*): the theological, the metaphysical, and the positivistic, with the last being the basis for scientific thought (cf., *Comte's paradox* which poses the question, How does the mind both function and observe its functioning at the same time?). Comte considered the psychology of his time (which emphasized the subjective analysis of one's consciousness via the introspective method) to be the last phase of theology. Comte argued that science itself is a matter of description, prediction,

114

and control, and the good scientist should avoid giving explanations to phenomena, particularly if there are unobservable entities involved. Postulation of unseen causes was regarded as a dangerous relapse into religion or metaphysical superstition. Since the time of Comte, *positivists* have organized the sciences hierarchically from the oldest and most basic (i.e., physics) up to the science of social planners (i.e., sociology). Comte's *theory of the hierarchy of sciences* states that each science is held to be reducible to the next lower level, with the overall effect that all sciences are, in principle, branches of physics (cf., Roeckelein, 1997). Comte's approach had a strong influence on the social theories of his time. He stressed that humans must rely on direct experience in a dynamic society where the aim of society (and "sociology") should be to remove the study of social factors from the influence of the theological and metaphysical stages of thought. Comte suggested that phenomena in the *social* sciences be examined and evaluated with the same criteria as used in discovering scientific laws in the *natural* sciences. Comte's notions have had a strong impact on modern *behaviorism*, and some psychologists consider Comte to have been the first *behaviorist*. Today, there is another type of *positivism*, inspired by Comte's original notion, called *logical positivism* which holds that the basic data of experience are the operations of scientific observation, and which led historically to the important prescriptions in science called *operationism* and *operational definitions* (i.e., approach in which concepts derive their meaning solely from the operations through which they are observed). In the doctrine called *logical empiricism*, developed by three American philosophers of science - the German-born Rudolph Carnap (1891-1970) and Hans Reichenbach (1891-1953) and the Czech-born Ernest Nagel (1901-1985) - it is asserted that the goal of research in both the *natural* and *social* sciences is the discovery and testing of general *scientific laws*. See also BEHAVIORIST THEORY; HERMENEUTICS THEORY; OPERATIONALISM DOCTRINE OF.

REFERENCES
Comte, A. (1853). *The positive philosophy*. London: Bell.
Bridgman, P. (1927). *The logic of modern physics*. New York: Macmillan.
Carnap, R., & Morris, C. (Eds.) (1948). *International encyclopedia of unified science*. Chicago: University of Chicago Press.
Brunswik, E. (1956). Historical and thematic relations of psychology to other sciences. *Scientific Monthly, 83*, 151-161.
Suppe, F. (1974). The structure of scientific theories. Urbana: University of Illinois Press.
Roeckelein, J. E. (1997). Psychology among the sciences: Comparisons of numbers of theories and laws cited in textbooks. *Psychological Reports, 80*, 131-141.

COMTE'S PARADOX. See COMTE'S LAW/THEORY.

COMTE'S THEORY OF THE HIERARCHY OF SCIENCES. See COMTE'S LAW/THEORY.

CONCENTRATION THEORY OF CUTA-NEOUS COLD. See ALRUTZ'S THEORY; NAFE'S VASCULAR THEORY OF CUTANEOUS SENSITIVITY.

CONCEPT LEARNING/CONCEPT FORMATION, THEORIES OF. A *concept* may be defined as a symbol or group of symbols that stands for a class of objects or events that possess common properties. Thus, *tree* is a concept because it is a symbol that stands for a larger group of objects, all of which possess common characteristics (e.g., a trunk, branches, leaves, etc.). Most words, with the exception of proper nouns that refer only to a particular/single object, are concepts [cf., the *doctrine of nominalism* - advanced by the English scholastic philosopher William of Ockham (c. 1285-1349), is the notion that only individual things exist and that universal concepts (such as "beauty") have no independent existence beyond being mere names; the doctrine posits, also, that scientific theories are never ultimately true or false, but they are only useful]. Concepts may be nonverbal as well as verbal; for instance, infants can have a concept of *mother* long before they have achieved language skills. The power of using concepts is that they help people and animals to think efficiently because they free them from having to create a unique label for each new instance of an object or event. The term *concept formation* refers to the problem-solving process one goes through to acquire concepts. Learning psychologists are interested, particularly, in understanding how individuals, both human and nonhuman, learn to identify objects or events as examples of specific concepts. The terms *concept formation* and *concept learning* are used, often, synonymously to refer to the process of abstraction of a quality, property, or set of features that may be taken to represent a concept; however, there is considerable latitude in actual usage. The literature in *cognitive psychology* abounds with synonymous terms that have been introduced to refer to these processes: concept acquisition, concept attainment, concept construction, concept development, concept discovery, concept identification, concept induction, and concept use. There seems to be little agreement about terminology concerning *concept learning/concept formation*, and perhaps the most useful advice is to read carefully and to reflect critically in this area. Several theories have attempted to account for the processes operating in *concept learning* and *concept formation*. The *behaviorist*, or *stimulus-response*, *theory* of concept learning was supported by the American psychologist Clark Hull (1884-1952). Although many of the participants in Hull's experiments on concept learning were able to learn the tasks, none of them were able to explain *how* they were classifying symbols and objects into different categories. Hull was impressed by persons' inabilities to describe their performance, and he emphasized the importance of analyzing individuals' behavior and not their introspective accounts of behavior. Thus, Hull's work advanced the *behaviorist* viewpoint; intro-spection was deemed unscientific, and speculations about what goes on "inside one's head" during concept learning were avoided. Other theories, however, are based on more *cognitive* notions, such as the assumption that people try to "solve concepts" by making up hypotheses or tentative guesses and then testing these hypotheses. J. S. Bruner, J. Goodnow, and G. Austin propose that people use "strategies" in order to learn concepts, where "strategy" is defined as an orderly method for making decisions that allows one to solve the concept accurately and quickly without taxing one's reasoning skills or memories. M. Levine formulated a *concept learning theory* which suggests that participants begin a concept formation task with a subset of hypotheses, one of which is the "working hypothesis;" if their feedback on the tasks is consistent with the "working hypothesis," they retain that hypothesis, but if the feedback is inconsistent, they shift their emphasis to a different "working hypothesis" that is selected from the original subset. *Componential theory* (also called *definitional theory* and *feature-list theory*) states that the meaning of a concept or word may be understood by analyzing it into its set of defining properties; this theory is a form of philosophical "essentialism" that was first enunciated by the Greek philosophers Plato and Aristotle over 2,000 years ago. Another theoretical approach is offered by G. Bower and T. Trabasso who argue that concept learning occurs in an *all-or-none* fashion, and is contrasted with the *incremental theory*, which holds that learning takes place gradually over a series of trials. According to the findings of Bower and Trabasso, it appears that concept learning may, at least sometimes, occur in a fashion resembling an *all-or-none* process, but a final answer with respect to the adequacy of the *all-or-none* conception must wait for further experimentation. Other approaches that attempt to explain concept learn-ing and concept formation invoke terms and procedures such as *decision trees, feature comparison models, prototype acquisition, animals' concept formation, rule learning and complexity, information-processing theories, quantitative and mathematical theories, abstracting ability, mediational theories,* and *cue-selection models.* See also BE-HAVIOR-IST THEORY; BRUNER'S CONCEPT FOR-MATION THEORY; FORGETTING AND MEMORY, THEO-RIES OF; FUZZY SET THEORY; GUPPY EFFECT; HULL'S LEARNING THEORY; INFORMATION AND INFORMATION-PROCESSING THE-ORY; LEARNING THEORIES AND LAWS; PAT-TERN/OBJECT RECOGNITION THE-ORY; PROTOTYPE THEORY; REAL-ISM, DOCTRINE OF; SET THEORY.

REFERENCES

Hull, C. L. (1920). Quantitative aspects of the evolution of concepts. *Psychological Monographs, 28*, No. 123.

Hovland, C. (1952). A "communication analysis" of concept learning. *Psychological Review, 59*, 461-472.

Bruner, J., Goodnow, J., & Austin, G. (1956). *A study of thinking.* New York: Wiley.

Bourne, L., & Restle, F. (1959). Mathematical theory of concept identification. *Psychological Review, 66*, 278-296.

Hunt, E. (1962). *Concept learning: An information-processing problem.* New York: Wiley.

Bower, G., & Trabasso, T. (1964). Concept identification. In R. Atkinson (Ed.), *Studies in mathematical psychology.* Stanford, CA: Stanford University Press.

Klausmeier, H., & Harris, C. (Eds.) (1966). *Analyses of concept learning.* New York: Academic Press.

Trabasso, T., & Bower, G. (1968). *Attention in learning.* New York: Wiley.

Fodor, J. (1975). *The language of thought.* New York: Crowell.

Levine, M. (1975). *A cognitive theory of learning.* Hillsdale, NJ: Erlbaum.

Anglin, J. (1977). *Word, object, and conceptual development.* New York: Norton.

Rosch, E., & Lloyd, B. (Eds.) (1978). *Cognition and categorization.* Hillsdale, NJ: Erlbaum.

CONCEPTUAL DEPENDENCY THE-ORY. See MEANING, THEO-RIES/ASSESS-MENT OF.

CONCOMITANT VARIATION, LAW OF. See PARSIMONY, LAW/PRINCIPLE OF.

CONCORDANCE DECISION-MAKING METHOD. See DECISION-MAKING THE-ORIES.

CONCORDANT TWIN THEORY. See PARANORMAL PHENOM-ENA/THEORY.

CONCORDE FALLACY/EFFECT. The British ethologist Richard Dawkins (1941 -) describes the *Concorde fallacy/effect* (also called the *sunk cost fallacy*) as the tendency to continue to invest in a project or activity merely to justify past investment in it, instead of evaluating the current reasons for investing and, also, regardless of what had happened previously (e.g., marriage partners often become caught up in escalating spirals of hostility and counter-hostility where they feel incapable of extricating themselves from the situation due to past emotional investments in the relationship). The *Concorde fallacy/effect* is named after the former Anglo-French supersonic airline, the Concorde, whose costs rose sharply during its development phase in the 1970s (so much so that it soon became an uneconomical and unprofitable enterprise), but the French and British governments continued to support the project in order to justify their past investment in it. In their ethological studies, R. Dawkins and H. J. Brockmann relate the *Concorde fallacy/effect* to the behavior of digger wasps regarding the latter's nesting activities where the findings are similar, generally, to humans' decision-making behaviors and strategies: individuals invest further in an activity because one has invested heavily in it in the past, rather than because of potential return on the investment [cf., the *dollar auction game* - a strategic decision game devised by the American economist Martin Shubik (1926-), designed to model and study strategic escalation and entrapment, and where typical results are that bidding in the auction invariably exceeds the value of the prize, goal, or target item]. In the psychological literature, the term *Concorde fallacy* has been applied strictly to lower animals, whereas the term *sunk cost effect* has been applied solely to humans. See also DECISION-MAKING THEORIES.

REFERENCES

Shubik, M. (1971). The Dollar Auction game. *Journal of Conflict Resolution, 15,* 109-111.

Dawkins, R., & Brockmann, H. J. (1980). Do digger wasps commit the Concorde fallacy? *Animal Behaviour, 28,* 892-896.

Shubik, M. (1987). What is an application and when is theory a waste of time? *Management Science, 33,* 1511-1522.

Staw, B. M., & Ross, J. (1989). Understanding behavior in escalation situations. *Science, 246,* 216-220.

Arkes, H. R., & Ayton, P. (1999). The sunk cost and Concorde effects: Are humans less rational than lower animals? *Psychological Bulletin, 125,* 591-600.

CONDILLAC'S THEORY OF ATTENTION. The French philosopher Etienne Bonnot de Condillac (1715-1780) successfully transported John Locke's method and theory of *empiricism* from England to France. The *theory* of empiricism states that all knowledge comes from experience, whereas the *method* of empiricism advocates the collection and evaluation of data where experimentation is emphasized, and induction via observation is favored over deduction from theoretical constructs. Condillac reacted against Rene Descartes' (1596-1650) *theory of innate ideas,* Nicolas de Malebranche's (1638-1715) *faculties theory,* and Gottfried Leibnitz's (1646-1716) *theory of the monad.* In 1754,

Condillac presented his famous analogy/parable of the *sentient statue* to emphasize that the whole of mental life may be derived in experience from sensation alone. One is asked to imagine a statue that is endowed with only a single sense, such as the simple sense of smell. The statue smells a rose (where the statue *is* a rose for the time being because there is nothing else to its existence than this odor) and is, thereby, said to be *attending* to the odor. Thus, one may see how *attention* comes into mental life: the first odor goes, and another odor comes; then the first returns, and the statue knows that what was can come again; this is "memory." When what recurs with what is, the statue may be said to be comparing: one odor is pleasant, another odor is unpleasant. Also, in the inherent values of the odors, the statue learns of desire and aversion. In like fashion, judgment, discernment, imagination, and other sorts of abstract notions are represented by Condillac as possible of development in experience with only a single sense as the medium. Later, the addition of other senses would still further enhance the statue's capacities. Thus, the essential point of Con-dillac's *statue analogy* is that all mental life, including *attention,* can be derived from sensory experience, and if a statue were endowed with only a single sense, it could develop all the mental processes currently possessed by humans (cf., Condillac's *constancy hypothesis* which assumes that there is a formal, one-to-one correspondence between a local stimulus and a percept). Condillac argued that the sum total of all human mental processes would develop without any need to presuppose the *laws of association,* and variations in the quality of sensations would necessarily produce all the qualities that are needed for human comprehension. Condillac's brand of *sensational empiricism* eventually failed because it was too simple: it was difficult to re-duce the mind to sensory experience alone. The 19th century French writers felt that Con-dillac's approach was too cold; 20th century psychologists could not ignore the "whole" person and tended to stress the notion that analysis without synthesis is open to failure in theorizing. However, on the positive side, Condillac fostered the *empirical* attitude, which had a strong impact on the French *materialism* movement and, like John Locke, he adopted a philosophical approach and strategy that paved the way for the development of the natural sciences. See also ASSOCIATION, LAWS AND PRINCIPLES OF; ATTENTION, LAWS/PRINCIPLES/THEORIES OF; DESCARTES' THEORY OF INNATE IDEAS; EMPIRICAL/EMPIRICISM, DOC-TRINE OF; EMPIRICIST VERSUS NATIVIST THEORIES; LEARNING THEORIES AND LAWS; LEIBNITZ'S MONAD THEORY; MALEBRANCHE'S THEORIES; MIND/MENTAL STATES, THEORIES OF.

REFERENCE

Condillac, E. (1754/1930). *Treatise on sensations*. Los Angeles: University of Southern California Press.

CONDITIONING OF TYPE R, LAW OF. See SKINNER'S DESCRIPTIVE BEHAV-IOR AND OPERANT CONDITIONING THEORY.

CONDITIONING OF TYPE S, LAW OF. See SKINNER'S DESCRIPTIVE BEHAV-IOR AND OPERANT CONDITIONING THEORY.

CONDUCT, LAWS OF. In 1937, the versatile Swiss psychologist Edouard Claparede (1873-1940) formulated the following 13 "functional" *laws of conduct* in an attempt to give psychology the "back-bone" it purportedly needs as a scientific endeavor: *law of need* - a need tends to evoke reactions proper to its satisfaction; *law of interest* - all conduct is dictated by interest, the goal being to secure objects and positions that attract us; *law of momentary interest* - every living being acts in accordance with his dominant interest of the moment, where the most imperative need of the moment dominates all others; *law of satiation and disgust* - once a need is satisfied, the reactions it evoked will cease and the former need-arousing objects will now arouse contrary reactions of repulsion and

disgust; *law of the extension of mental life* - mental life develops in proportion to the size of the gap between needs and their means of satisfaction; *law of awareness* - awareness of a process, relation, or object is delayed in proportion to the earliness and length of the period in which its automatic unconscious use has been implied in conduct; *law of anticipation* - any need, which by its very nature, is unlikely to be satisfied immediately appears early; *law of reproduction of the similar* - a need tends to reproduce reactions which have formerly proved desirable, and it tends to evoke, again, conduct which has already succeeded in similar circumstances; *law of trial and error* - a need will give rise to a series of exploratory reactions, of trial reactions, and of "gropings;" *law of economy of effort* - a need tends to seek satisfaction along the line of least resistance; *law of substitution* - when an end cannot be reached by one kind of behavior, another kind of behavior, likely to lead to the same end, is substituted in one of five different forms (simple, compensation, symbolic derivation, regression, or progression); *law of subjective dominance* - the self tends to subordinate the facts of reality to its own inclinations, aspirations, and needs; it tries to ignore reality and to deny it whenever it is in opposition to the desires of the self; and *law of functional autonomy* - one's capacity for reaction is adjusted to one's needs; functional autonomy consists of the functional unity and harmony of living beings. Claparede asserts that the *principle of autonomy* has revolutionized educational theory and practice; also, he suggests that education is no longer only a preparation for life, but it is a "life in itself" [cf., Ligon's (1939) eight "personality goals" (vision, love of righteousness and truth, faith in the friendliness of the universe, dominating purpose, being sensitive to the needs of others, forgiveness, magnanimity, and Christian courage) as another early approach toward instilling the "right/correct conduct" in individuals; and, also, the *eightfold-path doctrine/theory* of Buddhism which states that the "correct" way of living in order to achieve "nirvana" or "bliss" is to follow the eight percepts of conduct: right views, right concentration, right mindfulness, right effort, right intentions, right speech, right action, and right livelihood]. Generally, Claparede's early view of behavior initially was biological, and then later became functional and purposive, stressing the adap-tive response of the organism to the momentary situation (*law of momentary interest*). However, Claparede's choice of the term "laws" in his *laws of conduct* appears to be another instance of the early psychologists' loose, informal, and liberal use of the term *law* to describe general principles of behavior. Today, of course, usage of the term *law* in a scientific context, is restricted to more formal and empirically well-established descriptions of functional cause-and-effect relationships between, and among, variables (cf., Teigen, 2002). See also ALLPORT'S FUNCTIONAL AUTONOMY PRINCIPLE; BUDDHISM AND ZEN BUDDHISM, DOCTRINE OF; LEAST EFFORT, PRINCIPLE OF; MORAL DEVELOPMENT, PRINCIPLES/THEORY OF; MOTIVATION, THEORIES OF; NIRVANA PRINCIPLE.

REFERENCES

Claparede, E. (1937). Some major laws of conduct. *American Journal of Psychology, 50*, 68-78.

Ligon, E. M. (1939). *Their future is now.* New York: Macmillan.

Rahula. (1974). *What the Buddha taught.* New York: Grove Press.

Teigen, K. H. (2002). One hundred years of laws in psychology. *American Journal of Psychology, 115*, 103-118.

Emmons, R. A., & Paloutzian, R. F. (2003). The psychology of religion. *Annual Review of Psychology, 54*, 377-402.

CONFIGURAL SUPERIORITY EFFECT. See PERCEPTION (I. GENERAL), THE-ORIES OF; TOP-DOWN PROCESSING THEORIES.

CONFIGURATIONAL THEORIES OF HUMOR. The *configurational theories of humor* - which are allied closely to Gestalt psychology and Gestalt theory - are characterized, generally, by the perceptual experience of originally unrelated elements as suddenly falling into the "proper" place. Both the *configurational* and the *incongruity* theories of humor possess the common features of cognitive and perceptual attributes of humor. However, the *incongruity* approach emphasizes the perception of "disjointedness" in humor, whereas the *configurational* approach stresses "perceptual figure-ground shifts," the "falling into place," and "sudden insight" of originally ambiguous elements as the basis for the humor experience. See also FIGURE-GROUND RELATIONSHIPS, PRINCIPLE OF; GESTALT THEORY/LAWS; HUMOR, THEORIES OF; INCONGRUITY/INCON-SISTENCY THEORIES OF HUMOR; INCONGRUITY-RESOLUTION THEORIES; MAIER'S THEORY OF HUMOR.

REFERENCE

Roeckelein, J. E. (2002). *The psychology of humor*. Westport, CT: Greenwood Press.

CONFIRMATION, THEORY OF. See NULL HYPOTHESIS.

CONFIRMATION BIAS EFFECT. See PREJUDICE, THEORIES OF.

CONFIRMATION PARADOX. See NULL HYPOTHESIS.

CONFLICT, THEORIES OF. The term *conflict* is an extremely broad concept used to refer to any situation where there are mutually antagonistic events, motives, behaviors, impulses, or purposes. In the area of learning and motivation psychology, the American experimental psychologist Neal Elgar Miller (1909-2002) and his colleagues developed a precise formulation of *conflict theory* based on some preliminary ideas of the German-born American social psychologist Kurt Lewin (1890-1947). According to this approach, there are four major types of conflicts involving "approach" and "avoidance" behavioral tendencies: *approach-approach* - a situation in which the individual must choose between two positive goals of the same value [cf., *Buridan's donkey/ass* - an approach-approach decision-making dilemma, attributed to the French scholastic philosopher Jean Buridan (c. 1295-1356), in which a hungry donkey stands between two equidistant and equally-valued bales of hay, but the animal starves to death because reason gives no good grounds for choosing between the bales]; *avoidance-avoidance* - the individual must choose between two negative outcomes of approximately equal value; *approach-avoidance* - circumstances where achieving a positive goal will produce a negative outcome as well (cf., the *Rosencrantz/Guildenstern effect* which is a decision/cognitive entrapment experienced by one who is kept waiting while attempting to achieve a particular goal; an approach-avoid-ance dilemma dramatized in the British playwright Tom Stoppard's 1967 play, "Rosencrantz and Guildenstern are Dead"); and *double/multiple approach-avoidance* - the individual is required to choose between two, or more, alternatives each of which contains both positive and negative consequences. The concept of *ambivalence* (i.e., mixed positive and negative feelings regarding objects, people, places, or events) is a central characteristic of *approach-avoidance* conflicts and is translated, usually, into "partial approach." Within Miller's conflict paradigm, researchers (e.g., Epstein & Fenz, 1965; Epstein, 1982) have demonstrated the stressfulness of conflicts in their studies of parachute jumpers. The sympathetic autonomic arousal reaction of the jumpers rose dramatically to a peak at the moment of the jump, and then returned to normal levels immediately after they landed. In the area of *social conflict*, the study of conflict is an interdisciplinary enterprise, involving sociologists, political scientists, game theorists, and social psychologists. Some psychologists view *conflict* as a manifestation of individual aggression that is attributed, often, to frustrations experienced by the person; others see *conflict* as arising from images that persons or groups have of one another (e.g., in the mutual perception of

threat). During the late 1940s and early 1950s, conflict theorists began to study empirically the social phenomena of *cooperation* and *competition*. The terms *cooperation* and *competition* refer to collaborative efforts and rivalry, respectively, concerning mutually desired goals or the means of achieving individual or mutual goals. In a "pure cooperation" situation, the goal of one individual can be reached only if the other members also attain their goals. In the case of "pure competition," a person's goals can be attained only if the others do not attain their goals. However, the extremes of "pure cooperation" and "pure competition" are rarely encountered in realistic contexts, and most situations are a blend of both types. One theoretical approach uses *mathematical games and models* to describe the behavior of "rational" individuals in situations of interdependence. Other approaches study laboratory interactions of *bargaining and negotiation* situations, *prisoner's dilemma games*, *locomotion games*, and realistic *field scenarios*. In general, psychological research shows that *cooperative* activity most likely emerges when the interacting parties both share a common goal and a common means of attaining that goal, and *competition* most likely occurs when either the individual goals of the parties involved or the means of obtaining them are incompatible. Interest has been shown, also, by *conflict theorists* in the social sciences for practical methods of *conflict resolution*, such as bargaining and mediation (cf., *threshold theory* - refers to a conflict model in the area of group dynamics which states that conflict serves a useful purpose/function for groups as long as it does not exceed the tolerance threshold over a long period of time). Theories of conflict between groups, called *image theories*, have been proposed where diabolical images of the "other" or the "enemy," and virile or moral images of the "self" have been employed. Study of direct intergroup conflict concerning the variable of competition led to the formulation of the *realistic conflict theory of prejudice*, which states that prejudice arises from competition between social groups over scarce commodities or opportunities. The *realistic conflict theory* also suggests that as such competition persists, the members of the groups involved come to view each other in increasingly negative ways, much as indicated in the *image theories*. The concept of *conflict* has been invoked, also, in the history of psychology by the German philosopher/educator Johann Friedrich Herbart (1776-1841). Based on the popular assumption that elementary bits of ideas or experiences may combine harmoniously into wholes, Herbart taught that *ideas* themselves may come into relation with each other through *conflict* or struggle, as well. Thus, according to Herbart, ideas that are incapable of combining tend to compete with one another, and this competition occurs in order to gain a place in consciousness. Recent writers, including the psychoanalysts, emphasize that objects of thought do not conflict with each other because they are in logical opposition, as Herbart proposed, but because they lead to divergent lines of conduct; ideas are in conflict if they lead individuals to do opposite things. The concept of *conflict* may be found, also, in the area of *visual perception*. For example conflict of cues have been discussed relative to demonstrations of the influence of visual context upon monocular and binocular perception; surprising, sometimes startling, effects have been produced in the "Ames room demonstrations" [named after the American psychologist Adelbert Ames, Jr. (1880-1955) who set up demonstrations involving a series of illusions, and including distorted rooms so constructed that sizes and shapes in them appear to be distorted even though the actual trapezoidal room itself appears to be rectangular when viewed mon-ocularly; (see Appendix A, also)], such as seeing someone changed into a giant or a dwarf, and red spots on playing cards change to black - because of sheer congruity and the perceiver's "need for internal unity." In the Ames room situation, affective and familiarity factors may destroy the intended illusion. For example, the *Honi effect/phenomenon* refers to the failure of the well-known perceptual distortion effects of the Ames room to occur when a very familiar person such as a parent or spouse is placed in the room [in 1949, the American psychologist A. Hadley Cantril (1906-1969) observed that a woman, nicknamed "Honi," while viewing her husband in the Ames room reported that there was no distortion in her husband's size as he walked along the back wall of the room, which is contrary to one's perception of unfamiliar persons walking along the same route in the room; thus, the main factor that seems to determine whether a person will or will not seem to be distorted in the Ames room is whether or not that person produces anxiety in the observer; anxiety-producing persons appear to be less distorted]. The term *conflict*, when used in the area of *psychoanalysis*, refers to a painful emotional state that results from a tension between opposed and contradictory wishes and is due, theoretically, to the fact that an unconscious (repressed) wish is forcibly prevented from entering the conscious system (cf., *psychic/psychical conflict* - the condition under which two contradictory tendencies oppose each other in a person's mind; some such conflicts are conscious, as when a desire is opposed by a moral constraint, but it is *unconscious conflicts* that Sigmund Freud assumed to generate neurotic symptoms; also, according to psychoanalysis, such conflicts between ideas are traceable, theoretically, to conflicts between *instincts*). The term *major conflict* refers to the more dominant emotional state in a current conflict between opposed and contradictory wishes. *Actual conflict* is a presently occurring conflict where, in the psychoanalytic context, such conflicts are assumed to derive from "root conflicts" (i.e., the underlying conflict that is assumed to be primarily responsible for an observed psychological disorder; cf., *nuclear conflict*, which tends to be used in a broader fashion). *Nuclear conflict* is a fundamental dilemma occurring during infancy or early childhood that is assumed to be a root cause of a number of psychoneurotic disorders that may emerge only later in life. For Sigmund Freud, the *Oedipus complex* fulfilled this hypothesized role; for Karen Horney, it was a child's *feeling of helpless-*

ness; and for Alfred Adler, it was *feelings of inferiority*. The term *basic conflict* is Horney's term for the fundamental conflicts that emerge when "neurotic needs" are discoordinate. In *Horney's theory of personality*, the term *central conflict* is the psychic conflict between one's "real self" and one's "idealized self." The term *conflict-free ego sphere* is Heinz Hartmann's concept in his *ego theory* for the part of the ego called "primary autonomy," which includes the individual's perception, motility, and memory. In the area of measurement and statistics, the concept called *conflict index*, or *C*, is a statistic that gives an exact value for the total amount of energy that an organism (or other dynamic system) has bound up internally. Thus, *conflict theories*, and the versatile concept of *conflict*, have been used widely, among other things, to refer to individual or group preferences for incompatible actions in a given learning or motivation situation, to particular aspects of different psychoanalytic theories, to philosophical analyses concerning ideas, to perceptual demonstrations, to a statistical index, and to practical contexts involving resolution and resolution therapy, cooperation and competition, and negotiations and mediation situations. See also ADLER'S THEORY OF PERSONALITY; AGGRESSION, THEORIES OF; DECISION-MAKING THEORIES; DEUTSCH'S CRU-DE LAW OF SOCIAL RELATIONS AND RESOLUTIONS; EGO DEVELOPMENT, THEORIES OF; EQUITY THEORY; ERIKSON'S THEORY OF PERSONALITY; FESTINGER'S COGNITIVE DISSONANCE THEORY; FREUD'S THEORY OF PERSONALITY; HAWK-DOVE AND CHICK-EN GAME EFFECTS; HORNEY'S THEORY OF PERSONALITY; LEWIN'S FIELD THEORY; PREJUDICE, THEORIES OF.

REFERENCES

Lewin, K. (1935). *A dynamic theory of personality*. New York: McGraw-Hill.

Miller, N. E. (1944). Experimental studies in conflict. In J. McV. Hunt (Ed.), *Personality and the behavior disorders*. New York: Ronald Press.

Horney, K. (1945). *Our inner conflicts: A constructive theory of neurosis*. New York: Norton.

Neumann, J. von, & Morgenstern, O. (1947). *Theory of games and economic behavior*. Princeton, NJ: Princeton University Press.

Deutsch, M. (1950). A theory of cooperation and competition. *Human Relations, 2*, 129-152.

Miller, N. E. (1951). Comment on theoretical models illustrated by the development of a theory of conflict. *Journal of Personality, 20*, 82-100.

Ittelson, W. (1952). *The Ames demonstrations in perception*. Princeton, NJ: Prin-ceton University Press.

Hartmann, H. (1958). *Ego psychology and the problem of adaptation*. New York: International Universities Press.

Miller, N. E. (1959). Liberalization of basic S-R concepts: Extensions to conflict behavior, motivation, and social learning. In S. Koch (Ed.), *Psychology: A study of a science*. Vol. 2. New York: McGraw-Hill.

Deutsch, M., & Krauss, R. M. (1960). The effect of threat upon interpersonal bargaining. *Journal of Abnormal and Social Psychology, 61*, 181-189.

Siegel, S., & Fouraker, L. (1960). *Bargaining and group decision-making: Experiments in bilateral monopoly*. New York: McGraw-Hill.

Sherif, M., Harvey, O., White, B., Hood, W., & Sherif, C. (1961). *Intergroup conflict and cooperation: The Robber's Cave experiment*. Norman: University of Oklahoma Press.

Epstein, S., & Fenz, W. (1965). Steepness of approach and avoidance gradients in humans as a function of experience: Theory and experiment. *Journal of Experimental Psychology, 70*, 1-12.

Miller, N. E. (1971). *Selected papers on conflict, displacement, learned drives, and theory*. Chicago: Aldine.

Pruitt, D. (1972). Methods for resolving conflicts of interest: A theoretical an-alysis. *Journal of Social Issues, 28*, 133-154.

Toomey, M. (1972). Conflict theory approach to decision-making applied to alcoholics. *Journal of Personality and Social Psychology, 24*, 199-206.

Deutsch, M. (1973). *The resolution of conflict: Constructive and destructive processes*. New Haven, CT: Yale University Press.

Epstein, S. (1982). Conflict and stress. In L. Goldberger & S. Breznitz (Eds.), *Handbook of stress*. New York: Free Press.

Moore, C. W. (1986). *The mediation process: Practical strategies for resolving conflict*. San Francisco: Jossey-Bass.

Johnson, D. W., & Johnson, R. T. (1989). *Cooperation and competition: Theory and research*. Edina, MN: Interaction Book Co.

CONFLICT/COMMUNIST THEORY OF CRIMINALITY. See LOMBROSIAN THE-ORY.

CONFLICTING ASSOCIATIONS, LAW OF. See SKINNER'S OPERANT CONDITIONING THEORY.

CONFLUENCE THEORY. See ZAJONC'S AROUSAL THEORY.

CONFORMITY HYPOTHE-SIS/THEORY. See ALLPORT'S CONFORMITY HYPO-THESIS; ASCH CONFORMITY EFFECT.

CONGRUENCE-OF-IMAGES THE-ORY. See SELF-CONCEPT THEORY.

CONGRUENT TRANSCENDENCY THE-ORY. See LIFE, THEORIES OF.

CONGRUITY THEORY/PRINCIPLE. See FESTINGER'S COGNITIVE DISSO-NANCE THEORY.

CONJOINT MEASUREMENT THE-ORY. The American mathematical psychologist Robert Duncan Luce (1925-) and the American statistician John Wilder Tukey (1915-2000) developed *conjoint measurement theory* which involves a procedure/method for constructing measurement scales applied to objects having multiple attributes so that attributes may be traded off against one another, and where the scale value of each object is viewed as a function of the scale values of its component attributes. This approach may be used to determine whether apparent interaction effects come from actual interactions among the underlying attributes or if they are artifacts of the specific measurement model employed. Other general and specific terms related to *conjoint measurement theory* are the following: *axiomatic measurement theory* (or *abstract measurement theory*) - study of the correspondence between measurements of psychological or extra-psychological attributes/characteristics and the attributes themselves; *measurement model* - study of the relationship assumed to exist between numerical scales recorded as data in an empirical investigation and the attribute/characteristic being measured; *multiplicative model* - study of the expression of an effect as a weighted product of several independent/manipulated variables, so that if any of the independent variables is zero, then the value of the dependent/measured variable, also, is zero; *multiplicative models* may be divided into those that can be converted into *additive models* (via monotonic transformations of their independent and dependent variables) and those that cannot be converted ("non-additive models"); *axiomatic conjoint measurement theory* - study of the qualitative aspects of data to determine the optimal way to scale the data; *numerical conjoint measurement theory* (or *conjoint analysis*) - study of an assumed, particular composition rule and its relationship to scaled data while attempting to arrive at an *additive model* solution. See also MEASUREMENT THEORY.

REFERENCE
Luce, R. D. (1971/1989). *Foundations of measurement*. New York: Academic Press.

CONNECTION, LAWS OF. See REINFORCEMENT, THORNDIKE'S THEORY OF.

CONNECTIONISM, THEORY OF. See ASSOCIATION, LAWS/PRINCIPLES OF; PARALLEL DISTRIBUTED PROCESSING MODEL; REINFORCEMENT, THORN-DIKE'S THEORY OF; SCALAR TIMING THEORY.

CONNECTIONIST MODEL OF HUMOR. The American cognitive scientist Bruce F. Katz (1993) proposes a neural *connectionist model of humor* that purports to have advantages over the traditional "incongruity-resolution" theory. The neural model consists of two "disjoint" concepts/entities that are stored in a neural network and whereby the concepts are connected to two "external triggers" that simulate the role of internal and external factors that activate the concepts. According to this model, the appropriate timing of the triggers may result in a high, but unstable, arousal condition in which two incongruous concepts are possible for a brief period of time. Such a "boost/arousal" state may occur both in cases where an incongruity is resolved or merely where the incongruities are simultaneously present. Theoretically, when the thresholds of the neural units are lowered, humor effects (especially in cases of *tendentious humor* - humor that advances a definite point of view or, in psychoanalytical terms, humor that involves the release of libidinal drives) are associated with greater activation levels than are available normally. See also COGNITIVE THEORIES OF HUMOR; FREUD'S THEORY OF WIT AND HUMOR; HUMOR, THEORIES OF; INCONGRUITY/INCONSISTENCY THEORIES OF HUMOR; INCONGRUITY-RESOLUTION THEORIES.

REFERENCES
Zillman, D., & Bryant, J. (1980). Misattribution of tendentious humor. *Journal of Experimental Social Psychology, 16*, 146-160.
Katz, B. F. (1993). A neural resolution of the incongruity-resolution and incongruity theories of humour. *Connection Science: Journal of Neural Computing, Artificial Intelligence, and Cognitive Research, 5*, 59-75.

CONSCIOUS ILLUSION THEORY. See LIPPS' EMPATHY THEORY.

CONSCIOUSNESS, PHENOMENON OF. *Consciousness* is the ability to demonstrate awareness and to process sensations, thoughts, images, ideas, feelings, and perceptions; it is also the capacity of having experiences, the central affect of neural reception, the subjective aspect of brain activity, the relation of self to environment, and the totality of an individual's experiences at any given moment. Whereas E. B. Titchener (1867-1927), the major American proponent of the school of "Structuralism," declared that psychology is the "science of consciousness," J. B. Watson (1878-1958), the founder of the psychological school of "Behaviorism" (cf., *Meyers' psychological theories*), insisted on relegating the *phenomenon of consciousness* to the sphere of mythology or to the "rubbish heap of science" [Roback (1964); cf., Sutherland (1996) who suggests that nothing worth reading has been written on the issue or phenomenon of *consciousness*]. The consistent and pervasive fascination with the notion of *consciousness* within, as well as outside of, psychology derives from the strong and intuitive sense that it is one of the basic defining features of the human species. To be human, say some investigators, is to be able to study and reflect on our own conscious awareness and to "know that we know." Historically, the *phenomenon of consciousness* has been especially popular in the areas of Structuralism and psychoanalytic theory, but today is finding renewal as a topic for scientific study in the areas of neuropsychology, language, and cognition. E. R. Hilgard (1977) suggests that it is useful to assign two modes to *consciousness* (cf., Shallice, 1972): a *receptive* mode and an *active* mode, where the former is reflected in the relatively passive registration of events as they impinge on one's sense organs, and the latter is reflected in the active, planning, and voluntary aspects of behavior; both of these modes are demonstrated in the special problems of a "divided consciousness" or "divided control." Occasionally, the *phenomenon of consciousness* is equated with the term "self-consciousness" wherein to be conscious it is only necessary for one to be aware of the external world. Some skeptical writers, notably the behaviorists, assert that *consciousness* is an interesting, but elusive, phenomenon: it is impossible to specify what it is, what it does, or why it evolved [cf., Reese (2001, p. 229) who states that "very little, if any, progress has been made in a century of research on *consciousness*; we are not even closer to having a satisfactory definition of the term"]. See also BEHAVIORIST THEORY; DISSOCIATION THEORY; IMAGERY AND MENTAL IMAGERY, THEORIES OF; LIFE, THEORIES OF; MEYER'S PSYCHOLOGICAL THEORIES; MIND-BODY THEORIES; SELF-CONCEPT THEORY; UNCONSCIOUS INFERENCE, DOCTRINE OF.

REFERENCES

Roback, A. (1964). *History of American psychology*. New York: Collier.

Sperry, R. (1969). A modified concept of consciousness. *Psychological Review, 76*, 532-536.

Ornstein, R. (1972). *The psychology of consciousness*. San Francisco: Freeman.

Shallice, T. (1972). Dual functions of consciousness. *Psychological Review, 79*, 383-393.

Penfield, W. (1975). *The mystery of the mind: A critical study of consciousness and the human brain*. Princeton, NJ: Princeton University Press.

Tart, C. (1975). *States of consciousness*. New York: Dutton.

Globus, G., Maxwell, G., & Savodnik, I. (Eds.) (1976). *Consciousness and the brain*. New York: Plenum Press.

Schwartz, G., & Shapiro, D. (Eds.) (1976). *Consciousness and self-regulation. Advances in research.* Vol. 1. New York: Plenum Press.

Hilgard, E. R. (1977). *Divided consciousness: Multiple controls in human thought and action*. New York: Wiley.

Jaynes, J. (1977). *The origin of consciousness in the breakdown of the bicameral mind*. Boston: Houghton Mifflin.

Hilgard, E. R. (1980). Consciousness in contemporary psychology. *Annual Review of Psychology, 31*, 1-26.

Sutherland, S. (1996). *The international dictionary of psychology*. New York: Crossroad.

Baars, B. (1997). *In the theater of consciousness*. New York: Oxford University Press.

Hemeroff, S., Kaszniak, A., & Scott, A. (Eds.) (1998). *Toward a science of consciousness. II. The second Tucson discussions and debates.* Cambridge, MA: M.I.T. Press.

Tononi, G., & Edelman, G. (1998). Consciousness and complexity. *Science, 282*, 1846-1851.

Reese, H. W. (2001). Some recurrent issues in the history of behavioral sciences. *Behavior Analyst, 24*, 227-239.

Zeman, A. (2001). Consciousness. *Brain, 124*, 1263-1289.

Lambie, J. A., & Marcel, A. J. (2002). Consciousness and the varieties of emotion experience: A theoretical framework. *Psychological Review, 109*, 219-259.

CONSERVATION OF ENERGY, LAW/ PRINCIPLE OF. See GESTALT THEORY AND LAWS; JUNG'S THEORY OF PER-SONALITY; THERMODYNAMICS, LAWS OF.

CONSISTENCY THEORY OF WORK BEHAVIOR. See WORK/CAREER/OCCU-PATION, THEORIES OF.

CONSOLIDATION HYPOTHE-SIS/THE-ORY. See FORGET-TING/MEMORY, THE-ORIES OF.

CONSTANCY HYPOTHESIS. = perceptual constancy. This hypothesis, as employed in the area of perception psychology, states that perceived objects tend to remain constant in *size* where their distance from the observer (and, thus, the size of their retinal images) varies (cf., *theory of misapplied constancy* - states that the inappropriate interpretation of cues in the perception of certain illusions is the result of the observer's having previously learned strong cues for maintaining *size constancy*). Also, according to the *constancy hypothesis* in this perceptual context, objects tend to remain constant in *shape* (when the angle from which they are regarded - and, thus, the shape of their retinal images - varies), in *brightness* (when the intensity of illumination varies), and in *hue* (when the color composition of illumination varies). In general, *perceptual constancy* is the tendency for a perceived object to appear the same when the pattern of sensory stimulation (i.e., "proximal" stimulus) alters via a change in distance, orientation, or illumination, or some other extraneous variable. Thus, there are constancies regarding color, lightness, melody, object, odor, person, position, shape, size, velocity, and words. The term *Brunswik ratio* [named after the Hungarian-born American psychologist Egon Brunswik (1903-1955)] refers to an index of *perceptual constancy* expressed as: $(R-S)/(A-S)$, where R is the physical magnitude/intensity of the stimulus chosen as a match, S is the physical magnitude/intensity for a stimulus match with zero constancy, and A is the physical magnitude/intensity that could be chosen under 100 percent constancy; the ratio equals zero when there is *no* perceptual constancy, and 1.00 when there is perfect constancy; and the *Thouless ratio* [named after the English psychologist Robert H. Thouless (1894-1984)] which is a modification of the *Brunswik ratio*, taking *Fechner's law* (i.e., $S=k \log I$) into account, where the *perceptual constancy ratio* becomes: $(\log R - \log S)/(\log A - \log S)$. The *constancy hypothesis* hold up well with changing conditions if the observer has information about the changing conditions but, when one's ability to judge the total situation is reduced (e.g., as by a "reduction screen" such as looking at the object through the small peep hole made in your hand when you make a fist), then the constancy is reduced. The *constancy phenomena* have been known for a long time (cf., Boring, 1957). *Color constancy* was known to Ewald Hering in the 1860s, and *brightness constancy* was known to David Katz in the early 1900s. The idea of *size constancy* was known to the natural philosopher P. Bouguer before 1758, to the chemist J. Priestley in 1772, to the physicist/physiologist H. Meyer in 1842, to the physiologist C. F. W. Ludwig in 1852, to P. L. Panum in 1859, to G. Fechner in 1860, to E. Hering in 1861, to E. Emmert in 1881, to G. Martius in 1889, to F. Hillebrand in 1902, to W. Poppelreuter in 1911, to W. Blumenfeld in 1913, and to W. Kohler in 1915 - all of whom described or experimented on the phenomenon. See also BRUNSWIK'S PROBABALISTIC FUNCTIONALISM THEORY; CONDILLAC'S THEORY OF ATTENTION; CONSTANCY, PRINCIPLE OF; EMMERT'S LAW; FECHNER'S LAW; GESTALT THEORY/LAWS.

REFERENCES

Brunswik, E. (1929). Zur entwicklung der albedowahrnehmung. *Zeitschrift fur Psychologie, 109*, 40-115.

Thouless, R. H. (1931). Phenomenal regression to the real object. I., II. *British Journal of Psychology, 21*, 339-359; *22*, 1-30.

Leibowitz, H. (1956). Relation between the Brunswik and Thouless ratios and functional relations in experimental investigations of perceived shape, size, and brightness. *Perceptual and Motor Skills, 6*, 65-68.

Boring, E. G. (1957). *A history of experimental psychology*. New York: Apple-ton-Century-Crofts.

Myers, A. K. (1980). Quantitative indices of perceptual constancy. *Psychological Bulletin, 88*, 451-457.

CONSTANCY, PRINCIPLE OF. This general principle has at least two important meanings in psychological theory. In one case, for the areas of physiology, cognition, emotion, and motivation, the notion of *constancy* derives from the *first law of thermodynamics* (dealing with "conservation of energy") in physics and may be considered as a basis for the *principle of homeostasis* where organisms are motivated to maintain biological constancy of bodily functions and mechanisms (such as temperature regulation and hunger reduction), and psychological balance among mental/cognitive mechanisms. In another case, in the area of psychoanalysis, the *principle of constancy* refers to the proposition that the amount of "psychic energy" within the person's mental processes remains constant so that regulation of mental stability may be achieved either through discharge of excess energy (as via "abreaction" or release of emotional energy following the recollection of a painful memory that has been repressed), or through avoidance of an increase of excess energy (as via "ego defense mechanisms" or patterns of thought, behavior, or feeling that are reactions to a perception psychic tension or danger which enable the person to avoid conscious awareness of cognitive conflicts or anxiety-arousing wishes/ideas). In the latter usage, however, psychoanalysts have been suspect in their employment of the *principle of constancy* as being contradictory or ambiguous (cf., *quota of affect* - a quantity of instinctual energy that remains constant despite undergoing displacement and various qualitative transformations; in mental functions, a *quota of affect*, or "sum of excitation," possesses all the characteristics of a quantity which is capable of increase, decrease, and discharge/displacement and which, theoretically, is spread over the memory-traces of ideas, similar to an electric charge that spreads over the surface of the body). For example, Sigmund Freud (1920/1953) apparently confuses the reduction and extinction of psychic energy with its regulation; thus, in his application of the *nirvana principle* to psychoanalysis (that is, the tendency for the amount of energy in one's mental apparatus to reduce to zero), Freud defined this psychic-economy principle (derived from Buddhist/Hindu philosophy where "nirvana" is a psychic state achieved by the extinction of all earthly desires) in an ambiguous way as the principle of the mental apparatus for extinguishing - or at least of maintaining it at a low level - the amounts of excitation flowing into the mental apparatus. See also CONSTANCY HYPOTHESIS; FESTINGER'S COGNITIVE DISSONANCE THEORY; FREUD'S THEORY OF PERSONALITY; GENERAL SYSTEMS THEORY; HOMEOSTASIS, PRINCIPLE OF; HUNGER, THEORIES OF; HYDRAULIC THEORY; LIFE, THEORIES OF; SOLOMON'S OPPONENT-PROCESS THE-ORY OF EMOTIONS/FEELINGS/MOTIVA-TION; THERMODYNAMICS, LAWS OF.

REFERENCES

Freud, S. (1894/1964). The neuro-psychoses of defence. In *The standard edition of the complete psychological works of Sigmund Freud*. London: Hogarth Press.

Freud, S. (1920/1953). Beyond the pleasure principle. In *The standard edition of the complete psychological works of Sigmund Freud*. London: Hogarth press.

CONSTITUTIONAL THEORIES OF PERSONALITY. See KRETSCHMER'S THEORY OF PERSONALITY; SHELDON'S TYPE THEORY.

CONSTITUTIONAL-PREDISPOSITION THEORY OF SCHIZOPHRENIA. See SCHIZOPHRENIA, THEORIES OF.

CONSTRUCTIVISM, THEORIES OF. The *doctrine/theory of constructivism* refers to the way in which memories, perceptions, cognitions, and other complex mental structures are assembled *actively* (or "built") by one's mind, rather than merely being acquired in a *passive* manner. Two prominent versions of *constructivist theory* are the *radical constructivism* of the Swiss psychologist Jean Piaget (1896-1980) and the *social constructivism* of the foreign-born American sociologists Peter L. Berger (1929-) and Thomas Luckmann (1927-). *Piaget's theory* is based on the assumption that children construct mental schema and structures by observing the effects of their own actions on the environment (e.g., in "adaptive accommodation" and "assimilation," the psychological structures/processes of the child are modified to fit the changing demands of the situation, as when an infant in a crib reaches out and attempts to get a toy from outside the crib to the inside through the crib's vertical slats by simply turning the toy slightly sideways/vertically to get it past the slats and into the crib). *Social constructivist theory* emphasizes the manner in which people come to share interpretations of their social milieu (cf., *doctrine of liberal pluralism* - asserts that the individual is at the center of efforts to improve human welfare, and states that societies are to be created where people of diverse backgrounds may pursue their personal welfare and coexist with a minimum of conflict; and *doctrine of situated knowledge* - an approach that arose from cultural studies and feminist criticisms of science, as a challenge to the objectivity of scientific knowledge, on one hand, but aiming to avoid complete relativism, on the other hand; this doctrine represents a perspective of "positioned rationality," whereby knowledge allegedly may emerge only from multiple- and partial-positioned viewpoints; it is opposed to the notion of "transcendence" which asserts that knowledge is "universal;" the doctrine states that knowledge must be seen from the perspective of the knower, the relationships among knowers, and the relationship between the knower and the object of knowledge). Generally, social constructivists argue for rather extreme positions, including the idea that there is no such thing as a knowable objec-

tive reality - but, instead, maintain that all knowledge is derived from the mental constructions of the members of a particular social system [cf., *social-exchange theory* - first enunciated by the American sociologist George Caspar Homans (1910-), who presented a model of social structure based on the notion that most social behavior is founded on the individual's expectation that one's actions, with respect to others, will result in some degree of commensurate ("rewards" and "costs") return; *social Darwinism theory* - first described by the English philosopher Herbert Spencer (1820-1903), and proposes that social and cultural development may be explained by analogy with the *Darwinian theory of biological evolution*; thus, the theory suggests that society functions primarily through conflict and competition where the "fittest" survive and the "poorly adapted" are eliminated; *social identity theory* - formulated by the English-born Polish social psychologist Henri Tajfel (1919-1982), where this "social categorization" theory is based on the notion of "social identity" (i.e., the component of the "self-concept" that derives from group membership) and where social categories (including large groups such as nations, and small groups such as fraternal clubs) provide their members with a sense of one's "essential being" and even prescribes appropriate personal and social behaviors; also, members in such "social identity" groups view their groups as being superior to other groups; the *minimal group paradigm/situation* - studied by H. Tajfel and his colleagues in the early 1970s, refers to an experimental procedure in which the mere presence of social categorization produces intergroup discrimination; *theory of situated identities* - the suggestion that an individual will take on different social roles in different social settings and environments; the *aristocracy theory* - the notion that the social rank of some humans and animals is determined by their parents' rank; and the *minimal social situation effect* - studied by the American psychologist Joseph B. Sidowski (1925-), refers to an interactive decision in which each decision-maker is unaware of the interactive nature of the decision and even of the existence of another decision-maker whose behaviors influence the outcomes]. See also CONSTRUCTIVIST THEORY OF PERCEPTION; DARWIN'S EVOLUTION THEORY; EXCHANGE/SOCIAL EXCHANGE THEORY; INGROUP BIAS THEORIES; PIAGET'S THEORY OF DEVELOPMENTAL STAGES.

REFERENCES

Spencer, H. (1891). *The study of sociology.* New York: Appleton.

Homans, G. C. (1950). *The human group.* New York: Harcourt, Brace.

Piaget, J. (1954). *The construction of reality in the child.* New York: Basic Books.

Sidowski, J. B. (1957). Reward and punishment in a minimal social situation. *Journal of Experimental Psychology, 54,* 318-326.

Berger, P. L., & Luckmann, T. (1966). *The social construction of reality.* New York: Doubleday.

Tajfel, H., Billig, M., & Bundy, R. (1971). Social categorization and intergroup behavior. *European Journal of Social Psychology, 1,* 149-178.

Tajfel, H. (Ed.) (1982). *Social identity and intergroup relations.* New York: Cambridge University Press.

CONSTRUCTIVIST THEORY OF PERCEPTION. This approach toward explaining perceptual phenomena and processes focuses on how the mind *constructs* perceptions. *Constructivist theory* takes a number of different forms, including research on the connection between perception/neural processing and re-search on how perception is determined by mental processing. The idea of approaching perception by asking what the mind does during the perceptual process is an old notion whose roots go back to the 19th century, when the German physicist/physiologist Hermann L. F. von Helmholtz (1821-1894) proposed the *likelihood principle*: one perceives the object that is "most likely" to occur in "that particular situation." Also,

the English psychologist Sir Frederic Charles Bartlett (1886-1969) used *constructivist* concepts to explain results he observed in his studies on memory. Modern descendants of Helmholtz's *likelihood principle* are the English psychologist Richard Langton Gregory's (1923-) notion that perception is governed by a mechanism he calls *hypothesis testing*, and by the American psychologist Ulrich Neisser's (1928-) notion of *perceptual cycle*. *Hypothesis testing* refers to a function of sensory stimulation as providing data for hypotheses concerning the state of the external world. *Hypothesis testing* does not always occur at a conscious level, and perceivers are usually not aware of the complex mental processes that occur during a perceptual act. *Perceptual cycle*, also called the *cyclic model of perception*, refers to the set of cognitive schemata that direct perceptual processes, and the perceptual responses and feedback mechanisms through which perceptual information is sampled. The idea that mental operations occur during the perceptual process is illustrated by an early study by the German psychologist Oswald Kulpe (1862-1915): displays of various colors were presented to participants who were asked to pay attention to a particular aspect of the display (such as the positions of certain letters), but when they were asked, subsequently, to describe another aspect of the display (such as the color of a particular letter), they were not able to do it. This indicates that even though all of the information from the stimulus display reached the observer's eye, a selection process took place somewhere between the reception of this information and the person's perception so that only part of the information was actually perceived and remembered. Thus, perception seems to depend on more than simply the properties of the stimulus, and the observer/participant makes a contribution to the perceptual process. Another way that the *cognitive/constructivist* aspect of processing has been approached is by considering the *eye movements* that people make when observing an object. According to *eye movement theory* (e.g., Hochberg, 1971), as an observer looks at a scene, information is taken in by a series of "fixations" (i.e., pauses of the eye that occur one to three times per second as the person examines part of the stimulus) and "eye movements" that propel the eye from one fixation to the next. Such eye movements are necessary in order to see all of the details of the scene, because a single fixation would reveal only the details near the fixation point. Also, eye movements have another purpose: the information they take in about different parts of the scene is used to create a "mental map" of the scene by a process of "integration" or "piecing together." Thus, Helmholtz's *likelihood principle*, Gregory's idea of *hypothesis testing*, and Hochberg's *eye movement theory* all treat perception as involving an active, constructing observer who processes stimulus information. The *constructivist* approach also assumes that perception of a whole object is constructed from information taken in from smaller parts. The essence of all *constructivist theories* is that perceptual experience is viewed as more than a direct response to stimulation (cf., *direct perception theory*); it is, instead, viewed as an elaboration or "construction" based on hypothesized cognitive and affective operations and mech-anisms. See also ATTENTION, LAWS/PRINCIPLES/THEORIES OF; DIRECT PERCEPTION THEORY; MIND/MENTAL STATES, THEORIES OF; PERCEPTION (I. GENERAL), THEORIES OF; PERCEPTION (II. COMPARATIVE APPRAISAL), THEORIES OF; UNCONSCIOUS INFERENCE, DOCTRINE OF.

REFERENCES

Kulpe, O. (1904). Versuche uber abstraktion. *Berlin International Congress der Experimental Psychologie*, 56-68.

Bartlett, F. C. (1932). *Remembering: A study in experimental and social psychology*. Cambridge, UK: Cambridge, University Press.

Neisser, U. (1967). *Cognitive psychology*. New York: Appleton-Century-Crofts.

Hochberg, J. (1971). Perception. In J. Kling & L. Riggs (Eds.), *Woodworth and Schlosberg's experimental psychology*. New York: Holt, Rinehart, & Winston.

Gregory, R. L. (1973). *Eye and brain*. New York: McGraw-Hill.

CONSUMPTION PATTERNS, LAW OF. See MURPHY'S LAWS.

CONTACT HYPOTHESIS OF PREJUDICE. See PREJUDICE, THEORIES OF.

CONTEMPORANEITY, PRINCIPLE OF. This principle - derived from Kurt Lewin's *field theory* - states that "any behavior or any other change in a psychological field depends only upon the psychological field *at that time*." In other terms, the *contemporaneity principle*, also called the *contemporaneous-explanation principle* and the *billiard ball theory*, asserts that only present or current events can influence behavior and only these should be studied. Although this principle was emphasized by early field theorists, it was misunderstood, frequently, and interpreted to mean that field theorists are not interested in historical problems or in the influence of previous experiences. Lewin (1951) notes that nothing could be more mistaken and, in fact, field theorists are very interested in developmental and historical problems as evidenced by their efforts to enlarge the temporal scope of the psychological experiment; for example, they recommend expansion of the classical reaction-time experiment which typically lasts for only a few seconds, as well as extending the more experiential situations in which a systematically created history may run for hours or weeks for the experimental participants. See also LEWIN'S FIELD THEORY.

REFERENCE

Lewin, K. (1951). The nature of field theory. In M. H. Marx (Ed.), *Psychological theory: Contemporary readings*. New York: Macmillan.

CONTEMPORANEOUS-EXPLANATION PRINCIPLE. See CONTEMPORANEITY, PRINCIPLE OF.

CONTEMPORARY MODEL OF EMOTIONS. See EMOTIONS, THEORIES AND LAWS OF.

CONTEXT, LAW OF. See GESTALT THE-ORY/LAWS; INTERFERENCE THEORIES OF FORGETTING.

CONTEXT-DEPENDENT MEMORY EFFECT. See FORGETTING AND MEMORY, THEORIES OF; STATE-DEPEN-DENT MEMORY/LEARNING EFFECTS.

CONTEXT EFFECT. See HELSON'S ADAPTATION-LEVEL THEORY.

CONTEXT THEORY. See BERKE-LEY'S THEORY OF VISUAL SPACE PERCEPTION; GESTALT THE-ORY/LAWS.

CONTEXT THEORY OF DISTANCE. See BERKELEY'S THEORY OF VISUAL SPACE PERCEPTION.

CONTEXT THEORY OF MEANING. See MEANING, THEORIES AND AS-SESSMENTS OF.

CONTEXTUAL-CHANGE MODELS. See BLOCK'S CONTEXTUALISTIC MODEL OF TIME; PSYCHOLOGICAL TIME, MODELS OF.

CONTEXTUAL ENHANCEMENT EF-FECT. See INTERACTIVE ACTIVATON MODEL OF LETTER PERCEPTION.

CONTEXTUAL INTERFERENCE EF-FECT. See FORGETTING/MEMORY, THEORIES OF; INTERFERENCE THEORIES OF FORGETTING.

CONTEXTUALISM, DOCTRINE OF. See FORGETTING/MEMORY, THEO-RIES OF.

CONTIGUITY, LAW OF. See ASSO-CIATION, LAWS/PRINCIPLES OF; FORGETTING AND MEMORY, THEO-RIES OF; GESTALT THEORY AND LAWS; GUTH-RIE'S THEORY OF BE-HAVIOR; HABIT AND HABIT FORMA-TION, LAWS AND PRINCIPLES OF; LEARNING THEORIES AND LAWS; PAVLOVIAN CONDITIONING PRINCI-PLES, LAWS, AND THE-ORIES.

CONTIGUITY LEARNING THEORY. See ASSOCIATIVE SHIFTING, LAW OF; EFFECT, LAW OF; GUTHRIE'S THE-ORY OF BEHAVIOR; REINFORCE-MENT THEORY; TOLMAN'S THEORY;

CONTINGENCY THEORIES OF WORK MOTIVATION. See WORK/CAREER/OC-CUPATION, THEORIES OF.

CONTINGENCY THEORY OF LEAD-ERSHIP. See LEADERSHIP, THEORIES OF.

CONTINGENT AFTEREFFECT. See APPENDIX A.

CONTINUITY, LAW/PRINCIPLE OF. See GESTALT THEORY/LAWS.

CONTINUITY THEORY. See DEVEL-OPMENTAL THEORY; SPENCE'S THEORY.

CONTINUOUS ACTION THEORY OF TROPISMS. See LOEB'S TROPISTIC THEORY.

CONTRADICTION, PRINCIPLE OF. See THOUGHT, LAWS OF.

CONTRAFREELOADING EFFECT. See CRESPI EFFECT.

CONTRAST, LAW OF. See ASSOCIA-TION, LAWS/PRINCIPLES OF; COLOR VISION, THEORIES AND LAWS OF; FREQUENCY, LAW OF; GESTALT THEORY/LAWS; LEARNING, THEO-RIES AND LAWS.

CONTRAST EFFECTS. See CA-PALDI'S THEORY; COLOR VISION, THEORIES AND LAWS OF; CRESPI EFFECT.

CONTRAST ILLUSION. See APPEN-DIX A, BOURDON ILLUSION.

CONTROL/SYSTEMS THEORY. The terms *control theory* and *control theory psychology* are recent names for describing the development of a body of theory based on a *feedback-system model* or paradigm. *Control theory* posits that there are self-monitoring and self-functioning systems in living organisms similar to governors on motors that prevent them from going too fast; the control aspect essentially protects the organism from itself. Other current synonymous names for this approach include *cybernetic psychology*, *general feedback theory* of human behavior, and *systems theory psychology*. In the area of learning and conditioning, the *biofeedback principles* and procedures (i.e., the process of providing an organism with information about its biological functions such as alpha waves, heart rate, blood pressure, blood flow in the extremities) exemplify *control/systems* approaches in both laboratory and practical settings [cf., *Poiseuille's law* - named after the French physicist Jean L. M. Poiseuille (1797-1869) who verified the principle following earlier work by G. H. L. Hagen (1797-1884), sometimes called the *Poiseuille-Hagen law*, refers to a mathematical relationship among the variables of blood pressure, flow, and resistance]. The notion of self-regulating systems of the body is not new (cf., Bernard, 1865). However, the idea of applying the same principles to the study of the mind is relatively more recent (e.g., Ashby, 1952). Various unresolved issues confounded initial attempts to develop a comprehensive and precise feedback model, for instance, the concept of *homeostasis* (*internal* stability and balance) versus the concept of *adaptation* (*external* shaping and modifiability); that is, the dilemma was to be able to control behavior so as to accommodate *both* internal and external systems. Another problem was the development of mechanisms to account for integration of different feedback systems in the organism. W. Powers describes an *integration theory* and model involving a negative feedback control loop that consists of five elements: a *feedback* function consisting of a transducer/signal sensitive to identifiable environmental variables; a *comparator* function involving a feedback, reference, or error signal; a *compatibility* function between the reference and feedback signals; an error-signal *discrepancy* function between the feedback and reference signals; and an *output* function that exerts its effect upon the environment so as to make a match between the feedback and reference signals and reduce the error-signal to zero. A profound consequence of *integration theory* for psychology is the implication that living organisms do not control their environments by controlling their *outputs*; they control their *inputs*; that is, they control their "perceptions." Thus, according to this theoretical orientation, control over the environment results as a by-product of controlling one's perceptions. *Control theory* research breaks with more traditional approaches to research methodology in psychology (cf., *family-systems model/theory* - a paradigm emphasizing that families may be understood best via *systems theory*, and suggests that one conceive of the family as a complex of interrelating individuals where traits and disorders emerge based on the functionality and health of the family as a whole). Most current research in *control theory* is grounded in *causal models* where influence presumably flows in one direction, but *cybernetic theory* shows that the concept of *cause* becomes ambiguous when variables under the control of negative feedback systems are examined. Among other positive features, *control theory* provides a natural theoretical basis for *humanistic psychology*; that is, behavior originates not in stimuli from the environment but *within* the organism itself. See also HUMANIST THE-ORIES; GENERAL SYSTEMS THEORY; ORGANIZATIONAL, INDUSTRIAL, AND SYSTEMS THEORY; REACTANCE THEORY; TOTE MODEL/HYPOTHESIS.

REFERENCES

Bernard, C. (1865). *An introduction to the study of experimental medicine.* New York: Dover.

Wiener, N. (1948). *Cybernetics: Control and communication in the animal and the machine.* Cambridge, MA: M.I.T. Press.

Ashby, R. (1952). *Design for a brain.* New York: Wiley.

Slack, C. (1955). Feedback theory and the reflex arc concept. *Psychological Review, 62,* 263-267.

Maltz, M. (1960). *Psycho-cybernetics: A new way to get more living out of life.* Englewood Cliffs, NJ: Prentice-Hall.

Miller, G., Galanter, E., & Pribram, K. (1960). *Plans and the structure of behavior.* New York: Holt, Rinehart & Win-ston.

Smith, K., & Smith, M. (1966). *Cybernetic principles of learning and educational design.* New York: Holt, Rinehart & Winston.

Deutsch, K. (1968). Toward a cybernetic model of man and society. In W. Buckley (Ed.), *Modern systems theory for the behavioral scientist.* Chicago: Aldine.

Annett, J. (1969). *Feedback and human behavior.* Baltimore: Penguin Books.

Klir, G. (1969). *An approach to general systems theory.* New York: Van Nostrand Reinhold.

Miller, N. E. (1969). Learning of visceral and glandular responses. *Science, 163,* 434-445.

Powers, W. (1973a). *Behavior: The control of perception.* Chicago: Aldine.

Powers, W. (1973b). Feedback beyond behaviorism. *Science, 179,* 351-356.

Schwartz, G. (1973). Biofeedback as therapy: Some theoretical and practical issues. *American Psychologist, 28,* 666-673.

Miller, N. E. (1978). Biofeedback and visceral learning. *Annual Review of Psychology, 29,* 373-404.

Schwartz, G. (1978). Disregulation and systems theory: A biobehavioral framework for biofeedback and behavioral medicine. In N. Birbaumer & H. Kimmel (Eds.), *Biofeedback and self-regulation.* Hillsdale, NJ: Erlbaum.

Carver, C., & Scheier, M. (1982). Control theory: A useful conceptual framework for personality, social, clinical, and health psychology. *Psychological Bulletin, 92,* 111-135.

CONVERGENCE THEORY. See DARWIN'S EVOLUTION THEORY.

CONVERGENT EVOLUTION. See DAR-WIN'S EVOLUTION THEORY.

CONVERSION HYPOTHESIS. In logical reasoning, this is a speculation that some errors in judging the validity of syllogisms occur because people mentally translate a premise into one that appears to them to be equivalent but actually has a different logical meaning. For instance, the statement "If X, then Y" may be translated or converted mentally to "If and only if X, then Y," which may lead to the incorrect inference: "If not-X, then not-Y." Related to such erroneous logical mental conversions is the *atmosphere hypothesis* which holds that errors in judging the validity of syllogisms sometimes occur as the result of a bias in favor of judging a conclusion valid if it contains the same quantifiers or logical terms as are included ("atmosphere") in the premises. For instance, the following syllogism may erroneously be judged to be valid: Some soldiers are blond; Some blonds are gay; therefore, Some soldiers are gay. The repetition of the logical form "Some X are Y", plus the fact that the conclusion appears to be reasonable contribute to the seeming plausibility of this basically invalid syllogism. In *empirical/reality* terms (e.g., as via survey data), one may indeed discover the "truth" that "Some soldiers are gay," but in terms of *logic*, and errors in formal logic, the conclusion that "Some soldiers are gay" does not follow legitimately or validly from the given premises. In the contexts of Freudian analysis, clinical psychology, and psychotherapy, the notion of *conversion* (e.g., *conversion hysteria*) refers to the transformation or translation of psychic conflicts or psychological problems into physical symptoms such as apparent paralysis, blindness, deafness, or anaesthesia. See also FREUD'S THEORY OF PERSONALITY; GESTALT THEORY/LAWS; MIND/MEN-TAL SET, LAW OF; NULL HYPOTHESIS; PERCEPTION (II. COMPARATIVE APPRAISAL), THEORIES OF.

REFERENCES

Freud, S. (1909). Analysis of a phobia in a five-year-old boy. In *The complete psychological works of Sigmund Freud*. Vol. 10. London: Hogarth Press.

Colman, A. M. (2001). *A dictionary of psychology*. New York: Oxford University Press.

CONVERSION HYSTERIA PHENOMENON. See CONVERSION HYPOTHESIS; FREUD'S THEORY OF PERSONALITY.

COOLIDGE EFFECT. See LOVE, THEORIES OF.

COOPERATION/COMPETITION, THE-ORIES OF. See CONFLICT, THEORIES OF; DEUTSCH'S CRUDE LAW OF SO-CIAL RELATIONS/RESOLUTIONS.

COOPERATIVE PRINCIPLE. See PARALLEL DISTRIBUTED PROCESSING MODEL.

COPE MODEL. See COGNITIVE THEORIES OF EMOTIONS.

COPE'S LAW/RULE. See DEVELOPMEN-TAL THEORY.

COPY THEORY. See GESTALT THEORY/ LAWS.

CORE-CONTEXT THEORY. See PERCEPTION (II. COMPARATIVE APPRAISAL), THEORIES OF.

CORIOLIS ILLUSION. See APPENDIX A.

CORNSWEET ILLUSION. See APPENDIX A, CRAIK-O'BRIEN EFFECT.

CORPUSCULAR/PARTICLE THEORY. See VISION/SIGHT, THEORIES OF.

CORRESPONDENCE BIAS HYPOTHESIS. This conjecture in social psychology - formulated by the American psychologists Edward Ellsworth Jones (1926-1993) and Keith Eugene Davis (1936-) - concerns the tendency for one person to draw inferences about another person's unique and enduring dispositions from behaviors that may be explained entirely by the context(s) or situation(s) in which they occur. The major problem involved in interpreting and "making sense out of" other people is that we largely employ ("attribute") internal, invisible, intangible, and unobservable constructs such as character, belief, motive, intention, and desire when assessing another person - rather than using more observable, situational, and tangible factors such as the person's words and deeds. Accordingly, as we make inferences about other people based upon such invisible constructs, we risk making a mistake: when observing another's behavior, we may conclude (often erroneously) that the person who performed the behavior the behavior was "predisposed" (internal basis) to do so; that is, the person's behavior *corresponds* to the person's unique dispositions. Moreover, we may draw such conclusions even when a more rational and logical analysis (external basis) would suggest otherwise. Thus, the *correspondence bias hypothesis* states that humans have a pervasive tendency to *underestimate* the role of *external* situational factors and to *overestimate* the role of *internal* motives, dispositions, and factors when interpreting the behavior of other people. Among the mechanisms and factors that may produce distinct forms of *correspondence bias* are a lack of awareness, inflated categorizations, unrealistic expectations, and incomplete corrections. Other names for the *correspondence bias* are "correspondent inference," "fundamental attribution error," "dispositionist bias," and "overattribution bias." See also ATTRIBUTION THEORY; FUNDAMENTAL ATTRUBUTION ERROR; IMPRESSION FOR-MATION, THEORIES OF.

REFERENCES

Heider, F. (1958). *The psychology of interpersonal relations*. New York: Wiley.

Jones, E. E., & Davis, K. E. (1965). From acts to dispositions: The attribution processes in person perception. In L. Berkowitz (Ed.), *Advances in experimental social psychology*. Vol. 2. New York: Academic Press.

Gilbert, D. T., & Malone, P. S. (1995). The correspondence bias. *Psychological Bulletin, 117,* 21-38.

CORRESPONDENCE THEORY/LAW. See LOGAN'S MICROMOLAR THEORY.

CORRESPONDENT INFERENCE THEORY. See ATTRIBUTION THEORY.

CORRIDOR ILLUSION. See APPENDIX A.

COSINE LAW. See ABNEY'S LAW.

COST-REWARD MODELS. See BY-STAN-DER INTERVENTION EFFECT.

COUÉ METHOD/THEORY. See SELF-MONITORING THEORY/METHOD.

COUNTERINTUITIVE THEORY OF EMOTIONS. See JAMES-LANGE/LANGE-JAMES THEORY OF EMOTIONS.

COVARIATION THEORY. See DECISION-MAKING THEORIES; KELLEY'S COVARIATION THEORY.

COVARIATION/CORRELATION PRINCIPLE. See ATTRIBUTION THEORY.

CRAIK-O'BRIEN EFFECT. See APPEN-DIX A.

CREATIONISM/CREATION THEORY. See DARWIN'S EVOLUTION THEORY; LIFE, THEORIES OF.

CREATIVE SYNTHESIS/RESULTANTS, PRINCIPLE OF. See WUNDT'S THEORIES/DOCTRINES/PRINCIPLES.

CREATIVITY STAGE THEORY. See PROBLEM-SOLVING AND CREATIVITY STAGE THEORIES.

CRESPI EFFECT. The American psychologist Leo P. Crespi (1916-) is credited with the finding that in learning experiments on lower animals there is a disproportionate in-crease in a response with an increase in incentive. For example, if an animal presses a lever for one gram of food reinforcement and then is shifted suddenly to five grams of reinforcement, it will respond characteristically at a higher rate than a comparable animal that has been receiving five-gram reinforcements all along. This sudden shift in "attractiveness" of a reward is called the *Crespi effect* or the *contrast effect* [cf., *contrafreeloading effect* - paradoxical behavior where organisms work for reinforcement even though the identical reinforcement is available freely, as when a rat presses a lever repeatedly for food ("earned reinforcer") that is available simply to be taken with less effort from a nearby dish ("free reinforcer")]. Another example of the *Crespi effect* is seen in rats learning to run a maze: if a large amount of food provides the incentive, the rats run to the goal faster than if the amount of food is small. Thus, with practice, the rats in these two conditions (large reward versus small reward) show a significant difference in running speeds. Subsequently, once the levels of running are established in each condition, switching the amounts of food for the two groups has an immediate effect on maze-running performance. Rats that had received a large reward and now receive a small reward run more slowly. On the other hand, rats that had received a small reward and now receive a large reward run faster (cf., *compliance effects and techniques*). Additionally, the rats' performance with the changed reward often "overshoots" the mark expected from their earlier behavior. The rats switched from a large reward to a small one run more slowly than predicted, whereas those rats switched from a small reward to a large one run faster than expected. Increased performance as a result of going from small to a large reward is termed *positive contrast*, or an *elation effect*, whereas the poorer performance associated with going from a large to a small amount of reward is termed *negative contrast*, or a *depression effect* (cf., *nonreward hypothesis* - posits that an organism that expects a reward upon performing in a conditioning paradigm, but does not receive the reward, is frustrated and leads to greater efforts following subsequent stimuli). The replicability of Crespi's findings has been controversial. Although many studies support the *Crespi effect* and Crespi's earlier findings, a number of other researchers have not been able to obtain such effects. K. Spence (1956) failed to find *positive contrast effects* and suggested that the *positive contrast effect* obtained by Crespi was a function of the original high-reward group participants' not having reached their asymptote and that the shift-group responded to at the higher level because of the additional training trials. Spence does report, however, finding *negative contrast effects*. Thus, although the *negative contrast effect* seems to stand as a viable concept in the field, there have been questions about the validity of the *positive contrast effect*. Optimal explanations for the *contrast effects* may depend, ultimately, on whether only *negative contrast effects* are thought to be obtainable, or whether both *positive* and *negative contrast effects* may be considered as bona fide phenomena. If it is assumed that *both* types are obtainable, then a theory such as H. Helson's *adaptation-level theory* - as applied to conditioning and reinforcement - may be a feasible option. See also COMPLIANCE EFFECTS AND TECHNIQUES; HELSON'S ADAPTATION-LEVEL THEORY; LEARNING THEORIES/LAWS.

REFERENCES

Crespi, L. (1942). Quantitative variation of incentive and performance in the white rat. *American Journal of Psychology, 55*, 467-517.

Crespi, L. (1944). Amount of reinforcement and level of performance. *Psychological Review, 51*, 341-357.

Spence, K. (1956). *Behavior theory and conditioning*. New Haven, CT: Yale University Press.

Helson, H. (1964). *Adaptation-level theory: An experimental and systematic approach to behavior*. New York: Harper & Row.

CRIMINALITY, THEORY OF. See LOMBROSIAN THEORY.

CRITICAL PERIOD/STAGE HYPOTHESIS/PHENOMENON. See INFANT ATTACHMENT THEORIES.

CRITICAL THEORY. *Critical theory* is an analytical approach in political philosophy and psychology - especially associated with the University of Frankfurt in Germany and Columbia University in New York in the 1930s and advanced by Max Horkheimer (1895-1973), Theodor W. Adorno (1903-1969), and Herbert Marcuse (1898-1979) - that rejects the proposition of a value-free social science and examines the historical and ideological factors that determine culture and human behavior. *Critical theory* is proposed as a *practical/normative theory* (i.e., prescribing norms or standards, such as found in *decision theory* or *game theory* which seek to prescribe how rational decision-makers *ought* to choose in order to optimize or maximize their own interests) rather than as a *descriptive/positive theory* (i.e., propositions that seek to explain and predict the behavior of actual agents), and attempts to expose the contradictions inherent in individuals' belief systems and social mores or behaviors with the goal of changing them. See also DECISION-MAKING THEORIES; GAME THEORY.

REFERENCES

Marcuse, H. (1941). *Reason and revolution: Hegel and the rise of social theory*. London: Oxford University Press.

Horkheimer, M., & Adorno, T. W. (1947). *Dialektik der aufklarung*. Amsterdam: Querido.

Adorno, T. W. (1963). *Eingriffe: Neun kritische modelle*. Frankfurt am Main: Verlag.

Marcuse, H. (1968). *Negations: Essays in critical theory*. Trans. J. T. Shapiro. Boston: Beacon Press.

Adorno, T. W., Marcuse, H., & Habermas, J. (1970). *Das elend der kritischen theorie*. Freiburg: Rombach.

Horkheimer, M. (1970). *Traditionelle und kritische theorie*. Frankfurt am Main: Fischer-Bucherei.

Bell, D. E., Raiffa, H., & Tversky, A. (Eds.) (1988). *Decision making: Descriptive, normative, and prescriptive interactions*. New York: Cambridge University Press.

Marcuse, H. (2001). *Towards a critical theory of society*. (D. Kellner, ed.). New York: Routledge.

CROCKER-HENDERSON SYSTEM. See OLFACTION/SMELL, THEORIES OF.

CROSS-COUPLING EFFECT. See APPENDIX A, CORIOLIS ILLUSION.

CROSS-LINKAGE THEORY OF AGING. See AGING, THEORIES OF.

CROSSOVER EFFECT. See DEVELOPMENTAL THEORY.

CUE OVERLOAD PRINCIPLE. See LEARNING THEORIES/LAWS.

CUE-SELECTION MODELS. See CONCEPT LEARNING AND CONCEPT FORMATION, THEORIES OF.

CULTURAL ABSOLUTISM THEORY. See RECAPITULATION THEORY/LAW.

CULTURAL BIAS HYPOTHESIS. See INTELLIGENCE, THEORIES/LAWS OF.

CULTURAL DETERMINISM THEORY. See PERSONALITY THEORIES; RECAPITULATION THEORY/LAW.

CULTURAL-NORM HYPOTHESIS. See ATTRIBUTION THEORY.

CULTURAL RELATIVISM THEORY. See RECAPITULATION THEORY/LAW.

CULTURAL UNIVERSAL THEORY. See DEVELOPMENTAL THEORY.

CULTURE-BOUND EFFECTS/ PHENOM-ENA. Cross-cultural studies and research have indicated that there are several "culture-bound" (CB) phenomena/effects or behaviors that seem to be peculiar from the perspective of people in some of the more "advanced" or "developed" regions of the world, especially in the Western countries. For example, the following CB phenomena have been observed and documented: *latah* - found mainly in Malaysia and Indonesia, most often among middle-aged women, this behavior seems to be precipitated by sudden stress and has two major components: a startle reaction and subsequent imitative behavior including echolalia (repeating what someone *says*), echopraxia (repeating what someone *does*), automatic obedience coprolalia (involuntary speaking of obscene words), fear, a trance-like state, and altered consciousness; one theory of this behavior holds that certain Malaysian and Indonesian child-rearing practices predispose persons toward hypersuggestibility, which subsequently becomes related to sexual functioning (cf., Murphy, 1972); *amok* - originally, in the 16th century, occurred in religious zealots who had taken vows to sacrifice their lives in battle against the enemy; later, in Southeast Asia, the term referred to persons who emerge from periods of apathy and withdrawal with a sudden outburst of agitation, mania, and violent physical attacks on those nearby (i.e., the person "runs amuck"); among the theories of this behavior include the presence of febrile diseases (e.g., malaria), nonfebrile diseases (e.g., syphilis), opium addiction, chronic disorders (e.g., brain damage), sociopsychological distress, sleep deprivation, infections, sexual arousal, or excessive heat; this behavior appears to be similar to other-named behaviors in other cultures, such as "malignant anxiety" in Africa, "cathard" in Polynesia, "negi-negi" in New Guinea, and "pseudonite" in the Sahara desert region; *susto/espanto* - refers to "soul loss," is common among Hispanic populations especially in children and young women; this behavior typically follows some frightening ("susto" or "espanto") experience (sometimes weeks, or even months and years, later) in which one's soul is thought to have departed the body, resulting in weight loss, appetite loss, skin pallor, lethargy, fatigue, untidiness, and excessive thirst; theories of this behavior include the presence of unacceptable impulses, producing overreliance on the defense mechanisms of displacement, isolation, and projection; in children, this behavior may be due to insecurities and fears associated with parental abandonment, especially under circumstances of frequent migration and mobility; *koro/shook yong* - is found among Chinese peoples, mainly in men, in Southeast Asia and Hong Kong; this behavior is characterized by an intense fear that one's penis is shrinking and withdrawing into the body, and may cause one's death; in attempting to deal with this fear, the individual often holds onto his penis during the day and wears bamboo clamps on the penis while sleeping; in women, however, this fear may be experienced as a sensation that the breasts are shrinking or the labia are withdrawing into the body; theories of the behavior include the presence of faulty beliefs

about the balance of *yin* (female) and *yang* (male) forces related to sexual excesses, as well as perceived shame over one's actions, in particular if there is frequent resort to masturbation or prostitution; *locura* - a CB behavioral phenomenon resembling a chronic, schizophrenic-like psychosis, found in several Latin American countries, and consisting of incoherence, psychomotor agitation, visual and auditory hallucinations, and occasional outbursts of aggressive and violent behavior; *shenjing shuairuo* - a CB syndrome, found among Chinese communities in Southern/eastern Asia, and characterized by fatigue, headaches, dizziness, joint/muscle pain, sexual dysfunctions, and loss of concentration, and is similar to "mood disorders" and "anxiety disorders" in Western cultures; *shen-k'uei* - a CB phenomenon, found among men in Thailand and in ethnic Chinese communities in Southern/eastern Asia, and is characterized by anxiety and panic attacks, along with somatic symptoms such as sexual dysfunction, dizziness, insomnia, and fatigue, and is attributed often to loss of semen occasioned by increases or excesses in sexual intercourse, nocturnal emissions, or masturbation; it is similar to *dhat* - a CB effect, found in India and Sri Lanka, involving severe anxiety and hypochondria, and attributed to excessive discharge of semen; *shin-byung* - a CB phenomenon, found in Korea, and characterized by insomnia, dissociation, anxiety, dizziness, and fatigue, and attributed to possession by the spirits of dead relatives and ancestors; *taijin kyofusho* (also called *shinkei-shitsu*) - is a CB effect, found mainly in Japan, and characterized by intense/debilitating anxiety that one's body, or its parts and functions, are repugnant, embarrassing, displeasing, or offensive to others, and is similar to "social phobic" behavior in Western cultures (i.e., an anxiety/panic disorder characterized by an irrational fear of scrutiny by others, or of being the center of attention in social settings involving strangers); *uqamairineq* - a CB syndrome, found mainly in Eskimo communities of North America and Greenland, in which the sensation/experience of an unusual smell or

sound is followed by sudden paralysis, hallucinations, anxiety, or psychomotor agitation; this effect typically lasts only a few minutes and is attributed by those communities or cultures as being due to a loss of soul or possession by spirits, and it may be interpreted, also, by non-Eskimos as a form of dissociative disorder where there is a partial or total disconnection between past memories, self-awareness/identity, and immediate sensations precipitated by disturbed relationships, traumatic experiences, or problems perceived as insurmountable; *windigo* - a rare and controversial CB syndrome, found mainly among North American Indian tribes in the subarctic region, and is characterized by depression, suicidal/homicidal thoughts, and a compulsive desire to eat human flesh; if the afflicted individual does turn to cannibalism, he/she is considered by the culture to be a monster and is ostracized or put to death; *zar/sar* - a CB effect, found mainly in Ethiopia and other North African regions, as well as in certain Arab communities in various parts of the Middle East, and is characterized by episodes of personality dissociation attributed to spirit possession, and linked to behaviors such as excessive and inappropriate laughing, shouting, singing, and weeping, along with self-mutilation/injury, and is followed, often, by apathy and withdrawal from others; the CB effect is treated typically by elaborate exorcistic ceremonies involving dancing, singing, and drinking the blood of a sacrificed animal (much like many of the fraternity-induction ceremonies on many American college and university campuses); *bangungut* - a CB syndrome observed mainly in young Filipino and Laotian men in which the sufferer appears to have been frightened to death by severe nightmares. In general, theoretical approaches to CB phenomena may be viewed by Westerners as variants of "neurotic disorders" found in the Western world, or as forms of "reactive psychoses" related to paranoid or emotional/disordered consciousness problems; in either case, the CB behaviors and syndromes are viewed essentially as being psychogenic in origin and emphasize the role of cultural factors in the etiology, onset, manifestation /expression, course, and outcome of such effects/phenomena. See also LABELING/DEVIANCE THEORY; PSYCHOPATHOLOGY, THEORIES OF.

REFERENCES

Yap, P. M. (1951). Mental diseases peculiar to certain cultures. *Journal of Mental Science, 97,* 313-327.

Murphy, H. B. M. (1972). History and the evolution of syndromes: The striking case of *latah* and *amok*. In M. Hammer, K. Salzinger & S. Sutton (Eds.), *Psychopathology: Contributions from the biological, behavioral, and social sciences*. New York: Wiley.

Marsella, A. J., & White, G. (Eds.) (1982). *Cultural conceptions of mental health and therapy*. New York: Reidel.

CULTURE-EPOCH THEORY. See RECAPITULATION, THEORY/LAW OF.

CUMULATIVE ADVANTAGE, DOCTRINE OF. See MATTHEW EFFECT.

CUMULATIVE DEFICITS THEORY/ PHENOMENA. The American social psychologist Morton Deutsch (1920-) and the Nigerian psychologist Christopher Bakare (1935-) both suggested the *cumulative deficits phenonenon/theory*, and Bakare formulated a *theory of the cumulative cognitive deficit syndrome*. The *theory of cumulative deficits* refers to the condition where, with persistent influence from an impoverished environment, there is over time an increasingly larger negative effect on the behavior in question. Bakare studied the phenomenon in African children and developed a number of cognitive-stimulation materials for correcting such deficits once they are diagnosed (cf., M. Hutt's *theory of microdiagnosis* which proposes that in all exceptional cases an examiner should develop relevant hypotheses concerning test scores that would help to explain any suspected deviance from the "true score" of individuals). In addition to his study of the phenomenon, Deutsch has

conducted research on interracial housing, cooperation and competition, interpersonal conflict, and distributive justice. See also CONFLICT, THEORIES OF; INTELLI-GENCE, THEORIES/LAWS OF.

REFERENCES

Deutsch, M., & Brown, B. (1964). Social influences in negro-white intelligence differences. *Journal of Social Issues, 20*, 24-35.

Deutsch, M., & Krauss, R. (1965). *Theories of social psychology*. New York: Basic Books.

Bakare, C. (1972). Social class differences in the performance of Nigerian children on the Draw-a-Man test. In L. Cronbach, & P. Drenth (Eds.), *Mental tests and cultural adaptation*. The Hague: Mouton.

Hutt, M. (1980). Microdiagnosis and misuse of scores and standards. *Psychological Reports, 50*, 239-255.

CUPBOARD THEORY. The *cupboard theory* is one of the earliest explanations for the phenomenon of *infant attachment*. The theory refers to the mother's providing food when her infant is hungry, warmth when it is cold, and dryness when it is wet and uncomfortable. That is, the mother functions virtually as a *cupboard* of supplies for her infant. Through her association with the infant and giving such needed supplies, the mother herself becomes a positive stimulus (*conditioned reinforcer*) and, as a result of the association process, the infant clings to her and demonstrates other signs of attachment. A number of experiments conducted on the phenomenon of *infant attachment* in the monkey, however, indicate unequivocally that the *cupboard theory* cannot account exclusively for attachment behavior in infants. Rather, the clinging behavior (in the case of the monkeys, clinging to a soft, cuddly form) in infants appears to be an innate response. The American psychologist Harry Harlow (1905-1981) and his associates isolated baby monkeys from their mothers immediately after birth and raised them alone in a cage containing two inanimate "surrogate" (substitute) mothers, one that was made of bare wire mesh but providing milk nourishment, and the other padded and covered with terry cloth but providing no food nourishment If the *cupboard theory* were valid, the infants should have learned to cling to the surrogate mother that provided them with milk (the wire surrogate). However, the infant monkeys did not cling to the wire mother; they preferred to cling to the cuddly, cloth, warmer surrogate mother and went to the wire mother only to drink milk. Harlow's results suggest that close *physical contact* with a cuddly object is a biological need for infant monkeys (as well as for human infants), and infants cling and attach to their mothers not simply because the infant receives food from the mother but, also, because the *physical contact* with the mother is innately reinforcing. See also ANACLITIC THEORY; INFANT ATTACHMENT THEORIES; LOVE, THEORIES OF.

REFERENCES

Harlow, H. (1958). The nature of love. *American Psychologist, 13*, 673-685.

Harlow, H., & Zimmerman, R. (1959). Affectional responses in the infant monkey. *Science, 130*, 421-432.

Ainsworth, M., Blehar, M., Waters, E., & Wall, S. (1978). *Patterns of attachment*. Hillsdale, NJ: Erlbaum.

CYBERNETIC THEORY. See CONTROL/ SYSTEMS THEORY; TOTE MODEL/HY-POTHESIS.

CYBERNETIC THEORY OF AGING. See AGING, THEORIES OF.

CYBERNETIC THEORY OF PERCEPTION. See PERCEPTION (II. COMPARATIVE APPRAISAL), THEORIES OF.

CYCLIC MODEL OF PERCEPTION. See CONSTRUCTIVIST THEORY OF PERCEPTION.

CYCLOPEAN EYE. This speculation originally referred to a supposed/hypothetical structure in the brain

where the retinal images from both eyes are combined. Historically, the French philosopher Rene Descartes (1596-1650) asserted, erroneously, that such an entity resides in the pineal gland (because that structure is located in the center of the head); the German physiologist/physicist Hermann L. F. von Helmholtz (1821-1894) named the hypothetical structure the *Cyclopean eye* after the Greek mythological figure of the Cyclops, a member of a family of giants, who had a single round eye in the middle of its forehead; and, most recently, the Canadian-born American neurophysiologist David H. Hubel (1926-) and the Swedish neurobiologist Torsten N. Wiesel (1924-) located a region in the brain, containing the binocular cells/neurons of the visual cortex (approximately half the neurons in the primary visual cortex are binocular), where such retinal images combine to give one the sensation or experience of a single stereoscopic/three-dimensional depth perception. See also HOROPTER THEORY; PANUM PHENOMENON/EFFECT.

REFERENCES

Hubel, D. H., & Wiesel, T. N. (1959). Receptive fields of single neurones in the cat's striate cortex. *Journal of Physiology, 148,* 574-591.

Hubel, D. H., & Wiesel, T. N. (2000). Receptive fields and functional architecture of monkey striate cortex. In S. Yantis (Ed.), *Visual perception: Essential readings.* New York: Psychology Press.

CYNICS, LAW OF. See MURPHY'S LAWS.

D

DALE'S LAW/PRINCIPLE. See NEURON/ NEURAL/NERVE THEORY.

DALTONISM. See YOUNG-HELMHOLTZ COLOR VISION THEORY.

DARWIN-HECKER HYPOTHESIS OF LAUGHTER/HUMOR. This proposition - named after the English naturalist Charles Darwin and the German physiologist Ewald Hecker - states that humor and laughter (laughter induced by tickling) have common underlying mechanisms. In one test of the *Darwin-Hecker hypothesis* (Harris & Christenfeld, 1997), participants were tickled before and after viewing comedy videotapes; results showed that those who exhibited more pronounced laughter to comedy also laughed more vigorously to being tickled. However, there was no evidence that comedy-induced laughter increased subsequent laughter to tickle, nor that ticklish laughter increased laughter to comedy. Thus, it is suggested that humor and tickle are related only in that the two behaviors share a *final threshold* for elicitation of their common behavioral response (smiling and laughing), and the possibility is not ruled out that humor develops ontogenetically from tickling - but that after such a development has taken place, the two behaviors may share only a *final* common pathway. It may be possible, also, that tickle shares an internal state with other emotions (such as social anxiety), and that ticklish laughter might be more similar to nervous, rather than to mirthful, laughter. See also BEHAVIORAL THEORIES OF HUMOR AND LAUGHTER; DARWIN'S THEORY OF LAUGHTER AND HUMOR; HUMOR, THEORIES OF.
REFERENCES
Darwin, C. (1872/1965). *The expression of the emotions in man and animals.* London: Murray.
Hecker, E. (1873). *Die physiologie und psychologie des lachens und des komischen.* Berlin: Dummler.

Harris, C., & Christenfeld, N. (1997). Humour, tickle, and the Darwin-Hecker hypothesis. *Cognition and Emotion, 11*, 103-110.

DARWIN'S EVOLUTION THEORY/EVOLUTION, THEORY/LAWS OF. = Darwinism = biological evolution, doctrine of. The English naturalist Charles Robert Darwin (1809-1882) and the Welsh naturalist Alfred Russel Wallace (1823-1913) independently formulated the basic features/aspects of the *theory of evolution*, which was first publicly presented in 1858 at a meeting of the Linnaean Society (named in honor of the Swedish botanist and taxonomist Carolus Linnaeus, 1707-1778). In 1859, Darwin firmly established the *theory of organic evolution* known as *Darwinism*, and his name is better known than Wallace's today in connection with the origination of *evolutionary theory*. However, both men were exceptionally modest concerning "ownership" of the theory. At first, Wallace held that human evolution could be explained by his and Darwin's theory, but he later departed from Darwin on this point, asserting instead that a guiding "spiritual force" was necessary to account for the human soul. Wallace also considered "sexual selection" to be less important in evolution than did Darwin, holding that (unlike Darwin) it had no role in the evolution of human intellect. The *theory of evolution* holds that all naturally occurring populations are gradually and constantly changing as a result of *natural selection* that operates on individual organisms and varies according to their biological *fitness*. According to the theory, the process of evolution led to an enormous diversity in animal and plant forms where one of these lines evolved into hominids and, eventually, into humans. The implication of this *biological theory* for the discipline of psychology is that the human mind and behavior are as subject to natural law as is animal behavior (cf., *pangenetic theory* - Darwin's theory of heredity which holds that personal traits are transmitted from parents to the next generation via particles of each body organ, or part hidden in the spermatozoon and ovum of the parents; also, posits that mental traits, as well as physical characteristics, are inherited by *pangenesis*; thus,

Darwin viewed mental processes in humans and animals as products of evolution and a proper subject for scientific investigation). Darwin recognized that the evolutionary process is characterized by constant divergence and diversification where it could be likened to an enormously elaborate branching tree with living species represented by the tip of the branches, whereas the remainder of the tree denotes extinct species; it is estimated that as many as 98% of all species that ever existed are now extinct. One ramification of the branching tree analogy is that it is meaningless to place different species in an ordinal sequence from lower to higher. For instance, birds evolved from a line of reptiles different from those that evolved into mammals, and carnivores evolved along a different branch of the mammals than did primates. Therefore, birds, cats, monkeys, and humans do *not* form a continuum of evolution; they are *distinct types* of animals. Evolution has not been an orderly process that produced organisms of consistently increasing subtlety and complexity that culminated in the appearance of humans. Rather, the line of organisms leading to humans is only one branch among numerous other branches, and the human species, perhaps, does not deserve the universal evolutionary importance often given to it. Evolution is assumed, generally, to account for the variety of species on the earth today where (over millions of years) changes have taken place that are due to variation in the genes of a population and to survival and transmission of certain variations by natural selection. The *law of natural selection* is defined as the elimination of those individual organisms that are least well-adapted to the environment, with the survival and greater proportionate increase of those that are better adapted. The operative factor, according to *evolutionary theory*, is *competition* (or struggle) for existence where the result is *survival of the fittest* (cf., *optimal foraging theory* - refers to an organism's searching for food using strategies that are most efficient or cost-effective in terms of minimizing metabolic energy or maximizing Darwinian fitness). The phrase "survival of the fittest" was devised by the English philosopher/psychologist/sociologist Herbert Spencer (1820-1903) to describe the

results of biological competition and is equivalent to the phrase "survival of the best adapted organisms." Darwin (1859) postulated that *natural selection* interacts with genetic variation so that the fittest members of the population contribute most significantly to the gene pool of subsequent generations. Rate of evolutionary change is determined by rate of advantageous mutations and intensity of selection pressures. The process of evolution produces new species (called *speciation*) when two or more populations of a species become separated and isolated from each other in different environments; such populations evolve differently and, thus, become different species. The process of *adaptation* occurs when the environment remains fairly constant, and the entire species becomes better suited to the environment through *natural selection* and, thus, behaviors as well as anatomical structures evolve through the mechanism of *natural selection* [cf., *competitive exclusion principle*, also called *Gause's principle* - named after the Soviet biologist Georgyi F. Gause (1910-) - refers to the proposition that two distinct, but similar, species cannot occupy the same ecological niche indefinitely; the *Red Queen hypothesis* - named after the logic expressed by the character of the Red Queen in Lewis Carroll's 1872 book "Through the Looking Glass" - is the proposition that any evolutionary advance by one species is necessarily detrimental to other species in the same ecosystem, so that species are viewed as involved in a competitive evolutionary race whereby they must evolve continually just to survive and maintain their positions; *convergent evolution* - the development of similarities, not based on communality of descent, in two or more groups of organisms; a tendency of unrelated animals in a particular environment to acquire similar body structures that enable them to adapt optimally to the habitat; *convergence theory* - holds that individuals begin with hereditary givens or traits that are modified subsequently by environmental stimuli; and *neural Darwinism theory* - states that groups of neurons are selected by experience to form the foundation of cognitive operations - such as learning and memory - and where such *selectionism* is viewed as an explanation for the brain's functioning; also, it is the proposition that synaptic connections in the nervous system are shaped by competition where only those that are relatively useful are the ones that survive]. Evolutionary change does not need to be slow, gradual, and continuous, and there are not necessarily any "missing links" in the fossil record of the evolution of humans. Although evolution is a theory, it is a well-established one; it is not a hypothesis but a theory that is the end product of an empirical science that rests on masses of accumulated data. The terms *evolution, evolutionary theory*, and *theory of evolution* are used by most people as though they were synonyms and all indicating the Darwinian position. However, this pattern of usage tends to be misleading. *Evolution* is not theory but a fact; the *gradualist* position of origin of species by *natural selection* advanced by Darwin (*Darwinism*) is one attempt to explain that fact (cf., *catastrophism/neo-catastrophism* - the theory that gradual processes of evolution have been modified by the effects of great natural cataclysms). Defenders of *creationism/creation theory* (i.e., the doctrine that all things, including organisms, owe their existence to God's creation and not to evolution) often mistake disputes over the best characterization of the evolutionary process as indications that biologists themselves regard evolution as merely a "theoretical" concept (cf., *transformation theory* - states that one biological species becomes changed into another, basically different, species over the course of time). The influence of *evolutionary doctrine* in psychology has been both powerful and productive; it encouraged the study of individual differences, helped establish the fields of *comparative psychology* and *behavior genetics*, provided the useful concepts of *adaptation, purpose*, and *function* in 20th century psychology, and advanced the scientific study of *developmental psychology*. It is interesting to note that the *theory of evolution* is the *only* theory that is referenced and described in John Dewey's (1898) introductory psychology textbook. A comprehensive theory of evolution, called the modern synthesis or neo-Darwinism, was forged in the early 1940s and emphasizes the integration of the concepts of *natural selection, gradualism*, and *population genetics* as the fundamental units of evolu-

tionary change [cf., *evolutionarily stable strategy* - described by the English biologist John M. Smith (1920-) and the American chemist/physicist George R. Price (1922-1975), refers to any hereditary pattern of behavior that is fixed where - when most individuals in a population adopt it - no alternative behavior pattern has greater "Darwinian fitness" and so none other is favored over it by natural selection; *evolutionary bottleneck* - refers to a sudden decrease in the size of a population, typically due to an environmental catastrophe, and results in a loss or decrease in genetic variability and adaptability - even if the population is able to recover its original size; and *non-Darwinian evolution* - refers to changes in the relative frequencies of genes in a population resulting from "neutral mutation" and not from natural selection; also called *random/genetic drift*]. The relatively new area of study called *animal sociobiology*, which is the application of principles from evolutionary and population biology to animals' social behavior, has invoked the *modern synthetic theory of evolution*. This approach has stimulated scientists from various disciplines to reexamine the evolution of social behavior and to reconsider how the principle of *natural selection* works in this context. See also DOLLO'S LAW; EMPATHY-ALTRUISM HYPOTHESES; HAWK-DOVE/CHICKEN GAME EFFECTS; LAMARCK'S THEORY; MENDEL'S LAWS/PRINCIPLES; NATURAL SELECTION, LAW OF; PARSIMONY, LAW/PRINCIPLE OF; WEISMANN'S THEORY.

REFERENCES

Darwin, C. (1859). *On the origin of species by means of natural selection*. London: Murray.

Wallace, A. R. (1870). *Contributions to the theory of natural selection*. London: Macmillan.

Darwin, C. (1871). *The descent of man and selection in relation to sex*. London: Murray.

Spencer, H. (1892). *The principles of psychology*. New York: Appleton.

Dewey, J. (1898). *Psychology*. New York: Harper & Bros.

Fisher, R. A. (1929/1958). *The genetical theory of natural selection*. New York: Dover.

Hodos, W., & Campbell, C. (1969). *Scala naturae*: Why there is no theory in comparative psychology. *Psychological Review, 4,* 337-350.

Gruber, H. (1974). *Darwin on man: A psychological study of scientific creativity*. New York: Dutton.

Wilson, E. (1975). *Sociobiology: The new synthesis*. Cambridge, MA: Harvard University Press.

Denny, M. (1980). *Comparative psychology: An evolutionary analysis of animal behavior*. New York: Wiley.

Stanley, S. (1981). *The new evolutionary timetable*. New York: Basic Books.

DARWIN'S THEORY OF EMOTIONS.

Charles Darwin speculated that in prehistoric times - before communication that used words was common - one's ability to communicate with facial expressions increased an individual's chances of survival. Facial expressions could convey the various important messages of threat, submission, happiness, anger, and so on. *Darwin's theory of emotions* holds that the basic emotions demonstrated by facial expressions are a universal language among all humans no matter what their cultural setting. Today, however, it is an accepted belief that although cultures share a universal facial language, they differ in how, and how much, they express emotion. For example, as found in experimental studies, Americans grimace when viewing a film of someone's hand being cut off, whereas Japanese viewers tend to hide their emotions, especially in the presence of others. See also EKMAN-FRIESEN THEORY OF EMOTIONS; EMOTIONS, THEORIES/LAWS OF; FACIAL-FEEDBACK HYPOTHESIS; IZARD'S THEORY OF EMOTIONS.

REFERENCES

Darwin, C. (1872/1965). *The expression of the emotions in man and animals*. London: Appleton; Chicago: University of Chicago Press.

Markus, H., & Kitayama, S. (1991). Culture and the self: Implications for cognition, emotion, and motivation. *Psychological Review, 98,* 224-253.

Ekman, P. (1993). Facial expressions and emotion. *American Psychologist, 48,* 384-392.

DARWIN'S THEORY OF LAUGHTER/ HUMOR.

The English naturalist Charles Darwin (1809-1882) regarded laughter, generally, to be the expression of mere joy or happiness, but his theoretical account of the behavior states that the most common cause of laughter is experiencing something *incongruous* or unaccountable that excites *surprise* and a sense of *superiority* in the laugher. Darwin asserted that one may not understand why the sounds expressive of pleasure take the particular reiterated form of laughter, but it may readily be assumed that they should be as different as possible from the screams that express fear or distress. In Darwin's view, the physiological expression of distress takes the form of cries in which the body's expirations are continuous and prolonged (and the inspirations are short and interrupted), whereas pleasure is expressed by sound production in which short and broken expirations, together with prolonged inspirations, are observed. Concerning the specific physical features and shape of the mouth in laughter, Darwin notes that it must not be opened to its utmost extent and the retractions of the corners of the mouth are due to the necessity for a large orifice through which an adequate amount of sound may be issued; thus, because the mouth cannot be opened sufficiently in the vertical plane, the retraction of the corners of the mouth occurs. According to *Darwin's theory of laughter*, a physical/physiological continuum exists in laughter ranging from the most excessive laughter, through moderate laughter, to the broad smile, and finally to the faintest smile, where all these series of movements are expressions of pleasure to differing degrees. Darwin observes that the smile is the first stage in the development of the laugh, and suggests the following origins: the loud reiterated sounds of a certain type are the original expression of pleasure in which the utterance of these sound involves the retraction of the corners of the mouth; this smile reaction may, thus, have become a conditioned expression of pleasure when this was not sufficient to excite the more violent reaction of laughter. In the animal realm, on the phylogenetic scale, vocal laughter-like sounds are used either as a call or a signal by one sex for the other; and they may be employed, also, as the means for a joyful meeting between parents and their offspring or between the affiliated members of the same social unit. Darwin's "instinct-physiological" theory of humor assumes that the reaction of laughter is universal and widespread throughout the world as an expression of satisfaction, although other expressions of this same feeling exist as well. Darwin maintains, also, that laughter may be used in a forced way to conceal other emotions such as derision, contempt, shyness, shame, or anger (e.g., in derision, a real or feigned smile or laugh is blended with an expression of contempt whose function is to show the offending person that he or she evokes only amusement). Thus, *Darwin's theory of laughter/humor* contains several elements, including incongruity, superiority, physical/physiological features, instinctive behavior, and emotional or psychological behavior. See also DESCARTES' THEORY OF HUMOR/ LAUGHTER; HUMOR, THEORIES OF; MCDOUGALL'S THEORY OF HUMOR.

REFERENCE

Darwin, C. (1872/1965). *The expression of the emotions in man and animals.* London: Murray.

DEATH/DYING. See LIFE, THEORIES OF.

DECAY THEORY OF MEMORY. See FORGETTING/MEMORY, THEORIES OF.

DECISION-MAKING THEORIES. = rational choice theory. Decision-making research, generally regarded as a subarea within the field of *cognitive psychology*, investigates the issue of how organisms make *choices* between alternatives where the major focus is on human decision-making. *Decision theories* and *choice behavior theories* seek to explain decision-making and vary from the highly formal mathematical approaches based on *game theory* [i.e., the decision-making process that takes account of the actions, and options for action, of another individual whose deci-

sions are in conflict with one's own; variations on the basic theory have been directed at studies of interpersonal interactions, economics, labor-management negotiations/disputes, and international diplomacy, and involves terms such as *maximin* - a game strategy that insures the best of the worst possible payoffs, thereby maximizing the minimum possible payoff; *minimax* - a game strategy that minimizes the maximum payoff to a co-player; *zero-sum game* - a two-person game, or competitive game, containing a scenario in which the sum of the players' payoffs is equal to zero in every outcome of the game; *minimax theorem/principle* - a basic game theory result which posits that every finite, competitive game has an "equilibrium point" or "Nash equilibrium," whereby a "best reply" strategy gives the player choosing it at least as good a payoff as any other strategy; and *mixed strategy* - for each of two players, the game-theoretic solution is a randomized 50-50 mixed strategy in a two-alternative situation that assigns equal probabilities to each alternative); *probability theory* (i.e., the discipline within mathematics that deals with probability and forms the basis for all the statistical techniques of psychology where, given a relatively small number of observations in an experimental setting, one needs to make decisions about the likelihood of such observations in the long run); *classical strength theory* (cf., Neimark & Estes, 1967); and *utility theory* (i.e., utility is taken as the value to an individual of arriving at a particular decision, playing a game according to a particular strategy, or making a particular choice, such as reflected in *subjective expected utility* situations where the utility of any choice between alternatives is given by the sum of the person's *subjective probability estimates* of each alternative multiplied by the utility value of each one; and extending to the more informal or intuitive theories that deal with beliefs, attitudes, and other subjective factors]. In the *framing effect*, described by the Israeli psychologists Amos Tversky (1937-1996) and Daniel Kahneman (1934-), examination is made of the influence of the description, labeling, or framing/presentation of problems on decision-makers' responses; in *prospect theory*, as an alternative to *expected utility theory*, Tversky and Kahneman examine a *theory of preferences* among outcomes involving *risks*; according to *prospect theory*, people tend to evaluate outcomes as gains or losses relative to their current situation or the status quo rather than in terms of absolute value, and they tend to overweight very small probabilities and underweight moderate and high probabilities; also, they tend to attach greater weight to losses than to corresponding gains, and they tend to show "risk aversion" for gains by "risk seeking" for losses. In the *endowment effect*, people show the tendency to demand much more in order to give up an object than they are willing to pay to acquire it. Tversky and Kahneman also describe the *conjunction fallacy/effect* - as pervasive error in decisions and judgments whereby a combination of two or more attributes is judged to be more probable than either attribute when taken alone. In *psychological decision theory*, which is a normative and descriptive approach to decisions and judgments, the work of Tversky and Kahneman is complemented by the research of the American psychologists Sarah C. Lichtenstein (1933-), Baruch Fischhoff (1946-), and the American-based Israeli psychologist Paul Slovic (1938-); the latter two researchers define the *overconfidence effect* as an unwarranted belief in the correctness of one's judgments or beliefs, and is assessed via confidence ratings indicating one's own estimates of the probability of being correct on testing materials; and the *preference reversal effect*, which is the tendency, when facing a choice between gambles of nearly equal expected values, to prefer one gamble but to place a higher monetary value on the other; such reversals occur when one gamble offers a high probability of winning a small prize and the other offers a low probability of winning a large prize. The American psychologist Clyde Hamilton Coombs (1912-1988) formulated *portfolio theory* that is a conjecture of decision-making under *risk* based on the "unfolding technique" (i.e., a method of scaling a set of stimuli without relying on any presupposed scale of measurement). The *rational decision-making* viewpoint assumes that people calculate the costs and benefits of various actions and choose the best alternative in a fairly logical and reasoned way [cf*., the bounded ra-*

tionality principle, described by the American economist/decision theorist Herbert A. Simon (1916-2001), and refers to the human cognitive capacities and decision processes that are *not* strictly rational in nature and are *not* guaranteed to produce optimal results; and the *sure-thing principle*, first described by the American decision theorist Leonard J. Savage (1917-1971), and refers to a situation in which an alternative X is judged to be as good as another alternative Y in all possible states of the world, and better than Y in at least one, then a rational decision-maker will prefer X to Y]. Rational or normative/prescriptive decision-makers choose the alternative that gives them the greatest benefit at the least cost. Typical of this approach is the *behavioral decision theory* or the *expectancy-value theory* (cf., W. D. Edwards, 1954) which argues that decisions are made on the basis of the product of two factors: the value of the various possible outcomes of the decision and the probability or likelihood that each outcome will actually result from the decision (cf., *concordance decision-making method* - this approach consists of three features: *inclusion* in which the decision is made by people who know the most about it in order to guarantee quality, and those who are most affected by it in order to guarantee proper implementation; *control* where everyone has equal power and everyone has a veto vote; and *openness* where everyone is open and honest to each other and to themselves). Theories of decision-making in the area of political psychology include *conflict theory* that emphasizes the emotion-laden decisional conflicts, the various patterns of coping behavior common in such conflicts, the antecedents of coping patterns, and the various consequences for decisional rationality. Group decision-making may sometimes lead to the phenomenon called *groupthink*, first introduced by the American psychologist Irving L. Janis (1918-1990), which is an impairment in decision-making and sound judgment that may occur in highly cohesive groups with a strong, dynamic leader, and where group members isolate themselves from outside information, try to please the group leader, and agree on a decision even if it is irrational (cf., *Delphi method/technique*, named after the ancient Greek Delphic oracles who prophesized the future, is an approach developed in modern times by the Rand Corporation, and is employed in evaluation research for group decision-making where experts individually are presented with as much information as possible about a target issue; subsequently, the experts' recommendations are collected by a group facilitator who discloses them and attempts to achieve a group consensus concerning what is likely to occur in the future regarding the target issue). In the area of consumer purchasing behavior, and in regards to potentially irrational decisions, the *iceberg principle*, formulated by the Austrian-American motivational researcher and applied psychologist Ernest Dichter (1907-1992), refers to the notion that people - in purchasing merchandise - make some of their decisions based on *unconscious* goals and motives; the metaphor of the iceberg here is reminiscent of the Freudian dynamics regarding the presumed relationship between a person's conscious (rational) and unconscious (irrational) domains where a majority of the iceberg's mass is below the water line/surface (i.e., is mostly unconscious). Another group decision-making phenomenon is called the *risky-shift* or *choice-shift effect*, which reflects a more general process of "group polarization," and is defined as situations where people are more willing to support riskier decisions after taking part in a group discussion than they were before the discussion. *Risky-shift* may lead either to riskier or to more cautious decisions, depending on the initial views of group members. The *risky-shift effect* has been explained by the *social comparison effect* which is a cultural tendency for individuals to consider themselves at least as willing to take risks as their peers; and the *persuasive argumentation effect* which is a tendency in people to admire riskiness rather than caution, causing group members to be more willing to advance pro-risk than pro-caution persuasive arguments during group discussions [cf., *risk aversion effect* - a pervasive characteristic of human preferences, first noted by the Swiss mathematician/physicist Daniel Bernoulli (1700-1782) in 1738, whereby most people tend to value gains involving risk less than they do certain gains of equivalent monetary expectation; the corollary *risk seeking effect* - a ten-

dency among human decision-makers to prefer "risk-involvement losses" over "sure-thing losses" of equivalent monetary expectation; the *winner's curse effect* - a tendency for the highest bid at an auction to exceed the real or true market value of the auctioned object or prize, and is due, theoretically, to *risk aversion* among bidders where the *average* bid is usually less than the value of the auctioned object, but the *winning* bid usually exceeds the value of the object and illustrates the "winner's curse" such that "the winner is actually a loser;" and *covariation theory* - posits that when people attempt to determine the point or location of causality for a behavior, they seek to acquire information about the factors of consistency, distinctiveness, and consensus (cf., *Kelley's covariation theory*)]. In personal decision-making situations, the process frequently arouses *postdecision dissonance* or *cognitive dissonance*, which is the theoretical approach that assumes people have a drive toward consistency in their attitudes, beliefs, and decisions (cf., *hindsight bias effect* - the tendency for people, who know that a specific event has occurred, to overestimate, in hindsight, the probability with which they would have predicted the event in foresight). According to the *cognitive dissonance* approach, whenever one must decide between two or more alternatives, the final choice is, to some extent, inconsistent with some of the decision-maker's beliefs. That is, after the decision is made, all the *good* aspects of the *unchosen* alternative and all the *bad* aspects of the *chosen* alternative are dissonant with the person's decision. Theoretically, dissonance may be reduced by improving one's evaluation of the chosen alternative, because everything positive about it is consonant with the decision; dissonance may be reduced, also, by lowering the evaluation of the unchosen alternative, so that the less attractive it is, the less dissonance is aroused by rejecting it. Therefore, after people make decisions, there is a tendency for them to *increase* their liking for what they *chose* and to *decrease* their liking for that they did *not* choose. See also CONFLICT, THEORIES OF; EXPECTED UTILITY THEORY; FESTINGER'S COGNITIVE DISSONANCE THEORY; HAWK-DOVE/CHICKEN GAME EFFECTS; KELLEY'S CO-

VARIATION THEORY; ORGANIZATION-
AL, INDUSTRIAL, AND SYSTEMS THE-
ORY; PASCAL'S PROPOSITION/WAGER;
PROBABILITY THEORY AND LAWS;
THURSTONE'S LAW OF COMPARATIVE
JUDGMENT; UTILITY THEORY.

REFERENCES

Knight, R. H. (1921). *Risk, uncertainty, and profit*. Boston: Houghton Mifflin.

Cartwright, D., & Festinger, L. (1943). A quantitative theory of decision. *Psychological Review, 50*, 595-621.

Neumann, J. von & Morgenstern, O. (1947). *Theory of games and economic behavior*. Princeton, NJ: Princeton University Press.

Edwards, W. D. (1954). The theory of decision-making. *Psychological Bulletin, 51*, 380-417.

Festinger, L. (1957). *A theory of cognitive dissonance*. Evanston, IL: Row, Peterson.

Luce, R. (1959). *Individual choice behavior: A theoretical analysis*. New York: Wiley.

Luce, R., & Suppes, P. (1965). Preference, utility, and subjective probability. In R. Luce, R. Bush, & E. Galanter (Eds.), *Handbook of mathematical psychology*. Vol. 3. New York: Wiley.

Neimark, E., & Estes, W. (1967). *Stimulus sampling theory*. San Francisco: Holden-Day.

Simon, H. A. (1967). Motivational and emotional controls of cognition. *Psychological Review, 74*, 29-39.

Tversky, A. (1967). Utility theory and additivity analysis of risky choices. *Journal of Experimental Psychology, 75*, 27-36.

Lichtenstein, S., & Slovic, P. (1971). Reversals of preference between bids and choices in gambling decisions. *Journal of Experimental Psychology, 89*, 46-55.

Tversky, A., & Kahneman, D. (1974). Judgments under uncertainty: Heuristics and biases. *Science, 185*, 1124-1131.

Coombs, C. H. (1975). Portfolio theory and the measurement of risk. In M. F. Kaplan & S. Schwartz (Eds.), *Human judgment and decision processes*. New York: Academic Press.

Slovic, P., Fischhoff, B., & Lichtenstein, S. (1977). Behavioral decision theory. *Annual Review of Psychology, 28*, 1-39.

Feather, N. T. (1982). *Expectations and actions: Expectancy-value models in psychology*. Hillsdale, NJ: Erlbaum.

Janis, I. (1982). *Groupthink: Psychological studies of policy decisions and fiascoes*. Boston: Houghton Mifflin.

Isenberg, D. (1986). Group polarization: A critical review and meta-analysis. *Journal of Personality and Social Psychology, 50*, 1141-1151.

Cooper, W. S. (1987). Decision theory as a branch of evolutionary theory: A biological derivation of the Savage axiom. *Psychological Review, 94*, 395-411.

DECISION TREES. See CONCEPT LEARNING AND CONCEPT FORMATION, THEORIES OF.

DECLARATIVE MEMORY. See SHORT-TERM AND LONG-TERM MEMORY, THEORIES OF.

DECLINE EFFECT. See PARANORMAL PHENOMENA/THEORY.

DEFECT AND DEVELOPMENTAL THEORISTS. See DEVELOPMENTAL THEORY.

DEFENSE MECHANISMS. See CONSTANCY, PRINCIPLE OF; FREUD'S THEORY OF PERSONALITY.

DEFENSIVE TECHNIQUES THEORY. See GOOD BREAST/OBJECT AND BAD BREAST/OBJECT THEORY.

DEFINITIONAL THEORY. See CONCEPT LEARNING AND CONCEPT FORMATION, THEORIES OF; PROTOTYPE THEORY.

DEGENERACY THEORY. See SEXUAL ORIENTATION THEORIES.

DEGENERACY THEORY OF GENIUS. See LOMBROSIAN THEORY.

DEGRADATION, LAW OF. See WEBER'S LAW.

DEGREES OF CONSCIOUSNESS THEORY. See HERBART'S DOCTRINE OF APPERCEPTION.

DEINDIVIDUATION THEORY. The term *deindividuation* refers to the loss of one's sense of individuality during which the person behaves with little or no reference to personal internal values or standards of conduct. Deindividuated states are characterized as pleasurable wherein the person feels free to act on impulse and without regard to consequences. However, they can also be extremely dangerous in that they can result in violent and antisocial behavior. In the late 1800s, the French sociologist Gustave LeBon (1841-1931) postulated the phenomenon of a *group mind* and asserted that people in a crowd may lose their sense of personal responsibility and behave as if governed by a primitive, irrational, and hedonistic mind that seems to belong more to the group as a whole than to any one individual [cf., *shared autism theory* - holds that members of groups may have shared beliefs ("delusions") that have no foundation or validity in reality]. Thus, the state of *deindividuation* seems to be brought on by a combination of "reduced accountability" that comes from being a relatively anonymous member of a crowd and "shifting attention" away from the self and toward the highly arousing external stimulation associated with the mob's actions. Various theoretical approaches have been developed concerning the phenomenon of *deindividuation*. Festinger, Pepitone, and Newcomb (1952) suggest that the person's focus on the group (which is associated with their attraction to the group) lessens the attention given to individuals. Thus, the members of the group are *deindividuated* by their submergence and moral subordination to the group. Therefore, according to this view, *deindividuation* lowers the person's inhibi-

tions toward exercising counternormative actions. In another viewpoint, R. C. Ziller argues that persons learn to associate individuation with rewarding conditions and deindividuation with potentially punishing conditions. Thus, whenever the person expects punishment, there will be tendency to diffuse responsibility by submerging oneself into a group, whereas when one learns to expect rewards for jobs well done, she or he wants to appear uniquely and solely responsible for such behaviors. P. G. Zimbardo's *deindividuation theory* postulates that the expression of normally inhibited behavior may include creative and loving behavior as well as negative or counternormative behaviors. Zimbardo proposes that a number of factors may lead to *deindividuation*, in addition to focus on the group and avoidance of negative evaluation of moral responsibility: anonymity, group size, level of emotional arousal, altered time perspectives, novelty/ambiguity of the situation, and degree of involvement in group functioning. Such factors lead to a loss of identity or a loss of self-consciousness which, in turn, causes the person to become unresponsive to external stimuli and to lose cognitive control over motivations and emotions. Consequently, the *deindividuated* person becomes less compliant to positive or negative sanctions imposed from influences outside the group. E. Diener's theoretical approach emphasizes the association of *deindividuation* with *self-awareness*: deindividuated persons do not attend to their own behavior, and lack awareness of themselves as entities distinct from the group. With such little awareness of self, the individual is more likely to respond to immediate stimuli, motives, and emotions. According to Diener, the term *deindividuation* is a construct referring to a set of circumstances or relationships among emotional states, cognitive processes, situations, and behavioral reactions. In such circumstances, various antinormative behaviors - such as drug abuse, riots, lynchings, mob violence, and even reactions involving loss of inhibition in marathon, encounter, and other noncognitive therapy groups - are associated with a state of *deindividuation*. See also ALLPORT'S CONFORMITY HYPOTHESIS; ASCH CONFORMITY EFFECT; BYSTANDER INTER-

VENTION EFFECT; DECISION-MAKING THEORIES; SELF-CONCEPT THEORY; SOCIAL IMPACT, LAW OF.

REFERENCES

LeBon, G. (1896). *The crowd: A study of the popular mind.* London: E. Benn.

Festinger, L., Pepitone, A., & Newcomb, T. (1952). Some consequences of deindividuation in a group. *Journal of Abnormal and Social Psychology, 47,* 382-389.

Ziller, R. C. (1964). Individuation and socialization. *Human Relations, 17,* 341-360.

Singer, J., Brush, C., & Lublin, S. (1965). Some aspects of deindividuation and conformity. *Journal of Experimental Social Psychology, 1,* 356-378.

Zimbardo, P. G. (1970). The human choice: Individuation, reason, and order versus deindividuation, impulse, and chaos. In W. Arnold & D. Levine (Eds.), *Nebraska Symposium on Motivation.* Lincoln: University of Nebraska Press.

Diener, E. (1980). Deindividuation: The absence of self-awareness and self-regulation in group members. In P. Paulus (Ed.), *The psychology of group influence.* Hillsdale, NJ: Erlbaum.

DE JONG'S LAW. See TOTAL TIME HYPOTHESIS/LAW.

DELAY OF GRATIFICATION HYPOTHESIS. This hypothesis states that individuals may renounce, or choose to delay, immediate satisfaction or reward in order to obtain a larger reward or gratification on some future occasion. For example, a child may choose to delay her present response that would be instrumental in achieving a small toy now in favor of obtaining a larger toy that is promised to her for responding at a later time; also, an adult may choose to invest his money now and reap a larger benefit later, instead of spending the money immediately. See also MOTIVATION, THEORIES OF; REINFORCEMENT THEORY.

REFERENCE

Ross, M., Karniol, R., & Rothstein, M. (1976). Reward contingency and intrinsic motivation in children: A test of the delay of gratification hypothesis. *Journal of Personality and Social Psychology, 33,* 442-447.

DELAYED AUDITORY FEEDBACK EFFECT. See APPENDIX A; AUDITION AND HEARING, THEORES OF.

DELAYED-REACTION MODEL/PARADIGM. The *delayed-reaction model/paradigm* was introduced into experimental psychology by the American psychologist Walter S. Hunter (1889-1953) in 1913. In this approach, a human or infrahuman organism is presented with a limited number of behavior choices, such as three open compartments in one of which a reward (such as food) is placed. The organism is trained to find food in the one compartment that is lighted; after a pretest training period, the light is turned off, and the organism's choice is delayed forcibly for a number of seconds. The goal of the *delayed-reaction/response procedure* is to find out how *long* the animal or human can delay its behavioral reaction without forgetting where the light had been turned on. In other similar studies, Hunter used more "direct" methods where, for instance, immediate sight of food being placed into the compartment is substituted for the "indirect" method involving a light signal. This modified procedure apparently places less strain on the organism's symbolic processing capacities and indicates that much longer delays are obtainable with the "direct" than the "indirect" methods. The *delayed-reaction paradigm* is to be distinguished from the so-called "delayed-reward" procedure: in the former, the response is delayed but the reward immediately follows the appropriate response; in the latter (e.g., Wolfe, 1934), the correct response may be made promptly but time elapses before the reward is delivered. Other historical psychological paradigms and models in the experimental study of animal and human learning processes include the following: *habituation/negative adaptation* (i.e., learning *not* to respond to a repeated stimulus); *habit reversal/reversal* *learning* (i.e., learning situations in which an organism choosing repeatedly between two alternatives, X and Y, is initially rewarded for choosing X rather than Y until a preference for X is established, and then reversing by rewarding it for choosing Y rather than X until its preference for Y is established, etc.; in such a reversal paradigm, there is a species difference where birds and mammals show progressive improvement in switching from X to Y and back again, but fishes show little or no improvement); *non-reversal shift* (i.e., a form of serial learning in which the set of task stimuli is changed, but the rewarded and non-rewarded items are not merely interchanged; for example, the organism is trained to choose the red rather than the black objects, irrespective of their shapes, and are then presented with stimulus sets in which the reward is associated with the round rather than the square objects, irrespective of their colors; in this model, also called *transposition*, the organism demonstrates "insight" or its ability of "learning how to learn;" Spence, 1937; Harlow, 1949); *classical conditioning* (i.e., organisms' responses that are established originally by natural selection come under the control of novel stimuli; Pavlov, 1927); *instrumental* or *operant conditioning* (i.e., responses of an organism that produce reinforcing effects; Skinner, 1938); *puzzle/problem boxes* (i.e., discovery of an appropriate movement to lead to release from confinement or to resolve a problematic situation; Thorndike, 1911); *discrimination box/apparatus* (i.e., testing discriminatory capacities of organisms; Spence, 1937); *probability learning/matching* (a type of discrimination learning in which the positive stimulus is rewarded on a randomized proportion of trials; Humphreys, 1939); *alley* and *temporal mazes* (i.e., an obstacle - that is interposed between the organism and the desired goal - must be traversed; Tolman, 1932); *T-maze/labyrinth maze* (i.e., a simple two-choice T-shaped maze, or a more complex network of passages and blind alleys in a maze, used originally to study the "mental processes" of the rat; the laboratory labyrinth maze is often constructed to be an exact replica in miniature of the famous large-size maze for humans at Hampton Court in England; Small, 1900/1901); *detour/insight prob-*

lems (i.e., use of an indirect or circumventing path, or use of manipulable objects, to arrive at the solution of the organism's experimental problem; Kohler, 1925); *reasoning problems* (i.e., the organism is required to combine given segments/elements in novel ways to solve a problem; Kohler, 1925); *social learning paradigm* (i.e., study of the influence of one learner upon another observing individual, and may include copying or imitating responses, as well as competitive, cooperative, dominant, or submissive behaviors; Bandura, 1971). See also HABITUATION, PRINCIPLE/LAW OF; LEARNING THEORIES AND LAWS; OBJECT PERMANENCE PARADIGM/MODEL; PAVLOVIAN CONDITIONING PRINCIPLES, LAWS, AND THEORIES; TRANSPOSITION, THEORY OF; WORKING MEMORY, THEORY OF.

REFERENCES

Small, W. S. (1900/1901). An experimental study of the mental processes of the rat. I. and II. *American Journal of Psychology, 11*, 133-165; *12*, 206-239

Thorndike, E. L. (1911). *Animal intelligence.* New York: Macmillan.

Hunter, W. S. (1913). The delayed reaction in animals and children. *Behavior Monographs, 2*, No. 6.

Kohler, W. (1925). *The mentality of apes.* New York: Harcourt, Brace & World.

Pavlov, I. (1927). *Conditioned reflexes.* London: Clarendon Press.

Tolman, E. C. (1932). *Purposive behavior in animals and men.* New York: Appleton-Century-Crofts.

Wolfe, J. B. (1934). The effect of delayed reward upon learning in the white rat. *Journal of Comparative Psychology, 17*, 1-21.

Spence, K. W. (1937). The differential response in animals to stimuli varying within a single dimension. *Psychological Review, 44*, 430-444.

Skinner, B. F. (1938). *The behavior of organisms: An experimental analysis.* Englewood Cliffs, NJ: Prentice-Hall.

Humphreys, L. G. (1939). The effect of random alternation of reinforcement on the acquisition and extinction of conditioned eyelid responses. *Journal of Experimental Psychology, 25,* 141-158.

Harlow, H. F. (1949). The formation of learning sets. *Psychological Review, 56,* 51-65.

Bandura, A. (1971). *Social learning theory.* New York: General Learning Press.

DELBOEUF/UZNADZE ILLUSIONS. See APPENDIX A.

DELPHI METHOD/TECHNIQUE. See DECISION-MAKING THEORIES.

DELTA MOVEMENT EFFECT. See APPARENT MOVEMENT, PRINCIPLES AND THEORIES OF.

DEMAND CHARACTERISTICS OF THE SITUATION. See EXPERIMENTER EFFECTS.

DEMBER-EARL THEORY OF CHOICE/ PREFERENCE. = complexity discrepancy theory = theory of stimulus complexity. The American psychologists William N. Dember (1928-) and R. W. Earl formulated a *theory of choice* and *preference* that concerns the influence of stimulus complexity on organisms' behaviors. The theory holds that every stimulus object has a certain *complexity value* that is, also, its *information value.* One assumption behind the *theory of choice and preference* is that every individual (both human and nonhuman) has its own "ideal level" of complexity, that is, the level of stimulation for which it has a preference. Individuals seek out objects containing their ideal level of complexity, will choose them from among other objects, will work for them, and will learn what needs to be done in order to obtain them. Additionally, individuals will explore objects of a somewhat higher complexity level called "pacer stimuli." As organisms master the new level of complexity of the pacer stimuli, their own ideal level rises, and they are now ready to deal with new pacers and, again, raise their own ideal level. Thus, according to the *Dember-Earl theory of choice,* the need for stimulus variability in an individual's ex-

perience provides a basis and reinforcement for increasingly complicated kinds of learning. The results of several experiments confirm the predicted relation between complexity and preference in accordance with the *theory of choice and preference,* and attest to its generality over a wide range of stimulus materials and types of participants. For an account of *choice behavior* in a "foraging" and operant conditioning context, see Fantino and Abarca (1985); and for accounts of the *preference reversal phenomenon* (i.e., the effect in a gambling situation where people who choose gamble A over gamble B often ask for *less* money to sell A than B) and the *expression theory* (i.e., a postulate which assumes that the basic evaluation of a gamble is expressed on various scales via a subjective interpolation process), see Goldstein & Einhorn (1987). See also CHOICE THEORIES; DECISION-MAKING THEORIES; EXEMPLAR THEORY OF BEHAVIORAL CHOICE; PERCEPTION (I. GENERAL), THEORIES OF.

REFERENCES

Dember, W. N. (1956). Response by the rat to environmental change. *Journal of Comparative and Physiological Psychology, 49,* 93-95.

Dember, W. N., & Earl, R. W. (1957). Analysis of exploratory, manipulatory, and curiosity behaviors. *Psychological Review, 64,* 91-96.

Dember, W. N., Earl, R. W., & Paradise, N. (1957). Response by rats to differential stimulus complexity. *Journal of Comparative and Physiological Psychology, 50,* 514-518.

Hoben, T. (1971). Discrepancy hypotheses: Methodological and theoretical considerations. *Psychological Review, 78,* 249-259.

Coombs, C., & Avrunin, G. (1977). Single-peaked functions and the theory of preference. *Psychological Review, 84,* 216-230.

Fantino, E., & Abarca, N. (1985). Choice, optimal foraging, and the delay-reduction hypothesis. *Behavioral and Brain Sciences, 8,* 315-330.

Goldstein, W. M., & Einhorn, H. J. (1987). Expression theory and the preference reversal phenomenon. *Psychological Review, 94,* 236-254.

DEMING MANAGEMENT THEORY. See ORGANIZATIONAL, INDUSTRIAL, AND SYSTEMS THEORY.

DEMORALIZATION HYPOTHESIS. See DODO HYPOTHESIS.

DENERVATION, LAW OF. This principle, formulated by the American physiologist Walter Bradford Cannon (1871-1945) and the Mexican physiologist Arturo Rosenblueth (1900-1970), states that the *denervation* (i.e., the removal of the nerve supply to an organ or other tissue, where removal is either actual or "functional") results in a progressive sensitization of sites higher in the nervous system. The *law of denervation* has been cited in the contexts of sensory deprivation (SD) and perceptual deprivation (PD) experiments where the latter employ research formats and methods that lead to a "functional" form of denervation. A potential explanation for SD and PD is that they may sensitize the individual's sensory system and act to lower thresholds for subsequently presented stimuli (as well as resulting in the attribution of activity within higher sites) to an external stimulus affecting the unstimulated receptor. Also, the *phantom limb phenomenon*, occasionally observed in amputees, may be accounted for by neurophysiological theories that invoke the *law of denervation.* See also HABITUATION, PRINCIPLE/LAW OF; PHANTOM LIMB PHENOMENON.

REFERENCES

Cannon, W. B., & Rosenblueth, A. (1949). *The supersensitivity of denervated structures.* New York: Macmillan.

Zubek, J. (Ed.) (1969). *Sensory deprivation: Fifteen years of research.* New York: Appleton-Century-Crofts.

DEPRESSION, THEORIES OF. In general, *depression* is a mood state characterized by a sense of inadequacy, feelings of despondency, sadness, pessimism, and decrease in activity or reactivity. Depressive disorders involve a spectrum of psychological dysfunctions that vary in frequency, duration, and severity. At one end of the continuum is the experience of normal depression (a transient period, usually lasting no longer than two weeks), consisting of fatigue and sadness, and precipitated by identifiable stressors. At the other end of the spectrum is the longer-lasting period of depressed mood approaching clinical depressive disorders, which is accompanied by difficulties in sleeping, onset of eating problems, and growing thoughts of despair and hopelessness. In *psychotic depression,* the individual suffers deep despair and sadness and may lose contact with reality and develop delusions, hallucinations, and severe motor and psychological retardation. In this sense, depression may be a symptom of some other psychological disorder, a part or syndrome of related symptoms that appears as secondary to another disorder, or a specific disorder itself. A major difficulty in studying depression is that the term is often used indiscriminately for an entire spectrum of experiences where it has come to describe a mood, a symptom, and a syndrome. The theory and terminology of depression includes *dualistic* systems where the concepts of "reactive versus autonomous," "neurotic versus psychotic," "primary versus secondary," "exogenous versus endogenous," "unipolar versus bipolar," and "justified versus somatic" depression have been used. *Pluralistic* systems of depression classification describe many types of disorders. For example, Grinker, Miller, Sabshin, Nunn, and Nunnally (1961) propose four patterns of depression based on a factor analysis of moods, behaviors, and treatment responses: empty-, angry-, anxious-, and hypochondriacal-depression. Other *pluralistic* classification systems of depression are provided in the American Psychiatric Association's *Diagnostic and Statistical Manual* (2000), which lists more than a dozen different kinds of depressive disorders, including various depressive personality types, as well as schizoaffective and psychotic depressive disorders. Concerning the diagnosis of *depression,* the American psychiatrist Aaron Temkin Beck (1921-) designed the Beck Depression Inventory (BDI), which is based on observations of attitudes and symptoms characteristic of depressed patients. The BDI contains 21 categories of symptoms and attitudes, such as sense of failure, dissatisfaction, guilt, sense of punishment, self-accusations, and sleep disturbance. The various *theories of depression* may be grouped, generally, into *biological* or *psychological* types. The *biological theories* include the *genetic theories*, in which it is assumed that genetic factors interact with environmental factors and where heredity influences emotional lability, cellular functioning, basic arousal levels, stimulus threshold levels, and other physiological substrates of behavior; and the *biochemical theories*, which are further subdivided into *biogenic amine* (neurotransmitters) *theories*, including *catecholamine, indoleamine*, and *permissive amine hypotheses*; the *electrolyte metabolism theories*, which focus on sodium and potassium in the brain; and the *pituitaryadrenal axis theories*, which argue that the primary problem in depression disorders rests in the hypothalamic-pituitary-adrenal axis. The *psychobehavioral theories* may be subdivided into the *reconposre theory*, where the term *reconposre* stands for "response contingent positive reinforcement" and which argues that depression develops when individuals receive inadequate amounts of positive reinforcement in their lives; the *learned helplessness theory*, which proposes that when humans or animals are trapped in situations in which they cannot avoid threat or harm, and where uncontrollable aversive events produce an expectancy that one cannot control stressors, they develop a sense of helplessness, resignation, or hopelessness and act "depressed;" the *cognitive theories/models* (cf., the *cognitive vulnerability hypothesis* - states that negative cognitive styles confer vulnerability to depression when people confront negative life events), which emphasize the role of one's faulty thought processes, including factors such as logic errors, selective abstraction, arbitrary inferences, overgeneralizations, excessive magnification, and dichotomous/distorted thinking; and *psychoanalytic theory*, which argues that depression results from the loss of an ambivalently loved person or loss of a "love object," which leads to a self-directed hostility and constitutes the depressive experience; this approach suggests that the self-punishment that accompanies depression may actually be an unconscious effort to regain maternal love and support, or that in cases of traumatic experiences in childhood, there is resultant faulty ego and libido development with fixation at an earlier stage of insecurity and helplessness. The most current theories and perspectives of depression focus on the *interaction* of biological, psychological, and sociological levels of functioning. Such new approaches integrate the older theories and offer the promise of new insights into depression, its manifestations, diagnosis, and treatment. See also LEARNED HELPLESSNESS EFFECT/THEORY; PSYCHOPATHOLOGY, THEORIES OF.

REFERENCES

Grinker, R., Miller, J., Sabshin, M., Nunn, R., & Nunnally, J. (1961). *The phenomena of depressions*. New York: Hoeber.

Schildkraut, J. (1965). The catecholamine hypothesis of affective disorders: A review of supporting evidence. *American Journal of Psychiatry, 122*, 509-522.

Beck, A. T. (1967). *Depression: Clinical, experimental, and theoretical aspects*. New York: Harper & Row.

Masserman, J. H. (Ed.) (1970). *Depressions: Theories and therapies*. New York: Grune & Stratton.

Lewinsohn, P. (1974). A behavioral approach to depression. In R. Friedman & M. Katz (Eds.), *The psychology of depression*. Washington, D.C.: Winston.

Seligman, M. (1975). *Helplessness: On depression, development, and death*. San Francisco: Freeman.

Akiskal, H. (1979). A biobehavioral approach to depression. In R. Depue (Ed.), *The psychobiology of the depressive disorders*. New York: Academic Press.

Abramson, L. Y., Metalsky, G. I., & Alloy, L. B. (1989). Hopelessness depression: A theory-based subtype of depression. *Psychological Review, 96*, 358-372.

Segal, Z. V., & Dobson, K. S. (1992). Cognitive models of depression. *Psychological Inquiry, 3*, 219-224, 278-282.

American Psychiatric Association. (2000). *Diagnostic and statistical manual of mental disorders.* 4th Ed. Revised. Washington, D.C.: American Psychiatric Association.

DEPRESSION/NEGATIVE CONTRAST EFFECT. See CRESPI EFFECT.

DEPRESSIVE REALISM PHENOMENON/THEORY.

The American psychologists Lauren B. Alloy (1953-) and Lyn Y. Abramson (1950-) suggest the existence in individuals diagnosed with depression a reduction or absence of overconfidence and unrealistic optimism, with the result that such depressed people are more accurate (across situations and domains) in their processing of information related to themselves, as compared to nondepressed individuals who are typically positively biased regarding self-related information. Alloy and Abramson's *depressive realism theory* also has been labeled the "sadder but wiser" theory, where mental health is associated with overestimating personal control over successes (having an "illusion of control"), and where judging control accurately is associated with dysphoria (feelings of discomfort, sadness, anguish, or anxiety). See also DEPRESSION, THEORIES OF; OVERCONFIDENCE EFFECT.

REFERENCES
Alloy, L. B., & Abramson, L. Y. (1979). Judgment of contingency in depressed and nondepressed students: Sadder but wiser? *Journal of Experimental Psychology: General,* 108, 441-485.

Schwartz, B. (1981). Does helplessness cause depression, or do only depressed people become helpless? Comment on Alloy and Abramson. *Journal of Experimental Psychology: General,* 110, 429-435.

Cohen, D. M. (1998). The illusion of control revisited: A test of alternative explanations. *Dissertation Abstracts International,* 58 (11-B), 6230.

DER KLUGE HANS EFFECT. See CLEVER HANS EFFECT/PHENOMENON.

DERIVED PROPERTIES, POSTULATE OF. See GESTALT THEORY/LAWS.

DESCARTES' THEORY OF HUMOR/LAUGHTER.

The French mathematician and philosopher Rene Descartes (1596-1650) is regarded by many researchers to be the first writer to deal with laughter from the *physiological*, as well as from the *psychological*, point of view [however, other researchers attribute this honor to the French physician Laurent Joubert (1529-1582); cf., Roeckelein, 2002, p. 131]. *Descartes' theory of laughter* begins with a physiological account of what causes the audible explosion in laughter (the blood passes from the right cavity of the heart to the lungs, filling them, and drives out the air). According to Descartes, psychologically there are only six basic emotions (wonder, love, hatred, desire, joy, and sadness), and laughter is found to accompany three of them (wonder, mild hatred, and joy). Descartes asserted that derision is a kind of joy that is mixed both with surprise and hate, and when laughter is natural (and not feigned or artificial), it seems to be due partially to the joy derived from that which one recognizes as incapable of being injured by the malice that has excited an indignation, and partly to surprise at the novelty of that malice in such a manner that joy, hatred, and admiration are all contributory causes to the laughter. In his theoretical approach to humor, Descartes broke away from the literary tradition that had led all previous thinkers (following the classical writers) to deal with comedy as a literary form rather than with the wider issue of laughter, and although Descartes' account is inaccurate in *physiological* terms, it is nonetheless of interest because of the incidental *psychological* aspects contained in his theory. See also HUMOR, THEORIES OF; JOUBERT'S THEORY OF LAUGHTER AND HUMOR.

REFERENCES
Joubert, L. (1560/1579/1980). *Treatise on laughter.* Translated by G. D. de Rocher. University, AL: The University of Alabama Press.

Descartes, R. (1649/1909). *Les passions de l'ame.* Paris: Le Gras.

Roeckelein, J. E. (2002). *The psychology of humor*. Westport, CT: Greenwood Press.

DESCARTES' THEORY OF INNATE IDEAS/DESCARTES' THEORY. See CONDILLAC'S THEORY OF ATTENTION; LEARNING THEORIES/LAWS.

DETERMINING TENDENCY, PRINCIPLE OF. See ACH'S LAWS/PRINCIPLES/THEORY; WUNDT'S THEORIES, DOCTRINES, AND PRINCIPLES.

DETERMINISM, DOCTRINE/THEORY OF. The *doctrine of determinism* assumes that every event has causes, and is the theory or working principle according to which all phenomena are considered as necessary consequents of antecedent conditions (cf., *architectural determinism* - the notion that building design affects behavior, for instance, some building designs increase the possibility that people will congregate and meet with each other; *moral determinism* - the doctrine that the world is basically good because God made it so; and *moral nihilism* - the doctrine that there are no reasons for morals and that absolute pleasure at the expense of others is justified). The concept of *determinism* is central to science because it maintains that if one knew all the factors involved in a forthcoming event, it could be predicted exactly. *Determinism* implies a chain of events, each following the other, to produce a necessary conclusion where every thing and every event in the world (and the universe) is the result of natural laws that can be ascertained by the use of the scientific methods. A distinction is made often between *hard determinism* (or "nomological" laws, not allowing room for freedom of choice or indeterminism) and *soft determinism* (that is, attempts to reconcile determinism and free choice or indeterminism). For instance, concerning *hard determinism*, in *classical* mechanics in physics, it was assumed that if one knew the position and momentum of every particle of matter at one instant in time, then one could know its position and momentum at any other point in future time. This viewpoint, however, was "softened" somewhat with the development of *quantum* mechanics, where the levels of cause and effect are probabilistic in nature and which, consequently, shift the idea of perfect ("hard") prediction to probabilistic ("soft") prediction. In psychology, the issue of *determinism* generally revolves around the *humanist's* and *existentialist's* advocacy of "free will." However, if one wishes to study behavior and the mind in *scientific* terms, it must be assumed that there are deterministic and cause-effect relationships to take into serious consideration. Scientific psychology assumes a degree of *determinism* in behavior where three categories of determinants are studied, usually, as they interact to influence behavior: *biological* factors (includes heredity, bodily constitution, and physiological health and disease), *psychological* factors (includes emotions, drives, attitudes, learning experiences, and conscious and unconscious conflicts), and *social/cultural* factors (includes economic status, customs and mores, social status, and social conflicts). Deterministic relationships, or laws, are discovered in various ways. For example, the early Greek philosopher Aristotle (384-322 B.C.) first observed a phenomenon and then followed up by thinking about the event, classifying it, and putting it into a category so that predictions could be made (cf., *doctrine of ethical determinism* - a philosophical doctrine advanced by Socrates, but opposed by Aristotle, which suggests that humans will seek out automatically the good if they know that is "good"). Many methods of basic scientific inquiry are available, including observation, interpretation, conclusions, and hypotheses-testing, but they all depend on the fundamental notion of *deterministic causality* [cf., *psychical determinism doctrine* - the assumption made by psychologists that no psychological phenomena (including dreams, parapraxes, and symptoms; e.g., Freud, 1901) occur by chance, but they always have definite causes; on the other hand, Carl Jung (1953/1965) asserts that no psychological fact can ever be explained in terms of causality alone; and the *doctrine of particularism* - states that any human behavior needs to be understood in the context of that person's total history, including both heredity and environment]. The *doctrine of dialectical materialism* (i.e., the speculation that the ultimate reality is matter, which exists objectively and independently of mind or perception) developed by the German social theorist and philosopher Karl Marx (1818-1883), in the field of political science, is also in the *deterministic* tradition. Recent events in the field of physics, however, have modulated the scientific regnancy of *determinism*. In particular, it appears to be highly uncertain or impossible to determine, at the same time, the momentum of an electron particle as well as its position. The German theoretical physicist Werner Karl Heisenberg (1901-1976) came to this conclusion in 1927, which has come to be known today as *Heisenberg's principle of uncertainty* or the *Heisenberg indeterminacy principle*, and demonstrates that Newtonian physics does not apply at the level of analysis of atoms. In translating this principle to psychology, if one views an individual person as the equivalent of an atom, it is true that *determinacy* holds for the human species (which leads to *deterministic nomothetic laws*), but it is true, also, that indeterminacy holds for the human individual, whose "free will" behavior is only partially explainable in terms of antecedent events and, in which case, it makes it impossible to predict the individual's behavior at any given moment with complete accuracy (cf., Penrose, 1989, 1994). The *theory of indeterminism* means that one can act in relative independence of given stimuli and that the individual has freedom of choice or "free will." The laws of most societies, and the dogmas of many religions, are based on the ideas of individual responsibility and free will where the consequences of punishment, whether on earth or in heaven, are justified regarding a person's moral judgments and behavior. Psychologists appear to take a number of positions on the issue of *determinism* versus *indeterminism*, where rigid *behaviorists* tend to be strict *determinists*, and *humanistic existentialists* tend to be *indeterminists*, even though most psychologists seem to straddle the fence by asserting the necessity of *determinism* as part of scientific methodology, on one hand and, on the other hand, operating pragmatically day in and day out in terms of *indeterminism*. See also BEHAVIORIST THEORY; EXISTENTIAL ANALYSIS THEORY; FREUD'S THEORY OF PER-SONALITY; IDIOGRAPHIC AND NOMO-THETIC LAWS; MECHANISTIC THEORY; MIND/MENTAL STATES, THEORIES OF; NEURAL QUANTUM THEORY.

REFERENCES

Marx, K. (1867-1879). *Capital: A critique of political economy*. Chicago: Kerr.

Freud, S. (1901). The psychopathology of everyday life. In *The standard edition of the complete psychological works of Sigmund Freud*. London: Hogarth Press.

Hutchins, R. (Ed.) (1952). Aristotle's *Physics*. In *Great books of the Western world*. Vol. 8. Chicago: Encyclopedia Britannica.

Jung, C. G. (1953/1965). *The collected works of C. G. Jung*. Vol. 6. London: Routledge & Kegan Paul.

Heisenberg, W. (1958). *The physicist's conception of nature*. New York: Harcourt, Brace.

Penrose, R. (1989). *The emperor's new mind: concerning computers, minds, and the laws of physics*. New York: Oxford University Press.

Penrose, R. (1994). *Shadows of the mind: A search for the missing science of consciousness*. New York: Oxford University Press.

DEUTSCH'S CRUDE LAW OF SOCIAL RELATIONS/RESOLUTIONS. In research on conflict, the American social psychologist Morton Deutsch (1920-) and his colleagues found that a cooperative process leads to constructive conflict resolution whereas a competitive process leads to destructive conflict. Such findings have been useful to those concerned with the practical management of various types of personal and social conflict, including marital, labor-management, intergroup, and international relations. Deutsch's research on "mixed-motive" situations is generalized into *Deutsch's crude law of social relations and resolutions* which states that the typical effects of a given social situation tend to induce that social relation. In one case, this law was used to develop a framework for research on *distributive justice* which indicates that each distributive principle (e.g., equality or equity) has distinctive psychological orientations associated with it where, once induced, these also produce a preference for the related principle. Thus, *Deutsch's crude law* predicts that the typical aspects or effects of a given social relationship (such as cooperation) tend to instill that relationship in a social situation that is not yet strongly established. For instance, the typical ingredients, elements, or aspects of cooperation - such as trust, honest communication, and resource-sharing - will tend to induce cooperation when such aspects are introduced into a conflict situation whose specific character has not yet been determined. See also CONFLICT, THEORIES OF.

REFERENCES

Deutsch, M. (1949). An experimental study of the effects of cooperation and competition. *Human Relations, 2*, 199-232.

Deutsch, M., & Krauss, R. M. (1965). *Theories in social psychology.* New York: Basic Books.

Deutsch, M. (1969). Conflicts: Productive and destructive. *Journal of Social Issues, 25*, 7-41.

Deutsch, M. (1980). Fifty years of conflict. In L. Festinger (Ed.), *Retrospections on social psychology.* New York: Oxford University Press.

Deutsch, M. (1985). *Distributive justice.* New Haven, CT: Yale University Press.

Deutsch, M., & Coleman, P. T. (Eds.) (2000). *The handbook of conflict resolution: Theory and practice.* San Francisco: Jossey-Bass.

DEUTSCH'S STRUCTURAL MODEL. See TOLMAN'S THEORY.

DEVELOPMENTAL THEORY. *Development* is defined as the sequence and patterns of changes that occur over the full life span of an organism. The area of *developmental psychology* initially - via G. Stanley Hall in the early 1900s, who proposed a *biogenetic theory* of development - referred to the study of the full life span from birth to death, but today the tendency is to use the term, also, in more specific ways (e.g., developmental aphasia, developmental articulation disorder, developmental psycholinguistics, etc.). The "thing" that develops in *developmental theory* may be almost anything: molecular systems, bones and organs, emotions, ideas and cognitive processes, moral systems, personality, relationships, groups, societies, and cultures. Among the notions related to *developmental theory* are the following principles, laws, and effects: *Adam/Eve plan/principle* - the *Adam principle* is the argument that for a fetus to differentiate into a male individual, the basic *Eve plan* must be overridden via masculinization hormones and the suppression of an inhibiting hormone; the *Eve principle* is the tendency for sexual differentiation as a female individual to occur spontaneously, whereas differentiation into a male organism requires hormonal events to occur at the critical prenatal period; *law of acceleration* (see Bald-win, 1901/1905) - this developmental "law," enunciated independently by Alpheus Hyatt (1838-1902) and Edward Drinker Cope (1840-1897) in 1866, states that all modifications and variations in progressive series tend to appear first in the adolescent or adult stages of growth, and then to be inherited in successive descendents at earlier and earlier stages according to the *law of acceleration*, until they either become embryonic or are crowded out of the organization and replaced in the development by characteristics of later origin (cf., *Cope's law/rule* - states that phyletic lineages have a tendency to be founded on small-sized organisms, and that organisms tend to increase in size through evolutionary time, most likely due to larger organisms being better able to control resources, such as feeding territories, than smaller ones; and Hyatt's *anagenesis theory* - refers to "upward evolution" or the progressive evolution of species into new species, as well as the gradual transformation of one species into another from a single line of development). Charles Darwin referred to the *law of acceleration* as "earlier inheritance," and a very similar principle of ontogenetic acceleration was given by Ernst Haeckel (1834-1919) (called "heterochrony;" cf., Haeckel's *gastraea theory* - states that all organisms pass through a stage in which the gastraea/embryo consists of two layers, an inner one and an outer one; and his *prokaryotic theory of cellular evolution* - states that living cells lacking nuclei/bacteria were the first to appear on earth, where such cells gave rise to protista/algae, which then gave origin to early plants and animals) and by Sir Edwin Ray Lankester (1847-1929) (called "precocious segregation;" cf., Lankester's *degeneration theory* - states that species may become simpler over time, rather than evolving into more complex species or remaining the same) in 1877 to explain the early appearance of certain characteristics in embryos. In 1898, Ernst Meynert asserted that acceleration in the embryological development of an organ is correlated with the biological importance of that organ; cf., *crossover effect* - the phenomenon of two individuals or entities growing or developing with one being faster or larger than the other one but, subsequently, with the slower or smaller one passing the first one; occasionally observed in the case of a set of twins where one is taller up to a certain age, and then the shorter one passes the other one in height; *cultural universal theory* - posits that all children, regardless of their cultural background, progress in an identical fashion up to a certain point in their development; *reproductive phases theory* - proposed by the Austrian-American psychologist Charlotte B. Buhler (1893-1974), states that the primary psychosocial phases of lifespan development parallel the primary biological phases: progressive growth (birth to 15 years of age), emergence of sexual reproductive activity (16 to 25 years of age), stability (26 to 45 years of age), loss of reproductive capacity (46 to 65 years of age), and biological decline (66 years of age to death); *dialectic theory* - in lifespan developmental psychology, refers to any complex process of conceptual conflict or dialogue in which the generation, interpretation, and opposing viewpoints leads to a fuller mode of thought; *anterior-posterior development theory* - refers to the anatomical observation that there is a more rapid growth of the individual's head region as compared to the lower body areas during fetal development: in the "head-to-tail" development, the head (and its movements) develops first, then the upper trunk, arms and hands, followed by the lower trunk and leg, foot, and toe structures (and movements); *developmental theorist* - one who assumes that mental retardation is due to a slower than normal development of cogni-

tive processes and it is not different qualitatively from the cognitive processes of "normal" individuals; on the other hand, a *defect theorist* assumes that cognitive processes of individuals with mental retardation are qualitatively different than those of "normal" persons; *discrepancy principle* - states that infants and young children have a preference for experiences, objects, and situations that are moderately novel to them; *Dreikurs theory* [named after the Austrian-American Adlerian music and group therapist Rudolf Dreikurs (1897-1972)] - advances the notions of the "four goals of children" (i.e., they want to attract attention, to be powerful, to achieve revenge, and to assume inadequacy), "parenting training" (i.e., teaching parents to deal with undesirable behavior in their children), "democratic parenting" (i.e., a method employing periodic democratic family councils in which there is no punishment), "lifestyle analysis" (i.e., understanding clients' self-concepts before psychotherapy or counseling is attempted), and "logical and natural consequences" (i.e., teaching the child a sense of responsibility); *enrichment theory* - the speculation that during the infant's early development, the more stimuli and environmental events that she or he experiences, the more likely the child is to develop his or her potentialities; *focal-conflict theory* - states that one's current behavior in meeting current problems is determined by that particular person's method or style of dealing with conflicts early in life; *general developmental model* - defines the interrelationships of longitudinal, cross-sectional, and time-lag designs for collecting developmental data, and identifies the confounds in each design strategy due to cohort effects, time, and age factors; *left-right effect* - most children demonstrate a tendency to learn more easily the concepts of "up" and "down" than they do the concepts of "left" and "right;" *maturational hypothesis* - states that maturing individuals have particular mental and physiological abilities available to them that they do not actually use until they are needed; *maturation theory* - holds that some behaviors are largely hereditary, but do not appear until appropriate organs and neural mechanisms and systems have matured; *maturation-degeneration hypothesis* - posits that abilities and functions between birth and death may be plotted as a trajectory curve that asymptotes in the early years and declines gradually thereafter; *maximum contrast principle* - states that there is a tendency of infants and young children to pay attention to salient perceptual opposites and large contrasts rather than to small or subtle differences; the *organizing effect* - refers to the long-lasting influence of hormones during a critical period in the child's early development; *principle of anticipatory maturation, or anticipatory maturation principle* - holds that nearly all of an organism's functions may be elicited experimentally at some time prior to the normal appearance of the function, based on the observation that they develop before they are actually needed for interaction with the environment; *psychosexual neutrality theory* - posits that human infants are born without a gender/sexual identity; *reference man/woman model* - a theoretical model describing an average, 20-24 year-old, man and woman based on anthropometric studies of thousands of persons, giving mean values for mass or stature, head circumferences, skeletal diameters, and fat calculations, among other factors, in various groups; *secure-base phenomenon* - refers to a tendency in both human and animal infants and offspring to explore new or distant areas but always remaining close to their mothers; *teeter-totter effect* - refers to a tendency for two siblings, in particular those who have been in reciprocal competition when growing up, to show the result that if one is successful, the other one becomes a failure; *omnipotency theory* - a supposition held by many young people that they have mental control over other individuals, which makes the others carry out their biddings; in another sense, the theory refers to the attitude of many young people that they are invincible and free from harm, danger, or death and, as a result, they tend to engage in many risky behaviors and situations that older individuals may avoid; *omnipotency theory*, as postulated by Sigmund Freud, holds that thoughts alone can satisfy one's wishes without the use of external objects, and that one's thoughts can affect external events; both of these forms of the theory are assumed to be a natural stage in a child's development, and perhaps even at the foundation of beliefs in animism and magic; "omnipotence of thought" is observed, also, in many diverse psychiatric disorders; *timing-of-events model* - this theoretical model gives an account of adult social and emotional development as a response to whether the timing and occurrence of important life events is expected or unexpected]. The period of *early childhood* has received a great deal of theoretical attention in developmental psychology. Childhood is a culturally defined period in human development between infancy and adulthood where, only in the past 400 years or so [starting with the Moravian educator John Amos Comenius (1592-1670)], childhood has been a part of Western culture with the recognition of this special class of individuals and special growth phases, stages, and sequences of each person. M. Lewis (1990) notes that two views of human nature predominate in *theories of development*: the human is acted on by surrounding forces ("reactive view"), and the human acts on these forces ("active view"). The *reactive view* generates two major theoretical paradigms - biological and social control; the *active view* generates the *constructivist* or *developmental-cognitive* theoretical paradigm. In particular, Lewis explores three *models of intentionality* in children: mechanistic, emergent, and goal-directed systems/models. In general, *continuity theories of development* maintain that psychological development is a gradual, continuous process (cf., *perceptual theories of development* and, in particular, the issue of the origins of *self-perception* in infancy; Butterworth, 1992; and the construct of *psychological distance* - the distance between what the learner understands and what still has to be understood - as a *unifying theory of development*; Cocking & Renninger, 1993; cf., the theoretical notion of *personal space* - the area around a person's body into which other individuals may not normally intrude without provoking a negative reaction; Sommer, 1969; also, cf., *incremental theory of development* - asserts that mental and physical development occurs constantly and seamlessly; claims that *stage theories* are artificial but useful, and *incremental theories* are like a watch with a sweep second hand, whereas *stage theories* are like a watch with a digital readout). On the other hand, *stage*

162

theories of development maintain that psychological development is discontinuous, with plateaus (periods of relative stability) separated by periods of rapid change. *Psychoanalytic theories of development* hypothesize that early childhood is the critical period in development where major personality orientations emerge and continue into childhood, adolescence, and adulthood. An individual's sense of *self*, and one's *self-concept* and identity as a female or male, is formed in important ways during early childhood (as indicated in *psychoanalytic theories*, as well as in various *theories of ego development*). Two of the most prominent *psychoanalytic theories of development* are Sigmund Freud's *theory of psychosexual development*, which describes the oral, anal, phallic/oedipal, and genital stages of development, and Erik Erikson's *theory of psychosocial development*, which describes the "crises" of early childhood (such as trust versus mistrust, autonomy versus shame or doubt, industry versus inferiority). The *cognitive developmental theories* (e.g., J. Piaget; J. Bruner), also, emphasize early childhood as a period of critical construction of the child's knowledge and sense of reality. For example, according to Piaget, the child passes through *cognitive stages* of sensorimotor, preoperational, concrete operational, and formal operational modes of thinking that are based on a complex series of interactions of the child with the environment. Many of the *learning theorists* tend to consider developmental behavior as based on environmental, rather than organismic, factors and (like Freud) view the individual as a passive receptacle rather than active in its own development (cf., the *humanist's* "active" approach). The emergence of *social learning theory* may be viewed, in some respects for *developmental theory*, as a combination of *psychoanalytic* and *learning theory* conceptualizations. See also AGING, THEORIES OF; DARWIN'S EVOLUTION THEORY; EGO DEVELOPMENT, THEORIES OF; ERIKSON'S THEORY OF PERSONALITY; FREUD'S THEORY OF PERSONALITY; HUMANIST THEORIES; INTERPERSONAL ATTRACTION THEORIES; LEARNING THEORIES AND LAWS; LIFE, THEORIES OF; PIAGET'S THEORY OF DEVELOPMENTAL STAGES; SELF-CONCEPT THEORY; SELF PERCEPTION THEORY; SOCIAL LEARNING AND COGNITION THEORIES.

REFERENCES

Baldwin, J. M. (Ed.) (1901/1905). *Dictionary of philosophy and psychology*. 4 Vols. New York: Macmillan.

Freud, S. (1920). *A general introduction to psychoanalysis*. New York: Pocket Books.

Piaget, J. (1929). *The child's conception of the world*. New York: Littlefield, Adams.

Gesell, A., & Ilg, F. (1946). *The child from five to ten*. New York: Harper.

Erikson, E. (1950). *Childhood and society*. New York: Norton.

Rotter, J. (1954). *Social learning and clinical psychology*. New York: Johnson.

Bruner, J. (1968). *Processes of cognitive growth: Infancy*. Worcester, MA: Clark University Press.

Erikson, E. (1968). *Identity: Youth and crisis*. New York: Norton.

Sommer, R. (1969). *Personal space*. Englewood Cliffs, NJ: Prentice-Hall.

Bandura, A. (1977). *Social learning theory*. Englewood Cliffs, NJ: Prentice-Hall.

Ames, L., Gillespie, C., Haines, J., & Ilg, F. (1979). *The Gesell Institute's child from one to six*. New York: Harper & Row.

Gualtieri, T., & Hicks, R. E. (1985). An immunoreactive theory of selective male affliction. *Behavioral and Brain Sciences, 8*, 427-441.

Broughton, J. M. (1987). *Critical theories of psychological development*. New York: Plenum.

Lewis, M. (1990). The development of intentionality and the role of consciousness. *Psychological Inquiry, 1*, 231-247, 278-283.

Butterworth, G. (1992). Origins of self-perception in infancy. *Psychological Inquiry, 3*, 103-111, 134-136.

Cocking, R. R., & Renninger, K. A. (Eds.) (1993). *The development and meaning of psychological distance*. Hillsdale, NJ: Erlbaum.

Lerner, R. M. (2002). *Concepts and theories of human development*. Mahwah, NJ: Erlbaum.

Miller, P. H. (2002). *Theories of developmental psychology*. New York: Worth.

DEVIANCE/LABELING THEORY. See LABELING/DEVIANCE THEORY.

DEVIANT FILTER THEORY. See SCHIZOPHRENIA, THEORIES OF.

DEVIL EFFECT. See HALO EFFECT.

DIAGNOSIS OF PSYCHOPATHOLOGY. See PSYCHOPATHOLOGY, THEORIES OF.

DIALECTICAL MATERIALISM, DOCTRINE OF. See DETERMINISM, DOCTRINE/THEORY OF.

DIALECTICAL MONTAGE EFFECT. See PERCEPTION (I. GENERAL), THEORIES OF.

DIALECTIC THEORY. See DEVELOPMENTAL THEORY.

DIATHESIS-STRESS THEORY OF ABNORMALITY. See PSYCHOPATHOLOGY, THEORIES OF; SCHIZOPHRENIA, THEORIES OF.

DIFFERENCES, LAW OF. See PARSIMONY, LAW/PRINCIPLE OF.

DIFFERENTIAL EMOTIONS THEORY. See IZARD'S THEORY OF EMOTIONS.

DIFFERENTIAL FORGETTING, THEORY OF. See INTERFERENCE THEORIES OF FORGETTING.

DIFFERENTIAL INVERSION EFFECT. See APPENDIX A, MARGARET THATCHER ILLUSION.

DIFFERENTIAL K THEORY. See RECAPITULATION THEORY/LAW.

DIFFERENTIAL RISK THEORY. See SEXUAL ORIENTATION THEORIES.

DIFFERENTIATION HYPOTHESIS. See INTERFERENCE THEORIES OF FORGETTING.

DIFFUSION OF RESPONSIBILITY. See BYSTANDER INTERVENTION EFFECT.

DIMINISHING RETURNS, LAW/PRINCIPLE OF. See JOST'S LAWS.

DIMMING EFFECT AND DIMMING CONTRAST EFFECT. The American psychologist Leonard Thompson Troland (1889-1932) - who studied visual perception and retinal illuminance (the illuminance unit called the *Troland* is named after him, and is defined as the intensity of light falling on the retina, calculated as the product of luminance and pupil area), and who is the co-inventor of colored movies - described the *dimming effect* and the *principle of the dimming contrast effect* in 1917 in his investigations of afterimages produced under carefully controlled conditions. Troland found that if an afterimage, once formed and projected, is permitted to fade and, if then, the afterimage of the projection field itself be observed against a completely dark ground, a demarcation of the field into halves may be noted. This effect is always obtained with short pre-exposures and high intensities, but is absent for pre-exposures that approach in duration the "equilibrium time," or maximal duration of the image. If the intensity of the projection field is decreased, but not made zero, a similar rejuvenation of the afterimage contrast occurs. The pre-exposed half appears darker and complementary in hue as compared with the other half of the field. In its general form, this principle is that dimming the reaction light enhances the processes that are "antagonistic" to the original stimulation. However, to account for the increase of the afterimage, the principle requires a special mathematical form because if dimming influenced both halves of the field equally, the contrast would not be augmented, no matter how great the absolute alteration of the compared areas. Consequently, under these conditions, the *principle* *of the dimming contrast effect* refers to a very slight difference in the level of fatigue of two visual areas that furnishes the basis for a large difference in the magnitude of the *dimming effect* producible on the two respective areas. Such a contrast, which has been re-established by dimming, fades rapidly on the dimmed field, but - if after it has disappeared - the field is brightened to its original intensity and then dimmed again, the contrast returns. This process may be repeated successfully over a period sometimes twelvefold the life of the image on the undimmed field. The factor of the "relative durability" of the *dimming contrast effect* decreases rapidly to an asymptote with increase in the original pre-exposure time (i.e., the effect is less marked in conjunction with a generally low level of visual sensitivity than it is with higher levels). Troland stated that certain aspects of the dimming (and "reversal") phenomena are explainable by the earlier work of the German physiologist Ewald Hering (1834-1918), but Troland attempted to modify Hering's views (cf., Troland, 1915) and concluded that the *dimming effects* depend either upon the laws governing certain of the constants/parameters of the simple equations for retinal excitation, or else they rest on conditions present in the visual system posterior to the retina. See also ADAPTATION, PRINCIPLES/LAWS OF; VISION/SIGHT, THEORIES OF.

REFERENCES

Hering, E. (1878/1964). *Outlines of a theory of the light sense.* Cambridge, MA: Harvard University Press.

Troland, L. T. (1915). Adaptation of the chemical theory of sensory response. *American Journal of Psychology, 25,* 500-527.

Troland, L. T. (1917). The influence of changes of illumination upon afterimages. *American Journal of Psychology, 28,* 497-503.

DING-DONG THEORY. See LANGUAGE ORIGINS, THEORIES OF.

DIRCKS'/PEPPER'S GHOST/EFFECT.
The English civil engineer/patent agent Henry Dirchs (1806-1873) and the English analytical chemist John Henry Pepper (1821-1900) both devised and developed this spectral image demonstration that is produced by positioning a large sheet of clear glass at an angle, allowing objects and people to be seen through it while a brightly lit image of a person located elsewhere is reflected simultaneously from it. In 1858, Dircks worked out a concept for presenting a ghost on a theater stage, but his designs proved to be impractical. In 1862, "Professor" Pepper suggested that he and Dircks redesign the device/concept. In 1863, Dircks and Pepper jointly patented the device. The *Dircks'/Pepper's ghost/effect* was employed originally in Victorian theater productions to project an image of an actor from beneath the front of the stage, causing the image perceptually to appear or disappear depending on the lighting (bright or dim) cast on the actor; this theatrical "special-effect" is a hologram-like image that has the quality of an apparition/ghost through which other actors on the stage may pass. The "ghost" had some success in the theater, but getting the glass into position was a laborious process, and cut off the stage behind it acoustically. The effect was exploited successfully on the British fairgrounds, and by the late 1800s, the fairground "ghost show" had developed into one of the most popular forms of "walkup" show. However, within a few years of the introduction of motion pictures/films/movies in the 1890s, the "ghost show" became secondary to bioscope, panorama, diorama, and peep shows. See also IMAGERY/MENTAL IMAGERY, THEORIES OF; PERCEPTION (I. GENERAL), THEORIES OF; VISION/SIGHT, THEORIES OF.

REFERENCES

Pepper, J. H. (1890/1996). *The true history of the ghost and all about metempsychosis.* East Sussex, UK: Projection Box.

Ferguson, D. (1995). Pepper's ghost. [URL: *www.phantasmechanics.com/pepper.html*].

DIRECTION THEORY OF TROPISMS.
See LOEB'S TROPISTIC THEORY.

DIRECTIVE-STATE THEORY. See PERCEPTION (II. COMPARATIVE APPRAISAL), THEORIES OF.

DIRECT PERCEPTION THEORY. See PERCEPTION (I. GENERAL), THEORIES OF.

DISCONTINUITY HYPOTHESIS. See GESTALT THEORY/LAWS.

DISCONTINUITY THEORY. See SPENCE'S THEORY.

DISCOUNTING PRINCIPLE. See ATTRIBUTION THEORY.

DISCREPANCY-EVALUATION/CONSTRUCTIVITY THEORY. See SCHACHTER-SINGER'S THEORY OF EMOTIONS.

DISCREPANCY PRINCIPLE. See DEVELOPMENTAL THEORY.

DISCRIMINATION/GENERALIZATION HYPOTHESIS. See CAPALDI'S THEORY.

DISCRIMINATION LEARNING THEORY. See SPENCE'S THEORY.

DISEASE/MEDICAL MODEL. See WOLPE'S THEORY/TECHNIQUE OF RECIPROCAL INHIBITION.

DISEASE MODEL. See BEHAVIOR THERAPY/COGNITIVE THERAPY, THEORIES OF.

DISEASE, THEORY OF. See SEXUAL ORIENTATION THEORIES.

DISENGAGEMENT THEORY OF AGING. See AGING, THEORIES OF.

DISEQUILIBRIUM PRINCIPLE. See REINFORCEMENT THEORY.

DISINHIBITION, PRINCIPLE OF. See INHIBITION, LAWS OF.

DISPLACEMENT THEORY. See FORGETTING/MEMORY, THEORIES OF.

DISPOSITIONAL ATTRIBUTION EFFECT. See ATTRIBUTION THEORY.

DISPOSITIONAL (TYPE/TRAIT) THEORIES OF PERSONALITY. See PERSONALITY THEORIES.

DISPOSITION THEORY OF HUMOR/MIRTH. The proposition that the humor or mirth experience is determined largely by one's innate *disposition*, nature, attitudes, emotions, and character has enjoyed varying degrees of empirical and theoretical success (e.g., Zillman & Cantor, 1976/1996). The individual's *disposition* is the natural or prevailing aspect of one's mind, also, as demonstrated in behavior of relationships with other people. In terms of responsiveness to humorous stimuli, variables such as sexual humor, hostile/aggressive humor, gender of participants, sex-role attitudes, reference group, group membership, gender of disparaged victims, identification class, and ethnicity have been found to be influential and associative factors in determining one's responses in humorous and mirthful situations. Also, the *disposition theory of humor/mirth* attempts to account for the emotional, cognitive, and physiological impacts that amusement and humorous materials have on different audiences. See also HUMOR, THEORIES OF.
REFERENCES
Zillmann, D., & Cantor, J. R. (1976/1996). A disposition theory of humour and mirth. In A. J. Chapman & H. C. Foot (Eds.), *Humour and laughter: Theory, research, and application.* London: Wiley.
Raney, A. A. (2003). Disposition-based theories of enjoyment. In J. Bryant & D. Roskos-Ewoldsen (Eds.), *Communication and emotion: Essays in honor of Dolf Zillmann.* Mahwah, NJ: Erlbaum.

DISSOCIATION, LAW OF. See ASSOCIATION, LAWS/PRINCIPLES OF.

DISSOCIATION BY VARYING CONCOMITANTS, LAW OF. See ASSOCIATION, LAWS/PRINCIPLES OF.

DISSOCIATION THEORY. Early in the 20th century, the French neurologist and psychologist Pierre Janet (1859-1947) formulated *dissociation theory* to account for "automatism" (i.e., behavior carried out without conscious awareness or control, such as behavior during hypnosis, sleepwalking, fugue states, and some forms of epilepsy) and "hysteria" (i.e., behavior involving emotional outbursts, fainting, increased suggestibility, or clinical "conversion" symptoms such as various types of paralysis not founded in physiological substrata). According to Janet, such behaviors and disorders are the result of "dissociation" involving the partial or total disconnection between memories of the past (including identity awareness and immediate sensory awareness) and control of one's bodily movements; such dissociations are the result, theoretically, of early traumatic experiences, disturbed relationships, or stressful/chronic problems in the individual's life. More recently, the American psychologist Ernest Ropiequet (1904-2001) provides an historical account of *dissociation* and *hypnosis* that is grounded in the more general domain of the concept of *consciousness*. Hilgard notes that Janet's use of the term *dissociation* was borrowed from the *doctrine of association* that was prevalent in Janet's day: if thoughts and memories may be brought to the level of consciousness via the association of ideas, then if follows that those thoughts and memories that are *not* accessible to association must simply be "dissociated." In his defense of the concept of *dissociation*, and in advancing his own *neodissociation theory* and interpretation of the concept, Hilgard suggests that the activity of hypnosis involves a form of "divided consciousness" containing two modes: a *receptive* mode and an *active* mode where the former is reflected in the relatively passive registration of events as they impinge on one's sense organs, and the latter is reflected in the active, planning, and voluntary aspects of behavior. Memories may be separated so that reflection on experiences registered in the first mode may be disrupted and the voluntary and involuntary control systems may be reversed through "dissociation" with the result that an activity that is normally involuntary may be brought under voluntary control (e.g., as in some "compulsive" behaviors). See also ASSOCIATION, DOCTRINE OF; CONSCIOUSNESS, PHENOMENON OF; HYPNOSIS/HYPNOTISM, THEORIES OF; NEO-DISSOCIATION THEORY.

REFERENCES

Janet, P. (1899). *L'Automatisme psychologique*. Paris: Alcan.

Janet, P. (1907). *The major symptoms of hysteria*. New York: Macmillan.

Hilgard, E. R. (1977). *Divided consciousness: Multiple controls in human thought and action*. New York: Wiley.

Hilgard, E. R. (1994). Neodissociation theory. In S. J. Lynn & J. W. Rhue (Eds.), *Dissociation: Clinical and theoretical perspectives*. New York: Guilford Press.

DISSONANCE THEORY. See FESTINGER'S COGNITIVE DISSONANCE THEORY.

DISTORTED ROOM. See APPENDIX A, TRAPEZOIDAL/AMES WINDOW.

DISTRIBUTED-ACTIONS THEORY OF LEADERSHIP. See LEADERSHIP, THEORIES OF.

DISTRIBUTED MEMORY STORAGE THEORY. See SHORT-TERM AND LONG-TERM MEMORY, THEORIES OF.

DISTRIBUTED REPETITIONS, PRINCIPLE OF. See JOST'S LAWS.

DISTRIBUTIVE LAW. See PERCEPTION (I. GENERAL), THEORIES OF; PROBABILITY THEORY/LAWS.

DISUSE, LAW/THEORY OF. This law and theory is a generalization of conditioning formulated by the American psychologist Edward Lee Thorndike (1874-1949), and is derived from his *law of exercise*, which states that a learned stimulus-response bond or association will decrease and become weakened through disuse or through lack of practice. The *law of disuse* was invoked in early discussions in psychology of how forgetting occurs. That is, following the analogy that a muscle is weakened through disuse (and strengthened through exercise or use), lack of practice of learned materials may weaken the ability to recall those materials. However, the *law of disuse* is not widely held today because it is not supported by adequate data, and there are many common instances of its failure to predict the expected outcome (e.g., one may actually remember one's Spanish vocabulary and the names of high school classmates after 30 or 40 years, even if these materials have not been used during that time). See also EFFECT, LAW OF; EXERCISE, LAW OF; FORGETTING/MEMORY, THEORIES OF; USE, LAW OF.

REFERENCE

Thorndike, E. L. (1898/1911). *Animal intelligence*. New York: Macmillan.

DITCHBURN-RIGGS EFFECT. See VISION/SIGHT, THEORIES OF.

DNA MODEL. See LAMARCK'S THEORY.

DODO HYPOTHESIS. In 1936, the American psychologist Saul Rosenzweig (1907-2004) proposed that common factors are operative in the efficacy of psychotherapy and used the conclusion expressed by the Dodo bird in Lewis Carroll's 1865 book *Alice's Adventures in Wonderland* to emphasize the point. Thus, the *Dodo hypothesis* alludes to the Dodo bird's words to racers in a foot-race that *"everybody* has won, and *all* must have prizes!" This proposition, by extension, states that all mental health therapies are roughly equal - as proposed by Lester B. Luborsky, Barton Singer, and Lise Luborsky in 1975 (cf., the *demoralization hypothesis*, which states that because all forms of psychotherapy are helpful, their shared features must counteract a type of distress and disability common to most seekers of psychotherapy). Luborsky and his colleagues conducted reviews of studies of the efficacy of various psychotherapies and concluded that the *Dodo hypothesis* is essentially correct: *all* of the contenders in the "psychotherapy race" are successful. There is a huge amount of evidence that psychotherapy works, they say, but there is no evidence across a broad range of samples that any *one* mode of psychotherapy, or "talk therapies," is superior to the others (cf., *communion principle* - the theory that the first requisite of successful therapy is a sense of unity, trust, and mutuality between client/patient and therapist). Additionally, Luborsky and his group found support for an *allegiance effect*, which is the tendency of researchers to find evidence that favors the particular type of therapy that they themselves practice. However, another interpretation of the *Dodo hypothesis* is offered by the American psychiatrist E. Fuller Torrey (1992), who states that *everyone* has *lost*, and *none* must have prizes. Torrey criticizes psychoanalysis and all other "talk therapies" as *pseudoscience* and disputes the underlying assumption of such therapies that the human psyche is shaped by childhood experiences and can be reshaped through psychotherapy (cf., *psychobabble* - the use of excessive or superfluous psychological jargon, especially in connection with various forms of psychotherapy). Torrey asserts that drugs, gene therapy, and other biological remedies will make "talking cures" obsolete and, for now, psychotherapy should be excluded from health care coverage. According to Horgan (1996), bashing Freud and the "talk therapies" is not a novel pastime: the eminent Austrian-born English philosopher Karl Popper (1902-1994) recalled more than 60 years ago that "psychoanalysis is the treatment of the id by the odd." Thus, the debate continues concerning the efficacy of psychotherapy, in general, and Freudian psychoanalysis, in particular. See also FREUD'S THEORY OF PERSONALITY.

REFERENCES

Rosenzweig, S. (1936). Some implicit common factors in diverse methods of psychotherapy. *American Journal of Orthopsychiatry, 6,* 412-415.

Strupp, H. (1973). *Psychotherapy: Clinical, research, and theoretical issues.* New York: Aronson.

Luborsky, L. B., Singer, B., & Luborsky, L. (1975). Comparative studies of psychotherapies. *Archives of General Psychiatry, 32,* 995-1008.

Rosen, R. D. (1977). *Psychobabble: Fast talk and quick cure in the era of feeling.* New York: Atheneum.

Gross, M. (1979). *The psychological society.* New York: Simon & Schuster.

Torrey, E. F. (1992). *Freudian fraud*. New York: HarperCollins.

Dawes, R. (1994). *House of cards: Psychology and psychotherapy built on myth*. New York: Free Press.

Fisher, S., & Greenberg, R. (1996). *Freud scientifically reappraised*. New York: Wiley.

Horgan, J. (1996). Why Freud isn't dead. *Scientific American, 275*, 106-111.

Crits-Christoph, P. (1997). Limitations of the Dodo bird verdict and the role of clinical trials in psychotherapy research. *Psychological Bulletin, 122*, 216-220.

Wampold, B., Mondin, G., Moody, M., Stich, F., Benson, K., & Ahn, H. (1997). A meta-analysis of outcome studies comparing bona fide psychotherapies: Empirically, "All must have prizes." *Psychological Bulletin, 122*, 203-215, 226-230.

DOLLAR AUCTION GAME. See CONCORDE FALLACY/EFFECT.

DOLLO'S LAW. This principle, named in honor of the Belgian paleontologist Louis A. M. J. Dollo (1857-1931), states that an organism's function, or complex structure, that is lost in the course of evolution is never fully regained in its original form. Thus, *Dollo's law* implies that the process of evolution is irreversible. However, even though this may generally be true, there are exceptions to be found; for example, the eyes of snakes appear to have re-evolved from secondarily blind burrowing forms. See also EVOLUTION, LAWS OF.

REFERENCE

Jay, S. (Ed.) (1980). *Louis Dollo's papers on paleontology and evolution*. New York: Arno Press.

DOMAINS OF PROCESSING THEORY. See INFORMATION/INFORMATION-PROCESSING THEORY; SHORT-TERM AND LONG-TERM MEMORY, THEORIES OF.

DOMINATOR-MODULATOR THEORY. See GRANIT'S COLOR VISION THEORY.

DONDERS' LAW AND DONDERS' REACTION-TIME TECHNIQUES. The Dutch physiologist/ophthalmologist Franciscus Cornelis Donders (1818-1889) formulated this principle of visual fixation in 1846, according to which every position of the lines of regard in relation to the head corresponds to a definite, invariable angle of torsion of the eyes, regardless of the path by which that position has been reached. Another version of *Donders' law* states that the position of the eyes in looking at an object is independent of the movement of the eyes to that position; regardless of previous fixation points, every point on the line corresponds to a definite, invariable angle of the eyes, resulting in the fixation point being focused on the retina's fovea. Aided, in part, by Hermann von Helmholtz's invention of the ophthalmoscope in 1850, Donders established himself as a specialist in diseases of the eye, setting up a polyclinic for eye diseases at Utrecht University. Donders improved the efficiency of spectacles through the introduction of prismatic and cylindrical lenses, and wrote extensively on eye physiology. Donders is most remembered for his studies on *reaction time* (*RT*); that is, the minimum time between the presentation of a stimulus and the participant's response to it; e.g., *central RT* is the fraction of *RT* that remains after subtracting the time taken up by the passage of a nerve impulse from the sensory receptor to the brain and for another nerve impulse from the brain to the muscle; and the *subtraction method* refers to any of several methods for measuring the time it takes for particular psychological processes to occur. Donders studied three kinds of *RT* tasks: (1) *simple RT* - the minimum lag between a single simple stimulus, such as a tone or light, and the participant's making of a single simple response, such as pressing a button; (2) *discrimination RT* - there are two distinctive stimuli and the participant is asked to respond to only one of them and refrain from making a response to the other; and (3) *choice RT* - an extension of *simple RT* where the participant is confronted with two or more stimuli and two or more corresponding responses. By subtracting the time it took participants to carry out task (2) from the time it took to carry out task (3), Donders obtained an estimate of how long it took to make a *choice*; and by subtracting task (1) time from task (2) time, he obtained an estimate of the individual's *discrimination* time. In view of the originality and ingenuity of this first attempt to measure the speed of higher mental processes, it is astonishing to see the small amount of data upon which Donders based his judgments (30 trials or less with some of his participants). However, the validity of the *method of subtraction* has never been fully accepted by most investigators. Nevertheless, Donders' work is important for several reasons: he showed that some of the variability of results is not due to simple differences in speed of conduction but to central processes; he laid down the foundation for the analysis of the time relations of mental processes; and he found that the *RT* for the different senses show characteristic differences (cf., the *general theory of human reaction time* - is a "nonstage" theory, and posits that the strength of the excitatory tendency leading to response evocation grows continuously as a function of the time since stimulus onset; a response occurs when this strength reaches the value of a decision criterion that is normally distributed over trials). See also HICK'S LAW.

REFERENCES

Donders, F. C. (1869). Die schnelligkeit psychischer processe. *Archiv fur Anatomie und Physiologie, 6*, 657-681.

Brozek, J. (1970). Wayward history: F. C. Donders (1818-1889) and the timing of mental operations. *Psychological Reports, 26*, 563-569.

Teichner, W., & Krebs, M. (1972). Laws of the simple visual reaction time. *Psychological Review, 79*, 344-358.

Grice, G. R., Nullmeyer, R., & Spiker, V. A. (1982). Human reaction time: Toward a general theory. *Journal of Experimental Psychology: General, 111*, 135-153.

DOOR-IN-THE-FACE TECHNIQUE. See COMPLIANCE EFFECTS/TECHNIQUES.

DOPAMINE THEORY OF SCHIZOPHRENIA. See SCHIZOPHRENIA, THEORIES OF.

DOPPELGANGER PHENOMENON. See HYPNOSIS/HYPNOTISM, THEORIES OF.

DOPPLER EFFECT/PRINCIPLE/SHIFT. The Austrian physicist Christian Johann Doppler (1803-1853) enunciated this principle in 1842, which accounts for the variation of frequency observed (lower or higher than which is actually emitted) when a vibrating source of waves and the observer, respectively, recede from, or approach, one another. In other terms, the *Doppler effect* refers to the change in apparent frequency of a source due to relative motion of source and observer. An interesting experimental validation of the *Doppler effect* was conducted at Utrecht in the Netherlands in 1845: a locomotive pulling an open car containing several individuals playing trumpets passed by a group of musicians (who had perfect pitch) standing at a fixed location. The result was as expected: the apparent frequency of waves from the source (the trumpeters) when *moving toward* the observers (the musicians) was *increased,* whereas the apparent sound waves from the source (the trumpeters) when *moving away* from the observers (the musicians) was *decreased.* The *Doppler shift* (also called the *redshift* in the context of astronomy and wavelengths in the visible spectrum) refers to the magnitude of the change in frequency or wavelength of waves that results from the *Doppler effect.* C. J. Doppler's name is honored, also, in the concepts of "Doppler broadening" (thermal motion of molecules, atoms, or nuclei), "Doppler width" (distribution of velocities), and "Doppler radar." The *Doppler effect* has been used to measure the speed of the sun's rotation and Saturn's rings, to serve as the basis for police radar speed traps for vehicles, to act in "Doppler satellites" (used by aircraft and ships to locate their position), and to measure physiological events in echocardiography ("Doppler reflection") such as heart defects. In astronomy, the *Doppler effect* provides a basis for collecting valuable evidence for cosmological conceptions of the universe (e.g., an "expanding" universe) by studying the changes in spectral wavelengths as celestial bodies approach or recede from a fixed observation point on the earth. Doppler himself recognized that the *frequency effect* he described applied to light as well as to sound sources, and the French physicist Armand Fizeau (1819-1896) pointed out in 1848 that the spectral hues of stars should be shifted toward the red end of the spectrum according to the speed at which they are receding from us (i.e., the *Doppler shift*). Other astronomers have used the *redshift effect* to infer the speed of recession of other galaxies from the earth. See also AUDITION/HEARING, THEORIES OF; VISION/SIGHT, THEORIES OF.

REFERENCES

Doppler, C. J. (1842). [Sound pitch of a moving source and its position relative to the observer]. *Abhandlungen der Koniglichen Bohmischen Gesellschaft der Wissenschaften, 2,* 465.

Doppler, C. J. (1846). *Beitrage zur fixsternenkunde.* Prague: Haase.

DOUBLE-ASPECT THEORY. See MIND-BODY THEORIES.

DOUBLE-BIND HYPOTHESIS/THEORY. See SCHIZOPHRENIA, THEORIES OF.

DOUBLE-DEPLETION   HYPOTHESIS. See THIRST, THEORIES OF.

DOWNWARD DRIFT HYPOTHESIS. See SCHIZOPHRENIA, THEORIES OF.

DRAINAGE/DIVERSION HYPOTHESIS. See NEURON/NEURAL/NERVE THEORY.

DREAM THEORY. A *dream* may be defined as a more or less coherent imagery sequence that ordinarily occurs during sleep or, simply, as "imagery during sleep." Before 19th and 20th century scientific investigations took place, a *popular dream theory* was that they were divine messages with prophetic intent where the messages were coded, and the decoding task was performed by persons with a "gift" for dream interpretation (such as tribal leaders, chiefs, or witch doctors in uncivilized/primitive societies, or by psychoanalysts in modern/civilized societies). C. Hall divides the history of the scientific study and *theories of dreams* and dreaming into three periods: 1861-1900; 1900-1953; and 1953-present. In 1861, a French scientist, Alfred Maury, described the effects of external stimuli on his dreams (e.g., his dreaming of a guillotine sequence was interrupted by the headboard of his bed falling on his neck). Henri Bergson asserted that explanations of dreaming and dreams transcended a mere accounting of correlations between external and internal stimuli and anticipated the later interest in the influence of the *unconscious* on dreams. In 1900, Sigmund Freud initiated a period dominated by the clinical investigations of dreams where the functions of dreams were to help uncover the origins of patients' symptoms and to understand one's *unconscious* ("wish fulfillment") mental processes. According to Freud, a dream has different components: the *manifest content* - the dream as it is consciously recalled, and the *latent content* - the "true" meaning of the dream, which is unconscious. In Freud's approach, the dream as recalled represents a compromise between the fulfillment of a repressed wish and the desire to remain asleep; dreams were considered as guardians of sleep and protected the sleeper from being disturbed by unconscious conflicts and annoying external stimuli (cf., the *egoistic theory of dreams*, a basic psychoanalytic speculation which states that dreams are essentially egoistic in nature where any major "player" in a dream is likely to be the dreamer). Carl Jung distinguished "little dreams" (which are a continuation during sleep of one's waking preoccupations) from "big dreams' (which carry messages from the deepest layer of the unconscious, called the *collective unconscious* and, theoretically, are the same in every individual in every culture. The contents of the *collective unconscious* are defined as mental structures ("archetypes") inherited from previous generations. Jung developed the *method of amplification*, or "guided questioning," to identify the expression of an archetype in a "big dream." The symbols one uses in dreaming are not disguises, according to Jung, but are attempts of the archetypes to express themselves. Jung suggested that symbols reveal, rather than conceal, meaning - in contrast to Freud's viewpoint. On the other hand, both Jung and Freud agree that dreams are *compensatory* (cf., M. Boss, who argues that dreams are *neither* symbolic nor compensatory, but that they should merely be taken at "face value"). For Jung, dreams compensate for undeveloped archetypes, and for Freud dreams compensate for unfulfilled wishes. Other theoretical approaches to the *functions* of dreams are provided by B. Wolman who notes the wide variety and range of viewpoints: A. Adler suggests that dreams serve a problem-solving function offering cryptic solutions to difficulties the dreamer faces; Adler's idea is that the dream is always interpreted as a reflection of the dreamer's attitudes toward the future, especially one's drive toward superiority, and that they are "prodromic" (they foretell the future) where the dream is a kind of rehearsal for action; H. S. Sullivan asserts that dreams satisfy in symbolic ways the needs that may not be discharged in wakeful states and, thus, reduce tension; W. Dement and C. Fisher suggest that dreams are safety vales reducing the danger of emotional disturbance where deprivation of dreaming may produce psychosis; R. Hernandez-Peon considers dreams to be related to disinhibition of cortical and limbic neurons associated with the motivational and muscular systems where the neurons associated with memory functions determine the *manifest dream* content, and the limbic neurons determine the *latent dream* content; and M. Jouvet and J. Jouvet identify the causal-positive area in the thromboencephalic part of the brain as the locus and center of dreaming. An objective, laboratory-based analysis of dreaming is provided by E. Aserinsky and N. Kleitman who correlate the rapid, conjugate eye movements (REMs) that sleepers make periodically throughout the night with the experience of dreaming; they discovered that participants recall few dreams during non-REM (NREM) sleep and a great many dreams during REM periods of sleep. Other physiological characteristics of REM periods include high frequency/low amplitude brain waves during REM (but low frequency/higher amplitude during NREM), irregularities of breathing, blood pressure and heart-rate changes, and penile erections. The early *scanning hypothesis* of E. Aserinsky and N. Kleitman (which states that the dreamer's eye movements are correlated with the specific events the dreamer is "watching" in a dream) was not corroborated by later experiments. Later studies discovered, also, that dreams are recalled on awakening from *every* sleep stage, not just from REM awakenings. Thus, it appears that *all* sleep is "dreaming sleep." Another theoretical approach toward the study of dreams is the *content analysis* procedure of C. Hall, where different categories describe various elements in dream reports, such as human characters (distinguished by age, gender, family member, friends, strangers), animals, interactions among characters, objects, and emotions (cf., *salience hypothesis* - holds that emotionally-arousing dreams are more easily remembered than are non-arousing dreams). Generalizations from such *content analyses* indicate that women and men differ in their dreams: men dream more about male characters, strangers, physical aggression, sexuality, physical activities, tools/weapons, and outdoor settings than do women, whereas women dream more about female characters, familiar or known characters, verbal activities, clothes, and indoor settings than do men. Hall's data indicate that what an adult dreams about from one year to the next changes very little, and that there is considerable congruence or continuity between what one dreams about and one's preoccupations in waking life. The various theoretical approaches to dreaming have been challenged recently by a controversial, biologically-based approach called the *activation-synthesis theory*, which states that all dreams begin with random electrical discharges from deep within the brain. The signals emerge from the brain stem and go on to stimulate higher areas of the cortex. According to the *activation-synthesis theory*, the brain deals with this strange event by attempting to make sense out of all the input it receives, seeking to give order to chaos, and to "synthesize" the separate bursts of electrical stimulation into a coherent story by "creating" a dream (cf., *mental housecleaning hypothesis* - states that dreams clean the mind of what is redundant, bizarre, or useless and are, therefore, phenomena dedicated to the optimal and efficient functioning of the mind). Proponents of the *activation-synthesis theory* argue that REM sleep furnishes the brain with an internal source of activation (when external stimulation is minimal) to promote the growth and development of the brain. The content of a

172

dream results from such random stimulation, *not* unconscious wishes. In this view, the "meaning" of a dream comes as a "brainstorm afterthought" where meaningless activations, once synthesized, give a feeling of familiarity, coherence, and meaningfulness. The *activation-synthesis theory* helps to explain some of the "mysteries" of sleep where the essence of dreams may actually be a brain chemical (i.e., acetylcholine) that is turned "on" by one set of neurons in the brain stem during REM, and those neurons are "on" only when the others, which trigger the release of serotonin and norepinephrine, are "off." These two brain chemicals are necessary to store memories; people forget about 95 percent of their dreams because they are stored only temporarily in short-term memory, and they cannot be transferred to more permanent memory because serotonin and norepinephrine are shut off during the dream. This approach has opened the door to the molecular biology of sleep and closed it on the *psychoanalytic theory of dreams*. In another current theory, J. Antrobus' *neurocognitive theory*, dreams are regarded as variations of normal perceptual, cognitive, and motor activities. Under a high level of cortical arousal, produced by stimulation of the cortex by the reticular formation, together with a blocking of sensory input and motor input, various modules in the cortex interact with one another to produce the images and themes present in dreams, together with emotional responses to the dream content. It appears that humans are so competent at making sense out of chaos in waking life, they even do it in their sleep (cf., the *Poetzl phenomenon/effect* - following single tachistoscopic exposures of scenes, of about 1/100th second, the person's dreams the next night reflect with the greatest clarity those portions of the scene that the individual fails to report immediately after exposure or does not remember seeing). By understanding the mechanisms of *dreaming*, knowledge of the *waking* aspects of imagery and conscious thought processes, theoretically, may be enhanced. See also AROUSAL THEORY; FREUD'S THEORY OF PERSONALITY; IMAGERY AND MENTAL IMAGERY, THEORIES OF; JUNG'S THEORY OF PERSONALITY; POETZL/POTZL EFFECT; SHORT-TERM AND LONG-TERM MEMORY, THEORIES OF; SLEEP, THEORIES OF; UNCONSCIOUSNESS, PHENOMENON OF.

REFERENCES

Maury, A. (1861). *Le sommeil et les reves*. Paris: Didier.

Freud, S. (1900). The interpretation of dreams. In *The standard edition of the complete psychological works of Sigmund Freud*. Vols. 4, 5. London: Hogarth Press.

Bergson, H. (1901). *Dreams*. New York: Huebsch.

Warren, H. (Ed.) (1934). *Dictionary of psychology*. Cambridge, MA: Houghton Mifflin.

Jung, C. G. (1936). The concept of the collective unconscious. In *Collected works*. Vol. 9. Princeton, NJ: Princeton University Press.

Aserinsky, E., & Kleitman, N. (1953). Regularly occurring periods of eye motility and concomitant phenomena during sleep. *Science, 118*, 273-274.

Hall, C. (1953). *The meaning of dreams*. New York: McGraw-Hill.

Dement, W., & Kleitman, N. (1957). Cyclical variations in EEG during sleep and their relation to eye movements, bodily motility, and dreaming. *Electroencephalography & Clinical Neurophysiology, 9*, 673-690.

Boss, M. (1958). *The analysis of dreams*. New York: Philosophical Library.

Wolman, B. (Ed.) (1973). *Dictionary of behavioral science*. New York: Van Nostrand Reinhold.

Hobson, J., & McCarley, R. (1977). The brain as a dream state generator: An activation-synthesis hypothesis of the dream process. *American Journal of Psychiatry, 134*, 1335-1348.

Foulkes, D. (1978). *A grammar of dreams*. New York: Basic Books.

Hobson, J. (1988). *The dreaming brain*. New York: Basic Books.

Antrobus, J. (1991). Dreaming: Cognitive processes during cortical activation and high afferent thresholds. *Psychological Review, 98*, 96-121.

Bulkeley, K. (1997). *An introduction to the psychology of dreaming*. Westport, CT: Praeger.

DREIKURS' THEORY. See DEVELOPMENTAL THEORY.

DRIVE-REDUCTION THEORY/HYPOTHESIS. See AGGRESSION, THEORIES OF; HULL'S LEARNING THEORY; LEARNING THEORIES/LAWS; MOTIVATION, THEORIES OF; MOWRER'S THEORY; REINFORCEMENT THEORY.

DRIVE, THEORIES OF. See MOTIVATION, THEORIES OF.

DRIVE THEORY OF SOCIAL FACILITATION. See ZAJONC'S AROUSAL AND CONFLUENCE THEORIES.

DRY-MOUTH THEORY. See THIRST, THEORIES OF.

DUAL-AROUSAL THEORY. See SLEEP, THEORIES OF.

DUAL CODING HYPOTHESIS/MODEL/SYSTEM/THEORY. See IMAGERY/MENTAL IMAGERY, THEORIES OF.

DUAL-INSTINCT THEORY. See FREUD'S INSTINCT THEORY.

DUAL-INTELLIGENCE THEORY. See INTELLIGENCE, THEORIES OF.

DUALIST THEORY. See MIND-BODY THEORIES.

DUAL-MEMORY THEORY. See SHORT-TERM AND LONG-TERM MEMORY, THEORIES OF.

DUAL-PROCESS MODELS. In general, a *dual-process model* refers to any of several theories of social information processing (e.g., *elaboration likelihood model*) that originated in the 1980s and 1990s to explain phenomena such as social attitudes, person perception, stereotypes, memory, and decision-making. The basis of the *dual-process models* is trace-able to the American psychologist/philosopher William James (1842-1910), and these theories assert that there are two qualitatively different mechanisms of information-processing that are activated in forming judgments, making decisions, or solving problems. The first mechanism involves a rapid and easy processing mode based on an assumption of savings of energy/effort (*principle of least effort/energy*), and the second mechanism involves a slow and difficult rule-based, and systematic reasoning, processing mode. The first step in the dual-process often is unconscious and affective, and typically involves "automatic processing" (*automaticity*), whereas the second step is conscious and cognitive, and involves "controlled/deliberate processing." Recent work on *dual-process models* in psychology (e.g., Chaiken & Trope, 1999) makes the distinction between what people sometimes *think* they believe and what they *really* believe, that is, what resides at the *implicit* versus *explicit* levels of processing; for example, people may know that bad things happen in the world, but they simply do not believe that such things will happen to them. See also ATTITUDE/ATTITUDE CHANGE, THEORIES OF; AUTOMATICITY HYPOTHESIS; DECISION-MAKING THEORIES; ELABORATION LIKELIHOOD MODEL; FORGETTING/MEMORY, THEORIES OF; LEAST EFFORT, PRINCIPLE OF; LEAST-ENERGY EXPENDITURE, PRINCIPLE OF; PERSON PERCEPTION THEORY; SOCIAL PSYCHOLOGICAL DUAL-PROCESS MODELS.

REFERENCES

James, W. (1890). *The principles of psychology*. New York: Holt.

Chaiken, S., & Trope, Y. (Eds.) (1999). *Dual-process models in social psychology*. New York: Guilford.

DUAL-PROCESSES THEORY OF PREJUDICE. See PREJUDICE, THEORIES OF.

DUAL-ROUTE THEORY OF READING. One of the most influential current theories of word processing and reading is called the *dual-route theory* (cf., *dual-route cascaded model of reading*; Bates, Castles, Coltheart, Gillespie, Wright, & Martin, 2004) which proposes the existence of two functionally independent mechanisms of processing words: one involves access to "lexical knowledge," and the other involves access to "nonlexical grapheme-to-phoneme conversion." Thus, in the "strong version" of *dual-route theory*, it is held that in skilled readers there exist independent lexical and nonlexical routes for processing words (cf., Coltheart, 1981, 2004) where - in either of these routes - one may recognize or name words, and the dependence of word recognition or naming on either route is determined by their relative speed, the strategy adopted in the particular task, or both. One means of word processing, the lexical processing route, is thought to operate by a direct mapping of a word's visual characteristics onto a stored lexical representation. The other means, the nonlexical processing route, operates by translating the word's graphemic code into a phonological code on the basis of a small set of abstracted spelling-to-sound rules; such rules are nonlexical because their operation does not depend on word-specific spelling-to-sound knowledge. The *dual-route theory* has been used to examine issues such as the processing of "nonwords," the "spelling regularity effects," and the way in which reading may be impaired following "selective damage" to either of the two routes. Although the *dual-route theory of reading* has become highly popular in the area of word-processing analysis, the claims for an independent "nonlexical processing" route have been called into question recently (e.g., Humphreys & Evett, 1985). See also INFORMA-TION/INFORMA-TION-PROCESSING THEORY; PARALLEL DISTRIBUTED PROCESSING MOD-EL; PAT-TERN/OBJECT RECOGNITION THEORY.

REFERENCES

Coltheart, M. (1981). Disorders of reading and their implications for models of normal reading. *Visible Language, 15*, 245-286.

Humphreys, G. W., & Evett, L. J. (1985). Are there independent lexical and nonlexical routes in word processing? An evaluation of the dual-route theory of reading. *The Behavioral and Brain Sciences, 8*, 689-740.

Coltheart, M., Curtis, B., Atkins, P., & Haller, M. (1993). Models of reading aloud: Dual-route and parallel-distributed-processing approaches. *Psychological Review, 100*, 589-608.

Bates, T., Castles, A., Coltheart, M., Gillespie, N., Wright, M., & Martin, N. (2004). Behavior genetic analyses of reading and spelling: A component processes approach. *Australian Journal of Psychology, 56*, 115-126.

Coltheart, M. (2004). Are there lexicons? *Quarterly Journal of Experimental Psychology: Human Experimental Psychology, 57A*, 1153-1171.

DU BOIS-REYMOND, LAW OF. See NEURON/NEURAL/NERVE THEORY.

DUNCKER'S DISTANCE PARADOX/ EFFECT. See APPENDIX A.

DUPLICITY/DUPLEXITY THEORY. See VON KRIES' COLOR VISION THEORY.

DUPREEL'S SOCIOLOGICAL HUMOR/ LAUGHTER THEORY. The French sociologist Eugene Dupreel (1879-1967) argued that humor/laughter is purely a sociological problem and does not concern either psychology or metaphysics. *Dupreel's sociological humor/laughter theory* states that there are two kinds of laughter, both of which are *social*: the laughter of *companionship* (or "group-solidarity" and "inclusion"), and the laughter of *opposition* (or "exclusion"). In effect, Dupreel's two types of laughter demonstrate his general acceptance of Henri Bergson's "mechanization/automatism" view concerning the cause of laughter. However, although Dupreel accepts Bergson's view that the ludicrous always involves something mechanical (some automatism), this is the *consequence* - rather than the *cause* - of ridicule that excludes someone (i.e., the consequence that the "victim" appears to be "mechanical" and badly adjusted to the standards of the laughers in the group). See also BERGSON'S THEORY OF HUMOR/LAUGHTER; HUMOR, THEORIES OF; MARTINEAU'S SO-CIAL-COMMUNICATION MODEL OF HUMOR;

SOCIAL/COMMUNICATION THEORY OF LAUGHTER.
REFERENCE
Dupreel, E. (1928). Le probleme sociologique du rire. *Revue Philosophique, 106,* 213-260.

DURATION ESTIMATION PARADOX. See TIME, THEORIES OF.

DURATION, LAW OF. See ASSOCIATION, LAWS/PRINCIPLES OF; FREQUENCY, LAW OF.

DURATION, SENSE OF. See TIME, THEORIES OF.

DYADIC EFFECT. See COMMUNICATION THEORY.

DYNAMIC-EFFECT LAW. See MOTIVATION, THEORIES OF.

DYNAMIC INTERACTIONISM MODEL. See MOTIVATION, THEORIES OF.

DYNAMIC LAWS OF REFLEX STRENGTH. See SKINNER'S DESCRIPTIVE BEHAVIOR/OPERANT CONDITIONING THEORY.

DYNAMIC-SITUATIONS PRINCIPLE. See MOTIVATION, THEORIES OF.

DYNAMIC THEORY. See MOTIVATION, THEORIES OF; PERCEPTION (II. COMPARATIVE APPRAISAL), THEORIES OF; WUNDT'S THEORIES/DOCTRINES/PRINCIPLES.

DYNAMOGENESIS, LAW OF. See BALDWIN EFFECT; MOTIVATION, THEORIES OF; PERCEPTION (II. COMPARATIVE APPRAISAL), THEORIES OF.

DYSGENIC TREND THEORY. See INTELLIGENCE, THEORIES OF.

E

EARLY GREEK AND LATER PHILOSOPHICAL THEORIES OF TIME. Greek philosophers in the sixth- and fifth-centuries B.C. identified *dual aspects of time* (*being* - the "continuity" aspect of Parmenides; and *becoming* - the "transcience" aspect of Heraclitus) that, to this day, are concepts that are unreconciled. According to these early philosophers, time *extends* continuously from the past to the future (the *being* aspect), and things change in time (the *becoming* aspect). In the history of language, words for *time* are long preceded by words for *past, present,* and *future,* and the theoretical concept of *time* makes a relatively late appearance. The first attempt in the world to define and study, systematically and theoretically, the concept of *time* (and *motion*) derives from the ancient Greeks, primarily by the Eleatic school (a pre-Socratic philosophical school at Elea in Italy) founded by Parmenides (c.515 B.C.- ?) whose philosophy denied the reality of *change* on the basis that things either do, or do not, exist. The important notion of *change* is a fundamental assumption in modern-day theoretical treatments of temporal experience. Parmenides' point of view asserting that there are no "in-between" or "mediating" stages (such as the concept of *change* implies) served as an issue of debate among the early Greek philosophers, most notably Heraclitus (c.535-c. 475 B.C.) who taught that there is no permanent reality except the reality of *change,* and that permanence is an illusion of the senses. Although the early Greek philosophers apparently took the notion of *time* for granted, they generated significant questions involving *time.* In addition to the concept of *change* and its influence on the concept of *time,* the speculations of Pythagoras (c.582–c.507 B.C.) regarding the notion of *number* had a direct formative influence on Aristotle's (384–323 B.C.) later philosophy of *time,* and paradoxical problems such those posed by Zeno (c. 490-c.430 B.C.), directed attention critically toward the concept of *time.* According to an account by the Greek biographer and historian Plutarch (c.46-c.120 A.D.), when asked what *time* was, Pythagoras replied that it was the soul, or procreative element, of the universe. The degree to which Pythagoras and his followers were influenced by earlier conceptualizations of *time* - such as Asian/Oriental notions - is open to speculation. However, the Orphic (6th century B.C. religious cult in Greece) conception of *kronos* [related to *Cronus* - a Greek legendary figure (probably a god of agriculture of a pre-Hellenic people) who fathered mythologically the great gods Zeus, Poseidon, and Hades, among others] has features common with the Iranian notion of "Zurvan Akarana" (infinite or unending time). The concept of "Father Time" is believed to stem from Cronus, and later Greeks referred to him as Chronus, the god of time who - with his sickle - cuts down the passing years. Today, "Father Time" symbolizes the end of the year. Apparently, though, before the 5th century B.C., and the writings of the Athenian tragic poet Aeschylus (525-456 B.C.), the concept of *time* was relatively unimportant for the Greeks. Zeno of Elea - Parmenides' famous disciple - used a series of paradoxes (*Zeno's paradoxes*) to show logically the indefensibility of commonsense notions of reality [e.g., an arrow shot toward a target theoretically never reaches the target because a moving body (the arrow) can never come to the end of a line (the target) as it must first cover half the line, then half the remainder, and so on ad infinitum]. Although *Zeno's paradoxes* were concerned primarily with the problem of *motion,* they raised theoretical difficulties both for the notion of *time* as continuous or infinitely divisible, and the notion of *temporal atomicity.* Xenocrates (396-314 B.C), Anaxagoras (c.500-428 B.C.), and Democritus (c.460-c.370 B.C.) originated and advanced the *atomic theory* which occasionally figured in temporal problems and solutions of *Zeno's paradox*: if *time* consists of the indivisible moments, often referred to as "chrons," *motion* consists of imperceptible jerks that may explain how the arrow *actually* strikes the target. Plato (c.427-347 B.C.) conceived of *time* as a reality that is an "absolute flowing" apart from the events filling it. Parmenides' and Zeno's influence on Plato is apparent in the different treatment of *space* and *time* in Plato's various cosmological references: *space* exists in its own right as a given basis for the visible order of things, whereas *time* is merely an aspect of that order based on an "ideal" timeless archetype and involves static geometrical shapes ("eternity") of which *time* is the "moving image" and is governed by a regular numerical sequence occasioned by the *motions* of the heavenly bodies. Thus, Plato's intimate pairing of *time* with the universe led him to consider *time* as being produced, essentially, by celestial sphere revolutions (cf., Aristotle who rejected the idea that *time* is identified with any particular form of motion). It may be noted that *time* per se is nowhere contemplated psychologically by Plato; *time* is not one of Plato's "five categories" (Being, Rest, Motion, Sameness, and Difference). Among the Scholastic philosophers of the Middle Ages, St. Albertus Magnus (c.1193-1280 A.D.) held that natural philosophy, rather than metaphysics, is the primary discipline in which *time* is properly studied; he argued that because *time* is an attribute of the events of the physical world, *time's* mode of being is analogous to *motion's*. Magnus asserted that *time* does not possess *enduring* being (as do rocks, trees, and stars), but *time* does have *successive* being which flows and is always losing what was had and gaining what is to come. Magnus argued, also, that the present moment or "now," which is all of *time* that exists, is a flowing reality that is the end of the past and the beginning of the future. Magnus' concern was with the being and nature of *time* ("chronos"), rather than the measurement of time ("chronometrics"). Another Scholastic, St. Thomas Aquinas (1225-1274) - like his mentor St. Albertus Magnus - attempted to "Christianize Aristotle" by introducing Aristotle's scientific treatises and methods to Europe. Characteristic of the discussions of *time* during Aquinas' life were determinations of - and the differences between - *time, eternity,* and "aevum" (i.e., an attribute of the heavenly bodies and the angels; cf., *eternity* which is predicated only of God). Aquinas' best opinion was that *eternity* is a totality without the beginning, end, or succession essential to *time* and capable of being conjoined with "aevum." The most im-

portant theoretical theme in Aquinas' writings involving the notion of *time* is a *divine eternity* or "timelessness;" he interpreted the Biblical opposition between *time* and *eternity* in terms of its elaboration by neo-Platonic writers, notably St. Augustine (354-430). The last of the Scholastic philosophers, Francisco Suarez (1548-1617), made a distinction between "physical time" that measures the motions of the heavens, and "spiritual discrete time" that is composed of the indivisible, successive *instants of change* in the intellections and volitions of the angels, and is measured by the thought of the Supreme Angel. Suarez suggested that the seemingly successive parts of an action, and hence their real *duration*, may be conceived as a whole in a form that is nonsuccessive; he also considered the idea of *time* as a sort of space flowing from *eternity* as purely imaginary, and the location of a given *duration* in such a space as a purely mental act. However, Suarez did not seem to grasp the radical conception of *time* in totality as a mental construction. With the succeeding philosophers - such as Descartes, Hobbes, Spinoza, Locke, Leibnitz, Berkeley, Hartley, Hume, Kant, Fichte, Hegel, Schelling, and Herbart - the notions of *succession, duration, intuition, subjectivity, objectivity,* and *consciousness* take on additional meaning and importance for a cumulative and balanced understanding of the theories of *time*. See also ARISTOTLE'S TIME THEORY/PARADOX; BERGSON'S THEORY OF TIME; GUYAU'S THEORY OF TIME; PLOTINUS' THEORY OF TIME; ST. AUGUSTINE'S TIME THEORY/PARADOX; TIME, THEORIES OF.

REFERENCE

Roeckelein, J. E. (2000). *The concept of time in psychology*. Westport, CT: Greenwood Press.

EARLY SELECTION THEORIES. See ATTENTION, LAWS/PRINCIPLES OF.

EASTERBROOK HYPOTHESIS. See EMOTIONS, THEORIES/LAWS OF.

EASTMAN'S THEORY OF LAUGHTER. The American author Max Eastman (1883-1969) was an enthusiastic proponent of the *instinct* notion of humor and incorporated this into his *theory of laughter* where "human laughter finds its canine equivalent in the wagging of the tail." According to *Eastman's theory of laughter*, laughter is a means of social communication or pleasure that has acquired a kind of identity in humans' nervous systems with a state of satisfaction or joy. In Eastman's *instinct* approach, the activities of play and playfulness are a "hereditary gift" that are more spontaneous and instinctive than they are deliberate or conscious. Also, in *Eastman's theory of laughter*, ancient or primitive humans' initial laughter may have involved a "fighting-glory-laughter" sequence (i.e., triumphing over adversity) in which a primitive hunter would act like a ferocious gorilla, gnashing its teeth and thumping its chest, and laughing - after overcoming a formidable human or subhuman foe in combat. Thus the first savage who cracked his enemy over the head with a rock or heavy stick and cried "ha, ha!" was probably the world's first humorist, and began what may be called the "merry ha! ha!" form of humor - presumably the oldest and most primitive form of humor or laughter (cf., Leacock, 1935, 1937). Although, apparently, there are not yet any formal scientific "laws" of humor extant in psychology, Eastman (1921) formally offers his "first eight laws of a code for serious jokemakers" (e.g., "the feelings aroused in the person who is expected to laugh must not be too strong and deep"); he also informally devises "four laws of humor" (e.g., "things can be funny only when we are in fun") which - according to Eastman (1937) - defines "all there is in the science of humor as seen from a distance." See also COMMUNICATION THEORY OF LAUGHTER; HUMOR, THEORIES OF; INSTINCT THEORY; RAPP'S THEORY OF THE ORIGINS OF LAUGHTER AND HUMOR; THERAPEUTIC THEORY OF LAUGHTER AND HUMOR.

REFERENCES

Eastman, M. (1921). *The sense of humor*. New York: Scribner's.

Eastman, M. (1937). *Enjoyment of laughter*. Kent, UK: Hamish Hamilton.

Leacock, S. B. (1935). *Humour: Its theory & technique*. New York: Dodd, Mead.

Leacock, S. B. (1937). *Humour and humanity*. London: Butterworth.

EBBINGHAUS' DOCTRINE OF REMOTE ASSOCIATIONS. See SERIAL-POSITION EFFECT.

EBBINGHAUS/TITCHENER ILLUSION. See APPENDIX A.

ECCLESIASTES HYPOTHESIS. See MATTHEW EFFECT.

ECHOIC MEMORY/STORE. See SHORT-TERM AND LONG-TERM MEMORY, THEORIES OF.

ECHO PRINCIPLE. See LANGUAGE ORIGINS, THEORIES OF.

ECLECTIC INFLUENCE MODELS. See PERSUASION/INFLUENCE THEORIES.

ECOLOGICAL SYSTEMS MODEL. See PSYCHOPATHOLOGY, THEORIES OF.

ECONOMY OF EFFORT, LAW/PRINCIPLE OF. See CONDUCT, LAWS OF; LEAST EFFORT, PRINCIPLE OF.

ECONOMY, PRINCIPLE OF. See PARSIMONY, LAW/PRINCIPLE OF.

EDUCATIONAL THEORY. See HERBART'S DOCTRINE OF APPERCEPTION; LEARNING THEORIES/LAWS; MIND AND MENTAL STATES, THEORIES OF; TRANSFER OF TRAINING, THORNDIKE'S THEORY OF.

EFFECT, LAW OF. = empirical law of effect = Thorndike's law of effect = law of psychological hedonism. This is one of the major principles of the American psychologist Edward Lee Thorndike's (1874-1949) *learning theory*, which states that "satisfaction" strengthens a stimulus-response connection or bond, and "annoyance" weakens or gradually eliminates a stimulus-response bond. The *law of effect* is also called the *empirical law of effect* and the *law of selection* (cf., the most-likely law - posits that in predicting an organism's behavior that what has occurred most often in the past is what is most likely to happen in the future). In its original form, the *law of effect* states that of several responses made to the same situation, those that are accompanied or closely followed by satisfaction to the organism will, other things being equal, be more firmly connected with the situation, and those that are accompanied or closely followed by discomfort to the organism will, other things being equal, have their connections with that situation weakened. The greater the satisfaction (or discomfort), the greater the strengthening (or weakening) of the stimulus-response bond. Other forms of the *law of effect* are called *strong law of effect*, *weak law of effect*, and *negative law of effect*. The *weak law of effect* states that a response is more likely to recur if it is followed by a reinforcer, a "satisfier," or a "satisfying state of affairs." The *strong law of effect*, which is an extension of the *empirical* or *weak law of effect*, states that the necessary condition for a response to be learned is the explicit occurrence of a reinforcer(s) or a "satisfying state of affairs" after the response is exhibited (this is not a necessary requirement in other learning theories, such as E. R. Guthrie's *contiguity theory*). The *negative law of effect*, as a reciprocal of the *weak law of effect*, states that responses that are followed by an "annoying state of affairs" are less likely to be repeated. The *negative law of effect* was dropped by Thorndike in his later writings when he became convinced that punishment ("annoying state of affairs") did not simply "stamp out" behavior in the same way that reinforcers ("satisfiers") "stamp in" behavior. Historically, much confusion concerning the *law of effect* has resulted from failure to differentiate the law on three points: as an empirical statement; as a general theory of reinforcement; and as special hypotheses concerning the nature of reinforcers and their action characteristics. However, an implementation of the *law of effect* (cf., *minimal social situation effect*) may be seen in the *win-stay*, *lose-change strategy*, which is a simple strategy used in any sequential decision task/game where the first decision or move is chosen arbitrarily, and then whenever a choice leads to reward, the player repeats it on the following trial, and

whenever it leads to punishment or non-reward, the player switches to an alternate option on the following trial; e.g., Kelley, Thibaut, Radloff, & Mundy, 1962; cf., *three-door game show problem/effect*). Consistent criticism against the *law of effect* has focused on the tautology or circularity in reasoning inherent in the law (cf., *reinforcement retroactive paradox/hypothesis* - the contradictory notion that a reward *after* an activity can strengthen that activity, thus showing a "backward effect"). That is, it is difficult to explain an instance of learning in terms of its "effects" because the effects happen *after* the behavior or learning has already occurred, or the only way one can tell whether or not a given result is satisfying is by observing to see whether or not the organism repeats the behavior that produced the supposed reward. The circular reasoning is that a "satisfying state of affairs" is one that increases responding, and any event that increases responding is a "satisfying state of affairs." Thus, for example, an individual likes a stimulus (e.g., applause) because he or she repeats a behavior (e.g., acting on stage), and the individual repeats a behavior (e.g., acting on stage) because he or she likes the stimulus (e.g., applause). See also BELONGINGNESS, LAW/PRINCIPLE OF; EXERCISE, LAW OF; GUTHRIE'S THEORY; HEDONISM, THEORY/LAW OF; HERRNSTEIN'S MATCHING LAW; LEARNING THEORIES/LAWS; MINIMAL SOCIAL SITUATION EFFECT; READINESS, LAW OF; REINFORCEMENT, THORNDIKE'S THEORY OF; THREE-DOOR GAME SHOW PROBLEM/EFFECT.

REFERENCES

Thorndike, E. L. (1911). *Animal intelligence: Experimental studies*. New York: Macmillan.

Thorndike, E. L. (1927). The law of effect. *American Journal of Psychology*, *39*, 212-222.

Stephens, J. M. (1929). A mechanical explanation of the law of effect. *American Journal of Psychology*, *41*, 422-431.

Tolman, E. C., Hall, C., & Bretnall, E. (1932). A disproof of the law of effect and a substitution of the laws of emphasis, motivation, and disruption. *Journal of Experimental Psychology, 15,* 601-614.

Guthrie, E. R. (1935). *The psychology of learning.* New York: Harper.

Razran, G. (1939). The law of effect or the law of qualitative conditioning. *Psychological Review, 46,* 445-463.

Mowrer, O. H. (1946). The law of effect and ego psychology. *Psychological Review, 53,* 321-334.

Postman, L. (1947). The history and present status of the law of effect. *Psychological Bulletin, 44,* 489-563.

Meehl, P. E. (1950). On the circularity of the law of effect. *Psychological Bulletin, 47,* 52-75.

Kelley, H. H., Thibaut, J. W., Radloff, R., & Mundy, D. (1962). The development of cooperation in the "minimal social situation." *Psychological Monographs, 76,* 1-19.

Herrnstein, R. (1970). On the law of effect. *Journal of the Experimental Analysis of Behavior, 13,* 243-266.

EGAN EFFECT. See AUDITION/HEARING, THEORIES OF.

EGO-ALTER THEORY. See ORGANIZATIONAL/INDUSTRIAL/SYSTEMS THE-ORY; SELF-CONCEPT THEORY.

EGO DEVELOPMENT, THEORIES OF. See ALLPORT'S THEORY OF PERSONALITY; DEVELOPMENTAL THEORY.

EGOISTIC THEORY OF DREAMS. See DREAM THEORY.

EGO PSYCHOLOGY. See ERIKSON'S THEORY OF PERSONALITY.

EGO-STATE THEORY. See HYPNOSIS/HYPNOTISM, THEORIES OF.

EHRENSTEIN BRIGHTNESS AND SQUARE ILLUSIONS. See APPENDIX A; SPILLMAN'S ILLUSION.

EICHMANN EFFECT. See SOCIAL IMPACT, LAW OF.

EIDOTROPICS, LAW OF. See GESTALT THEORY/LAWS.

EIGHTFOLD-PATH DOCTRINE/THEORY. See CONDUCT, LAWS OF.

EINSTEIN'S THEORY OF RELATIVITY. See NEWTON'S LAW/PRINCIPLES OF COLOR MIXTURE.

EINSTELLUNG EFFECT. See LEARNED HELPLESSNESS EFFECT; MIND/MENTAL SET, LAW OF; PERCEPTION (II. COMPARATIVE APPRAISAL), THEORIES OF.

EKMAN-FRIESEN THEORY OF EMOTIONS. This current *theory of emotions* by the American psychologists Paul Ekman (1934-), William V. Friesen, and their associates, combines a *somatic theory of emotions* (the somatic nervous system controls many bodily muscles, including facial muscles) with an *evolutionary theory of emotions* (based on the *Darwinian theory* which states that some ways of expressing emotions are inborn). The *Ekman-Friesen theory* argues that there are distinct facial expressions that accompany a number of emotions, including fear, joy, surprise, anger, excitement, scorn, and sadness. When an environmental event occurs, the person's facial muscles react with an emotional expression. The information of how the face is responding is transmitted to the brain, which then labels a specific emotional state. In this way, autonomic arousal may occur either before or after the labeling of an emotion. When it occurs before the labeling process, it may be incorporated into the label and influence the interpretation of the intensity of the emotion. This theory has been proposed to account for emotional behavior across cultures, and Ekman and Friesen found many similarities in the way people from different cultures express specific emotions. However, although such cross-cultural studies demonstrate some degree of universality in emotional expression, research continues to help decide if emotional expression is inborn as the *Darwinian evolutionary theory* suggests. See also DARWIN'S EVOLUTION THEORY; DARWIN'S THEORY OF EMOTIONS;

EMOTIONS, THEORIES/LAWS OF; FA-
CIAL FEEDBACK HYPOTHESIS; IZARD'S
THEORY OF EMOTIONS; JAMES-LANGE/
LANGE-JAMES THEORY OF EMOTIONS;
PLUTCHIK'S MODEL OF EMOTIONS.

REFERENCES

Langfeld, H. (1918). The judgment of emotion
by facial expression. *Journal of Abnormal and Social Psychology, 13,*
172-184.

Feleky, A. (1922). *Feelings and emotions.*
New York: Pioneer Press.

Frois-Wittmann, J. (1930). The judgment of
facial expressions. *Journal of Experimental Psychology, 13,* 113-
151.

Munn, N. (1940). The effect of knowledge of
the situation upon judgment of emotions from facial expressions. *Journal of Abnormal and Social Psychology, 35,* 324-338.

Andrew, R. (1965). The origins of facial expressions. *Scientific American, 4,*
88-94.

Ekman, P., & Friesen, W. V. (1971). Constants across culture in the face and
emotions. *Journal of Personality
and Social Psychology, 17,* 124-129.

Ekman, P., & Friesen, W. V. (1975). *Unmask-
ing the face.* Englewood Cliffs, NJ:
Prentice-Hall.

Ekman, P., & Friesen, W. V. (1978). *The Facial Action Coding System: A technique for the measurement of facial
movement.* San Francisco: Consulting Psychologists Press.

Ekman, P., Levenson, R., & Friesen, W. V.
(1983). Autonomic nervous system
activity distinguishes among emotions. *Science, 221,* 1208-1210.

Ekman, P. (1993). Facial expressions and
emotion. *American Psychologist,
48,* 384-392.

Ekman, P. (1994). Strong evidence for universals in facial expressions: A reply to
Russell's mistaken critique. *Psychological Bulletin, 115,* 268-287.

ELABORATION LIKELIHOOD MODEL.
See ATTITUDE/ATTITUDE CHANGE,
THEORIES OF; PERSUASION AND IN-
FLUENCE THEORIES.

ELATION EFFECT. See CRESPI EFFECT.

**ELECTRODERMAL ACTIVITY AND
PHENOMENA.** The term *electrodermal activity* (EDA) is used by psychophysiologists to
refer to the electrical activity of the skin on
the palms of the hand or on the fingers. The
first researchers to use this measure thought
that it indicated the "secrets" of mental life.
However, today, EDA is considered merely as
a state of the individual's interaction with the
environment. The terms used to describe EDA
have changed over the years. The term *psy-
chogalvanic reflex* (PGR) was used during the
early 1900s, and later the term *galvanic skin
response* (GSR) became popular [named in
honor of the Italian physiologist Luigi Galvani
(1737-1798), who discovered animal electric-
ity]. The difficulty found, later, with the term
GSR was that it came to describe several different aspects of EDA (e.g., basal level, response amplitude), and most psychophysiologists today seem to prefer the term EDA. The
electrical activity of the skin may be measured
in two ways: the *Fere method* and the
Tarchanoff method. The French neurologist
Charles S. Fere (1852-1907) used an "exoso-
matic" method, often referred to as the *Fere
effect/phenomenon,* where a small current is
passed through the skin from an external
source, following which the resistances to the
passage of current are measured. The Russian
physiologist Ivan R. Tarchanoff (1846-1908)
used an "endosomatic" method, often referred
to today as the *Tarchanoff effect/phenomenon,*
where the electrical activity is measured at the
surface of the skin with no externally imposed
current. The *Fere method* has been modified
today into the measurement of *skin conduc-
tance* (SC), which is the reciprocal of skin
"resistance." *Tarchanoff's method* is still used
today to measure *skin potential* (SP). The
galvanometer is an instrument that measures
electric current and provides a measure of the
electrical response of the skin. Thus, Fere's
measure records changes in the resistance of
the skin to the passage of a weak electric current, and Tarchanoff's measure records weak
current actually produced by the body. Because the Fere measure increases with increasing amounts of perspiration, it is assumed,
often, to be an indication of emotional tension

or anxiety (as employed in the so-called "lie detection" or "polygraph" procedure). However, this assumption has proven difficult to substantiate, and it is probably best to consider it merely as a general measure of physiological arousal. See also EMOTIONS, THEORIES/LAWS OF.

REFERENCES

Fere, C. S. (1888). Note sur les modifications de la resistance electrique sous l'influence des excitations sensorielles et des emotions. *Comptes Rendus Societe Biologique Memoir, 40*, 217-219.

Tarchanoff, I. R. (1890). Uber die galvanischen erscheinungen in der haut des menschen bei reizungen der sinnesorgane und bei verschiedennen formen der psychischen thatigkeit. *Pflugers Archiv Gesamte Physiologie , 46*, 46-55.

Newmann, E., & Blauton, R. (1970). The early history of electrodermal research. *Psychophysiology, 6*, 453-475.

Stern, R., Ray, W., & Davis, C. (1980). *Psychophysiological recording.* New York: Oxford University Press.

ELECTROLYTE METABOLISM THEORY OF DEPRESSION. See DEPRESSION, THEORIES OF.

ELECTRON-PROTON THEORY. See LIFE, THEORIES OF.

ELICITED OBSERVING RATE HYPOTHESIS. This conjecture describes the complex relation between observing activity, decision processes, and vigilance in sustained attention tasks. This hypothesis attempts, also, to formulate the issue of vigilance within the framework of *signal detection theory.* The *elicited observing rate hypothesis* makes the assumption that during vigilance activities (e.g., a sailor's monitoring a sonar screen to detect enemy submarines) the observer constantly makes sequential decisions as to emit or not to emit an observing response toward a display that is being monitored. In general terms, observing responses are termed *unitary attentive acts* and may involve "internal" message selection by the central nervous system. The hypothesis states that signal detection failures (e.g., an enemy sub was present, but the sailor didn't see or hear it) occur when the individual does not emit the observing responses and, also, proposes that the effort involved in observing has a quantifiable energy "cost" where decisions to observe or not to observe are based on their *utility* (i.e., the "cost" of observing relative to the "reward" of correct signal detection). Poor vigilance, according to the hypothesis, results from the decrement in quality and quantity of elicited observing behavior over a period of time and where factors such as fatigue and low motivation account for the high "costs" of the observing activity. Definitive tests of the *elicited observing rate hypothesis* are difficult because of the imprecise specification of the nature of the "internal" observing mechanism. See also ATTENTION, LAWS/PRINCIPLES/THEORIES OF; DECISION-MAKING THEORIES; SIGNAL DETECTION, THEORY OF; UTILITY THEORY; VIGILANCE, THEORIES OF.

REFERENCES

Baker, C. (1960). Observing behavior in a vigilance task. *Science, 132*, 674-675.

Jerison, H., & Pickett, R. (1964). Vigilance: The importance of the elicited observing rate. *Science, 143*, 970-971.

Jerison, H. (1970). Vigilance, discrimination, and attention. In D. Mostofsky (Ed.), *Attention: Contemporary theory and analysis.* New York: Appleton-Century-Crofts.

Jerison, H. (1977). Vigilance, biology, psychology, theory, and practice. In R. Mackie (Ed.), *Vigilance: Theory, operational performance, and physiological correlates.* New York: Plenum.

ELIMINATION BY ASPECTS THEORY. = lexicographic choice theory. The Israeli psychologist Amos Tversky (1937-1996) formulated this *theory of multiattribute decision-making* whereby a *choice* is reached via an iterated series of eliminations, and where at each iteration, the decision-maker chooses an attribute (quality, property, aspect, or feature) of a phenomenon. In this approach, the probability of choosing is proportional to the perceived importance of the attribute, and there is elimination of all alternatives that lack the attribute in question. Subsequently, selection is made of the next most important attribute and proceeds in a similar manner, on and on, until all but one of the alternatives have been eliminated. In a variation method of multiattribute decision-making, called the *linear additive value-maximization model*, a person purchasing a house, for example, may choose a house by comparing alternatives according to variables/attributes such as location, price, proximity to schools, and number of rooms in the house. According to this variation, the decision-maker simply gives weights to the attributes based on their perceived importance, then sums the weights, and finally chooses the alternative with the highest aggregate weight. Although these various approaches are not guaranteed to produce an optimal choice, empirical and experimental tests indicate that they are fairly typical of human multiattribute decision-making. See also BOUNDED RATIONALITY PRINCIPLE; CHOICE THEORIES; DECISION-MAKING THEORIES.

REFERENCE

Tversky, A. (1972). Elimination by aspects: A theory of choice. *Psychological Review, 79*, 281-299.

EMBOITEMENT, THEORY OF. This biologically-based theory is stated by the English philosopher Herbert Spencer (1820-1903) as follows: "[I]n the germ of every living creature the future adult exists...and within this exist the immeasurably more minute forms of adults which will eventually descend from it, and so on *ad infinitum*" (Spencer, 1892, p. 655). The term *emboitement*, ac-cording to Webster's 1986 unabridged dictionary is defined as "encasement; to put into a box; encase; fit together." Although it does have a certain intuitive appeal (much like the *theory of recapitulation*), as a theory in psychology the notion of *emboitement* appears to be somewhat archaic and is mentioned only infrequently by authors of psychology textbooks. For example, in a study that sampled 136 textbooks published from 1885 to 1996 (Roeckelein, 1996), only one writer (Spencer,

1892) makes reference to the *theory of emboitement*. See also RECAPITULATION, THEORY/LAW OF.

REFERENCES

Spencer, H. (1892). *The principles of psychology*. New York: Appleton.

Roeckelein, J. E. (1996). Citation of *laws* and *theories* in textbooks across 112 years of psychology. *Psychological Reports, 79*, 979-998.

EMERGENCY THEORY. See CANNON/ CANNON-BARD THEORY.

EMINENCE, THEORIES AND MEASURES OF. *Eminence* may be defined, generally, as a condition of prominence or superiority by reason of rank, office, or personal attainments. In the context of psychology, the notion of *eminence* is defined and measured using various theoretical and empirical approaches. For example, the English naturalist/psychologist Sir Francis Galton (1822-1911) asserted that there is a general tendency for *eminence* to run in certain families and such abilities are inherited. Galton selected his "eminent men" via biographical protocols that were then paired with the person's number of eminent relatives. The American psychologist J. M. Cattell's approach employed the method of the "order of merit" that included a calculation of the average ranking for each scientist's name, followed by a final rank order of names. E. L. Annin, E. G. Boring, and R. I. Watson measured *eminence* by a rating scale that was given to a panel of nine judges who rated names on a 3-point familiarity/evaluation scale with total possible scores ranging from 0 to 27. Criticizing the Annin, et al. study on methodological grounds, L. Zusne conducted an improved study and found an extremely skewed distribution of ratings more in agreement with the theoretically expected shape of such a frequency distribution. Subsequently, Zusne recommended the use of a ranking, rather than a rating, method for assessing *eminence*. Zusne demonstrated that a hyperbolic function describes the relationship between page-space given to particular psychologists in the history of psychology textbooks and their rank in terms of that space (cf., Coleman, 1991). Such a hyperbolic function was found, also, by J. E. Roeckelein who assessed space given to psychologists' names (cf., *eponymy theory* - study of the influence and impact of naming/surnames in the history of psychology) in introductory psychology textbooks when drawn from different time periods. S. J. Haggbloom, et al. measured psychological *eminence* - and provide a rank-ordered list of the 100 most eminent psychologists of the 20th century - using scores on three *quantitative* (e.g., citation frequency counts of names in psychological publications) and three *qualitative* (e.g., membership in professional organizations) variables or factors (cf., Wispe, 1965; Feist, 1993). In his approach to *eminence theory*, D. K. Simonton proposes that a latent factor - that he calls "Galton's G" (analogous to the traditional "Spearman's g" in *intelligence theory*) and which cuts across various alternative measures of *eminence* - may account for individual differences in attained distinction and *eminence*. Thus, based on diverse, alternative measurements made on psychologists' names, it appears, empirically, that those who are highly *eminent* in psychology receive a *disproportionate* share of attention, praise, and citation space in the psychological literature. See also LOTKA/LOTKA-PRICE LAW; MATTHEW EFFECT; NATURALISTIC THEORY OF HISTORY; PERSONALISTIC THEORY OF HISTORY.

REFERENCES

Galton, F. (1869/1962). *Hereditary genius: An inquiry into its laws and consequences*. London: Collins.

Cattell, J. M. (1927). The origin and distribution of scientific men. *Science, 66*, 513-516.

Wispe, L. (1965). Some social and psychological correlates of eminence in psychology. *Journal of the History of the Behavioral Sciences, 1*, 88-98.

Annin, E. L., Boring, E. G., & Watson, R. I. (1968). Important psychologists, 1600-1967. *Journal of the History of the Behavioral Sciences, 4*, 303-315.

Roeckelein, J. E. (1972). Eponymy in psychology. *American Psychologist, 27*, 657-659.

Zusne, L. (1975). Contributions to the history of psychology: XXI. History of rat-ing eminence in psychology revisited. *Psychological Reports, 36*, 492-494.

Zusne, L. (1985). Contributions to the history of psychology: XXXVIII. The hyperbolic structure of eminence. *Psychological Reports, 57*, 1213-1214.

Coleman, S. R. (1991). Contributions to the history of psychology: LXXX. The hyperbolic structure of eminence updated, 1975-1986. *Psychological Reports, 68*, 1067-1070.

Feist, G. J. (1993). A structural model of scientific eminence. *Psychological Science, 4*, 366-371.

Roeckelein, J. E. (1996). Contributions to the history of psychology: CIV. Eminence in psychology as measured by name counts and eponyms. *Psychological Reports, 78*, 243-253.

Haggbloom, S. J., Warnick, R., Warnick, J., Jones, V., Yarbrough G., Russell, T., Borecky, C., McGahhey, R., Powell, J., Beavers, J., & Monte, E. (2002). The 100 most eminent psychologists of the 20th century. *Review of General Psychology, 6*, 139-152.

Simonton, D. K. (2002). *Great psychologists and their times: Scientific insights into psychology's history*. Washington, D.C.: American Psychological Association.

EMMERT'S LAW. = size-distance invariance hypothesis. This generalized principle is named in honor of the Swiss ophthalmologist Emil Emmert (1844-1911) and refers to the tendency of a projected image (usually an *afterimage*) to increase in size in proportion to the distance to which it is projected onto a background surface. *Emmert's law* is also called the *afterimage law*; cf., U. Ebbecke (1929) who proposed a *theory of positive and negative afterimages*. Another *afterimage* phenomenon is the *McCollough effect/color-contingent aftereffect* - named after the American psychologist Celeste Faye McCollough (1926-) - which is a persistent afterimage produced by saturating the eye with red and green patterns of different angularity: in a typical demonstration, a pattern of bright red and black horizontal lines is alternated with a pattern of bright green and black vertical lines every five seconds for several minutes. Following these exposures, a pattern of black and white lines at various angles is presented and, when the afterimage appears, the horizontal white lines are seen as tinged with green and the vertical with red. If the head is tilted 90 degrees, the colors change, taking on the appropriate coloration. The *McCollough effect* may last up to four or five days. *Emmert's law* is based on the use of size as a cue in estimating distance and involves the geometry of visual size and depth that suggests the following equation (this equation is also called *Euclid's law* - named after the Greek mathematician Euclid, c. 300 B.C.): $a = A/D$, where a is the retinal image of an object, A is the actual size of the object, and D is the distance from the object to the retina. This equation says, at face value, that the farther away an object is, the smaller it should look ("retinal size"). However, there is an apparent exception to *Euclid's law*. In 1881, Emmert reported that an *afterimage* actually looks bigger if it is projected on a more distant surface; that is, the judged size of the image is proportional to the distance (*Emmert's law*). Thus, *Emmert's law*, essentially, is a special case of *Euclid's law*. The relationship of the variable of size to the variable of distance was studied earlier by the Italian physicist Benedetto Castelli (1578-1643), and by the German physiologist and psychologist Hermann von Helmholtz (1821-1894), the latter who argued that observers learn through experience that an object's physical size remains the same (invariant), although its retinal image size varies with distance. Thus, one's perceptual system records the size of the retinal image and then changes or corrects this information in light of available cues about distance to arrive at judgments of object size. Helmholtz suggested, also, that in perceiving object size, people implicitly solve the equation: object size = retinal size x distance (cf., *Euclid's law*). More recently, this view of size constancy constitutes the *size-distance invariance hypothesis*, which implies that accurate perception of an object's distance leads to accurate perception of its size. Thus, the link between the *size-distance invariance hypothesis* and *Em-*

mert's law is the use in the latter of an *afterimage* of an object that is projected onto a background surface. The basic principles concerning the relationship between perceived size and perceived distance remain the same in either case. The *size-distance invariance hypothesis* has been generally useful in the psychology of perception. For instance, it is the most widely cited account of the phenomenon of *size constancy*, but it has also generated controversy, and there are limits to its applicability [cf., *shape-slant invariance hypothesis*, also called "shape-tilt invariance," refers to a conjecture (that is apparently obvious yet contradicted by empirical evidence) that impressions of the shape, slant, or orientation of an object are mutually dependent, with the result that misperceptions of shape produce misperceptions of slant, and vice versa]. *Emmert's law* and the *size-distance invariance hypothesis* have been invoked as a possible explanation for one of the classical illusions, the *moon illusion* (i.e., the experience where the perceived size of a full moon observed on the horizon seems much larger than the same moon when viewed overhead at its zenith a few hours later; also called the *celestial illusion* because the effect may also occur with respect to the sun), which has been a puzzle since antiquity and has been discussed repeatedly in ancient and medieval literature. However, there seems to be no single final answer or explanation, such as *Emmert's law*, for the ancient puzzle and curiosity of the *moon illusion*. See also PERCEPTION (I. GENERAL), THEORIES OF; PERCEPTION (II. COMPARATIVE APPRAI-SAL) THEORIES OF; VISION/SIGHT, THEORIES OF.

REFERENCES

Emmert, E. (1881). Grossenverhaltnisse der nachbilder. *Klinical Monatsblatter der Augenheilkunde*, 443-450.

Helmholtz, H. von (1856-1866). *Handbuch der physiologischen optik*, Leipzig: Voss.

Ebbecke, U. (1929). [Afterimage theory]. *Archiv fur die Gesamte Physiologie*, *221*, 160-212.

Boring, E. G. (1943). The moon illusion. *American Journal of Physics*, *11*, 55-60.

Edwards, W. (1950). Emmert's law and Euclid's optics. *American Journal of Psychology, 63,* 607-612.

Boring, E. G., & Edwards, W. (1951). What is Emmert's law? *American Journal of Psychology, 64,* 416-422.

Kilpatrick, F., & Ittelson, W. (1953). The size-distance invariance hypothesis. *Psychological Review, 60,* 223-231.

Epstein, W., Park, J., & Casey, A. (1961). The current status of the size-distance hypothesis. *Psychological Bulletin, 58,* 491-514.

Boring, E. G. (1962). On the moon illusion. *Science, 137,* 902-906.

Kaufman, L., & Rock I. (1962). The moon illusion. *Scientific American, 207,* 120-130.

Wallach, H. (1962). On the moon illusion. *Science, 137,* 900-902.

McCollough, C. (1965). Color adaptation of edge-detectors in the human visual system. *Science, 149,* 1115-1116.

Weintraub, D., & Gardner, G. (1970). Emmert's laws: Size constancy vs. optical geometry. *American Journal of Psychology, 83,* 40-51.

Ross, H., & Ross, G. (1976). Did Ptolemy understand the moon illusion? *Perception, 5,* 377-385.

Dodwell, P. C., & Humphrey, G. K. (1990). A functional theory of the McCollough effect. *Psychological Review, 97,* 78-89.

EMOTIONAL CONTAGION/PRIMITIVE EMOTIONAL CONTAGION, THEORY OF. See FACIAL FEEDBACK HYPOTHESIS.

EMOTIONAL EXPRESSION, PRINCIPLES OF. See WUNDT'S THEORIES/DOCTRINES/PRINCIPLES.

EMOTIONAL INTELLIGENCE, THEORY OF. = social intelligence. The American psychologists Peter Salovey (1958-) and John D. Mayer (1953-) speculated that the following four groups of abilities and competencies comprise the notion of *emotional intelligence*: the appraisal, perception, and expression of emotions accurately; the ability to access and elicit emotions when they aid in the cognitive processes; the ability to understand emotional messages and make use of emotional information; and the regulation of one's own emotions in order to achieve and promote growth, health, and well-being. Other criteria employed in *emotional intelligence theory* include the addition of various other factors such as interpersonal skills, and the ability to adapt to changing situations and environments; cf., the concept of *emotional quotient* or *EQ* (analogous to the IQ index of conventional *intelligence theory*) which is assessed via self-report measures of persons' perceptions and appraisals of their own competencies/experiences and levels of functioning, among other measures. The concept of *EQ* here is not to be confused with the concept of *encephalization quotient* (also known as *EQ*) that is an index of the *comparative intelligence* of animal species (where brain volume of a given animal is divided by the brain volume of a standard comparison animal belonging to the same class and corrected for body size), and as developed by the Polish-born American psychologist Harry J. Jerison (1925-) [cf., *progression index* - also a mea-sure of the comparative intelligence of mammalian species, based on a modification of the *encephalization quotient* involving volume of animals' neocortex; and *association/sensation (A/S) ratio* - the Canadian psychologist Donald O. Hebb (1904-1985) formulated this index of the comparative intelligence of mammalian species, defined as brain volume dedicated to "association areas" of the brain divided by brain volume dedicated to "sensory/ motor" areas]. See also EMOTIONS, THEORIES/LAWS OF; INTELLIGENCE, THEORIES/LAWS OF.

REFERENCES

Hebb, D. O. (1947). *Organization of behavior.* New York: Wiley.

Leuner, B. (1966). Emotional intelligence and emancipation. *Praxis der Kinderpsychologie und Kinderpsychiatrie, 15,* 196-203.

Payne, W. L. (1986). A study of emotion: Developing emotional intelligence; self-integration; relating to fear, pain, and desire. *Dissertation Abstracts International, 47(1-A),* 203.

Salovey, P., & Mayer, J. D. (1989-1990). Emotional intelligence. *Imagination, Cognition, and Personality*, 9, 185-211.

Salovey, P., & Sluyter, D. J. (Eds.) (1997). *Emotional development and emotional intelligence: Educational implications*. New York: Basic Books.

Ciarrochi, J., Forgas, J., & Mayer, J. D. (Eds.) (2001). *Emotional intelligence in everyday life: A scientific inquiry*. Philadelphia, PA: Psychology Press.

Barrett, L. F., & Salovey, P. (Eds.) (2002). *The wisdom in feeling: Psychological processes in emotional intelligence*. New York: Guilford Press.

EMOTIONAL QUOTIENT. See EMOTIONAL INTELLIGENCE, THEORY OF.

EMOTIONS, THEORIES/LAWS OF. The term *emotion* derives from the Latin *emovere*, meaning to excite, to move, to agitate, or to stir up. Historically, the term *emotion* has defied exact definition, even though it is widely used as if implicit agreement existed, and most textbook authors employ it as the title of a chapter, allowing the material presented to be a substitute for a precise definition. Despite the long history of the concept of *emotion*, which goes back to the early Greek philosophers, as well as to Descartes' analysis of emotions into *six passions of the soul* (i.e., wonder, love, hate, desire, joy, sadness), there had been little discussion of emotion as theory. Modern interest in *theories of emotion* began with the writings of the American philosopher/psychologist William James (1842-1910), and there are currently a number of specific theoretical orientations toward emotion (see cross-referenced terms below). Current usage of the term *emotion* falls into two categories: the identification of several subjectively experienced states (e.g., fear, anger, love, surprise, disgust), and the reference to a field of scientific research that examines the physiological, behavioral, cognitive, and environmental factors underlying the subjective aspects of emotion (cf., the *Easterbrook hypothesis* - the speculation that emotional arousal narrows one's focus of attention; Easterbrook, 1959; and the *excitation transfer*

theory - holds that residual arousal from one setting may be attributed mistakenly to a subsequent emotional setting and, consequently, increasing the emotional response; also, cf., *generalization principles*; and the *isopathic principle*, also called the *homeopathic principle*, which states that a symptom may be relieved by the simple expression of the emotion that has been repressed, such as the mitigation of guilt - caused by hate - via an overt demonstration of hate). The definitions of terms in the second category amount to *minitheories of emotion*, where there seems to be consensus on at least four generally important factors for study: (1) *instigating stimuli* - both exogenous (external stimuli such as environmental events) and endogenous (internal stimuli such as images or thoughts); (2) *physiological correlates* - general biological systems (such as central and autonomic nervous system events) and specific action patterns (such as hypothalamic-thalamic interactions, that yield theories of emotion such as *Papez's theory* - named after the American psychologist J. W. Papez (1883-1958), and *MacLean's theory* - named after the American psychologist P. D. MacLean (1913-); (3) *cognitive appraisal* - individualistic or personal significance of potential and actual emotional events (such as exhibiting fear reactions to caged lions at a zoo); and (4) *motivational aspects* - the organismic arousal associated with emotions is consistently associated with the activation involved in motivation (such as becoming angry for some reason and then displacing aggression onto an innocent bystander). In general, emotional states have other characteristics that distinguish them from allied concepts in the history of psychology. For example, emotions are *acute* (i.e., they are momentary conditions of high intensity), which sets them apart from *sentiments* (i.e., general complex dispositions toward action), *feelings* (i.e., general sensing or experiencing of events in the world such as happiness or well-being), and *organized behaviors* (i.e., nonerratic, non-chaotic, well-integrated, and controlled behavioral responses to the environment). Also, in general, emotions tend *not* to be cyclical or regular (aside from psychopathological conditions such as the *affective disorders*, which show inappropriate, chronic expression of an emotional state), but seem in "normally" functioning individuals to be dependent on specific situations and are tied to one's particular personal perception and meaning. The difficulty in studying emotions is due to a number of causes and problems, prominent among which is the pervasive tendency by investigators to separate emotion from cognition or rational thought processes (cf., the *aha experience/effect* - an emotional response that occurs, typically, at the moment of sudden insight, generally following a long and tedious process of problem-solving; in psychotherapy, it is the sudden insight one has into one's unconscious motives). The physiological and psychological processes involved in emotion are most likely interrelated, and separation by theorists of emotion from these other aspects of experience may not be productive; rather, integration of the psychological and physiological realms in the study of emotions is a desideratum. It is interesting to note that recently, in only 30 years from 1954 to 1984, it is estimated that there have been at least 20 new *theories of emotions* advanced by psychologists. D. Coon provides a synthesis (*contemporary model of emotions*) of the main factors of several of the most popular theories of emotions in psychology. In this model, the following feedback sequence occurs in an emotional episode: an emotional stimulus triggers a cognitive appraisal of the situation, which then gives rise to arousal, behavior, facial/postural expressions, and emotional feelings. Arousal, behavior, and expressions then add to emotional feelings. Emotional feelings influence appraisal, which further affects arousal, behavior, expressions, and feelings. Sound circular? Some few writers argue that the study of emotions has achieved the status of lawful phenomena where the *laws of emotion* may now be cited. For example, N. H. Frijda describes the following set of *laws of emotion*: law of situational meaning; law of concern; law of reality; laws of change, habituation, and comparative feeling; law of hedonic asymmetry; law of conservatism of emotional momentum; law of closure; and the laws of care for consequence, of lightest load, and of greatest gain. Time will tell, perhaps, which of these *laws of emotion*, if any, will be acknowledged and honored by psychologists.

See also ACTIVATION/AROUSAL THEORY; ARNOLD'S THEORY OF EMOTIONS; BEHAVIORISTIC THEORY; CANNON/CANNON-BARD THEORY; COGNITIVE-APPRAISAL THEORY; DARWIN'S THEORY OF EMOTIONS; EKMAN-FRIESEN THEORY OF EMOTIONS; FACIAL-FEEDBACK HYPOTHESIS; GENERALIZATION, PRINCIPLES OF; IZARD'S THEORY OF EMOTIONS; JAMES-LANGE/LANGE-JAMES THEORY OF EMOTIONS; MOTIVATION, THEORIES OF; PLUTCHIK'S MODEL OF EMOTIONS; SCHACHTER-SINGER'S THEORY OF EMOTIONS; SOLOMON'S OPPONENT-PROCESS THEORY OF EMOTIONS; UNIVERSAL MODEL OF HUMAN EMOTIONS.

REFERENCES

Descartes, R. (1650). *Les passions de l'ame*. Paris: Loyson.

Bain, A. (1859). *The emotions and the will*. London: Longmans.

James, W. (1890). *The principles of psychology*. New York: Holt.

Paulhan, F. (1930). *The laws of feeling*. New york: Harcourt, Brace & Company.

Duffy, E. (1934). Emotion: An example of the need for reorientation in psychology. *Psychological Review, 41*, 184-198.

Gardiner, H. M., Metcalf, R. C., & Beebe-Center, J. G. (1937). *Feeling and emotion: A history of theories*. New York: American Book Company.

Papez, J. W. (1937). A proposed mechanism of emotion. *Archives of Neurological Psychiatry, 38*, 725-743.

Duffy, E. (1948). Leeper's "motivational theory of emotions." *Psychological Review, 55*, 324-328.

MacLean, P. D. (1958). Contrasting functions of limbic and neocortical systems of the brain and their relevance to psychophysiological aspects of medicine. *American Journal of Medicine, 25*, 611-626.

Easterbrook, J. A. (1959). The effect of emotion on cue utilization and the organization of behavior. *Psychological Review, 66*, 183-201.

Averill, J. (1980). A constructionist view of emotion. In R. Plutchik & H. Kellerman (Eds.), *Emotion: Theory, research, and experience.* New York: Academic Press.

Frijda, N. H. (1986). *The emotions.* London: Cambridge University Press.

Frijda, N. H. (1988). The laws of emotion. *American Psychologist, 43,* 349-358.

Ortony, A., & Turner, T. J. (1990). What's basic about basic emotions? *Psychological Review, 97,* 315-331.

Barlow, D. H. (1991). Disorders of emotion. *Psychological Inquiry, 2,* 58-71.

Ekman, P. (1992). Are there basic emotions? *Psychological Review, 99,* 550-571.

Mesquita, B., & Frijda, N. H. (1992). Cultural variations in emotions: A review. *Psychological Bulletin, 112,* 179-204.

Strongman, K. T. (1996). *The psychology of emotion: Theories of emotion in perspective.* New York: Wiley.

Coon, D. (1997). *Essentials of psychology.* Pacific Grove, CA: Brooks/Cole.

Nussbaum, M. C. (2001). *Upheavals of thought: The intelligence of emotions.* New York: Cambridge University Press.

Russell, J. A., Bachorowski, J.-A., & Fernandez-Dols, J.-M. (2003). Facial and vocal expressions of emotion. *Annual Review of Psychology, 54,* 329-349.

EMPATHY-ALTRUISM HYPOTHESIS.
This emotional/motivational, social/prosocial, and genetic/psychological speculation challenges the traditional "egoistic" assumption that people help or benefit others because, ultimately, to do so benefits themselves. The *empathy-altruism hypothesis* holds that empathic emotion evokes truly altruistic motivation with an ultimate goal of benefiting not the self but the individual for whom empathy is felt. This hypothesis makes logical and psychological distinctions between the concepts of *egoism* (i.e., a motivational state with the ultimate goal of increasing one's *own* welfare) and *altruism* (i.e., a motivational state with the ultimate goal of increasing *another's* welfare), and provides a conceptual framework for empirical tests for the existence of *altruism.* In

the special case of *reciprocal altruism* (i.e., situations in which one's performance is conditional on the recipient behaving altruistically in return), a "tit-for-tat" strategy may be observed - such as that typically found in playing a game repeatedly (e.g., repeating a "prisoner's dilemma" game) where a preprogrammed strategy directs the program/player to cooperate on the first trial and then, on each subsequent trial, to choose the strategy chosen by the co-player on the previous trial. In the area of *evolutionary theory* and *genetics,* however, the notion of *altruism* as the "unselfish concern for the well-being of others" takes on a slightly different, and paradoxical, connotation. That is, *evolutionary theory* - based on differential reproduction of genetic alternatives (or "survival of the fittest") - seems to require some type of "ultimate *selfishness*" in order to be successful in the domain of reproductive competition. See also BYSTANDER INTERVENTION EFFECT; DARWIN'S EVOLUTION THEORY; EGO DEVELOPMENT, THEORIES OF; EMPATHY THEORY; LIPPS' EMPATHY THEORY; MACHIAVELLIAN THEORY; PRISONER'S DILEMMA GAME.

REFERENCES

Hamilton, W. D. (1963). The evolution of altruistic behavior. *American Naturalist, 97,* 354-356.

Krebs, D. L. (1970). Altruism - An examination of the concept and review of the literature. *Psychological Bulletin, 73,* 258-303.

Trivers, R. L. (1971). The evolution of reciprocal altruism. *Quarterly Review of Biology, 46,* 35-57.

Campbell, D. T. (1972). On the genetics of altruism and the counter-hedonic components in human culture. *Journal of Social Issues, 28,* 21-37.

Batson, D., & Coke, J. (1981). Empathy: A source of altruistic motivation for helping. In *Altruism and helping behavior.* Hillsdale, NJ: Erlbaum.

Batson, D., & Shaw, L. L. (1991). Evidence for altruism: Toward a pluralism of prosocial motives. *Psychological Inquiry, 2,* 107-122.

Preston, S. D., & deWaal, F. (2002). Empathy: Its ultimate and proximate bases.

The Behavioral and Brain Sciences,
25, 1-72.

EMPATHY THEORY. The notion of *empathy* refers to one person vicariously experiencing the perception, emotions, feelings, and thoughts of another person. Traditionally, *empathy* has been viewed as the basis for all positive social relationships. Various theorists define the concept of *empathy* differently. For example, *clinical* psychologists/therapists include in the definition the therapist's intellectual understanding of the client, the therapist's sharing of the client's feelings, the effectiveness and ease of communication, and the therapist's positive attitude toward the client. Other psychologists (e.g., *cognitive* psychologists) emphasize the cognitive aspects of *empathy*, and focus on the ability of one person to understand intellectually the inner experience of another person. *Developmental* psychologists may approach *empathy* as a direct sharing of feelings between parent and infant, and consider it to be a major factor in the maturation process. Experimental *social* psychologists have studied *empathy* in laboratory settings under conditions controlled for possible non-empathetic sources of emotional arousal, and have discovered that empathetic emotional arousal is reflected both in self-reports and in certain physiological changes. Among the empirical and theoretical findings on *empathy* (e.g., Stotland, Shaver, & Sherman, 1971), the key antecedent condition for *empathy* appears to be the empathizer imagining herself or himself as having the same experience as the other person and, thus, imaginatively taking the *role* of the other person. Such a theoretical approach toward mental processes contrasts with viewing the other person in more objectified or intellectualized ways. Therefore, *empathy* in adults may be viewed as having a long developmental history, where infants, at first, do not distinguish between *self* and *other* and, consequently, empathize readily; only gradually do infants come to learn that *self* and *other* are distinct and separate entities (cf., Hoffman, 1977). Recently, in the *shared-manifold hypothesis*, actions are analyzed as to their potential connection to neurobiological factors (e.g., *mirror neurons*) in which the capacity for understanding others as intentional agents is grounded in the relational nature of action and, ultimately, on neuropsychological mechanisms. Such an account of "intersubjectivity" is put in relation to *empathy*, invoking one of the classical tenets of phenomenology, and indicates an alternative approach to *empathy* that is not dependent exclusively on mentalistic or linguistic abilities or factors. See also BYSTANDER INTERVENTION EFFECT; DEVELOPMENTAL THEORY; EMPATHY-ALTRUISM HYPOTHESIS; LIPPS' EMPATHY THEORY; MACHIAVELLIAN THEORY; MIND/MENTAL STATES, THEORIES OF; MIRROR NEURONS THEORY; SELF-CONCEPT THEORY.

REFERENCES

Dymond, R. (1949). A scale for measurement of empathetic ability. *Journal of Consulting Psychology, 14,* 127-133.

Truax, C. (1961). A scale for the measurement of accurate empathy. *Psychiatric Institute Bulletin, 1,* 12.

Berger, S. (1962). Conditioning through vicarious instigation. *Psychological Review, 69,* 450-466.

Feshback, N., & Roe, K. (1968). Empathy in six- and seven-year olds. *Child Development, 39,* 133-145.

Stotland, E., Shaver, K., & Sherman, S. (1971). *Empathy and birth order.* Lincoln, NE: University of Nebraska Press.

Hoffman, M. (1977). Empathy, its development and prosocial implications. *Nebraska Symposium on Motivation, 25,* 169-211.

Stotland, E., Mathews, K., Sherman, S., Hansson, R., & Richardson, B. (1978). *Fantasy, empathy, and helping.* Beverly Hills, CA: Sage.

Gallese, V. (2001). The "shared-manifold" hypothesis: From mirror neurons to empathy. In E. Thompson (Ed.), *Between ourselves: Second-person issues in the study of consciousness.* Charlottesville, VA: Academic.

EMPIRICAL/EMPIRICISM, DOCTRINE OF. This is the philosophical doctrine /theory that sense experience is the only source of knowledge (cf., *doctrine of sensationalism*, also called the *doctrine of sensationism* - posits that all knowledge originates in sensations, and that even reflective ideas and intuitions may be traced back to elementary sense impressions; this doctrine denies that there are innate ideas). One meaning of the term *empirical* stresses the reliance on practical experience without reference to scientific principles, whereas the term *empirical method* emphasizes observation and experiment rather than theory. The British philosopher John Locke (1632-1704) was the major leader of the British *empiricistic* tradition (cf., *Hobbes' psychological theory*). *Locke's psychological theory* of "environmental determinacy" is summarized in the notion that there is nothing in the mind that was not first in the senses. Locke rejected other sources of knowledge that were thought to be innately endowed through God or otherwise; rather, all knowledge is derived from experience. Locke distinguishes between sensations (physical entities) and perceptions (reflected products of sensation). According to Locke, the units of the mind called "ideas" are derived from sensations through self-reflection. Locke asserted, also, that physical objects have inherent primary, and perceived secondary, qualities. The primary qualities are properties of objects as they exist (such as length, volume, motion, and number), but the secondary qualities are produced by the perceiver and attributed to objects (such as odors, sounds, colors, and tastes). Locke's form of *empiricism*, called *rational empiricism*, had a definite need for the concept of *mind* and posited two operations for the *mind*: reflection and association. Through reflection, the operations of *mind* in themselves produce new or compound ideas based on the simple ideas obtained from sensations. Through association, the *mind* links sensations together to form perceptions where associations, by chance, are spontaneous linkages without an apparent logical basis (cf., Hobbes' "contiguity" approach), and constitute what today is called "superstitious behavior/reinforcement." In psychology, *empiricism* is the approach that views knowledge as resulting from experience, induction, and learning and where, in its once extreme form, it asserted that *mind* at birth was a "blank slate"

or *tabula rasa* upon which experience writes its messages. Locke's inconsistency concerning his *doctrine of tabula rasa* has been criticized often (e.g., he inserted the notion that the *mind* has "faculties" and these can be modified; he also conceded that the *mind* could arrive at new ideas by reflecting on sensory input. Thus, Locke admitted, indirectly, that not every idea comes directly from experience. Another of Locke's concepts, called "archetypes" (i.e., development of complex ideas via reflecting on sensations), comes close to supporting Descartes' opposing position of *innate ideas* rather than upholding a purely *empirical* approach. *Empiricism* is commonly contrasted with the *doctrine of nativism* (innate capacities). Modern scientific psychology espouses *empiricism* through an inductive method and emphasis upon experimental methods, as well as sense experience and observable data, over a purely theoretical or deductive approach. See also A POSTERIORI/A PRIORI DISTINCTION; ASSOCIATION, LAWS/PRINCIPLES OF; DESCARTES' THEORY OF INNATE IDEAS; EMPIRICIST VERSUS NATIVIST THEORIES; HOBBES' PSYCHOLOGICAL THEORY; MIND/MENTAL STATES, THEORIES OF; NATIVISTIC/NATIVISM THEORIES/DOCTRINE; RATIONALISM/RATIONALIST, DOCTRINE OF; SUPERSTITION AND SUPERSTITIOUS EFFECTS; UNCONSCIOUS INFERENCE.

REFERENCES

Locke, J. (1690). *An essay concerning human understanding*. London: Dent.

Brennan, J. (1991). *History and systems in psychology*. Englewood Cliffs, NJ: Prentice-Hall.

EMPIRICAL LAW OF EFFECT. See EFFECT, LAW OF; ESTES' STIMULUS SAMPLING THEORY.

EMPIRICIST VERSUS NATIVIST THEORIES. The "empiricist-nativist" distinction in psychology is as old as the history of psychology itself. The *empiricist/empiricism* theoretical position - deriving from the "British Empiricists": the English philosopher John Locke (1632-1704), the Irish philosopher Bishop George Berkeley (1685-1753), and the

Scottish philosopher David Hume (1711-1776) - holds that all elements of knowledge basically emanate from experience ("nurture") or contact with the environment. On the other hand, the *nativist/nativism doctrine* or theoretical orientation ("nature") holds that the mind innately contains knowledge that is not derived from the senses, and emphasizes hereditary factors and biological constitution as determinants of one's behavior, perceptions, attitudes, and personality. Historically, the *nativist-empiricist* distinction is epitomized in the theoretical dispute between the German psychologists Ewald Hering (1834-1918) and Hermann L. F. von Helmholtz (1821-1894) concerning, in particular, the issue of *visual space perception*. The key question was: Is the spatial ordering of visual perception given as "native/inborn endowment" or is it somehow "acquired/learned"? Hering adopted the *nativst* position, whereas Helmholtz advanced the *empiricist* position. Hering argued that each retinal point is innately endowed with three "local signs" (height, right-left position, and depth). Helmholtz, on the other hand, proposed that space forms are "built-up" in experience and that the location of the "local signs" has to be learned. Thus, Helmholtz, as *empiricist*, was following R. M. Lotze and the British *empiricistic* tradition, whereas Hering (who was not the first to conceive of, or originate, *nativism*) was following Johannes Muller who, in turn, was influenced by Immanuel Kant's conception of space as a "native intuition." Ultimately, the *empiricist/nativist* dichotomy and philosophy goes back to John Locke's *empiricism* and Rene Descartes' *innate ideas*. As one psychological historian (E. G. Boring) points out, the Helmholtz-versus-Hering difference has not yet fully surrendered to the conception that nature (*nativism*) and nurture (*empiricism*) always work together, and neither of them works alone. See also A POSTERIORI/A PRIORI DISTINCTION; BERKELEY'S THEORY OF VISUAL SPACE PERCEPTION; DESCARTES' THEORY OF INNATE IDEAS; EMPIRICAL AND EMPIRICISM, DOCTRINE OF; LEARNING THEORIES/LAWS; LOTZE'S THEORY OF LOCAL SIGNS; NATIVISTIC/NATIVISM THEORIES AND DOCTRINE; NATURE VERSUS NURTURE THEORIES; RATIONALISM/RATIONALIST, DOCTRINE OF; SPEECH THEORIES; UNCONSCIOUS INFERENCE, DOCTRINE OF.

REFERENCE
Boring, E. G. (1957). *A history of experimental psychology.* 2nd ed. New York: Appleton-Century-Crofts.

EMPTY ORGANISM THEORY. See SKINNER'S OPERANT CONDITIONING THEORY.

ENANTIODROMIA, PRINCIPLE OF. See JUNG'S THEORY OF PERSONALITY.

ENCEPHALIZATION QUOTIENT. See EMOTIONAL INTELLIGENCE, THEORY OF.

ENCODING SPECIFICITY HYPOTHESIS/PRINCIPLE. See CODING THEORIES.

ENCODING THEORY OF TASTE QUALITY. See GUSTATION/TASTE, THEORIES OF.

ENCODING VARIABILITY PRINCIPLE. See CODING THEORIES.

ENERGIZATION THEORY. See MOTIVATION, THEORIES OF.

ENERGY CONSERVATION THEORY. See SLEEP, THEORIES OF.

ENERGY METABOLISM THEORY. See HUNGER, THEORIES OF.

ENESTRUENCE/EVENT-STRUCTURE, THEORY OF. See ALLPORT'S THEORY OF ENESTRUENCE; PERCEPTION (II. COMPARATIVE APPRAISAL), THEORIES OF.

ENGRAM THEORY. See SHORT-TERM AND LONG-TERM MEMORY, THEORIES OF.

ENRICHMENT THEORY. See DEVELOPMENTAL THEORY.

ENTROPY PRINCIPLE. See GENERAL SYSTEMS THEORY; JUNG'S THEORY OF PERSONALITY; THERMODYNAMICS, LAWS OF.

ENVIRONMENTAL DETERMINISM, DOCTRINE OF. See NATURE VERSUS NURTURE THEORIES.

ENVIRONMENTAL SECURITY HYPO-THESIS. This conjecture (Pettijohn & Tesser, 1999) states that exposure to highly threatening, stressful, pessimistic, or stagnant environmental conditions (e.g., social/economic conditions in the U.S. from 1932-1945) causes people to show a relatively greater preference for individuals with "mature" facial features (e.g., small eye size, thin cheeks, large chins), as compared to preferences for individuals with "non-mature/neonate" facial features (e.g., large eye size, round cheeks, small chins) under less threatening, less stressful, and more prosperous/optimistic existing environmental conditions. The *environmental security hypothesis* predicts that under high threat conditions, people choose "mature-face features" because the attributes associated with such features - such as independence, maturity, and competence - fulfill the functional roles and characteristics people value when stressed or threatened. However, results from investigations (via photographs) of facial feature choices and preferences of popular American actors across social and economic "hard times" indicate that facial preferences in *male* actors are not as systematically determined as facial features in *female* actors. See also CHOICE THEORIES.

REFERENCES

Pettijohn, T. F., II. & Tesser, A. (1999). Popularity in environmental context: Facial feature assessment of American movie actresses. *Media Psychology, 1*, 229-247.

Pettijohn, T. F., II. (2000). An investigation of facial feature preferences under conditions of threat. *Dissertation Abstracts International, 61, (6-B)*, 3324.

Wapner, S. (2000). *Theoretical perspectives in environment-behavior research.* New York: Kluwer Academic.

ENVIRONMENTAL STRESS OR LOAD THEORY. See SELYE'S THEORY/MODEL OF STRESS; SCHIZOPHRENIA, THEORIES OF.

ENZYME THEORY OF TASTE. See GUSTATION/TASTE, THEORIES OF.

EPAM THEORY/MODEL/PROGRAM. The American cognitive psychologist, economist, and philosopher Herbert Alexander Simon (1916-2001) and the cognitive/computer scientist Edward A. Feigenbaum (1936-) proposed and developed this unified theory simulating perception and memory called EPAM ("elementary perceiver and memorizer") in 1959, which is a computer program that explains behavior in a number of experimental paradigms, including the classical experimental domain of verbal memory, and learning to categorize stimuli. Thus, EPAM - as a computer simulation of human perceptual, recognition, and memory processes, and the symbolic structures that support them - has been successful in predicting a large range of experimental/empirical findings about human perception, verbal and concept learning, and short-term and long-term memory. The most recent version of this model is called EPAM IV and has been adapted to handle short- and long-term memory tasks as well as expert memory tasks. The major current modifications include a retrieval structure, or a long-term memory schema, created by the expert's learning operations and complemented by the addition of an associative search process in long-term memory. See also ADAPTIVE CONTROL OF THOUGHT THEORY/MODEL; INFORMATION AND INFORMATION-PROCESSING THEORY; SHORT-TERM AND LONG-TERM MEMORY, THEORIES OF.

REFERENCES

Simon, H. A., & Newell, A. (1964). Information processing in computer and man. *American Scientist, 52*, 281-300.

Feigenbaum, E. A. (1965). Memory mechanism and EPAM theory. In D. Kimble (Ed.), *The anatomy of memory.* New York: Science and Behavior Books.

Simon, H. A., & Barenfeld, M. (1969). Information processing analysis of perceptual processes in problem solving. *Psychological Review*, *76*, 473-483.

Newell, A. (1990). *Unified theories of cognition*. Cambridge, MA: Harvard University Press.

Richman, H. B., Staszewski, J. J., & Simon, H. A. (1995). Simulation of expert memory using EPAM IV. *Psychological Review*, *102*, 305-330.

EPIGENETIC THEORY. See ERIKSON'S THEORY OF PERSONALITY; GALTON'S LAWS; WEISMANN'S THEORY.

EPIMENIDES' PARADOX. See GODEL'S THEOREM/PROOF.

EPIPHENOMENALISM, THEORY OF. See MIND-BODY THEORIES.

EPISODIC MEMORY. See FORGETTING/ MEMORY, THEORIES OF; SHORT-TERM AND LONG-TERM MEMORY, THEORIES OF.

EPONYMY THEORY. See EMINENCE, THEORIES AND MEASURES OF; NATURALISTIC THEORY OF HISTORY.

EPSILON MOVEMENT EFFECT. See APPARENT MOVEMENT, PRINCIPLES/ THEORIES OF.

EQUAL DISTRIBUTION OF IGNORANCE, PRINCIPLE OF. See PROBABILITY THEORY/LAWS.

EQUALITY, LAW OF. See GESTALT THEORY/LAWS; PERCEPTION (I. GENERAL), THEORIES OF.

EQUALIZATION, PRINCIPLE OF. See GOLDSTEIN'S ORGANISMIC THEORY.

EQUAL-LOUDNESS CONTOUR EFFECT. See APPENDIX A.

EQUILIBRIUM HYPOTHESIS. = affiliative conflict theory = hypothesis of compensation. The English social psychologists Michael Argyle (1925-) and Janet Dean suggest that participants in a social interaction situation who feel that the level/degree of intimacy transmitted by particular channels of nonverbal communication is inappropriate to the level of intimacy of the relationship in question, will tend to compensate by reducing the intimacy transmitted through other channels (e.g., in a crowded elevator where people are forced to stand closer together than is ordinarily appropriate with strangers, individuals tend to reduce the level of intimacy by making less eye contact with each other; thus, in such cases, *increased* proximity is related to *decreased* nonverbal eye contact). In experimental studies, Argyle and Dean found that the intimacy-proximity/nonverbal behavior effect was greatest for opposite-sex pairs of participants and, also, that individuals tend to stand closer to another person when the latter's eyes are shut. The *equilibrium hypothesis*, in this social context (cf., the concept/the-ory of *personal space* - the hypothetical area around an individual's body into which other individuals or conspecifics may not normally intrude without eliciting feelings of uneasiness or provoking a negative reaction), indicates that people move towards an "equilibrium distance" and adopt a particular level of nonverbal behavior, such as degree/level of eye contact, when placed in close physical proximity to other unfamiliar persons or strangers [cf., Coutts & Schneider (1976), and Patterson (1973, 1975) for cautions, clarifications, and qualifications of the phenomenon]. See also EXCHANGE/SOCIAL EXCHANGE THEORY.

REFERENCES

Argyle, M., & Dean, J. (1965). Eye-contact, distance, and affiliation. *Sociometry*, *28*, 289-304.

Stephenson, G. M., & Rutter, D. R. (1970). Eye-contact, distance, and affiliation: A re-evaluation. *British Journal of Psychology*, *61*, 385-393.

Patterson, M. L. (1973). Compensation in nonverbal immediacy behaviors: A review. *Sociometry*, *36*, 237-252.

Patterson, M. L. (1975). Eye contact and distance: A re-examination of measurement problems. *Personality and*

Social Psychology Bulletin, *1*, 600-603.

Coutts, L. M., & Schneider, F. W. (1976). Affiliative conflict theory: An investigation of the intimacy equilibrium and compensation hypothesis. *Journal of Personality and Social Psychology*, *34*, 1135-1142.

EQUILIBRIUM, LAW OF. See NEWTON'S LAW/PRINCIPLES OF COLOR MIXTURE.

EQUILIBRIUM THEORY OF LEARNED PERFORMANCE. See EXCHANGE/SOCIAL EXCHANGE THEORY; PREMACK'S PRINCIPLE/LAW.

EQUIPOTENTIALITY THEORY. See LASHLEY'S THEORY; PERCEPTION (II. COMPARATIVE APPRAISAL), THEORIES OF.

EQUITY THEORY. The essential structure of *equity theory* is that it consists of four interdependent, or interlocking, propositions: (1) people attempt to maximize outcomes (where an outcome equals reward minus punishment); (2) people in groups may maximize collective reward by devising systems for equitable apportionment of resources and will reward group members who treat others in an equitable fashion but will punish group members who treat each other inequitable; (3) people who find themselves participating in inequitable relationships will become distressed at a level that is directly proportionate to the level of inequitability; and (4) people will attempt to eliminate distress and restore equity when they find themselves in an inequitable situation. *Equity theory* has been applied to areas of human interaction such as intimate and exploitative interpersonal relationships, philanthropic and altruistic relationships, and business relationships. Equity theory research indicates that people who discover that they are in an inequitable relationship attempt to reduce their resultant distress by restoring either "actual" or "psychological/perceived" equity to their relationship. Actual equity may be restored by altering one's own or one's partner's relative gains in certain ways. For instance, if a worker discovers that he is getting paid less than was contracted for, he may establish equity in a number of different ways: lower one's own personal effort or input into the job; raise one's outcomes by stealing from the company; raise the employer's inputs by making deliberate job-related mistakes; or lower the employer's outcomes by deliberately damaging company equipment. An employee can insist, also, that equity be restored to the employee-employer relationship by demanding various types of restitution. Other research on *equity theory* indicates that the "overbenefited" often voluntarily compensate the "underbenefited." Psychological equity may be used, also, to restore equity in an unbalanced relationship: the individual may distort reality and convince herself that the unjust relationship really is perfectly fair [cf., *relative deprivation* - the notion regarding the discrepancy one perceives between what one has and what one should have, as opposed to "absolute deprivation" of the crucial necessities for living; the British sociologist Walter G. Runciman (1934-) suggests that workers' feelings of deprivation and class consciousness tend to be "relative" rather than "absolute"]. The chief arguments made by proponents of *equity theory* are that such diverse topics/issues as cooperation, perceived deprivation, aggression, power, altruism, and other social psychological phenomena can be satisfactorily accounted for by an analysis of *outcomes, inputs, equity*, and *inequity* in various interpersonal relationship situations. See also CONFLICT, THEORIES OF; EXCHANGE/SOCIAL EXCHANGE THEORY; FESTINGER'S COGNITIVE DISSONANCE THEORY; ORGANIZATIONAL/INDUSTRIAL/SYSTEMS THEORY; SEXUAL ORIENTATION THEORIES; WORK/CAREER/OCCUPATION, THEORIES OF.

REFERENCES

Adams, J. S. (1963). Toward an understanding of inequity. *Journal of Abnormal and Social Psychology*, *67*, 422-436.

Adams, J. S. (1965). Inequity in social exchange. In L. Berkowitz (Ed.), *Advances in experimental social psychology*. Vol. 2. New York: Academic Press.

Runciman, W. G. (1966/1980). *Relative deprivation and social justice*. London: Routledge.

Walster (Hatfield), E., Walster, G., & Berscheid, E. (1978). *Equity: Theory and research*. Boston: Allyn & Bacon.

Hatfield, E., Utne, M., & Traupmann, H. (1979). Equity theory and intimate relationships. In R. Burgess & T. Huston (Eds.), *Social exchange in developing relationships*. New York: Academic Press.

EQUITY THEORY OF WORK. See WORK/CAREER/OCCUPATION, THEORIES OF.

EQUIVALENCE PRINCIPLE. See JUNG'S THEORY OF PERSONALITY.

ERIKSON'S THEORY OF PERSONALITY. The German-born American psychoanalyst Erik Homburger Erikson (1902-1994) attempted to revive the structure of psychoanalysis after the death of Sigmund Freud in 1939. Erikson considered himself to be a Freudian psychoanalyst in spite of some opinions that he fell outside the Freudian tradition. Erikson helped to establish the theoretical approach called *ego psychology*, along with the Austrian-born American psychoanalyst Heinz Hartmann (1894-1970), the German psychologist Ernst Kris (1901-1957), and the Hungarian-born American psychologist David Rapaport (1911-1960). The theme of *ego psychology* is that the "ego" is capable of functioning autonomously and is not confined to internal conflicts with the "id" and the "super-ego" as in Freudian doctrine. Erikson's major contributions to contemporary *psychoanalytic theory* include a *psychosocial theory of development* and psychohistorical analyses of famous persons. According to Erikson's theoretical approach, the term *psychosocial* refers to the stages of an individual's life from birth to death and focuses on the social/environmental influences that interact with the physical and psychological growth of the person. Erikson's *psychosocial theory*, which describes "stages" of development, supplements S. Freud's *psychosexual stage of development*

theory, J. Piaget's *cognitive stage development theory*, and H. S. Sullivan's *interpersonal stage development theory*. The notion of "stage" in developmental theories refers to the more or less clearly defined *ages* at which new forms of behavior appear in response to new maturational and social variables. Erikson coined the term *identity crisis* and posited that development proceeds in eight consecutive stages, where the first four stages occur during infancy and childhood, the fifth stage occurs during adolescence, and the final three stages occur during adulthood up to old age. Each stage contributes to an individual's whole personality in an *epigenetic* sense (i.e., overall development unfolds via interaction with the environment), but different people may have different timetables for entering and progressive through each stage (cf., *psychosocial moratorium* - denotes a "time-out" from life during which a person may retain a "fluid identity," such as young adults taking time out to travel before settling into more fixed identities constrained by relationships and work responsibilities). Erikson asserted that each of the eight stages is characterized by a specific psychological *conflict* that seeks resolution. The eight stages are: *basic trust versus basic mistrust* - infancy period, when very young children develop attitudes of trust or mistrust concerning people; *autonomy versus shame/doubt* - early childhood, when the child grows older and, in its attempt to gain control over muscles and bones, develops attitudes of autonomy, independence, and success, or of shame, doubt, and failure; *initiative versus guilt* - occurs during preschool age, when the child is about four years old and is seeking behavior roles to imitate; if she learns the socially acceptable behaviors, then initiative is required, but if there is failure, a sense of lasting guilt develops; *industry versus inferiority* - when the child begins school, he attempts to master the world in certain social ways, and success is characterized by industry or competence, whereas failure is associated with the development of inferiority feelings; *identity versus identity confusion/diffusion* - when the young adult approaches adolescence and puberty, she must decide "who she is" and "where she is going" (Erikson's *role confusion hypothesis* states that role confusion arises from an individual's failure to establish a *sense of identity* during this fifth stage); at this stage, also, decisions concerning sexual identity, occupation, and adult life-plans generally are made; *intimacy versus isolation* - during young adulthood, when the person has "found himself" and knows where he's going, then intimacy with another person is possible; however, if adolescence has passed without proper role identity and resolution, isolation from others may be the result; *generativity versus stagnation* - while in middle or full adulthood, the person must choose to continue her mental growth, health, creativity, and productivity or else risk the chance of stagnation and loss of growth; *integrity versus despair* - this last stage is a "crisis of old age or maturity" that challenges a person to choose between maintaining feelings of worth and integrity that have been built up or to yield to opposing feelings of despair and resignation where one senses that life has been a futile waste of time and energy. Also, according to Erikson's *psychosocial theory*, each individual's personality may be viewed as the result of an encounter between the *person's* needs and the *society's* needs at, or during, a particular chronological or historical time frame ("epoch") wherein each person develops a unique *psychohistory*. Erikson defines *psychohistory* as "the study of individual and collective life with the combined methods of psychoanalysis and history." His interest in psychoanalyzing famous historical personages include Martin Luther, William James, and Thomas Jefferson. Evaluations by psychologists of Erikson's theoretical approach often indicate a positive attitude toward the face validity of his formulations, which are a rich source of hypotheses that may be tested, eventually, and also indicate a preference for Erikson's *psychosocial stage theory* over Freud's *psychosexual stage theory*. Some psychologists feel that Erikson has done for *personality-development theory* what Piaget has done for *cognitive/intellectual development theory*. On the other hand, however, Erikson has been criticized for "watering down" *Freudian theory*, for creating an overly optimistic view of the concept of *ego* and of human beings (just as Freud has been criticized for his overly pessimistic view of people), and for the poor quality of the empirical foundations (i.e., personal/subjective observation method) of his theory. *Erikson's theory*, taken as a heuristic scheme, has had a marked impact on contemporary developmental psychology, especially the psychology of adolescence, and investigations of adolescent identity formation have started to move in the direction of testing specific predictions based on his theory. See also DEVELOPMENTAL THEORY; FREUD'S THEORY OF PERSONALITY; PERSONALITY THEORIES; PIAGET'S THEORY OF DEVELOPMENTAL STAGES; PSYCHO-ANALYTIC THEORY; SULLIVAN'S THEORY OF PERSONALITY.

REFERENCES

Erikson, E. H. (1950/1963). *Childhood and society*. New York: Norton.

Erikson, E. H. (1958). *Young man Luther*. New York: Norton.

Erikson, E. H. (1968). *Identity: Youth and crisis*. New York: Norton.

Erikson, E. H. (1974). *Dimensions of a new identity*. New York: Norton.

Erikson, E. H. (1975). *Life history and the historical moment*. New York: Norton.

ERROR, LAW OF. See PROBABILITY THEORY/LAWS.

ERRORLESS DISCRIMINATION LEARNING, PHENOMENON OF. See SPENCE'S THEORY.

ESSENTIAL IDENTITY LAW. See ALL-OR-NONE LAW/PRINCIPLE.

ESTES' STIMULUS SAMPLING THEORY. = statistical-learning theory/model = stochastic learning theory. The American psychologist William Kaye Estes (1919-) formulated a *mathematical learning theory* that seeks to predict the exact numerical details of experimental results. The term *mathematical learning theory* denotes a type of approach to theory construction rather than a single, specific set of postulates that could technically be called a theory. Estes developed a form of *mathematical learning theory* in the 1950s called *stimulus sampling theory* (*SST*). *SST* started as a form of stimulus-response (S-

R) *associationism* that assumed that organisms learn by attaching new adaptive behaviors to stimulus situations where they formerly had inappropriate behaviors (cf., *S-S learning model/theory* - a learning approach that focuses on the association between stimuli, including both intervening variables and cognitive structures). Estes accepted E. L. Thorndike's *empirical law of effect* (i.e., reinforcers strengthen and guide behavior), although he does not subscribe to the "satisfaction" or "drive-reduction" properties of rewards. In *SST*, learning and performance are treated explicitly as a *probabilistic* or *stochastic* process (i.e., as a sequence of events that can be analyzed in terms of probability). The main dependent variable of *statistical learning theory* is the probability of various responses of a participant at any point in time (within a given learning theory), and a *statistical learning model* consists of assumptions about how the participant's probability of a correct response changes from trial to trial as a result of the outcomes experienced on each trial. In *SST*, the stimulus situation is represented as a population of independent variable components and the total environment ("stimulus elements"). At any given moment, only a sample of elements from the total population is effective or active, where the less variable the experimental conditions, the less variable are the successive trial samples of stimulus elements. The assumption of *SST* concerning responses is that their probabilities are determined by the proportions of stimulus elements in the sample connected to the various responses. The early experimental work in *SST* employed the probability-learning paradigm where the participant's task was to predict on each trial which of two events was going to occur; after the predictive response was made, the actual event was shown. Events in these *probability learning* experiments occurred in a random sequence with no information available to help in predicting perfectly which event will occur. The phenomena of forgetting and spontaneous recovery were interpreted by Estes in terms of random changes in factors in the stimulating environment from one experimental session to the next (e.g., factors such as temperature, humidity, participants' receptor sensitivity and attitudes). Estes' *fluctuation theory of stimulus change* accounts for the shapes of forgetting and recovery curves; it has been applied, also, to the phenomena of retroactive and proactive inhibition and verbal short-term memory. *SST* considers *stimulus generalization* in a manner similar to Thorndike's *identical elements theory*: a response associated with a stimulus population will generalize to a test stimulus to the extent that the second population shares common stimulus elements with the first population. Concerning *discrimination learning, SST* adopts the concept of *selective attention* and its associative relevant cues to help explain behavioral outcomes. Estes indicates that different learning models follow from *SST* when a small number of stimulus elements is assumed. Such "small-element models" fit the experimental data as well as do the original large-element models. Recent developments in *Estes' theory* have changed in a direction closer to cognitive psychology and away from his original Guthrian stimulus-response approach. For example, Estes deals with the issue of participants' decision-making in preferential choice situations through his *scanning model*, which provides a viable approach to a *process theory of decision-making*. Estes also developed a *hierarchical associations theory of memory* that compares favorably with the "duplex" ideas of British *associationism* and with the "higher-order memory nodes" in J. Anderson and G. Bower's *theory of memory*. Although *SST* today has relatively few adherents as a "total" theory, the basic ideas of *SST* have been assimilated into a common stock of useful theoretical constructs. To date, Estes' *SST* is probably the most significant and rational attempt at a global *quantitative learning theory* in psychology. See also ASSOCIATION, LAWS/PRINCIPLES OF; ATTENTION, LAWS/PRINCIPLES/THEORIES OF; DECISION-MAKING THEORIES; DISCRIMINATION/GENERALIZATION HYPOTHESIS; FORGETTING AND MEMORY, THEORIES OF; GENERALIZATION, PRINCIPLES OF; GUTHRIE'S THEORY OF BEHAVIOR; HULL'S LEARNING THEORY; IDENTICAL ELEMENTS THEORY; INTERFERENCE THEORIES OF FORGETTING; PROBABILITY THEORY/ LAWS; THORNDIKE'S LAW OF EFFECT.

REFERENCES
Estes, W. (1955a). Statistical theory of distributional phenomena in learning. *Psychological Review, 62*, 369-377.
Estes, W. (1955b). Statistical theory of spontaneous recovery and regression. *Psychological Review, 62*, 145-154.
Restle, F. (1955). A theory of discrimination learning. *Psychological Review, 62*, 11-19.
Estes, W. (1959). The statistical approach to learning theory. In S. Koch (Ed.), *Psychology: A study of a science.* Vol. 2. New York: McGraw-Hill.
Bower, G. (1972). Stimulus-sampling theory of encoding variability. In E. Martin & A. Melton (Eds.), *Coding theory and memory*. Washington, D.C.: Hemisphere.
Anderson, J., & Bower, G. (1973). Human associative memory. Washington, D.C.: Winston.
Estes, W. (1976). The cognitive side of probability learning. *Psychological Review, 83*, 37-64.

ETHICAL DETERMINISM, DOCTRINE OF. See DETERMINISM, DOCTRINE/THEORY OF.

ETHICAL-RISK HYPOTHESIS. See KOHLBERG'S THEORY OF MORALITY.

ETHOLOGICAL MODELS OF PERSONAL SPACE. See INTERPERSONAL ATTRACTION THEORIES.

ETHOLOGICAL THEORY. See AGGRESSION, THEORIES OF; HABIT AND HABIT-FORMATION, LAWS/PRINCIPLES OF; HYDRAULIC THEORY; INFANT ATTACHMENT THEORIES; McDOUGALL'S HORMIC/INSTINCT THEORY/DOCTRINE.

EUCLID'S LAW. See EMMERT'S LAW.
EUDEMONISM, DOCTRINE OF. See HEDONISM, THEORY/LAW OF.

EUGENICS, DOCTRINE OF. See GALTON'S LAWS.

EUSTRESS THEORY. See SELYE'S THEORY/MODEL OF STRESS.

EVENT-STRUCTURE THEORY. See ALLPORT'S THEORY OF ENESTRUENCE; PERCPETION (II. COMPARATIVE APPRAISAL), THEORIES OF.

EVERSION THEORY OF AGING. See AGING, THEORIES OF.

EVIDENCE, THEORY OF. See MEINONG'S TEORIES.

EVOLUTION, LAWS OF. See DARWIN'S EVOLUTION THEORY.

EVOLUTIONARILY STABLE STRATEGY. See HAWK-DOVE/CHICKEN GAME EFFECTS.

EVOLUTIONARY/CIRCADIAN THEORY. See SLEEP, THEORIES OF.

EVOLUTIONARY HIERARCHICAL MODEL. See FRASER'S INTERDISCIPLINARY TIME THEORY.

EVOLUTIONARY THEORY. See DARWIN'S EVOLUTION THEORY.

EVOLUTIONARY THEORY OF COLOR VISION. See LADD-FRANKLIN/FRANKLIN COLOR VISION THEORY.

EWALD'S SOUND-PATTERN THEORY. See AUDITION/HEARING, THEORIES OF.

EXAFFERENCE, PRINCIPLE OF. See REAFFERENCE THEORY/PRINCIPLE.

EXCHANGE/SOCIAL EXCHANGE THEORY. The terms *exchange* and *social exchange* refer to a model of social structure that is based on the principle that most social behavior is predicated in the individual's expectation that one's actions with respect to others will result in some type of commensurate return. *Exchange theory* is a body of theoretical work in sociology and social psychology that emphasizes the importance of the reward-cost interdependence of group members in shaping their social interaction patterns as well as their psychological responses to one another (cf., *behavior-exchange model/theory* - the conjecture that human behavior, especially interactive behavior, may be understood as an exchange of rewards and costs). The most comprehensive *social exchange theories* are those of the American social psychologists John W. Thibaut (1917-1986) and Harold H. Kelley (1921-2003) and the American sociologists George C. Homans (1910-1989) and Peter M. Blau (1918-2002). *Social exchange theories* involve an analogy between economic relationships and other kinds of social relationships where an exchange is assumed to occur when each of the parties involved controls goods valued by the others, and each values at least some of the goods that others control more than at least some of the goods that she or he controls (goods may be any commodity, condition, person, or act that has value for the individual). *Social exchange theories* differ in their conceptual language and in the explicit reference to economic or behavioral psychology concepts. *Homans' theory* borrows concepts and language (e.g., *frequency, value, reward, satiation,* and *extinction*) from B. F. Skinner's behavioral psychology, and focuses on concepts of *equilibration* in exchange, attempting to explain social interaction in small groups. Homans also uses the concepts of *expectancy* and *distributive justice* in which the parties to an exchange should receive rewards proportional to their costs and investments. *Blau's theory,* although similar to Homans', makes more explicit use of economic concepts such as *indifference curves, power,* and *normative obligation.* Much of *Blau's theory* is concerned with the roots of emergent social structure in social exchange patterns in small groups. *Thibaut and Kelley's theory* uses the language of group problem solving (with two-person, dyadic groups) in which many of the assumptions are common to the reinforcement concepts of behavioral psychology. Thibaut and Kelley make extensive use of *reward-cost matrices* derived from *game theory,* which led to the development of various indices of individuals' interdependence, such as definition of parties' power over each other and their conflicts of interest ("correspondence" versus

"noncorrespondence" of outcomes). Thibaut and Kelley also invoke the concept of *reflexive control,* which refers to the extent that an individual can unilaterally affect her or his own outcomes in a relationship via chosen behaviors. Through analyzing the particular aspects of power in a given encounter, Thibaut and Kelley were able to predict the likely course of social interaction. They also analyzed persons' attractions to relationships based on how the outcomes received in a relationship compare to the individual's "comparison level" (i.e., a standard for evaluating the goodness of outcomes from a relationship based on a central tendency of the distribution of all outcomes from previous salient relationships). Although Thibaut and Kelley's analyses are concerned primarily with dyadic relationships, their same principles have been applied to larger groups in studying topics such as coalition formation, status, and role differentiation in groups. Some theoretical approaches to *social exchange* argue that the concrete nature of the outcome sought affects the nature of the exchange. For example, U. Foa and E. Foa advance a classification of rewards based on "concreteness" versus "abstractness" and on situational specificity in which some outcomes are not exchangeable (e.g., love will be exchanged for love, but not for money). According to I. Altman and D. Taylor's *social penetration theory,* which addresses the nature and quality of social exchange and close bonds, relationships progress from superficial exchanges to more intimate ones as people begin to give more of themselves to one another; their exchanges become both broader (including more areas of their lives) and deeper (involving more intimate and personally meaningful areas). The *social penetration* process may involve a greater sharing of possessions or physical intimacy, but the most important commodity of all may be the sharing of innermost thoughts and feelings with another in the act of "self-disclosure." In his *gain-loss theory,* E. Aronson also has applied the principles of *social exchange theory* to the factors that promote interpersonal attraction. For example, long-distance relationships may have the potential to be as rewarding as proximal ones; however, the former have higher costs associated with them in terms of time, effort, and financial expenditure and, thus, people usually choose to have relationships with individuals who live close by. See also ATTRIBUTION THEORY; EQUILIBRIUM HYPOTHESIS; EQUITY THEORY; GAME THEORY; INTERPERSONAL ATTRACTION THEORIES; LOVE, THEORIES OF; SEXUAL ORIENTATION THEORIES.

REFERENCES

Skinner, B. F. (1938). *The behavior of organisms: An experimental analysis.* New York: Appleton-Century.

Thibaut, J. W., & Kelley, H. H. (1959). *The social psychology of groups.* New York: Wiley.

Homans, G. C. (1961). *Social behavior: Its elementary forms.* New York: Harcourt, Brace, & World.

Blau, P. M. (1964). *Exchange and power in social life.* New York: Wiley.

Altman, I., & Taylor, D. (1973). *Social penetration: The development of interpersonal relationships.* New York: Holt, Rinehart & Winston.

Simpson, R. (1973). *Theories of social exchange.* Morristown, NJ: General Learning Press.

Foa, U., & Foa, E. (1974). *Societal structures of the mind.* Springfield, IL: Thomas.

Heath, A. (1976). *Rational choice and social exchange: A critique of exchange theory.* Cambridge, UK: Cambridge University Press.

Thibaut, J. W., & Kelley, H. H. (1978). *Interpersonal relations: A theory of interdependence.* New York: Wiley.

Gergen, K., Greenberg, M., & Willis, R. (Eds.) (1980). *Social exchange: Advances in theory and research.* New York: Plenum.

Aronson, E. (1972/1984). *The social animal.* San Francisco: Freeman.

Alessio, J. (1990). A synthesis and formalization of Heiderian balance and social exchange theory. *Social Forces, 68,* 1267-1286.

EXCITATION TRANSFER THEORY. See EMOTIONS, THEORIES/LAWS OF.

EXCLUDED MIDDLE/THIRD, LAW/PRINCIPLE OF. In the context of formal logic, the *principle of excluded middle* (or *third*) formulates one aspect of the simple and universal condition of knowledge: every judgment must be either true or false. That is, between the assertions that express the truth and the falsity of any significant judgment, there is no medium- or middle-ground; one or the other must be true. J. M. Baldwin suggests that in order to avoid confusion regarding the scope and nature of the *principle of excluded middle/third*, one must take care to insure that the assertions do no more than express the truth or falsity of some relations represented in thought - a requirement not easily met if there is any ambiguity in the subject of the particular assertions that are in question or under analysis. See also EXCLUSION, LAW OF; KOLMOGOROV'S AXIOMS/THEORY; THOUGHT, LAWS OF.

REFERENCE

Baldwin, J. M. (Ed.) (1901-1905). *Dictionary of philosophy and psychology.* New York: Macmillan.

EXCLUSION, LAW OF. In the context of experiments on phenomena such as recognition and tonal memory, the *law of exclusion* was used to explain how a perceiver's judgment concerning comparison stimuli occurs. The German psychologist Oswald Kulpe (1862-1915) - who is the author of the first experimental psychology textbook (1895) in the world, and who, in opposing the "structuralist" theories of Wilhelm Wundt, founded the Wurzburg "imageless thought" school - asserted that in a stimulus comparison situation, there is no mediation of a comparison by a memory image, but the judgment is passed immediately after the perception of the second stimulus just as occurs in direct recognition. Also, Kulpe maintained that such judgments of stimuli are passed independently of any centrally excited sensations. Thus, through a *law of exclusion* of intermediate terms (which plays a large part in the determination of ideational connection in general), direct comparison and direct recognition involve a transformation process where the direct form is a derivative of the indirect. The *law of exclusion* (a sort of "short-cut" through experience) may be formulated as follows: When a simultaneous or successive connection of three contents, *A*, *B*, and *C*, has established a "liability" of reproduction between *A* and *C*, *C* gradually comes to be excited directly by *A*, without the intermediation of *B*. See also EXCLUDED MIDDLE/THIRD, LAW OR PRINCIPLE OF; PSYCHOPHYSICAL LAWS/THEORY; THOUGHT, LAWS OF.

REFERENCE

Kulpe, O. (1895). *Outlines of psychology*. London: Sonnenschein.

EXCLUSION, METHOD OF. This method of investigation is a portion of the English philosopher Francis Bacon's (1561-1626) general view of *induction* (i.e., the formulation of general rules or explanations) that consists of elimination by comparison of cases, particularly negative cases, all that is nonessential (the "residue"). Bacon's radical empiricist *method of exclusion* for discovering forms of nature was to prepare exhaustive and comparative listings of apparently unrelated concrete instances and, by stripping away all nonessential characteristics, to arrive at the one common underlying cause or form of the phenomenon under study. See BACONIAN METHOD; PARSIMONY, LAW OR PRINCIPLE OF.

REFERENCE

Bacon, F. (1620/1960). Novuum organum. In F. Anderson (Ed.), *The new organon and related writings*. New York: Liberal Arts Press.

EXEMPLAR THEORY OF BEHAVIOR CHOICE. = exemplar choice theory of behavior = exemplar choice theory. This particular version of *choice theory*, called *exemplar choice theory* (*ECT*), applied to human social behavior, posits that the person/actor (when he or she chooses what to do in a given situation) relies on stored memory representations of past instances or examples of actions observed previously (cf., *general exemplar theory* - holds that particular desirable characteristics or traits may be personified by certain individuals; e.g., the patience/faithfulness of Job in the scriptures). *ECT* attempts to achieve a theoretical integration in various areas in psychology including motor learning, perception, categorization- and concept-learning, priming phenomena, and social judgment. *ECT* is a "social" theory, in the broad sense that the observed actions may have been performed by persons other than the observer (i.e., the observed actions are sources of "social influence") and, in a particular sense, *ECT* may be viewed as a theory of "imitation" (i.e., the manifest symptom of "social influence" may be that the actor chooses to do the same thing as the observed fellow actor). Just as some of the early "imitation" theories of psychologists and sociologists (such as William McDougall and C. L. Morgan) held "imitativeness" to be an innate/instinctive tendency, *ECT* proposes the existence of an innate "imitative" motivational mechanism. The basic claim of the new *ECT* is that human beings are "intelligent imitators;" that is, they try to behave the way a prototypical (or "average") individual/actor would have done in the same situation. *ECT* may be viewed, also, as an updated, and more general, version of the old doctrine of "ideomotor action" (i.e., an overt act initiated by an idea in early *ideomotor theory*) such as that described by William James in the late 1800s. Specifically, *ECT* differs from the older/classical *ideomotor theories* in its account of how the actor stores and uses information about observed acts (e.g., the content of "movement ideas," the memory representations of movements, how the ideas are derived from experiences with actual movements, and the ways in which the movements are "encoded" by the actor). However, the *ECT* shares enough certain common or basic structural features with the classical *theory of ideomotor action* (e.g., both theories essentially are "information-processing" models that attempt to explain behavior in terms of stored-action representations) that it poses a great challenge for *ECT* to distinguish itself as a truly novel approach in the area of *choice theory*. See also CHOICE THEORIES.

REFERENCES

James, W. (1890/1950). *The principles of psychology*. New York: Holt/Dover.

Kvadsheim, R. (1992). *The intelligent imitator: Towards an exemplar theory of behavioral choice*. Amsterdam: North-Holland.

EXERCISE, LAW OF. In his *law of exercise*, Edward Lee Thorndike (1898) recognized and renamed an older generalization in psychology and education concerning learning called the *law of frequency*. The *law of exercise* states that, other things being equal, the repeated occurrence of any act makes that behavior easier to perform and is less vulnerable or subject to error; that is, "practice makes perfect." Thorndike regarded his *law of exercise* and his *law of effect* to be of equal importance until 1931, when the *law of exercise* was given a subordinate position in his system. Thus, Thorndike was led by his own research to renounce his former position and to argue against "exercise" as a factor working independently of "effect." The phrase "other things being equal" in the definition of the *law of exercise* has been the topic of debate among learning theorists for decades. Another criticism of the *law of exercise* is that it does not take into account the important factor of "incentive" (i.e., reinforcement value). See also DISUSE, LAW/THEORY OF; EFFECT, LAW OF; FREQUENCY, LAW OF; USE, LAW OF.

REFERENCE

Thorndike, E. L. (1898). Animal intelligence: An experimental study of the associative processes in animals. *Psychological Review Monograph Supplement, 2*, No. 8.

EXISTENTIAL ANALYSIS THEORY. The Swiss psychiatrist/existentialist Ludwig Binswanger (1881-1966) developed this theoretical form of psychoanalysis in the 1930s that is based on the philosophical/phenomenological movement called *existentialism* - advanced by the Danish philosopher Soren A. Kierkegaard (1813-1855), the German philosopher Martin Heidegger (1889-1976), and the French philosopher/writers Albert Camus (1913-1960), Jean-Paul Sartre (1905-1980), and Simone de Beauvoir (1908-1986) - which emphasizes the existence of the individual as a free entity burdened with personal responsibility (cf., the existentialist notion of *bad faith* - a form of self-deception in which individuals refuse to accept responsibility for their own freely chosen actions and depict themselves as the passive victims of worldly circumstance).

Philosophical existentialism is an approach holding that one's existence cannot be studied objectively, but is revealed via reflection on existence in space and time; it tends, also, to reject objective values and to discredit scientific knowledge and methodology. *Psychoanalytical existentialism* ("daseinsanalysis") seeks to reconstruct the inner experience of patients, not necessarily to cure symptoms; the goal of this therapeutic approach is to get patients to confront their existence and to exercise their personal freedom and autonomy. Binswanger's case study of "Ellen West" - the pseudonym of a young woman patient with anorexia nervosa who experienced extreme mental distress, ending in her tragic death - is one of the most disturbing, and celebrated, case studies in the literature of existential analysis and psychiatry. See also FREUD'S THEORY OF PERSONALITY; MEANING, THEORY AND ASSESSMENT OF.

REFERENCES

Binswanger, L. (1942/1953). *Grundformen und erkenntnis menschlichen daseins*. Zurich: Niehaus.

Binswanger, L. (1958). The existential analysis school of thought. In R. May, E. Angel, & H. F. Ellenberger (Eds.), *Existence*. New York: Basic Books.

Binswanger, L. (1973). *Being-in-the-world: Selected papers of Ludwig Binswanger*. New York: Basic Books.

Vandereycken, W. (2003). New documentation on the famous case of Ellen West. *History of Psychiatry, 14,* 133.

EXISTENTIAL/PHENOMENOLOGICAL THEORIES OF ABNORMALITY. See PSYCHOPATHOLOGY, THEORIES OF.

EXPECTANCY EFFECT. See EXPERIMENTER EFFECTS.

EXPECTANCY-REINFORCEMENT THEORY. See ROTTER'S SOCIAL LEARNING THEORY; TOLMAN'S THEORY.

EXPECTANCY THEORY. See LEARNING THEORIES/LAWS; TOLMAN'S THEORY; VIGILANCE, THEORIES OF.

EXPECTANCY THEORY OF WORK. See WORK/CAREER/OCCUPATION, THEORIES OF.

EXPECTANCY-VALUE THEORY/MODEL. See DECISION-MAKING THEORIES; REASONED ACTION AND PLANNED BEHAVIOR THEORIES; ROTTER'S SOCIAL LEARNING THEORY; TOLMAN'S THEORY.

EXPECTED UTILITY THEORY. = utility theory. The Hungarian-born American mathematician John von Neumann (1903-1957) and the German-born American economist Oskar Morgenstern (1902-1977) formulated the modern version of *expected utility theory* of decision-making which indicates that a human decision-maker chooses strategies/actions that maximize "expected utility" (i.e., the average subjective desirability of an outcome/event associated with one's decision or preference for it - calculated by multiplying each of the possible outcomes of the decision by its probability and then summing the resulting products), and where *utilities* are determined by "revealed preferences" (i.e., a preference inferred from observations of a decision-maker's actual choices) [cf., *maximizing/op- timizing hypothesis* - posits that people act so as to gain as much utility (regarding happiness, money, etc.) as possible; this is in contrast to the American economist/psychologist Herbert Alexander Simon's (1916-2001) *satisficing hypothesis* which holds that people act to gain only a certain satisfactory utility level]. When the probabilities are phrased in subjective terms, it is called *subjective expected utility theory* - formulated by the American decision-theorist Leonard J. Savage (1917-1971) and named by the American psychologist Ward Denis Edwards (1927-) - which suggests that a decision-maker chooses an alternative or strategy that maximizes the expected utility of an event/outcome calculated from "subjective probabilities" (degree of belief; cf., *taxicab problem*) rather than from "objective probabilities" (relative frequencies of observable events). The general notion of *utility* for decision-making was first indicated in 1738 by the Swiss physicist /mathematician Daniel Bernoulli (1700-1782)

who discussed "moral worth" and explained that the value of something to a person is not simply equivalent to its monetary value, but is based, also, on its subjective "moral worth" (i.e., utility). See also ALLAIS PARADOX/ EFFECT; DECISION-MAKING THEORIES; PASCAL'S PROPOSITION OR WAGER; PROBABILITY THEORY/LAWS; PROSPECT THEORY; TAXICAB PROBLEM/ EFFECT; WELLS EFFECT.

REFERENCES

Bernoulli, D. (1738/1968). *Hydrodynamica*. New York: Dover.

Neumann, J. von, & Morgenstern, O. (1947). *Theory of games and economic behavior*. Princeton, NJ: Princeton University Press.

Edwards, W. D. (1954). The theory of decision-making. *Psychological Bulletin, 51*, 380-417.

Savage, L. J. (1954). *The foundations of statistics*. New York: Wiley.

Simon, H. A. (1957). *Models of man: Social and rational*. New York: Wiley.

Lurie, S. (1987). A parametric model of utility for two-person distributions. *Psychological Review, 94*, 42-60.

Rapoport, A. (1987). Research paradigms and expected utility models for the provision of step-level public goods. *Psychological Review, 94*, 74-83.

Luce, R. D. (2000). *Utility of gains and losses: Measurement, theoretical, and experimental approaches*. Mahwah, NJ: Erlbaum.

EXPERIENTIAL LEARNING THEORY. See LEARNING STYLE THEORY.

EXPERIENTIAL THEORY. See SCHIZOPHRENIA, THEORIES OF.

EXPERIMENTAL HYPOTHESIS. See NULL HYPOTHESIS; ORGANIZATIONAL/INDUSTRIAL/SYSTEMS THEORY.

EXPERIMENTALLY-INDUCED FALSE MEMORIES. See APPENDIX A.

EXPERIMENTER BIAS. See EXPERIMENTER EFFECTS.

EXPERIMENTER EFFECTS. = experimenter bias effects. When a researcher conducts an experiment, she or he hypothesizes that one or several variables will have a particular outcome. The experiment is planned to test the hypotheses under investigation and to eliminate as many alternative or "rival" explanations as possible (cf., *investigator paradigm effect* - the tendency in researchers, at any one time and place, to be influenced by popular fads or conceptualizations and paradigms in vogue, that determine what particular research questions are asked, what kind of data is collected, and what conclusions are stated; *perturbation theory* - provides means for disposing of extraneous factors among true psychological factors, controlling for errors such as observer's biases, instrument calibration errors, and participant sampling errors; *situational effect* - occurs when participants are placed in different settings or situations, such as in a bare room versus a well-furnished office; often, performance in the former type of setting tends to be inferior to that in the latter type of surroundings; in the *doctrine of situationalism*, it is posited that the environment and one's immediate situational factors primarily determine one's behavior). A major set of rival explanations in this process is called *experimenter effect* [also known as *observer effect* or *Rosenthal effect* - named after the German-born American psychologist Robert Rosenthal (1933-)], which refers to a number of possible effects upon participants in an experiment that may be traced to the biases or behaviors of the experimenter. One such effect is called the *experimenter-expectancy effect* or *expectancy effect*, which refers to an experimenter artifact that results when the hypothesis held by the experimenter leads unintentionally to behavior toward the participants that, in turn, increases the likelihood that the hypothesis will be confirmed; this is also called *self-fulfilling prophesy*. The phenomenon called *experimenter bias* (where experimenters may unwittingly influence participants' behavior in the direction of the fomer's expectations) is illustrated by the classic case of "Clever Hans" (Pfungst, 1911/1965), which points out that researchers often give cues to participants unintentionally through facial expressions and tones of voice. With this in mind, researchers are attempting constantly to eliminate experimenter-participant interactions that may lead to biased data and conclusions (cf., *biosocial effect* - an experimenter bias effect in which possible differential influences may be placed on different participants by virtue of the experimenter's differing attitudes and moods; and *performance cue effect* - knowledge of how a group performed previously may influence an experimenter's/rater's judgments of the group's current or subsequent performance). Another type of experimenter effect focuses on the factor of attention, especially on how attention paid to participants by the experimenter may bias the research results. The classic illustration here is the study by F. Roethlisberger and W. Dickson (cf. Mayo, 1933), who are credited with discovering the *Hawthorne effect*. This effect (named after the locale of the research - the Hawthorne plant of the Western Electric Company in Cicero, Illinois, near Chicago - where ways to increase worker productivity were studied) refers to the positive influence of attention on participants' performance. In the Hawthorne study (whose results and interpretation today are sometimes controversial), the effects of attention were so powerful that performance improved even when the objective working conditions worsened. Thus, the *Hawthorne effect* has come today to refer generally to the fact that one's performance in an experiment/study is affected by knowledge that one is participating in an experiment and refers to a change in behavior that results from participants' awareness that someone is interested in them. A phenomenon similar to the *Hawthorne effect* is called the *novelty/disruption effect*, which refers to a treatment effect that may result when an experimental treatment condition involves something new or unusual. For instance, inserting a red-colored nonsense syllable in the most difficult position in a serial list of black-on-white nonsense syllables facilitates the learning of that novel stimulus. When the novelty or disruption diminishes, the treatment effect may disappear. Experimenters may also provide the conditions for the *pretesting effect*, which refers to the influence that administering a pretest may have on the experimental treatment effect: it may sensitize the participant in such a way to behave differently than participants who did not receive the pretest. Another category of effects that may occur in psychological experiments is called *subject/participant effects*, which refer to any response by subjects or participants in a study that does not represent the way they would normally behave if not under study (cf., *Hawthorne effect*). Two powerful *subject/participant effects* are the *placebo effect* (i.e., in a treatment study, any observed improvement in response to a sham treatment that is probably due to the participant's *expectations* for treatment effectiveness; cf., *tomato effect* - a person may be affected negatively by something if he/she believes it to be harmful even though it is not; the name here comes from the introduction of tomatoes into Europe and where tomatoes had the bad reputation of causing numerous illnesses); and the *demand characteristics of the situation* [i.e., cues inadvertently given to individuals in a study concerning how they are *expected* to behave, including not only characteristics of the setting and procedures but also information, and even rumors, about the researcher and the nature of the research; cf., *John Henry effect* - named after the hardworking African-American folktale hero of the late 19th century - is a tendency for participants in a control group to adopt a competitive attitude towards the experimental group in certain experiments and, thereby, vitiating the validity of the control group; and the *good subject/participant effect*, or the *Orne effect* - named after the Austrian-American psychiatrist/hypnotist Martin Theodore Orne (1927-2000), refers to the situation where if participants in a study know what a researcher is looking for, they will typically behave accordingly in the predicted way]. Researchers conducting psychological experiments should, ideally, include *controls* for these and other possible *experimenter* and *subject/participant effects* to prevent "confounding" (i.e., cases where an extraneous variable systematically varies with variations in the independent variables under study) and to guard against the reduction of a study's validity. Yet other non-experimenter effects that may affect the validity of an experiment include: *order effects* - the order in which two or more experimental treatments are adminis-

tered may be significant and needs to be balanced or counterbalanced to control for an artificial progressive change over time; *sequence effects* - in multiple-treatment experimental designs, the different combinations of treatments should be counterbalanced across participants to insure that the sequence in which treatments are given is not the causative factor, but only the treatments themselves; *self-selection* or *selective sampling bias/effect* - when a number of people are asked to participate in an experiment, those likely to volunteer are probably *not* representative of the total group or population; random assignment of participants to treatments/groups may circumvent this bias/effect; and the *leniency effect*, proposed by the Austrian-born American psychologist Fritz Heider (1896-1988), refers to a judgmental error especially likely to occur in personality assessment situations where well-known or sympathetic individuals are evaluated more favorably than less familiar or less sympathetic persons. See also CLEVER HANS EFFECT/ PHENOMENON; HALO EFFECT; PYGMALION EFFECT.

REFERENCES

Pfungst, O. (1911/1965). *Clever Hans (the horse of Mr. von Osten): A contribution to experimental animal and human psychology.* New York: Holt, Rinehart, and Winston.

Mayo, E. (1933). *The human problems of an industrial civilization.* New York: Macmillan.

Roethlisberger, F., & Dickson, W. (1939). *Management and the worker.* Cambridge, MA: Harvard University Press.

Barber, T. X., & Silver, M. (1968). Fact, fiction, and the experimenter bias effect. *Psychological Bulletin Monograph Supplement, 70,* 1-29.

Parsons, H. (1974). What happened at Hawthorne? *Science, 183,* 922-932.

Barber, T. X. (1976). *Pitfalls in human research: Ten pivotal points.* New York: Pergamon.

Rosenthal, R. (1976). *Experimenter effects in behavioral research.* New York: Irvington.

Rosenthal, R., & Rubin, D. (1978). Interpersonal expectancy effects: The first 345 studies. *The Behavioral and Brain Sciences*, *3*, 377-386.

Ross, M., & Olson, J. M. (1981). An expectancy-attribution model of the effects of placebos. *Psychological Review*, *88*, 408-437.

Rice, B. (1982). The Hawthorne defect: Persistence of a flawed theory. *Psychology Today*, *16*, 70-74.

EXPRESSION THEORY. See DEMBER-EARL THEORY OF CHOICE/PREFERENCE.

EXTENSION OF MENTAL LIFE, LAW OF THE. See CONDUCT, LAWS OF.

EXTENSIONS-OF-WAKING-LIFE THEORY. See SLEEP, THEORIES OF.

EXTENSION THEOREM OF SEMANTIC ENTAILMENT. See SET THEORY.

EXTINCTION, LAWS OF. See GENERALIZATION, PRINCIPLES OF.

EXTINCTION OF CHAINED REFLEXES, LAW OF. See SKINNER'S DESCRIPTIVE BEHAVIOR/OPERANT CONDITIONING THEORY.

EXTINCTION OF TYPE R, LAW OF. See SKINNER'S DESCRIPTIVE BEHAVIOR/OPERANT CONDITIONING THEORY.

EXTINCTION OF TYPE S, LAW OF. See SKINNER'S DESCRIPTIVE BEHAVIOR/OPERANT CONDITIONING THEORY.

EXTINCTION THEORY. See AMSEL'S HYPOTHESIS/THEORY; CAPALDI'S THEORY; GUTHRIE'S THEORY OF BEHAVIOR.

EXTRA-SENSORY PERCEPTION THEORY. See PARANORMAL PHENOMENON AND THEORY.

EYE MOVEMENT THEORY. See APPARENT MOVEMENT, PRINCIPLES/THEORIES OF; CONSTRUCTIVIST THEORY OF PERCEPTION; MUNSTERBERG'S THEORY OF PERCEPTUAL FLUCTUATIONS.

EYE PLACEMENT PRINCIPLE. See GESTALT THEORY/LAWS.

EYEWITNESS MISINFORMATION EFFECT. = misinformation effect. The American psychologists Elizabeth F. Loftus (1944-) and John C. Palmer (1954-) described this phenomenon whereby misleading post-event information may distort recall of an event by an eyewitness. The *eyewitness misinformation effect* may be caused by the post-event information "overwriting" the original memory, or by the eyewitness becoming confused about the sources of different items of information, without the original memory invariably being impaired [cf., *experimentally-induced false memory technique* (also called the "Deese/Roediger-McDermott paradigm") - any repeatable method/procedure for generating false memories and which creates a powerful "cognitive/memory illusion" causing participants to believe that they can remember experiences, materials, or events that did not actually occur - first reported by the American psychologist James Deese (1921-1999) and later studied by the American psychologists Henry L. Roediger III (1947-) and Kathleen B. McDermott (1968-)]. E. F. Loftus also describes the so-called "Piaget kidnapping memory" incident which is a classic example of a *false memory* deriving from the second year of life of the Swiss psychologist Jean Piaget (1896-1980), where his nurse fabricated a story about him being kidnapped and Piaget himself developed an elaborate *false visual memory* over the years of the alleged event. Other related memory concepts in this area are: *deferred action* - a psychoanalytic term denoting the revision of memories (i.e., "after the event" or memory with "hindsight") to fit in with new experiences and information or the achievement of later developmental stages; *reconstructive memory* - dynamic memory processes whereby various strategies are used during memory retrieval to rebuild information from memory, and filling in missing elements while attempting to remember material (cf., *confabulation* - a memory disorder related to amnesia, but involving the fabrication of events, facts, and experiences, either consciously or unconsciously, in order to compensate for memory loss; sometimes called "honest lying"); *recovered memory* - the recall of some event, usually involving a traumatic experience (such as being sexually abused as a child), retrieved after having been repressed or forgotten for many years; often such recovered memories, unless verified by reliable sources, turn out to be *false memories*, "pseudomemories," or "pseudomnesia;" *constructive memory* - memories produced under the influence of prior experience or expectations where existing "schemas" or new information determine how the information is stored in memory; and *changed-trace hypothesis* - posits that new information can change old information in memory and helps explain the *misinformation effect* (cf., *multiple trace hypothesis* which states that new information interferes with, rather than changes, old information). See also APPENDIX A; CONSTRUCTIVISM, THEORIES OF; FORGETTING/MEMORY, THEORIES OF; INTERFERENCE THEORIES OF FORGETTING; SHORT-TERM AND LONG-TERM MEMORY, THEORIES OF.

REFERENCES

Deese, J. (1959). On the prediction of occurrence of particular verbal intrusions in immediate recall. *Journal of Experimental Psychology, 58*, 17-22.

Loftus, E. F., & Palmer, J. C. (1974). Reconstruction of automobile destruction: An example of the interaction between language and memory. *Journal of Verbal Learning and Verbal Behavior, 13*, 585-589.

Loftus, E. F. (1979). *Eyewitness testimony*. Cambridge, MA: Harvard University Press.

Roediger, H. L. III, & McDermott, K. B. (1995). Creating false memories: Remembering words not presented in lists. *Journal of Experimental Psychology: Learning, Memory, and Cognition, 21*, 803-814.

Wickens, T. D., & Hirshman, E. (2000). False memories and statistical design theory. *Psychological Review, 107*, 377-383.

Wells, G. L., & Olson, E. A. (2003). Eyewitness testimony. *Annual Review of Psychology, 54*, 277-295.

Watson, J. M., McDermott, K. B., & Balota, D. A. (2004). Attempting to avoid false memories in the Deese/Roediger-McDermott paradigm. *Memory and Cognition, 32*, 135-141.

EYSENCK'S THEORY OF PERSONALITY. The German-born English psychologist Hans Jurgen Eysenck (1916-1997) viewed personality as organized in a hierarchy where *types* are located at the most general level, *traits* at the next level (similar to R. B. Cattell's *source traits*), *habitual responses* at the next level, and *specific responses* at the bottom of the hierarchy. Eysenck analyzed personality at the *type* level along the following three dimensions: "extraversion-introversion," "neuroticism-stability," and "normality-psychoticism" by using ratings, situational tests, questionnaires, and physiological measures. For example, a person who scores high on the "psychoticism" dimension tends to be hostile, egocentric, and antisocial, and is generally considered to be "peculiar" by other people. Eysenck developed an innovative aspect of *factor analysis* called *criterion analysis*, in which a given factor is adjusted in such a way as to give maximal separation in the analysis to a specific criterion group (e.g., the factor of "neuroticism" may be aligned to differentiate it maximally between a group of nonneurotic persons versus a group of neurotic individuals). Thus, the use of the technique of *factor analysis* (cf., *Cattell's personality theory*) within an articulated theoretical framework is characteristic of Eysenck's approach to personality study. There is a duality to *Eysenck's personality theory*: (1) *theory of personality structure*, consisting of the extraversion-intro-version, neuroticism, and psychoticism dimensions, where the first two dimensions have been studied most and may be assessed via the Eysenck Personality Inventory; and (2) *theory of cause*, which proposes that behaviors are caused by characteristic brain functions or other neurophysiological functions. Eysenck's model for the causation of high degrees of neuroticism, for example, holds that the hypothalamus is likely to discharge excessive stimulation into the cerebral cortex and into the autonomic nervous system in such cases, and his model of extraversion-introversion holds that when the balance of inhibition versus excitation of the cortex is disrupted, the behavior of turning outward or turning inward occurs. *Eysenck's personality theory* and his view of humans are governed by the idea that people are biosocial organisms whose actions are determined equally by *biological* (genetic, physiological, endocrine) and *social* (historical, economic, interactional) factors. His insistence on seeing individuals as a product of *evolution* was regarded by Eysenck, also, as essential for a proper understanding of people. See also CATTELL'S PERSONALITY THE-ORY; DARWIN'S EVOLUTION THEORY; PERSONALITY THEORIES.

REFERENCES

Eysenck, H. J. (1947). *Dimensions of personality*. London: Routledge & Kegan Paul.

Eysenck, H. J. (1952). *The scientific study of personality*. London: Routledge & Kegan Paul.

Eysenck, H. J. (1953). *The structure of human personality*. London: Routledge & Kegan Paul.

Eysenck, H. J. (1955). A dynamic theory of anxiety and hysteria. *Journal of Mental Science, 101*, 28-51.

Cattell, R. B. (1965). *The scientific analysis of personality*. Baltimore, MD: Penguin Books.

Eysenck, H. J., & Eysenck, S. (1968). *Manual for the Eysenck Personality Inventory*. San Diego, CA: Educational and Industrial Testing Service.

Eysenck, H. J. (1969). *Personality structure and measurement*. San Diego, CA: Knapp.

Cartwright, D. (1979). *Theories and models of personality*. Dubuque, IA: Brown.

Eysenck, H. J. (1979). The conditioning model of neurosis. *The Behavioral and Brain Sciences, 2*, 155-199.

Eysenck, H. J. (1993). Creativity and personality: Suggestions for a theory. *Psychological Inquiry, 4*, 147-178.

F

FACE-GOBLET/FACE-VASE/REVERSIBLE GOBLET ILLUSION. See APPENDIX A, RUBIN FIGURE/ILLUSION.

FACE RECOGNITION/FACIAL IDENTITY THEORY. The various models and theories of face-recognition and facial identity attempt to explain the different types of information that is extracted from the faces one sees in the world. In one integrative approach, the *Bruce-Young functional model of face recognition*, it is proposed that three of the major aspects of face perception - recognition of facial *identity*, recognition of facial *expression*, and recognition of facial *speech* - are all *independently* achieved by the perceiver. According to this model, one does not have to recognize a person's identity in order to be able to "speech-read" their lips and, at an intuitive level, information extracted from a face that allowed it to be classified as "familiar" would not be the same as that which needs to be extracted for making use of facial speech cues. Evidence supporting such a face-recognition model of functional organization comes primarily from two sources: experiments carried out on "normal" participants where one kind of performance is affected, while there is little or no effect on another; and data from "brain-damaged" patients where different patterns of selective impairment of different face-processing tasks are reported. Essentially, in a number of reports, the independence of facial *expression* and facial *identity* processing has been supported by converging evidence from studies with normal adults, neuropsychological dissociations, and neurophysiological recordings; moreover, independence of *memory* for faces and facial *speech* has been observed in autistic individuals. Other studies showing a double dissociation between facial *speech* and facial *identity* processing suggest that these two functions are independent where each activates a different cortical processing mechanism. However, data from yet other studies indicate that the *Bruce-Young functional model of face recognition* is not entirely supported regarding the notion of independence of the processing of facial *speech* and the processing of facial *identity*. See also McGURK EFFECT/ILLUSION.

REFERENCES
Bruce, V., & Young, A. (1986). Understanding face recognition. *British Journal of Psychology, 77*, 305-327.
Young, A. W., Hellawell, D., & Hay, D. C. (1987). Configurational information in face perception. *Perception, 16*, 747-759.

FACIAL FEEDBACK HYPOTHESIS. This hypothesis refers to the notion that emotional activity causes genetically-programmed alterations to occur in facial expression where the face subsequently provides cues ("feedback") to the brain that help a person to determine what emotion is being felt. In other terms, the *facial feedback hypothesis* states that having facial expressions and becoming aware of them are what lead to an emotional experience. Indeed, according to the *facial feedback hypothesis*, when people deliberately form various facial expressions, emotion-like transformations occur in their bodily activity (cf., *social smile theory* - posits that a smile on the face of an infant or an adult affects others in a favorable way and, hence, the behavior of smiling has survival value for the individual and the species). Thus, "making faces" can actually cause emotion. The idea that sensory feedback from one's own facial expression can influence one's emotional feeling suggests a possible mechanism through which emotional "contagion" can occur: people may automatically mimic the facial expressions of others, and then, perhaps, feedback from one's own body alters the emotions to coincide with the expressions that are being mimicked. Recently, E. Hatfield, J. Cacioppo, and R. Rapson proposed this *theory of primitive emotional contagion* in which the mimicry of expressions does not involve higher cognitive processes. A considerable amount of research shows that people do automatically mimic the emotional expressions of others. The ability to synchronize emotions quickly with other people may have been an advantage in our evolution, and may still be today, by helping to promote our acceptance of those around us (cf., *other-race face-perception effect* - refers to the finding that face-recognition memory is better for faces of the same "race" that the observer belongs to, as compared to the faces of people of other "races"). Perhaps overt facial expressions of emotion, coupled with an automatic tendency to mimic those expressions, came about in evolution partly to facilitate social acceptance. See also EKMAN-FRIESEN THEORY OF EMOTIONS; EMOTIONS, THEORIES OF; IZARD'S THEORY OF EMOTIONS.

REFERENCES

Meltzoff, A., & Moore, M. (1977). Imitation of facial and manual gestures by human neonates. *Science, 198,* 75-78.

Buck, R. (1980). Nonverbal behavior and the theory of emotion: The facial feedback hypothesis. *Journal of Personality and Social Psychology, 38,* 811-824.

Strack, F., Martin, L., & Stepper, S. (1988). Inhibiting and facilitating conditions of the human smile: A nonobtrusive test of the facial feedback hypothesis. *Journal of Personality and Social Psychology, 54,* 268-272.

Adelmann, P., & Zajonc, R. (1989). Facial efference and the experience of emotion. *Annual Review of Psychology, 40,* 249-280.

Izard, C. (1990). Facial expressions and the regulation of emotions. *Journal of Personality and Social Psychology, 58,* 487-498.

Ekman, P. (1993). Facial expression and emotion. *American Psychologist, 48,* 384-392.

Hatfield, E., Cacioppo, J., & Rapson, R. (1993). *Emotional contagion.* Madison, WI: Brown.

FACILITATION, LAW OF. See SKINNER'S DESCRIPTIVE BEHAVIOR/OPERANT CONDITIONING THEORY.

FACTOR THEORY. See HULL'S LEARNING THEORY.

FACTOR THEORY OF LEARNING. See LEARNING THEORIES/LAWS.

FACULTY THEORY. See MALEBRANCHE'S THEORIES; MIND/MENTAL STATES, THEORIES OF; TRANSFER OF TRAINING, THORNDIKE'S THEORY OF.

FAILURE, LAW OF. See MURPHY'S LAWS.

FALSE-CONSENSUS EFFECT. This form of *social psychological assimilation* (i.e., examining the discrepancy between one's own attitude and that of a persuasive message or source) was introduced by the Canadian psychologist Lee David Ross (1942-). The *false-consensus effect* refers to an intuitive tendency for the individual to *overestimate* the extent to which other people share one's own attitudes, behaviors, and beliefs. For example, in the context of social perception/attribution, one tends to assume that his/her own responses and behaviors are more common than, in fact, they really are; and, also, to consider alternative responses or behaviors (to one's own) as uncommon, inappropriate, or deviant from the norm. The *false-consensus effect,* as a tendency to assume that personal traits are common in others, usually occurs because a person tends to connect or affiliate with others of similar status who tend to have opinions in common. See also ASSIMILATION-CONTRAST EFFECT; ASSUMED SIMILARITY BIAS EFFECT; ATTRIBUTION THEORY; ORGANIZATIONAL/INDUSTRIAL/SYSTEMS THEORY.

REFERENCES

Ross, L. D. (1977). The intuitive psychologist and his shortcomings: Distortions in the attribution process. In L. Berkowitz (Ed.), *Advances in experimental social psychology.* New York: Academic Press.

Ross, L. D., Lepper, M. R., Strack, F., & Steinmetz, J. (1977). Social explanation and social expectation: Effects of real and hypothetical explanations on subjective likelihood. *Journal of Personality and Social Psychology, 35,* 817-829.

FALSIFICATION/FALSIFIABILITY THEORY. See NULL HYPOTHESIS.

FAMILY-SYSTEMS MODEL/THEORY. See CONTROL/SYSTEMS THEORY.

FAN EFFECT. In the context of memory research, the *fan effect* refers to a tendency for the amount of time required to retrieve a specific fact about a concept to increase with the number of facts that are known about that particular concept (i.e., the greater the number of links to a concept, the more time is required to verify any one link). The *fan effect* has been observed in diverse study areas such as face recognition, retrieval of various types of knowledge, age-related memory deficits, and increase of information retrieval time with advanced age. It may be suggested that the *fan effect* is either due to "multiple mental models" or to "suppression of concepts." However, when invoking the Adaptive Control of Thought-Rational (ACT-R) theory or model (Anderson & Lebiere, 1998) - which embodies associative interference - experimental results are consistent with the "multiple mental models" interpretation over the "concept suppression" approach. Thus, the ACT-R theory or model provides a good quantitative fit to results of the *fan effect* experiments. See also ADAPTIVE CONTROL OF THOUGHT THEORY/MODEL; INFORMATION/INFORMATION PROCESSING THEORY; SHORT-TERM AND LONG-TERM MEMORY, THEORIES OF.

REFERENCES

Anderson, J. R., & Lebiere, C. (1998). *The atomic components of thought.* Mahwah, NJ: Erlbaum.

Anderson, J. R., & Reder, L. M. (1999). The fan effect: New results and new theories. *Journal of Experimental Psychology: General, 128,* 186-197.

Radvansky, G. A. (1999). The fan effect: A tale of two theories. *Journal of Experimental Psychology: General, 128,* 198-206.

FASHIONING EFFECT. See PERCEPTION (II. COMPARATIVE APPRAISAL), THEORIES OF; SELF-CONCEPT THEORY.

FEATURE ANALYSIS/DETECTION/EXTRACTION THEORY. See PATTERN/OBJECT RECOGNITION THEORY.

FEATURE-COMPARISON MODEL. See CONCEPT LEARNING AND CONCEPT FORMATION, THEORIES OF.

FEATURE INTEGRATION THEORY. See PATTERN/OBJECT RECOGNITION THEORY.

FEATURE-LIST THEORY. See CONCEPT LEARNING AND CONCEPT FORMATION, THEORIES OF; PROTOTYPE THEORY.

FEATURE THEORY/MODEL OF MEMORY. See FORGETTING/MEMORY, THEORIES OF.

FECHNER-HELMHOLTZ LAW. See FECHNER'S LAW.

FECHNER'S COLORS. See FECHNER'S LAW.

FECHNER'S LAW. The German physiologist, physicist, mathematician, and philosopher Gustav Theodor Fechner (1801-1887) is best remembered in psychology for his development of *psychophysics*, that is, the study of the relationships between the mental world ("mind") and the material world ("body"). From his work in *psychophysics*, Fechner formulated a lawful connection between mind (mental sensation) and body (material stimulus). This quantitative relationship, called *Fechner's law*, is stated in the equation: $S = k \log I$, where S is the mental sensation, I is the material stimulus, log is the logarithmic value of a given I, and k is a constant referring to a particular sensory modality (e.g., vision, audition, touch). According to *Fechner's law*, as the stimulus intensity increases in geometrical series, the mental sensation increases in arithmetical series; cf., *Fechner-Helmholtz law,* also know as the *coefficient law* - a visual stimulus reduces the excitability of the visual system so that the effect of an equal subsequent stimulus is diminished by approximately the same amount as would have been the case had the stimulus intensity itself been diminished proportionately; and the *parallel law* - Fechner's assertion that when two stimuli of different intensity are presented for a period of time, although through adaptation the apparent magnitude of each will lessen, the ratio of their apparent magnitudes will remain the same. Fechner advanced the field of *psychophysics* by systematizing three methods: *average error* - where a mean represents the best approximation of a large number of measures; *constant stimuli* - determines the amount of difference in stimulation needed to indicate a sensory difference; and *limits* - determines the thresholds of sensory stimulations (also called *just noticeable differences* or *JND*). Although the German physiologist/psychophysicist Ernst Weber's (1795-1878) investigations using the *JND* method preceded Fechner's work, Fechner's contribution is based in his mathematical statement of the relationship between the mental and the physical domains. Apparently, Weber himself did not recognize the general significance of his *JND law*, and he formulated no specific law. Fechner later realized that his own principle was essentially what Weber's earlier results showed, and Fechner gave the empirical relationship mathematical form and he called it *Weber's law*. In recent times, there has been a tendency to correct Fechner's generosity and to give the name *Fechner's law* to what Fechner called *Weber's law*, reserving the latter term for Weber's simple statement that the *JND* in a stimulus bears a constant ratio to the stimulus (k = delta I/I). The immediate result of Fechner's idea was the formulation of the program of what he later called *psychophysics*. Inasmuch as *Fechner's law* was derived from *Weber's law*, the combination term *Weber-Fechner law* is used occasionally by writers to encompass both generalizations. There is come confusion, also, in the older literature over whose law is called by which name [cf., *Bouguer-Weber law* - a rarely published name for the *Weber-Fechner law*, based on the theory that the phenomenon of the *Weber-Fechner law* was anticipated by the earlier work of the French physicist Pierre Bouguer (1698-1758); Bouguer also discovered the "law of absorption," sometimes unjustly known as *Lambert's law*]. *Fechner's law* may be indicted on several grounds based on the data accumulated in the century since its formulation: Fechner's summated *JND* technique may introduce serious error into the form of the psychophysical relation between stimulus magnitude and subjective magnitude. Fechner's choice of the *absolute threshold* as an arbitrary starting point for scale of psychological magnitude may not have been a good one because the nature of the *absolute threshold* is, in itself, open to question; and Fechner's assumption that all *JND* are subjectively equal to each other (and, therefore, that each *JND* contributes an equal increment to perceived magnitude) is contradicted by empirical evidence [cf., *absolute/absolute threshold* - in philosophy and pre-scientific psychology, *absolute* refers to: (1) an ultimate principle that is all-comprehensive or universal (as in the philosophical systems of neo-Hegelianism,, Idealism, and Pantheism); (2) an immediate or unknowable event that escapes all possible definitions or distinctions (as in the systems of Kantianism and Agnosticism); and (3) a world-ground, first-cause, or "relative absolute" (as in the epistemological systems of Realism, Materialism, Spiritualism, and Theism). In meaning (1), the concept of *absolute* is necessarily psychic in nature; in meaning (3), the term *absolute* (via the British philosophers Sir William Hamilton and Herbert Spencer) has been taken as implying freedom from all relation, including the internal relation of the parts to the whole or to each other, and the freedom from external and necessary relation (that is, independence). In modern scientific psychology, the term *absolute* has been joined with the concept of *threshold* ("absolute threshold"). Around 1860, Fechner assumed that as the magnitude of a stimulus increased from zero, a point would be reached where the stimulus could be detected consciously. Thus, according to Fechner, the *absolute threshold* is the intensity of a stimulus at, or above, which a sensation results and below which no detectable sensation occurs. Fechner's position is consonant with the orientations of the earlier philosophers Gottfried Leibnitz ("petites perceptions") and Johann Herbart ("thresholds of consciousness"); for each of these individuals, the effects of stimulation cumulate and, at some point - the *absolute threshold* - are capable of causing a conscious sensation]. The German physiologist, philosopher, and psychologist Wilhelm Wundt (1832-1920) is credited by most historians as the "founder" of modern experimental psychology in 1879, but some writers consider Fechner's publication in 1860 of his *Elemente der Psychophysik* (Elements of Psychophysics) to be a significant and noteworthy event in the development and advancement of psychology as a *science*. In addition to *Fechner's law*, Fechner's name is associated with *Fechner's colors* (subjective colors seen in slowly rotating discs having black and white patterns), and *Fechner's paradox* (condition in which a visual target viewed with two eyes appears brighter if one eye is suddenly covered up). See also ABNEY'S LAW; HERBART'S DOCTRINE OF APPERCEPTION; HICK'S LAW; LEIBNITZ'S MONAD THEORY; MERKEL'S LAW; STEVENS' POWER LAW; WEBER'S LAW; WUNDT'S THEORIES/DOCTRINES/PRINCIPLES.

REFERENCES

Weber, E. (1842-1853). Der tastsinn und das gemeingefuhl. In R. Wagner (Ed.), *Handworterbuch der physiologie*. Braunschweig: Vieweg.

Fechner, G. T. (1860). *Elemente der psychophysik*. Leipzig: Breitkopf, Hartel.

Stevens, S. S. (1957). On the psychophysical law. *Psychological Review, 64,* 153-181.

FECHNER'S PARADOX. See FECHNER'S LAW.

FEEDBACK-SYSTEM MODEL. See CONTROL/SYSTEMS THEORY.

FEELINGS, THEORY OF. See WUNDT'S THEORIES/DOCTRINES/PRINCIPLES.

FEMINIST THEORY. See SEXUAL ORIENTATION THEORIES.

FERBER TECHNIQUE/EFFECT. The American pediatric sleep researcher Richard Ferber (1944-) developed this procedure (sometimes called "Ferberization") for training an infant to be self-reliant and to sleep on its own. The *Ferber technique/effect* requires that the care-giver place the infant in its crib, then leave the room and ignore the infant's crying for at least 20 minutes. Subsequently, the care-giver returns to the crib, pats the infant on the back, but doesn't pick it up, and then leaves the room quickly. This procedure is repeated every night, increasing the waiting period by five minutes per night before responding to the infant's crying with patting. This often controversial child-care practice is similar, theoretically, to a modification of the operant/behavioral conditioning procedure called "fading" used in stimulus control and errorless discrimination learning situations (where discriminative stimuli are "faded out" gradually) but, in this case, fading occurs by slowly extending (fading out) the waiting time period before the reinforcing stimulus (pat or attention given by the care-giver) is administered. The *Ferber technique/effect* seems to work for some infants, but not for others. See also BEHAVIORIST THEORY; ERRORLESS DISCRIMINATION LEARNING, PHENOMENON OF; LEARNING THEORIES/LAWS; PUNISHMENT, THEORIES OF; REINFORCEMENT THEORY.

REFERENCES

Terrace, H. S. (1963). Errorless transfer of a discrimination across two continua. *Journal of the Experimental Analysis of Behavior, 6,* 223-233.

Ferber, R. (1985/1986). *Solve your child's sleep problem*. New York: Simon & Schuster/Fireside.

FERE EFFECT/PHENOMENON. See ELECTRODERMAL ACTIVITY/PHENOMENA.

FERENCZI'S CATASTROPHE THEORY. See CATASTROPHE THEORY/MODEL.

FERRY-PORTER LAW. = Porter's law. This principle - named in honor of the American physicist Ervin Sidney Ferry (1868-1956) and the English scientist Thomas Cunningham Porter (1860-1933) - states that *critical flicker frequency* (*cff*) increases by equal amounts for equal increases in the logarithm of the brightness/intensity of the stimulus. This generalization is independent of the wavelength composition or color of the stimulus. *Cff* is the frequency of intermittence of a visual stimulus just necessary to eliminate the sensation of "flicker," where the *flicker phenomenon* is defined as a rapid periodic change perceived in a visual impression due to a corresponding rapid periodic change in the intensity or some other feature of the stimulus. Flicker disappears when the frequency of the stimulus change exceeds the *cff* rate, which is about 25 to 30 hertz [1 hertz, or HZ, = one cycle per second; this unit of measurement is named in honor of the German physicist Heinrich Rudolph Hertz (1857-1894)]. The *cff* rate is somewhat higher at higher intensity levels and lower for lower intensities, and the rate is lowered, also, with decrease in the intensity difference between parts of the sequence or period. The *Ferry-Porter law* holds only over a very limited range of conditions, and this is particularly evident when considering the variations in the character of temporal modulation of the extant stimulus. The law does not hold at all for very low modulation amplitudes. See also TALBOT-PLATEAU LAW; VISION/SIGHT, THEORIES OF.

REFERENCES

Ferry, E. S. (1892). Persistence of vision. *American Journal of Science, 44,* 192-207.

Porter, T. C. (1902). Contributions to the study of flicker. II. *Proceedings of the Royal Society of London, 70A,* 313-329.

Porter, T. C. (1912). Contributions to the study of flicker. III. *Proceedings of the Royal Society of London, 86A,* 495-513.

Brown, J. (1965). Flicker and intermittent stimulation. In C. Graham (Ed.), *Vision and visual perception.* New York: Wiley.

FESTINGER'S COGNITIVE DISSONANCE THEORY. = cognitive dissonance theory = dissonance theory. The American psychologist Leon Festinger (1919-1989) developed the *theory of cognitive dissonance,* which is based on the tenet that an individual is motivated to maintain consistency, consonance, or balance (i.e., *congruity the-*

ory/principle, or *cognitive consistency theory*) among pairs of cognitive beliefs, ideas, perceptions, or attitudes about oneself, behavior, or the environment. According to the theory, when inconsistency occurs between cognitions, the person is assumed to be psychologically uncomfortable, and internal pressure is exerted both to reduce the dissonance and to avoid information and events that would increase the dissonance. Festinger's position is similar to the American psychologist George Kelly's (1905-1966) approach, which assumes that cognitions are the basic elements relevant to achieving consistency. *Festinger's theory* concerns *psychological* inconsistency, not *formal logical* inconsistency. For example, the behavior-cognition pair "I smoke" and "Smoking is unhealthy" will produce dissonance only with the assumption that the smoker does not want to be unhealthy or to contact cancer. Such ambiguity concerning type of inconsistency both increases the scope of *dissonance theory* and also makes it difficult to predict when dissonance will occur. *Festinger's theory of cognitive dissonance* is an elaboration, also, of the German-born American psychologist Kurt Lewin's (1890-1947) field theory, in which the situation existing prior to one's making a decision about events differs from the situation after a decision has been made. Festinger's experimental research on cognitive dissonance demonstrates that people are more likely to change their beliefs to conform to their public statements if they are under rewarded than if they are given large rewards, a surprising finding that is at odds with traditional *reinforcement theory* (cf., *less-leads-to-more effect,* also called *negative incentive effect* - refers to a tendency in people who have been rewarded minimally to state positions contrary to their true beliefs to generate more attitude change than occurs with larger rewards). Whereas *reinforcement theory* indicates that one dislikes things associated with pain, *cognitive dissonance theory* suggests that persons come to like those things for which they suffer (cf., *cognitive evaluation theory* - posits that if a person is rewarded for good behavior, the behavior will either get better or worse depending on whether the person sees the reward as the result of improved "effectance" or as a means for the rewarder to assert control over the respondent; and *commodity theory* - holds that goods and products are perceived to have more value when there is a cost attached to them). Festinger identified four types of dissonance: postdecision dissonance (cf., double approach-avoidance situation of *conflict theory*); forced compliance dissonance; maximized dissonance/consequent attitude change; and social support system dissonance. Occasionally, people behave in ways that run counter to their attitudes, but subsequently may be faced with their dissonant cognitions (such as saying "I believe *this*, but I did *that*"). They can't undo their deed, but they can relieve their dissonance by changing, even reversing, their attitudes to justify an action. This phenomenon is called the *insufficient-justification effect* and is defined as a change in attitude that occurs because, without the change, the individual cannot justify the already completed action. Hundreds of field studies and experiments have demonstrated the power of the *theory of cognitive dissonance* to change behavior and attitudes. Additionally, Festinger was among the first to point out that group membership fills needs for social comparison. Festinger's *theory of social comparison* holds that in an ambiguous situation (i.e., when one is not certain about what to do or how to feel) the individual will affiliate with people with whom one can compare feelings and behaviors (cf., Donald W. Fiske and Salvatore R. Maddi's *personality theory* that is based on a consistency model concerning the match and mismatch between one's customary or actual levels of *activation/tension* rather than of *cognitions*). By the 1970s, the *theory of cognitive dissonance* was recognized as one of the most important and influential developments in social psychology up to that time. Detractors of *cognitive dissonance theory* (e.g., Daryl J. Bem's *self-perception theory*) indicate that dissonance phenomena may be more parsimoniously accounted for by assuming that actors infer their beliefs from observations of their own behavior. The strength of *cognitive dissonance theory*, also, has been its weakness: the postulation of cognitive mechanisms has had a positive impact, but the intricate experimental procedures used have led to alternative interpretations of results. Recently, there has been a decline of interest in *cognitive dissonance theory*. Perhaps, part of the reason for this has to do with its focus on the motivational concept of *tension-reduction*. By the mid- and late-1970s, psychologists' attraction to the theory began to wane as interest in the entire topic of *motivation* faded, and the journals were overwhelmed by studies concerning the purely cognitive approaches (absent motivational constructs such as *drive-reduction* and *tension-reduction*) and it was fashionable to pretend that *motivation* did not exist as an issue. However, it may be speculated that *dissonance theory* will soon make a comeback (cf., Aronson, 1992). See also ATTITUDE/ATTITUDE CHANGE, THEORIES OF; ATTRIBUTION THEORY; BEM'S SELF-PERCEPTION THEORY; CONFLICT, THEORIES OF; DECISION-MAKING THEORIES; KELLY'S PERSONAL CONSTRUCT THEORY; LEWIN'S FIELD THEORY; MOTIVATION, THEORIES OF; REINFORCEMENT THEORY.

REFERENCES

Lewin, K. (1935). *A dynamic theory of personality*. New York: McGraw-Hill.

Heider, F. (1946). Attitudes and cognitive organization. *Journal of Psychology, 21*, 107-112.

Festinger, L. (1954). A theory of social comparison processes. *Human Relations, 7*, 117-140.

Kelly, G. (1955). *The psychology of personal constructs*. New York: Norton.

Festinger, L. (1957). *A theory of cognitive dissonance*. Stanford, CA: Stanford University Press.

Fiske, D. W., & Maddi, S. R. (Eds.) (1961). *Functions of varied experience*. Homewood, IL: Dorsey Press.

Festinger, L. (1964). *Conflict, decision, and dissonance*. Stanford, CA: Stanford University Press.

Bem, D. J. (1967). Self-perception: An alternative interpretation of cognitive dissonance phenomena. *Psychological Review, 74*, 183-200.

Cooper, J., & Fazio, R. (1984). A new look at dissonance theory. In L. Berkowitz (Ed.), *Advances in experimental social psychology*. New York: Academic Press.

Aronson, E. (1992). The return of the repressed: Dissonance theory makes a comeback. *Psychological Inquiry, 3*, 303-311.

FIAMBERTI HYPOTHESIS. See SCHIZOPHRENIA, THEORIES OF.

FIELD DEPENDENCE/INDEPENDENCE. See WITKIN'S PERCEPTION THEORY.

FIELD EFFECTS. See PERCEPTION (I. GENERAL), THEORIES OF.

FIELD THEORY. See LEWIN'S FIELD THEORY.

FIELD THEORY OF PERSONALITY. See PERSONALITY THEORIES.

FIGHT OR FLIGHT THEORY. See CANNON/CANNON-BARD THEORY.

FIGURE-GROUND RELATIONSHIPS, PRINCIPLE OF. See APPENDIX A, RUBIN'S FIGURE OR ILLUSION; GESTALT THEORY/LAWS.

FILAR THEORY. See LIFE, THEORIES OF.

FILIAL REGRESSION, LAW OF. See GALTON'S LAWS.

FILLED-DURATION ILLUSION. See APPENDIX A.

FILLED-SPACE EFFECT/ILLUSION. See OPPEL'S EFFECT/ILLUSION.

FILLING-IN ILLUSION. See APPENDIX A.

FILTER THEORY/MODEL. See ATTENTION, LAWS/PRINCIPLES/THEORIES OF.

FILTER THEORY OF MATE SELECTION. See INTERPERSONAL ATTRACTION THEORIES.

FINAL THEORY. The notion of a *final theory* (also known as: "single theory," "grand unified theory," "theory of everything," and "ultimate theory") is popular among many physicists (cf., Weinberg, 1993) who assert that a unification is imminent (e.g., via - as of yet - a highly untestable "string theory" or "superstring theory") of various separate branches of theoretical physics, including *general relativity theory* (describing *large, telescopic* entities such as galaxies and the universe, and involving the concept of *gravity*) and *quantum mechanics/field theory* (describing *small, microscopic* entities such as electromagnetism, subatomic particles, and strong and weak nuclear forces). *String* and *superstring theories*, along with *M theory* and a *supersymmetry principle*, view the universe as filled with energy entities such as vibrating strings, superstrings, gravitons, membranes, branes, supermembranes, and sparticles, as well as other theoretical constructs/entities, and invoke ancillary phenomena such as parallel universes, and extra-dimensions (totaling eleven). *String theory* deals with elementary particles and attempts to overcome the problems inherent in *general relativity theory* that occur when a quantum account of *gravity* is advanced. *String theory* states that instead of point-like particles, the basic aspects or entities are finite lines/strings or closed loops (like rubber bands). Advocates of a *final theory* assume that ultimate *natural laws* will be discovered and expressed by the same mathematical formalism that is associated with contemporary physics (cf., *uniformity of nature theory* - refers to a final collection or summary of all laws formulated for natural events/phenomena in a given branch of science, such as physics or chemistry, and which asserts that given the same or similar antecedent conditions, the same or similar consequents always will follow). However, in fields such as evolutionary biology, mathematical logic, and interbehavioral psychology, arguments have been made indicating that certain inconsistencies are inherent in the *final theory* concept of a "terminal stage" of scientific discovery. For example, the contention made by interbehavioral psychologists (e.g., Kantor, 1938) that science consists of human contact with ever-changing objective events presupposes that *scientific theory* is tied to a particular stage of organic evolution, including cultural evolution. Considered in such a biological, psychological, and interbehavioral context, a *final theory* implies that there will be an abrupt end in the evolution of organisms, as well as culture, on earth. Such a result seems to many social and behavioral scientists to be as imponderable as the difficult problems in physics that a *final theory* is supposed to solve (cf., Zimmerman, 1996). Thus, the critics of a *final theory* suggest that it is far more likely - in a future of changing science - that societies, language, cognitive structures, and even brains, themselves, will change with the result that such transformations obfuscate, disarm, or discredit a *final theory* inasmuch as such changes may be linked to newer and more highly developed *scientific theories* issuing from the extended contact that humans make with objective environmental events. See also EINSTEIN'S THEORY OF RELATIVITY; INTERBEHAVIORAL THEORY.

REFERENCES

Kantor, J. R. (1938). The nature of psychology as a natural science. *Acta Psychologica, 4*, 1-61.

Weinberg, S. (1993). *Dreams of a final theory*. New York: Random House.

Zimmerman, D. W. (1996). Is a final theory conceivable? *Psychological Record, 46*, 423-438.

Greene, B. (2003). *The elegant universe*. New York: W. W. Norton.

FIRO THEORY OF INTERPERSONAL BEHAVIOR. The American social/educational/personality psychologist William C. Schutz (1958) proposed a "three-dimensional theory of interpersonal behavior" called *FIRO* ("Fundamental Interpersonal Relations Orientation") that is based on openness and honesty in human relations and which examines the basic notion that every person orients herself or himself in characteristic ways towards other people. *FIRO* is a *formal theory*, ranging across three kinds of interpersonal behavior: *prior* - relations between early interpersonal relations and present ones; *present* - relations between elements of the present interpersonal situation; and *consequent* - relations between present interpersonal orientations and other behaviors and attitudes. The theory provides several postulates and derived principles and theorems (e.g., in the postulate of "interpersonal needs," it is stated that every individual has three interpersonal needs: *inclusion, control*, and *affection*; in the postulate of "relational continuity," the principles of "constancy" and "identification" are developed; and in the postulate of "group development," the principles of "group integration" and "group resolution" are defined). *FIRO* states that the compatibility of two or more persons depends on the following factors: their ability to satisfy, reciprocally, each other's interpersonal needs; their complementarity vis-à-vis originating and receiving behavior in each need area; and their similarity with respect to the amount of interchange they desire with other people in each need area. The three-dimensional *FIRO theory* claims that every interpersonal relation follows the same general developmental sequence: it starts with *inclusion* behavior, is followed by *control* behavior and, finally, *affection* behavior. This cycle may recur, however, when the relation approaches termination; it reverses direction, and investment from the relation is withdrawn in the order: *affection, control*, and *inclusion*. Theoretically, according to *FIRO*, it is possible to *predict* the course of a relation if one knows the interpersonal orientations of the individual members of the relation as well as the interpersonal description of the circumstances under which they will interact. See also: COMPLEMENTARY NEEDS, THEORY OF; EXCHANGE AND SOCIAL EXCHANGE THEORY; MACHIAVELLIANISM; SOCIAL COMPARISON/EVALUATION THEORY; SOCIAL FACILITATION THEORY.

REFERENCES

Schutz, W. C. (1958). *FIRO: A three-dimensional theory of interpersonal behavior*. New York: Holt, Rinehart, and Winston.

Macrosson, W., & Semple, J. (2001). FIRO-B, Machiavellianism, and teams. *Psychological Reports, 88*, 1187-1193.

FIRST NIGHT, LAW OF THE. See COMPLIANCE EFFECTS/TECHNIQUES.

FIRST QUANTITATIVE LAW OF PSYCHOLOGY. See WEBER'S LAW.

FISKE AND MADDI'S PERSONALITY THEORY. See FESTINGER'S COGNITIVE DISSONANCE THEORY.

FIT THEORY OF COLLEGE SATISFACTION. A number of studies in educational psychology have assessed whether the degree of "fit" between student characteristics and college environment variables predicts one's college satisfaction. Results supporting the *fit theory of college satisfaction* include the following aspects: level of college satisfaction is related directly to the degree of *congruence* between student orientations and attributes of the college; students' *perceptions* of the degree of fit between themselves and their college; the educational *orientations* of students and faculty; and students regarding their *major* field of study. Other factors that influence college satisfaction are: social integration and structure, social support, quantity of student's peer relationships, extracurricular activities, and informal faculty-student contact. See also BUFFERING MODEL/HYPOTHESIS OF SOCIAL SUPPORT; SELF-CONSISTENCY AND SELF-ENHANCEMENT THEORIES; STUDENT RETENTION/ATTRITION MODEL.
REFERENCES
Okun, M. A., & Weir, R. M. (1990). Toward a judgment model of college satisfaction. *Educational Psychology Review, 2,* 59-76.
Weir, R. M. (1990). The joint effects of positive college events, social support, and self-esteem on college satisfaction. Unpublished doctoral dissertation, Arizona State University, Tempe, AZ.

FITTS' LAW. See HICK'S LAW; INFORMATION/INFORMATION-PROCESSING THEORY.

FIXATION, LAW OF. See TOTAL TIME HYPOTHESIS/LAW.

FLETCHER-MUNSON/ISOPHONIC CONTOUR. See APPENDIX A, EQUAL-LOUDNESS CONTOUR EFFECT.

FLOATING-FINGER ILLUSION. See APPENDIX A.

FLOOR/BASEMENT, OR BASEMENT/FLOOR, EFFECT. See MEASUREMENT THEORY; NORMAL DISTRIBUTION THEORY.

FLOUREN'S THEORY. See WHORF-SAPIR HYPOTHESIS/THEORY.

FLUCTUATION THEORY OF STIMULUS CHANGE. See ESTES' STIMULUS SAMPLING THEORY.

FLYNN EFFECT. See INTELLIGENCE, THEORIES/LAWS OF.

FOCAL-CONFLICT THEORY. See DEVELOPMENTAL THEORY.

FOOD-SATIATION THEORY. See HUNGER, THEORIES OF.

FOOT-IN-THE-DOOR TECHNIQUE. See COMPLIANCE EFFECTS/TECHNIQUES.

FORBES' COLOR VISION THEORY. See COLOR VISION, THEORIES/LAWS OF.

FORBES-GREGG HYPOTHESIS. See NEURON/NEURAL/NERVE THEORY.

FORCED COMPLIANCE. See COMPLIANCE EFFECTS/TECHNIQUES.

FORCED MOVEMENT THEORY. See LOEB'S TROPISTIC THEORY.

FORGETTING, LAW OF. See FORGETTING/MEMORY, THEORIES OF.

FORGETTING/MEMORY, THEORIES OF. Four major theories of forgetting and memory have been described consistently in the psychological literature: *decay/trace theory, interference theory, reconstruction theory,* and *theory of motivated forgetting* (cf., the *law of forgetting* - the principle that forgetting increases linearly with the logarithm of the time since learning occurred). According to the *decay/trace theory* (often called the "power law of forgetting"), which is a classical, intuitive, and commonsense approach to forgetting, memories that are not used tend gradually to fade, deteriorate, and die over time (cf., the *obliteration theory*, which posits a sudden, rather than a gradual, destruction of a memory trace occurs). The *decay theory* had been discarded by psychologists as being incorrect until recent years. The acceptance by most psychologists today of some version of the *storage-and-transfer model of memory* or the *three-stage theory of memory* (i.e., the stages of "sensory register," "short-term memory," and "long-term memory") has revived the *decay theory* somewhat. Apparently, the simple passage of time may be a cause of for-getting both in the sensory register and in short-term memory, but it does not appear that time-passage decay is a cause of forgetting in long-term memory. Memory "traces" seem to be permanent once they have been consolidated into long-term memory - the *consolidation hypothesis/theory (cf., long-term potentiation theory* - the hypothetical process whereby consolidation of certain types of memory traces, occurring primarily in the brain's hippocampal region, involve cells that show increased sensitivity to new stimulation as a result of prior excitation; thought to be promoted by noradrenalin, opiates, and dopamine); and forgetting in long-term memory is probably due to other factors such as irretrievability of stored materials rather than simply to their disuse over time (cf., *molecular model of memory* - holds that permanent memory recall is a self-regeneration operation involving a sensory stimulus that triggers an electrical impulse code to produce a specific ribonucleic acid, which then produces a particular protein used in the consolidation process). The *interference theory of forgetting* refers to the blocking or disruption of memories due to the relative similarity of learned materials and acts on the storage or retrieval of information. When interference is built up by *prior* learning, it is called *proactive interference/inhibition* and when interference is created by *later* learning, it is called *retroactive interference/ inhibition*. Interference may cause forgetting in long-term memory by retrieval failure (called *retrieval failure theory*), but it may also cause forgetting in short-term

memory in a different way, either by overloading the capacity of short-term memory or by weakening or completely "knocking out" an item from storage (cf., *word-length effect* - refers to the results of immediate-memory studies where lists of short words are more easily remembered than lists of long words; the effect is due to the time needed to hear or speak the word and not the number of letters in the word). A great deal of experimental evidence supports the *interference theory of forgetting* in both long-term and short-term memory for isolated facts and materials (cf., *contextual interference effect* - refers to the improvement in retention of, but decrement in acquisition of, new information as a function of increased similarity in items/materials to be learned; however, the *displacement theory*, which is a "limited-mind" effect, states that the mind's capacity for learning/memory is limited, and when the limit is reached, new learning or memories are possible only if older learning or memories are lost). However, other factors - such as "meaning" - may be operating in the forgetting of information. One interesting phenomenon related to interference in memory is called the *tip-of-the-tongue phenomenon* (*TOT*), which is a type of effortful retrieval that occurs when people are confident that they know something but just can't quite retrieve it from long-term memory (cf., *ugly sister effect* - named after the fairy tale in which Prince Charming attempts to see the beautiful Cinderella but is blocked by her ugly sisters who suddenly appear in her place - is a common aspect of the *TOT*, when a different but related "blocking memory" suddenly appears in consciousness and impedes or blocks access to the required memory; *loss of access theory* - holds that forgetting is a process of losing accessibility to the information due to inadequate retrieval cues; and the *suffix effect* - refers to the situation whereby an extraneous stimulus, or a "suffix," is presented immediately after the complete list of materials to be learned serves to depress the recall of that material; such a *depression effect* occurs even when the participant is told in advance that the "suffix" stimulus is irrelevant to the task at hand and should be ignored). *TOT* seems to become more frequent during stressful situations, as people get older, and with words that are seldom used. The *reconstruction theory of forgetting* was first stated by the British psychologist Sir Frederic Charles Bartlett (1886-1969) in 1932, and states that forgetting is due to changes in the structure of a memory that make it inaccurate when retrieved, and where some memory traces become so distorted over time that they are unrecognizable (cf., *successive reproduction technique/method of repeated reproduction* - Bartlett's method for studying reconstructive memory, in which the participant reproduces learned material on a sequence of occasions over a period of time). According to this approach, memories change with time in such a way as to become less complex, more congruent, and more consistent with what the person already believes or knows. *Reconstruction theory* seems to be intuitively appealing but, until recently, it seems to have had little impact on memory research, perhaps because of the vague terminology in Bartlett's original statements. More recent versions of *reconstruction theory* (also called the *theory of productive memory*), tend to employ the distinction made by the Estonian-born Canadian psychologist Endel Tulving (1927-) between *episodic* and *semantic* memory where the "meaning" of events in *semantic* memory is stored better than the *episodic* details. In this approach, meaning takes precedence over details, where details may be created (reconstructed and distorted) in order to be consistent with the remembered meaning of events. The way *reconstruction theory* explains forgetting and memory is similar to the way in which the brain "constructs" full and complete perceptions out of a minimum, or inadequate amount, of sensory information (cf., the "filling-in" of the blind spot in visual perception). People sometimes construct their memories from minimal information. The *theory of motivated forgetting* (also called the *theory of intentional forgetting*) was enunciated originally by Sigmund Freud and states that forgetting is based on the threatening, anxiety-arousing, or upsetting nature of the forgotten information. In Freudian terms, the concept of *repression* refers to forgetting that occurs when the conscious mind deals with unpleasant information by pushing it into unconsciousness (cf., *reactivation of memory hypothesis* - states that forgotten or lost memories may be recalled if the appropriate "triggers" are supplied). Support for the *motivated forgetting theory* largely comes from clinical case studies rather than from laboratory investigations. However, case study evidence is not a good source of support for the theory because there is absence of precise experimental control, the effect of a stressful event may be to disrupt the biological process of consolidating the memory trace in long-term memory (rather than to cause repression of the memory), and it does not explain events in ordinary life but just in unusually stressful situations. Currently, psychologists are examining distinctions between visual versus verbal information types of memory (cf., *modality effect* - refers to the differential effects on memory depending on sensory modality used; for example, auditory presentation usually produces better retention for the last few items in a series than does visual presentation). According to the *propositional theory* (also called the *feature theory/model* in the context of analyzing the mental representation of a "concept"), memories for visual scenes are similar to memories for verbal information where both types of memories are assumed to be stored as sets of *propositions* that are elementary units of meaningful information. However, according to the *analogue theory* (also called the *prototype theory* in the context of analyzing mental representations of "concepts"), visual memories are fundamentally different from verbal memories where it is assumed that visual information is stored in a way that preserves the spatial gradients of the original scene. That is, visual memory is produced in a way that is functionally equivalent or *analogous* to a picture. Another line of theorizing in memory research continues the *associationisitic* tradition begun by Aristotle (384-322 B.C.), especially when invoking his *association principles* of *contiguity* and *similarity*. Today, cognitive psychologists depict the mind's storehouse of knowledge as a vast network of mental concepts (or "schemas") linked by *associationistic* ties (cf., *context-dependent memory effect* - refers to the result in memory tests that memory may be worse when tested in a new or different context relative to performance in conditions where the surrounding context is the same as that of the original learning; and the *doctrine of contextualism* - postulates that the memory of experiences is not the result merely of linkages between events, as stated in *associationistic doctrine*, but is due to the "meanings" of the "psychological space" in which they occur). One such network model of memory organization is the *spreading-activation model of memory organization*, which hypothesizes that the degree to which one word speeds up the ability to recognize or recall another word reflects the strength of the mental association between the two words or concepts (cf., *generation effect* - refers to the result that when participants are asked simply to read an item aloud on some lists/trials, versus generating or creating an item on other lists/trials, memory is typically better for the generated/created items). See also ASSOCIATION, LAWS/PRINCIPLES OF; BARTLETT'S SCHEMATA THEORY; CONCEPT LEARNING/CONCEPT FORMATION, THEORIES OF; IMAGERY/MENTAL IMAGERY, THEORIES OF; INFORMATION/INFORMATION-PROCESSING THEORIES; INTERFERENCE THEORIES OF FORGETTING; LEWIN'S FIELD THEORY; MEANING, THEORIES/ASSESSMENT OF; SERIAL POSITION EFFECT; SHORT-TERM AND LONG-TERM MEMORY, THEORIES OF.

REFERENCES

Ebbinghaus, H. von (1885/1964). *Memory: A contribution to experimental psychology.* New York: Dover.

Burnham, W. (1888). Memory, historically and experimentally considered. *American Journal of Psychology, 2,* 39-90.

Kennedy, F. (1898). On the experimental investigation of memory. *Psychological Review, 5,* 477-554.

Freud, S. (1915/1959). Repression. In E. Jones (Ed.), *Collected papers.* Vol. 4. New York: Basic Books.

Bartlett, F. C. (1932). *Remembering: A study in experimental and social psychology.* New York: Cambridge University Press.

Brown, R. W., & McNeill, D. (1966). The "tip of the tongue" phenomenon. *Journal of Verbal Learning and Verbal Behavior, 5,* 325-337.

Atkinson, R. C., & Shiffrin, R. M. (1968). Human memory: A proposed system and its control processes. In K. Spence & J. Spence (Eds.), *The psychology of learning and motivation.* Vol. 2. New York: Academic Press.

Tulving, E. (1972). Episodic and semantic memory. In E. Tulving & W. Donaldson (Eds.), *Organization and memory.* New York: Academic Press.

Anderson, J., & Bower, G. (1974). A propositional theory of recognition memory. *Memory and Cognition, 2,* 406-412.

Collins, A., & Loftus, E. (1975). A spreading-activation theory of semantic processing. *Psychological Review, 82,* 407-428.

Salter, D., & Colley, J. G. (1976). The stimulus suffix: A paradoxical effect. *Memory and Cognition, 5,* 257-262.

Klatzky, R. (1980). *Human memory: Structures and processes.* San Francisco: Freeman.

Schacter, D. L. (1982). *Stranger behind the engram: Theories of memory and the psychology of science.* Hillsdale, NJ: Erlbaum.

Anderson, J. (1983). A spreading activation theory of memory. *Journal of Verbal Learning and Verbal Behavior, 27,* 261-295.

Tulving, E. (1985). How many memory systems are there? *American Psychologist, 40,* 385-398.

Baddeley, A. (1990). *Human memory: Theory and practice.* Boston: Allyn & Bacon.

Brown, A. (1991). A review of the tip-of-the-tongue experience. *Psychological Bulletin, 109,* 204-223.

Collins, A., Gathercole, S., Conway, M., & Morris, P. (1993). *Theories of memory.* Hove, UK: Erlbaum.

Verhave, T. (1993). Network theories of memory: Before Wundt and Herbart. *Psychological Record, 43,* 547-552.

Nairne, J. S. (2002). Remembering over the short-term: The case against the standard model. *Annual Review of Psychology, 53*, 53-81.

Tulving, E. (2002). Episodic memory: From mind to brain. *Annual Review of Psychology, 53*, 1-25.

FORGETTING/TRANSFER, LAWS OF. See INTERFERENCE THEORIES OF FORGETTING.

FORMAL BEHAVIORIST THEORY. See BEHAVIORIST THEORY.

FORMAL DISCIPLINE AND TRAINING, THEORY/DOCTRINE OF. See ALGORITHMIC-HEURISTIC THEORY.

FORWARD CONDUCTION LAW. See NEURON/NEURAL/NERVE THEORY.

FOUNDER EFFECT. See HARDY-WEINBERG LAW.

FOUR-ELEMENT THEORY. See SOMESTHESIS, THEORIES OF.

FOURIER'S LAW/SERIES/ANALYSIS. The French mathematician Jean Baptiste Joseph Fourier (1768-1830) formulated the mathematically demonstrable generalization (*Fourier's law*) that any complex periodic pattern (such as sound waves) may be described as a particular sum of a number of "sine waves" (i.e., a wave form characterized by regular oscillations with a set period and amplitude such that the displacement amplitude at each point is proportional to the sine of the phase angle of the displacement; a "pure tone" is propagated as a sine wave). The sine waves so used are called a *Fourier series*, and the description itself is called a *Fourier analysis*. Thus, a *Fourier analysis* is a mathematical procedure whereby any intensity pattern may be broken down into a number of sine-wave components, and such an analysis may be applied to visual stimulation as well as to auditory phenomena. That is, any visual stimulus can be broken down into sine waves with different spatial frequencies, amplitudes, contrasts, and phases. *Fourier's theorem* is a

mathematical proof that any periodic function can be decomposed by *Fourier analysis* into a *Fourier series* that is a sum of sine and cosine terms with suitable constants. The notion behind *Fourier analyses* in vision is that the visual system carries out an analysis by breaking a scene down into a number of sine-wave components. This information is contained in the firing of spatial frequency detectors (neurons that fire best to specific frequencies). The visual system then uses the information from these neurons to carry out the reverse process, called *Fourier synthesis*, in which the information is combined to create the visual scene. See also AUDITION/HEAR-ING, THEORIES OF; OHM'S ACOUSTIC/ AUDITORY LAW; SET THEORY; VISION/ SIGHT, THEORIES OF.

REFERENCES

Fourier, J. B. J. (1822/1955). *Theorie analytique de la chaleur*. New York: Dover.

Herivel, J. (1975). *Joseph Fourier: The man and the physicist*. Oxford, UK: Oxford University Press.

Kaufman, L. (1979). *Perception: The world transformed*. New York: Oxford University Press.

Bloomfield, P. (2000). *Fourier analysis of time series*. New York: Wiley.

FOURIER'S THEOREM. See FOURIER'S LAW/SERIES/ANALYSIS.

FOVEAL CONE HYPOTHESIS. Many theories concerning the mechanisms of color vision have been proposed over several decades. D. B. Judd provides a summary table of a few of the better-known visual theories, including the following information: theorists' names, the anatomical location, fundamental colors, and chief limitations of the theories. Regarding retinal cone function and color response, there are two major contending hypotheses of the functioning of foveal cones: the *single-receptor theory* - states that all receptors are able to respond to all parts of the color spectrum; and the *triple-receptor theory* - states that the receptors belong to one of three groups, those that are sensitive either to red, or green, or blue. Additionally, two other color vision hypotheses have been proposed:

R. Granit and H. Hartridge's *polychromatic hypothesis*, and H. Hartridge's *cluster hypothesis*. See also COLOR VISION, THEORIES/LAWS OF; GRANIT'S COLOR VISION THEORY; HARTRIDGE'S POLYCHROMATIC VISION THEORY; VISION/SIGHT, THEORIES OF.

REFERENCE

Judd, D. B. (1951). Basic correlates of the visual stimulus. In S. S. Stevens (Ed.), *Handbook of experimental psychology*. New York: Wiley.

FRAISSE'S THEORY OF TIME. The French experimental psychologist Paul Fraisse (1911-1996) asserts that humans have no specific "time sense" (i.e., one has no direct experience of time as such), but only an appreciation of particular sequences or rhythms. According to *Fraisse's theory of time*, it is not time itself, but what goes on *in time* that produces temporal effects, experiences, or perceptions. Fraisse typically takes a unified, empirical, and systematic approach toward the study of time. He differentiates among three main groups of an organism's reactions to temporal conditions: *conditioning* to time (change), *perception* of time (change), and *control* over time (change). Basic to *Fraisse's theory* is the notion that all activity itself is nothing but a succession of changes that, in turn, implies the temporal unit of "duration." Moreover, Fraisse maintains that the idea of time applies to two different concepts that may be recognized clearly from one's personal experience of change: the concept of *succession* (which corresponds to the fact that two or more events may be perceived as different and organized sequentially, and is based on one's experience of the continuous changing through which the "present" becomes the "past"), and the concept of *duration* (which refers to the interval between two successive events). Fraisse contends that *duration* has no existence in and of itself, but is the intrinsic characteristic of that which "endures," and there is no *duration* without *succession*. Thus, according to Fraisse, *events* are perceivable, but *time* is not. In his analyses of the perception of "filled" and "empty" time, Fraisse describes the similarities between spatial and temporal aspects of perception. Fundamental

gestalt-like laws of spatial structure apply, also, to temporal structure. For instance, the spatial-organizational *law of assimilation* (i.e., the tendency to minimize small differences) and the *law of contrasts* (i.e., the tendency to exaggerate appreciable differences) apply equally well to the temporal organization of stimulus materials. Regarding "empty" time, Fraisse formulates the following theoretical generalizations: perception of the duration of an interval depends on the nature of its limit(s) and cannot be dissociated from it; through the *laws of assimilation* and *contrast*, the relationship between intervals and limits is one of inclusiveness or isolation, respectively; interval-limits effects may be different depending on whether the time is more or less than 0.75 second; the average duration of the complete process of perception is set at about 0.5 second; the processes that organize limits are affected by the nature of the stimuli and by the attitude of the individual; with stimuli of equal physical duration, larger perceived intervals are associated with longer sensory processes; with auditory stimuli of brief duration, more intense stimuli are associated with shorter perceived intervals, and with longer durations, the phenomenon is less marked; with short durations, if the first stimulus of a delimiting set of stimuli is more intense than the second, the interval seems shortened, but if the second stimulus is more intense than the first, the interval seems longer; intervals delimited by auditory stimuli of higher pitch are perceived as longer than those of lower pitch; the greater the difference in pitch between two limiting auditory stimuli, the longer is the perceived interval; if one of two delimiting auditory stimuli is long and the other is brief, the interval between them is overestimated when the long one comes first and underestimated when the long one comes second; and increased durations of the delimiting auditory stimuli are associated with longer perceived durations of the interval. Concerning "filled" time, Fraisse cites the following *laws/principles*: a divided interval of time appears to be longer than an empty interval of the same duration [this generalization is analogous to the visual-spatial perception of dots in space under the same divided-interval versus empty-interval conditions; also called *Oppel's effect/illusion* -

named after the German physicist Johann Joseph Oppel (1815-1894)]; an interval of time with more divisions seems longer than one with fewer divisions; of two divided intervals, the one that is evenly divided seems to be longer than that which is divided irregularly or unevenly; and with auditory stimuli, more intense sounds seem to be longer than less intense sounds (this effect decreases, however, as the judged duration increases; thus, this *law* for "filled" time appears to be exactly opposite to the one for "empty" time when only *short* durations are employed). See also ASSIMILATION, LAW OF; ASSOCIATION, LAWS/PRINCIPLES OF; GUYAU'S THEORY OF TIME; MICHON'S MODEL OF TIME; OPPEL'S EFFECT/ILLUSION; ORNSTEIN'S THEORY OF TIME; TIME, THEORIES OF; VIERORDT'S LAW OF TIME ESTIMATION.

REFERENCES

Fraisse, P. (1963). *The psychology of time.* New York: Harper & Row.

Funke, J. (1988). Changes or effort? A test of two time-estimation theories. *Zeitschrift fur Experimentelle und Angewandte Psychologie, 35,* 218-241.

FRAMING EFFECT. See DECISION-MAKING THEORIES.

FRANKLIN EFFECT/EXPERIMENT. See APPENDIX A.

FRASER'S INTERDISCIPLINARY TIME THEORY. The American philosopher and independent scholar Julius Thomas Fraser (1923-) is a leading contemporary figure in the interdisciplinary study of time, and his original theoretical contribution to time study is the idea that one must abandon the search for the "ultimate clock" and, instead, begin to conceptualize time as a *hierarchy* of different, but deeply interconnected, *temporalities.* Whereas time has been understood, typically, as the agent of change (i.e., time is what a clock measures), Fraser maintains that time, itself, is dynamical. Also, Fraser asserts that the "correct" model for time is that of an *evolutionary hierarchical model* consisting of more and more complex *temporalities* where the focus of attention goes beyond the simple

dialectic between human subjective time and quantified public time (such as indicated in the earlier time theories of Henri Bergson, Edmund Hussert, and Marcel Proust who emphasize the "flows" and "eddies" of internal time consciousness without reference to other forms of temporality). Essentially, Fraser offers a *five-level hierarchical theory of time,* and associated causality, focusing on the following levels: *no temporality* (noetic intentionality); *biotemporal* (the temporal reality or "nowness" of living organisms), *eotemporal* (the time of the universe of large-scale matter; the physicist's "t"); *prototemporal* (the time of elementary objects such as photons and quarks); and *atemporal* ("black hole" time with no mode of causality). Fraser (1978) also discusses the notion of "chronons" as the basic "atoms" of time, including the theoretical concepts of physical, physiological, and perceptual chronons. See also TIME, THEORIES OF.

REFERENCES

Fraser, J. T. (Ed.) (1966). *The voices of time.* New York: Braziller.

Fraser, J. T. (1975). *Of time, passion, and knowledge.* Princeton, NJ: Princeton University Press.

Fraser, J. T. (1978). *Time as conflict: A scientific and humanistic study.* Basel, Switzerland: Birkhauser Verlag.

Fraser, J. T. (1989). *Time and mind: Interdisciplinary issues. The study of time, VI.* Madison, CT: International Universities Press.

Soulsby, M. P., & Fraser, J. T. (Eds.) (2000). *Time: Perspectives at the millennium. The study of time, X.* Westport, CT: Bergin & Garvey.

FRASER SPIRAL/TWISTED-CORD ILLUSION. See APPENDIX A.

FRATERNAL BIRTH ORDER EFFECT. See SEXUAL ORIENTATION THEORIES.

FREGOLI'S PHENOMENON. See APPENDIX A, CAPGRAS ILLUSION.

FREQUENCY, LAW OF. A correlate of the *law of use,* the *law of frequency* attempted to explain that exercise - up to a certain physiological limit - is cumulative in effect, and if one response strengthens the connection somewhat, then two responses have a greater effect than one, and so on. The *law of frequency*, also known as the *law of repetition*, states that, other things being equal, the more frequently a connection has been exercised, the stronger the connection and the more resistant it is to extinction. The concept of *frequency*, as an important factor in experimental psychology and learning, has been traced back formally to 1820 and to the British school of association psychologists, in particular to the Scottish meta-physician Thomas Brown (1778-1820), who maintained that there are three *primary laws of association* (Aristotle's *laws of similarity, contrast*, and *contiguity in time and space*). Additionally, Brown formulated several *secondary laws* (or as he called them, *laws of suggestion*): *duration, liveliness/vividness*, and *frequency*. From his simpler instances of "suggestion," Brown distinguished relative "suggestions," such as resemblance, difference, and proportion, which anticipated the acknowledgement by future psychologists that mere association does not account for all cognitions; relative "suggestions" supplemented the modulating effect of the *secondary laws* on the *primary* ones. Modern learning experiments explore the effects on learning of the very aspects hypothesized by Brown; of Brown's *secondary laws of association* - a major contribution to the *associationistic doctrine* - only *frequency* had been suggested earlier (e.g., by Aristotle). Thus, *frequency* as a general principle - operating in philosophical and psychological descriptions of individual differences and behavior - formally (via Brown) goes back more than 180 years, if not 2,000 years in an informal (via Aristotle) sense. See also EXERCISE, LAW OF; FRAISSE'S THEORY OF TIME; READINESS, LAW OF; USE, LAW OF.

REFERENCE

Brown, T. (1820). *Lectures on the philosophy of the human mind*. Edinburgh: Tait.

FREQUENCY/REPETITION, PRINCIPLE OF. See ASSOCIATION, LAWS/ PRINCIPLES OF; FREQUENCY, LAW OF; SKINNER'S DESCRIPTIVE BEHAVIOR/ OPERANT CONDITIONING THEORY.

FREQUENCY/TELEPHONE THEORY. See AUDITION/HEARING, THEORIES OF.

FREQUENCY THEORIES OF HEARING. See AUDITION/HEARING, THEORIES OF.

FREUD'S DOCTRINE OF CATHARSIS. See FREUD'S INSTINCT THEORY; FREUD'S THEORY OF PERSONALITY.

FREUD'S INSTINCT THEORY. The Austrian neurologist and psychoanalyst Sigmund Freud (1856-1939) argued that all animals, human and nonhuman, are born with powerful biological urges, in particular *aggression instincts* [cf., Freud's notions of *sexual instincts, libido*, and *component instincts* as any of the basic elements of *sexual instinct* as defined by instinctual *sources*, instinctual *aims*, and instinctual *objects*; and his *dual-instinct theory* - posits that humans act primarily in terms of pervasive instinctive drives toward both *love* ("eros") and *aggression* ("thanatos")]. The *aggression instinct* creates a drive to engage in acts of aggression that must be satisfied. Through the operation of a type of "pressure-building" mechanism, the instincts create an uncomfortable tension within the individual that must be released, often in the form of overt acts of aggression. According to Freud's *instinct theory*, the way to curb violence and other antisocial aggressive acts is to find non-violent ways to release the aggressive energy, such as engaging in competitive activities, reading about violent crimes, or watching aggressive sporting events. Freud's viewpoint that the behavior of aggression is inborn has been reinforced by a number of other researchers, often ethologists and biologists, who suggest that violence is an element of *evolutionary theory* and is necessary for the survival of the fittest. Perhaps the most debatable aspect of *Freud's instinct theory* is his assertion that instinctual aggressive energy needs to be released in some fashion. Freud referred to the process of releasing instinctual energy as *catharsis* (from the Greek word *katharsis*, meaning "purgation or cleansing, especially of guilt"), and suggested that societies should develop methods whereby the nonviolent catharsis of aggressive energy may occur. Some psychologists agree generally with Freud that aggression is an inborn aspect of human behavior but do not agree, in particular, that it stems from an overwhelming instinctual urge to aggress. The counterview is that aggression is a natural reaction to the blocking ("frustration") of important motives and goals. Thus, the *frustration-aggression theory* suggests that not only people but entire nations as well - whose intended motives and goals are frustrated - will react with aggression and anger. Other psychologists, often social psychologists, argue that *Freud's catharsis theory* and notions of the ways in which catharsis may be exhibited actually have the opposite effect of increasing aggression, rather than dissipating it. Such *social learning theory* approaches suggest that individuals are aggressive only if they have learned that it is to their benefit to be aggressive. Thus, the *social learning theorists* disagree with Freud concerning the concept of *catharsis*. Where *Freudian theory* emphasizes that cathartic outlets need to be found for aggressive energy in order to keep it from appearing as actual aggression, *social learning theory* posits that cathartic outlets such as yelling when angry, hitting or punching a bag, or watching violent sporting events will not decrease violence but will actually increase it by teaching violence to the person. See also AGGRESSION, THEORIES OF; AIM-INHIBITION THEO-RY; BANDURA'S THEORY; DARWIN'S EVOLUTION THEORY; FREUD'S THEORY OF PERSONALITY.

REFERENCES

Freud, S. (1907/1959). *The collected papers of Sigmund Freud*. New York: Basic Books.

Freud, S. (1934). Instincts and their vicissitudes. In *Collected papers*. Vol. 4. London: Hogarth Press.

Geen, R., & Quanty, M. (1977). The catharsis of aggression: An evaluation of a hypothesis. In L. Berkowitz (Ed.), *Advances in experimental social psychology*. Vol. 10. New York: Academic Press.

FREUD'S THEORY OF PERSONALITY. Sigmund Freud (1856-1939) had early associations with the Austrian physician Josef Breuer (1842-1925) and the French physician Jean-Martin Charcot (1825-1893), who gave him an appreciation of the value of the "talking cure," "catharsis," and "hypnosis" for treating hysterical neuroses and, also, of the sexual etiology of neuroses. These experiences with Breuer and Charcot served as the basis for the development of the *Freudian theory of personality* and the method called *psychoanalysis*, formally initiated in 1895 (cf., *basic rule* - the fundamental tenet of psychoanalysis that the analyst must aid the patient to put spontaneous feelings, thoughts, and memories into words and, thereby, bring unconscious impulses to the surface for analysis). For over 40 years, Freud examined the structure and function of one of his most important concepts, the *unconscious* (cf., *perception-consciousness system* - Freud's hypothesized subsystem of the mental apparatus characterized by consciousness receiving input from the outside world via the sensory receptors and from the "preconscious" via the activation of memories, and playing a dynamic role in avoidance of unacceptable impulses, ideas, or thoughts and control of the "pleasure principle") through the methods of free association and dream analysis, and developed the first comprehensive *theory of personality* (cf., *primal-horde theory* - Freud's speculative reconstruction of the original human family consisting of a dominant, powerful man governing over a subordinate group of women and younger men, and accounting for the origin of behaviors such as the incest taboo, guilt, totemism, and marriage outside one's own social group). The psychoanalytic movement was advanced greatly in 1902 by Freud, who invited Alfred Adler (1870-1937), Otto Rank (1884-1939), and Carl Jung (1875-1961) to join him in regular discussions concerning problems of neurosis and the applied techniques of the new method. This group became known as the Vienna Psychological Society and, later, the Vienna Psychoanalytical Association. The group was disrupted, however, over theoretical differences after about 10 years, with Adler's leaving the group in 1911, and Jung's leaving in 1914. The three major systems or mechanisms in Freud's *structure of personality* (i.e., the *structural hypothesis/ model/theory*) are called the *id* - instinctual, biological, animal-like sexual and aggressive urges of self-gratification under the aegis of the *pleasure principle* (i.e., the governing of one's psychological processes and actions by the gratification of needs and the avoidance or discharge of unpleasurable tension); the *ego* - the objective aspect of personality and reason, operating under the *reality principle* (i.e., the psychic mechanism that meets the conditions imposed on the individual by external reality and acts to moderate and control the *pleasure principle*; cf., *splitting of the ego* - the hypothesized coexistence within the *ego* of two attitudes towards external reality, functioning side by side without affecting each other, one taking reality into account and the other rejecting reality); and the *superego* - the idealistic, moral, and social aspect of the *conscience* that strives for perfection (cf., *talion law/principle* - refers to retaliation, especially in kind, such as the biblical injunction "an eye for an eye, and a tooth for a tooth;" this law includes the general notion of retribution for defying the directives of the *superego*). According to Freud's *psychic energy theory*, an individual's behavior is almost always the product of an interaction among the three systems of the *id, ego,* and *superego*, where they work together as a team under the administrative leadership of the *ego*. Theoretically, a state of anxiety results whenever the *ego* becomes too overwhelmed with the triple impact of the *id's* powerful psychic energies, the *ego's* tension-reduction need to manipulate reality, and the *superego's* relentless quest for perfection. Freud proposed the *structural theory* to replace the earlier topographic division of the mind into the three domains or regimes of the *unconscious*, the *preconscious*, and the *conscious*. Freud's *dynamics of personality* involve the concepts of *instincts* - inborn and constant psychological representations of inner somatic sources of excitation that are the sole motives for human behavior (includes *life instincts* operating via sexual energy or *libido*, and *death instincts/wishes* with corresponding self-destructive aggressiveness); *distribution of psychic energy* - diversion of psychic energy

from the *id* into the *ego* via operation of the *identification* mechanism, which matches subjective mental representations with objective physical reality, and use of various coping strategies (cf., *defense mechanisms*); *bound energy* - psychic energy in the "secondary process," or conscious/rational mode of mental functioning based on the *reality principle*, and accumulated and contained within particular groups of neurons, its flow being subject to control through *binding* (an operation that restricts the flow of *libidinal* energy, usually by the *ego* exerting restraint on the "primary process" or unconscious/irrational mode of mental functioning based on the *pleasure principle*; cf., *nirvana principle* - the tendency for the quantity of energy in the mental apparatus to reduce to zero); and *anxiety* - a state of tension that may be one of three types: *reality anxiety* or fear of external world dangers, *neurotic anxiety* or fear of punishment, and *moral anxiety* or fear of the *conscience* involving violations of moral codes. Freud's *development of personality* involves the concepts of *identification* - the modeling of one's behavior after that of another person, usually a parental figure; *displacement* - the development of a new "cathexis" or *libidinal energy fixation* when "anticathexis" or blocking actions and events occur (*sublimation* may result, also, when the displacement produces a higher social/cultural achievement); *ego defense mechanisms* - the unconscious, reality-distorting measures taken by the *ego* to reduce psychic pressure and relieve anxiety that include *repression* (information kept below conscious awareness), *projection* or displacing unacceptable urges onto someone else, *reaction formation* or replacing an anxiety-producing impulse with an opposite impulse, *fixation/regression* or arrested personality growth at a particular stage such as an earlier, more secure or comfortable stage of development, and *undoing* or dealing with an action-related emotional conflict by negating the action via substituting an appropriate opposite action; and the *psychosexual stages of development* - the psychodynamically-differentiated stages during the person's first few years of life that are decisive, allegedly, in the permanent formation of one's personality, and include the *oral stage*, where primary pleasure is gained by activity in the oral cavity [cf., the *oral-sadistic phase* of the later *oral stage*, suggested by the German psychoanalyst Karl Abraham (1877-1925) in 1924, corresponding to the teething period and characterized by biting, as opposed to sucking in the earlier *oral stage*; some psychoanalysts - such as Melanie Klein (1882-1960) - reject Abraham's distinction between the early sucking and later biting phases of the *oral stage*, and declare the *oral stage* to be sadistic from the start where aggression, theoretically, forms part of the infant's earliest relation to the mother's breast]; the *anal stage*, where successful toilet training must occur for one's proper socialization (and where imperfect negotiation of this stage leads, theoretically, to the "anal triad" of the three personality traits of parsimony/meanness, obstinacy, and orderliness - sometimes called the "three Ps": parsimony, pedantry, and petulance; cf., *cloacal/cloaca theory* - an *infantile birth theory* and *sexual theory*, often adopted by children, that confuses the female vagina and the anus; young children of both sexes tend to believe that a baby is evacuated like a piece of excrement from the mother); the *phallic stage*, where the *castration complex* (i.e., a male child's fantasies of his penis being cut off, occasioned by the child's discovery of the anatomical differences between the sexes, where it is experienced as a "loss" in a female child but as "anxiety" in a male child; in boys, it is a fear of being castrated by their fathers for having sexual feelings for their mothers, and in girls, it is the unconscious fantasy that the penis has been removed as a punishment for which they blame their mother) and *Oedipus complex* (i.e., the child's feelings involving both love and hatred/hostility towards its parents and involving sexual desires as well as hatred or jealousy of the parents; at ages 3-5, it is the erotic feelings of a son toward his mother, accompanied by fear, rivalry, and hostility toward the father, and in the daughter at this age, it is the corresponding relationship between her and her father, sometimes called the "female Oedipus complex" or the "Electra complex") must be resolved for proper sexual development to occur (cf., *polymorphous perversity theory* - refers to the varied bodily sources and styles of libidinal gratification in the course of early psychosexual development); the *latent stage*, where physical/chemical changes take place in the body serving as a transition from childhood to adulthood, and the *genital stage*, where truly socialized and adult relationships with others are developed. *Freud's theory* and method of treating personality problems identified certain resistance and repressions ("motivated forgetting") that an individual uses to get protection from pain [cf., *conversion hysteria* - another term for "dissociative disorder" that denotes a form of *hysteria* (a term derived from the Greek meaning "wandering womb/uterus"); in this case, it is characterized by the presence of physical symptoms (such as paralyses, blindness) that are judged to be of psychological origin]. In Freud's approach, the "talking techniques" of dream analysis, free association of ideas (the free association technique is referred to as the *fundamental* or *basic rule* or *principle of psychoanalysis*), and working through *transference* (where the patient shifts his/her emotional attitudes from parental figures onto the therapist) were employed to cure patients' neurotic behaviors (cf., the case of the "Rat Man" - the nickname of an early patient of Freud's - who was tormented by fantasies of rats gnawing at his father's anus and that of a women to whom he was attracted; the case is a classic study on the *psychoanalytic theory of obsessive-compulsive disorder*). Freud's approach, theories, and methods have been criticized for several reasons: the unsystematic and uncontrolled manner of data collection and interpretation; an overemphasis on biological factors, especially sex, as the major force in personality development, and an excessive deterministic or mechanistic view of the influence of past behavior on a person's present functioning. On the other hand, although many of the methods and mechanisms of psychoanalysis have not been absorbed completely into the mainstream of general psychological thought, various Freudian conceptualizations (such as unconscious motivation, emphasis on important childhood experiences, defense mechanisms, and the case study method, including *psychohistory* - a form of history in which the empirical and theoretical discoveries of psychology are used explicitly to explain past events, and entails the application of psychoanalytic theory to the interpretation of historical events as well as historical personalities) have gained wide acceptance in the contemporary psychological community. References to Freud's work (via use of the eponyms *Freud's theory*, *Freudian*, and *Freudianism*) have steadily increased in citation frequency in psychology textbooks, and Freud's name continues to be one of the most popular referents in psychology for more than 75 years (Roeckelein, 1995, 1996). See also ANAL-EXPULSIVE THEORY; DETERMINISM, DOCTRINE/THEORY OF; DODO HYPOTHESIS; FREUD'S INSTINCT THEORY; GOOD BREAST OR OBJECT-BAD BREAST OR OBJECT THEORY; PARAPRAXIS THEORY; PERSONALITY THEORIES.

REFERENCES

Freud, S., & Breuer, J. (1892). On the psychical mechanism of hysterical phenomena. In *Collected papers*. Vol. 1. London: Hogarth Press.

Breuer, J., & Freud, S. (1895). *Studies on hysteria*. New York: Basic Books.

Freud, S. (1895). Project for a scientific psychology. In J. Strachey (Ed.) (1953-1964), *The standard edition of the complete psychological works of Sigmund Freud*. London: Hogarth Press.

Freud, S. (1920). Beyond the pleasure principle. In J. Strachey (Ed.) (1953-1964), *The standard edition of the complete psychological works of Sigmund Freud*. London: Hogarth Press.

Freud, S. (1923). *The ego and the id*. New York: Norton.

Abraham, K. (1924). *A study of the developmental history of the libido*. Leipzig: IPV.

Freud, S. (1937). *The ego and mechanisms of defense*. New York: International Universities Press.

Jones, E. (1953-1957). *The life and work of Sigmund Freud*. 3 vols. New York: Basic Books.

Turiell, E. (1967). A historical analysis of the Freudian concept of the superego. *Psychoanalytic Review, 54*, 118-140.

Stannard, D. E. (1980). *Shrinking history: On Freud and the failure of psychohistory*. New York: Oxford University Press.

Kline, P. (1981). *Fact and fantasy in Freudian theory*. London: Routledge.

Roeckelein, J. E. (1995). Naming in psychology: Analyses of citation counts and eponyms. *Psychological Reports, 77*, 163-174.

Roeckelein, J. E. (1996). Contributions to the history of psychology: CIV. Eminence in psychology as measured by name counts and eponyms. *Psychological Reports, 78*, 243-253.

FREUD'S THEORY OF PRIVATION. See CATASTROPHE THEORY/MODEL.

FREUD'S THEORY OF WIT/HUMOR. The Austrian physician/psychiatrist Sigmund Freud (1856-1939) viewed sexual and aggressive humor as important psychodynamic "release valves" in the "psychic economy" of the individual. Freud's approach toward wit and humor analysis may be placed, generally, within the "motivational-content" theories that emphasize the thematic aspects of jokes and humor stimuli such as cartoons. Freud refers to *tendentious humor* whereby humor functions as a *defense mechanism* in which the acute, fleeting pleasure of laughter stems from gratifying a drive/motive that otherwise would have remained pent up in the person. Generally, studies of the *motivational theory of humor* have yielded inconsistent relationships between experimentally-induced drive/motive states and the enjoyment of sexual and aggressive humor. This situation led to the development in psychology of micro-theories that link humor and aggression, for instance, to situation-specific variables. Basically, *Freud's theory of wit and humor* is based on the *hydraulic theory of psychic energy* that was popular in the 1800s. In a fashion similar to Herbert Spencer's earlier theory of laughter and humor (i.e., usage of theoretical concepts of "overflow of surplus energy" and "descending incongruity"), Freud regarded laughter as an outlet for nervous or psychic energy/tension. In this sense, *Freud's theory of wit and humor* may be classified as a "relief/tension-release" theory, but his approach is more complex and filled with many more diverse psychodynamic mechanisms than are found in previous "relief theories" of humor. In his theoretical viewpoint, Freud distinguishes among three kinds of laughter situations: wit/jokes, humor, and the comic, where each type of situation involves a savings of psychic energy that is available for a given task but is not needed, subsequently, for that purpose. Thus, according to *Freud's humor theory*, the "superfluous energy" is that which is discharged via the muscular movements of laughter, and in the "joking" situation, the energy saved is that which would normally be used to *repress* sexual or hostile thoughts and feelings. In Freud's "release/economy" humor theory - involving the principle of "economy of psychic expenditure" - the situation of "wit/joking," like dreaming, functions as a "safety valve" for forbidden thoughts and feelings, and when the person expresses what is *inhibited* normally, the energy of repression is released in the form of laughter. In the case of the "comic," the energy saved is energy of *thought* - the person is spared some mental or cognitive processing (which normally involves energy that is required for performance) and the surplus energy now is discharged in laughter. For the "humor" situation, the energy that is saved is energy of *emotion* - the person prepares for feeling a negative emotion (such as fear or pity) - with the subsequent realization that there is no real need for concern and where the energy summoned up for the emotion is suddenly superfluous and now available for discharge in the form of laughter. Freud asserts that the three laughter situations - wit/jokes, humor, and the comic - have one feature in common: they all represent ways of bringing back from the psychic realm a state of pleasure that is lost in the development of that very realm (in which the sought-after euphoria is a mental state of bygone times involving psychic work having a minimum of energy expenditure), and is reflective of a state of one's childhood in which one did not know about the "comic," was incapable of "wit/jokes," and did not need "humor" to achieve happiness. It may be noted that Freud's definition and use of the term "humor" is much narrower in scope than that

usually expressed today where contemporary usage includes *both* the "comic" and the "wit/joking" situations. See also COGNITIVE-SALIENCE MODEL OF HUMOR; CONNECTIONIST MODEL OF HUMOR; FREUD'S THEORY OF PERSONALITY; HUMOR, THEORIES OF; HYDRAULIC THEORY; MOTIVATIONAL THEORIES OF HUMOR; RELIEF/TENSION-RELEASE THEORIES OF HUMOR AND LAUGHTER; SPENCER'S THEORY OF LAUGHTER/HUMOR.

REFERENCES

Freud, S. (1905/1916). *Wit and its relation to the unconscious*. New York: Moffat Ward.

Freud, S. (1960). *Jokes and their relation to the unconscious*. New York: Norton.

FROEBELISM THEORY. See PLAY, THEORIES OF.

FROMM'S THEORY OF PERSONALITY. In the development of his "dialectic humanistic" *personality theory*, the German-born American psychoanalyst Erich Fromm (1900-1980) departed from the standard *Freudian theory* by stressing the effect of social forces on personality, and was greatly influenced by the German social philosopher Karl Heinrich Marx (1818-1883) who, in *Marxist psychological theory*, argues that society is in a constant state of change where persons are products of their society and of the social forces imposed on them; in all stratified societies, according to this theory, there is inherent potential for social conflict where economic conditions affect power relationships. The fundamental notion that underlies most of Fromm's writings is that individuals feel lonely and isolated because they have become separated from other people and from nature. Embedded in this theme is a basic dilemma of humans that consists of a person's being both a part of nature and separate from it, where the individual is both an animal and a social human being. In his *personality theory*, Fromm suggests that as humans have gained more freedom throughout the centuries, they also have felt more alone, and freedom then becomes an aversive condition from which people try to escape. There are two solutions to such a dilemma: to submit to authority and conform to society or to join with others in a spirit of love and social productivity. Fromm chose "productive love" as an important theme in his theory. He proposed, also, five *needs* that arise from the condition of being human and through which humans attempt to resolve the contradictions of existence: *relatedness* (also called *frame of devotion*), *transcendence, rootedness, identity*, and *frame of orientation*. Fromm discusses the concept of *character* from two points of view: individual and social. From an individualistic viewpoint, *character* is dynamic and structured in infancy, and it involves the functions of facilitation of personal action, selection of world-confirming judgments and ideas, adaptation to one's own culture, and orientations toward death and life (Fromm defines the notion of *individuation* as the gradual attainment by a growing child of the awareness of being an individual entity or person). From a societal viewpoint, *character* is seen as ways in which persons relate to the world and to each other, and includes the following five *social character types* (Fromm's "typology"): receptive, exploitative, hoarding, marketing, and productive. Of these five types, Fromm regarded only the *productive* type to be a healthy condition of character development. He emphasized the role that socioeconomic factors play in one's life, maintaining that through a kind of "dialectic" process - that is, the process through which an idea or event (thesis) generates its opposite (antithesis), leading to a reconciliation of opposites (synthesis) - one's socioeconomic class influences social character which, in turn, influences the adaptation of free individuals to the prevailing social milieu. Thus, in other terms, social character internalizes the external needs and orients individuals toward tasks required by the particular socioeconomic system. Fromm's formulations in his *personality theory* - where an individual's relationship to society is a key theme - may be summed up in the following assumptions: humans fundamentally have an inborn nature; society is created by humans in order to fulfill this essential nature; no society that has yet been devised meets the basic needs of human existence; and it is possible to create such a society. Fromm's name for such an ideal society is "humanistic communitarian socialism." Fromm's *personality theory* consistently focuses on the thesis that character or personality influences, and is influenced by, social structure and social change. His major contribution to *personality theory* is the idea that through the *productive* type of character, people may realize their own potentialities and, in so doing, may subordinate themselves to the well-being and welfare of all humans. See also ADLER'S THEORY OF PERSONALITY; FREUD'S THEORY OF PERSONALITY; HORNEY'S THEORY OF PERSONALITY; JUNG'S THEORY OF PERSONALITY; MASLOW'S THEORY OF PERSONALITY; PERSONALITY THEORIES; ROGERS' THEORY OF PERSONALITY.

REFERENCES

Fromm, E. (1941). *Escape from freedom*. New York: Avon Books.

Fromm, E. (1947). *Man for himself: An inquiry into the psychology of ethics.* New York: Holt, Rinehart, & Winston.

Fromm, E. (1950). *The sane society.* New York: Holt, Rinehart, & Winston.

Fromm, E. (1956). *The art of loving.* New York: Harper & Row.

Fromm, E. (1962). *Beyond the chains of illusion: My encounter with Marx and Freud.* New York: Simon & Schuster.

Fromm, E. (1970). *The crisis of psychoanalysis.* New York: Holt, Rinehart, & Winston.

Fromm, E. (1980). *Greatness and limitations in Freud's thought.* New York: Harper & Row.

FRUSTRATION-AGGRESSION HYPOTHESIS. See AGGRESSION, THEORIES OF; FREUD'S INSTINCT THEORY.

FRUSTRATION-FIXATION HYPOTHESIS. See AGGRESSION, THEORIES OF.

FRUSTRATION-REGRESSION HYPOTHESIS. See AGGRESSION, THEORIES OF.

FRUSTRATION THEORY. See AMSEL'S HYPOTHESIS/THEORY.

FUCHS PHENOMENON. See PERCEPTION (I. GENERAL), THEORIES OF.

FULLERTON-CATTELL LAW. This generalized formulation, called the *square root law* in the area of psychophysics, is credited to the American psychologists George Stuart Fullerton (1859-1925) and James McKeen Cattell (1860-1944), and states that the error of observation and *least noticeable difference*, or *just noticeable difference* (*JND*), are proportional to the square root of the value of the stimulus rather than to the stimulus value itself. Thus, in a psychophysical experiment, the error of a participant's observation is seen to increase with the square root of the intensity of the stimulus that is being administered. The *Fullerton-Cattell law* of 1892 was proposed as a substitute for Ernst Weber's earlier law of 1834 on the basis that one's observation errors may more validly be viewed as psychological processes (involving "confidence" in judgments and "guessing" responses) than as the results of the classical "introspective" methodology (i.e., looking into one's own experience and reporting on it) to determine actual *JND*. The American psychologist Robert Sessions Woodworth (1869-1962) proposed that a compromise between the two laws was sound theoretically, where much psychophysical data do fall between the values predicted by the two laws. However, some writers suggest that the *Fullerton-Cattell law* may not be a more universal or accurate law of psychophysical judgment as compared to the *Weber law*. See also FECHNER'S LAW; PSYCHOPHYSICAL LAWS/THEORY; WEBER-FECHNER LAW; WEBER'S LAW.

REFERENCES

Fullerton, G. S., & Cattell, J. McK. (1892). On the perception of small differences, with special reference to the extent, force, and time of movement. *Philosophical Series*, No. 2, Philadelphia: University of Pennsylvania Press.

Woodworth, R. S. (1914). Professor Cattell's psychophysical contributions. *Archives of Psychology, New York*, No. 30.

Guilford, J. (1932). A generalized psychophysical law. *Psychological Review*, *39*, 73-85.

FUNCTIONAL ANALYTIC CAUSAL MODEL (FACM). See PSYCHOPATHOLOGY, THEORIES OF.

FUNCTIONAL ASYMMETRY HYPOTHESIS. See PERCEPTION (II. COMPARATIVE APPRAISAL), THEORIES OF.

FUNCTIONAL AUTONOMY PRINCIPLE/LAW. See ALLPORT'S FUNCTIONAL AUTONOMY PRINCIPLE; CONDUCT, LAWS OF.

FUNCTIONAL EQUIVALENCE HYPOTHESIS. See IMAGERY/MENTAL IMAGERY, THEORIES OF.

FUNCTIONAL FIXITY OR FIXEDNESS PHENOMENON. See MIND AND MENTAL SET, LAW OF; PROBLEM-SOLVING AND CREATIVITY STAGE THEORIES.

FUNCTIONALISM THEORY. See REFLEX ARC THEORY/CONCEPT.

FUNCTIONAL PLASTICITY THEORY. See LASHLEY'S THEORY.

FUNCTIONAL SYSTEMS THEORY. See GENERAL SYSTEMS THEORY.

FUNCTIONAL THEORIES OF ATTITUDE CHANGE. See ATTITUDE/ATTITUDE CHANGE, THEORIES OF.

FUNCTIONAL THEORY OF COGNITION. See INFORMATION INTEGRATION THEORY.

FUNCTIONAL THEORY OF INCEST TABOO. See INCEST TABOO THEORIES.

FUNDAMENTAL ATTRIBUTION ERROR. See ATTRIBUTION THEORY; IMPRESSION FORMATION, THEORIES OF.

FUNDAMENTAL POSTULATE. See KELLY'S PERSONAL CONSTRUCT THEORY.

FUZZY SET/LOGIC THEORY. *Fuzzy set/logic theory* refers to a generalized concept of a logical set in which the elements have continuously graded degrees of set membership that range from the values 0 to 1 (rather than either belonging or not belonging to the set as in conventional *set theory*). *Fuzzy logic* is a form of algebra useful in drawing conclusions from insufficient, imprecise, or conflicting data sets and, presumably, mimics the way in which the brain arrives at conclusions. *Fuzzy set theory* was first proposed by the Azerbaijanian systems theorist/computer scientist Lofti A. Zadeh (1921-) in 1965, and was used, initially, to demonstrate that many natural characteristics (such as height, baldness, beauty) contain indistinct and undifferentiated boundary lines. The notions of *guppy effect* and *prototype theory* indicate potential areas of weakness for *fuzzy set theory*. The *guppy effect* (described by the American psychologists D. N. Osherson and E. E. Smith in 1981) refers to an inconsistency or deviation in *prototype theory* in which a term is more prototypical of a conjunctive concept than of either, or any, of its constituent concepts (e.g., the term "guppy" - as well as the term "goldfish" - is assumed to be more prototypical of the conjunctive concept "pet fish" than of either of the separate constituent terms "pet" or "fish"). If *prototype theory* (i.e., a theoretical perspective concerning concepts and concept formation) is formulated within the parameters of *fuzzy set theory*, a potential contradiction occurs which implies that either *fuzzy set theory* or *prototype theory* is basically flawed. See also CONCEPT LEARNING/CONCEPT FORMATION, THEORIES OF; MIND/MENTAL SET, LAW OF; NEURAL NETWORK MODEL OF INFORMATION PROCESSING; PROTOTYPE THEORY; SET THEORY.

REFERENCES

Zadeh, L. A. (1965). Fuzzy sets. *Information and Control, 8,* 338-353.

Osherson, D. N., & Smith, E. E. (1981). On the adequacy of prototype theory as a theory of concepts. *Cognition, 9,* 35-58.

Zadeh, L. A. (1982). A note on prototype theory and fuzzy sets. *Cognition, 12,* 291-297.

Zetenyi, T. (Ed.) (1988). *Fuzzy sets in psychology.* Oxford, UK: North-Holland.

G

GAEA/GAIA HYPOTHESIS. See LIFE, THEORIES OF.

GAIN-LOSS THEORY. See EXCHANGE/ SOCIAL EXCHANGE THEORY; INTER-PERSONAL ATTRACTION THEORIES.

GALEN'S DOCTRINE OF THE FOUR TEMPERAMENTS. The ancient Greek physician/philosopher Claudius Galen (c. 130-200) formulated the *doctrine of the four temperaments of personality* based on the earlier *doctrine of bodily humors* as outlined by the Greek philosopher Empedocles (c. 495-435 B.C.) and the Greek physician Hippocrates (c. 460-377 B.C.). Empedocles posited that the universe is made up of the four basic elements of: *earth, fire, air,* and *water,* where combinations of these four elements, in one way or another, can explain all know substances. Each of the four elements has corresponding "qualities": *earth* - cold and dry; *fire* - warm and dry; *air* - warm and moist; and *water* - cold and moist. When the qualities are taken with respect to the human body, they assume the form of four substances or *humors*: blood, yellow bile, black bile, and phlegm. Hippocrates considered these *humors* to be the basic constituents of the body where - depending on their deficiency, excess, or balance - they could cause both disease and health. In this sense, Hippocrates' naturalistic approach and explanations of cause-effect relationships anticipated modern medicine and psychology, rather than appealing to the presence of "evil spirits" as the cause of diseases. Later, Galen systematized the relationship of the Empedoclean/ Hippocratic notions of elements/humors into a general *personality theory of temperaments* where an excess of blood characterized the *sanguine* (warmhearted, cheerful) person, a preponderance of black bile related to the *melancholic* (sad, fearful) personality, an excess of yellow bile led to the *choleric* (fiery, highly reactive) person, and an excess of phlegm typified the *phlegmatic* (slow, slug-

gish) individual. *Galen's doctrine of the four humors* and their corresponding *temperaments* was viable until about A.D. 1400, when the Renaissance and the rebirth of medicine took place, and the doctrine faded. Although Galen's doctrine now is chiefly of historical interest only, certain vestiges of terminology remain in our language, such as the expressions "bad humor," "good humor," and "humorless." Galen was one of the first investigators to speculate that the *front* part of the brain receives *sensory* impressions and the *back* part has *motor* functions, in the anticipation or initiation of *brain-localization theories.* Galen's *doctrine of the temperaments* served, also, as the intellectual basis for certain contemporary *theories of personality* that formulated and advanced the concept of *types,* such as W. Sheldon's triad of personality types: *visceratonic* - outgoing, cheerful, happy; *somatotonic* - athletic, energetic, vigorous; and *cerebrotonic* - inward, bookish, shy. In another case, A. Adler related his hypothesized four *styles of life* to *Galen's four temperaments.* The work of Hippocrates and Galen may have inspired some modern investigators to look for biochemical sources of variations in human personality and behavior, and the *four temperament type*s themselves, detached from the *humoral doctrine,* have continued to interest prominent psychologists such as W. Wundt, I. Pavlov, and H. Eysenck. See also ADLER'S THEORY OF PERSONALITY; EMOTIONS, THEORIES AND LAWS OF; EYSENCK'S THEORY OF PERSONALITY; KRETSCHMER'S THEORY OF PERSONALITY; LEARNING THEORIES AND LAWS; PERSONALITY THEORIES; SHELDON'S TYPE THEORY.

REFERENCES

Spranger, E. (1920). *Types of men.* Halle, East Germany: Niemeyer.

Kretschmer, E. (1922). *Physique and character: An investigation of the nature of constitution and of the theory of temperament.* London: Paul, Trench, Trubner.

Adler, A. (1927). *The practice and theory of individual psychology.* New York: Harcourt, Brace, & World.

Sheldon, W., & Stevens, S. S. (1942). *Varieties of human temperament: A psy-*

chology of constitutional differences. New York: Harper.

Galen, C. (1956). *On anatomical procedures.* London: Oxford University Press.

GALTON'S LAWS. The English natural scientist/psychologist Sir Francis Galton (1822-1911) has been called the "father of differential psychology" and was one of the foremost progenitors of the field of *psychometrics* (i.e., the quantitative measurement of psychological characteristics through psychological tests and statistical techniques). Galton's contributions to *differential psychology* (i.e., the branch of psychology that studies the differences and variations in certain fundamental characters as manifested in different races and social groups, or in individuals of the same group) reflected his conviction that all human characteristics, both physical and mental, could ultimately be described in quantitative terms (cf., *doctrine of eugenics* - a term coined by Galton, refers to the notion that human qualities, such as character and intelligence, are inherited and that society should take deliberate steps to produce "good," "fine," or "superior" offspring; *positive eugenics* is the reproduction of desirable types, whereas *negative eugenics* is the attempt to prevent undesirable persons from reproducing offspring; the rise of racism, and the doctrines and goals of Nazism in particular in the 1930s and 1940s, caused *eugenics* to fall out of vogue). Galton's long-term concern and study of heredity led him to anticipate the *polygenic theory of inheritance* of continuous characteristics that was later developed by the English geneticist/statistician Sir Ronald Fisher (1890-1962). Galton anticipated, also, the formalized *motor theory of thought* via his finding that many scientists seemed to have no visual imagery at all (Galton, himself, apparently had clear visual imagery). In attempting to explain how his "men of science" could have ideas without visual images, Galton asserted that the missing faculty was replaced by other modes of conception, chiefly that of the "incipient motor sense," not only of the eyeballs but of the muscles generally (cf., *synethesia effect* - an experience of imagery where stimulation of one sensory modality, such as auditory words/sounds, arouses sensations in another sensory system, such as visual colors; thus, musical notes may arouse certain colors in the listener, or numbers may be experienced as sounds in the viewer). Galton was the first scientist to formulate clearly the so-called *nature-versus-nurture* question, that is, the relative contributions of heredity and environment to individual and group differences in human abilities, traits, and talents. He was the first, also, to note the methodological importance of monozygotic and dizygotic twins for estimating the relative effects of genetic and environmental factors in human variation (cf., *epigenetic theory* and its reference to changes in an organism that are due to environmental factors or to gene-environment interaction rather than purely to genetic factors). Galton investigated the inheritance of general ability by studying nearly 1,000 men who had achieved *eminence*, and recorded the frequency of eminent men among all their relatives (cf., Roeckelein, 1996). He found that as the degree of genetic kinship decreased, the percentage of eminent relatives also decreased in a markedly stepwise fashion - as predicted from Galton's *model of genetic inheritance*, which also explained in hereditary terms physical traits such as fingerprints and stature. From these data, Galton argued that mental ability is inherited in the same way as are many physical traits. For example, Galton's *law of filial regression to mediocrity* is demonstrated in the trait of stature: the offspring of a deviant parent (i.e., a parent who is either very tall or very short) are, on average, less deviant from the mean of the population than is the parent regarding the trait in question. Thus, the offspring of two very tall or two very short parents would be more nearly of average height than the parents themselves. A corollary to this law is Galton's *law of reversion*, which refers to the reappearance of a recessive genetic trait that had not been present in the phenotypes for one or more generations. Galton explained the phenomenon of *regression* in terms of his *law of ancestral inheritance*, by which the genetic contribution of each parent to an offspring is 1/4, of each grandparent is 1/16, of each great-grandparent is 1/64, and so on. Presumably, each further-removed ancestral generation comes closer to being a random sample of the general population. Therefore, the offspring's total genetic inheritance for the trait studied, being the sum of this infinite series of decreasing fractions, comes closer to the population mean than does that of the parents. This explanation for *regression*, however, has been rejected totally by modern geneticists. The concept of *regression* developed by Galton served as the basis for the statistical *correlation* methods formulated by the English statistician Karl Pearson (1857-1936). Galton first studied statistically the relationship between the heights of fathers and their sons; Galton hired Pearson as a statistician to work with him and his father on a series of investigations involving the contributions of heredity to the development of human attributes. In addition to *regression* and *correlation*, Galton's contributions to statistics and psychometrics include formulations and developments of the bivariate scatter diagram, multiple correlation, standardized or scale-free scores, percentile ranks, the use of median and geometric mean as measures of central tendency, and rating scales. The possible causes of *regression* among parents and offspring (or any other kinship) may be classified into three categories: errors of measurement, genetic factors, and environmental factors. There is nothing in the phenomenon of *regression* per se that proves either genetic or environmental causes or some combination of these. However, the complex methods of quantitative genetics that partition the total population variance in a trait into its genetic and environmental components may give an estimate of how much observed regression is attributable to genetic factors, to the environment, and to measurement error. See also EMINENCE, THEORIES/MEASURES OF; HARDY-WEINBERG LAW; IMAGERY/MENTAL IMAGERY, THEORIES OF; INTELLIGENCE, THEORIES AND LAWS OF; MENDEL'S LAWS AND PRINCIPLES; NATURE VERSUS NURTURE THEORIES.

REFERENCES

Galton, F. (1869/1962). *Hereditary genius: An inquiry into its laws and consequences*. London: Collins.

Galton, F. (1872). Statistical inquiries into the efficacy of prayer. *The Fortnightly Review, 12*, 125-135.

Galton, F. (1874). *English men of science: Their nature and nurture*. London: Macmillan.

Galton, F. (1879-1880). Psychometric experiments. *Brain, 2*, 149-162.

Galton, F. (1883). *Inquiries into human faculty and its development*. London: Macmillan.

Galton, F. (1889/1973). *Natural inheritance*. New York: AMS Press.

Hartung, J. (1985). Matrilineal inheritance: New theory and analysis. *The Behavior and Brain Sciences, 8*, 661-688.

Roeckelein, J. E. (1996). Contributions to the history of psychology: CIV. Eminence in psychology as measured by name counts and eponyms. *Psychological Reports, 78*, 243-253.

GAMBLER'S FALLACY. See PROBABILITY THEORY/LAWS.

GAME THEORY. See DECISION-MAKING THEORIES; INNER EYE THEORY OF LAUGHTER.

GAMMA MOVEMENT EFFECT. See APPARENT MOVEMENT, PRINCIPLES/THEORIES OF.

GARCIA EFFECT. The American psychologist John Garcia (1917-1986) and his colleagues conducted extensive work in the area of learning, specifically on classically conditioned taste aversion. The *Garcia effect* (also called *bait-shyness effect, toxicosis effect, flavor-aversion effect, conditioned food/taste aversion, food avoidance learning /conditioning, taste-aversion effect*, and *learned taste/flavor aversion*), refers to an acquired syndrome in which an organism learns to avoid a particular food because of a conditioned aversion response to its smell or taste. A *toxicosis* reaction can be formed in a single trial during which consumption of a novel food is followed by nausea and sickness - even when the toxic reaction itself is not experienced for some hours after eating (cf., cheese effect - acute attack of hypertension in a person taking a monoamine oxidase inhibitor drug who eats cheese, caused by an interaction of the drug with tyrosine in the cheese; other substances producing this effect include red wine, pickled herring, and yeast extract; and *sauce Bearnaise effect* - refers to a single-trial learning response involving an association to a highly specific stimulus and a delayed negative consequence based on an analogy to becoming sick some hours after a meal that included sauce Bearnaise and, regardless of the cause of the illness, the sauce becomes identified with the aversive episode). Specifically, laboratory rats quickly acquire an aversion to a sweet-tasting liquid when it is followed by an injection that makes them ill, but they do not readily acquire an aversion to the sweet taste when it is followed by an electric shock. In contrast, rats learn to avoid a light/noise stimulus combination when it is paired with shock but not when it is followed by a nausea-inducing injection. These findings indicate that classical conditioning cannot be established equally well for all stimuli. The key to conditioning in these types of studies is that the original association must be with an internal, digestively-linked stimulus (either the smell or taste of the food substance), and the aversive outcome must be associated with alimentary function such as nausea. The *Garcia effect* is a particularly interesting phenomenon because it can be formed over such a long interval of time, whereas in all other forms of classical conditioning the optimal interval between the operative stimuli is approximately only a half a second. See also GUSTATION/TASTE, THEORIES OF; OLFACTION/SMELL, THEORIES OF; PAVLOVIAN CONDITIONING PRINCIPLES/LAWS.

REFERENCES

Garcia, J., & Koelling, R. (1966). Relation of cue to consequence in avoidance learning. *Psychonomic Science, 4,* 123.

Garcia, J., Hankins, W., & Rusiniak, K. (1974). Behavioral regulation of the milieu internal in man and rat. *Science, 185,* 824-831.

Revusky, S. (1977). Learning as a general process with an emphasis on data from feeding experiments. In N. Milgram, L. Krames, & T. Alloway (Eds.), *Food aversion learning.* New York: Plenum.

Braverman, N., & Bronstein, P. (1985). Experimental assessments and clinical applications of conditioned food aversions. *Annals of the New York Academy of Sciences, 43,* 1-41.

GARDNER'S MULTIPLE INTELLIGENCES THEORY. See INTELLIGENCE, THEORIES/LAWS OF.

GAS CHROMATOGRAPHIC MODEL. See OLFACTION/SMELL, THEORIES OF.

GATE-CONTROL THEORY. = pain theory. The American psychologist Ronald Melzack (1929-) and the American-based English biologist and anatomist Patrick D. Wall (1925-) formulated the *gate-control theory of pain*, which states that the spinal cord contains a type of neurological "gate" that either blocks or allows pain signals to pass on to higher centers in the brain. The spinal cord contains small nerve fibers ("C-fibers") that conduct most pain signals and larger fibers ("A-delta fibers") that transmit most other sensory information. When some bodily tissue is injured, the small fibers activate and open the "neural gate," and the person feels "pain." Larger fiber activity, on the other hand, serves to close the pain gate and turns pain off. Thus, according to the *gate-control theory of pain*, one way to treat chronic pain is to stimulate (via small electrical currents or by acupuncture) the "gate-closing" activity in the large neural fibers. This is called the "counterirritant" method for reducing pain. For example, ice applied to an arm bruise not only controls swelling but also triggers "cold messages" that close the gate on the pain signals. Patients suffering from arthritis may carry a small, portable electrical stimulation unit next to a chronically painful area, and when the unit stimulates nerves in that area, the individual feels a vibrating sensation rather than pain. The effectiveness of acupuncture (*acupuncture theory of pain*) may be adequately explained by *gate-control theory* where inserting needles into the large neural fibers transmits sensory signals that compete with pain signals of the small neural fibers and, thus, close the "pain gate." The *gate-control theory of pain* has been revised recently to account for the importance of several brain mechanisms in the perception of pain, such as one's current emotional state interacting with the onset of a painful stimulus, which may alter the pain intensity one feels. Thus, the brain itself may affect pain perception by sending messages that either close the spinal gate (as when one relaxes) or keep it open (as when one is anxious). Opiate-like chemicals, called endorphins and enkephalins, that are produced in the body naturally may interact with the spinal gate, also, to lessen the sensations of pain. Certain areas of the spinal cord are rich in opiate receptors and endorphin-loaded neurons, and these substances may close the spinal gate by inhibiting the release of excitatory substances for neurons transmitting signals about pain. It has been suggested that social and cognitive-behavioral factors can strongly affect pain, even though pain is a basic sensory experience, and the specific mechanisms accounting for such factors are still being researched. In the illusory sensation called *phantom limb phenomenon* or *phantom extremity effect* (which is experienced by an amputee of the limb still being attached to the body even though all sensory nerve fibers associated with the limb have been removed) the allied sensations include pain perception experienced by a majority of amputees; the accompanying sensations of tingling, itching, or burning may be due to stimulation of the nerve ends or due to psychological reactions; such an experience may occur, also, in *phantom breast effect* occasioned by a woman's breast(s) having been amputated due to cancer or disease. See also COGNITIVE THERAPY, THEORIES OF.

REFERENCES

Melzack, R., & Wall, P. (1965). Pain mechanism: A new theory. *Science, 150,* 971-979.

Melzack, R. (1976). Pain: Past, present, and future. In M. Weisenberg & B. Tursky (Eds.), *Pain: New perspectives in therapy and research*. New York: Plenum.

Nathan, P. (1976). The gate control theory of pain. *Brain, 99,* 123-158.

Melzack, R., & Wall, P. (1982). *The challenge of pain*. New York: Basic Books.

Weisenberg, M. (1984). Cognitive aspects of pain. In P. Wall & R. Melzack (Eds.), *Textbook of pain*. Edinburgh: Churchill Livingstone.

Melzack, R. (1992). Phantom limbs. *Scientific American, 266,* 120-126.

GATTI ILLUSION. See APPENDIX A.

GAUSE'S PRINCIPLE. See DARWIN'S EVOLUTION THEORY.

GAUSSIAN DISTRIBUTION. See NORMAL DISTRIBUTION THEORY.

GAUSSIAN LAW. See PROBABILITY THEORY/LAWS.

GEGENSTANDS THEORIE/THEORY OF OBJECTS. See MEINONG'S THEORY.

GELB EFFECT/PHENOMENON. See PERCEPTION (I. GENERAL), THEORIES OF.

GENDER CONSTANCY THEORY. See SEXUAL ORIENTATION THEORIES.

GENDER SCHEMA THEORY. See SEXUAL ORIENTATION THEORIES.

GENDER/SEX THEORIES. See SEXUAL ORIENTATION THEORIES.

GENERAL DEVELOPMENTAL MODEL. See DEVELOPMENTAL THEORY.

GENERAL FEEDBACK THEORY. See CONTROL/SYSTEMS THEORY.

GENERALIZABILITY THEORY. See MEASUREMENT THEORY.

GENERALIZATION-DIFFERENTIATION THEORY. See INTERFERENCE THEORIES OF FORGETTING.

GENERALIZATION, PRINCIPLES OF. The *principle of response generalization* states that an increase (or decrease) in the strength of one response through a reinforcement (or extinction) procedure is accompanied by a similar, but smaller, increase (or decrease) in the strength of other responses that have properties common with the first response. The *principle of stimulus generalization* is the tendency for stimuli similar to the original stimulus in a learning situation to produce the response originally acquired (cf., the *unit hypothesis* - the amount of generalization along a continuum decreases with the number of test stimuli that lie between the training stimulus and a given test stimulus and increases with the number that lie beyond it). Although there has been a tendency to regard *stimulus generalization* as a "fundamental" process, it has been noted that when it occurs, it may be viewed simply as the failure of the organism to have established a "discrimination" (i.e., the ability to perceive and respond differentially to differences between two or more stimuli) between the original stimulus and the new one(s). *Stimulus generalization* was first demonstrated by Ivan Pavlov in 1927 in laboratory experiments with dogs: after the dog experiences a succession of pairings between a stimulus such as a tone (e.g., 200 Hz) and food reinforcement, a stimulus similar in character (e.g., 400 Hz) and yet discriminably different from the original tone is presented without reinforcement. This procedure results in the establishment of the *excitatory gradient of generalization*, which shows that the intensity of the animal's response to the test stimulus is directly proportional to its similarity to the training stimulus (cf., *octave effect* - refers to the result that occurs when an organism is conditioned to respond to a tone, and the response generalizes more to a pitch that is an octave higher, or lower, than to one that is actually closer to the original tone). Pavlov placed great importance on *stimulus generalization* and saw it as biologically adaptive: animals generalize their responses to stimuli other than the original one to compensate for the instability of the environment. The early emphasis on the adaptive value of *stimulus generalization* led later theorists (e.g., K. W. Spence; C. L. Hull) to treat it as a fundamental and irreducible aspect of learning. The later theorists derived other, more complex psychological phenomena from the concept of *gener-*

alization. The *theories of generalization* began with Pavlov's *physiological theory*, in which he argued that *generalization* from the training (original) stimulus to the testing (similar) stimuli was due to a *spreading wave of excitation* across the cortex. Pavlov's theory may be dismissed, however, with the observation that there is no physiological evidence for cortical waves then or now. Later, Hull wrote about generalization in terms of the *spread of habit strength* in a way similar to Pavlov's *spread of cortical excitation*. The common aspect to both *Pavlov's theory* and *Hull's theory* concerning *generalization* is that it was seen as an innate propensity of the brain that was hypothesized to occur naturally via cortical waves or habit structures once a training stimulus came to elicit a response reliably. The theoretical development of *generalization* lay dormant for a number of years until the appearance of the *Lashley-Wade hypothesis* - named after the American neuropsychologist Karl Spencer Lashley (1890-1958) and the American psychologist Marjorie Wade (1911-) - which suggested that the view of innate *generalization* is incorrect. Rather, *generalization* occurs because of failure to discriminate the training stimulus from the test stimulus. According to Lashley and Wade, the dimensions of a stimulus series are determined by comparison of two or more stimuli and do not exist for the organism until established by differential training. Thus, the *Lashley-Wade hypothesis* asserts that there is no *generalization* (or *generalization gradient*) without discrimination learning, and the organisms learns about the dimensions of stimuli by training to discriminate differences between them. There is both a strong and a weak interpretation of the *Lashley-Wade hypothesis*. The strong interpretation is that *all* generalization is a function of discrimination experience with *no* contribution from innate sources. The weak interpretation is that there *may be* influences from innate sources but, nevertheless, training in discriminating the values of a stimulus dimension will affect generalization. Conclusions from research concerning the strong interpretation have been negative, whereas studies focusing on the weak interpretation have shown positive evidence. In addition to discrimination training, other variables such as schedules of reinforcement and amount of training are important for amount of generalization. Generalization can be *excitatory* (in which the spread of responding occurs with respect to the training stimulus that has been reinforced), or it can be *inhibitory* (in which there is a spread of non-responding with respect to the stimulus that has not been reinforced). Recently, a *cognitively* oriented explanation of *stimulus generalization* rivals the earlier interpretations. In this approach, *stimulus generalization* is regarded as a special case of stimulus classification: the organism categorizes discriminably different events as equivalent and responds to them in terms of their class membership rather than to their peculiarities. In another area of research, the *behavioral contrast effect/phenomenon* - where a behavioral change occurs as a consequence of a transition from one condition of reinforcement to another - has attracted the interest of psychologists because it appears to be an exception to the *laws of extinction* and *stimulus generalization*. The issue as to whether *behavioral contrast* can be incorporated into existing laws of conditioning, or whether new laws must be formulated to account for the phenomenon, is still unresolved. Apparently, although psychologists are closer now than they once were to a comprehensive explanation of *generalization*, they are still lacking a fundamental theory. See also AMSEL'S HYPOTHESIS/THEORY; ASSOCIATIVE SHIFTING, LAW OF; CAPALDI'S THEORY; DISCRIMINATION/GENERALIZATION HYPOTHESIS; DISCRIMINATION LEARNING THEORY; HULL'S LEARNING THEORY; INTERFERENCE, THEORIES OF; LASHLEY'S THEORY; PAVLOVIAN CONDITIONING PRINCIPLES/LAWS/THEORIES; SPENCE'S THEORY.

REFERENCES

Pavlov, I. (1927). *Conditioned reflexes*. New York: Oxford University Press.

Spence, K. W. (1936). The nature of discrimination learning in animals. *Psychological Review*, *43*, 427-449.

Hull, C. L. (1943). *Principles of behavior*. New York: Appleton-Century-Crofts.

Lashley, K., & Wade, M. (1946). The Pavlovian theory of generalization. *Psychological Review*, *53*, 72-87.

Guttman, N., & Kalish, H. (1956). Discriminability and stimulus generalization. *Journal of Experimental Psychology*, *51*, 79-88.

Pearce, J. M. (1987). A model for stimulus generalization in Pavlovian conditioning. *Psychological Review*, *94*, 61-73.

Thomas, D. R. (1993). A model for adaptation-level effects on stimulus generalization. *Psychological Review*, *100*, 658-673.

GENERAL RELATIVITY THEORY. See FINAL THEORY.

GENERAL SYSTEMS THEORY. The Austrian-born biologist Ludwig von Bertalanffy (1901-1972) is considered widely to be the father of general systems theory, which he viewed comprehensively as "a science of science." Other precursors of *general systems theory* include the development of Gestalt psychology, and development of the "holistic" approach in psychology. The goal of *general systems theory* is to find models that are applicable across many diverse disciplines such as agriculture, metallurgy, music, business, psychology, sociology, and others (cf., periodic attempts to establish a *unity of science* orientation across disciplines). One of the most popular of such general models is the *open versus closed system model* where each system may be seen in terms of degree of "openness/closedness," and in terms of how self-sufficient or independent it is regarding outside influences. Diverse examples of such systems are: an eddy in a stream (open system); the solar system (closed system); an ant's behavior (closed system); a well-adjusted person (open system); learning theory in psychology (a limited, or open-closed, system), and personality psychology (a unisystem centering on the concepts of self-consistency, integrity, and balance). Other system models in psychology include the concepts of *homeostasis* - the maintenance of constancy in internal functioning; *self-concept* - constancy/consistency of personality; and *stress* - changes in personality structure as a result of psychological stress that are similar to changes in physiological structure as a result of biological stress. Other concepts in *general systems theory* include *entropy* (degree of disorder of a closed system), *negative entropy* (information in *information theory*), *feedback* (return of part of a system's output to its input), *adaptation* (temporary reduction in the responsiveness of a sensory receptor as a result of continuous stimulation), and *equifinality* (difficulty in determining a causative process from the shape of a land form alone). Distinctions are made between the terms *systems*, *general systems*, and *systems analysis* where *systems* applies to a model within a discipline (such as a communication system, a governmental system, an administrative system, etc.), *general systems* refers to common models that are incorporated into two or more fields, and *systems analysis* refers to the analysis of the structure of specific systems (cf., *functional systems theory* - states that given an intact organism, interactions with its environment result in adjustments in the individual's physiological or internal processes due to the influence of the invariant environment; across the evolutionary period of organisms, such adjustments become more complex). *General systems theory* tends to de-emphasize the tenets of elementarism and reductionism, which ignore the significance of "wholes" or "systems" (cf., K. Lewin's *field theory*, which recognizes the importance of holistic, organismic, and field-emergent influences when analyzing human behavior). Any failures in the wide acceptance and application of general systems theory may be connected to some of the theory's shortcomings: it doesn't have a formulation of the system that is acceptable to a majority of investigators, it hasn't revealed an organizing factor where the transfer into the system of the chaos of a great number of components - into an organized multitude - has occurred, and the system is portrayed as a homogeneous entity without any "operational architectonics" that would permit the evaluation of the system. However, it has been proposed recently (e.g., Schwartz, 1991) that concepts and methods from *systems theory* provide a powerful integrative tool for researchers and clinicians in behavioral medi-

cine. For example, the *risk-factor interaction hypothesis* is a special case of the *biobehavioral interaction hypothesis*, a fundamental conjecture in behavioral medicine; the hypothesis is that biological and psychosocial variables are not merely additive classes of factors that contribute independently to health and illness, but they may interact with each other ("synergistically") and, therefore, act interdependently; the *biobehavioral interaction hypothesis*, in turn, is a special case of what may be called the *generic interaction hypothesis*, which is a fundamental hypothesis in *general systems theory* in general, and *living systems theory* in particular (cf., Miller, 1978). See also ADAPTATION, PRINCIPLES/LAWS OF; CHAOS THEO-RY; CONTROL/SYSTEMS THEORY; GESTALT THEORY/LAWS; INFORMATION/INFORMATION-PROCESSING THEORY; LEARNING THEORIES/LAWS; LEWIN'S FIELD THEORY; ORGANIZATIONAL/INDUSTRIAL/SYSTEMS THEORY; SELF-CONCEPT THEORY; SELYE'S THEORY/MODEL OF STRESS.

REFERENCES

Lewin, K. (1936). *Principles of topological and vectoral psychology*. New York: McGraw-Hill.

Neurath, O., Carnap, R., & Morris, C. (Eds.) (1938). *International encyclopedia of unified science*. Chicago: University of Chicago Press.

Lecky, P. (1945). *Self-consistency: A theory of personality*. Garden City, NY: Doubleday/Anchor.

Bertalanffy, L. von (1950a). An outline of general systems theory. *British Journal of Philosophy and Science, 1*, 134-165.

Bertalanffy, L. von (1950b). The theory of open systems in physics and biology. *Science, 111*, 23-29.

Stagner, R. (1951). Homeostasis as a unifying concept in personality theory. *Psychological Review, 58*, 5-17.

Bertalanffy, L. von (1955). General systems theory. *Main Currents in Modern Thought, 11*, 75-83.

Bertalanffy, L. von (1968). *General systems theory*. New York: Braziller.

Miller, J. G. (1978). *Living systems*. New York: McGraw-Hill.

Schwartz, G. E. (1991). Addition versus interaction hypothesis: The $64,000 question. *Psychological Inquiry, 2*, 262-263.

GENERAL THEORY OF BEHAVIOR. In his search for a *general theory of behavior*, the American social/behavioral scientist Richard D. Alexander (1975) offers the desideratum that such a future theory must correspond with current knowledge concerning *evolutionary theory*, and he suggests that a useful, predictive, and *general theory of behavior* is unlikely to be constructed by building upward toward greater complexity starting from the "engram," the "reflex," or some other simple theoretical unit of activity. Alexander describes several principal/critical elements that may be included, eventually, in a *general theory of behavior*: *group-living* (when individuals congregate, they increase the intensity and directness of competition for existing resources, including mates); *sexual competition* (sex-ratio selection is such that approximately equal numbers of adult males and females are produced in all human and primate societies, regardless of the proportion of either sex that goes mateless); *incest avoidance* (avoidance of close inbreeding is one of the salient universals in human society); *nepotism* (the reproductive interests of different individuals will overlap to the degree that their genetic makeup overlaps); *reciprocity* (the degree and extent to which humans have "traded benefits" to mutual reproductive advantage); and *parenthood* (the evolution of adult humans so as to assist the reproduction of their offspring, and the use of their individual offspring so as to maximize the parents' overall reproduction). Alexander emphasizes that scientists' theories of human behavior (as well as their theories of animal behavior) must be *evolutionary* in the sense that modern biologists understand the process of natural selection - not in the terms of progress or movement from level to level characteristic of "anthropological evolutionism," not in the "social Darwinist" sense of natural laws that should not be violated (or instincts that cannot be thwarted), and not in the poorly focused

and inadequate terms of the biology of the first two-thirds of the 20th century. According to Alexander, failure of the behavioral sciences to develop an adequate *general theory of behavior* is seen as a result of the difficulty in deriving a sub-theory or set of sub-theories, from *evolutionary theory*. Alexander's recommendation, and prescriptive first step, is to combine the approaches and data of biologists and social scientists in analyzing the notion of *reciprocity* in social interactions. See also EVOLUTIONARY THEORY.

REFERENCE

Alexander, R. D. (1975). The search for a general theory of behavior. *Behavioral Science, 20*, 77-100.

GENERAL THEORY OF HUMAN REACTION TIME. See DONDERS' LAW.

GENERAL THEORY OF VERBAL HUMOR. = semantic script theory of humor. In language-based research on humor, Salvatore Attardo and Victor Raskin propose a *general theory of verbal humor* as represented, psycholinguistically, by verbal jokes, puns, and the relationship between the linguistic form and content of humorous texts. According to this approach, jokes may be analyzed in terms of their formal/semantic degrees of similarity and difference; also, various "knowledge resources" (such as "script opposition" and "logical mechanism") may be placed in a hierarchical organization on the basis of logical binary relations of dependence, the content- and tool-related nature of knowledge resources, and hypothesized perception concerning the degree of similarity among jokes or humor stimuli. The *general theory of verbal humor* has been compared favorably, in particular, with the more traditional *incongruity-resolution models of humor* where the notions of "script opposition" and "logical mechanism" correspond, respectively, to the "incongruity phase" and the "resolution phase" in the older models. See also COGNITIVE THEORIES OF HUMOR; HUMOR, THEORIES OF; INCONGRUITY AND INCONSISTENCY THEORIES OF HUMOR; INCONGRUITY-RESOLUTION THEORIES.

REFERENCES
Raskin, V. (1985). *Semantic mechanisms of humor*. Dordrecht: Reidel.
Attardo, S., & Raskin, V. (1991). Script theory revis(it)ed: Joke similarity and joke representation model. *Humor: International Journal of Humor Research, 4*, 293-347.
Ruch, W., Attardo, S., & Raskin, V. (1993). Toward an empirical verification of the General Theory of Verbal Humor. *Humor: International Journal of Humor Research, 6*, 123-136.
Attardo, S. (1994). *Linguistic theories of humor*. Hawthorne, NY: Mouton de Gruyter.
Attardo, S. (1997). The semantic foundations of cognitive theories of humor. *Humor: International Journal of Humor Research, 10*, 395-420.

GENERATION EFFECT. See FORGETTING/MEMORY, THEORIES OF.

GENETIC BALANCE THEORY. See MENDEL'S LAWS/PRINCIPLES.

GENETIC CONTINUITY, PRINCIPLE OF. See WEISMANN'S THEORY.

GENETIC DRIFT EFFECT. See HARDY-WEINBERG LAW.

GENETIC INHERITANCE, MODEL OF. See GALTON'S LAWS.

GENETIC MEMORY/STORAGE THEORY. See WEISMANN'S THEORY.

GENETIC PROGRAMMING THEORIES OF AGING. See AGING, THEORIES OF.

GENETICS, LAWS OF. See MENDEL'S LAWS/PRINCIPLES.

GENETIC THEORIES OF DEPRESSION. See DEPRESSION, THEORIES OF.

GENETIC THEORY OF COLOR VISION. See LADD-FRANKLIN/FRANKLIN COLOR VISION THEORY.

GEONS HYPOTHESIS. See PATTERN/OBJECT RECOGNITION THEORY.

GERM-PLASM/CONTINUITY THEORY. See WEISMANN'S THEORY.

GERM THEORY. See MIND/MENTAL STATES, THEORIES OF.

GESCHWIND'S THEORY. The American behavioral neurologist Norman Geschwind (1926-1984) speculated that excessive intrauterine exposure to androgens inhibits development in the individual's thymus and left cerebral hemisphere; Geschwind attempted to explain why learning disabilities and left-handedness are associated with autoimmune disorders and, also, to explain why they are more prevalent in men than in women. Thus, according to *Geschwind's theory*, the brain's "architecture" and certain patterns of behavior (such as dyslexia) are related to exposure during fetal life, in particular, to high levels of the male hormone testosterone. See also LANGUAGE ACQUISITION THEORY; LATERALITY THEORIES; MIND/MENTAL STATES, THEORIES OF; RIGHT-SHIFT THEORY; SPEECH THEORIES; WERNICKE-GESCHWIND THEORY.

REFERENCES
Geschwind, N., & Levitsky, W. (1968). Human brain: Left-right asymmetries in temporal speech region. *Science, 161*, 168-177.
Geschwind, N. (1970). The organization of language and the brain. *Science, 172*, 940-945.
Geschwind, N. (1974). *Selected papers on language and the brain*. Boston: Reidel.
Geschwind, N., & Galaburda, A. M. (1986). *Cerebral lateralization: Biological mechanisms, associations, and pathology*. Cambridge, MA: M.I.T. Press.

GESTALTEN, LAWS OF. See PERCEPTION (II. COMPARATIVE APPRAISAL), THEORIES OF.

GESTALT THEORY/LAWS. = laws of perceptual organization. The German word

Gestalt may be translated into English as "form" or "configuration." *Gestalt theory* is an example of a "rationalist" (i.e., progressing from abstract ideas to interpretations and demonstrations of the phenomena under study) theory in psychology that was developed initially by the German psychologists Wolfgang Koh-ler (1887-1967), Kurt Lewin (1890-1947), Kurt Koffka (1886-1941), and Max Wertheimer (1880-1943). Forerunners of *Gestalt psychology/theory* were the German poet Johann Wolfgang von Goethe (1749-1832), the Austrian physicist/ philosopher/psychologist Ernst Mach (1838-1916), and the German philosopher Christian von Ehrenfels (1859-1932). However, Max Wertheimer is considered by many to be the official founder of *Gestalt psychology*. Gestalters - those who advocate the Gestaltist approach - were concerned originally with the predominant nature of perception, thinking, problem-solving processes (including "insight"), and the structure of psychological experience, *without* primary reference to learning phenomena (cf., *shift of level principle* - Koffka's speculation that when a change of circumstances alters the position of two stimuli on a continuum, the two tend to retain the same relation to each other; and *rapid-change theory* - holds that behavioral, cognitive, and emotional changes may be instantaneous or abrupt and permanent; in sociology, it is the notion that the status of older persons in previously static societies declines if there are sudden sociopolitical changes in those societies). Gestalters suggested that what was learned in a learning/memory context is a product of the *laws of perceptual organization*. They argued that traces of perceptual events are stored in memory and, because *organizational laws* determine the structuring of perception, those laws also determine the structure of what information is laid down in memory. The *laws of perceptual organization*, or *laws of grouping-configuration*, indicate the priority of perception in *Gestalt theory* and show how a perceiver groups together certain stimuli and, thereby, how one structures and interprets a visual field (cf., *autochthonous laws* - the innate understanding of perceptions or proper behavior that individuals obey without experience or instruction). A few of these

subsidiary laws are: *figure-ground, proximity, similarity, common direction/good continuation, continuity, inclusiveness, simplicity,* and *common fate* (cf., *eye-placement principle* - discovered by the British-born American psychologist Christopher W. Tyler (1943-), refers to a principle of composition in portrait painting that involves the artist's placement of one of the subject's eyes somewhere on the vertical axis running down the center of the frame; it is suggested that this is an unconscious behavior in portrait painters). The *principle of figure-ground relationships* refers to the contrast between the *figure* - the area of a visual stimulus that is the focus of attention and appears closest to the perceiver, such as letters printed on paper - and the *ground* - the area of the visual stimulus that recedes beyond the figure and constitutes the background upon which a figure is superimposed, such as the white paper upon which letters or symbols are printed [cf., the *Liebmann effect* - named after the German psychologist Susanne E. Liebmann (1897-1990) - states that as the luminosity of a colored figure increases, the contrast between the figure and the ground on which it lies begins to diminish and, if the figure is complex, it becomes simpler; when the figure-ground luminosities are equal, the figure cannot be distinguished from the ground; the *law of surroundedness* - where one figure surrounds another, the surrounding figure is likely to be seen as *background* and the enclosed figure as *figure*; and the *successive contrast effect* - the tendency of a sensation such as color, lightness, or warmth to induce the opposite sensation in a stimulus that follows it]. Sometimes, what is figure and what is ground in a given visual stimulus is ambiguous, where the perceiver may organize it in one way at a given time and then, a few seconds later, switch to seeing it another way (cf., the *Schafer-Murphy effect* - the alleged phenomenon that when participants are rewarded for seeing an *ambiguous/reversible figure* in one way, they are more likely to see it in that way in the future). The relevance of the *principle of figure-ground relationships* for *learning theory* is the notion that people learn primarily about the figure they focus in attention, rather than the background, and what becomes an important figure can be influenced by various factors (such as instructions given to human participants). In the context of learning/memory, it is emphasized that it is "perceptually interpreted" objects, not the raw stimuli themselves, that are learned. The *law of proximity* refers to the tendency for the perceiver to group together elements of a visual or auditory field based on their nearness/proximity to one another. The factor of *proximity* (cf., E. L. Thorndike's *principle of belongingness*) is used in the communication processes of reading, writing, or talking, as well as with relatively discrete, isolated, neutral, or meaningless stimuli. The *law of similarity/resemblance* states that items similar in respect to some feature (such as color, shape, texture) will tend to be grouped together by the perceiver (cf., *law of equality* - states that as the several components of a perceptual field become more similar, they will tend to be perceived as a unit). The *similarity principle* is utilized consistently when a person speaks or reads. For example, in the *cocktail party effect* it is possible to pick out and listen to a particular speaker against a noisy background because of the consistent voice quality of the speaker from one moment to another (cf., *chatterbox effect* - a tendency of some hydrocephalic patients to appear fluent in conversation, but they are unable to communicate meaningfully; also called *cocktail-party conversationalism*; such individuals fabricate incidents and events to hold the attention of listeners, but later are unable to recall what was discussed). The *law of common direction/ good continuation/continuity* refers to the perceiver's tendency to group together a set of points if some appear to continue or complete a "lawful" series or complete a simple curve. The *law of simplicity* (also called the *precision law*) states that, other things being equal, the perceiver will see the visual field as organized into simple, regular figures (called "good gestalts" of symmetry, regularity, and smoothness; also called the *symmetry law*). For example, figures containing "gaps" yield perceptions of closed, complete figures where the perceiver fills in the gap with the redundant, predictable extrapolation of the simplest description of the figure (this is referred to, also, as *closure*, in which closed areas or complete figures perceptually give more stability than

unclosed areas or incomplete figures). The *law of inclusiveness* states that there is a tendency for one to perceive only the larger figure and not the smaller figure when a smaller figure is included/embedded in a larger figure. The *law of common fate* states that elements that move in the same direction will be perceived as belonging together and forming a figure. For example, an animal in the forest is hidden if its surface is covered with the same elements found in the background because its boundary is unclear: there is no basis for grouping the elements or spots on the animal as long as the animal is stationary and it remains well hidden. However, once it moves, the elements on the animal's surface will move together, and the animal's form is perceived quickly. A practical application of the *laws of perceptual organization*, one that is especially relevant to the *law of common fate*, is illustrated in the art of "camouflage" where a significant figure is buried or hidden by supplementing its lines, shape, color, and contours so that attention is defocused from the original shape. An additional, and more general, law called the *law of pragnanz* (meaning "compact and significant;" "good figure") was formulated, also, to describe the common features of the subsidiary laws of grouping. The *law of pragnanz* (also known as the *law of eidotropics*), similar to the *law of simplicity*, states that people have a tendency to see things in the simplest form possible (cf., *law of good shape* - states that people generally perceive stimulus units and patterns in a uniform and methodical manner). Consistent with the *law of pragnanz* is the Gestalt principle called the *law of least action*, which states that an organism tends to follow the course of action that requires the least effort or expended energy under prevailing conditions. In a personality-psychology context, course of action and energy expenditure can be influenced by the individual's personality characteristics so that an objectively easy course of action may be difficult for a person because of the amount of emotional investment required. The *law of least action* is called, also, the *principle of least-energy expenditure* and the *least-effort principle*. The German physicist and mathematician Hermann von Helmholtz (1821-1894) formulated the mathematical foundation for the *law of conservation of energy* (cf., Sir William Hamilton's *principle of least action/law of resistance/law of least constraint/law of least energy/law of greatest economy*; Thorndike, 1907). Up until the appearance of *Gestalt psychology* and *Gestalt theory* in America in the late 1920s and the early 1930s, the traditional method of scientific analysis was to describe the parts of a complex phenomenon and arrive at the whole by adding up the discrete descriptions (cf., the *and-summation hypothesis* - the "reductionist" conjecture that wholes may be constructed by the mere addition of distinct parts, in contrast to the approach which states that elements becoming part of a whole lose their particular identity; the *bundle hypothesis* - the study of consciousness and sensory experience as composed of elements held together by "and-connections," "senseless agglutinations," and "hookups;" the *discontinuity hypothesis* - focuses on the role of perceptual reorganization and sudden insight in discrimination learning and problem solving; states that a correct answer is recognized when its relation to the problem as a whole is discovered, and is distinguished from the trial-and-error, step-by-step approach of the *associationist hypothesis*; and the *postulate of derived properties* - emphasizes that parts of a stimulus cannot easily be disjointed or separated from other parts). Developments in the fields of biology, physics, psychology, and sociology, however, began to indicate that such an approach does not account adequately for "field processes" (i.e., entities composed of interacting forces). The contribution of *Gestalt theory* to psychology lies in its emphasis on the value of accounting for field forces in scientific methodology in general. In particular, the *Gestalt theorists* emphasized that the whole perception one obtains in a perceptual field "emerges" from the relationships among the parts of the form, where the parts may lose their former properties and take on new properties determined by the form of the whole pattern (cf., Kohler's *principle of intimacy* - states that in visual perception, in particular, the individual elements of a "whole" are dependent on each to give the true picture of the "whole"). In short, "the whole of perceptual experience is *more* than the sum of the parts." An example of

"emergent" properties of *physical* parts is the liquid nature of water when the gaseous elements of hydrogen and oxygen are combined. An example of "emergent" properties in *psychological* parts is the apparent motion (called the *phi phenomenon/ movement*) created in a perceiver when rapidly flipping a series of overlapping still photographs (cf., *short-circuit theory* - suggests that apparent or phenomenal movement is due to a short-circuit between the regions of the brain aroused by each stimulus and, consequently, generates newly-structured unities or perceptions). The Gestaltist emphasis on the "wholism" of perceptual experience has been accepted largely in modern *perceptual theories*, where it often is called *top-down* (or *context-determined*) *processing* of stimulus information. In a learning/memory context, the Gestalt conception of *memory* is comparable to Aristotle's earlier theory that perception is "stamp-ed in" as a corresponding *memory trace*; cf., the German philosopher Friedrich Eduard Beneke's (1798-1854) early *doctrine of traces* which states that an idea, upon its disappearance from the mind, leaves a trace; the subsequent revival/retrieval of this trace constitutes memory; and *copy theory*, also called *passive registration theory*, which states that what is perceived is a replica of real objects and that memory is an accurate storehouse of reality. Gestalters argue that the neural processes active during perception may endure in a mitigated form as a *trace* and, thus, information is stored in substantially the same form by the same neural processes as in the original perception (cf., *phenomenon/hypothesis of isomorphism* - the notion that there is a structural similarity between excitatory fields in the cortex and conscious experience). The old *laws of association* (such as *contiguity, similarity/resemblance*, and *contrast*), enunciated by the early philosophers, are analogous to the Gestalt laws of perceptual organization (such as *proximity, similarity*, and *good continuation*). In recent years, studies in perception have attempted to quantify the *laws of perceptual organization* as the Gestalters originally described them (cf., *stepwise phenomenon* - Wertheimer's principle that a sequence of separate steps along a continuum is perceived normally as an organized smooth progression, and occurs with "prothetic" but not with "metathetic" continua; cf., *Stevens' power law*). The typical approach is to create a number of perceptual stimulus arrays, present them to individuals, and then ask the people to rank them numerically along certain stimulus dimensions (such as good continuation or similarity). Much of this work has provided experimental confirmation of many of the propositions of *Gestalt theory*. However, researchers are not able to explain *how* these *perceptual organization laws* work. Current investigations in the field of artificial intelligence are seeking to model and design human perceptual systems, including the *laws of perceptual organization*, but, to date, this work has met with only limited success. See also ASSOCIATION, LAWS/PRINCIPLES OF; BELONGINGNESS, LAW/PRINCIPLE OF; COCKTAIL PARTY EFFECT; CODING THEORIES; CONSTANCY HYPOTHESIS; EMPIRICIST VERSUS NATIVIST THEORIES; INFORMATION AND INFORMATION-PROCESSING THEORY; LEARNING THEORIES/LAWS; LEAST EFFORT, PRINCIPLE OF; LEWIN'S FIELD THEORY; PERCEPTION, THEORIES OF; REDINTEGRATION, PRINCIPLE/LAWS OF; STEVENS' POWER LAW; TOP-DOWN PROCESSING THEORIES; von RESTORFF EFFECT; ZEISING'S PRINCIPLE.

REFERENCES

Beneke, F. E. (1832). *Lehrbuch der psychologie als naturwissenschaft*. Berlin: Mittler.

Thorndike, E. L. (1907). *The elements of psychology*. New York: Seiler.

Wertheimer, M. (1912). Experimental studies of the perception of movement. *Zeitschrift fur Psychologie, 61*, 161-265.

Wertheimer, M. (1923/1958). Principles of perceptual organization. In D. Beardslee & M. Wertheimer (Eds.), *Readings in perception*. Princeton, NJ: Van Nostrand Reinhold.

Beebe-Center, J. G. (1929). The law of affective equilibrium. *American Journal of Psychology, 41*, 54-69.

Kohler, W. (1929). *Gestalt psychology*. New York: Liveright.

Koffka, K. (1935). *The principles of Gestalt psychology*. New York: Harcourt, Brace, and World.

Wertheimer, M. (1938). Laws of organization in perceptual forms. In W. Ellis (Ed.), *A sourcebook of Gestalt psychology*. London: Paul, Trench, Trubner.

Santos, J. F., & Garvin, E. A. (1962). A further examination of the Schafer-Murphy effect. *American Journal of Psychology, 75*, 259-264.

Heider, R. (1970). Gestalt theory: Early history and reminiscences. *Journal of the History of the Behavioral Sciences, 6*, 131-139.

Restle, F. (1982). Coding theory as an integration of Gestalt psychology and information processing theory. In J. Beck (Ed.), *Organization and representation in perception*. Hillsdale, NJ: Erlbaum.

Wertheimer, M. (1982). Gestalt theory, holistic psychologies, and Max Wertheimer. *Zeitschrift fur Psychologie, 190*, 125-140.

Zusne, L. (1987). *Eponyms in psychology*. Westport, CT: Greenwood Press.

Tyler, C. W. (1995). Empirical aspects of symmetry perception. *Spatial Vision, 9*, 1-7.

Tyler, C. W. (1998). Painters centre one eye in portraits. *Nature, 392*, 877-878.

GHOST THEORY. See KOHLBERG'S THEORY OF MORALITY.

GIBSON EFFECT. See PERCEPTION (I. GENERAL), THEORIES OF.

GIBSON'S DIRECT PERCEPTION THEORY. See PERCEPTION (I. GENERAL), THEORIES OF.

GLASSER'S CHOICE THEORY. In addition to formulating "reality therapy" (a clinical approach that emphasizes one's basic needs such as the needs to belong, to be loved, and to gain self-worth and recognition), the American psychiatrist William Glasser (1925-..) asserts that most human misery is caused by people trying to control *others*, whereas, in fact, the only behavior controllable is one's *own* behavior. Likewise, according to Glasser, others cannot make us do anything we really don't want to do. For all practical purposes, *choice theory* proposes that we choose everything we do, including the unhappiness we may feel. Other people can neither make us miserable, nor make us happy - all we can get from others, or give to them, is information. *Choice theory* states that we choose all of our actions and thoughts as well as, indirectly, almost all of our feelings and much of our physiology. Glasser's *behavioral choice theory* helps individuals to avoid confrontation by having them ask pertinent questions, and views both conscious and unconscious desires for external control as the main problem in the four major personal relationships: husband-wife, teacher-student, parent-child, and manager-worker. *Choice theory* advances the notion that all personal problems are both "present" problems and "relationship" problems, and suggests that anyone in a relationship should ask - before taking action - whether that action will help to keep the two related persons at least as close together as they are presently (if it will, the action may be worth taking). Moreover, in terms of *choice theory*, one is not depressed but, rather, one chooses "to depress." Glasser points out that choices about human relationships are at the heart of almost all psychological problems and that what governs such interactions, traditionally, is "external-control psychology;" and people - in seeking to achieve their goals - generally try to manipulate or coerce others. *Choice theory* challenges the ancient tradition of "I know what's right for you," and attempts to help people figure out how to be free to live their own lives the way they want to live them and still get along well with the people they need in their lives (cf., *paradox of choice* - too many options, or too many choices, may produce paralysis in the individual, rather than liberation). According to the prescriptions of Glasser's *choice theory*, what is needed today in one's relationships at home, work, and school is a total absence of effort to control or even judge others where the focus solely is on improving the relationships themselves. Such an orientation, however, may tend to legitimize an "ultra-laissez faire" attitude in human

interactions and the theory, also, may appear to be too unidimensional in character for adoption by many clinical psychologists and therapists. In more positive terms, on the other hand, *choice theory* is a "non-controlling psychology" that promotes personal freedom in an effort to understand and sustain in people the relationships that lead to healthy and productive lives. See also CHOICE THEORIES; ELIMINATION BY ASPECTS THEORY; EXEMPLAR THEORY OF BEHAVIORAL CHOICE.

REFERENCES

Glasser, W. (1998). *Choice theory: A new psychology of personal freedom.* New York: HarperCollins.

Schwartz, B. (2004). *The paradox of choice: Why more is less.* New York: HarperCollins.

GLUCOSTATIC THEORY. See HUNGER, THEORIES OF.

GLUTAMATE HYPOTHESIS. See SCHIZOPHRENIA, THEORIES OF.

GOAL-SETTING THEORY. See ORGANIZATIONAL/INDUSTRIAL/SYSTEMS THEORY.

GODEL'S THEOREM/PROOF. The Czech Republic-born American logician and mathematician Kurt Godel (1906-1978) formulated his "incompleteness theorem" in 1931, which states that in any formal system that employs arithmetic, it is possible to develop statements that are true but that cannot be proved within the system. Another way to express *Godel's theorem* is: All consistent axiomatic formulations of number theory include undecidable propositions. This "theorem of incompleteness" means that all mathematics is based on a set of axioms; some mathematical truths cannot be derived from these axioms, and the set of axioms, therefore, is incomplete. In its barest form, Godel's formulation involves the translation of an ancient paradox (i.e., *Epimenides' paradox,* or the *liar paradox*) in philosophy into mathematical terms. Epimenides (c. 6th century, B.C.) was a Cretan prophet who made one immortal statement: "All Cretans are liars" (cf., Titus 1:12 in the

New Testament of the Bible). Other versions of this statement are, simply, "I am lying;" or "This statement is false." This latter version of *Epimenides paradox* violates the usually assumed dichotomy of statements into categories of "true" and "false," because if you tentatively think the statement is "true," then it immediately backfires on you and makes you think it is "false." On the other hand, once you have decided the statement is "false," a similar backfiring returns you to the idea that it must be "true." *Godel's theorem* had a significant effect on logicians, mathematicians, and philosophers interested in the foundations of mathematics because it showed that no fixed system - no matter how complicated - could represent the complexity of the whole numbers (0, 1, 2, 3, etc.). *Godel's theorem/proof*, also, has had a bearing on psychology, especially in the area of *artificial intelligence (AI)*. For instance, computers must be programmed for *AI*, but there is only a finite number of possible programs. Humans, on the other hand, are capable of an unlimited number and variety of behaviors. Therefore, any set of existing computer programs would be incomplete and, consequently, this fact indicates that it is impossible to construct a machine (*AI*) that behaves like a human being. *Godel's theorem/proof* has been used to argue against both the "strong *AI*" position (that "conscious awareness/thought" may be explained in terms of computational principles) and the "weak *AI*" position (that "conscious awareness/thought" may be simulated by computational procedures). In this context, then, *Godel's theorem/proof* argues in favor of the viewpoint that a fundamental difference exists between "human intelligence" and "artificial intelligence." See also ARTIFICIAL INTELLIGENCE; CELLULAR AUTOMATON MODEL.

REFERENCES

Godel, K. (1931). Uber formal unentscheidbare satze der *Principia Mathematica* und verwandter systeme I. *Monatshefte fur Mathematik und Physik, 38*, 173-198.

Godel, K. (1962). *On formally undecidable propositions*. New York: Basic Books.

Hofstadter, D. R. (1979). *Godel, Escher, Bach: An eternal golden braid*. New York: Basic Books.

GOLDEN SECTION HYPOTHESIS AND PRINCIPLE. See ZEISING'S PRINCIPLE.

GOLDSTEIN'S ORGANISMIC THEORY. = holistic theory. The German-American neuropsychiatrist Kurt Goldstein (1878-1965) was the leading exponent of *organismic theory* (cf., *organismic model* - in developmental psychology, an approach which holds that the cognitive organization of the child is influenced by the same adaptive factors that account for the evolution of physical/bodily forms), even though there had been previous advocates (including writers and philosophers such as Aristotle, Goethe, Spinoza, and William James) of the *organismic* approach (i.e., treating the organism as a unified, organized whole rather than "atomizing" the individual into elementary particles of feelings, images, and sensations). The *holistic/organismic* viewpoint has appeared in studies in the fields of psychobiology, psychosomatics, developmental biology, neurology, physiology, philosophy, and psychology. *Organismic psychology* may be regarded as the extension of Gestalt principles to the organism as a whole. The central features of *organismic theory*, as regards a theory of personality are the following: an emphasis on the unity, consistency, coherence, and integration of the personality - where organization is normal, and disorganization is pathological; a belief that the organized system of the organism may be analyzed by differentiating the whole into its constituent membership parts - where the whole organism functions according to the laws that cannot be found in study of the isolated parts separately; an assumption that the person is motivated by sovereign drive ("self-actualization/realization") rather than by a plurality of drives - where a singleness of purpose gives direction to the person's life; a tendency to stress the inherent potentialities of the organism for growth - where the influence of the external environment on normal development is minimized; and a belief in the advantages of studying comprehensively one individual rather than studying one isolated psychological function in many persons. The primary organization of organismic functioning, according to *Goldstein's theory*, is that of *figure* (any foreground process or conscious action that emerges and stands out as a contour against a background surface) and *ground* (the continuous, often unconscious, background or surrounding environment). Goldstein distinguishes between different kinds of structural behavior: *performances* – consciously experienced, voluntary activities; *attitudes* - inner experiences such as moods and feelings; *processes* - indirect experiencing of bodily functions; *concrete behavior* – automatically responding to a stimulus; and *abstract behavior* - the organism acting on a stimulus after cognitively considering it. Goldstein described the dynamics of the organism by developing the concepts of *equalization* - an "average" state of tension in the organism that acts as the "center" of the individual; the *principle of equalization* - explains the orderliness, coherence, and consistency of behavior; *self-actualization/self-realization* - the predominant motive that an organism possesses whereby all other drives, such as power, sex, hunger, and curiosity, are merely subordinate entities; *self-actualization* is the fulfillment and replenishment of one's needs; and *coming to terms with the environment* - the interaction between the organism and the environment where the person attempts to master the challenges of the environment, such as overcoming the physical and psychological threats and pressures that jeopardize one's drive toward *self-actualization*. If the discrepancy between the organism's goals and the realities of the environment becomes too great, the person either breaks down or makes compromises whereby some lower level of functioning is accepted for *self-actualization*. Many of Goldstein's theoretical notions were applied in his treatment and study of the behavior patterns and symptoms of brain-damaged persons. He and his colleagues also developed a number of psychological tests for diagnosing the degree of impairment in an individual's ability to abstract things about the environment, to plan ahead, and to think in symbolic terms. One charge that has been made against *Goldstein's theory* is that it is not sufficiently "holistic" (cf., the *organismic*

paradox - the organismic theorist denies the validity of partitive concepts yet is forced to use them) where it treats the organism as a segregated unit that is set apart from the rest of the world. Other critiques of *Goldstein's theory* assert that Goldstein does not distinguish adequately between what is in the organism versus what is culturally determined; cf., Skinner (1940) who suggests that Goldstein's main concept of *self-actualization* is too metaphysical in character and not open to experimental testing. However, for better or for worse, Goldstein is credited with being a major forerunner to the human potential/growth movement popularized by Abraham Maslow and Carl Rogers in the 1960s and 1970s. See also ANGYAL'S PERSONALITY THEORY; MASLOW'S THEORY OF PERSONALITY; MURPHY'S BIOSOCIAL THEORY; PERSONALITY THEORIES; REFLEX ARC THEORY/CONCEPT; ROGERS' THEORY OF PERSONALITY.

REFERENCES

Goldstein, K. (1934/1939). *The organism.* New York: American Book.

Skinner, B. F. (1940). Review of K. Goldstein's "The organism." *Journal of Abnormal and Social Psychology, 35*, 462-465.

GOMPERTZ HYPOTHESIS. See LIFE, THEORIES OF.

GONADOSTAT THEORY. See HUNGER, THEORIES OF.

GOOD BREAST/OBJECT AND BAD BREAST/OBJECT THEORY. The English-based Austrian psychoanalyst Melanie Klein (1882-1960) hypothesized that infants psychically defend against *ambivalence* (i.e., the coexistence in the infant of two opposing desires, emotions, behavioral tendencies, or beliefs that are directed toward the same object, such as it mother and, in particular, involving both love and hate) and *anxiety* by *splitting* the mother as an *instinctual object* into "good breast" ("good object") and "bad breast" ("bad object"). Through an infantile fantasy process, the gratification of hunger, for example, tends to produce an idealized image ("imago") of a "good breast," whereas withdrawal of the mother from the infant produces the "bad breast" via a vicious cycle involving the mechanism of "projection" (i.e., attributing unacceptable impulses, feelings, or thoughts to other individuals) whereby the infant comes to believe that the mother's breast is withdrawn because of the mother's hatred of the infant. The Scottish psychoanalyst W. Ronald Fairbairn (1889-1964) proposed a *theory of defensive techniques*, or *theory of mental disorders*, which includes the notion the location (internally or externally) of the "good breast" and the "bad breast" determines the particular defensive technique that is adopted by an individual if, or when, a mental disorder is exhibited. Fairbairn's *defensive techniques* denote any of four different processes that occur during normal development (as the infant makes the transition from total dependency to quasi-independence), or as a consequence of *splitting the object* (e.g., the mother or the breast) into a "good object" that satisfies, or a "bad object" that frustrates. Fairbairn's four *defensive techniques* are: hysterical reaction (*externalization* of the "good object" and internalization of the "bad object," whereby the hysterical individual considers *internal* impulses to be "bad"); obsessive reaction (*internalization* of both the "good object" and the "bad object," causing the obsessional individual to consider "bad objects" as alien *internal* forces requiring control); paranoid reaction (*internalization* of the "good object" and *externalization* of the "bad object," causing the paranoid individual to feel persecuted by *external* forces); and phobic reaction (*externalization* of both the "good object" and the "bad object," causing the phobic individual to feel threatened by *external* forces). See also DODO HYPOTHESIS; FREUD'S THEORY OF PERSONALITY; OBJECT-RELATIONS THEORY; PSYCHOPATHOLOGY, THEORIES OF.

REFERENCES

Klein, M. (1932). *The psycho-analysis of children*. London: Hogarth Press.
Fairbairn, W. R. D. (1952). *Psychoanalytic studies of the personality*. London: Tavistock.

GOOD CONTINUATION, PRINCIPLE OF. See GESTALT THEORY/LAWS.

GOOD-ENOUGH MOTHER HYPOTHESIS. See SELF-CONCEPT THEORY.

GOODMAN'S PARADOX. See NULL HYPOTHESIS.

GOOD SHAPE, LAW OF. See GESTALT THEORY/LAWS.

GOOD SUBJECT/PARTICIPANT EFFECT. See EXPERIMENTER EFFECTS.

GRACEFUL DEGRADATION, PRINCIPLE OF. See INFORMATION/INFORMATION-PROCESSING THEORY.

GRADIENT THEORY. See GENERALIZATION, PRINCIPLES OF.

GRAND THEORY. See ORGANIZATIONAL/INDUSTRIAL/SYSTEMS THEORY.

GRANIT-HARPER LAW. See GRANIT'S COLOR VISION THEORY.

GRANIT'S COLOR VISION THEORY. The viewpoint exemplified by the Finnish-Swedish neurophysiologist Ragnar Arthur Granit's (1900-1991) research in color vision has been characterized as *theory-neutral* and not so much of a theory as an approach that has established some limiting conditions for any good *theory of color vision*. Some aspects of Granit's research might be interpretable in a context of *trichromatic theory* (e.g., *Young-Helmholtz theory*), whereas other aspects may be taken within a context of *opponent-colors theory* (e.g., *Hering-Hurvich-Jameson theory*). Granit recorded the electrical reactions via microelectrodes in single and grouped optic nerve fibers and ganglion cells in the retinas of different animals when stimulated by lights of different wavelengths. Granit presented "scotopic dominator curves" (giving rod sensitivity), "photopic dominator curves" (giving cone sensitivity), and "modulator curves" based on wavelength stimulation of the retinas of various species, including snakes (which have cone receptors only), frogs, cats, pigeons, fish, and tortoises. *Granit's dominator-modulator vision theory* asserts that the photopic dominator curve may be attributed to the combined activity of several modulator curves and where, at a more complex level, photopic visibility and hue discrimination may be explained by various modulator combinations. According to Granit, it is likely that the photopic and scotopic dominators (which demonstrate the *Purkinje effect* between them) are responsible for the average spectral distributions of photopic and scotopic luminances. Thus, the photopic dominator may be considered as corresponding to the *Hering-Hurvich-Jameson* achromatic black-white process, and the modulators considered as cue-providers for wavelength discriminations. Granit describes various mechanisms of color blindness, as well as the relationships of the *scotopic-dominator, photopic-dominator*, and *modulator theory* to the data of color vision, and indicates how modulators may combine to yield the human photopic luminosity curve (cf., the *Granit-Harper law* - named after Ragnar A. Granit and Phyllis Harper - which is the generalization, formulated in 1930, that "critical fusion frequency" and the logarithm of the areas of the stimulus are related linearly over a luminance range of 1,000 to 1, and circular stimulus areas ranging from 0.98 to 5.0 degrees in diameter for retinal locations up to 10 degrees away from the fovea). S. Bartley discusses hypotheses that are related to Granit's work, called the *polychromatic hypothesis* of Granit and H. Hartridge, and the *cluster hypothesis* of H. Hartridge. See also COLOR VISION, THEORIES/LAWS OF; FOVEAL CONE HYPOTHESIS; HARTRIDGE'S POLY-CHROMATIC VISION THEORY; HERING-HURVICH-JAMESON COLOR VISION THEORY; PURKINJE EFFECT/PHENOMENON/SHIFT; YOUNG-HELMHOLTZ COLOR VISION THEORY.

REFERENCES

Granit, R. A. (1943). A physiological theory of colour perception. *Nature, 151,* 11-14.

Granit, R. A. (1947). *Sensory mechanisms of the retina.* New York: Oxford University Press.

Bartley, S. (1951). The psychophysiology of vision. In S. S. Stevens (Ed.), *Handbook of experimental psychology.* New York: Wiley.

GRANIT'S DOMINATOR-MODULATOR VISION THEORY. See GRANIT'S COLOR VISION THEORY.

GRANULAR THEORY. See LIFE, THEORIES OF.

GRAPHOLOGY, THEORY OF. The theoretical relationship between the features of one's handwriting and his/her personality or character has been studied extensively in modern times by the French abbot Jean Hippolyte Michon (1806-1881) and by the German philosopher/psychologist Ludwig Klages (1872-1956). Based on analyses of the characteristics and variables in personal handwriting - such as modulations in size of letters, layout, connectedness, slant, regularity, speed, forms, shading, and angularity - graphologists (those who analyze the physical features and patterns of handwriting and who formulate *graphology theory*) have speculated on persons' traits, qualities, and attributes. Some graphologists use the "analytic" approach, in which relatively isolated aspects of the handwriting (e.g., curvature, angularity, width, slant of individual letters) are presumed indicators of specific personality traits of the writer. Other graphologists assert that personality characteristics are reflected only by the "patterns" of isolated elements of the writer's script. Scientific attempts to relate a number of such variables of handwriting to objective measures/scores on personality inventories and tests, however, have produced only weak and unstable correlations and conclusions. Perhaps, it is fair to say that most scientists generally regard graphology as a "pseudoscience" and, in psychology in particular, it falls in an area called *pseudopsychology* that includes other "scientifically-suspect" areas of investigation, such as astrology, numerology, color preference, phrenology, physiognomy, palmistry, "cold reading," parapsychology, demonology/witchcraft, and some orientations toward dream analysis. Apparently, the value of *graphology theory* and the validity of graphological/handwriting analyses depends on the examiner and not on the procedure itself. See also ASTROLOGY, THEORY OF; BARNUM EFFECT; PERSONALITY THEORIES; PSEUDOSCIENTIFIC/UNCONVENTIONAL THEORIES.

REFERENCES
Michon, J. H. (1875/1944). *Systeme de graphologie*. Paris: Payot.

Klages, L. (1910). *Die principien der charakterologie*. Leipzig: Barth.

Klages, L. (1916). *Handschrift und charkter*. Leipzig: Barth.

GRASSMANN'S LAWS. This is a set of principles concerning the normal visual system summarized by the German-Polish physicist/mathematician Hermann Gunther Grassmann (1809-1877), and was foreshadowed by Isaac Newton's (1642-1727) *laws of color mixture*. The basic assumption of *Grassman's laws* is that if a light composed of known amounts of three primary color components is equivalent in color to another light, the three known amounts may be used as a color specification for this light. Such amounts are called *tristimulus values* of the color. *Grassmann's laws* state the following: when equivalent lights are *added* to equivalent lights, the *sums* are equivalent also; when equivalent lights are *subtracted* from equivalent lights, the *differences* are equivalent also; and lights equivalent to the same light are equivalent to each other. Thus, *Grassmann's laws* indicate relationships among the three primary colors that follow algebra-like rules under conditions where a person matches colors by adjusting the amounts of each of the three primary colors needed to match perceptually ("subjective equivalence") a test color. The term *color equation* describes the conditions and results of such a color-matching task. The principles expressed in *Grassmann's laws* have been established by numerous experiments conducted over a wide range of retinal illuminance for all kinds of vision, both normal and abnormal. However, the principles tend to weaken for very high retinal illuminance and for illuminance conditions of 10 minutes or more where retinal rod vision is initiated. Between these two extremes, *Grassmann's laws* hold independent of the particular adaptive state of the viewer's eye. In a completely different context, in the area of *linguistics*,

however, *Grassmann's law* refers to a modification of *Grimm's law* [named after the German philologist Jakob L. K. Grimm (1785-1863) who proposed in 1822 that various shifts occur in the pronunciation of certain consonants between different languages] in 1863 which asserts that a sequence of two audible breath/ speech sounds in a word is sufficient to block the "sound shift" phenomenon of consonants expressed in *Grimm's law*. See also COLOR MIXTURE, LAWS/THEORY OF; COLOR VISION, THEORIES OF; NEWTON'S LAWS/PRINCIPLES OF COLOR MIXTURE.

REFERENCES
Grassmann, H. G. (1853). [Laws of color mixture]. *Annalen der Physik und Chemie, 165*, 69-84.

Grassmann, H. G. (1854). On the theory of compound colours. *Philosophy Magazine, 7*, 254-264.

GREATEST ECONOMY, LAW OF. See GESTALT THEORY/LAWS.

GREAT MAN/GREAT PERSON THEORY. See LEADERSHIP, THEORIES OF; NATURALISTIC THEORY OF HISTORY.

GREAT MAN/GREAT WOMAN THEORY OF LEADERSHIP. See LEADERSHIP, THEORIES OF.

GREENSPOON EFFECT. The American psychologist Joel Greenspoon (1921-) conducted studies indicating that verbal *awareness* of the learning situation or of the new responses in not a necessity for behavior to be altered. In the experimental condition showing the *Greenspoon effect*, participants were asked to say all the words they could think of in 50 minutes. The experimenter sat behind the individuals and uttered "mmm-hmm" (an assenting murmur) every time a plural noun was spoken. With other participants, the experimenter murmured "huh-uh" (dissenting) when plural nouns were spoken. Upon debriefing, most of the individuals were unable to see any connection between the behavior of the experimenter and the words they were saying. Nevertheless, "mmm-hmm" *increased* the number of plural nouns that were said, and "huh-uh" *decreased* the number of emitted plural nouns. The *Greenspoon effect* has been taken by some psychologists, particularly behaviorists, as evidence that language can be brought under operant control and, by extension, as evidence that language learning takes place through a process of social reinforcement. The verbal conditioning paradigm in the *Greenspoon effect* seems to provide a valuable tool and method for bridging the gap between the clinical psychologist and the general-experimental psychologist. However, it may be suggested that more basic research in verbal conditioning needs to be conducted. See also CHOMSKY'S PSYCHOLINGUISTIC THEORY; SKINNER'S DESCRIPTIVE BEHAVIOR/OPERANT CONDITIONING THEORY.

REFERENCES

Greenspoon, J. (1955). The reinforcing effect of two spoken sounds on the frequency of two responses. *American Journal of Psychology, 68,* 409-416.

Krasner, L. (1958). Studies of the conditioning of verbal behavior. *Psychological Bulletin, 15,* 148-171.

Salzinger, K. (1959). Experimental manipulation of verbal behavior: A review. *Journal of Genetic Psychology, 61,* 65-95.

Spielberger, C., & DeNike, L. (1962). Operant conditioning of plural nouns: A failure to replicate the Greenspoon effect. *Psychological Reports, 11,* 355-366.

Greenspoon, J. (1963). Reply to Spielberger and DeNike: Operant conditioning of plural nouns: A failure to replicate the Greenspoon effect. *Psychological Reports, 12,* 29-30, 103-106.

GREIG'S THEORY OF LAUGHTER. The British humor researcher J. Y. T. Greig (1923/1969) proposed that study of the earliest laughter of infants leads to the conclusion that the essential element in situations provoking laughter is personal whereby one's laugh is a response within the "ill-coordinated" behavior or instinct of *love.* According to *Greig's theory of laughter,* laughter appears to arise when an obstruction of some kind is first encountered, and then suddenly is overcome. Laughter marks the escape of psycho-physical energy mobilized to meet the obstruction, but not actually required for that purpose and, therefore, for the moment, may be considered as "surplus." Greig asserts that *love* is a primary (and *hate* is a secondary) development issuing from laughter, and he attempts to trace this double strain in laughter from its simplest to its most complex manifestations - from the smile of the infant in its cradle to the highest and most ethereal forms of adult wit and humor. *Greig's theory of laughter* has been called both an "ambivalent/conflicting-emotions theory," and an "interrupted love-reaction theory." See also HUMOR, THEORIES OF; LOVE, THEORIES OF; McDOUGALL'S THEORY OF HUMOR.

REFERENCE

Greig, J. Y. T. (1923/1969). *The psychology of laughter and comedy.* New York: Dodd-Mead/Cooper Square.

GRIMM'S LAW. See GRASSMANN'S LAWS.

GROOS' THEORY OF PLAY. See PLAY, THEORIES OF.

GROUNDED THEORY. See NULL HYPOTHESIS.

GROUP CONFLICT THEORY. See IN-GROUP BIAS THEORIES.

GROUPING/CONFIGURATION, LAWS OF. See GESTALT THEORY/LAWS.

GROUP MIND PHENOMENON. See DEINDIVIDUATION THEORY.

GROUPTHINK PHENOMENON. See DECISION-MAKING THEORIES.

GROWTH/ACTUALIZATION THEORY. See MASLOW'S THEORY OF PERSONALITY; MOTIVATION, THEORIES OF.

GROWTH PRINCIPLE. See ROGERS' THEORY OF PERSONALITY.

GRUNER'S GAME THEORY OF HUMOR. The theoretical proposition advanced by the American humor researcher Charles R. Gruner (1931-) is that all humor - including, in particular, "puns" (which involves the *game* of "word play") - is actually a disguised succession of *games* that are there to be won. The very notion of *games* implies fun, leisure, entertainment, recreation, and affable human interaction, but it also implies, according to *Gruner's game theory of humor*, a sort of competition, a kind of score-keeping, and a winner/loser outcome. Gruner observes that the Greeks used the word "paronomasia" (i.e., "equal word") for what is today called a "pun." Three major kinds of *puns* are the *homograph* (i.e., "same writing;" e.g., "How did Samson die? From fallen *arches*"), the *homophone* (i.e., "same sound;" e.g., "The man with a squeaking shoe became a songwriter because he had music in his *sole*"), and the *double-sound pun* (i.e., "punning on a pun;" e.g., "Get thee to a *punnery*"). Gruner argues that the modern *pun* descended from the *conundrum* (i.e., "punning riddle") that, in turn, descended from the ancient common *riddle*. Thus, in Gruner's view - with the exception of good-natured play - humor is rarely as "innocent" as it first appears, but it is consistent with accounts based on the traditional *superiority theory of humor* where there are adversaries, triumphs, victories, winners, losers, and implicit "self-others" comparisons. See also HOBBES' THEORY OF HUMOR/ LAUGHTER; HUMOR, THEORIES OF; SUPERIORITY THEORIES OF HUMOR.

REFERENCES

Gruner, C. R. (1978). *Understanding laughter: The workings of wit and humor.* Chicago: Nelson Hall.

Gruner, C. R. (1997). *The game of humor: A comprehensive theory of why we laugh.* New Brunswick, NJ: Transaction.

G-SPOT OR GRAEFENBERG SPOT/EFFECT. = Gräfenberg spot. The German gynecologist, and developer of the intrauterine device (IUD), Ernst Graefenberg (1881-1957) described an erotically sensitive area presumably located in the anterior wall of the woman's vagina and, supposedly, when the area is stimulated, the woman more easily releases female ejaculate and/or achieves orgasm. The *G-spot* is usually located about halfway between the back of the pubic bone and the cervix, along the course of the urethra and near the neck of the bladder. It swells when it is stimulated, although it is difficult to palpate when in an unstimulated state. In 1981, the *G-spot* was named by John Perry and Beverly Whipple to commemorate the research of Graefenberg who - in 1944, along with Robert L. Dickinson - described a zone of erogenous feeling located along the suburethral surface of the anterior vaginal wall. Although Graefenberg and others had written about this phenomenon/effect, it was virtually ignored until Perry and Whipple gave renewed attention to it. Initially, Graefenberg benefited from the much earlier work in the 1600s of the Dutch physician/anatomist Regnier de Graaf (1641-1673) who referred to such an area/spot and its effects. The *G-spot* is not felt normally during a gynecological exam, because the area must be sexually stimulated in order for it to swell and be palpable; physicians, of course, do not sexually arouse their patients and, therefore, do not typically find the woman's *G-spot*. In the final analysis, however, despite the evidence that specific anatomical structures correspond to the area defined as the *G-spot*, its exact anatomical identity in all women, universally, remains inconclusive. See also SEXUAL ORIENTATION/BEHAVIOR THEORIES.

REFERENCES

Graefenberg, E. (1950). The role of the urethra in female orgasms. *International Journal of Sexology, 3,* 145-148.

Ladas, A., Whipple, B., & Perry, J. D. (1982). *The G-spot and other recent discoveries about human sexuality.* New York: Holt, Rinehart, and Winston.

Alzate, H., & Hoch, Z. (1986). The "G-spot" and "female ejaculation": A current appraisal. *Journal of Sex and Marital Therapy, 12,* 211-220.

Davidson, J. K., Darling, C. A., & Conway-Welch, C. (1989). The role of the Graefenberg spot and female ejaculation in the female orgasmic response: An empirical analysis.

Journal of Sex and Marital Therapy,
15, 102-120.

GUDDEN'S LAW. In 1870, the German psychiatrist Johan Bernhard Aloys von Gudden (1824-1886) enunciated this *neurological degeneration principle/law* which may be stated in several ways, but all carrying the same meaning: in the division of a nerve, degeneration in the proximal portion is toward the nerve cell; the degeneration of the proximal end of a divided nerve is cellulipetal; and lesions of the cerebral cortex do not result in an atrophying of peripheral nerves. See also NEURON/NEURAL/NERVE THEORY.

REFERENCE

Gudden, J. B. A. von (1870). Experimentale untesuchungen uber das peripherische und centrale nervensystem. *Archiv fur Psychiatrie, 2,* 1-24.

GUILFORD'S STRUCTURE-OF-INTEL-LECT MODEL/THEORY. See INTELLI-GENCE, THEORIES/LAWS OF.

GUPPY EFFECT. See FUZZY SET THEO-RY.

GUSTATION/TASTE, THEORIES OF. In terms of *evolutionary theory*, when life moved from sea to land, the undifferentiated chemical receptor systems of *taste* and *smell* became differentiated and began to serve different functions where the *taste* system served as a "close-up" sense that provided the last check on the acceptability of food, and *smell* served as a useful "distance" sense, although it also retained an important function in dealing with food. The physical stimuli for the *taste* system are substances that can be dissolved in water and, as is common for physical stimuli, the amount of a chemical substance present is related to the intensity of the experienced *taste* (cf., A. Baradi & G. Bourne's *enzyme theory of taste*). However, which properties result in the various different *taste qualities* is still unknown in detail, even though there are several guesses, such as the size of the substances' individual molecules, how the molecule breaks apart when dissolved in water, or how molecules interact with cell membranes. Complete agreement on the basic *dimensions* of taste is still lacking, but there seems to be general agreement on at least *four primary taste qualities* [cf., H. Henning's *taste theory/taste pyramid*, or *Henning's tetrahedron* - a classification of tastes using a pyramid with a triangular base whose corners represent the primary tastes, named after the German psychologist Hans Henning (1885-1946)]: sweet, salty, sour, and bitter (L. Bartoshuk suggests a fifth quality: that of water). When considering the question of how *taste quality* is neurally coded, it was originally thought that there would be different receptors for different *taste qualities*. However, most receptor cells on the tongue seem to respond to all four of the basic kinds of taste stimuli but at different rates. One *theory of taste*, called the *across-fiber pattern theory* [formulated by the American psychologist Carl Pfaffmann (1913-1994)] holds that if the condition of various neural units having different stimulus-specific response rates is met, then the code for *taste quality* could be an *across-fiber pattern* of neural activity. According to this theory, unique taste fibers respond in a different pattern to each *taste quality*, even though all of the fibers respond to all taste inputs to some extent. Another *theory of taste quality encoding*, called the *labeled-line theory* of C. Pfaffmann, suggests that each taste fiber encodes the intensity of a single basic *taste quality*. This theory states that to the extent that a stimulus activates the "sweet" fibers, for example, it tastes sweet, and to the extent that it activates the "bitter" fibers, it tastes bitter. The theory suggests, also, that "simple" stimuli could have a complex taste if they activate several types of fiber. The *labeled-line theory* is compatible with the *across-fiber pattern theory* except that in the former the code for *taste quality* is a profile across a few fiber types rather than a pattern across many thousands of unique fibers. Different gustatory fibers seem to be "tuned" to certain taste stimuli, much as auditory nerve fibers are tuned to certain sound frequencies. Such fibers respond most intensely to their "best" substances and less intensely to others. In the future, it may be possible to classify such *taste fibers* into a few classes, corresponding to the basic *taste qualities*. Although it is unknown at present whether *labeled-lines* exist along the entire taste pathway, cortical neurons most responsive to the four basic tastes seem to be localized in different parts of the taste cortex. Also, it is likely that some recoding of the taste information takes place in the cortex, where specific cortical cells give an "on" or "off" response to different taste stimuli, much like the feature-specific cells in the visual cortex. See also EVOLUTIONARY THEORY; GARCIA EFFECT; OLFACTION/SMELL, THEORIES OF; VISION/ SIGHT, THEORIES OF.

REFERENCES

Henning, H. (1916). Die qualitatenreihe des geschmaks. *Zeitschrift fur Psychologie, 74*, 203-219.

Lewis, D. (1948). Psychological scales of taste. *Journal of Psychology, 26*, 437-446, 517-524.

Baradi, A., & Bourne, G. (1951). Localization of gustatory and olfactory enzymes in the rabbit, and the problems of taste and smell. *Nature, 168*, 977-979.

Pfaffmann, C. (1955). Gustatory nerve impulses in rat, cat, and rabbit. *Journal of Neurophysiology, 18*, 429-440.

Pfaffmann, C. (1965). De gustibus, *American Psychologist, 20*, 21-33.

Bekesy, G. von (1966). Taste theories and the chemical stimulation of single papillae. *Journal of Applied Physiology, 21*, 1-9.

Schiffman, S. S., & Erickson, R. P. (1971). A psychophysical model for gustatory quality. *Physiology and Behavior, 1*, 617-633.

Funakoshi, M., Kasahara, Y., Yamamoto, T., & Kawamura, Y. (1972). Taste coding and central perception. In D. Schneider (Ed.), *Olfaction and taste IV*. Stuttgart: Wissenshaftliche Verlagsgesellschaft MBH.

Bartoshuk, L. (1974). NaCl thresholds in man: Thresholds for water taste or NaCl taste? *Journal of Comparative Physiological Psychology, 87*, 310-325.

Pfaffmann, C. (1974). Specificity of the sweet receptors of the squirrel monkey. *Chemical Senses and Flavor, 1*, 61-67.

Pfaffmann, C., Frank, M., & Norgren, R. (1979). Neural mechanisms and behavioral aspects of taste. *Annual Review of Psychology, 30*, 283-325.

Rozin, P. (1982). "Taste-smell confusions" and the duality of the olfactory sense. *Perception and Psychophysics, 31*, 397-401.

Erickson, R. P. (1985). Definitions: A matter of taste. In D. Pfaff (Ed.), *Taste, olfaction, and the central nervous system*. New York: Rockefeller University Press.

GUTHRIE'S THEORY OF BEHAVIOR.

The American behavioral psychologist Edwin Ray Guthrie (1886-1959) formulated an objective stimulus-response association psychology system (*contiguous conditioning*). Guthrie's one primary law of association or learning is devised around the *contiguity* (nearness) of cue and response; that is, a combination of stimuli that is accompanied by a movement will - on its recurrence - tend to be followed by that movement. In his *one-trial learning theory*, Guthrie proposed that learning may take place on a single trial, and improvement with practice represents the acquisition of simple/individual elements that make up more complex behaviors. In Guthrie's approach, E. L. Thorndike's concept of *associative shifting* (i.e., the shifting of a response to one stimulus onto another stimulus paired with it) is a central feature of his *behavior theory*. Guthrie did not accept, however, the more prominent *law of effect* as stated by Thorndike. Guthrie's major emphasis on the single *principle of associative/contiguity learning* also separated him, on theoretical grounds, from Ivan Pavlov and the principles and procedures of "classical conditioning." Pavlov criticized Guthrie for his solitary focus on the *contiguity* concept without concern for the many complexities of conditioning. In his *extinction theory*, Guthrie explained the phenomena of *extinction* and *forgetting* (weakening of behaviors) through the process of associative competition or interference where the learning of a different and incompatible response to the initial stimulus situation occurred. He suggested three methods that contribute to the weakening of behaviors: the toleration method, the exhaustion (flooding) method, and the method of counter conditioning (cf., J. Wolpe's modern technique of *systematic desensitization* that is based on Guthrie's earlier methods). In *Guthrie's theory*, motives act to provide "maintaining stimuli" to keep the organism active until a goal is reached, and conduct is organized into sequences in which the individual makes plans and carries them out. Guthrie followed the lead of C. S. Sherrington and R. S. Woodworth in considering sequences of behavior as composed of preparatory responses followed by consummatory responses where these "anticipatory responses" are conditioned to maintaining stimuli. According to Guthrie, *reward* is a secondary principle and is effective because it removes the organism from the stimulating situation in which the "correct" response has been made. Reward does not strengthen the correct response but prevents its weakening because no new response can become attached to the cues that led to the correct response. The effects of punishment for learning are determined by what it causes the organism to do and suggests the principle that the best predictor of learning is the response that *last* occurred in the situation (cf., *postremity principle* - Guthrie's notion that the organism always does what it *last* did in a given stimulus situation). When learning transfers to new situations, it is because of the common elements within the old and new, and when forgetting occurs, it is due to the learning of new responses that replace the old responses. Criticisms of *Guthrie's learning theory* include uneasiness by some psychologists concerning Guthrie's assured answers to all the problems of learning, where either the theory is extraordinarily inspired or it is not stated very precisely and, hence, it is not very sensitive to experimental data. In addition to circular reasoning in the theory, critics have suggested that the simplicity of *Guthrie's theory* may be illusory, and that many reviews of Guthrie in the psychological literature have probably mistaken incomplete-ness for simplicity. Guthrie essentially was an *associationist*, at heart, with a strong behavioristic bias (e.g., in attempting to get rid of subjective terms, he referred to "inner speech" and "movement-produced stimuli" instead of the more mentalistic term "thinking"). Although

the *associationist* tradition doubtless will continue on, Guthrie's particular version of it seems to have lost its appeal to succeeding generations of learning theorists. See also ASSOCIATION, LAWS/PRINCIPLES OF; ASSOCIATIVE SHIFTING, LAW OF; LEARNING THEORIES AND LAWS; PAVLOVIAN CONDITIONING PRINCIPLES/LAWS/THEORIES; THORNDIKE'S LAW OF EFFECT; WOLPE'S THEORY/ TECHNIQUE OF RECIPROCAL INHIBITION.

REFERENCES

Sherrington, C. S. (1906). *The integrative action of the nervous system.* New Haven, CT: Yale University Press.

Woodworth, R. S. (1918). *Dynamic psychology.* New York: Columbia University Press.

Guthrie, E. R. (1930). Conditioning as a principle of learning. *Psychological Review, 37,* 412-428.

Pavlov, I. (1932). The reply of a physiologist to a psychologist. *Psychological Review, 39,* 91-127.

Guthrie, E. R. (1934). Pavlov's theory of conditioning. *Psychological Review, 41,* 199-206.

Guthrie, E. R. (1934). Reward and punishment. *Psychological Review, 41,* 450-460.

Guthrie, E. R. (1935). *The psychology of learning.* New York: Harper & Row.

Guthrie, E. R. (1940). Association and the law of effect. *Psychological Review, 47,* 127-148.

Seward, J. (1942). An experimental study of Guthrie's theory of reinforcement. *Journal of Experimental Psychology, 30,* 247-256.

O'Connor, V. (1946). Recency or effect? A critical analysis of Guthrie's theory of learning. *Harvard Educational Review, 16,* 194-206.

Sheffield, F. D. (1949). Hilgard's critique of Guthrie. *Psychological Review, 56,* 284-291.

GUYAU'S THEORY OF TIME. The French social philosopher Jean-Marie Guyau (1854-1888) shifted philosophical attention from *time* as an a priori feature of the mind (as in Immanuel Kant's approach) to a focus on the actual or *empirical* development of the concept of *time*, and to a theoretical view that relates time experience to human information-processing activities. Guyau maintained that *time* itself does not exist in the universe, but rather that *time* is a purely mental construction arising from the events that take place, and held that temporal experience is constructed based on the intensity, number, associations of stimuli as well as the attention paid to the stimuli, the extent of the differences between the stimuli, and the expectations called up by the stimuli. According to Guyau, acquiring the idea of *time* is an important functional adaptation to one's environment, and is the result of a long process of evolution in a social context. In support of this theory, Guyau specifies five mechanisms that allow the individual to achieve the memory organization that is requisite to temporal appreciation: schema formation, matching, spatial analogy, chunking, and narrative closure. *Guyau's theory of time* holds that with more "images," and more changes and more mental content, the experience of "duration" is lengthened. In this sense, Guyau regarded *time* not as an a priori condition, but as a consequence of one's experience of the world, and the result of a long evolutionary history. According to Guyau, *time* essentially is a product of human imagination, memory, and will. Also, in Guyau's view, even though one may use *time* and *space* to measure each other, nevertheless they are distinct ideas with their own characteristics; the idea of *space* originally developed before the idea of *time*. Guyau suggested that the idea of *time* arose when humans became conscious of their reactions toward pleasure and pain, and of the succession of muscular sensations associated with such reactions. Thus, Guyau held that the original source of the human idea of *time* is an accumulation of sensations that produces an internal perspective directed towards the future. See also FRAISSE'S THEORY OF TIME; MICHON'S MODEL OF TIME; ORNSTEIN'S THEORY OF TIME; TIME, THEORIES OF.

REFERENCES

Guyau, J.-M. (1890). *La genese de l'idee de temps*. Paris: Alcan.

Michon, J., Pouthas, V., & Jackson, J. (1988). *Guyau and the idea of time*. Amsterdam, Netherlands: North-Holland.

H

HABIT/HABIT FORMATION, LAWS/ PRINCIPLES OF. The *principle of habit* may be defined as any instrumentally learned response that occurs with regularity and occurs in response to particular environmental events (cf., *redundancy principle* - states that there are frequent, established, and repetitive behavioral sequences that occur between individuals; for instance, greeting a person with the words "Good morning" every time you meet the same individual day after day). In some cases, the habit is connected to a number of frequently occurring stimuli whereas, in other cases, habits may be connected to stimuli that infrequently occur [cf., *law of accommodation* - accommodation is the determination of a function as modified by the incorporation of new elements; a single case of such incorporation is an "accommodation," and the generalization that the mind's progress and growth occurs by such modifications is the *law of accommodation*. The true *theory of accommodation* dates from the French philosopher Rene Descartes in the 17ᵗʰ century. J. M. Baldwin notes that as the concept of *accommodation* is the adaptive principle of "modification of type," so the concept of *habit* is the principle of mental "conservation of type"]. The concept of *habit/habit formation* has a long history in psychology - Aristotle considered habit to be of basic importance in the development of one's morality - where it originally referred only to motor or physical patterns of behavior (e.g., W. James and J. M. Baldwin), and has appeared most recently in the *learning theories* of C. L. Hull and K. W. Spence as a central term in their approaches where *habit* ("response tendency") interacts with *drive* to produce behavior and where learning is considered to be the organization and accumulation of response habits. However, currently, the concept of *habit* is given less attention because most psychologists today acknowledge that it is better defined in terms of operational definitions, processes of acquisition, and generalization, as well as

other factors that directly influence *habits*, especially the role of various environmental cues in *habit formation*. When *habit* is defined within the context of personality psychology, it refers to a pattern of activity that has, through repetition, become fixed, automatic, and easily carried out. In this case, *habit* is close in meaning to the concept of *trait* (i.e., any enduring characteristic of an individual that may serve in the role of a theoretical entity as an explanation for the observed regularities or consistencies in behavior. When *habit* is defined within the context of *ethology* (i.e., the study of animal behavior), it usually refers to a pattern of action that is characteristic of a particular species of animal and where an innate or species-specific behavior pattern is implied (as opposed to a "learned" behavior). The term *habit formation* presents some semantic problems, historically, where it has often been used as a synonym for *learning*, but today most psychologists would avoid such an equivalency and insist, instead, that all learning is not merely the formation of habits. Also, the term *formation* is ambiguous because it may apply to the actual acquisition of a new habit or the novel use of a previously acquired habit. Thus, the *principle of habit* has served historically as a generally useful (i.e., covers a wide range of disciplines) concept throughout the development of the social and behavioral sciences, perhaps coming close to the overall influence and utility of other omnibus terms such as *adaptation, assimilation, association, accommodation, activation,* and *contiguity.* See also ACCOMMODATION, LAW/PRINCIPLE OF; ACTIVATION/AROUSAL THEORY; ADAPTATION, PRINCIPLES/LAWS OF; ASSIMILATION, LAW OF; ASSOCIATION, LAWS/PRINCIPLES OF; CONTIGUITY, LAW OF; HULL'S LEARNING THEORY; LEARNING THEORIES/LAWS; SPENCE'S THEORY.

REFERENCES

James, W. (1890). *The principles of psychology.* New York: Holt.

Baldwin, J. M. (1894). *Handbook of psychology.* New York: Holt.

Hull, C. L. (1943). *Principles of behavior.* New York: Appleton-Century.

Hull, C. L. (1952). *A behavior system: An introduction to behavior theory con-*

cerning the individual organism. New Haven, CT: Yale University Press.

Spence, K. W. (1956). *Behavior theory and conditioning.* New Haven, CT: Yale University Press.

Spence, K. W. (1960). *Behavior theory and learning.* Englewood Cliffs, NJ: Prentice-Hall.

HABITUATION, PRINCIPLE/LAW OF. The *principle of habituation* refers to the elimination of a response as a result of a continuous exposure to the stimulus that originally elicited the response. Another term for *habituation* is *negative adaptation*. The concept of *habituation* has been used to refer both to an empirical result and to a hypothetical construct, depending on the context, character, and depth of its study. Factors such as injury, fatigue, adaptation, and drugs are not usually included under *habituation*, even though these variables may produce a decline in responsiveness. An example of *habituation* is the *orienting reflex response*, which is an attentional response of an organism that functions to put it into a physical position or orientation whereby it is exposed optimally to the source of stimulation, such as a strange noise that alarms an animal, which then stops whatever its was doing, becomes motionless, and scans its surroundings in search of the sound source. After a few seconds, if there is no danger, the animal resumes its initial activity, perhaps eating behavior. If similar noises are made subsequently, and again not danger is present, the animal makes progressively weaker and shorter alerting responses whereupon *habituation* is said to have occurred to those types of noises. Distinctions have been made among the terms *specific habituation, general habituation,* and *acclimatization/acclimation. Specific habituation* is the localization or restriction of a habitual response to a particular area or part of the body. *General habituation* is the change in one's psychological or mental *set* that results in a generalized reduction in response to a repeated stimulus. The term *acclimatization* refers to the compensation that results over a period of time (days or weeks) in response to a complex of changes, and *acclimation* is the same type of adjustment but,

in this case, only to a simple, or single, environmental condition. Also, the following characteristics have been associated with *habituation*: spontaneous recovery of an originally strong response will occur after a long enough absence of stimulation; habituation is faster when the evoking stimulus is given more frequently and regularly; habituation is slower when the eliciting stimulus is stronger, and near-threshold stimuli may not habituate; habituation is prolonged and spontaneous recovery is delayed when additional stimulation is given beyond the level that completely abolishes the original habituated response; habituation may generalize its effects to other, similar stimuli; "dishabituation" or restoration of an original response may occur when a stimulus is presented that is stronger (or, sometimes, weaker) than is customarily given; habituation will not occur if the eliciting stimulus is converted through conditioning into a signal of biological importance (such as pairing a click with a painful shock or with food). Various models have been proposed to explain the nature of the neural mechanisms involved in *short-term habituation*. For example, the *synaptic depression model* states that sensory input energizes the small interneurons located in the periphery of the brain stem reticular formation (BSFR) and, assuming that synaptic depression occurs in this region, these neurons then activate the neurons in the BSRF core, which then lead to cortical arousal (in higher-order mammals). Another model of habituation, called the *match-mismatch model* (Sokolov, 1963), states that a stimulus elicits a neural representation ("engram") of itself in higher-order mammals that is relatively permanent and where the neural consequences of subsequent stimuli are compared with the representation of the original alerting stimulus. In this case, if there is a match between the subsequent stimuli and the original stimulus, then no BSRF arousal occurs, and the result is *habituation*. The term *sensitization* is distinguished from *habituation* where the former refers to an *initial* increase in the habituated response after a stimulus has been repeatedly presented, and where the alerting response has first increased and then decreased. The *principle of sensitization* has led to a good deal of empirical and theoretical controversy regarding the equivalence of responses in different species, in the parts of the nervous system involved, and in the time frames for the *sensitization* and *habituation* processes. The *principle of habituation* within the context of neurophysiological research is being actively and vigorously pursued. See also ADAPTATION, PRINCIPLES AND LAWS OF; ATTENTION, LAWS/PRINCIPLES/THEORIES OF; DENERVATON, LAW OF; HABIT/HABIT FORMATION, LAWS/PRINCIPLES OF; MIND/MENTAL SET, LAW OF; VIGILANCE, THEORIES OF.

REFERENCES

Dodge, R. (1923). Habituation to rotation. *Journal of Experimental Psychology*, 6, 1-35.

Humphrey, G. (1930). Extinction and negative adaptation. *Psychological Review*, 37, 361-363.

Sharpless, S., & Jasper, H. (1956). Habituation of the arousal reaction. *Brain*, 79, 655-680.

Sokolov, E. (1963). Higher neuron functions: The orienting reflex. *Annual Review of Physiology*, 25, 545-580.

Thompson, R., & Spencer, W. (1966). Habituation: A model phenomenon for the study of neuronal substrates of behavior. *Psychological Review*, 173, 16-43.

Mackworth, J. (1968). Vigilance, arousal, and habituation. *Psychological Review*, 75, 308-322.

Groves, P., & Thompson, R. (1970). Habituation: A dual process theory. *Psychological Review*, 77, 419-450.

HAECKEL'S GASTRAEA THEORY. See DEVELOPMENTAL THEORY.

HAECKEL'S PROKARYOTIC THEORY. See DEVELOPMENTAL THEORY.

HALO EFFECT. The *halo effect* (also called the *atmosphere effect* and *halo error*) is a person-perception phenomenon that refers to the tendency (favorable or unfavorable) to evaluate an individual high on many other traits because of a belief, or evidence, that the individual is high on one particular trait; that is, the rated trait seems to "spill over" onto other traits. The *halo effect* most often emerges as a bias on personal rating scales, but may also appear in the classroom (e.g., R. Nash, 1976). The effect was first reported in 1907 by the American psychologist Frederick L. Wells (1884-1964), and was first supported empirically by E. L. Thorndike in 1920. The *halo effect/error* is detrimental to rating systems because it masks the presence of individual variability across different rating scales. Many suggestions have been offered to control or counteract the effect. For example, rating all people on one trait before going on to the next, varying the anchors of the scale, pooling raters with equal knowledge, and giving intensive training to the raters (this technique appears to be the most effective). Related closely to the *halo effect* is the concept of the *devil effect* (also called the *horns effect* or *reverse halo effect*), where a rater evaluates an individual low on many traits because of a belief, or evidence, that the person is low on one trait that is assumed to be critical, or is an unwarranted extension of an overall negative impression of an individual based on specific attributes/traits. The *halo effect* and the *devil effect* usually increase to the degree that the rated characteristic is vague or difficult to measure. See also EXPERIMENTER EFFECTS; PYGMALION EFFECT.

REFERENCES

Wells, F. L. (1907). A statistical study of literary merit. *Columbia University Contributions to Philosophy and Psychology*, 16, 3; *Archives of Psychology*, No. 7.

Thorndike, E. L. (1920). A constant error on psychological ratings. *Journal of Applied Psychology*, 4, 25-29.

Nash, R. (1976). *Teacher expectations and pupil learning*. London: Routledge & Kegan Paul.

HAMILTON'S HYPOTHESIS OF SPACE. See BERKELEY'S THEORY OF VISUAL SPACE PERCEPTION.

HAMILTON'S PRINCIPLE OF LEAST ACTION/LAW OF LEAST RESISTANCE. See GESTALT THEORY/LAWS.

HANDEDNESS. See LATERALITY THEORIES; RIGHT-SHIFT THEORY.

HARD/SOFT DETERMINISM, DOCTRINE OF. See DETERMINISM, DOCTRINE/THEORY OF.

HARD-TO-GET EFFECT. See RECIPROCITY OF LIKING EFFECT.

HARDY-WEINBERG LAW. The English mathematician Godfrey H. Hardy (1877-1947) and the German physician Wilhelm Weinberg (1862-1937) independently formulated that principle in 1908. The *Hardy-Weinberg law of population genetics* states that the relative gene frequencies in a population remain stable from generation to generation under the conditions that mating occurs randomly and that selection, migration, and mutation do *not* occur. In other words, the *Hardy-Weinberg law* does not apply under five conditions: mutation, gene migration, genetic drift, nonrandom mating, and natural selection. The *Hardy-Weinberg equilibrium* [also called a *balanced polymorphism*, and the *Castle-Hardy-Weinberg equilibrium*, named after The American biologist William Ernest Castle (1867-1962)] or *genetic equilibrium* states that if two individuals - who are heterozygous (e.g., Bb) for a trait - are mated, it is found that 25-percent of their offspring are homozygous for the dominant allele (BB), 50-percent are heterozygous like their parents (Bb) and 25-percent are homozygous for the recessive allele (bb) and, thus, unlike their parents, express the recessive phenotype. Related terms in the area of *population genetics* include: the *founder effect* - the tendency for an isolated offshoot of a population to develop genetic differences from the parent population due to the distribution of "alleles" or "allelomorphs" (one of two or more alternative versions of a gene that can occupy a particular place on a chromosome where each is responsible for a different characteristic) in its founder members, not being perfectly representative of the distribution in the parent population; and *genetic drift effect* (also called *random drift* and *non-Darwinian evolution*) - the change in the relative frequencies of genes in a population resulting from neutral mutation, but not from natural selection. See also DARWIN'S EVOLUTION THEORY; EUGENICS, DOCTRINE OF; GALTON'S LAWS; MENDEL'S LAWS/PRINCIPLES; WEISMANN'S THEORY.

REFERENCES

Castle, W. E. (1903). The laws of Galton and Mendel and some laws governing race improvement by selection. *Proceedings of the American Academy of Arts and Sciences, 35,* 233-242.

Hardy, G. H. (1908). Mendelian proportions in a mixed population. *Science, 28,* 49-50.

Weinberg, W. (1908). Uber den nachweis der verebung beim menschen. *Naturk in Wuttemberg, 64,* 368-382.

Stern, C. (1943). The Hardy-Weinberg law. *Science, 97,* 137-138.

HARP THEORY. See AUDITION/HEARING, THEORIES OF.

HARTLEY'S THEORY OF HUMOR AND LAUGHTER. The English physician and philosopher David Hartley (1705-1757) defined *laughter* as a "nascent cry" where the first occasion of children's laughter is based in *surprise* - momentary fear at first, and then becoming momentary joy as a result of the removal of the fear (e.g., in the case of *tickling*, a momentary pain and apprehension of pain is experienced with the immediate removal of that pain). According to Hartley, young children do not laugh aloud for some months after birth, and they have to learn to laugh as well as learn to control or abate their laughter; also, laughter - even in adults - is facilitated by the presence of other individuals who are laughing. Hartley's observations on humor and laughter may not constitute a novel *theory of humor*, but they are of interest in the way they bring together the elements of traditional *humor theories*, and for their approximate speculations concerning the ethics, physiology, and sociology of humor. *Hartley's theory of humor/laughter* makes contact with *incongruity theory* when he discusses surprise, inconsistencies, and improprieties as causes of laughter, and contact with *relief theory* when he notes that laughter sometimes results from the sudden dissipation of fear and other negative emotions. It has been noted (Morreall, 1987) that Hartley develops an interesting theoretical approach via his notion of an element of "irrationality" to humor. That is, those people who are always looking for the humorous aspects of their experiences thereby disqualify themselves from the larger search for truth. Hartley's *nascent cry theory of laughter* may be considered to be important because it represents the first scientific elucidation of the connection between fear or unhappiness and laughter. Also, Hartley was the pioneer in the formal scientific recording of the development of laughter in children; the only other observer on this issue before Hartley was the Roman naturalist Pliny (A.D. 23-79) who informally, but specifically, stated in the 1st century that the child's first laugh takes place 40 days after birth. HUMOR, THEORIES OF; INCONGRUITY/INCONSISTENCY THEORIES OF HUMOR; RELIEF/TENSION-RELEASE THEORIES OF HUMOR/LAUGHTER; SURPRISE THEORIES OF HUMOR.

REFERENCES
Hartley, D. (1749). *Observations on man, his frame, his duty, and his expectations*. London: Johnson.
Morreall, J. (1987). *The philosophy of laughter and humor*. Albany: State University of New York Press.

HARTRIDGE'S POLYCHROMATIC VISION THEORY. The British physiologist Hamilton Hartridge (1886-1976) proposed a *polychromatic theory of vision* in the late 1940s and early 1950s that was interpreted to be consistent with existing *dominator-modulator* concepts and factors of the human fovea (cf., R. Granit for an account of the relations of the *dominator-modulator theory* to the data of color vision). *Hartridge's theory* is based on evidence - first observed by the Swedish physiologist Alarik Holmgren (1831-1897) in 1884 and the German physiologist A. Fick in 1889 - that a small white stimulus moving slowly over the retina is seen as having different colors at different positions. Based on the results of a number of such experiments, Hartridge concluded that there are seven types of color receptors. *Hartridge's polychromatic theory* postulates two kinds of

units in addition to a tricolor unit of the single-receptor theory. One of these is called the "Y-B unit" and possesses receptors most responsive to wavelengths for yellow and blue; the other unit is called the "R-BG-R unit" and contains two kinds of receptors responding most vigorously to wavelengths in the red and blue-green part of the color spectrum (the red receptors also have a secondary quality of being sensitive in the extreme violet part of the spectrum and is indicated as the extra R in the symbol for the unit). Whereas R. Granit developed his theory from electrical recordings from the retina via microelectrodes, Hartridge obtained most of his evidence from sensory data that occurred when he studied the fovea, the periphery, and several levels of illumination as variables. The *polychromatic theory* has received little support, generally, because the problem arises of evaluating the influence of *eye movements* occurring during experimental trials and, also, a special speculation - called the *cluster hypothesis* - requires more empirical verification and validation. According to the *cluster hypothesis of cone function*, receptors of a given variety tend to group together in a "non-uniform distribution" where, at one retinal point, there may be a cluster of "dominators" and, at another point, some blue-sensitive receptors, and at still another point, some green-sensitive receptors. See also COLOR VISION, THEORIES/LAWS OF; DOMINATOR-MODULATOR THEORY; GRANIT'S COLOR VISION THEORY.

REFERENCES
Granit, R. (1947). *Sensory mechanisms of the retina*. New York: Oxford University Press.
Hartridge, H. (1948). Recent advances in color vision. *Science, 108*, 395-404.
Hartridge, H. (1949). *Colours and how we see them*. London: G. Bell & Sons.
Hartridge, H. (1950). *Recent advances in the physiology of vision*. London: Churchill.

HARVEY'S PRINCIPLE. See VISION/SIGHT, THEORIES OF.

HAUNTED SWING ILLUSION. See APPENDIX A.

HAWK-DOVE/CHICKEN GAME EF-FECTS. The English biologist John Maynard Smith (1920-) and the American physicist and chemist George R. Price (1922-1975) empirically assessed the *hawk-dove*, or *chicken*, *game* as it relates to biology, conflict, and evolution [the "chicken game" was named and described by the Welsh philosopher Bertrand A. W. Russell (1872-1970) in 1959, but it may be traced as far back as the 8th century B.C. to the Greek epic poet Homer and his reputed poem "The Iliad"]. The *chicken game* is a two-person strategic game, or a strategic model of "brinkmanship," where - in its simplest version - two motorists speed towards each other, where each driver has the option of swerving to avoid a collision or to drive straight ahead. If both drivers swerve, the outcome is a draw with "second-best" payoffs going to each driver; if both persons drive straight ahead, they risk death and each receives the "worst/fourth-best" payoff; but if one "chickens out" (i.e., is a "cowardly person") by swerving and the other proceeds by driving straight on, then the swerver loses face and earns the "third-best" payoff, whereas the nonswerver wins a victory and earns the "best" payoff. In a biological context, the *hawk-dove game* states that the "hawk" strategy involves "escalated" fighting until the individual adopting it is forced to withdraw or its opponent gives up, and the "dove" strategy involves "conventional" fighting where the individual adopting it retreats before getting injured if its opponent causes an escalation in fighting. The highest payoff - in terms of evolution and Darwinian fitness - goes to the "hawk" strategy when going against a "dove," the second-highest payoff goes to "dove" against "dove," the third-highest payoff goes to "dove" against a "hawk," and the lowest payoff goes to "hawk" against "hawk." The *evolutionarily stable strategy* in these gaming scenarios/effects is a *mixture* of "hawk and dove" strategies. In the *hawk-dove-retaliator game*, which is an extension of the *hawk-dove game*, the additional strategy is available of fighting "conventionally" and escalating only if one's adversary escalates. In this version, a "retaliator" typically plays "dove" but responds to a "hawk" opponent by playing "hawk;" in this case, the *evolutionarily stable*

strategy is that of the "retaliator" strategy. In another psychological two-person game called the *Prisoner's Dilemma Game* - initially studied by the American mathematicians Albert W. Tucker (1905-1995) and Merrill M. Flood (1908-), and the Polish-born American mathematician Melvin Dresher (1911-1992) - one finds the best-known "mixed motive" game (i.e., involving *both* competitive and cooperative aspects; cf., *zero-sum games* which are situations of complete competition between the players, and *coordination games* which are situations in which the possible decision combinations are given exactly the same preference-ordering by both players) in psychology, where each player has two choice alternatives, and each player's welfare depends on the resultant combination of choices [cf., *N-person Prisoner's Dilemma* - developed by the American psychologist Robyn M. Dawes (1936-), the American mathematician Henry Hamburger (1940-), and the American economist Thomas C. Schelling (1921-) in 1973 - which is a generalization of the *Prisoner's Dilemma Game* that includes more than two players, and is an interactive multi-person social dilemma/decision game in which each player faces a choice between a cooperative strategy and a non-cooperative/defecting strategy]. The prototype situation/scenario for the two-player *Prisoner's Dilemma Game* involves two prisoners held by the police for a particular crime. The police separate the two prisoners, and inform each of them that if he/she gives evidence against the other, he/she may go free. The prisoners are aware that if only one gives evidence, the other will receive the maximum penalty, but if both give evidence, each will receive a moderate sentence. However, if neither prisoner gives evidence, each will be tried on a minor charge with a money penalty and a very short prison sentence for each individual. Basically, both prisoners would prefer to go free, but if both give evidence, both will go to jail for a moderate number of years. On the other hand, opting for the minor charges by refusing to give evidence may result in the most severe penalty if the other person gives evidence. In this game, refusing to give evidence is defined as a *cooperative* response, because both parties must do so for the choice to give mutually beneficial payoffs. Giving evidence, on the other hand, is viewed as *competitive* - as a strategy to obtain the best outcome for oneself at the expense of the other person (or as *defensive*, in an effort to thwart the competitive intention of the other person). Persons who play this game typically make *competitive* choices despite the collectively poor payoffs embodied in this strategy. The *Prisoner's Dilemma Game* is used widely by social psychologists in studying interpersonal conflict, decision-making, and policy-making (such as in weapons/nuclear arms races). See also CONFLICT, THEORIES OF; DARWIN'S EVOLUTION THEORY; DECISION-MAKING THEORIES; EVOLUTION, THEORY/LAWS OF.

REFERENCES

Russell, B. (1959/2001). *Common sense and nuclear warfare*. London: Routledge.

Rapoport, A., & Chammah, A. M. (1965). *Prisoner's dilemma: A study in conflict and cooperation*. Ann Arbor: University of Michigan Press.

Maynard Smith, J., & Price, G. R. (1973). The logic of animal conflict. *Nature, 246*, 15-18.

Myers, D. G., & Bach, P. J. (1974). Discussion effects on militarism-pacifism: A test of the group polarization hypothesis. *Journal of Personality and Social Psychology, 30*, 741-747.

Pruitt, D. G., & Kimmel, M. J. (1977). Twenty years of experimental gaming: Critique, synthesis, and suggestions for the future. *Annual Review of Psychology, 28*, 363-392.

Taylor, P. D., & Jonker, L. (1978). Evolutionarily stable strategies and game dynamics. *Mathematical Bioscience, 40*, 145-156.

Maynard Smith, J. (1982). *Evolution and the theory of games*. New York: Cambridge University Press.

Weibull, J. W. (1995). *Evolutionary game theory*. Cambridge, MA: M.I.T. Press.

HAWTHORNE EFFECT. See EXPERIMENTER EFFECTS.

HEAD'S THEORY OF DUAL CUTANEOUS SENSIBILITIES. See SOMESTHESIS, THEORIES OF.

HEALTH BELIEF MODEL. In the area of health psychology, the most *established* model of health-related behavior is the *health belief model* (cf., Janz & Becker, 1984), which proposes that individuals - in response to a cue or action such as the experience of a symptom or invitation to attend a health checkup - will act on the basis of their beliefs about the advantages and disadvantages of taking a particular course of action (cf., the less widely used but more *successful* model, called the *theory of reasoned action*, which proposes that the best predictors of individuals' voluntary action are their behavioral *intentions* that are determined by one's attitude and beliefs regarding the behavior, and the *subjective* norm regarding the behavior, including normative beliefs concerning *others'* opinions about the behavior). According to the *health belief model*, persons' perceptions of the particular threat depends on their beliefs about its seriousness and their vulnerability and/or susceptibility to it. For example, for some health-related behaviors (such as "safe" sexual behavior), individuals may acknowledge the gravity of the associated health threat (such as becoming infected by HIV) but may not see themselves as being vulnerable; in contrast, for other behaviors (such as dental health care), individuals may well acknowledge their susceptibility to health threat (such as cavities or gum disease) but may not regard it as sufficiently serious to take the appropriate preventive action. The *health belief model* has been used for numerous studies of health-related behaviors, particularly those concerned with prevention. However, it has not been entirely successful and, as a result, other variables (e.g., "efficacy beliefs") have been added to the model to increase its explanatory power; but, even with the supplement of such variables, the overall results are still modest. This condition may reflect, in part, the general problem of trying to predict behavior from *attitudes*, as well as the more specific problem that people may not necessarily think about health issues in the way suggested by the *health belief model*. See also REASONED ACTION AND PLANNED BEHAVIOR THEORIES.

REFERENCES

Janz, N. K., & Becker, M. (1984). The health belief model: A decade later. *Health Education Quarterly, 11*, 1-47.

Duberstein, P. R., & Masling, J. M. (2000). *Psychodynamic perspectives on sickness and health.* Washington, D.C.: American Psychological Association.

HEALTH SWEEP IMAGERY TECHNIQUE. See IMAGERY/MENTAL IMAGERY, THEORIES OF.

HEARING THEORIES. See AUDITION/ HEARING, THEORIES OF.

HEBB'S CELL ASSEMBLY THEORY. See PERCEPTION (II. COMPARATIVE APPRAISAL), THEORIES OF.

HEBB'S RULE. See PERCEPTION (II. COMPARATIVE APPRAISAL), THEORIES OF.

HEBB'S THEORY OF PERCEPTUAL LEARNING. See PERCEPTION (II. COMPARATIVE APPRAISAL), THEORIES OF.

HECHT'S COLOR VISION THEORY. = Hecht's photochemical theory. The Austrian-American physiologist Selig Hecht (1892-1947) conducted research in the areas of physical chemistry, physiology, and biophysics and studied, among other issues, the basic functioning of the eye, the sensitivity curve to different wavelengths under low illumination viewing with the rods, and a hypothetico-deductive approach to the chemical breakdown and recombination in the rods and cones. *Hecht's color vision theory* is a mathematical account of the component physiological processes that intervene between visual data and a mathematical space and elaborates on the *line-element theory* of H. von Helmholtz and W. S. Stiles. The theory assumes that there are three kinds of cones present in the retina and that in the fovea they exist in approximately equal numbers. The sensations that result from the action of the three types of cones are qualitatively specific and are described as blue, green, and red. Given a specific cone that contains a photosensitive substance whose spectral absorption is greater in the blue or in the green or in the red, and when the substance is altered by light and initiates a nerve impulse, the nerve will register, respectively, blue, green, or red in the brain. The type of *color vision theory* proposed by Hecht exhibits many desirable features; for example, it formulates mechanisms that offer many researchers a flexible basis for further exploration of visual processes. Certain aspects of color vision, however, are not accounted for by *Hecht's theory*, such as the data generated by some studies of *color blindness*, as well as some of the data in the *two-color threshold* domain of vision research. See also COLOR VISION, THEORIES/LAWS OF; HELMHOLTZ'S COLOR VISION THEORY; PUR-KINJE EFFECT/PHENOMENON/SHIFT; STILES' COLOR VISION THEORY.

REFERENCES

Hecht, S. (1928). On the binocular fusion of colors and its relation to theories of color vision. *Proceedings of the National Academy of Sciences, 14*, 237-241.

Hecht, S. (1930). The development of Thomas Young's theory of color vision. *Journal of the Optical Society of America, 20*, 231-270.

Hecht, S. (1931). The interrelations of various aspects of color vision. *Journal of the Optical Society of America, 21*, 615-639.

Hecht, S. (1935). A theory of visual intensity discrimination. *Journal of General Physiology, 18*, 767-789.

Hecht, S. (1937). Rods, cones, and the chemical basis of vision. *Physiological Review, 17*, 239-290.

Hecht, S. (1944). Energy and vision. *American Scientist, 32*, 159-177.

Graham, C. (1965). Color: Data and theories. In C. Graham (Ed.), *Vision and visual perception.* New York: Wiley.

HEDONIC RELATIVITY PRINCIPLE. See HERRNSTEIN'S MATCHING LAW.

HEDONISM, THEORY/LAW OF. The ethical/philosophical *theory of hedonism* (the notion that pleasure is the person's ultimate goal) goes back to the Greek writings of Aristippus (435-360 B.C.) and Epicurus (341-270 B.C.). Aristippus developed the first coherent exposition of *hedonism*, which held pleasure to be the highest good, and virtue to be identical with the ability to enjoy (cf., the *doctrine of eudemonism* - states that the major goal of living should be the achievement of happiness). Epicurus defined philosophy as the art of making life happy and strictly subordinated metaphysics to ethics, naming pleasure as the highest, and only, good. Thus ancient *hedonistic theory* was expressed in two ways: the *cruder* form proposed by Aristippus, who asserted that pleasure was achieved by the complete gratification of all one's sensual desires, and the more *refined* form of Epicurus, who accepted the primacy of pleasure but equated it with the absence of pain, and taught that it could best be attained through the rational control of one's desires. As a more modern *psychological theory, hedonism* is the assumption that individuals act so as to attain pleasant, and avoid unpleasant, feelings. *Motivational hedonic theory* states that people have tendencies to approach pleasure and to avoid pain. The English philosopher Jeremy Bentham (1748-1832) was one of the main proponents of the *motivation theory of hedonism*, which holds that human activity arises out of a desire to avoid pain and to seek pleasure. Bentham defined principles of utility, happiness, good, and pleasure, and proposed that the object of legislation should be the general happiness of the majority of people. The influence of Bentham's philosophies of *hedonism* and *utility* was widespread: it affected the writings of John Stuart Mill (1806-1873) and Herbert Spencer (1820-1903); Christian theologians emphasized the pleasures of heaven and the pain of hell; Sigmund Freud (1856-1939) - borrowing from Gustav Fechner (1801-1887) - described the *pleasure principle* as activity of the unconscious *id*; Edward Thorndike (1874-1949) formulated his *law of effect*, in which the *hedonic principle* operates - actions that lead to satisfying consequences are "stamped in;" and Clark Hull (1884-1952) and B. F. Skiinner

(1904-1990) developed the *principle of reinforcement*, in which hedonic expression, also, is found. H. Warren elevated the theoretical status of *hedonic doctrine* somewhat by his references to *hedonic law*. Other writers in psychology refer to *pleasure-pain theories, pleasure principle, law of pleasure, law of pleasure-pain,* and *doctrine of pleasure-pain.* J. M. Baldwin refers to this concept as *Aristotle's theory of pleasure-pain.* M. Maher gives an historical perspective and progression of *theories of pleasure-pain,* but he also describes the *laws of pleasure-pain.* According to Maher, other laws that are subsidiary to the *pleasure laws* are the *law of change* (concerns the relativity of pleasures), the *law of accommodation* (pleasures may become habituated), and the *law of repetition* (diminished pleasures may be revitalized). Maher represents an interesting "turn-of-the-20th-century" amalgam of the disciplines of philosophy and psychology concerning the *doctrine of hedonism.* See also EFFECT, LAW OF; FREUD'S THEORY OF PERSONALITY; REINFORCEMENT THEORY.

REFERENCES

Bentham, J. (1789). *Principles of morals and legislation.* Oxford, UK: Clarendon Press.

Bentham, J. (1798). *Theory of legislation.* Oxford, UK: Clarendon Press.

Baldwin, J. M. (1894). *Handbook of psychology.* New York: Holt.

Maher, M. (1900). *Psychology: Empirical and rational.* New York: Longmans, Green.

Warren, H. C. (1919). *Human psychology.* Boston: Houghton Mifflin.

HEIDER'S BALANCE THEORY. See ATTRIBUTION THEORY.

HEISENBERG'S PRINCIPLE OF UNCERTAINTY/INDETERMINACY. See DETERMINISM, DOCTRINE/THEORY OF.

HELIOCENTRIC THEORY. See SELF-CONCEPT THEORY.

HELLIN'S LAW. See PROBABILITY THEORY/LAWS.

HELMHOLTZ CHESSBOARD ILLUSION. See APPENDIX A.

HELMHOLTZ ILLUSION AND IRRADIATION ILLUSION. See APPENDIX A.

HELMHOLTZ'S COLOR VISION THEORY. See YOUNG-HELMHOLTZ COLOR VISION THEORY.

HELMHOLTZ'S LIKELIHOOD PRINCIPLE. See CONSTRUCTIVIST THEORY OF PERCEPTION.

HELMHOLTZ'S THEORY OF ACCOMMODATION. See YOUNG-HELMHOLTZ COLOR VISION THEORY.

HELMHOLTZ'S THEORY OF HEARING. See AUDITION/HEARING, THEORIES OF.

HELPING BEHAVIOR. See BYSTANDER INTERVENTION EFFECT.

HELPLESSNESS/HOPELESSNESS THEORY OF DEPRESSION. See DEPRESSION, THEORIES OF.

HELSON'S ADAPTATION-LEVEL THEORY. = AL theory = adaption-level theory = adaptation-level affect/phenomenon = context effect. The American psychologist Harry Helson (1898-1977) developed this *psychological* and *perceptual theory*, which postulates a momentary state and subjective evaluation of the individual in which stimuli are judged to be indifferent or neutral on any given attribute. Stimuli above this *point of subjective equality* have specific features and those below this point have complementary qualities. As an example, when one goes through the transition in a set of stimuli from pleasant stimuli (e.g., substances having a sweet taste) to unpleasant stimuli (e.g., substances having a sour taste), there is a stimulus (or group of stimuli) that is neutral (i.e., neither pleasant nor unpleasant). This transitional zone, called the *adaptation-level* (*AL*), represents the stimuli to which the individual is adapted concerning the particular magnitude, quality, or attributes of those stimuli. Another common example of the operation of *AL* is where cool water may be made to feel warm if the person first adapts to rather cold water. The *AL* may be defined operationally as the stimulus value that elicits a neutral response when a person judges a set of stimuli in terms of numerical (quantitative or qualitative) rating scales. *Helson's theory of AL* attempted to evaluate the variables that affect the neutral zone of stimuli in terms of their *background*, *focal*, and *residual* levels. Because the *AL* is rarely observed to be at the arithmetic mean (center point) of a stimulus series, the phenomenon of *AL* has been called *decentering*. It is an accepted feature of *AL* that it is a weighted geometric mean consisting of *background*, *focal*, and *residual* stimuli. *Background* stimuli are "contextual" or "ground" (in the sense of a Gestalt "figure versus ground" relationship); *focal* stimuli are "attentional" or "figural" (in the sense of Gestalt *figure* versus *ground* relationships); and *residual* stimuli are "extra-situational" stimuli computed from differences between *background* and *focal* stimuli. Thus, *AL theory* maintains that the neutral or adapted background stimuli provide a basis, frame of reference, or standard against which new stimuli are perceived. See also ADAPTATION, PRINCIPLES/LAWS OF; ASSIMILATION-CONTRAST THEORY; CRESPI EFFECT; PERCEPTION (II. COMPARATIVE APPRAISAL), THEORIES OF; WEBER-FECHNER LAW.

REFERENCES

Helson, H. (1947). Adaptation-level as frame of reference for prediction of psychophysical data. *American Journal of Psychology*, 60, 1-29.

Helson, H. (1948). Adaptation-level as a basis for a quantitative theory of frames of reference. *Psychological Review*, 55, 297-313.

Michels, W., & Helson, H. (1949). A reformulation of the Fechner law in terms of adaptation-level applied to rating-scale data. *American Journal of Psychology*, 62, 355-368.

Helson, H. (1964). *Adaptation-level theory: An experimental and systematic approach to behavior*. New York: Harper & Row.

Corso, J. (1971). Adaptation-level theory and psychophysical scaling. In M. Appley (Ed.), *Adaptation-level theory: A symposium*. New York: Academic Press.

HEMORRHAGE AND THIRST HYPOTHESIS. See THIRST, THEORIES OF.

HEMPEL'S PARADOX. See NULL HYPOTHESIS.

HENNING'S THEORY OF SMELL. See OLFACTION/SMELL, THEORIES OF.

HENNING'S THEORY/PARADOX OF TASTE. See GUSTATION/TASTE, THEORIES OF.

HERBART'S DOCTRINE OF APPERCEPTION. The German philosopher, psychologist, and mathematician Johann Friedrich Herbart (1776-1841) viewed psychology as a science that is based on experience, metaphysics, and mathematics. However, Herbart did not consider psychology to be experimental, because he could not conceive of ways to experiment on the mind. Herbart was in agreement with the German philosopher Immanuel Kant (1724-1804) concerning the nature of a unitary mind or soul, but he proposed, also, that the mind could be an entity composed of smaller units. That is, Herbart thought of the mind as an *apperceptive mass* made up of psychic states. Unconscious ideas existed in a kind of static state that has "forces" or "intensities." According to Herbart, when the "forces" become strong enough, they can overcome the "counterforces" already present in the *apperceptive mass*, cross the threshold, and enter into consciousness. The interaction of psychic states, in and out of consciousness, constitutes Herbart's *psychic dynamics theory*. In its original sense, the concept of *apperception* dates back to the German philosopher/mathematician Gottfried Wilhelm von Leibnitz (1646-1716), who referred to it as a final or clear phase of perception in which there is recognition, identification, or comprehension of what has been perceived. According to *Leibnitz's monad theory* (a "monad" is his term for the essential unit or individuality of all substances), the world consists of an infinite number of independently acting *monad*s, which are points of "force" rather than substance, and where all *monad*s have various degrees of clarity and consciousness ranging from the relatively unclear and unconscious to the most conscious and perceptible. Leibnitz called the *lower* degrees of consciousness (unconscious) the "little perceptions," which, when actualized, become *apperceptions*. Leibnitz was probably the first person to develop a *theory of degrees of consciousness*, and it became the cornerstone of Sigmund Freud's conception of the *tripartite personality* (i.e., id, ego, and super-ego) and mental apparatus of opposing forces (i.e., *cathexis* and *anticathexis*), as well as Alfred Adler's and Carl Jung's approaches to degrees of consciousness and unconsciousness in their personality theories. For Herbart, however, *apperception* was considered to be the fundamental process of acquiring knowledge wherein the perceived qualities of a new object, event, or idea are assimilated with already existing knowledge. In some form or another, the basic notion of *apperception* - that learning and understanding depend on recognizing relationships between new ideas and existing knowledge - is axiomatic of nearly all *educational theory* and practice. The mathematics involved in Herbart's *psychic dynamics* focused on what could and could not enter consciousness where calculations concerned the amount of one force that was going to oppose another force. It was possible, also, for two forces or ideas to combine and suppress the ideas that are weaker [it was Herbart (1824) who introduced the psychodynamic term *repression* into psychology, where the term was elaborated later, and more fully, by Freud and the psychoanalysts]. Herbart's contribution to psychology is the notion that it could be quantified and, even though he denied that psychology could be experimental in nature, ironically his advocacy of quantification was crucial to the modern development of experimental psychology itself. See also ADLER'S THEORY OF PERSONALITY; FREUD'S THEORY OF PERSONALITY; JUNG'S THEORY OF PERSONALITY; PERSONALITY THEORIES; WUNDT'S THEORIES/DOCTRINES.

REFERENCES

Leibnitz, G. (1714/1898). *Monadology*. Oxford, UK: Oxford University Press.

Kant, I. (1781/1929). *Critique of pure reason.* New York: St. Martin's Press.

Herbart, J. F. (1816). *A textbook of psychology: An attempt to found the science of psychology on experience, metaphysics, and mathematics.* New York: Appleton.

Herbart, J. F. (1824). *Psychologie als wissenschaft.* 2 vols. Konigsberg: Unzer.

HEREDITY PREDISPOSITION THEORY. See LAMARCK'S THEORY.

HERING-HURVICH-JAMESON COLOR VISION THEORY. = Hering's color theory = Hurvich-Jameson color vision theory = opponent-process color vision theory = tetrachromatic theory. The German physiologist Karl Ewald Hering (1834-1918) based his original *color vision theory* on the fact that individuals uniformly select four colors when asked to designate unique colors: primary *blue* (about 480 nanometers, or nm where 1 nm = one-billionth of one meter), primary *green* (about 510 nm), primary *yellow* (about 580 nm), and primary *red* (about 700 nm). *Hering's theory*, therefore, assumes that *yellow* is a fourth primary color in addition to the three primary colors of *red, green,* and *blue.* This is one of the factors that distinguishes his theory from other *trireceptor* (red, blue, green) theories, such as the *Young-Helmholtz theory.* Another distinguishing feature of *Hering's theory* is an *opponent-process* aspect where each of three sets of receptor systems in the retina responds to either of two complementary colors: blue-yellow, red-green, and black-white (each system is assumed to function as an antagonistic pair), and where other colors are formed by the combined stimulation of more than one type of color receptor. The term *opponent-processes* refers to the opposing reactions that occur among the different substances in the retina where a "catabolism" or "breakdown" reaction corresponds to excitation of the red, yellow, and white substances, and an "anabolism" or "buildup" reaction corresponds to excitation of the opposite color substances of green, blue, and black.

The intermediate hues (e.g., the color *violet*) depend on the interaction between the anabolic processes and the catabolic components (e.g., for *violet*, the combination of catabolic *red* with anabolic *blue*). *Hering's theory* is able to explain the red-green type of color blindness (called *deuteranopia* for green light vision deficiency and *protanopia* for red light vision deficiency) by assuming some dysfunction in the red or green visual receptors, whereas the blue or yellow receptors remain unaffected. This accounts for the fact that red-green color-blind persons can still discriminate the colors blue and yellow. The theory also explains the phenomena of *color contrast* and *negative afterimages* - where opposite reactions to an initial stimulation are observed. The term *tetrachromatism* is used to refer to color vision that is characterized by the ability to distinguish or discriminate among all four of the Hering primaries (red, green, yellow, and blue). The American psychologists Leo M. Hurvich (1910-) and Dorothea Jameson (1920-1998) expanded *Hering's antagonistic/ opponent-process* (or opponent-colors) *theory* by giving it a more quantitative basis. They assume, as did Hering, that there are four basic hues, along with their corresponding receptor-processes, paired in three sets of receptors: yellow-blue, red-green, and black-white. The Hurvich-Jameson modification of *Hering's theory* accounts for the facts of color mixture, for most color-vision defects, and for the appearances of "dissimilarity," "similarity," and "purity" among the hues of the color circle. The effect of light, according to the *Hering-Hurvich-Jameson theory*, depends not only on its physical properties but also on the condition of the visual mechanism. According to this viewpoint, a phenomenon such as the *Bezold-Brucke effect* (where a change in hue is a function of brightness) may be ascribed to mechanisms and conditions of visual adaptation and compensation. The phenomenon of *simultaneous color contrast* can be viewed, also, as a condition where antagonistic processes are set up in areas adjacent to a stimulated zone, and the addition of complementary lights results in addition of brilliance, but also a subtraction process occurs where opponent colors react to each other and yield the color white. Today, the *Hering-Hurvich-Jameson theory* is regarded as a better approximation to the true explanation and state of color vision than is the *Young-Helmholtz theory*. However, it is cautioned that any good color vision theory must eventually deal with the fact that the retina organizes and processes visual stimuli differently from the cortical and subcortical visual centers. See also BEZOLD-BRUCKE EFFECT; COLOR MIXTURE, LAWS/THEORY OF; COLOR VISION, THEORIES/LAWS OF; NEWTON'S LAWS/PRINCIPLES OF COLOR MIXTURE; YOUNG-HELMHOLTZ COLOR VISION THEORY.

REFERENCES

Hering, E. (1878). *Zur lehre vom lichtsinn.* Vienna: Gerolds.

Hering, E. (1890). Beitrage zur lehre vom simultankontrast. *Zeitschrift fur Psychologie, 1,* 18-28.

Hering, E. (1920). *Grundzuge der lehre vom lichtsinn.* Berlin: Springer.

Hurvich, L., & Jameson, D. (1949). Helmholtz and the three-color theory: An historical note. *American Journal of Psychology, 62,* 111-114.

Hurvich, L., & Jameson, D. (1951). The binocular fusion of yellow in relation to color theories. *Science, 114,* 199-202.

Hurvich, L., & Jameson, D. (1955). Some quantitative aspects of an opponent-colors theory. II. Brightness, saturation, and hue in normal and dichromatic vision. *Journal of the Optical Society of America, 45,* 602-616.

Jameson, D., & Hurvich, L. (1955). Some quantitative aspects of an opponent-colors theory. I. Chromatic responses and spectral saturation. *Journal of the Optical Society of America, 45,* 546-552.

Jameson, D., & Hurvich, L. (1957). An opponent-process theory of color vision. *Psychological Review, 64,* 384-404.

Hurvich, L., & Jameson, D. (1974). Opponent-processes as a model of neural organization. *American Psychologist, 29,* 88-102.

Hurvich, L. (1981). *Color vision.* Sunderland, MA: Sinauer.

Jameson, D., & Hurvich, L. (1989). Essay concerning color constancy. *Annual Review of Psychology, 40,* 1-22.

HERING ILLUSION. See APPENDIX A.

HERING IMAGE. See PURKINJE EFFECT/PHENOMENON/SHIFT.

HERING'S COLOR THEORY. See HERING-HURVICH-JAMESON COLOR VISION THEORY.

HERING'S LAW OF EQUAL INNERVATION. See VISION/SIGHT, THEORIES OF.

HERMANN GRID ILLUSION. See APPENDIX A.

HERMENEUTIC INTERPRETATIVE THEORY. See HERMENEUTICS THEORY.

HERMENEUTICS THEORY. = hermeneutic interpretative theory. The German philosopher Wilhelm Dilthey (1833-1911) first described this viewpoint concerning the ability and art of interpreting human speech, writing, and behavior in terms involving difficult or "fuzzy" concepts such as *intentions* and *meanings* (cf., the existentialists' study of the "meaning of life"). The approach in *hermeneutics theory* employs methods of investigation that are inappropriate, typically, for studying the phenomena of the natural sciences. The term *hermeneutics* originally (about 1654) was used, specifically, to denote the interpretation of Scriptural writings, but it is employed today more broadly to refer to any interpretative process, operation, or procedure. In *hermeneutic interpretative theory* (i.e., the theory of human understanding in its interpretative aspect, in particular, a *hermeneutic* is a set of practices or recommendations for revealing an intelligible meaning in an otherwise unclear text or text-analogue), debate revolves around three issues; whether interpretation occurs in an already fixed or existing world or in an evolving world; whether interpretation is a process taking place within a formal system of already-existing categories or whether it is a more

274

fundamental process that works to provide - prior to any explicit understandings - a specific structure of "pre-understanding" (cf., Heidegger, 1962) upon which all the more explicit, categorical understandings rest; and distinctions are made between "dualistic" and "monistic" positions in the sense that the hermeneutical "task" may either be considered as directed towards grasping a spiritual or an objective "inner reality" in one's "outer" aggressions, or towards a more practical aim. The first formulation of a difference between systematic "historical hermeneutics" and a "psychological hermeneutics" (i.e., the reconceptualization of hermeneutics as concerned with the general problem of understanding) was made by the German Protestant theologian Friedrich D. E. Schleiermacher (1768-1834) who asserted that hermeneutics must accomplish by conscious effort and technique what ordinary conversationalists achieve effortlessly, that is, a grasp of the contents of one another's "minds" (cf., Palmer, 1969). In his invocation of the German word *Verstehen* ("to understand"), Dilthey advanced the notion of the interpretation and understanding of other people through an "intuitive" account of symbolic relationships obtained from adopting the point of view of the individuals being studied. Dilthey argued that the ultimate goal of the mental/human sciences is "understanding," but that of the natural/physical sciences is "explanation." Also, Dilthey claimed that the "natural" and the "human" sciences require radically different methodologies [cf., P. Duhem (1906-1962) who noted around the turn of the 20th century that natural scientific assertions are not tested one by one against experience, but require interpretation within a *theory* as a whole; and T. S. Kuhn (1962) who argues that the proper interpretation of *theoretical* statements requires reference to the context of scientific traditions and practices within which they have their expression]. Currently, on a related issue (i.e., the status of "psychology as a *science*"), the debate continues as to whether psychology *is* a science at all, and *if* it is, does it approximate more closely the *natural* sciences (e.g., physics, chemistry) or is it nearer to the *social/cultural* sciences (e.g., sociology, anthropology) (cf., Roeckelein, 1997a,b). See also COMTE'S

LAW/THEORY; FUZZY SET/LOGIC THEORY; INTENTIONALISM, PSYCHOLOGICAL THEORY OF; MEANING, THEORY/ASSESSMENT OF; MIND AND MENTAL STATES, THEORIES OF.

REFERENCES

Dilthey, W. (1894/1977). Ideas concerning a descriptive and analytic psychology. In R. M. Zaner & K. I. Heiges (Eds.), *Descriptive psychology and historical understanding*. The Hague: Nijhoff.

Duhem, P. (1906/1962). *The aim and the structure of physical theory*. New York: Atheneum.

Heidegger, M. (1962). *Being and time*. New York: Harper & Row.

Kuhn, T. S. (1962). *The structure of scientific revolutions*. Chicago: University of Chicago Press.

Palmer, R. E. (1969). *Hermeneutics: Interpretation theory in Schleiermacher, Dilthey, Heidegger, and Gadamer*. Evanston, IL: Northwestern University Press.

Messer, S. B., & Sass, L. A. (1988). *Hermeneutics and psychological theory*. New Brunswick, NJ: Rutgers University Press.

Roeckelein, J. E. (1997a). Hierarchy of the sciences and the terminological sharing of laws among the sciences. *Psychological Reports, 81*, 739-746.

Roeckelein, J. E. (1997b). Psychology among the sciences: Comparisons of numbers of theories and laws cited in textbooks. *Psychological Reports, 80*, 131-141.

HERRINGBONE ILLUSION. See APPENDIX A, POGGENDORFF/ZOLLNER ILLUSION.

HERRNSTEIN'S MATCHING LAW. The *matching law* was formulated by the American experimental psychologist Richard J. Herrnstein (1930-1994) who observed and recorded the behavior of pigeons pecking two keys for food reinforcement delivered on concurrent variable interval (i.e., an average, non-fixed amount of elapsed time) schedules. The pigeons yielded response curves that conformed closely to a predicted line of perfect matching where response ratios are matched to ratios of obtained reinforcements. The *matching law* is defined as the matching of response ratios to reinforcement ratios where the match is most robust when dealing with concurrent variable interval/variable interval and concurrent variable interval/variable ratio reinforcement schedules of operant behavior. Experiments using pigeons, rats, and people as participants show that the *matching law* applies when they choose between alternative sources of food, brain stimulation, and information, respectively. The three species, doing different things for different consequences, all crowd the theoretical "matching line." The acknowledged qualifications on the *matching law* involve three empirical issues: the equivalence of responses, the equivalence of rewards, and the interactions among drives. Much is unsettled about *matching* as a general principle, but various quantitative conclusions can be drawn regarding the law. For example, experiments consistently show that a response rises in rate either when its reward increases or when the reward for other concurrent responses decreases. Inversely, a response declines either when its reward decreases or when other available responses gain reward. Because pleasures and pains are always felt relative to a context ("total rewards that are available"), the traditional *law of effect* may more properly be called the *law of relative effect*. In this way, the *law of relative effect* is considered to be a *principle of hedonic relativity* where individuals that are subject to its workings allocate their behavior according to the relative gain connected with each. Therefore, an animal or person may work at a maximal rate for a pittance, if the alternatives are poor enough. In contrast, when the alternatives improve, even generous rewards may fail to produce much of any sort of activity. The *relativity* of the *law of effect* explains why context is so important for how people behave. Herrnstein defined the *law of relative effect* as the rate of a given response that is proportional to its rate of reinforcement relative to the reinforcement for all other responses. However, although the *relative law of effect* predicts well for simple variable interval reinforcement schedules, it has failed to

serve as a basis for a more general principle of reinforcement. See also EFFECT, LAW OF; SKINNER'S OPERANT CONDITIONING THEORY.

REFERENCES

Herrnstein, R. J. (1961). Relative and absolute strength of response as a function of frequency of reinforcement. *Journal of the Experimental Analysis of Behavior, 4*, 267-272.

Herrnstein, R. J. (1970). On the law of effect. *Journal of the Experimental Analysis of Behavior, 13*, 243-266.

Herrnstein, R. J. (1971). Quantitative hedonism. *Journal of Psychiatric Research, 8*, 399-412.

Rachlin, H. (1971). On the tautology of the matching law. *Journal of the Experimental Analysis of Behavior, 15*, 249-251.

Herrnstein, R. J. (1974). Formal properties of the matching law. *Journal of the Experimental Analysis of Behavior, 21*, 159-164.

HERSEY-BLANCHARD SITUATIONAL LEADERSHIP THEORY. See LEADERSHIP, THEORIES OF.

HESS EFFECT. See PERCEPTION (I. GENERAL), THEORIES OF.

HESS IMAGE. See PURKINJE EFFECT/ PHENOMENON/SHIFT.

HEURISTIC THEORY OF PERSUASION. See ATTITUDE AND ATTITUDE CHANGE, THEORIES OF; PERSUASION/ INFLUENCE THEORIES.

HEYMAN'S LAW. See INHIBITION, LAWS OF.

HICK-HYMAN LAW. See HICK'S LAW.

HICK'S LAW. The English physician William Edmund Hick (1912-1974) "reformulated" this principle [it was first described in 1885 by the German physiologist Julius Merkel (1834-1900)], which states that the rate of processing a signal is a linear increasing function of stimulus information (e.g.,

276

choice reaction time increases as a linear function of *stimulus uncertainty*), or that the rate of gain of information is a constant. The time between the occurrence of a stimulus and the initiation of a response is called reaction time (RT). The study of RT represents one of the oldest problems in psychology, dating from 1850 when Hermann von Helmholtz developed the RT experiment. A Hirsch measured the physiological time of the eye, ear, and sense of touch; F. Donders invented the *disjunctive RT experiment*; S. Exner introduced the term *reaction time*; Wilhelm Wundt's students began studies of single and complex RTs in 1879; and J. McK. Cattell and his students worked extensively on RT investigations. One of the first experimental studies of the effects of *stimulus uncertainty* on *choice RT* was made by Julius Merkel who found a predictable regularity in the nature of RT [cf., *Merkel's law*, which is the generalization that to equal differences between stimuli at above-threshold strength, there correspond equal differences in sensation; however, today, this is considered to be an incorrect assumption or generalization]. It was not until many years later, and the advent of *information theory*, that the general applicability of Merkel's initial finding be-came apparent. W. E. Hick realized that the uncertainty produced by variations in the number of stimulus alternatives could be viewed in *information theory* terms by expressing the number of alternatives in *bits* (i.e., "binary digit" where a *bit* is the amount of information needed to reduce the alternatives in a choice situation by one half). Hick found that RT increases as a linear function of the log (base 2) of the number of stimulus alternatives and, thus, in *information theory* terms, RT is proportional to stimulus uncertainty. Hick's discovery was not in itself new but was a confirmation of Merkel's earlier finding in 1885, using a different scale for describing the number of stimulus alternatives. Hick's approach makes it possible to map a number of ways to manipulate stimulus uncertainty onto a common scale. Although there is some disagreement, the general trend of the data seems to indicate that *choice RT* is proportional to stimulus information (cf., *symbolic distance effect* - when a participant has to gauge from memory the relative posi-

tion of two items on a dimension - such as length - the smaller the difference between the two items on the dimension, the longer is the participant's RT). Within limits, it does not seem to matter if uncertainty is manipulated through variations in the number of stimulus alternatives or through variations in stimuli probabilities or their sequential dependencies. A variation of *Hick's law*, called the *Hick-Hyman law* - named after W. E. Hick and the American psychologist Ray Hyman (1928-), is the generalization that RT increases as a function of the amount of information transmitted in making a response. Apparently, *Hick's law* possesses generality because it applies to vigilance tasks as well as to the *choice RT* tasks for which it was originally formulated. See also DONDERS' LAW; FECHNER'S LAW; FITTS' LAW; INFORMATION AND INFORMATION-PROCESSING THEORY; REACTION-TIME PARADIGMS/MODELS; SYSTEMS THEORY. VIGILANCE, THEORIES OF.

REFERENCES

Hirsch, A. (1861-1865). Experiences chronoscopiques sur la vitesse des differentes sensations et de la transmission nerveuse. *Societe Science National Bulletin, 6*, 100-114.

Donders, F. (1868). Die schnelligkeit psychischer processe. *Archiv fur Anatomie und Physiologie, 2*, 657-681.

Exner, S. (1873). Experimentelle untersuchung der einfachsten psychischen processe. *Pflugers Archiv Gesamte Physiologie, 7*, 601-660.

Merkel, J. (1885). Die zeitlichen verhaltnisse der willensthatigkeit. *Philosophische Studien, 2*, 73-127.

Cattell, J. McK. (1886a). Psychometrische untersuchungen. *Philosophische Studien, 3*, 305-335, 452-492.

Cattell, J. McK. (1886b). The time taken up by the cerebral operations, *Mind, 11*, 220-242, 377-392, 524-538.

Hick, W. E. (1952). On the rate of gain of information. *Quarterly Journal of Experimental Psychology, 4*, 11-26.

Hyman, R. (1953). Stimulus information as a determinant of reaction time. *Journal of Experimental Psychology, 45*, 188-196.

Garner, W. (1962). *Uncertainty and structure as psychological concepts*. New York: Wiley.

Kornblum, S. (1968). Serial-choice reaction time: Inadequacies of the information hypothesis. *Science, 159*, 432-434.

Smith, E. (1968). Choice reaction time: An analysis of the major theoretical positions. *Psychological Bulletin, 69*, 77-110.

Alluisi, E. (1970). Information and uncertainty: The metrics of communications. In K. DeGreene (Ed.), *Systems psychology*. New York: McGraw-Hill.

Teichner, W., & Krebs, M. (1974). Laws of visual choice reaction time. *Psychological Review, 81*, 75-98.

HIERARCHICAL ASSOCIATIONS THEORY. See ESTES' STIMULUS SAMPLING THEORY.

HIERARCHICAL INSTINCT THEORY. See McDOUGALL'S HORMIC/INSTINCT THEORY/DOCTRINE.

HIERARCHICAL MODEL OF WORD IDENTIFICATION. Typical *hierarchical models* of word perception emphasize that identification of a word is mediated by identification of its component letters. In one version of such a *hierarchical model* (Johnston & McClelland, 1980), evidence and an explanation are offered as to why people are more accurate in perceiving a briefly-presented letter when it appears in a word than when it appears alone (this is called the "word-letter phenomenon" or WLP). This model makes predictions that are consistent with the results of previous studies of WLP, but makes two new predictions: the sizeable WLP obtainable using a vector/visual mask made up of letter features are reduced greatly if the mask consist of complete letters; and the size of the WLP is the same whether or not mask letters spell out a word. Although both of these predictions run counter to the traditional principle in the area of verbal learning (i.e., that interference increases with the similarity of target and mask aspects), experimental results con-

firm both predictions in conditions that test letter features against word masks. See also INTERACTIVE ACTIVATION MODEL OF LETTER PERCEPTION; INTERFERENCE THEORIES OF FORGETTING; PERCEPTION (I. AND II.), THEORIES OF; TOP-DOWN PROCESSING THEORIES; WORD-SUPERIORITY EFFECT.

REFERENCE

Johnston, J. C., & McClelland, J. L. (1980). Experimental tests of a hierarchical model of word identification. *Journal of Verbal Learning and Verbal Behavior, 19*, 503-524.

HIERARCHY OF NEEDS THEORY OF WORK MOTIVATION. See WORK/CAREER/OCCUPATION, THEORIES OF.

HIERARCHY OF THE SCIENCES, THEORY OF. See COMTE'S LAW/THEORY.

HIERARCHY THEORY OF MOTIVATION. See MASLOW'S THEORY OF PERSONALITY.

HIGHER CORTICAL FUNCTIONING, LAWS OF. See LURIA'S LAWS OF CORTICAL FUNCTIONING.

HILGARD'S HIDDEN OBSERVER HYPOTHESIS. See HYPNOSIS/HYPNOTISM, THEORIES OF.

HINDSIGHT BIAS EFFECT. See DECISION-MAKING THEORIES.

HISTORICAL MODELS OF EXPERIMENTAL PSYCHOLOGY. In the history of psychology, the common textbook model suggests that experimental psychology began, consensually, as a *science* with the work of the German physiologist, psychologist, and philosopher Wilhelm Maximilian Wundt (1832-1920) and his establishment of the world's first recognized psychological laboratory at the University of Leipzig in 1879. Following 1879, an extended debate in the United States and Europe over the nature, scope, and methods of psychology took place where influences from different lines of research played an important role in the debate and where the so-called "schools," "-isms," and "systems" developed (e.g., structuralism, functionalism, behaviorism). Beyond this period, two main historical models appeared: one model states that the psychological schools or systems were modified by the debate of the first two decades of the 20th century (some schools may have dropped out, but the others continue to exert influence in modified forms up to the present time); and the other model states that the schools gradually disappeared, or were absorbed, and what emerged is called the "mainstream of psychology." A different kind of historical model for psychology (e.g., Mueller, 1979) has two components: one aspect is the recognition of Wundt's achievements in establishing the first experimental psychology laboratory and the first psychological journal (*Philosophische Studien*) in 1881, and credits Wundt with institutionalizing psychology as a separate discipline; the second component is that since 1904 there has been no discernible long-term systematic direction that has emerged following the appearance of the "schools," and there is no agreed-upon systematic "mainstream psychology." Although this position may seem to be unduly pessimistic, it is suggested that there has been real *scientific progress* in psychology following the popularity of the "schools." C. G. Mueller notes that it is only when psychologists try to articulate what their science is all about that they encounter difficulty and, although most psychologists have a need to think along systematic lines and to put their research into some broader context, it is when psychologists attempt to do this with some unity that the situation becomes analogous to the physicists' perspectives on the *laws of thermodynamics* (where every physicist knows exactly what the first and second laws mean, but no two physicists agree about them). Mueller notes, also, that there is a paradox inherent in the fact that psychology selected as the founder of its science (i.e., Wundt) a man whole line of methodological inquiry (i.e., mainly, the introspective method) brought with it no single consensually acceptable experimental method. Thus, the Wundtian and related traditions brought to the 20th century some interesting psychological questions and issues, yet they brought *no* method

for demonstrating whether the questions were for science or philosophy. Historically, other non-Wundtian lines of inquiry were needed to furnish psychology with the methods to become a science, as well as help resolve the relative facts of, and importance of, psychology's origins. Recently, the notions of *psychologic (PL)* and *overarching psychological theory* are offered as ways to explain and formalize the basic conceptual structure of psychology. The *PL* theoretical (e.g., Smedslund, 1991) contains 26 axioms, 83 definitions, and more than 150 corollaries and theorems; *PL* allows one to distinguish between the a priori/noncontingent and the empirical/contingent as a way to discover, and prevent, "pseudoempirical" research. Also, the *PL* paradigm (cf., Kuhn, 1962/1970) suggests that there can be no general and empirical psychological laws, only local or historically-determined regularities. The eclectic *overarching psychological theory* (e.g., Walters, 2000) rests upon the physical model of *nonlinear dynamical systems theory* and integrates philosophical *existentialism* into its structure, as well as being grounded in *evolutionary biological theory*, *symbolic interactionalism theory*, *object-relations theory*, *cognitive constructionalism theory*, and *learning/motivation theories*; also, the concept of *lifestyle* (cf., *Adler's theory*) is incorporated into *overarching psychological theory* along with the three main models that constitute *lifestyle theory* (structural-, functional-, and change-models). See also ADLER'S THEORY OF PERSONALITY; A POSTERIORI/A PRIORI DISTINCTION; GREAT MAN/ GREAT PERSON THEORY; NATURALIST THEORY OF HISTORY; PARADIGM SHIFT DOCTRINE; THERMODYNAMICS, LAWS OF.

REFERENCES

Kuhn, T. S. (1962/1970). *The structure of scientific revolutions*. Chicago: University of Chicago Press.

Kruglanski, A. W. (1976). On the paradigmatic objections to experimental psychology. *American Psychologist*, *31*, 655-663.

Mueller, C. G. (1979). Some origins of psychology as science. *Annual Review of Psychology*, *30*, 9-29.

Smedslund, J. (1991). The pseudo empirical in psychology and the case for psychologic. *Psychological Inquiry*, 2, 325-338, 376-382.

Walters, G. D. (2000). *Beyond behavior: Construction of an overarching psychological theory of lifestyles*. Westport, CT: Praeger.

HISTORIC THEORIES OF ABNORMALITY. See PSYCHOPATHOLOGY, THEORIES OF.

HOBBES' PSYCHOLOGICAL THEORY. The English philosopher Thomas Hobbes (1588-1679), often referred to as the founder of British empiricism (cf., *Locke's psychological theory*), asserted in his primary principle of psychology that all knowledge is derived through sensations. By suggesting that nothing exists internal or external to the individual (except matter and motion), Hobbes grounded his psychology firmly in the philosophical positions called "materialism" and "mechanism" (cf., Brennan, 1991). The *materialistic approach* stresses that the only means through which reality is known is through an understanding of physical matter (cf., *mentalism* which emphasizes the necessity for using mental units or phenomena in explaining human behavior, and *vitalism* which maintains that a nonchemical, nonphysical, and nonmechanical "vital force" is responsible for life). The *mechanistic approach* holds that all events, phenomena, or behavior may be explained in mechanical terms; for instance, Hobbes' *theory of sensation* states in Newtonian mechanistic terms that one's sense organs are agitated by external motions without which there could be no sensations, and emphasizes the belief that "all is body or body in motion." In his psychological treatment of the process of *imagination*, Hobbes echoes Aristotle who earlier described memories as motions within the body and who treated associations as following the sequence in which the original events occurred; and in his *theory of motivation*, Hobbes argues that humans behave in the long run so as to maximize pleasure and minimize pain - an idea that was later developed by Sigmund Freud (1856-1939) in his "reality principle." In his philosophy of

materialistic monism (i.e., there is only *one* type of ultimate reality; cf., *dualism* which asserts that there are *two* separate states of reality or *two* sets of basic principles in the universe), Hobbes found no evidence for the existence of a soul and, thereby, had no need to explain the way in which body and soul (mind) interacted. Like the later behaviorists, Hobbes simply ignored the question of conscious awareness as a matter of concern to psychologists. Thus, Hobbes' psychology portrayed the individual as a machine operating in a mechanized world where sensations arise from motion and result in ideas, according to the *laws of association*. However, a major inconsistency in Hobbes' position lies in explaining consciousness: his sequence of thought implies an awareness of a cognitive content, but he is unclear on the manner of movement from physically-based sensations to nonphysical thought. See also ASSOCIATION, LAWS/PRINCIPLES OF; BEHAVIORIST THEORY; EMPIRICAL/EMPIRICISM, DOCTRINE OF; FREUD'S THEORY OF PERSONALITY; LOCKE'S PSYCHOLOGICAL THEORY; LOEB'S TROPISTIC THEORY; VITALISM THEORY.

REFERENCES

Hobbes, T. (1651). *Leviathan*. Cambridge, UK: Cambridge University Press.

Stagner, R. (1988). *A history of psychological theories*. New York: Macmillan.

Brennan, J. (1991). *History and systems of psychology*. Englewood Cliffs, NJ: Prentice-Hall.

HOBBES' THEORY OF HUMOR AND LAUGHTER. The "sudden-glory" and "superiority" theory of humor by the English philosopher Thomas Hobbes (1588-1679) represents the first systematic *psychological theory of laughter* ever proposed. In general, Hobbes' philosophy proceeds from a mechanistic view of life where humans by nature are selfish and are constantly at war with each other. Moreover, the fear of violent death is the principle motive that causes men to create a state by contracting to surrender their natural rights and to submit to the absolute authority of a sovereign power. Specifically, *Hobbes' theory of humor* declares that there is a passion which "has no name" (and its outward sign is a distortion of the face known as laughter) and which is always joy. *Hobbes' humor theory* - which is basically a "superiority/social-comparison" theory - states that this passion is nothing else but the "sudden glory" arising from a sudden conception of some eminency in ourselves, or by comparing ourselves with the infirmity of others, or by comparing our present with our past infirmities. Such a *superiority theory of laughter* (which originated in the humor theories of Plato and Aristotle) was cast into its strongest form by Hobbes where individuals are all constantly watching for signs that they are better off than others, or that others are worse off than oneself. In this analysis, the behavior of laughter is nothing but an expression of our "sudden glory" where we realize that in some way we are "superior" to someone else. According to *Hobbes' humor/laughter theory*, those things which cause laughter must be new and unexpected; also, a person who is laughed at essentially is "triumphed over" and, thus, we do not laugh when we or our friends are made the subjects/targets or the butt of jokes and jests. Hobbes disputes the older theory that laughter is mere appreciation of wit; people laugh at indecencies and mishaps where there is no apparent jest or wit at all. Involved in such an analysis, as some of Hobbes' critics have pointed out, is a potential logically-circular argument: Hobbes suggests that there must be some *inner* reason in laughter itself to account for it. However, on the positive side, it was only after some 2,000 years of recorded history concerning the theories of laughter that Hobbes' unique viewpoint emerged. Thus, *Hobbes' theory of humor and laughter* was novel and thought-provoking in that he located - in a *psychological* sense - the "gravitational center" of the laugh *within* the laugher himself or herself. See also ARISTOTLE'S THEORY OF HUMOR; HUMOR, THEORIES OF; PLATO'S THEORY OF HUMOR; SUPERIORITY THEORIES OF HUMOR.

REFERENCES

Hobbes, T. (1650/1839). Human nature. In W. Molesworth (Ed.), *Hobbes' English works*. Cambridge, UK: Cambridge University Press.

Hobbes, T. (1651/1839/1904). *Leviathan*. Cambridge, UK: Cambridge University Press.

HODOLOGICAL/VECTOR PSYCHOLOGY. See LEWIN'S FIELD THEORY.

HÖFFDING STEP/PHENOMENON. See PATTERN/OBJECT RECOGNITION THEORY.

HÖFFDING'S THEORY OF HUMOR/ LAUGHTER. The German philosopher and psychologist Harald Höffding (1843-1931) advanced the notion that laughter - as an expression of pleasant feelings - is possible at a lower stage of consciousness than is involved in the "upper-level" of the appreciation of the ridiculous. According to *Höffding's theory of humor/laughter*, laughter may be aroused, also, by certain physical conditions without being the expression of any emotion (e.g., intense cold may produce laughter as well as shivering). In Höffding's analysis, smiling does not appear until the fourth week after birth, when it is accompanied by various "bleating" sounds; such sounds - together with the smile - develop later into laughter which is considered originally as an expression of satisfaction. Höffding's position on laughter approaches *Hobbes' humor theory* when the former examines how laughter is aroused by the perception of the ludicrous: laughter is primarily an expression of pleasure in general, but - because in the struggle for existence where self-preservation plays a leading role - laughter comes to be the specific expression of the satisfaction of the "instinct" of self-preservation (which Höffding identifies with the love of self). Thus, in *Höffding's theory*, the original sentiment of pure "superiority" may be tempered somewhat by contempt, or by sympathy (in the latter case, one may observe humor). In this sense, *Höffding's humor/laughter theory* may be viewed as a "Hobbes-plus" theory of laughter in which the pure superiority emphasis of Hobbes may be augmented by Höffding's "plus" element of sympathy. One of the most significant features of *Höffding's theory of the ludicrous* is his choice of the *affective* - over the *cognitive* - nature of the contrast involved in a potentially humorous situation. Höffding maintains that in humor one feels great and small at the same time, and sympathy makes laughter humorous, just as it changes fear into reverence. See also HOBBES' THEORY OF HUMOR/LAUGHTER; HUMOR, THEORIES OF.

REFERENCE

Höffding, H. (1887/1891/1896). *Outlines of psychology*. London: Macmillan.

HOLE-IN-THE-HAND ILLUSION. See APPENDIX A.

HOLISTIC THEORY. See GOLDSTEIN'S ORGANISMIC THEORY.

HOLLOW SQUARES ILLUSION. See APPENDIX A, MUNSTERBERG ILLUSION.

HOLMES' REBOUND PHENOMENON/ EFFECT. = rebound phenomenon of Gordon Holmes = Holmes' phenomenon/sign = Gordon Holmes' rebound phenomenon. The Irish clinical neurologist Sir Gordon Morgan Holmes (1876-1965) observed in patients with cerebellar lesions that the forcible motion of the person's limb towards the source of pressure occurs when that pressure is removed suddenly; it is proposed in undiagnosed persons that the *Holmes' rebound effect* may be considered to be a sign of cerebellar damage, and the reaction tests whether cerebellar ability to control coordinated movement has been lost. See also INHIBITION, LAWS OF; LASHLEY'S THEORY; NEURON/NEURAL/NERVE THEORY.

REFERENCE

Holmes, G. M. (1918). [Rebound phenomenon]. *British Journal of Ophthalmology, 2*, 449-468, 506-516.

HOLOGRAPHIC/HOLONOMIC BRAIN THEORY. See PRIBRAM'S HOLOGRAPHIC MODEL.

HOMANS' EXCHANGE THEORY. See EXCHANGE/SOCIAL EXCHANGE THEORY.

HOMEOPATHIC PRINCIPLE. See EMOTIONS, THEORIES/LAWS OF; HOMEOPATHY THEORY.

HOMEOPATHY THEORY. The German physician Christian Friedrich Samuel Hahnemann (1755-1843) developed this unconventional/alternative approach to drug therapy for treating physical and mental disorders that goes back to the Greek physician Hippocrates (c. 460-377 B.C.). The controversial method employed in *homeopathy theory* is based on the practice of administering a drug (that produces a particular pattern of symptoms/disorders in a healthy person) by giving it in an extremely dilute form over time to treat maladies (characterized by similar symptoms/disorders in the healthy individual). In this "like-for-like" or "like-cures-like" form of therapy, one is typically given successive dilutions of the drug where the therapeutic solution eventually contains no ingredients of the original active substance at all. Through such a substance-dilution process, the drugs/solutions are considered to have therapeutic benefits for the recipient or patient. The principles of *homeopathy theory* are diametrically opposed to those of *allopathy theory*, which is a more "orthodox" pharmacological and therapeutic approach for physical and mental disorders, that involves the use of drugs having effects that are *opposite* to those of the disorder, rather than the use of drugs having effects that are *similar* to those of the disorder, as in *homeopathy theory*. Many of Hahnemann's drugs were herbal in origin, and homeopathists today continue to emphasize natural remedies for many physical and mental disorders. See also PLACEBO EFFECT; PYGMALION EFFECT.

REFERENCE

Hahnemann, C. F. S. (1833). *The homeopathic medical doctrine*. Dublin: Wakeman.

HOMEOSTASIS, PRINCIPLE OF. See CONTROL/SYSTEMS THEORY; HUNGER, THEORIES OF.

HOMOEROTICISM THEORIES. See SEXUAL ORIENTATION THEORIES.

HOMOSEXUALITY THEORIES. See SEXUAL ORIENTATION THEORIES.

HOMUNCULUS/SENSORY HOMUNCULUS HYPOTHESES. See WEISMANN'S THEORY.

HONI EFFECT/PHENOMENON. See CONFLICT, THEORIES OF.

HOPELESSNESS THEORY. See SUICIDE, THEORIES OF.

HORIZONTAL-VERTICAL ILLUSION. See APPENDIX A, WUNDT ILLUSION.

HORMIC PSYCHOLOGY. See McDOUGALL'S HORMIC/INSTINCT THEORY/DOCTRINE.

HORMONAL THEORY OF HUNGER. See HUNGER, THEORIES OF.

HORNER'S LAW. See COLOR VISION, THEORIES/LAWS OF.

HORNEY'S THEORY OF PERSONALITY. The German-born American physician and psychiatrist Karen Clementine Danielson Horney (1885-1952) was trained originally in the method of *Freudian psychoanalysis/theory* but she broke away eventually from the standard Freudian orthodoxy over the issue of female sexuality. Where Freud emphasized the concepts of penis envy, jealousy of the male, *libido theory*, and feelings of genital inferiority as determinants in the psychology of women, Horney argued that lack of confidence and overemphasis on the love relationship are at the heart of feminine psychology. Horney retained many of the basic Freudian concepts and methods, such as free association, transference, repression, and resistance, but she - like other analysts (e.g., A. Adler, E. Fromm, and H. S. Sullivan) - stressed the importance of environmental and social factors in developing the personality. She also kept the Freudian doctrine of unconscious motivation and psychic determinism. Horney redefined the meaning of the Freudian oedipal complex (it was anxiety that grew out of the parent-child relationship, not a sexual- aggres-

sive conflict) and aggression (it was security-protection, not an inborn trait). Horney also criticized the Freudian notions of the id, ego, superego, anxiety, masochism, and repetition compulsion. The primary concepts in *Horney's personality theory* are *basic anxiety* and *idealized image*, which are pervasive learned characteristics of the child that result from feeling isolated and helpless in a hostile environment. A powerful drive for parental security and safety arises in the child out of the feeling of *basic anxiety*; the *idealized image* is a fictitious, self-deceiving creation of the individual that expresses discontent with one's "real" self. Horney presented a list of ten *neurotic* (irrational) *needs* that are acquired as a consequence of trying to find solutions to disturbed human relationship problems. These are *neurotic needs* for approval and affection, a partner who will take over one's life, restriction of one's life within narrow borders, power, exploitation of others, prestige, personal admiration, personal achievement, self-sufficiency/independence, and perfection/unassailability. According to Horney, the *neurotic needs* are "insatiable" (the more one gets, the more one wants) and are sources from which inner conflicts develop. Horney classified the *neurotic needs* under the three orientations/headings of "moving toward people," "moving away from people," and "moving against people." It is these orientations where inner conflict develops. Although the "normal" individual is able to resolve the inner conflicts posed by these orientations concerning others by integrating all three orientations, the "neurotic" person develops and utilizes artificial or irrational solutions (cf., Horney's term *shallow living* - a neurotic method of dealing with a conflict by immersing oneself in trivial and distracting activities). Such inner conflicts, however, are avoidable and resolvable if the child is reared in a home that has warmth, trust, love, respect, and tolerance of mistakes. Thus, Horney did not feel that conflict is innate, but that it stems from relationships with parents and other social conditions. *Horney's theory of personality* deals essentially with the dynamics and causes of *neurosis*. She incorporated into her theory a unique synthesis of some of the formulations and concepts both of Sigmund Freud and Alfred Adler. See also ADLER'S THEORY OF PERSONALITY; FREUD'S THEORY OF PERSONALITY; JUNG'S THEORY OF PERSONALITY; LIBIDO THEORY; PERSONALITY THEORIES.

REFERENCES

Freud, S. (1905/1931). Three essays on the theory of sexuality/Female sexuality. In *The standard edition of the complete psychological works of Sigmund Freud*. Vols. 7, 21. London: Hogarth Press.

Horney, K. (1937). *The neurotic personality of our times*. New York: Norton.

Horney, K. (1939). *New ways in psychoanalysis*. New York: Norton.

Horney, K. (1950). *Neurosis and human growth: The struggle toward self-realization*. New York: Norton.

Horney, K. (1967). *Feminine psychology*. New York: Norton.

HORNS EFFECT. See HALO EFFECT.

HOROPTER THEORY. See BERKELEY'S THEORY OF VISUAL SPACE PERCEPTION; PANUM PHENOMENON/EFFECT.

HORWICZ'S THEORY OF ATTENTION. See ATTENTION, LAWS/PRINCIPLES/THEORIES OF.

HULL'S LEARNING THEORY. The American psychologist Clark Leonard Hull (1884-1952) formulated a hypothetico- deductive, behavioristic, reductive, mechanistic, and Darwinian/adaptive learning theory that uses *habit* as its core concept, along with a number of intermediary (*mediational theories*) theoretical constructs called *intervening variables*. The notion of *intervening variables* was first described by the American psychologist Edward C. Tolman (1886-1959) in 1938 [cf., *hypothetical construct* - a conjectured process, event, or entity that contains "surplus meanings" and is not observed directly but is used to explain an observable and measurable phenomenon; in 1948, the American psychologists Kenneth MacCorquodale (1919-1985) and Paul E. Meehl (1920-2003) made a distinction between *hypothetical constructs* and *intervening variables* where the latter refer to variables whose values are determined by a specified manipulation of independent variables *without* any hypotheses about the existence of unobserved entities or processes]. In Hull's system, it is assumed that a given psychological state usually involves multiple causes and multiple effects, and this necessitates the postulation of various *intervening variables* that mediate between observable cause and observable effect events within the organism. For example, Hull describes the *intervening variable* of "thirst" as mediating the input variable of "hours of water deprivation" and the output variable of "amount of water drunk." In his theory, Hull postulates about eight *intervening variables* (such as "habit" or "thirst") and describes their causal input variables. Several *intervening variables* are combined to determine the organism's final behavior observed in problem-solving and conditioning tasks. Among Hull's other theoretical concepts and constructions are *habit strength, drive level, positive associative response strength, negative/inhibitory response strength, conditioned inhibition, reaction potential, net response strength, incentive motivation, drive stimuli, fatigue, general drive pool, evoking-stimulus goodness, anticipatory goal responses, gradient of reinforcement, habit-family hierarchy*, and *fractional anticipatory goal reaction* (cf., Hull's *multiple response principle* - states that an organism will react to a new/novel situation with a number of potential responses already within its behavioral repertoire). In his ambitious behavior theory and program of experimentation, Hull developed sequences of calculational stages, equations, and mathematical derivations that describe both the acquisition and extinction of conditioned responses that, in the abstract, are similar to Ivan Pavlov's notions of behavior as being determined by the subtraction of internal inhibition from excitation and, also, to E. R. Guthrie's ideas of the competition among conditioned responses vis-à-vis the interfering movements evoked by the conditioned stimulus. Hull went beyond E. L. Thorndike's *law of effect* and hypothesized that all primary/biological reinforcers serve to reduce their corresponding drive/need; he concluded that any reduction of a drive may act as a reinforcing event. In his *factor theory* *of learning*, Hull characterizes the complex phenomena of learning in terms of two factors: classical and operant/instrumental conditioning principles that are necessary to explain learning (cf., *factor theory* - based on the work of Sir Francis Galton, any school or theory that analyzes behavioral phenomena in terms of different aspects or factors, and also describes theories based on two separately identifiable processes; for example, physiological and cognitive processes). Criticisms against *Hull's theory* are that it does not have a tractable mathematical system, it has too many parameters to be measured and too weak a measurement theory to get leverage on the quantitative details of his experimental data, and its mathematical derivations are suspect in detail where ad hoc rules are often invented to handle special problems arising in each derivation. On the positive side, Hull's quantitative system and program - which arguably was the most influential of the learning theories between 1930 and 1955 - set the stage for later development in the area of *mathematical learning theory*. Hull also influenced profoundly a number of his students (the "neo-Hullians") and other prominent re-searchers and writers in learning psychology, such as N. E. Miller, O. H. Mowrer, K. Spence, A. Amsel, and F. Logan. See also AMSEL'S HYPOTHESIS AND THEORY; EFFECT, LAW OF; GALTON'S LAWS; GUTHRIE'S THEORY OF BEHAVIOR; LEARNING THEORIES/LAWS; LOGAN'S MICROMOLAR THEORY; MOWRER'S THEORY; PAVLOVIAN CONDITIONING PRINCIPLES/LAWS/THEORIES; SPEN-CE'S THEORY; TOLMAN'S THEORY.

REFERENCES

Hull, C. L. (1932). The goal-gradient hypothesis and maze learning. *Psychological Review, 39*, 25-43.

Hull, C. L. (1938). The goal-gradient hypothesis applied to some "field-force" problems in the behavior of young children. *Psychological Review, 45*, 271-299.

Tolman, E. C. (1938). The determiners of behavior at a choice point. *Psychological Review, 45*, 1-41.

Hull, C. L. (1943). *Principles of behavior.* New York: Appleton-Century-Crofts.

Meehl, P. E., & MacCorquodale, K. (1948). On a distinction between hypothetical constructs and intervening variables. *Psychological Review, 55*, 95-107.

Hull, C. L. (1951). *Essentials of behavior.* New Haven, CT: Yale University Press.

Hull, C. L. (1952). *A behavior system: An introduction to behavior theory concerning the individual organism.* New Haven, CT: Yale University Press.

Seward, J. (1954). Hull's system of behavior: An evaluation. *Psychological Review, 61*, 145-159.

Cotton, J. (1955). On making predictions from Hull's theory. *Psychological Review, 62*, 303-314.

HULL-SPENCE THEORY OF DISCRIMINATION. See SPENCE'S THEORY.

HUMAN DIALOGIC INTERACTION THEORY. See MIRROR NEURONS THEORY.

HUMANIST THEORIES. See MASLOW'S THEORY OF PERSONALITY; ROGERS' THEORY OF PERSONALITY.

HUMAN PROBLEM SOLVING THEORY. See PROBLEM SOLVING AND CREATIVITY STAGE THEORIES.

HUME'S PROBLEM. See NULL HYPOTHESIS.

HUMORAL/HUMORS THEORY. See GALEN'S DOCTRINE OF THE FOUR TEMPERAMENTS.

HUMOR ELICITATION, THEORY OF. See WYER AND COLLINS' THEORY OF HUMOR ELICITATION.

HUMOR, THEORIES OF. In considering the psychological nature of humor, a distinction often is made among the concepts *humor,*

wit, and *laughter/smiling*. In the simplest terms, *wit* refers to intellectual brilliance and quickness in perception that is frequently associated with expressing ideas in an entertaining fashion. *Humor*, on the other hand, refers to a disposition to view the comical, the ludicrous, the ridiculous, or the absurd in a suggestive and sympathetic way regarding human frailties and failings. Although both *humor* and *wit* are internal, dispositional states (technically called "intervening variables" or "hypothetical constructs"), the occurrence of laughter/smiling is an external, observable response or behavior (technically called a "dependent variable"). Historically, theories of *humor*, *wit*, and *laughter* abound and cut across many disciplines including literature, anthropology, sociology, philosophy, and psychology. *Theories of humor* have been assigned to various functional categories such as behavioral theories, cognitive/perceptual theories, psychodynamic/psychoanalytical theories, social/cultural theories, superiority theories, incongruity theories, release-from-tension/restraint theories, ambivalence theories, biological/instinct/evolution theories, surprise theories, configurational theories, neoclassical theories, modern theories, conflict theories, dualistic theories, and semantic/content analytical theories. Humor may derive, also, from self-disparagement, as well as disparagement of others (cf., the German word *Schadenfreude*, which refers to malicious enjoyment of someone else's misfortunes, and embodies a type of humor). In so-called "gallows humor," humor may occur in the context of death or disaster, and involve macabre or comical types of inappropriate behavior. A brief survey (alphabetically arranged with major proponents in parentheses) of a few dozen *humor theories* - expressed epigrammatically with general, or slogan-like, labels (Bergler, 1956) - are listed in Appendix B. See also APTE'S THEORY OF HUMOR/LAUGHTER; APTER'S REVERSAL THEORY OF HUMOR; ARISTOTLE'S THEORY OF HUMOR; BAIN'S THEORY OF HUMOR/LAUGHTER; BEHAVIORAL THEORIES OF HUMOR/LAUGHTER; BERGLER'S THEORY OF HUMOR AND LAUGHTER; BERGSON'S THEORY OF HUMOR AND LAUGHTER; CICERO'S THEORY OF HUMOR; COGNITIVE THEORIES OF HUMOR; COGNITIVE AND PERCEPTUAL THEORIES OF HUMOR; COGNITIVE-SALIENCE MODEL OF HUMOR; CONFIGURATIONAL THEORIES OF HUMOR; CONNECTIONIST MODEL OF HUMOR; DARWIN-HECKER HYPOTHESIS OF LAUGHTER/HUMOR; DARWIN'S THEORY OF LAUGHTER AND HUMOR; DESCARTES THEORY OF HUMOR/LAUGHTER; DUPREEL'S SOCIOLOGICAL HUMOR AND LAUGHTER THEORY; EASTMAN'S THEORY OF LAUGHTER; FREUD'S THEORY OF WIT AND HUMOR; GREIG'S THEORY OF LAUGHTER; GRUNER'S GAME THEORY OF HUMOR; HARTLEY'S THEORY OF HUMOR/LAUGHTER; HOBBES' THEORY OF HUMOR/LAUGHTER; HÖFFDING'S THEORY OF HUMOR/LAUGHTER; HUTCHESON'S THEORY OF HUMOR; INCONGRUITY/INCONSISTENCY THEORIES OF HUMOR; INNER EYE THEORY OF LAUGHTER; JOUBERT'S THEORY OF LAUGHTER/HUMOR; KIERKEGAARD'S THEORY OF HUMOR; KOESTLER'S THEORY OF HUMOR/LAUGHTER; LANGUAGE ORIGINS, THEORIES OF; LATTA'S COGNITIVE-SHIFT THEORY OF HUMOR; LUDOVICI'S THEORY OF LAUGHTER; MARTINEAU'S SOCIAL/COMMUNICATION MODEL OF HUMOR; McDOUGALL'S THEORY OF HUMOR; MORREALL'S THEORY OF HUMOR/LAUGHTER; MOTIVATIONAL THEORIES OF HUMOR; NONPSYCHOANALYTIC HUMOR AND LAUGHTER THEORIES; ORING'S THEORY OF HUMOR; PIDDINGTON'S COMPENSATORY HUMOR THEORY; PLATO'S THEORY OF HUMOR; QUINTILIAN'S THEORY OF HUMOR; RAPP'S THEORY OF THE ORIGINS OF LAUGHTER/HUMOR; RELIEF AND TENSION-RELEASE THEORIES OF HUMOR AND LAUGHTER; SANTAYANA'S THEORY OF HUMOR; SCHOPENHAUER'S THEORY OF HUMOR; SIDIS' LAW OF LAUGHTER; SOCIAL/COMMUNICATION THEORY OF LAUGHTER; SPENCER'S THEORY OF LAUGHTER AND HUMOR; SULLY'S THEORY OF LAUGHTER/HUMOR; SUPERIORITY THEORIES OF HU-

MOR; SURPRISE THEORIES OF HUMOR; THERAPEUTIC THEORY OF LAUGH-TER/HUMOR; VEATCH'S THEORY OF HUMOR; WEISFELD'S ADAPTIVE/EVO-LUTIONARY AND ETHOLOGICAL HU-MOR THEORY; WYER AND COLLINS' THEORY OF HUMOR ELICITATION.

REFERENCES

Bergler, E. (1956). *Laughter and the sense of humor.* New York: International Medical Book Corporation.

Schmidt, H. E., & Williams, D. I. (1971). The evolution of theories of humor. *Journal of Behavioral Science, 1,* 95-106.

Roeckelein, J. E. (2002). *The psychology of humor.* Westport, CT: Greenwood Press.

HUMPHREY'S LAW. See STROOP EF-FECT/INTERFERENCE EFFECT/STROOP TEST.

HUMPHREY'S PARADOX. See ARPEG-GIO PARADOX.

HUNGER-PANG THEORY. See HUN-GER, THEORIES OF.

HUNGER, THEORIES OF. An operational definition of the term *hunger* is the internal state that results from food deprivation and whose severity is measured by the duration of the deprivation. In terms of physiology, the state of hunger results from particular imbalances in nutrients in the body whose severity is determined by the degree of imbalance. The American physiologist Walter Bradford Cannon (1871-1945) introduced the useful *principle of homeostasis* (i.e., the body's natural tendency to maintain equilibrium among its various states, such as temperature and glucose level) to help understand the motivational aspects of organisms. Early *theories of hunger* focused on the *peripheral factors* in eating such as the way in which eating behavior is regulated where the obvious locus is the stomach and the digestive tract. It had been known for a long time that an empty stomach displays vigorous contractions in addition to the peristaltic movements that occur normally during the digestion/processing of food. One of the

first formal theories of hunger, called the *stomach-contraction theory*, the *local stimulus theory*, or the *hunger-pang theory* (Cannon & Washburne, 1912) asserts that the stomach's contractions are signals to the central nervous system concerning hunger where the behavioral regulation of food intake results from such *peripheral* information from the stomach. However, Cannon's commonsense *stomach-contraction theory* has been discredited by evidence from animal studies where the sensory pathways leading from the stomach muscles to the brain and motor pathways leading from the brain to the stomach muscles were severed surgically. Stomach contractions do occur, under normal circumstances, when one experiences hunger and may become important conditioned stimuli for eating, but they do not appear to be essential. It seems that hunger and satiety originate in brain mechanisms that collect information about the body's energy supply. Along these lines, the most widely accepted theory of hunger, the *lateral hypothalamus/feeding center theory*, or the *hypothalamic theory* (Stellar, 1954), holds that hunger is proportional to the neural activity in the lateral hypothalamus (LH) region of the brain, an area that is implicated, also, in the regulation of thirst (cf., the *gonadostat theory* - posits that there is a hypothetical mechanism in which testicular or ovarian hormones regulate secretions in the pituitary and hypothalamic regions). Satiety, according to the *food-satiation theory*, is caused by the activation of the immediately adjacent medial/ventromedial hypothalamus (VMH). In simple terms, the LH area is seen as a "turn-on" eating center, and the VMH is viewed as a "turn-off" eating center. Many puzzling questions have been asked about the *hypothalamic theory* of hunger and energy regulation. Damage to the LH abolishes eating in experimental animals; however, it is not clear that the effect is necessarily attributed to destruction of a hunger center rather than to an interruption of some of the major pathways through the area. The *hypothalamic theory* is widely accepted today because no viable alternatives have been offered. Concerning the question of how the hypothalamus is apprised of the state of constantly changing nutrients, the *glucostatic theory* (Mayer, 1955; cf., G. Kennedy's hy-

pothesized *lipostat mechanism*) suggests that the extent of glucose utilization in body cells is monitored by special "glucoreceptors" in the VMH (an earlier hypothesis - that simply the level of glucose in the bloodstream is important - had to be discarded because evidence from diabetic individuals showed them actually to eat more, rather than less as the *blood-glucose theory* would have predicted). Another theory of hunger, the *thermostatic theory* (Brobeck, 1948) proposes that animals eat to maintain their body temperature and stop eating to prevent hyperthermia. However, although environmental temperature does affect food and water regulation, there is no evidence that internal temperature changes are responsible for such regulation. The *restrained-eating hypothesis* states that people who are obese are oversensitive to external food cues, and are more likely to eat foods that are available easily even when they are not hungry, as compared to individuals who are not obese and who can ignore food cues, and who generally eat only when hungry (cf., Schachter, 1968, 1971). The *yo-yo effect* - in the context of eating/hunger, refers to the recurrent changes and reversions to the original where the person loses weight and then regains it; this effect is frequently due to the fact that weight gain occurs more easily with repeated cycles of weight loss. A *hormonal theory of hunger* (Davis, Gallagher, Ladove, & Turausky, 1969) holds that there is a hormonal inhibition of eating that is mediated through the blood supply. The *chemical profile theory* (Myers, 1975) suggests that a whole range of substances, making up a chemical "profile" reflecting the metabolic condition of the body, affect brain mechanisms controlling feeding and hunger. Another theory, the *energy metabolism theory* (Friedman & Stricker, 1976), maintains that the stimulus for hunger should be sought among changes that occur in the supply of metabolic fuels rather than in the utilization of specific nutrients or in levels of fuel reserves. The *peripheral theories of hunger* point to a variety of oropharyngeal and postingestional, gastric, and humoral factors in hunger. Each of these undoubtedly plays some role in the regulation of food intake; none of these, however, can be considered as critical or as the sole

determinant of hunger. One theory that integrates the diverse findings on hunger, eating, and weight, called the *set-point theory* (Keesey, 1980), suggests that a homeostatic mechanism that regulates food intake, fat reserves, and metabolism operates to keep an organism at its predetermined weight. According to *set-point theory*, which was first suggested by research with laboratory rats, no single area in the brain keeps track of weight. Rather, an interaction of metabolism, fat cells, and hormones keeps people at the weight for which their bodies are designed. A common, persistent psychological theory holds that being overweight is a sign of emotional disturbance, but research has failed to support this popular belief. However, tension and irritability can result from constant dieting (being hungry much of the time), and unhappiness can result from being heavy in a society that discriminates against people who weigh more than the cultural ideal. Culture and ethnic background contribute, also, to understanding hunger and eating behavior; for example, how often one eats, what foods one eats, and with whom one eats are important social-cultural influences in the dynamics of hunger. See also THIRST, THEORIES OF.

REFERENCES

Cannon, W. B., & Washburne, A. (1912). An explanation of hunger. *American Journal of Physiology, 29*, 444-454.

Cannon, W. B. (1934). Hunger and thirst. In C. Murchison (Ed.), *Handbook of general experimental psychology*. Worcester, MA: Clark University Press.

Brobeck, J. (1948). Food intake as a mechanism of temperature regulation in rats. *Federation Proceedings, American Physiological Society, 7*, 13.

Kennedy, G. (1953). The role of depot fat in the hypothalamic control of food intake in the rat. *Proceedings of the Royal Society of London, 140*, 578-592.

Stellar, E. (1954). The physiology of motivation. *Psychological Review, 61*, 15-42.

Mayer, J. (1955). Regulation of energy intake and the body weight: The glucostatic theory and the lipostatic the-

ory. *Annals of the New York Academy of Sciences, 63*, 15-42.

Teitelbaum, P., & Epstein, A. (1962). The lateral hypothalamic syndrome: Recovery of feeding and drinking after lateral hypothalamic lesions. *Psychological Review, 69*, 74-90.

Schachter, S. (1968). Obesity and eating. *Science, 161*, 751-756.

Davis, J., Gallagher, R., Ladove, R., & Turausky, A. (1969). Inhibition of food intake by a humoral factor. *Journal of Comparative and Physiological Psychology, 67*, 407-414.

Schachter, S. (1971). Some extraordinary facts about obese humans and rats. *American Psychologist, 26*, 129-144.

Grossman, S. (1975). Role of the hypothalamus in the regulation of food and water intake. *Psychological Review, 82*, 200-224.

Myers, R. (1975). Brain mechanisms in the control of feeding: A new neurochemical profile theory. *Pharmacology, Biochemistry, and Behavior, 3*, 75-83.

Friedman, M., & Stricker, E. (1976). The physiological psychology of hunger: A physiological perspective. *Psychological Review, 83*, 409-431.

Keesey, R. (1980). A set-point anslysis of the regulation of body weight. In A. Stunkard (Ed.), *Obesity*. Philadelphia: Saunders.

Polivy, J., & Herman, C. P. (2002). Causes of eating disorders. *Annual Review of Psychology, 53*, 187-213.

HUNTER-McCRARY LAW. See SERIAL-POSITION EFFECT.

HURVICH-JAMESON COLOR VISION THEORY. See HERING-HURVICH-JAMESON COLOR VISION THEORY.

HUTCHESON'S THEORY OF HUMOR. In his theory of humor, the British philosopher Francis Hutcheson (1694-1746) distinguishes between *laughter* and *ridicule* in which the latter is only a subspecies of the former. In Hutcheson's view, the occasion of laughter is the opposition or contrast of dignity and meanness. *Hutcheson's theory of humor* is based on the association of ideas (a phenomenon that was much discussed in the 18th century), and it suggests that comic genius is largely the ability to use somewhat inappropriate metaphors and similes to produce ideas that clash with each other. In this sense, then, Hutcheson may be said to have at least the beginnings of an *incongruity theory of humor*. Concerning the functions and value of humor, Hutcheson maintained that humor gives pleasure, it promotes mental flexibility, and it acts as a social facilitator. On occasion, Hutcheson took elaborate pains to refute *Hobbes' theory of humor*, using many counterexamples to show that there is *no* essential connection between having feelings of *superiority* and laughing or being amused. Thus, according to Hutcheson's approach, having feelings of *superiority* is neither a necessary nor a sufficient condition for experiencing humor. See also HOBBES' THEORY OF HUMOR/ LAUGHTER; HUMOR, THEORIES OF; IN-CONGRUITY/ INCONSISTENCY THEORIES OF HUMOR; SUPERIORITY THEORIES OF HUMOR.

REFERENCE

Hutcheson, F. (1750). *Reflections upon laughter*. Glasgow: Urie.

HUTT'S MICRODIAGNOSIS THEORY. See CUMULATIVE DEFICITS PHENOMENON/THEORY.

HUYGEN'S WAVE THEORY OF LIGHT. See VISION/SIGHT, THEORIES OF.

HYATT'S ANAGENESIS THEORY. See DEVELOPMENTAL THEORY.

HYBRID THEORY. See LOGAN'S MICROMOLAR THEORY.

HYDRAULIC THEORY. This general notion - which underlies several theories that model the phenomena under study using a *hydraulic* or *pressure principle* - refers to the assumption that things behave like fluids under pressure and are ready to break through any weak spots in a boundary, barrier, or border should the pressure exceed some critical level. Examples of such *hydraulic theories* are

the German-American psychologist Max Meyer's (1873-1967) *theory of hearing*, Sigmund Freud's *personality theory*, and the *ethological theory* of the Austrian ethologist Konrad Z. Lorenz (1903-1989) and the Dutch ethologist Nikolaas Tinbergen (1907-1988). In one case, in *Lorenz's hydraulic model of aggression*, it is hypothesized that stored instinctual energy needs to be discharged and, once discharged, a refractory period is required for buildup because the full store of emotional energy is flushed (comparable to flushing a toilet). Lorenz claimed that aggressive behavior may detonate spontaneously, even in the absence of a stimulus, because of the operation of a hypothetical "innate releasing mechanism." See also AGGRESSION, THEORIES OF; ALEXANDER'S PRINCIPLE OF SURPLUS ENERGY; AUDITION/ HEARING, THEORIES OF; FREUD'S THEORY OF PERSONALITY; INFANT ATTACHMENT THEORIES; SPENCER'S THEORY OF LAUGHTER/HUMOR.

REFERENCES

Meyer, M. (1928). The hydraulic principles governing the function of the cochlea. *Journal of General Psychology, 1*, 239-265.

Freud, S. (1953-1964). *The standard edition of the complete psychological works of Sigmund Freud.* J. Strachey (Ed.), 24 vols. London: Hogarth Press.

Lorenz, K. Z. (1966). *On aggression.* New York: Harcourt Brace Jovanovich.

HYDRAULIC THEORY OF HUMOR. See FREUD'S THEORY OF WIT/HUMOR; HYDRAULIC THEORY; SPENCER'S THEORY OF LAUGHTER/HUMOR.

HYPHEN PSYCHOLOGIST. See SKINNER'S OPERANT CONDITIONING THEORY.

HYPNIC-JOLTS EFFECT/PHENOMENON. See SLEEP, THEORIES OF.

HYPNOSIS/HYPNOTISM, THEORIES OF. The British surgeon James Braid (1795-1860) is credited by some writers to be the discoverer of *hypnosis* (Braid actually first introduced the term *hypnosis* in 1852), and

others hold that the German physician Franz Anton Mesmer (1734-1815) should be recognized as the founding father of modern *hypnosis* (which Mesmer called *animal magnetism*). It was Braid's idea that *hypnosis* is really nothing more than suggestion, and his significance for psychology is that he took the phenomenon out of the area of mystical explanation and placed it on a physical basis (cf., *special process hypothesis* - holds that an individual's behavior when under hypnosis is different qualitatively than that of when the person is not under hypnosis). Mesmer applied the *principles of magnetism* developed in physics to the problems of mental health; his method was to have patients grasp metal rods that protruded from a tub of water filled with iron filings, join hands with other patients, and wait for Mesmer to "lay hands on" them as they became "hypnotized." However, a number of experiments conducted in Paris in 1784, headed by the American statesman and ambassador Benjamin Franklin (1706-1790), led to the demise of Mesmer's *animal magnetism theory*. The phenomenon of *hypnosis* was known, also, and practiced by the British surgeon James Esdaile (1808-1859) in India, where he performed over 1,000 operations using hypnosis as his only anesthesia; by the English physician John Elliotson (1791-1868), who employed hypnosis in the treatment of a wide variety of medical disorders; by the Frenchmen A. Liebeault, H. Bernheim, and J. M. Charcot, who experimented and published papers on the use of hypnosis in therapy; and by Sigmund Freud and Josef Breuer in Vienna, who used hypnosis to help patients emotionally relive their early childhood traumas (a process called *abreaction*). Bernheim, like Braid, viewed hypnosis as a manifestation of suggestibility, and this persistent idea became the subject matter of a major research program on hypnosis conducted by the American learning theorist Clark Hull. Other notable practitioners of hypnosis and hypnotherapy were G. Simmel in Germany and J. Hadfield in England, who treated war neuroses during World War I; J. Watkins, who treated battle casualties during World War II; and M. Erickson, who made refinements in the use of hypnosis and expanded its use for a number of personality and behavioral disorders, including dentistry. Many modern counterparts to all the early developments in *hypnosis theory* still exist today and contribute to both the skepticism and enthusiasm of the phenomenon (cf., *nonstate theories of hypnosis* - hold that some people do things automatically by suggestion, which is similar to being under hypnosis, and that such individuals are not in a unique state of consciousness but, rather, are under the power of social pressure factors and influence; *state theories of hypnosis* - posit that for hypnosis to be genuine, the individual must first be placed in a "trance"). Few terms in the psychological lexicon are so thoroughly wrapped in confusion and mysticism as is the term *hypnosis*. The logical positivist and the cautious scientist find that it is difficult to give a satisfactory definition of *hypnosis*, and many of the arguments over the nature of the *theory of hypnosis* depend on which aspects one emphasizes: the hypnotist-patient/subject relationship, the type of suggestions given regarding cognitive, perceptual, and affective distortion, or the ability of some individuals to "relinquish control" temporarily. I. Kirsch and S. J. Lynn suggest that all current *theories of hypnosis*, including the social-cognitive model, are provisional and incomplete; however, the *multiple streams of consciousness hypothesis* and the *hypnotic state hypothesis* need to be abandoned because they are not well supported by data or research in social/cognitive psychology and, in their place, it is suggested that theoretical formulations be employed that are based on concepts such as "response sets," "hierarchical control systems," "associative memory networks," "automatic activation of behavior," "response expectancy," "intention," and "motivation" (cf., Kihlstrom, 1998; Woody & Sadler, 1998). Given such qualifications, a number of standardized scales have been developed and used to measure hypnotic states (e.g., the Stanford Hypnotic Susceptibility Scales; the Harvard Group Scale of Hypnotic Susceptibility). Also, dreams may be initiated when under hypnosis, and persons may report dreams in detail that were forgotten apparently in the conscious, waking state. Research by the American psychologist Ernest R. Hilgard (1904-2001) on "hypnotic analgesia" - which deals with the conscious perception of pain -

led to his formulation of the *neodissociation theory of hypnosis*, involving the concepts of *divided consciousness* and *hidden observer* whereby multiple control systems of thought and action are hypothesized as operating independently of each other. A *hidden observer* is a conjectured, concealed consciousness that is inferred to experience events differently from the hypnotized consciousness, although they operate in a parallel fashion. Hilgard's notion of a *hidden observer* impacts directly on certain central issues in cognitive psychology, such as the problem of serial versus parallel processing of information. The phenomenon of a *hidden observer* appears to be similar to the concept of *ego-state/ego-state theory* (Watkins, 1994). The typical hypnotizable individual does not seem to be weak-willed, gullible, hysterical, passive, or submissive to the dominant personage of the hypnotist. Rather, he or she (there seem to be no gender/sex differences on this issue) is an individual who has the capacity to become totally absorbed in some particular fantasy or ongoing experience and has a considerable ability to empathize with other people, both real and fictitious (cf., *Doppelganger phenomenon* - the delusion or fantasy that an exact double, twin, or alter ego exists and who looks, and acts, the same as the person who has the fantasy; *real-simulator model* - an experimental design in which some participants are instructed to simulate hypnosis or some other psychological state, whereas other participants genuinely experience the phenomenon; and *role-enactment theory* - states that people who are hypnotized and requested to behave in ways they may not ordinarily act, may be complying with the hypnotist's directives without conscious intent, rather than truly being in a "trance;" Sarbin & Coe, 1972). Cognitive flexibility seems to be the hallmark of the hypnotizable person. Due to its methodological sophistication, contemporary hypnosis research is significant in its contributions to general psychological theory (e.g., Barber, 1969; Sheehan & Perry, 1976; Orne, 1979). *Hypnotherapy* has been used successfully as a treatment for many diverse clinical maladies, among which are the control of pain in general, relief of anxiety, postsurgical depression, impotence, and frigidity. When used in a research context, there are potential limitations to the validity of hypnosis-related data, such as possible *deception or faking* on the part of the participant concerning the execution of hypnotic instructions, possible *demand characteristics of the situation* where participants are unconsciously predisposed to perform in ways they believe the experimenter expects, possible lack of *external validity* (i.e., generalizability of results to the population at large) through the use of specially selected participants (e.g., using only high-scoring persons on standard tests of hypnotic susceptibility), and the extensive use of *small sample sizes* in studies involving hypnosis. See also DISSOCIATION THEORY; EXPERIMENTER EFFECTS; FREUD'S THEORY OF PERSONALITY.

REFERENCES

Mesmer, F. A. (1799). *Memoir*. New York: Eden Press.

Braid, J. (1843). *Neurohypnology, or the rationale of nervous sleep considered in relation with animal magnetism*. London: Redway.

Elliotson, J. (1843). *Numerous cases of surgical operations without pain in the mesmeric state*. Philadelphia: Lea & Blanchard.

Esdaile, J. (1847). *Hypnosis in medicine and surgery*. New York: Julian Press.

Liebeault, A. (1866). *Du sommeil et das etats analogues, consideres surtout au point de vue de l'action du moral sur le physique*. Paris: Masson.

Bernheim, H. (1886/1964). *Hypnosis and suggestibility in psychotherapy: A treatise on the nature and use of hypnosis*. New Hyde Park, NY: University Books.

Charcot, J. (1890). *Complete works*. Vol. 9. *Metalotherapie et hypnotisme*. Paris: Fourneville & Brissand.

Freud, S., & Breuer, J. (1892). On the psychical mechanism of hysterical phenomena. In *Collected papers*. Vol. 1. London: Hogarth Press.

Hull, C. L. (1933). *Hypnosis and suggestibility*. New York: Appleton-Century.

Barber, T. X. (1969). *Hypnosis: A scientific approach*. New York: Van Nostrand Reinhold.

Sarbin, T. R., & Coe, W. C. (1972). *Hypnosis: A social psychological analysis of influence communication*. New York: Holt, Rinehart, and Winston.

Sheehan, P., & Perry, C. (1976). *Methodologies of hypnosis: A critical appraisal of contemporary paradigms of hypnosis*. New York: Wiley.

Hilgard, E. R. (1977). *Divided consciousness: Multiple controls in human thought and action*. New York: Wiley.

Orne, M. (1979). On the simulating subject as a quasi-control group in hypnosis research: What, why, and how. In E. Fromm & R. Shor (Eds.), *Hypnosis: Developments in research and new perspectives*. New York: Aldine.

Kihlstrom, J. F. (1998). Dissociations and dissociation theory in hypnosis. *Psychological Bulletin, 123*, 186-191.

Kirsch, I., & Lynn, S. J. (1998). Dissociation theories of hypnosis. *Psychological Bulletin, 123*, 100-115, 198-202.

Woody, E., & Sadler, P. (1998). On reintegrating dissociated theories. *Psychological Bulletin, 123*, 192-197.

HYPNOTHERAPY, THEORIES OF. See HYPNOSIS/HYPNOTISM, THEORIES OF.

HYPOCRISY THEORY. See PERSUASION/INFLUENCE THEORIES.

HYPOTHALAMIC THEORY. See HUNGER, THEORIES OF.

HYPOTHESIS-TESTING THEORY. See CONSTRUCTIVIST THEORY OF PERCEPTION; NULL HYPOTHESIS.

HYPOTHESIS THEORY. See PERCEPTION (II. COMPARATIVE APPRAISAL), THEORIES OF.

HYPOTHETICAL CONSTRUCTS. See HULL'S LEARNING THEORY.

HYPOTHETICO-DEDUCTIVE LEARNING THEORY. See BEHAVIORIST THEORY; HULL'S LEARNING THEORY.

I

ICEBERG PRINCIPLE. See DECISION-MAKING THEORIES.

ICEBLOCK THEORY. See LEWIN'S FIELD THEORY.

ICONIC MEMORY/STORE. See SHORT-TERM AND LONG-TERM MEMORY, THEORIES OF.

IDEALISM, DOCTRINE OF. See REALISM, DOCTRINE OF.

IDEAS, THEORY OF. See ARISTOTLE'S DOCTRINES/THEORIES.

IDENTICAL ELEMENTS AND COMPONENTS THEORY. See ESTES' STIMULUS SAMPLING THEORY; TRANSFER OF TRAINING, THORNDIKE'S THEORY OF.

IDENTICAL VISUAL DIRECTION, LAW OF. See VISION/SIGHT, THEORIES OF.

IDENTIFIABILITY PRINCIPLE. See TRANSFER OF TRAINING, THORNDIKE'S THEORY OF.

IDENTIFICATION THEORY. The Austrian-born psychoanalysts Sigmund Freud (1856-1939) and Anna Freud (1895-1982) both described and developed *identification theory*. In the former case (Sigmund), *identification* refers to the deliberate adoption of another person's behavior as one's own and, in the jargon of psychoanalysis, it is called a "defense mechanism" (i.e., a psychic guard against anxiety) whereby one unconsciously incorporates the attributes of another person (usually a parental figure) into one's own personality. In the latter case (Anna), the term *identification with the aggressor* is a "defense mechanism" employed in situations whereby an individual facing an external threat (e.g., disapproval or criticism from a parent or au-

thority figure) identifies with the source of the threat, either by seizing/embracing the aggression or by adopting other aspects of the threatening figure (e.g., some prisoners in Nazi concentration camps during World War II came to identify with their guards). Psychoanalysts typically argue that the *identification* mechanism plays an important role in the early development of the "superego" (conscience) before criticism is turned inward at a later stage of psychosexual development. Other theoretical psychoanalytic terms related to *identification* are: *primary identification* - a primitive form of identification that occurs during the oral stage of psychosexual development before any other kind of "object-relationship" (i.e., a relationship experienced, or an emotion directed, by the person's ego towards an "instinctual object") is formed; *secondary identification* - the identification that may occur after the establishment of an initial "object-relationship;" *projective identification* - according to the Austrian psychoanalyst Melanie Klein (1882-1960), a childish fantasy in which one inserts oneself into an "instinctual object" in order to control, possess, or harm it (e.g., a child's fantasy of invading its mother's body and sadistically attacking it); *introjection* - according to the Hungarian psychoanalyst Sandor Ferenczi (1873-1933), a defense mechanism whereby an "instinctual object" is symbolically (or in fantasy) absorbed by an individual, or "instinctual energy" is turned inward (e.g., a depressed person may turn aggression back on the self); and *incorporation* - a defense mechanism whereby an individual mentally ingests/swallows another person; it has an "instinctual goal" that is characteristic of the oral stage of psychosexual development, and it provides a model for the mechanisms of *identification* and *introjection*. See also FREUD'S THEORY OF PERSONALITY.

REFERENCES

Freud, S. (1921/1960). *Group psychology and the analysis of the ego*. New York: Bantam Books.

Freud, S. (1923/1962). *The ego and the id*. New York: Norton.

Klein, M. (1932). *The psychoanalysis of children*. London: Hogarth Press.

Freud, A. (1937/1946). *The ego and the mechanisms of defense.* New York: International Universities Press.

Bettelheim, B. (1943). Individual and mass behavior in extreme situations. *Journal of Abnormal and Social Psychology, 38,* 417-452.

Ferenczi, S. (1950-1955). *Selected papers.* 3 vols. New York: Basic Books.

Balint, M. (1952). *Primary love and psychoanalytic technique.* London: Hogarth Press.

Klein, M. (1952). On the theory of anxiety and guilt. In J. Riviere (Ed.), *Developments in psychoanalysis.* London: Hogarth Press.

IDENTITY DISRUPTION MODEL. The *identity disruption model* (Brown & McGill, 1989) is a variant of "self-consistency theory" and states that life events impact negatively on one's health because they disrupt the individual's identity, causing disturbances in the *self-concept.* The model - when applied to positive life events - proposes that the occurrence of such events threatens the self-view of *low* self-esteem persons, and thus places them at risk for health problems. For example, if a student with a poor academic image experiences a positive college event (such as personal academic achievement), such an event would lead to a disruption of the "poor student" identity - creating uncertainty regarding the self - and have possible negative health consequences. However, for *high* self-esteem persons, the *identity disruption model* predicts increases in health for positive life events. See also SELF-CONCEPT THEORY; SELF-CONSISTENCY/SELF-ENHANCEMENT THEORIES.

REFERENCE

Brown, J. D., & McGill, K. L. (1989). The cost of good fortune: When positive life events produce negative health consequences. *Journal of Personality and Social Psychology, 57,* 1103-1110.

IDENTITY HYPOTHESIS THEORY/ PRINCIPLE. See MIND-BODY THEORIES; THOUGHT, LAWS OF.

IDEOMOTOR THEORIES. See EXEMPLAR THEORY OF BEHAVIORAL CHOICE.

IDIODYNAMICS DOCTRINE. See IDIOGRAPHIC/NOMOTHETIC LAWS.

IDIOGENETIC THEORY. See MIND-BODY THEORIES; MIND AND MENTAL STATES, THEORIES OF.

IDIOGRAPHIC/NOMOTHETIC LAWS. The term *idiographic* (from the Greek word meaning "separate" or "distinct" relates to the unique and individualistic approach in science and is usually contrasted with the term *nomothetic* (from the Greek word meaning "general," "universal," or "abstract"), which refers to general scientific laws of nature. In simple terms, *idiographic* refers to the specific case, and *nomothetic* refers to the general perspective (cf., the *idiodynamics doctrine* - states that an individual attends to the environmental factors considered to be relevant to behavior, where the person selects out stimuli and organizes responses and, thus, demonstrates that one is in charge of one's own life even at the habit level). In the psychological literature, the synonymous terms *idiographic laws, idiographic theory, ideographic approach, idiographic psychology,* and *idiographic science* are used, as well as the counterpart terms *nomothetic laws, nomothetic theory, nomothetic approach, nomothetic psychology,* and *nomothetic science.* In terms of research strategy, psychologists may choose to take an *idiographic* or a *nomothetic* approach concerning the descriptions, explanations, and interpretations of their subject matter. The *idiographic-nomothetic* distinction is due originally to the German philosopher Wilhelm Windelband (1848-1915) who distinguished studying phenomena from a *nomothetic* versus an *idiographic* standpoint where the former concentrates on general laws or theories such as demonstrated by the empirical natural sciences, and the latter approach stresses the uniqueness and particularities of the individual case. This distinction has been used recently (Meissner, 1971) to describe Freud's method of psychoanalysis as a scientific hybrid tied into the two combined poles of *nomothetic,* which uses rules, laws, mathematics, physics, and energy, and *idiographic*, which represents ideas by various unique symbols and metaphors for understanding psychological phenomena. An examination of the history of the terms *idiographic* and *nomothetic* shows a conflict between these two models of science where the origins of the debate are traceable to the 18th and 19th centuries in academic disciplines including anthropology, sociology, psychology, history, religion, and geography. Today, there seems to be a renewal of interest in the *idiographic-nomothetic* debate where the basic assumptions concerning the philosophy of science, the goals and purposes of the sciences, and the nature of scientific inquiry are questioned. In the discipline of psychology, the question is asked whether psychology should be a cause-effect (lawful) science that seeks general relational statements (laws) of behavior, or whether it should be a personalistic/interpretive science capable of describing single cases. In the area of personality psychology, the American psychologist Gordon Allport (1897-1967) acknowledged that there is a fundamental difference between the intuitive and scientific views concerning the explanation of human behavior where the terms *idiographic* and *nomothetic* are invoked to emphasize and describe such a dichotomy. Allport attempted to combine and reconcile the two viewpoints where *nomothetic* characteristics may be measured by objective personality tests given to many people, and the *idiographic* approach may employ the individual case study method such as analyzing a person's diary or imaginative writings. The search for uniformity in patterns of human behavior is at the bottom of both the *idiographic* and *nomothetic* approaches, and such uniformities may be discovered and formulated ultimately in a diversity of ways (e.g., correlational, mathematical, structural, descriptive, analytical), and the unyielding adherence to only one theoretical approach or method may be unwise. See also PERSONALISTIC/NATURALISTIC THEORIES OF HISTORY; PERSONALITY THEORIES.

REFERENCES

Dilthey, W. (1894). Ideas concerning a descriptive and analytic psychology. In R. Zaner & K. Heiges (Eds.), *Descriptive psychology and historical understanding*. The Hague: Nijhoff.

Windelband, W. (1921). *An introduction to philosophy*. London: Unwin.

Allport, G. (1929). The study of personality by the intuitive method. *Journal of Abnormal and Social Psychology, 24*, 14-27.

Meissner, W. (1971). Freud's methodology. *Journal of the American Psychoanalytic Association, 19*, 265-309.

Lamiell, J. T. (1998). "Nomothetic" and "idiographic": Contrasting Windelband's understanding with contemporary usage. *Theory and Psychology, 8*, 23-38.

IDIOSYNCRASY-CREDIT MODEL. See LEADERSHIP, THEORIES OF.

ILLUMINATION, LAW OF. See VISION/SIGHT, THEORIES OF.

ILLUSION OF CONTROL THEORY. See ATTRIBUTION THEORY.

ILLUSION OF DOUBLES/FALSE RECOGNITION. See APPENDIX A, CAPGRAS ILLUSION/SYNDROME.

ILLUSIONS/EFFECTS. See APPENDIX A.

ILLUSIONS OF POSITIVE/NEGATIVE DOUBLES. See APPENDIX A, CAPGRAS ILLUSION/SYNDROME.

ILLUSORY CORRELATION EFFECT. See APPENDIX A; PREJUDICE, THEORIES OF.

IMAGELESS THOUGHT THEORY. See WUNDT'S THEORIES/DOCTRINES/PRINCIPLES.

IMAGEN THEORY. See SHORT-TERM AND LONG-TERM MEMORY, THEORIES OF.

IMAGERY LAW OF COMPENSATION/RIVALRY. See IMAGERY/MENTAL IMAGERY, THEORIES OF.

IMAGERY/MENTAL IMAGERY, THEO-RIES OF. In the context of *cognitive* experiences, the term *image* refers to a mental representation of an earlier sensory stimulus or experience and represents a less vivid copy of that event [cf., *imagery law of compensation/rivalry* - proposed by the English psychologist Charles W. Valentine (1879-1964), states that in the aesthetic appreciation of poetry, visual imagery displaces, or is displaced by, auditory imagery, or by emphasized attention to rhythm, sound, or meaning]. When *image* is used to mean a "picture in one's head," it is assumed that this representation is not a literal one but merely acts "as if" one had a mental picture that is an analog of a real-world scene. Also, the *image* in this sense is assumed to be a "construction" or a "synthesis" of an earlier event and not merely a copy of some previously experienced sensory (visual, auditory, tactile, gustatory, or olfactory) stimulus [cf., the discredited *reproduction theory of imagery* proposed by the German psychologist Oswald Kulpe (1862-1918), which holds that an image is a copy or point-by-point reproduction of the original stimulus; the *functional equivalence hypothesis* which is a general proposition that *imagery* - although it does not result from sensory organ stimulation - is basically the same as *perception* in the manner in which it functions; and the *theory of imagery types* (beginning with the work of Sir Francis Galton in 1880) indicates that some persons are strongest in visual imagery, whereas others are strongest in auditory or motor imagery, etc.]. Four different *classes of mental images* have been described: *afterimages* - a perceptual experience that occurs after the original source of stimulation has been removed; *eidetic images* - prolonged mental imagery that is vivid and persistent, commonly called "photographic memory;" *memory/thought images* - images that are fragmented, pallid, indefinitely localized, and of brief duration; and *imagination images* - images that are influenced by motivational states and generally involve concentrated quasi-hypnotic attention along with inhibition of associations; this class includes hypnagogic, perceptual isolation, hallucinogenic drug, and sleep deprivation images. *Afterimages/aftereffects* include the following: *postural aftereffect* - a subjective phenomenon resulting from adoption of an eccentric or abnormal body position for a period of time, and then assuming a normal position whereupon one has the sensation of an abnormal posture that is in the opposite direction to the prior abnormal posture; such an aftereffect is a result of the *perdeviation effect* - a form of postural adaptation where an eccentric body posture held for some time yields the sensation that the posture is normal; the *Kohnstamm effect* [named after the German physician Oskar Kohnstamm (1871-1917)] - refers to a postural aftereffect involving involuntary upward movement of one's arm after standing close to a wall and pressing the back of the hand hard against the wall for about two minutes and then standing away from the wall with the arm hanging loosely; typically, one's arm spontaneously rises into the air in this effect. Around the turn of the 20th century, mental images were mentioned frequently in controversies over cognitive experiences, such as whether *images* are critical to thinking and problem-solving processes. After the waning of interest in *imagery* due to the early influence of behaviorism in psychology in the 1920s, it has become one of the most significant issues in current cognitive psychology. In his *dual-coding model*, A. Paivio suggests that there are two main modes of coding experience: *verbal processes* - which involve a functional symbolic system and are assumed to be auditory/motor; and *imaginal processes* - which constitute the representational mode for nonverbal thinking. Paivio's *dual coding hypothesis* states that higher imagery conditions are so effective in learning and memory because they increase the probability that both imaginable and verbal processes play a mediational role in item retrieval. Both verbal-sequential and imagery-spatial-parallel processing are needed for optimal human functioning. However, because of its concrete/ contextual nature, the *imagery* system appears to be more akin to perception (cf., the *Perky effect* - named after the American female psychologist Cheves West Perky (1874-1940), and refers to the subjective impression of imagery with the objective presence of a physical stimulus; when a person is asked to form a mental image of an object, and a very faint image of the object then is presented on a screen, the projected image may be taken to be the mental image; thus, this is an act of mistaking a physical stimulus for an image of imagination). It has been demonstrated that an image and a percept cannot be distinguished from each other on the basis of their intrinsic qualities. In addition to Paivio's *dual-coding theory*, a number of other *theories/models of mental imagery* have been proposed. For a listing of *theories of imagery*, see Appendix C. All these *theories/models of imagery* may be placed into one of two groups: the *iconophiles* - those who endow mental imagery representations with a special nature, and the *iconophobes* - those who hold that images have no special status concerning intrinsic spatial or pictorial characteristics. The current theoretical differences concerning *mental imagery* focus generally on two related issues: the degree of direct and functional relationships between imagery and thinking, and the nature and extent of the physical/isomorphic processes that underlie mental images in the brain (cf., *health sweep imagery technique* - a method whereby the person conjures up mental pictures of a liquid or other substance flowing through his/her body, typically beginning at the head and going down to the toes; in this way, the individual's malady or disease is imagined as being cleansed from the body; some other similar "sweepings" placed the person's imagery at the cellular level where "good/healthy" cells are imagined - as little soldiers - to be engaging in battle/combat against the "bad/diseased" cells/soldiers; and *psychoneuromuscular theory* - posits that imagery facilitates subsequent performance by innervating one's muscles, analogous to the innervation that is needed for actual performances). Throughout the history of psychology the notions of *mental image* and *mental imagery* have been scrutinized, debated, argued, and criticized. Today, however, there seems to be convincing evidence both for the importance of *mental images* in psychology in general, and for their practical applications in clinical and diagnostic settings, in particular. In a review of the imagery research literature, Roeckelein (2004) cites the following *imagery-related theories*: creativity, emotion, hallucinations, recognition, sex- versus gender-differences, consciousness, imagery types, identical points, image complexes, image formation, imagistic representation, mind, perceptual development, projection, reflection, rhetoric, thinking, and visual perception; and the following *imagery-related laws*: afterimages, coexistence, comparative judgment, compensation/rivalry, contiguity, development, mnemic causality, perseveration, physical causality, reintegration, similarity, succession, transition, association, ideation, relationships, and reproductive imagination. See also FORGETTING/MEMORY, THEORIES OF; HEBB'S THEORY; NEW STRUCTURALISM THEORY/PARADIGM; PERCEPTION (II. COMPARATIVE APPRAISAL), THEORIES OF.

REFERENCES

Galton, F. (1880). Statistics of mental imagery. *Mind, 5*, 301-318.

Perky, C. W. (1910). An experimental study of imagination. *American Journal of Psychology, 21*, 422-452.

Valentine, C. W. (1923). The function of images in the appreciation of poetry. *British Journal of Psychology, 14*, 164-191.

Holt, R. (1964). Imagery: The return of the ostracized. *American Psychologist, 19*, 254-264.

Paivio, A. (1971). *Imagery and verbal processes*. New York: Holt, Rinehart, & Winston.

Sheehan, F. (1972). *The function and nature of imagery*. New York: Academic Press.

Paivio, A. (1982). The empirical case for dual coding. In J. Yuille (Ed.), *Imagery, cognitions, and memory*. Hillsdale, NJ: Erlbaum.

Pinker, S., & Kosslyn, S. (1983). Theories of mental imagery. In A. Sheikh (Ed.), *Imagery: Current theory, research, and application*. New York: Wiley.

Richardson, A. (1983). Imagery: Definition and types. In A. Sheikh (Ed.), *Imagery: Current theory, research, and application*. New York: Wiley.

Ahsen, A. (1987). *Image psychology and the empirical method*. New York: Brandon House.

Roeckelein, J. E. (2004). *Imagery in psychology*. Westport, CT: Praeger.

IMAGERY TYPES, THEORIES OF. See IMAGERY/MENTAL IMAGERY, THEORIES OF.

IMAGE-SOMATIC RESPONSE-MEANING MODEL. See MOTOR LEARNING/PROCESS THEORIES; NEW STRUCTURALISM THEORY/PARADIGM.

IMAGE THEORIES. See IMAGERY/MENTAL IMAGERY, THEORIES OF; WUNDT'S THEORIES, DOCTRINES, AND PRINCIPLES.

IMAGE THEORY OF CONFLICT. See NEW STRUCTURALISM THEORY/PARADIGM.

IMITATION, THEORY OF. See LANGUAGE ORIGINS, THEORIES OF.

IMMATERIALISM, THEORY OF. See MIND-BODY THEORIES.

IMPASSE-PRIORITY THEORY. See PERSONALITY THEORIES.

IMPLICIT THEORY OF PERSONALITY. See PERSONALITY THEORIES.

IMPOSSIBLE FIGURES/PERSPECTIVE REVERSAL. See APPENDIX A, NECKER CUBE ILLUSION.

IMPOVERISHED MIND, THEORY OF. See MIND/MENTAL STATES, THEORIES OF.

IMPRESSION FORMATION, THEORIES OF. The original research on *impression formation* (i.e., how one person perceives another person) is credited to the Polish-born American psychologist Solomon E. Asch (1907-1996), who addressed two major issues in his work: the *meaning* people give to their observations of others, and how to *measure* exactly a perceiver's impressions of another person. Asch used three methods to measure impressions: he asked the perceiver to write out in a brief paragraph impressions about another person (these then were evaluated in terms of the presence of consistent themes); the perceiver was asked to make up a list of words or phrases (i.e., a "free association" style) that came to mind when thinking about the other person; and the perceiver was given a list of prechosen adjectives and asked to place a check mark by the adjectives that applied to the other person. Recent research on impression formation employs a fourth approach - the use of a rating scale defined by end labels such as "very favorable" and "very unfavorable." Asch's main theoretical concern was the importance of understanding how people cope with the diverse information they receive about another individual (cf., the *trait centrality phenomenon* and *warm/cold effect* - a tendency for certain personality traits, such as the "warm/cold" trait, to have a significant effect on personality impression formation, even to the extent of influencing the interpretation of *other* traits associated with the person being assessed, and which also may be called an *atmosphere effect*). This concern sometimes is called the *information integration problem*. Two major theoretical approaches toward impression formation and the information integration problem are the *Gestalt approach* and the *cognitive algebra approach*. The *Gestalt theory* maintains that people adopt a configural strategy where they appraise the entire information array and, subsequently, form a theoretical interpretation that integrates all the separate pieces of data into a coherent whole. This approach often involves the reinterpretation of some data and the discounting of other information. The *cognitive algebra theory* holds that each item of information contributes independently to one's overall impression. This approach (unlike the Gestalt view) assumes that the information items are not actively interrelated into a single thematic or meaningful configuration but, rather, each item is evaluated separately and may be combined with any pre-existing evaluations to yield a current evaluative impression of the person. This viewpoint is called the *cognitive algebra approach* because information items are combined through algebra rules such as multiplying, adding, or averaging. Although the *Gestalt theory* and the *cognitive algebra* *theory* are different in their conceptual assumptions, they seem to be equally capable of accounting for the empirical findings in research on impression formation, including a variety of characteristics regarding the information items such as *primacy-recency effects* - occurs when perceivers' attention is paid either to the first, or last, part of a list of items; *meaning shift effects* - refers to the rating of one item in a set in a particular way depending on the nature of other items in the set; and *set size effects* - refers to the influence of the relative number of positive items to the number of negative items in a set. Another area linked theoretically to impression formation is the study of *interpersonal perception.* Person perception is a complex topic involving inferences and attributions made by an observer about others. Theoretical approaches in this area include those by F. Heider (1958), H. H. Kelley (1973), and E. E. Jones and K. E. Davis (1965). According to Heider and *attribution theory*, causes for behavior are attributed to either the environment or the person. When an action can be attributed to environmental causes, the actor is not held responsible for the positive or negative effects of her behavior, but when the actor is perceived as the originator, she is held accountable for the effect. Kelley proposed a *discounting principle* to account for causes of behavior where it is hypothesized that observers have a tendency to accept the first sufficient cause as the reason for behavior, but the impact of any particular cause in producing an effect is "discounted" if other plausible causes are present. Kelley suggests, also, an *augmentation principle* where the more "costs" the actor risks in order to act as he does, the more likely the observer is to attribute the behavior to "person causes." Kelley's rule of thumb is that the more the actor's behavior deviates from what the perceiver believes most people would do, the more likely the action is associated with an actor-specific feature or factor. The focus of attention on the actor to the exclusion of the environment is called the *fundamental attribution error* - first identified by the Polish-born Austrian social psychologist Gustav Ichheiser (1897-1969) in 1933 (and described by Fritz Heider in 1944, E. E. Jones in 1965, and L. D. Ross in 1977) - and is a phenomenon leading observers to make stronger personal attributions than do actors, and is a tendency to *underestimate* the importance of *external* situational pressures and to *overestimate* the importance of *internal* motives and dispositions in interpreting others' behaviors. Jones and Davis argue that once an observer makes an attribution to personal causes, a *correspondent inference* will be made from the observed behavior and the motive that is inferred as underlying that behavior. According to this approach, the observer notes effects that occur in the environment and traces these back to the behavior of an actor; if the behavior is attributed to environmental factors, the information processing stops. However, if a personal attribution is made, the observer assumes the actor intended the effects observed (cf., *misattribution theory* - posits that due to favorable emotional outcomes, events or factors that just happen to be present may gain value they would not otherwise possess). Most of the literature on interpersonal perception assumes that a stimulus person is inert basically, and the observer draws inferences from the behavior exhibited. However, the actor may have something to gain or lose by the impressions generated by behavior and may be motivated to influence them in some way such as engaging in a number of possible "impression management strategies" to negotiate an identity in the eyes of the observer. The study of *interpersonal perception* has not yet fully incorporated the dynamic interactions proposed by *impression management theory*, and the attribution process appears to be relatively static with an overreliance on rational models of information processing. See also ATTITUDE/ATTITUDE CHANGE, THEORIES OF; ATTRIBUTION THEORY; BALANCE, PRINCIPLES/THEORY OF; CORRESPONDENCE BIAS HYPOTHESIS; IMPRESSION MANAGEMENT THEORY; INFORMATION/INFORMATION-PROCESSING THEORY; INFORMATION INTEGRATION THEORY; PERCEPTION (I. GENERAL), THEORIES OF.

REFERENCES

Ichheiser, G. (1933). Die vieldeutigkeit im begriff des erfolges. *Zeitschrift fur Padogogische Psychologie und Jugenkunde, 34*, 97-104.

Heider, F. (1944). Social perception and phenomenal causality. *Psychological Review, 51,* 358-374.

Asch, S. E. (1946). Forming impressions of personality. *Journal of Abnormal and Social Psychology, 41,* 258-290.

Heider, F. (1958). *The psychology of interpersonal relations.* New York: Wiley.

Anderson, N. (1965). Averaging versus adding as a stimulus-combination rule in impression formation. *Journal of Experimental Psychology, 70,* 394-400.

Jones, E. E., & Davis, K. E. (1965). From acts to dispositions: The attribution process in person perception. In L. Berkowitz (Ed.), *Advances in experimental social psychology.* Vol. 2. New York: Academic Press.

Kelley, H. H. (1973). The process of causal attribution. *American Psychologist, 28,* 107-128.

Ostrom, T. (1977). Between theory and within theory conflict in explaining context effects in impression formation. *Journal of Experimental Social Psychology, 13,* 492-503.

Mellers, B., Richards, V., & Birnbaum, M. H. (1992). Distributional theories in impression formation. *Organizational Behavior & Human Decision Processes, 51,* 313-343.

IMPRESSION MANAGEMENT THEORY. See SELF-CONCEPT THEORY.

IMPRINTING PHENOMENON. See INFANT ATTACHMENT THEORIES; LANGUAGE ORIGINS, THEORIES OF.

INBREEDING-DEPRESSION THEORY. See INCEST TABOO THEORIES.

INCENTIVE THEORY. See MOTIVATION, THEORIES OF; REINFORCEMENT THEORY.

INCEST TABOO THEORIES. The notion of *incest,* that is, the law/custom in all societies prohibiting sex and marriage between members of the "nuclear family" (the basic family unit consisting of a mother and father with their immediate children) is embedded in a universal principle/practice that is difficult, typically, to explain. However, the following *incest taboo theories* have been offered to explain the phenomenon: the *functional theory* - holds that the taboo creates and maintains networks of social relationships that are necessary to prevent societies from disintegrating into separate nuclear families; this theory is based on the debatable assumption that without the incest taboo, people would normally want to mate with close relatives; also, this theory fails to account for reasons why the taboo governs sexual intercourse rather than marriage; the *inbreeding-depress-ion theory* - states that the practice of inbreeding results in the genetic deterioration and elimination of any society allowing it because deleterious recessive genes are more likely to flourish, and the taboo may have evolved via the *principle of natural selection*; however, this viewpoint does not answer the questions as to why few infrahuman animals demonstrate incest taboos and why some successful human societies have an explicit obligation to marry cousins; and the *prepubertal interaction theory* - this conjecture is based on empirical psychological evidence that intimate contact between children at a critical period (approximately 2-6 years of age) before puberty results in the elimination of sexual attraction between them in their adulthood. See also DARWIN'S EVOLUTION THEORY; GALTON'S LAWS; MENDEL'S LAWS/ PRINCIPLES; NATURAL SELECTION, LAW OF; PSYCHOPATHOLOGY, THEORIES OF.

REFERENCES
Westermarck, E. A. (1889/1921). *The history of human marriage.* Helsingfors, Finland: Erenakell/London: Macmillan.

Westermarck, E. A. (1906). *The origin and development of moral ideas.* London: Macmillan.

INCLUSIVENESS, LAW OF. See GESTALT THEORY/LAWS.

INCOME DISTRIBUTION, LAW OF. See LOTKA/LOTKA-PRICE LAW.

INCONGRUITY/INCONSISTENCY THE- ORIES OF HUMOR. The *incongruity/ inconsistency theories of humor* are characterized generally by cognitions involving disjointed ideas, ill-suited ideational pairings of situations, and/or presentations of ideas or situations that diverge from habitual or expected customs. According to the *principle of incongruity* (i.e., the incompatibility of contexts or materials), the perception of contrast, contrariness, expectancy violations, inconsistency, incongruity, and/or uncommon or novel mixtures of relations is central to the humor experience. See also ARISTOTLE'S THEORY OF HUMOR; BERGSON'S THEORY OF HUMOR; COGNITIVE THEORIES OF HUMOR; HARTLEY'S THEORY OF HUMOR/LAUGHTER; HUMOR, THEORIES OF; HUTCHESON'S THEORY OF HUMOR; KANT'S THEORY OF HUMOR/ LAUGHTER; KIERKEGAARD'S THEORY OF HUMOR; MORREALL'S THEORY OF HUMOR; MOTIVATIONAL THEORIES OF HUMOR; SCHOPENHAUER'S THEORY OF HUMOR; SPENCER'S THEORY OF LAUGHTER/HUMOR.
REFERENCE
Roeckelein, J. E. (2002). *The psychology of humor*. Westport, CT: Greenwood Press.

INCONGRUITY, PRINCIPLE OF. See INCONGRUITY/INCONSISTENCY THEORIES OF HUMOR.

INCONGRUITY-RESOLUTION THEO- RIES. See COGNITIVE THEORIES OF HUMOR; INCONGRUITY/INCONSISTENCY THEORIES OF HUMOR.

INCREMENTAL LEARNING THEORY. See CONCEPT LEARNING/CONCEPT FORMATION, THEORIES OF.

INCREMENTAL THEORY OF DEVEL- OPMENT. See DEVELOPMENTAL THEORY.

INCUBATION OF AVOIDANCE THE- ORY. See NAPALKOV PHENOMENON; PUNISHMENT, THEORIES OF.

INCUBATION THEORY. See NAPAL-KOV PHENOMENON.

INDEPENDENCE HYPOTHESIS. See INTERFERENCE THEORIES.

INDEPENDENT ASSORTMENT, LAW OF. See MENDEL'S LAWS/PRINCIPLES.

INDETERMINISM, DOCTRINE/THEO- RY OF. See DETERMINISM, DOCTRINE/ THEORY OF.

INDIFFERENCE INTERVAL. See VIER-ORDT'S LAWS.

INDIFFERENCE PRINCIPLE. See BAYES' THEOREM; REINFORCEMENT THEORY.

INDIVIDUALITY THEORY. See INTEL-LIGENCE, THEORIES OF.

INDIVIDUATION, LAW OF. See PERCEPTION (I. GENERAL), THEORIES OF.

INDIVIDUATION THEORY. See FROMM'S THEORY OF PERSONALITY.

INDOLEAMINE HYPOTHESIS OF DE- PRESSION. See DEPRESSION, THEORIES OF.

INDUCED EMOTION, THEORY OF. See LAZARUS' THEORY OF EMOTION.

INDUCED MOVEMENT EFFECT. See APPARENT MOVEMENT, PRINCIPLES/ THEORIES OF.

INDUCTION, LAW OF. See SKINNER'S DESCRIPTIVE BEHAVIOR AND OPER-ANT CONDITIONING THEORY.

INDUCTION PROBLEM. See NULL HY-POTHESIS.

INDUCTIVE METHOD. See BACONIAN METHOD; BRUNER'S CONCEPT FOR-MATION THEORY; EXCLUSION, METH-OD OF.

INERTIA, LAW OF. See INTELLIGENCE, THEORIES/LAWS OF.

INFANT ATTACHMENT THEORIES. The English psychiatrist John Bowlby (1907-1990) introduced the term *attachment* into psychology and psychiatry, even though Sigmund Freud laid the foundation for theoretical "attachment concepts" by suggesting the *cathexis* (i.e., an "investment" or "holding") of libidinal energy onto a "love object" in order to establish an emotional connection for behavioral stability and organization. Bowlby argued that *attachment* is an expression of the biology of a species that is exhibited by species-specific behaviors (such as sucking, crying, smiling, clinging, and following responses) that occur at different ages and are focused on the infant's mother. *Theories of infant attachment* have appeared as subtheories and supporting concepts in *ethological theory, psychoanalytic theory*, and *learning theory*. In the area of *ethology* (the study of animal behavior), lasting attachments are created via the *imprinting phenomenon* or process whereby a newborn organism "attaches" itself to the first moving object, usually the parent (e.g., by exhibiting following behavior), it sees shortly after birth during a *critical period*. Thus, *ethological theory* - in particular, as proposed by the Austrian zoologist Konrad Z. Lorenz (1903-1989) - assumes that genetically programmed behaviors (via a hypothetical "hard-wired" device in the animals' central nervous system, called an *innate-releasing mechanism*, that causes a "sign stimulus" or "releaser" to elicit a fixed-action behavior pattern) interact with the environment during a *critical stage* of growth to develop bonding in the young organism with other individuals/organisms. In humans, attachments are generally more complex, require a longer time-span for development, and are dependent on bonding "networks" of behavior (such as "body-contact" and "eye-face-contact"). According to *psychoanalytic theory*, and *anaclitic theory*, attachment occurs during the nurturing-affectionate caretaking activities (such as feeding) where the infant's instinctual biological urge for oral gratification is met through sucking responses and contact with the mother's breast, which is then transferred into psychological attachment to the mother as a "love object." The Austrian psychoanalyst Rene A. Spitz (1887-1974) described the disorder called *anaclitic depression* in infants that may result from parent-child separation after a relatively long (about six months) attachment period. Spitz also defined *hospitalism* as the physical and psychological effects on an infant (up to 18 months of age) of prolonged and total separation from its mother, due to hospitalization, or some other similar condition; the effects include disruption of perceptual-motor skills and language, and retarded physical development. In the area of *learning theory*, the behavior of feeding is the major "drive-reducing reinforcement" mechanism for learned attachment to the mother. In addition to oral satisfaction through feeding, the behaviors of touching, holding, and physical contact are considered necessary for the development of comfort and attachment in the young child. Bowlby's work on mother-child separation indicates that the infant reacts to "loss" of the mother in three distinct stages: protests of anger/crying to get the mother back; a period of despair, withdrawal, depression, and decreased activity if the mother does not return as a result of the initial protests; and a *detachment* phase where the infant is relatively unresponsive to people and intensely hates the mother figure [cf., *mignon delusion* - named after the heroine (who dies without her longings being fulfilled) of an 1866 French opera by Ambroise Thomas (1811-1896), refers to a fixed false belief or delusion that one is the child of a distinguished family; it usually arises on the basis of disillusionment with one's real parents who have failed to demonstrate the omnipotence and qualities with which the child has endowed them, or as a defense against the aggressive sexual elements of the Freudian Oedipal period]. Bowlby asserts that *attachment theory*, vis-à-vis its relationship to psychopathology in the individual, is a scientifically valid approach that combines concepts from the fields of psychoanalysis, cognitive theory, control theory, and ethology. See also ANACLITIC THEORY; COGNITIVE CONSISTENCY THEORY; CONTROL/SYS-TEMS THE-ORY; CUPBOARD THEORY; ETHOLOGI-CAL THEORY; FREUD'S THE-ORY OF

PERSONALITY; GOOD BREAST/ OBJECT AND BAD BREAST/OBJECT THEORY; LEARNING THEORIES/LAWS; LOVE, THEORIES OF; PARENTAL INVESTMENT THEORY.

REFERENCES

Lorenz, K. Z., & Tinbergen, N. (1938). Taxis und instinkthandlung in der eiroll-bewegung der graugans. *Zeitschrift fur Tierpsychologie, 2*, 1-29.

Spitz, R. (1945). Hospitalism: An inquiry into the genesis of psychiatric conditions in early childhood. *Psychoanalytic Studies of the Child, 1*, 53-74.

Bowlby, J. (1958). The nature of the child's tie to his mother. *International Journal of Psychoanalysis, 39*, 350-373.

Bowlby, J. (1960). Separation anxiety. *International Journal of Psychoanalysis, 41*, 89-113.

Bowlby, J. (1969-1980). *Attachment and loss.* 3 vols. London: Hogarth Press.

Harlow, H. (1971). *Learning to love.* New York: Ballantine Books.

Ainsworth, M. (1973). The development of infant-mother attachment. In B. Caldwell & H. Ricciuti (Eds.), *Review of child development research.* Vol. 3. Chicago: University of Chicago Press.

INFANTILE BIRTH THEORY. See CLO-ACAL/CLOACA THEORY.

INFECTION THEORY/EFFECT. The viewpoint of *infection theory* is that theories in psychology generally cluster around some fundamental concept disseminated by researchers who are in personal touch with one another, but especially with the individual who originally proposed or developed the hypothesis. The *infection effect* is most noticeable in centers and institutes of learning and research (particularly in prestigious graduate schools) when a teacher shares ideas with high-ability students and with other professional colleagues. Promising students - who are "infected" - research their teachers' ideas, advance and perpetuate those ideas throughout their own careers, and strengthen them with published experimental research (cf., *social impact theory* - the larger the number of people influencing someone in the same direction, the more important they are, and the more immediate their influence, then the greater their influence will be). Once these students become influential in their field, their mentors' hypotheses and theories are cited in the psychological literature and, consequently, become known and supported in the discipline. A *snowball effect* occurs in this process where particular hypotheses and theories are published in one textbook, and then other authors pick them up and include them in their books, thus giving those hypotheses and theories greater circulation. According to *infection theory*, theoretical orientations such as those of Kurt Lewin and B. F. Skinner achieved wide audiences because many graduate students under their influence engaged in psychological research and prolific writing. One undesirable consequence of the *infection effect* is the inbreeding of ideas. Instead of a free and open exchange of ideas, hypotheses, and theories, authors with more personal contacts tend to have their orientations magnified or augmented. The *infection effect* tends to make psychology (and other disciplines) *less* diverse and varied. For example, the area of *personality theory* tends to contain a limited set of ideas due to the restricted interests of influential psychologists where the full spectrum of personality - involving study of traits such as humor, love, faith, and aesthetic sensitivity - is left virtually unexplored. See also DODO HYPOTHESIS; INOCULATION THEORY; PERSONALITY THEORIES.

REFERENCES

Sahakian, W. (1980). The infection theory in social psychology. *Society for the Advancement in Social Psychology Newsletter, 6*, 3-4.

Sahakian, W. (1994). Infection theory. In R. J. Corsini (Ed.), *Encyclopedia of Psychology.* New York: Wiley.

INFERENCE THEORY. See APPARENT MOVEMENT, PRINCIPLES AND THEORIES OF; UNCONSCIOUS INFERENCE, DOCTRINE OF.

INFORMAL BEHAVIORIST THEORY. See BEHAVIORIST THEORY.

INFORMATION/INFORMATION-PRO-CESSING THEORY. In general, *informa-tion-processing (IP) theory* is concerned with the way organisms attend to, select, and inter-nalize information and how the information is used subsequently to make decisions and di-rect their behavior. *Information theory* was developed independently in the late 1940s and early 1950s by the English statistician Ronald A. Fisher (1890-1962) and the American mathematicians Norbert Wiener (1894-1964) and Claude E. Shannon (1916-); and was pioneered, also, by the English mathematician Alan Mathison Turing (1912-1954). *IP theo-ries* have generated research in various areas of psychology, including memory, perception, attention, language, problem-solving, and thinking. *Information theory* was introduced into psychology by the American psycholo-gists George A. Miller (1920-) and Frederick C. Frick (1918-1992) in 1949. The term *IP theory* refers to some common presuppositions and research methods involving specialized scientific language and concepts in which the primary empirical domain is intelligent behav-ior and mental processes. At the broadest level, *IP* research and theory are aimed at studying the properties of adaptive mecha-nisms concerning the apprehension, storage, retrieval, and use of information that may be initiated in either internal states or external environments (cf., the *information-processing/ levels of processing model of memory*; and the *domains of processing theory* - the specula-tions that the more elaboration is involved in information processing at a given processing level, the more superior will be its recall; the *principle of graceful degradation* - a notion developed by the English psychologist David C. Marr (1945-1980) that in any information-processing system, the effects of an error should be restricted and should not produce completely false results; the human mind ap-pears to obey this principle (most computers do not), because few of the errors it makes are catastrophic; *serial processing theory*, also called *sequential processing* and *intermittent processing theories* - holds that rapid shifting between different information sources ac-counts for the apparent ability to carry on separate cognitive functions simultaneously; it also states that two sets of stimuli cannot be

processed simultaneously; on the other hand, *parallel processing theory* states that two separate sets of stimuli can be attended to simultaneously and, thus, accounts for the ability to carry on different cognitive func-tions at the same time; *single channel model* - posits that at any one time there can be only one cognitive aspect/function occurring for any individual; thus, it is impossible allegedly to have two thoughts simultaneously, even though with extremely rapid transitions be-tween thoughts the person may believe that many thoughts are occurring simultaneously; and the *principle of least commitment* - the generalization that a task will be more effi-ciently executed if no decisions are taken that may subsequently have to be reversed, i.e., at each point in processing, a decision should be taken only when there is enough evidence to warrant it. *IP theories* that mainly originated in psychology derive from the behavioristic studies of K. Spence, the verbal learning ex-periments of J. McGeoch, the experimental analyses of attention and perception by D. Broadbent, and studies of human engineering and performance; cf., *Fitt's law* - named after the American psychologist Paul Morris Fitts (1912-1965) - is an equation that describes the movement between two similar targets, each of which must be touched in turn, where movement time decreases with the size of the target and increases with the amplitude of the movement (cf., Kvalseth, 1980, 1993). Other *IP theories* that originated outside psychology include M. Minsky's mathematical logic/computer science, N. Chomsky's trans-formational linguistics, and C. Shannon's communication engineering/information the-ory. Thus, *IP theory* has been influenced gen-erally by viewpoints and advancements in the areas of behaviorism, engineering/information theory, linguistics, and computer science. In particular, in a learning context, *IP theory* has progressed through *robotology* (e.g., Ashby, 1952; cf., Ashby's *law of requisite variety*, which is a mathematical statement about *IP* that describes the procedure for choosing cor-rect alternatives and rejecting incorrect ones), to *computer models* dealing with experimental synthesis of complex human behaviors and using specialized computer languages (e.g., Newell & Simon, 1963; cf., Miller, Galanter,

& Pribram, 1960) and "artificial intelligence" (e.g., Newell & Simon, 1972; Hunt, 1975). Since the 1950s and 1960s, and the major beginnings of modern information-processing models, there has been a proliferation of models, theories, simulations, and programs dealing with pattern recognition, perceptual learning, problem solving, language, and learning/memory. The development of computer technology has provided a valuable tool for understanding the complexities of human thought and information processing. See also ALGORITHMIC-HEURISTIC THEORY; ATTITUDE/ATTITUDE CHANGE, THEORIES OF; COMMUNICATION THEORY; CONTROL/SYSTEMS THEORY; DECISION-MAKING THEORIES; HICK'S LAW; INFORMATION INTEGRATION THEORY; LEARNING THEORIES AND LAWS; NETWORK MODEL OF INFORMATION PROCESSING; PARALLEL DISTRIBUTED PROCESSING MODEL; PATTERN/OBJECT RECOGNITION THEORY; SHORT-TERM AND LONG-TERM MEMORY, THEORIES OF.

REFERENCES

Turing, A. M. (1936). On computable numbers, with an application to the Entscheidungsproblem. *Proceedings of the London Mathematical Society*, *42*, 230-265.

McGeoch, J. (1942). *The psychology of human learning: An introduction*. New York: Van Rees Press.

Shannon, C. (1948). A mathematical theory of communication. *Bell System Technical Journal*, *27*, 379-423, 623-656.

Wiener, N. (1948). *Cybernetics*. New York: Wiley.

Miller, G. A., & Frick, F. (1949). Statistical behavioristics and sequences of responses. *Psychological Review*, *56*, 311-324.

Shannon, C., & Weaver, W. (1949). *The mathematical theory of communication*. Urbana: University of Illinois Press.

Ashby, W. (1952). *Design for a brain*. New York: Wiley.

Fitts, P. M. (1954). The information capacity of the human motor system in controlling the amplitude of movement. *Journal of Experimental Psychology*, *47*, 381-391.

Miller, G. A. (1956). The magical number seven, plus or minus two: Some limits on our capacity for processing information. *Psychological Review*, *63*, 81-97.

Quastler, H. (1956). *Information theory in psychology*. New York: Free Press.

Spence, K. (1956). *Behavior theory and conditioning*. New Haven, CT: Yale University Press.

Broadbent, D. (1958). *Perception and communication*. London: Pergamon Press.

Attneave, F. (1959). *Applications of information theory to psychology*. New York: Holt, Rinehart, and Winston.

Miller, G. A., Galanter, E., & Pribram, K. (1960). *Plans and the structure of behavior*. New York: Holt, Rinehart, and Winston.

Newell, A., & Simon, H. (1963). Computers in psychology. In R. Luce, R. Bush, & E. Galanter (Eds.), *Handbook of mathematical psychology*. Vol. 1. New York: Wiley.

Chomsky, N. (1965). *Aspects of the theory of syntax*. Cambridge, MA: M.I.T. Press.

Minsky, M. (1967). *Computation: Finite and infinite machines*. Englewood Cliffs, NJ: Prentice-Hall.

Newell, A., & Simon, H. (1972). *Human problem solving*. Englewood Cliffs, NJ: Prentice-Hall.

Garner, W. (1974). *The processing of information and structure*. Englewood Cliffs, NJ: Prentice-Hall.

Hunt, E. (1975). *Artificial intelligence*. New York: Academic Press.

Norman, D. (1977). *Memory and attention: An introduction to human information processing*. New York: Wiley.

Marr, D. C. (1982). *Vision*. San Francisco: Freeman.

INFORMATION INTEGRATION THEORY. The American social/cognitive psychologist Norman H. Anderson (1981, 1982, 1990, 2004) describes the *theory of information* *integration (IIT)*, which is an attempt to develop a *cognitive theory* of everyday life and language, to serve as the basis for a *scientific theory* of social psychology, and to provide a *unified theory* (cf., Newell, 1990/1994) and general approach to social and developmental psychology. Thus, *IIT* covers many substantive areas in psychology ranging from psychophysics, perceptual illusions, psychological measurement, memory, social stereotypes, interpersonal attraction (cf., *reinforcement theory*), person cognition, language processing, and judgment/decision-making (cf., *sequential decision theory* - decisions made in sequences or separate steps, usually at each step of a procedure, to determine the acceptability of the data). The essential notion in *IIT* is that thought and action typically arise from multiple causes that occur together. In one case, *IIT* conceptualizes group decision-making and bargaining in terms of a theorem concerning "social averaging" that provides exact predictions about group compromise and decisions that focus on information communication and information integration. In another case, a *functional theory of cognition* is proposed that is founded on the axiom of purposiveness and grounded in *cognitive algebra theory* in which the functional nature of cognition manifests itself in an approach-avoidance axis of thought and action (represented by positive and negative values). Overall, the *averaging model* inherent in *IIT* provides a basis for developing heuristics for making parameter estimations, and for defining and measuring various psychological concepts (e.g., the notion of "weight" or "stimulus importance") that generates research and may be subjected to empirical validation and reliability testing. See also DECISION-MAKING THEORIES; IMPRESSION FORMATION, THEORIES OF; INFORMATION/INFORMATION-PROCESSING THEORY; INOCULATION THEORY; PERSUASION/INFLUENCE THEORIES; REINFORCEMENT THEORY.

REFERENCES

Kaplan, M. F., & Anderson, N. H. (1973). Information integration theory and reinforcement theory as approaches to interpersonal attraction. *Journal of Personality and Social Psychology*, *28*, 301-312.

Anderson, N. H. (1981). *Foundations of information integration theory*. New York: Academic Press.

Anderson, N. H. (1982). *Methods of information integration theory*. New York: Academic Press.

Kerkman, D. D. (1988). An exegesis of two theories of compensation development: Sequential decision theory and information integration theory. *Developmental Review*, *8*, 323-360.

Anderson, N. H. (Ed.) (1990). *Contributions to information integration theory. Vol. 1: Cognition; Vol. 2: Social; Vol. 3: Developmental*. Hillsdale, NJ: Erlbaum.

Newell, A. (1990/1994). *Unified theories of cognition*. Cambridge, MA: Harvard University Press.

Anderson, N. H. (1996). *A functional theory of cognition*. Hillsdale, NJ: Erlbaum.

Anderson, N. H. (2004). Unified theory. In J. T. Jost & M. R. Banaji (Eds.), *Perspectivism in social psychology: The yin and yang of scientific progress*. Washington, D. C.: American Psychological Association.

INFORMATION-PROCESSING/LEVELS OF PROCESSING MODELS. See INFORMATION/INFORMATION-PROCESSING THEORY; PIAGET'S THEORY; SHORT-TERM AND LONG-TERM MEMORY, THEORIES OF.

INFORMATION-PROCESSING MODEL OF THE INTERNAL CLOCK. See SCALAR TIMING THEORY.

INFRARED THEORY. See OLFACTION/SMELL, THEORIES OF.

INGROUP BIAS THEORIES. The concept of *ingroup bias*, or "ethnocentrism," refers to the relationship between intergroup behavior at the societal level and perceptions/attitudes at the personal level and, thus, provides a link between sociological theories of group relations/dynamics and psychological theories of interpersonal attraction. The following four theoretical approaches have been the most influential in attempts by psychologists and sociologists to explain and understand the widespread tendency toward ingroup favoritism/bias: *realistic group conflict theory* - stresses the role of conflict, competition, and the struggle for existence when resources and goods are scarce in a given geographical region; *psychoanalytic theory* - ingroup biases are traced to the motives and needs of individuals, rather than to group processes; in the case of one specific concept ("authoritarianism"), it is posited that generalized hatred and distrust toward persons in outgroups (particularly prejudice against religious and racial minorities) stems from projection of repressed hostilities that originate in childhood experiences with parental authority and, thus, ingroup bias is a result of the individual's efforts to develop and maintain one's ego and self-esteem; *categorization theory* - emphasizes the general cognitive processes by which humans structure, simplify, and give significance to their social and physical environments; in this approach, intergroup perceptions develop from the same processes of categorization and classification that apply to the perception of physical objects; for instance, the *assimilation-contrast effect* refers to the superimposition of a classification on a set of stimuli which vary systematically along some physical dimension and leads to a marked tendency to accentuate intercategory differences and intracategory similarities on that dimension; when extrapolated to social differentiation processes, this effect indicates that members of the same social group will be perceived as more similar to one another and more different from members of other groups than they actually are; thus, members of one's own group (ingroup) are viewed as generally similar to oneself, whereas members of outgroups are viewed as different [cf., *ingroup extremity effect* - the tendency of those strongly identifying with a group to evaluate members of their own group (ingroup) more extremely than those in other groups; however, on the other hand, the *outgroup extremity effect* is said to be present when the individual's evaluations of outgroup members are more extreme than their evaluations of members of their own ingroup; cf., *minimum-resource/ power theory*

- in group dynamics, provides an explanation for coalitions among members that is based on individuals' prior resources, payoffs, and power types where attempts are made to maximize control over others in the group, and where the most likely "minimum resource" coalitions are those that are sufficient to prevail under conditions where the members own the minimum resources for that purpose; and *outgroup homogeneity bias effect* - refers to a tendency for members of a particular group to assume there is more similarity among members of an outgroup than is actually the case]; and *social identity theory* - this perspective combines the basic aspects of categorization theory with those of motivational theories such as group-conflict and psychoanalytic theories; according to this theoretical approach, the perceptual effects of category differentiation are linked with social comparisons and an assumed drive for "positive self-identity;" *social identity theory* reverses the causal events of realistic group conflict theory (i.e., ingroup solidarity and identification are the products of intergroup competition) by suggesting that social competition is generated via group differentiation where ingroup-outgroup differences highlight social comparisons that favor the ingroup for the purpose of achieving positive self-identity. See also ASSIMILATION-CONTRAST THEORY/EFFECT; ATTITUDE/ATTITUDE CHANGE, THEORIES OF; COALITION FORMATION THEORIES; INTERPERSONAL ATTRACTION THEORIES; PREJUDICE, THEORIES OF.

REFERENCES

Levine, R. A., & Campbell, D. T. (1972). *Ethnocentrism: Theories of conflict, ethnic attitudes, and group behavior*. New York: Wiley.

Hewstone, M., Rubin, M., & Willis, H. (2002). Intergroup bias. *Annual Review of Psychology, 53*, 575-604.

Major, B., & O'Brien, L. T. (2005). The social psychology of stigma. *Annual Review of Psychology, 56*, 393-421.

INGROUP EXTREMITY EFFECT. See INGROUP BIAS THEORIES.

INHERITABLE ACQUIRED CHARAC-TERISTICS, PRINCIPLE OF. See LA-MARCK'S THEORY.

INHERITANCE, LAWS OF. See MEN-DEL'S LAWS/PRINCIPLES.

INHERITANCE, POLYGENIC THEORY OF. See GALTON'S LAWS.

INHIBITION, LAWS OF. The term *inhibition* has different meanings depending on the context in which it is used. In general, *inhibition* is the restraining, repressing, preventing, decreasing, or prohibiting of any process or the process that brings about such restraining. In the context of physiology, *inhibition* is the partial or complete arrest of an already active function, especially of a muscular contraction; it is also that condition of a tissue or organ in which a function cannot be excited by the usual stimulus. In the area of psychoanalysis, *inhibition* refers to a mental condition that, through an opposing force, tends to check or prevent certain modes of expression, especially such as would expose to others the individual's thoughts or character (synonymous terms are *repression* and *suppression*). In the context of learning/memory, *inhibition* (or "interference") is the reduction in, or prevention of, a response due to the operation of some other process, such as *retroactive inhibition* or *proactive inhibition* (see *interference theories of forgetting*). The term *central inhibition* is used whenever the assumed inhibitory action is taking place within the central nervous system; cf., *reciprocal inhibition*, where inhibition is shown by antagonistic muscles when the neural message to one muscle to contract is accompanied by a relaxation of the other, resulting from an inhibition of its motor nerve cells; and *reflex inhibition*, which is the prevention of one reflex by a mutually incompatible one. The terms *external inhibition* and *internal inhibition* refer, respectively, to the inhibition of a conditioned response produced when a novel or irrelevant stimulus is presented along with the conditioned stimulus, and to the inhibition that depends on a conditioning process such as *extinction* (cf., I. Pavlov's *inhibition of inhibition*, or *disinhibition*, which refers to the removal of an inhibi-tion by an extraneous stimulus). The term *latent inhibition* refers to inhibition that is established by nonreinforced exposure to a stimulus; for example, an animal learns not to attend to that stimulus so that when it is presented in a reinforcing situation, learning is inhibited; also called the *stimulus preexposure effect*. The terms *reactive inhibition* and *inhibitory potential* were used by C. L. Hull to refer, respectively, to the hypothesized inhibitory tendency that builds up as a result of effortful responding, and to the hypothesized state that results from the performance of a response that reflects the organism's tendency to inhibit the making of the response. Among his *static laws of the reflex*, B. F. Skinner describes the *law of inhibition*, where the strength of a reflex may be decreased through presentation of a second stimulus that has no other relation to the effector involved. The *Wedensky inhibition principle/effect* - named after the Russian physiologist Nikolai E. Wedensky (1852-1922), refers to the situation where a critical frequency for stimulating a nerve in a nerve-muscle preparation is found, and at which rate the muscle responds with a very rapid series of twitches (e.g., 200 per sec.), whereas if the rate of stimulation is increased somewhat, the muscle responds with a single contraction followed by complete relaxation; this phenomenon is related to the *theory of neuromuscular inhibition* via its interference or "over-crowding" of nerve pulsations. *Heymans' law of inhibition* - named after the Dutch psychololgist Gerardus Heymans (1857-1930) who set up the first psychological laboratory in Holland, refers to visual stimulation where the threshold value of a given stimulus is increased proportionately to the intensity of the inhibitory stimulus, when an inhibitory stimulus is offered. The *Ranschburg inhibition effect* - named after the Hungarian psychiatrist Paul Ranschburg (1870-1945), is the generalization that under tachistoscopic viewing conditions (i.e., where materials are presented only for a very brief exposure period) more individual stimuli can be recognized if all are different than if some are identical; that is, the effect refers to the inhibition among identical materials (cf., *repetition effect* - a special case of *Ranschburg inhibition* in serial recall of a string of items, where generally superior performance is observed when none of the items occurs more than once versus some items being repeated). See also FREUD'S THEORY OF PERSONALITY; HULL'S LEARNING THEORY; INTERFERENCE THEORIES OF FORGETTING; PAVLOVIAN CONDITIONING PRINCIPLES/LAWS/THEORIES; SKINNER'S DESCRIPTIVE BEHAVIOR/ OPERANT CONDITIONING THEORY; WOLPE'S THEORY/TECHNIQUE OF RECIPROCAL INHIBITION.

REFERENCES

Heymans, G. (1901). [Mental inhibition]. *Zeitschrift fur Psychologie und Physiologie der Sinnesorgane, 26*, 305-382.

Ranschburg, P. (1905). [Retroactive inhibition]. *Jahrbucher fur Psychiatrie und Neurologie, 5*, 560-578.

Pavlov, I. (1927). *Conditioned reflexes.* New York: Dover.

Skinner, B. F. (1938). *The behavior of organisms: An experimental analysis.* New York: Appleton-Century.

Hull, C. L. (1943). *Principles of behavior.* New York: Appleton-Century.

Hull, C. L. (1952). *A behavior system.* New Haven, CT: Yale University Press.

Wolpe, J. (1958). *Psychotherapy by reciprocal inhibition.* Stanford, CA: Stanford University Press.

INHIBITORY POTENTIAL, PRINCIPLE OF. See HULL'S LEARNING THEORY; INHIBITION, LAWS OF; PAVLOVIAN CONDITIONING PRINCIPLES, LAWS, AND THEORIES; SKINNER'S OPERANT CONDITIONING THEORY; SPENCE'S THEORY.

INITIAL VALUE(S), LAW OF. = Wilder's law of initial value(s). The Romanian-born Canadian/American pharmacist/neuropsychiatrist Joseph Wilder (1896-1993) originally formulated in 1931 the *law of initial values* (*LIV*) which is an empirical and statistical rule that may be stated as follows: the response to agents stimulating the function under investigation depends to a very large extent on the initial level of that function; if that level is low, there is a tendency to marked increase, and if the value is high, often there is a minimal or no increase, and often a paradoxical drop in the examined function; the exact opposite is true for inhibitory agents. In other terms, the *LIV* states that the response to the stimulus of a physiological function is almost always related to the initial level of intensity of that function where the higher the initial level, the lesser will be the sensitivity to a new stimulus. Essentially, the *LIV* is a completely general and positivistic assertion with two emphases: regarding the full range of a variable, there is a negative correlation between initial scores and change scores; and regarding only the extreme (high and low initial scores) of a variable, there is frequent occurrence of null reactions, or even paradoxical reactions. Thus, the *LIV* effectively points out that the reaction of the organism to a stimulus is not dependent solely on the nature and intensity of that stimulus. In 1958, Wilder reported that the *LIV* was widely known and taught in European medical schools about 25 years before it came to the attention of American researchers. The *LIV* has been applied to study of the autonomic concomitants of psychic processes (such as anxiety, hostility, depression, and emotion); to the areas of psychophysics, somatopsychic and psychosomatic medicine; to study of blood pressure and heart beat before and after the administration of drugs such as adrenalin, atropine, and pilocarpine; to study of Ivan Pavlov's theory of excitation-inhibition of the central nervous system, and Hans Eysenck's personality theory of introversion-extraversion. Even though the *statistical* aspects of the *LIV* were recognized in America, it was not until 1956 when J. I. Lacey published an important monograph on the issue that American psychophysiologists began to take an interest in the *LIV*. Since that time, the *LIV* has been widely accepted and studied in psychophysiology, although some confusion still exists as to its importance and generality. Although the *LIV* has *both* statistical and psychophysiological aspects, many researchers today assert that the *LIV* belongs more exclusively to the domain of the psychophysiologist than to the statistician. See also REDINTEGRATION, PRINCIPLE/LAW OF.

REFERENCES

Wilder, J. (1931). Das "ausgangswert-gesetz," ein unbeachtetes biologisches gesetz und seine bedeutung fur forschung und praxis. *Zeitschrift fur die Gesamte Neurologie und Psychiatrie, 31,* 317-338.

Lacey, J. I. (1956). The evaluation of autonomic responses: Toward a general solution. *Annals of the New York Academy of Sciences, 67,* 123-164.

Wilder, J. (1957). The law of initial value in neurology and psychiatry. *Journal of Nervous and Mental Disorders, 125,* 73-86.

Wilder, J. (1958). Modern psychophysiololgy and the law of initial value. *American Journal of Psychotherapy, 12,* 199-221.

Block, J. D., & Bridger, W. H. (1962). The law of initial value in psychophysiology: A reformulation in terms of experimental and theoretical considerations. *Annals of the New York Academy of Sciences, 98,* 1229-1241.

Wilder, J. (1962). Basimetric approach (law of initial value) to biological rhythms. *Annals of the New York Academy of Sciences, 98,* 1211-1220.

Wilder, J. (1967). *Stimulus and response: The law of initial value.* Bristol, UK: Wright.

Heilizer, F. (1975). The law of initial values (LIV) in personality. *Journal of General Psychology, 92,* 273-290.

Myrtek, M., Foerster, F., & Wittmann, W. (1977). The problematic law of initial values: Theoretical discussion and empirical investigations. *Zeitschrift fur Experimentelle und Angewandte Psychologie, 24,* 463-491.

Campbell, M. E. (1981). Statistical procedures with the law of initial values. *Journal of Psychology, 108,* 85-101.

Berntson, G., Cacioppo, J., & Quigley, K. (1991). Autonomic determinism: The modes of autonomic control, the doctrine of autonomic space, and the laws of autonomic constraint. *Psychological Review, 98,* 459-487.

Geenen, R., & Van de Vijver, F. (1993). A simple test of the law of initial values. *Psychophysiology, 30,* 525-530.

Jamieson, J. (1993). The law of initial values: Five factors or two? *International Journal of Psychophysiology, 14,* 233-239.

INNATE LANGUAGE SPECIFIC THEORY. See LANGUAGE ORIGINS, THEORIES OF.

INNATE RELEASING MECHANISM HYPOTHESIS. See INFANT ATTACHMENT THEORIES.

INNER EYE THEORY OF LAUGHTER. In his *inner eye theory of laughter* (cf., Humphrey, 1986), the American psychologist Wonil Edward Jung (2003) proposes a three-component set of jointly necessary and sufficient "trigger criteria" for all cases of involuntary laughter; the theory employs concepts both from the *theory of mind* in cognitive science and *game theory* in information-processing, decision-making, and social-exchange contexts. The three "trigger criteria" in Jung's theory are: *falsification* by the person of a belief representation held by self and others - laughter requires the falsification of a particular belief, or a null belief (ignorance), regarding events present in the actual or eventual state of the world, where the greater the strength of the falsification, the stronger is the laughter; *empathy* - appreciation, sensing, feeling, and thinking in imagination from the perspective of another person, where the objective is understanding (cf., "sympathy" which implies empathy plus caring for the well-being of the sympathized); and *sympathetic instant utility* - the pleasurable or painful attribute of an experience at a particular moment, involves the comparison of two different states of the world (the state believed, expected, or intended from the perspective with the false belief versus the actual or eventual state); this criterion always requires the laugher to use his/her "mindreading" ability. The three "trigger criteria" may be complemented by modulating factors of laughter, such as attention, mood, and the laughter of others. The goal of the *inner eye theory of laughter* is to encourage the scientific investigation of laughter as an evolutionarily de-signed signal that is used to facilitate coopera-tion among individuals (cf., Weisfeld, 1993). The theory seeks, also, to examine what types of mental representations are possessed - and may be falsified - by children, adults, autistic persons, and nonhuman primates. See also DECISION-MAKING THEORIES; EX-CHANGE/SOCIAL EXCHANGE THEORY; GAME THEORY; INFORMATION/INFOR-MATION-PROCESSING THEORY; MIND/ MENTAL STATES, THEORY OF.

REFERENCES

Humphrey, N. (1986). *The inner eye*. London: Faber and Faber.

Weisfeld, G. E. (1993). The adaptive value of humor and laughter. *Ethology and Sociobiology, 14*, 141-169.

Jung, W. E. (2003). The inner eye theory of laughter: Mindreader signals coop-erator value. *Evolutionary Psychol-ogy, 1*, 214-253.

INNER SENSES, THEORY OF. This early theory - deriving from attempts to elaborate on Aristotle's psychological notions concerning the "inner senses" - was formulated by the medieval Islamic, and later Christian, scholars and was advanced by a medical account de-veloped around the fourth century. The *theory of inner senses* postulates that the several cog-nitive processes - such as the imagination, common sense, and memory - are performed in the ventricles of the brain. In one version of this antique theory - developed by the Arab physician/philosopher Avicenna (c. 1037) - there are presumed to be three ventricles ar-ranged linearly in the head, all filled with a fluid or "spirit." According to this account, sensory information is sent to the front ventri-cle, which has connections to the middle ven-tricle which, in turn, connects to the rear ven-tricle. Of course, accounts of the assumed anatomy in this hypothesis differ significantly from present-day accounts. See also ARIS-TOTLE'S DOCTRINES/THEORIES; COG-NITIVE THEORY OF EMOTIONS.

REFERENCES

Avicenna. (1952). *Avicenna's psychology*. F. Rahman, Trans. London: Oxford University Press.

Kazdin, A. E. (Ed.) (2000). *Encyclopedia of psychology*. Vol. 6. New York: Ox-ford University Press.

INNERVATION, PRINCIPLE OF. See NEURON/NEURAL/NERVE THEORY; WUNDT'S THEORIES/DOCTRINES/PRIN-CIPLES.

INOCULATION THEORY. The American social psychologist William James McGuire (1925-) formulated this theory of resistance to persuasion based on the premise that most ordinary beliefs and attitudes are relatively resistant to change due to having been ex-posed to repeated mild cognitive/attitude "at-tacks" in one's everyday environment. The reasoning in *inoculation theory* is similar to that in a biological context where an individ-ual who has been raised in a sterile and germ-free environment (and who appears on the "surface" to be healthy) is, in fact, highly vulnerable to infection because she or he has not had the opportunity to develop chemical and biological defenses (such as antibodies) to ward off diseases (cf., Meichenbaum, 1985). Thus, in this context, an injection or "chemical inoculation" is used to provide biological resistance to diseases. So too, in psychological and social contexts, if the attitudes and beliefs (especially those regarding "personal-cultural truisms" - such as "early to bed, early to rise, makes one healthy, wealthy, and wise") of the individual have never been challenged (i.e., beliefs and attitudes exist in a vacuum or "sterile" environment), and there have not been any opportunities to develop defensive arguments, the person's resistance to persua-sion and attitude-change may, similarly, be increased by a process of "cognitive inocula-tion." *Inoculation theory* proposes that expos-ing the person to relatively weak "attacking" arguments (against certain of her atti-tudes/beliefs, along with rebuttals that are externally or internally generated) acts as an inoculation to strengthen the individual against stronger and more persuasive attacks concerning those attitudes/beliefs in the fu-ture. Also, *inoculation theory* indicates that the person so exposed/inoculated generally becomes more resistant to persuasion in the future even when the newer "attacking" arguments are different from those that were presented in the inoculation process. In his experiments, McGuire developed two types of "defense messages": the "supportive defense" - positive reassuring information supporting one's belief; and "refutational defense" - presentation of arguments against a belief/truism and then extensively refuting those arguments. McGuire found that the "supportive defense" increased the participant's belief in the given truism, whereas the "refutational defense" left the belief unchanged. However, when a message attacking the given truism was presented, it was found that the "supportive defense" gave much *less* resistance than the "refutational defense." The supposedly stronger attitude induced by the "supportive defense" was, in fact, *more* vulnerable to attack. McGuire labeled this paradoxical pattern the *paper tiger effect* and interpreted it in terms of a "motivation-practice" theoretical framework; cf., Farkas & Anderson (1976) who discovered that the seeming paradox of the *paper tiger effect* vanishes when viewed from the perspective of *information integration theory*, and suggest that there is no need to invoke the motivational concepts of belief threat and refutational practice employed in *inoculation theory*. See also INFECTION THEORY/EFFECT; INFORMATION INTEGRATION THEORY; PERSUASION/INFLUENCE THEORIES.

REFERENCES

McGuire, W. J. (1961). The effectiveness of supportive and refutational defenses in immunizing and restoring beliefs against persuasion. *Sociometry, 24,* 184-197.

McGuire, W. J. (1964). Inducing resistance to persuasion: Some contemporary approaches. In L. Berkowitz (Ed.), *Advances in experimental social psychology.* New York: Academic Press.

Farkas, A. J., & Anderson, N. H. (1976). Integration theory and inoculation theory as explanations of the "paper tiger effect." *Journal of Social Psychology, 98,* 253-268.

Meichenbaum, D. (1985). *Stress inoculation training.* New York: Pergamon.

INSTANCE/EPISODE/EXEMPLAR THEORY. See TRANSFER OF TRAINING, THORNDIKE'S THEORY OF.

INSTINCTIVE/INSTINCTUAL DRIFT. See McDOUGALL'S HORMIC/INSTINCT THEORY/DOCTRINE.

INSTINCTIVE THEORY OF PLAY. See PLAY, THEORIES OF.

INSTINCT THEORY. See McDOUGALL'S HORMIC/INSTINCT THEORY/DOCTRINE.

INSTINCT THEORY OF LAUGHTER/ HUMOR. See EASTMAN'S THEORY OF LAUGHTER; HUMOR, THEORIES OF; McDOUGALL'S THEORY OF HUMOR.

INSTRUCTIONAL THEORY. See ALGORITHMIC-HEURISTIC THEORY.

INSTRUMENTAL CONDITIONING, PRINCIPLE OF. See REINFORCEMENT THEORY; REINFORCEMENT, THORNDIKE'S THEORY OF; SKINNER'S DESCRIPTIVE BEHAVIOR/OPERANT CONDITIONING THEORY.

INSTRUMENTALITY THEORY. See WORK, CAREER, AND OCCUPATION, THEORIES OF.

INSUFFICIENT DETERRENCE HYPOTHESIS. See PUNISHMENT, THEORIES OF.

INSUFFICIENT-JUSTIFICATION EFFECT. See FESTINGER'S COGNITIVE DISSONANCE THEORY.

INSUFFICIENT REASON. See BAYES' THEOREM.

INTEGRATION THEORY. See CONTROL/SYSTEMS THEORY.

INTEGRITY THERAPY THEORY. See MOWRER'S THEORY.

INTELLIGENCE, THEORIES/LAWS OF. The concept of *intelligence* is broad in nature and refers to a person's complex mental abilities that include, among other things, the variables of amount of knowledge available at a given time; speed with which new knowledge is acquired; the ability to adapt to new situations; and the ability to deal with new and old concepts, abstract symbols, and cognitive relationships. The process of developing general mental "schemas" to classify events in the environment is called *abstract intelligence/ reasoning* (cf., *concretistic reasoning* or solving specific problems with specific materials) and *formal operations* (cf, Piaget, 1963), and may be measured in various ways. Many of the *theories of intelligence* are tied to particular tests, methods, and assessments of this complex concept, and these constitute what might be called *measured intelligence*. Some researchers in this area refer, also, to the "adaptive ability" (e.g., grades in school, performance and success at work) of the person as an indication of *general intelligence*. The modern concept of *measured intelligence* in psychology began with the French psychologist Alfred Binet (1857-1911), who was called upon in 1904 by the Paris minister of public instruction to develop a test that would identify subnormal children in the Paris schools for the purpose of placing and educating them in special schools. In 1905, Binet presented a scale for the measurement of intelligence, along with the French psychologist Theodore Simon (1873-1961). The scale consisted of tasks that were arranged in increasing difficulty according to the age at which an "average" child (i.e., criterion of 60-90% students passing the tasks) could master them. Using this method, Binet and Simon could identify a "mentally retarded" child, who performed below the average child for his or her particular age group. A total *mental age* (*MA*) score was calculated for each student and compared with his or her *chronological age* (*CA*). Binet's work on intelligence was developed further after 1911 by the German psychologist Lewis William Stern (1871-1938), who formulated the concept of *intelligence quotient, or IQ*, where overall *IQ score* equals *MA* divided by *CA* x 100 (cf., *Heinis' constant/law of mental growth*; Zusne, 1987). Thus, in the case of Binet, Simon, and Stern, intelligence was considered to be one *general* or *common*

factor of global functioning based on the person's test score on their standardized test. The Binet-Simon Test was translated from French into English and brought to the United States by the American psychologist Henry Goddard (1866-1957) in 1908. In 1916, the American psychologist/psychometrician Lewis Terman (1877-1956) at Stanford University adapted the Binet-Simon Test to create the Stanford-Binet Test, which provided a single score of intelligence. In 1904, the English psychologist and psychometrician Charles Spearman (1863-1945) proposed a slightly different theoretical viewpoint (called the *two-factor theory*) concerning intelligence, where he showed the presence of one *general factor* (*g*) in classroom tests of intellectual ability and achievement (cf., *law of inertia* - posits that persons who are slow in starting a mental process take a long time to finish, and such people have difficulty in going back and forth between two ideas, as well as difficulty in applying an earlier learned skill to new ideas; also, J. Raven's *progressive matrices theory*), as well as a number of *specific factors* (*s*). The question of whether intelligence is basically a single ability (*g*) or a group of specific abilities (*s*) has been debated by psychologists for more than three generations and still remains unresolved [cf., the notion of *fluid intelligence/ability*, derived from *factor analysis* by the English-born American psychologist Raymond B. Cattell (1905-1998), referring to nonverbal reasoning abilities requiring rapid understanding of novel relationships; *fluid intelligence*, along with *crystallized intelligence* comprises Cattell's *dual-intelligence theory*]. The Romanian-American psychologist David Wechsler (1896-1981) developed a set of individually administered intelligence tests that measured several factors such as comprehension, vocabulary, similarities, block design, and object assembly on scales that provide an overall intelligence score as well as subscale scores on *verbal* and *performance* abilities (cf., *multimodal theory of intelligence*, or *multiple-factor theory*, which generally postulates that more than one common factor can account for a given phenomenon and, in particular, assumes that intelligence is made up of a number of different factors or abilities). The American psychologist/psychometrician Louis

Leon Thurstone (1887-1955) devised a ratio scale for the measurement of intelligence in 1928 after he pointed out the psychometric inadequacies of the Binet-Simon-Stern concept of *MA* as a scale for mental ability and of the *IQ* concept when used as the ratio of *MA* to *CA*. That is, the concept of *MA* is ambiguous and can mean two different things: the average age of children obtaining a given score or the average test score of children of a given age. Thurstone's theoretical approach emphasizes the use of percentile ranks or standard scores instead of *MA* and *IQ*. This viewpoint is the basis for all modern intelligence tests, and such intelligence scores today are actually standard scores with a population mean of 100 and standard deviation of 15 or 16. Thurstone's approach is based, also, on the statistical method of *factor analysis*, wherein he extracted a number of factors he called *primary mental abilities*. Thurstone developed "factor-pure" tests for the seven factors of reasoning, verbal comprehension, word fluency, number, spatial visualization, perceptual speed, and associative memory. Currently, however, it is thought that each "factor-pure" test measures not only one of Thurstone's *primary abilities* but, also, Spearman's *g* factor to some degree. The American psychologist Joy Paul Guilford (1897-1987) made numerous *factor analytic* studies of intellectual abilities and developed an ambitious and creative model called the *structure-of-intellect model/theory*, which suggests the existence of as many as 150 separate and distinct functions or abilities. In at least 120 of these "intelligences," Guilford conceives of a stack of building blocks six blocks high, four blocks wide, and five blocks deep, and where each block, theoretically, is a separate "intelligence." This novel approach (also called *Guilford's cube*) suggests there are five "operations" (evaluation, convergent production, divergent production, memory, cognition), four "contents" (figural, symbolic, semantic, behavioral), and six "products" (units, classes, relations, systems, transformations, implications). According to Guilford, a person uses various operations, contents, and products whenever she or he is engaged in intellectual activities (cf., *Sternberg & Lubart's theory of creativity*). Thus, to oversimplify the range of *classical*

theories of intelligence, one may go from the Binet-Simon-Stern concept of one general/global factor, to the Spearman-Wechsler concept of one general plus several specific factors, to Jean Piaget's emphasis on cognitive development, to Thurstone's seven (or eight) factors/abilities and, finally, to Guilford's theoretical approach that invokes 150 distinct abilities or "intelligences" [cf., *aggregation theory* - refers to a conjecture by the American psychologist James McKeen Cattell (1860-1944) that intelligence is a function of the number of neurons in the brain and the interconnections among them]. The more *modern/contemporary theories of intelligence* focus on concepts such as *multiple intelligences* (Gardner, 1983), *triarchic* (componental, experiential, and contextual, or analytic, creative, and practical) *intelligence* (Sternberg, 1985, 1988), *emotional/social intelligence* (Goleman, 1995), and *mental self-government* (Sternberg, 1986). A general class of theories that attempts to account for individual differences ranging from reaction time, through intelligence, to study of personal values is called *individuality theory*. Questions concerning *intelligence* that remain to be answered by further theoretical and empirical developments before the "laws of intelligence" may be stated are: Is intelligence truly one general ability or several specific abilities? Is intelligence a matter of rapid information processing? In intelligence genetically, environmentally, or culturally defined? The American psychologist Arthur Robert Jensen (1923-) developed an *information-processing theory of intelligence* and succeeded - where Francis Galton (1822-1911) failed earlier - in showing a relationship between general intelligence and measures derived from choice reaction-time tasks; Jensen studied, also, several physical and neurological correlates of general intelligence [cf., *Flynn effect* - named after the American-born New Zealand political scientist James Robert Flynn (1934-), refers to a mysterious increase in average *IQ* scores, about three *IQ* points per decade, that has been occurring in many industrial societies since the introduction of *IQ* tests; and *collective memory theory* - attempts to explain the general rise of *IQ* scores over time, whereas the general level of intelligence remains relatively

314

constant for any given population; the theory assumes that intelligence test items become more familiar longitudinally - vis-à-vis popular tests - as an increasing number of people learn the answers to questions over time; cf., *dysgenic trend theory* - claims that the general level of intelligence is falling/decreasing over time; the *overlap hypothesis* - attempts to explain the increasing consistency of *IQ* scores as individuals become older by stating that knowledge and skills remain constant and, thus, overlap increasingly with time; and *resource depletion theory* - a questionable proposition which states that with a reduction of resources in families - dependent on the number of children - the possible result, among other things, would be lower intelligence test scores for children in large families]. One popular explanation for the observed social class and racial differences on intelligence tests is called the *cultural bias hypothesis*, which states that the typical experiences involving the acquisition of skills and knowledge are different for different subpopulations, and the content of test items is selected much more from the experiences of certain groups of individuals such as whites, Anglo-Saxons, Protestants, and "middle" class persons than from the experiences of other groups of persons such as blacks, poor, and "lower" class individuals (cf., Herrnstein & Murray, 1994) . See also EMOTIONAL INTELLIGENCE, THEORY OF; GALTON'S LAWS; NATURE VERSUS NURTURE THEORIES; PERSONALITY THEORIES; PIAGET'S THEORY OF DEVELOPMENTAL STAGES.

REFERENCES

Spearman, C. (1904). "General intelligence," objectively determined and measured. *American Journal of Psychology, 15*, 201-292.

Stern, W. (1912). *The psychological methods of testing intelligence.* Baltimore: Warwick & York.

Binet, A., & Simon, T. (1915). *A method of measuring the development of intelligence of young children.* Chicago: Medical Books.

Terman, L. (1916). *The measurement of intelligence.* Boston: Houghton Mifflin.

[Symposium]. (1921). Intelligence and its measurement. *Journal of Educational Psychology, 12*, 123-147, 195-216, 271-275.

Thurstone, L. (1926). The mental age concept. *Psychological Review, 33*, 268-278.

Thurstone, L. (1938). Primary mental abilities. *Psychometric Monographs*, No. 1. Chicago: University of Chicago Press.

Thurstone, L. (1947). *Multiple-factor analysis: A development and expansion of the vectors of the mind.* Chicago: University of Chicago Press.

Guilford, J. P. (1956). The structure of intellect. *Psychological Bulletin, 53*, 267-293.

Raven, J. (1960). *Guide to the standard progressive matrices.* London: Lewis.

Piaget, J. (1963). *The origins of intelligence in children.* New York: Norton.

Guilford, J. P. (1967). *The nature of human intelligence.* New York: McGraw-Hill.

Jensen, A. R. (1969). How much can be boost IQ and scholastic achievement? *Harvard Educational Review, 39*, 1-123.

Eysenck, H. J. (1971). *The IQ argument: Race, intelligence, and education.* New York: Library Press.

Wechsler, D. (1974). *Wechsler Intelligence Scale for Children, revised.* New York: Psychological Corporation.

Flynn, J. R. (1980). *Race, IQ, and Jensen.* London: Rutledge & Kegan Paul.

Jensen, A. R. (1980). *Bias in mental testing.* New York: Free Press.

Gould, S. J. (1981). *The mismeasure of man.* New York: Norton.

Gardner, H. (1983). *Frames of mind: The theory of multiple intelligences.* New York: Basic Books.

Sternberg, R. (1985). *Beyond IQ: A triarchic theory of human intelligence.* New York: Cambridge University Press.

Sternberg, R. (1986). Intelligence is mental self-government. In R. Sternberg & D. Detterman (Eds.), *What is intelligence? Contemporary viewpoints on its nature and definition.* Norwood, NJ: Ablex.

Zusne, L. (1987). *Eponyms in psychology.* Westport, CT: Greenwood Press.

Sternberg, R. (1988). *The triarchic mind: A new theory of human intelligence.* New York: Viking.

Sternberg, R., & Lubart, T. (1991). An investment theory of creativity and its development. *Human Development, 34,* 1-31.

Herrnstein, R. J., & Murray, C. A. (1994). *The bell curve: Intelligence and class structure in American life.* New York: Free Press.

Goleman, D. (1995). *Emotional intelligence: Why it can matter more than IQ.* New York: Bantam.

INTENSITY THEORY OF TROPISMS. See LOEB'S TROPISTIC THEORY.

INTENSITY/VIVIDNESS, LAW OF. See ASSOCIATION, LAWS/PRINCIPLES OF.

INTENTIONAL FORGETTING, THEORY OF. See FORGETTING/MEMORY, THEORIES OF.

INTENTIONALISM/INTENTIONALITY, PSYCHOLOGICAL THEORY OF. See DEVELOPMENTAL THEORY; MIND-BODY THEORIES.

INTERACTION AND MAIN/TREATMENT EFFECTS. The *interaction effect* is a pattern of data in statistics obtained from multifactorial analysis of variance in which the influence/effect of a manipulated [or independent variable (IV)] factor varies across different levels of another IV, or across combinations of levels of other IVs or factors. Under such conditions, variation in the measured [or dependent variable (DV)] factor is *not* the result of a simple additive combination of the IVs/factors; for example, the IV of "task difficulty" and the DV of measured "arousal level" often *interact* whereby increased "arousal" increases performance on "easy tasks," but decreases it on "difficult tasks;" cf., *Yerkes-Dodson law*). The principal difficulty with *interaction effects*, once discovered in data, is that they are very difficult to interpret, and where a graphing of the levels and

factors on an "interaction graph" is somewhat helpful. In contrast to an *interaction effect*, the concept of a *main effect/treatment effect* refers to a statistically significant difference between two or more means/averages; a *two-way interaction* is a statistically significant difference between two or more *differences* between means/aver-ages; and a *three-way interaction* is a statistically significant difference between two or more differences between two or more *differences* between means/averages, and so on; however, the data interpretations beyond *three-way interactions* are extremely complex both in understanding and in graphing results. In graphing *interaction effects*, say for a *two-way interaction*, the vertical axis represents scores on the DV, and the horizontal axis represents different levels of one IV, and each line on the graph denotes a different level of another IV; if the lines so constructed are *parallel*, it signifies that there is *no* interaction effect present, but if the lines cross or are non-parallel, it signifies that there *is* an interaction effect present, at which time the data may be tested further for statistical significance using specialized "post-hoc" statistical procedures or tests. See also AROUSAL THEORY; YERKES-DODSON LAW.

REFERENCE

Ray, W. J. (2003). *Methods toward a science of behavior and experience.* 7th ed. Belmont, CA: Wadsworth/Thomson.

INTERACTION/INTERACTIONISM, THEORY/DOCTRINE OF. See MIND-BODY THEORIES.

INTERACTION OF REFLEXES, LAW OF. See SKINNER'S DESCRIPTIVE BEHAVIOR/OPERANT CONDITIONING THEORY.

INTERACTION PRINCIPLE. See LEWIN'S FIELD THEORY.

INTERACTION PROCESS ANALYSIS TECHNIQUE. The American social psychologist Robert F. Bales (1916-) developed the *interaction process analysis* approach to study behavior in small groups where observers of the group interaction process record the actions of each of the group member's responses into one of 12 categories: shows *solidarity* - the target person raises others' status, gives help, gives rewards; *shows tension-release* - the individual laughs, jokes, or shows satisfaction; *shows agreement* - the person indicates passive acceptance, understanding, or compliance; *gives suggestion* - the person gives directions, or implies autonomy for others; *gives opinion* - the person gives evaluation, analysis, feelings, or wishes; *gives orientation* - the individual gives information, repeats, confirms, or clarifies information; *asks for orientation* - the person asks for information, confirmation, or repetition of past information; *asks for opinion* - the person asks for evaluation, analysis, or expression of feeling; *asks for suggestion* - the person asks for direction or possible ways of action; *disagrees* - the individual shows passive rejection or withholds help; *shows tension* - the person asks for help or withdraws from the situation; *shows antagonism* - the person deflates the status of others, and defends or asserts himself. The researcher may combine some of the 12 categories in certain ways and, thereby, define and elaborate on various subsets of interaction "climates." For example, in defining a social-emotional climate as "positive," categories 1-3 would score highest; task climate is "neutral" when categories 4-9 score highest; and a "negative" social-emotional climate is defined by high scores in categories 10-12. Also, by combining the scores in certain categories, one may quickly identify and analyze various types of specific issues (such as problems of communication, evaluation, control, decision-making, tension-reduction, and reintegration) in a group interaction situation. When the *interaction process analysis* data is organized according to "initiators" and "targets," one obtains a "matrix;" when it is organized according to "acts," one obtains a "profile;" and when it is organized according to "time," one obtains a "phase sequence." Further analyses of the summary forms of organization indicate certain regularities of group interaction (e.g., "matrices" show a tendency for group members to reach a balance regarding the relative amount of activity they initiate and receive; "profiles" reveal a tendency for attempted answers to out-number

their related questions and for positive reactions to out-number their related negative reactions; and "phase sequences" reveal progressive shifts from emphasis on the problem-orientation to emphasis on the problems of evaluation and control). Typically, protocol analyses of the *interaction process analysis* technique reveal that two major types of group *leader* emerge in the interactive group: a "task-oriented specialist," and a "social-oriented specialist," where the group's leadership role is shared, mostly by the two individuals who fill such "specialist" roles. Bales is the author and inventor, also, of the "System for the Multiple Level Observation of Groups" (SYMLOG) which is a *field theory* emphasizing the multiple contexts in which people live; SYMLOG has been employed successfully in the following training and developmental areas: individual coaching/counseling; leadership; management/organization; human resources; strategic planning; organizational culture; program evaluation and refinement; market research/customer relations; team development; global/cross-cultural work force development; and family/group counseling. See also COMMUNICATION THEORY; DECISION-MAKING THEORIES; DEINDIVIDUATION THEORY; GROUP MIND PHENOMENON; GROUPTHINK PHENOMENON; LEADERSHIP, THEORIES OF; ORGANIZATIONAL, INDUS-TRIAL, AND SYSTEMS THEORY.

REFERENCES

Bales, R. F. (1950). *Interaction process analysis: A method for the study of small groups*. Reading, MA: Addison-Wesley.

Polley, R. B., Hare, A. P., & Stone, P. J. (1988) *The SYMLOG practitioner: Applications of small group research*. New York: Praeger.

Hare, A. P. (1992). *Groups, teams, and social interaction: Theories and applications*. New York: Praeger.

INTERACTIVE ACTIVATION MODEL OF LETTER PERCEPTION. This model describes perception resulting from excitatory and inhibitory interactions of detectors for visual features, letters, and words. According to the *interactive activation model of letter perception*, a visual input excites detectors for visual features in a display, and for letters consistent with the active features; *letter* detectors, in turn, excite detectors for consistent *words*. The model, along with its computer-simulation form, proposes that active word detectors mutually inhibit each other and send feedback to the letter level and, thereby, strengthen activation as well as facilitating the perception of a word's constituent letters. The model demonstrates the "perceptual advantage" for letters-in-words over that of unrelated contexts, and is consistent with the basic findings concerning "word advantage;" also, the model facilitates perception for letters in pronounceable pseudowords as well as regular words. Thus, the *interactive activation model* indicates that *context* aids the perception of target letters as they are processed in the perceptual system (the *contextual enhancement effect*), in addition to accounting for rule-governed performance in situations where there are no apparent or actual rules present. See also HIERARCHICAL MODEL OF WORD IDENTIFICATION; INFORMATION/INFORMATION-PROCESSING THEORY; PERCEPTION (I. AND II.), THEORIES OF; TRACE MODEL OF DISTRIBUTED MEMORY AND SPEECH PERCEPTION; WORD-SUPERIORITY EFFECT.

REFERENCES

McClelland, J. L., & Rumelhart, D. E. (1981). An interactive activation model of context effects in letter perception: I. An account of basic findings. *Psychological Review*, 88, 375-407.

Rumelhart, D. E., & McClelland, J. L. (1982). An interactive activation model of context effects in letter perception: II. The contextual enhancement effect and some tests and extensions of the model. *Psychological Review*, 89, 60-94.

INTERBEHAVIORAL THEORY. *Interbehavioral theory*, or "interbehaviorism," is a naturalistic and behavioral system of psychology developed by the American psychologist Jacob Robert Kantor (1888-1984) that attempts to indicate the appropriate way of dealing with different scientific concepts. Interbehaviorism rejects traditional mental fictions ("mentalism") that result from humans operating and reacting in a *dualistic* (mind-body) culture, as well as rejecting most of the other hypothetical entities so popular in mainstream psychology. *Interbehavioral theory* asserts that there is no scientific basis for imaginary constructs, such as "executive" or "storage" centers of the mind/brain, and "psychological events" are considered to be part of nature and not apart from nature. In Kantor's approach, the behaving organism may be viewed as a stimulus object where it interacts with other behaving organisms so that the action of each is considered to be coordinate, reciprocal, and mutual. In *interbehavioral theory*, emphasis is placed on a field approach and rationale where the setting and conditions surrounding the interaction or interbehavior of the organism and other stimulus objects is paramount. Similar to the discipline of ecology - where analyses are made of the relationships of organisms to their environment and to one another – *interbehavioral theory* views the joint activity of organisms and their environments as a "system" or "field" where the interaction of the various complex and interdependent factors constitute a "psychological event" for the organism. In particular, *interbehavioral theory* rests largely on the principle that "present events are a function of antecedent events;" also, it relies only on observable entities where past events - even though not now observable - were observable at one time and, therefore, are not merely imaginary phenomena. Several of the distinct features of "psychological events" - as theorized by the *interbehaviorist* - include the following: they are historical and show a greater specificity than biological events; they show integration and variability; they are modifiable and show inhibition as well as delayability. Additionally, the *interbehaviorist* distinguishes among the concepts of object, stimulus object, response function, and stimulus function; for instance, an object, as such, has no psychological significance until it begins to participate in a "psychological event;" also, different response configurations may serve equivalent functions and even the *same* response configuration may serve different functions. Essentially, *interbehavioral theory*, or *interbehavioral psychol-*

318

ogy, is distinguished by the following characteristics: it abandons *mind-body dualism*; it
adopts a *naturalistic* approach; it advances a
field theory paradigm that requires detailed
analyses and variables-specifications involved
in the field; and it distinguishes *psychological*
from *physiological* data. See also FINAL
THEORY; LEARNING THEORIES/ LAWS;
LEWIN'S FIELD THEORY; SKINNER'S
DESCRIPTIVE BEHAVIOR/OPER-ANT
CONDITIONING THEORY.

REFERENCES

Kantor, J. R. (1924/1926). *Principles of psy-
chology.* 2 vols. New York: Knopf.
Kantor, J. R. (1933). *A survey of the science of
psychology.* Bloomington, IN: Prin-
cipia Press.
Kantor, J. R. (1958). *Interbehavioral psychol-
ogy.* Bloomington, IN: Principia
Press.
Kantor, J. R. (1963). *The scientific evolution
of psychology.* Chicago: Principia
Press.
Kantor, J. R. (1971). *Aim and progress of
psychology and other sciences.* Chi-
cago: Principia Press.
Kantor, J. R. (1982). *Cultural psychology.*
Chicago: Principia Press.

INTEREST, LAW OF. See CONDUCT,
LAWS OF.

**INTERFERENCE THEORIES OF FOR-
GETTING.** *Interference theory* states that
forgetting occurs because similar memories
interfere with the storage or retrieval of information. Interference is an *active* theory of forgetting; without interfering events there is no
forgetting. An early functionalist's view of the
conditions that affect the transfer and forgetting of verbal materials is provided by the
American psychologist John Alexander Mc-
Geoch (1897-1942), who accepted two major
laws of forgetting and transfer: the *law of
context*, which states that the degree of retention of material, as measured by performance,
is a function of the *similarity* between the
original learning situation and the retention
situation; and the *law of proactive and retroactive inhibition*, which states that the retention of material is a function of *activities* occurring prior to, and subsequent to, the origi-

nal learning (cf., *perseveration theory* of G.
Muller and A. Pilzecker - refers to the consolidation of memory where the preservation
of a neural process is viewed as necessary for
a permanent trace to be established; thus, a
new experience creates neural activity in the
brain and, if the event is to be remembered, a
process that changes the brain must occur).
The evolution of hypotheses regarding *similarity effects* in retroaction and transfer is
traced by G. Bower and E. R. Hilgard (1981):
the early experiments, demonstrating retroactive inhibition and the possible role of *similarity* as a factor (e.g, J. A. McGeoch); E.
Robinson's somewhat crude dimensional hypothesis, which led to a series of experiments
that revealed multiple sources and kinds of
intertask similarities requiring a generalization
more complex than the *Skaggs-Robinson hypothesis* (E. Skaggs and E. Robinson); C.
Osgood's synthesis (via his *transfer and retroaction surface*), incorporating the results of
transfer and retroactive interference; and E.
Martin's proposed "component transfer surfaces" to compensate for Osgood's simplistic
synthesis. This type of succession of hypothesized generalizations, according to Bower and
Hilgard - with an interplay between data, analytical criticism, and theory - demonstrates a
maturing functional analysis, as well as indicating some potential frustrations of a func-
tionalistic approach. The most serviceable
theory of forgetting that has emerged from
laboratory experiments is the *interference
theory* that is connected to the functionalists'
analysis of negative transfer and interference.
The *interference theory* is an "association"
theory; that is, its basic primitive concept is an
associative bond, or functional connection,
between two or more elements where elements may be ideas, words, situational stimuli,
or responses. Changes in *interference theory*
have occurred over the years. For example, L.
Postman's formulations may be compared
with J. McGeoch's earlier statements where
new concepts have been added, unsupported
conjecture dropped, and new experimental
methods devised to measure more exactly the
relevant dependent variables. One major shift
in *interference theory* consists of the powerful
role assigned to *proactive* sources of interference in forgetting. The history of research on

verbal interference shows several subtheories of interference. In the 1930s, a viable theory of interference was the *independence hypothesis*, which suggested that interfering responses compete at recall, and the strongest one in the competition is the one that actually occurs. In a *retroactive interference paradigm* where the learning of material A and B is followed by the recall of A, the decrement in recall of A was explained by the dominance of B. The successor to the *independence hypothesis* was the *unlearning hypothesis*, which holds that the decrement in A at recall is due to the fact that the learning of B brings about the *extinction* of A in part. Later, there is the *differentiation hypothesis/theory of differential forgetting* (McGeoch, 1942), which asserts that interference reduces the discriminability, or differentiation, of the material where the learning of B reduces the discriminability of A, and decreases its availability at recall (cf., *generalization-differentiation theory*; Gibson, 1940; Tighe & Tighe, 1968). The early studies of interference used "meaningless" materials such as *nonsense syllables* or randomly unrelated words as information to be learned. However, recent research provides evidence that similar interference processes operate in the learning and forgetting of meaningful text materials (e.g., single sentences and interrelated sets of sentences or paragraphs) as well. See also ASSOCIATION, LAWS/PRINCIPLES OF; FORGETTING/MEMORY, THEORIES OF; FUNCTIONALISM THEORY; INHIBITION, LAWS OF; SKAGGS-ROBINSON HYPOTHESIS; TRANSFER OF TRAINING, THORNDIKE'S THEORY OF.

REFERENCES

Muller, G., & Pilzecker, A. (1900). Experimentelle beitrage zur lehre vom gedachtnis. *Zeitschrift fur Psychologie*, Ergbd. I.

Skaggs, E. (1925). Further studies in retroactive inhibition. *Psychological Monographs, 34*, No. 161.

Robinson, E. (1927). The "similarity" factor in retroaction. *American Journal of Psychology, 39*, 297-312.

McGeoch, J. A. (1932). Forgetting and the law of disuse. *Psychological Review, 39*, 352-370.

Gibson, E. (1940). A systematic application of the concepts of generalization and differentiation to verbal learning. *Psychological Review, 47*, 196-229.

McGeoch, J. A. (1942). *The psychology of human learning*. New York: Longmans, Green.

Osgood, C. (1949). The similarity paradox in human learning: A resolution. *Psychological Review, 56*, 132-143.

Underwood, B. (1957). Interference and forgetting. *Psychological Review, 64*, 49-60.

Underwood, B., & Postman, L. (1960). Extra-experimental sources of interference in forgetting. *Psychological Review, 67*, 73-95.

Postman, L. (1961). The present status of interference theory. In C. Cofer (Ed.), *Verbal learning and verbal behavior*. New York: McGraw-Hill.

Martin, E. (1965). Transfer of verbal paired associates. *Psychological Review, 72*, 327-343.

Tighe, T., & Tighe, L. (1968). Differentiation theory and concept-shift behavior. *Psychological Bulletin, 70*, 756-761.

Lewis, D. J. (1979). Psychology of active and inactive memory. *Psychological Bulletin, 86*, 1054-1083.

Bower, G., & Hilgard, E. R. (1981). *Theories of learning*. Englewood Cliffs, NJ: Prentice-Hall.

Sarason, I. G., & Pierce, G. R. (1996). *Cognitive interference: Theories, methods, and findings*. Mahwah, NJ: Erlbaum.

INTERJECTIONAL/POOH-POOH/EXCLAMATION THEORY. See LANGUAGE ORIGINS, THEORIES OF.

INTERMEDIATE GENE EFFECTS. See MENDEL'S LAWS/PRINCIPLES.

INTERMITTENT PROCESSING THEORY. See INFORMATION/INFORMATION-PROCESSING THEORY.

INTERPERSONAL ATTRACTION THEORIES. *Interpersonal attraction* refers to a favorable attitude toward, or feeling of liking for, another person. People are attracted to others for a variety of reasons, and there are many different kinds of attraction. One generalization concerning interpersonal attraction is the *reward theory*, which states that we like people whose behavior provides us with maximum reward at minimum cost. The *gain-loss theory* suggests that increases in positive, rewarding behavior from another person will have more impact on an individual than constant, invariant reward from that person. Thus, if one considers "being liked" as a reward, a person whose liking for us *increases* over time will be liked more than one who has *always* liked us. Four other theories/principles that describe interpersonal attraction are *similarity*, *beauty/physical appearance*, *proximity*, and *social exchange*. The *similarity-attraction theory* suggests that we like other people whose attitudes, values, and beliefs appear to be similar to our own (cf., *matching hypothesis* - holds that one tends to interact with, and be attracted to, others who are relatively equal to oneself in factors such as physique, age, intelligence, and ethnicity, and seems to be true for both same-sex and opposite-sex relationships). The *principle of beauty/physical appearance* refers to the rather obvious prediction that we tend to prefer physically attractive to physically unattractive individuals. Within a given *culture*, there is considerable agreement in judgments of a person's physical attractiveness, but little is known about the particular attributes that define "beauty." However, there is strong evidence indicating a gender distinction where physical appearance has a greater influence on the attraction of men to women than vice versa. The principle of *proximity* states that we are more likely to be attracted to people who live and work close to us rather than to those who live/work farther away. Use of the term *proximity* in the area of study called *proxemics*, including *body-buffer zone theory* (where emphasis is placed on the nonverbal expression involving spatial *distance* between interacting people, and their orientation toward each other, as reflected in *distance* separating them; according to this approach, the greater the "body-buffer zone," the more aggressive is the individual), involves the related issues/concepts of "crowding," "territoriality," and "personal space" [cf., *ethologi-*

cal models of personal space - suggest that "personal space bubbles" (i.e., the proximity with-in which creatures of one species will not allow other members of the same species to come near them) have been used by various species throughout evolutionary history to protect individual organisms against aggression; allegedly, persons living near the equator have relatively small person-space limits, whereas those living in northern areas have a need for relatively larger limits]. *Proximity* is, perhaps, the most important determinant of whom people choose as friends, lovers, and spouses; often, people end up marrying mates who live only a few blocks away. In general, the closer in distance people are to others, the more opportunities they have of becoming familiar with them: knowledge often leads to attraction and love. According to the *filter theory of mate selection*, people consciously or unconsciously search for mates based on a series of standards in a "filter hierarchy;" filters include age, appearance, education, nationality, vocation, personal resources, personality, friends, and family; the *likeness and completeness marital success theories* suggest that the factors of "likeness" and "group completeness," as reflected in participants' responses on marital inventories/tests, are characteristic of more successful marriages; and the *stage theory of mate selection* emphasizes the *process* by which persons are attracted to one another, fall in love, and marry; the process is described in terms of discrete stages relating to the stabilization of the relationship and by stimulus variables and social-role expectations. The *theory of social exchange* states that a relationship between two persons will be formed and maintained if, for each person, the *rewards* from the interaction are greater than the *costs*. A variation on the *social-exchange theory*, called *equity theory*, shifts the emphasis from the individual to that of the factors of mutual costs and benefits where a group of people can maximize their outcome in any interaction situation by working out an arrangement for equitably dividing the benefits and costs among group members. There is some evidence, also, that attraction and liking are influenced by such *nonverbal* behaviors as smiling, eye contact, physical touch, and body posture. See also COOP-

ERATION/COMPETITION, THEORIES OF; DEVELOPMENTAL THEORY; EQUITY THEORY; EXCHANGE AND SOCIAL EXCHANGE THEORY; INGROUP BIAS THEORIES; LOVE, THEORIES OF; SULLIVAN'S THEORY OF PERSONALITY.

REFERENCES

Heider, F. (1958). *The psychology of interpersonal relations.* New York: Wiley.

Thibaut, J., & Kelley, H. (1959). *The social psychology of groups.* New York: Wiley.

Aronson, E., & Linder, D. (1965). Gain and loss of esteem as determinants of interpersonal attractiveness. *Journal of Experimental Social Psychology, 1*, 156-171.

Berscheid, E., & Walster, E. (1969). *Interpersonal attraction.* Reading, MA: Addison-Wesley.

Byrne, D. (1971). *The attraction paradigm.* New York: Academic Press.

Huston, T., & Levinger, G. (1978). Interpersonal attraction and relationships. *Annual Review of Psychology, 29*, 115-156.

INTERPERSONAL PERCEPTION THEORY. See IMPRESSION FORMATION, THEORIES OF.

INTERPERSONAL STAGE DEVELOPMENT THEORY. See ERIKSON'S THEORY OF PERSONALITY.

INTERPERSONAL THEORY. See SULLIVAN'S THEORY OF PERSONALITY.

INTERPRETER EFFECT. See COMMUNICATION THEORY.

INTERVENING VARIABLES THEORY. See HULL'S LEARNING THEORY; LEARNING THEORIES/LAWS.

INTERVIEW CONTRAST EFFECT. See COMMUNICATION THEORY.

INTERVIEWER BIAS/EFFECT. See COMMUNICATION THEORY.

INTIMACY, PRINCIPLE OF. See GESTALT THEORY/LAWS.

INTRAPSYCHIC THEORIES. See PSYCHOPATHOLOGY, THEORIES OF; RANK'S THEORY OF PERSONALITY.

INTUITION, THEORIES OF. The phenomenon of *intuition* refers to a mode of knowing that emphasizes direct and immediate understanding and which occurs without conscious thought or judgment. The following theoretical orientations toward *intuition* are described by the Canadian psychologist Malcolm R. Westcott (1968; 1984): various *philosophical* viewpoints are covered by K. W. Wild who provides over two dozen definitions of *intuition*, including its status as the most primitive mental function (on which all perception and reason depend), its function as the realization of "fundamental truth," its ability demonstrated in some persons for arriving at conclusions without formulation of the premises, its connection to ultimate human values such as goodness, beauty, and truth, its facility of knowing what is beyond proof or demonstration, and its role in reason as that which follows, rather than precedes, rational thought; Wild suggests that *intuition* should not be viewed as antagonistic to reason, but the two are merely "alien" to each other (cf., Bunge, 1962). Among the *psychological* conceptions of *intuition*, and *theories of intuition*, are the following: in the 19th century, H. von Helmholtz argued that intuitions are rapid "unconscious inferences" developed from common experiences; in *Gestalt theory*, the notion was advanced that intuition helps to apprehend events and stimuli as totalities, which was opposed by *associationistic theory* which argued that totalities are built up or constructed as inferences from separate sensory events; in *personality theory*, G. W. Allport argued for the "total apprehension" of a personality via intuition, but R. B. Cattell suggested that as an independent method of arriving at psychological knowledge, intuition seems to be "pure illusion;" C. G. Jung presents intuition as one of four basic mental functions (the others are feeling, sensation, and thinking) that all individuals possess, but developed only to greater or lesser degree across people; also, according to *Jung's theory*, intuition focuses on a nonjudgmental perception of principles, possibilities, and implications at the expense of details, and it may exist in extraverts as well as introverts. Although other psychologists have given accounts of intuition, only the Australian-Jamaican educator Tony Bastick (1982) has attempted to place the concept in a central role in a *general theory*; Bastick reviews a great variety of definitions and descriptions of intuition from diverse fields, and derives almost two dozen different properties that characterize the process, such as emotional involvement, subjective certainty, empathy, and speed. In his *theory of intuition*, Bastick argues, also, that intuitive processes are involved in all thought and action; the theory suggests that important/great intuitions occur when there is high initial dissonance in a situation where such a state is resolved by a new combination of "emotional sets," and where the thoughts, feelings, and actions associated with the new "emotional set" constitutes the intuition. In support of his *theory of intuition*, Bastick integrates research from a wide array of fields/topics such as projective testing, psychophysiology, cognition, personality, and demographic/cultural variables. Such an approach serves to highlight the two broad notions, or theoretical views, of intuition among psychologists: intuition is conceived of as solving problems and making judgments via informal, inexplicit, and/or obscure information processes (cf., *intuitive physics* - involves assumptions about the motion of objects that are commonly believed but that sometimes violate the established laws of Newtonian mechanics; e.g., dropping an object while walking fast results in the object continuing to move forward, hitting the ground alongside the walker, but most people believe that the object will drop straight down, hitting the ground directly below the point at which it was released); and intuition is conceived of as a cognitive/emotional step that goes beyond judgment, decision-making, or learning to achieve a full appreciation and understanding of a personality, subject matter, or situation, sometimes involving the modification of one's phenomenal field or set. See also ASSOCIATION, LAWS/PRINCIPLES OF; DISSONANCE THEORY; EMPATHY THEORY; GESTALT THEORY/LAWS; INTUITIVE THEORY OF EMOTIONS; JUNG'S THEORY OF PERSONALITY; PERSONALITY THEORIES; PROBLEM-SOLVING AND CREATIVITY STAGE THEORIES; UNCONSCIOUS INFERENCE, DOCTRINE OF.

REFERENCES

Jung, C. G. (1921/1976). *Psychological types*. Princeton, NJ: Princeton University Press.

Allport, G. W. (1929). The study of personality by the intuitive method. *Journal of Abnormal and Social Psychology*, 24, 14-27.

Cattell, R. B. (1937). Measurement versus intuition in applied psychology. *Character and Personality*, 6, 114-131.

Wild, K. W. (1938). *Intuition*. London: Cambridge University Press.

Bunge, M. (1962). *Intuition and science*. Englewood Cliffs, NJ: Prentice-Hall.

Westcott, M. R. (1968). *Toward a contemporary psychology of intuition*. New York: Holt, Rinehart, and Winston.

Bastick, T. (1982). *Intuition: How we think and act*. Chichestser, UK: Wiley.

Westcott, M. R. (1984). Intuition. In R. J. Corsini (Ed.), *Encyclopedia of psychology*. Vol. 2. New York: Wiley.

Bastick, T. (2003). *Intuition: Evaluating the construct and its impact on creative thinking*. New York: Stoneman & Lang.

INTUITIVE THEORY OF EMOTIONS. See JAMES-LANGE/LANGE-JAMES THEORY OF EMOTIONS.

INVERSE SQUARE LAW. See NORMAL DISTRIBUTION THEORY; VISION/SIGHT, THEORIES OF.

INVERTED IMAGES EFFECT/ILLUSION. See APPENDIX A.

INVERTED QUALIA. See MIND/MENTAL STATES, THEORIES OF.

INVERTED-U HYPOTHESIS. This hypothesis, also known as the *Yerkes-Dodson law*, refers to the results observed in a situation where performance on a task (e.g., taking a test) is seen as a function of one's arousal level (e.g., degree of motivation or anxiety), and where behavior is optimal at *moderate* levels but drops off with either decreases or increases in the individual's arousal level. When graphed, the distribution of potential results under such circumstances appears to be a curve in the shape of an upside down (inverted) letter U. Because the phenomenon described by the inverted-U relationship - in this case between performance and arousal level - may be categorized as either a *law* or a *hypothesis*, a semantic/labeling/identity problem arises and becomes a decision for the reader or researcher to make concerning the scientific validity and/or utility of the *hypothesis* (or *law*). See also AROUSAL THEORY; CATASTROPHE THEORY/MODEL; REINFORCEMENT THEORY; YERKES-DOD-SON LAW.

REFERENCE

Naatanen, R. (1973). The inverted-U relationship between activation and performance: A critical review. In S. Kornblum (Ed.), *Attention and performance.* IV. New York: Academic Press.

INVESTIGATOR PARADIGM EFFECT. See EXPERIMENTER EFFECTS.

IRRADIATION THEORY. See LEARNING THEORIES/LAWS; REINFORCEMENT, THORNDIKE'S THEORY OF.

ISAKOWER PHENOMENON. See SLEEP, THEORIES OF.

ISM MODEL. See MOTOR LEARNING/PROCESS THEORIES; NEW STRUCTURALISM THEORY/PARADIGM.

ISOLATION EFFECT. See ORGANIZATIONAL/INDUSTRIAL/SYSTEMS THEORY; von RESTORFF EFFECT.

ISOMORPHISM, PHENOMENON/HYPOTHESIS OF. See GESTALT THEORY/LAWS.

ISOPATHIC PRINCIPLE. See EMOTIONS, THEORIES/LAWS OF.

ISSAWI'S LAWS. See MURPHY'S LAWS.

ITEM RESPONSE THEORY. See CLASSICAL TEST/MEASUREMENT THEORY.

IZARD'S THEORY OF EMOTIONS. The American psychologist Carroll E. Izard"s (1923-) approach to the study of emotions is influenced strongly by the *evolutionary theory* of Charles Darwin (1809-1882), who argued that certain basic patterns of emotional expression are part of one's biological inheritance. Such patterns of emotion evolved because of their high survival value in giving humans mutual and beneficial systems of communication. For example, humans – including nonhuman animals such as dogs and baboons - grimace and bare their teeth when they become threatened and, thus, convey their dispositions and level of arousal to others of the species. *Izard's theory* is called a *differential emotions theory* because it emphasizes 10 distinct and discriminable emotions: joy, excitement, anguish, rage, startle, revulsion, scorn, humiliation, remorse, and terror. To this list of distinctive emotions - including various other physiological and cognitive components of emotion - Izard adds the variable of *facial expression* for displaying emotional expressiveness and suggests that each of the specific emotions has its own separate facial pattern. For example, when one experiences *rage*, a specific pattern of muscle firings that is physiologically connected to anger "informs" the person's brain that it is *rage* that he/she is feeling and not some other emotion such as shame or fear. Thus, according to *Izard's theory*, facial patterning and facial muscle tension initiates, sustains, and increases one's experience of emotion, and the facial-muscular movement that occurs with each emotion is part of a biological and evolutionary program that is "wired" into the individual. *Evolutionary emotion theories*, such as Izard's and R. Plutchik's, hold that emotion evolved before thought and that emotions originate in subcortical brain structures (such as the limbic system and the hypothalamus), which evolved before the cortical areas that are associated with more complex thought. The principal goal of the *neo-evolutionary theories of emotion* is to come up with a list of the basic or primary emotions. Of course, not all theorists come up with the same list of emotional terms and concepts, but there is considerable overlap. See also DARWIN'S THEORY OF EMOTIONS; EKMAN-FRIESEN THEORY OF EMOTIONS; EMOTIONS, THEORIES/ LAWS OF; FACIAL-FEEDBACK HYPO-THESIS; LUDOVICI'S THEORY OF LAUGHTER; PLUTCHIK'S MODEL OF EMOTIONS.

REFERENCES

Darwin, C. (1872). *The expression of emotions in man and animals*. London: Appleton.

Izard, C. E. (1971). *The faces of emotion*. New York: Appleton-Century-Crofts.

Izard, C. E. (1977). *Human emotions*. New York: Plenum.

Mandler, G. (1984). *Mind and body*. New York: Norton.

Plutchik, R. (1984). Emotions: A general psychoevolutionary theory. In K. Scherer & P. Ekman (Eds.), *Approaches to emotion*. Hillsdale, NJ: Erlbaum.

Izard, C. E. (1990). The substrata and function of emotional feeling: William James and current theory. *Personality and Social Psychology Bulletin, 16*, 625-635.

Mesquita, B., & Frijda, N. (1992). Cultural variations in emotions: A review. *Psychological Bulletin, 112*, 179-204.

Izard, C. E. (1994). Innate and universal facial expressions: Evidence from developmental and cross-cultural research. *Psychological Bulletin, 115*, 288-299.

J

JACKSON'S LAW. See NEURON/NEUR-AL/NERVE THEORY.

JAMES-LANGE/LANGE-JAMES THEO-RY OF EMOTIONS. This theory is credited to both the American philosopher/psychologist William James (1842-1910) and the Danish psychologist Carl Georg Lange (1834-1900), who independently proposed the theory. The term *James-Lange theory* is seen more frequently in the psychological literature, but the *Lange-James theory* has been used as well. The theory is sometimes called the *counterintuitive theory of emotions* because it states that overt, external action (e.g., laughter) precedes the internal/emotional response (e.g., happiness). The older, classical, popular, *commonsense*, or *intuitive theory of emotions* states the sequence of events occurs in the opposite order: the internal event (e.g., happiness) precedes the external action (e.g., laughter). The *commonsense theory* states we laugh because we're happy, whereas the *James-Lange theory* holds that we're happy because we laugh. The empirical works by James and Lange were among the first proposing a theory that identified a physiological mechanism and neural basis for emotionality. However, the ancient Greeks set up four non-empirically based categories of physiological states (involving a predominant ingredient in one's bodily fluids) for emotionality: the *sanguine, melancholic, choleric,* and *phlegmatic* temperaments. The key idea behind the *James-Lange theory* is that an emotion is not a direct reaction to an environmental happening, but rather it is a reaction to how the body responds to the environmental event. James (1890, p. 450) stated that "we feel sorry because we cry, angry because we strike, afraid because we tremble, and not that we cry, strike, or tremble because we are sorry, angry, or fearful, as the case may be." *James' theory* posits that the bodily changes directly follow the perception of the exciting fact, that one's feeling of the same changes as they occur *is*

the emotion, and that every one of the bodily changes is *felt* acutely or obscurely the moment it occurs. *Lange's theory* posits that a stimulus object or situation immediately leads to vasomotor changes wherever blood vessels are found. According to Lange, the secondary changes that occur in the bodily tissues give rise to the sensations that constitute the emotion. Overall, the *James-Lange theory* does more than simply focus attention on bodily (somatic and autonomic) responses that occur during stress; it proposes that these bodily responses form the essential basis for an emotional experience/episode. The strongest objections to the *James-Lange theory* were raised by the American physiologist Walter B. Cannon (1871-1945), who cited five principal criticisms: total separation of the viscera from the central nervous system does not alter emotional behavior; the same visceral changes occur in diverse emotional states and in non-emotional states; the viscera are relatively insensitive structures; the visceral changes are too slow to be a direct source of emotional feeling; and artificial induction of the visceral changes typical of strong emotions does not produce them. In the light of such criticisms, some writers suggest that the *James-Lange theory* by its very nature and formulation is not a theory per se but rather an untestable hypothesis. It is clear today that greater attention is given to the influence of the central nervous system on emotions and one's cognitions and interpretation of events, rather than merely on the examination of visceral processes to achieve the most comprehensive view of emotionality. See also CANNON/CAN-NON-BARD THEORY; COGNITIVE THE-ORIES OF EMOTION; GALEN'S DOC-TRINE OF THE FOUR TEMPERAMENTS; EMOTIONS, THEORIES/LAWS OF.

REFERENCES

James, W. (1884). What is an emotion? *Mind,* 9, 188-205.

Lange, C. G. (1885). *Om sindsbevaegelser.* Leipzig: T. Thomas.

James, W. (1890). *The principles of psychology.* New York: Holt.

Cannon, W. B. (1927). The James-Lange theory of emotions: A critical examination and an alternative theory.

American Journal of Psychology, 39, 106-124.

Cannon, W. B. (1931). Again the James-Lange and the thalamic theories of emotion. *Psychological Review, 38*, 281-295.

JAMES' TIME THEORY. The American philosopher/psychologist William James (1842-1910) described a *psychic law of time perception* (based on the work of Paul Janet) by which the apparent length of an interval at a given epoch of a person's life is proportional to the total length of the person's life itself. Thus, for example, the law states that a 10-year old child feels one year as one-tenth of his whole life, whereas a 50-year old adult feels one year as one-fiftieth of his whole life, where the "whole life" apparently preserves a constant length. James adds to Janet's "law" the theoretical notion of the foreshortening of the years (as one grows older) as being due to the monotony of memory's content and the consequent simplification of the "backward-glancing" view. In his general account of *time and thinking*, James invokes various cognitive processes and phenomenal events. His theoretical conjectures and constructs of the *specious/sensible present* [cf., Whitrow (1980) for the origin of the terms *psychological present* and *specious present* (mainly via E. R. Clay in 1882) - refers to the "true present" that is durationless, a moment of time sharply dividing past from future and clearly distinct from both], the transitional processes from *simultaneity* to *successiveness*, and the differences between experiences of "time in passing" (*prospective time*) and "time in memory" (*retrospective time*) are still recognized and cited by contemporary psychologists studying time. Thus, James' generalized notions are valid today concerning the issue of "duration" estimation: *experienced* duration ("prospective judgment") lengthens as attention to time increases, whereas *remembered* duration ("retrospective judgment") lengthens as memory contents change. See also BLOCK'S CONTEXTUALISTIC MODEL OF TIME; TIME, THEORIES OF.

REFERENCES

James, W. (1890). *The principles of psychology*. Vol. 1. New York: Holt.

Whitrow, G. J. (1980). *The natural philosophy of time*. 2nd ed. Oxford, UK: Clarendon.

JANIS-FEYERABEND HYPOTHESIS. See COMMUNICATION THEORY.

JASTROW ILLUSION. See APPENDIX A.

JENKINS' CONCENTRATION THEORY OF CUTANEOUS COLD. See NAFE'S VASCULAR THEORY OF CUTANEOUS SENSITIVITY.

JET LAG EFFECT. See TIME, THEORIES OF.

JOB-CHARACTERISTICS MODEL. See WORK/CAREER/OCCUPATION, THEORIES OF.

JOINT AGREEMENT/DISAGREEMENT, LAW OF. See PARSIMONY, LAW/PRINCIPLE OF.

JOHN HENRY EFFECT. See EXPERIMENTER EFFECTS.

JOST'S LAWS. The German psychologist Adolph Jost (1874-1920) formulated these laws based on his work, as well as the earlier research by the German psychologist Hermann von Ebbinghaus (1850-1909) in 1885 in the area of human learning and retention. The earlier studies reported that when lists of materials are learned on successive days ("distributed practice") using the same criterion each day, the number of trials to learn becomes progressively less. Jost expanded on this idea and proposed the following principles (*Jost's laws*): (1) given two associations of the same strength, but of different ages, the older one has greater value on a new repetition; (2) given two associations of the same strength, but of different ages, the older falls off less rapidly in a given length of time. Jost's data were rather meager for founding "laws," but more recent experiments have helped to corroborate his findings. For example, A. Youtz confirmed the fact that an older habit shows a larger learning increment after a single relearning trial and that when comparable parts of the materials are equated initially, as on the first recall, the amount of increment from new repetitions tends to increase in a logarithmic fashion. Thus, older associations (materials) require fewer trials to relearn than do younger associations. Inasmuch as younger habits show an excess of errors in the middle of a series of materials, the ratio of errors in the central position to those in the end position was used as one of the indicators of age. Subsequently, Youtz (1941, p. 46) restated *Jost's first law* in the following terms: "[O]f two series of associations which are overtly remembered to the same degree, the one exhibiting the most extensive dissipation of intralist inhibition will profit more on a new repetition." A principle in learning related to *Jost's law*, called the *law of diminishing returns* (Thorndike, 1907), states that in memorizing a series of items, each successive repetition increases the amount recalled less than does the one preceding it (cf., *diminishing-returns principle* - a person's perceived value of anything lessens the more the person has of that item; for example, if one has only one dollar, another dollar would be a big difference, but if one has 100 dollars, that same dollar does not seem to be as important or valuable; and the *principle of distributed repetitions* - in the learning process, this refers to the acquisition of an ability where a smaller number of repetitions is distributed over a longer period of time as compared to them being crowded together; the repetitions are often spaced gradually farther and farther apart as in "progressively distributed practice"). As part of *Spearman's theory of intelligence*, the *law of diminishing returns* states that the more ability (e.g., intelligence) a person already has available, the less advantage accrues to his or her ability from further increments of it. All the studies conducted in psychology on the distribution of learning (and on the relations of retention, recall, and relearning) seem to fit together adequately and probably embody some fundamental law - that would likely supersede *Jost's laws* - even though that law has not yet been formulated. *Jost's laws* are largely obsolete today, and the principles have been incorporated into the more modern area of human memory that employ newer concepts and terms such as *short-term memory* and *long-term memory*. See also FORGETTING/MEMORY, THEORIES OF; LEARNING THEORIES/LAWS; SHORT-TERM AND LONG-TERM MEMORY, THEORIES OF; SPEARMAN'S TWO-FACTOR THEORY.

REFERENCES

Ebbinghaus, H. von (1885). *Uber das gedachtnis: Untersuchungen zur experimentellen psychologie.* Leipzig: Duncker & Humbolt.

Jost, A. (1897). Die assoziation festigkeit in ihrer abhangigkeit von der verteilung der wiederholungen. *Zeitschrift fur Psychologie, 14*, 436-472.

Thorndike, E. L. (1907). *The elements of psychology.* New York: Seiler.

Britt, S. H., & Bunch, M. E. (1934). Jost's law and retroactive inhibition. *American Journal of Psychology, 46*, 299-308.

Youtz, A. (1941). An experimental evaluation of Jost's laws. *Psychological Monographs*, No. 238.

JOUBERT'S THEORY OF LAUGHTER/ HUMOR. The French physician Laurent Joubert (1529-1582) emphasized the *physiological mechanisms* causing the convulsions of laughter; he also considered laughter to be a mixture of opposite emotions - joy and sorrow - where he set the conflict of emotions (as Plato enunciated centuries earlier) clearly in the heart, not in the mind. *Joubert's theory of laughter* states that the contrary emotions stirred in the heart involve alternating contractions and dilations, with sadness causing the contractions and joy causing the dilations. Such an alternating movement is transferred to the pericardium - an organ that is attached firmly by a large tissue to the diaphragm. According to *Joubert's theory*, the diaphragm (which undergoes the same alternations as the heart) causes the breath in the person's lungs to be expelled, and results in a "hearty" laugh. Thus, Joubert characterizes the phenomenon of laughter in such anatomical and physiological terms; he argues, also, that animals do *not* laugh because their pericardium is *not* firmly attached to the diaphragm as it is in humans. In his *humor theory*, Joubert relates laughter at the ridiculous to the laughter arising from the action of tickling whose "strange touch" brings some pain and annoyance to the parts of the body unaccustomed to it, but it also causes a kind of "false pleasure" that is not offensive. Of course, *Joubert's physio-psychological theory of laughter/humor* is outdated today and is eclipsed by more modern assessments of the role of physiology in the explanation of laughter. See also DESCARTES' THEORY OF HUMOR/LAUGHTER; HUMOR, THEORIES OF.

REFERENCE
Joubert, L. (1560/1579/1980). *Treatise on laughter*. G. D. de Rocher, Transl. University, AL: The University of Alabama Press.

JUKE-BOX THEORY OF EMOTIONS. See SCHACHTER-SINGER'S THEORY OF EMOTIONS.

JULESZ'S OBJECT PERCEPTION THEORY. See PATTERN/OBJECT RECOGNITION THEORY.

JUNG'S THEORY OF PERSONALITY. The Swiss-born psychiatrist/psychoanalyst Carl Gustav Jung (1875-1961) first met Sigmund Freud in 1907 and was soon named Freud's successor ("my crown prince") by Freud, but by 1914 Jung and Freud parted company - never to see one another again - essentially due to theoretical differences concerning the interpretation of psychoanalysis, the influence of *determinism* on personality (Freud asserted that personality was basically set or determined in the first few years of childhood; Jung maintained that personality was more malleable and changeable in later life by future goals), and the concepts of *libido* (Freud stated that it was "sexual energy," whereas Jung regarded it as a generalized "life energy") and *unconscious* (Freud stated that it was the prime source of motivation with one-way master control over one's conscious thoughts and behavior; Jung partitioned it into the "personal" and "collective" unconscious where life's experiences are progressive and more flexibly selected and guided under their influence; cf., Jung's *principle of psychosynthesis* - the unification of various components of the unconscious, dreams, fantasies, and instincts with the personality; Jung used the

term "constructive" as opposed to Freud's term "reductive" in this unification process). Jung's *psychic energy theory* of personality, psychoanalysis, and therapeutic practice became widely known as *analytical psychology*, wherein he formulated his unique notions about the myths and symbols that people have used throughout centuries of recorded history (e.g., the term *mana* denotes a supernatural life force, usually originating from the spirit world and that may be concentrated in other people or objects and inherited/transmitted between people, conferring ritual power or high social status; *numinosum* - Jung's term for a type of involuntary mystical/religious experience, or dynamic agency/effect, not caused by an arbitrary act of will, whereby the individual is seized and controlled by the force/energy whatever its causes; *uroboros* - an ancient circular symbol depicting a snake or dragon swallowing its own tail, and represents unity/infinity; this symbol was interpreted by Jung as a metaphor for early development where the infant does not distinguish the feeder from the fed or love from aggression; *biological memory* - the notion that humans inherently have a memory of the history of the race, a memory that is not typically available to them; and *mnemic theory* - states that heredity is a form of memory based on inherited "engrams"). The structure of "total personality" (i.e., the mind or *psyche*) in *Jung's theory* consists of a number of differentiated, but interacting, systems: the *ego* or conscious mind; the *personal unconscious* or repressed, suppressed, ignored, or forgotten experiences that may form "complexes;" and the *collective, transpersonal unconscious* or storehouse of latent memory traces inherited from one's ancestral past. The notion of *individuation* is defined by Jung as the process of coming to "selfhood" or the tendencies toward "self-actualization." The *theory of the collective unconscious* is one of the most original and controversial features of *Jung's personality theory* (cf., *psychoid* - Jung's term applied to the *collective unconscious*, and which cannot be perceived or represented directly, in contrast to the perceptible psychic phenomena; and *mediumistic hypothesis* - posits that schizophrenics are close to the *collective unconscious* and, thereby, are in a position to see and accept the course of events and indications of their disintegration). One of the components of the collective unconscious (or "objective psyche") is called *archetypes* (other names for this component are *dominants, primordial images, imagoes, mythological images*, and *behavior patterns*), which are universal ideas that are emotion-laden and create images/visions that correspond allegedly to some aspect of the conscious situation in normal waking life (cf., *theory of phylogenesis* - refers to the origin and biological development of a species as a whole, but Jung extended this theory within psychology to include the development of the *psyche* and *archetypes*; the *theory of racial memory/unconscious* - holds that people inherit the common body of experiences and memories of *all* past humans, and that in human consciousness such elements continue from generation to generation; thus, humans not only inherit their physical aspects from their ancestors, but their memories as well). Other components of the *collective unconscious* are called the *persona* - the masked or public face of personality; the *anima* and *animus* - a bisexual aspect where the feminine archetype in men is the *anima*, and the masculine archetype in women is the *animus* (cf. Jung's use of the term *syzygy* - the juxtaposition of opposites, or a pair of opposites, especially the *anima* and *animus*; the term derives from astronomy, in which the Earth and the moon lie in a straight line on opposite sides of the sun; Jung was impressed by the apparent ubiquity of cultural symbols of *syzygy*, such as the Chinese complementary principles of the universe called "yin" and "yang," or the melding of a man and woman into a "divine couple"); the *shadow* - the animal instincts that humans have inherited in their evolution from lower life forms and that may be manifested as recognition of original sin, the devil, or an enemy (Jung's term *inflation of consciousness* refers to the expansion of a person's consciousness beyond its normal limits stemming from identification with an *archetype*, the *persona*, or a famous person that results in an exaggerated sense of importance that may be compensated for by feelings of inferiority); and the *self* - comprising all aspects of the unconscious, it attempts to achieve equilibrium, integration, individuation, self-actualization, and unity, and is expressed in the symbols of the mandala and the circle. According to Jung, the well-adjusted person is one who seeks a compromise between the demands of the *collective unconscious* and the actualities of the external world. Jung also distinguishes between the *extraversion* attitude - orientation of the person toward the external/objective world, and the *introversion* attitude - orientation of the person toward the internal/subjective world. He describes four fundamental *psychological types/functions/styles: thinking* (ideational), *feeling* (evaluative), *sensing* (perceptual), and *intuiting* (unconscious or subliminal) aspects of processing information in the world [cf., the *Myers-Briggs Type Indicator* - developed in 1943 and named after the American writer Isabel M. Myers (1897-1980) and her mother, the self-taught American psychologist Katharine E. Briggs (1875-1968), designed to implement/measure *Jung's theory of functional types*; cf., *clouding effect* - a tendency for people who are classified as different functional types to have problems understanding each other where, allegedly, women and men differ in their communication "styles"]. Jung wrote broadly on such diverse topics as mythology, symbols, occult sciences, word associations, religion, dreams, telepathy, clairvoyance, spiritualism, and flying saucers. Jung borrowed concepts from the physical sciences (e.g., the principles of *equivalence, entropy*, and *synchronicity* in chemistry and physics) in describing the psychodynamics of personality. The *principle of entropy* - as adapted by Jung [the term *entropy*, originally coined by the German physicist Rudolf J. E. Clausius (1822-1888), refers to a measure of the degree of disorder of a closed system and relates to the *second law of thermodynamics* in physics] - states that the distribution of energy in the psyche seeks an equilibrium or balance. When Jung asserted that self-realization is the goal of psychic development, he meant that the dynamics of personality move toward a perfect balance of forces. The *principle of equivalence* states that if energy is expended in bringing about a certain condition, the amount expended will appear somewhere else in the system. This principle is similar to the *first law of thermodynamics* in physics [this law was discovered by the Ger-man physician/physicist Julius Mayer (1814-1878) and states that when a system changes from one state to another, energy is converted to a different form but the total energy remains unchanged/conserved; this law virtually makes a "perpetual-motion" device theoretically impossible], and to Hermann von Helmholtz's (1821-1894) adaptation in psychology of the physical *principle of the conservation of energy*. The *principle of synchronicity* is a general statement concerning event interpretation that applies to events that occur together in time but that are not the cause of one another. Jung borrowed the *principle of enantiodromia* from the Greek philosopher Heraclitus (c. 540-c. 480 B.C.), which refers to the notion that everything eventually changes into its opposite, and which Jung described as the principle that governs all cycles of natural life, both large and small. Today, in spite of a few detractors and a lack of contact with scientific psychology, *Jungian theory* seems to have a number of devoted proponents and admirers throughout the world, and his influence has spread into many extrapsychological disciplines, including history, literature, literary criticism, anthropology, religion, and philosophy, among others. Perhaps Jung's *analytical psychology* has been dismissed by many psychologists because his theories are based on psychoanalytical and clinical findings (which include mythical and historical sources) rather than on experimental research. It may be suggested that what *Jungian theory* needs to make it more acceptable to scientific psychology is to test experimentally some of his hypotheses. See also ANAGOGIC THEORY; ANIMISM THEORY; DETERMINISM, DOCTRINE/THEORY OF; FREUD'S THEORY OF PERSONALITY; PERSONALITY THEORIES; THERMODYNAMICS, LAWS OF.

REFERENCES

Jung, C. G. (1912). *The psychology of the unconscious*. Leipzig: Deuticke.

Jung, C. G. (1913). The theory of psychoanalysis. In *Collected works*. Vol. 4. Princeton, NJ: Princeton University Press.

Jung, C. G. (1921). Psychological types. In *Collected works*. Vol. 6. Princeton, NJ: Princeton University Press.

Jung, C. G. (1936). The concept of the collective unconscious. In *Collected works*. Vol. 9. Part 1. Princeton, NJ: Princeton University Press.

Jung, C. G. (1940). *The integration of the personality*. London: Routledge & Kegan Paul.

Glover, E. (1950). *Freud or Jung*. New York: Norton.

Jung, C. G. (1953). *Modern man in search of a soul*. New York: Harcourt, Brace.

Read, H., Fordham, M., & Adler, G. (Eds.) (1953-1978). *C. G. Jung, Collected works*. 20 vols. Princeton, NJ: Princeton University Press.

Jung, C. G. (1957). *The undiscovered self*. Boston: Little, Brown.

Jung, C. G. (1960). A review of the complex theory. In *Collected works*. Vol. 8. Princeton, NJ: Princeton University Press.

Myers, I. (1962). *The Myers-Briggs Type Indicator*. Princeton, NJ: Educational Testing Service.

Jung, C. G. (Ed.) (1964). *Man and his symbols*. New York: Dell.

Jung, C. G. (1968). *Analytical psychology: Its theory and practice*. New York: Random House.

Progoff, I. (1973). *Jung, synchronicity, and human destiny*. New York: Julian.

McGuire, W. (Ed.) (1974). *The Freud/Jung letters: The correspondence between Sigmund Freud and C. G. Jung*. Princeton, NJ: Princeton University Press.

Coan, R. (1994). Archetypes. In R. J. Corsini (Ed.), *Encyclopedia of psychology*. New York: Wiley.

JUSTIFICATION THEORY. See MOTIVATION, THEORIES OF.

JUST-NOTICEABLE DIFFERENCES, PRINCIPLE OF. See WEBER'S LAW.

JUST-WORLD HYPOTHESIS. See ATTRIBUTION THEORY.

K

KALAM THEORY OF ATOMIC TIME.

This *theory of time* was developed by Arab philosophers in the tenth- and eleventh-centuries A.D. and sought to demonstrate the total dependence of the material world on the will of the Supreme Being or "sole agent." In Islam, the term *kalam* is derived from the phrase *kalam Allah* (Arabic: "word of God"), which refers to the Qur'an, the sacred scripture of Islam. The *kalam theory of atomic time* states that temporal entities called "atoms" are isolated by "voids," and their configurations are governed not by natural events or forces but by the will of the "sole agent;" thus, according to this viewpoint, *time* is ultimately under the control of the Supreme Being or the "sole agent.". See also ARISTOTLE'S TIME THEORY/PARADOX; EARLY GREEK AND LATER PHILOSOPHICAL THEORIES OF TIME; PLOTINUS' THEORY OF TIME; ST. AUGUSTINE'S PARADOX OF TIME; TIME, THEORIES OF.

REFERENCES

Maimonides, M. (1927). *The guide for the perplexed*. New York: Dover.

Harrison, E. (1994). Atomicity of time. In S. Macey (Ed.), *Encyclopedia of time*. New York: Garland.

KAMIN EFFECT. See BLOCKING, PHENOMENON OF; MOWRER'S THEORY.

KANIZSA TRIANGLE ILLUSION. See APPENDIX A.

KANT'S THEORY OF HUMOR/LAUGHTER.

In his work on aesthetics, the German philosopher Immanuel Kant (1724-1804) articulated a *theory of jokes* that may be taken as a *general theory of humor*. Kant's theoretical approach to humor is a kind of *incongruity theory* (i. e., laughter is a reaction to the disparity between expectations and perceptions), although he emphasizes the physical- over the mental- side of amusement. According to *Kant's theory of humor/laughter*, the pleasure one takes in humor is not as great a pleasure as one's delight in beauty or in moral goodness. Even though amusement is caused by the play of ideas, it is more a type of sensory gratification based on feelings of health and well-being. Kant maintained that in listening to a joke the person develops a certain expectation as to how it will turn out; then, at the "punch line," the expectation suddenly vanishes. The sudden mental activity is not enjoyed by one's reason, and the desire to understand is frustrated. Accompanying the mental movement/gymnastics at the "punch line" is the activity of the person's internal organs (producing the resultant feeling of health). Thus, according to *Kant's humor theory*, the *incongruity* one experiences in humor gives the body a sort of "wholesome shock." In Kant's approach, the transformations accompanying laughter (that is, the sudden transformation of a strained expectation into "nothing") must be into nothing and not into the positive opposite of expectation. This is because it is not enjoyable to one's understanding directly, but only indirectly, by throwing the body's organs into a state of oscillation, then restoring them to equilibrium, and thus promoting health. *Kant's humor theory* has been called the "nothing theory of humor" where the "nothing" refers to holes that are *not* filled with explanations concerning wit and laughter. Thus, many a "strained expectation" - which *fails* to materialize - leads to a letdown, and not to laughter, in the listener. See also HUMOR, THEORIES OF; INCONGRUITY/INCONSISTENCY THEORIES OF HUMOR; SCHOPENHAUER'S THEORY OF HUMOR.

REFERENCE

Kant, I. (1790/1892/1914). *Critique of judgment*. London: Macmillan.

KAPPA- AND TAU-EFFECTS. See TAU- AND KAPPA-EFFECTS.

KARDOS EFFECT. See PERCEPTION (I. GENERAL), THEORIES OF.

KASPAR HAUSER EFFECT/EXPERIMENT.

This phenomenon is named after a German teenage boy, Kaspar Hauser (c. 1812-1833), who suddenly and mysteriously appeared in the German town of Nuremberg in 1828. Apparently, Hauser was a "feral child" [i.e., an individual/child/infant who is raised, supposedly, by wild animals and has little or no contact or involvement with other humans; cf., "Wild Child/Boy of Aveyron" - a boy, about 10 years old, who was discovered in 1798 by a group of hunters near Aveyron, France; the feral ("wild") child apparently had been abandoned at a young age and was living in the forest, roaming about almost naked, and had no human contact. The child was studied clinically by the French physician Jean Marie Gaspard Itard (1775-1838); an engaging, documentary-type movie - called "L'enfant sauvage" (or the "Wild Child" in the U.S., and the "Wild Boy" in the U.K.) - about the case was made in 1970 by the talented French filmmaker Francois Truffaut (1932-1984); in the film, Truffaut himself plays the role of the doctor who tries to teach language to the boy and to civilize and socialize him]. The *Kaspar Hauser experiment/effect* refers to a study/experiment/technique in which an animal is reared in *isolation* from members of its own species. The British ethologist William Homan Thorpe (1902-1986) conducted such experiments in the 1950s with birds reared in *isolation* in order to determine which aspects of their songs are "innate" and which ones are "learned." See also EMPIRICIST VERSUS NATIVIST THEORIES; LANGUAGE ACQUISITION THEORY; NATURE VERSUS NURTURE THEORIES; SPEECH THEORIES.

REFERENCES

Itard, J. M. G. (1962). *The wild boy of Aveyron*. New York: Appleton-Century-Crofts.

Thorpe, W. H. (1963). *Learning and instinct in animals*. London: Methuen.

Malson, L. (1972). *Wolf children and the problem of human nature*. New York: Monthly Review Press.

Thorpe, W. H. (1972). *Duetting and antiphonal songs in birds: Its extent and sig-nificance*. Leiden: Brill.

Thorpe, W. H. (1974). *Animal nature and human nature*. London: Methuen.

KELLEY'S ANALYSIS OF VARIANCE (ANOVA) MODEL. See ATTRUBUTION THEORY; KELLEY'S COVARIATION THEORY.

KELLEY'S ATTRIBUTION THEORY. See ATTRIBUTION THEORY.

KELLEY'S COVARIATION THEORY. In attempting to answer the question what makes people attribute a behavior to internal versus external factors, the American social psychologist Harold H. Kelley (1921-) speculates that people use a principle of *covariation* in interpreting other's behaviors. The *covariation principle* is the tendency to ascribe behavior to a cause that is present only when the behavior occurs, or that is observed to vary over time with the behavior. Thus, in this context, one should observe what potential causes are present or absent when a behavior does and doesn't occur, and draw conclusions accordingly. *Kelley's theory* focuses on the use of three variables or types of information in deciding whether to make internal or external attributions: *consistency* (the degree to which one reacts to an event in the same way on many different occasions), *distinctiveness* (the degree to which one does *not* react the same way to different events), and *consensus* (the degree to which others react to an event in the same way as the person who is being observed). Theoretically, each of the three variables may be judged to be high or low, resulting in eight possible combinations, often portrayed as a $2 \times 2 \times 2$ cube (called *Kelley's cube model/theory*, or *Kelley"s ANOVA model*). According to Kelley's approach, persons tend to attribute behavior to internal or dispositional causes within another person when *consensus* is low, *distinctiveness* is low, and *consistency* is high. On the other hand, *Kelley's theory* predicts that persons tend to attribute behavior to external or situational causes when *consensus* is high, *distinctiveness* is high, and *consistency* is low. See also ATTRIBUTION THEORY; CORRESPONDENCE BIAS HYPOTHESIS.

REFERENCES

Kelley, H. H. (1967). Attribution theory in social psychology. In D. Levine (Ed.), *Nebraska symposium on motivation* (pp. 192-328). Lincoln, NB: University of Nebraska Press.

Kelley, H. H. (1972). Attribution in social interaction. In E. E. Jones, D. E. Kanouse, H. H. Kelley, R. E. Nisbett, S. Valiens, & B. Weiner (Eds.), *Attribution: Perceiving the causes of behavior*. Morristown, NJ: General Learning Press.

KELLEY'S CUBE MODEL/THEORY. See ATTRIBUTION THEORY; KELLEY'S COVARIATION THEORY.

KELLEY'S PRINCIPLE OF COVARIATION/CORRELATION. See ATTRIBUTION THEORY; KELLEY'S COVARIATION THEORY.

KELLY'S PERSONAL CONSTRUCT THEORY. = role-construct theory. The American psychologist George A. Kelly (1905-1967) developed the *personal construct theory of personality*, which emphasizes the ways in which individuals interpret or construe events, and advances the viewpoint that each person unwittingly takes the role of "scientist" by observing events, formulating concepts to organize phenomena, and attempting to predict future events (cf., *Kelly's fundamental postulate* - the conjecture that behavior is determined and directed by the way in which people *construe* their worlds and reality). According to Kelly, people conduct mental "miniexperiments" in order to interpret and understand their own experiences. In this sense, people are actively engaged in the construction of their own subjective worlds, and one's perceptual processes are directed by the way one anticipates future events. The theory states that people are active and future-oriented rather than passive or merely reactive, that they develop certain concepts, categories, and constructs that they use to describe themselves, and that a concept such as *hostility* may be defined as a continuing and futile effort to find positive evidence for something that has already been recognized as a failure. *Kelly's theory* has two key features: it deals both with change and stability - including the aspects of process and structure in the individual; and it focuses on the uniqueness of the person (*idiographic*) as well as on the characteristics and processes that are common to all

people (*nomothetic*). Kelly's major theoretical concept is the *construct*, which refers to a bipolar way of interpreting and perceiving events. For instance, the *construct/dimension* of "good-bad" is used often by individuals as they assess events and other people. Examples of other *constructs* - where the bipolar terms are not necessarily the logical opposite of each other - are "receive-give," "take-give," "unassertive-assertive," "hate-love," and "lust-love." When a *construct* becomes part of an individual's cognitive structure, it may be applied to anything or anyone. Kelly distinguishes among different types of *constructs*: *core constructs* (such as "weak-strong") versus *peripheral constructs* (such as "humorous-serious"); *verbal* versus *preverbal constructs* and *superordinate* versus *subordinate constructs*. An individual's *personal constructs* are organized to form a *construct system* ranging from a *simple system* (containing only one or two levels of organization) to a *complex system* (containing multiple levels of organization). *Complex construct systems* allow greater differentiation and detailed predictions in one's perception of the world, whereas *simple construct systems* indicate that the person lumps all people and things into a few categories such as "good-bad" or "successful-unsuccessful" where the person's predictions are the same without regard to the situation or circumstances. An individual's *personal construct system* may be assessed by Kelly's "Role Construct Repertory Test" (or Rep Test). Interpreting the results from this test is a subjective and laborious process because it is as much a projective test as a rating scale. In the absence of an objective scoring system, the Rep Test has not been widely used for either clinical or research purposes, and its validity is largely unknown. Although Kelly influenced later personality theorists, the *theory of personal constructs* has advanced little since its initial development. Originally, *Kelly's theory* was set down in a formal postulate fashion with 11 corollaries in his 1955 book, and it is difficult to classify or contrast it with other approaches. L. Sechrest (1977) describes *Kelly's theory* as having many second cousins, but no siblings. Kelly's ideas arose from his clinical experience rather than from experimental research or systematic correlational studies, and there is relatively little current research based on *Kelly's theory* that is reported in the psychological literature. See also FESTINGER'S COGNITIVE DISSONANCE THEORY; IDIOGRAPHIC/NOMOTHETIC LAWS; PERSONALITY THEORIES.

REFERENCES

Kelly, G. A. (1955). *The psychology of personal constructs*. New York: Norton.

Kelly, G. A. (1963). *A theory of personality*. New York: Norton.

Sechrest, L. (1977). Personal constructs theory. In R. J. Corsini (Ed.), *Current personality theories*. Itasca, IL: Peacock.

Pervin, L. (1996). *The science of personality*. New York: Wiley.

KENNARD PRINCIPLE. The American physician Margaret A. Kennard (1899-1976) was a pioneer in the experimental study of "sparing" and "recovery" of function in organisms. Her most famous studies were performed on monkeys and apes at Yale University during the late 1930s and early 1940s. In her investigations, she described the behavioral effects of brain damage on infantile, juvenile, and older primates, and drew attention to the importance of developmental state at the time of neural insult. Kennard also conducted experiments showing that even adult primates may exhibit significant recovery of function, especially if brain lesions are made in stages rather than all at once. The *Kennard principle* states that it is easier to recover from brain damage if the individual is young at the time of the damage than if the damage occurs later in life; for many years, the idea persisted in the medical field that equivalent brain damage to a child and an adult would lead to less problems in a child than in the adult. *Kennard's principle* suggests that a child's brain, while evolving/developing, exhibits "neuroplasticity," enabling it to work around, or adapt to, organic brain damage. However, many recent studies indicate that the Kennard principle is inaccurate and that, in reality, the outcome for children suffering traumatic brain injury/insult may be far worse than the outcome for an equally injured adult. See also LASHLEY'S THEORY; NEURON/NEURAL/NERVE THEORY.

REFERENCES

Kennard, M. A. (1936). Age and other factors in motor recovery from precentral lesions in monkeys. *American Journal of Physiology, 115*, 138-146.

Kennard, M. A. (1940). Relation of age to motor impairment in man and subhuman primates. *Archives of Neurology and Psychiatry, 44*, 377-397.

Schneider, G. E. (1979). Is it really better to have your brain lesion early: A revision of the "Kennard principle." *Neuropsychology, 17*, 557-583.

Finger, S., & Wolf, C. (1988). The "Kennard effect" before Kennard: The early history of age and brain lesions. *Archives of Neurology, 45*, 1136-1142.

Webb, C., Rose, F., Johnson, D., & Attree, E. (1996). Age and recovery from brain injury: Clinical opinions and experimental evidence. *Brain Injury, 10*, 303-310.

KENSHALO/NAFE QUANTITATIVE THEORY. See NAFE'S VASUCLAR THEORY OF CUTANEOUS SENSITIVITY.

KERCKHOFF-DAVIS HYPOTHESIS. See LOVE, THEORIES OF.

KERNEL OF TRUTH HYPOTHESIS. See PREJUDICE, THEORIES OF.

KERR EFFECT. In the general area of visual research and, in particular, regarding the issue of experimenter control of stimulus duration, Riggs (1965) describes the use of the *Kerr effect* (eponym origination unknown) to achieve an electro-optical shutter. A cell with transparent walls is inserted in a position such that the rays of a stimulus light are parallel, and crossed polarities are placed on either side of the cell so that a minimum amount of light passes through the system. The cell is then filled with a liquid and a current is passed through the liquid in a direction perpendicular to the optic axis. The result is a rotation of the plane of polarization such that some of the light now passes through the stimulating mechanism. The main problems with this system of stimulation are that some light passes through the polarizers when no current flows; and a rather limited transmission is given at peak current. However, the major advantage of the *Kerr effect* is its practicality regarding an unlimited range of possible stimulus exposure times. See also VISION/SIGHT, THEORIES OF.

REFERENCE

Riggs, L. A. (1965). Light as a stimulus for vision. In C. H. Graham (Ed.), *Vision and visual perception*. New York: Wiley.

KIERKEGAARD'S THEORY OF HUMOR. In his *theory of humor*, the Danish philosopher Soren Kierkegaard (1813-1855) presents a version of the *incongruity theory* in which humor is analyzed in terms of the "comical" and suggests that the primary element in the comical is "contradiction." Kierkegaard examines *humor*, and its close relative *irony*, for their relations to the three "spheres of existence" or the three "existential stages of life" - the aesthetic, the ethical, and the religious realms. Kierkegaard claims that *irony* marks the boundary between the ethical and the aesthetic spheres, whereas *humor* marks the boundary between the ethical and the religious spheres. He asserts that *humor* is the last stage of existential awareness before faith. Kierkegaard indicates, also, that a strong connection exists between having a religious view of life and possessing a sense of humor. He suggests that the humorous is present throughout Christianity, and that Christianity is the most humorous view of life in the history of the world. See also HUMOR, THEORIES OF; INCONGRUITY/INCONSISTENCY THEORIES OF HUMOR.

REFERENCE

Kierkegaard, S. (1846/1941). *Concluding unscientific postscript*. Princeton, NJ: Princeton University Press.

KINESTHETIC AFTEREFFECT ILLUSION/HALLUCINATION. See APPENDIX A.

KINETIC AFTEREFFECT ILLUSION. See APPENDIX A.

KINETIC DEPTH EFFECT. The German-born American perceptual psychologist Hans Wallach (1904-1998) described the *kinetic depth effect* in which a moving two-dimensional shadow that is cast by a three-dimensional object (e.g., a rod) appears to be three-dimensional when the object is positioned obliquely and rotated about its center. This causes complex transformations making the shadow appear to move in the front of, and behind, the surface on which it is cast. If the object stops moving (or if it rotates in a plane that is perpendicular to the surface on which the shadow is cast - causing the shadow to shorten and lengthen as the object rotates), then the *kinetic effect* disappears. This effect is related closely to the visual *windmill illusion* - first noted by the English mathematician Robert Smith (1689-1768) - in which the blades of a windmill (seen from a distance and silhouetted against the sky) appear to reverse their direction of rotation. See also ALIASING/STROBOSCOPIC PHENOMENON; APPENDIX A; PERCEPTION (I. GENERAL), THEORIES OF; PERCEPTION (II. COMPARATIVE APPRAISAL), THEORIES OF.

REFERENCES

Smith, R. (1738). *A compleat system of opticks in four books*. Cambridge, UK: R. Smith.

Wallach, H., & O'Connell, D. N. (1953). The kinetic depth effect. *Journal of Experimental Psychology, 45*, 205-217.

KINNEY'S LAW. See WHORF-SAPIR HYPOTHESIS/THEORY.

KIRSCHMANN'S LAW OF CONTRAST. See COLOR VISION, THEORIES/LAWS OF.

KJERSTAD-ROBINSON LAW. See SKAGGS-ROBINSON HYPOTHESIS.

KLEIN'S THEORY. See GOOD BREAST/OBJECT-BAD BREAST/OBJECT THEORY; OBJECT-RELATIONS THEORY.

KNOWLEDGE-ACROSS-SITUATIONS HYPOTHESIS. See ATTRIBUTION THEORY.

KNOWLEDGE OF RESULTS PRINCIPLE. See LEARNING THEORIES/LAWS.

KOESTLER'S THEORY OF HUMOR/LAUGHTER.

The English writer Arthur Koestler (1905-1983) speculated that the ancient Greeks' humorous attitude toward the stammering barbarian - much like the primitive person's laughter over a dying animal's anguished kicking and convulsing that presumably (in the savage's perception) "pretends" to suffer pain - may be inspired by the conviction that the foreigner is not really human but only "pretends" to be. *Koestler's theory of humor/laughter* suggests that as laughter emerged from the ancient/primitive form of humor, it was so aggressive that it has been likened to a dagger. In ancient Greece, the dagger was transformed into a pen/quill - dripping with poison at first and then diluted and infused later with amusing lyrical and fanciful elements. Koestler notes that the fifth century B.C. saw the first rise of humor into art, starting with parodies of Olympian heroics and reaching a peak in the comedies of Aristophanes. According to Koestler, from this point onward, the evolution of humor and comedy in the western world merged with the history of literature and art. Thus, in *Koestler's theory*, the overall trend in humor - from the ancient/primitive to later sophisticated forms - was away from aggression-based humor and toward the "humanization" of humor and laughter. See also HUMOR, THEORIES OF.

REFERENCES

Koestler, A. (1964). *The act of creation*. London: Hutchinson.

Koestler, A. (1997). Humour and wit. In *The New Encyclopaedia Britannica, Macropaedia*. Vol. 20. Chicago: Encyclopaedia Britannica, Inc.

KOHLBERG'S THEORY OF MORALITY.

The American psychologist Lawrence Kohlberg (1927-1987) proposed a *stage-dependent theory of moral development*, which is largely cognitive in nature and considers morality as a universal cognitive process that proceeds from one stage to the next in a definite and fixed manner at a pace that is determined by the individual's particular experiences and opportunities. According to Kohlberg, the typical child progresses through three general levels of moral development: a *preconventional level* (cf., *ethical-risk hypothesis* - posits that moral/immoral behavior depends on a child's evaluation of the risk involved, i.e., getting caught; as the possibility of discovery increases, the occurrence of the behavior decreases) in which morality essentially is a matter of external rather than internal standards - this "premoral" level is indicated when the physical consequences of an action determine its "goodness" or "badness" regardless of the human meaning or value of the consequences and, also, where "right" action consists of things that instrumentally satisfy one's own needs (and mutuality, reciprocity, or concern for others is present only to the degree that they help the child fulfill her or his own needs); a *conventional level* in which morality derives from the child's performance of correct roles - this "conventional" level is exhibited when "good" behavior occurs in order to please or help others, and conformity-type behaviors occur where the child has the "intention" of doing "good" (also, at this level, fixed laws and authority figures are obeyed where "right" behavior consists of doing one's duty, respecting authority, and maintaining social conventions and rules for their own sake); and a *postconventional level* in which morality is basically one of shared standards, duties, and rights - this "self-accepted" morality level is shown when "right" action is defined by the standards agreed upon by the whole society and is designed to take account of an individual's rights, and where there is awareness that personal values differ where people must reach a consensus on certain social issues (also, this level is characterized by the orientation that "right" is defined by "conscience" in accord with universal principles of justice and respect for others). Kohlberg's three levels consist of two orientations each and, thus, his *theory of morality* identifies *six* separate states (three general levels × two orientations each): obedience-reward; instrumental exchange; conformist; law and order;

social-contract; and universal-ethical principle. The central tenet of Kohlberg's original formulation (i.e., the presence of a universally fixed sequence of *six moral stages*) has not been supported by empirical investigations. On the other hand, research does indicate that an invariant level-to-level sequence may occur where *preconventional morality* is a prerequisite for *conventional reasoning* and where both must precede the appearance of *postconventional morality*. Critics of *Kohlberg's theory* have emphasized the role that social-cultural factors may play in the development of *postconventional reasoning*, especially experiences within the context of a particular jurisprudence system of justice. Thus, although Kohlberg's model may not provide *the* universal view of a moral person, it may be relevant to an individual living in the United States of America who has a constitutionally based legal system. However, in the final analysis, the notion of *morality* - as it derives from a social codification of "right" and "wrong" - may be viewed as either *internal* (part of an individual's personal code) or *external* (imposed by society) and, although certain truths seem to be self-evident, it is probably *not* the case that a universal code of morality either exists or can be established (cf., *theories of religion/ethics*, such as *ghost theory* which posits that religions originated from aboriginal or primitive peoples' beliefs in ghosts or disembodied spirits; the *doctrine of mysticism* which asserts that the ultimate spiritual truth is to be found in *internal* states such as meditation, contemplation, and intuition rather than through *external* sense experience such as minister/priest-mediated rituals or social/religious gatherings; *religious instinct hypothesis* which holds that all humans have an innate tendency to want to believe in a religion, to practice certain rituals, and to behave according to the tenets and principles of some particular religion; and *secular humanism doctrine* which is a nontheistic approach that rejects supernaturalism, advances the notion of a person's capacity for self-realization through reason, is typically opposed to traditional religion but often holds many of the ethical tenets of religion, and places great respect for humans as the center of moral/ ethical interest). See also PIAGET'S THEORY OF DEVELOPMENTAL STAGES; SOCIAL LEARNING/COGNITION THEORIES.

REFERENCES

Broad, C. D. (1930/1956). *Five types of ethical theory*. London: Routledge & Kegan Paul.

Kohlberg, L. (1969). *Stages in development of moral thought and action*. New York: Holt.

Goldiamond, I. (1972). Moral behavior: A functional analysis. *Readings in psychology today*. Del Mar, CA: CRM.

Kurtines, W., & Greif, E. (1974). The development of moral thought: Review and evaluation of Kohlberg's approach. *Psychological Bulletin, 81*, 453-470.

Kohlberg, L. (1978). Revisions in the theory and practice of moral development. In W. Damon (Ed.), *New directions for child development: Moral development*. San Francisco: Jossey-Bass.

Colby, A. (1979). *Measurement of moral judgment: A manual and its results*. New York: Cambridge University Press.

Blasi, A. (1980). Bridging moral cognition and moral action: A critical review of the literature. *Psychological Bulletin, 88*, 1-45.

Rich, J. M.,& DeVitis, J. L. (1985). *Theories of moral development*. Springfield, IL: C. C. Thomas.

Spilka, B., & McIntosh, D. (1997). *The psychology of religion: Theoretical approaches*. Boulder, CO: Westview Press.

Cunningham, G. (1999). *Religion and magic: Approaches and theories*. New York: New York University Press.

Forsyth, J. (2003). *Psychological theories of religion*. Upper Saddle River, NJ: Prentice Hall.

KOHLER-RESTORFF PHENOMENON. See von RESTORFF EFFECT.

KOHNSTAMM EFFECT. See IMAGERY/ MENTAL IMAGERY, THEORIES OF.

KOLMOGOROV'S AXIOMS/THEORY.
The Soviet mathematician Andrei Nikolaevich Kolmogorov (1903-1987) formulated the *axiomatic theory of probability* (also known as *Kolmogorov's axioms*) that provides four propositions concerning probabilities from which all major theorems may be derived: the probability of *any* event is equal to, or greater than, zero; the probability of a *particular* event is 1.00; if A and B are two mutually exclusive events (cf., *principle of the excluded middle* or *excluded middle law* - the law/principle which states that for any proposition *p*, the proposition *p or not p* is true according to logical necessity), then the probability of the *disjunction* (i.e., the probability of *either* A *or* B occurring) is equal to the *sum* of their individual probabilities; and the probability of a *conjunction* of two events A and B (i.e., the probability that *both* A and B occur) is equal to the probability of A (assuming that B occurs) *multiplied* by the probability of B. See also BOOLEAN SET THEORY; DECISION-MAKING THEORIES; EXCLUDED MIDDLE, PRINCIPLE OF; PROBABILITY THEORY/LAWS; SET THEORY.

REFERENCE
Kolmogorov, A. N. (1933). *Grundbegriffe der wahrscheinlichkeitsrechnung.* Berlin: Springer.

KONIG'S THEORY. See COLOR VISION, THEORIES/LAWS OF.

KORTE'S LAWS. The German Gestalt psychologist Adolf Korte (1915) developed a series of general statements or laws that describe the optimal conditions for *apparent motion* when demonstrating the *phi phenomenon* (i.e., perceived motion produced when two stationary lights are flashed successively, where the sensation of *apparent movement* of the light from the first location to the second location occurs if the time interval between the flashing of the two lights is about 150 milliseconds). *Korte's principles of apparent movement (phi)* are: (1) when the intensity of the lights is held constant, the time interval for optimal *phi* varies directly with the distance between the stimuli; (2) when time is held constant, the distance for optimal *phi* varies directly with the intensity of the lights; and (3) when distance between the stimuli is held constant, the intensity for optimal *phi* varies inversely with the interval of time that is used. Thus, *Korte's laws* state that it is more difficult to perceive *apparent motion* or *phi* when the spatial separation between lights is too wide, when illumination is too low, and when interstimulus interval is too short, even though decrements in one (or two) of the variables can be adjusted by increments in the other(s). The *phi phenomenon* may be observed in non-laboratory settings such as in motion pictures ("movies"), television, animated displays, and various neon sign displays where the sensation of motion is overwhelming and "irresistible." *Korte's laws* have been revised and extended in recent experiments (cf., Kolers, 1964), and several other stimulus variables that determine optimal *apparent movement* have been described. See also APPARENT MOVEMENT, PRINCIPLES/THEORIES OF; PHI PHENOMENON; UNCONSCIOUS INFERENCE, DOCTRINE OF.

REFERENCES
Stratton, G. (1911). The psychology of change: How is the perception of movement related to that of succession? *Psychological Review, 18,* 262-293.

Korte, A. (1915). Kinematoskopische untersuchungen. *Zeitschrift fur Psychologie, 72,* 193-296.

Neuhaus, W. (1930). Experimentelle untersuchung deer scheinbewegung. *Archiv fur die Gesamte Psychologie, 75,* 315-458.

Fernberger, S. (1934). New phenomenon of apparent visual movement. *American Journal of Psychology, 46,* 309-314.

Neff, W. (1936). A critical investigation of the visual apprehension of movement. *American Journal of Psychology, 48,* 1-42.

Kolers, P. (1964). The illusion of movement. *Scientific American, 211,* 98-106.

Graham, C. (1965). Perception of movement. In C. Graham (Ed.), *Vision and visual perception.* New York: Wiley.

Bell, H., & Lappin, J. (1973). Sufficient conditions for the discrimination of motion. *Perception & Psychophys-ics*, *14*, 45-50.

Pantle, A., & Picciano, L. (1976). A multistable movement display: Evidence for two separate motion systems in human vision. *Science, 193*, 500-502.

Beck, J., Elsner, A., & Silverstein, C. (1977). Position uncertainty and the perception of apparent movement. *Perception & Psychophysics, 21*, 33-38.

KRAEPELIN'S THEORY/CLASSIFICATION. See PSYCHOPATHOLOGY, THEORIES OF.

KRETSCHMER'S THEORY OF PERSONALITY. = somatotype theory = typology theory. The German psychiatrist Ernst Kretschmer (1888-1964) devised a *theory of personality* based on the relationship of physical characteristics to personality attributes. Before *Kretschmer's theory* appeared, various other viewpoints were advanced by early investigators concerning the association between physical and personality traits. The Greek physician Hippocrates (460-370 B.C.) suggested both a *typology of physique* and a *typology of temperament*, as well as indicating the relationships between the body's *humors* (liquid substances), temperament, and behavior that anticipated the modern importance of endocrine secretions as determinants of behavior. Hippocrates suggested a dichotomy concerning physiques that separated people into those who were "thick and short" versus those who were "thin and long." He also indicated that these body types are accompanied by characteristic diseases and disorders. For example, the first type of person (thick and short) is prone to apoplexy, and the second type (thin and long) is prone to consumption. Kretschmer inaugurated *constitutional psychology* into the modern era based on observations he made in his psychiatric practice concerning the relationships between physique and manifest behavior, especially the behaviors displayed in manic-depressive psychosis and schizophrenia. As a result of his measurements of physique, Kretschmer described three fundamental types: *asthenic* - refers to a linear, frail physique (later called *leptosomic*); *athletic* - refers to a muscular, wide-shoulder physique; and *pyknic* - refers to a plump, round-figured physique. A fourth, "mixed" type, *dysplastic* - referring to a "rare or ugly" physique, was described, also, that applied to a small group of "deviant" cases. Kretschmer related the incidence of *physique types* to the two kinds of psychosis in his patients and concluded that there was a strong biological affinity between *manic-depression* and the *pyknic* body build and a similar association between *schizophrenia* and the *asthenic, athletic*, and *dysplastic* body builds. Criticisms of *Kretschmer's theory*, in this case, focus on his failure to control adequately for differences in age between manic-depressives and schizophrenics. Thus, the common observation is suggested that with increasing age most people increase in weight and, thereby, are more likely to resemble Kretschmer's *pyknic* type. Also, inasmuch as manic-depression typically occurs later in life than does schizophrenia, this may account for the particular relationships Kretschmer observed between physique and psychosis. See also GALEN'S DOCTRINE OF THE FOUR TEMPERAMENTS; PERSONALITY THEORIES; SHELDON'S TYPE THEORY; TYPE THEORIES OF PERSONALITY.

REFERENCES

Lavater, J. (1804). *Essays on physiognomy: For the promotion of the knowledge and the love of mankind*. London: Whittingham.

Kretschmer, E. (1921). *Korperbau und charakter*. Berlin: Springer.

Kretschmer, E. (1925). *Physique and character*. New York: Harcourt.

Sheldon, W. (1944). Constitutional factors in personality. In J. McV. Hunt (Ed.), *Personality and the behavior disorders*. New York: Ronald Press.

Kefir, N., & Corsini, R. J. (1974). Dispositional sets: A contribution to typology. *Journal of Individual Psychology, 30*, 163-178.

KUBLER-ROSS' STAGES OF DYING THEORY. See LIFE, THEORIES OF.

KUNDT'S RULES/EFFECTS. See OPPEL'S EFFECT/ILLUSION.

L

LABELED-LINE THEORY. See GUSTA-TION/TASTE, THEORIES OF; OLFAC-TION/SMELL, THEORIES OF.

LABELING/DEVIANCE THEORY. The *labeling theory of deviant behavior*, also called *societal-reaction theory*, postulates an interaction between individuals and their social environment where society both defines and produces *deviance*. That is, *labeling theory* focuses on society's reaction to personal behavior as a fundamental aspect of a deviance-producing process. Whereas other models of deviance may place the source of deviance solely within the individual or solely within society, the *labeling theory* emphasizes the interactive processes between society and the individual (cf., the *residual deviance hypothesis* - holds that behavioral disorders are due, after all other reasons have been exhausted or excluded, to the individual's intention to break society's rules; and the *transgenerational hypothesis* - holds that deviant behavior may be explained on the basis of its having been acquired or learned from previous generations). According to *labeling theory*, deviance is created by other individuals' reactions to a given act or event where those with the ability and power to label are called the "influential audience." Certain behaviors are designated as il-logical, deviant, or mentally ill when they have been codified appropriately and when a group has power to impose standards of codification [for example, consider the marginal and controversial issue/practice of *nudism*, or the public display of the naked human body, where *rational nudism theories* (such as rebellion against Victorian modesty and hypocrisy; a man's desire to display his masculinity in reaction to castration anxiety; a woman's desire to display her body to indicate her ability to attract men; or a rejection of religious prudishness via a "back-to-nature" philosophy) struggle for expression, often, against inflexible and established standards and social norms]. Thus, both the behavior and the person exhibiting the behavior become labeled as *deviant*. In general, the study of deviance has been approached from two different theoretical aspects: deviance is an exceptional and consistent variation from statistical norms of the overall population (cf., *communitarianism theory* - a social theory which holds that human behavior is determined largely by the culture and norms of the place where people live; this approach is in contrast to theories that explain behavior and deviance in individualistic/intrapsychic terms that do not take into account the role of the social context in understanding human intentions and deviant behaviors); and deviance is defined by the occurrence of single "critical" events (e.g., violence, high-intensity behavior, emotions, or cognitions). In particular, theoretical positions on deviance include: *internal factors* and *differences among individuals* with use of typologies and classification schemes such as insanity, criminality, mental illness, and learning disabilities; *social structural differences* where social alienation, enmity, and differential access to both legitimate and illegitimate opportunity are critical aspects of deviance; *interactionist* viewpoint, or *differential labeling theory* - where deviance arises from an interaction between individuals' performances and society's reaction to those performances; and *learning theory* - argues that all behaviors, including both normal and deviant, are learned according to the laws of punishment, reinforcement, and modeling. Various critics of *deviance theory* in general, and *formal labeling theory* in particular, suggest that the labeling of deviance (such as "criminal" and "mentally ill") is an unjust and irrational process, and argue from research that shows that deviance is not absolute in character but may be attributed to an act, depending on the variance of the act from the experience of the audience, on the observability and location of the act, and on the implied motivation of the act. See also BEHAVIOR THERAPY/COGNITIVE THERAPY, THEO-RIES OF; MEDI-CAL/DISEASE MODEL; PERSONALITY THEORIES; PSYCHOPATHOLOGY, THEORIES OF; PYGMALION EFFECT; SELF-FULFILLING PROPHESY.

REFERENCES

Merton, R. (1949). *Social theory and social structure.* New York: Free Press.

Becker, H. (1963). *Outsiders: Studies in the sociology of deviance.* New York: Free Press.

Scheff, T. (1974). The labeling theory of mental illness. *American Sociological Review, 39,* 444-452.

Gibbons, D., & Jones, J. (1975). *The study of deviance: Perspectives and problems.* Englewood Cliffs, NJ: Prentice-Hall.

Prentky, R. (1994). Mental illness: Early history. In R. J. Corsini (Ed.), *Encyclopedia of psychology.* New York: Wiley.

LACK OF SELF KNOWLEDGE THEORY. See PLATO'S THEORY OF HUMOR.

LADD-FRANKLIN/FRANKLIN COLOR VISION THEORY. The American-German psychologist Christine Ladd-Franklin (née Christine Franklin) (1847-1930) proposed a *color vision theory* in 1892 that is a compromise between the *Young-Helmholtz* and the *Hering* (later, the *Hering-Hurvich-Jameson*) *theories,* and that has been called both a *genetic theory* and an *evolutionary theory* of color vision. The *Ladd-Franklin theory* assumes that light energy liberates respective red-, green-, and blue-stimulating substances from a complex photosensitive molecule in the retinal nerve endings. When the red- and green-stimulating substances are present, they combine to form a yellow-stimulating substance that, in turn, may combine with blue to form a white-stimulating substance. According to this theory, blue and red (or blue and green) cannot combine and, thereby, do not individually disappear in the mixtures of blue-red (or blue-green). Thus, the *Ladd-Franklin theory* postulates four primary colors (red, green, yellow, and blue) where separate cone mechanisms for each primary are assumed. This *four-receptor theory* is linked to various evolutionary facts (such as the evolutionary development of achromatic rod vision into chromatic cone vision and the relatively rapid evolution of the foveal area of the eye as compared to the periphery) and is able to give a convincing account of both color blindness and perimetry (stimulation of retinal perimeter areas) data. The genetic and evolutionary aspects of the *Ladd-Franklin genetic theory* may be stated in terms wherein various portions of the retina "recapitulate" the course of evolution and where all four types of color receptors are present near the fovea, but not at the periphery of the retina. The *Ladd-Franklin evolutionary theory of color vision* had much to recommend it, but it was never as popular as the *Young-Helmholtz theory.* See also COLOR VISION, THEORIES/LAWS OF; HERING-HURVICH-JAMESON COLOR VISION THEORY; RECAPITULATION, THEORY OF; YOUNG-HELMHOLTZ COLOR VISION THEORY.

REFERENCES

Ladd-Franklin, C. (1892). Eine neue theorie der lichtempfindungen. *Zeitschrift fur Psychologie und Physiologie Sinnesorgange, 4,* 211.

Ladd-Franklin, C. (1929). *Colour and colour theories.* New York: Harcourt, Brace.

LADD-FRANKLIN GENETIC THEORY. See LADD-FRANKLIN/FRANKLIN COLOR VISION THEORY.

LAG EFFECT. See TOTAL TIME HYPOTHESIS/LAW.

LAING'S THEORY OF SCHIZOPHRENIA. See SCHIZOPHRENIA, THEORIES OF.

LAMARCKIAN-LYSENKO DOCTRINE. See LAMARCK'S EVOLUTION THEORY.

LAMARCK'S EVOLUTION THEORY. = Lamarckian-Lysenko doctrine = Lamarckianism = Lamarckism. The French naturalist/evolutionist Jean-Baptiste Pierre Antoine de Monet Lamarck (1744-1829) presented his *theory of evolution* in 1800 in a public lecture in which he proposed the first coherent theory of the process of evolution prior to *Darwin's theory of natural selection* (Lamarck also proposed the *heredity predisposition theory,* which is used often in relation to pathological conditions, such as schizophrenia, to explain the conduct of a person who appears to have inherited a predisposition towards a particular trait or characteristic; such pathology is presumed to develop only in the appropriate environmental context). Lamarck formulated four "laws" in this theory: (1) there is a natural tendency toward increasing organic complexities; (2) new organs evolve by indirect environmental influences; (3) there is a *use-disuse principle* operative in changes to an organ where parts of the body used extensively to cope with the environment become larger and stronger and - where new habits are acquired - useless organs disappear; and (4) acquired characteristics are inheritable. Lamarck published his *theory of evolution* in 1809, the year Charles Darwin was born. Out of his interest in zoology and by comparing current species to fossil forms, Lamarck observed several lines of descent where each line was a chronological series of older to younger fossils leading to a modern species. To illustrate his *use-disuse principle*, Lamarck cited examples of the blacksmith who develops a bigger bicep in the arm that works the hammer and a giraffe stretching its neck to new lengths in pursuit of tree-leaves to eat. The *principle of inheritable acquired characteristics* presumes that the modifications an organism acquires during its lifetime may be passed along to its offspring. However, there is no convincing evidence to support this principle, and most scientists today agree that acquired traits do *not* change genes transmitted by gametes to offspring - notwithstanding recent developments and techniques in biology called *genetic engineering*, *recombinant DNA*, and *gene cloning* where genetic manipulations can cause profound organismic changes and where the term *acquired characteristics* may require redefinition. Modern geneticists have affirmed that inheritance is determined solely by the reproductive cells and is unaffected by somatic (body) cells. Therefore, belief in the *inheritance of acquired characteristics* is rejected, generally, today. Although the *Lamarckian theory of evolution* may be ridiculed by some people today because of its *inheritable acquired characteristics* assumption, that aspect of inheritance was accepted widely in Lamarck's time, and even Darwin himself could offer no acceptable alternative. Also, the con-

cept of inheritable acquired characteristics seems to have some survival value where it has been revived in certain contexts and in various guises (cf., the notion of *meme* - a self-replicating cultural element or pattern of behavior analogous to a gene but transferred from one individual to another via memory and imitation rather than genetic transmission) by several early and modern biologists and psychologists, for example, Jean Piaget, Herbert Spencer, William McDougall, and Carl Jung. In the 1930s, the Soviet geneticist and agronomist Trofim Denisovich Lysenko (1898-1976) formulated a *neo-Lamarckian theory of genetics* (also called *Lysenkoism*) that suggested that environment may alter the hereditary material. Lysenko rejected the popular *doctrine of neo-Mendelism*, and his theories were offered as Marxist orthodoxy, which won the official support of the Soviet government. However, during the 1950s, Soviet physicists and mathematicians had gained status and strength with the growth of the Soviet space program and, as scientific support grew for Francis Crick and James Watson's model of DNA in 1953, criticism mounted against Lysenko and his ideas. Lysenko was forced to resign his position as director of the Institute of Genetics and the Soviet Academy of Sciences in 1965. In the final analysis, Lamarck probably deserves some credit for his unorthodox theory, which was visionary in may respects: it claimed that evolution is the best explanation for both the fossil record and the current diversity of life, it emphasized the great age of Earth, and it stressed adaptation to the environment as a primary product of evolution. See also DARWIN'S EVOLUTION THEORY; MENDEL'S LAWS/PRIN-CIPLES; USE, LAW OF; WEISMANN'S THEORY.

REFERENCES

Lamarck, J. (1809). *Zoological philosophy: An exposition with regard to the natural history of animals*. London: Macmillan.

Lysenko, T. D. (1948). *Agrobiology*. Moscow: Foreign Languages Publication House.

Watson, J., & Crick, F. (1953). Molecular structure of nucleic acids. A structure for deoxyribose nucleic acid. *Nature, 171,* 737-738.

Dawkins, R. (1999). *The extended phenotype. The long reach of the gene.* New York: Oxford University Press.

LAMBERT'S LAW/COSINE LAW. See ABNEY'S LAW; FECHNER'S LAW.

LAND EFFECT. See COLOR VISION, THEORIES/LAWS OF.

LANDOLT CIRCLES/RINGS. See APPENDIX A.

LAND'S RETINEX THEORY. See COLOR VISION, THEORIES/LAWS OF.

LANGUAGE ACQUISITION THEORY. See CHOMSKY'S PSYCHOLINGUISTIC THEORY.

LANGUAGE AND THOUGHT THEORY. See WHORF-SAPIR HYPOTHESIS/THEORY.

LANGUAGE ORIGINS, THEORIES OF. The French word *langage* (the root of our word *language*) was introduced early in the 20th century by the Swiss linguist Ferdinand de Saussure (1857-1913) to denote the faculty of speech present in all humans and acquired through heredity, and divided roughly into the two aspects of "competence" (*langue*) and "performance" (*parole*) (cf., Saussure, 1959). *Langue* denotes language as an abstract communicative system, and *parole* denotes language as concrete utterances of particular speakers. The following general theories and speculations of the *phylogenetic* (i.e., development in the species or group of people) *origins of language* were developed most fully during the 1800s (even though the earliest written records are about 4,000 years old, language probably originated much more recently): the *natural response theory* - holds that automatic vocal responses/reactions to specific environmental stimuli are the initial verbal communications; the *yo-he-ho theory* - suggests that language and speech began as outcries under the strain of work; and as workers struggled in groups against the harsh

environment; the *onomatopoetic theory* (also called the *ding-dong theory,* the *animal-cry theory,* the *bow-wow theory* (from "dogs barking"), the *splish-splash theory,* and the *nativist theory*) - holds that imitations of sounds of animals and natural events constitute the origins of human language (cf., the *echo principle* - a tendency for children to imitate the linguistic patterns/behaviors of their parents; the *theory of imitation* and the *autism theory of language learning* by the American psychologist Orval Hobart Mowrer (1907-1982) which states that a word initially acquired on an "autistic," or "self-satisfying," basis then may become instrumental in producing subsequent and predictable behavior on the part of others); the *interjectional theory* (also called the *pooh-pooh* and *exclamation theories*) - suggests that humans' emotional exclamations (such as "ow," "ah," "oh," and "oof") were the first words of humankind; the *ta-ta theory* holds that language began in combinations of tongue movements and gestures; and the *sing-song theory* asserts that language evolved from inarticulate chants of a ritualistic nature. Collectively, these various *phylogenetic* points of view lack in their explanatory power, and today there is no well-formulated or unanimously-accepted *phylogenetic theory of language origination.* However, there is much research being conducted currently by psychologists, linguists, anthropologists, and biologists on the issue of *ontogenetic* (i.e., occurrence of language in the individual) *language origins,* including the topics of language acquisition and language development. For instance, in a grammatical context, children start off producing single-word utterances and, with increasing age, grammatical sophistication increases, with predictable patterns of mastery on linguistic structures such as questions, negation, passives, and relative clauses. Because language learning occurs so rapidly, and with such apparent ease, some researchers (e.g., Chomsky, 1968; Fodor, 1975) propose that language learning is fundamentally different from other cognitive skills, and involves an "innate, language-specific component." Theorists advancing this ontogenetic approach claim that the linguistic input that a child receives does not contain enough information to allow a child to deduce (within the given time period) the grammatical structure of the language correctly. One influential *innate language-specific theory* is called the *theory of parameter setting*, which proposes that an infant is born with a set of "switches/parameters" that code all possible linguistic variations. Such parameters begin with a "default setting;" linguistic input then triggers the parameters to be set to the value appropriate for that language. Setting the parameter in this way subsequently enables mastery of particular syntactic structures of that language and, thus, through the combination of the innate parameters and triggers from the linguistic input, grammatical mastery is achieved. In contrast to this viewpoint, other theorists consider language acquisition and development to be an issue of general learning - involving the traditional *learning theory principles* (e.g., Skinner, 1957) - where the child brings general learning processes to language and applies these to the linguistic input, eventually figuring out the grammar involved. Although both the *innate theory* and the *learning theory* approaches toward language development have their advocates, a third viewpoint - called the *interaction theory* - holds that the interaction between the infant and caregiver, or between one person and another, is at the heart of language acquisition and development. Another speculation is that language origination/acquisition/development is analogous to the ethologist's *imprinting phenomenon* (cf., Hess, 1959; Lorenz, 1970-71) - that is, a form of rapid learn-ing (via innate ability) that takes place during a "critical period" of development, where the environment provides the requisite stimulation to release or trigger the behavior [cf., the *waggle dance of bees*, described by the Austrian zoologist Karl von Frisch (1886-1982), that comes closer to being a language than any other nonhuman communication system; and *Yerkish* - named after the American psychologist Robert Yerkes (1876-1956) who experimented with primates - refers to an artificial language using a computer console with keys containing geometrical symbols for words in the effort to communicate with, and study language development in, chimpanzees; Rumbaugh, Savage-Rumbaugh, & Scanlon, 1982]. Thus, each theory essentially contributes to

current understanding of language origination, *ontogenetically* considered: humans seem to be *innately* sensitized to master language, where they *learn* the particularities of a language via reinforcement and punishment, and where the specific responsiveness and *interaction* of other people further influences and fine-tunes language achievement in the individual. The *origins* of language may be distinguished from the *evolution* of language where, in chronologically-based terms, study of the *evolution* of language *starts* from the time when language first emerged, whereas the study of the *origin* of language *ends* at the point when language emerged. Such a distinction is necessary due to the fundamentally different ways casual, spoken language changes and the ways hominid communicative behavior changes. Theoretically, the early hominid communicative behavior, not human language, was subject to the constraints of *Darwinian evolution*. In this latter context, the *origins* of language also rest on the evolutionary *processes* leading to actual language production (such as gastrointestinal tract reduction, vertebral canal enlargement, descent of the larynx, and increase in encephalization), as well as evolutionary *mechanisms* underlying language emergence (such as duplication of human genes, change of developmental clock, casual role of behavior in evolution), and the beginnings of symbolic and abstract communication and thinking. See also CHOMSKY'S PSYCHOLINGUISTIC THEORY; DARWIN'S EVOLUTION THEORY; HUMOR, THEORIES OF; LANGUAGE ACQUISITION THEORY; LEARNING THEORIES/LAWS; MIRROR NEURONS THEORY; RIGHT-SHIFT THEORY; WHORF-SAPIR HYPOTHESIS/THE-ORY.

REFERENCES

Hales, F. N. (1904). Materials for the psychogenetic theory of comparison. *British Journal of Psychology*, *1*, 205-221.

Mowrer, O. H. (1952). The autism theory of speech development and some clinical applications. *Journal of Speech and Hearing Disorders*, *17*, 263-268.

Skinner, B. F. (1957). *Verbal behavior*. New York: Appleton-Century-Crofts.

Hess, E. (1959). Imprinting: An effect of early experience. *Science, 130*, 133-141.

Saussure, F. de (1959). *Course in general linguistics*. New York: Philosophical Library.

Mowrer, O. H. (1960). *Learning theory and the symbolic processes*. New York: Wiley.

Frisch, K. von (1967). *The dance language and orientation of bees*. Cambridge, MA: Harvard University Press.

Chomsky, N. (1968). *Language and the mind*. New York: Harcourt, Brace & World.

Lorenz, K. Z. (1970-71). *Studies on animal behavior*. Cambridge, MA: Harvard University Press.

McNeill, D. (1970). *The acquisition of language: The study of developmental psycholinguistics*. New York: Harper & Row.

Fodor, J. A. (1975). *The language of thought*. New York: Crowell.

DeCasper, A. J., & Fifer, W. P. (1980). Of human bonding: Newborns prefer their mother's voices. *Science, 208*, 1174-1176.

Rumbaugh, D. M., Savage-Rumbaugh, E. S., & Scanlon, J. L. (1982). The relationship between language in apes and human beings. In J. L. Fobes & J. E. King (Eds.), *Primate behavior*. New York: Academic Press.

Biakerton, D. (1984). The language bioprogram hypothesis. *The Behavioral and Brain Sciences, 7*, 173-221.

Hirsh-Pasek, K., & Golinkoff, R. M. (1996). *The origins of grammar*. Cambridge, MA: M.I.T. Press.

Saffran, J. R., Aslin, R. N., & Newport, E. L. (1996). Statistical learning by 8-month old infants. *Science, 274*, 1926-1928.

Jusczyk, P. W. (1997). *The discovery of spoken language*. Cambridge, MA: M.I.T. Press.

Li, C. N., & Hombert, J.-M. (2002). On the evolutionary origin of language. In M. Stamenov & V. Gallese (Eds.), *Mirror neurons and the evolution of brain and language*. Amsterdam, Netherlands: J. Benjamins.

Martin, R. C. (2003). Language processing: Functional organization and neuroanatomical basis. *Annual Review of Psychology, 54*, 55-89.

LANKESTER'S DEGENERATION THEORY. See DEVELOPMENTAL THEORY.

LARGE NUMBERS, LAW OF. See PROBABILITY THEORY/LAWS.

LASHLEY'S THEORY. The American behaviorist and physiological psychologist Karl Spencer Lashley (1890-1958) developed two principles of brain operation and organization in his work on localization of functions: the *principle/theory of mass action* and the *principle/theory of equipotentiality*. The concept of *mass action* refers to the operation of the cortex as a coordinated system where large masses of tissue are involved in all complex functioning (cf., Lashley's *multiple control principle* - states that any particular part of the brain is likely to be implicated in the performance of many different types of behavior; also, conversely, a single behavior involves a number of brain states; the principle maintains that the brain functions as an integrated whole). The *mass action principle* contrasts with the competing theory that specific local areas of the brain mediate specific behaviors. Lashley's argument for *mass action* is based on the demonstration that the degree of disruption of a learned behavior is due not simply to the *location* of brain lesions but to the *amount* of tissue involved. Lashley was not suggesting that there is no localization of function but that such localization was only part of the explanation. In its classical form, *localization theory*, as proposed by the French physiologist Pierre Jean Marie Flourens (1794-1867), states that each area within the brain is responsible for specific psychological skills; thus, in this approach, for instance, the *location* of brain injury is the salient factor in assessing loss of skills and behaviors. As an example of *mass action*, Lashley taught cats to escape from a puzzle box, then removed various parts of the cortex of their brains. After the cats had recovered from the operation, they were placed in the box again. Lashley found that the cats could no longer perform the previously learned escape behavior, but with further training they were able to relearn the escape behavior even in cases where both frontal lobes had been removed entirely. Lashley concluded that the *principle of mass action* shows that learning is not dependent on specific neural connections in the brain but on the brain as a whole, where the rate of relearning is a function of the total mass of brain tissue involved. The *principle of equipotentiality* within neuropsychology and neurophysiology refers to the speculation that all the neurons that mediate a given sensory modality have a common competing function in addition to their specific functions (i.e., each has equal potential for participating in a sensory event within that modality). By extension, the principle applies, also, to the notion that within certain limits one portion of the cerebral cortex can take on the functions of another part (cf., *functional plasticity theory*, *vicarious brain process hypothesis*, or *alternative brain process theory* - conjecture that in some cases of damage to a part of the brain, another part will take over the function of the damaged part; and *reciprocal blow effect* - refers to the case where an external injury to an area on one side of the head causes a brain injury on the opposite side; this is caused by pressure waves traveling to the right and left of the impact site and producing a summation of force around the person's skull from the point 180-degrees away; thus, an injury to the left side of the head may disrupt motor functions on the right side of the body rather than the left side). Thus, the *principle of equipotentiality* states that each part of the brain is just as important as any other, and if some parts are removed, other parts can carry on their functions. For instance, when Lashley removed the visual area of rats' brains - al-though they lost visual patterning - the rats could still discriminate differences in light intensity and could follow a moving-light stimulus. The two theories of *equipotentiality* and *localization* form the basis for the major theoretical schools within neuropsychology. However, psychological research has not wholly supported either the *localization* or the *equipotentiality theory*. See also BEHAVIORIST THEORY; BRAIN-LOCALIZATION THEORY; SPENCE'S THEORY.

REFERENCES

Flourens, P. J.-M. (1824). *Recherches experimentales sur les proprietes et les fonctions du systeme nerveaux dans les animaux vertebres*. Paris: Academie Royale.

Lashley, K. S. (1924). Studies of cerebral function in learning. V. The retention of motor habits after destruction of the so-called motor areas in primates. *Archives of Neurological Psychiatry, 12*, 249-276.

Lashley, K. S. (1929). *Brain mechanisms and intelligence*. Chicago: University of Chicago Press.

Lashley, K. S. (1950). In search of the engram. *Symposium of the Society of Experimental Biology, 4*, 454-482.

Lashley, K. S., Chow, K., & Semmes, J. (1951). An examination of the electrical field theory of cerebral integration. *Psychological Review, 58*, 123-136.

Luria, A. (1973). *The working brain*. New York: Basic Books.

LASHLEY-WADE HYPOTHESIS. See GENERALIZATION, PRINCIPLE OF.

LATENCY, LAW OF. See SKINNER'S DESCRIPTIVE BEHAVIOR AND OPERANT CONDITIONING THEORY.

LATENT INHIBITION, PRINCIPLE OF. See INHIBITION, LAWS OF.

LATENT OR INCIDENTAL LEARNING THEORY. See TOLMAN'S THEORY.

LATENT TRAIT THEORY. See CLASSICAL TEST/MEASUREMENT THEORY.

LATERAL AND VERTICAL THINKING THEORIES. See LATERALITY THEORIES.

LATERAL EYE MOVEMENT THEORY. See LATERALITY THEORIES.

LATERAL HYPOTHALAMUS/FEEDING CENTER THEORY. See HUNGER, THEORIES OF.

LATERAL INHIBITION THEORY. See LATERALITY THEORIES.

LATERALITY THEORIES. The term *lateral/laterality* refers to something situated at the side, or oriented towards the side - away from the median axis; for example, the term *lateral dominance* denotes "handedness" (preferred use of left versus right hand, or both as in "ambidexterous") or to "cerebral dominance" (right versus left side of cerebral cortex). The *cerebral dominance theory* posits that cortical activity relating to higher functions is dominated normally by the cerebral hemisphere that controls the most-used hand. In *lateral eye movement* (LEM), there is a deflection of one's gaze to the left or right side (or up versus down in *vertical eye movement* or VEM). *LEM theory* states that one's direction of gaze indicates an increase of activity in the contralateral cerebral hemisphere, such that a person tends to give a *rightward* deflection of gaze when preparing to answer a question requiring *verbal* processing, whereas a *leftward* gaze deflection indicates that the person is thinking about a *spatial* problem. However, it is recommended that one exercise caution when extrapolating from LEMs to cognitive-affective processes (cf., Ehrlichman & Weinberger, 1978; Raine, 1991). In *brain laterality theory*, it is posited that there is a functional asymmetry of the two cerebral hemispheres of the brain and, even though the two halves of the brain work together as a coordinated and integrated whole, many functions are subserved more by one hemisphere than by the other (e.g., the *left* side of the brain in most right-handed people subserves the *language* function, whereas the *right* side of the brain seems to control *visual-spatial* reasoning/memory, tactile/visual recognition of *form*, musical ability, and copying/drawing geometric figures; also, the *left* hemisphere seems to be the "analytic" side and functions in a sequential, rational way, whereas the *right* hemisphere seems to be the "synthetic" side and functions in a more "holistic" and non-rational fashion). However, it is suggested that the *laterality* of the brain provides a means of processing different components of information, rather than performance of separate types of activity. In *lateral inhibition theory*, there is

suppression by a neuron of the response of a nearby neuron at the same level in a sensory system, and occurs in various neural structures where receptor cells are arranged to represent points along a continuum (e.g., the retina of the eye; the organ of Corti of the cochlea of the inner ear); in this phenomenon, excitation at one point produces inhibition at adjacent points, leading to augmentation of differences between neighboring neural regions. In *lateral thinking theory*, creative problem-solving occurs via reformulation or restructuring of the problem, or assessing it from a new and fresh perspective (cf., *vertical thinking* which involves the discovery of methods for overcoming obstacles in the accepted cognitive approach). See also INHIBITION, LAWS OF; RIGHT-SHIFT THEORY.

REFERENCES

Bryden, M. P. (1965). Tachistoscopic recognition, handedness, and cerebral dominance. *Neuropsychologia, 3*, 1-8.

Sperry, R. W. (1968). Hemisphere deconnection and unity in conscious awareness. *American Psychologist, 23*, 723-733.

DeBono, E. (1970). *Lateral thinking: Creativity step by step.* New York: Harper & Row.

Gazzaniga, M. S. (1970). *The bisected brain.* New York: Appleton-Century-Crofts.

Nebes, R. D. (1974). Hemispheric specialization in commisurotomized man. *Psychological Bulletin, 81*, 1-14.

Wada, J. A., Clarke, R., & Hamm, G. (1975). Cerebral hemispheric asymmetry in humans. *Archives of Neurology, 32*, 239-246.

Lake, D. A., & Bryden, M. P. (1976). Handedness and sex differences in hemispheric asymmetry. *Brain and Language, 3*, 266-282.

Ehrlichman, H., & Weinberger, A. (1978). Lateral eye movements and hemispheric asymmetry: A critical review. *Psychological Bulletin, 85*, 1080-1101.

Galaburda, A. M., LeMay, M., Kemper, T. L., & Geschwind, N. (1978). Right-left

348

asymmetries in the brain. *Science*, *199*, 852-856.

Bryden, M. P. (1979). Evidence for sex-related differences in cerebral organization. In M. A. Wittig & A. C. Petersen (Eds.), *Sex-related differences in cognitive functioning: Developmental issues*. New York: Academic Press.

Kinsbourne, M. (1982). Hemispheric specialization and the growth of human understanding. *American Psychologist*, *37*, 411-420.

Raine, A. (1991). Are lateral eye movements a valid index of functional hemispheric asymmetries? *British Journal of Psychology*, *82*, 129-135.

LATE SELECTION THEORIES. See ATTENTION, LAWS/PRINCIPLES/THEORIES OF.

LATTA'S COGNITIVE-SHIFT THEORY OF HUMOR. Robert L. Latta (1998) proposed a *cognitive-shift theory of humor* (which he calls "Theory L," named after himself) that is intended to be an argument against the traditional *incongruity theories of humor*. *Latta's theory* - expressed in logical and syllogistical terms - may be classified as a "response-side" theory, and states that the response aspect of the basic humor process demonstrates a particular pattern. Specifically, the person responds to stimuli in a way that entails "unrelaxation;" that is, the individual makes a cognitive shift (which implies "relaxation"), and then responds to the situation the shift creates by relaxing again through the mechanism of laughter. Latta argues that his approach accomplishes the following: it meets the challenges often raised against *relief theories of humor*; it allows for the occurrence of a wide variety of humor processes; it incorporates the genuine insights of other theories of humor; it explains the psychodynamics of diverse examples of humor; it provides a basis for answers to questions regarding the global phenomenon of humor; it is consistent with evolutionary theory; it accounts for the specious appeal of *incongruity theory*; and it explains why humor has remained such a mysterious phenomenon for such a long time. See also COGNITIVE-PERCEPTUAL THEORIES OF HUMOR; HUMOR, THEORIES OF; INCONGRUITY/INCONSISTENCY THEORIES OF HUMOR; RELIEF/TENSION-RELIEF THEORIES OF HUMOR.

REFERENCE
Latta, R. L. (1998). *The basic humor process: A cognitive-shift theory and the case against incongruity*. Berlin: Mouton de Gruyter.

LAUGHTER, THEORIES OF. See HUMOR, THEORIES OF.

LAVATORY-WALL ILLUSION. See APPENDIX A, MUNSTERBERG ILLUSION.

LAY EPISTEMIC THEORY. The American social psychologist Arie W. Kruglanski (1980, 1981, 1990) describes a *theory of lay epistemics* that is applied to a wide range of topics within social-cognitive psychology. The theory concerns the process whereby human knowledge is formed and modified, and emphasizes the *epistemic* (i.e., pertaining to the need to know, often considered to be a basic drive, and observable, in particular, in young children who are curious and want to "know everything") functions of *hypothesis generation* and *hypothesis validation*. Generally, *knowledge* is defined in terms of propositions in which an individual has a given degree of confidence, and where such a definition imposes two functional requirements on a model of *knowledge formation*: hypothesis generation and hypothesis validation. It is assumed that *hypothesis generation* depends on persons' cognitive capability and their epistemic motivations, and *hypothesis validation* is based on preexisting inference rules in the person's mind that connect given categories of evidence with given hypotheses. *Hypothesis generation* and *validation models* have been employed previously to depict epistemic activities on levels of perception, concept formation, problem solving, and scientific discovery. The *lay epistemic* approach has been employed, also, in analyses of various social-cognitive phenomena where the same knowledge-acquisition process is assumed to exist, such as attribution, attitude formation, dissonance, and judgmental accuracy. In this way, the *lay epistemic analysis* may integrate apparently diverse social psychological issues under the same fundamental principles. In other areas of application, the *lay epistemic theory* seems to be capable of synthesizing conceptions of normal and neurotic inference, of adaptive and maladaptive thinking, and of lay and scientific inference. See also ATTITUDE/ATTITUDE CHANGE, THEORIES OF; ATTRIBUTION THEORY; CONCEPT LEARNING/CONCEPT FORMATION, THEORIES OF; DISSONANCE THEORY; PROBLEM-SOLVING AND CREATIVITY STAGE THEORIES.

REFERENCES

Kruglanski, A. W. (1980). Lay epistemologic process and contents: Another look at attribution theory. *Psychological Review, 87*, 70-87.

Kruglanski, A. W. (1981). The epistemic approach in cognitive therapy. *International Journal of Psychology, 16*, 275-297.

Kruglanski, A. W. (1989). *Lay epistemics and human knowledge: Cognitive and motivational bases.* New York: Plenum.

Kruglanski, A. W. (1990). Lay epistemic theory in social-cognitive psychology. *Psychological Inquiry, 1*, 181-197, 220-230.

LAY PERSONALITY THEORY. See PERSONALITY THEORIES.

LAZARUS' THEORY OF EMOTIONS. The American psychologist Richard S. Lazarus (1922-) proposed a *cognitive theory of emotions* that makes the concept of *appraisal* the keystone for analyzing and synthesizing the events that occur in an emotional episode (cf., *theory of induced emotion* - holds that the perception of emotional behavior or expression is sufficient to excite the same emotion in the person who perceives it). Lazarus argues that each emotion one experiences is based on a specific kind of *cognitive appraisal* that is accompanied by motor, behavioral, and physiological changes. Lazarus and his associates found that the appraisal of an event or situation - and, therefore, a person's emotional reaction - could be manipulated experimentally. According to Lazarus, *appraisal* falls into various categories: *primary* - initial evaluation leading to an incipient emotional response; *secondary* - an evaluation of one's relation to the environment leading to an altered emotional response; and *reappraisal* - evaluation of the significance of the secondary appraisal, or a psychological attempt to cope with stress in the situation. *Reappraisal* may not be based on the facts at hand but may be a "defensive reappraisal" where the person attempts to express a more compatible, friendly, or sympathetic point of view toward the situation or events. In Lazarus' approach, the notion of *coping* (in the *reappraisal* phase) functions as a mediator between events in the environment and one's emotional reaction. Thus, an individual may cope with a situation by reflecting on it, but it is the appraisal of one's conclusion (and not the reflection itself) that may alter the person's subsequent emotion. For example, you may *feel* uneasy over something that you have done or said long before you actually *think* about it, and subsequently you decide that you have behaved badly. See also ARNOLD'S THEORY OF EMOTIONS; COGNITIVE THEORIES OF EMOTIONS; EMOTIONS, THEORIES AND LAWS OF; SCHACHTER-SINGER'S THEORY OF EMOTIONS.

REFERENCES

Lazarus, R. S. (1966). *Psychological stress and the coping process.* New York: McGraw-Hill.

Lazarus, R. S., Averill, J., & Opton, E. (1970). Towards a cognitive theory of emotion. In M. Arnold (Ed.), *Feelings and emotions.* New York: Academic Press.

Lazarus, R. S. (1991). Progress on a cognitive-motivational-relational theory of emotion. *American Psychologist, 46*, 819-834.

Lazarus, R. S. (1993). From psychological stress to the emotions: A history of changing outlooks. *Annual Review of Psychology, 44*, 1-21.

LEADERSHIP, THEORIES OF. The earliest investigation of *leadership* that is regarded as uniquely psychological is attributed to the Italian statesman Niccolo Machiavelli (1469-

1527) in his 16th century book "The Prince." As defined in psychological research, the term *leadership* involves the notion of persuading people to ignore their individual concerns and devote themselves instead to a common goal that is important for the welfare of the group. In another definition, *leadership* refers to the direction, supervision, or management of a group or an organization. Originally, *leadership* was thought to be a fixed attribute of a person, trait, or a series of traits. Leaders may be "emergent" (i.e., informally acknowledged and elected by the group) or "appointed" (i.e., chosen by the organization of which the group is a part). Empirical research on *leadership* has evolved from the simplistic search for leadership traits (and the best way to relate to group members) to the relatively complex view that different situations require different types of leader personalities or behaviors. *Theories of leadership* may be classified as those stressing leader *traits/behaviors*, those emphasizing *contingencies/environmental influences*, those dealing with *transactional encounters*, and those emphasizing *cognitive processes*. From the early 1900s to about 1940, *leadership* research focused on the traits and personal characteristics that distinguish leaders from followers. The general *trait theory* viewpoint also has been called the *great man/great woman theory of leadership*. For instance, in the *great woman theory* proposed by the American psychologist Florence Harriet Lewion Denmark (1932-), an attempt is made to account for the observable sex differences in the number of men and women who are recognized leaders by emphasizing the significance of personality traits and qualities where cultural and social, rather than gender, factors are predominant. There have been studies in support of the *trait theory of leadership*, some of which have yielded positive results, but the differences found between leader and followers were quite small and of little practical or theoretical value. In one case (Lewin, Lippitt, and White, 1939), it was indicated that a democratic, participative leadership style produced better involvement and member satisfaction than either an autocratic or laissez-faire leadership style. In another case (Stogdill and Coons, 1957), using leader behavior rating scales, two behavior factors

emerged (*consideration* - concern for the welfare of subordinates, and *structuring* - assigning roles, setting standards, and evaluating performance) that helped to understand the leader's role in shaping the group's interaction. In a *humanistic* approach (McGregor, 1960), *Theory X* is described which contains an assumption about the nature of the worker (i.e., that human nature is basically lazy and externally motivated) and, also, *Theory Y* is described which contains the assumption that human nature is basically responsible and self-directed. Another more recent orientation describes *Theory Z* (Ouchi, 1981), which combines some of the positive features of the Japanese workplace with some of the realities of the American workplace. *Theory Z* suggests that American firms - such as the Japanese "paternalistic" firms - offer workers long-term (if not lifetime) employment when possible and restructuring (when necessary) to avoid layoffs, both of which would enhance workers' loyalty. Many of the *leader behavior theories* have had a major impact on management thinking, but they have not been consistently supported by empirical research. The *Hersey-Blanchard situational leadership theory* is based on the amount of direction (task behavior) a leader must provide given the situation and the "level of maturity" of the followers. The *contingency leadership theories* (e.g., Fiedler, 1967) assert that the leader's environment is an important determinant of the leader's performance. The *contingency model* views the leadership situation as giving high, moderate, or low degree of power, influence, and control to the leader. In this approach, the effectiveness of the leader is contingent on both the leader's personality and the characteristics of the situation (cf., *idiosyncrasy-credit model* - a leadership model which assumes that a leader is able to depart from group standards to the degree that the leader has built up and amassed "credits" or prestige over a period of time by adherence and conformity to group norms; and *sawtoothed theory* - holds that task-oriented leaders are most effective when faced with highly unfavorable or highly favorable conditions, and relations-oriented leaders are most effective when situations are only moderately favorable; contributing factors in these leadership situations are esteem and power of the leader and structure of the particular setting). Although the *contingency theories* have generated controversy, there appears to be substantial support for this approach. The *path-goal theory* (House, 1971) is a contingency model involving the interaction of behavior and situation that states that the leader must motivate the subordinate individuals by stressing the relationship between the subordinates' needs and the organizational goals and by facilitating the "path" that subordinates must take to fulfill their own needs and the organization's goals. Research supports this approach concerning employee job satisfaction and motivation, but the theory's predictions concerning performance have not been well supported. Another contingency model, called the *normative decision theory* (Vroom & Yetton, 1973), deals with the conditions under which leaders should take an autocratic role when making decisions. This theory assumes that individual decisions are more time-effective than group decisions, that subordinates who participate in the formulation of a decision are more committed to it, and that complex/ambiguous tasks require more information and consultation to achieve high-quality decisions. Further research is needed concerning the predictive validity of the *normative decision theory*, but the theory does indicate the best leadership style to use under various decision-making conditions. The newer *transactional theories of leadership* have replaced the older *situational theory* approach, which argued that leaders are best viewed in terms of the task faced by the group and the general situation within which it must operate. The *situational theory* tended to see leadership as a kind of "one-way" street; that is, it assumed that leaders influence and direct their groups but are not, in turn, affected by their followers. Many recent studies suggest, however, that leaders' behaviors are often strongly affected by the actions and demands of other group members. With more current transactional theories, leadership is viewed as a reciprocal process of social influence in which leaders both direct followers and are, in turn, influenced by these individuals (cf., *attribution theory of leadership* - suggests that leaders are influenced by their subordinates,

with leaders showing sensitivity to the attitudes of subordinates and continuously adjusting to them; *cognitive resource theory* - holds that leadership performance depends on the leader's control over the group's processes and outcomes; and *distributed-actions theory of leadership* - refers to the performance of acts that help the group to complete its task and to maintain optimal working relationships among group/team members). *Transactional theory* also calls attention to the importance of the perceptions of both leaders and followers regarding the relationship between them (e.g., do the followers perceive the leader's position as legitimate or illegitimate?). The *transactional* viewpoint argues, also, that both characteristics of the leader and situational factors (such as the task faced by the group) must be taken into account. Thus, the *transactional* approach adopts a highly sophisticated account of the leadership process, and is much more complex than previous approaches. Also, leadership theorists have begun increasingly to study the *cognitive processes* inherent in leadership situations. Leadership theory and research is likely to continue in the study of both noncognitive and cognitive variables in the leader-member relationship, as well as show increasing interest in the role of task characteristics in the determination of effective group and member performance. See also ATTRIBUTION THEORY; MACHIAVELLIAN THEORY; OCCUPATION THEORIES; ORGANIZATIONAL/INDUSTRIAL/SYSTEMS THEORY; PERSONALITY THEORIES.

REFERENCES
Lewin, K., Lippitt, R., & White, R. (1939). Patterns of aggressive behavior in experimentally created social climates. *Journal of Social Psychology, 10*, 271-299.

Coffin, T. (1944). A three-component theory of leadership. *Journal of Abnormal and Social Psychology, 39*, 63-83.

Stogdill, R., & Coons, A. (1957). *Leader behavior: Its description and measurement.* Columbus: Ohio State University, Bureau of Business Research.

McGregor, D. (1960). *The human side of enterprise.* New York: McGraw-Hill.

Fiedler, F. (1967). *A theory of leadership effectiveness*. New York: McGraw-Hill.

House, R. (1971). A path-goal theory of leader effectiveness. *Administrative Science Quarterly, 16*, 321-338.

Vroom, V., & Yetton, P. (1973). *Leadership and decision making*. Pittsburgh: University of Pittsburgh Press.

Stogdill, R. (1974). *Handbook of leadership*. New York: Free Press.

Osborn, R., & Hunt, J. (1975). An adaptive-reactive theory of leadership. *Organization & Administrative Sciences, 6*, 27-44.

Denmark, F. H. (1977). Styles of leadership. *Psychology of Women Quarterly, 2*, 99-113.

Ouchi, W. (1981). *Theory Z: How American business can meet the Japanese challenge*. Reading, MA: Addison-Wesley.

Strube, M., & Garcia, J. (1981). A metatheoretical analysis of Fiedler's contingency model of leadership effectiveness. *Psychological Bulletin, 90*, 307-321.

Hersey, P. (1985). *The situational leader*. New York: Warner.

Hogan, R., Curphy, G., & Hogan, J. (1994). What we know about leadership: Effectiveness and personality. *American Psychologist, 49*, 493-504.

Hersey, P., Blanchard, K. H., & Johnson, D. E. (2000). *Management of organizational behavior*. Englewood Cliffs, NJ: Prentice-Hall.

Olmstead, J. A. (2000). *Executive leadership: Building world-class organizations*. Houston, TX: Cashman Dudley.

Olmstead, J. A. (2002). *Leading groups in stressful times: Teams, work units, and task forces*. Westport, CT: Quorum books.

LEARNED HELPLESSNESS EFFECT/ PHENOMENON/HYPOTHESIS/THEO-RY.

The American psychologist Martin E. P. Seligman (1942-) and his associates demonstrated that when reinforcing outcomes are independent of an organism's responses, the individual learns that it will get the same outcomes whether it responds or not and, thereby, finds that responding is useless. In effect, the organism has learned to be inactive or to feel "helpless." Constant and unavoidable punishment eventually causes organisms to give up and quietly submit to the punishment. In the original experiments on *learned helplessness*, dogs were first restrained in harnesses and given a series of severe, inescapable shocks. The next day, the dogs were placed in a simple, discriminated-avoidance situation. On each trial, when a conditioned stimulus (such as a tone) came on, shock followed after 10 seconds unless the dogs jumped over a low barrier. If they failed to jump, the conditioned stimulus remained on, and shocks continued for 50 seconds. Using this procedure, the dogs had an opportunity either to avoid or escape from the shock by jumping the barrier. Dogs that did not have "day-before" exposure to inescapable shock had no difficulty learning first to escape from shock and then to avoid it by jumping as soon as they heard the conditioned stimulus. On the other hand, the dogs that were pre-trained with inescapable shock almost invariably failed to jump at all. Similar effects have been shown in experimental situations with a variety of species and different aversive stimuli. The effects often generalize from one highly aversive stimulus (such as water immersion) to another stimulus (such as shock). This pattern indicates that the aversiveness of the situation is the crucial aspect for most animals. The *learned helplessness* effects may be thought of as involving the long-known phenomenon of *Einstellung* (or *set*), which is defined as rigidity produced by earlier experience with testing/training conditions (e.g., Luchins, 1942). A certain amount of controversy occurred for a number of years concerning whether *learned helplessness* is simply an effect of the suppression of punishment (of effective responses), or whether in some *cognitive* sense the organisms actually learn or really "know" that they have no control over what happens to them. The *cognitive* interpretation is called the *learned helplessness (LH) hypothesis* and is distinguished from the experimentally-based *learned-helplessness effect*. There is no doubt about the "effect," but the status of the "hypothesis" is less certain. Apparently, a great deal of interest in *learned helplessness* derives from Seligman's arguments that *learned helplessness* presents a model for understanding the ubiquitous malady of human *depression*. The *theory of learned helplessness* has been challenged, however, by other investigators who have explained the phenomenon in other ways. The issue is whether learning to be helpless in a particular situation generalizes only to similar situations or to a wide variety of them. For instance, McReynolds (1980) observed that when people experience a situation in which reinforcements are not contingent on their responding, their responding extinguishes. If the situation then changes to one where responding will be reinforced, the individuals will continue not to respond unless they perceive that the schedule of reinforcement has changed. The more similar the second situation is to the first, the more likely the person will act "helpless." Thus, the phenomenon of *learned helplessness* may be viewed as a failure to discriminate between the situation under which responding is reinforced and the situation under which it is not reinforced. Further research may determine whether *learned helplessness* is a stable personality trait, as Seligman argues, or whether it can be explained by instrumental/operant conditioning principles. See also DEPRESSION, THEORIES OF; MIND/MENTAL SET, LAW OF; SKINNER'S DESCRIPTIVE BEHAVIOR/OPERANT CONDITIONING THEORY.

REFERENCES

Luchins, A. (1942). Mechanization in problem solving: The effect of Einstellung. *Psychological Monographs, 54*, No. 248.

Overmeier, J., & Seligman, M. E. P. (1967). Effects of inescapable shock upon subsequent escape and avoidance learning. *Journal of Comparative and Physiological Psychology, 63*, 23-33.

Seligman, M. E. P., & Maier, S. (1967). Failure to escape traumatic shock. *Journal of Experimental Psychology, 74*, 1-9.

Seligman, M. E. P. (1975). *Helplessness: On depression development and death*. San Francisco: Freeman.

Maier, S., & Seligman, M. E. P. (1976). Learned helplessness: Theory and evidence. *Journal of Experimental Psychology: General, 105*, 3-46.

Abramson, L. Y., Seligman, M. E. P., & Teasdale, J. (1978). Learned helplessness in humans: Critique and reformulation. *Journal of Abnormal Psychology, 87*, 49-74.

Huesmann, L. (Ed.) (1978). Learned helplessness as a model of depression. (Special Issue). *Journal of Abnormal Psychology, 87*, 1.

McReynolds, W. (1980). Learned helplessness as a schedule-shift effect. *Journal of Research in Personality, 14*, 139-157.

Roth, S. (1980). Learned helplessness in humans: A review. *Journal of Personality, 48*, 103-133.

Seligman, M. E. P., & Weiss, J. (1980). Coping behavior: Learned helplessness, physiological activity, and learned inactivity. *Behavioral Research Theory, 18*, 459-512.

LEARNED TASTE AVERSION EFFECT. See GARCIA EFFECT.

LEARNING STYLE THEORY. The American organizational/educational psychologist David A. Kolb (1939-) developed his Learning Style Inventory (LSI) based on his *experiential learning theory* (ELT) (Kolb, 1984) and on *learning styles theory* (cf., Cassidy, 2004). ELT provides a holistic model of the learning process and a multi-linear model of adult development; it emphasizes the central role that experience plays in the learning process, differentiating it from both *cognitive learning theories* and *behavioral learning theories*. The ELT model advances two dialectically related modes of experience: concrete experience and abstract conceptualization; and the related modes of transforming experience: reflective observation and active experimentation. According to Kolb's ELT, a four-stage learning cycle is involved where immediate/concrete experiences are the basis for observations and reflections; the reflections are assimilated and distilled into abstract concepts from which new implications for action may be drawn. Kolb's LSI contains four primary learning styles (doing, thinking, watching, and feeling), and four learning style types (accommodator, diverger, converger, and assimilator). A major hypothesis of *Kolb's learning style theory* is that individuals use and prefer different learning strategies or styles that correspond to how effective and comfortable they are when learning. Critics of Kolb's LSI cite the following aspects or arguments against its use: it contains flawed methodology; its statistical procedure is misapplied; there are logical inconsistencies in the theory construction; and there is a general lack of support for reliability and validity (cf., Atkinson, 1989; Koob & Funk, 2002; Wilson, 1986). See also COGNITIVE STYLE MODELS; LEARNING THEORIES/LAWS.

REFERENCES

Kolb, D. A. (1971/1976/1981/1985). *The Learning Style Inventory*. Boston: McBer.

Kolb, D. A., & Fry, R. (1975). Toward an applied theory of experiential learning. In C. Cooper (Ed.), *Theories of group process*. London: Wiley.

Kolb, D. A. (1984). *Experiential learning: Experience as the source of learning and development*. Englewood Cliffs, NJ: Prentice Hall.

Wilson, D. K. (1986). An investigation of the properties of Kolb's Learning Style Inventory. *Leadership and Organization Development Journal, 7,* 3-15.

Atkinson, G. (1989). Kolb's Learning Style Inventory - 1985. *Psychological Reports, 64,* 991-995.

Cornwell, J. M., & Manfredo, P. A. (1994). Kolb's learning style theory revisited. *Educational and Psychological Measurement, 54,* 317-327.

Kolb, A., & Kolb, D. A. (2000). *Bibliography of research on experiential learning and the Learning Style Inventory*. Cleveland, OH: Case Western Reserve University.

Kolb, D. A., Boyatzis, R., & Mainemelis, C. (2001). Experiential learning theory: Previous research and new directions. In R. J. Sternberg & L. Zhaig (Eds.), *Perspectives on thinking, learning, and cognitive styles*. Mahwah, NJ: Erlbaum.

Koob, J. J., & Funk, J. (2002). Kolb's Learning Style Inventory: Issues of reliability and validity. *Research on Social Work Practice, 12,* 293-308.

Cassidy, S. (2004). Learning styles: An overview of theories, models, and measures. *Educational Psychology, 24,* 419-444.

LEARNING THEORIES/LAWS. The term *learning* may be defined as a relatively permanent change in behavior or in behavioral potentiality as a result of experience and cannot be attributed to temporary body states such as those induced by illness, fatigue, or drugs [cf., the *alpha-, beta-,* and *gamma-hypotheses* of the American psychologist Knight Dunlap (1873-1949), which refer, respectively, to the enhancement, non-enhancement, or hindering of learning through frequency/repetition of a behavior; and the *factor theory of learning* - states that there are two or more factors/processes involved in learning: conditioning, comprehension, and attention factors]. *Learning* is a general term to describe behavioral changes, whereas the term *conditioning* is a more specific term used to describe actual procedures that can modify behavior (e.g., *classical conditioning; instrumental/operant conditioning*). In a chronological sequence of ideas in philosophy, the history of *learning* starts with the Greek philosopher Plato (c. 427-347 B.C.) and his *rationalist* position (i.e., knowledge is available only through reasoning) concerning the conception of the universe in *dualistic* terms (abstract/ideation/nonsensory versus sensory experience). Plato maintained a *nativist* position in his *reminiscence theory of knowledge* [i.e., the belief that all knowledge is present in the human soul at birth and, thus, "to know" is to remember the contents of the soul; cf., *neo-Platonism theory* - is a revision of Plato's philosophy, especially as developed by the Roman introspectionist philosopher Plotinus (c. 205-270) who blended the themes of Plato, Pythagoras, Aristotle, and the Stoics to produce a philosophy consistent with the Christian religious doctrine of the time]. Plato's famous student Aristotle (384-322 B.C.) held that knowledge is gained both from sensory experience and from thinking/reasoning. However, for Aristotle (unlike Plato), the laws and forms in the universe did *not* have an existence independent of their *empirical* aspects but are simply observed relationships in nature. Thus, Aristotle's position was that of an *empiricist* (where knowledge is based on sensory experience), and he formulated his *laws of association* (such as the *laws of similarity, contrast,* and *contiguity*) within this empiricist context. According to Aristotle, sensory experience gives rise to ideas, and the ideas stimulate other ideas in accordance with the *principles of association.* Later, in philosophy, the attempt to explain the relationship between ideas using the *laws of association* came to be known as *associationism.* Aristotle's ideas regarding *associationism* were so significant that they operate even today in all the major *contemporary learning theories.* Next, the French philosopher Rene Descartes (1596-1650) inferred from his famous edict, "I think, therefore I am," that sensory experience must be a reflection of a greater objective reality. Descartes also postulated (in *Cartesian dualism*) a separation between the *mind* (which is free and capable of choice) and the *body* (which is similar to a predictable machine) where the pineal gland is the point of contact between the *mind* and *body.* According to Descartes, the mind can move the gland from side to side to open or close the "pores" of the brain (allowing "animal/vital spirits" to flow throughout the body and cause bodily movements in a *reflex action* fashion). Descartes relied heavily on *innate ideas* (such as the concepts of God, self, space, and time) that are not derivable from experience but are an integral part of the mind. Thomas Hobbes (1588-1679), however, opposed the notion that innate ideas are the source of knowledge. Instead, Hobbes held that sense impressions are the source of all knowledge and, with this belief, helped to pave the way for the renewal of the concepts of *empiricism* and *associationism.* According to Hobbes, human behavior is controlled by "appetites" (events that are "good" and are approached by the individual) and "aversions" (events that are "evil" and avoided by the person); cf., Jeremy Bentham's (1748-1832) concept of the *pleasure principle,* which was

hypothesized to control human behavior and which was later employed by Sigmund Freud as well as the *reinforcement theorists.* John Locke (1632-1704) also opposed the notion of *innate ideas* and suggested that the mind at birth is a blank tablet ("tabula rasa") upon which experiences writes. Thus, according to Locke, there is nothing in the mind that is not first in the senses. Locke distinguished between *primary qualities* (characteristics of physical objects such as size, weight, solidity, mobility, and shape) and *secondary qualities* (things in the mind of the perceiver such as colors, odors, and tastes). Locke held that ideas are the elements that constitute the mind where the *laws of association* explain how the ideas come to be combined. George Berkeley (1685-1753) amended Locke's viewpoint by claiming that there are no primary qualities, only secondary qualities where the only reality is the mind. Because Berkeley asserted that the contents of the mind are derived from experience, he may still be considered an *empiricist.* Next, the philosopher David Hume (1711-1776) carried Berkeley's argument another step further and insisted that persons can know nothing for sure about ideas, and mind is no more than a stream of ideas, memories, feelings, and imaginings. Hume, also an *empiricist,* argued that the "laws of nature" are constructs of the imagination where the "lawfulness" observed in nature is in one's head and not in nature (cf., *Hume's fork* - Hume's argument that the only legitimate sources of knowledge/belief are reason and empirical evidence; this argument was adopted by the *logical positivists* who rejected metaphysics, theology, and ethics as meaningless). Immanuel Kant (1724-1804) attempted to reconcile the viewpoints of *rationalism* (the manipulation of concepts) and *empiricism* (the examination of sensory experience). Kant suggested that *innate categories of thought* (such as unity, totality, reality, existence, and causality) exist where innate mental faculties are superimposed over one's sensory experiences, thereby giving them meaning and structure. Thus, according to Kant, the mind makes an active contribution to one's experience involving organization and meaning of sensory information (cf., *Gestalt theory* and *cognitive-developmental theory*). In this sense,

Kant kept the *doctrine of rationalism* vital by indicating the importance of *mind* as the source of knowledge. John Stuart Mill (1806-1873) accepted the earlier notion of Hobbes and Locke that complex ideas are combinations of simpler ideas but also added the innovative notion that a new totality - which bears little resemblance to its parts - may emerge in the process (cf., the later *Gestaltists'* assertion that "the whole is more than the sum of its parts"). Other historical influences on *modern learning theory* are Thomas Reid's (1710-1796) suggestion that there are 27 discrete areas of the brain where each corresponds to a specific *innate faculty*, that is, a power of the mind that influences how one perceives the world; Franz Joseph Gall's (1758-1828) assertion that a person's strong and weak faculties could be detected by analyzing the depressions and bumps on the person's skull, a system of analysis, known as *brain-localization theory* or *phrenology*; Charles Darwin's (1809-1882) demonstration of the utility of behavior in adjusting to a changing environment and his evolutionary notion that human development is biologically continuous with that of lower animals; and Hermann Ebbinghaus' (1850-1909) original experimental studies of learning and memory using "nonsense syllables," which demonstrated how the *law of frequency* operates in the formation of new verbal associations (cf., the *cue overload principle* - states that there are a limited number of items that can be associated with a cue before it begins to lose its effectiveness, and where the more items that are connected with a cue, the less effective the cue in eliciting the item in the future; and *reduced cue hypothesis* - holds that upon further repetitions of conditioning, less and less of the original stimulus is required to elicit the response). The so-called schools or "isms" in the history of psychology also influenced the shape of *modern learning theory*: *structuralism* (via Wilhelm Wundt and Edward B. Titchener), whose goal was to discover and examine the basic elements of thought ("sensations") through the method of *trained introspection* (self analysis using predetermined modes of language or vocabulary); *functionalism* (via John Dewey, William James, and James R. Angell), whose goal was to discover how mental and behav-

ioral processes are related to an organism's adaptation to its environment by analysis of the person's acts and functions; and *behaviorism* (via John B. Watson), whose stated goal was to be totally objective and scientific in its study of external behavior, and where the study of inner consciousness was rejected completely. Of these schools of psychological thought, the approach of *behaviorism* probably had the most profound overall effect on American *learning theory*. Numerous theories dominated *modern learning theories* from about 1900 to 1960. Most of these may be called *intervening variable theories*, or *mediational theories*, because they attempted to explain hypothetical processes that intervene between observable environmental and behavioral events (cf., *S-O-R theory/model* – advances the study of intervening variables and hypothetical constructs as contained in the *O* or "organism" component of the model where *S* is the stimulus input and *R* is the response output; some *S-O-R theorists* emphasize the "organisms" contributions to learning, and others focus on the importance of "perception" in learning). One exception to the intervening variable approach is a metatheoretical/atheoretical area of study in learning called the *experimental analysis of behavior*, which refers to an emphasis on examination, development, and application of the *principles of operant conditioning*. The *model of operant conditioning*, along with its many experimentally produced concepts, is considered to play an extremely important role in *learning theory* because it helps to explain how new and complex behaviors and phenomena are developed in individuals. Among the *intervening variable theories* (that attempt to deal with topics that the experimental analysis of behavior approach tends to avoid, such as memory, motivation, and cognition) are E. C. Tolman's *expectancy theory* - where "expectanies" were hypothesized to develop in the organism due solely to the temporal succession, or contiguity, of environmental events and not necessarily on the consequences of responding (cf., *cognitive sign principle* - the conjecture that true learning involves an awareness that the various steps to the achievement of a goal is a unified pattern, and that every step is a totality rather than merely a series of connections); I.

Pavlov's *physiological theory* - in which the relation between events and intervening variables invoke physiological referents to explain how learning occurs (cf., D. Hebb's *neuropsychological theory* and *irradiation theory* - a hypothesis that assumes that during learning excitation spreads into neighboring structures such as nerves or muscles; more generally, *irradiation theory* refers to learning that involves selective reinforcement of one of many responses within a "response hierarchy;" and C. L. Morgan's *trial and error theory of learning* - proposes that learning consists of the process of succeeding in attempts by trying repeatedly, and gaining knowledge subsequently from one's failures; phenomena such as "sudden solutions" and "insight" in problem-solving serve to qualify this approach somewhat); E. R. Guthrie's *molecular /contiguity theory* - where temporally contiguous events, molecular stimulus events called "cues," molecular responses called "movements," and molar behaviors called "acts" are examined to understand an organism's behavior; R. S. Woodworth's *massed-spaced theory of learning* - refers to the relative advantages and disadvantages of learning material in an intensive session; factors such as the volume of material to be learned, the nature of the learning theory, the context in which the material is learned and reinforced, and learner/ individual differences are experimentally manipulated in studies of this theory; and C. L. Hull's and K. Spence's *drive-reduction theory* - in which contiguity of stimulus with response, in addition to various drive-reduction concepts such as "habit," was hypothesized to account for learned behavior (cf., *linear-operator model of learning* - holds that learning is based on an organism responding to part of the total stimulus where responses occur due to fractional elements of the total stimulus; in this model, learning is increased by reward but reduced by the effort required by the learning process; cf., Bush & Mosteller, 1955). Supplemental modern learning theories developed in the 1950s, 1960s, and 1970s have been called "miniature" theories, and they typically involve quantitative characteristics with a circumscribed range of content. Such *miniature theories* are illustrated by W. Estes' *mathematical learning/stimulus sampling theory*; R. Atkinson and R. Shiffrin's *information-processing/memory theory*; H. Simon and L. Gregg's *stochastic/computer model theory*; and R. D. Luce's *probability theory of learning* - states that when a choice of behavior exists, the probability of a response tends toward the probability of reinforcement. Currently, the work by intervening variable theorists on *classical conditioning* and by experimental analysts on *operant conditioning* may be viewed as converging on a common understanding of mutually employed concepts such as the key concept of *reinforcement* in *learning theory*. However, various important questions concerning learning processes and phenomena remain unanswered (Hergenhah, 1982): How does learning vary as a function of *maturation*? Does learning depend on *reward*? How does learning vary as a function of *species*? How does learned behavior relate to *instinctive* behavior? Can some *associations* be learned more easily than others? How does learning vary as a function of *personality* characteristics? To what extent is learning a function of the total *environment*? and How do internal and external variables *interact* with type of learning? (cf., the areas of *applied learning theory* in educational psychology called *instructional theory* and instructional design; Gagne, 1985; Reigeluth, 1983; cf., *knowledge of results principle* - states that immediate/prompt feedback given to a learner concerning performance is more effective than delayed feedback, also called *performance re-view effect*; *practice effect* - refers to any change or improvement in learning that results from repetition or practice of the task materials; and *testing effect* - refers to any of a number of consequences of taking tests, ranging from developing a strong attitude, positive or negative, towards tests to learning how to take tests to obtain unwarranted positive results). Most of what is now known about learning came out of the great debates among learning theorists that took place in the 1930s and 1940s. Such an atmosphere still exists in psychology, but the debate among learning theorists does not seem to be as intense today as it was during that earlier era. See also ASSOCIATION, LAWS/PRINCIPLES OF; BANDURA'S THEORY; BEHAVIORIST THEORY;

COMTE'S LAW/THEORY; DARWIN'S EVOLUTION THEORY; EMPIRICAL/EMPIRICISM, DOCTRINE OF; EMPIRICIST VERSUS NATIVIST THEORIES; ESTES' STIMULUS SAMPLING THEORY; FORMAL DISCIPLINE THEORY; GESTALT THEORY AND LAWS; GUTHRIE'S THEORY OF BEHAVIOR; HEBB'S THEORY OF PERCEPTUAL LEARNING; HULL'S LEARNING THEORY; INFORMATION/INFORMATION-PROCESSING THEORY; INTERBEHAVIORAL THEORY; MIND-BODY THEORIES; MIND/MENTAL STATES, THEORIES OF; MOTOR LEARNING THEORIES; MOWRER'S THEORY; PAVLOVIAN CONDITIONING PRINCIPLES/LAWS/THEORIES; PIAGET'S THEORY OF DEVELOPMENTAL STAGES; PUNISHMENT, THEORIES OF; REINFORCEMENT THEORY; REINFORCEMENT, THORNDIKE'S THEORY OF; SKINNER'S DESCRIPTIVE BEHAVIOR/OPERANT CONDITIONING THEORY; SPENCE'S THEORY; THORNDIKE'S LAW OF EFFECT; TOLMAN'S THEORY; WUNDT'S THEORIES/DOCTRINES.

REFERENCES

Bentham, J. (1830). *Works*. J. Bowruy (Ed.). Edinburgh: Hait.

Gall, F. (1835). *Works: On the functions of the brain and each of its parts*. Boston: Marsh, Capen, & Lyon.

Reid, T. (1849). *Essays on the intellectual powers of the mind*. Edinburgh: Macachian, Stewart.

Darwin, C. (1859). *On the origin of species by means of natural selection*. London: Murray.

Ebbinghaus, H. von (1885). *Uber das gedachtnis*. Leipzig: Duncker.

Wertheimer, M. (1912). Experimentelle studien uber das sehen von be-wegung. *Zeitschrift fur Psychologie, 61*, 161-265.

Pavlov, I. (1927). *Conditioned reflexes*. London: Oxford University Press.

Symonds, P. M. (1927). Laws of learning. *Journal of Educational Psychology, 18*, 405-413.

Tolman, E. C. (1932). *Purposive behavior in animals and men*. New York: Appleton-Century-Crofts.

Dashiell, J. (1935). A survey and synthesis of learning theories. *Psychological Bulletin, 32*, 261-275.

Guthrie, E. R. (1935). *The psychology of learning*. New York: Harper.

Skinner, B. F. (1938). *The behavior of organisms: An experimental analysis*. New York; Appleton-Century-Crofts.

Hull, C. L. (1943). *Principles of behavior*. New York: Appleton-Century-Crofts.

Pitts, W. (1943). A general theory of learning and conditioning. *Psychometrika, 8*, 1-18.

Hilgard, E. R. (1948). *Theories of learning*. New York: Appleton-Century-Crofts.

Hebb, D. O. (1949). *The organization of behavior*. New York: Wiley.

Estes, W. (1950). Toward a statistical theory of learning. *Psychological Review, 57*, 94-107.

Spence, K. (1951). Theoretical interpretations of learning. In S. S. Stevens (Ed.), *Handbook of experimental psychology*. New York: Wiley.

Hull, C. L. (1952). *A behavior system: an introduction to behavior theory concerning the individual organism*. New Haven, CT: Yale University Press.

Bush, R. R., & Mosteller, F. (1955). *Stochastic models for learning*. New York: Wiley.

Spence, K. (1956). *Behavior theory and conditioning*. New Haven, CT: Yale University Press.

Gregg, L., & Simon, H. (1967). Process models and stochastic theories of simple concept formation. *Journal of Mathematical Psychology, 4*, 246-276.

Atkinson, R., & Shiffrin, R. (1968). Human memory: A proposed system and its control processes. In K. Spence & J. Spence (Eds.), *The psychology of learning and motivation*. Vol. 2. New York: Academic Press.

Piaget, J. (1970). Piaget's theory. In P. Mussen (Ed.), *Carmichael's manual of child psychology*. Vol. 1. New York: Wiley.

Seligman, M. E. P. (1970). On the generality of the laws of learning. *Psychological Review, 77*, 406-418.

Bower, G., & Hilgard, E. R. (1981). *Theories of learning.* Englewood Cliffs, NJ: Prentice-Hall.

Hergenhahn, B. (1982). *An introduction to theories of learning.* Englewood Cliffs, NJ: Prentice-Hall.

Reigeluth, C. M. (1983). *Instructional-design theories and models.* Hillsdale, NJ: Erlbaum.

Gagne, R. M. (1985). *The conditions of learning and theory of instruction.* New York: Holt, Rinehart, and Win-ston.

Mowrer, R. R., & Klein, S. B. (2001). *Handbook of contemporary learning theories.* Mahwah, NJ: Erlbaum.

LEARNING THEORY, THORNDIKE'S. See REINFORCEMENT, THORNDIKE'S THEORY OF.

LEAST ACTION, LAW OF. See GESTALT THEORY/LAWS.

LEAST COMMITMENT, PRINCIPLE OF. See INFORMATION/INFORMATION-PROCESSING THEORY.

LEAST CONSTRAINT, LAW OF. See GESTALT THEORY/LAWS.

LEAST-EFFORT, GESTALT PRINCIPLE OF. See GESTALT THEORY/LAWS.

LEAST EFFORT, PRINCIPLE OF. = law of simplest path. This general principle states that when there are a number of possibilities for action, a person will select the one that requires the *least amount of effort*, or the one that involves the minimum expenditure of cognitive energy (cf., Allport, 1954). The principle has been invoked in a wide range of disciplines and in a diverse range of problems from rats learning to run mazes (cf., Tsai, 1932) to the operation of economic systems. In the area of personality and social psychology, a principle called *least interest* found expression similar to that of *least effort*: in a personal relationship, whichever member of a couple is less interested in the relationship is the one who is able to set its terms. The American philologist George Kingsley Zipf (1902-1950) enumerated various functional relationships in the area of the lawfulness of language phenomena that exemplify the *principle of least effort*: the frequency of occurrence of words is inversely related to their length; that is, there is a universal tendency for people to use short words (e.g., "TV") more often than long ones (e.g., "television"); the lower the rank order in word frequency, the more different words are found at that rank (e.g., in a sample of 1,000 words there are many different words that occur once, and there are only a very few words that occur as frequently as 40 times per 1,000 words); the more "effortful" a sound is, the less frequent its occurrence tends to be; and the average number of different meanings per word is proportional to its frequency of occurrence. Zipf presented analyses and evidence indicating that there is a "grand harmony" or balance in the use of language. A related principle, called *economy of effort*, or *adaptive adaptation*, refers to the tendency of an organism in repeated performances to minimize the expenditure of energy by eliminating useless movements. See also LANGUAGE ORIGINS, THEORIES OF; ZIPF'S LAW.

REFERENCES

Tsai, L. S. (1932). The law of minimum effort and maximum satisfaction in animal behavior. *Monographs of the National Research Institute of Psychology, Academica Sinica, 1*, 1-47.

Zipf, G. K. (1949). *Human behavior and the principle of least effort.* Cambridge, MA: Addison-Wesley.

Allport, G. W. (1954). *The nature of prejudice.* Cambridge, MA: Addison-Wesley.

LEAST-ENERGY EXPENDITURE, PRINCIPLE OF. See GESTALT THEORY/LAWS.

LEAST INTEREST, PRINCIPLE OF. See LEAST EFFORT, PRINCIPLE OF.

LEAST SQUARES, LAW OF. See PROBABILITY THEORY/LAWS.

LEE-BOOT EFFECT. See OLFACTION/ SMELL, THEORIES OF.

LEE-HENDRICKS MODEL. See LOVE, THEORIES OF.

LEFT-RIGHT EFFECT. See DEVELOP-MENTAL THEORY.

LEIBNITZ'S MONAD THEORY. See HERBART'S DOCTRINE OF APPERCEP-TION.

LENIENCY EFFECT. See EXPERIMEN-TER EFFECTS.

LENS MODEL. The Hungarian-born American psychologist Egon Brunswik (1903-1955) proposed this metaphor to emphasize the probabilistic relationship between "ecological/ distal criterion" (an aspect or feature of an environmental context to which an organism must adapt functionally, and which the organism cannot perceive directly but judges it as best it can from sensory cues) and the sensory cues of "imperfect ecological validity" (a dimension/aspect of a proximal/near stimulus, such as the monocular and binocular depth cues one employs in making depth perception assessments) whereby an organism judges the ecological criterion. In the *lens model*, sensory cues are hypothesized as being focused by cognitive processes in a manner similar to a lens with rays of light falling onto the object or surface of the ecological criterion. Brunswik refers to the correlation between the sensory cue(s) and the imperceptible ecological criterion as the "ecological validity" of the cue(s). See also PERCEPTION (II. COM-PARATIVE APPRAISAL, THEORIES OF; PROBABILISTIC FUNCTIONALISM, THE-ORY OF.

REFERENCE

Brunswik, E. (1952). *The conceptual frame-work of psychology*. Chicago: University of Chicago Press.

LEONARDO'S PARADOX. See VISION/ SIGHT, THEORIES OF.

LEPLEY HYPOTHESIS/LEPLEY-HULL HYPOTHESIS. See SERIAL POSITION EFFECT.

LESS-LEADS-TO-MORE EFFECT. See FESTINGER'S COGNITIVE DISSONANCE THEORY.

LEVEE EFFECT. See SELYE'S THEORY/ MODEL OF STRESS.

LEVELS OF PROCESSING THEORY. See INFORMATION/INFORMATION-PRO-CESSING THEORY; SHORT-TERM AND LONG-TERM MEMORY, THEORIES OF.

LEWIN'S FIELD THEORY. = topological psychology = hodological/vector psychology. The German-born American psychologist Kurt Lewin (1890-1947) developed a *field theory of personality* that was influenced by Gestalt psychology and psychoanalysis. The concept of *field*, a major principle of Gestaltists, refers to the determination of one's behavior by the psychophysical field, consisting of an organized system of stresses or forces, that is analogous in its dynamics to an electromagnetic/gravitational field in physics. In the *field theory* approach, a person's perception of an object is determined by the total field in which the object is contained. According to Lewin, *field theory* provides a method of analyzing causal relations among mutually interdependent facts and of developing scientific constructs. The principal features of *Lewin's field theory* are study of behavior as a function of the field that exists at the time the behavior occurs; analysis of behavior in the situation as a whole and from which the component parts may be distinguished; focus on the concrete person in a concrete situation that can be represented mathematically; and a preference for psychological, as opposed to physical or physiological, descriptions of the field in which underlying forces or needs determine behavior. Lewin's conceptualization of the structure of personality is cast in terms of spatial representations because such accounts can be treated in nonmetrical-mathematical ways, whereas ordinary verbal definitions do not lend themselves to such treatments. For example, the separation of the person from the rest of the universe is depicted by simply drawing an enclosed figure such as a circle, square, or triangle. The boundary of the figure defines the limits of the *person* where everything inside the boundary is "P" (the person) and everything outside the boundary is "non-P." Drawing another larger figure around the initial figure defines Lewin's concept of *psychological environment*, and the total area within both figures is called the *life space*. All the space outside the two figures represents the non-psychological aspects of the universe. Thus, according to Lewin, *life space* (L) equals the *person* (P) plus the *psychological environment* (E). The L (also called *total psychological field*) is surrounded by a "foreign hull" that is part of the non-psychological or objective environment. Lewin's spatial representation separates the regions of P and the environment by "boundaries" that have degrees of "permeability" and various dimensions such as "nearness/remoteness." Regions of L are interconnected so that a "fact" in one region may affect a "fact" in another region (an influence between "two facts" is called an *event*). Connections between regions are said to exist when the person can perform a "locomotion" between regions, and regions of P are considered connected when they can "communicate" with one another. The L also has the dimensions of "reality-unreality" and "past-future." All of Lewin's spatial concepts and relationships can be handled by the branch of mathematics called *typology*, and his structural concepts of personality are called *topological psychology*. Lewin's invention of a new type of spatial representation is called *hodology* (the "science of paths"), wherein he was able to deal with various dynamic concepts such as *force*, *distance*, and *direction* (e.g., *interhodological distances* may be defined, psychologically, not by the shortest path, but by the path of *least effort*, given the positive and negative valences of the regions comprising the space). Lewin's account of the dynamics of his personality theory is called *vector psychology*, which includes development of the concepts of *need*, *psychical energy*, *tension*, *force* (vector), and *valence*. These dynamical constructs, in conjunction with his structural constructs, determine the particular locomotions of P and the way P structures her or his environment (cf., Lewin's *interaction principle* - states that behavior and environment have a reciprocal effect on each other where

one cannot be studied or explained without reference to the other). Locomotions and restructurings are ways P reduces tension by satisfying needs. The ultimate goal of all psychological processes, according to Lewin, is to return P to a state of equilibrium. *Lewin's learning theory*, as part of his *personality development theory*, consists of descriptions of the changes that occur in behavior and employed concepts such as *cognitive restructuring*, *differentiation*, *motivation*, *changes in boundary conditions*, *integration*, and *organization*. Based on the amount of experimentation that Lewin's *personality theory* generated since its inception, it may be considered a "good" theory. In particular, *Lewin's field theory* instigated a great deal of experimental work in the areas of aspiration level, achievement motivation, interrupted or incompleted activities, regression, conflict, aggression, and cognitive dissonance concerning interpersonal relations. *Lewin's field theory* led to the development of an active area of investigation called *group dynamics* in social psychology (cf., *iceblock theory* - Lewin's speculation that in behavior change efforts in the context of group dynamics, involving "training groups/sensitivity training," the person's attitudes and behavior first need to be "unfrozen," and then new attitudes and behaviors are to be created and then "frozen" into new habit patterns), and also provided the impetus for development of ecological/environmental psychology. Lewin's *theory of the person*, however, has made no important advances since the early 1940s, even though many of his concepts - such as *life space, vector, valence, barrier*, and *tension system* - have been assimilated into the mainstream of psychology. Formal criticisms of *Lewin's field theory* have focused on four issues: Lewin's topological and vectorial systems do not provide anything new about the behavior they are supposed to explain; psychology should not ignore the objective environment; Lewin does not account for the individual's past history; and Lewin misuses mathematical and physical concepts. See also ACHIEVEMENT MOTIVATION, THEORY OF; CONTEMPORANEITY, PRINCIPLE OF; FESTINGER'S COGNITIVE DISSONANCE THEORY; GESTALT THEORY/LAWS; HEIDER'S

BALANCE THEORY; PSYCHOANALYTIC THEORIES OF PERSONALITY; ZEIGARNIK EFFECT.

REFERENCES

Lewin, K. (1935). *A dynamic theory of personality*. New York: McGraw-Hill.

Lewin, K. (1936). *Principles of topological psychology*. New York: McGraw-Hill.

Garrett, H. (1939). Lewin's "topological" psychology: An evaluation. *Psychological Review, 46*, 517-524.

Leeper, R. (1943). *Lewin's topological and vectoral psychology: A digest and a critique*. Eugene: University of Oregon Press.

Lewin, K. (1951). *Field theory in social science: Selected theoretical papers*. New York: Harper & Row.

Deutsch, M. (1968). Field theory in psychology. In G. Lindzey & E. Aronson (Eds.), *Handbook of social psychology*. Vol. 1. Cambridge, MA: Addison-Wesley.

Wheelan, S. A., Pepitone, E. A., & Abt, V. (Eds.) (1990). *Advances in field theory*. Newbury Park CA: Sage.

LEWINSOHN'S THEORY OF DEPRESSION. See DEPRESSION, THEORIES OF.

LEXICOGRAPHIC CHOICE THEORY. See ELIMINATION BY ASPECTS THEORY.

LIAR PARADOX. See GODEL'S THEOREM/PROOF.

LIBERALIZED STIMULUS-RESPONSE THEORY. See BEHAVIORIST THEORY.

LIBERAL PLURALISM, DOCTRINE OF. See CONSTRUCTIVISM, THEORIES OF.

LIBIDO THEORY. See ANXIETY, THEORIES OF; FREUD'S THEORY OF PERSONALITY; HORNEY'S THEORY OF PERSONALITY; JUNG'S THEORY OF PERSONALITY; SULLIVAN'S THEORY OF PERSONALITY.

LIEBMANN EFFECT. See GESTALT THEORY/LAWS.

LIFE-SPAN DEVELOPMENT THEORIES. See AGING, THEORIES OF.

LIFESTYLE THEORY. See ADLER'S THEORY OF PERSONALITY; HISTORICAL MODELS OF EXPERIMENTAL PSYCHOLOGY.

LIFE, THEORIES OF. The concept of *life* may be defined as matter having a type of organization, and having the properties of self-perpetuation (for a longer or shorter time) and of reproduction in some form. It is also distinguished by certain characteristics described as "vital" properties of living matter (such as nutrition involving processes of anabolism and catabolism, and irritability involving conductivity and contractibility). Living substance has been analyzed in terms of chemical protoplasm (consisting largely of water, proteins, lipids, carbohydrates, and inorganic salts, and is differentiated into nucleoplasm and cytoplasm), as well as in terms of its physiological and morphological properties. There are *four classical theories of protoplasmic structure* (Baldwin, 1901-1905): the *granular theory* - basic biological units of lower order than the cell, including Spencer's "physiological units," Nageli's "micellae," and Darwin's "gemmules"); the *filar theory* - Flemming's conceptualization that spongioplasm is composed of interlacing threads (that do not unite) to form a reticulum; the *reticular theory* - protoplasmic structure is thought to be a mass of threads that are combined into a more or less regular network; and the *alveolar theory* - Butschli's viewpoint that protoplasm is a microscopic foam or emulsion of two liquids of different densities. The nature of the bond which holds the diverse substances of living matter together is the so-called "problem of life" (cf., *constancy principle* - states that what is alive will be dead someday, and all organic matter will return to inorganic matter; and the discredited *theory of spontaneous generation*, or *abiogenesis theory*, which states that living organisms may develop from nonliving matter, based on observations such as the development of maggots on decaying meat, but which occurred, in fact, as a result of flies' laying eggs on the meat). Across the centuries, *theories of life* have focused predominantly on the form of organization displayed, as compared to the other forms, such as the chemical bases (cf., *electron-proton theory* - the "atomistic" or "reductive" approach which states that everything about a living organism, both overt and covert, is nothing more than a grouping of electrons and protons in a dynamic structure). For example, according to *Aristotle's theory*, the soul is the "form" or "formal cause" of the organized body, the matter of which is the "material cause" of the living creature. Later, in the 10th through the 15th centuries, the *Scholastic theory* postulated a "vital force" or *vitality principle* [cf., *pneumatism theory*, proposed by the early Greek physician Erasistratus (c. 310-250 B.C.), is the semi-mystical proposition that breathing is caused by a "vital principle" or "holy spirit;" Erasistratus also asserted that the soul resides in the brain, and was the first to suggest a distinction between sensory and motor nerves], in addition to those of mechanical action and chemical organization (cf., *principle of conservation of energy* and *law of natural selection* which subsequently challenged this position). Historically, in addition to mechanical and chemical factors, the ignorance concerning the precise and essential nature of life and living matter was cloaked in the term *vitalism* (cf., *vital fluids theory* - posits that the loss of seminal fluids drains vital fluids from the body and/or brain, and deprives one of one's strength; and *doctrine of creationism* - asserts that all living organisms were created separately and suddenly by a supreme spiritual power, known under various names; this position is maintained by a number of cultural and religious groups, including Aztecs, Native Americans, various African tribes, Buddhists, Christians, Hindus, and ancient Egyptians, Greeks, and Romans). The question as to whether or not vital changes (such as those of development and growth) can be adequately accounted for as transformations of the known forms of energy led to the *vitalistic* or *neo-vitalistic* viewpoint which holds that some sort of "new force" or "new energy" (e.g., the "genetic energy" of Williams; the "growth force" of Cope) is operative, some property of "self-adaptation" or "direction" occurs, or some form of a "directive force" serves to guide physical energy [cf., *theory of congruent transcendency* - posits that life form, for example, one's personality is governed by a kind of master plan that permits integration of present status with the "ultimate life form;" Van Kaam (1964/1980; 1966); *transmigration theory* - holds that one state of existence or essence may change into another one, specifically the notion that the soul of a person leaves the body at death and goes into another body, such as allegedly occurs in the process of "resurrection" or "reincarnation" in certain religious belief systems; and the *Gaea/Gaia hypothesis* (named after the ancient mythological Greek goddess of the earth) - posits that the earth is a separate self-regulating and functioning organism with all flora and fauna determining the planet's health in interaction with the atmosphere and oceans to maintain its existence; according to this hypothesis, the earth is neutral in regard to its inhabitants; the hypothesis was first proposed by the British organic chemist James E. Lovelock (1919-) and the British molecular biologist Lynn Margulis (1938-), where the stability of atmospheric components over many eons is cited as evidence for this controversial notion]. It is notable for theory development in psychology that the "directive force" approach gave the concept of *consciousness* a new and important role in the discussion and represented a tendency to restate the older philosophical question of *life* in terms of a *dualism* between *matter* and *mind* rather than between *matter* and *life*. On the related issue of *death/dying*, theoretical conjectures focus on the *dying process* (i.e., psychological processes occurring in a dying person are usually feelings of anger, fear, sadness, and shame) and on *stages of dying* [according to the Swiss psychiatrist Elisabeth Kubler-Ross (1926-2004), there are five major attitudes/stages experienced by dying persons: denial, anger, bargaining, depression, and acceptance, and where "hope of survival" persists through all the stages; cf., *Gompertz hypothesis* (named after the self-educated English mathematician Benjamin Gompertz (1779-1865) - states that the probability of mortality increases geometrically as a function of the length of time the person has lived]. See also CONSCIOUSNESS, PHENOMENON OF; CONSERVATION OF ENERGY, LAW/PRINCIPLE OF; DARWIN'S EVOLUTION THEORY; DEVELOPMENTAL THEORY; LOEB'S TROPISTIC THEORY; NATURAL SELECTION, LAW OF.

REFERENCES

Baldwin, J. M. (Ed.) (1901-1905). *Dictionary of philosophy and psychology.* New York: Macmillan.

Van Kaam, A. (1964/1980). *Religion and personality.* Denville, NJ: Dimension books.

Van Kaam, A. (1966). *Existential foundations of psychology.* Pittsburgh, PA: Duquesne University Press.

Kubler-Ross, e. (1969/1997). *On death and dying.* New York: Macmillan/Scribners.

Lovelock, J. (1988). *The ages of Gaia: A biography of our living earth.* New York: Oxford University Press.

LIGHT REFRACTION, LAWS OF. See VISION/SIGHT, THEORIES OF.

LIGHT, THEORIES OF. See VISION/SIGHT, THEORIES OF.

LIKELIHOOD PRINCIPLE. See CONSTRUCTIVIST THEORY OF PERCEPTION; UNCONSCIOUS INFERENCE, DOCTRINE OF.

LIKENESS AND COMPLETENESS THEORIES OF MARITAL SUCCESS. See INTERPERSONAL ATTRACTION THEORIES.

LIKING, THEORIES OF. See LOVE, THEORIES OF.

LIMITED-CAPACITY RETRIEVAL HYPOTHESIS. See SHORT-TERM AND LONG-TERM MEMORY, THEORIES OF.

LINDSLEY'S ACTIVATION THEORY. The American psychologist and neuroscientist Donald Benjamin Lindsley's (1907-2003) germinal work on activation in the general area of emotion shows the importance of the brain-stem portion of the brain called the *reticular substance.* Lindsley's *activation theory* is based, in particular, on research involving the electroencephalogram (EEG) and its relevance toward understanding the interaction of the cerebral cortex and the subcortical structures. The *activation theory* was advanced not only as an explanatory concept for emotional behavior, but it was related also to the phenomenon of sleep-wakefulness, to EEG recordings of cortical activity, and to different types of abnormal behavior involving various psychiatric symptomatologies. The *activation theory* states: (1) the EEG in emotion shows an *activation pattern* with reduction in alpha (synchronized) rhythms and induction of low-amplitude, fast activity; (2) the EEG *activation pattern* is reproducible by electrical stimulation of the brain-stem reticular formation (BSRF); (3) destruction of the rostral end of the BSRF abolishes EEG activation and allows restoration of rhythmic discharges in the thalamus/cortex; (4) the behavior associated with destruction of the rostral end of the BSRF is the opposite of emotional excitement, namely, apathy, somnolence, lethargy, and catalepsy; (5) the combined mechanism of the basal diencephalon and lower BSRF is identical with, or overlaps, the EEG activating mechanism, and this mechanism causes the objective features of emotional expressiveness to appear. Lindsley (1951) concludes that it is not legitimate on the basis of the existing experimental evidence to attempt to account for all the varieties of emotional expression, and further research is advised on the influences of learning, habituation, and memory on emotional expression. The *activation theory* is able to account for the extremes of emotional behavior but is not able to explain completely the intermediate and mixed states of emotional expressiveness. See also ACTIVATION/AROUSAL THEORY; EMOTIONS, THEORIES/LAWS OF; MOTIVATION, THEORIES OF; SLEEP, THEORIES OF.

REFERENCES

Moruzzi, G., & Magoun, H. W. (1949). Brain stem reticular formation and activation of the EEG. *Electroencephalography and Clinical Neurophysiology, 1,* 455-473.

Lindsley, D. B. (1951). Emotion. In S. S. Stevens (Ed.), *Handbook of experimental psychology*. New York: Wiley.

Lindsley, D. B. (1982). Neural mechanisms of arousal, attention, and information processing. In J. Orbach (Ed.), *Neuropsychology after Lashley*. Hillsdale, NJ: Erlbaum.

LINEAR ADDITIVE VALUE-MAXIMIZATION MODEL. See ELIMINATION BY ASPECTS THEORY.

LINEAR-OPERATOR LEARNING MODEL. See LEARNING THEORIES/LAWS.

LINEAR TIMING HYPOTHESIS. See SCALAR TIMING THEORY.

LINE-ELEMENT THEORY. See HECHT'S COLOR VISION THEORY; STILES' COLOR VISION THEORY; YOUNG-HELMHOLTZ COLOR VISION THEORY.

LINGUISTIC DETERMINISM. See WHORF-SAPIR HYPOTHESIS/THEORY.

LINGUISTIC RELATIVITY HYPOTHESIS. See WHORF-SAPIR HYPOTHESIS/THEORY.

LIPOSTATIC THEORY. See HUNGER, THEORIES OF.

LIPPS' EMPATHY THEORY. The German philosopher and psychologist Theodor Lipps (1851-1914) formulated an *empathy theory* of aesthetic enjoyment in which aesthetic feeling is based in four different types of projection of the observer onto the perceived objects (cf., *conscious illusion theory* - holds that art-experience is a process of illusion or esthetic play resulting in a pleasurable free and conscious oscillation between semblance and reality): (1) a *general apperceptive empathy*, which involves the animation of the forms of common objects (e.g., perceiving a line as movement); (2) *empirical empathy*, which refers to the humanizing of natural objects (e.g., the phrase "babbling brook" may be used to describe a stream); (3) *mood empathy*,

where one ascribes or incorporates feelings into colors or music (e.g., the painting was described as a "cheerful yellow," or the music had a "sad" and "melancholic" melody); and (4) *sensible appearance empathy*, where gestures and other bodily movements of persons may be interpreted as indicators of their inner lives. Lipps maintained through these four types of empathy that *beauty* is a function of both the beholder/observer as well as the object itself. See also EMPATHY-ALTRUISM HYPOTHESIS; ZEISING'S PRINCIPLE.

REFERENCES

Lipps, T. (1897). *Raumasthetik und geometrisch-optische tauschungen*. Leipzig: Barth.

Lipps, T. (1905). *Psychological studies*. Baltimore: Williams & Wilkins.

LIPPS' ILLUSION. See APPENDIX A.

LISTING'S LAW. See VISION/SIGHT, THEORIES OF.

LIVELINESS, LAW OF. See ASSOCIATION, LAWS/PRINCIPLES OF; FREQUENCY, LAW OF.

LLOYD MORGAN'S/MORGAN'S CANON. See PARSIMONY, LAW OF.

LOCALIZATION THEORY. See LASHLEY'S THEORY.

LOCALIZED MEMORY STORAGE/THEORY. See SHORT-TERM AND LONG-TERM MEMORY, THEORIES OF.

LOCAL SIGN THEORY. See LOTZE'S THEORY OF LOCAL SIGNS.

LOCAL STIMULUS THEORY. See HUNGER, THEORIES OF.

LOCAL THEORY OF THIRST. See THIRST, THEORIES OF.

LOCK-AND-KEY THEORY. See OLFACTION/SMELL, THEORIES OF.

366

LOCKE'S PSYCHOLOGICAL THEORY.
See EMPIRICAL/EMPIRICISM, DOC-
TRINE OF.

LOCUS OF CONTROL THEORY. See
ROTTER'S SOCIAL LEARNING THEORY.

LOEB'S TROPISTIC THEORY. The German-born zoologist/physiologist Jacques Loeb
(1859-1924) formulated a *theory of the tropism* as applied to animal behavior. The term
tropism refers to any unlearned movement or
orientation of an organic unit as a whole toward a source of stimulation [cf., *phototro-
pism*, which means "turning toward light;"
heliotropism is "movement toward the sun,"
geotropism is a simple orienting response,
either negative or positive, to the lines of force
of gravity, and *galvanotropism* is a simple
orienting response, either negative or positive,
to electrical stimulation; the *genotropism doctrine* - first proposed by the Hungarian genet-
ist/psychoanalyst Leopold Szondi (1893-
1977), states that latent recessive genes determine instinctive or spontaneous choices,
such as those in friendship, love, occupation,
illness, and manner of death, and underlie the
attraction between people who share the same
genes]. Modern convention reserves the term
tropism for plants and the term *taxis* for such
automatic movements when made by animate
organisms. The *tropism*, according to Loeb, is
a turning process - toward or away from specific objects in the environment - that is the
key to instinct and to life in general. The
tropistic theory states that an animal's response is a direct function of the stimulus, and
the behavior is "forced" (*forced movement
theory*) and does not require any explanation
in terms of consciousness. Loeb's *continuous
action theory of tropisms* holds that the orienting responses of animals depend on the continuous application of the stimulus and not on
mere changes in intensity (cf., *intensity theory
of tropisms*, which holds that the tropic orientation of an organism to a stimulus is due to
unequal intensity of stimulation of symmetrical points on the body; and the *direction theory of tropisms*, which asserts that the tropic
orientation is determined by the direction or
point in space from which the stimulus acts,
rather than by its duration and intensity; Loeb,

more than any other one person, formalized a
mature and complete *mechanistic theory* or
mechanistic psychology [i.e., the study of the
problems of mind are reduced to the form of
general problems; cf., the *vitalism theory* approach of the French philosopher Henri Bergson (1859-1941) which holds that a "vital
force" not subject to physical, mechanical, or
chemical laws is responsible for life] in the
closing years of the 19th century. As one of the
early animal psychologists, Loeb influenced
the thinking of John B. Watson, the founder of
behaviorism. Loeb's basic impact on psychology was as a forerunner of an objective, scientific, and naturalistic psychology. His work
emphasized experimental methods and de-
emphasized the role of consciousness in behavior. See also BEHAVIORIST THEORY;
LIFE, THEORIES OF; MECHANISTIC
THEORY.

REFERENCES

Loeb, J. (1890). *Der heliotropismus der tiere*.
Wurzburg: Hertz.

Loeb, J. (1907). Concerning the theory of
tropisms. *Journal of Experimental
Zoology, 4*, 151-156.

Loeb, J. (1908). *Forced movements, tropisms,
and animal conduct*. Philadelphia:
Lippincott.

Bergson, H. (1911). *Creative evolution*. New
York: Holt.

Loeb, J. (1912). *The mechanistic conception
of life: Biological essays*. Chicago:
University of Chicago Press.

Szondi, L. (1944). *Analysis of destiny*. Basel:
Schwabe.

**LOGAN'S HYBRID THEORY OF
LEARNING.** See LOGAN'S MICROMO-
LAR THEORY.

LOGAN'S MICROMOLAR THEORY.
The American psychologist Frank A Logan
(1924-   ) formulated *micromolar theory*,
which defines the quantitative aspects of various types of responses - such as speed, volume, and amplitude - where such aspects or
dimensions become part of what the person
actually learns (cf., *correspondence theory/
law* - borrowed from the works of the Danish
physicist Niels Bohr (1885-1962), this approach states that whatever is true of "molecu-

lar" behavior is true, also, of "molar" behavior, and that a unifying principle may be discovered ultimately). In the classical view of response parameters, as exemplified in C. L. Hull's *macromolar theory*, response classes are defined in terms of their achievements (e.g., running a maze, pressing a lever), and variations in the response (e.g., speed and amplitude) during training are taken to be indices of the strength of the "response tendency." Logan's *micromolar theory*, on the other hand, identifies a dimension (e.g., speed) as containing different responses that are learned selectively and influenced by differential reinforcement. *Logan's theory* is essentially a *utility* analysis where the *net utility* of a particular response, such as speed, is given by its *positive utility* minus its associated *negative utility*. The profile of *net utility* across a particular response (e.g., speed) continuum is used then to calculate the probability distribution of the various responses (e.g., speeds). In experiments within the context of the *Hull-Spence stimulus-response incentive theory*, Logan found that humans' performance speed (and "learning to learn") is dependent on practice speed. Logan also described the *hybrid theory of learning* that combines the features of various existing theories into a single system. Among the unique aspects of the *hybrid theory* is the hypothesization of two kinds of learning process: a cognitive-associative process for *classical conditioning* and a stimulus-response process for *operant conditioning*. The importance of Logan's *micromolar theory* has been primarily that of "conceptual housecleaning" within *learning theory* where several theoretical puzzles connected with the problem of how reinforcement shapes behavior have been unraveled and better understood. See also HULL'S LEARNING THEORY; LEARNING THEORIES/LAWS; PAVLOVIAN CONDITIONING/PRINCIPLES/LAWS/THEORIES; SKINNER'S DESCRIPTIVE BEHAVIOR/OPERANT CONDITIONING THEORY; SPENCE'S THEORY.

REFERENCES

Hull, C. L. (1943). *Principles of behavior*. New York: Appleton-Century-Crofts.

Logan, F. (1956). A micromolar approach to behavior theory. *Psychological Review, 63*, 63-73.

Logan, F. (1977). Hybrid theory of classical conditioning. In G. Bower (Ed.), *The psychology of learning and motivation*. Vol. 2. New York: Academic Press.

Logan, F. (1979). Hybrid theory of operant conditioning. *Psychological Review, 86*, 507-541.

LOGICAL EMPIRICISM DOCTRINE. See COMTE'S LAW/THEORY.

LOGOGEN THEORY. See SHORT-TERM AND LONG-TERM MEMORY, THEORIES OF.

LOGOTHERAPY THEORY. See MEANING, THEORIES/ASSESSMENT OF.

LOMBROSIAN THEORY. Attempts to determine, or predict, who will be a criminal, are not new. Various anthropological and psychological theories based on mental ability have provided explanations for criminal behavior [cf., the American sociologist Robert K. Merton's (1910-2003) *anomie theory of crime* - the conjecture that people with culturally-approved goals of success, who cannot achieve them in a normal way, develop innovative and usually criminal ways of achieving them; the *bonding theory of criminality* - the notion that career criminals who have separated themselves from conventional society no longer accept its legitimacy and, thus, establish their own independent norms; and the *victim precipitation hypothesis* - postulates that a victim of a crime, especially in cases of incest or rape, is responsible partially for it, and is called "victim-blaming"]. The Italian anthropologist/criminologist Cesare Lombroso (1836-1909) - who wrote on the connection between genius and insanity - proposed a *theory of criminality* in the late 19th century (cf., Lombroso's *atavistic theory* - the outdated conjecture that some people are more like their distant ancestors than they are to their parents). According to Lombroso's *type theory*, criminals are throwbacks to prehuman evolution; he considered the *physical charac-*

teristics of criminals to resemble the characteristics of prehistoric humans. For example, Lombroso argued that people with a receding chin, flattened nose, and low, flat forehead or other features of earlier forms of human life are more likely to be criminals. Lombroso showed that there is a relatively high incidence of these features among persons in jail. According to this approach, criminals are deformed physically and may, therefore, be identified easily. A variation on *Lombroso's theory* in 1888 is called the *degeneracy theory of genius* and refers to the overdevelopment of certain capacities or traits that are accompanied by various defects, indicating an instability of organization pointing toward degeneration. In this version, Lombroso suggested the innate disposition to criminal behavior as being associated with degeneration of hereditary cells, and he maintained that most criminals have physical signs ("stigmata of degeneration") indicating the innate, constitutional disposition to crime. Surprisingly, for a while, the *Lombrosian theory* was widely accepted, in spite of the fact that there was an equally high incidence of "criminal features" among non-criminal populations as there was among criminal populations. Eventually, however, *Lombroso's theory* was abandoned (cf., *cold effects* - the effects of cold temperatures on physical and mental health; studies of cold effects on social behavior produce both increased and decreased aggression; however, *criminal* activity generally appears to decline in cold weather; and *conflict/communist theory of criminality* - holds that the rich and powerful make laws to maintain the status quo and to repress the poor and powerless). See also ANOMIE THEORY; KRETSCHMER'S THEORY OF PERSONALITY; SHELDON'S TYPE THEORY; TYPE THEORIES OF PERSONALITY.

REFERENCES

Lombroso, C. (1876/1911). *Criminal man.* New York: Putnam.
Dugdale, R. (1877). The Jukes: *A study in crime, pauperism, disease, and heredity.* New York: Putnam.
Goddard, H. (1910). *The criminal imbecile.* New York: Macmillan.
Hawkins, J. D. (1996). *Delinquency and crime: Current theories.* New York: Cambridge University Press.
Knepper, P. (2001). *Explaining criminal conduct: Theories and systems in criminology.* Durham, NC: Carolina Academic Press.

LONG-TERM MEMORY, THEORY OF. See SHORT-TERM AND LONG-TERM MEMORY, THEORIES OF.

LONG-TERM POTENTIATION THEORY. See FORGETTING/MEMORY, THEORIES OF.

LORENZ'S HYDRAULIC MODEL OF AGGRESSION. See HYDRAULIC THEORY.

LOSS OF ACCESS THEORY. See FORGETTING/MEMORY, THEORIES OF.

LOST-LETTER TECHNIQUE/EFFECT. This technique was introduced by the American social psychologist Stanley Milgram (1933-1984) and his colleagues as an "unobtrusive measure" [i.e., an indirect method for collecting data without the conscious awareness or cooperation of the research participants, and includes a number of techniques popularized by the American psychologist Eugene J. Webb (1933-) and several co-authors in the 1960s, even though the original notion of the technique is traceable to the work of the English natural scientist Sir Francis Galton (1822-1911) in the 1870s] of attitudes whereby stamped, addressed envelopes (cf., postcards) are scattered in various public places (as if left by accident). The proportion of the envelopes that are posted/returned to the envelope addresses by individuals of the public are taken as providing a rough index of attitudes in the community. For instance, if half of the envelopes are addressed to a "pro-stem cell research" organization and half to an "anti-stem cell research" organization, and if equal numbers of each type of envelope are distributed, but more of the "pro-stem cell research" envelopes are returned, then it may be concluded, tentatively, that members of the community are more favorably disposed towards the "pro-stem cell research" than the "anti-stem cell research" cause. This *returned envelope effect*, although only an indirect measure of public attitudes, possesses the salient feature or criterion of generality in that the technique may be employed in a number of different physical locations (cf., the similar "lost email technique"), and has been used for assessing a wide range of different social, psychological, and economic issues (e.g., gay/lesbian marriage; battered/abused women; abortion; small-town versus large-city living; religious beliefs; impeachment/election of presidents; violence/aggression in public settings; evolution theory versus creationism; oil-drilling and environmental issues; alcohol issues; altruism; personality deviance; prejudices; interracial marriage; sex education in the schools; and international attitudes towards America). See also ATTITUDE/ATTITUDE CHANGE, THEORIES OF.

REFERENCES
Milgram, S., Mann, L., & Harter, S. (1965). The lost-letter technique. *Public Opinion Quarterly, 29*, 437-438.

Webb, E. J., Campbell, D. T., Schwartz, R. C., & Sechrest, L. (1966). *Unobtrusive measures: Nonreactive research in the social sciences*. Chicago: Rand-McNally.

Milgram, S. (1977). *The individual in a social world*. Reading, MA: Addison-Wesley.

Stern, S. E., & Faber, J. E. (1997). The lost e-mail method: Milgram's lost-letter technique in the age of the internet. *Behavior Research Methods, Instruments, and Computers, 29*, 260-263.

LOTKA/LOTKA-PRICE LAW. This law was developed originally by Alfred J. Lotka (1880-1949), who was a demographer for the New York Metropolitan Life Insurance Company in the 1920s. *Lotka's law* states that the number of scientists publishing n papers is roughly proportional to n-squared where the constant of proportionality varies with the discipline. This law is somewhat similar to the Italian sociologist/economist Vilfredo Pareto's (1848-1923) *law of income distribution* in economics. The English-born American "father of scientometrics/bibliometrics" Derek de

Solla Price (1922-1983) subsequently refined *Lotka's law*, which now states that half of all scientific publications are made by the square root of the total number of scientific contributors. The *Lotka-Price law of historiometry* indicates the inequality of scientific productivity, and is depicted as highly skewed, hyperbolic-shaped distributions of creative output. See also EMINENCE, THEORIES/ MEASURES OF; EPONYMY THEORY; PERSONALISTIC THEORY OF HISTORY; STIGLER'S LAW OF EPONYMY.

REFERENCES
Lotka, A. (1926). The frequency distribution of scientific productivity. *Journal of the Washington Academy of Sciences, 16*, 317-323.

Price, D. (1963/1986). *Little science, big science...and beyond*. New York: Columbia University Press.

Price, D. (1976). A general theory of bibliometric and other cumulative advantage processes. *Journal of the American Society of Information Sciences, 27*, 292-306.

Furnham, A., & Bonnett, C. (1992). British research productivity in psychology 1980-1989. Does the Lotka-Price law apply to university departments as it does to individuals? *Personality and Individual Differences, 13*, 1333-1341.

LOTZE'S THEORY OF LOCAL SIGNS. The German physiologist and psychologist Rudolph Hermann Lotze (1817-1881) developed a *theory/doctrine of local signs*, or *locality sign theory*, that was typical of 19th century thought in which philosophical concepts, rather than empirical concepts, dominated the area of the physiology of sense organs. However, Lotze sought to unify physiological and psychological material in a coherent system in which both empirical findings and philosophical interpretations may be reconciled. Lotze argued that psychology must deal with the organism where the nervous system and the mind should be seen in relation to each other. On the other hand, Lotze maintained that it is foolish to suppose that the mere existence of physical and chemical processes is an "explanation" of mind. He argued that exact science can give no clue as to the ultimate nature of mental processes where, in particular, the meanings of life, the reality of pleasures and pain, and the reality of one's ideals and dreams are not affected by the discovery of mechanical laws. A *local sign* is defined as an inherent qualitative factor by means of which one visual or tactual sensation can be distinguished from others with respect to position in space. *Locality sign*, another term for *local sign*, is similarly defined as a specific character assumed to be inherent in the sensory experience aroused by a single receptor or by a single afferent neuron (and to differ for each receptor or for each afferent neuron). *Locality sign* or *local sign* is so call-ed because it furnishes a cue to the position of the receptor-unit stimulated and, hence, to the location of the stimulus. The concept of *local signs* is applicable to most *nativistic* (i.e., inherent knowledge; cf., Helmholtz, 1856) *theories of space* (e.g., Hering, 1878) and *genetic theories* (e.g., Wundt, 1862). According to *Lotze's theory*, every tactual and visual sensation has its own specific *local sign* or "signature," which is an experiential intensity that is particular for the point stimulated - either on the retina for visual stimulation or on the skin for tactile stimulation. In the case of *space perception*, Lotze theorized that it is produced by the relationship between the *local signs* as the stimulation shifts across the receptor system. Lotze's *theory of local signs* was an attempt to find a compromise between the various views on *space perception*: the *theory of perceptual innateness* of I. Kant (1724-1804), the *experiential theory* of J. Herbart (1776-1841), and the theory of J. Muller (1801-1858), who taught that *space perception* is *innate*, but the elaboration of the world of space must be *learned*. Lotze's view, both in visual and cutaneous space, is that psychological space is built up from sensations that in isolation would not be spatial but whose order of stimulation corresponds to transition of the stimulus from one point in physical space to another. Lotze's *theory of local signs* not only was highly important as an application of physiological findings and *associationist theory* to a complex problem but was one of the boldest, most fruitful attempts to make muscular sensations play their part in mental life. Later,

however, organismic and Gestalt approaches to psychology challenged Lotze's analytic, atomistic, and associationist conceptions such as those embedded in his *local sign theory*. See also BERKELEY'S THEORY OF SPACE PERCEPTION; EMPIRICIST VERSUS NATIVIST THEORIES; GESTALT THEORY/LAWS.

REFERENCES

Lotze, R. H. (1852). *Medicinische psychologie oder, physiologie der seele*. Leipzig: Weidmann.

Helmholtz, H. von. (1856). *Handbuch der physiologischen optik*. Leipzig: Voss.

Wundt, W. (1862). *Beitrage zur theorie der sinneswahrnehmung*. Leipzig: Wunter'sck Verlaghandlung.

Lotze, R. H. (1864). *Microcosmus: An essay concerning man and his relation to the world*. Edinburgh: Clark.

Hering, E. (1878). *Zur lehre vom lichtsinn*. Vienna: Gerolds.

Lotze, R. H. (1879). *Metaphysic, in three books: Ontology, cosmology, and psychology*. Oxford, UK: Clarendon Press.

LOVE, THEORIES OF. In general, two contemporary notions of *love* that may, or may not, carry sexual connotations are: internal feelings of strong liking/affection for some specific thing or person, and enduring sentiments toward a person providing a desire to be with that person and a concern for the happiness, welfare, and satisfactions of that person. An earlier conception of *love*, however, seemed strongly to imply a sexual component: a feeling or sentiment of attachment toward some person, often growing out of sexual attraction, relations, or situations, and exhibiting a great diversity of psychological and physiological manifestations; cf., the *Coolidge effect* - named after the 30th American president John Calvin Coolidge (1872-1933) and based, perhaps fictitiously, on a semi-salacious joking interchange (concerning the mating/sexual behavior of roosters) between Coolidge and his wife - refers to the high continuous sexual performance shown by males of many species for extended periods of time with the introduction of new, receptive females). Many dictionaries of psychological terms, interestingly, do not even attempt to give a definition of *love*. Other approaches toward defining *love* are provided in *psychoanalytic theory* where it is used variously as any affective state defined as the opposite of "hatred," as an emotion liable to sublimation or inhibition, and an equivalent to Eros and an "instinctive force" close either to the "life instincts" or to the "sexual instincts," depending on early or late *Freudian* formulation. Only recently have social scientists systematically gathered information about *love*. Using *love* in a scientific context leads to several types of conflicts or questions: Can love exist independent of sex/sexual expression? Is love innate, or is it an acquired emotional response? Can the feeling of love be dissociated from the behavior, or does the emotion always contaminate the behavior? The American social psychologist Zick Rubin (1944-) distinguishes between the conditions/states of *liking* and *loving*. According to Rubin, *romantic love* generally includes such aspects as responsibility for the other person, tenderness, and self-disclosure. On the other hand, *liking* refers to an attraction for the other person that includes respect and the perception that the other person is similar to oneself. Rubin developed a *liking scale* and a *loving scale* to distinguish between the theoretical aspects of interpersonal attraction. Specifically, Rubin's *love scale* is constructed to evaluate three components: affiliative/dependent needs, predispositions to help, and exclusiveness. His *liking scale* is based on two primary components: a feeling that the liked person is similar to oneself, and an overall favorable evaluation of the liked person. Another theoretical approach toward *love* is provided by E. Hatfield and G. Walster who distinguish between *passionate love* - a profound physiological arousal and an intensely emotional state with a confusion of feelings, tenderness and sexuality, elation and pain, anxiety and relief, and altruism and jealousy; and *companionate love* - a combination of friendly affection and deep attachment. In yet another approach, called the *Lee-Hendrick model*, a distinction is made among six types/styles of *love*: *eros* - romantic and sexual love; *mania* - obsessive and demanding love; *ludis* - self-centered and playful

love; *storge* - companionship and close-friends love; *agape* - saintly and "thou-centered" love; and *pragma* - logical and practical love. The *theory of complementary needs* argues that people fall in love with those individuals who complement their own personalities and needs. However, researchers do not agree completely with such an argument and suggest, instead, that people tend to select mates who possess similar (rather than complementary) personalities and needs (cf., the *Kerckhoff_Davis hypothesis* - discusses the relationship between the "filtering factors" of similarity and complementarity concerning mate selection). The *attitude similarity hypothesis*, also called the *similarity-attraction hypothesis*, states that people are attracted to other persons who share their attitudes and values in significant life areas and issues (cf., the *assumed similarity bias effect* - refers to a tendency for people to assume that they are similar to most other people). In another *theory of love* (Stoller, 1978), it is asserted that hostility (i.e., the overt or hidden desire to harm another person) generates and enhances sexual excitement and passionate love. According to this approach, the absence of hostility leads to sexual indifference and boredom. In D. Tennov's theoretical approach, it is argued that *both* pleasure and pain are associated with love, and love may be stimulated by either condition. According to *Sternberg's triangular theory of love*, love may be conceived of as a three-dimensional triangular model where the three points of the figure are *intimacy* (the closeness two people feel toward one another, including reciprocal sharing and valuation), *commitment* (the decision to remain in the relationship), and *passion* (feelings of romance and physical/sexual attraction). In the American psychologist Robert Sternberg's (1949-) approach, relationships can involve different combinations of the models' three components where seven distinct love relationships (plus one of "nonlove") may be formed: liking, infatuated love, romantic love, empty love, companionate love, fatuous love, and consummate love. Generalizations from research on *love* indicate that there are subtle gender differences in how women and men experience love: men tend to be more "romantic" than women; men seem to fall *in* love *faster* and to fall *out of* love *slower* than women; women are more likely to experience the "agony" and the "ecstasy" of love than men; and women are more likely than men to disclose their feelings, both positive and negative, in casual relationships. Individuals in love exhibit, invariably, several behavioral cues such as paying attention to physical appearance and "preening," gazing deeply into each other's eyes, and touching and standing close to each other. The areas of *love* and *intimacy* are relatively unexplored scientifically, and psychologists have just begun to investigate the conditions, feelings, emotions, and behaviors that occur when one person loves another. See also CUPBOARD THEORY; FREUD'S THEORY OF PERSONALITY; INFANT ATTACHMENT THEORIES; INSTINCT THEORY; INTERPERSONAL ATTRACTION THEORIES.

REFERENCES

Ellis, H. (1897/1936). *Studies in the psychology of sex.* 4 vols. New York: Random House.

Winch, R. (1958). *Mate selection: A study of complementary needs.* New York: Harper & Row.

Kerckhoff, A. C., & Davis, K. E. (1962). Value consensus and need complementarity in mate selection. *American Sociological Review, 27,* 295-303.

Levinger, G., Senn, D., & Jorgensen, B. (1970). Progress toward permanence in courtship: A test of the Kerckhoff-Davis hypothesis. *Sociometry, 33,* 427-443.

Rubin, Z. (1970). Measurement of romantic love. *Journal of Personality and Social Psychology, 16,* 265-273.

Rubin, Z. (1973). *Liking and loving.* New York: Holt, Rinehart, and Winston.

Lee, J. (1977). *The colors of love.* New York: Bantam.

Stoller, R. (1978). *Sexual excitement.* New York: Pantheon.

Tennov, D. (1979). *Love and limerence.* New York: Stein & Day.

Pope, K. (1980). *On love and loving.* San Francisco: Jossey-Bass.

Hatfield, E., & Walster, G. (1981). *A new look at love.* Reading, MA: Addison-Wesley.

Hendrick, C., & Hendrick, S. (1986). A theory and method of love. *Journal of Personality and Social Psychology, 50,* 392-402.

Sternberg, R. J. (1986). A triangular theory of love. *Psychological Review, 93,* 119-135.

Sternberg, R. J., & Barnes, M. L. (Eds.) (1988). *The psychology of love.* New Haven, CT: Yale University Press.

Sternberg, R. J. (1988). *The triangle of love: Intimacy, passion, commitment.* New York: Basic Books.

LOWBALL TECHNIQUE. See COMPLIANCE EFFECTS/TECHNIQUES.

LUDOVICI'S THEORY OF LAUGHTER. The outspoken English-born writer, Nietzschean philosopher, and intellectual Anthony Mario Ludovici (1882-1971) - who once described himself as taking "a fearless approach to the truth" - provides a "new theory of laughter" in which the roots of laughter are seen to lie in the triumph one attains over other people or circumstances. Such an ideational/theoretical basis for humor/laughter is included in a genre called *superiority theories of humor.* Ludovici maintains that laughter may be traced back to the snarls of triumph or mocking behavior that early humans made over a defeated adversary, and describes why assertion of superiority takes this particular form in behavior. Ludovici asserts that in the specific act of the "baring of the teeth" - where this behavior evolutionarily carried the function and nonverbal message in primitive humans and animals of warding off an enemy or establishing dominance - an interpretation may be made in modern humans that involves the notion of "superior adaptation." Based on such an evolutionary pattern involving aggression and attack, *Ludovici"s theory of laughter* refers to the audible aspect of laughter as "spiritualized snarlings" where human beings, also, show their teeth (as in the act of laughing) in all those situations in which they feel themselves to be "superiorly adapted." Thus, according to *Ludovici's theory*, the essence of laughter is the baring of the teeth, and he repeatedly uses the phrase "show teeth" as a synonym for "laugh" in his theory. However, a criticism of *Ludovici's theory* and its attendant "superior adaptation" notion may be found in the observations by ethologists that animals, at least, show their fangs most often when they are brought into a corner by a power, object, or animal that they fear is superior to themselves. Ludovici - who had no graduate degrees or university professorships - was virtually alone among Western thinkers; he wrote on the following diverse issues: the sickness afflicting modern art; arguments why men should not have given women the right to vote; arguments why democracy culminates in anarchy; discussion of evolutionary ethics that mankind needs for survival in a hostile universe; marriage should take place only among members of the same race ("like should marry like" - in personality, physiognomy, and racial type); interpretations of Nietzsche's writings; the Jewish role in Western societies; and the proper relationship between church and state. See also HUMOR, THEORIES OF; IZARD'S THEORY OF EMOTIONS; SUPERIORITY THEORIES OF HUMOR.

REFERENCE

Ludovici, A. M. (1932). *The secret of laughter*. London: Constable & Co.

LULLABY EFFECT. See PAVLOVIAN CONDITIONING/PRINCIPLES/LAWS/THEORIES.

LUNEBURG'S THEORY. See PERCEPTION (I. GENERAL), THEORIES OF.

LURIA'S LAWS OF CORTICAL FUNCTIONING. The Russian neuropsychologist Aleksandr Romanovich Luria (1902-1977) developed innovative methods for restoring brain functioning in damaged brain structures, based on his view of the brain as a complex functional system rather than a single entity. Luria's position may be summarized in his three basic *laws of higher cortical functioning*: there exists a *hierarchical structure* of cortical zones; there is *diminishing specificity* in cortical functioning; and there is *progressive lateralization* in cortical processes. Overall, Luria

contributed substantially to the development and refinement of clinical tests for brain damage that correlate well with surgical and pathological studies. The strengths in Luria's approach include the following: it is based on an *explicit* theoretical formulation of cerebral organization (however, some parts of his model have been contradicted by empirical evidence); it emphasizes the *qualitative* aspects of performance (i.e., *how* something is performed, not just an absolute level of performance); and it is *flexible* in its diagnosis of mental deficits. On the negative side, there have been no rigorous or extensive assessments of Luria's procedures so that a healthy skepticism remains of the psychometric properties of his "clinical-analytical" approach. See also FORGETTING/MEMORY, THEORIES OF; LANGUAGE ACQUISITION THEORY; SPEECH THEORIES.

REFERENCES

Luria, A. R. (1958). Brain disorder and language analysis. *Language and Speech, 1*, 14-34.

Luria, A. R. (1963). *Restoration of function after brain injury*. New York: Macmillan.

Luria, A. R. (1966). *Higher cortical function in man*. New York: Basic Books.

Luria, A. R. (1968). *The mind of a mnemonist*. New York: Basic Books.

Luria, A. R. (1970). The functional organization of the brain. *Scientific American, 222*, 66-78.

Luria, A. R. (1973). *The working brain*. New York: Penguin.

LYSENKO'S THEORY/LYSENKOISM. See LAMARCK'S THEORY.

M

MACH BANDS. See APPENDIX A, CRAIK-O'BRIEN EFFECT.

MACH-BREUER-BROWN THEORY OF LABYRINTHINE FUNCTIONING. See WITKIN'S PERCEPTION THEORY.

MACH-DVORAK PHENOMENON. See PERCEPTION (I. GENERAL), THEORIES OF.

MACHIAVELLIAN HYPOTHESIS. See MACHIAVELLIAN THEORY.

MACHIAVELLIAN THEORY. This approach involves an alleged/hypothetical *personality trait* (typically assessed via scores on the "Mach Scale/Questionnaire" or the "Machiavellianism Scale") reflecting one's use of a social conduct strategy whereby other people are manipulated - via deception, opportunism, and deviousness - in order to gain a personal advantage for oneself, often resulting in the detriment of the exploited person(s). The notion of *Machiavellianism* is named after the Florentine political philosopher and statesman Niccolo Machiavelli (1469-1527) who advanced the strategy of power and control through manipulative political behavior, and was popularized by the American psychologists Richard Christie (1918-1992) and Florence L. Geis (1933-) in the late 1960s, especially through their "Mach Scale" in which the respondent if asked to agree or disagree with a series of statements (e.g., "the best way to handle people is to tell them what they want to hear"), many of which are actual, direct quotes from Machiavelli's own writings. The "Mach Scale" has been used in conjunction with the study of a wide range of psychological, social, political, and economic behaviors/issues such as: just-world beliefs; celebrity worship; bully/victim problems of school children; car salesperson's tactics; Alzheimer's disorder; adolescent aggression; theory of mind; schizophrenia; business ad-

ministration education; social functioning of children; leadership performance; stockbrokers' behaviors; sexual aggression; bargaining-game behavior; team performance; personal honesty; and interpersonal communication processes (cf., the *Machiavellian hypothesis*, or the *cognitive arms race hypothesis* - posits that the major selective mechanism in the evolution of intelligence has been social competitiveness). See also EMPATHY- ALTRUISM HYPOTHESIS; EMPATHY THEORY; JUST-WORLD HYPOTHESIS; MIND/MENTAL STATES, THEORIES OF; PERSONALITY THEORIES; SCHIZOPHRENIA, THEORIES OF.

REFERENCES

Machiavelli, N. (1532/1992). *Il principe (The prince)*. Transl. N. H. Thompson. New York: Dover.

Christie, R., & Geis, F. L. (Eds.) (1970). *Studies in Machiavellianism*. New York: Academic Press.

McIlwain, D. (2003). Bypassing empathy: A Machiavellian theory of mind and sneaky power. In B. Repacholi & V. Slaughter (Eds.), *Individual differences in theory of mind*. New York: Psychology Press.

MACHINE THEORY. See PERCEPTION (II. COMPARATIVE APPRAISAL), THEORIES OF.

MACH'S THEORY OF BODILY ROTATION. See WITKIN'S PERCEPTION THEORY.

MacLEAN-PAPEZ THEORIES. See EMOTIONS, THEORIES/LAWS OF.

MACROMOLAR THEORY. See LOGAN'S MICROMOLAR THEORY.

MAIER'S LAW. This is a cynical "law" stated by the American psychologist Norman R. F. Maier (1900-1977) suggesting that "if the data do not fit the theory, the data must be disposed of." Apparently, in this proposition, Maier is chiding his colleagues for excessive concern with their own particular theoretical models. See also REBER'S LAW; ROECKELEIN'S LAW.

REFERENCE
Maier, N. R. F. (1960). Maier's law. *American Psychologist, 15*, 208-212.

MAIER'S THEORY OF HUMOR. The American psychologist Norman Raymond Frederick Maier (1900-1977) proposed a *Gestalt theory of humor* whereby the sudden change in interpretation that occurs when a joke is understood implies that the meaning of particular elements changes because the meaning of an element depends on the nature of the "configuration" in which it operates. According to *Maier's theory of humor*, humor implies objectivity in that the attitude with which one approaches the content of a joke is one in which emotions and sympathies are "unengaged." The two aspects of jokes/humor (objectivity and sudden change in configuration) are characteristic equally of productive thinking, so the essence of the ridiculous, according to Maier, must be found elsewhere. For instance, it may be found in the isolation of a humorous situation in which humorous configurations are not to be taken seriously and not to be judged by tests used in non-humorous situations. Thus, the appreciation of a joke may be viewed as analogous to the sudden perceptual or cognitive *shifts* that occur with the relevant figure-ground relationships or configurations in the stimulus materials. See also FIGURE-GROUND RELATIONSHIPS, PRINCIPLE OF; GESTALT THEORY/LAWS; HUMOR, THEORIES OF; MORREALL'S THEORY OF HUMOR/ LAUGHTER.

REFERENCE
Maier, N. R. F. (1932). A Gestalt theory of humour. *British Journal of Psychology, 23*, 69-74.

MAJOR EVENTS EFFECT. See SUICIDE, THEORIES OF.

MALEBRANCHE'S THEORIES. In his most important work, *The Search After Truth* (*De la recherché de la verite*) published in 1674-75, the French philosopher/priest Nicolas de Malebranche (1638-1715) investigates various sources of human error and provides a basis for the perception of truth about oneself, about the world, and about God. Male-branche's three most famous conceptualizations are his doctrines of: *occasionalism* (i.e., all finite created entities are absolutely devoid of causal efficacy where God is the only true causal agent); *vision in God* (i.e., persons are as cognitively dependent on the divine understanding as bodies in motion are dependent ontologically on the divine will); and *theodicy* (i.e., explanation of how God's wisdom, power, and goodness are to be reconciled with the evils and imperfections in the world). Malebranche's *theodicy* suggests that God always acts in the simplest way possible - a notion that anticipated the *psychological law of parsimony* - and acts only by means of law like general volitions. Among Malebranche's detractors and critics was the Cartesian philosopher Antoine Arnauld (1612-1694) who was part of the great Malebranche-Arnauld debate that was one of the great intellectual events of the 17th century and attracted the attention of other great thinkers such as Leibnitz, Spinoza, Locke, and Newton. Malebranche's pre-scientific conceptions were in theoretical agreement with the French philosopher/mathematician Rene Descartes (1569-1650) concerning separation of the mind and body, but were in disagreement with Descartes as to how the two entities interact. In Malebranche's approach, unlike Descartes' *theory of mind-body interaction*, God mediated mind and body interactions. For example, a person's wish to do something becomes an occasion (*occasionalism doctrine*) for God to cause the individual's body to act. Thus, Malebranche's view of the mind-body relationship may be called a "mind-body parallelism" (such as two separate clocks keeping time together with no influence of one on the other) with divine intervention. *Malebranche's theory of psychology* asserts that mind is something distinct from the body and is made up of certain objective elements that, although in constant flux, are definitely observable. The mind, according to Malebranche, is composed of "psychic objects." The physical world of the body, on the other hand, is made up of "physical objects" consisting of a different stuff or sort of material from the "psychic objects." Other minor conceptualizations in Malebranche's psychology involve the non-observability of relations; the notions of ideas, sensations, and images; and a characteristic view of the *method of introspection* (i.e., observing consciousness by looking into one's own subjective experience and reporting on it) that anticipated W. Wundt's later influential employment of the method in the development of experimental/ scientific psychology. The American psychologist Knight Dunlap (1875-1949) observed that Malebranche postulated a mental object for each physical object but failed to provide a mental relation to correspond to a physical relation. Dunlap indicated, also, Malebranche's importance for psychology (especially among the psychoanalysts) in the former's reference to a general school of *psychological theory* that he called "Malebrachian" or "introspectional," and in which the notion of an "unconscious mind" was advanced. See also FREUD'S THEORY OF PERSONALITY; MIND-BODY THEORIES; MIND/MENTAL STATES, THEORIES OF; OCCASIONALISM, THEORY OF; PARSIMONY, LAW/PRINCIPLE OF.

REFERENCES

Dunlap, K. (1926). The theoretical aspect of psychology. In C. Murchison (Ed.), *Psychologies of 1925: Powell lectures on psychological theory*. Worcester, MA: Clark University Press.

Robinet, A. (Ed.) (1958-1967). *Oeuvres completes de Malebranche*. 20 vols. Paris: J. Vrin.

Lennon, T., & Olscamp, P. (1980). *Nicolas Malebranche: The search after truth; elucidations of the search after truth*. Columbus, OH: Ohio State University Press.

MALEVOLENT PERSONALITY THEORY. See PSYCHOPATHOLOGY, THEORIES OF.

MALTHUS' THEORY. = Malthusian theory = Malthusianism. This pessimistic speculation by the English political economist, demographer, and clergyman Thomas Robert Malthus (1766-1834) states that in any species the population tends to increase geometrically whereas the supply of food increases only arithmetically. Thus, in order to keep a balance or check on the system of population size, some disastrous events must occur such as war, pestilence, plagues, disease, and/or famine. Modern deliberate attempts to control over-population (called *neo-Malthusianism*) include limitations in family size and voluntary birth control measures. The worst-case scenario, according to *Malthusian theory*, is that humanity is destined to live in poverty and hunger. The controversial theory is dismissed largely by many researchers who cite its failure to take into account technological advances in agriculture and food production methods. However, some modern biologists and population experts still argue cautiously concerning the eventuality of Malthus' dire speculations (cf., Ehrlich, 1968; Ehrlich & Ehrlich, 1990). See also MENDEL'S LAWS/ PRINCIPLES; SYSTEMS THEORY.

REFERENCES

Malthus, T. R. (1798/1803/1890). *Essay on the principle of population*. London: J. Johnson/Ward, Lock, & Co.

Ehrlich, P. R. (1968). *The population bomb*. New York: Ballantine Books.

Ehrlich, P. R., & Ehrlich, A. H. (1990). *The population explosion*. New York: Simon & Schuster.

Brown, L. R., Gardner, G., & Halweil, B. (1998). *Beyond Malthus: Nineteen dimensions of the population challenge*. Washington, D.C.: Worldwatch Institute.

MANDLER'S THEORY OF EMOTION. See SCHACHTER-SINGER'S THEORY OF EMOTIONS.

MARBE'S LAW. See ASSOCIATION, LAWS/PRINCIPLES OF.

MARBE-THUMB LAW. See ASSOCIATION, LAWS/PRINCIPLES OF.

MARGARET THATCHER ILLUSION. See APPENDIX A.

MARKEDNESS HYPOTHESIS. See CHOMSKY'S PSYCHOLINGUISTIC THEORY.

MARK II CELL ASSEMBLY THEORY.
See PERCEPTION (II. COMPARATIVE
APPRAISAL), THEORIES OF.

MARR'S COMPUTATIONAL THEORY.
See VISION/SIGHT, THEORIES OF.

**MARTINEAU'S SOCIAL-COMMUNICA-
TION MODEL OF HUMOR.** The American
sociologist W. H. Martineau (1967, 1972)
provides a review of the literature on the sociology of humor and presents a *social-
communication model of humor* that involves
the social functions of humor both in in-
tragroup and intergroup situations. Martineau's model contains a number of theorems
that are relevant to the sociological literature,
and its basic premise is that humor is a social
mechanism with definite social functions. The
model considers humor as a distinctive type of
persuasive social process and medium of
communication by which acting units in the
social system convey information during the
ongoing process of interaction. Martineau's
model attempts to combine some of the salient
variables involved in the social-
communication process (e.g., the actor, the
audience/recipient, the butt of the humor, the
judgment of the humor, the cultural context,
and the social position of the involved individuals). Rather than emphasizing the functions of humor directly, Martineau's approach
reverses the procedure: the model identifies
some conditions under which the functions of
humor may be specified further (e.g., humor
may be analyzed in an intergroup situation
with a focus on the internal *structure* of one
group). Essentially, Martineau's *model of
humor* derives from several structural situations, each of which is described in terms of
other identified variables which, when combined in sets, are used to delineate theorems
representing the social functions. Thus, according to this approach, humor as a basic
condition of communication assumes many
forms and its social functions achieve complexity under the influence of other social
processes and existing social structures. Martineau's model systematically deals with several social processes in an effort to generate
researchable hypotheses as well as to develop
an overall framework for additional theoretical formulations of humor function. See also
DUPREEL'S SOCIOLOGICAL HU-
MOR/LAUGHTER THEORY; HUMOR,
THEORIES OF; SOCIAL/COM-
MUNICATION THEORY OF LAUGHTER.
REFERENCES
Martineau, W. H. (1967). A model for a theory of the function of humor. *Research Reports in the Social Sciences, 1,* 51-64.
Martineau, W. H. (1972). A model of the social functions of humor. In J. H.
Goldstein & P. E. McGhee (Eds.),
*The psychology of humor: Theoret-
ical perspectives and empirical is-
sues.* New York: Academic Press.

MARXIST PSYCHOLOGICAL THEORY.
See FROMM'S THEORY OF PERSONAL-
ITY.

**MASLOW'S THEORY OF PERSONAL-
ITY.** The American psychologist Abraham
Harold Maslow (1908-1970) advanced a holistic, organismic, dynamic, and humanistic
viewpoint of personality that has features
similar to the theories of Kurt Goldstein and
Andras Angyal. However, where Goldstein's
and Angyal's theories are derived from the
study of mentally unhealthy and brain-damaged individuals, *Maslow's theory of personality* derives from the study of creative,
healthy, and "self-actualized" persons. Consequently, Maslow's approach toward personality tends to be optimistic, health-oriented, and
growth/potential-oriented. Maslow distinguishes between the terms *basic needs* and
meta-needs where needs are organized in a
hierarchy (*need-hierarchy theory*) or pyramid
with the *basic needs* (such as food, air, water,
sex, affection, and security) at the bottom and
requiring satisfaction before moving up the
pyramid to the *metaneeds* at the top. The list
of *metaneeds* includes: *wholeness* and *perfection* - the need for unity and completeness;
justice - the need for fairness; *aliveness* and
richness - the needs for spontaneity and complexity; *beauty* - the need for rightness and
form; *goodness* - the need for benevolence;
uniqueness - the need for individuality; *truth* -
the need for reality; and *self-sufficiency* - the
need for autonomy. According to Maslow's

model, persons cannot be concerned with a lofty principle such as *justice* unless their "lower" need for food is met first. However, *metaneeds* are as important as *basic needs* in order to achieve a desirable state of *self-actualization*. When *metaneeds* are not fulfilled, the individual typically becomes cynical, alienated, and apathetic toward the world. Maslow identified certain *peak experiences* of living (such as maternal child-birth) that are characterized by profound feelings of spontaneity and harmony with the universe. Maslow cites various historical figures as illustrations of *self-actualized persons*: Beethoven, Einstein, Lincoln, Jefferson, Thoreau, Eleanor Roosevelt, and Walt Whitman. According to Maslow, such individuals possessed the requisite personality characteristics of *self-actualization*: realistic orientation of themselves within the world, complete acceptance of themselves and others, problem-oriented rather than self-oriented, highly private and detached, high levels of spontaneity and independence, and nonconformity to their culture. As a critic of science, Maslow assert-ed that the classical *mechanistic* approach of science (e.g., the *behavioristic* viewpoint in psychology) was inappropriate for characterizing the whole individual, and he advocated a *humanistic* approach, which he called the *third force* in American psychology, following the *psychoanalytic* and *behavioristic* viewpoints/forces. Criticisms of *Maslow's humanistic theory of personality* include the points that it is more of a secular replacement for religion than it is a scientific psychology, that it accepts as true that which is yet only hypothetical, that it confuses theory with ideology, and that it substitutes rhetoric for research. See also ANGYAL'S PERSONALITY THEORY; BEHAVIORIST THEORY; FREUD'S THEORY OF PERSONALITY; GOLDSTEIN'S ORGANISMIC THEORY; MOTIVATION, THEORIES OF; PERSONALITY THEORIES; ROGERS' THEORY OF PERSONALITY.

REFERENCES

Maslow, A. H. (1943). A theory of human motivation. *Psychological Review*, *50*, 370-396.
Maslow, A. H. (1954). *Motivation and personality*. New York: Harper & Row.
Maslow, A. H. (1962). *Toward a psychology of being*. Princeton, NJ: Van Nostrand.
Maslow, A. H. (1967). A theory of metamotivation: The biological rooting of the value-life. *Journal of Humanistic Psychology*, *7*, 93-127.
Maslow, A. H. (1970). *Religions, values, and peak experiences*. New York: Penguin Books.

MASS ACTION, PRINCIPLE/THEORY OF. See LASHLEY'S THEORY.

MASSED-SPACED THEORY OF LEARNING. See LEARNING THEORIES/LAWS.

MATCHING HYPOTHESIS. See INTERPERSONAL ATTRACTION THEORIES.

MATCHING LAW. See HERRNSTEIN'S MATCHING LAW.

MATCH-MISMATCH MODEL. See HABITUATION, PRINCIPLE/LAW OF.

MATERIALISM AND MECHANISM, DOCTRINES OF. See HOBBES' PSYCHOLOGICAL THEORY; MECHANISTIC THEORY.

MATHEMATICAL LEARNING THEORY. See ESTES' STIMULUS SAMPLING THEORY; HULL'S LEARNING THEORY; LEARNING THEORIES/LAWS.

MATTHEW EFFECT. This phenomenon in the sociology of science, described by the American sociologist Robert King Merton (1910-2003), refers to a scientist's lifetime productivity in terms of his/her publications, and involves a by-product called "cumulative advantage." That is, scientists who publish early in their careers and continue their productive output seem to attract surplus resources and advantages, such as grant support, greater number of student disciples, and affiliation at major research organizations, universities, and institutions. Such a result allows the prolific scientist to publish even more which brings even more additional rewards and incentives, whereas the less-published scientist falls by the wayside. Thus, in common terms, "the rich get richer, and the poor get poorer." This phenomenon has been called the *Matthew effect*, fashioned after the biblical passage of the Parable of the Talents in the Gospel According to St. Matthew (Matthew 25:29) which states that "For to everyone who has, *more* shall be given, and he will have an abundance; but from the one who does not have, even what he does have shall be taken away." An interesting implication of such a *doctrine of cumulative advantage*, as noted by D. K. Simonton, is that individuals who begin their scientific careers with roughly equivalent capabilities will eventually find themselves separated out into losers and winners by the "luck of the draw" (i.e., not everyone can publish in the most prestigious journals, win the most financially-rewarding grants, or receive premier appointments at prestigious universities, so that someone has to come out on the bottom of the heap). Such a possibility, in turn, has been referred to as the *Ecclesiastes hypothesis*, named after the following biblical passage (Ecclesiastes 9:11): "I returned and saw under the sun that the race is not to the swift, Nor the battle to the strong, Nor bread to the wise, Nor riches to men of understanding, Nor favor to men of skill; But time and chance happen to them all." See also EMINENCE, THEORIES AND MEASURES OF; LOTKA/LOTKA-PRICE LAW; PERSONALISTIC THEORY OF HISTORY.

REFERENCES

Merton, R. K. (1968). The Matthew effect in science. *Science, 159*, 56-63.

Turner, S. P., & Chubin, D. E. (1976). Another appraisal of Ortega, the Coles, and science policy: The Ecclesiastes hypothesis. *Social Science Information, 15*, 657-662.

Turner, S. P., & Chubin, D. E. (1979). Chance and eminence in science: Ecclesiastes II. *Social Science Information, 18*, 437-449.

Simonton, D. K. (2002). *Great psychologists and their times: Scientific insights into psychology's history.* Washington, D.C.: American Psychological Association.

MATURATIONAL HYPOTHESIS. See DEVELOPMENTAL THEORY.

MATURATION-DEGENERATION HYPOTHESIS. See DEVELOPMENTAL THEORY.

MATURATION THEORY. See DEVELOPMENTAL THEORY.

MAXIMIZATION THEORY. The speculations of *maximization theory* in behavioral psychology (e.g., Rachlin, Battalio, Kagel, & Green, 1981) - which are borrowed from theoretical notions in the field of economics - provides techniques for predicting the behavior of organisms, including humans as well as animals. *Maximization theory* posits the construction of a theoretical "behavioral space" in which each point represents a given combination of various behavioral alternatives. For example, with two alternatives - behavior X and behavior Y - each point within the space represents a certain amount of time spent performing behavior X and a certain amount of time spent performing behavior Y. Particular environmental situations may be described as constraints on available points ("circumscribed area") within the space. *Maximization theory* assumes that organisms always choose the available point having the highest numerical value, and the task of the theory is to assign values to points in the "behavioral space" that remain constant across various environmental situations where, as those situations change, the point actually chosen is always the one having the highest assigned value. The general goal of *maximization theory* in behavioral psychology is to serve as an alternative to *reinforcement theory* as a description of "steady-state" behavior, and includes applications to reinforcement situations such as rats pressing levers, and pigeons pecking keys, in Skinner boxes, as well as to human economic behavior assessments and human self-control situations. Inasmuch as *maximization theory* takes situational/contextual factors into account, it purportedly has greater predictive power than does the traditional, and more molecular, *reinforcement theory* (cf., the *maximum likelihood principle* - in the field of statistics, this conjecture refers to the use of any population estimate that serves as the basis for predicting the total parameter; and, in the area of subjective judgments, this speculation refers to making a prediction on the basis of what seems to be the most reasonable estimate under the given circumstances). See also LEWIN'S FIELD THEORY; OPERANT CONDITIONING/BEHAVIOR, LAWS/THEORY OF; REINFORCEMENT THEORY.

REFERENCE

Rachlin, H., Battalio, R., Kagel, J., & Green, L. (1981). Maximization theory in behavioral psychology. *Behavioral and Brain Sciences, 4,* 371-417.

MAXIMIZING/OPTIMIZING HYPOTHESIS. See EXPECTED UTILITY THEORY.

MAXIMUM CONTRAST, PRINCIPLE OF. See DEVELOPMENTAL THEORY.

MAXIMUM LIKELIHOOD PRINCIPLE. See MAXIMIZATION THEORY.

MAXWELL DISK OR COLOR-MIXING WHEEL. See TALBOT-PLATEAU LAW.

MAXWELLIAN VIEW. See VISION/SIGHT, THEORIES OF.

MAXWELL'S DEMON. See THERMODYNAMICS, LAWS OF.

McCOLLOUGH EFFECT. See EMMERT'S LAW.

McDOUGALL'S COLOR VISION THEORY. See von KRIES' COLOR VISION THEORY.

McDOUGALL'S HORMIC/INSTINCT THEORY/DOCTRINE. The British-born American social psychologist William Mc-Dougall (1871-1938) formulated the system of psychology called *hormic* (meaning "animal impulse" or "urge") *psychology*, which is based on goal-oriented and purposeful behaviors that are assumed to be motivated by innate propensities or instincts. For McDougall, goal-seeking behavior became the core of a psychology of all living organisms, and he defined purposive/goal-seeking behavior as being spontaneous, persistent, variable, and repetitive. Although McDougall emphasized the instinctive/innate nature of goal-seeking, he did admit that some learning may occur. McDougall developed a *theory of instincts* that became an important part of his *hormic psychology*, where instincts have three essential aspects: for any given instinct there is a perceptual predisposition to notice certain stimuli and not others (e.g., food odors are perceived by the organism when the hunger instinct is engaged); there is a predisposition for the organism to make movements toward the appropriate goal; and there is an "emotional core," "energy," or "driving force" in the organism between the perception of, and the movement toward, the goal. In the early 1900s, McDougall originally listed 12 major *instincts* in humans (i.e., hunger, rejection of particular substances, curiosity, escape, pugnacity, sex, maternal/paternal instinct, gregariousness, self-assertion, submission, construction, and acquisition), but by 1932 the list of *instincts* (or *propensities*) had increased to 17 (the five new instincts were laughter, crying out/appeal, comfort, rest/sleep, and migration). In addition to these *instincts*, there are other tendencies posited by McDougall such as breathing, sneezing, and coughing. According to McDougall, complex forms of human behavior involve a combination (called *sentiments*) of two or more *instincts* (e.g., the sex and maternal/paternal instincts combine to account for a man's love for his wife). McDougall accepted the *doctrine of native capacities* where humans are endowed with certain potentials such as high intelligence and artistic, musical, and athletic talents, but the presence of an *instinct* is required and operates as a "push" toward their fulfillment (cf., *apertural hypothesis* - the conjecture that the psychological representations of the primary instinctual functions focus on the apertures of organs that serve elementary instincts, such as the mouth, anus, urethra, and vagina; in a psychoanalytical context, this approach asserts that the phase of a woman's hormonal cycle may be predicted via analysis of her fantasies and dreams). McDougall's (1905) definition of psychology as the positive science of the *conduct* of living creatures - that equates the term *conduct* with that of *behavior* – anticipated the *behaviorist* J. B. Watson's (1913) definition (i.e., the science of *behavior*). However, ironically, McDougall was one of the more vigorous critics of Watsonian *behaviorism* and, at one time, he attracted numerous proponents to his system of *hormic psychology*, particularly among social psychologists, sociologists, and anthropologists, many of whom viewed Watson's position as too simplistic and sterile (i.e., Watson "threw the baby out with the bath water"). McDougall's *hormic theory* contains several shortcomings, the primary one being a lack of precision in the definition and use of the concept of *instinct*. *Hormic psychology* and McDougall's *instinct theory* are mostly of historic interest and, as far as *human* behavior (as distinguished from *animal* or *sub-human* behavior) is concerned, the *instinct doctrine* is not generally accepted today (except by Freudians). However, McDougall's ideas led to a revival of interest in the concept of *instinct* among animal ethologists, in particular [cf., *hierarchical instinct theory* - in the Dutch-English ethologist Nikolaas Tinbergen's (1907-1988) approach, the theory/model states that motivational energy accumulated in the organism's neural centers (whereby patterns of specific behavioral responses are generated via the hypothalamic, cortical, and sensory systems) is released by an appropriate environmental stimulus, and flows through motor-system pathways to produce behavior that is optimal to the organism's goal-achievement; and *instinctive/instinctual drift* - the tendency of an animal (that has been trained with food reward) to ignore or disregard the reinforced behavior and return back to a more basic, primitive, or instinctive behavior, such as a dog burying a stick (thrown by the trainer) instead of returning it to the trainer for a reward]; and his notion of purposive/goal-directed behavior was advocated by some learning theorists (e.g., E. C. Tolman). See also ALLPORT'S THEORY OF PERSONALITY; BEHAVIORIST THEORY; FREUD'S THEORY OF PERSONALITY; LAMARCKIAN/LYSENKO DOCTRINE; OBJECT-RELATIONS THEORY; SOUL THEORY; TOLMAN'S THEORY.

REFERENCES

McDougall, W. (1905). *Physiological psychology*. London: Dent.

McDougall, W. (1908). *An introduction to social psychology*. Boston: Luce.

Watson, J. B. (1913). Psychology as the behaviorist views it. *Psychological Review, 20*, 158-177.

Wilm, E. C. (1925/1971). *The theories of instinct: A study in the history of psychology*. New Haven, CT: Yale University Press.

Watson, J. B., & McDougall, W. (1929). *The battle of behaviorism*. New York: Norton.

McDougall, W. (1932). *Energies of men: A study of the fundamental dynamics of psychology*. London: Methuen.

Tolman, E. C. (1932). *Purposive behavior in animals and men*. New York: Appleton-Century-Crofts.

Tinbergen, N. (1951). *The study of instinct*. New York: Oxford University Press.

McDOUGALL'S THEORY OF HUMOR/ LAUGHTER. The British-born American psychologist William McDougall (1871-1938) developed an *instinct theory of humor and laughter* whose major premise is the *denial* that laughter is an expression of pleasure. McDougall claims that *all* laughter-provoking situations are unpleasant, and actually would be annoying if they were not laughed at (his theory has been referred to as the "anti-annoyance" theory of humor). Thus, *McDougall's theory of humor* is in direct contradiction to the scores of theories that view laughter as a proof of joy. According to McDougall, the functions of laughter are various *physiological* advantages (such as stimulation of circulation and respiration, blood pressure increase, and increase of blood flow to the brain) and *psychological* benefits (such as an increase in euphoria via the interruption of every train of thought and every sustained physical and mental activity). *McDougall's theory* indicates that laughter has evolved in the human species as an "antidote to sympathy" or as a protective reaction that shields one from the depressive influence of others' shortcomings and weaknesses. Curiously, McDougall attaches considerable importance to the topic of *tickling* in the history of laughter, and suggests that laughter on being tickled is the crudest and earliest form of humor. In admitting laughter to the group of "minor instincts," McDougall maintains that it differs from all other instincts in that its impulse seeks no goal beyond itself, but secures its own satisfaction by means of bodily processes that influence nothing in the external environment. Thus, *McDougall's instinct theory of humor* asserts that laughter evolved as a necessary corrective of the effects of interpersonal sympathy where the human species might not have survived without laughter and a sense of the ludicrous and humorous. See also DARWIN'S THEORY OF LAUGHTER/ HUMOR; HUMOR, THEORIES OF; LUDOVICI'S THEORY OF LAUGHTER.

REFERENCES

McDougall, W. (1903). The theory of laughter. *Nature, 67*, 318-319.

McDougall, W. (1922). A new theory of laughter. *Psyche, 2*, 292-303.

McGREGOR'S THEORIES X AND Y. See LEADERSHIP, THEORIES OF.

McGURK EFFECT/ILLUSION. The *McGurk effect/illusion,* named after the Scottish psychologist Harry McGurk (1936-1998), is a phenomenon in audiovisual speech perception in which synchronous, but conflicting, auditory and visual phonetic information is presented to participants who typically report - under such circumstances - hearing a "blend" or a "combination" of the seen and heard utterances. The original procedure employed in demonstrating this effect had normal-hearing participants repeat the consonant-vowel syllables they heard while watching and listening to the videotaped face of a speaker. The videotape was created such that the seen (visual "face-articulated") and heard (auditory) speech syllables had conflicting consonants, but were nevertheless presented in synchrony. For example, a visual, "face-articulated" stimulus "ga" accompanied by an auditory/heard stimulus "ba" was reported by participants as being heard as a "da" or "tha;" and a visual, "face-articulated" stimulus "ba" accompanied by an auditory/heard stimulus "ga" was reported as being heard as "bga." In

another case, when the videotaped face visually articulates "gi" and the auditory stimulus that is presented is "bi," participants typically report hearing "di." Furthermore, the audiovisual integration of the effect occurs even when participants are told explicitly of the dubbing procedure involving visual and auditory stimuli, or when they are asked to attend to only one (i.e., auditory or visual) of the information streams. Since the original report on the *McGurk effect* - the influence of vision on speech perception - there have been numerous replications of the phenomenon as well as results concerning a number of basic facts about audiovisual integration in the effect, including the following: it is influenced by the vowel context in which the consonants are spoken; vowels themselves may show the effect; the visual information for place of articulation may influence the auditory perception of consonants that differ in voicing; participants may be sensitive to the concordance of the time-varying aspects of speech but they do not require temporal coincidence of that information; the effect is sustained under substantial changes in the visual stimulus; it occurs with the use of both elaborate and schematic synthetic visual stimuli; an integration may occur over auditory and visual signals generated by speakers of different gender - indicating that the two information streams need not appear to emanate from the same source; and images that involve no identifiable facial features (e.g., use of only a few illuminated dots on a darkened face) may also influence heard speech. Moreover, the *McGurk effect* has been found in participants of different ages, as well as with various native-language backgrounds. Thus, the *McGurk effect/illusion* appears to be "robust" to the extent that it holds over substantial visual stimulus changes, is maintained regardless of what the participant knows about the stimuli, and is not decreased when the participant has had considerable practice at selectively attending. See also FACE RECOGNITION/FACIAL IDENTITY THEORY; SPEECH THEORIES.

REFERENCES

McGurk, H., & MacDonald, J. (1976). Hearing lips and seeing voices. *Nature, 264*, 746-748.

Massaro, D. W. (1987). *Speech perception by ear and eye: A paradigm for psychological inquiry*. Hillsdale, NJ: Erlbaum.

Dodd, B., & Campbell, R. (Eds.) (1987). *Hearing by eye: The psychology of lip-reading*. Hillsdale, NJ: Erlbaum.

McNAUGHTON RULES/PRINCIPLES. See PSYCHOPATHOLOGY, THEORIES OF.

MEANING SHIFT EFFECTS. See IMPRESSION FORMATION, THEORIES OF.

MEANING, THEORIES AND ASSESSMENT OF. The American psychologists Charles Egerton Osgood (1916-1991) and George John Suci (1925-), and the Canadian-born American psychologist Percy Hyman Tannenbaum (1927-), developed a popular paper-and-pencil measurement device called the *semantic differential technique* that attempts to assess quantitatively the affective/connotative *meaning* ("signification") of words, as well as measuring attitudes towards other objects, entities, and concepts. Thus, in this approach, the *theory of meaning* is coterminous with its *measurement* (cf., Evans, 1975). The *semantic differential* consists of several seven-point bipolar rating scales (e.g., good-bad; active-passive; strong-weak) on which the individual rates the word, concept, or item under study. The technique led to the conclusion (via factor analysis) that there are three basic dimensions, theoretically, of affective/connotative *meaning*: evaluation, activity, and potency [cf., the English-born American structuralist Edward B. Titchener's (1867-1927) *context theory of meaning* which holds that meaning depends on the mental images associated with a specific collection or body of sensations, as in the concept of "fire;" the *motor theory of meaning* proposed by the American behaviorist John Broadus Watson (1878-1958) which holds that meaning consists of *covert* movements and motor sets or motor readiness, that is, of the tendencies toward action that are aroused partially by an object; for example, the "meaning" of the red object on the table is its naming in internal speech as "apple," plus the motor readiness to

overtly pick up the object and eat it; the *conceptual dependency theory* - introduced by the American linguist/cognitive scientist Roger C. Schank (1946-) in the area of knowledge representation - refers to the way in which meaning is represented, whereby propositions are reduced to a small number of semantic primitives, such as agents, actions, and objects, and which are interpreted according to knowledge stored as "scripts;" *logotherapy theory* - a type of psychotherapy developed by the Austrian psychiatrist Viktor E. Frankl (1905-1997) which focuses on the patient's "will to *meaning*" (rather than on a "will to power" or a "will to pleasure") and seeks to restore in the individual a sense of *meaning* via creative activities/experiences of art, culture, and nature, and encourages the person's self-acceptance and his/her meaningful place in the world; among the techniques here is "paradoxical intention" (or "negative practice") especially useful for treating obsessive-compulsive disorders in which the person deliberately rehearses a particular habit, behavior, or undesirable pattern of thought, with the goal of developing a less fearful attitude towards it, controlling it, and/or extinguishing it; and *psycholexicology* - a rarely-used term that refers to the psychological study of words and their *meanings*; the term purportedly was coined by G. A. Miller and P. N. Johnson-Laird in the 1970s, and remains closely related to the notion of "procedural semantics" which emphasizes the importance of perceptual and other computational operations that language users supposedly employ in determining the applicability of words]. See also ATTITUDE/ATTITUDE CHANGE, THEORIES OF; EXISTENTIAL ANALYSIS THEORY; EXISTENTIAL/PHENOMENOLOGICAL THEORIES OF ABNORMALITY; LANGUAGE ORIGINS, THEORIES OF.

REFERENCES

Osgood, C. E. (1952). The nature and measurement of meaning. *Psychological Bulletin, 49*, 197-237.

Osgood, C. E., Suci, G. J., & Tannenbaum, P. H. (1957). *The measurement of meaning*. Urbana, IL: University of Illinois Press.

Frankl, V. E. (1962/1980). *Man's search for meaning: An introduction to lo-*

gotherapy. New York: Simon & Schuster.

Evans, R. B. (1975). The origins of Titchener's doctrine of meaning. *Journal of the History of the Behavioral Sciences, 21,* 334-341.

Miller, G. A., & Johnson-Laird, P. N. (1976). *Language and perception.* Cambridge, MA: Harvard University Press.

Schank, R. C., & Abelson, R. P. (1977). *Scripts, plans, goals, and understanding: An inquiry into human knowledge structures.* Hillsdale, NJ: Erlbaum.

Narens, L. (2002). *Theories of meaningfulness.* Mahwah, NJ: Erlbaum.

MEASUREMENT MODEL. See CONJOINT MEASUREMENT THEORY.

MEASUREMENT THEORY. The notion of *measurement* refers to the systematic assignment of numbers to represent quantitative aspects/attributes of events or objects. The American experimental psychologist Stanley Smith Stevens (1906-1973) proposed the following *scales of measurement level* that includes the assignment of numbers "according to rules:" *nominal scale* - a discrete (rather than continuous) form of data classification where elements/items are not quantified but are merely assigned to different, often numbered, named/labeled categories (e.g., assigning individuals to "hair-color" categories based on the color of their hair); *ordinal scale* - data are arranged in order/ranking of magnitude but the scale possesses no standard measurement of degrees of difference between the elements/items (e.g., the rank ordering of women in a "beauty contest" on the basis of perceived attractiveness; or the medals awarded to athletes in the Olympic Games); *interval scale* - differences among elements/items/scores can be quantified more or less in "absolute" terms, but the zero point on the scale is fixed arbitrarily; in this scale, the "equal differences" between scores correspond to equal differences in the attribute/characteristic being measured, but there is no score corresponding to the total absence of the attribute (e.g., calendar dates where each day is 24 hours long, but there is no zero point/score representing an absence of time/days); *ratio scale* - differences among values of elements/items/scores can be quantified in "absolute" terms where a "fixed zero point" is specified or defined; in this scale, equal differences between scores represent equal differences in the measured attribute, and a zero score represents the complete absence of the attribute; when measurement is on a *ratio scale*, it is meaningful to describe a score in terms of ratios (e.g., "she is twice as old as he is," or there is a ratio of 2:1 in their ages; one's age as measured in years is a *ratio scale* measure where birth represents the "fixed zero point"). Some psychologists prefer to avoid Stevens' theoretical approach to *measurement* and *scales* for the following reasons: it overlooks a crucial defining feature of measurement, that is, its connection with quantity or magnitude; it involves "rule-governed" assignments of numbers that do not truly represent quantities or magnitudes (e.g., the assignment of telephone numbers to individuals); "naming" is merely describing and not quantifying (as in the *nominal scale*); there is no real/true "absolute zero" point in measurement (as implied in the *ratio scale*); and some psychological researchers are easily led to conclude erroneously that there is a direct relationship between *level of measurement scale* used and type of *statistical test* to be employed (cf., Gaito, 1980). Among other speculations, effects, and issues related to *measurement theory* and psychological measurement ("psychometrics") are: *generalization theory* - the use of statistical analytical techniques to estimate the extent to which the scores derived from a particular test/data collection situation are applicable *beyond* the specific conditions under which those data were obtained; also called *external* or *ecological validity* [cf., *internal validity* - the extent to which a dependent variable/measure is determined by the independent variable(s) in an experiment]; *reliability theory* - study of the internal consistency and stability with which a measuring device performs its intended function in an accurate fashion (e.g., getting the same results from a group of participants who take the same test, or equivalent forms of the same test, on two separate occasions under virtually the same testing conditions); *scale attenuation effects* - refers to a reduction in the range of scale values utilized by participants in a study and may originate from difficulties in interpreting results when participants' responses on the dependent variable are either nearly perfect (as in the *ceiling effect*) or nearly absent (as in the *floor effect*); *basement/floor effect* - refers to the inability of measuring instruments or statistical procedures to determine differences at the *bottom* of data when the difference between scores/data is *small*; *ceiling effect* - refers to the inability of measuring instruments or statistical procedures to determine differences at the *top* of data when the difference between scores/data is *large*, or the inability of a test to measure or discriminate above a certain point, usually because the items are too easy for some people; and the *testing effect* - refers to the influence that taking a test actually has on the variables/traits which the test was designed to assess, and is a major source of error in psychological testing that is likely to occur, especially, where the use of pre-tests may alter the phenomenon that is measured/tested subsequently. See also CLASSICAL TEST/MEASUREMENT THEORY; CONJOINT MEASUREMENT THEORY.

REFERENCES

Stevens, S. S. (1946). On the theory of scales of measurement. *Science, 103,* 677-680.

Suppes, P., & Zinnes, J. L. (1963). Basic measurement theory. In R. D. Luce, R. R. Bush, & E. Galanter (Eds.), *Handbook of mathematical psychology.* Vol. 1. New York: Wiley.

Gaito, J. (1980). Measurement scales and statistics: Resurgence of an old misconception. *Psychological Bulletin, 87,* 564-567.

MECHANISTIC THEORY. In the history of psychology, and philosophy, the *doctrine of mechanism* is the notion that all animals, including humans, may be viewed as machines, with the added fiat that although living organisms may be complex, nevertheless they essentially are machines requiring no special, additional, or surplus principles to account for their behavior. Traditionally, the controversial *mechanistic theory* has been contrasted with

the *theory of vitalism* (which holds that a "vital force," not explicable by chemical, mechanical, or physical principles, is the basic cause of life) and the *theory of organicism* (a version of "holism" that emphasizes the notion that the parts of living organisms are only what they are due to their contributions to the whole being.) The *theory of vitalism* had its origins in the field of chemistry, in particular in the classification of compounds in 1675 by the French chemist Nicolas Lemery (1645-1715), and by the French chemist Antoine Laurent Lavoisier (1743-1794). In 1815, the Swedish chemist Johan J. Berzelius (1779-1848) proposed a distinction between "organic" and "inorganic" compounds which are governed by different laws; for example, organic compounds are produced under the influence of a "vital force," and are incapable of being prepared artificially. In 1828, this distinction was eclipsed when the German chemist Friedrich Wohler (1800-1882) synthesized the organic compound "urea" from an inorganic substance. In the field of philosophy, in one case [according to the German philosopher Hans Driesch (1867-1941)], the *life-force principle* may take the form of "entelechies" (i.e., actualities or realizations) within living things thought to be responsible for their growth and development. In another case [according to the French philosopher Henri Bergson (1859-1941)], the general "life force" takes on the features of an "élan vital" (life/vital force or spurt) which rejects the type of *vitalism* that postulates individual "entelechies." *Mechanistic theory* is associated, often, with both the *doctrine of determinism* (which posits that all events, physical or mental, including all forms of behavior, are the result of prior causal factors) and the *doctrine of materialism* (hypotheses asserting that physical matter is the only ultimate reality), but must be distinguished from such allied doctrines. For example, the "mechanist" (one who denies the existence of anything such as a "soul" or "mind" in living beings) is always a "materialist," but a "materialist" is not always a "mechanist;" also, a "vitalist" may promote "materialism," but discovers in organic tissue a special type of matter whose functions may not be explained in "mechanical" terms. A "mechanist" is a "determinist," because machines are defined often as "determined entities;" however, a "determinist" may not be a "mechanist" [e.g., the Dutch philosopher Benedictus/Baruch Spinoza (1632-1677) was a "pantheist" (the belief that God is the transcendent reality of which the material universe and man are only manifestations; it involves a denial of God's personality and expresses a tendency to identify God with nature), but he subscribed, also, to a vigorous "determinism" and a denial of free will]. The origins of the *psychological doctrine of mechanism* lie in the mechanistic viewpoint of the world as triggered by the scientific revolution of the 17th century [e.g., the English physicist/mathematician Sir Isaac Newton (1642-1727) proposed in 1687 that the universe is a "celestial clockwork" that adheres to precise and mathematically-stated natural laws]. It was an easy, and inevitable, step to go from the "celestial clockwork" of physics to the "behavioral clockwork" of psychology. However, along the way, the philosophers once again made contributions to *mechanistic theory*. For instance, the French philosopher Rene Descartes (1569-1650) advanced a rigorous mechanical conception of nature, and proposed that animals are mere machines whose behavior is determined by the mechanical functioning of their nervous systems. For Descartes, people are considered likewise to be machines, but they also possess "free souls" (that can "think") separate from bodily deterministic mechanisms. However, functions/capabilities such as memory, perception, and imagination were viewed by Descartes as physiological phenomena that are discernible or accountable by *mechanical laws*. The French philosopher Julien Offray de LaMettrie (1709-1751) asserted that "man is a machine," and although he denied the existence of a "soul," he was not a "mechanist" in all respects, inasmuch as he espoused *vitalism* by distinguishing between inorganic and organic matter. In the 19th and 20th centuries, various scientific and theoretical obstacles to *mechanistic theory* were overcome slowly; for example, the development of the *sensory-motor conception* of nervous function overshadowed investigators' search for the "soul" in the human body, and the development of the *theory of evolution* - along with the discovery of the DNA molecule -

helped to explain how vital life processes may be accounted for by mechanical reproduction, transmission, and communication systems. It may be observed that *mechanistic theory*, today, still disturbs those individuals (and religious groups) who believe that "mechanism," by embracing *determinism*, works to undermine belief in "free will" and "moral responsibility." The debate continues. See also BEHAVIORIST THEORY; DESCARTES' THEORY; DETERMINISM, DOCTRINE/THEORY OF; EVOLUTIONARY THEORY; EXISTENTIAL ANALYSIS THEORY; HOBBES' PSYCHOLOGICAL THEORY; HOLISTIC THEORY; LEARNING THEORIES/LAWS; LOEB'S TROPISTIC THEORY; MIND-BODY THEORIES.

REFERENCES

Newton, I. (1687). *Philosophiae naturalis; principia mathematica.* London: Pepys.

Driesch, H. (1905/1914). *The history and theory of vitalism.* Leipzig: Engelmann.

Bergson, H. (1911). *Creative evolution.* New York: Holt.

Young, D. (1970). *Mind, brain, and adaptation in the nineteenth century.* Oxford, UK: Clarendon Press.

MEDIATIONAL THEORIES. See CONCEPT LEARNING/CONCEPT FORMATION, THEORIES OF; HULL'S LEARNING THEORY; LEARNING THEORIES/LAWS.

MEDICAL/DISEASE MODEL. See WOLPE'S THEORY/TECHNIQUE OF RECIPROCAL INHIBITION.

MEDIUMISTIC HYPOTHESIS. See JUNG'S THEORY OF PERSONALITY.

MEEHL'S SIXTH LAW OF SOFT PSYCHOLOGY. The American clinical psychologist, statistician, and theoretician Paul Everett Meehl (1920-2003) provides a critique of the process of *null hypothesis testing* that is commonly employed in the "softer" areas of psychology. Among the ten factors identified by Meehl as obscuring most literature surveys that are base on correlational evidence is the *sixth law* (also called the "crud factor").

Meehl's sixth law of soft psychology states that "everything correlates to some extent with everything else." Thus, the "background noise level" in a typical study involves a matrix of correlations that - although small in magnitude - tend to be statistically significant rather than non-significant (particularly when large sample sizes are involved). Consequently, according to this law, setting up a *null hypothesi*s of zero correlation between two chosen variables (or of zero difference between two sample means) - to be refuted by at some level of significance - may be a specious exercise: the *null hypothesis*, in some sense, is always literally untrue. It is suggested that the researcher *not* overly rely on significance levels for correlational data. Also, it is recommended that one reduce the typical emphasis in psychological research on significance levels (involving the setting up of a "straw man" - via the *null hypothesis* - to be refuted), and to devote more attention to "power" and "strength of effect" analyses, tests, and strategies. See also NULL HYPOTHESIS.

REFERENCES

Meehl, P. E. (1990). Appraising and amending theories: The strategy of Lakatosian defense and two principles that warrant it. *Psychological Inquiry*, *1*, 108-141, 173-180.

Meehl, P. E. (1990). Why summaries of research on psychological theories are often uninterpretable. *Psychological Reports*, *66*, 195-244.

Standing, L., Sproule, R., & Khouzam, N. (1991). Empirical statistics: IV. Illustrating Meehl's sixth law of soft psychology: Everything correlates with everything. *Psychological Reports*, *69*, 123-126.

MEINONG'S THEORIES. The Austrian philosopher/psychologist Alexius Ritter von Handschuchsheim Meinong (1853-1920) studied under Franz Brentano (1838-1917), the founder of *act psychology* (i.e., a philosophical psychological system that was a precursor to *functionalism* and focused on the *acts* or *processes* of mind as the fundamental source of empirical data; cf., the *structuralist's* approach, which argued that the basic subject matter of psychology was the *conscious con-tent* of mind). Meinong's field was theoretical psychology, including the *theory of knowledge*, and he formulated a *theory of assumptions*, a *theory of evidence*, a *theory of value*, and a *theory of objects*; cf., *Gegenstandstheorie* ("theory of objects") - a branch of science originated by Meinong, designed to study the properties and relations of objects, as such, that the other sciences, particularly psychology, neglected. In his *theory of objects*, Meinong accepted Plato's conceptions of ideal objects that subsist and other objects that exist, but he added a third aspect: objects that are non-existing but have objective characteristics (cf., Meinong's *founding processes* - an intellectual activity by which conscious contents are consolidated to form objects of higher order, termed *complexes*). Thus, it is possible to speak of impossible-to-exist entities such as "round squares;" one may make true statements about many more things than the objects that exist. In his *theory of value*, Meinong appealed to the psychology of humans where people's emotional reactions, for example, are not balanced or consistent (e.g. one may show more sorrow in the non-existence of the good than show pleasure in its existence or take displeasure in the existence of evil than joy in its non-existence). Meinong's *value theory* anticipated contemporary study of psychological-ethical thought with his various subdivisions of good and bad (e.g., good that is meritorious, good that is merely required, bad that is excusable, and bad that is inexcusable). See also DECISION-MAKING THEORIES; FUNCTIONALISM THEORY; MIND/ MENTAL STATES, THEORIES OF; OBJECT-RELATIONS THEORY; PATTERN/ OBJECT RECOGNITION THEORY; PERCEPTION (I. GENERAL), THEORIES OF; STRUCTURALISM/ STRUCTURALIST THEORY.

REFERENCES

Meinong, A. (1891). Zur psychologie der komplexionen und relationen. *Zeitschrift fur Psychologie*, *2*, 245-265.

Meinong, A. (1894). *Psychologisch-ethische untersuchungen zur werththeorie*. Graz, Austria: Leuschner & Lubensky.

Meinong, A. (1914). *Abhandlungen zur psychologie*. Leipzig: Barth.

MELODIC/SEMITONE/TRITONE PARADOX EFFECTS. See APPENDIX A.

MEMBRANE THEORY OF NERVE CONDUCTION. See NEURON/NEURAL/NERVE THEORY.

MEMORY ILLUSION. See APPENDIX A.

MEMORY, THEORIES OF. See FORGETTING AND MEMORY, THEORIES OF; SHORT-TERM AND LONG-TERM MEMORY, THEORIES OF.

MEMORY TRACE THEORY. See GESTALT THEORY/LAWS.

MENDELIAN RATIO. See MENDEL'S LAWS/PRINCIPLES.

MENDEL'S LAWS/PRINCIPLES. = Mendelian ratio = Mendel's theory of heredity = Mendelism. The Austrian botanist and experimental biologist Gregor Johann Mendel (1822-1884) was ordained as a priest in 1847, studied science in Vienna from 1851 to 1853, and returned later to the Brno monastery, becoming abbot in 1868. Mendel bred peas in the experimental garden of the monastery and grew almost 30,000 plants between 1856 and 1863. He artificially fertilized plants with specific characteristics; he crossed species that produced tall plants with those that produced short plants and counted the numbers of tall and short plants that appeared in the subsequent generations. All the plants of the first generation were tall, and the next generation consisted of some tall and some short in proportions of 3:1. Mendel suggested that each plant received one character from each of its parents, tallness being *dominant* and shortness being *recessive* or hidden and appearing only in later generations. The term *Mendelian ratio* refers to biparental offspring where the ratio is between those that possess a given unit character or combination of unit characters (dominants) and those that do not possess (recessives) the character. For a single *unit character* the ratio in the first filial generation is three dominants to one recessive. The term *Mendelism* refers to a theory of inheritance (based on *Mendel's law*) according to which

the constitution of the offspring is determined by a certain number of independent factors, called unit characters, contributed by the parents. *Mendel's law*, then, is a principle of hereditary transmission according to which the characters of the parents are transmitted to the offspring in units without change, some becoming perceptible in individuals of the first generation and others in those of later generations, with a definite ratio for each generation (cf., *genetic balance theory* - indicates how sex chromosomes and autosomes together determine the individual's sex at the molecular, cellular, and organ levels in the embryo stage; and *intermediate gene effects* - refers to the ability of some genes to "cooperate" and work together with other genes, rather than some being dominant over others, with the result that each gets expressed in some aspect of the organism). Mendel's experiments led to the formulation of his *law of segregation* and *law of independent assortment*. Mendel's *first law/ law of segregation* states that during meiosis (the process whereby a nucleus divides by two divisions into four nuclei), the two members of any pair of alleles (different sequences of genetic material occupying the same gene locus) possessed by an individual separate (segregate) into different gametes and subsequently into different offspring, neither having blended with or altered the other in any way although together in the same cell. Mendel's *second law/law of independent assortment of genes* states that during meiosis all combinations of alleles are distributed to daughter nuclei with equal probability, the distribution of members of one pair having no influence on the distribution of members of any other pair. *Mendel's first law* is a consequence of the behavior of all chromosomes during meiosis; his *second law* is a consequence of the independent behavior of non-homologous chromosomes during meiosis (cf., *non-Mendelian gene* - any gene not conforming to a Mendelian mechanism of inheritance, or is not inherited according to Mendel's laws, in particular, the genes encoded in "plasmids" and "mitochondrial DNA;" *trans-methylation hypothesis* - holds that due to some genetic or metabolic defect, certain normal body chemicals are converted into LSD-like substances in the brain; and *selfish gene hypothesis* - holds that a living organism is merely the result of the genes of that individual attempting to replicate themselves). The English zoologist William Bateson (1861-1926) contributed to the establishment of the Mendelian concept of heredity and variations, and gave the name *genetics* to the new science. Bateson experimented on hybridization in order to understand the transmission of inherited characteristics from parents to immediate offspring. In 1865, after Mendel's initial work in breeding peas was conducted, little further attention was given to *Mendel's laws* or *genetics* [cf., *Malthus' law* - a genetic/statistical principle proposed by Thomas Robert Malthus (1766-1834) which states that the population of any given region in respect to any given species tends to increase in geometrical progression, whereas the means of subsistence increases at a less rapid rate]. However, Bateson "rediscovered" Mendel's findings - after being neglected by biologists for 35 years - and reinterpreted them in the light of more recent evidence. Bateson founded the *Journal of Genetics* in 1910 and served as a spokesman for the new science of *genetics*. Bateson also de-vised a *vibratory theory of inheritance* founded on the concepts of force and motion, but it never received much favor among his contemporary scientists. During the 1920s, genetic research focused on mutations and, as an alternative to *Darwin's theory of natural selection*, a widely accepted hypothesis held that evolution occurs in *rapid leaps*; cf., *punctuated equilibrium theory* - the notion that evolution occurs in bursts with long periods of little change between them as a result of radical changes in phenotype caused by mutations. This idea contrasts sharply with Darwin's view of *gradual evolution* due to environmental selection acting on continuous variations among individuals of a population. An important turning point for *evolution theory* was the birth of the field/study of *population genetics*, especially in the 1930s, when *Mendelism* and *Darwinism* were reconciled, and the genetic basis of variation and natural selection was worked out. The results of Mendel's original experiments on garden peas have been extended to genetics and heritability in humans, where it has been discovered that certain genetic disor-ders - such as sickle-cell anemia, Tay-Sachs disease, and cystic fibrosis - are inherited as simple recessive traits from phenotypically normal, heterozygous carriers. See also DARWIN'S EVOLUTION THEORY; GALTON'S LAWS; HARDY-WEINBERG LAW; MALTHUS' THEORY.

REFERENCES

Mendel, G. J. (1901/1965). *Versuche uber pflanzenhybriden*. Edinburgh: Oliver & Boyd.

Bateson, W. (1902). *Mendel's principles of heredity*. Cambridge, UK: Cambridge University Press.

Bateson, W. (1914). *Mendel's vererbungstheorien*. Berlin: Teubner.

MENDEL'S THEORY OF HEREDITY. See MENDEL'S LAWS/PRINCIPLES.

MENTAL-FACULTY THEORY. See TRANSFER OF TRAINING, THORNDIKE'S THEORY OF.

MENTAL HOUSECLEANING HYPOTHESIS. See DREAM THEORY.

MENTAL IMAGERY THEORIES. See IMAGERY/MENTAL IMAGERY, THEORIES OF.

MENTAL LAWS OF ASSOCIATION. See ASSOCIATION, LAWS/PRINCIPLES OF.

MENTAL MODEL. See MIND/MENTAL STATES, THEORIES OF.

MENTAL SELF-GOVERNMENT THEORY. See INTELLIGENCE, THEORIES/LAWS OF.

MERE EXPOSURE EFFECT. This phenomenon was first studied quantitatively by the American-based Polish psychologist Robert B. Zajonc (1923-) in 1968, even though the effect was suggested initially much earlier both by the German philosopher/psychologist Gustav Theodor Fechner (1801-1887) in 1876, and the American philosopher/psychologist William James (1842-1910) in 1890. The *mere exposure effect* refers to the tendency for repeated exposure to a stimulus to be adequate to enhance or increase an individual's liking or positive attitude towards it. In Zajonc's study, pairs of antonyms were examined, and it was found that positively-toned words were more frequent in the language according to word counts than were negatively-toned words (e.g., the English word "beauty" occurs 41 times more frequently than does the word "ugly"). In investigations of other non-English languages, Zajonc also found that there are direct relationships between exposure frequency and rated favorability of words in languages such as German, French, Russian, and Spanish; cf., the *Pollyanna effect* [named by the American psychologist Charles E. Osgood (1916-1991) in the 1960s, in honor of the overly-optimistic character "Pollyanna Whittier" in American writer Eleanor H. Porter's (1868-1920) novels in the early 1900s] - refers to a tendency for individuals to pay more attention to positive than negative aspects or conceptual terms in their speech and thoughts, and the tendency to process the positive information more easily than the negative information; cf., however, *trait negativity bias* - a tendency for unfavorable information about a person to carry more impact on impressions of that person than favorable information; it is hypothesized (from *information theory*), that inasmuch as information about people typically tends to be mostly positive (or neutral), the presence of negative information tends to have more "information" and "salience;" and the *preference-feedback hypothesis* [formulated by the South African-born English psychologist Andrew M. Colman (1944-), the English psychologist David J. Hargreaves (1948-), and the Polish-born British psychologist Wladyslaw Sluckin (1919-1985)] - is the speculation that for certain classes of stimuli (e.g., surnames), the relationship between rated "familiarity" and "attractiveness" is a curve having an inverted U shape, with both very familiar and very unfamiliar surnames receiving lower ratings of "attractiveness" than surnames of intermediate familiarity; however, for other classes of stimuli (e.g., first names), the relationship is a monotonic curve with "attractiveness" increasing indefinitely with "familiarity;" also, the hypothesis suggests the operation of a "feedback mechanism" (which partly explains the *mere exposure effect*), and the role of human choice in the "exposure-familiarity" association, especially as regards the class of stimuli consisting of first names. See also INFORMATION AND INFORMATION-PROCESSING THEORY; IMPRESSION FORMATION, THEORIES OF; INTERPERSONAL ATTRACTION THEORIES; ZAJONC'S AROUSAL AND CONFLUENCE THEORIES.

REFERENCES

Fechner, G. T. (1876/1897). *Verschule der aesthetik*. Leipzig: Breithopf & Haertel.

James, W. (1890/1950). *The principles of psychology*. Vol. 2. New York: Dover.

Zajonc, R. B. (1968). Attitudinal effects of mere exposure. *Journal of Personality and Social Psychology Monograph Supplement, 9*, 1-27.

Boucher, J., & Osgood, C. E. (1969). The Pollyanna hypothesis. *Journal of Verbal Learning and Verbal Behavior, 8*, 1-8.

Colman, A. M., Hargreaves, D. J., & Sluckin, W. (1981). Preferences for Christian names as a function of their experienced familiarity. *British Journal of Social Psychology, 20*, 3-5.

Colman, A. M., Sluckin, W., & Hargreaves, D. J. (1981). The effect of familiarity on preferences for surnames. *British Journal of Psychology, 72*, 363-369.

Zajonc, R. B., & Moreland, R. L. (1982). Exposure effects in person perception: Familiarity, similarity, and attraction. *Journal of Experimental Social Psychology, 18*, 395-415.

MERKEL'S LAW. See HICK'S LAW.

MESMER'S THEORY/MESMERISM. See HYPNOSIS/HYPNOTISM, THEORIES OF.

METABOTROPIC EFFECT. See NEURON/NEURAL/NERVE THEORY.

METACOGNITION/METAMEMORY. See MIND/MENTAL STATES, THEORIES OF.

MEYER'S PSYCHOBIOLOGY THEORY.
See MURPHY'S BIOSOCIAL THEORY.

MEYER'S PSYCHOLOGICAL THEO-RIES. About eight years prior to John B. Watson's (1919) publication of his influential "Psychology from the Standpoint of a Behaviorist," the German-American psychologist Max Frederick Meyer (1873-1967) provided the rudiments of a *behavioristic psychology* in his "Fundamental Laws of Human Behavior" (1911), followed up by a more systematic account in his "Psychology of the Other One" (1921) wherein he stated that the task of psychology is the study of public data. Meyer asserted, in particular, that the concept of *consciousness* can be studied scientifically only if it is made public. Meyer's major contributions to empirical psychology were in the areas of audition and musical acoustics where he published for over 50 years (1899-1950). Meyer proposed a *theory of hearing* - that almost equaled *Helmholtz's audition theory* in popularity - in which he made the variable of *pitch* a function of frequency of sound waves and excluded the variable of *resonance*. *Meyer's theory* also dealt with the perception of loudness of complex sound waves by placing the locus for analysis of such waves in the inner ear rather than in the brain. In 1912 and 1913, Meyer - who was an uncompromising neurophysiological reductionist and anticipated the development of modern cognitive neuropsychology - considered the problem of mind and body, and used mechanical analogies to prove that the *behavioristic* conception of nervous function is superior to others. Later, Meyer devised a scheme of abnormal psychology based on *behavioristic* principles. See also AUDITION/HEARING, THEORIES OF; BEHAVIORIST THEORY; CONSCIOUSNESS, PHENOMENON OF; EMPIRICAL/EMPIRICISM, DOCTRINE OF; EMPIRICIST VERSUS NATIVIST THEORIES.

REFERENCES

Roback, A. A. (1964). *History of American psychology*. New York: Collier.

Zusne, L. (1984). *Biographical dictionary of psychology*. Westport, CT: Greenwood Press.

MEYER'S THEORY OF HEARING. See AUDITION/HEARING, THEORIES OF.

MICHELANGELO PHENOMENON. See SELF-CONCEPT THEORY.

MICHELSON-MORLEY EXPERIMENT. See NEWTON'S LAWS/PRINCIPLES OF COLOR MIXTURE.

MICHON'S MODEL OF TIME. The Dutch experimental psychologist John A. Michon (1935-) notes that in its first century the experimental study of *human time experience* is almost entirely a "psychophysics of duration," and it is only recently (with the emergence of cognitive psychology) that a much broader array of temporal phenomena has become the topic of empirical study, including the perception of rhythmic patterns, the planning of future actions, and the narrative structure of complex events. Michon argues for a model of time wherein duration is an advanced abstraction, a form of "representation," which derives functionally from a much more basic biological requirement: the need to stay in tune with a dynamic, unfolding outside world. According to *Michon's model of time*, mental representations of time enable the person to achieve behavioral and cognitive coherence of successions of real events and episodes. If such events pertain to the individual's personal history, this "narrative closure" leads to the identity of what is called the "self." In this approach, cognitive representations of time range from highly concrete, dynamic scenes to semi-abstract analogical schemes, and involve formalized or axiomatic theories of time. Michon asserts that the instability of time's "rate of flow" is the chief characteristic of subjective time and the principal dependent variable of the "psychophysics" of time; it is derived from the use one makes of the various types of representation as one "tunes in" on the sequential contingencies of the environment. Michon suggests that although there is not yet a "received view" concerning a general account of the psychology of time, there appears to be enough commonality among psychologists to specify some of the basic assumptions ("metatheoretical criteria") underlying theory construction regarding psychological time: a *psychological time theory* should specify the *functional stimuli* for one's "sense of time;" the *hierarchical levels of explanation* used in the theory should be specified; the theory should account for the distinction between *implicit and explicit temporality* of human action; the theory should explain the various *modes of representation* of time and their *operational rules*; the theory should specify the role of *space* for the representation of time; the role of *memory* in the theory should be specified; and the theory should specify the *ontogenesis of time* or how one experiences time via development of cognitive mechanisms across the life span. See also FRAISSE'S THEORY OF TIME; GUYAU'S THEORY OF TIME; TIME, THEORIES OF.

REFERENCES

Michon, J. A. (1990). Implicit and explicit representations of time. In R. Block (Ed.), *Cognitive models of psychological time*. Hillsdale, NJ: Erlbaum.

Michon, J. A. (1993). Concerning the time sense: The seven pillars to time psychology. *Psychologica Belgica, 33,* 329-345.

Michon, J. A. (1994). Psychology of time. In S. Macey (Ed.), *Encyclopedia of time*. New York: New York: Garland.

MICROGENETIC THEORY. See BROWN'S THEORY OF TIME AWARENESS.

MICROMOLAR THEORY. See LOGAN'S MICROMOLAR THEORY.

MIGNON DELUSION. See IMPRESSION FORMATION, THEORIES OF.

MILL'S CANONS. See PARSIMONY, LAW/PRINCIPLE OF.

MIND BLINDNESS THEORY. See MIND/MENTAL STATES, THEORIES OF.

MIND-BODY THEORIES. Philosophers and scholars in all disciplines have struggled for centuries to define the nature of the human being. A prominent issue in this endeavor deals with the *mind/soul* and the *body* and the relationship between them, or what is called the *mind-body problem*, leading to *mind-body theories*. Plato (c. 428-347 B.C.) was a *dualist* who divided the human being in his *dualist theory* into *material body* and *immaterial soul* (cf., *monist/monism theory* - postulates that the human organism consists of a single unified identity; some empirical "monistic reductionists" equate the mind to the activity of the brain and the nervous system). For Plato, the body is a hindrance to the soul in the acquisition of knowledge and, as a *rationalist*, he abandoned the body and the senses for the activity of the soul capable of accounting for absolute being. Plato spoke of the soul as a unity that has three aspects: *reason* (located in the head), *spirit/courage* (located in the chest), and *appetite* (located in the abdomen). Basically, Plato favored rational/deductive science over the empirical/inductive approach. Aristotle (384-322 B.C.) attempted to solve the *mind-body problem* as presented in Platonic dualism by formulating a concrete, functional view of organic life. Later, Rene Descartes (1596-1650) proposed that matter (body) is "extended substance" and that the soul (mind) is "unextended substance" (cf., *soul theory* - holds that mental phenomena are the manifestations of a specific substance, usually assumed to be distinct from material substance; *mind-dust theory* - the view that atoms or particles of mind exist extensively in the universe and are combined to form actual minds; and the *mind-stuff theory* - the view that mind is formed by the combination of atoms and particles that are held to be the same as those elements that appear to the observer as matter). Descartes held that these two kinds of substance interact with each other in the human organism, body affecting mind and mind affecting body; Descartes' dualistic approach is known as the *mind-body theory of interactionism* [also called the "ghost in the machine" dogma by the English philosopher Gilbert Ryle (1900-1976)] - in which events and processes in the mental and physical realm influence or interact with each other. Other early attempts to solve the *mind-body problem* are the *theory of occasionalism* - the view propounded by A. Geulincx (1624-1669) and N. Malebranche (1638-1715) that the concomitance between conscious and bodily processes is due to the intervention of the Deity, who determines that a specific conscious process shall occur on the occasion of a specific bodily process, and vice versa; and the *theory of preestablished harmony* - which refers to the relation between mental and physical events that assumes that they occur independently, that is, without either affecting the other causally, but that they harmonize and constitute parallel event series due to a fundamental or original characteristic of reality; this approach was one phase of a more general theory originated by G. W. Leibnitz (1646-1716); cf., Leibnitz's *law of sufficient reason*, which states that - given sufficient knowledge and time - one might discover why any specific occurrence is such as it is and not otherwise. More recent approaches to the *mind-body problem* are the *double-aspect theory*, which assumes that conscious experiences and brain processes are fundamentally identical, the two groups of phenomena being two manifestations or aspects of a single set of events (a synonym for this theory is the *identity hypothesis/theory*); the *theory of parallelism*, or *psychophysicalism*, which is confused often with the *double-aspect theory*, and states that for every variation in conscious processes or experiences there is a concomitant variation in neural processes [this theory makes no assumption of a causal relation between the mind and the body; the *theory of parallelism* was formulated by B. Spinoza (1632-1677), and the *psychophysical* aspect was added by G. Fechner (1803-1887)]; the *theory of epiphenomenalism*, which maintains that conscious processes are not in any sense causal agents, even with respect to one another, but are merely correlated with certain causally effective physiological processes; the *theory of phenomenalism*, which holds that human knowledge is limited to phenomena or one's experience and does not reach the real nature of things [proponents and precursors to this theory were E. Husserl's (1859-1938) and F. Brentano's (1838-1917) *psychological theory of intentionalism*, which defines the distinguishing feature of psychical phenomena, such as acts of perception or judgment, as their "intention" or reference to an object; this theory is synonymous with *act psychology*, in which the data are psychic activities, usually of a subject upon an object; cf., F. Brentano's *idiogenetic theory*, which holds that the function of judgment is an original or primordial mental fact; and A. E. Jones' *non-common effects principle* - states that the disposition of intention begun by an action is most readily seen by acknowledging the "non-common" consequences of alternative actions; the fewer non-common effects of the action and alternative actions, the more readily an attribution of intention of disposition may be made]; and the *theory of immaterialism* - maintains that the existence of matter cannot be affirmed confidently inasmuch as all perceptual experiences are aspects of consciousness. There is general agreement by writers that *body* refers to the material, physical, or physiological characteristics of the organism and such activities can be studied by the traditional empirical methods of science. However, the *mind, psyche*, or *soul* entity of the *mind-body problem* presents the most difficulty, where questions remain concerning whether such an entity even exists (cf., *synergy theory*, which holds that mental synthesis consists in a unitary response, whether perceptual or motor, aroused by the aggregate of sensory or other elements that are conceived as stimuli converging upon a single response mechanism; the *theory of mind/mind mechanism*, which is the use of one's existing concepts of people's mental states to explain their behavior; and the *law of span*, which states that every mind tends to keep its total simultaneous cognitive output constant in quantity, however varying in quality). Questions remain, also, about how best to define the mind and how to apply the empirical methods of science to obtain descriptions and functional laws for such an inferred entity (cf., *doctrine of psychologism* - posits that everything should be viewed from the reference point of the psychology of the individual, and advances the notion that the problem of the validity of human knowledge may be solved by the study of mental processes). See also FECHNER'S LAW; MALEBRANCHE'S THEORIES; MIND/MENTAL STATES, THEORIES OF; RATIONALISM/RATIONALIST, DOCTRINE OF; WEBER-FECHNER LAW.

REFERENCES

Bain, A. (1873). *Mind and body: The theories of their relation*. New York: Appleton.

Brentano, F. (1874). *Psychologie vom empirischen standpunkt*. Leipzig: Dun-ker & Humblot.

Baldwin, J. M. (1905). Sketch of the history of psychology. *Psychological Review, 12*, 144-165.

Ryle, G. (1949). *The concept of mind*. London: Hutchinson.

Husserl, E. (1962). *Phenomenological psychology*. The Hague: Nijhoff.

Polten, E. (1973). *Critique of the psychophysical identity theory*. The Hague: Mouton.

Cheng, D. (1975). *Philosophical aspects of the mind-body problem*. Honolulu: University of Hawaii Press.

Levin, M. (1979). *Metaphysics and the mind-body problem*. Oxford, UK: Clarendon Press.

MIND-DUST THEORY. See MIND-BODY THEORIES.

MIND/MENTAL SET, LAW OF. = set, law of. The term *set* is defined in the present context as a temporary condition of the organism that facilitates a certain specific type of activity; cf., the *set-theoretical model*, which refers to any model that treats the entities under consideration as elements arranged in a series or aggregate and formally represents the relations between the elements in terms of *set theory* that may be applied, among other things, to mathematical characterization, semantic features, word meaning, or human long-term memory (cf., *resonance theory of learning*, proposed by the American psychologist Harry F. Harlow (1905-1981), which holds that items belonging to a certain set are more likely to be recalled/responded to during the time that set is being dealt with). The related terms *mental/determining set* and *perceptual set* refer, respectively, to any condition, disposition, or tendency on the organism's part to respond in a particular manner, and to a kind of cognitive readiness for a particular stimulus or class of stimuli (called *Einstellung* in German). When *set* is associated with a problem-solving or task-oriented situation, the German word *Aufgabe* ("task") is used to capture the idea that each particular task or set of instructions for performing a particular task carries with it a cluster of constraints indicating the use of particular processes (cf., N. Ach's *determining tendency*; R. Wheeler refers to the law of *Aufgabe*). Thus, the *law of set/mental set*, in a psychological context, refers to a temporary condition of responding that can arise from the task requirements (via overt or covert instructions), context, prior experiences, or expectations (cf., *rational principle* - refers to a *mind set* concerning how one intends to solve a problem or determine a fact, such as deciding to use deductive versus inductive reasoning in problem-solving). At higher cognitive levels, *set* can alter the pattern of information pickup, the nature of what is perceived, and the probability that a particular problem may be solved; (cf., *fuzzy set theory*, which is the *mathematical theory of sets* that does not have sharp boundaries and, because most concepts are fuzzy in this sense - for example, "bald," "bad" - some believe the *mathematical theory* could throw light on cognition). Other ways in which *set* interacts with cognitive processes are called *attentional set*, which refers to a condition whereby the observer is prepared to receive information of a particular type (or from a particular channel), and the *functional fixedness phenomenon* [or *functional fixity* - first described by the German-born American psychologist Karl Duncker (1903-1940)], which is a *conceptual set* whereby objects that have been used for one function tend to be viewed as serving only that function, even though the situation may call for the use of the object in a different manner. See also ACH'S LAWS/PRINCIPLES/THEORY; FUZZY SET THEORY; MIND/MENTAL STATES, THEORIES OF; WUNDT'S THEORIES/ DOCTRINES.

REFERENCES

Ach, N. (1905). *Uber die willenstatigkeit und das denken*. Gottingen: Vardenboek.

Wheeler, R. (1929). *The science of psychology: An introductory study*. New York: Crowell.

Duncker, K. (1935/1945). Zur psychologie des produktiven denkens . *Psychological Monographs, 58* , No. 5.

Gibson, J. (1941). A critical review of the concept of set in contemporary experimental psychology. *Psychological Bulletin, 38,* 781-817.

Luchins, A. (1942). Mechanization in problem solving - The effect of Einstellung. *Psychological Monographs, 54,* No. 248.

Bruner, J. (1957). On perceptual readiness. *Psychological Review, 64,* 123-152.

MIND/MENTAL STATES, THEORIES OF. In its generalized form, *mind theory* refers to people's beliefs, cognitions, and intuitive understanding of their own, and other people's, mind/mental states that develop over a period of time beginning at a very early age (cf., *solipsistic doctrine* - a philosophical speculation that there can be no proof that phenomena exist outside of the mind inasmuch as everything is assumed to be dependent on personal perception; also, it is the extreme view that only the self exists, where everything and everyone else is a product of one's imagination). Although children typically have a well-developed *theory of mind* by about the age of three years, they do not yet possess the understanding that people's beliefs may be false (cf., Piaget, 1929). In some atypical and intrapersonal cases, such as children diagnosed with autism, there is an inability to understand the notion of mental states and the way in which such states modify or control behavior (cf., *theory of impoverished mind* - attempts to account for the condition of autism in children, suggesting that autistic individuals have an "impoverished mind" in which they have difficulty imagining others as holding beliefs, ideas, and expectations; however, such persons can identify emotional states via cues such as facial expression and other observable behaviors in other people). In other interpersonal cases, the inability of one person to appreciate the mental states of other people is called the *mind-blindness theory*. In general, however, people possess the ability to attribute mental states (beliefs, desires) to themselves and others; D. Premack and G. Woodruff called this ability as having a *theory of mind* and, thus, possessing a *theory of mind* enables an individual to explain and predict others' behavior in terms of their mental states. This orientation suggests that when persons in a society or culture lack a *theory of mind/mental states*, social behavior is affected adversely and where, in particular, cooperation among members in the group is disrupted (cf., Vygotsky, 1978). In a larger philosophical context, the notion of *category mistake* - described by the English philosopher Gilbert Ryle (1900-1976) - refers to a statement about something that belongs to one category but is intelligible only of something belonging to another category (e.g., as in the case where the *mind* is referred to as if it were a *physical* entity). Philosophers also use the notion of *inverted qualia* (a hypothetical situation in which an individual experiences "qualia," or sensory data/events, such as the experience of the "redness" of roses, in the opposite way to another person) - with the apparent impossibility of knowing if, indeed, *inverted qualia* exist - as an argument that mental experiences are not reducible to physical entities/states. The versatile German physician, painter, naturalist, and psychologist Carl Gustav Carus (1789-1869) developed a *topographic hypothesis/model of the mind* in which one's awareness of mental contents and functions is divided into four aspects: conscious, preconscious, general absolute, and partial absolute where the elements possess interactional characteristics; Sigmund Freud initially adopted Carus' model but replaced it, subsequently, with his own *structural hypothesis/model/theory* consisting of the three aspects/components of unconscious, preconscious, and conscious (cf., *doctrine of universalism* - philosophical speculation that some aspects of the human mind are universal; for example, the notion that humans recognize some behaviors as being intrinsically bad or evil such as killing other humans against their will). In the obsolete school of psychology called *faculty psychology* - developed and popularized by the German philosopher and mathematician Christian Wolff (1679-1754) in the 1730s - it was suggested that the mind is divided into arbitrarily posited powers or capacities (called "faculties"), such as reason, will, and instinct, through which all mental functions and phenomena supposedly occur and interact. In the early *act psychology* [i.e., an anti-elementalism, anti-content approach that emphasized the unity of interactions with the environment (and which argued that "psychological acts," such as emotions, judgments, and ideations, are intentional, and all analytical attempts to study the individual destroy the acts being studied) of the German psychologist Franz Brentano (1838-1917)], the *idiogenetic theory* posits that the function of judgment/ideation is a primordial, and original, mental capacity of humans. *Faculty psychology* served as the basis for the foundation of the later theoretical, and discredited, approach called *phrenology* - founded by the German physiologist Franz Joseph Gall (1758-1828) who called it "craniology" and the Austrian physician Johann K. Spurzheim (1776-1832) who called it "phrenology" - that was a doctrine of mental faculties allegedly located in specific areas of the brain and detectable via bumps at corresponding points on the outside of the skull. Another basis for *phrenology* is found in the *doctrine of the modularity of mind*, traceable back to the Greek philosopher Aristotle (384-322 B.C.) who indicated that cognitive processes are controlled by subsystems that operate as distinct units and with a large degree of independence from one another (cf., Fodor, 1983). Today, in *educational theory, modularity theories* assume that the human mind is composed of various independent units/modules that may be made to operate in several ways where, over time, the modules relate to each other to establish a type of integrative synthesis [cf., *regional-localization theory* - states that the brain has special areas that control particular functions, such as the occipital lobes in the back area of the brain as being instrumental in vision; *Broca's area* - named after the French physician/physiologist Paul Broca (1824-1880) - located in the left cerebral cortex, is essential to the production/motor aspects of *spoken* language; and *Wernicke's area* - named after the German neurologist Carl Wernicke (1848-1905) - located in the left cerebral cortex, is essential to the comprehension of *meaning* in language; cf., *Wernicke-Geschwind theory* - named after Carl Wernicke and the American neurologist

Norman Geschwind (1926-1984), attempts to explain how the brain processes information related to speech and other verbal behaviors]. In the modern *computational theory of mind* (e.g., Pinker, 1988; cf., Horst, 1996) - which is a central strategy/dogma at the heart of cognitive science, and is analogous to the *doctrine of atomism* in physics, the *germ theory* of disease in medicine, and *plate tectonics theory* in geology - it is posited that mental processes are formal manipulations of symbols/programs consisting of sequences of elementary processes made accessible by the information-processing capabilities of neural tissue; accordingly, *images* may be viewed as patterns of activation in a three-dimensional array of cells accessed by two overlaid coordinate systems (i.e., a *fixed* viewer-centered spherical coordinate system, and a *movable* object-centered or world-centered coordinate system); such a theoretical framework allows the researcher to generate, inspect, and transform *images*, as well as attend to locations and recognize shapes. The term *mental model* - introduced in 1943 by the Scottish psychologist Kenneth J. W. Craik (1914-1945) - refers to an internal representation having the same structure (in an abstract sense) as the aspect or portion of external reality that it represents; for example, the English psychologist David C. Marr's (1945-1980) *3-D model of visual perception*; the British psychologist Philip N. Johnson-Laird's (1936-) proposition that *mental models* are constructed by people to carry out inductive and deductive reasoning on the basis of propositions that are not themselves mental models by typically lead to mental models; and other psychologists' suggestions that *mental models* are needed to comprehend discourse, to experience consciousness, and the have a body image. The terms *metacognition* and *meta-memory* [which, again, may be traced back to Aristotle, and popularized more recently in the 1970s by the American psychologists John H. Flavell (1928-), Richard E. Nisbett (1941-), and Timothy D. Wilson (1951-)] - refer to beliefs and knowledge about one's own cognitive/mnemonic processes, and may be applied to regulation of one's cognitive functions, including planning, checking, and monitoring processes - such as planning for a cognitive strategy when memorizing material, checking accuracy in performing mental arithmetic, or monitoring one's comprehension during reading. Research in this area indicates, generally, that people often are unaware of the variables that influence their own choices, behavior, and evaluations, and typically - when questioned - produce verbal re-ports that may be misleading and filled with errors. The *theory of mental self-government*, developed by the American psychologist Robert J. Sternberg (1949-), is a model that attempts to reconcile intelligence and personality, and proposes a set of intellectual styles that are stated in terms of the various functions, forms, levels, and aspects of government, such as the legislative/executive, mon-archic/anarchic, and global/local dimensions. See also COOPERATIVE PRINCIPLE; EMPATHY THEORY; FREUD'S THEORY OF PERSONALITY; GESCHWIND'S THEORY; IMAGERY/MENTAL IMAGERY, THEORIES OF; INTELLIGENCE, THEORIES/LAWS OF; LEARNING THEORIES/ LAWS; MIND-BODY THEORIES; MIND/ MENTAL SET, LAW OF; PIAGET'S THEORY OF DEVELOPMENTAL STAGES.

REFERENCES

Piaget, J. (1929). *The child's conception of the world*. New York: Littlefield, Adams.

Aristotle. (1941). De anima (On the soul). In R. McKeon (Ed.), *The basic works of Aristotle*. New York: Random House.

Craik, K. J. W. (1943). *The nature of explanation*. Cambridge, UK: Cambridge University Press.

Morris, C. W. (1946). *Six theories of mind*. Chicago: University of Chicago Press.

Ryle, G. (1949). *The concept of mind*. London: Hutchinson.

Scher, J. M. (Ed.) (1966). *Theories of mind*. New York: Free Press.

Nisbett, R. E., & Wilson, T. D. (1977). Telling more than we can know: Verbal reports on mental processes. *Psychological Review, 84*, 231-259.

Premack, D., & Woodruff, G. (1978). Does the chimpanzee have a theory of mind" *The Behavioral and Brain Sciences, 4*, 515-526.

Vygotsky, L. S. (1978). *Mind in society: The development of higher psychological processes*. New York: Cambridge University Press.

Flavell, J. H. (1979). Metacognition and cognitive monitoring. *American Psychologist, 34*, 906-911.

Hebb, D. O. (1980). *Essay on mind*. Hillsdale, NJ: Erlbaum.

Sternberg, R. J. (1980). Sketch of a componential theory of human intelligence. *The Behavioral and Brain Sciences, 3*, 573-584.

Fodor, J. A. (1983). *The modularity of mind*. Cambridge, MA: M.I.T. Press.

Johnson-Laird, P. N. (1983). *Mental models: Towards a cognitive science of language, inference, and consciousness*. Cambridge, MA: Harvard University Press.

Leslie, A. M. (1987). Pretense and representation: The origins of "Theory of Mind." *Psychological Review, 94*, 412-426.

Richards, R. J. (1987). *Darwin and the emergence of evolutionary theories of mind and behavior*. Chicago: University of Chicago Press.

Astington, J., & Harris, P. L. (1988). *Developing theories of mind*. Cambridge, UK: Cambridge University Press.

Pinker, S. (1988). A computational theory of the mental imagery medium. In M. Denis, J. Engelkamp, & J. T. E. Richardson (Eds.), *Cognitive and neuropsychological approaches to mental imagery*. Dordrecht, The Netherlands: M. Nijhoff.

Wellman, H. M. (1990). *The child's theory of mind*. Cambridge, MA: M.I.T. Press.

Newell, A. (1991). Metaphors for mind, theories of mind: Should the humanities mind? In J. J. Sheehan & M. Sosna (Eds.), *Boundaries of humanity: Humans, animals, machines*. Berkeley, CA: University of California Press.

Whiten, A. (1991). *Natural theories of mind*. Oxford, UK: Blackwell.

Fodor, J. A. (1992). A theory of the child's theory of mind. *Cognition, 44,* 283-296.

Carruthers, P., & Smith, P. K. (1996). *Theories of theories of mind.* New York: Cambridge University Press.

Horst, S. (1996). *Symbols, computation, and intentionality: A critique of the computational theory of mind.* Berkeley/Los Angeles: University of California Press.

Lillard, A. (1998). Ethnopsychologies: Cultural variations in theories of mind. *Psychological Bulletin, 123,* 3-32.

Sigel, I. E. (1999). *Development of mental representation theories and applications.* Mahwah, NJ: Erlbaum.

Velde, van der, C. D. (2004). *The mind: Its nature and origin.* New York: Prometheus Books.

MIND/MIND MECHANISM, THEORY OF. See MIND-BODY THEORIES.

MIND'S EYE THEORY. See VISION/SIGHT, THEORIES OF.

MIND-STUFF THEORY. See MIND-BODY THEORIES.

MIND-TWIST HYPOTHESIS. See SCHIZOPHRENIA, THEORIES OF.

MINIMAL GROUP PARADIGM/SITUATION. See CONSTRUCTIVISM, THEORIES OF.

MINIMAL SOCIAL SITUATION EFFECT. See CONSTRUCTIVISM, THEORIES OF.

MINIMAX THEOREM/PRINCIPLE. See DECISION-MAKING THEORIES.

MINIMUM-RESOURCE/POWER THEORY. See INGROUP BIAS THEORIES.

MINITHEORIES OF EMOTION. See EMOTIONS, THEORIES/LAWS OF.

MIRROR NEURONS THEORY. Recent physiological research indicates that *mirror neurons,* first located in the rostral part of monkeys' ventral premotor cortex (called "area F5"), discharge under conditions both when the animal performs a goal-directed hand action and when it observes another individual performing the same, or a similar, action (i.e., "imitation gestures" and "affordances"). Also, in the same cortical area, *mirror neurons* have been found that respond to the observation of mouth actions. In humans, it has been shown that the observations of actions performed with the hand, the mouth, and the foot leads to activation of different sectors of Broca's area [a cortical region involved in the production of language - named after the French surgeon and anthropologist Paul Broca (1824-1880) who discovered its function in 1861] and premotor cortex, according to the effector involved in the observed action, and follows a somatotopic pattern resembling the classical motor cortex "homunculus." Such observations and results support the *mirror neuron theory* regarding the hypothesized existence of an execution-observation matching system (mirror neuron system). According to the *mirror neuron theory,* the mirror-neuron substrates promote language abilities in humans, where the neurons appear to represent a system that matches observed events to similar, internally generated actions and, in this way, forms a link between the observer and the actor. In one case (Weigand, 2002), a *theory of human dialogic interaction* is proposed that contains a methodology focusing on how the constitutive features of language are confirmed by the discharging of *mirror neurons.* Mirror neurons theory also hypothesizes that there is a very general, evolutionarily ancient mechanism, called the "resonance mechanism," through which pictorial descriptions of motor behaviors are matched directly on the observer's motor "representations" of the same behaviors. The "resonance mechanism" is posited to be a fundamental mechanism at the basis of inter-individual relations, including some behaviors commonly described as "imitative." Thus, *mirror neurons theory* has implications for several classes of behavior and related issues, including imitation, autism, language origins and production, motor activity, implicit-procedural memory, and learning. Inasmuch as the *mirror neurons* show activity in relation both to specific actions performed by self and matching actions performed by others, the theory provides a potential neurophysiological and neuropsychological "bridge between minds." See also AFFORDANCE THEORY; EMPATHY THEORY; HOMUNCULUS/SENSORY HOMUNCULUS HYPOTHESES; LANGUAGE ORIGINS, THEORIES OF; MIND/MENTAL STATES, THEORIES OF; NEURON/NEURAL/NERVE THEORY; RIGHT-SHIFT THEORY; SPEECH THEORIES.

REFERENCES

Miklosi, A. (1999). From grasping to speech: Imitation might provide a missing link. *Trends in Neurosciences, 22,* 151-152.

Wolf, S., Gales, M., Shane, E., & Shane, M. (2000). Mirror neurons, procedural learning, and the positive new experience: A developmental systems self psychology approach. *Journal of the American Academy of Psychophysics and Dynamic Psychiatry,* 28, 409-430.

Rizzolatti, G., Craighero, L., & Fadiga, L. (2002). The mirror system in humans. In M. Stamenov & V. Gallese (Eds.), *Mirror neurons and the evolution of brain and language.* Amsterdam, Netherlands: J. Benjamins.

Rizzolatti, G., Fadiga, L., Fogassi, L., & Gallese, V. (2002). From mirror neurons to imitation: Facts and speculations. In A. N. Meltzoff & W. Prinz (Eds.), *Imitative mind: Development, evolution, and brain bases.* New York: Cambridge University Press.

Vihman, M. M. (2002). The role of mirror neurons in the ontogeny of speech. In M. Stamenov & V. Gallese (Eds.), *Mirror neurons and the evolution of brain and language.* Amsterdam, Netherlands: J. Benjamins.

Weigand, E. (2002). Constitutive features f human dialogic interaction: Mirror neurons and what they tell us about human abilities. In M. Stamenov & V. Gallese (Eds.), *Mirror neurons and the evolution of brain and language.* Amsterdam, Netherlands: J. Benjamins.

Buccino, G., & Binkofski, F. (2004). The mirror neuron system and action recognition. *Brain & Language, 89,* 370-376.

MIRROR-REVERSAL PHENOMENON/ EFFECT. The issue of why a mirror - when we look into it - appears to reverse right and left, but not up and down, has been debated ever since the Greek philosopher Plato (c. 427-347 B.C.) answered it incorrectly in the 4th century B.C. More recently, explanations for the *mirror-reversal effect* have been proposed by the American science-writer Martin Gardner (1914-) and the English psychologist Richard L. Gregory (1923-). In the former case, Gardner suggests that because the image appears behind the mirror, the viewer performs a mental rotation of it, using the *vertical* axis of rotation; however, this explanation is lacking because the operation of mental rotation under these conditions takes too much time to account for the experienced phenomenon. In the latter case, Gregory offers a seemingly more satisfying and correct solution to the issue: a mirror doesn't reverse left and right or top and bottom, but in order to see the reflection of an object/person, the viewer has to rotate it physically about the *horizontal* axis to face the mirror; when this is done, the image appears left-right reversed because the object/person is left-right reversed relative to the orientation of the reflected image. Looking into a mirror, a mirror image of one's own face appears left-right reversed for the same reason; in order to look into a mirror, one perceptually turns horizontally through 180-de-grees relative to the reflected image that is about to be produced. In terms of *unconscious inference,* one cannot face the same way as the reflected image, because then the person would be facing away from the mirror (cf., Holmes, Roeckelein, & Olmstead, 1968). See also PERCEPTION (I. GENERAL), THEORIES OF; PERCEPTION (II. COMPARATIVE APPRAISAL), THEORIES OF; UNCONSCIOUS INFERENCE, DOCTRINE OF; VISION/SIGHT, THEORIES OF.

REFERENCES
Plato. (1953). Timaeus. *The dialogues of Plato*. 4 vols. Oxford, UK: Clarendon Press.
Gardner, M. (1964). *The ambidextrous universe*. New York: Basic Books.
Holmes, D. S., Roeckelein, J. E., & Olmstead, J. A. (1968). Determinants of tactual perception of finger-drawn symbols: Reappraisal. *Perceptual and Motor Skills*, *27*, 659-672.
Gregory, R. L. (1997). *Mirrors in mind*. New York: W. H. Freeman.

MISAPPLIED CONSTANCY, THEORY OF. See CONSTANCY HYPOTHESIS.

MISATTRIBUTION THEORY. See IMPRESSION FORMATION, THEORIES OF.

MISINFORMATION EFFECT. See EYEWITNESS MISINFORMATION EFFECT.

MISORIENTATION EFFECT. See PERCEPTION (I. GENERAL), THEORIES OF.

MISSING FUNDAMENTAL ILLUSION. See APPENDIX A.

MIXED CEREBRAL DOMINANCE THEORY. See NEURON/NEURAL/NERVE THEORY.

MNEMIC THEORY. See JUNG'S THEORY OF PERSONALITY.

MNEMON. See SHORT-TERM AND LONG-TERM MEMORY, THEORIES OF.

MODALITY EFFECTS. See FORGETTING/MEMORY, THEORIES OF; SHORT-TERM AND LONG-TERM MEMORY, THEORIES OF.

MODEL OF TIME AND BRAIN CONSCIOUSNESS. This theoretical *model of time and brain consciousness* describes how, where, and when the human brain receives and analyzes different perceptual stimuli. In particular, the model advances the notion that when stimuli occur very fast the brain perceives and remembers the more *useful* stimuli, and not necessarily in the sequence in which they occur. See also CONSCIOUSNESS, PHENOMENON OF; TIME, THEORIES OF.
REFERENCE
Dennett, D., & Kinsbourne, M. (1992). Time and the observer. The where and when of consciousness in the brain. *The Behavioral and Brain Sciences*, *15*, 183-201.

MODEL OF TIME IN ADOLESCENTS. This model for qualitative logic analysis in adolescents is based on the Newtonian concept of "absolute" or "physical" time. In this approach, within a psychological context, children's cognitive development is viewed as alternating between structurally stable and unstable cognitive systems where consistency or inconsistency of general and referred knowledge provides the foundation for the *model of time in adolescents*. See also DEVELOPMENTAL THEORY; TIME, THEORIES OF.
REFERENCE
Crepault, J. (1983). Models, reasoning, and notion of time in adolescents. *Cahiers de Psychologie Cognitive*, *3*, 387-392.

MODERN/CONTEMPORARY THEORIES OF INTELLIGENCE. See INTELLIGENCE, THEORIES/LAWS OF.

MODERN SYNTHETIC THEORY OF EVOLUTION. See DARWIN'S EVOLUTION THEORY/EVOLUTION, THEORY/LAWS OF.

MODIFICATION BY EXERCISE, LAW OF. See USE, LAW OF.

MODULARITY HYPOTHESIS/THEORY. See TRANSFER OF TRAINING, THORNDIKE'S THEORY OF.

MODULARITY OF MIND, DOCTRINE OF. See MIND/MENTAL STATES, THEORIES OF.

MODULARITY THEORIES. See MIND/MENTAL STATES, THEORIES OF.

MOLECULAR/CONTIGUITY THEORY.
See LEARNING THEORIES/LAWS.

MOLECULAR MODEL OF MEMORY.
See FORGETTING/MEMORY, THEORIES
OF.

MOLYNEUX'S QUESTION. See NATURE
VERSUS NURTURE THEORIES.

MOMENTARY INTEREST, LAW OF. See
CONDUCT, LAWS OF.

MONAD THEORY. See HERBART'S
DOCTRINE OF APPERCEPTION.

MONIST/MONISM THEORY. See MIND-
BODY THEORIES.

MONOAMINE HYPOTHESIS. See DE-
PRESSION, THEORIES OF.

MONOTONICITY. See SET THEORY.

MONOTYPIC EVOLUTION THEORY.
See RECAPITULATION THEORY/LAW.

**MONTAGUE'S THEORY OF TIME
PERCEPTION.** The American psychologist
W. Montague (1904) formulated a *theory of
time perception* that - although dependent on a
rather artificial view of consciousness -
marked a new stage at the turn of the 20th
century in the analysis of time by its conception of time as *change*, by a revised account of
the "specious present" (of William James) as
the relation of old content to new content, and
of the elaboration of "recognition" as the resultant of a "two-fold specious present" (cf.,
Dunlap, 1904). See also FRAISSE'S THE-
ORY OF TIME; JAMES' TIME THEORY;
TIME, THEORIES OF.
REFERENCES
Dunlap, K. (1904). Time. *Psychological Bulletin, 1*, 363-365.
Montague, W. (1904). A theory of time-
perception. *American Journal of
Psychology, 115*, 1-14.

MONTE CARLO FALLACY. See PROB-
ABILITY THEORY/LAWS.

MONTESSORI METHOD/THEORY. The
Italian physician (Italy's first *woman* physician) and educator Maria Montessori (1870-
1952) established an educational system in
Italy in the early 1900s that emphasized the
self-education of preschool children via the
development of initiative by means of freedom of action. The *Montessori method theory*
involves training in sense perception using
objects of different colors, shapes, and sizes,
and the development of eye-hand coordination
in exercises and games. Montessori's educational model offers a "prepared environment"
emphasizing the values of care for oneself and
one's property, and includes materials to promote sensory, motor, and language skills education, proceeding in strict sequence according to the teacher's demonstration and facilita-
tive leadership, and which combines work and
play for the children (cf., *synectics model* - an
educational strategy that focuses on creative
problem-solving and the development and
implementation of teaching methods that increase students' creativity, such as stressing
students' metaphorical thinking abilities).
Additionally, in the Montessori approach,
children have the freedom to select any materials to which they are attracted spontaneously; each learner's choices reveal the individual's unique potentialities, and children
may work independently or in groups. The
Montessori class typically carries no grades,
and rules are intended to encourage mutual
cooperation, rather than competition; pupils
are responsible for maintaining cleanliness
and order, and normally acquire self-discipline
rapidly. Typically, by age four or five years
old, Montessori children spontaneously burst
into writing activities; they learn spelling via a
movable alphabet. The Montessori curriculum
consists of science, history, geography, geometry, and arithmetic, and is based on the
finding that preschool children can solve problems and accomplish a great deal of intellectual work before actually entering formal
schooling (i.e., children from birth to six years
of age demonstrate that they possess an "absorbent mind"). In the Montessori nursery
schools, children are encouraged to establish
good student-teacher relationships that are
expected to generalize to subsequent relationships between the child and other adults in

society. See also INSTRUCTIONAL THE-ORY; LEARNING THEORIES/LAWS.

REFERENCES

Montessori, M. (1949). *The absorbent mind.* Madras, India: Theosophical Publications.

Montessori, M. (1964). *The Montessori method.* New York: Schocken Books.

Montessori, M. (1976). *Education for human development: Understanding Montessori.* New York: Schocken Books.

MONTY HALL PROBLEM/DILEMMA. See THREE-DOOR GAME SHOW PROBLEM/EFFECT.

MOON ILLUSION THEORY. Although any normal, healthy, sensory-intact individual may readily experience the *moon illusion* (i.e., the full moon on the horizon appears to be larger than the same moon when viewed directly overhead at its apex), there have been various speculations - ever since the ancient Greeks - as to how the illusion occurs. Foremost among such "best guesses" is the *moon illusion theory* that states that perceptual factors such as apparent size, afterimage, and distance act in the person's unconscious perceptual constructions by placing the horizon *sky* (which acts as a "background" surface for the "figure" of the moon) at a further distance than it really is (due to "familiar" cues on the horizon such as trees, the skyline, and buildings that serve as bases for distance estimations). Also, the moon on the horizon is perceived as being behind the various depth cues that are present, so the depth perception cue of "overlap" adds to the "erroneous" perception that the moon on the horizon is farther away. The *moon illusion* involves, also, the misapplication of the *principle of size constancy*; that is, much like the *afterimage* of the stimulus of a glowing light bulb that "appears" to be larger on a distant wall as compared to the *afterimage* on a near wall, the moon "appears" to be larger when the perception of its distance increases. In actuality, the perceiver's retinal size/image of the full moon is the same in all locations whether near or far. Thus, even though one's retinal image of the moon re-mains constant in size, the viewer makes a "perceptual error" and perceives the moon as being larger because it seems to be farther away on the erroneously-estimated distant horizon. Theoretical notions about illusions, such as the *moon illusion*, emphasize the fact that what humans "see" is not merely a simple objective ("veridical") reflection of the world, but involves one's subjective perceptual interpretation - often including "perceptual errors" - of stimuli in the environment. In a sense, illusions - such as the *moon illusion* - are "irresistible;" that is, in spite of the fact that we *know* - in a rational or intellectual way - about certain facts or features of our environment, we nevertheless make "perceptual errors" about our surroundings that are beyond our resistance or control and seem to be unavoidable. See also AFTERIMAGE LAW; CONSTANCY HYPOTHESIS; EM-MERT'S LAW; FIGURE-GROUND RELATIONSHIPS, PRINCIPLE OF.

REFERENCES

Boring, E. G. (1962). On the moon illusion. *Science, 137,* 902-906.

Kaufman, L., & Rock, I. (1962). The moon illusion. *Scientific American, 207,* 120-130.

Kaufman, L., & Kaurman, J. H. (2000). Explaining the moon illusion. *Proceedings of the National Academy of Sciences, USA, 97,* 500-505.

MORAL DETERMINISM, DOCTRINE OF. See DETERMINISM, DOCTRINE/THEORY OF.

MORAL DEVELOPMENT, PRINCIPLES/THEORY OF. See KOHLBERG'S THEORY OF MORALITY.

MORAL NIHILISM, DOCTRINE OF. See DETERMINISM, DOCTRINE/THEORY OF.

MORENO'S SOCIAL GROUP TECHNIQUES/THEORY. The Romanian-born American psychiatrist Jacob Levy Moreno (1889-1974) developed a number of techniques for studying and assessing the dynamics of *social group processes* and interpersonal relationships, among which are the following: *sociodrama* - a group-training and role-taking method that is a supplement to Moreno's *psychodrama technique* (i.e., a therapeutic format whereby people act out their own emotional problems/conflicts in front of an audience for the purpose of achieving objectivity and understanding of those issues), but that differs from *psychodrama* in its greater emphasis on audience participation and its greater focus on problems common to all members of the group rather than just one individual; the job of the director or leader of the *sociodrama* session is to keep the audience members continually on-track and involved; in *psychodrama*, which heralded the beginning of the various group therapy techniques, the person enacts on a stage a particular life situation that relates to the present maladjustment, where other individuals are assigned the roles of "significant others" in the person's life ("auxiliary egos"); theoretically, in acting out the situation, the individual reveals her personality structure, conflicts, and motivations, and cure is achieved via *catharsis* and the acquisition of greater spontaneity in meeting life's problems; *sociogram* - a chart/diagram indicating the network of the interrelationships of members in a social group, which is constructed typically by having group members indicate their choices/preferences and rejections of each other; in particular, the chart/diagram shows each member as represented by a circle, with an arrow pointing from each circle to another one, revealing which persons choose which others, and indicates those individuals who are chosen by many others, those who are chosen by only a few others, and cliques of mutually-chosen persons; and *sociometry* - refers to the quantitative assessment of the interrelations between members of a social group via the use of a *sociogram*. At a theoretical level concerning therapy, Moreno objected to the traditional Freudian approach as consisting of an artificial world of dreams and words occurring in therapists' offices; rather, in his *psychodrama technique*, Moreno focused on behaviors and activities that occur in natural settings, including the use of role-playing/train-ing techniques, and emphasized the factors of time, reality, and space. *Psychodrama* has several variations, among which are: *sociodrama* (centers on the active structuring of social worlds and collective ideologies; may involve role-playing for instruction and information rather than for therapy); *physiodrama* (blends physical conditioning with psychodrama); *axiodrama* (deals with understanding ethics and philosophical issues such as truth, beauty, and justice); *hypnodrama* (combines psychodrama with hypnosis); *psychomusic/psychodance* (integrates spontaneous music and/or dance into the psychodrama procedure); *group psychodrama* (in which all the actors are in the therapy group); and *family groups* (in which difficult familial and domestic issues and conflicts are acted out). See also CATHARSIS THEORY; FREUD'S THEORY OF PERSONALITY; PSYCHOPATHOLOGY, THEORIES OF; PSYCHOSOCIAL DEVELOPMENT, THEORY OF.

REFERENCES

Moreno, J. L. (1934/1953). *Who shall survive?* Beacon, NY: Beacon House.

Moreno, J. L. (1946/1959). *Psychodrama.* Beacon, NY: Beacon House.

Moreno, J. L. (1951). *Sociometry, experimental method, and the science of society.* Beacon, NY: Beacon House.

MORGAN'S CANON OR LLOYD MORGAN'S CANON. See PARSIMONY, LAW/PRINCIPLE OF.

MORINAGA MISALIGNMENT ILLUSION. See APPENDIX A.

MORITA THERAPY THEORY. The Japanese psychiatrist Shoma Morita (1874-1938) introduced this form of psychotherapy - based on *Buddhist doctrine* and beliefs - to psychology. The therapy initially involves four to seven days of complete bed rest without any activities/behaviors such as talking or even reading. Following this extended rest period, a program of progressively difficult and demanding activities and work is administered, often in a communal setting. The Morita approach has been employed, in particular, in treating individuals exhibiting somatoform disorders/symptoms, such as hypochondriasis, as manifested in intense preoccupation and anxiety about one's health. See also BUDDHISM/ZEN BUDDHISM, DOCTRINE OF;

CONDUCT, LAWS OF; PSYCHOSO-
MATICS THEORY.
REFERENCE
Morita, S. (1921). *Theory of nervosity and
neurasthenia*. Tokyo: Nibon Seish-
iningskuki.

**MORREALL'S THEORY OF HUMOR/
LAUGHTER.** The American philosopher/
teacher John Morreall (1982, 1983, 1987)
initially examines laughter by considering the
three traditional theories of laughter (i.e., superiority, incongruity/inconsistency, and re-
lief/tension-relief) in great length/detail, and
then attempts to construct a novel, comprehensive theory based on the older approaches.
Morreall suggests that three general features
of laughter situations should form the basis of
any new comprehensive theory: the *change of
psychological state* that the laughter undergoes; the *suddenness of psychological shifts*
and changes in laughter; and the *pleasantness
of psychological shifts* in laughter episodes.
By combining the three features together into
a general "formula" statement for characterizing laughter situations, Morreall contends that
laughter results from a "pleasant psychological shift or sudden change." According to
Morreall's approach, when we react to incongruity with emotions such as anger or fear (or
in cases when we try to make sense out of
incongruity), it disturbs us and we feel uneasy
about it. Such uneasiness partially comes from
a feeling of loss of control, and acts as a moti-
vator to regain control by doing something. In
the case of a negative emotion, the person
attempts to change the incongruous situation,
whereas in the case of "reality assimilation"
(that is, "puzzlement at the strange"), the person attempts to change his/her *understanding*
of it. Morreall argues that amusement contrasts sharply with both negative emotion and
reality assimilation: when amused, one is not
disturbed by incongruity, is not motivated to
change the incongruous situation in any way,
and does not feel a loss of control. Morreall
(1987) provides accounts of other contemporary *theories of laughter and humor*, viz, theories by Michael Clark (*theories of humor* are
distinguished from *theories of laughter*; develops the notion of the "formal object" of
amusement in a new version of the *incongru-*

ity theory); Roger Scruton (discusses a "pattern of thought" that is characteristic of
amusement and which consists of the enjoyable devaluing and demolition of something
human); and Mike W. Martin (challenges two
common perspectives about humor: that
amusement is the enjoyment of incongruity,
and that amusement is a type of aesthetic ex-
perience; suggests that the enjoyment of in-
congruity for its own sake is a *necessary* - but
not a *sufficient* - condition for amusement).
See also HUMOR, THEORIES OF; INCON-
GRUITY/INCONSISTENCY THEORIES OF
HUMOR; RELIEF/TENSION-RELIEF THE-
ORIES OF HUMOR; SUPERIORITY THEO-
RIES OF HUMOR.
REFERENCES
Morreall, J. (1982). A new theory of laughter.
Philosophical Studies, 42, 243-254.
Morreall, J. (1983). *Taking laughter seriously*.
Albany: State University of New
York Press.
Morreall, J. (Ed.) (1987). *The philosophy of
laugher and humor*. Albany: State
University of New York Press.

MOSAIC THEORY OF PERCEPTION.
See PERCEPTION (I. GENERAL), THEO-
RIES OF.

MOST LIKELY LAW. See EFFECT, LAW
OF.

**MOTIVATED FORGETTING, THEORY
OF.** See FORGETTING/MEMORY, THEO-
RIES OF.

MOTIVATIONAL HEDONIC THEORY.
See HEDONISM, THEORY/LAW OF.

**MOTIVATIONAL THEORIES OF HU-
MOR.** According to American psychologist
Jacob Levine (1969), *theories of humor* that
are based largely on experimental evidence
have employed, generally, three basic research
models to explain *motivational* (i.e., goal-
directed, drive-energized behaviors) sources
of humor: *cognitive-perceptual theory* (involves the resolution of incongruities); *behavior theory* (emphasizes the stimulus-response
aspects of learning and the reduction of basic
drives); and *Freudian/psychoanalytic theory*

(focuses on the gratification of the primary unconscious drives of aggression and sex in conjunction with the pleasures of mental activity). Levine notes that the most comprehensive humor theory - *Freudian/psychoanalytic theory* - has been the richest source of ideas for experimentalists who have employed parts of the theory to support either *cognitive-perceptual hypotheses* or *drive-reduction* assumptions regarding the humor experience. The American psychologists R. S. Wyer and J. E. Collins describe the following categories of *motivational theories of humor*: *arousal and arousal-reduction theories* - one set of theories here assumes that humor responses reflect a release/reduction in arousal (e.g., Sigmund Freud argued that humorous reactions to stimuli are motivated by needs to release tension or arousal, often aggression- or sex-related, that one inhibits from expressing directly; thus, individual differences in the humor elicited by different jokes or witticisms are assumed to reflect differences in the intensity of suppressed or repressed emotions that have become associated with stimuli of the type to which the jokes/witticisms are relevant); another approach in this category is the general conception of humor proposed by the American psychologist D. E. Berlyne who assumes an inverted-U relation between psychological arousal and the experience of pleasure (i.e., pleasure first increases with arousal increases up to some optimal value and then decreases, finally reaching a point at which the arousal becomes aversive; thus, a joke is conceived of as consisting of a scenario that induces arousal beyond its optimal level of pleasure, followed by a "punch line" that rapidly decreases the arousal to a more pleasurable level, and where the rapid increase in pleasantness is experienced as "humor;" unfortunately, there is little empirical evidence that decreases in physiologically measured arousal following a joke's "punch line" are correlated with subjective estimates of the humor elicited by the joke; *superiority and disparagement theories* – assume that people derive pleasure from feelings of mastery or control, where laughter or amusement at another person's deformities or misfortunes reflects an attempt to maintain or re-establish such feelings; thus, this approach regards amusement as a by-product of "downward social comparison;" further, it is suggested in this class of theories that humor is more apt to be elicited by the misfortunes of "socially-undesirable" people than by the misfortunes of "socially-esteemed" people; *incongruity resolution theories* - this common viewpoint assumes that humor is stimulated by the sudden awareness of an incongruity between two objects or events, or the concepts associated with them; *reversal theory* - this approach (e.g., Apter, 1982) takes both motivational and cognitive factors into account; it is applicable to many different types of humor-eliciting experiences, it states explicitly the conditions that are both necessary and sufficient for humor elicitation to occur, and it emphasizes processes of revising perceptions of people and objects in light of new information (including the assumptive factors of "non-replacement" and "diminishment"); and *comprehension-elaboration theory* - this approach (e.g., Wyer & Collins, 1992) consists of a series of eight postulates that relate to the comprehension of semantic and episodic information; the theory specifies the conditions in which humor is experienced in both non-social and social contexts, and takes into account the interpretation of a stimulus event that is necessary to elicit humor, the problem of identifying the humor-eliciting aspects of the interpretation, and the cognitive elaboration of the event's implications. See also APTER'S REVERSAL THEORY OF HUMOR; AROUSAL THEORY; BEHAVIORAL THEORIES OF HUMOR/LAUGHTER; COGNITIVE-PERCEPTUAL THEORIES OF HUMOR; FREUD'S THEORY OF WIT/HUMOR; HUMOR, THEORIES OF; SUPERIORITY THEORIES OF HUMOR; WYER AND COLLINS' THEORY OF HUMOR ELICITATION.

REFERENCES

Freud, S. (1905/1960). *Jokes and their relation to the unconscious.* New York: Norton.

Levine, J. (1956). Responses to humor. *Scientific American, 194,* 31-35.

Berlyne, D. E. (1969). Laughter, humor, and play. In G. Lindzey & E. Aronson (Eds.), *Handbook of social psychology.* Vol. 3. Reading, MA: Addison-Wesley.

Levine, J. (Ed.) (1969). *Motivation in humor.* New York: Atherton.

Apter, M. J. (1982). *The experience of motivation: The theory of psychological reversals.* London: Academic Press.

Wyer, R. S., & Collins, J. E. (1992). A theory of humor elicitation. *Psychological Review, 99,* 663-688.

MOTIVATION, THEORIES OF. The term *motivation* comes from the same Latin stem "mot-" (meaning "move") as does the term *emotion.* The term *motive* applies to any internal force that activates and gives direction to behavior. Other related terms emphasize different aspects of motivation. For example, *need* stresses the aspect of lack or want; *drive* emphasizes the impelling and energizing aspect; and *incentive* focuses on the goals of motivation (cf., *incentive theory* and *energization theory* - hold that the strength of an incentive varies with the energy level mobilized to obtain or avoid the incentive, where the higher the energization the greater the subjective desirability of a positive outcome; and *need-drive-incentive pattern theory* - posits that physiological needs are created by a state of deprivation that generates a drive to satisfy those needs and creates incentives that, in turn, lead to consummatory responses to achieve the things that reduce the drive). In general, *motivation theories* deal with the reasons that behaviors occur and refer to the internal states of the organism as well as the external goals (rewards and reinforcers) in the environment (cf., *process theories of motivation* - theories that attempt to account for the various factors that motivate individuals, and try to explain the mechanisms underlying motivation). Typically, motivation involves the energization of behavior and goal direction where a distinction is made between the organism's *disposition* and its *arousal.* For example, a generalized state of hunger, anxiety, or fear may be called the individual's *disposition,* whereas the specific act of behaving toward, or away from, a particular goal is the result of its *arousal.* The concept of *motivation,* as a fundamental influence in many phenomena, cuts across the various areas in psychology of intelligence, learning, personality, and thinking. Research on motivation has studied both the type and intensity (formerly called *dynamogenesis*) of motives. Various *theories of motivation* have originated in the area of *dynamic psychology,* which is a traditional approach used to study behavior by examining its underlying forces. The *dynamic* approach is contrasted with the *descriptive* approach, which is concerned with naming, classifying, and diagnosing - whereas the *dynamic* approach is concerned with tracing behavior to its origins in prior experience. The American psychologist Robert Sessions Woodworth (1869-1962) developed the eclectic approach called *dynamic psychology,* which focused on the motivational forces of behavior where a variety of viewpoints (e.g., behaviorism, Gestalt psychology, functionalism, and structuralism) were brought together to study the common/central concepts of *drive* and *motive* (cf., *structured learning theory* - a dynamic approach that predicts learning from the dynamic structure of the individual in terms of the stimulus and the ambient situation). *Dynamic psychology* argues that humans are not motivated simply by a few universal drives or instincts but that each person has a unique spectrum of natural capacities, wishes, needs, purposes, and emotions that set the personality in motion (cf., *dynamic-effect law* - holds that goal-directed behaviors become habitualized as they effectively achieve the goal under consideration, and emphasizes the importance of planning and the attainment of sub-goals within a plan rather than reinforcement of specific responses; the *dynamic interactionism model* - focuses attention on the reciprocal interplay between environmental/situational/stimulus events and the individual's or group's behaviors; and the *dynamic-situations principle* - states that any stimulus pattern undergoes changes continuously due to factors such as visceral changes, varied responses, and uncontrolled variables). The Freudian *psychoanalytical* approach emphasizes the interplay among drives as expressed in dynamic concepts such as *conflict,* *anxiety,* and *defense mechanisms.* The term *dynamic* attains its broadest meaning in the theoretical approach called *general systems theory,* even though *general systems theory* says little, specifically, about motivation and the motives that instigate and direct action. A great variety of *motivation theories* have been developed over the years and may be placed in three general categories: (1) *Hedonic/pleasure theories* - this forms the largest category of motivation theories and emphasizes the role of pleasure in organizing one's activities [(cf., *optimal level theories* - posit that the best methods of arousal are those that are pleasurable, and the best way to motivate an organism is via stimuli that are naturally motivating; and the *principle of optimal stimulation* - states that an organism tends to learn those responses that produce an optimal level of stimulation or excitation; either drive-arousal or drive-reduction may lead to the optimal stimulation level); the concept of *tension-reduction* is important here, where pleasure is derived from reduction of tension through the discharge of energy, expression of an instinct, or reduction in drive level; R. S. Woodworth introduced the term *drive* into American psychology, and it was used until the 1960s; distinctions have been made between the terms *needs* versus *drives/motives*, *innate* versus *acquired* drives, *primary* versus *secondary* drives, *viscerogenic* versus *psychogenic* drives, and *intrinsic* versus *extrinsic* motivation (cf., *justification theory* - states that rewards given by others, if the rewarded person views the reward as a bribe, tend to decrease the rewarded person's motivation); C. L. Hull and K. Spence use the concept of *drive* extensively in their *stimulus-response learning theory*, where the organism is viewed as having primary/innate drives such as pain and hunger, as well as learned or secondary drives such as fears and the desire for money; J. Dollard and N. Miller extended Hull's work and emphasized the role of learned, secondary *drives* in behavior; they also integrated *Hullian learning theory* concepts with *Freudian theory* concepts; the concept of *need* was studied, also, within the tension-reduction, hedonistic/pleasure approach]. (2) *Cognitive/ need-to-know theories* - although some cognitive approaches to motivation retain tension-reduction models (e.g., L. Festinger's *theory of cognitive dissonance*), other cognitive theories emphasize the motivation inherent in the *information-processing* activity of the organism (e.g., G. Kelly's *cognitive theory of motivation*). (3) *Growth/actualization theories* -

representative theories in this category are A. Angyal, K. Goldstein, A. Maslow, and C. Rogers, who share the common rejection of tension-reduction as the whole basis for human activity. Rather, these theorists emphasize the activities that lead to growth, self-fulfillment, and self-actualization in the individual's personality (cf., *Porter-Lawler integrated model of motivation* - named after the American organizational psychologists Lyman W. Porter and Edward E. Lawler, is a process theory suggesting that levels of motivation are based on the value that people place on rewards, and involving the concepts of *valence* and *expectancy*; this model interrelates process theory factors, performance rewards, and job satisfaction). In general, most psychologists agree that the more active is an organism, the higher the level of motivation; they agree, also, that motivation energizes the human and nonhuman organism, but they often disagree as to just how motivation causes the energization [cf., *action theory* - a theoretical position advanced by the American physician/ psychiatrist Abram Kardiner (1891-1981) in which the body is presumed to have an action-system/mechanism for fulfilling desires or needs; Kardiner assumed that traumatic neuroses were caused by damage to an action-system]. A fourth category of *motivation theory* concerns the role of *brain structures* and *neural mechanisms* in motivated behavior. Research in this area typically falls in the areas of *psychobiology*, *biopsychology*, or *neurobiology*. In one case, a part of the brain called the *reticular activating system* provides a physiological basis for the energizing effects of heightened motivation. Studies by G. Moruzzi and H. Magoun, and D. B. Lindsley, focused attention on the combined regions of the thalamus, reticular formation, and cortex in explaining both the specific and general arousal aspects of motivated organisms. On the other hand, the presumption of a single arousal system has been debated by researchers at both behavioral and physiological levels. The current impetus in research on motivation has shifted away from the study of generalized arousal/general motivation and toward the study of specific motives and motivations. See also ACHIEVEMENT MOTIVATION, THEORY OF; ACTIVATION/

AROUSAL THEORY; ADLER'S THEORY OF PERSONALITY; AGGRESSION, THEORIES OF; ANGYAL'S PERSONALITY THEORY; CONTROL/SYSTEMS THEORY; DRIVE, THEORIES OF; DYNAMOGENESIS, LAW OF; EMOTIONS, THEORIES/ LAWS OF; FESTINGER'S COGNITIVE DISSONANCE THEORY; FREUD'S THEORY OF PERSONALITY; GENERAL SYSTEMS THEORY; GOLDSTEIN'S ORGANISMIC THEORY; HEDONISM, THEORY/ LAW OF; HULL'S LEARNING THEORY; HUNGER, THEORIES OF; JUNG'S THEORY OF PERSONALITY; KELLY'S PERSONAL CONSTRUCT THEORY; LEARNING THEORIES/LAWS; LEWIN'S FIELD THEORY; MASLOW'S THEORY OF PERSONALITY; McDOUGALL'S HORMIC/ INSTINCT THEORY/DOCTRINE; PERSONALITY THEORIES; REINFORCEMENT THEORY; ROGERS' THEORY OF PERSONALITY; THIRST, THEORIES OF; WORK/CAREER/OCCUPATION, THEORIES OF.

REFERENCES

Woodworth, R. S. (1918). *Dynamic psychology*. New York: Columbia University Press.

Leeper, R. (1948). A motivational theory of emotion to replace "emotion as disorganized response." *Psychological Review*, 55, 5-21.

Webb, W. (1948). A motivational theory of emotions. *Psychological Review, 55*, 329-335.

Moruzzi, G., & Magoun, H. (1949). Brain stem reticular formation and activation of the EEG. *Electroencephalography and Clinical Neurophysiology, 1*, 455-473.

Dollard, J., & Miller, N. (1950). *Personality and psychotherapy: An analysis in terms of learning, thinking, and culture*. New York: McGraw-Hill.

Lindsley, D. B. (1951). Emotion. In S. S. Stevens (Ed.), *Handbook of experimental psychology*. New York: Wiley.

Allport, G. (1953). The trend in motivational theory. *American Journal of Orthopsychology, 23*, 107-119.

Leuba, C. (1955). Toward some integration of learning theories: The concept of optimal stimulation. *Psychological Reports*, 1, 27-33.

Koch, S. (1956). Behavior as "intrinsically" regulated: Work notes towards a pretheory of phenomena called "motivational." In M. Jones (Ed.), *Current theory and research in motivation*. Vol. 4. Lincoln: University of Nebraska Press.

Spence, K. (1958). A theory of emotionally-based drive (D) and its relation to performance in simple learning situations. *American Psychologist, 13*, 131-141.

Hunt, J. (1965). Intrinsic motivation and its role in psychological development. In D. Levine (Ed.), *Nebraska symposium on motivation*. Vol. 13. Lincoln: University of Nebraska Press.

Routtenberg, A. (1968). The two-arousal hypothesis: Reticular formation and limbic system. *Psychological Review, 75*, 51-80.

Arnold, W., & Levine, D. (Eds.) (1969). *Nebraska symposium on motvation*. Lincoln: University of Nebraska Press.

Bolles, R. (1975). *Theory of motivation*. New York: Harper & Row.

Mook, D. (1987). *Motivation: the organization of action*. New York: Norton.

Eccles, J. S., & Wigfield, A. (2002). Motivational beliefs, values, and goals. *Annual Review of Psychology, 53*, 109-132.

Beck, R. C. (2004). *Motivation: Theories and principles*. Upper Saddle River, NJ: Pearson/Prentice Hall.

MOTORIC REPRODUCTION PROCESS HYPOTHESIS. See MOTOR LEARNING/ PROCESS THEORIES.

MOTOR LEARNING/PROCESS THEORIES. In his emphasis on the role of *feedback* in movement regulation, the American psychologist J. A. Adams (1971) gave a new direction to the topic of *motor learning* and initiated his *closed loop theory*, which was developed on the basis of motor-learning empirical laws employing simple and slow movements of linear positioning. The critical aspects of Adams' theory rest upon the following: the feedback production capacity; the comparison of the latter to a "correctness reference" called the *perceptual trace*; and the error correction resulting from the difference between the received feedback and the "correctness reference." According to Adams, "knowledge of results" is an obligatory source of information for the correction of motor responses, and motor learning improvement depends on the degree of accuracy – qualitatively and quantitatively - in knowledge of results. Such a structure gives Adams' theory its "closed-loop" quality, and reveals its historical continuity with *closed-loop theory* from the field of engineering, which uses peripheral feedback as a source of information about the system's response. However, Adams' theory does not seem to be able to solve the two main problems of motor learning: the novelty and the storage problems; the theory is limited, also, to linear positioning studies that are simple, slow, and generally executed in the laboratory. Additionally, the theory ties motor learning to the stereotyped repetition of movement in identical environmental conditions, which causes a practice-organization problem (cf., the *motoric reproduction process hypothesis* - suggests that the reproduction of motoric processes calls for capacities permitting a person to translate what is learned through observation into actual performance, such as reproducing the notion of rolling a bowling ball down the alley following a demonstration by an experienced bowler). In reacting to Adams' theory, the American psychologist R. A. Schmidt (1975) developed his *motor schema theory*, which includes his notion of a "generalized motor program" that is formed in the central nervous system and which contains stored muscle commands with all of the details necessary to execute a movement. Schmidt's "generalized motor program" is an abstract mnemonic structure that, once activated, allows for the execution of similar movements; and the selection of movement parameters devolves to a "motor schema" function, which represents a rule and determines the category of stimuli belonging to the proper group. The relationship between Schmidt's "generalized motor program" and the "motor schema" is hierarchical, where the former selects the appropriate program for the execution of a movement, and the latter assigns the principal parameters needed for its application with regard to learning situation requirements (cf., Henry & Rogers, 1960). However, the problems of storage and novelty seem to be as applicable to Schmidt's theory as they are to Adams' theory. Another theory, developed by the Pakistan-born American psychologist Akhter Ahsen, and called *Ahsen's Triple Code Model (ISM)*, has been offered as an active *mental imagery model for motor learning and performance* (cf., Washburn, 1916). In Ahsen's model, three important operational principles are represented by the acronym *ISM* (image-somatic response-meaning); the model is a theoretical approach that is holistic, experiential, and grounded in imagery, and provides a meaningful framework for research in the field of motor learning and performance. *ISM* represents not only the separate roles of the three active components that describe the operations of mental imagery, but also posits their coalescence as an integrated dynamic experience (cf., Ahsen, 1984). In Ahsen's view, mental imagery is a kind of simulator of action/motor expression that is based on real-life actions and potential actions in which a person may engage; as a simulator, mental imagery provides a kinesthetic feel to it that is not merely the output of some abstract computational machine, but provides the full-bodied experiences that have the qualities of texture and a felt-sense of three-dimensional depth. Essentially, Ahsen's model is able to account for not only why mental practice/mental imagery affects motor performance, but also which components may be employed during mental rehearsal in order to produce successful outcomes. Thus, Ahsen's model suggests that mental practice (of come motor performance/learning) is compos-ed of three components: the *imagery* (*I*) of the act itself (and the manner in which the person interacts with the image *as if* they were acting in the real world); the *meaning* (*M*) which refers to the way the performer understands how the motor/skill *should* be done; and the *somatic* (*S*) response the person has when becoming aware of what is required of him or her. Ashen's *ISM* has been identified as an approach that provides solutions in each of the areas where Adams' and Schmidt's motor learning theories have been found to be deficient (cf., Taktek & Hochman, 2004). In the subject areas of motor coordination, kinematics, human locomotion, visual motion, motion perception, handwriting/drawing movements, and arm-pointing movements, the *two-thirds power law* (e.g., Lacquanti, Terzuolo, & Viviani, 1983) has been invoked as a quantitative descriptive/explanatory device. For example, the *two-thirds power law*, a specific power law/function, describes the data/results of studies where the velocity of execution of handwriting/drawing movements depends on the global metric properties of the motor movement (e.g., size, linear extent), and where the instantaneous velocity depends, also, on the local curvature of the trajectory (i.e., on the differential geometrical properties of the person's movement). In such cases, the velocity of movement execution increases with the radius of curvature, implying the presence of a built-in tendency of a person's motor-control system to keep angular velocity relatively constant, and describable by a specific exponent of the power law. Thus, in general terms, the *two-thirds power law* describes and quantifies the relationship between movement/motor velocity and curvature of the endpoint path of movement, and is able to integrate both mechanical and neural factors in motor learning/process contexts. See also IMAGERY/MENTAL IMAGERY, THEORIES OF; LEARNING THEORIES/LAWS; MOTOR THEORY OF THINKING/CONSCIOUSNESS; NEW STRUCTURALISM THEORY/PARADIGM; STEVENS' POWER LAW.

REFERENCES

Washburn, M. F. (1916). *Movement and mental imagery: Outlines of a motor theory of the complexer mental processes*. Boston: Houghton Mifflin.

Henry, F. M., & Rogers, D. E. (1960). Increased response latency for complicated movements and a "memory drum." Theory of neuro-motor reaction. *Research Quarterly*, *31*, 448-458.

Adams, J. A. (1971). A closed-loop theory of motor learning. *Journal of Motor Behavior*, *3*, 111-150.

Schmidt, R. A. (1975). A schema theory of discrete motor skill learning. *Psychological Review*, *82*, 225-260.

Lacquaniti, F., Terzuolo, C., & Viviani, P. (1983). The law relating the kinematic and figural aspects of drawing movements. *Acta Psychologica*, *54*, 115-130.

Soechting, J. F., & Lacquaniti, F. (1983). Modification of trajectory of a pointing movement in response to a change in target location. *Journal of Neurophysiology*, *49*, 548-564.

Ahsen, A. (1984). ISM: The triple code model for imagery and psychophysiology. *Journal of Mental Imagery*, *8*, 15-42.

Flach, R., Knoblich, G., & Prinz, W. (2004). The two-thirds power law in motion perception. *Visual Cognition*, *11*, 461-481.

Taktek, K., & Hochman, J. (2004). Ahsen's triple code model as a solution to some persistent problems within Adams' closed loop theory and Schmidt's motor schema theory. *Journal of Mental Imagery*, *28*, 115-158.

MOTOR-PRIMACY THEORY. See NEURON/NEURAL/NERVE THEORY.

MOTOR SCHEMA THEORY. See MOTOR LEARNING/PROCESS THEORIES.

MOTOR THEORY OF MEANING. See MEANING, THEORIES/ASSESSMENT OF.

MOTOR THEORY OF SPEECH PERCEPTION. See SPEECH THEORIES.

MOTOR THEORY OF THINKING/CONSCIOUSNESS. See WHORF-SAPIR HYPOTHESIS/THEORY.

MOWRER'S THEORY. The American psychologist Orval Hobart Mowrer (1907-1982) was a neo-Hullian who developed a *two-factor learning theory* that describes the operation of two principles of reinforcement: *instrumental responses* involving the skeletal musculature that are mediated by the central nervous system and are reinforced and strengthened by drive reduction; and *emotions* such as fear and nausea involving the smooth musculature (e.g., glands, viscera, vascular tissue) that are mediated by the autonomic nervous system and are learned by sheer temporal contiguity of a conditioned stimulus to the elicitation of the emotional response. An example of *two-factor learning theory* in animal learning is the pairing of a buzzer with painful shocks in order to set up an association between the animal's state of fear and the buzzer and, at the same time, provide the opportunity for the animal to make some active avoidance response (such as jumping across a barrier separating two compartments in the cage) that, when performed, becomes reinforced through the hypothesized operation of *fear-reduction*. Mowrer also offered an analysis of *punishment* that involves a *passive* state in the organism where the animal reduces fear and avoids shock by doing nothing in the punishment situation. This is in contrast to the *active* avoidance situation where the animal reduces fear and avoids shock by doing something such as jumping out of the shock-compartment of the cage (cf., the *Kamin effect* - animals trained on an avoidance task, when tested at different times after training, show a U-shaped curve of performance: they perform well at first and much worse after an hour or so; performance recovers after about two hours). In his later work, Mowrer refined his analysis of *instrumental behavior* where positive habits are interpreted in the same way as punished habits, except the sign of the anticipated outcome is reversed. That is, the *proprioceptive feedback* from making a correct response is in "favorable" contiguity to the positive reinforcement (i.e., drive-reduction) so that it acquires secondary reinforcing capabilities via *contiguity conditioning*. Analogous to the way incipient punished responses are deterred, the incipient rewarded responses are pushed on through to completion because their proprioceptive response pat-tern is conditioned to the emotion of "hope" (that is, the anticipation/hope of reward). In Mowrer's revision, there is not a direct associative con-

nection between the external stimulus and the *instrumental response* but, rather, feedback stimulation from the correct response becomes conditioned to a positive emotion ("hope") that excites, or gives energy to, the completion of that response (cf., Mowrer's *integrity therapy theory*, in a wider clinical context, which posits that neuroses are a form of moral failure or "sins," where individuals should be concerned with taking responsibility for their committed misdeeds, and strive to live up to an acceptable ethical code). Today, it appears that even though Mowrer's classification system for reinforcers and punishers is *not* discredited, it is very likely that his *drive-reduction hypothesis* may be somewhat empirically inadequate. See also CONTIGUITY, LAW OF; EMOTIONS, THEORIES/LAWS OF; GUTHRIE'S THEORY OF BEHAVIOR; HELSON'S ADAPTATION-LEVEL THEORY; HULL'S LEARNING THEORY; INSTRUMENTAL CONDITIONING, PRINCIPLES OF; KAMIN EFFECT; MOTIVATION, THEORIES OF; PRE-MACK'S PRINCIPLE/LAW; PUNISHMENT, THEORIES OF.

REFERENCES

Mowrer, O. H. (1947). On the dual nature of learning - A re-interpretation of "conditioning" and "problem-solving." *Harvard Educational Review*, *17*, 102-148.

Mowrer, O. H. (1956). Two-factor learning theory reconsidered, with special reference to secondary reinforcement and the concept of habit. *Psychological Review*, *63*, 114-128.

Mowrer, O. H. (1960a). *Learning theory and behavior*. New York: Wiley.

Mowrer, O. H. (1960b). *Learning theory and the symbolic processes*. New York: Wiley.

Sheffield, F. (1965). Relation between classical conditioning and instrumental learning. In W. Prokasy (Ed.), *Classical conditioning: A symposium*. New York: Appleton-Century-Crofts.

MOZART EFFECT. This conjecture, called the *Mozart effect*, states that a temporary increase in one's *spatial* abilities occurs immediately after listening to the music of Wolfgang Amadeus Mozart. *Spatial reasoning* abilities are involved in any task that requires the actual or imagined (mental imagery) manipulation of objects in space (e.g., the mental rotation of objects such as the movement of pieces of a jigsaw puzzle, or the mental activity involved in reading a map). Recently, a team of researchers (Rauscher, Shaw, & Ky, 1993, 1995) found that three dozen college students increased their average *spatial reasoning* scores (with a supposed equivalency of about 8 to 9 IQ points) after listening to one of Mozart's sonatas ("Sonata for Two Pianos in D Major"). The increase in students' *spatial reasoning* ability, however, was only temporary (lasting fewer than 15 minutes). Moreover, when the same students sat in silence, or listened to a relaxation tape, the effect did not occur (i.e., there was *no* increase in their *spatial reasoning* abilities). Even though there have been numerous subsequent studies that have failed to demonstrate the *Mozart effect* (cf., Steele, Brown, & Stoecker, 1999), the mass media hastily reported that "simply listening to Mozart can make people smarter." The cumulative research regarding the *Mozart effect*, so far, underscores the importance in scientific psychology of the successful replication of experimental results, and highlights the self-correcting nature of the scientific process. To date, the numerous replication *failures* in finding the *Mozart effect* seriously challenges the validity of this supposed phenomenon.

REFERENCES

Rauscher, F., Shaw, G., & Ky, K. (1993). Music and spatial task performance. *Nature, 365*, 611.

Rauscher, R., Shaw, G., & Ky, K. (1995). Listening to Mozart enhances spatial-temporal reasoning. *Neuroscience Letters, 185*, 44-47.

Steele, K. M., Brown, J. D., & Stoecker, J. A. (1999). Failure to confirm the Rauscher and Shaw description of recovery from the Mozart effect. *Perceptual and Motor Skills, 88*, 843-848.

MRS. PARKINSON'S LAW. See MURPHY'S LAW.

M THEORY. See FINAL THEORY.

MULLER EFFECT. See VISION/SIGHT, THEORIES OF.

MULLER-LYER ILLUSION. See APPENDIX A.

MULLER-SCHUMANN LAW. See SKAGGS-ROBINSON HYPOTHESIS.

MULLER'S COLOR VISION THEORY. See COLOR VISION, THEORIES/LAWS OF.

MULLER'S DOCTRINE OF SPECIFIC NERVE ENERGIES. = specific nerve energies, law of. The German physiologist Johannes Peter Muller (1801-1858) formulated the *doctrine/theory/law of specific nerve energies* in 1826, which holds that each sensory nerve, however stimulated, gives rise to only one type of sensory process and a single quality of sensation. Thus, the *law of specific energies of nerve fibers* holds that the quality of sensation depends on the type of fiber excited, not on the form of physical energy that initiates the process [cf., *Bowditch's law* - named after the American physiologist Henry Pickering Bowditch (1840-1911), is the principle that the nerves cannot be fatigued: they will keep transmitting nerve impulses no matter how many consecutive times they are stimulated]. Muller's *law of specific nerve energies* is expressed vividly by the imaginary or hypothetical scenario that if one crosses the auditory and optic nerves, one would then be able to *see thunder* and *hear lightning*. Earlier (in 1811), the Scottish anatomist Sir Charles Bell (1774-1842) suggested that each sensory nerve conveys one kind of quality or experience (e.g., visual nerves carry only visual impressions, auditory nerves carry only auditory impressions, etc.). Some researchers have argued that Bell's name, rather than Muller's, should be attached to the law. However, Muller's contribution lies in giving the notion of *specific energies of nerves* explicit and precise formulation. Application of the law occupies almost two-percent of an entire volume of Muller's *Handbuch* (Muller, 1833-1840). Muller actually formulated the *doctrine of* *specific nerve energies* under ten laws, but the essential generalization is that the various qualities of experience derive not from differences in the physical and environmental stimuli that impinge on us but from the specific neural structures that each excites. Muller's particular form of the *doctrine of specific nerve energies* was discredited eventually by later physiological research. The plasticity of Muller's idea, however, gave it long life. The concept of *specific nerve energies*, at one time or another, has been explicitly referred to as a *doctrine*, a *hypothesis*, a *theory*, and a *law/principle*, and it has a rather consistent and even record of citation in textbooks across 112 years of psychology (cf., Roeckelein, 1996). The *doctrine of specific nerve energies* made attempts at precision in the quest for neural foundations for sensory experience and, consequently, it was highly useful as a guiding hypothesis in experimental psychology. See also ALL-OR-NONE LAW/PRINCIPLE.

REFERENCES

Bell, C. (1811). *Idea of a new anatomy of the brain*. London: Strahan & Preston.

Muller, J. P. (1833-1840). *Handbuch der physiologie des menschen*. 3 vols. Coblenz: Holscher.

Muller, J. P. (1842). *Elements of physiology*. London: Taylor & Walton.

Roeckelein, J. E. (1996). Citation of *laws* and *theories* in textbooks across 112 years of psychology. *Psychological Reports, 79*, 979-998.

MULLER'S ZONE THEORY. See COLOR VISION, THEORIES/LAWS OF.

MULTIATTRIBUTE DECISION-MAKING, THEORY OF. See ELIMINATION BY ASPECTS THEORY.

MULTIFACTOR THEORY OF THIRST. See THIRST, THEORIES OF.

MULTIMODAL THEORY OF INTELLIGENCE. See INTELLIGENCE, THEORIES/LAWS OF.

MULTIPLE CONTROL PRINCIPLE. See LASHLEY'S THEORY.

MULTIPLE FACTOR THEORY. See INTELLIGENCE, THEORIES/LAWS OF.

MULTIPLE INTELLIGENCES THEORY. See INTELLIGENCE, THEORIES/LAWS OF.

MULTIPLE OSCILLATOR MODEL. See SCALAR TIMING THEORY.

MULTIPLE RESPONSE PRINCIPLE. See HULL'S LEARNING THEORY.

MULTIPLE TRACE HYPOTHESIS. See EYEWITNESS MISINFORMATION EFFECT.

MULTIPLICATIVE LAW OF PROBABILITY. See PROBABILITY THEORY/LAWS.

MULTIPLICATIVE MODEL. See CONJOINT MEASUREMENT THEORY.

MULTISTAGE THEORIES. See ERICKSON'S THEORY OF PERSONALITY; FREUD'S THEORY OF PERSONALITY; KOHLBERG'S THEORY OF MORALITY; PIAGET'S THEORY OF DEVELOPMENTAL STAGES.

MUNSTERBERG ILLUSION. See APPENDIX A.

MUNSTERBERG'S THEORY OF PERCEPTUAL FLUCTUATIONS. The German-born American applied psychologist Hugo Munsterberg (1863-1916) proposed that in visual-perception experimental situations, participants - when asked to regard a weak, barely-visible light under instructions to report when the light is visible and when it is not - typically show responses that have an alternating character where positive responses (e.g., "the light is visible") alternate with negative responses (e.g., "the light is not visible"). Oscillating behavior of this sort traditionally has been called *fluctuation of attention*, and may continue in a more or less rhythmical way for many cycles in a given experiment. *Fluctuations of behavior* occur not only to weak visual stimuli but to weak stimuli in the other senses, as well. *Munsterberg's theory* is significant mainly because of his conclusion that *fluctuations* to visual stimuli are due to changes in *accommodation* and *fixation*, even though later studies indicate that *accommodation* changes do not account exclusively for the oscillations. Other *theories of perceptual fluctuations* include those of E. Pace who introduced the concept of *light adaptation* as a determinant of fluctuations, and B. Hammer and C. E. Ferree who added the factor of *eye movements* as complementary influences to fluctuations. Presumably, *eye movements* - in causing stimulation to shift to new portions of the retina - operate to restore sensitivity that is diminished, in turn, by *adaptation*. However, as evidence against *eye movement theory* in such cases, H. S. Liddell failed to find any relation between *eye movements* and *fluctuations*, a fact that was verified later by J. P. Guilford. See also ACCOMMODATION, LAW/PRINCIPLE OF; ADAPTATION, PRINCIPLES/LAWS OF; APPARENT MOVEMENT, PRINCIPLES/THEO-RIES OF; CONSTRUCTIVIST THEORY OF PERCEPTION; EYE-MOVEMENT THEO-RY; PERCEPTION (I. AND II.), THEORIES OF.

REFERENCES

Munsterberg, H. (1889). *Beitrage zur experimentellen psychologie.* Freiburg, Germany: Mohr.

Pace, E. (1893). Zur frage der schwankungen der aufmerksamkeit mach versuchen mit der massonschen scheibe. *Philosophische Studien, 8*, 388-401.

Hammer, B. (1905). Zur experimentellen kritik der theorie der aufmerksamkeitsschwankungen. *Zeitschrift fur Psychologie, 37*, 363-376.

Ferree, C. E. (1913). Fluctuation of liminal visual stimuli of point area. *American Journal of Psychology, 24*, 378-409.

Liddell, H. S. (1919). Eye-movement during the fluctuation of attention. *American Journal of Psychology, 30*, 241-252.

Guilford, J. P. (1927). "Fluctuations of attention" with weak visual stimuli. *American Journal of Psychology, 38*, 534-583.

MURPHY'S BIOSOCIAL THEORY. = biosocial theory. The American psychologist Gardner Murphy (1895-1979) formulated a *biosocial theory of personality* that was popular in the 1950s and was eclectic in nature by combining holistic, evolutionary, functional, and biosocial concepts into a comprehensive psychological system [cf., the Swiss-American physician Adolf Meyer's (1866-1950) integrative *theory of psychobiology*, which emphasizes the importance of biological, social, and psychological influences on the individual; and the American physician (and the first American to become a psychoanalyst) Trigant Burrow's (1875-1950) *phyloanalytic/phylobiological theory* that attempts to unite biological and social factors to form a total personality view of individuals, as well as a total view of human societies]. Although Murphy's approach overlaps with the theories of other psychologists, his systematization efforts include some core ideas that are his own. For example, Murphy emphasizes sensory and activity needs in describing biological aspects of motivation, and he suggests that an organism's curiosity-behavior emanates from a brain drive. Other concepts that are adopted and expanded by Murphy are: *autism* - where cognitions move toward satisfaction of needs; *field theory* - in which personality is viewed as an organized field within a larger field involving a reciprocity of incoming and outgoing energies; *feedback* - where reality-testing based on outside information helps one escape from "autistic self-deception;" a *three-phase developmental theory* - in which all reality moves from an undifferentiated, homogeneous state, through a differentiated, heterogeneous reality, to an integrated and structured reality; and *canalization* - where needs tend to become more specific as a result of being satisfied in specific ways. Murphy's *canalization hypothesis* (cf., Edwin Holt's *canalization hypothesis*) is one of his most important *learning theory* formulations and refers to the progressive differentiation ("narrowing") of the general and preferred ways in which one's drives may be satisfied. The idea of progressive "narrowing" of drives is invoked, also, in Sigmund Freud's concept of *cathexis*. Murphy borrowed the term *canalization* from the French physician and psychiatrist Pierre Janet (1859-1947), and it has come today to have many meanings, depending on the context in which it is used. In the area of neurology, *canalization* refers to the formation and neural connections that facilitate the flow of the neural current. In evolutionary genetics, *canalization* is the idea that a particular epigenetic capability or behavior pattern continues to be observed in situations of less-than-optimal environments or, if disrupted by extreme conditions, to be relatively easy to restore when conditions are once more made appropriate (cf., the developmental biologist Conrad H. Waddington's (1905-1975) definition of *canalization* that refers to the capacity to produce a particular definite end-result in spite of a certain variability both in the initial selection and in the course of development of organs and tissues). In the area of learning, comparative, and physiological psychology, the *canalization hypothesis* of E. Holt and G. Murphy were attempts to break away from the *associationistic model* and *the Pavlovian conditioning* procedure as explanations for deeply ingrained and strongly motivated action patterns. Murphy's *canalization hypothesis* provides a conceptualization of drive modification as a function of repeated satisfaction by stimuli within a limited range and is distinguished from the phenomenon of *conditioning*, which involves what the English physiologist Charles S. Sherrington (1861-1952) called *preparatory responses* - whereas Murphy's *canalization hypothesis* involves *consummatory responses*. Essentially, the *canalization hypothesis* attempts to account for the process whereby an originally neutral stimulus acquires positive value as a satisfier and for narrowing the range from within which a drive may be satisfied. The hypothesis accounts for the acquisition of tastes and preferences, it illuminates conceptions of motivation and learning, it represents the biosocial process of development, and it gives important insights into numerous psychological phenomena such as *conflict* and *ambivalence*. See also ASSOCIATION, LAWS/PRINCIPLES OF; CONFLICT, THEORIES OF; FREUD'S THEORY OF PERSONALITY; GOLDSTEIN'S ORGANISMIC THEORY; MULTISTAGE THEORIES; PAVLOVIAN CONDITIONING PRINCIPLES, LAWS, AND THEORIES.

REFERENCES

Janet, P. (1898). *Nevroses et idees fixes*. Paris: Alcan.

Sherrington, C. S. (1906). *The integrative action of the nervous system*. New Haven, CT: Yale University Press.

Janet, P. (1923). *La medecine psychologique*. Paris: Flammarion.

Holt, E. (1931). *Animal drive and learning process: An essay toward radical empiricism*. New York: Holt.

Murphy, G. (1947). *Personality: A biosocial approach to origins and structure*. New York: Harper.

Meyer, A. (1957). *Psychobiology: A science of man*. Springfield, IL: Thomas.

Waddington, C. H. (1975). *The evolution of an evolutionist*. Ithaca, NY: Cornell University Press.

MURPHY'S LAW(S). These principles are most likely based on a fictional, apocryphal or legendary Irish character and, in the first sense, these "laws" seem to share a common connotative ground consistent generally with the lexicological concept of *Murphy* (any of a number of confidence games in which a victim, for example, is left with a sealed envelope supposedly containing money, but which contains only scrap paper cut to the same dimensions as bone fide paper money) in which one person is duped adroitly by another person. In a second sense, *Murphy's laws* contain the following fatalistic observations and pessimistic predictions/aphorisms: "Anything that can possibly go wrong will go wrong;" "Anything one plans will cost more and take longer in its execution;" and "Anything that goes wrong will do so at the worst possible time." Numerous psychologists, especially experimental psychologists, may corroborate the veracity of *Murphy's laws* based on their own personal research activities and experiments. If one surfs the "world wide web" and enters the term *Murphy's law(s)* into a search engine, such as "Google," it may be seen that there are several speculations as to the origins of the law, and there are virtually thousands of epigrammatic versions of *Murphy's law*, ranging from "A" to "Z," often in eponymous form.

Examples here include: Ade's Law - anybody can win, unless there happens to be a second entry; Baker's Law - misery no longer loves company; nowadays it insists on it; Bartz's Law - the more ridiculous a belief system, the higher the probability of its success; Beauregard's Law - when you're up to your nose, keep your mouth shut; Berkeley's Law - most general statements are false, including this one; Clapton's Law - for every credibility gap there is a gullibility fill; Cohen's Law - what really matters is the name you succeed in imposing on the facts, not the facts themselves; Cole's Law - thinly sliced cabbage; and Wyszowski's First Law - no experiment is reproducible. The Egyptian-born American economist Charles Philip Issawi (1916-) formulated several "laws," among which are the following: *Law of Consumption Patterns* - other people's patterns of expenditure and consumption are highly irrational and slightly immoral; *Law of Cynics* - cynics are right nine times out of ten; what undoes them is their belief that they are right ten times out of ten; *Law of the Social Sciences* - by the time a social science theory is formulated in such a way that it can be tested, changing circumstances have already made it obsolete; *Law of Social Motion* - in any dispute, the intensity of feeling is inversely proportional to the value of the stakes at issue; that is why academic politics are so bitter [cf., *Sayre's law* - named after the American political scientist Wallace S. Sayre (1905-1972) - states that academic politics is the most vicious and bitter form of politics, because the stakes are so low]. And, of course, there is the famous *Parkinson's law* - named after the English political scientist C. Northcote Parkinson (1909-1993) - states that work expands so as to fill the time available for its completion. In this milieu, also, are the following: *Mrs. Parkinson's law* - heat produced by pressure expands to fill the mind available from which it can pass only to a cooler mind; the *Peter principle* - named after the Canadian sociologist Laurence J. Peter (1920-1990) - states that in a hierarchy every employee tends to rise to his level of incompetence; and *Putt's law* - named after a pseudonym "Archibald Putt" (?) - states that every technical hierarchy, in time, develops a competence inversion; and technology is dominated by two types of people: those who understand what they do not manage, and those who manage what they do not understand; also, along with *Putt's law* is *Putt's canon*, containing a plethora of other laws and corollaries (sample: *Law of failure* - technology abhors little failures, but rewards big ones; and its *corollary*: if you must fail, fail big). The prolific Putt also provides *Putt's corollary to Murphy's law* - if nothing can go wrong, it will go right; as well as *Putt's parallels to Murphy's law* - anything that can go wrong will go faster with computers; and whenever a computer can be blamed, it should be blamed. See also CONTROL/SYSTEMS THEORY; EXPERIMENTER EFFECTS; ORGANIZATIONAL/INDUSTRIAL/SYSTEMS THEORY; REBER'S LAW; ROECKELEIN'S LAW; WORK/CAREER/OCCUPATION, THEORIES OF.

REFERENCES

Sayre, W. S. (1937). *An outline of American government*. New York: Barnes & Noble.

Parkinson, C. N. (1957). *Parkinson's law, or the pursuit of progress*. London: Murray.

Parkinson, C. N. (1968). *Mrs. Parkinson's law*. Boston: Houghton Mifflin.

Peter, L. J., & Hull, R. (1969). *The Peter principle*. New York: W. Morrow.

Issawi, C. P. (1973/1991). *Issawi's laws of social motion*. New York: Hawthorn/Princeton, NJ: Darwin Press.

Parkinson, C. N. (1980). *Parkinson: The law*. Boston: Houghton Mifflin.

Putt, A. (1981). *Putt's law and the successful technocrat*. Smithtown, NY: Exposition Press.

Reber, A. S. (1995). *The Penguin dictionary of psychology*. New York: Penguin Press.

Brannon, L. A., Hershberger, P. J., & Brock, T. C. (1999). Timeless demonstrations of Parkinson's first *law*. *Psychonomic Bulletin & Review, 6*, 148-156.

MURRAY'S THEORY OF PERSONALITY. = need-press theory = personology theory. The academically versatile American psychologist Henry Alexander Murray (1893-

1988) argued that the fundamental goal of psychology should be to study *personality*, and this idiographic viewpoint, accordingly, has been called *personology*. Murray's wide-ranging, diverse, humanistic, and optimistic *personality theory*, or *personological system*, is characterized by the following tenets: (1) personality is shaped by numerous conscious and unconscious forces, by early childhood experiences, by individuals' habits, motivations, complexes, ambitions, wishes, needs, sentiments, dreams, and fantasies; (2) a taxonomic approach where personality is precisely dissected and categorized; for instance, twenty human psychological needs were described (later expanded to thirty needs), including the needs for aggression, achievement, affiliation, and abasement, where the person reacts to *press* (determinants of behavior) from the environment and other people, and where combinations of needs, *press*, and *press-need patterns* lead to *themas*, that is, characterizations of one's life; (3) a concern with time that involves longitudinal studies of personality and lives in progress; (4) a multiform system of personality assessment including development of projective tests such as the Thematic Apperception Test (TAT) and a multifaceted orientation based on the works of Sigmund Freud, Carl Jung, Kurt Koffka, Kurt Lewin, Alfred North Whitehead, Talcott Parsons, Clyde Kluckhohn, and William McDougall; (5) a capacity for studying personages who are living, dead, fictional, historical, or arche-typal; and (6) a concern for diverse issues ranging from global problems such as prevention of nuclear war to reconciliation between religion and science. Murray's *theory of motivation and needs*, which is related closely to his accounts of the dynamics of personality, includes various novel concepts such as *press, press-need patterns, need-press theory, need integration, thema, unity thema, value-vector scheme*, and *regnancy*. Even though Murray's theories have undergone constant reexamination and modification, his approach has always emphasized the importance on personality of unconscious sources of motivation and of the relationship between brain processes and psychological processes. Some critics of Murray's *personology theory* (e.g., Walsh, 1973) have argued that it loses power in being too broad in scope, that it gives a disproportionate amount of attention to the topic of motivation over that of learning, that it does not adequately explain the processes by which motives develop in one's personality, and that its concepts lack interface with empirical data. In general, Murray's writings and his research do not seem to be fashionable today within the psychological mainstream, and he has been characterized, fairly, as being too much of a poet and too little of a logical positivist. See also ACHIEVEMENT MOTIVATION, THE-ORY OF; IDIO-GRAPHIC/NOMOTHETIC LAWS; PERSONALITY, THEORIES OF.

REFERENCES

Morgan, C., & Murray, H. A. (1935). A method for investigating fantasies. *Archives of Neurological Psychiatry, 34*, 289-306.

Murray, H. A. (1936). Basic concepts for a psychology of personality. *Journal of General Psychology, 15*, 241-268.

Murray, H. A. (1938). *Explorations in personality: A clinical and experimental study of fifty men of college age.* New York: Oxford University Press.

Murray, H. A. (1943). *Manual of Thematic Apperception Test.* Cambridge, MA: Harvard University Press.

Murray, H. A. (1960). Two versions of man. In H. Shapley (Ed.), *Science ponders religion.* New York: Appleton-Century-Crofts.

Murray, H. A. (1962). Prospect for psychology. *Science, 136*, 483-488.

Murray, H. A. (1968). Components of an evolving personological system. In D. Stills (Ed.), *International encyclopedia of the social sciences.* New York: Macmillan & Free Press.

Walsh, W. (1973). *Theories of person-environment interaction: Implications for the college student.* Iowa City, IA: American College Testing.

MYELINOGENETIC LAW. See NEURON/NEURAL/NERVE THEORY.

MYSTICISM, DOCTRINE OF. See KOHLBERG'S THEORY OF MORALITY.

N

NAFE'S PATTERN THEORY OF FEEL-ING. See SOMESTHESIS, THEORIES OF.

NAFE'S VASCULAR THEORY OF CU-TANEOUS SENSITIVITY. The sense of touch consists of several partly independent senses [first identified by the Austrian physiologist Maximilian R. F. von Frey (1852-1932) in 1904]: pressure on the skin, warmth, cold, pain, vibration, movement across the skin, and stretch of the skin. These sensations (*cutaneous senses*) depend on several kinds of receptors in the skin; the cutaneous senses are known sometimes by the broader term *somatosensory system*. Two hypotheses (the *specific terminal hypothesis* and the *specific tissue hypothesis*) have been proposed for the thermal receptors although there is little or no direct evidence in support of either [cf., C. E. Osgood's account and evaluation of *thermal sensitivity theories*: the *gradient theory*; M. von Frey's *specific receptor theory*; J. P. Nafe's *vascular theory*; and W. Jenkins' *concentration theory* - states that the perception of cold intensity depends on the average concentration of active spots of encapsulated nerve endings beneath the area of the stimulated skin; in this approach, however, there are insufficient encapsulated endings to satisfy the theory, but this hypothesis stimulated much work on the primary functional sensory systems in the skin regarding the aspects of warmth, cold, pain, and touch]. The *specific terminal hypothesis* assumes a molecular configuration or other specific feature of the terminal membrane that governs differential responsiveness to thermal and mechanical stimuli. The *specific tissue hypothesis* assumes that afferent nerves are alike, essentially, but they end in non-neural tissues whose characteristics are responsible for the stimulus specificities observed in the activity of the associated axon. An example of this latter type of hypothesis is the *vascular theory* proposed by J. P. Nafe, and reviewed by D. R. Kenshalo, in which the smooth muscles of the cutaneous

vascular system contract when cooled and relax when warmed. According to this viewpoint, the movement of the vessels initiates activity in the afferent nerves that terminate in the vessel walls. Another current theory, the *quantitative theory of cutaneous sensitivity* is representative of several of the so-called *pattern theories of cutaneous sensory coding*. This theory holds that the qualities of cutaneous sensation are partly a function of the mechanical and thermal properties of the tissue in which the sensory nerves terminate and partly a function of variations in the temporal and spatial patterns of neural discharge of those nerves. The *pattern theories of somatosensory coding* may require a great deal of experimental validation. However, on the basis of currently available data, it may be assumed that every different cutaneous sensation that can be discriminated is the result of a unique pattern of neural activity arriving at the points in the brain where it is interpreted. See also AL-RUTZ'S THEORY; CODING THEORIES; GATE-CONTROL THEORY; SOMESTHE-SIS, THEORIES OF.

REFERENCES

von Frey, M. R. F. (1904). *Vorlesungen uber physiologie.* Berlin: Springer-Verlag.

Nafe, J. P. (1934). Pressure, pain, and temperature senses. In C. Murchison (Ed.), *A handbook of general experimental psychology.* Worcester, MA: Clark University Press.

Jenkins, W. (1939). Nafe's vascular theory and the preponderance of evidence. *American Journal of Psychology, 52,* 462-465.

Walshe, F. (1942). The anatomy and physiology of cutaneous sensibility: A critical review. *Brain, 65,* 48-112.

Osgood, C. E. (1953). *Method and theory in experimental psychology.* New York: Oxford University Press.

Kenshalo, D. R., & Nafe, J. P. (1962). A quantitative theory of feeling - 1960. *Psychological Review, 69,* 17-33.

Kenshalo, D. R. (1970). Cutaneous temperature receptors: some operating characteristics for a model. In J. Hardy (Ed.), *Physiological and behavioral temperature regulation.* Springfield, IL: Thomas.

NAÏVE PERSONALITY THEORIES. See PERSONALITY THEORIES.

NAÏVE REALISM DOCTRINE. See PERCEPTION (I. GENERAL), THEORIES OF.

NAPALKOV PHENOMENON. This phenomenon is named after the contemporary Russian neurophysiologist Anatolii Viktorovich Napalkov (? - ?), and refers to an exception to the usual conditioned reflex experimental paradigm and results that occur in some phobic individuals, in which the conditioned stimulus (such as a traumatic event) does *not* immediately produce a fear reaction. On the contrary, the fear increases over time, rather than being extinguished as it would ordinarily during exposure to the unreinforced conditioned stimulus (cf., H. J. Eysenck's *incubation theory* - states that under certain conditions exposure to a fear-eliciting conditioned stimulus may result in a delayed growth of fear, and the theory has been used to explain extreme avoidance/symptom maintenance in extinction procedures; and *incubation of avoidance theory* - based on evidence of the delayed appearance of conditioning in laboratory animals exposed to a traumatic event, such as electroconvulsive shock, this theory posits that avoidance learning requires a consolidation or incubation period before it becomes established in memory). See also EYSENCK'S THEORY OF PERSONALITY; PAVLOVIAN CONDITIONING PRINCIPLES/LAWS/THEORIES.

REFERENCES

Eysenck, H. J. (1955). A dynamic theory of anxiety and hysteria. *Journal of Mental Science, 101,* 28-51.

Napalkov, A. V., & Karas, A. I. (1957). Elimination of conditioned pathological bonds in experimental hypertensive conditions. *Zhurnal Vysshei Nervnoi Deyatel'nosti Im I. P. Pavlova, 7,* 402-409.

Napalkov, A. V. (1963). Information processes of the brain. In N. Weiner & J. P. Schade (Eds.), *Progress in brain research: Nerve, brain, and memory*

models. Amsterdam, Netherlands: Elsevier.

Malloy, P. F., & Levis, D. J. (1990). A human laboratory test of Eysenck's theory of incubation: A search for the resolution of the neurotic paradox. *Journal of Psychopathology and Behavioral Assessment (Historical Archive), 12,* 309-327.

NATIVE CAPACITIES, DOCTRINE OF. See McDOUGALL'S HORMIC/INSTINCT THEORY/DOCTRINE.

NATIVIST VERSUS EMPIRICIST THEORIES. See EMPIRICIST VERSUS NATIVIST THEORIES.

NATIVISTIC/NATIVISM THEORIES/ DOCTRINE. See EMPIRICIST VERSUS NATIVIST THEORIES; LOTZE'S THEORY OF LOCAL SIGNS.

NATURAL LAW. See NATURE VERSUS NURTURE THEORIES.

NATURAL LAW THEORY. See NATURE VERSUS NURTURE THEORIES.

NATURAL RESPONSE THEORY. See LANGUAGE ORIGINS, THEORIES OF.

NATURALISTIC THEORY OF HISTORY. Two general approaches may be taken to explain how a science, such as psychology, develops: the *naturalistic* (or *Zeitgeist* - "spirit of the times") *theory* and the *personalistic* (or "great man/person") *theory.* The *naturalistic theory* holds that "the *times* make the person" or at least make possible the acceptance of what she or he has to say [cf., the *Ortgeist theory* ("spirit of the place") - states that a given culture, place, or location determines the characteristics of theories and research, as contrasted with a given historical time or era as supposed by the *Zeitgeist theory*]. The *personalistic theory* suggests that scientific events would not have happened had it not been for the appearance of the great men and women; this theory maintains that "the *person* makes the times." Are the great men/great women the *causes* of progress, or are they merely its *symptoms*? The American psychologist/historian Edwin Garrigues Boring (1886-1968) suggests that they are neither; rather, they are the *agents* of progress. The *naturalistic theory* stresses the role of the social, cultural, and intellectual climate within which the investigator works and lives (cf., *doctrine of social determinism* - holds that history is influenced primarily by broad social and cultural forces rather than by individuals). However, the acceptance and use of a discovery may be limited by the dominant pattern of thought in a culture, region, or era. An idea that is too novel or unique to gain acceptance in one period of civilization may be readily accepted a generation or a century later. Slow change seems to be the pattern of scientific progress. For example, the Scottish physiologist Robert Whytt (1714-1766) first suggested the concept of *conditioning of responses* in 1763, but it was well over 100 years later - at a time when psychology was moving toward greater objectivity - that the Russian physiologist Ivan Pavlov (1849-1936) expanded and developed the concept in 1927 into a systematic body of knowledge. The great scholars, themselves, have become *eponyms*; that is, their names have been given to systematic positions or *laws* (the study/science of names and naming is called *onomastics* and is divided into "anthroponomastics" - the study of *personal* names, and "toponymy" - the study of *place* names); and this *personalistic* process fosters the belief that a scientific discovery is the result of one person's sudden insight. According to Boring (1963), *eponymy* may "distort" history by not taking proper account of the *Zeitgeist* and of earlier neglected contributions by other scientists. In the final analysis, however, the history of psychology should probably be considered in terms of *both personalistic* and *naturalistic theories* of history, with a major role being assigned to the influence of the *Zeitgeist*. See also HISTORICAL MODELS OF EXPERIMENTAL PSYCHOLOGY; PAVLOVIAN CONDITIONING PRINCIPLES/LAWS/THEORIES; PERSONALITY THEORIES; STIGLER'S LAW OF EPONYMY.

REFERENCES

Boring, E. G. (1957). *A history of experimental psychology*. New York: Appleton-Century-Crofts.

Boring, E. G. (1963). *History, psychology, and science: Selected papers*. New York: Wiley.

Curti, M. (1973). Psychological theories in American thought. Vol. 4. In P. Wiener (Ed.), *Dictionary of the history of ideas*. New York: Scribners.

Roeckelein, J. E. (1995). Naming in psychology: Analyses of citation counts and eponyms. *Psychological Reports*, *77*, 163-174.

NATURAL RESPONSE THEORY. See LANGUAGE ORIGINS, THEORIES OF.

NATURAL SELECTION, LAW OF. This generalization, first proposed by the English naturalist Charles Darwin (1809-1882) and the British biologist Alfred Russel Wallace (1823-1913) in 1858, asserts that of the range of inheritable variations of traits in a population, those that contribute to an individual's survival will be the ones that have the highest probability of being passed on to the next generation of individuals or organisms. *Natural selection* assumes that the contributions to succeeding generations of organisms do not appear in a random fashion, but are "selected out" on the basis of the viability and utility of the trait(s). The *law of natural selection* is recognized today, generally, as the essential biological mechanism operative in evolutionary processes. See also DARWIN'S EVOLUTION THEORY/EVOLUTION, THEORY/ LAWS OF.

REFERENCES

Darwin, D. (1859). *On the origin of species by means of natural selection*. London: Murray.

Wallace, A. R. (1905). *My life: A record of events and opinions*. New York: Dodd, Mead & Company.

NATURE VERSUS NURTURE THEORIES. The *nature versus nurture* dichotomy originated with the Greek philosopher Socrates (c. 470-399 B.C.), and was popularized later by the English schoolmaster Richard

Mulcaster (1530-1611) and the English naturalist/psychologist Sir Francis Galton (1822-1911). In psychology, the *nature versus nurture theories* reflect the historical controversy over whether psychological abilities, traits, characteristics, and behaviors are inborn/inherited/hereditary (*nature* position) or whether they are mainly learned/acquired through experience and contact with the environment (*nurture* position, or *doctrine of environmental determinism*). Traditionally, several areas in psychology have been involved intimately in the *nature versus nurture* controversy (cf., *natural law* - in the "hard" or "tough-minded" sciences, such as physics and chemistry, this principle refers to a general statement of the factors whereby the phenomena of the universe proceed; and in the "soft" or "tender-minded" sciences, such as psychology and sociology, it refers to any sanction of social behavior based on established custom, norms, or divine sanction, rather than on legislative enactment; and *natural law theory* - in the disciplines of philosophy and theology, this principle refers to the notion of the supremacy of nature in defining the purpose of all natural phenomena). For example, on the issue of *intelligence*, the question has been asked, "Is intelligence genetically, environmentally, or culturally defined?" On the issue of *visual space perception*, the question has been asked, "Is our perception of a three-dimensional world based on the fact that we are born with such a spatial knowledge, or does it occur because we learn to see such spatial relationships through experience?" [cf., *visual cliff phenomenon/apparatus/test* - a device used to test depth perception in very young organisms, animals as well as humans; it consists of a large box with a heavy glass top and a narrow board across the center of the glass; the board separates a shallow "safe" side from an apparent and dangerous drop (the "visual cliff"); the participant is placed on the board, and its consistent movement toward the shallow side indicates, presumably, an *innate* ability to perceive depth; results with this apparatus consistently show that most young species that can locomote at birth show an immediate avoidance of the "dangerous" cliff side; also, human neonates - who can self-locomote - indicate by their consistent avoid-ance of the cliff side that they seem to have an *innate* appreciation of depth and possess a natural ability for visual depth perception]. In this regard, in 1688, the Irish philosopher, astronomer, and politician William Molyneux (1656-1698) posed a question (called *Molyneux's Question*, today) to the English philosopher John Locke (1632-1704), asking whether a congenitally blind adult - upon suddenly acquiring vision - would be able to distinguish between a ball (globe) and a cube by sight alone, without touching them. Both Molyneux and Locke (who was an *empiricist*) agreed the answer to the question was "no." [Note: However, psychological research in the 1960s on the topic of "cross-modal transfer" found results supporting a "yes" answer to *Molyneux's Question*]. Molyneux's simple question went straight to the heart of the early philosophical debate over "innate ideas," and is still of interest to psychologists today in terms of theories of the form and extent of the brain's biological/genetic programming and circuitry, especially concerning language, perception, intelligence, and social behavior. See also BEHAVIORAL THEORIES OF HUMOR/LAUGHTER; BERKELEY'S THEORY OF VISUAL SPACE PERCEPTION; CATTELL'S THEORY OF PERSONALITY; CHOMSKY'S PSYCHOLINGUISTIC THEORY; EMPIRICAL/EMPIRICISM, DOCTRINE OF; EMPIRICIST VERSUS NATIVIST THEORIES; GALTON'S LAWS; INTELLIGENCE, THEORIES/LAWS OF; LOCKE'S PSYCHOLOGICAL THEORY; PERCEPTION (I. GENERAL), THEORIES OF; SPEECH THEORIES.

REFERENCES

Locke, J. (1690/1965). *Essay concerning human understanding*. London: Dent.

Davis, J. W. (1960). The Molyneux problem. *Journal of the History of Ideas, 21*, 392-408.

Morgan, M. J. (1977). *Molyneux's question: Vision, touch, and the philosophy of perception*. Oxford, UK: Cambridge University Press.

Weisfeld, G. E. (1982). The nature-nurture issue and the integrating concept of function. In B. B. Wolman (Ed.), *Handbook of developmental psy-*

422

chology. Englewood Cliffs, NJ: Prentice-Hall.

Heil, J. (1987). The Molyneux question. *Journal for the Theory of Social Behavior, 17*, 227-241.

Evans, G. (2002). Molyneux's question. In A. Noe & E. Thompson (Eds.), *Vision and mind*. Cambridge, MA: M.I.T. Press.

NECKER CUBE ILLUSION. See APPENDIX A.

NEED ACHIEVEMENT THEORY. See ACHIEVEMENT MOTIVATION, THEORY OF.

NEED-DRIVE-INCENTIVE PATTERN THEORY. See MOTIVATION, THEORIES OF.

NEED-HIERARCHY THEORY. See MASLOW'S THEORY OF PERSONALITY.

NEED, LAW OF. See CONDUCT, LAWS OF.

NEED-PRESS THEORY. See MURRAY'S THEORY OF PERSONALITY.

NEED-REDUCTION THEORIES. See MOTIVATION, THEORIES OF.

NEED THEORIES. See MOTIVATION, THEORIES OF.

NEGATIVE ADAPTATION, PRINCIPLE OF. See HABITUATION, PRINCIPLE/LAW OF.

NEGATIVE AFTERIMAGES PHENOMENON. See EMMERT'S LAW; HERING-HURVICH-JAMESON COLOR VISION THEORY.

NEGATIVE CONTRAST EFFECT. See CRESPI EFFECT.

NEGATIVE INCENTIVE EFFECT. See FESTINGER'S COGNITIVE DISSONANCE THEORY.

NEGATIVE LAW OF EFFECT. See EFFECT, LAW OF.

NEGATIVE RECENCY EFFECT. See PROBABILITY THEORY/LAWS.

NEGATIVE SELF-VERIFICATION THEORY. See SELF-CONCEPT THEORY.

NEGATIVE STATE RELIEF MODEL. See BYSTANDER INTERVENTION EFFECT.

NEGATIVE TRANSFER OF TRAINING EFFECT. See ASSIMILATION, LAW OF.

NEOBEHAVIORIST THEORY. See BEHAVIORIST THEORY.

NEOCATASTROPHISM THEORY. See DARWIN'S EVOLUTION THEORY.

NEO-DISSOCIATION THEORY. See DISSOCIATION THEORY; HYPNOSIS/HYPNOTISM, THEORIES OF.

NEO-EVOLUTIONARY THEORIES OF EMOTION. See IZARD'S THEORY OF EMOTIONS.

NEO-FREUDIAN/NEO-ANALYTIC/PSYCHODYNAMIC/PSYCHOANALYTIC THEORIES. See PERSONALITY THEORIES.

NEO-LAMARCKIAN THEORY OF GENETICS. See LAMARCK'S THEORY.

NEO-MALTHUSIANISM. See MALTHUS' THEORY.

NEO-MENDELISM, DOCTRINE OF. See LAMARCK'S THEORY.

NEO-PLATONISM THEORY. See LEARNING THEORIES/LAWS.

NERNST HEAT THEOREM. See THERMODYNAMICS, LAWS OF.

NERNST-LILLIE THEORY. See NEURON/NEURAL/NERVE THEORY.

NETWORK EFFECT. See PSYCHOPA-THOLOGY, THEORIES OF.

NETWORK MODEL. See NEURAL NETWORK MODELS OF INFORMATION PROCESSING; PARALLEL DISTRIBUTED PROCESSING MODEL.

NEURAL DARWINISM THEORY. See DARWIN'S EVOLUTION THEORY.

NEURAL NETWORK MODELS OF IN-FORMATION PROCESSING. According to these *models of information processing,* a system of interconnected neurons (either physiologically-real or computer-simulated) provides the basis for mental experiences via the interaction of multiple neurons or comput-ing units - each in a particular activating/firing state and each possessing the capacity to in-fluence others by either inhibitory or excita-tory connections/synapses. The entire neural network/system is activated initially by a stimulus that affects a subset of the units, and continues to travel through the network until an equilibrium state of minimum energy is reached. The notion of a *neural network model* was first anticipated by William James (1842-1910) in the late 1800s; the first *neural logic (binary code) circuit* was proposed by Nicholas Rashevsky (1899-1972) in 1938; the first *detailed neural network* was developed by Warren Sturgis McCulloch (1898-1968 and Walter Pitts (1923-1969) in 1943; the first *neural network* with the ability to *learn* was developed by Alan Mathison Turing (1912-1954) in 1948 and Donald Olding Hebb (1904-1985) in 1949; the *perceptron* - a pat-tern-recognition machine and an early exam-ple of a *neural network* - was developed by Frank Rosenblatt (1928-) in 1958; and a *connectionist model of human memory* was developed and popularized by James Lloyd McClelland (1948-) in 1981. *Neural network models* have been referred to, also, as *neural nets* and *artificial neural networks* that indi-cate their artificial, rather than their natural, structures. Some versions of *neural networks* employ *fuzzy logic* - a form of logic in which propositions contain "truth values" that range from 0 to 1 rather than being either false (0) or true (1) as employed in more conventional Boolean logic systems. See also ADAPTIVE CONTROL OF THOUGHT THEORY/MOD-EL; BOOLEAN SET THEORY; CASCADE PROCESSING MODEL; FORGETTING/ MEMORY, THEORIES OF; FUZZY SET THEORY; INFORMATION/INFORMA-TION-PROCESSING THEORY; NOMO-LOGICAL NETWORK THEORY; PARAL-LEL DISTRIBUTED PROCESSING MOD-EL.

REFERENCES

Rosenblatt, F. (1958). The perceptron: A probabilistic model for information storage and organization in the brain. *Psychological Review, 65,* 386-408.

Parks, R. W., & Levine, D. S. (Eds.) (1998). *Fundamentals of neural modeling: Neuropsychology and cognitive neuroscience.* Cambridge, MA: M.I.T. Press.

Rolls, E. T., & Treves, A. (1998). *Neural net-works and brain function.* Oxford, UK: Oxford University Press.

NEURAL QUANTUM THEORY. In psy-chology, the *classical theory of sensory dis-crimination* has been contrasted historically with the *neural quantum theory* in a contro-versy sometimes called the *sensory continuity-noncontinuity* issue, with origins in the area of psychophysics. Some early researchers in psychophysics (e.g., R. Lotze; G. Fechner) argued for the *noncontinuity* (or *discontinuity*) position that involves the concept of *thresh-old,* whereas other researchers (e.g., G. Mul-ler; J. Jastrow) maintained that the sensory continuum consists of a *continuous* series of intermediate degrees of sensation where there is no "true" threshold. The center of the con-troversy was whether the changes on the psy-chological continuum occur in a smooth or continuous manner as the value of the physi-cal stimulus increases continuously along a specified dimension, or whether there is an abrupt, step like change from "no sensation" to "sensation" or from "sensation" to a "dif-ference in sensation." The early *theory of threshold* (Fechner, 1860) holds that the brain in its waking state is physiologically active and, consequently, for an increasing stimulus to be detected, it has to generate neurological excitations that are larger than those already present as the result of the brain's spontaneous activity (cf., Herbart, 1824). The *sensory continuity-noncontinuity* issue deals with the challenging question of how sensory mechanisms - that are composed of discrete neural elements that obey the *all-or-none law* of physiology - can convert continuous energy from the environment into an apparently continuous change in sensory experience. The Hungarian-American biophysicist Georg von Bekesy (1899-1972) showed in the 1930s that *discrete* steps can be obtained in studies of sensory discrimination and, thereby, offers evidence for the *quantal* nature of sensory functions; cf., Corso (1961) who suggests that both the *quantal theory* and the *phi-gamma hypothesis* - which represents the *classical theory of sensory discrimination* and predicts the general form of the psychometric function to be the integral of the normal probability distribution - are equally acceptable in predicting the same results, and indicates that support of one theory to the exclusion of the other is not reasonable. The *neural quantum theory* in psychology was first introduced by S. S. Stevens, C. Morgan, and J. Volkmann in 1941 within the context of *auditory* discrimination; cf., J. Corso (1956) and H. Blackwell (1953) for *neural quantum theory* in the context of *visual* discrimination. Unlike the *classical theory of sensory discrimination*, which states that the proper form of the psychometric function for sensory discrimination is a normal ogive, the *neural quantum theory* asserts that the relationship between the proportion of judgments and corresponding stimulus values is represented best by a linear function, which implies that sensory discrimination is characterized by finite, discrete, or quantal steps. The *neural quantum theory* is intended to be consistent with the *all-or-none principle* because it is maintained, generally, that discriminatory judgments are mediated by the activities of underlying neural structures. In the *psychological theory of neural quantum*, the term *quantum* refers, specifically, to a "functionally distinct" unit in the neural mechanisms that are involved in sensory discrimination and, in this context, the term *quantum* implies a *perceptual* unit, not a *physical* unit (such as used in the science of *physics* to refer to distinct

physical-energy units). Another version of this approach, the *quantal hypothesis*, asserts that continuous increments in a physical variable produce discrete (quantal) increases in sensation (cf., the *law of quanta* - states that with a conscious responding system, the system makes a quantity of a certain kind of energy into a thing or object unlike the thing or object "out there"). It appears, in the final analysis and on the basis of the existing data, that it is not determinable whether the *theory of neural quantum* provides a better explanation of sensory discrimination than the *classical theory*. It may be concluded, fairly, that unequivocal support of the *neural quantum theory* is lacking, and the tenability of the *quantal hypothesis*, as opposed to the *phi-gamma hypothesis*, is extremely difficult to evaluate due to the severe restrictions in methodology and to the statistical limitations in the treatment of data. See also ALL-OR-NONE LAW/PRINCIPLE; PSYCHOPHYSICAL LAWS/THEORY; QUANTUM THEORY; SIGNAL DETECTION, THEORY OF.

REFERENCES
Herbart, J. (1824). *Psychologie als wissenschaft, neu gegrundet auf erfahrung, metaphysik, und mathematik.* Konisberg, Germany: Unzer.

Lotze, R. (1852). *Medicinische psychologie, oder physiologie der seele.* Leipzig, Germany: Weidmann.

Fechner, G. (1860). *Elemente der psychophysik.* Leipzig, Germany: Breitkopf & Hartel.

Muller, G. (1878). *Zur grundlegung der psychophysik.* Berlin, Germany: Gruben.

Jastrow, J. (1888). A critique of psychophysic methods. *American Journal of Psychology, 1,* 271-309.

Thurstone, L. L. (1928). The phi-gamma hypothesis. *Journal of Experimental Psychology, 11,* 293-305.

Bekesy, G. von (1930). Uber das Fechner'sche gesetz und seine bedeutung fur die theorie der akustischen beobachtungsfehler und die theorie des horens. *Annals der Physik, 7,* 329-359.

Stevens, S. S., Morgan, C., & Volkmann, J. (1941). Theory of the neural quantum in the discrimination of loudness and pitch. *American Journal of Psychology, 54,* 315-335.

Miller, G., & Garner, W. (1944). Effect of random presentation in the psychometric function: Implications for a quantal theory of discrimination. *American Journal of Psychology, 57,* 451-467.

Blackwell, H. (1953). Evaluation of the neural quantum theory in vision. *American Journal of Psychology, 66,* 397-408.

Corso, J. (1956). The neural quantum theory of sensory discrimination. *Psychological Bulletin, 53,* 371-393.

Neisser, U. (1957). Response-sequences and the hypothesis of the neural quantum. *American Journal of Psychology, 70,* 512-527.

Corso, J. (1961). The quantal hypothesis and the threshold of audibility. *American Journal of Psychology, 74,* 191-204.

Corso, J. (1963). A theoretico-historical review of the threshold concept. *Psychological Bulletin, 60,* 356-370.

Norman, D. (1964). Sensory thresholds, response biases, and the neural quantum theory. *Journal of Mathematical Psychology, 1,* 88-120.

NEURAL TIMING THEORY. The American experimental/mathematical and cognitive psychologist Robert Duncan Luce (1925-) and the sensory/auditory/experimental and physiological psychologist David M. Green (1932-) formulated a psychophysiological *theory of neural timing* (and a *theory of neural attention*) based on the assumption that - at a hypothetical neural decision-center - signal/sound intensity is represented by a number of independent and parallel Poisson processes whose rates are the same power function of physical intensity. Information concerning signal intensity is based on the observed times between successive neural firings/pulses. *Response time* is defined as the result of the decision-latency that depends, in turn, on the signal intensity, decision rule, and residual latency. The theory posits decision rules for contexts involving magnitude estimation, discrimination, recognition, and detection

tasks (cf., Treisman, 1984). See also PSYCHOLOGICAL TIME, MODELS OF; PSYCHOPHYSICAL LAWS/THEORY; TIME, THEORIES OF.

REFERENCES

Luce, R. D., & Green, D. M. (1972). A neural timing theory for response times and the psychophysics of intensity. *Psychological Review, 79,* 14-57.

Luce, R. D., & Green, D. M. (1973). *Neural coding and psychophysical discrimination data.* Irvine, CA: University of California Press.

Green, D. M., & Luce, R. D. (1974). Variability of magnitude estimates: A timing theory analysis. *Perception & Psychophysics, 15,* 291-300.

Luce, R. D., & Green, D. M. (1978). Two tests of the neural attention hypothesis for auditory psychophysics. *Perception & Psychophysics, 23,* 363-371.

Luce, R. D., Baird, J. C., Green, D. M., & Smith, A. F. (1980). Two classes of models for magnitude estimation. *Journal of Mathematical Psychology, 22,* 121-148.

Treisman, M. (1984). A theory of criterion setting: An alternative to the attention band and response ratio hypotheses in magnitude estimation and cross-modality matching. *Journal of Experimental Psychology: General, 113,* 443-463.

NEUROBIOTAXIS, LAW OF. See NEURON/NEURAL/NERVE THEORY.

NEUROCOGNITIVE THEORY OF DREAMING. See DREAM THEORY.

NEURODEVELOPMENTAL HYPOTHESIS. See SCHIZOPHRENIA, THEORIES OF.

NEUROLINGUISTIC THEORY. See CHOMSKY'S PSYCHOLINGUISTIC THEORY.

NEUROMUSCULAR INHIBITION, THEORY OF. See INHIBITION, LAWS OF.

NEURON/NEURAL/NERVE THEORY.

The *neuron* (or *neurone, nerve cell*) is the basic structural and functional unit of the nervous system and consists of three main parts: a *cell body* ("soma") that contains the nucleus, an *axon*, and one or more *dendrites*. A distinction is made between the terms *neuron* and *nerve* where a *neuron* is a single cell consisting of three parts (one of which is an *axon*), whereas a *nerve* is a bundle of many neural *axons* [cf., *Waller's law* - formulated by the English physician/physiologist Augustus V. Waller (1816-1870) in 1850 - which states that if posterior roots of the spinal cord are cut on the central side of the ganglia, those portions of the cut nerves that lie within the spinal cord degenerate, whereas the peripheral portions of the same nerves (not being severed from the ganglia) do not degenerate]. Neurons are cells that transmit information throughout the body, as well as within the brain [cf., *Dale's law/principle* - formulated by the English physiologist Sir Henry H. Dale (1875-1968) - proposes that only one kind of neurotransmitter substance is produced by a given neuron; however, today, it is known that there are exceptions to this principle; the *drainage/diversion hypothesis* asserts that facilitation of neural conduction over certain neurons and its inhibition over others are due to a drainage of energy from paths of higher resistance into those of lower resistance; the *chemoaffinity hypothesis* proposes that molecules of particular chemical substances guide neurons in the formation of appropriate synapses during development and regeneration; and *Du Bois-Reymond's law* - formulated by the German electrophysiologist Emil Du Bois-Reymond (1818-1896) - states that the excitatory efficiency of an electric current that passes through neural tissue is dependent on the rate of current density *change* and not on the current's absolute value]. Many of the neurons in the human nervous system are extremely small (some axons are only about 0.1 millimeter long; other axons stretch up to a meter through the adult nervous system). It is estimated that the nervous system contains about 100 billion neurons. The *neuron theory* holds that any sensorimotor neural pathway is not a continuous tissue but consists of separate nerve cells (the neurons) that are merely contiguous end-to-end (cf., the *law of forward conduction* - states that nerve impulses always travel from the postsynaptic membrane of the dendrites to the terminal knob of the axon; the *law of neurobiotaxis* states that dendrites of developing nerve cells grow in the direction of the axons of nearby active neurons; and the *motor-primacy theory* posits that bodymechanisms associated with motor-nerve functions develop before sensory-nerve mechanisms, and their degree of maturation governs their ability to respond to stimulation). According to the *neuron theory*, the neuron is the basic and essential histological/metabolic unit of the nervous system. The *neuron theory* (also called the *neuron doctrine*) was first named by the German histologist and anatomist Wilhelm Waldeyer-Hartz (1839-1921) - who also coined the words *neuron* and *chromosome*; the theory is founded on a viewpoint of the nervous system held by the Spanish physician and histologist Santiago Ramon y Cajal (1852-1934) whose major work was on the microstructure of the nervous system (cf., *avalanche law* - the principle that neural impulses spread from a stimulus receptor site to a number of other neurons, resulting in an effect that is disproportionate to the initial stimulus, such as may be observed in an epileptic seizure; and *autocorrelation theory* - suggests that groups of individual nerve fibers collaborate to transmit *auditory* nerve impulses, based on the finding that because a single fiber is unable to transmit impulses faster than 1,000 cycles per second, fibers must function as a team with one firing at one cycle, another at the next cycle, and so on; cf., *volley theory of audition*). Ramon y Cajal utilized the specialized histological staining techniques of the Italian histologist Camillo Golgi (1843-1926). However, the two men disagreed in their interpretations of neural structure; Ramon y Cajal maintained that nerve cells are discrete and that there is no physical continuity between one cell and another. The revolutionary "Golgi stain technique" (that impregnates neural tissue with silver) was crucial, histologically, for the eventual confirmation of the *neuron theory*, which holds that neurons act as units and communicate via synapses rather than as a continuous network-like circuit (this latter notion, called the *reticularist theory*, is disregarded today). The dispute over this neural issue between Ramon y Cajal and Golgi became so heated that Golgi's 1906 Nobel Prize acceptance speech consisted of a fiery denunciation of the *neuron doctrine*. The controversy over the *neuron theory/doctrine* continued for more than 25 years afterward, despite the accumulation of evidence in its favor. Only with the advent of electron microscopic pictures in the 1950s were the opponents finally satisfied. The *neuron theory* is one of the most important neurological contributions for the history of psychology because it brought together numerous data concerning the nature of nervous physiology that psychologists could apply in their own disciplinary specialties and interests, notably in the areas of *learning theory* and the *theory of association*; cf., the *theory of psychoneural parallelism* which holds that every fact of consciousness is concomitant with some neural change without implication of the reverse relation, namely, that all neural conditions are concomitant with conscious processes. Other relevant issues and theories related to functioning of the neurons, nerves, and the nervous system are the *synaptic theory of facilitation and inhibition*, and the *membrane theory of nerve conduction* (cf., *segmental theory* - posits that each segment of the nervous system, in segmented animals, controls and regulates largely the activities of the corresponding segment of the body; and *stimulation effects on neurons* - refers to physiological changes created when a stimulus changes the electrical potential of a neuron by producing an irritating effect on the cell membrane which, in turn, disrupts the ionic balance on either side of the membrane; the potential change travels along the nerve fiber to a terminal point or synapse which then passes the impulse along to a nearby fiber; when neurons are exposed to electrical stimulation in test tube experiments, increased temperature and oxygen consumption, as well as other metabolic effects, are observed). According to the *synaptic theory*, the actual pathway activated depends on the physiological properties of the synapse at the time, and the choice between alternatives that nerve impulses can take depends on slight and momentary factors such as *refractory phases* and *summation* (cf., *metabotropic effect* - refers to

a neurological event at a synapse in which neurotransmitters generate a slow, pro-longed effect via metabolic, rather than ionic, changes). In 1895, the neurologist/psychoanalyst Sigmund Freud set out his assumptions about how the nervous system works (cf., *Jackson's law* - named after the English neurologist John Huglings Jackson (1835-1911) and formulated in 1898 - states that when mental abilities are lost because of a neurological disorder, the abilities that appeared *last* in the course of evolution are lost *first* because it is the higher nervous centers (that is, those appearing last phylogenetically) that are first affected, and the lower/older centers are the last affected; also, *Jackson's mixed cerebral dominance theory* states that speech disorders and some other maladjustments may be due to the fact that one cerebral hemisphere does not lead consistently the other hemisphere in controlling bodily movement). Freud hypothesized that neural elements are separated from one another by "contact barriers" (the notion of *synapses* was contested hotly when Freud proposed this idea), and one element can excite the next one only when the "contact barrier" (i.e., synapse) is crossed (cf., *Hebb's theory*). With the English neurophysiologist Sir Charles Scott Sherrington's (1857-1952) contributions, as well as those made earlier by the Austrian physiologist Sigmund Exner (1846-1926), the supposition was greatly strengthened that processes of *facilitation* and *inhibition* are *synaptic functions* [cf., *drainage hypothesis* - posited by the British-American psychologist William McDougall (1871-1938), states that facilitation of neural conduction over particular neurons, and its inhibition over certain others, is due to a "drainage of energy" (analogous to a *hydraulic mod-el*) from paths of higher resistance into those of lower resistance]. The nature of synaptic function, however, was not disclosed completely by Sherrington's methods. The work of W. H. Nernst, R. S. Lillie, and K. Lucas added theoretical and empirical understanding to the neural-related issues of depolarization, refractory phase, hyperexcitability, inhibition, and facilitation. The *membrane theory of nerve conduction* was developed along with the other discoveries of the nature of synapses and conduction (cf., *sensitization theory* - states

428

that once a synapse has fired repeatedly it eventually becomes more active or more effective in exciting the postsynaptic cell). The German physical chemist Wilhelm Ostwald (1853-1932) first proposed the *membrane theory* in 1890; Julius Bernstein amplified and established it in 1902; and R. S. Lillie began a series of experiments that supported it in 1909. The *membrane theory of conduction* is an explanation of the propagation of the nerve impulse in terms of the electrochemical properties of surface films or membranes [cf., *Forbes-Gregg hypothesis* - named after the American physiologist Alexander Forbes (1882-1965) and the American physician Alan Gregg (1890-1957), states that stimulus strength is translated by nerve fibers into frequency of discharge; this hypothesis was offered to explain how the nervous system handles varying stimulus intensities in spite of the honored *all-or-none law* that precludes variability of the strength of discharge in a nerve fiber; and the *rate law* - states that the strength of a stimulus is indicated by the rate of firing of the affected axons]. The eponymous *Nernst-Lillie theory of excitation and conduction* - named after the German physical chemist Walther H. Nernst (1864-1941) and the American physiologist R. S. Lillie (? - ?), holds that excitation of a living cell results from a change in the electrical polarization of a protoplasmic membrane, following local change of ionic concentration at the membrane surface (cf., *myelinogenetic law* - states that a nerve is not ready to function, usually, until its myelin sheath has developed). The effect in the *Nernst-Lillie theory* is transmitted automatically because of resulting secondary changes, such as permeability, in the properties of the membrane itself. The *membrane theory* accounts for the facts of *refractory phase* and *all-or-none transmission*, and was well on its way toward general acceptance among physiologists by 1920. See also ALL-OR-NONE LAW/PRINCIPLE; ASSOCIATION, LAWS/PRINCIPLES OF; AUDITION/HEARING, THEORIES OF; HEBB'S THEORY OF PERCEPTUAL LEARNING; HYDRAULIC THEORY; LEARNING THEORIES/LAWS; MIRROR NEURONS THEORY; REFLEX ARC THEORY/CON-CEPT; SPECIFIC NERVE ENERGIES, LAW OF.

REFERENCES

Exner, S. (1882). [Facilitation and inhibition]. *Archiv fur die Gesamte Physiologie, 28*, 1-49.

Waldeyer-Hartz, W. (1891). Uber einige neuere forschungen im gebiete der anatomie des centralnervensystems. *Deutsche Medizinische Wochenschrift, 17*, 1213-1218.

Jackson, J. H. (1895). [Jackson's law]. *Lancet, 1*, 79-87.

Ramon y Cajal, S. (1899-1904). *Textura del sistema nervioso del hombre y de los vertebrados*. Madrid: Moya.

Sherrington, C. S. (1906). *The integrative action of the nervous system*. New Haven, CT: Yale University Press.

Nernst, W. H. (1908). Sur theorie des elektrischen reizes. *Archiv fur die Gesamte Physiologie, 132*, 275-314.

Lucas, K. (1917). *The conduction of the nervous impulse*. London: Longmans, Green.

Lillie, R. S. (1923). *Protoplasmic action and nervous action*. Chicago: University of Chicago Press.

Bishop, G. (1956). Natural history of the nerve impulse. *Physiological Review, 36*, 376-399.

Williams, R., & Herrup, K. (1988). The control of neuron number. *Annual Review of Neuroscience,11*, 423-453.

Milner, P. M. (1999). *The autonomous brain: A neural theory of attention and learning*. Mahwah, NJ: Erlbaum.

NEUROPSYCHOLOGICAL THEORY. See HEBB'S THEORY OF PERCEPTUAL LEARNING; LEARNING THEORIES AND LAWS.

NEUROTRANSMITTER/BIOGENIC AMINE THEORY OF DEPRESSION. See DEPRESSION, THEORIES OF.

NEW STRUCTURALISM THEORY/ PARADIGM. The Pakistan-born American psychologist, psychotherapist, and imagery authority Akhter Ahsen (1986) formulated a synthesis of several earlier *imagery paradigms* in his *New Structuralism theory* [cf., the original, or "old," school of *Structuralism* – established by the German psychologist Wilhelm Wundt (1832-1920) and the English-born American psychologist Edward B. Titchener (1867-1927) - was based on the assumption that all human mental experience should be viewed as combinations/blends of simple processes, or sensations; *structuralism*, as an older and more general paradigm, was employed, also, in the field of linguistics, most notably by the Swiss linguist Ferdinand de Saussure (1857-1913); in the area of anthropology by the French anthropologist Claude Levi-Strauss (1908-); and in developmental psychology, most notably by the Swiss psychologist Jean Piaget (1896-1980)]. The earlier, traditional strategies/paradigms used in psychology to study *imagery* include: the experimental-cognitive approach (G. Fechner; W. Wundt; F. Galton); the psychoanalytical-dissociationist approach (S. Freud; J. M. Charcot;; P. Janet); the neuropsychological approach (P. Flourens; A. Luria; D. O. Hebb); and the developmental approach (J. Piaget; B. Inhelder). The *New Structuralism theory/ paradigm* includes the experimental methods of the laboratory, but it bases its assumptions on the insights originally obtained through clinical research and therapy. The *New Structuralism* methodology differs radically from other paradigms in that it explicitly sets out to obtain as complete a phenomenological report as possible of the participant's imagery that is produced via standard instructions; the results obtained in this approach show that introspection provides a highly reliable and valid indicator of imagery quality, content, and structure. Among Ahsen's other theoretical formulations are the following: an *image theory of conflict* - in which the image is examined as a composite phenomenon where the somatic or physiological response and meaning (lexical/verbal aspect) are reportable dimensions; meaning is viewed as a covert image, and the possible divergence between the original overt image and the covert image in meaning is the primary domain of possible conflict; this theory suggests that an image produces a conflict only when contradicted by a covert image from the verbal process/do- main, and is resolvable only when the individual compares the original and covert images, and corrects the misrepresentation of the original image in verbal report; and the *triple code model of imagery* (also known as the *image-somatic response-meaning*, or tripartite *ISM model*) - in which the *structural* aspects define the whole metaphorical process: the image, the feeling, and the meaning (i.e., *ISM*) which produce a single, undivided, and unified effect. In the *ISM model*, the feeling and emotion (*S*) stand between the image (*I*) and the meaning (*M*); in this formulation, the basic minimal unit of psychological experience that involves imagery is the *ISM sequence*: the interconnected operations may be found in this three-dimensional unity that is composed of a vivid image (*I*), a somatic/body response (*S*), and a meaning (*M*) where it is suggested that normal imagery experiences tend to occur mostly in the *I-S-M order/sequence*. However, for various reasons, the *ISM* may *not* occur in the proper order for the individual. Hypothetically, there are six basic operational sequences/variations of the *ISM*: *ISM*, *IMS*, *MIS*, *MSI*, *SIM*, and *SMI*, each one of which affords the opportunity for therapeutic analysis and/or discussions of psychological theories, in general, as well as the particular theoretical issues of metaphor, rhetoric, literary analysis, and imagination. See also IMAGERY AND MENTAL IMAGERY, THEORIES OF; MOTOR LEARNING/PROCESS THEORIES; PARADIGM SHIFT DOCTRINE.

REFERENCES

Ahsen, A. (1984). ISM: The Triple Code Model for imagery and psychophysiology. *Journal of Mental Imagery, 8*, 15-42.

Ahsen, A. (1986). The New Structuralism: Images in dramatic interlock. *Journal of Mental Imagery, 10*, 1-92.

Ahsen, A. (1990). An image theory of conflict. *Journal of Mental Imagery, 14*, 53-61.

NEWTON'S ETHER THEORY. See NEWTON'S LAW/PRINCIPLES OF COLOR MIXTURE.

NEWTON'S LAW/PRINCIPLES OF COLOR MIXTURE. In 1704, the English physicist, mathematician, and philosopher Sir

Isaac Newton (1642-1727) presented the first fruitful system for describing the data of *color mixture*. In an imaginative leap of speculation, Newton suggested that colors be arranged in a circle with white at the center and the spectral colors/hues (red, orange, yellow, green, blue, indigo, and violet) around the circumference, where the more "desaturated" a color, the closer it is to the center of the circle. Newton also had the idea of representing a given color's quantity by a small circle drawn about the position of the color on the large circle, and the area of the small circle was thought to be proportional to the quantity of the color. According to Newton, the position of a mixture of colors could be determined by calculating the center of gravity of the weighted individual components. Even though Newton had no way in 1704 of actually quantifying a color, his account contains generally all the *principles of color mixture* as developed by other scientists (e.g., H. Grassman) 150 years later. Newton's *color mixture law* states that if two color mixtures yield the same sensation of hue, then the mixture of these two mixtures will also yield the same hue sensation. Newton's synonymous *law of equilibrium in color mixing* refers to the mixture of two hues to yield an intermediate hue. For example, if A and B are the hues that are mixed in proportions of m and n, then the resultant hue will be at a point on a line joining A and B so that AO/OB = n/m. Newton's famous *prismatic experiment* demonstrates how color mixture using light waves may be analyzed. If a white light is passed through a glass prism, it breaks up into all the "rainbow" colors of the spectrum, and if the entire spectrum of light wavelengths is recombined subsequently, the result is a white light again. In another area of theoretical interest to Newton, his *theory of ether* suggested that *ether* was a hypothetical medium that filled all space, and was invoked as the medium to carry light waves and possesses the properties of elasticity and density. However, in the *Michelson-Morley experiment* [named after the German-born American physicist Albert Abraham Michelson (1852-1931) and the American chemist/physicist Edward Williams Morley (1838-1923)], a test was made in 1887 of *Newton's ether theory* in which the time it took for a light beam to be reflected directly back from a straight-ahead mirror was compared to the time it took for reflection from a beam traveling the same distance at right angles to the first beam; the result of this experiment was that there was no difference in any direction and, thus, it was concluded that there was no *ether*; this experiment paved the way for Albert Einstein's *theory of relativity* - that gives a unified account of the *laws of mechanics and electromagnetism*, and rejects the Newtonian concepts of absolute space and time and the 19th century idea that an electromagnetic *ether* exists with respect to which motion can be determined absolutely. See also COLOR MIXTURE, LAWS/THEORY OF; COLOR VISION, THEORIES/LAWS OF; GRASSMAN'S LAWS; VISION/SIGHT, THEORIES OF.

REFERENCES

Newton, I. (1704). *Opticks*. London: Innys.

Grassman, H. (1853). Zur theorie der farbenmischung. *Poggendorf Annales der Physik, 89,* 69.

Grassman, H. (1854). On the theory of compound colours. *Philosophy Magazine, 7,* 254-264.

Graham, C. (1965). Color mixture and color systems. In C. Graham (Ed.), *Vision and visual perception*. New York: Wiley.

NEXT-IN-LINE EFFECT. See ZAJONC'S AROUSAL AND CONFLUENCE THEORIES.

NIRVANA PRINCIPLE. See CONSTANCY, PRINCIPLE OF; FREUD'S THEORY OF PERSONALITY.

NOMINALISM, DOCTRINE OF. See CONCEPT LEARNING/CONCEPT FORMATION, THEORIES OF; REALISM, DOCTRINE OF.

NOMOLOGICAL NETWORK THEORY. The American psychologists Lee J. Cronbach (1916-2001) and Paul Everett Meehl (1920-2003) proposed that a lawful pattern of interrelationships exists between *hypothetical constructs* (i.e., a suggested mechanism whose existence is inferred but for which objective evidence is not yet available) and observable entities/attributes, and which guides researchers in establishing the *construct validity* (i.e., procedures that capture the hypothetical quality of designated construct/trait) of a psychological test or measure [cf., *trait validity* - the "goodness" of a test determined by the extent to which the test correlates more highly with different methods of measuring the same construct than it does with similar methods of measuring different constructs; proposed by the American psychologist Donald T. Campbell (1916-1996); cf., *reliability* - the "stability" or "dependability" of a test determined by the consistency with which the test yields the same approximate results when given repeatedly under similar conditions]. The *nomological network theory* includes a presumed framework for what is being measured and the specification of associations between different hypothetical constructs, between different observable attributes, and between joint hypothetical constructs/observable attributes. According to this approach, it may be concluded that qualitatively different measurement operations measure the same attributes if their locations in the same *nomological network* link them to the same hypothetical construct variable. See also CLASSICAL TEST/MEASUREMENT THEORY; HYPOTHETICAL CONSTRUCTS; MEASUREMENT THEORY; NEURAL NETWORK MODELS OF INFORMATION PROCESSING.

REFERENCES

Cronbach, L. J., & Meehl, P. E. (1955). Construct validity in psychological tests. *Psychological Bulletin, 52,* 281-302.

Cronbach, L. J., & Merwin, J. C. (1955). A model for studying the validity of multiple-choice items. *Educational and Psychological Measurement, 15,* 337-352.

Campbell, D. T. (1960). Recommendations for APA test standards regarding construct, trait, or discriminant validity. *American Psychologist, 15,* 546-553.

Cronbach, L. J., Rajaratnam, N., & Gleser, C. (1963). Theory of generalizability: A liberalization of reliability theory. *British Journal of Statistical Psychology, 16,* 137-163.

NOMOTHETIC LAWS. See IDIOGRAPHIC/NOMOTHETIC LAWS.

NON-COMMON EFFECTS PRINCIPLE. See MIND-BODY THEORIES.

NONCONTINUITY THEORY. See NEURAL QUANTUM THEORY; SPENCE'S THEORY.

NONCONTRADICTION, LAW OF. See PARSIMONY, LAW/PRINCIPLE OF.

NONLINEAR DYNAMICAL SYSTEMS THEORY. See ORGANIZATIONAL/INDUSTRIAL/SYSTEMS THEORY.

NONPSYCHOANALYTIC HUMOR AND LAUGHTER THEORIES. Taken collectively, or comparatively, the various traditional *nonpsychoanalytic humor/laughter theories* (cf., *psychoanalytic/Freudian theory of wit/humor*) may be distinguished on the following theoretical bases, issues, or points of disagreement: whether laughter is of a *pleasurable* nature or not; whether laughter is an inborn *instinct* or an individually-acquired behavior; whether or not laughter contains *aggressive* and/or *sexual* components; whether laughter contains *moralistic* notions of goodness and spontaneous appearance; is there a lack of standardized *terminology* (where, for example, the terms *humor, wit,* the *comic, self-derision,* and *grim humor* are confused invariably); whether a laughter theory needs to explain the *causes* of laughter and the "transformation of energy;" whether the use of laughter for *social* purposes is primary or secondary; whether laughter is a purely *aesthetic* issue or involves a *psychological* problem; whether laughter is exclusively a *human* attribute; the alleged reasons and mechanisms that *produce* laughter; the *functions* that humor and laughter serve; and whether the notion of the *unconscious* plays any role at all in laughter and humor. See also FREUD'S THEORY OF WIT/HUMOR; HUMOR, THEORIES OF.

REFERENCE

Bergler, E. (1956). *Laughter and the sense of humor.* New York: International Medical Book Company.

432

NONREWARD HYPOTHESIS. See CRES-PI EFFECT.

NONSTATE THEORIES OF HYPNOSIS. See HYPNOSIS/HYPNOTISM, THEORIES OF.

NORMAL/BELL-SHAPED CURVE. See NORMAL DISTRIBUTION THEORY.

NORMAL DISTRIBUTION THEORY. As is the case with many theoretical functions, a *normal distribution* is specified completely only by its mathematical statement or rule. Another name for the theoretical *normal distribution* is the *Gaussian distribution*, named in honor of the German mathematician, physicist, and astronomer Johann Carl Friedrich Gauss (1777-1855) who studied its basic characteristics. The *normal distribution* is a bell-shaped and symmetrical probability distribution (also called *normal curve, bell-curve,* and *bell-shaped curve*) showing the most probable scores from various tests or situations as concentrating around the central, average, or mean point, and indicating progressively less probable scores as being further from the mean, or central, point. For a mathematical expression of the *normal distribution,* or *normal density function,* see Hays (1994, p. 238). In technical terms, concerning this theoretical distribution, approximately 68 percent of scores fall within one "standard deviation" (i.e., a measure of the extent of variability, dispersion, or "scatter" in a set of scores - defined as the "square root of the variance") on either side of the mean; approximately 95 percent of scores fall within two standard deviations; and approximately 99 percent of scores fall within three standard deviations. In practical terms - and as explained by the *central limit theorem* - the normal distribution approximates the empirical, actual, or observed frequency distribution found in numerous psychological events, variables, behaviors, or situations (e.g., intelligence measurements) and - by virtue of this "natural" fact - is a widely-employed probability distribution in psychological statistics, especially in the area of "inferential statistics" that deals with making "best guesses" about the features of a population based on only a limited number of cases, scores, or sample data. Other related principles and effects in statistics and *measurement theory* are the following: the *inverse square law* - states that the *sampling error* (i.e., deviations of the summary values yielded by samples, from the values yielded by the entire population) tends to be inversely proportional to the square root of the size of the sample; *floor/basement effect* - an artificial *lower* limit on the value that a variable may have, causing the distribution of scores to be skewed or "peaked left" (often observed in tests that are too *difficult* where most of the respondents obtain very low scores or scores of zero); and *ceiling effect* - an artificial *upper* limit on the value that a variable may have, causing the distribution of scores to be skewed or "peaked right" (often observed in tests that are too *easy* where most of the respondents obtain perfect, or very high, scores). See also CENTRAL LIMIT THEOREM; PROBABILITY THEORY/LAWS.

REFERENCES

Gauss, J. C. F. (1966). *Disquisitiones arithmeticae.* Trans. A. A. Clarke. New Haven, CT: Yale University Press.

Hays, W. L. (1994). *Statistics.* Fifth edition. New York: Harcourt Brace.

NORMALIZATION PRINCIPLE. See PSYCHOPATHOLOGY, THEORIES OF.

NORMATIVE DECISION THEORY. See LEADERSHIP, THEORIES OF.

NORM OF RECIPROCITY, PRINCIPLE OF. See RECIPROCITY OF LIKING EFFECT.

NOVELTY/DISRUPTION EFFECT. See EXPERIMENTER EFFECTS.

NUDISM THEORIES. See LABELING/ DEVIANCE THEORY.

NULL HYPOTHESIS. = statistical hypothesis. The term *null hypothesis* refers to any statement, proposition, or assumption that serves as a tentative explanation of certain facts where the assumption of *no difference* exists between the studied groups (e.g., the effects of a tested drug will be the *same* for both the *experimental* and *control* groups of participants). When statistical analyses are used to test hypotheses, experimenters typically set up the *null hypothesis* prior to collecting data. This predetermined postulation allows for an evaluation of research results on the basis of sampling distribution and normal curve *probability theory*. A *null hypothesis* deals with the relationship between variables and is stated so that either it or its negation will result in information that may be used to advance a particular research hypothesis (cf., *partial null hypothesis* - a null hypothesis stating that there is no difference between any pair of group means on the dependent variable in a study containing several groups). In the standard *hypothesis-testing* approach in science, one attempts to demonstrate the *falsity* of the *null hypothesis* (in a "straw-man" type of reasoning strategy called *falsification*; for example, a tested drug shows that there *is* a difference between the experimental and control groups of participants), leaving one with the implication that the *alternative* (or mutually exclusive/opposite) hypothesis is the "correct" or acceptable one. The *alternative hypothesis* (also called the *experimental* or *research hypothesis*) functions as an alternative to the *null hypothesis* and typically asserts that the independent variable has an influence on the dependent variable, an effect that cannot be accounted for by chance alone. After the data in a study are collected, and the actual statistics are calculated, the researcher must decide whether or not to reject the *null hypothesis* [cf., *Simpson's paradox* - named after the British mathematician Edward H. Simpson (1927-), refers to a statistical paradox where the sets of data, when considered separately, each support a particular conclusion, but when taken together support the opposite conclusion]. In the *hypothesis-testing* activity, several hypothetical, or potential, statistical errors may be identified vis-à-vis the *null hypothesis* decision: *Type I error* - refers to the rejection of the null hypothesis when it is actually true; *Type II error* - refers to the failure to reject the null hypothesis when it is actually false; and a related interpretative error, *Type III error* - is an error arising from a misinterpretation of the nature of the scores being compared in a statistical significance test (cf., *grounded theory* -

refers to a systematic approach in theory development that advances the notion of close observation of the world without any prior theoretical framework or bias; such a theory is developed via the use of conceptualizations that link facts together rather than the use of inferences and hypothesis-testing strategies; this approach finds its value in the inductive generation of associations and categories that facilitate the attack of topical issues that are difficult to explore in the normal laboratory setting). The concept of the *null hypothesis* was developed by the English geneticist/statistician Sir Ronald Aylmer Fisher (1890-1962) and approximates the Austrian-born British philosopher Sir Karl Popper's (1902-1994) philosophy of science approach that views science to be a process for the *elimination of false theories* (i.e., the major role of science should be the *falsification* of incorrect theories). According to these reasoning viewpoints or strategies, science - particularly psychology - never "proves" hypotheses. Science shows only that certain hypotheses (e.g., the *null hypothesis*) have been "disproved" [cf., the American philosopher of science Thomas S. Kuhn's (1922-1996) *anti-confirmationism* viewpoint which states that proving a hypothesis has little meaning, but *disconfirming* a hypothesis may be very meaningful]. Therefore, the *null hypothesis* itself cannot be proved without knowing the "true" state of affairs, but it can be disproved if the obtained results in a study are too unlikely to be compatible with it. Decisions based on statistical *hypothesis-testing* procedures are usually cast in terms of levels of probability, or levels of confidence, as to the correctness of various outcomes vis-à-vis the *null hypothesis*. Other related forms of the *theory of confirmation* and *inductive reasoning* (i.e., inferring a general law/principle from particular observed instances) include the following: *problem of induction/Hume's problem* - named after the Scottish philosopher David Hume (1711-1776) - is an apparent inconsistency of inductive reasoning that is solved by using empirical evidence to falsify, rather than to confirm, hypotheses; *confirmation paradox/Hempel's paradox* - named after the German-born American philosopher Carl Gustav Hempel (1905-1997) - is confirmation of a statement via a process that contains no logical flaw in reasoning but has psychological difficulties arising from "misguided intuition;" for example, proving the statement that "all presidents live at the White House" tends to be confirmed (falsely) by finding or observing, say, a kennel containing a dog, because this is an instance of a dwelling that is *not* the White House which is the home of a *non*-president - which is a logically equivalent statement; the resolution of *Hempel's paradox* is to restrict the universe in which the data search is made; *Goodman's paradox* - named after the American philosopher Nelson Goodman (1906-1998) - is an apparent paradox, or refutation, of induction; for example, suppose that you note that all rubies that have ever been observed are red, and argue inductively that to conclude that all rubies are red; next, suppose one defines "roja" as the property of being red up to some time *t* (say, the end of the year 2040) and yellow thereafter; all the inductive evidence supports the conclusion that all rubies are "roja" just as it supports the conclusion that all rubies are red; therefore, one has no grounds for preferring either conclusion. See also MEEHL'S SIXTH LAW OF SOFT PSYCHOLOGY; PROBABILITY THEORY/LAWS.

REFERENCES

Fisher, R. A. (1925). *Statistical methods for research workers*. New York: Hafner.

Popper, K. (1935). *The logic of scientific discovery*. New York: Basic Books.

Hempel, C. G. (1937). Le probleme de la veacuterite. *Theoria, 3.* 3.

Goodman, N. (1955/1983). *Fact, fiction, and forecast*. Fourth edition. Cambridge, MA: Harvard University Press.

Schoffler, I. (1963). *The anatomy of inquiry*. New York: Knopf.

Kuhn, T. S. (1977). Objectivity, value judgment, and theory choice. In T. S. Kuhn (Ed.), *The essential tension: Selected studies in scientific tradition and change*. Chicago: University of Chicago Press.

Campbell, D. T. (1990). The Meehlian corroboration-verisimilitude theory of science. *Psychological Inquiry, 1,* 142-172.

NUMERICAL CONJOINT MEASUREMENT THEORY. See CONJOINT MEASUREMENT THEORY.

O

OBEDIENCE EFFECT. See SOCIAL IM-PACT, LAW OF.

OBJECTIVE TIME. See TIME, THEORIES OF.

OBJECT PERCEPTION. See PATTERN/OBJECT RECOGNITION THEORY.

OBJECT PERMANENCE PARADIGM/MODEL. This model/paradigm was employed originally by the Swiss biologist, philosopher, and psychologist Jean Piaget (1896-1980) to test the cognitive ability, working memory, and awareness in children that a physical object is permanent, and that it continues to exist even when the child no longer is in direct contact with it. That is, *object permanence* is the individual's understanding that an object still has existence even when it is temporarily out of sight. *The object permanence paradigm/test* involves the following procedure: the child is shown two containers, one of which holds a desirable object such as a toy, then the containers are closed and the child's attention is diverted elsewhere for a short time; later, the child is asked to choose the container having the toy. After several trials during which the child makes correct choices, the toy object is switched to the other container while the child observes. Then, further trials are conducted to determine whether the child is able to transfer choice-responses based on the new information. Theoretically, the *object permanence paradigm* (along with other tests such as the *delayed-reaction paradigm*) tests the child's working memory and cognitive development which depends on the neurological maturity of a part of the child's brain, the prefrontal cortex, that is presumed to be critical in successful performance on such "delayed" tasks. Generally, the prefrontal cortex of children under the age of about 8-9 months (in Piaget's terms: later in the "sensorimotor period" of the child's cognitive developmental stages) is not yet fully ma-

tured, and they perform poorly on the *object permanence* and *delayed-reaction* tasks. Further evidence of the importance of maturity of the prefrontal cortex for successful responding under such "delayed" tasks is available from studies of primates that have undergone surgical ablations/lesions in this cortical region. See also DELAYED-REACTION PARADIGM/MODEL; PIAGET'S THEORY OF DEVELOPMENTAL STAGES; WORKING MEMORY, THEORY OF.
REFERENCE
Piaget, J. (1929/1963). *The child's conception of the world.* New York: Littlefield, Adams.

OBJECT-RELATIONS THEORY. = object theory. The British-based Austrian psychoanalyst Melanie Klein (1882-1960), the British-based Hungarian psychiatrist Michael Balint (1896-1970, the English psychoanalyst Donald W. Winnicott (1896-1971), and the Scottish psychoanalyst W. Ronald D. Fairbairn (1889-1964) all contributed to the development of *object-relations theory* that deals with the emotional bonds that individuals form with so-called "instinctual objects" (i.e., anything whereby an instinct attempts to attain its "instinctual aim," or instinctually-driven behavior/activity, including "objects" such as a person, or part of a person - such as the mother's breast - in the individual's fantasy, and as distinguished from love/interest in oneself. *Object-relations theory* examines the capacity for one person to develop loving relationships with other people where such bonds are called "object-relationships." The concepts of *instinctual aim, instinctual object,* and *instinctual source* were introduced by the Austrian neurologist/psychoanalyst Sigmund Freud (1856-1939) in 1905. In *Freudian theory*, the notion of "instinct" ("Trieb" in German) refers to a dynamic force/drive of biological origin, represented psychically by ideas/images containing an emotional valence called *cathexis*, and generating psychological or mental pressure directing an individual toward its (instinctual) aim. The concept of *instinct/drive* was originally associated by Freud with *libido* (sexual drive/energy), but later with the psychic mechanisms/notions of *eros* (life instincts, including both the sexual and ego/self-preservation instincts), and *thanatos* (the unconscious drive towards dissolution/death, initially turned inwards on oneself and tending to self-destruction, and later turn-ed outwards in the form of aggression). See also FREUD'S THEORY OF PERSONALITY; GOOD BREAST/OBJECT AND BAD BREAST/OBJECT THEORY; INSTINCT THEORY.

REFERENCES

Freud, S. (1905). Three essays on the theory of sexuality. In *The standard edition of the complete psychological works of Sigmund Freud*. London: Hogarth Press.

Freud, S. (1920). Beyond the pleasure principle. In *The standard edition of the complete psychological works of Sigmund Freud*. London: Hogarth Press.

Klein, M. (1932). *The psycho-analysis of children*. London: Hogarth Press.

Freud, S. (1934). Instincts and their vicissitudes. In *Collected papers*. Vol. 4. London: Hogarth Press.

Freud, S. (1940/1969). *An outline of psychoanalysis*. New York: Norton.

Klein, M. (1948). *Contributions to psychoanalysis, 1921-1945*. London: Hogarth Press.

OBJECTS, THEORY OF. See MEINONG'S THEORIES.

OBJECT SUPERIORITY EFFECT. See TOP-DOWN PROCESSING THEORIES.

OBJECT THEORY. See OBJECT-RELATIONS THEORY.

OBLITERATION THEORY. See FORGETTING/MEMORY, THEORIES OF.

OBSERVATIONAL LEARNING THEORY. See BANDURA'S THEORY.

OBSERVER EFFECT. See EXPERIMENTER EFFECTS.

OCCAM MODEL. This computational *model of learning*, regarding predictive and explanatory knowledge, called the *OCCAM model* (Pazzani, 1990, 1991), integrates three separate learning methods: similarity-based learning (SBL), explanation-based learning (EBL), and theory-driven learning (TDL). The goal of this integration via *OCCAM* is to provide a "learning architecture" that accounts for the effects of prior knowledge on human learning, and helps to explain how an individual may learn rapidly when new experiences are consistent with prior knowledge, as well as still retaining the ability to learn in novel domains. See also CONCEPT LEARNING/CONCEPT FORMATION, THEORIES OF; LEARNING THEORIES/LAWS.

REFERENCES

Pazzani, M. (1990). *Creating a memory of causal relationships: An integration of empirical and explanation-based learning methods*. Hillsdale, NJ: Erlbaum.

Pazzani, M. (1991). Learning to predict and explain: An integration of similarity-based, theory-driven, and explanation-based learning. *The Journal of the Learning Sciences, 1*, 153-199.

OCCAM'S/OCKHAM'S RAZOR. See PARSIMONY, LAW/PRINCIPLE OF.

OCCASIONALISM, THEORY OF. See MIND-BODY THEORIES.

OCCUPATION THEORIES. See WORK/CAREER/OCCUPATION, THEORIES OF.

OCTAVE EFFECT. See GENERALIZATION, PRINCIPLES OF.

OCULOGYRAL/OCULOGRAVIC ILLUSIONS. See APPENDIX A.

OHM'S ACOUSTIC/AUDITORY LAW. = Ohm's law of hearing. The German physicist Georg Simon Ohm (1787-1854) formulated this principle in 1843, which states that a complex tone is analyzed by the perceiver into its frequency components; in this way, for example, when one listens to an orchestra, the separate instruments may be distinguished even though the ears receive only a single complex sound wave. In addition to the ability to objectively break down a complex sound into sine-wave components by means of a mathematical procedure (known as a *Fourier analysis*), the ear is able to carry out this analysis as well. The ear can carry out an analysis of complex tones into simpler components because of the way structures inside the ear vibrate in response to different frequencies and because individual neurons are tuned to respond to a narrow range of frequencies. Such an analysis takes place early in the auditory system and - then at higher levels in the system - neural information about these frequency components is combined to create one's perception of sound. Although this analysis is not normally part of one's awareness, with training a hearer can learn to perceive individual *harmonics* (i.e., an overtone or "partial," the frequency of which is a multiple of the fundamental tone or sine wave with the lowest frequency) in a complex sound. *Ohm's acoustic law* is a theoretical statement about the perceiver/hearer and is differentiated from a *Fourier analysis*, which is a theoretical statement about the physical stimulus. The word *acoustic* in *Ohm's acoustic law* (which was added to distinguish it from *Ohm's electrical law* of 1827, the latter stating that I = E/R, where I is current in amperes, E is volts, and R is resistance) may be an unfortunate choice because it confuses the issue: it may have been better to call the acoustic principle here *Ohm's auditory law*. See also AUDITION/HEARING, THEORIES OF; FOURIER'S LAW/SERIES/ANALYSIS.

REFERENCES

Ohm, G. S. (1827). *Die galvanische kette mathematisch bearbeitet.* Berlin: Juncker.

Ohm, G. S. (1843). [Acoustic principle/law]. *Annalen der Physik und Chemie, 135,* 497-565.

OHM'S ELECTRICAL LAW. See OHM'S ACOUSTIC/AUDITORY LAW.

OLD WOMAN/YOUNG GIRL FIGURE. See APPENDIX A, RUBIN FIGURE/ILLUSION.

OLFACTION/SMELL, THEORIES OF. Several interesting things about *olfaction* include the ideas that much of one's perceptual processing of odors is unconscious, that it is very difficult to recall smells, and that it is difficult to name them. However, curiously, the experience of a particular smell at a particular moment can stimulate numerous memories, often highly emotional, of episodes in which that smell was present [cf., *Proust phenomenon/effect* - named after the French novelist Marcel Proust (1871-1922), refers to the main character in his novel "Remembrance of Things Past" (1922-32) in which the individual recalls past events evoked by smells; of the various senses, smells are most likely to call up past memories]. Smell seems to act according to two separate modes of action that may result in different perceptual and informational experiences: the "near" experience of flavors in food and the "far" experience of air-borne smells (e.g., insects and some higher animals secrete volatile chemicals called *pheromones*, whose molecules travel through the air to other members of the species; cf., the *Lee-Boot effect* - named after the Dutch biologists S. van der Lee and I. M. Boot who reported the effect in 1955, refers to the gradual slowing down of the estrus cycles of a group of female mice that are housed together; if they are then exposed to the odor of a male mouse or to his urine, their cycles begin again; this latter effect, called the *Whitten effect* - named after the Australian biologist Wesley Kingston Whitten who described it in 1959, is caused by a *pheromone* in the male's urine; and the *Vandenbergh effect* - named after the American biologist John G. Vandenbergh, refers to the acceleration of the onset of puberty in female mice caused by a *pheromone* in the urine of a mature male mouse). Molecules that evoke the sensation of smell may be described as having a specific size, shape, weight, and "vibration frequency" (i.e., atoms in a given molecule move around in a characteristic pattern at predictable speeds that are different for different substances). Also, the particular atoms that make up a molecule (and the number of electrons available for chemical bonding with other molecules on the smell receptors) are likely to be important components of smell stimuli. However, as yet, there is no consensus as to which of these factors is critical. As is the case with other senses, the mechanism by which the stimulus molecules cause an electrical response (the *transduction process*) in the receptors in the upper nasal passages (the "olfactory epithelium") is still something of a mystery. There are probably at least two classes of *transduction mechanisms* in olfaction/smell: highly selective processes where specific receptor-cell proteins ("specialists") form reversible chemical bonds with specific parts of odorant molecules, and less selective processes where chemicals directly affect the receptor cell membrane anywhere they contact it ("generalist" smell receptors). Several of the current *theories of olfaction* concerning the more selective ("specialist") mechanisms are the *lock-and-key theory* (also called the *stereochemical theory*) - which holds that variously shaped molecules fit into special sites on the receptor membrane like a key fitted into a lock: when a molecule fits into a receptor site, a change in the structure of the cell membrane occurs, allowing ions into or out of the cell and, consequently, generating an electrical current [cf., the Swedish-American Carl Emil Seashore's (1866-1949) *law of complementary odors*]; the *vibration/vibrational theory* - maintains that the stimulus molecule ruptures certain chemical bonds in the cell membrane, causing the release of stored-up energy which, in turn, generates an electrical current and action potentials; which bonds are ruptured in which cells depends on the unique vibration frequency of each stimulus molecule; and the *gas chromatographic model* - states that the rate of movement of an odorant molecule across the receptor surface determines the neural coding of its smell; that is, some molecules travel slowly across the receptor surface whereas others travel more rapidly, with the result that each molecule stimulates a different spatiotemporal pattern of receptors [cf., the earlier *infrared theory* of L. Beck & W. Miles - states that the olfactory sense organ functions, partly at least, through the filtering or absorption of infrared radiation from substances that emit odors. In the *Raman effect/shift* - named after the Indian physicist C. V. Raman (1888-1970), there is a shift in the frequency of light caused by the interaction of a photon with the energy level changes of an atom/molecule

exposed to the photon; Raman showed that the interaction of vibrating molecules with photons passing through them alters the spectrum of the scattered light, either increasing or decreasing it by a fixed amount; thus, the *Raman effect* enables the probing of molecular energy levels and became an important spectroscopic technique that is used universally]. The *gas chromatographic* approach is based on the observation that the same sort of "across-fiber patterns" that are found in the sense of *taste* seem to be present in the olfactory/smell system, where it is likely that the "code" for smell qualities will be found in these patterns. However, a *label-ed-line theory*, such as applied to taste, may not be feasible for olfaction because it has many more types of labeled lines where there is no small list of primary smells for olfaction as there is for taste/gustation. Thus, at present, there is no evidence of olfactory fibers falling into groups as the taste fibers seem to display. The *stereochemical/lock-and-key theory*, or *steric theory of odor*, is based on the identification of *seven primary odors*, each associated with a particular molecule shape [cf., the German psychologist Hans Henning's (1885-1946) *smell theory/smell prism* that proposes *six primary qualities* of olfaction: *foul, fruity, burnt, resinous, spicy,* and *flower*]. The seven odors presumed by the *steric theory of odor*, along with their proposed shapes, and typical stimuli/examples are: *camphoraceous* (spherically shaped; e.g., camphor or mothballs); *eth-ereal* (small, flat, thin; e.g., dry-cleaning flu-id); *floral* (key-shaped; e.g., rose); *musky* (disk-shaped; e.g., angelica root oil); *minty* (wedge-shaped; e.g., peppermint candy); *pungent* (shape unknown; e.g. vinegar); and *putrid* (shape unknown; e.g., rotten eggs). Among other theoretical systems for identifying and classifying odors are: the *Crocker-Henderson smell system* - named after the American chemists Ernest C. Crocker (1888-1964) and Lloyd F. Henderson (? - ?), identifies *four primary odors* (*fragrant, acid, burnt,* and *caprylic*); and the *Zwaardemaker smell system* - named after the Dutch physiologist Hendrik Zwaardemaker (1857-1930), classifies smells on *nine primary dimensions/odors*: *ethereal* (e.g., fruits, wine), *aromatic* (e.g., spices), *fragrant* (e.g., flowers, vanilla), *ambrosiac* (e.g., musk), *alliaceous* (e.g., garlic), *empyreumatic* (e.g., coffee), *hircine* (e.g., rancid fat, cheese), *foul* (e.g., belladonna), and *nauseous* (e.g., rotten meat, feces). The phenomenon of *adaptation* is among the "laws" of olfaction (other "laws" of smell include *fusion, compensation, selectivity*, and *modulation*; cf., Boring, Langfeld, & Weld, 1939). The perceived *intensity* of an odor is affected by *adaptation* where only a brief period of exposure is sufficient to render an odor undetectable. In practical terms, *adaptation* may be beneficial to workers in an animal laboratory, an animal slaughter-house, or a zoo, but non-beneficial to coal miners who might need to detect an increase in the intensity of a potentially lethal gas. See also ADAPTATION, PRINCIPLES/LAWS OF; GUSTATION/TASTE, THEORIES OF.

REFERENCES

Henning, H. (1915). Der geruch. *Zeitschrift fur Psychologie, 73*, 161-257.

Seashore, C. E. (1923). *Introduction to psychology*. New York: Macmillan.

Boring, E. G., Langfeld, H., & Weld, H. (1939). *Introduction to psychology*. New York: Wiley.

Beck, L., & Miles, W. (1947). Some theoretical and experimental relationships between infrared absorption and olfaction. *Science, 106*, 511.

Amoore, J., Johnson, J., & Rubin, M. (1964). The stereochemical theory of olfaction. *Scientific American, 210*, 42-49.

Pfaffman, C. (Ed.) (1969). *Olfaction and taste*. New York: Rockefeller University Press.

Mozell, M. (1970). Evidence for a chromatographic model of olfaction. *Journal of General Physiology, 56*, 46-63.

Amoore, J. (1982). Odor theory and odor classification. In E. theimer (Ed.), *Fragrance chemistry - the science of the sense of smell*. New York: Academic Press.

Engen, T. (1982). *Perception of odors*. New York: Academic Press.

Vandenbergh, J. G. (Ed.) (1983). *Pheromones and reproduction in animals*. New York: Academic Press.

Gibbons, B. (1986). The intimate sense of smell. *National Geographic, 170*, 324-361.

Getchell, T., & Getchell, M. (1987). Peripheral mechanisms of olfaction: Biochemical and neurophysiology. In T. Finger & W. Silver (Eds.), *Neurobiology of taste and smell*. New York: Wiley.

Gilbert, A., & Wysocki, C. (1987). The smell survey: Results. *National Geographic, 172*, 514-525.

OMNIPOTENCY THEORY. See DEVELOPMENTAL THEORY.

ONE-TRIAL LEARNING THEORY. See GUTHRIE'S THEORY OF BEHAVIOR.

ONOMATOPOETIC/DING-DONG/ANIMAL CRY/BOW-WOW THEORY. See LANGUAGE ORIGINS, THEORIES OF.

ONTOLOGICAL ECONOMY, PRINCIPLE OF. See PARSIMONY, LAW/PRINCIPLE OF.

OPEN SYSTEMS THEORY. See ORGANIZATIONAL/INDUSTRIAL/SYSTEMS THEORY.

OPERANT CONDITIONING/BEHAVIOR, LAWS/THEORY OF. See SKINNER'S DESCRIPTIVE BEHAVIOR/OPERANT CONDITIONING THEORY.

OPERANT RESERVE, LAW OF. See SKINNER'S DESCRIPTIVE BEHAVIOR/OPERANT CONDITIONING THEORY.

OPERATIONALISM, DOCTRINE OF. In the 1920s, the American philosopher of science Percy W. Bridgman (1882-1961) advanced the *logical positivist* viewpoint (i.e., the rejection of metaphysics, theology, and ethics as meaningless areas of study, and the suggestion that the only valid propositions are those consisting of elementary propositions that are empirically verifiable) and, in this context, the *doctrine of operationalism* refers to the requirement that all theoretical terms in science (i.e., those that do not refer to something directly observable) be given *operational definitions*. The basis of *operational definition* was proposed independently by Bridgman (who named it) and by the *logical positivists*, who called it *explicit definition*. In 1935, the American experimental psychologist and psychophysicist Stanley Smith (S. S.) Stevens (1906-1973) introduced *operationalism* to psychology where it played an important role in the development of *behaviorism*. Most scientists agree that the enterprise of science needs theory and theoretical terms, and *operationalists* attempt to guarantee the cognitive significance of theoretical terms by giving them *operational definitions*. In an *operational definition*, a theoretical term (e.g., "intelligence") is defined by relating the term to some publicly-verifiable operation, procedure, measurement, or manipulation (e.g., a score on the Stanford-Binet Intelligence Test); also, the operation is one that may be performed on the environment (e.g., the concept "drive" may be *operationally defined* as "the withholding of food from an animal for a specified number of hours"). According to this approach, an ill-defined concept - such as the Freudian notion of *superego* - may be challenged as fundamentally non-scientific because there is no explicit way of defining it in terms of something observable. In spite of its initial attraction, however, *operationalism* has been controversial within psychology and the philosophy of science, as it has been difficult to *operationalize* all the terms of a science, even physics, thereby leading the *logical positivists* eventually to largely abandon the *doctrine of operationalism*. Within psychology, although the requirement to *operationalize* theoretical terms remains strong, the doctrine has been criticized for its narrowing of psychology's perspective by insisting that *behaviorism* is the only viable methodology or strategy for gaining psychological knowledge. See also BEHAVIORIST THEORY; COMTE'S LAW/THEORY; SKINNER'S DESCRIPTIVE BEHAVIOR/OPERANT CONDITIONING THEORY; STEVENS' POWER LAW.

REFERENCES

Bridgman, P. W. (1927). *The logic of modern physics*. New York: Macmillan.

Steven, S. S. (1935). The operational basis of psychology. *American Journal of Psychology*, 47, 323-330.

Suppe, F. (1972). Theories, their formulations, and the operational imperative. *Synthese*, *25*, 129-165.

Suppe, F. (Ed.) (1974). *The structure of scientific theories*. Urbana, IL: University of Illinois Press.

Leahy, T. H. (1980). The myth of operationism. *Journal of Mind and Behavior*, *1*, 127-143.

OPPEL-KUNDT EFFECT/ILLUSION. See OPPEL'S EFFECT/ILLUSION.

OPPEL'S EFFECT/ILLUSION. = Oppel-Kundt effect/illusion = filled-space illusion = filled-duration effect/illusion = Kundt's rules/effects. These spatial and temporal effects/illusions were first described in 1860-61 by the German physicist Johann Joseph Oppel (1815-1894) and later studied in 1863 by the German physicist August Adolph Kundt (1839-1894). In the area of *spatial perception*, the effect is called the *filled-space effect/illusion*, and refers to a misperception of magnitude that occurs when a given line, volume, or area - when occupied/filled by a number of distinct elements/units, such as dots or dashes - is perceived to be *larger* than if the line, volume, or area is empty. The original illusion, called the *geometric-optical illusion* by Oppel 1854, consisted of a number of parallel upright line segments continuous with an empty space of the same length whose end was marked by a single upright segment. In the *area of temporal perception*, the effect is called the *filled-duration effect/illusion*, and refers to a misperception of magnitude that occurs when a given period of time - if that time is occupied/ filled by may stimuli, events, materials, such as auditory tones or sounds - is perceived to be *longer* than if the temporal interval is relatively empty. In the case of *Kundt's rules/effects*, there are two misperceptions: (1) a given space or distance - when divided into parts - appears to be greater than that same space or distance when it is not divided; and (2) when one is asked to bisect/divide a given line - while using one eye only - there is a tendency to place the halfway mark closer to the nasal side of the *open* eye. For the description of various other effects/illusions, see Appendix A, especially the *filled-duration illusion*. See also FRAISSE'S THEORY OF TIME; TIME, THEORIES OF; VIERORDT'S LAW OF TIME ESTIMATIONS.

REFERENCES

Oppel, J. J. (1860-61). Uber geometrisch-optische tauschungen. *Jahresbericht des Physikalischen Vereins Frankfurt-an-Main, 1,* 27-47.

Kundt, A. A. (1863). [Perception of visual extent]. *Poggendorffs Annalen der Physik und Chemie, 120,* 118-158.

OPPONENT-PROCESS COLOR VISION THEORY. See COLOR VISION, THEORIES/LAWS OF; HERING-HURVICH-JAMESON COLOR VISION THEORY.

OPPONENT-PROCESS THEORY OF EMOTION/MOTIVATION. See SOLOMON'S OPPONENT-PROCESS THEORY OF EMOTIONS, FEELINGS, AND MOTIVATION.

OPPOSITION-COHERENCE THEORY OF HUMOR. The *opposition-coherence theory of humor* (Chen, Cheng, & Cho, 2001) postulates that there are three key components that influence the degree of humor appreciation in humor stimuli: fixity of dominant schema; backward-inference difficulty; and degree of opposition of two opposing schema. Data generated from such a model of humor have been analyzed in terms of additive and multiplicative assumptions within *information integration theory*. Typical results in such analyses show that the three components of the *opposition-coherence theory of humor* operate in an additive/serial manner, and the "degree of opposition of two opposing schemata" generated by humorous text is the most salient of the three components. See also HUMOR, THEORIES OF; INFORMATION INTEGRATION THEORY.

REFERENCES

Anderson, N. H. (Ed.) (1990). *Contributions to information integration theory. Vol. 1: Cognition; Vol. 2: Social;*

Vol. 3: Developmental. Hillsdale, NJ: Erlbaum.

Chen, H.-C., Cheng, C.-M., & Cho, S.-L. (2001). An opposition-coherence theory of humor. *Chinese Journal of Psychology, 43,* 137-153.

OPTIMAL FORAGING THEORY. See DARWIN'S EVOLUTION THEORY.

OPTIMAL LEVEL THEORIES. See MOTIVATION, THEORIES OF.

OPTIMAL SELF-ESTEEM THEORY. See SELF-CONCEPT THEORY.

OPTIMAL STIMULATION, PRINCIPLE OF. See MOTIVATION, THEORIES OF.

OPTOKINETIC EFFECT. See APPENDIX A, SIZE-WEIGHT ILLUSION.

ORBISON ILLUSION. See APPENDIX A.

ORDER EFFECTS. See EXPERIMENTER EFFECS.

ORGANIC EVOLUTION, THEORY OF. See DARWIN'S EVOLUTION THEORY.

ORGANICISM THEORY. See MECHANISTIC THEORY.

ORGANISMIC PSYCHOLOGY. See GOLDSTEIN'S ORGANISMIC THEORY.

ORGANISMIC THEORY/MODEL. See GOLDSTEIN'S ORGANISMIC THEORY.

ORGANIZATIONAL/INDUSTRIAL/SYSTEMS THEORY. The branch of applied psychology called *organizational/industrial psychology* covers various areas such as industrial, military, economic, and personnel psychology and researches problems of tests and measurements, organizational behavior, personnel practices, human engineering/factors, and the effects of work, fatigue, pay, satisfaction, and efficiency. In the present context of *theory*, the term *organization* is defined as a complex social system made up of individuals, their facilities, and the products created, where the following criteria may be applied: there must be coordination of personnel effort, personnel must have some set of common goals or purposes, there has to be some division of labor within the larger structure, and there has to be some degree of integrated functioning, including a hierarchy of authority. The area called *systems theory* emphasizes the interaction and interrelated nature of behavior (cf., *ego-alter theory*, which attempts to account for the origin or existence of social organizations in terms of innate egoism or altruism; and *open systems theory* which holds that an organization may be viewed as an "open system" where it "imports energy" via hiring and "transforms energy" via making products); according to *systems theory*, an individual's behavior does not occur in a vacuum but rather is influenced by, and in turn influences, the environment in which it occurs [cf., *chaos theory* (also known as *nonlinear dynamical systems theory*) described by the American science writer James Gleick as a viewpoint imported from the mathematics of nonlinear systems that is applied to the behavior of complex systems such as humans, the weather, and wildlife populations; the *butterfly effect* (also known as the *sensitive dependence phenomenon*) is the tendency for two sets of initial conditions (that differ by an arbitrarily small degree at the outset) to diverge dramatically over a long period; the *catastrophe theory*, which is a mathematical approach developed by the French mathematician Rene Thom (1923-) that attempts to formalize the nature of abrupt discontinuities in functions, and may be used to model psychological phenomena, such as gradually increasing anger, leading abruptly to a temper tantrum/behavioral display; and the American economist Julian L. Simon's (1932-1998) economics-based *grand theory* that represents an "anti-entropy" position, emphasizing the notion that evolving humans *create* more than they use or destroy]. The general term *organizational dynamics* is used to refer collectively to the various dynamic patterns of shifting elements within an organizational unit where at least seven conceptual elements may be viewed in interrelationships: organizational processes, external environment, employees, formal structure, internal social system, tech-

nology, and coalitions within the organization [cf., *Taylor system/theory* - named after the American engineer Frederick W. Taylor (1856-1915), refers to the prototype/rational system of scientific management development in the 1880s whose goal was the improvement of industrial efficiency via the use of *time-and-motion* studies, and the use of regular rest periods, among other techniques; *Deming management theory* - named after the American business/organizational consultant and statistician W. Edwards Deming (1900-1993), who developed the area of *total quality management* (TQM), that is, an integrated and pervasive *management theory* that attempts to maximize the quality of an organization's services and products; Deming formulated a set of 14 guidelines for optimal organizational behavior and quality management: constancy of purpose; the new philosophy; cease dependence on mass inspection; end lowest tender contracts; improve every process; institute training on the job; institute leadership; drive out fear; break down departmental barriers; eliminate exhortations and slogans; eliminate arbitrary numerical targets; permit pride of workmanship; encourage education; and foster top management commitment and action]. Three topics of special theoretical interest to contemporary organizational psychologists concern managerial/leadership style, worker motivation/attitudes, and job satisfaction. Four different theories about the nature of individuals (includes both genders, *women* as well as *men*, even though the theories typically, and historically, refer exclusively to "man") that are held by managers and leaders are: the *rational-economic man theory* - argues that humans are primarily motivated by money; the leader's task is to manipulate the worker to perform his/her best within the limits of what one can be paid; workers' feelings, which are viewed as irrational, must be prevented from obstructing the expression of the workers' rational self-interest [cf., the American social and industrial psychologist Douglas Murray McGregor's (1906-1964) *Theory X* - a traditional approach to control in organizations where it is assumed, among other things, that the average person dislikes work and will avoid it if possible, and people need to be directed, coerced, controlled, and threatened with punishment by management]; *social man theory* - holds that people are basically motivated by social needs that determine their sense of identity and meaning through relationships with others; *self-actualizing man theory* - maintains that people are intrinsically motivated, as in the worker who has deeply personal, internalized reasons for doing a good job; and *complex man theory* - argues that different workers have different needs and capabilities, and managers/leaders must be sensitive to individual differences in the desires, needs, fears, and abilities of workers. The issue of worker motivation has been approached by three theories, among others: *goal-setting theory*, *equity theory*, and *expectancy theory*. Research on *goal-setting theory* (i.e., the proposal that specific and difficult goals lead to higher performance) suggests that goals provide both direction and mobilization of behaviors where the specificity of the goal acts as an internal stimulus. According to *equity theory* in a work setting, a worker is driven to perform by a need to maintain equilibrium or balance - that is, employees prefer jobs in which the "output" is equal to the "input;" if imbalances occur, workers adjust their input, output, or their psychological perceptions of work; Currently, one of the most popular theories of worker motivation and attitudes is *expectancy theory*, which holds that workers' efforts are determined by expectancy of outcomes, their desirability, and the energy needed to achieve them (cf., *prospect theory* - an algebraic decision theory that attempts to explain departures from *expected utility theory*; it includes the *certainty effect* - the tendency to overweight outcomes that are certain relative to outcomes that are merely probable; *reflection effect* - the tendency to consider and deliberate over alternative solutions to problems; and *isolation effect* - the tendency to show superior recall in the learning of items having a high degree of salience or distinctiveness; note, also, the *false-consensus effect*, which is the tendency to overestimate the degree to which one's opinions and beliefs are shared by others; and the *assimilation-contrast theory* that is based on the assumption that attitudes are modified by changes in the relationship between one's originally held position, the opin-

ion of the person effecting the change, and the source credibility). *According to expectancy theory*, workers ask themselves three questions: What can I reasonably expect from my efforts? Do I really want the rewards offered by management? If I give maximum effort, will it be reflected in my job evaluation? Another important issue in organizational psychology is the problem of job satisfaction. Among the theories of job satisfaction is the *personality-job fit theory*, which asserts that a good fit, or match, between an individual's personality and an occupation results in maximal job satisfaction (cf., the *Peter principle*, which states that one gets promoted up through the ranks of an organization until one reaches one's level of incompetence!). See also ASSIMILATION-CONTRAST THEORY/EFFECT; CATASTROPHE THEORY/MODEL; CONTROL/SYSTEMS THEORY; DECISION-MAKING THEORIES; EQUITY THEORY; EXCHANGE AND SOCIAL EXCHANGE THEORY; EXPECTED UTILITY THEORY; FALSE CONSENSUS EFFECT; GENERAL SYSTEMS THEORY; HAWTHORNE EFFECT; LEADERSHIP, THEORIES OF; MURPHY'S LAW(S); RISKY-SHIFT EFFECT; WORK/CAREER/OCCUPATION, THEORIES OF.

REFERENCES

Taylor, F. W. (1911). *The principles of scientific management*. New York: Harper.

McGregor, D. M. (1960). *The human side of enterprise*. New York: McGraw-Hill.

Argyris, C. (1964). *Integrating the individual and the organization*. New York: Wiley.

Schein, E. (1965). *Organizational psychology*. Englewood Cliffs, NJ: Prentice-Hall.

Deming, W. E. (1966*). Some theory of sampling*. New York: Dover.

Locke, E. (1968). Toward a theory of task motivation and performance. *Organizational Behavior & Human Performance, 4*, 309-329.

Blau, P. M. (1970). A formal theory of differentiations in organizations. *American Sociological Review, 35*, 201-218.

Silverman, D. (1971). *The theory of organizations: A sociological framework.* New York: Basic Books.

Thom, R. (1972). *Stabilite structurelle et morphogenese: Essai d'une theorie generale des modeles.* Paris: E.S.F.

Tausky, C., & Parke, E. (1976). Job enrichment, need theory, and reinforcement theory. In R. Dubin (Ed.), *Handbook of work, organization, and society.* Chicago: Rand-McNally.

Argyris, C., & Schon, D. (1978). *Organizational learning: A theory of action perspective.* Reading, MA: Addison-Wesley.

Blake, R., & Mouton, J. (1978). *The new managerial grid.* Houston, TX: Gulf.

Kopelman, R. (1979). Directionally different expectancy theory predictions of work motivation and job satisfaction. *Motivation & Emotion, 3,* 299-317.

Holland, J. (1985). *Making vocational choices: A theory of vocational personalities and work environments.* Englewood Cliffs, NJ: Prentice-Hall.

Deming, W. E. (1986). *Out of the crisis.* Cambridge, MA: M.I.T. Press.

Gleick, J. (1987). *Chaos: Making a new science.* New York: Penguin Books.

Walton, M., & Deming, W. E. (1988). *The Deming management method.* New York: Perigee.

Abraham, F. D., & Gilgen, A. R. (Eds.) (1995). *Chaos theory in psychology.* Westport, CT: Greenwood Press.

Wilpert, B. (1995). Organizational behavior. *Annual Review of Psychology, 46,* 59-90.

Simon, J. L. (1996). *The ultimate resource 2.* Princeton, NJ: Princeton University Press.

Cooper, C. L. (1998). *Theories of organizational stress.* New York: Oxford University Press.

Rapoport, D. C. (2001). *Inside terrorist organizations.* London: F. Cass.

Brief, A. P., & Weiss, H. M. (2002). Organizational behavior: Affect in the workplace. *Annual Review of Psychology, 53,* 279-307.

Olmstead, J. A. (2002). *Creating the functionally competent organization: An open systems approach.* Westport, CT: Quorum Books.

Ilgen, D., Hollenbeck, J., Johnson, M., & Jundt, D. (2005). Teams in organizations: From input-process-output models to IMOI models. *Annual Review of Psychology, 56,* 517-543.

ORGANIZING EFFECT. See DEVELOPMENTAL THEORY.

ORGAN SPECIFICITY HYPOTHESIS. See PSYCHOSOMATICS THEORY.

ORGONE THEORY. See REICH'S ORGONE/ORGONOMY THEORY.

ORING'S THEORY OF HUMOR. According to Elliott Oring's (1945-) *theory of humor,* humor depends on the discernment of an "appropriate incongruity" and suggests that humor is based on the perception or apprehension by the individual of a *structure* of ideas rather than a reaction to particular ideas, motives, or events. Such a hypothesis is reflective, formally, of classical metaphysics and mythic formulae in which, for example, Aristotle's assertion that all definitions should include a "genus" and a "differentia" is found in Oring's notion of humor where it may be viewed more "genus" (i.e., a given entity is located within a particular set) than "differentia" (i.e., distinction of a given member of a set from other members). Oring argues that as *sentiments,* in particular, have become suppressed in modern society, they have been rechanneled through humor. Also, according to Oring, humor serves as a vehicle for *sentiments* because it is a form of "intellectual play," it tends to be a distraction from underlying thoughts, and it tends to devalue emotions. In Oring's approach, three communicative cases or situations are illustrated in which humor is used *socially* to convey affection: dyadic traditions, greeting cards, and "social roasts." See also HUMOR, THEORIES OF; INCONGRUITY/INCONSISTENCY THEO-

RIES OF HUMOR; SOCIAL/COMMUNI-
CATION THEORY OF LAUGHTER.

REFERENCES
Oring, E. (1981). *Israeli humor: The content and structure of the Chizbat of the Palmah*. Albany, NY: State University of New York Press.
Schrempp. G. (1995). Our funny universe: On Aristotle's metaphysics, Oring's theory of humor, and other appropriate incongruities. *Humor: International Journal of Humor Research*, 8, 219-228.
Oring, E. (1997). *The jokes of Sigmund Freud: A study in humor and Jewish identity*. Northvale, NJ: Jason Aronson.
Oring, E. (2003). *Engaging humor*. Urbana, IL: University of Illinois Press.

ORNE EFFECT. See EXPERIMENTER EFFECTS.

ORNSTEIN'S THEORY OF TIME. In his account of the experience of the passage of *time*, the American psychologist Robert Ornstein (1942-) proposed that the subjective or phenomenal passing of time is primarily dependent on the amount of cognitive activity going on in a given physical time period, where - by counting the number of "cognitive markers" or individual mental events that occur - an approximate measure of experienced duration is possible. See also BLOCK'S CONTEXTUALISTIC MODEL OF TIME; FRAISSE'S THEORY OF TIME; GUYAU'S THEORY OF TIME; TIME, THEORIES OF.

REFERENCE
Ornstein, R. (1969). *On the experience of time*. Harmondsworth, UK: Penguin Books.

ORTGEIST THEORY. See NATURALISTIC THEORY OF HISTORY.

ORTHOGENETIC PRINCIPLE. See PERCEPTION (I. GENERAL), THEORIES OF.

ORTHOMOLECULAR THEORY. The American chemist Linus C. Pauling (1901-1994) developed this approach to the treatment of psychopathology or mental disorders based on the tenet that every disorder may be alleviated with the administration of specific chemical substances. This therapeutic viewpoint is known, also, as *megavitamin therapy*, *orthomolecular psychiatry*, and *vitamin therapy*. In general, biological/biochemical theories of mental illness and mental retardation are gaining in recognition and popularity (cf., Frazer & Winokur, 1977). Advanced research, also, has aided in identifying certain types of mental illness as a *somatopsychic effect* of biological conditions, including genetic, biochemical, environmental, and nutritional factors. The field called *somatopsychics* ("body-mind") refers to psychological or psychiatric symptomatology of primary physical etiology; cf., *psychosomatics* ("mind-body") in which physical conditions/maladies result from psychological stress. Thus, in simple terms, in *somatopsychics theory*, the *body's* state of health affects the *mind's* well-being, whereas in *psychosomatics theory*, the *mind's* state of health influences the *body's* well-being. Both *orthomolecular theory* and *somatopsychics theory* deal with the awareness that mental and emotional disorders may be caused by biological/chemical deficiencies of certain nutritional elements (vitamins, protein, minerals), as well as by malnutrition in general. However, it is highly debatable just how far *somatopsychics* and biology/chemistry will advance and be able, ultimately, to replace the therapeutic methods of psychology. See also PSYCHOPATHOLOGY, THEORIES OF; PSYCHOSOMATICS THEORY.

REFERENCES
Pauling, L. (1968). Orthomolecular psychiatry. *Science*, 160, 265-271.
Pauling, L. (1974). On the orthomolecular environment of the mind: Orthomolecular theory. *American Journal of Psychiatry*, 131, 1251-1257.
Frazer, A., & Winokur, A. (Eds.) (1977). *The biological bases of psychiatric disorders*. New York: Spectrum.

OSGOOD'S TRANSFER SURFACE/MODEL. See SKAGGS-ROBINSON HYPOTHESIS.

OTHER-RACE FACE-PERCEPTION EFFECT. See FACIAL FEEDBACK HYPOTHESIS.

OUCHI ILLUSION. See APPENDIX A, AUDITORY, COGNITIVE, TACTILE, AND VISUAL ILLUSIONS/EFFECTS.

OUTGROUP EXTREMITY EFFECT. See INGROUP BIAS THEORIES.

OUTGROUP HOMOGENEITY BIAS EFFECT. See INGROUP BIAS THEORIES.

OUTSHINING HYPOTHESIS. See PERCEPTION (I. GENERAL), THEORIES OF.

OUTWARD MOBILITY, LAW OF. See VIERORDT'S LAWS.

OVERARCHING PSYCHOLOGICAL THEORY. See HISTORICAL MODELS OF EXPERIMENTAL PSYCHOLOGY.

OVERATTRIBUTION EFFECT. See ATTRIBUTION THEORY.

OVERCONFIDENCE EFFECT. See DECISION-MAKING THEORIES.

OVERFLOW OF NERVOUS ENERGY THEORY OF HUMOR. See SPENCER'S THEORY OF LAUGHTER/HUMOR.

OVERJUSTIFICATION EFFECT/HYPOTHESIS. See REINFORCEMENT THEORY.

OVERLAP HYPOTHESIS. See INTELLIGENCE, THEORIES/LAWS OF.

OVERLEARNING REVERSAL EFFECT. See SPENCE'S THEORY.

P

PAIN THEORY. See GATE-CONTROL THEORY; PLEASURE-PAIN, DOCTRINE/ THEORY/LAW OF.

PAIRING HYPOTHESIS. See REINFOR- CEMENT THEORY.

PANDEMONIUM MODEL/THEORY. See PATTERN/OBJECT RECOGNITION THE- ORY.

PANGENETIC THEORY. See DARWIN'S EVOLUTION THEORY.

PANUM PHENOMENON/EFFECT. = Panum's limiting case = Wheatstone-Panum limiting case. In 1858, the Danish physician/ physiologist Peter Ludvig Panum (1820-1885) described this visual sensation concerning three-dimensional depth that occurs when two lines - one to each of the person's eyes - are given at positions that permit binocular fusion to occur. Then, at the same time, a third line is presented to one of the person's eyes at a dif- ferent position. This stimulus-condition results in a perception where the fused line appears nearer than the single line. The effect is called a *limiting case* because it is similar to the stimulus pattern that occurs when two stimu- lus objects at different distances are viewed from an angle such that one of the objects is hidden behind the other one from the vantage point of one eye (whereas the other eye sees both of the objects). The effects described in the *Panum phenomenon* were discovered ini- tially by the English inventor/physicist Sir Charles Wheatstone (1802-1875) in 1838, a year in which he described, also, his famous "stereoscope," a prism device used even today in psychological experiments to study three- dimensional perception ("stereopsis"). An- other term *Panum's fusion area*, also named in honor of Peter Panum, refers to an area or volume of space (relative to the *horopter* - the curved surface of points in space that, for a given degree of ocular convergence, are pro-

jected on to corresponding retinal points, and where all points on the *horopter* are perceived as the same distance away as the point being fixated) within which different points pro- jected onto the right and left retinas result in binocular fusion and produce a sensation of visual depth. Points far from the *horopter* - outside *Panum's fusion area* - do not result in binocular fusion, but produce double images in a condition of double-vision called "diplo- pia." See also CYCLOPEAN EYE; HOROP- TER THEORY; PERCEPTION (I. GEN- ERAL), THEORIES OF.
REFERENCES
Panum, P. L. (1858). *Physioloogische unter- suchungen uber das sehen mit zwei augen.* Leipzig: Breitkopf, Hartel.
Wade, N. J. (Ed.) (1983). *Brewster and Wheatstone on vision.* London: Ac- ademic Press.

PANUM'S LIMITING CASE. See PANUM PHENOMENON/EFFECT.

PAPER TIGER EFFECT. See INOCULA- TION THEORY.

PAPEZ-MacLEAN THEORIES. See EMO- TIONS, THEORIES/LAWS OF.

PARADIGM OF ASSOCIATIVE INHIBI- TION. See MULLER-SCHUMANN LAW.

PARADIGM SHIFT DOCTRINE. In 1962, the American historian/philosopher of science Thomas S. Kuhn (1922-1996) presented his *doctrine of the paradigm shift* in science. In general, a *paradigm* is a model, pattern, or diagram of the functions and interrelationships of a process, and includes a conceptual frame- work within which theories in a specific re- search area are organized and constructed. In particular, Kuhn proposed that systematic pat- terns to organize and conduct research within different spheres of knowledge, or disciplines, occur periodically [cf., *scientist-practitioner/ Boulder model* - an educational paradigm for the training of clinical psychologists; the *Boulder model* is based on recommendations reached at a 1949 United States Public Health Service conference held in Boulder, Colorado stating that practitioners/clinicians in psychology should be trained essentially as scientists who appreciate, and carry out, scientific research and methodologies; *Planck's principle* - named after the German physicist Max Karl Ernst Ludwig Planck (1858-1947), states that new scientific data/facts may survive not by convincing opponents of their validity, but because the opponents die and the newer generations accept those facts and principles; the *doctrine of post-constructionism*, also called *social constructionism*, is a philosophical doctrine advanced by the controversial Algerian-born French philosopher Jacques Derrida (1930-2004) suggesting that all theories, concepts, and scientific principles are merely linguistic constructions and lack actual being or existence; *doctrine of post-modernism* - a re-cent international movement in the social sciences and humanities, suggesting that claims about social and psychological knowledge cannot be objective, and theories and research findings in the social sciences cannot transcend the time and/or place in which they were produced; the doctrine attempts to assess the role played in science by the values and subjectivity of the researcher - as well as the existing politics - surrounding the discovery and formulation of social knowledge; and *theory-begging fallacy* - the logical error of the labeling of a theoretical assumption as a behavioral fact, involving the intellectual dishonesty of making some improved or unprovable statement and then relating it with some fact to create in the audience belief in the original statement]. In psychology, for example, *paradigmatic shifts* occurred when *introspection* gave way to *behaviorism* early in the 20th century and, again later, shifts occurred from *behaviorism* to *cognitive processes/psychology* [cf., *third-force theory /therapy* - this is a relatively recent paradigm in psychological theory and psychotherapy that contrasts both with the *behavior-therapy* and *psychoanalytic* theoretical approaches, and includes several existential, humanistic, and experiential therapies and theories; *third-force therapy* centers on the individual's direct experience, the "here-and-now," responsibility for self-change, the use of group dynamics/ interactions, the development of trust in natural processes, the expression of spontaneous feelings over reason, the emphasis on personal growth over cure or adjustment, and the self-discovery/self-exploration of one's potentialities; *third-force theory*, or *humanist theory* and *self-growth/ self-actualization psychology*, was advanced by the American psychologist Abraham Maslow (1908-1970), among several others]. Thus, the *paradigm shift doctrine* states that - occasionally in science - there is a system-wide alteration in thinking, procedures, and orientation, where a fundamental reorganization occurs (sometimes abruptly) concerning how people think about an entire topic/issue; for instance, the evidence advanced by the Polish astronomer Nicolas Copernicus (1473-1543) - that the earth revolves around the sun - caused a *paradigm shift* in the discipline of astronomy, and replaced the older paradigm or notion of the Egyptian astronomer and geographer Ptolemy (c. 90-168 A.D.) that the earth is the stationary center of the universe. In his writings, Kuhn distinguishes, also, between the concepts of *normal science* (a period in the development of any scientific discipline where there is general acceptance and agreement concerning the basic concepts and where there is steady, cumulative progress) and *scientific revolution* (a period in which paradigms compete with one another in a scientific discipline until a new paradigm replaces the old - by a process analogous to Darwin's *evolutionary principle of survival of the fittest* - causing a *paradigm shift* to occur in the science). See also BEHAVIORIST THEORY; DARWIN'S EVOLUTION THEORY; HISTORICAL MODELS OF EXPERIMENTAL PSYCHOLOGY; MASLOW'S THEORY OF PERSONALITY.

REFERENCE

Kuhn, T. S. (1962/1970). *The structure of scientific revolutions*. Chicago: University of Chicago Press.

PARADOXICAL COLD PHENOMENON. See ALRUTZ'S THEORY.

PARALLEL AND SERIAL THEORIES OF TIMING. See SCALAR TIMING THEORY.

PARALLEL DISTRIBUTED PROCESSING MODEL. This model of knowledge- and information-processing represents units and items of information as patterns of connections of differing strengths between locations within a *network model* (i.e., any model consisting of a collection of units, each joined to one or more other units that it may inhibit or excite). In this model, also generally known as a *distributed network model*, information processing assumes the form of the parallel processing of collections of activated links. The *parallel distributed processing model* (PDP) is tied closely to one of the definitions of *connectionism* - the design of "intelligent" systems in the area of *artificial intelligence* where neural networks consist of patterns of activation over collections of units and where the patterns are adaptive in function as they are capable of "learning" from previous experience. The notion of PDP - in which separate subprocesses are distributed within a *single* entity - is distinguished from that of "distributed cognition" which refers to information processing that is shared among *several* separate entities. An example of "distributed cognition" may be seen in the *cooperative principle* - a concept described by the English philosopher Herbert Paul Grice (1913-1988) wherein individuals normally attempt to cooperate when communicating by following conversational rules of truth/quality, information/ quantity, relevance/explanation, and clarity/ manner, and according to which conversation between humans proceeds, typically, on the assumption that the rules are being followed implicitly by the communicating individuals. The *back-propagation algorithm/model* is a special PDP method whereby the adjustment of the output of a multi-leveled neural network is used to produce a desired state for a given input by first checking the input and computing the required output for that input, and then comparing the present output with the required output and adjusting the "connection weights" (via the "Delta rule" or the "Hebbian synapse rule" - that is, the use of a "teacher unit" having a predetermined level of activation that governs the activation levels of other units to achieve a desired target level) in order to decrease the discrepancy between the required output and the present output, and then repeating these steps of adjustment for the next level down in the system and for each lower level of the system, in turn, down to the lowest level (this "causes" the system to "learn" to produce the required output). The term *anneal* (literally, "to burn" or "set on fire") refers to the use of random shocks to the system to alter the states of units in a network of connected units until they are all responding consistently to signals received from one another and no further adjustments lead to further improvements in the network. In general, the *PDP models* are *associationist networks* that are an improvement over previous paradigms, such as *Markov chaining* - a theory that central motor mechanisms involve a chain reaction in which each movement depends on a preceding movement which sends a feedback signal - that were once the strongest modeling available. However, some researchers assert that calling *PDP models* "neural networks" does not necessarily make them into models of brain function; thus, *PDP models* are suggestive of cognitive structures for mental functions, but are not necessarily substitutes for human study at the neuronal or cognitive levels. See also FUZZY SET THEORY; INFORMATION/INFORMATION-PROCESSING THEORY; MEANING, THEORIES/ASSESSMENT OF; NEURAL NETWORK MODELS OF INFORMATION PROCESSING.

REFERENCES

Grice, H. P. (1957). Meaning. *The Philosophical Review, 64*, 377-388.

McClelland, J. L., & Rumelhart, D. E. (1986). *Parallel distributed processing: Explorations in the microstructure of cognition.* Cambridge, MA: M.I.T. Press.

Morris, R. G. M. (Ed.) (1989). *Parallel distributed processing: Implications for psychology and neurobiology.* New York: Oxford University Press.

Parks, R. W., Long, D. L., Levine, D. S., & Crockett, D. J. (1991). Parallel distributed processing and neural networks: Origins, methodology, and cognitive functions. *International Journal of Neuroscience, 60*, 195-214.

Davis, S. (Ed.) (1992). *Connectionism: Theory and practice.* London: Oxford University Press.

PARALLELISM/PSYCHOPHYSICAL, THEORY/DOCTRINE OF. See MIND-BODY THEORIES.

PARALLEL LAW. See FECHNER'S LAW.

PARALLEL PROCESSING THEORY. See INFORMATION/INFORMATION-PRO-CESSING THEORY.

PARAMETER-SETTING THEORY. See LANGUAGE ORIGINS, THEORIES OF.

PARANORMAL PHENOMENA/THEO-RY. = extra-sensory perception = parapsychology = psi phenomena. The *paranormal* class of effects refers to supernatural events/ results ("beyond the normal") that are inexplicable by the usual laws of science and/or reason. The related terms *extra-sensory perception* (ESP) (including clairvoyance, precognition, and telepathy) and *psychokinesis* (PK) are generic terms for various hypothetical paranormal phenomena that involve experiences having no direct sensory contact, or refer to perception without the use of sense organs (cf., *concordant twin theory* - the proposition that identical twins will be able to communicate via ESP to a higher degree than concordant twins, and that - even if separated either at birth or soon after - such twins in the future will have similar preferences and lifestyles as well as identical physical ailments). The American parapsychologist Joseph B. Rhine (1895-1980) claimed to have coined the term *extra-sensory perception* in 1934, but the Haitian-born German physician/psychical researcher Gustav Pagenstecher (1855-1942) anticipated the notion in his book published in 1924 [cf., the German ophthalmologist and psychical researcher Rudolf Tischner (1879-1961) who studied the ESP phenomena of telepathy and clairvoyance in the 1920s; the term ESP was used, also, by the adventurer/ scholar Sir Richard Burton (1821-1890) in 1870; and the French psychical researcher Paul Joire (1856-1931) used the term ESP in 1892 to describe the ability of persons who have been hypnotized to externally sense things without using their ordinary senses; the phenomena of ESP may even have been indicated in Biblical times]. The first systematic study of ESP was conducted in 1882 when the Society for Psychical Research was founded in London, England (the American Society for Psychical Research was founded in 1885). However, the first ESP studies were rarely experimental in nature, and consisted mostly of researchers merely bombarding "sensitives/ psychics" with questions under conditions that resembled prosecuting lawyers questioning a defendant in a court of law. The following paranormal phenomena have received the most attention: *clairvoyance or remote viewing* - the extra-sensory *visual* perception of events/objects; *clairaudience* - the ability to sense *sounds* that are beyond the range of normal hearing; *pre-cognition* - the perception of events/objects in the future (or of another person's future mental processes) without the use of the sense organs (cf., *pre-recognition hypothesis* - posits that an expectation of an event occurs as the result of previous experiences in similar situations, and that future events "cast their shadow" before they happen, allowing certain "sensitive" people with psychic abilities to predict disasters and catastrophes); *psychokinesis/telekinesis/parakinesis* - the movement or change of physical objects simply by mental processes without the use of physical force or direct intervention; *telesthesia* - perception of events or objects that are beyond the range of the individual's sense organs; *telegnosis* - know-ledge of distant objects/events obtained without the use of the sense organs; and *telepathy* - perception of another person's mental processes without the use of the sense organs. One of the major requirements or criteria for valid scientific findings/results is that of *replicability* (i.e., obtaining the same results across studies that are repeated using the same procedures); however, unfortunately, the majority of research on *paranormal phenomena* lacks reproducibility/replicability and, accordingly, many psychologists remain skeptical concerning the existence of such hypothesized events [cf., *change effect* - a tendency for scores to drop temporarily following the change in experimental conditions in parapsychological tests; *decline effect* - the tendency for scores on psi phenomena tests to decline within a run, a session, or an experiment; *preferential effect* - in ESP research, this refers to a class of differential effects in which the positive scoring, i.e., "hitting," on one of the two contrasting conditions is associated with the individual's preference for that condition; *sheep-goat effect* - the tendency for individuals who believe in the possibility of ESP (the "sheep") to obtain scores *above* the mean chance expectation, as compared to those who do not believe in ESP (the "goats") who tend to score *below* the expected mean in ESP tests]. See also PSEUDOSCIENTIFIC/ UNCONVENTIONAL THEORIES.

REFERENCES

Pagenstecher, G. (1920). A notable psychometric test. *Journal of the American Society for Psychical Research, 14,* 386-417.

Pagenstecher, G. (1924). *Aussersinnlicher wahrnehmung (Extra-sensory perception).* Leipzig: Mutze.

Tischner, R. (1925). *Telepathy and clairvoyance.* London: Kegan, Paul, Trench, & Trubner.

Rhine, J. B. (1934). *Extrasensory perception.* Boston: SPR/Humphries.

Zusne, L., & Jones, W. H. (1982). *Anomalistic psychology.* Hillsdale, NJ: Erlbaum.

PARAPRAXIS THEORY. The Austrian physician and psychoanalyst Sigmund Freud (1856-1939) proposed *parapraxis theory* in which minor errors in speech or action (such as "slips" of the tongue, of the pen, or of action) are viewed *not* as random events, but often as representative of fulfillments of the individual's unconscious desires or wishes. The notion of "parapraxis" (in Greek, "beside or beyond a deed," and in German, "faulty performance") in *parapraxis theory* may be examined in the psychoanalytic milieu/context for possible clues concerning repressed thoughts and desires by the use of a therapeutic technique similar to dream analysis involving free association and interpretation of latent content of verbal and behavioral protocols. *Parapraxes* have been referred to, also, by psychologists as "motivated errors," and by laypersons as "Freudian slips." See also FREUD'S THEORY OF PERSONALITY.

REFERENCE

Freud, S. (1901). The psychopathology of everyday life. In *The standard edition of the complete psychological works of Sigmund Freud.* London: Hogarth Press.

PARAPSYCHOLOGY. See PARANORMAL PHENOMENA/THEORY.

PARENTAL IMPERATIVE HYPOTHESIS. See PARENTAL INVESTMENT THEORY.

PARENTAL INVESTIMENT THEORY. The American biologist Robert L. Trivers (1943-) introduced the notion of *parental investment* into the field of ethology, and defined the concept as any contribution that a parent makes towards an offspring, and which tends to increase that individual offspring's chances of survival and reproduction at the expense of the parent's ability to contribute to other offspring, including the production of sex cells, and the feeding and guarding/protection of the young (cf., *parental imperative hypothesis* - holds that biological and cultural factors cause humans to suppress certain behaviors and traits during parenthood where - when the demands of parenthood end - the suppressed characteristics and behaviors may appear; for example, many marriages may disintegrate where the parents/couples tend to return to earlier modes of behavior when their children leave home and the parents become "empty-nesters," or when "midlife crises" surface in the parents). *Parental investment theory* suggests that in species in which female organisms/women provide more parental investment than male organisms/men, the latter compete among themselves for the female mates, as well as having consequences showing that the female organisms/women are more vulnerable to mate desertion (cf., the notion of *sexual selection,* a form of natural or evolutionary selection operating via the differential process of individuals of different genotypes in acquiring mates, working largely through mate choices that are made by members of the opposite sex, and based on variables/characteristics such as plumage, size, behavior, power, health, etc.). Species seem to vary in degree of *parental investment*; for instance, sea turtles offer very little to their offspring, whereas many birds and humans offer a great deal of investment). In most sexually-reproducing species, the sexes are asymmetrical concerning *parental investment* where the female organism invests more than the male, although there are exceptions to this rule (e.g., the male stickleback fish demonstrates more involvement than does the female stickleback). See also DARWIN'S EVOLUTION THEORY; DEMBER-EARL THEORY OF CHOICE/PREFERENCE; INFANT ATTACHMENT THEORIES.

REFERENCE

Trivers, R. L. (1972). Parental investment and sexual selection. In B. Campbell (Ed.), *Sexual selection and the descent of man, 1871-1971*. Chicago: Aldine.

PARETO PRINCIPLE/CHART/OPTIMALITY. The French-born Italian mathematical economist and sociologist Vilfredo Pareto (1848-1923) suggested that all societies must change eventually by means of revolutions because they tend to be governed by a minority of the rich and powerful. Pareto often employed a *Pareto chart* (i.e., a vertical bar chart that shows the frequency of relative importance of conditions or issues) to explain and illustrate his ideas; the chart is designed as an analytic tool ("Pareto analysis") to indicate a starting point for process-improvement by visually aiding in the discrimination and separation of the few important and vital issues from the many trivial issues. In *Pareto optimality*, an income-distribution situation is described in which the distribution of economic welfare cannot be improved for one individual without reducing that of another person; on the other hand, *the Pareto principle* states that a legitimate welfare improvement occurs only when any change improves the welfare of at least one person. See also DECISION-MAKING THEORIES; MEASUREMENT THEORY.

REFERENCES

Pareto, V. (1906/1909). *Manuale d'economia politica*. Milan/Paris: V. Giard & E. Briere.

Pareto, V. (1935). *Mind and society*. New York: Harcourt, Brace & Co.

Pareto, V. (1968/1979). *The rise and fall of the elites*. New York: Arno Press.

PARKINSON'S LAW. See MURPHY'S LAW(S).

PARSIMONY, LAW/PRINCIPLE OF. = Lloyd Morgan's/Morgan's canon = Occam's razor = Occam's principle = economy, principle of. The *law of parsimony* states that if two scientific propositions, or two theories, are equally tenable, the *simpler* one is to be preferred. Another name for this law is called *Lloyd Morgan's canon* in honor of the English zoologist/physiologist Conway Lloyd Morgan (1852-1936). Morgan articulated the principle in 1894 (cf., the German psychologist Wilhelm Wundt who anticipated *Morgan's principle* in the former's lectures in 1863) and cautioned against the explanatory excesses of the emerging field of comparative psychology by stating that in interpreting an animal's behavior, it is always preferable to adopt the psychologically *simplest* interpretation (cf., the *parsimony principle* in biology/evolution, which is the proposition that closely related organisms, having diverged relatively recently in evolutionary history, have fewer differences in their DNA than more distantly related organisms). Thus, *Morgan's canon* refers to the use of a lower, more "primitive" explanation of phenomena than to assume the activity of a higher, more "mentalistic" functioning [cf., the tendency of the English naturalist George J. Romanes (1848-1894) to *anthropomorphize* animals' behavior). The canon was very influential in the development of the early *behaviorists'* programs and doctrines such as those proposed by J. B. Watson and E. L. Thorndike. During Morgan's time, when the proof of *Darwin's evolutionary theory* was uppermost in the minds of psychologists and biologists, demonstration of *Morgan's canon* and the *law of parsimony* was a definite advancement in scientific thinking [note, also, the British philosopher/economist *John Stuart Mill's* (1806-1873) earlier *canons*, which are principles that govern inductive reasoning about cause-effect relationships and include the *laws of agreement, differences, joint* *agreement/disagreement, residues,* and *concomitant variation*; cf., *law of noncontradiction* - a canon of rational thinking stating that if a certain proposition is true, its exact opposite or contradictory is false]. A third name for the *law of parsimony* is called the *principle of economy* and refers to a working rule for treatment of scientific data, according to which the simplest available explanation is to be preferred, that is, the explanation that involves the fewest or least complexly related concepts that are adequate. This was known, also, as the *law of simplicity* (and the *principle of ontological economy*) that was advanced originally by the English scholastic philosopher William of Occam (or Ockham) (c. 1285- c. 1349). Occam allegedly argued that reality exists only in individual things or events, and he further enjoined "economy" in explanation (e.g., "What can be done with fewer assumptions is done in vain with more"). Today, *Occam's principle* is also called *Occam's razor* - the principle of scientific thinking that the simplest adequate explanation of a thing is to be preferred to any more complex explanations. See also BEHAVIORIST THEORY; DARWIN'S EVOLUTION THEORY; MALEBRANCHE'S THEORIES.

REFERENCES

Mill, J. S. (1874). *A system of logic.* New York: Harper.

Romanes, G. (1884). *Mental evolution in animals.* New York: Appleton.

Morgan, C. L. (1890/1891). *Animal life and intelligence.* London: Arnold.

Morgan, C. L. (1894). *An introduction to comparative psychology.* London: Scott.

Thorndike, E. L. (1898). *Animal intelligence.* New York: Macmillan.

Watson, J. B. (1919). *Psychology from the standpoint of a behaviorist.* Philadelphia, PA: Lippincott.

PARTIAL NULL HYPOTHESIS. See NULL HYPOTHESIS.

PARTIAL REINFORCEMENT EXTINCTION EFFECT. See CAPALDI'S THEORY; REINFORCEMENT THEORY.

PARTICIPATION, LAW OF. See WHORF-SAPIR HYPOTHESIS/THEORY.

PARTICULARISM, DOCTRINE OF. See DETERMINISM, DOCTRINE/THEORY OF.

PASCAL'S PROPOSITION/WAGER. The French mathematician, philosopher, and physicist Blaise Pascal (1623-1662) proposed the rational argument/wager concerning the belief in a deity that it is in one's self- or best-interest to assume that God exists because no matter how small the probability is that God does not exist (provided that the probability is not zero), the infinite gain from belief (and the infinite punishment from disbelief) outweighs any advantage of disbelief if God does not exist. Essentially, *Pascal's proposition/wager* purports to show - in more modern decision-making, or rational-choice, terms - that the *expected utility* of assuming that God exists must be greater than the *expected utility* of believing that God does not exist. Formally, *expected utility* is the average utility (i.e., measure of the subjective desirability of an outcome/event, corresponding to the person's preference for it) calculated by multiplying each of the possible outcomes of the decision by its probability and then summing the resulting products. A major rational criticism of *Pascal's proposition/wager*, and one that serves to undermine the argument, is that there are more than two possibilities concerning the issue of the existence of the Christian God: God exists, God does not exist, and an infinite number of other possibilities. See also DECISION-MAKING THEORIES; EXPECTED UTILITY THEORY; UTILITY THEORY.

REFERENCES

Pascal, B. (1670/1961). *Pensees.* Paris: Desprez/Garden City, NY: Doubleday.

Benn, A. W. (1905). Pascal's wager. *International Journal of Ethics, 15,* 305-323.

Rosenthal, R. (1967). Psychology of the scientist: XXIII. Experimenter expectancy, experimenter experience, and Pascal's wager. *Psychological Reports, 20,* 619-622.

PASSING STRANGERS/STRANGER ON A TRAIN EFFECT. See RECIPROCITY OF LIKING EFFECT.

PASSIVE REGISTRATION THEORY. See GESTALT THEORY/LAWS.

PATH-GOAL THEORY. See LEADERSHIP, THEORIES OF.

PATTERN-MATCHING THEORY. See PATTERN/OBJECT RECOGNITION THEORY.

PATTERN/OBJECT RECOGNITION THEORY. The perception of shape/form, including figural pattern and detail, is generally achieved by organisms through analysis of stimulus features from the sensory input [cf., the *Höffding step/phenomenon* - named after the Danish philosopher and psychologist Harald Höffding (1843-1931), is the Gestaltist's term for the mental step through which the perception of an image makes contact with a memory trace]. Contour and edge perceptions are hypothesized to take place at the retinal level, and some vision experts propose that contour and edges are the basis of complex *form perception*. An *information-processing theory* or analysis of vision requires an initial stage of figural synthesis, which is the way that stimulus information is transferred from the icon and synthesized into a form. In order for *pattern/shape recognition* to occur, the synthesized information is transferred, subsequently, to memory to produce a unique response (cf., *pattern-matching theory* - assumes that individuals can recognize differences and similarities between certain patterns actually presented to them and contain patterns deposited in their "memory store"). One of the major problems for *pattern recognition* and perception theorists is to understand how the organism consistently recognizes forms/shapes when they are presented in different sizes and retinal locations, are degraded by poor or "noisy" environmental conditions, and are partially outlined in cartoon or picture-like formats. The *pandemonium model/theory* was an early and influential computer model of *pattern perception*. In its simplest form, it was based on a number of

perceiving elements called "demons" that were tuned to detect specific features (e.g., a straight line, a half circle, etc.). Each low-level demon that was activated "shouted out," and the higher level demons decided what stimulus was presented by sifting through the "wild uproar" or *pandemonium* (named after the capital of Hell in John Milton's book *Paradise Lost*). One general approach in *pattern recognition theory* is the *feature extraction/ feature detection theory*, which involves *template-matching theory* processes - and which assumes that various internal representations (i.e., "templates") of objects are stored in memory, and new stimuli are processed by comparing them with the templates until a match is found. However, as a *theory of human pattern recognition*, it is too simple and it cannot, for example, account for the ability to recognize that a, A, *A*, and α are all examples of the same letter. Most research on *form/ shape recognition* and perception includes basic visual functions concerning luminance distribution that produce lines or Mach bands, discriminable differences in forms, figural aftereffects, visual illusion changes due to unspecified cues, and estimation of the vertical orientation. F. Attneave and M. Arnoult studied the psychophysics of form and demonstrated that judgments of attributes of abstract forms could be related to stimulus *domain features* such as *complexity* and *area*. J. J. Gibson describes *three-dimensional perception* and suggests that object perception can be based only on *form perception*; he argues that *features* are important where what counts is not the form per se but the *dimensions* of variation of form. L. Zusne makes the terminological distinction that *form* is the more general term, and *shape* is more specific, even though the terms *form* and *shape* frequently are used interchangeably. B. Julesz hypothesizes that the "primitives" for object perception are units called *textons* that operate during the initial ("preattentive") stage of vis-ion. According to Julesz, texture formation in object perception is automatic and happens almost instantaneously. In her *feature integration theory* (*FIT*), A. Treisman suggests that the "primitives" of object perception operate in five stages. Treisman's *FIT* focuses on how different attributes such as shape, color, texture, and size are integrated into a simple object. However, Treisman does not spell out exactly how the process of feature combination works in her *FIT*. Another approach, I. Biederman's *recognition by components* (*RBC*) *theory*, is based on "primitives," also, but rather than being elementary properties such as color and shape, the "primitives" in *RBC theory* are volumetric primitives (such as spheres, cubes, and cylinders) called *geons* (for geometric ion). The basic idea behind *RBC theory* is that objects are recognized by perceiving their *geons*. According to the *principle of componential recovery*, one can easily recognize an object if its *geons* can be identified. The basic message of *Biederman's theory* is that if enough information is available to enable one to identify an object's basic *geons*, the perceiver will be able to identify the object. The theories by Julesz concerning *textons*, Treisman concerning *FIT*, and Biederman regarding *RBC* all have in common the notion that the perception of objects involves a number of stages, beginning with "primitives" and ending with the combination of primitives into the complete perception of an object. See also ARTIFICIAL INTELLIGENCE; CONCEPT LEARNING/CONCEPT FORMATION, THEORIES OF; GESTALT THEORY/LAWS; INFORMATION/INFORMATION-PROCESSING THEORY; MACH BANDS; PERCEPTION (I. GENERAL), THEORIES OF; PERCEPTION (II. COMPARATIVE APPRAISAL), THEORIES OF.

REFERENCES

Höffding, H. (1889). [Mediating mental step]. *Vierteljahrsschrift Wissenschaftlicher Philosophie*, *13*, 420-458.

Attneave, F., & Arnolult, M. (1956). The quantitative study of shape and pattern perception. *Psychological Bulletin*, *53*, 452-471.

Selfridge, O. (1959). Pandemonium: A paradigm for learning. In D. Blake & A. Uttley (Eds.), *Proceedings of the symposium on the mechanization of thought processes*. London: HM Stationery Office.

Uhr, L. (Ed.) (1966). *Pattern recognition: Theory, experiment, computer simulations, and dynamic models of form perception and discovery*. New York: Wiley.

Minsky, M. L., & Papert, S. (1969). *Perceptrons*. Oxford, UK/Cambridge, MA: M.I.T. Press.

Zusne, L. (1970). *Visual perception of form*. New York: Academic Press.

Gibson, J. J. (1979). *The ecological approach to visual perception*. Boston: Houghton Mifflin.

Julesz, B. (1981). Textons, the elements of texture perception, and their interactions. *Nature*, *290*, 91-97.

Biederman, I. (1987). Recognition-by-components: A theory of human image understanding. *Psychological Review*, *94*, 115-147.

Treisman, A. (1993). The perception of features and objects. In A. Baddeley & L. Weiskrantz (Eds.), *Attention: Selection, awareness, and control*. Oxford, UK: Clarendon.

PATTERN THEORIES OF CUTANEOUS/ SOMATOSENSORY CODING. See NAFE'S VASCULAR THEORY OF CUTANEOUS SENSITIVITY.

PAVLOVIAN CONDITIONING PRINCIPLES/LAWS/THEORIES. The Russian physiologist Ivan Petrovich Pavlov (1849-1936) - [note: Pavlov's name was spelled in various ways (such as "Pavloff," "Pawlow," and "Pavlow") by some American writers in the 1920s and 1930s] - was the first to explore extensively the characteristics of *classical conditioning*, even though he was not the first to discover the *conditioned response* (also called the *conditional response*, the *conditioned reflex*, and the *conditional reflex*). Aristotle's *laws of association* anticipated the *principle of conditioning*; the Scottish physiologist Robert Whytt (1714-1766) and J. A. Unzer (1727-1799) laid down the foundations for the *doctrine of reflex action*; and Whytt (1763) recognized *psychic secretions* over a century before Pavlov described them. The American psychologist Edwin Burket Twitmyer (1873-1943), in a doctoral dissertation in 1902 at the University of Pennsylvania, discovered the *conditioned response* (without actually using the term) in the course of an investigation of the knee jerk response. Pavlov, along with another Russian scientist, Vladimir M. Bekhterev (1857-1927) - who is best known for his work on "associated reflexes" and the conditioning of motor withdrawal responses - both worked within the conditioning framework laid down by their Russian predecessor Ivan M. Sechenov (1829-1905). Sechenov freely used the expression *psychic reflexes* and interpreted a person's voluntary behavior in reflex terms. Pavlov acknowledged the importance of having read Sechenov as he began to study psychic processes by physiological means. The procedure of *Pavlovian conditioning*, which is a particular form of learning, consists of the pairing of two stimuli, each of which initially produces a response that is different from the other one. Pavlov's *classical conditioning* experiment involved placing meat powder in a dog's mouth, whereupon salivation took place; the food was called the unconditioned stimulus (UCS), and the salivation was called the unconditioned reflex (URC). Subsequently, an arbitrary stimulus, such as a light or bell, was combined with the presentation of the food. Eventually, after repetition and the optimal time relationships, the light or bell evoked salivation independently of the food; the light or bell became a conditioned stimulus (CS), and the response to it was called a conditioned reflex (CR) (cf., the *Rescorla-Wagner theory/ model* - states that the increment in the CS-CR association on any one trial is a decreasing function of the predictability of the CS). Many such conditioning studies indicate that the CR is seldom, if ever, an exact replica of the UCR and may differ markedly from it. This fact was recognized early by American researchers and led to the substitution of the term *response* for *reflex* inasmuch as the concept of *reflex* implies a fixed and stereotyped movement. Pavlov developed a number of concepts and principles in his systematic study and theorizing about conditioning: *reinforcement*; *extinction* (cf., *overtraining* - the continuation of conditioning beyond the point at which the organism has no further increase in responsiveness; *overtraining extinction effect* - the tendency for an organism that has been overtrained to show more rapid extinction than one who has not been overtrained; *overtraining*

reversal effect - the tendency for an organism that has been overtrained, and then is presented with a habit reversal learning task, to learn to reverse its responses more quickly than an organism that has not been overtrained; and the *lullaby effect* - the process whereby an organism becomes adapted to a new stimulus that is given repeatedly; for example, the sudden onset of a thumping sound may initially elicit a startle reaction in the individual, but is diminished if it is repeated and the stimulus loses its effectiveness); *spontaneous recovery*; *generalization* (cf., the *law of coexistence* and the *law of contiguity*, which state that if two mental events occur at the same time, the recurrence of one tends to call forth the idea corresponding to the other); *differentiation* (cf., the *law of cohesion* - states that acts that occur in close succession tend to become combined or unified and form an integrated act of more complex character); *forward/backward /simultaneous/delayed* and *trace conditioning*; *inhibition*; *association, irradiation*; *concentration*; *reciprocal induction* (this phenomenon has been rediscovered in recent times and renamed *behavioral contrast*); *first and second signal systems*; *experimental neurosis*; and *higher-order conditioning*. Pavlov's conditioning paradigm has come to be known as *classical conditioning* and is distinguished from other types of conditioning and learning (cf., E. R. Hilgard and D. Marquis who coined the labels *classical* and *instrumental conditioning*). Other writers have used different labels for the two types of conditioning where the first term in the following pairs is the equivalent of *classical conditioning*, and the second term is the equivalent of *instrumental conditioning* (cf., *bifactorial theory of conditioning* - asserts that *attitudes* determine *probabilities* of conditioning, whereas the properties of *stimuli* affect the *magnitude* of responses in conditioning): *associative shifting* versus *trial and error learning*; *Type I* versus *Type II*; *Type S, respondent* versus *Type R, operant*; *conditioning* versus *success learning*; and *conditioning* versus *problem-solving*. Pavlov has had a major impact on psychology, particularly *learning theory*, due to his preferences for important topics of research. In G. Kimble's (1961) list of terms relevant to *con-*

ditioning and *learning*, 31 terms are attributed to Pavlov, and only 21 other terms are attributed to all other psychologists combined. G. Razran estimated that by the year 1965 some 6,000 experiments had been conducted using Pavlov's exact *classical conditioning model*, and were reported in at least 29 different languages. Even after the paradigm of *instrumental conditioning/learning* was introduced and developed, it was found that most of the phenomena studied in the *classical conditioning* paradigm (e.g., reinforcement, generalization, extinction) still held up well. The first experiments on the phenomenon of *intermittent reinforcement* were conducted in Pavlov's laboratory and, thereby, anticipating modern and more extensive investigations of the topic of *schedules of reinforcement*. As judged by formal evaluation studies and surveys (e.g., Coan & Zagona, 1962; Roeckelein, 1995), Pavlov ranks high - along with Freud and Wundt - as a major influence in American psychology today. See also ASSOCIATION, LAWS OF; ASSOCIATIVE LEARNING IN ANIMALS, THEORIES OF; ASSOCIATIVE LEARNING, PRINCIPLE OF; BEHAVIORAL CON-TRAST EFFECT/PHENOMENON; BLOCKING, PHENOMENON/EFFECT OF; COHESION LAW; CONNECTIONISM, THEORY OF; DELAYED-REACTION PARADIGM/MODEL; INHIBITION, LAWS OF; LEARNING THEORIES; REFLEXOLOGY THEORY; RESCORLA-WAGNER THEORY/MODEL.

REFERENCES

Whytt, R. (1763). *An essay on the vital and other involuntary motions of animals*. Edinburgh: Balfour.

Sechenov, I. (1863/1965). *Refleksy golovnogo mozga*. St. Petersburg. Translated as *Reflexes of the brain*. Cambridge, MA: M.I.T. Press.

Pavlov, I. (1927). *Conditioned reflexes*. New York: Dover.

Bekhterev, V. (1928). *General principles of human reflexology*. New York: International.

Pavlov, I. (1932). The reply of a physiologist to psychologists. *Psychological Review, 39*, 91-127.

Konorski, J., & Miller, S. (1937). On two types of conditioned reflex. *Journal of General Psychology, 16*, 264-272.

Schlosberg, H. (1937). The relationship between success and the laws of conditioning. *Psychological Review, 44*, 379-394.

Skinner, B. F. (1937). Two types of conditioned reflex: A reply to Konorski and Miller. *Journal of General Psychology, 16*, 272-279.

Hilgard, E. R., & Marquis, D. (1940). *Conditioning and learning*. New York: Appleton-Century-Crofts.

Mowrer, O. H. (1947). On the dual nature of learning - a reinterpretation of "conditioning" and "problem-solving." *Harvard Educational Review, 17*, 102-148.

Ferster, C., & Skinner, B. F. (1957). *Schedules of reinforcement*. New York: Appleton-Century-Crofts.

Kimble, G. (1961). *Hilgard and Marquis' conditioning and learning*. New York: Appleton-Century-Crofts.

Reynolds, G. (1961). Behavioral contrast. *Journal of the Experimental Analysis of Behavior, 4*, 57-71.

Coan, R., & Zagona, S. (1962). Contemporary ratings of psychological theorists. *Psychological Record, 12*, 315-322.

Razran, G. (1965). Russian physiologists' psychology and American experimental psychology. *Psychological Bulletin, 63*, 42-64.

Skinner, B. F. (1969). *Contingencies of reinforcement: A theoretical analysis*. New York: Appleton-Century-Crofts.

Miller, R., Barnet, R., & Grahame, N. (1995). Assessment of the Rescorla-Wagner model. *Psychological Bulletin, 117*, 363-386.

Roeckelein, J. E. (1995). Naming in psychology: Analyses of citation counts and eponyms. *Psychological Reports, 77*, 163-174.

Domjan, M. (2005). Pavlovian conditioning: A functional perspective. *Annual Review of Psychology, 56*, 179-206.

PERCEPTION (I. GENERAL), THEO-RIES OF. The area in psychology called *perception* refers to the study of the *central* processes that give coherence and unit to sensory (*peripheral* processes) input. Involved in these processes are physical, physiological, neurological, sensory, cognitive, and affective components of behavior (cf., *orthogenetic principle* - proposed by the German zoologist J. Wilhelm Haacke (1855-1912), states that the perception of objects, shapes, forms, and stimuli follow a predictable, specific life-span trend, for instance, children perceive the world in a global/diffuse way initially and, as they mature, they learn to integrate the parts of stimulus patterns with the whole pattern simultaneously as they relate to each other). *Theories of perception*, much like *theories of learning*, are very far-reaching and encompass nearly every area of psychology. Most *theories of perception* start with the recognition that what is perceived is not uniquely determined by physical stimulation but is a complex process dependent on a number of other factors, such as *attention* - focusing on selectively chosen stimuli [e.g., the *Broadbent filtering effect* - named after the English psychologist Donald Eric Broadbent (1926-1993), refers to the phenomenon, in a dichotic listening task, of not hearing the message in the unattended ear when the hearer complies with instructions to listen only to the message presented to the other ear]; *constancy* – stabilization of the perceptual world despite changes in sensory input; *motivation* - physical and psychological drive level of the person (cf., *perceptual defense/vigilance effects* - refers to perceptually selective processes in which one *defensively* blocks or distorts perceptions that are considered to be disagreeable to oneself; and, in tachistoscopic *vigilance* experiments, it is the phenomenon whereby participants require shorter viewing exposure durations to recognize threatening stimuli, as contrasted with non-threatening visual material);

organization - sensory elements are grouped and ordered into coherent wholes (see R. Wheeler's *organismic laws* - where parts of behavior are accounted for in terms of the whole; and his *law of individuation* - the principle that parts come into existence from wholes through a process of individuation; cf.,

distributive law - the principle that an operation performed on a complex whole affects each part of this complex in the same way as if performed on that part separately); *set* – cognitive and emotional predispositions toward a stimulus array; *learning* - the degree to which perceptions are acquired from experience versus innate origins and the degree that learning adapts to, and changes, perception; *distortion/ hallucination* - misperceptions due to emotional feelings, drugs, lack of sleep, sensory deprivation, stress, and mental disorders, and that may be classified as *top-down processes*; and *illusion* - normal perceptions concerning unpredictability and information often due to conflicting sensory cues [e.g., the *shrinkage illusion* of the *Ansbacher effect* - named after the German-American psychologist Heinz L. Ansbacher (1904-), also called the *Ansbacher shrinkage effect/H. C. Brown shrinkage effect* - refers to a situation where a lighted arc placed at the edge of a disc that is rotated in a dark room appears to be shorter the greater is the velocity of the rotation; note, also, the *texture illusion* of the *Spillman-Redies effect* - named after the German psychologist Lothar Spillman (1938-) and the German biophysicist Christoph Redies (1958-); the *geometric illusion* of the *Bourdon effect* - named after the French psychologist Benjamin Bourdon (1860-1943); the *subliminal illusion* of the *Poetzl effect* - named after the Austrian psychiatrist Otto Poetzl (1877-?); the *movement illusion* of the *Ternus phenomenon* - named after the German Gestalt psychologist Josef Ternus (1892-1959); and the *barber's pole effect* - when viewing a rotating pole (painted with spiral stripes of alternating colors) through a horizontal slit, one perceives it as marks moving horizontally, and if viewed through a vertical slit, one perceives it as marks moving vertically)]. One major theoretical approach, the *classical theory* of perception, has dominated perceptual inquiry for many years. The *classical theory* began with the physiological studies of the German physiologist Johannes Muller (1801-1858) concerning the division of sensory experience into the modalities of vision, touch, and smell. Muller argued that the organized perceived world is actually composed of separate channels of experience, each of which depends on the action of some specific and identifiable part of the sensory nervous system (cf., *mosaic theory of perception* - states that each nerve fiber of a peripheral organ communicates directly with a specific neuron in the brain, and complex sensations are produced by combinations of sensory-fiber impulses; and the *perceptual cycle hypothesis* - suggests that perception occurs in a three-part cycle consisting of an anticipatory schema, a stimulus-field sampling, and environmental stimulation where the cycle repeats as perception continues). Later, the German physicist Hermann von Helmholtz (1821-1894) subdivided the sensory modalities themselves into elementary sensations, each of which reflects the normal activity from the stimulation of specific receptor nerve cells by particular physical energies (cf., *naïve realism* - the doctrine that perception of a physical object is a direct awareness of the object itself, rather than of a representation of it; this view is challenged by the phenomena of *perceptual vigilance* and, in particular, *visual illusions*; see Appendix A for a listing of various *visual illusions*). The German physicist/psychologist Gustav Fechner (1801-1887) developed the *classical psychophysical methods* to measure the effects on experience of small stimulation differences and which provided the tools for perceptual analysis in sensory research. The analytic approach of these early researchers accounted for many major theoretical features of sensory experience. For example, *Helmholtz's visual perception theory* (which receives little support today) related the three fundamental visual sensations of red, green, and violet to the physical aspect of long-, middle-, and short-wavelengths of light, respectively. Helmholtz also proposed a *perceptual theory of audition* (that also receives little support today) where the fundamental sensations for differences in pitch were attributed to differing receptor cell activity and responses made to the frequency components of sound waves entering the ear. The early studies in the physiology of sensation and perception continue today as a vital area devoted to sensory research, principally in the domains of visual and auditory science. The *classical perceptual theory* of the 1800s set the stage for subsequent investigations of perceptual

experience involving the properties of things and events such as shape, brightness, distance, movement, and space [cf., *Lune-burg's theory of visual space* - named after the German-American mathematician Rudolph K. Luneburg (1903-1949), refers to a geometric theory that binocular visual space, in contrast to physical space, is best described as a Riemannian space of constant Gaussian curvature]. In one case, the perception of *three-dimensional space* posed a problem to early researchers because three dimensions are not directly specified by the two-dimension array of light that enters the eye [cf., the *Hess effect* - named after the German ophthalmologist Carl von Hess (1863-1923), and the *Pulfrich phenomenon/effect* - named after the German physicist Carl P. Pulfrich (1858-1927), is a visual stereoscopic effect in which a regularly swinging pendulum is perceived to follow an elliptical path when viewed monocularly through a medium-density filter; the *Mach-Dvorak phenomenon* - named after the Austrian physicist Ernst Mach (1838-1916) and the Czech physicist Vinko Dvorak (1848-1922), refers to the perception of stereoscopic depth as a result of delaying the presentation of a moving object to one eye as compared to the other; and the *Panum phenomenon* - named after the Danish physiologist Peter L. Panum (1820-1885), refers to an effect observed in the stereoscopic image produced by three equal, parallel lines, two of them close together and presented to one eye, the third line presented to the other eye; if the single line is made to overlap one of the other two lines, the combined line appears to be closer to the viewer than the other line in the pair]. A traditional *theory of depth perception* is that cues about the third dimension of space are provided by an *unconscious inference* process concerning the proximity/distance of objects in the environment. This viewpoint emphasizes the notion that - because the use of such depth cues involves no conscious process - depth cues are available in a direct manner rather than being mediated by conscious deduction. Cues for depth, such as linear/size perspective, interposition, aerial perspective, and atmospheric conditions of haze, were known and used by painters for generations before research in perception took place. In the early *classical perceptual theory*, it was assumed that depth perception was achieved through the learned association of such visual cues with memories of previous muscle-stretch and touch sensations. However, Gibson and Walk (1960) found - via their *visual cliff apparatus* - that some organisms respond to visual depth cues *without* previous visual experience, indicating that depth perception, at least, is innate rather than learned through experience. Thus, concerning *space perception*, for instance, there appears to be a need to identify some innate visual mechanisms for depth response where a fundamental revision of the *classical theory* is required. Three other major sets of phenomena present problems for the *classical perceptual theory*: constancies, illusions, and *perceptual organization*. Historically, the most systematic opposition to the *classical theory of perception* was *Gestalt theory*, which argued that the configuration ("gestalt") of the stimulating energies, not the energies themselves, is the essential stimulus attribute to which the nervous system responds [cf., *configural superiority effect* - the tendency for observers to perceive a difference among integrated stimuli more readily than differences among simple *stimuli; reorganization principle* - states that new perception or learning requires a reorganization of understanding or perception such that something that seemed arbitrary, or made no sense, previously is now reorganized into a structure that does make sense; and *reorganization theory* - states that the primary process involved in *learning* is the alteration of existing mental structures and is found, commonly, in opposition to *associationistic theory*, which holds that structural reorganization is *not* necessary in learning new responses; cf., the *Gelb phenomenon/effect* - named after the German psychologist Adhemar M. Gelb (1887-1936), refers to the situation where a spinning black wheel illuminated by a circle of light in a dark room looks white, but looks blacker if a white piece of paper is put into the light just in front of it; the effect suggests that *brightness constancy* is, in part, determined by the gradients of luminance between neighboring surfaces; and the *Kardos effect* - named after the Hungarian psychologist Lajos Ludwig Kardos (1899-1985), is the phenomenon concerning brightness constancy

where a white rotating disc exactly covered by a shadow looks dark gray or black; both the *Gelb* and *Kardos effects* are examples of *context* and *field effects*, that is, the influence of surrounding events, fields, objects, or information on a person's response to a stimulus, or the influence of spatial or temporal setting on the appearance of an image or part of an image; other *context effects* are the *dialectical montage effect* used in films that enables an actor to convey an emotion without actually expressing it; and the *outshining hypothesis*, which (in recognition tasks) holds that if an item is a strong cue or has very salient features, it tends to over-power the context cue/factor effect; note, also, the *Fuchs phenomenon* - named after the German psychologist Wilhelm Fuchs, is an effect observed when viewing an object through a transparent filter against a homogeneous background; if the object is displaced completely outside the contours of the filter, the filter appears to be opaque]. The Gestalt *laws of perceptual organization* - such as *figure-ground*, *proximity*, *similarity* (also called the *law of equality*), and so on - presented relevant demonstrations of perceptual experience, even though they were not quantitatively or objectively studied (cf., *law of precision*, which states that organization occurs in such a way that its products, namely, the whole field - perceptual, ideational, and behavioral - become as well articulated as possible). Attempts to formulate a theory from the Gestaltist demonstrations focused on radically different notions of the nervous system and attempts to formulate objectively the *laws of perceptual organization* (largely based on the *principle of simplicity*) have not flourished. Current versions of the *classical theory of perception* can better explain the Gestaltist demonstrations than can *Gestalt theory* or its successors. An early view from *classical theory* concerning the *illusions* and *constancies* is that they both are aspects of one process, and *Helmholtz's theory of unconscious inference*, based on "unnoticed sensations," has been revitalized, even though the theory is difficult to test. Theories of *direct perception* and the *constancy hypothesis* - the notions that perceptions are direct responses to physical properties of the environment [e.g., J. J. Gibson's "global psychophysics;" cf., *Gibson effect* - named after the American psychologist J. J. Gibson (1904-1980), refers to the situation where vertical lines appear curved when viewed through a wedge prism; the apparent curvature diminishes with prolonged viewing, but when the prism is removed, vertical lines appear again but now curved in the opposite direction] - make Helmholtz's inference-like mental processes and the concept of *unconscious inference* unnecessary (cf., the *constructivist theory of perception* - holds that perceptual experience is more than a direct response to stimulation). However, although a few mathematical analyses of the direct theoretical approach have been offered (e.g., explanation of the *phenomenon of motion parallax*), there is no good evidence to support completely the *direct perception theory*, and the *classical theory* concerning explanations of various *constancy/illusion phenomena* remains strong among contemporary perceptual psychologists. Three avenues of research have been preeminent in providing opportunities to test and amend the *classical theory*: infant perception/perceptual development; perceptual adaptation/rearranged sensory input (cf., *misorientation effect* - refers to difficulty in reorganizing an object that is in an orientation different from that presented during the initial exposure or familiarity trials); and complex sensory channels. J. Hochberg (1994) reviews evidence concerning mental structure and inference in perception, and concludes that what we perceive is not fully determined by direct sensory response to object properties alone but requires the addition of cognitive factors as well - as the *classical theory* proposed - to understand completely the perceptual process. See also APPARENT MOVEMENT, PRINCIPLES/THEORIES OF; ATTENTION, LAWS/PRINCIPLES/THEORIES OF; CONSTRUCTIVIST THEORY OF PERCEPTION; FECHNER'S LAW; GESTALT THEORY/LAWS; LEARNING THEORIES/LAWS; MIND/MENTAL SET, LAW OF; NATURE VERSUS NURTURE THEORIES; PANUM PHENOMENON/EFFECT; PERCEPTION (II. COMPARATIVE APPRAISAL), THEORIES OF; PULFRICH PHENOMENON/EFFECT; SUBLIMINAL PERCEPTION EFFECTS/PHENOMENA; TOP-DOWN PROCESSING/THEORIES; UNCONSCIOUS INFERENCE, DOCTRINE OF; VISION AND SIGHT, THEORIES OF; YOUNG-HELMHOLTZ COLOR VISION THEORY.

REFERENCES

Muller, J. (1842). *Elements of physiology*. London: Taylor & Walton.

Helmholtz, H. von (1856-1866). *Handbuch der physiologischen optik*. Leipzig: Voss.

Fechner, G. (1860/1966). *Elements of psychophysics*. (D. Howes & E. G. Boring, eds.). New York: Holt, Rinehart, & Winston.

Helmholtz, H. von (1863). *Lehre von dem tonempfindungen als grundlage fur die theorie der musik*. Leipzig: Voss.

Hering, E. (1878/1964). *Outlines of a theory of the light sense*. Cambridge, MA: Harvard University Press.

Wheeler, R. (1930). The individual and the group: An application of eight organismic laws. In R. Wheeler (Ed.), *Readings in psychology*. New York: Crowell.

Gibson, J. J. (1950). *The perception of the visual world*. Boston: Houghton Mifflin.

Hamlyn, D. W. (1957). *The psychology of perception: A philosophical examination of Gestalt theory and derivative theories of perception*. New York: Humanities Press.

O'Neill, W. (1958). Basic issues in perceptual theory. *Psychological Review, 65*, 348-361.

Gibson, E., & Walk, R. (1960). The "visual cliff." *Scientific American, 202*, 64-71.

Mundle, C. W. K. (1971). *Perception: Facts and theories*. London: Oxford University Press.

Avant, L., & Helson, H. (1973). Theories of perception. In B. B. Wolman (Ed.), *Handbook of general psychology*. Englewood Cliffs, NJ: Prentice-Hall.

Rock, I. (1977). In defense of unconscious inference. In W. Epstein (Ed.), *Sta-

bility and constancy in visual perception. New York: Wiley.

Walk, R. (1981). *Perceptual development.* Monterey, CA: Brooks/Cole.

Hochberg, J. (1994). Perception. In R. J. Corsini (Ed.), *Encyclopedia of psychology.* New York: Wiley.

Walk, R. (1994). Illusions. In R. J. Corsini (Ed.), *Encyclopedia of psychology.* New York: Wiley.

PERCEPTION (II. COMPARATIVE APPRAISAL), THEORIES OF. The American psychologist Floyd Henry Allport (1890-1978) reviewed and critiqued the major *theories of perception* and, subsequently, proposed his won *perceptual theory of structure* (called *event-structure* or *enestruence*), which holds that social structure has no anatomical or physical basis but consists of cycles of events that return on themselves to complete and maintain the cycle. Allport (1955) appraises the following 13 theories of perception: core-context, Gestalt, topological field, cell-assembly, sensory-tonic field, set and motor adjustments, adaptation-level, probabilistic functionalism, transactional functionalism, directive state, hypotheses, behavior, and cybernetic theories. The *core-context theory of perception* - formulated by the English-born American psychologist Edward Bradford Titchener (1867-1927), states that a perception consists of three items in its earlier stage: a number of sensations consolidated into a group under the laws of attention and the special properties of sensory connection; images from past experiences that supplement the sensations; and meaning (i.e., "context;" cf., *atmosphere/context effects* and *context theory*, which maintain that all behavior must be analyzed within the context in which it occurs). Allport considers the *core-context theory* to be parsimonious and in agreement with the limited range of facts used to support it; though the theory centers on "object meaning," it has a potentiality for generalization. The theory is weak, however, in logical consistency and explanatory value, but its chief merit is that it recognizes the part played in perception by "object" and "situational" meaning. The *Gestalt theory of perception* employs basic principles such as form-concept and isomorphism, field/forces, flexibility, transposition, symmetry, goodness of form, transformation, and organization. Within the area of Gestalt psychology, W. Kohler proposed the *dynamic theory* ("psychic dynamism"), according to which physiological processes are determined by dynamic conditions (e.g., by forces involved in the central nervous system field as a whole) rather than by structural conditions (e.g., neural structures and connections). The dynamic theory may be contrasted with the machine theory that states that physiological processes are machinelike and determined by constant conditions (e.g., by neural topography) rather than by dynamic conditions. Also, with the Gestalt psychology domain, M. Wertheimer proposed the *short-circuit theory* that states that phenomenal movement - such as the *phi phenomenon* - is due to a short-circuit between the regions of the brain excited by each stimulus, thereby giving rise to a new structured unity. Six major principles cover most of the *Gestalt laws*, and the Gestalt approach, demonstrations, and experimental exhibits. However, as many as 114 *laws of gestalten* have been formulated by various writers, but eventually they were edited down to a list of 14 principles. The *Gestalt theory of perception* is consistent, parsimonious, and based on a large number of experiments that support its phenomenological generalizations. However, concerning one of its speculations, called *brain-field theory*, the Gestalt approach has difficulties with the facts of brain physiology and has problems, also, with some genetic and clinical observations. K. Lewin's *topological field theory of perception* is an offshoot of the Gestalt movement in psychology and, although it makes use of the concept of *fields* and other related Gestalt principles and terms, it has no direct concern with physiological bases or *isomorphism* (i.e., the hypothesis that there is a point-by-point relationship between the two systems of excitatory fields in the cortex and conscious experience or between the perception of the stimulus and the brain). According to Allport, *Lewin's field theory* is short on logical consistency because it does not discriminate well between phenomenological and physicalistic data. The *cell-assembly theory of perception*, also called *Hebb's theory of perceptual learning* - named after the Canadian psychologist Donald Olding Hebb (1904-1985), holds that perception is not an innate process but has to be learned. The theory maintains that a particular perception depends on the excitation of particular brain cells (*cell assemblies*) at some point in the central nervous system. In his theory, *Hebb's rule* states that the cellular basis of learning is determined by the strengthening of synapses that are active and practiced repeatedly when the postsynaptic neurons fire; cf., *Mark II cell assembly theory* - a supplement to *Hebb's cell assembly theory* that adds a model of inhibitory mechanisms and sensitization to establish the association of ideas. The cell assembly is Hebb's basic unit of perception and represents the physiological basis of the simplest percept (cf., *reverberating circuit theory* - states that a cell assembly may function as an independent unit within the brain, and may continue to respond to a stimulus even after the stimulus has been terminated; and the *short-circuiting law* - Hebb's speculation that the neurophysiological mechanism underlying the process of a physical activity or a mental process tends to become automatic, and no conscious effort of attention is used to perform a particular mental activity). In Hebb's *phase sequence hypothesis*, complex perceptions (called *phase sequences*) are formed out of the basic assemblies by the principles of mutual facilitation in conduction and consolidation in timing. The *cell-assembly theory*, according to Allport, is fairly logical, parsimonious, and built on facts of neurophysiology, genetic development, and brain pathology; however, the theory has difficulty with the concept of *equipotentiality* (i.e., that all neurons mediating a given sensory modality have a common function), and does not handle well the aspects of dimension, constancy, and frame of reference. The *sensory-tonic field theory of perception* deals with the relationship between *tonic events* (e.g., changes in postural/muscular tension) and *sensory events* (e.g., a conscious experience such as a sensory quality). The attempt of *sensory-tonic theory* is to show that tonic factors interact with sensory factors in perception and that a "field" is present in which the body and the perceived object interact (cf., *sensory conflict theory* - is a proposed account of mo-

tion sickness according to which passive movement produces a mismatch between cues or information relating to orientation and movement provided by the visual and the vestibular systems, whereby such a mismatch creates feelings of nausea; and *functional asymmetry hypothesis* - is a poorly documented postulate that there is superiority in perception of ears or eyes on one side of the body for certain types of stimuli; for instance, the right ear excels in receiving verbal sounds whereas the left ear is better in receiving environmental sounds, or the left half-field of the eyes is better for face recognition, whereas the right half-field is better for reading tasks). The *sensory-tonic theory* is well supported by experimental findings, but it fails to explain the interrelation of sensory and tonic factors in a clear and logical manner. The *set and motor adjustments theory of perception* holds that *set* (i.e., a disposition to respond in a particular way; includes perceptual set, or *Einstellung*, and task-oriented set, or *Aufgabe*) - and the actual behaviors that prepare the organism - provides a basis for understanding the motor aspects of perception (cf., *warm-up effects* - in learning theory, this refers to the influence of preparation and set on the transfer and retention of materials to be learned). The *set and motor adjustments theory* is logical, unified, and based on experimental findings, and is in general agreement with motor physiology; however, according to Allport, the theory fails to unite exteroceptive sensory and motor elements in the perceptual process (cf., an early, curious, and nonperceptual principle concerning the relationship between sensory and motor events, called the *law of dynamogenesis*, which states that any change in sensory stimulation has a corresponding effect in altering muscular activity or tension; Baldwin, 1894; Triplett, 1898). The *adaptation-level (AL) theory of perception* is a formulation of sensory-context effects that maintains that the neutral, adapted background provides a standard against which new stimuli are perceived (cf., psychological *law of relativity*, which states that an experience is understood only in its relation to other experiences, as when the visual localization of an object depends on the perception of the relation of the object to the existing frame of reference). The *AL theory* has been extended from explanations in the area of sensory processes to those of attitudes and attitude change. *AL theory* states that the concept of *adaptation-level* represents a weighted geometric mean of all the stimuli that have been judged on a particular dimension. According to Allport, *AL theory* is logical, supported by experimental facts, and has good generalizability and parsimony; however, the theory does not seem applicable to the phenomena of configuration, and it falls short in interpreting the non-quantitative aspects of perceptual aggregates, including object and situational meaning. The *probabilistic functionalism theory of perception* – formulated by the Hungarian-born American psychologist Egon Brunswik (1903-1955) - argues that the veridical distal relationship with objects in the environment is dependent on the statistical validity of the cue-to-object relationships where the attainment of distal objects is never better than an approximate or "probable" achievement. The theory stresses that perception is a process of discovering which aspects of the stimulus provide the most useful or functional cues. The *transactional theory of perception* [most notably presented by the American psychologist/painter Adelbert Ames (1880-1955) in his famous "Ames distorted room" and "trapezoidal window" demonstrations, and traceable to the writings on vision in 1709 by the Irish philosopher Bishop George Berkeley (1685-1753)] is based on the notion that perception results from acquired, but unconscious, assumptions about the environment, represented as probabilities of transactions occurring within it. Thus, the relationship between *probabilistic theory* and *transactional theory* is very close: both deal with the "dimensional" aspect of perception, both are "molar," both rely on past experience, both give a strategic position to cues and their probabilistic weighting, both involve unconscious inferences or judgments of the perceiver, and both hold an intermediate ground between the stimulus object and some activity of the organism. The main difference, on the other hand, between the theories is that *probabilistic theory* is concerned with phenomenological "attainment" of perceptual objects, but *transactional functionalism* contains a more spe-

cific statement of the perceptual significance of action and purpose. The *directive-state theory of perception* divides the determinants of perception into two contrasting categories: the *autochthonous* (structural) aspects - including the stimulus and effects of stimulation on the receptors, afferent neurons, and sensory cortical areas; and the *behavioral* (motivational or "New Look") aspects - including the needs, tensions, values, defenses, and emotions of the perceiver (cf., the *fashioning effect* of *role theory* whereby the role adopted by the perceiver influences both that person's behavior and her/his self-perceptions). Corresponding to these are two contrasting programs of experiment and theory: the *formal* and the *functional*; taken together, the behavioral determinants form a *central directive state* where they may be viewed as independent variables in an experimental setting. Experimental evidence (which has not gone unchallenged) for the *directive-state theory* derives from six areas: the effect of bodily needs on what is perceived; the effect of reward and punishment on perceptual content; the influence of values on speed of object-recognition; effects of needs and values on the dimensionality of the percept; personality as a perceptual determinant; and the effect on perception of the emotionally disturbing nature of the stimulus-object. The *directive-state theory*, although it opened a new field of dynamic possibilities, doesn't offer enough agreement with the available facts; however, according to Allport, the theory does show the importance of taking individual cases into account. The *hypothesis-theory of perception* is a reformulation of the *directive-state theory* and argues that all cognitive processes, whether they take the form of perceiving, thinking, or recalling, represent *hypotheses* that are usually unconscious and that the organism sets up in a given situation. Such hypotheses require "answers" in the form of further experience that will either confirm or disprove them (for the same notion in a *learning* context, see Restle, 1962). Adjustment of the organism to the environment proceeds by such a process of hypothesis confirmation or rejection. The *hypothesis theory* is in accord with experimental findings and draws together many of the discordant results of the *directive-state* experiments and moves, generally, in the direction of a *unified theory*. However, according to Allport, it is deficient in explanatory principles for hypothesis checking, stimulus-transformation, monopoly, and other similar concepts and processes [cf., D. M. Armstrong's *knowledge-based theory of perception*, and his discussion of three other theories of perception: *realism, representationalism*, and *phenomenalism*; Armstrong asserts that any complete *theory of perception* must be able to answer questions concerning the nature of bodily sensations, dreams, and mental imagery]. The *behavior theory of perception* is based on the association, or stimulus-response (*S-R*), notion of the linkage of a stimulus or stimulus-pattern to a response/reaction and the gradual strengthening of such a connection. In this approach, learning involves the increasing of *habit strength* where the strengthening takes place through repeated trials accompanied by reinforcement (i.e., need-state or drive-reduction). Another notion in *learning theory* (e.g., Tolman, 1932) has relevance to *perception theory* where the organism learns *meanings* and *relationships* rather than the specific movements required in a situation; i.e., the *field*, or stimulus-stimulus (*S-S*), type of theory. The *S-S type of learning* is related to perception by the similarity of acquisition of elements: in *learning*, cognitions are expected suddenly; and in *perception*, a percept is a very brief, all-or-none event as well. Thus, the cognitive and other aspects of *S-S learning theory*, in particular, seem to fit a phenomenological or perceptual frame of reference better than a physicalistic or *S-R* framework. However, *S-S, field*, or *cognition-like theories* have not succeeded in becoming general for all the phenomena of perception. Some of the *S-S theories* have almost completely discounted the evidence that past experience is an important determinant of perceptual behavior. In Allport's assessment, the *S-S learning models of perception* seem to lack in explicit reference, explanatory value, parsimony, and generalizability. The *cybernetic theory of perception* is based on the modern development of technological communication and control systems (the term *cybernetic* means "helmsman," or "one who steers"). The specific contributions of *cybernetics* to the study of perception are relatively few, but the following *cybernetic* concepts and principles may prove fruitful, ultimately, to perceptual theory: *open systems* (involving terms such as "irreversibility," "steady state," and "negative entropy"), *information, coding, feedback loops, negative feedback, oscillation, scanning, teleological mechanisms*, and *repeating circuits*. The correspondence between some *cybernetic* concepts and perceptual/imagery phenomena is good, but other notions - such as digitalization of information in the nervous system, time limitations of the reverberating circuit, and scanning device - seem more dubious. On the whole, however, Allport suggests that the *cybernetics theory* has contributed valuable structural ideas and models for the *theory of open systems* and neurophysiology. After his appraisal of the major *theories of perception*, Allport concludes that most of the theories contain certain common generalizations - such as internal relatedness, self-closedness or circularity, and space/time building - and he asserts that such generalizations represent the most substantial insights that psychologists have into the nature of the perceptual act, and they account for the best explanations of why things appear as they do to the perceiver. See also ALLPORT'S THEORY OF ENESTRUENCE; ATTITUDE/ATTITUDE CHANGE, THEORIES OF; BERKELEY'S THEORY OF VISUAL SPACE PERCEPTION; CONTROL SYSTEMS AND THEORY; DYNAMOGENESIS, LAW OF; GESTALT THEORY/LAWS; HELSON'S ADAPTATION-LEVEL THEORY; HULL'S LEARNING THEORY; INFORMATION AND INFORMATION-PROCESSING THEORY; LASHLEY'S THEORY; LEWIN'S FIELD THEORY; PARSIMONY, LAW/PRINCIPLE OF; PERCEPTION (I. GENERAL), THEORIES OF; PHI PHENOMENON; SPENCE'S THEORY; TOLMAN'S THEORY.

REFERENCES

Baldwin, J. M. (1894). *Handbook of psychology*. New York: Holt.

Triplett, N. (1898). The dynamogenic factors in peacemaking and competition. *American Journal of Psychology, 9*, 507-533.

466

Titchener, E. B. (1909). *Experimental psychology and the thought processes*. New York: Macmillan.

Wertheimer, M. (1912). Experimentelle studien uber das sehen von bewegung. *Zeitschrift fur Psychologie, 61*, 161-265.

Kohler, W. (1929). *Gestalt psychology*. New York: Liveright.

Tolman, E. C. (1932). *Purposive behavior in animals and men*. New York: Century.

Helson, H. (1933). The fundamental propositions of gestalt psychology. *Psychological Review, 40*, 13-32.

Koffka, K. (1935). *Principles of gestalt psychology*. New York: Harcourt.

Lewin, K. (1936). *Principles of topological psychology*. New York: McGraw-Hill.

Freeman, G. (1939). The problem of set. *American Journal of Psychology, 52*, 16-30.

Boring, E. G. (1942). *Sensation and perception in the history of experimental psychology*. New York: Appleton-Century-Crofts.

Walthall, W. J. (1946). The Kohler effect. *American Journal of Psychology, 59*, 152-155.

Helson, H. (1948). Adaptation-level as a basis for a quantitative theory of frames of reference. *Psychological Review, 55*, 297-313.

Wiener, N. (1948). *Cybernetics*. New York: Wiley.

Hebb, D. O. (1947). *The organization of behavior*. New York: Wiley.

Werner, H., & Wapner, S. (1949). Sensorytonic field theory of perception. *Journal of Personality, 18*, 88-107.

Spence, K. (1951). Theoretical interpretations of learning. In C. Stone (Ed.), *Comparative psychology*. New York: Prentice-Hall.

Ittelson, W. (1952). *The Ames demonstrations in perception*. Princeton, NJ: Princeton University Press.

Kilpatrick, F. (Ed.) (1952). *Human behavior from the transactional point of view*. Princeton, NJ: Institute for Associated Research.

Von Foerster, H. (Ed.) (1950-1952). *Cybernetics*. New York: J. Macey Foundation.

Werner, H., & Wapner, S. (1952). Toward a general theory of perception. *Psychological Review, 59*, 324-338.

Allport, F. (1955). *Theories of perception and the concept of structure*. New York: Wiley.

Brunswik, E. (1956). *Perception and the representative design of psychological experiments*. Berkeley, CA: University of California Press.

Armstrong, D. M. (1961). *Perception of the physical world*. New York: Humanities Press.

Restle, F. (1962). The selection of strategies in cue learning. *Psychological Review, 69*, 329-343.

Armstrong, D. M. (1965). A theory of perception. In B. B. Wolman (Ed.), *Scientific psychology: Principles and approaches*. New York: Basic Books.

Royce, J. R. (1970). *Toward unification in psychology*. Toronto: University of Toronto Press.

PERCEPTION-CONSCIOUSNESS SYSTEM. See FREUD'S THEORY OF PERSONALITY.

PERCEPTUAL CONSTANCY. See CONSTANCY HYPOTHESIS; PERCEPTION (I. GENERAL), THEORIES OF.

PERCEPTUAL CYCLE HYPOTHESIS. See CONSTRUCTIVIST THEORY OF PERCEPTION; PERCEPTION (I. GENERAL), THEORIES OF.

PERCEPTUAL DEFENSE/VIGILANCE EFFECTS. See PERCEPTION (I. GENERAL), THEORIES OF.

PERCEPTUAL FLUCTUATION THEORIES. See MUNSTERBERG'S THEORY OF PERCEPTUAL FLUCTUATIONS.

PERCEPTUAL MEMORY. See SHORT-TERM AND LONG-TERM MEMORY, THEORIES OF.

PERCEPTUAL ORGANIZATION, LAWS OF. See GESTALT THEORY/LAWS.

PERCEPTUAL THEORIES OF ATTI-TUDE CHANGE. See ATTITUDE/ATTI-TUDE CHANGE, THEORIES OF.

PERCEPTUAL THEORIES OF DEVEL-OPMENT. See DEVELOPMENTAL THE-ORY.

PERDEVIATION EFFECT. See IM-AGERY/MENTAL IMAGERY, THEORIES OF.

PERFORMANCE-CUE EFFECT. See EX-PERIMENTER EFFECTS.

PERFORMANCE REVIEW EFFECT. See LEARNING THEORIES/LAWS.

PERFORMATIVITY THEORY. See SEX-UAL ORIENTATION THEORIES.

PERIODICITY THEORY. See AUDITION/HEARING, THEORIES OF.

PERIPHERAL THEORIES OF HUNGER/THIRST. See HUNGER, THEORIES OF; THIRST, THEORIES OF.

PERKY EFFECT. See IMAGERY/MEN-TAL IMAGERY, THEORIES OF.

PERLOCUTIONARY EFFECT. See PER-SUASION/INFLUENCE THEORIES.

PERMISSIVE AMINE THEORY OF DE-PRESSION. See DEPRESSION, THEORIES OF.

PERSEVERATION THEORY. See IN-TERFERENCE THEORIES OF FORGET-TING.

PERSONAL CONSTRUCT THEORY. See KELLY'S PERSONAL CONSTRUCT THE-ORY.

PERSONAL EQUATION PHENOMEN-ON. This phenomenon of idiosyncrasy con-cerning one's observational ability or reactiv-ity refers, in particular, to a person's charac-teristic *reaction time* (or a correction for it), and was reported initially in 1799 by the Eng-lish astronomer Nevil Maskelyne (1732-1811) who found discrepancies in time estimations (of the transit times of stars across a hair-line, measured by counting the ticks of a pendulum clock) between himself and his assistant (the assistant, as a result of making such "persis-tent errors," was fired subsequently from his job). Later, in 1823, the German astronomer and mathematician Friedrich Wilhelm Bessel (1784-1846) examined Maskelyne's earlier report and discovered that even experienced and skilled astronomers vary considerably and consistently in their reported estimations re-garding stars' transit times. Accordingly, Bes-sel introduced the notion of the *personal equation* to apply to individuals who perform calibrating tasks, and that reflect such be-tween-person differences in what eventually came to be called *personal reaction time* to some stimulus (such as a star's transit time). Consequently, the determination of *personal equations* (i.e., A-B = X sec., where A and B are different observers) became an important aspect of astronomical observations and, in the 1860s and 1870s, Bessel's work was ex-tended to include the dependence of *reaction time* on variables such as the brightness of the celestial object and its rate of motion. Bessel's contribution to psychology was to highlight the psychological nature of the *reaction time* problem and to advance the study of the role of the so-called "complications" or mental processes in experiments involving more than one sense modality. Related to the *personal equation phenomenon* is the *prior entry law*, which states that if two events/stimuli occur simultaneously (such as a star's transit and a ticking clock), then an individual who attends primarily to one of them will usually perceive that event/stimulus as occurring before the other; thus, in regard to the *personal equation* issue, the *prior entry law* appears to be one factor that accounts for the personal observa-tion differences in astronomy where, in par-ticular, some observers of star transits may be attending primarily to one stimulus (such as the star), whereas other observers may be attending primarily to another stimulus (such as a ticking clock). See also ATTENTION,

LAWS/PRINCIPLES/THEORIES OF; ELIC-
ITED OBSERVING RATE HYPOTHESIS;
REACTION TIME PARADIGMS; VIGI-
LANCE, THEORIES OF.

REFERENCES

Maskelyne, N. (1799). [Kinnebrook's persistent error]. *Astronomical Observations at Greenwich, 3*, 319-340.

Bessel, F. W. (1823). [Personal equation].
*Astronomische Beobachtungen im
Konisberg, 8*, 3-8; *11*, 4.

Dunlap, K. (1910). The complication experiment and related phenomenon. *Psychological Review, 17*, 157-191.

Stone, S. A. (1926). Prior entry in the audi-
tory-tactual complication. *American
Journal of Psychology, 37*, 184-191.

Boring, E. G. (1957). The personal equation.
In *A history of experimental psychology*. Chapter 8. New York: Appleton-Century-Crofts.

**PERSONALISTIC THEORY OF HIST-
ORY.** See NATURALISTIC THEORY OF
HISTORY.

PERSONALITY DISINTEGRATION. See
SELF-CONCEPT THEORY.

PERSONALITY-JOB FIT THEORY. See
ORGANIZATIONAL/INDUSTRIAL/SYS-
TEMS THEORY.

PERSONALITY THEORIES. A *theory of
personality* is a set of unproven speculations
about various aspects of human behavior that
often invites argument from research-oriented
psychologists who decry the lack of quantification and the proliferation of untestable hypotheses found in most personality theories,
whereas personality theorists, in turn, criticize
the laboratory approach toward understanding
behavior as being too artificial and trivial. C.
Hall and G. Lindzey discuss in detail what
personality is, what a theory is, what a theory
of personality is, and assess over 15 major
personality theories. The personality theorist
typically devises a variety of interrelated concepts, constructs, and terms that provide convenient descriptions of behavior and establish
a framework for organizing large amounts of
data. However, the definition of the term *personality* itself seems to be so resistant to a
consensual-agreement statement, and so broad
in usage, that most psychology textbooks
(other than textbooks on personality theories)
use it strategically as the title of a chapter and
then expound freely on it without incurring
any of the definitional or positivistic responsibilities attached to it (cf., *implicit personality
theory/lay personality theory* and *implicit
theory of personality* - first described by J. S.
Bruner, R. Tagiuri, and L. J. Cronbach, which
refers to the unconsciously held ideas that
most laypeople have about the personalities of
others, where they establish a complex web of
assumptions about the traits and behaviors of
others and assume that they will act in accordance with those assumptions). One approach
toward understanding the term *personality* is
to examine it according to the role it has
played in psychological theory, in general,
rather than to list its numerous definitions.
Thus, the following roles, or theory-
categories, of personality may be cited: (1)
type theories - persons are described and classified based on a pattern of traits or other dispositional characteristics (e.g., the ancient
Greek physician Hippocrates hypothesized the
four basic temperament types of: sanguine,
choleric, melancholic, and phlegmatic; W.
Sheldon proposed personality characteristics
as related to the three body types or "somato-
types" of: endomorph, mesomorph, and ecto-
morph; C. Jung classified individuals as to
introvert versus extravert types); (2) *trait theories* assume that personality may be described as a compendium of particular ways
("traits") and dispositions of behaving (cf.,
dispositional theory - holds that the readiness
of a person to act selectively in social situations depends mainly on how that individual
has acted in the past in similar settings; according to this approach, such dispositions are
based on a hierarchy consisting of generalized
attitudes, interests, and value systems), thinking, feeling, and reacting (e.g., G. W. Allport's *cardinal*, *central*, and *secondary traits*;
the factor analytic approach of R. B. Cattell,
who identified 16 basic dimensions as the
"core" of personality; and H. J. Eysenck's
approach of two fundamental dimensions - introversion versus extraversion and stability
versus unstability - as the core of personality

(cf., *role theory of personality* - describes personality development as the gradual acquisition of roles as prescribed by a particular social unit or culture; *doctrine of cultural determinism* - states that environment, culture, and the combined aspects of a given society's economic, political, social, and religious organization determines personality to a greater degree than do hereditary factors; the current *big five model of personality traits* that identifies the basic five factors in personality as: extroversion, agreeableness, conscientiousness, neuroticism, and openness to experience; and the *little thirty traits* that are specific personality traits associated with the *big five factors*, where each of the latter is described by six traits on which it loads most heavily; e.g., extroversion is associated with warmth, positive emotions, sociability, activity, excitement-seeking, and assertiveness); (3) *psychodynamic/psychoanalytic theories*, which characterize personality by the "integration" of systems (such as the manner in which unconscious mental forces interplay with thoughts, feelings, and behavior), the motivation of the person, and the concern with the development of personality over time (e.g., the personality theories of S. Freud, C. Jung, A. Adler, R. Laing, F. Perls, W. R. D. Fairbairn, and the "neo-Freudians" such as E. Fromm, H. S. Sullivan, and K. Horney; (4) *behavioristic theories*, which extend *learning theory* to the study of personality and assess personality from an outside (rather than an internal) perspective by measuring observable behaviors and reinforcement contingencies (e.g., the approaches of J. B. Watson and B. F. Skinner); (5) *social learning/social cognitive theories* (including *situationism/situationist critique* - a criticism by W. Mischel of one of the assumptions of personality theory that people display consistent behavior patterns across situations, and *interactionism* - proposes that human behavior is dependent partly on internal personality factors, partly on external situational factors, and partly on interactions between the two), which examine factors, in addition to external observable behaviors, such as complex social roles, memory, retention processes, modeling, observational learning, and self-regulatory processes as they contribute to the functioning of personality (e.g., the approaches of J. Dollard and N. E. Miller, A. Bandura, J. Rotter, W. Mischel, A. Staats, H. J. Eysenck, and J. Wolpe; (6) *humanistic theories* (also called the *phenomenological perspective*, and the *third force in psychology* - so called because it developed as a reaction to both psychoanalytic and learning theories) emphasize internal experiences, feelings, thoughts, and the basic self-perceived worth of the individual human being where self-actualization/self-realization are the overall goals (e.g., the theories of C. Rogers and A. Maslow); and (7) *field theories of personality* - posit that humans' behaviors depend on their constitutional-birth programming and their specific social experiences, both factors interacting to produce one's particular reactions to the world. S. R. Maddi, R. J. Corsini, C. Hall and G. Lindzey, R. Ewen, D. Schultz, and L. Pervin all show the range that personality theorists cover concerning the core and structure of personality, the development and dynamics of personality, and the criteria of the healthy personality. The contributions that *personality theories* have made to psychology include the following: insights into dream interpretation, the causes and dynamics of psychopathology, new and creative developments in psychotherapy, facilitation of learning in work and educational settings, expanded methods of literary analysis, and fuller understanding of the nature of religious beliefs and prejudices. Some of the constructs that originated in *personality theory* and have enjoyed widespread acceptance in psychology include the following: the phenomena of the unconscious, parapraxes ("Freudian slips"), anxiety-reducing defense mechanisms, narcissism, transference of emotions, resistance in therapy, anxiety, introversion and extraversion, inferiority and superiority complexes, lifestyle, body language, compensation, identity crisis, intrapsychic conflict, traits, and needs for self-esteem, self-hate, self-actualization, and achievement [cf., *as-if personality* - a pattern of behavior that seems to be well-adjusted and normal, but the individual is unable to behave in a spontaneous, genuine, or warm manner; the *as-if hypothesis* - a conjecture that human actions and thoughts are guided by unproven or contradictory assumptions that are treated as if they were true; and *impasse-priority theory* - suggests that per-sons may show four "impasses" or efforts to avoid certain conditions: controller (avoids ridicule), pleaser (avoids insignificance), moral superiority (avoids rejection), and avoider (escapes stress)]. General criticisms and evaluations of *personality theory* include the suggestions that the field of personality would benefit enormously from: an increased sophistication in methodology, more sensitive discrimination between effective literary style and powerful theorizing, more freedom concerning an obligation to justify theoretical formulations that depart from normative or customary views of behavior, and an avoidance of theoretical "imperialism." Also, it may be suggested that personality theorists have been far too free with *neologisms* (i.e., coining new words or terms, or using existing terms in novel ways), and that the inability of personality theorists to resolve the most fundamental issues (such as the nature of human motivation) may lead people to question the merits of the entire field of personality psychology (cf., *naïve personality theories* - refer to informal judgments that serve as premature personality assessments, and are based largely on common sense, intuition, and uncontrolled observations of self and others). On balance, however, despite such negative assessments, the area of *personality theory* seems to represent a potentially useful contrast and adjunct to the sometimes narrow scope of modern empirical research in psychology. See also ADLER'S THEORY OF PERSONALITY; ALLPORT'S THEORY OF PERSONALITY; ANGYAL'S PERSONALITY THEORY; CATTELL'S THEORY OF PERSONALITY; ERIKSON'S THEORY OF PERSONALITY; EYSENCK'S THEORY OF PERSONALITY; FREUD'S THEORY OF PERSONALITY; FROMM'S THEORY OF PERSONALITY; GALEN'S DOCTRINE OF THE FOUR TEMPERAMENTS; GOLDSTEIN'S ORGANISMIC THEORY; HORNEY'S THEORY OF PERSONALITY; INTELLIGENCE, THEORIES/LAWS OF; JUNG'S THEORY OF PERSONALITY; KELLY'S PERSONAL CONSTRUCT THEORY; KRETSCHMER'S THEORY OF PERSONALITY; LEARNING THEORIES/LAWS; MASLOW'S THEORY OF PERSONALITY; MURPHY'S BIOSOCIAL THEORY; MURRAY'S THEORY OF PERSONALITY; RANK'S THEORY OF PERSONALITY; REICH'S ORGONE/ORGONOMY THEORY; ROGERS' THEORY OF PERSONALITY; SHELDON'S TYPE THEORY; SULLIVAN'S THEORY OF PERSONALITY.

REFERENCES

Fairbairn, W. R. D. (1954). *An object-relations theory of the personality.* New York: Basic Books.

Cronbach, L. J. (1955). Processes affecting scores on "understanding of others" and "assumed similarity." *Psychological Bulletin, 52,* 177-193.

Mischel, W. (1968). *Personality and assessment.* New York: Wiley.

Maddi, S. R. (1972). *Personality theories: A comparative analysis.* Homewood, IL: Dorsey.

Corsini, R. J. (Ed.) (1977). *Current personality theories.* Itasca, IL: Peacock.

Hall, C., & Lindzey, G. (1978). *Theories of personality.* New York: Wiley.

Ewen, R. (1980). *An introduction to theories of personality.* New York: Academic Press.

Schultz, D. (1981). *Theories of personality.* Monterey, CA: Brooks/Cole.

Pervin , L. (1985). Personality: Current controversies, issues, and directions. *Annual Review of Psychology, 36,* 83-114.

Digman, J. (1990). Personality structure: Emergence of the five-factor model. *Annual Review of Psychology, 41,* 417-440.

Goldberg, C. R. (1993). The structure of phenotypic personality traits. *American Psychologist, 48,* 26-34.

Pervin, L. (1993). *Personality: Theory and research.* New York: Wiley.

Wiggins, J. S. (1996). *Five-factor model of personality: Theoretical perspectives.* New York: Guilford Press.

Hergenhahn, B. R., & Olson, M. H. (2003). *An introduction to theories of personality.* Upper Saddle River, NJ: Prentice Hall.

PERSONAL SPACE THEORY. See DEVELOPMENTAL THEORY; EQUILIB-

RIUM HYPOTHESIS; INTERPERSONAL ATTRACTION THEORIES.

PERSON-CENTERED THEORY. See ROGERS' THEORY OF PERSONALITY.

PERSONOLOGY THEORY. See MURPHY'S BIOSOCIAL THEORY.

PERSON PERCEPTION. See IMPRESSION FORMATION, THEORIES OF.

PERSUASION/INFLUENCE THEORIES. The phenomenon of *persuasion* refers to the social-cognitive process by which attitude change occurs, and typically involves the presentation of a message(s) containing arguments in favor of, or against, the person, issue, or object that is the target of the change process (cf., *hypocrisy theory* - predicts that if one person attempts to persuade another person to stop performing an activity/behavior that the first person actually continues to engage in, the attempt typically does not succeed; the adage "Do as I say, and not as I do" captures such hypocrisy). Among the theoretical approaches to persuasive/attitude change effects are the following *persuasion theories* [cf., *pithiatism theory* - proposed by the Polish-French physician Joseph Babinski (1857-1932) as a way for removal of hysterical symptoms by persuasion based on the notion that such symptoms are produced by suggestion and, therefore, may be eliminated by suggestion; the Swiss-French physician Paul-Charles Dubois (1848-1918), the founder of modern psychotherapy, also advocated the use of persuasion to cure nervous and mental disorders]: *social judgment theory* - hypothesis that the effect of persuasive communication depends on the way in which the receiver or target evaluates the position advocated and the clarity with which the message identifies its position; also, effectiveness rests on assimilation of contrast effects (cf., *perlocutionary effect* - the response/reaction of an audience to a speech, such as responses of fear, anger, pleasure, or inspiration; and *sleeper effect* - a tendency to be influenced by a message, especially a persuasive communication following a time delay rather than immediately after the message is received; the *sleeper effect* is the "hidden impact" that a mass communication or propaganda message may have on its audience, where the attitude change produced by the message often is not detectable until a period of time has elapsed); *information-integration models of attitude* - the main theme of these models - which includes Martin Fishbein's "summative/expectancy-value model of attitude" and Norman. H. Anderson's "weighted-averaging model" - is that one's attitudes toward an object is a function of the way in which one integrates and combines the information one possesses about the object; *cognitive dissonance theory* - although not a systematic theory of persuasion, the notion of cognitive consistency/inconsistency - that persons seek to maximize the internal psychological consistency of their cognitions, beliefs, and attitudes - has yielded a number of useful findings bearing on persuasion processes; *theory of reasoned action* - is based on the idea that the most immediate determinant of a person's behavior is that individual's "behavioral intention," that is, what the person "intends" to do; the theory proposes that the intention to perform or not perform a given behavior is a function of two factors: the individual's attitude toward the behavior in question, and the person's "subjective norm," which represents his/her general perception of whether "important others" desire the performance or nonperformance of the behavior; thus, intentions are influenced both by personal attitudinal judgments (one's own personal evaluation) and by social-normative considerations (one's assessment of what other people think one should do); *elaboration likelihood model* - this approach toward persuasion, developed by Richard Petty, John Cacioppo, and their associates, suggests that important variations in the nature of persuasion are a function of the likelihood that receivers/targets will engage in "elaboration" of information relevant to the persuasive issue; with variations in the degree of elaboration, different factors influence persuasive outcomes. In a current strategic approach (Trenholm, 1989), it is suggested that one employ *eclectic influence models* in the understanding and explanation of persuasion/social influence by *combining* various theoretical approaches, such as *learning theories* (humans act to maximize rewards and minimize punishments); *information-processing theories* (obtaining new information will change beliefs, attitudes, and behaviors; cf., the *big lie theory* - the speculation, used in propaganda efforts, that if a false statement of extreme magnitude is repeated constantly to the public, it is more impressive and persuasive - and less likely to be challenged - than if a lesser falsehood is repeated); *attributional theories* (humans naturally form impressions and attribute motives to self and others); *cognitive consistency theories* (humans feel discomfort when cognitive elements conflict; such discomfort may be reduced by changing attitudes or actions); *group/social identity theories* (people need the approval and validation provided by groups; acting in socially acceptable ways assures continued affiliation and social power). The guiding assumptions of such *eclectic models/approaches* are that human behavior is complex, that individuals are driven by multiple motivations and, therefore, may adopt behaviors and beliefs for many diverse reasons, and that influence agents must match their methods to the conditions under which attitudes and actions are adopted initially. Thus, the pragmatic *eclectic influence models* attempt to understand individual circumstances and particular motivations in the persuasion/influence/attitude-change process. See also ATTITUDE AND ATTITUDE CHANGE, THEORIES OF; ATTRIBUTION THEORY; BRAINWASHING TECHNIQUES AND THEORY; COGNITIVE DISSONANCE THEORY; COMPLIANCE EFFECTS/TECHNIQUES; ELABORATION LIKELIHOOD MODEL; INFORMATION INTEGRATION THEORY; INOCULATION THEORY; REASONED ACTION AND PLANNED BEHAVIOR THEORIES; SOCIAL IMPACT, LAW OF.

REFERENCES

Roloff, M. B., & Miller, G. R. (Eds.) (1980). *Persuasion: New directions in theory and research*. Beverly Hills, CA: Sage.

Petty, R. E., & Cacioppo, J. T. (1981). *Attitudes and persuasion: Classic and contemporary approaches*. Dubuque, IA: Brown.

Petty, R. E., Ostrom, T. M., & Brock, T. C. (Eds.) (1981). *Cognitive responses in persuasion*. Hillsdale, NJ: Erlbaum.

Reardon, K. K. (1981). *Persuasion: Theory and context*. Beverly Hills, CA: Sage.

Smith, M. J. (1982). *Persuasion and human action: A review and critique of social influence theories*. Belmont, CA: Wadsworth.

Smith, M. J. (1982). The contingency rules theory of persuasion: An empirical test. *Communication Quarterly, 30*, 359-367.

Cialdini, R. B. (1985/1993/2001). *Influence: Science and practice*. Glenview, IL: Scott, Foresman/New York: Harper Collins/Boston: Allyn and Bacon.

Trenholm, S. (1989). *Persuasion and social influence*. Englewood Cliffs, NJ: Prentice-Hall.

O'Keefe, D. J. (1990/2002). *Persuasion: Theory and research*. Thousand Oaks, CA: Sage.

Cialdini, R. B. (1993). Influence: *The psychology of persuasion*. New York: Morrow.

Petty, R. E., & Wegener, D. T. (1999). The elaboration likelihood model: Current status and controversies. In S. Chaiken & Y. Trope (Eds.), *Dual-process theories in social psychology*. New York: Guilford Press.

Wood, W. (2000). Attitude change: Persuasion and social influence. *Annual Review of Psychology, 51*, 539-570.

PERSUASIVE ARGUMENTATION EFFECT. See DECISION-MAKING THEORIES.

PERTURBATION THEORY. See EXPERIMENTER EFFECTS.

PETER PRINCIPLE. See MURPHY'S LAW(S); ORGANIZATIONAL/INDUSTRIAL/SYSTEMS THEORY.

PHALLIC OATH/PENIS HOLDING. See PHALLUS THEORY.

PHALLUS THEORY. The French psychoanalyst Jacques Lacan (1901-1981) formulated the *phallus theory* according to which the phallus/penis is a symbol of desire where the Freudian *Oedipal complex* is revised to involve a conflict between "being" versus "not being" a phallus (or "having" versus "not having" a phallus), and where it plays a different role in the desires of each of the three parties (child, mother, and father) of the complex (cf., *phallic oath/penis holding* – according to anthropological evidence, this refers to the swearing of an oath, or a greeting, accompanied by one's own hand on one's own penis or testicles, or on someone else's penis, as a sign of respect and/or a gesture of solemnity). The erect phallus/penis is considered, traditionally, as a symbol of masculinity, potency, or generation (cf., the term *linga*, which is the Hindu equivalent for the phallus and is manifested in the phallic image of the Hindu god Shiva). According to *Freudian theory*, during the phallic stage of psychosexual development, libido/sexual energy is focused on the child's genital organs, but the child, whether male or female, is cognizant of only the male organ and the difference between the sexes is interpreted simply as "phallic" versus "castrated." It is during the phallic stage, also, that the *castration complex* predominates whereas the *Oedipus complex* flourishes and then dissolves. According to Freudian "penis envy" - which is a key aspect of female psychology and originates in a girl's discovery of the anatomical differences between the sexes - the female child comes to feel deprived because she has no penis and, later during the Oedipal phase, she develops a desire, theoretically, for a penis which is manifested symbolically as a desire to have a child or to possess a penis during the act of sexual intercourse. See also FREUD'S THEORY OF PERSONALITY.

REFERENCES

Freud, S. (1905). Three essays on the theory of sexuality. In *The standard edition of the complete psychological works of Sigmund Freud*. London: Hogarth Press.

Freud, S. (1924). The dissolution of the Oedipus complex. In *The standard edition of the complete psychological works of Sigmund Freud*. London: Hogarth Press.

Freud, S. (1925). Some psychical consequences of the anatomical distinction between the sexes. In *The standard edition of the complete psychological works of Sigmund Freud*. London: Hogarth Press.

Georgin, R. (1977). *Lacan: Theorie et pratiques. Lausanne*: Editions L'Age d'homme.

Lacan, J. (1982). *Feminine sexuality*. New York: W. W. Norton.

PHANTOM BREAST EFFECT. See GATE-CONTROL THEORY.

PHANTOM EXTREMITY EFFECT. See GATE-CONTROL THEORY.

PHANTOM LIMB PHENOMENON. See DENERVATION, LAW OF; GATE-CONTROL THEORY.

PHASE SEQUENCE HYPOTHESIS. See PERCEPTION (II. COMPARATIVE APPRAISAL), THEORIES OF.

PHENOMENALISM, THEORY OF. See MIND-BODY THEORIES.

PHENOMENISTIC THOUGHT/CAUSALITY. See PIAGET'S THEORY OF DEVELOPMENTAL STAGES.

PHENOMENOLOGICAL (HUMANISTIC) THEORIES OF PERSONALITY. See PERSONALITY THEORIES.

PHI GAMMA HYPOTHESIS. See NEURAL QUANTUM THEORY.

PHI PHENOMENON. See APPARENT MOVEMENT, PRINCIPLES/THEORIES OF; GESTALT THEORY/LAWS; KORTE'S LAWS.

PHLOGISTON THEORY. See THERMODYNAMICS, LAWS OF.

PHONATORY THEORY. See SPEECH THEORIES.

PHONEMIC RESTORATION/PHAN-TOM EFFECT. See APPENDIX A; WHORF-SAPIR HYPOTHESIS/THEORY.

PHONOLOGICAL LOOP MODEL. See WORKING MEMORY, THEORY OF.

PHOTOCHEMICAL THEORY. See VISION/SIGHT, THEORIES OF.

PHOTOGRAPHIC LAW. See BUNSEN-ROSCOE LAW.

PHRENOLOGY, DOCTRINE OF. See LEARNING THEORIES/LAWS; MIND/MENTAL STATES, THEORIES OF; PSEUDOSCIENTIFIC/UNCONVENTIONAL THEORIES.

PHYLOANALYTIC/PHYLOBIOLOGICAL THEORY. See MURPHY'S BIOSOCIAL THEORY.

PHYLOGENETIC THEORY AND PRINCIPLE. See JUNG'S THEORY OF PERSONALITY; RECAPITULATION THEORY/LAW.

PHYSICAL CORRELATE THEORY. See STEVENS' POWER LAW.

PHYSICAL SYMBOL SYSTEM HYPOTHESIS. This hypothesis, advanced by Alan Newell (1927-1992) and Herbert Alexander Simon (1916-2001), attempts to give a formulation connecting the abstract and concrete levels of human ideation, mental capacities, and brain processes. The hypothesis identifies such processes and capacities with physical symbol systems containing symbolic re-presentations that are altered by precisely de-fined symbol-manipulating operations. Thus, "mental events" may be described in a theoretical system that applies, also, to concrete, physical entities. In this way, one may construct rigorous theoretical depictions of hypothetical mental/brain processes in terms at least as real and concrete as the physical entities of molecules and atoms in physical chemistry. Newell and Simon's hypothesis presupposes that important aspects of the human mind, the brain, and the computer are

separate instances of the same kind of system. The *physical symbol system hypothesis* - whether or not stated explicitly - is at the foundation of much of the theory and research in the area of psychological information-processing. At its base, the hypothesis attempts to identify and define the presence of "intelligence" in a system and may explain how an "intelligent system," whether artificial or real/human, can "learn" and create new knowledge. See also INFORMATION/INFORMATION-PROCESSING THEORY; NEURAL NETWORK MODELS OF INFORMATION PROCESSING.

REFERENCES

Newell, A., Shaw, J. C., & Simon, H. A. (1958). Elements on a theory of human problem solving. *Psychological Review, 65*, 151-166.

Newell, A., & Simon, H. A. (1961). Computer simulation of human thinking. *Science, 134*, 2011-2017.

Simon, H. A. (1979). *Models of thought*. New Haven, CT: Yale University Press.

Newell, A. (1980). Physical symbol system. *Cognitive Science, 4*, 135-183.

PHYSIOLOGICAL LAWS OF ASSOCIATION. See ASSOCIATION, LAWS/PRINCIPLES OF.

PHYSIOLOGICAL THEORY OF GENERALIZATION. See GENERALIZATION, PRINCIPLE OF.

PIAGET'S PRINCIPLE OF CONSERVATION. See PIAGET'S THEORY OF DEVELOPMENTAL STAGES.

PIAGET'S THEORY OF DEVELOPMENTAL STAGES. The Swiss biologist, psychologist, and genetic epistemologist Jean Piaget (1896-1980) formulated a *theory of cognitive development* where development is considered to be a continuous and creative interaction between the child and the environment, and where both the child's body and sensory activities contribute to the development of intelligence and thinking skills [cf., the American developmental psychologist Jerome S. Bruner's (1915-) *theory of cognitive development* containing three stages/

modes of cognitive development: *enactive* (movement-based), *iconic* (based on stored memory), and *symbolic* (based on symbols and words); and *skill theory* - a reinterpretation of Piaget's stages in terms of information-processing operations whereby each stage is considered to be an extended period of skill acquisition demonstrated by children achieving new competencies, integrating them with others, and transforming them into more efficient, higher-order skills]. According to Piaget, four major and distinct stages occur sequentially in development where each child must pass through all four stages (cf., *multistage theories* - posit that certain processes go through a number of changes where, in some cases, the stages are clear - as in information-processing - and in other cases, the stages are somewhat arbitrarily set; the individual moves from one phase to another in a continuous manner even though events may move in an abrupt fashion). However, Piaget's stages are not rigidly fixed in a time sequence, but they can overlap, and the ages are only approximate concerning the appearance of a given stage. Piaget's stages are: (1) the *sensorimotor stage* - occurs from birth to approximately two years of age; the infant at this stage is learning to use its body, and all experience is gained immediately through the senses where adequate sensory stimulation is important in developing the child's abilities; the term *practical intelligence* is used to describe behavior at this stage, where the infant learns to act in the world without thinking about what is happening; (2) the *preoperational stage* - occurs from about two to seven years of age during the child's preschool years when she/he can begin to use words - from one or two-word sentences at age two to about eight or ten-word sentences at age five - and can understand that objects can be moved from place to place and maintain an existence even when not perceiving the movements of the object; a more complete understanding of *object permanence* occurs during this period where the child's image-based thinking improves and develops with a capacity called *representation* (cf., Piaget's concept of *centration* - the tendency of young children to focus attention on only one salient aspect of an object, problem, or situation at a time, and excludes other poten-

tially relevant aspects; *decentration* refers to the cognitive development process by which the child advances from *centration* to a more objective way of perceiving the world); with *representation*, the child can think about some actions when they are not being performed, can think about events when they are not actually happening, and can think of objects when they are not present; (3) the *concrete operations stage* - appears from about 7 to 11 years of age during the child's school age where the child continues to use "intuitive" thought that characterized the preoperational period; during this stage the child also begins to develop an understanding of "concrete operations" such as *conservation* of liquid and addition and multiplication of classes of objects where the child is able to carry out transformations mentally without carrying them out physically; (4) the *formal operations stage* - occurs from about 11 to 15 years of age during the beginning of adolescence and continues to develop throughout adulthood; the individual at this stage is able to think in a hypothetical way and to carry out systematic tests of the various possible explanations of a phenomenon or a specific event; rational patterns of thinking now develop where symbolic meanings are understood, and abstract mental strategies are possible. Although adults may behave at the *sensorimotor level* (e.g.. ice-skating or bicycle riding where deep understanding of what is happening is not necessary), the difference between the infant and the adult is that the infant does not yet recognize a distinction between one's own knowledge or actions and the objects in the world that are acted upon. One of the limitations of the *concrete-operations stage* is that although the child may be able to deal with concrete objects and events in an "actual" situation, the child cannot deal with such things in a "hypothetical" situation. The development of "higher-order" systems of thought takes time, and all capacities do not develop simultaneously (cf., *phenomenistic thought* - Piaget's term for the reasoning of young children whose cognitive processes center on the physical appearances of objects; *phenomenistic causality* - in the child's reasoning, events/processes that occur together are viewed as being causally related, as when a child believes that trains go fast because they are big; and *animistic thinking* - a stage in Piaget's *cognitive developmental theory* in which friendly or hostile intentions/attributes are assigned by the child to inanimate objects such as cars, buildings, or rocks). This fact was viewed by Piaget particularly in the sequential (not simultaneous) development of the different types of *conservation* (i.e., the understanding that quantitative aspects of a set of materials or other stimulus display are not changed or affected by transformations of the display itself); *conservation of number* develops first, followed by *conservation of amount*, followed by *conservation of weight*, and so on. Inasmuch as the *concrete-operations* child cannot yet tie together and coordinate her or his various operational systems, each type of conservation problem seems like a new and separate problem to the child. During the *formal-operations stage*, the child is able to coordinate and integrate two separate dimensions together (such as "weight" and "distance"), as well as to understand and appreciate abstract principles and hypothetical cases, both of which are prerequisite to study in fields such as mathematics, science, ethics, and languages. According to Piaget, a child's intelligence and understanding of events seem to be *constructed* as a result of encounters between the child and the environment where the child experiences a discrepancy between what is already understood and what the environment is presenting. The concept of *adaptation*, in this context, refers to the modification of an individual's psychological processes and structures in response to the demands of the environment. Piaget employs the concepts of *schemes, assimilation, accommodation,* and *equilibrium* in his discussions of the "construction of an understanding." A *scheme* is an organized action or mental structure that the child holds at a particular time. The terms *assimilation* and *accommodation* refer to the interaction and adjustment that the individual makes between his/her scheme and the objects and events in the world. *Assimilation* is the person's active attempt to apply particular schemes to events, and *accommodation* is the person's adjustment of her/his schemes to the events to be known. The term *equilibrium* was used by Piaget to summarize the joint effects of assimilation and accommodation. The mind constantly seeks a psychological equilibrium between these two processes, much like the internal physiological processes of the body that naturally seek equilibrium, balance, or homeostasis. The fundamental problem for *Piaget's theory*, say some developmentalists, and one for which no convincing answer has yet been found is the issue of spontaneity and novelty in the child's development: How does "new" knowledge arise out of a cognitive structure that did not, in any distinctive or discernible way, contain the "new" knowledge and, once "new" knowledge does emerge, how does it come to be regarded as necessarily connected to other knowledge? (cf., *theory-theory* - an approach concerning the mental development of children that challenges *Piaget's theory*; this viewpoint assumes that children attempt - at much earlier ages than posited by Piaget - to try to make coherence out of life by generating their own theories and testing them out; cf., *Kelly's construct theory*). A current alternative to *Piaget's theory of cognitive development* is the *information-processing model*, which describes the process of taking in, remembering or forgetting, and using information. This approach draws an analogy between the mind and the computer to explain cognitive development. See also ACCOMMODATION, LAW/PRINCIPLE OF; ANIMISM THEORY; CONSTRUCTIVISM, THEORIES OF; CONSTRUCTIVIST THEORY OF PERCEPTION; INFORMATION/INFORMATION-PROCESSING THEORY; OBJECT PERMANENCE PARADIGM/MODEL; PLAY, THEORIES OF.

REFERENCES

Piaget, J. (1926). *The language and thought of the child*. New York: World.

Piaget, J. (1929). *The child's conception of the world*. New York: Littlefield, Adams.

Piaget, J. (1936/1953). *Origins of intelligence*. New York: International Universities Press.

Piaget, J. (1941/1952). *The child's conception of number*. London: Routledge & Kegan Paul.

Piaget, J. (1954). *The construction of reality in the child*. New York: Basic Books.

Piaget, J., & Inhelder, B. (1956). *The child's conception of space*. London: Routledge & Kegan Paul.

Bruner, J. S. (1968). *Processes of cognitive growth*. Worcester, MA: Clark University Press.

Piaget, J. (1970). Piaget's theory. In P. Mussen (Ed.), *Carmichael's manual of child psychology*. New York: Wiley.

Vuyk, R. (1981). *Overview and critique of Piaget's genetic epistemology 1965-1980*. New York: Academic Press.

McShane, J. (1991). *Cognitive development: An information processing approach*. Oxford, UK: Blackwell.

PIANO THEORY OF HEARING. See AUDITION/HEARING, THEORIES OF.

PIDDINGTON'S COMPENSATORY HUMOR THEORY. The English anthropologist Ralph Piddington refers to his theoretical approach toward humor as the *compensatory theory of humor*, which is a concept derived from the relationship between elementary laughter and laughter at the ludicrous in which the *principle of psychic compensation* (i.e., a hypothesized mechanism by which one seeks to make up for a real or imagined psychological defect by developing or exaggerating a psychological strength) is invoked. According to Piddington, laughter serves a social function by a process that is analogous to "exaggeration of the opposite character." The reasoning behind *Piddington's compensatory humor theory* is that all ludicrous situations are potentially subversive to the social order, and the reaction of laughter (affirming the "satisfying nature of the situation, breaking up all trains of thought, and producing bodily euphoria) is the socially appropriate response to the stimulus of the ludicrous. Also, it is the response that expresses the "suitable" attitude for members of society to take towards ludicrous situations, and its primary function is to prevent any disturbance of the system of social values on which the society depends for its existence and strength. In his approach, Piddington compares his "compensatory" notion against various other intellectualist, degradation, corrective, play-mood, biological and aesthetic theories. Piddington also refers to B. Malinowski's *theory of needs* and W. L. Warner's *theory of species behavior* as a foundation for inclusion in his humor theory of both the biological needs and the psychological drives upon which social behaviors (such as kinship and family) are based. Piddington's treatment of laughter is neither entirely psychological nor entirely biological, and he attempts to assess the psychology of the original reaction of laughter and to relate this to the various functions that it subserves in society. *Piddington's humor theory* may be called the "two contradictory social situations theory," whereby the ludicrous basically involves two contradictory social evaluations in which the laughter that is aroused is a socially-conditioned reaction that signifies satisfaction under some otherwise socially-disturbing conditions. See also HUMOR, THEORIES OF; SOCIAL/COMMUNICATION THEORY OF LAUGHTER.

REFERENCES

Piddington, R. (1933/1963). *The psychology of laughter: A study in social adaptation*. London: Figurehead.

Malinowski, B. (1944). *A scientific theory of culture and other essays*. Chapel Hill, NC: University of North Carolina Press.

Warner, W. L. (1959/1975). *The living and the dead: A study of the symbolic life of Americans*. New Haven, CT: Yale University Press.

PIECEMEAL ACTIVITY, LAW OF. See REDINTEGRATION, PRINCIPLE/LAW OF.

PIERON'S LAW. The French physiological/sensory psychologist Henri Pieron (1881-1964) stated in 1907 - before the American behavioral psychologist John B. Watson's pronouncements in 1913 and 1919 - that the proper subject matter of psychology should be *behavior*; also, Pieron was the originator of the French school of *behaviorism*, or *psychologie du comportement*. It's been known since the 1880s that *simple reaction time* or SRT decreases when the intensity of a given stimulus increases. *Pieron's law* describes this principle by the following power function: $SRT-t_o = \beta \, I^{-\alpha}$, where SRT is simple reaction time, t_o is an asymptotic reaction time (RT) reached at higher stimulus intensities, β is the range of changes between the t_0 value and the maximum RT determined at threshold, I is the intensity of the stimulus, and α is the exponent of the function. The parameters of α and t_0 in *Pieron's law* appear to be specific for a given sensory modality, and t_0 appears to represent the combination of two constant parameters: the duration of the motor component and a specific processing time for a given sensory modality. Inasmuch as t_0 varies between sensory modalities, its functional significance is apparently more *sensory* than *decisional*. However, its estimation is difficult and depends on the range and/or the number of intensities. When the range of intensities does not extend high enough, it may be safer to reduce Pieron's function to two parameters (α and β), although the generality of the exponent may not be guaranteed. *Pieron's law* seems to hold for *choice reaction time* (CRT), as well as for SRT, tasks and describes RT as a power function of stimulus intensity, with similar exponents, regardless of the complexity of the experimental task. See also BEHAVIORIST THEORY; REACTION-TIME PARADIGMS/MODELS; WATSON'S THEORY.

REFERENCES

Pieron, H. (1914). On the laws of variation of sensory processing time as a function of the excitatory intensity. *L'Annee Psychologique, 20,* 17-96.

Pieron, H. (1920). Further evidence on the laws of sensory processing time as a function of the excitatory intensity. *L'Annee Psychologique, 26,* 58-142.

Pins, D., & Bonnet, C. (1996). On the relation between stimulus intensity and processing time: Pieron's law and choice reaction time. *Perception & Psychophysics, 58,* 390-400.

Pins, D., & Bonnet, C. (2000). The Pieron function in the threshold region. *Perception & Psychophysics, 62,* 127-136.

PINEL'S CLASSIFICATION SYSTEM. See PSYCHOPATHOLOGY THEORIES.

PIPER'S LAW. See RICCO'S/PIPER'S LAW.

PITHIATISM THEORY. See PERSUASION/INFLUENCE THEORIES.

PITUITARY ADRENAL AXIS THEORIES. See DEPRESSION, THEORIES OF.

PLACEBO EFFECT. See EXPERIMENTER EFFECTS.

PLACE/PLACE-VOLLEY/PLACE-FREQUENCY THEORY. See AUDITION/HEARING, THEORIES OF.

PLANCK'S PRINCIPLE. See PARADIGM SHIFT DOCTRINE.

PLANNED BEHAVIOR THEORY. See REASONED ACTION AND PLANNED BEHAVIOR THEORIES.

PLATEAU SPIRAL/TALBOT-PLATEAU SPIRAL. See APPENDIX A.

PLATO'S LEARNING THEORY. See ASSOCIATION, LAWS/PRINCIPLES OF; LEARNING THEORIES/LAWS.

PLATO'S THEORY OF HUMOR. The early Greek philosopher Plato (c. 427-c. 347 B.C.) proposed that what people laugh at is vice, particular as revealed in the "self-ignorance" (or "lack of self-knowledge") that occurs in those who are relatively powerless. According to *Plato's theory of humor*, human amusement is a type of malice or derision toward such powerless people, and is based on situations that make the observer feel *superior* in some way. It is noteworthy that Plato cautioned that rational people should generally suppress their laughter and should be wary of amusement - especially in cases where one's emotions are activated - because under such influences one tends to lose rational control of oneself. Plato's *lack-of-self-knowledge theory* is the most ancient of the theories of laughter to have been passed down to modern times. In his *Philebus 47-50*, Plato is the first person to suggest that envy or malice is at the root of comic enjoyment. *Plato's theory of humor* asserts that self-deception (or the vain conceit of wisdom, wealth, or beauty) - when it is powerful - is to be hated, but - when it is feeble and unable to do hurt to others - it is ridiculous and laughable. Thus, according to Plato, we laugh at the misfortunes of our friends under circumstances where we experience mixed feelings of both pain and pleasure and, thereby, Plato also advances a *pleasure-pain theory of humor*. By previously defining "lack-of-self-knowledge" as a misfortune, Plato reasons as follows: laughter is a pleasure and to laugh at the conceit of someone is to gloat over his/her misfortune; however, such gloating implies malice that is painful. In other terms, Plato compares the appreciation of the ludicrous to the relief that one derives from scratching an itch where we have a "mixed feeling of the body" - pain caused by the itch and pleasure evoked by the remedial treatment of scratching. Moreover, in the case of the appreciation of the ludicrous, one has a corresponding "mixed feeling of the soul" whereby pleasure and pain are combined (i.e., the ludicrous consists of a negation of the Delphic/Socratic precept, "know thyself," or constitutes a lack of self-knowledge. Thus, in Plato's reasoning, lack of self-knowledge is a misfortune and, because laughter is a pleasure, to laugh at the conceit of one's friends is, therefore, to rejoice in their misfortunes and that implies malice which is painful. The German language contains the humor-related word *Schadenfreude* (i.e., malicious delight and the notion of enjoyment obtained from the mishaps of others or, literally, "joy through damage/injury") that is similar to this state of affairs in *Plato's humor theory* where the logical conclusion is that laughter involves simultaneously *both* pleasure and pain. See also ARISTOTLE'S THEORY OF HUMOR; HOBBES' THEORY OF HUMOR/LAUGHTER; HUMOR, THEORIES OF; SUPERIORITY THEORIES OF HUMOR.

REFERENCES

Piddington, R. (1933/1963). *The psychology of laughter: A study in social adaptation*. London: Figurehead/New York: Gamut.

Plato (1937). *The works of Plato*. Translated by B. Jowett. New York: Tudor.

Morreall, J. (Ed.) (1987). *The philosophy of laughter and humor*. Albany, NY: State University of New York Press.

PLAY-PRACTICE, THEORY OF. See PLAY, THEORIES OF.

PLAY, THEORIES OF. The term *play* has many different meanings (at least 55 distinguishable definitions). At the core of most definitions is the notion that *play* involves diversion or recreation and is an activity not necessarily to be taken seriously. Play is activity for its own sake and may be viewed, at least for children, as what they do when allowed to freely choose activity. An early theory of play - the *instinctive theory*, also called the *theory of play-practice*, formulated by the German-Swiss philosopher/psychologist Karl Theodor Groos (1861-1946) - states that play allows animals to perfect their instinctive skills and asserts that the very existence of youth is largely for the sake of play (cf., *surplus energy theory* - holds that play activities of human and subhuman young are due to the superabundance of energy in growing organisms. A more recent, similar theory, called *competence theory* - formulated by the American psychologist Robert White (1904- ?) - argues the need for developmental competence or effectiveness in one's environment where play is one form of activity that helps in the maturation process. Another earlier theory, the *recapitulation theory* - developed by the American psychologist Granville Stanley Hall (1844-1924) - maintains that play is an evolutionary link between the child and all biological and cultural stages that have preceded human beings on the phylogenetic scale. The *autotelic theory*, or *motivational model*, stresses that play is an activity that is done for its own sake with the reward residing in the process itself. Although this approach recognizes ultimately useful outcomes of playful activity, it is concerned mainly with immediate satisfactions such as pleasure, fun, spontaneity, and reduction of uncertainty. An opposing viewpoint is that play is a useful activity that enhances the growth and development of an individual toward maturity and adulthood. Consistent with this perspective is Jean Piaget's *stage theory of cognitive development*,

480

which posits that at each stage of development certain types of play become predominant (cf., *Froebelism* - named after the German educator Friedrich W. A. Froebel (1782-1852) - refers to the use of *instructive play* at the kindergarten level). C. Hutt and H. Day describe a typology/taxonomy that distinguishes five forms of play: exploratory, creative, diversive, mimetic, and cathartic play (cf., *practice theory of play*, which states that the function of play is to give the organism practice on tasks that it will have to perform in earnest in later life); a principle is proposed, also, by which all activities can be measured along a *playfulness-workfulness* continuum where the concept of *playfulness* may be employed as a method of comparing all forms of behavior including those observed on jobs and in games with the goal of identifying the motivation to participate in such activities. See also BEHAVIORAL THEORIES OF HUMOR/LAUGHTER; HYDRAULIC THEORIES; PIAGET'S THEORY OF DEVELOPMENTAL STAGES; RECAPITULATION, THEORY/LAW OF.

REFERENCES

Groos, K. (1898). *The play of animals*. New York: Appleton.

White, R. (1959). Motivation reconsidered: the concept of competence. *Psychological Review*, 66, 297-333.

Piaget, J. (1963). *The origins of intelligence in children*. New York: Norton.

Berlyne, D. (1969). Laughter, humor, and play. In G. Lindzey & E. Aronson (Eds.), *Handbook of social psychology*. Vol. 3. Reading, MA: Addison-Wesley.

Ellis, M. (1973). *Why people play*. Englewood Cliffs, NJ: Prentice-Hall.

Bruner, J., Jolly, A., & Sylva, K. (Eds.) (1976). *Play - Its role in development and evolution*. New York: Basic Books.

Day, H. (1979). Why people play. *Loisir et Societe*, 2, 129-147.

Sutton-Smith, B. (1980). Children's play: Some sources of play theorizing. In K. Rubin (Ed.), *New directions for child development - children's play*. San Francisco: Jossey-Bass.

Hutt, C. (1981). Toward a taxonomy and conceptual model of play. In H. Day (Ed.), *Advances in intrinsic motivation and aesthetics*. New York: Plenum.

Bates, C. (2002). *Play in a godless world: The theory and practice of play in Shakespeare, Nietzsche, and Freud*. New York: Open Gate Press.

PLEASURE-PAIN, DOCTRINE/THEORY/LAW OF. See HEDONISM, THEORY/LAW OF.

PLEASURE-PAIN THEORY OF HUMOR. See PLATO'S THEORY OF HUMOR.

PLEASURE/REALITY PRINCIPLE. See ANXIETY, THEORIES OF; FREUD'S THEORY OF PERSONALITY; HEDONISM, THEORY/LAW OF; LEARNING THEORIES/LAWS; MOTIVATION THEORIES OF.

PLOTINUS' THEORY OF TIME. The Roman neo-Platonist philosopher Plotinus (c. 205-270) hypothesized that *time* is generated by the restless energy of the soul seeking to express in matter the infinite and eternal "fullness of being," and it is that which is accomplished in a successive series of acts, not in a single stroke. According to Plotinus, *time* is the life of the soul much like eternity is the life of intelligible being in its full, unbroken, and absolutely unchangeable totality. In such a view (that may be found in various modifications in the history of the notion of *dynamic idealism* - that is, all reality is the creation of spirit or mind), *time* is "objective" only because the object that it qualifies is subjectively determined. However, according to Plotinus, both subject and object are included in a comprehensive unity that is timeless. See also ARISTOTLE'S TIME THEORY AND PARADOX; EARLY GREEK AND LATER PHILOSOPHICAL THEORIES OF TIME; IDEALISM, DOCTRINE OF; ST. AUGUS-TINE'S TIME THEORY AND PARADOX; TIME, THEORIES OF.

REFERENCE

Baldwin, J. M. (Ed.) (1901-1905). *Dictionary of philosophy and psychology.* New York: Macmillan.

PLUTCHIK'S MODEL OF EMOTIONS.

The American psychologist Robert Plutchik - like C. E. Izard and S. Tomkins - independently developed an approach toward the understanding of emotions that is based largely on the *evolutionary theory* of Charles Darwin (1809-1882). *Plutchik's model*, also known as the *multidimensional model of the emotions* (*MME*), shows how "primary" emotions such as surprise and fear may blend into "secondary" emotions such as awe, as well as indicates how various emotions such as fear, terror, and apprehension may involve one "primary" emotion experienced at several different levels of intensity. *Plutchik's model* is shown both as a two-dimensional circle and a three-dimensional ellipse so that, when viewed as a two-dimensional circle (analogous to a *color wheel*), it indicates how the eight primary emotions (joy, acceptance, fear, surprise, sadness, disgust, anger, anticipation) may be mixed/blended to give various secondary emotions (awe, disappointment, remorse, contempt, aggressiveness, optimism, love, submission). When the model is viewed as a three-dimensional ellipse (analogous to a *color spindle*), emotional intensity may be assessed for the primary and secondary emotions. According to Plutchik, diversity in human emotion is a product of variations in emotional intensity, as well as a blending of primary emotions. Each vertical slice in his model is a primary emotion that can be subdivided into emotional expressions of varied intensity ranging from most intense at the top of the model to least intense at the bottom. Plutchik joins the ranks of those *evolutionary theorists* of emotion who assume that evolution equips us with a small number of primary emotions that have proven to be adaptive and have survival value. *Plutchik's model*, when viewed as two- and three-dimensional figures, appears to be a combination of the earlier model of emotion by H. Schlosberg and of the earlier model of activation and arousal by D. Lindsley, as well as some basis in the historical "Galen-Wundt theory of personality structure" (cf., Eysenck, 1970). In his current *circumplex model of emotion and personality*, Plutchik focuses on determining how traits and emotions are similar structurally, and offers an economical description of that relationship. See also ACTIVATION/AROUSAL THEORY; DARWIN'S EVOLUTION THEORY; EKMAN-FRIESEN'S THEORY OF EMOTIONS;; EMOTIONS, THEORIES/ LAWS OF; FACIAL-FEEDBACK HYPOTHESIS; IZARD'S THEORY OF EMOTIONS; UNIVERSAL MODEL OF HUMAN EMOTIONS.

REFERENCES

Darwin, C. (1872). *Expression of the emotions in man and animals.* London: Murray.

Lindsley, D. (1951). Emotion. In S. S. Stevens (Ed.), *Handbook of experimental psychology.* New York: Wiley.

Eysenck, H. J. (1953). *The structure of human personality.* New York: Wiley.

Schlosberg, H. (1954). Three dimensions of emotion. *Psychological Review, 61,* 81-88.

Plutchik, R. (1962). *The emotions: Facts, theories, and a new model.* New York: Random House.

Plutchik, R. (1980). *Emotion: A psychoevolutionary synthesis.* New York: Harper & Row.

Tomkins, S. (1980). Affect as amplification: Some modifications in theory. In R. Plutchik & H. Kellerman (Eds.), *Emotion, theory, research, and experience.* New York: Academic Press.

Izard, C. E. (1984). Emotion-cognition relationships and human development. In C. E. Izard, J. Kagan, & R. Zajonc (Eds.), *Emotions, cognition, and behavior.* Cambridge, UK: Cambridge University Press.

PNEUMATISM THEORY. See LIFE, THEORIES OF.

POETZL/PÖTZL EFFECT/PHENOMENON. See DREAM THEORY; PERCEPTION (I. GENERAL), THEORIES OF.

POGGENDORFF/ZÖLLNER ILLUSION. See APPENDIX A.

POINT-LIGHT DISPLAY ILLUSION. See APPENDIX A.

POISEUILLE-HAGEN LAW. See CONTROL/SYSTEMS THEORY.

POISEUILLE'S LAW. See CONROL/SYSTEMS THEORY.

POLLYANNA EFFECT. See MERE EXPOSURE EFFECT.

POLYCHROMATIC THEORY/HYPOTHESIS OF VISION. See FOVEAL CONE HYPOTHESIS; GRANIT'S COLOR VISION THEORY; HARTRIDGE'S POLYCHROMATIC VISION THEORY.

POLYMORPHOUS PERVERSITY THEORY. See FREUD'S THEORY OF PERSONALITY.

PONZO/RAILROAD/RAILWAY ILLUSION. See APPENDIX A.

POPULATION STEREOTYPE. See THREE-SEVEN EFFECT/PHENOMENON.

PORTER-LAWLER INTEGRATION THEORY. See MOTIVATION, THEORIES OF.

PORTER'S LAW. See FERRY-PORTER LAW.

POSITIVE/NEGATIVE CONTRAST EFFECTS. See CRESPI EFFECT.

POSITIVE TRANSFER OF TRAINING EFFECT. See ASSIMILATION, LAW OF.

POSITIVISM, DOCTRINE OF. See BEHAVIORIST THEORY; COMTE'S LAW/THEORY.

POSITIVITY BIAS/EFFECT. See ATTRIBUTION THEORY.

POSTCATEGORICAL ACOUSTIC MEMORY/STORE. See SHORT-TERM AND LONG-TERM MEMORY, THEORIES OF.

POSTCONSTRUCTIONISM, DOCTRINE OF. See PARADIGM SHIFT DOCTRINE.

POSTMODERNISM, DOCTRINE OF. See PARADIGM SHIFT DOCTRINE.

POSTREMITY PRINCIPLE. See GUTHRIE'S THEORY OF BEHAVIOR.

POSTSTRUCTURALISM, DOCTRINE OF. See PARADIGM SHIFT DOCTRINE.

POSTTRAUMATIC GROWTH MODELS. The concept of *posttraumatic growth* (e.g., Tedeschi & Calhoun, 1996, 2004) refers to the experience of positive change that occurs as a result of the struggle with highly challenging life crises (e.g., near-death experiences, terminal diseases), and is manifested in a number of ways, including an increased appreciation for life in general, more meaningful interpersonal relationships, an increased sense of personal strength, changed priorities, and a richer spiritual and existential life. Three explanatory *posttraumatic growth models* (cf., Janoff-Bulman, 2004) are: *strength through suffering* - knowing that survivors have experienced pain and suffering and have come through their trials is sufficient for understanding their new-found strength; *psychological preparedness* - posits that by virtue of coping successfully with their experience, survivors are not only better prepared for subsequent tragedies but, as a consequence, are apt to be less traumatized by them as well; coping involves rebuilding a viable "assumptive world," and it is change at this level that provides the survivor with psychological protection; and *existential reevaluation* - in the face of loss, and potential loss, survivors recognize the preciousness of life and, when faced with the powerful possibility of nonexistence, they become aware of the amazing fact of, and value of, existence; life takes on new meaning and value, and appreciation involves an appraisal or reevaluation of increased value/worth. Although the term *posttraumatic growth* is new, the idea is ancient that "great good may come from great suffering." However, in *posttraumatic* conditions, the positive and negative aspects are linked inextricably. The long-term legacy of trauma involves both losses and gains; as in the case of *reversible figures* in perception psychology, the survivor may focus on one or the other, but both are present. In the aftermath of trauma, survivors experience both disillusionment and appreciation, unpredictability and preparedness, and vulnerability and strength. It is suggested that the notion of *posttraumatic growth* mutually interacts with "life-wisdom" and the development of the "life narrative," and that it is a *dynamic* and ongoing process, rather than a *static* outcome. See also DUAL PROCESS MODELS; INOCULATION THE-ORY; STRESS THEORY.

REFERENCES

Tedeschi, R. G., & Calhoun, L. G. (1996). The Posttraumatic Growth Inventory: Measuring the positive legacy of trauma. *Journal of Traumatic Stress, 9*, 455-471.

Janoff-Bulman, R. (2004). Posttraumatic growth: Three explanatory models. *Psychological Inquiry, 15*, 30-34.

Tedeschi, R. G., & Calhoun, L. G. (2004). Posttraumatic growth: Conceptual foundations and empirical evidence. *Psychological Inquiry, 15*, 1-18.

POWER LAW. See STEVENS' POWER LAW.

POWER LAW OF PRACTICE. See PROBLEM-SOLVING AND CREATIVITY STAGE THEORIES; TOTAL TIME HYPOTHESIS/LAW.

PRACTICE EFFECT. See LEARNING THEORIES/LAWS.

PRACTICE THEORY OF PLAY. See PLAY, THEORIES OF.

PRAGNANZ, LAW OF. See GESTALT THEORY/LAWS.

PRECATEGORICAL ACOUSTIC MEMORY/STORE. See SHORT-TERM AND LONG-TERM MEMORY, THEORIES OF.

PRECEDENCE EFFECT. See APPENDIX A, AUDITORY FUSION/BINAURAL FUSION.

PRECISION, LAW OF. See GESTALT THEORY/LAWS; PERCEPTION (I. GENERAL), THEORIES OF.

PREESTABLISHED HARMONY, THEORY/DOCTRINE OF. See MIND-BODY THEORIES.

PREFERENCE-FEEDBACK HYPOTHESIS. See MERE EXPOSURE EFFECT.

PREFERENCE REVERSAL EFFECT/PHENOMENON. See DECISION-MAKING THEORIES; DEMBER-EARL THEORY OF CHOICE/PREFERENCE.

PREFERENCE, THEORY OF. See DECISION-MAKING THEORIES; DEMBER-EARL THEORY OF CHOICE/PREFERENCE; PERCEPTION (I. GENERAL), THEORIES OF.

PREFORMISM/PREFORMATIONISM, THEORY OF. See WEISMANN'S THEORY.

PREGNANCY BLOCKAGE EFFECT. See BRUCE EFFECT.

PREJUDICE, THEORIES OF. The term *prejudice* refers to an act of "prejudging" or "preconception" and is the formation of an attitude toward some issue prior to having sufficient information on that issue. A *prejudice* may be either negative or positive in evaluative terms concerning any particular thing, person, event, idea, or issue. A *prejudice* may be defined, also, as an attitude, either for or against a certain unproved hypothesis, and one that prevents the individual from evaluating new evidence correctly. The term *prejudice* carries an emotional implication, whereas the synonymous term *bias* lacks an emotional component. More commonly, in social psychology, *prejudice* refers to a negative attitude toward a particular group of persons based on negative traits assumed to be uniformly displayed by all members of that group (cf., *doctrine of racialism* - the debatable notion that although the races of people may be identical in all respects, except appearance, the races nevertheless should be kept separate; and *racism* is the action-backed belief that some races are superior to others; cf., *systemic counseling theory* - focuses on changing the social environment in group settings where the goal is to resolve racial conflicts that interfere with the growth and adjustment of minority individuals in a group, and where the counseler is a facilitator who acts as an advocate or agent of change). A related term, *discrimination*, refers to external, observable behaviors, whereas *prejudice* is applied more to internal, inferred attitudes. Another related term, *stereotype*, refers to a set of relatively fixed, simplistic overgeneralizations about a group or class of people (cf., *confirmation bias/effect* - the tendency to test one's beliefs by seeking evidence that might confirm/verify them and to ignore evidence that might disconfirm/refute them; *illusory correlation effect* - an apparent correlation that does not actually exist in the data being judged, and helps to bolster superstitions, stereotypes, and prejudices; and *scapegoat theory* - states that people with prejudices target innocent people or groups as outlets for their own anger due to frustration). *Stereotypes* and *prejudices* differ in two ways: the former are more cognitive and concerned with *thinking*, whereas the latter are more affective and concerned with *feelings*. Consequently, *stereotypes* can be relatively neutral, whereas *prejudices* are essentially positive or negative, usually negative. *Stereotype theories* include social cognition perspectives such as *categorization theory*, *schema theory*, *implicit personality theories*, the *cognitive miser theory* (*principle of least effort*) and *hypothesis-to-be-tested theories*. One of the oldest theories of prejudice, the *realistic conflict theory*, maintains that prejudice stems from competition between social groups over valued commodities or opportunities where the greater the competition, the greater the members of the groups come to assess each other in more and more negative ways (cf., *kernel of truth hypothesis* - posits that a prejudice at one time or another may have had a factual basis for either a particular prejudiced person or for a group

of people; and *reference-group theory* - states that prejudices and attitudes are determined largely by the normative or reference group from which individuals establish their interpersonal and social standards). Another theoretical approach, the *us-versus-them effect* or the *self-categorization theory*, assumes that people have a tendency to divide the social world into two distinct categories - *us* or *them*. That is, individuals view other persons as belonging either to their own social group (usually termed the *ingroup*) or to another group (called the *outgroup*). Such distinctions are based on many dimensions such as religion, race, age, sex/gender, ethnicity, geographical location, and occupation. The *dual-processes theory of prejudice* is based on the distinction between uncontrolled/automatic versus controlled/conscious mental processes. This theory states that stereotypes pervade the culture and exert an automatic/unconscious influence on one's perceptions of members of stereotyped groups. Once implication of the *dual-processes theory* is that overcoming prejudice is like attempting to resist any well-learned habit. The *contact hypothesis* suggests that patterns of prejudice and stereotypes can be broken by direct intergroup contact: there are potential benefits for resisting prejudice when there is close acquaintance with members of other groups. Social research indicates that intergroup contact reduces prejudice only under certain conditions: when the groups that interact are roughly equal in social, economic, or task-related status, when the contact situation involves cooperation and interdependence where the groups work toward shared goals, when contact between the groups is informal and on a one-to-one basis, when contact occurs in a setting where existing norms favor group equality, and when the persons involved view each other as typical members of their respective groups. See also ATTITUDE/ATTITUDE CHANGE, THEORIES OF; FESTINGER'S COGNITIVE DISSONANCE THEORY. INGROUP BIAS THEORIES.

REFERENCES

Lippmann, W. (1922). *Public opinion*. New York: Harcourt Brace.

Allport, G. (1954). *The nature of prejudice*. Cambridge, MA: Addison-Wesley.

Dovidio, J., & Gaertner, S. (Eds.) (1986). *Prejudice, discrimination, and racism.* Orlando, FL: Academic Press.

Stephan, W. (1987). The contact hypothesis in intergroup relations. *Review of Personality and Social Psychology, 9,* 41-67.

Turner, J., Hogg, M., Oakes, P., Reicher, S., & Wetherell, M. (1987). *Rediscovering the social group: A self-categorization theory.* Oxford, UK: Blackwell.

Kurcz, I. (1995). Inevitability and changeability of stereotypes: A review of theories. *Polish Psychological Bulletin, 26,* 113-128.

Schneider, D. J. (2004). *The psychology of stereotyping.* New York: Guilford Press.

PREMACK'S PRINCIPLE/LAW. The American psychologist David Premack (1925-) offers a reappraisal of the concepts of *reinforcement* and *Thorndike's law of effect* that serves to increase the generality of these terms. *Premack's principle/law* states that any response that occurs with a fairly high frequency may be used to reinforce a response that occurs with a relatively lower frequency. *Premack's principle* is based on the implicit assumption that the organism's responses/activities that are to be reinforced are neutral and have no intrinsic value. With the counterassumption that an organism engages in a variety of activities that vary in their intrinsic value, Premack ties the reinforcement relation to a preference ranking of the activities where a given activity can be used to reinforce those of lesser value but not those of higher value. Premack proposed that a generally valid index of value for both humans and nonhumans would be *response rate* in a free-operant situation in which the activity is freely available. Premack presents data from children, monkeys, and rats that suggest his predictions concerning the reinforcing effects of certain behaviors over others are generally accurate. He also demonstrated that it is possible to reverse the reinforcement relation between two activities by altering level of deprivation or motivation. *Premack's principle* has the merit of being operational, of generating novel experiments, and of describing many social behaviors/activities that may be used as reinforcers for humans. However, there have been some criticisms and difficulties with *Premack's principle* (also called the *probability-differential theory of reinforcement* and the *prepotent response theory*). For example, W. Timberlake and J. Allison's *response-deprivation theory of reinforcement* and W. Timberlake's *equilibrium theory of learned performance* provide a more *general theory* to handle all results consistent with *Premack's theory* as well as consider other results and studies that disconfirm his theory. See also REINFORCEMENT THEORY; REINFOR-CEMENT, THORNDIKE'S THEORY OF; THORNDIKE'S LAW OF EFFECT.

REFERENCES

Premack, D. (1959). Toward empirical behavior laws. I. Positive reinforcement. *Psychological Review, 66,* 219-233.

Premack, D. (1962). Reversibility of the reinforcement relation. *Science, 136,* 255-257.

Premack, D. (1965). Reinforcement theory. In M. Jones (Ed.), *Nebraska symposium on motivation.* Lincoln: University of Nebraska Press.

Timberlake, W., & Allison, J. (1974). Response deprivation: An empirical approach to instrumental performance. *Psychological Review, 81,* 146-164.

Timberlake, W. (1980). A molar equilibrium theory of learned performance. In G. Bower (Ed.), *The psychology of learning and motivation.* New York: Academic Press.

PREPOTENCY, LAW OF. See SKINNER'S DESCRIPTIVE BEHAVIOR/OPERANT CONDITIONING THEORY.

PREPOTENT RESPONSE THEORY. See PREMACK'S PRINCIPLE/LAW; REINFORCEMENT THEORY.

PREPUBERTAL INTERACTION THEORY. See INCEST TABOO THEORIES.

PRERECOGNITION HYPOTHESIS. See PARANORMAL PHENOMENA/THEORY.

PRETESTING EFFECT. See EXPERI-MENTER EFFECTS.

PRIBRAM'S HOLOGRAPHIC MODEL. = Pribram's holonomic brain theory = holographic brain theory. The Austrian-born American physician and neuropsychologist Karl Harry Pribram (1919-) developed a *holographic model of memory* ("holographic memory") constituting a hypothetical concept of the neurophysiological aspects of memory that resemble a hologram having a three-dimensional feature. In photography, the term *holography* refers to a method of producing three-dimensional images by using light wave interference patterns, and has been suggested by Pribram as an explanation for the process whereby images may be formed in the mind. The term *hologram* refers to the film used in *holography*, and is constructed typically by photographically recording wave-fronts of laser light reflected from actual objects. The map of the neurological pathways in the human brain is complex and interactions occur at many levels. *Pribram's model* suggests that the map be viewed not as a representation in Euclidian geometry but as Rimanian, viewing a scene in three dimensions rather than two in order to understand the variety of frames of reference when they interact. Concerning the brain's memory storage, the deep structure for this capacity is distributed over some extent within each brain system and is composed of "patches" within the synaptodendritic processing web - patches that are organized by experience. Thus, propositional, categorical, object, allo-, and ego-centric frames access the deep store somewhat like a computer program addresses the memory store in a computer. How-ever, in the brain the process seems to be *content* oriented rather than *location* oriented. Pribram asserts that a neural holographic process does not imply that input information is distributed randomly over the entire depth and surface of the brain, but only those limited regions where reasonably stable junctional designs are initiated by the input participate in the distribution. According to Pribram, the capability to directly "address" *content* with-out reference to *location*, so readily accomplished by the holographic process, eliminates the need for keeping track of where information is stored. Thus, *Pribram's holographic model* involves "content-addressable" holographic-like matching between current input and stored memory, where the model is based on evidence obtained with microelectrode recordings made within the brain's hippocampal system and within the somatosensory cortex of the parietal lobe. In effect, *Pribram's model* is a holographic process that is based on the distribution of, and enfolding of, information over and within an "extent" (i.e., a spatial and temporal envelope) that is structurally and functionally similar to the "marketplace" in economics. For example, an economic marketplace may be viewed as a holographic structure in which each transaction enfolds the values of the whole, which are distributed throughout the extent of the whole. Thus, when one spends a unit of currency, say a dollar, the current value of that unit/currency represents the productivity of some nation, the adjustments of nations to a common market and common currency, the status of stock markets, etc. In the same way, in Pribram's approach, the current valuation of an event occurs within the "marketplace" of the episode within which the event is generated, and valuation depends on the values attributed to the variety of transactions that compose the episode. See also MEMORY, THEORIES OF; TOTE MODEL/HYPOTHESIS.

REFERENCES

Pribram, K. H. (1960). A review of theory in physiological psychology. *Annual Review of Psychology, 11*, 1-40.

Pribram, K. H. (1971/1977/1982). *Languages of the brain: Experimental paradoxes and principles in neuropsychology.* Englewood Cliffs, NJ: Prentice-Hall.

Pribram, K. H. (1975/1985). *The hippocampus.* 4 vols. New York: Plenum.

Pribram, K. H. (1991). *Brain and perception: Holonomy and structure in figural processing.* Hillsdale, NJ: Erlbaum.

Pribram, K. H. (1998/2003). *The holographic brain* (video). Karl Pribram (#5490). Berkeley, CA: Thinking Allowed Productions.

PRIMACY EFFECT. See IMPRESSION FORMATION, THEORIES OF.

PRIMACY EFFECT/LAW. See SERIAL-POSITION EFFECT.

PRIMAL FANTASY. See SEDUCTION THEORY.

PRIMAL HORDE THEORY. See FREUD'S THEORY OF PERSONALITY.

PRIMARY LAWS OF ASSOCIATION. See ASSOCIATION LAWS/PRINCIPLES OF.

PRIMARY MEMORY HYPOTHESIS. See SHORT-TERM AND LONG-TERM MEMORY, THEORIES OF.

PRIMARY MENTAL ABILITIES THEORY. See INTELLIGENCE, THEORIES/LAWS OF.

PRIMITIVE EMOTIONAL CONTAGION, THEORY OF. See FACIAL FEEDBACK HYPOTHESIS.

PRINCIPLE OF ANTICIPATORY MATURATION. See DEVELOPMENTAL THEORY.

PRIOR ENTRY, LAW OF. See PERSONAL EQUATION PHENOMENON; VIGILANCE, THEORIES OF.

PRISONER'S DILEMMA GAME. See CONFLICT, THEORIES OF; HAWK-DOVE/CHICKEN GAME EFFECTS.

PRIVATION, THEORY OF. See CATASTROPHE THEORY/MODEL.

PROACTIVE INHIBITION, LAW OF. See FORGETTING/MEMORY, THEORIES OF; INTERFERENCE THEORIES OF FORGETTING.

PROBABILISTIC FUNCTIONALISM, THEORY OF. See PERCEPTION (II. COMPARATIVE APPRAISAL), THEORIES OF.

PROBABILITY-DIFFERENTIAL THEORY OF REINFORCEMENT. See PREMACK'S PRINCIPLE/LAW.

PROBABILITY THEORY/LAWS. The mathematical foundation of *probability theory* forms the basis for all the statistical techniques of psychology. *Probability theory* originated in games of gambling where, on the basis of a relatively small number of trials (e.g., roulette-wheel spins, dice throws, poker hands), some decisions needed to be made about the likelihood of particular events occurring in the long run, given the basic assumption of the uniformity of nature and the mutual cancellation of complementary errors. The earliest contributions to *probability* refer to the *probability principles* as *laws of chance* (cf., *aleatory theory* - the belief that changes in society over time are due largely to chance), and were made by the French mathematician/astronomer Pierre Simon de Laplace (1749-1827), who is credited with founding the modern form of *probability theory* [cf., the *theory of accidentalism* (J. M. Baldwin, 1901-1905) - this early theory asserts that events may occur absolutely without cause. In the area of ethics, it is called *indeterminism*, and in the area of metaphysics, it is known as *tychism*. A related notion, the *theory of absolute chance*, states that the occurrence of an event due to chance is one that has no assignable cause and, hence, commonly supposed to have no cause. Historically, the concept of *chance*, itself, was hypothesized eventually as a source of uncaused events. The *theory of absolute chance*, or *pure accidentalism*, was abandoned largely and remains as a metaphysical speculation called *tychism* - a term introduced by C. S. Peirce to denote the theories that give to chance an objective existence in the universe instead of regarding it as due to one's lack of knowledge. *Tychism* (in Greek means "chance") was a theory that gave both chance and necessity a share in the process of evolution. Today, the notion of a chance event is accounted for after it has happened, or predicted before it happens, by the *law(s) of probability*. Thus, the *law(s) of probability* provide a statement of the degree of probability, called "the chance," of an event's happening on the basis of what is already known about such events]. In the early 1800s, Laplace postulated seven general principles of the calculus of probabilities. Laplace was also the pioneer of the *theory of errors* (i.e., the assumption that "error" behaves in a random way as an additive component of any score and where random error is distributed in a "normal" way), but the contributions of the German mathematician Carl Friedrich Gauss (1777-1855) were so striking that the normal *law of error* is sometimes (and, incorrectly, it would seem) called the *Gaussian law*. As the *theory of probability* developed, in addition to serving as a model of games of chance, it served also as a model for many other kinds of things having little obvious connection with games - such as results in the sciences. One feature is common to most applications of *probability theory*: the observer is uncertain about what the outcome of some observation will be and, eventually, must infer or guess what will happen [cf., the *gambler's fallacy* or the *Monte Carlo fallacy* - the mistaken belief that, in a series of *independent* chance events, future events can be predicted invariably from past ones (e.g., the fallacious belief that if a coin has come down heads many times in succession, it has an increased probability of coming down tails on the next throw); the *negative recency effect* - in predicting events, this is the tendency to select an event that could have happened but didn't, using the argument that it *should* have and is, as a consequence, more likely to do so in the near future; such an argument, of course, is fallacious; the *base-rate fallacy* - is the tendency to ignore the base-rate at which events occur when making decisions; the *regression fallacy* - is an erroneous interpretation of regression towards the mean as being caused by something other than chance; the *sample size fallacy* - is a failure to take account of sample size when estimating the probability of obtaining a particular value in a sample drawn from a known population; the *a priori theory of probability* - refers to the ability to state in advance the probability of certain events happening; and the *principle of equal distribution of ignorance*, formulated by the English mathematician George Boole (1815-1864) in 1854, which states that when the relative probabilities of two or more events are un-

known, the chances of their occurrences are equal]. In *probability theory*, in particular, the observer needs to know what will happen "in the long run" if observations could be made indefinitely (cf., the *law of averages*, which states that the arithmetic mean of a group of observations has a probability of occurrence that is greater than that of any single observation). The logical machinery of "in the long run" is formalized in the *theory of probability*. The theory alone does not tell anyone how to decide on events (cf., the mathematical *law of least squares* that refers to deciding on the most acceptable values from among a series of unknown quantities by taking the minimum sum of the squared residual errors of the observations), but it does give ways of evaluating the degree of *risk* one takes for some decisions. There are diverse views of the nature of probability and the topic is not without controversy. Three approaches to probability have been employed: the *subjective/personalistic* approach (e.g., "It will probably rain today"), the *formal mathematical* approach (e.g., "The probability of an event is the ratio of the number of favorable cases to the total number of equally likely cases"), and the *empirical relative-frequency* approach (e.g., "A population of events is defined where probability is the relative frequency in the population and is a population parameter") [cf., *Hellin's law* - named after the Polish pathologist Dyonizy Hellin (1867-1935) - is the principle that as the number of infants in a multiple birth increases, the relative frequency of occurrence compared to total births in a population decreases geometrically; thus, twins occur once in 89 births, triplets occur once in 89^2 births, etc.]. In recent years, interest in *subjective probability*, and in *Bayesian statistics*, has increased [cf., *Bayes' theorem* - named after the English clergyman/mathematician Thomas Bayes (1702-1761), states the relation among the various conditional probabilities of various events]. The basic *laws/theorems of probability* (cf., *law of large numbers* - states that the larger the sample taken from a population, the more likely is the sample's mean to approximate that of the whole population; and the *central-limit theorem* - states that as the size of any sample of scores becomes large, the sampling distribution of the mean approaches the normal distribution) that are central to *probability theory* are the *additive law of probability*, which states that in a given set of mutually exclusive events the probability of occurrence of one event *or* another event is equal to the sum of their separate probabilities; and the *multiplicative law of probability*, which states that the probability of the *joint* occurrence of two or more independent events is the *product* of their individual probabilities (cf., *distributive law* - states that an operation performed on a complex whole influences each part of the complex in the same way, as if performed on each part separately). See also BAYES' THEOREM; CENTRAL LIMIT THEOREM; DECISION-MAKING THEORIES; ESTES' STIMULUS SAMPLING THEORY; HYPOTHESIS-TESTING THEORY; KOLMOGOROV'S AXIOMS/THEORY; NORMAL DISTRIBUTION THEORY; NULL HYPOTHESIS.

REFERENCES

Laplace, P. S. (1812). *Theorie analytique des probabilities*. Paris: Courcier.

Laplace, P. S. (1818). *Essai philosophique sur les probabilities*. Paris: Courcier.

Gauss, C. F. (1870). *Carl Friedrich Gauss werke*. Gottingen: Kaestner.

Baldwin, J. M. (Ed.) (1901-1905). *Dictionary of philosophy and psychology*. New York: Macmillan.

Boring, E. G. (1957). *A history of experimental psychology*. New York: Appleton-Century-Crofts.

De Finetti, B. (1978). Probability: Interpretations. In W. Kruskal & J. Turner (Eds.), *International encyclopedia of statistics*. New York: Free Press.

PROBABILITY THEORY OF LEARNING. See LEARNING THEORY/LAWS.

PROBLEM-SOLVING AND CREATIVITY STAGE THEORIES. The American cognitive psychologist and computer scientist Allen Newell (1927-1992) and Herbert Alexander Simon (1916-2001) formulated a *theory of human problem solving* that examines the processes of human problem solving, and their theory is based on four propositions: the fundamental characteristics of the information processing system, the "problem space," the structure of the task environment, and the nature of the problem solving process. The heuristic value of this theory is relevant to theories of learning, perception, and concept formation. A. Newell also proposed a *unified theory of cognition*, and presented an exemplar of such a theory, called the *Soar theory/system*, consisting of a computer program that simulates human cognition and, thus, represents a pioneer computer system in *artificial intelligence*. The *Soar system/theory* is the first problem solver to create its own subgoals and to learn continuously from its own experience; *Soar* is able to operate within the real-time constraints of intelligent behavior, such as immediate-response to item-recognition tasks, and illustrates important aspects of the human cognitive structure and of problem-solving characteristics. Allen Newell and Paul S. Rosenbloom describe the *power law of practice* that applies to cognitive skill acquisition, learning, and problem-solving tasks, and states that there is a positive correlation between the number of times a task has been practiced and increase of skill in that area; stated another way, the *power law of practice* predicts that the speed of performance of a task will improve as a *power* of the number of times that the task is performed. However, the validity of the *power law of practice* (e.g., some task-acquisition data may deviate systematically from *power-function* fits) has been challenged recently, along with suggested theoretical alternatives and/or supplements, such as "aggregated learning," "power law of retention," "problem-solving fan-effect," "component power laws," "strategy shifting," and "in-stance theory of automaticity." Historically, the classic work of the German psychologist Karl Duncker (1903-1940) on problem solving and creativity is noteworthy. Duncker was the first person to propose the notion of *functional fixity/fixedness* in problem solving (i.e., the inability to find the solution to a new problem because one attempts to use old methods that are not suitable in the new situation). In his famous 1935 monograph on problem solving, Duncker gives a detailed description of the organization of problem solving, the establishment of the general range of the problem and its possible solutions, the stage of functional solutions, and the stage of specific solutions. The mental processes involved in *creative thinking* lead to a new solution, invention, or synthesis in a given area on a particular problem; "creative solutions" typically employ preexisting objects and/or ideas, but uniquely create new relationships between the elements used, such as new social techniques, mechanical inventions, scientific theories, or artistic creations. The English psychologist Graham Wallas (1858-1932) proposed that the following four stages comprise the successive phases/operations that may be observed in the general process of problem-solving, including creative thinking: *preparation* - setting the appropriate mental conditions for solving a particular problem (such as mastering the techniques of one's art/skill and includes all the random and direct/formal educational exposures that the person has experienced; preparation for the scientist in problem-solving seems to be a more deliberate process than it is for the artist or poet); *incubation* - characterized by creative thinking while the issue/problem is "turned over" in one's mind, often unconsciously, and where there's a great amount of inactivity with no obvious or apparent progress being made (the person may deliberately relax, sleep, or initiate a change of pace in activities in order to reduce or eliminate occasional sources of interference to the intuitive-creative process); *illumination/ inspiration/insight* - the process by which the meaning and significance of a pattern, or the overall solution to a problem, suddenly becomes clear (often via an "aha" or "eureka!" revelatory experience or feeling); this stage is characterized by the three factors of "sudden illumination," "feelings of elation," and "delivery via a mysterious external source;" inspiration seems to occur when there is the greatest degree of discouragement or lack of apparent/palpable progress; and *verification* - this phase is characterized by hard work wherein the individual attempts to "materialize" all that has occurred previously in the unseen thought processes. Thus, the "creative act" is a combination of knowledge, imagination, timing, and evaluation. In another theoretical approach to problem-solving stages, the American philosopher/psychologist John Dewey (1859-1952) proposed the following five stages that comprise the sequencing of operations: *suggestion* (a loosely organized intuition or set of propositions/definitions concerning the particular issue at hand); *translation* (transformation of any difficulties into "well-defined problems" where the starting position or initial state, the permissible operations, and the goal/end state are specified precisely and clearly); *framing of a hypothesis* (specification of potential cause-effect relationships within the framework or domain of the issue/problem at hand); *reasoning* (application of formal rules of logic or some other rationally-based methodology to the proposition, such as deductive or inductive reasoning); and *testing* (submission of the resultant reasoned/stated hypotheses to formal test and assessment conditions and devices). Other general, but formal, approaches offered by research psychologists to solving problems include the following sequential/orderly activities: *define* the problem exactly; *evaluate* the definition; *remember* the problem; search for *hypotheses*; enumerate several or *alternative hypotheses*; *choose* the *best* hypothesis; *evaluate* the *best* hypothesis; and *implement* the *best* hypothesis. See also ARTIFICIAL INTELLIGENCE; DECISION-MAKING THEORIES; INTUITION, THEORIES OF.

REFERENCES

Dewey, J. (1910/1933). *How we think*. Boston: Heath.

Wallas, G. (1926). *The art of thought*. New York: Harcourt, Brace.

Duncker, K. (1935/1945). Zur psychologie des produktiven denkens (On the psychology of productive thought). *Psychological Monographs, 58*, 5.

Newell, A., Shaw, J. C., & Simon, H. A. (1958). Elements of a theory of human problem solving. *Psychological Review, 65*, 151-166.

Newell, A., & Simon, H. A. (1961). Computer simulation of human thinking. *Science, 134*, 2011-2017.

Wason, P. C., & Johnson-Laird, P. N. (Ed.) (1968). *Thinking and reasoning*. Harmondsworth, UK: Penguin.

Simon, H. A., & Newell, A. (1971). Human problem solving: The state of the theory in 1970. *American Psychologist, 26*, 145-159.

Simon, H. A., & Newell, A. (1972). *Human problem solving*. Englewood Cliffs, NJ: Prentice-Hall.

Newell, A., & Rosenbloom, P. S. (1981). Mechanisms of skill acquisition and the law of practice. In J. R. Anderson (Ed.), *Cognitive skills and their acquisition*. Hillsdale, NJ: Erlbaum.

Newell, A., & Simon, H. A. (1988). The theory of human problem solving. In A. M. Collins & E. E. Smith (Eds.), *Readings in cognitive science: A perspective for psychology and artificial intelligence*. San Mateo, CA: Kaufmann.

Shrager, J., Hogg, T., & Huberman, B. (1988). A graph-dynamic model of the power law of practice and the problem-solving fan-effect. *Science, 242*, 414-416.

Newell, A. (1990). *Unified theories of cognition*. Cambridge, MA: Harvard University Press.

Newell, A. (1992a). Precis of unified theories of cognition. *The Behavioral and Brain Sciences, 15*, 425-492.

Newell, A. (1992b). Unified theories of cognition and the role of Soar. In J. A. Michon & A. Akyurek (Eds.), *Soar: A cognitive architecture in perspective: A tribute to Allen Newell*. New York: Kluver/Plenum.

Colonius, H. (1995). The instance theory of automaticity: Why the Weibull? *Psychological Review, 102*, 744-750.

Logan, G. D. (1995). The Weibull distribution, the power law, and the instance theory of automaticity. *Psychological Review, 102*, 751-756.

Rickard, T. C. (1997). Bending the power law: A CMPL theory of strategy shifts and the automatization of cognitive skills. *Journal of Experimental Psychology: General, 126*, 288-311.

Palmeri, T. J. (1999). Theories of automaticity and the power law of practice. *Journal of Experimental Psychology: Learning, Memory, and Cognition, 25*, 543-551.

Haider, H., & Frensch, P. A. (2002). Why aggregated learning follows the power law of practice when individual learning does not. *Journal of Experimental Psychology: Learning, Memory, and Cognition, 28*, 392-406.

PROCEDURAL MEMORY. See SHORT-TERM AND LONG-TERM MEMORY, THEORIES OF.

PROCEDURAL REINSTATEMENT HYPOTHESIS. See CODING THEORIES.

PROCESS INTERACTION SYSTEM/ THEORY. See COMMUNICATION THEORY; INTERACTION PROCESS ANALYSIS TECHNIQUE.

PROCESS THEORIES OF MOTIVATION. See MOTIVATION, THEORIES OF.

PROCESS THEORY OF DECISION-MAKING. See ESTES' STIMULUS SAMPLING THEORY.

PRODUCTIVE MEMORY. See FORGETTING/MEMORY, THEORIES OF.

PROGRESSION INDEX. See EMOTIONAL INTELLIGENCE, THEORY OF.

PROGRESSION, LAW OF. See WEBER'S LAW.

PROGRESSIVE MATRICES THEORY. See INTELLIGENCE, THEORIES/LAWS OF.

PROGRESSIVE RELAXATION THEORY/TECHNIQUE. See WOLPE'S THEORY/TECHNIQUE OF RECIPROCAL INHIBITION.

PROGRESSIVE TELEOLOGICAL-REGRESSION HYPOTHESIS. See SCHIZOPHRENIA, THEORIES OF.

PROOF-READER'S ILLUSION/EFFECT. See STROOP EFFECT/STROOP TEST.

PROPORTION, PRINCIPLE OF. See ZEISING'S PRINCIPLE.

PROPOSITIONAL THEORY OF MEM-ORY. See FORGETTING/MEMORY, THE-ORIES OF.

PROSPECTIVE TIME ESTIMATION. See TIME, THEORIES OF.

PROSPECT THEORY. See DECISION-MAKING THEORIES; ORGANIZATION-AL/INDUSTRIAL/SYSTEMS THEORY.

PROTOPLASMIC STRUCTURE THEO-RIES. See LIFE, THEORIES OF.

PROTOTYPE ACQUISITION. See CON-CEPT LEARNING/CONCEPT FORMA-TION, THEORIES OF.

PROTOTYPE THEORY. The *prototype theory of concepts and concept formation* was developed by the American psychologist El-eanor Rosch/Heider (1938-) in 1973, chal-lenging the classical *componential theory* (also called *definitional theory* and *feature-list theory*) of the Greek philosophers Plato and Aristotle who maintained that concepts are stored in the mind as logical lists of sufficient and necessary conditions defining member-ship ("defining properties") of a given cate-gory. *Prototype theory* rejects this older no-tion that every concept has a defining attribute or essence that determines its identity, and suggests that most everyday concepts have a graded internal structure that is characterized by a "prototype" (i.e., a "reference point" or an "optimal example") at their core and "fuzzy boundaries" (i.e., loose lines of differ-entiation between positive and negative in-stances) at their periphery. In a manner sug-gestive of the Austrian-born British philoso-pher Ludwig Wittgenstein (1889-1951) - who proposed, in one case, that although a rope consists of many strands, no single strand runs the entire length of the rope - Rosch notes that concept-defining attributes do not need to be shared by all instances of a given concept. Rather, all members of a mental category may be shown to have a "family resemblance" to each other, and such resemblance may be recognized *perceptually* instead of being de-fined *logically* (e.g., not all "cups" have han-dles or are used for the purpose of drinking).

Prototype theory indicates that the meaning of many everyday concepts, or "natural catego-ries," is derived not from their defining char-acteristics but from the features that describe their most typical member. Thus, a *prototype* is the member of a category that shares a maximum of attributes with other members and a minimum of attributes with members of different categories. The theory suggests that people decide whether or not an item/object belongs to a specific category by comparing the item with the prototype of that category. According to this approach, an item/object will be classified as an instance of a category if it is "similar" to the prototypical member of that category, but some researchers question how "similarity" is assessed. *Prototype theory* is somewhat vague on this issue (as well as on the issue of the degree to which our concep-tual structures are culture-bound), and some investigators suggest that one use several "ex-emplars," rather than a single prototype, to establish "similarity." However, the value of *prototype theory* resides in its attempts to explain how people can form concepts of groups that consist of rather loosely-structured items or objects. See also CONCEPT LEARNING AND CONCEPT FORMA-TION, THEORIES OF; FUZ-ZY SET THE-ORY.

REFERENCES

Wittgenstein, L. (1953). *Philosophical inves-tigations*. Translated by G. E. M. Anscombe. New York: Macmillan.

Rosch, E. (1973). Natural categories. *Cogni-tive Psychology*, *4*, 328-350.

Rosch, E. (1981). Categorization of natural objects. *Annual Review of Psychol-ogy*, 32, 89-115.

Margolis, E. (1994). A reassessment of the shift from the classical theory of concepts to prototype theory. *Cogni-tion*, *51*, 73-89.

PROUST PHENOMENON/EFFECT. See OLFACTION/SMELL, THEORIES OF.

PROVISIONAL EXPECTANCIES/HYPO-THESES THEORY. See TOLMAN'S THE-ORY.

PROXEMICS THEORY. See INTER-PERSONAL ATTRACTION THEORIES.

PROXIMITY, LAW OF. See GESTALT THEORY/LAWS.

PSEUDOSCIENTIFIC AND UNCONVENTIONAL THEORIES. The term *pseudoscience* refers to a system of theories and methods that claims falsely to be scientific, or is a system that is falsely regarded by some people to be scientific. The term *pseudopsychology* is an approach to psychology that employs unscientific, even fraudulent, methods in it investigations; and the term *unconventional theory* (in particular, in psychology, in reference to *therapeutic* theoretical approaches) refers to those methods of treating mind, body, or mind-body interactions, that are not considered by the scientific and professional community to be mainstream approaches. Among the *pseudoscientific theories/methods* that impact on, or challenge, scientific psychology are the following: *astrology* (the belief that the location of the stars and planets at the time of one's conception and/or birth influences their lives subsequently); *biological rhythms/biorhythms* (periodic variations in one's physiological and psychological functions that, when charted, are used by some individuals to predict and/or control their feelings and behaviors); *characterology* (one's basic "character" is assessed or "read" by external signs of body features, such as hair- or eye-color); *clairvoyance* (an alleged "extra-sensory" ability of some "psychics" used to reveal information about one's past, present, or future); *dianetics/scientology* (an amalgamation/system of philosophical and psychological theories that employs concepts from psychoanalysis, cybernetics, and other disciplines to help the individual achieve an optimal life, and is based on a central hypothetical entity called the *engram* that allegedly affects behavior and is regarded as the cause of mental and psychosomatic illness; *engrams* are thought to be the result of painful past experiences and psychological shocks suffered in the present and previous "incarnations;" this approach is aimed at healing illness by erasing the appropriate *engrams*); *iridology* (assumes that the iris of the eye gives information that enables one to make diagnoses of nutritional imbalances); *dowsing* (a person, known as a "dowser" or "diviner," who uses a "magic wand," staff, rod, or forked stick to allegedly locate underground water, oil, precious metals, or minerals); *exorcism* (a religious/superstitious ritual consisting of prayers, incantations, and "devil-threats" performed by a shaman or priest who attempts to expel "demons" from "possessed" persons); *extrasensory perception* (also called ESP, "paranormal cognition," or "parapsychology;" the alleged awareness of external events by means other than the normal sensory channels or receptors, includes telepathy, clairvoyance, precognition, and psychokinesis); *mediums* (per-sons who allegedly communicate with dead individuals through rituals called "séances" where a group of persons sit around a table in a darkened room and "speak" with the decreased); *numerology* (study of the occult meaning of numbers, such as birth dates or digits derived from the letters of a name, used to interpret one's future and life); *occultism* [belief that nature, natural processes, or people may be controlled by secret or magic methods and rituals (cf., five types of research-oriented "occultism categories" are: *protoscientific* - scientific attempts are made but the data are not accepted as valid; *quasi-scientific* - false attempts are made to appear scientific; *pragmatic* - beliefs approximate science but no claims are made; *shared mystical* - similar private experiences exist among members of a group; and *private mystical* - validation is made only on a personal or private basis)]; *orgonomy* (belief in the concept of "orgone energy" that allegedly is concentrated in the sexual organs during sexual activity); *Ouija board* (belief that a special board painted with letters and numbers, and containing a movable pointer, is influenced by supernatural forces); *out-of-body experience* (imagining that one's spirit or soul has left the body and is perceiving/acting on its own); *palmistry* (the lines and other skin surface features of one's palms are interpreted as signs of one's personality traits, and are used in predicting the person's future); *phrenology* (also called "craniology," attempts to identify one's psychological aspects, faculties, or characteristics by analysis of the swellings, bumps, and hollows on the surface of one's skull); *physiognomy* (evaluation of one's personality from facial features, such as chin, forehead, and eye orientation and structure); and *poltergeists* (purported ghosts, spirits, or demons, usually mischievous and noisy, that are heard but not seen typically). Among the *unconventional therapies* are: *aroma therapy* (the inhalation of aromatic oils of various plants to promote physical and/or psychological health); *crystal-healing* (belief that healing may occur via natural quartz crystals that purportedly retain energy and provide vibrations that are transferred to one's body for various salubrious effects); and *homeopathy* (a physical-treatment approach toward disease, in which "like cures like" and "less is more," and involves the administration of minute doses of extracts of natural substances - such as herbs and minerals - to patients, or "vaccines" may be given to healthy persons to prevent various diseases). The theories/systems of *acupuncture* [i.e., the ancient Chinese practice of inserting needles into specific parts of the body to control pain or cure illness, based on the idea that pathways of energy flow between places on the skin (and, perhaps, in peripheral nerves) and the body's organ systems] and *acupressure* [i.e., a variation of *acupuncture*, in which healing supposedly occurs by applying pressure with thumbs (instead of needles) on various points of the body] are considered, also, as *unconventional therapies* and some individuals claim to have gained relief from pain by these methods, but potential explanatory effects such as the *placebo effect* and various other *experimenter effects* (such as *demand characteristics of the situation*) may need to be invoked as possible causative factors in such claims. See also ASTROLOGY, THEORY OF; BIORHYTHM THEORY; CYBERNETIC THEORY; ENGRAM THEORY; EXPERIMENTER EFFECTS; GRAPHOLOGY, THEORY OF; INOCULATION THEORY; PARANORMAL PHENOMENA AND THEORY; PHRENOLOGY, DOCTRINE OF; PLACEBO EFFECT; REICH'S ORGONE/ORGONOMY THEORY; SUPERSTITION AND SUPERSTITIOUS EFFECTS.

REFERENCES

Christopher, M. (1970). *ESP, seers, and psychics*. New York: Crowell.

Hansel, C. E. M. (1980). *ESP and parapsychology: A critical evaluation*. Buffalo, NY: Prometheus.

Randi, J. (1980). *Flim-flam*. New York: Harper & Row.

Gardner, M. (1982). *Science: Good, bad, and bogus*. Buffalo, NY: Prometheus.

Ridgway, J. M., & Benjamin, M. (1987). *Psi Fi: Psychological theories and science fictions*. Leicester, UK: British Psychological Society.

PSEUDOSCOPE/PSEUDOPHONE EFFECTS. See APPENDIX A.

PSI PHENOMENA. See PARANORMAL PHENOMENA/THEORY.

PSYCHICAL DETERMINISM DOCTRINE. See DETERMINISM, DOCTRINE/THEORY OF.

PSYCHICAL REALITY THEORY. See SEDUCTION THEORY.

PSYCHIC COMPENSATION, PRINCIPLE OF. See PIDDINGTON'S COMPENSATORY HUMOR THEORY.

PSYCHIC DYNAMICS THEORY. See HERBART'S DOCTRINE OF APPERCEPTION.

PSYCHIC ENERGY THEORY. See FREUD'S THEORY OF PERSONALITY; JUNG'S THEORY OF PERSONALITY.

PSYCHIC LAW OF TIME PERCEPTION. See JAMES' TIME THEORY.

PSYCHIC RESULTANTS, LAW OF. See WUNDT'S THEORIES/DOCTRINES/PRINCIPLES.

PSYCHOANALYTICAL/LIBIDINAL THEORY OF DEPRESSION. See DEPRESSION, THEORIES OF.

PSYCHOANALYTIC THEORIES OF PERSONALITY. See FREUD'S THEORY OF PERSONALITY; PERSONALITY THEORIES.

PSYCHOANALYTIC THEORY OF DREAMS. See DREAM THEORY.

PSYCHOANALYTIC THEORY OF HUMOR/WIT. See FREUD'S THEORY OF WIT/HUMOR; HUMOR, THEORIES OF; MOTIVATIONAL THEORIES OF HUMOR.

PSYCHOANALYTIC THEORY OF INGROUP BIAS. See INGROUP BIAS THEORIES.

PSYCHOBIOLOGY, THEORY OF. See MOTIVATION, THEORIES OF; MURPHY'S BIOSOCIAL THEORY.

PSYCHODYNAMIC THEORIES OF PERSONALITY. See FREUD'S THEORY OF PERSONALITY; PERSONALITY THEORIES.

PSYCHOGENIC THEORIES OF ABNORMALITY. See PSYCHOPATHOLOGY, THEORIES OF.

PSYCHOHISTORY. See ERIKSON'S THEORY OF PERSONALITY; FREUD'S THEORY OF PERSONALITY.

PSYCHOLEXICOLOGY THEORY. See MEANING, THEORY/ASSESSMENT OF.

PSYCHOLINGUISTICS THEORY. See CHOMSKY'S PSYCHOLINGUISTICS THEORY; LANGUAGE ACQUISITION THEORY; SPEECH THEORIES.

PSYCHOLOGICAL DISTANCE. See DEVELOPMENTAL THEORY.

PSYCHOLOGICAL HEDONISM, LAW OF. See EFFECT, LAW OF; HEDONISM, THEORY/LAW OF.

PSYCHOLOGICAL LAW OF RELATIVITY. See WUNDT'S THEORIES/DOCTRINES/PRINCIPLES.

PSYCHOLOGICAL MOMENT. See JAMES' TIME THEORY; TIME, THEORIES OF.

PSYCHOLOGICAL REVERSAL THEORY. See APTER'S REVERSAL THEORY OF HUMOR.

PSYCHOLOGICAL THEORY OF INTENTIONALISM. See MIND-BODY THEORIES.

PSYCHOLOGICAL THEORY OF LAUGHTER, FIRST. See HOBBES' THEORY OF HUMOR/LAUGHTER.

PSYCHOLOGICAL TIME, MODELS OF. The current *models of psychological time* may be categorized into two classes of mutually incompatible models or theories: the *biological theories* - propose timing *with* a timer (e.g., clock-counter models) and the *cognitive theories* - propose timing *without* a timer (e.g., attentional models). *Biological theories* speculate that psychological time is a product of brain mechanisms that include one or more "internal clocks" by which the individual has *direct* access to time behavior and aids in judging duration (cf., *neural timing theory*; Luce & Green, 1972). On the other hand, *cognitive theories* suggest that psychological time is a product of information-processing events, especially those involving memory, attention, and judgment. R. Block and D. Zakay (1996) attempt to reconcile these two influences by proposing an *attentional-gate model* that apparently seems capable of combining a psychobiological "pacemaking mechanism" with cognitive and motivational processes within a single model. These researchers (Zakay & Block, 1997) examine, also, the issue of *prospective* (the "experience" of duration, "time in passing") versus *retrospective* (the "memory/remembrance" of duration, "time in retrospect") judgments in the estimation of relatively short durations. They suggest that the two different types of timing involve different cognitive processes requiring separate models, and propose the *attentional-gate* and *contextual-change models*, respectively, for *prospective* and *retrospective* timing. Additionally, D. Zakay's (1989) *resource-allocation model of time estimation* generates experimental data that support the hypothesis that *prospective* timing creates a dual-task condition where magnitude of duration judgments are indicative of the amount of attentional resources that are allocated for the processing of time/temporal information and data. See also BEHAVIORAL THEORY OF TIMING; BLOCK'S CONTEXTUALISTIC MODEL OF TIME; SCALAR TIMING THEORY; TIME, THEORIES OF.

REFERENCES

Luce, R. D., & Green, D. M. (1972). A neural timing theory for response times and the psychophysics of intensity. *Psychological Review*, *79*, 14-57.

Poynter, W. D. (1989). Judging the duration of time intervals: A process of remembering segments of experience. In I. Levine & D. Zakay (Eds.), *Time and human cognition: A life-span perspective*. Amsterdam, Netherlands: North-Holland.

Zakay, D. (1989). Subjective time and attentional resource allocation: An integrated model of time estimation. In I. Levine & D. Zakay (Eds.), *Time and human cognition: A life-span perspective*. Amsterdam, Netherlands: North-Holland.

Block, R. (1990). *Cognitive models of psychological time*. Hillsdale, NJ: Erlbaum.

Brown, S., & West, A. (1990). Multiple timing and the allocation of attention. *Acta Psychologica*, *75*, 103-121.

Block, R., & Zakay, D. (1996). Models of psychological time revisited. In H. Helfrich (Ed.), *Time and mind*. Seattle, WN: Hogrefe & Huber.

Zakay, D., & Block, R. (1997). Temporal cognition. *Current Directions in Psychological Science*, *6*, 12-16.

PSYCHOLOGIC THEORY/DOCTRINE. See HISTORICAL MODELS OF EXPERIMENTAL PSYCHOLOGY.

PSYCHOLOGISM, DOCTRINE OF. See MIND-BODY THEORIES.

PSYCHONEURAL PARALLELISM, THEORY OF. See NEURON/NEURAL/NERVE THEORY.

PSYCHONEUROMUSCULAR THEORY. See IMAGERY/MENTAL IMAGERY, THEORIES OF.

PSYCHOPATHOLOGY, THEORIES OF. The general term *psychopathology* refers to the scientific study of mental disorders that includes findings from the fields of psychology, psychiatry, pharmacology, neurology, and endocrinology, among others, and is distinguished from the actual practice of clinical psychologists and psychiatrists in the treatment of individuals with mental disorders (cf., *functional analytic causal model*, or FACM, which is a vector diagram/functional analysis of a patient to clarify, organize, and symbolize various types and factors concerning the individual's behavioral problems; the model constitutes an alternative mode of conceptualizing a clinical case study, its history, and prescriptive actions). The specific terms *psychopathy*, *sociopathy*, *sociopathic personality*, and *psychopathic personality* refer to a personality disorder characterized by amorality, a lack of affect, and a diminished sense of anxiety/guilt associated with antisocial behaviors. These terms, once popular, are now little used, and the term *antisocial personality disorder* is more preferred in mainstream psychology today but with the absence of the clinical features of anxiety/guilt under the newer term. The process of *diagnosis of psychopathology* refers to classifying information relevant to an individual's behavioral and emotional state and the subsequent assignment of a name or label to that state taken from a commonly accepted classification system (cf., *anchoring effect* - a tendency for clinicians, after they have made a diagnostic decision, usually early in the therapeutic process, to adhere to that diagnosis as time passes, and resisting revisions, even though later evidence argues that the original diagnosis was incorrect). The *psychodiagnostic process* has been criticized, often, because of the labeling practice where, once identified as a patient, the individual may then feel the "victim" of an illness and, as a consequence, may fail to take responsibility for resolution of problems (cf., the *question method/phenomenon* - refers to a "strategic question" that a therapist might pose to a client to determine whether the person's problem is medical/physiological or psychological/ functional; for instance, if the therapist asks the client, "If you did *not* have this symptom/condition, what would you do?" A client's reply such as "I would go back to work to provide for my family" may reveal that the symptom/condition is psychological, but a reply such as "I would feel comfortable and not be in so much pain" may indicate that the problem is medical). Different historical perspectives and *theories of psychopathology* have been proposed, ranging from beliefs in demons, witches, and supernatural powers inhabiting the afflicted person, to use of mental status examinations by judges to distinguish mental retardation from mental illness [cf., *malevolent personality theory* - holds that "evil personalities" are not explained by reference to the devil or to mental illness, but rather by choices the person makes between good and bad behaviors, beginning early in life; "malevolent personalities" are said to possess traits such as contempt for others, magical thinking, justification, rationalization, shame, and unwillingness to examine one's own "dark side;" *McNaughten rules/principles* (altenative spellings are: *McNaughton*, and *M'Naughten*) - refers to a set of four rules established in English law in the case *Regina v. McNaughten* (1843), according to which legal proof of "insanity" and, thus, lack of criminal responsibility, requires evidence that the accused either did not know what he/she was doing or was incapable of knowing "right" from "wrong;" the case involved the defendant Daniel McNaughten who shot and killed the secretary of the British prime minister Sir Robert Peel, but was found to have been of "unsound mind" at the time; and *uterine theory* - a discredited theory first proposed by the Greek physician Hippocrates (c. 460-377 B.C.), stating that *hysteria* is exclusively a fe-male disorder caused by a displaced or "wandering" womb/uterus]. The comprehensive *di-agnostic system of psychopathology* used today began with the German-born psychiatrist Emil Kraepelin (1856-1926), the "father of modern psychiatry," who made careful observations of patients and statistical tabulations of symptoms. In his approach, *Kraepelin's theory/classification* concludes that there are two major mental disorders

largely caused by physiological or biological factors: *dementia praecox* [a term in Latin meaning "early madness," and coined by the English physician and anatomist Thomas Willis (1621-1673)] - was subdivided into the categories of simple, hebephrenia, catatonia, and paranoia types; and *manic-depressive psychosis* that had many subdivisions depending on the regularity or irregularity of the cycles of mania and depression [cf., *Pinel's classification system* - named after the French physician Phillippe Pinel (1745-1826) who categorized mental disorders into four types: melancholic/depressive, mania/delirium, mania/no delirium, and dementia/mental deterioration; Pinel argued against the *doctrine of phrenology*, and he also helped in establishing more humane treatment methods in mental hospitals]. Kraepelin's nosological term *dementia praecox* was criticized severely for almost 50 years on the basis that the alleged irreversible behavioral deterioration in this condition was actually reversible. Later, the Swiss psychiatrist Eugen Bleuler (1857-1939) advanced Kraepelin's basic subtypes of disorder but substituted the term *schizophrenia* for *dementia praecox*. In 1945, the U.S. Army Medical Department developed a revised classification system where *schizophrenic* patients were no longer forced into the Kraepelin-type system. Today, the *Diagnostic and Statistical Manual of Mental Disorders* (developed and published by the American Psychiatric Association) is used by the majority of psychologists and psychiatrists treating the *psychopathologies* in the United States; cf., *International Classification of Diseases* (via the World Health Organization) as the recognized international classificatory sys-tem. The American personality theorist Theodore Millon (1967) describes a number of *theories of psychopathology* under the rubrics of: *biophysical theories* (e.g., E. Bleuler and W. Sheldon), *intrapsychic theories* (e.g., S. Freud, E. Erikson, K. Horney, H. S. Sullivan, E. Fromm, and C. Jung), *behavioral theories* (e.g., B. F. Skinner, H. Eysenck, J. Dollard, N. Miller, and A. Bandura), and *existential/phenomenological theories* (e.g., C. Rogers, R. May, R. D. Laing, and A. Maslow). Millon states that the term *psychopathology* is defined in the context of the theory one employs (cf., *network effect* - relates to the interactions and relationships in a patient's environment that play a significant role in the production of psychiatric disorders). For instance, an *idiographically-oriented* humanist theorist who emphasizes the importance of phenomenological experience will include uniqueness and self-discomfort in the definition, whereas a *nomothetically-oriented* biochemical theorist will formulate a definition in terms of biochemical dysfunctions. According to Millon, once a particular theory has been selected, the definition of *psychopathology* follows logically and inevitably. No single definition of *psychopathology* conveys the wide range of observations and orientations with which psychopathology may be examined (cf., *normalization principle* - holds that persons with mental and/or physical disabilities should not be denied social or sexual relationships because of their maladies, where such relationships may include a range of physical and emotional contacts from friendships to sexual activity; and *social stress theories of pathology* - regards the relation between social class and mental illness, and states that the greater aspects of environmental stress that typically confront the poor of society lead to their greater frequency of personal and social pathology). Current models/theories in psychopathology and therapy include *physiological/biochemical*; *psychoanalytic* [cf., *Fairbairn's revised psychopathology* - the theory of mental disorder proposed by the Scottish psychoanalyst W. R. D. Fairbairn (1889-1964), including his theory of the "defensive technique;" *retreat from reality hypothesis* - holds that a person with a mental disorder is unable to cope with the undesirable and unpleasant aspects of life, and is able to "escape" by losing touch with reality and other people; the hypothesis states that such individuals avoid getting well because a return to reality would require them to face their problems and confront life's disappointments and unpleasantries; *sociogenic hypothesis* - suggests that sociological factors, such as living in an impoverished environment, contribute to the cause of behavioral and mental disorders (e.g., criminal behavior; schizophrenia); and *understimulation theory* - holds that severe anxiety and other psychological disorders may be caused by an inadequate or insufficient stimulation in the individual's life or environment, and has been used as a rationale, as well, to explain vandalism and other crimes that occur in urban settings where youngsters lack exposure to a large variety of stimuli; cf., *sensory deprivation effects*]; *learning*; *environmental* (cf., the *ecological-systems mod-el* - speculates that mental disorders are reflections of environmental disequilibrium, not merely of personal imbalance, and may be prevented and treated by studying and modifying the environmental factors surrounding the affected individual); *cognitive*; *humanistic*; and *predispositional/diathesis-stress paradigms* (cf., *stress-decompensation model* - suggests that abnormal behavior originates as a result of stress that leads to "decompensation," i.e., a gradual progressive deterioration of normal behavior) where the definition of *abnormal/abnormality* yields several criteria (e.g., statistical rarity, subjective distress, disability, and norm violations), but no single criterion, by itself, is completely satisfactory. At this stage and time, too little is known about *psychopathology* and its treatment to settle conclusively on any one paradigm. See also EXISTENTIAL ANALYSIS THEORY; GOOD BREAST/OBJECT-BAD BREAST/ OBJECT THEORY; IDIOGRAPHIC/NOMO-THETIC LAWS; LABELING/DEVIANCE THEORY; MEDICAL/DISEASE MODEL; PERSONALITY THEORIES; SCHIZOPHRENIA, THEORIES OF; SENSORY DEPRIVATION EFFECTS.

REFERENCES

Kraepelin, E. (1883/1907). *Clinical psychiatry*. New York: Macmillan.

Bleuler, E. (1916). *Textbook of psychiatry*. New York: Macmillan.

Zilboorg, G., & Henry, G. (1941). *A history of medical psychology*. New York: Norton.

Fairbairn, W. R. D. (1952). *Psychoanalytic studies of the personality*. London: Tavistock.

Szasz, T. S. (1961/1967). *The myth of mental illness*. New York: Dell/Delta.

Millon, T. (Ed.) (1967). *Theories of psychopathology*. Philadelphia: Saunders.

Zubin, J. (1967). Classification of behavior disorders. *Annual Review of Psychology, 18*, 373-406.

Neugebauer, R. (1979). Medieval and early modern theories of mental illness. *Archives of General Psychiatry, 36*, 477-483.

McReynolds, P. (1989). Diagnosis and clinical assessment: Current status and major issues. *Annual Review of Psychology, 40*, 83-108.

Wakefield, J. C. (1992). The concept of mental disorder: On the boundary between biological facts and social values. *American Psychologist, 47*, 373-388.

Wilson, M. (1993). DSM-III and the transformation of American psychiatry: A history. *American Journal of Psychiatry, 150*, 399-410.

Millon, T., Blaney, P. H., & Davis, R. D. (Eds.) (1999). *Oxford textbook of psychopathology.* New York: Oxford University Press.

American Psychiatric Association. (2000). *Diagnostic and statistical manual of mental disorders.* 4th edition TR. Washington, D. C.: American Psychiatric Press.

Widiger, T. A., & Sankis, L. M. (2000). Adult psychopathology: Issues and controversies. *Annual Review of Psychology, 51*, 377-404.

Plomin, R., & McGuffin, P. (2003). Psychopathology in the post-genomic era. *Annual Review of Psychology, 54*, 205-228.

PSYCHOPHYSICAL LAWS/THEORY. See FECHNER'S LAW; STEVENS' POWER LAW; WEBER'S LAW.

PSYCHOPHYSICAL PARALLELISM, DOCTRINE OF. See MIND-BODY THEORIES.

PSYCHOSEXUAL DEVELOPMENT, THEORY OF. See DEVELOPMENTAL THEORY; ERIKSON'S THEORY OF PERSONALITY; FREUD'S THEORY OF PERSONALITY.

PSYCHOSEXUAL NEUTRALITY THEORY. See DEVELOPMENTAL THEORY.

PSYCHOSOCIAL/PSYCHOLOGICAL THEORIES OF PERSONALITY. See DEVELOPMENTAL THEORY; ERIKSON'S THEORY OF PERSONALITY.

PSYCHOSOMATICS THEORY. The term *psychosomatics* (i.e., interactions between psychological behaviors, such as feelings/thoughts and physical illness) was coined in the early 1800s and has undergone several terminological and theoretical changes (cf., Dunbar, 1943; Margetts, 1950; Lipowski, 1968; Henker, 1982). Originally, *psychosomatics* referred to particular disturbances, such as obsessions and phobias. Today, however, *psychosomatics* may be characterized as a "holistic" medical approach and includes investigations of the scientific relationship between psychological and biological events, as well as the consultation activities between mental health workers and physically ill clients. Contemporary theories concerning psychosomatics may be classified into *specificity theories* and *nonspecificity theories*. *Specificity theories* state that definite psychological patterns/symptoms produce each psychosomatic disorder, where there are four general groups of *specificity hypotheses*: *personality-specific* - holds that definite personality traits lead to specific physical symptoms (e.g., the "A-type" behavior pattern and its link to coronary artery disease); *conflict-specific* - an extension of the psychoanalytic concept of "conversion" where unconscious conflicts are resolved via "conversion" into bodily/somatic symptoms, such as peptic ulcers, bronchial asthma, rheumatoid arthritis, and hypertension; *emotion-specific* - suggest that specific emotions lead to definite somatic changes or disturbances (e.g., anxiety may be distinguished from anger; cf., *specific-attitudes theory* - holds that certain psychosomatic disorders are associated with particular attitudes on the part of the sufferer); and *response pattern-specific* - emphasize individual differences in stress-response patterns (e.g., blood-pressure reactors are prone to hypertension; cf., *specific-reaction theory* - states that psychosomatic symptoms result from an innate tendency of the autonomic nervous system to react to a stressful situation in a particular way). In the *organ specificity hypothesis*, it is held that the individual suffering from psychosomatic disorders unconsciously chooses a particular organ, or part of the body (such as the skin for hives, or the stomach for ulcers), to be the physical locus or manifestation of her/his tension or stress that has not been discharged in other more customary or healthy ways. The *associated specificity theory* states that through learned mediation or "accidental conditioning," an association may be formed between a physiological response and an idea, emotion, or thought. Research gives only partial support to all the *specificity hypotheses*, and does not support completely any single approach. The *nonspecificity theories* maintain the etiological primacy of psychological factors in at least some cases of certain physical diseases, but do not attempt to explain symptom choice; rather, the term "organ vulnerability" may be employed as an "explanation." An example of a *nonspecificity theory* is the *alexithymia hypothesis*, which states that certain individuals find it difficult to express or experience emotions as do most other people. As with the *specificity theories*, the *nonspecificity theories of psychosomatics* may only partially explain some behaviors, but not all instances of such behavior. See also MORITA THERAPY THEORY; ORTHOMOLECULAR THEORY; SELYE'S THEORY/MODEL OF STRESS; SOMATOPSYCHICS THEORY.

REFERENCES

Dunbar, H. F. (1943). *Psychosomatic diagnosis*. New York: Hoeber.

Alexander, F. G., & French, T. M. (1948). *Studies in psychosomatic medicine*. New York: Ronald Press.

Margetts, E. L. (1950). The early history of the word "psychosomatic." *Canadian Medical Association Journal, 63*, 402-404.

Lipowski, Z. J. (1968). Review of consultation psychiatry in psychosomatic medicine. III. Theoretical issues. *Psychosomatic Medicine, 30*, 395-422.

Christie, M. J., & Mellett, P. G. (Eds.) (1981). *Foundations of psychosomatics*. New York: Wiley.

Henker, F. O. (1982). Conflicting definitions of the term "psychosomatic." *Psychosomatics, 23*, 8-11.

PSYCHOSYNTHESIS, PRINCIPLE OF. See JUNG'S THEORY OF PERSONALITY.

PUBERTAL SEXUAL RECAPITULATION THEORY. See RECAPITULATION THEORY/LAW.

PULFRICH PHENOMENON/EFFECT. The German physicist/psychologist Carl Pulfrich (1858-1927) described this visual stereoscopic effect/illusion in 1922; ironically, Pulfrich was born blind in one eye and never himself experienced stereoscopic vision or "stereopsis." The *Pulfrich illusion/effect* may be experienced when a pendulum - such as a string with a weight attached to one end - is swung from side to side in a plane perpendicular to the viewer's line of vision. If such a stimulus is viewed from a distance with a dark lens (as with a pair of sunglasses or dark filter over one eye but with both eyes open, and attending to the center of the swing), the pendulum seems to move in an ellipse that is parallel to the floor. The pendulum appears to swing *clockwise* when viewed from above if the dark lens covers the left eye, but *counterclockwise* if the dark lens covers the right eye. Also, a "kinephantom," or misperception of visual movement, may occur when any object moves across the viewer's line of vision (and where the dark filter covers the left eye), with the result that objects moving from left to right (say on a television screen) appear to *recede*, whereas objects moving from right to left on a screen seem to be displaced *forward*. For the description of various other effects and illusions, see Appendix A. See also PERCEPTION (I. GENERAL), THEORIES OF.

REFERENCES

Pulfrich, C. (1922). Die stereoskopie im dienste der isochromen und heterochromen photometrie. *Naturwissenschaften, 10*, 533-564, 569-601, 714-722, 735-743, 751-761.

Rosemann, H., & Buchmann, H. (1953). The explanation of the Pulfrich effect. *Zeitschrift fur Biologie, 106*, 71-76. [See also (1952), *105*, 134-146].

Weale, R. A. (1954). Theory of the Pulfrich effect. *Ophthalmologica (Basel)*, *128*, 380-388.

Morgan, M. J., & Thompson, P. (1975). Apparent motion and the Pulfrich effect. *Perception*, *4*, 3-18.

Mahmud, S. H. (1990). The Pulfrich effect: A new look. *Psychological Studies*, *35*, 104-108.

Ito, H. (2003). The aperture problems in the Pulfrich effect. *Perception*, *32*, 367-375.

PUNCTUATED EQUILIBRIUM THEORY. See MENDEL'S LAWS/PRINCIPLES.

PUNISHMENT, THEORIES OF. In the context of *operant conditioning* (i.e., learning from consequences), the term *reinforcement* refers to an *increase* in the frequency of a behavior, whereas the term *punishment* denotes a *decrease* in the frequency of a behavior. One way that punishment may be administered, called *positive punishment*, is via the application of some aversive stimulus (e.g., give a spanking, an electric shock, etc.) contingent on the occurrence of a particular behavior. Another method, called *negative punishment*, for decreasing a particular behavior is the elimination or removal of a desired stimulus (e.g., take away TV/movie privileges, etc.) contingent on the occurrence of the behavior. It is useful to distinguish between the terms *punishment* (i.e., the procedure or process) and *punisher* (i.e., the thing or stimulus used in decreasing a given behavior). The punishing stimulus itself may be short in duration, simple to administer, and well defined (as in most laboratory studies where electric shock is used), but it may also be an extended, complex event (as in cases where society incarcerates a legal offender). Punishers may be given, also, for the performance of some response (e.g., for a rat that presses the "wrong" bar) or for the nonperformance of a response (e.g., a rat's failure to press the bar). The term *punishment* is confused, often, by the layperson with the term *negative reinforcement*: correct usage has the former term referring to a *decrease* in behavior, whereas the latter term refers to an *increase* in behavior due to the removal of an aversive stimulus. A number and variety of theories have been proposed to account for the fact that punishment and aversive stimuli change an organism's behavior. An early theory by E. L. Thorndike holds that a punishing stimulus that is contingent on a response simply decreases the strength of that stimulus-response connection. However, contemporary theories stress both the contribution of an emotional state (e.g., fear) elicited by the noxious stimulus and the learning of avoidance responses that interfere with a previously learned response. Another theoretical position, the *two-stage process theory* of O. H. Mowrer assumes that the response followed by punishment produces certain internal and external stimuli that, by virtue of their contiguity with the aversive stimulus, acquire the capacity to arouse fear (cf., the *single-factor theory* of W. Estes). According to *Mowrer's theory*, two learning processes are involved: fear conditioning via classical conditioning, and the subsequent learning of an instrumental response that eliminates or controls the fear. Another *theory of punishment* is J. Dinsmoor's *avoidance hypothesis*, which explains the reduction in the frequency of the punished behavior in terms of simple stimulus-response principles of *avoidance learning* (cf., *incubation of avoidance theory* - states that avoidance learning requires a consolidation period, or incubation, before it becomes grounded in memory; this theory was formulated based on evidence of a delayed feature in conditioning of experimental animals exposed to electroconvulsive shock/stimulation). The *avoidance learning theory* holds that there is an interference between the behaviors where punished behaviors decrease and are suppressed because of an increase in *other* behaviors that *compete* with the punished response (cf., *insufficient deterrence hypothesis* - posits that the severity of a minimally sufficient deterrent is inversely related to the degree of internalization of the prohibition: the milder the threatened punishment, the more likely that the prohibitions will be internalized, assuming the person stops performing the forbidden behavior). Current thinking on how effective a given punishment situation is depends on various factors, such as the characteristics of the punishing stimulus, the desire to merely suppress an undesirable behavior temporarily or to eliminate it permanently, the specific behavior being punished, and the particular individual being punished. See also ESTES' STIMULUS SAMPLING THEORY; LEARNING THEORIES/LAWS; MOWRER'S THEORY; REINFORCEMENT THEORY; SKINNER'S DESCRIPTIVE BEHAVIOR/OPERANT CONDITIONING THEORY.

REFERENCES

Thorndike, E. L. (1932). Reward and punishment in animal learning. *Comparative Psychology Monographs*, *8*, No. 39.

Skinner, B. F. (1938). *The behavior of organisms: An experimental analysis.* New York: Appleton-Century-Crofts.

Estes, W. (1944). An experimental study of punishment. *Psychological Monographs*, No. 263.

Skinner, B. F. (1953). *Science and human behavior.* New York: Macmillan.

Dinsmoor, J. (1954). Punishment. I. The avoidance hypothesis. *Psychological Review*, *61*, 34-46.

Dinsmoor, J. (1955). Punishment. II. An interpretation of empirical findings. *Psychological Review*, *62*, 96-105.

Mowrer, O. H. (1960). *Learning theory and behavior.* New York: Wiley.

Solomon, R. (1964). Punishment. *American Psychologist*, *19*, 239-253.

Azrin, N., & Holz, W. (1966). Punishment. In W. Honig (Ed.), *Operant behavior: Areas of research and application.* New York: Appleton-Century-Crofts.

Estes, W. (1969). Outline of a theory of punishment. In B. Campbell & R. Church (Eds.), *Punishment and aversive behavior.* New York: Appleton-Century-Crofts.

Dunham, P. (1971). Punishment: Method and theory. *Psychological Review*, *78*, 58-70.

Walters, G., & Grusec, J. (1977). *Punishment.* San Francisco: Freeman.

PUPILLOMETRICS THEORY. In the late 1800s and early 1900s, the Polish physician Jan Piltz (1870-1931) researched the cortical control of the pupils of the eyes, as well as the symptomatology of nervous disorders, in particular, pupillary symptoms. The term *Piltz's reflex* refers to a reflexive change in the size of the pupil when attention is fixed suddenly on an event, issue, or object. Piltz suggested that the reflex is mediated by emotional arousal; for instance, positive arousal results in a dilated pupil and negative arousal results in a constricted pupil. In the normal *physiological pupillary reflex* (or "light reflex"), as studied originally by the Scottish physician Robert Whytt (1714-1766), there is an automatic, involuntary change in the size of the pupil in response to light changes or a change of fixation point. More recently, concerning the *psychological* (versus *physiological*) aspects of *pupillary changes*, the American psychologist Eckhard H. Hess (1916-1986) and his colleague James M. Polt tested the *pupillometrics theory* that large pupils in individuals makes them more attractive to others by asking male participants to rate four photographs of two women. The photos were retouched so that each woman had small pupils in one photo and large pupils in another. The participants were asked to select which woman - in a series of pairs of these photos - appeared to be more friendly, charming, attractive, etc. Hess found that his participants were likely to attribute more of the attractive traits to the women with large pupils. Other studies - using both male and female participants - subsequently replicated Hess' results. See also ACTIVATION/AROUSAL THEORY; VISION/SIGHT, THEORIES OF.

REFERENCES

Hess, E. H., & Polt, J. M. (1960). Pupil size as related to interest value of visual stimuli. *Science*, *132*, 349-350.

Hess, E. H., & Polt, J. M. (1964). Pupil size in relation to mental activity during simple problem solving. *Science*, *143*, 1190-1192.

Hess, E. H. (1965). Attitude and pupil size. *Scientific American*, *212*, 46-54.

Hess, E. H. (1975a). The role of pupil size in communication. *Scientific American*, *233*, 110-119.

Hess, E. H. (1975b). *The tell-tale eye: How your eyes reveal hidden thoughts and emotions*. Oxford, UK: Van Nostrand Reinhold.

Tryon, W. W. (1975). Pupillometry: A survey of sources of variation. *Psychophysiology, 12*, 90-93.

Niedenthal, P. M., & Cantor, N. (1986). Affective responses as guides to category-based influences. *Motivation and Emotion, 10*, 217-232.

PURE MEANING, CONCEPT OF. See WHORF-SAPIR HYPOTHESIS/THEORY.

PURKINJE EFFECT/PHENOMENON/ SHIFT. In the early 1800s, the Czech-born German physiologist Jan Evangelista Purkinje (1787-1869) (also spelled "Purkyne") described the change in color sensitivity as a visual stimulus moves from the center of the visual field to the periphery - where colors become gray at the periphery of the field and different colors change at different visual field locations. In 1825, Purkinje also reported that *visual accommodation* is caused by changes in the shape of the eye's lens. The *Purkinje effect/phenomenon/shift* refers to the manner in which colors emerge from darkness at dawn: initially there is only black and gray (with red as the darkest), next the blues appear, and finally the reds appear. The *Purkinje effect* occurs when the illumination of objects is reduced, and the red and orange hues (at the long wavelength end of the electromagnetic spectrum) lose their perceived brightness faster than the green and blue hues (at the short wavelength end of the spectrum). Consequently, the reds are relatively bright in strong light, and the greens and blues are bright in dim light. The greens and blues in dim light are not only relatively bright but are also "whitish" because of the colorless contribution of the rods under such viewing conditions. The *Purkinje shift* is caused by the differential activity of the rods, which have a greater overall sensitivity than the cones: at sunset we shift from cone to rod vision, and at sunrise we shift from rod to cone vision. The *Purkinje effect* fails to occur under conditions where the stimulus light is confined strictly to the rod-free region of the retina and when considering cases of *night blindness* or *nyctalopia* - that is due, often, to a deficiency of vitamin A or to a congenital retinal defect. In addition to the *Purkinje effect*, Purkinje's name is honored in the terms *Purkinje figures* - the network of interwoven blood vessels of the retina that may be perceived under conditions of low ambient illumination and when a small bright light is positioned just under the eye as the person stares at a blank screen or wall; *Purkinje-Sanson images* - named after Purkinje and the French surgeon Louis Joseph Sanson (1790-1841), refers to the perception by one person (by looking at a second person's eye) of three separate images of an object that the second person looks at, where one image is from the surface of the cornea, one is from the back of the lens, and one is from the front of the lens; and the *Purkinje afterimage* - is the *second* positive afterimage that follows stimulation by a bright light that is a hue complement to the original stimulus [the *first* in the sequence of three visual afterimages following a brief exposure to a bright light is called a *Hering image* - named after the German physiologist and psychologist Ewald Hering (1834-1918); the *second* afterimage is the *Purkinje image*; and the *third* afterimage is called a *Hess image* - named after the German ophthalmologist Carl von Hess (1863-1923)]. Purkinje's other research in sensory psychology included work on *afterimages* [or *Bidwell's ghost* - named in honor of the English physicist Shelford Bidwell (1848-1909), and is another term often used loosely for the *Purkinje afterimage*], *dark adaptation*, the location and nature of the *blind spot* in the retina, a comparison of *monocular* and *binocular vision*, the "flight of colors" (i.e., the succession of colors that occurs in a visual afterimage), and the *physiology of optics*. The *Purkinje shift* led the German scientist Johannes von Kries (1853-1928) to postulate the existence of two separate visual systems (rods and cones), and the *Purkinje effect* helped the Austrian-American physiologist Selig Hecht (1892-1947) to establish firmly von Kries' *duplicity theory* (or *duplexity theory*) of rod and cone visual systems for modern theories of vision. See also HECHT'S COLOR VISION THEORY; IMAGERY AND MENTAL IMAGERY, THEORIES OF; VISION/SIGHT, THEORIES OF; von KRIES' COLOR VISION THEORY.

REFERENCES

Purkinje, J. E. (1819). *Beitrage zur kenntniss des sehens in subjectiver hinsicht.* Prague: Calve.

Purkinje, J. E. (1825). *Neue beitrage zur kenntniss des sehens in subjectiver hinsight.* Berlin: Reimer.

PURPOSIVE/COGNITIVE THEORY. See BEHAVIORIST THEORY; REINFORCEMENT THEORY; TOLMAN'S THEORY.

PUTT'S LAWS. See MURPHY'S LAW(S).

PYGMALION EFFECT. = pygmalionism. This phenomenon is derived from the name of a 1912 play (called *Pygmalion*) by the Ireland-born British playwright, dramatist, and critic George Bernard Shaw (1856-1950). Originally, the name *Pygmalion* came from a Greek legend in which Pygmalion, a king of Cyprus, and a sculptor, made a statue of a beautiful maiden (named Galatea). Aphrodite - the goddess of love and beauty - gave the statue life after she discovered that Pygmalion fell in love with the statue. In psychiatry and clinical psychology, the term *pygmalionism* refers to a pathological condition in which one falls in love with one's own creation. The *Pygmalion effect*, on the other hand, is the observed effect whereby people come to behave in ways that correspond to others' expectations concerning them (cf., *upward Pygmalion effect* - the influence that an individual's behavior creates in others, especially on those in superordinate positions or positions of control over the person). The *Pygmalion effect* is similar, functionally, to the concept of *self-fulfilling prophecy/prediction,* that is, things turn out just as one expected or prophesied that they would, not necessarily because of one's prescience but because one behaved in a manner that optimized those very outcomes [cf., *Oedipus effect* - the influence of a prediction on the predicted event, where the prediction either causes or prevents the event that it predicts; the term was coined in 1936 by the Austrian-born British philosopher Karl R. Popper (1902-1994) who concluded from it that "exact/detailed" scientific social predictions are impossible; the use of the term *Oedipus* derives from the mythological Greek character Oedipus who unwittingly killed his father, as a direct result of the prophecy that had caused his father, originally, to abandon him; and the *self-defeating prophecy* - a prediction that becomes false as a consequence of its having been made originally]. The *Pygmalion effect* is particularly relevant to the social and psychological dynamics in the classroom between teacher and students. R. Rosenthal and L. Jacobson were the first to use the term *Pygmalion effect* (in their book "Pygmalion in the Classroom"), in situations concerning the effects of teachers' expectations on students' behaviors. See also EXPERIMENTER EFFECTS; HALO EFFECT; HEISENBERG'S PRINCIPLE OF UNCERTAINTY OR INDETERMINACY; LABELING/DEVIANCE THEORY.

REFERENCES

Merton, R. (1948). The self-fulfilling prophesy. *Antioch Review, 8,* 193-210.

Popper, K. R. (1957). *The poverty of historicism.* New York: Basic Books.

Rosenthal, R., & Jacobson, L. (1968). *Pygmalion in the classroom: Teacher expectation and pupils' intellectual development.* New York: Holt, Rinehart, & Winston.

Nash, R. (1976). *Teacher expectations and pupil learning.* London: Routledge & Kegan Paul.

PYTHAGORAS' THEORY OF VISION. See VISION/SIGHT, THEORIES OF.

Q

QUANTA, LAW OF. See NEURAL QUAN-
TUM THEORY.

QUANTAL HYPOTHESIS. See NEURAL
QUANTUM THEORY.

QUANTITATIVE LEARNING THEORY.
See ESTES' STIMULUS SAMPLING THE-
ORY.

**QUANTITATIVE THEORY OF CUTAN-
EOUS SENSITIVITY.** See NAFE'S VAS-
CULAR THEORY OF CUTANEOUS SEN-
SITIVITY.

QUANTUM THEORY. See VISION/
SIGHT, THEORIES OF.

QUESTION METHOD/PHENOMENON.
See PSYCHOPATHOLOGY, THEORIES
OF.

QUINTILIAN'S THEORY OF HUMOR.
The Roman rhetorician Quintilian (c. 35-96
A.D.) - like both Cicero and Aristotle – em-
braces the theories/aspects of the "deformity"
and the "baseness" in humor in his theoretical
approach. *Quintilian's theory of humor/laugh-
ter* proposes that laughter is always associated
with something low ("humile") that may take
any of six forms: urbanity, gracefulness, pi-
quancy, pleasantry, jesting, or verbal attacks.
In concert with Cicero, Quintilian calls attention to those laughs that arise from *surprise*
("the happiest jokes of all"), the laughs from
the deceit and defeat of *expectation*, and the
laughs that are involved in situations where
the turning of another person's words express
a *meaning* not originally intended by the
speaker. Quintilian suggests that the rhetorical
value of humor resides in its ability to "dissi-
pate melancholy," to "unbend the mind" in
intense situations, and to "gain renewed
strength" following excesses or fatigue. According to R. Piddington, Plato and Aristotle
place emphasis on the ethical implications of
laughter, and Cicero focuses on the use of
ridicule in rhetoric, whereas *Quintilian's theory of humor* is of interest because it represents the first attempt to produce a psychological analysis of the effects of laughter. See
also ARISTOTLE'S THEORY OF HUMOR;
CICERO'S HUMOR THEORY; GREIG'S
THEORY OF LAUGHTER; HUMOR,
THEORIES OF; PIDDINGTON'S COM-
PENSATORY HUMOR THEORY.

REFERENCES
Quintilian, M. F. (1714/1821-1825). *De insti-
    tutione oratoria*. London: Heine-
    mann/Paris: Lamaire.
Greig, J. Y. T. (1923/1969). *The psychology of
    laughter and comedy*. New York:
    Dodd, Mead/Cooper Square.
Piddington, R. (1933/1963). *The psychology
    of laughter: A study in social adap-
    tation*. London: Figurehead/New
    York: Gamut.

QUOTA OF AFFECT. See CONSTANCY,
PRINCIPLE OF.

QUOTIENT HYPOTHESIS. See WEBER'S
LAW.

R

RACIALISM, DOCTRINE OF. See PREJUDICE, THEORIES OF.

RACIAL MEMORY/UNCONSCIOUS, THEORY OF. See JUNG'S THEORY OF PERSONALITY.

RADICAL BEHAVIORIST THEORY. See BEHAVIORIST THEORY.

RANDOM/GENETIC DRIFT. See DARWIN'S EVOLUTION THEORY.

RANGE-OF-AFFECT HYPOTHESIS. See WORK/CAREER/OCCUPATION, THEORIES OF.

RANK'S THEORY OF PERSONALITY. The Austrian psychoanalyst Otto Rank (1884-1939) formulated a theory of personality that may be characterized as *an intrapsychic conflict model* where all functioning of the individual is expressive of the dual tendency to minimize both the *fear of life* and the *fear of death*. According to Rank, life is equivalent to the processes of separation and individualization, whereas death is the opposite processes of union and fusion. The two opposing fears of life and death are experienced as uncomfortable tension states, much as the concept of *anxiety* is emphasized by other conflict theorists. However, Rank prefers the more definitive term *fear* over the diffuse term *anxiety*. Although the individual does possess biological instincts, they do not provide the intrinsic basis for conflict. More important for conflict is the tendency for living things to individuate and separate. Rank asserts that the mere act of being born is a deeply traumatic experience because the newborn must relinquish the warm and relatively constant environment of the womb where one's needs were met automatically. Rank initially considered the *birth trauma* to be the most significant event in one's life (e.g., the shock of birth creates a reservoir of anxiety, and all neuroses allegedly

derive from birth anxiety). However, later in his career, Rank came to consider birth only the first in a long series of separation experiences that are caused by biological, psychological, and social factors that are indistinguishable from life [cf., Rank's term *vagina dentata*, also described by the Hungarian psychoanalyst Sandor Ferenczi (1873-1933), refers to a fantasy of a "toothed vagina" that is a legendary danger associated with sexual intercourse and is, theoretically, a cause of anxiety among neurotic men; the counterpart of this concept in women is *penis dentata*, or "tooth-ed penis," and is a less commonly experienced neurotic sexual fear in women]. Another important core characteristic in *Rank's theory* is the concept of *will*, which is analogous to S. Freud's concept of *ego*, and to H. S. Sullivan's concept of *self*. Rank's concept of *will* refers to an organized sense of self-identity and functions consciously to aid in the development of a basis for minimizing both the life and death fears. Rank argued that the highest form of living involves a mature expression of *will* - over those forces of counterwill and guilt - where it provides the basis for successful expression of the core tendency of minimizing both fear of life and fear of death. In general, *Rank's personality theory* has never been very popular in mainstream psychology. However, Rank's theorizing has proven useful for explanation of some empirical research results "after the fact," even though such research was not planned a priori or explicitly to measure or validate Rank's conceptualizations or formulations. In the final analysis, the overall fruitfulness of Rank's theoretical position has not yet been demonstrated empirically. See also CONFLICT, THEORIES OF; FREUD'S THEORY OF PERSONALITY; PERSONALITY THEORIES; SULLIVAN'S THEORY OF PERSONALITY.

REFERENCES

Rank, O. (1924/1929). *The trauma of birth*. New York: Harcourt, Brace.

Rank, O. (1929/1945). *Will therapy and truth and reality*. New York: Knopf.

RANSCHBURG INHIBITION/EFFECT. See INHIBITION, LAWS OF.

RAPID-CHANGE THEORY. See GESTALT THEORY/LAWS.

RAPP'S THEORY OF THE ORIGINS OF LAUGHTER/HUMOR. The American historian/classics educator Albert Rapp (1899- ?) proposed that the notions of ridicule, release, and communication were at the heart of laughter in early/primitive human beings. *Rapp's theory of laughter* regarding primitive humans indicates that laughter in the form of ridicule was probably directed at other persons at an earlier time than was laughter arising from riddles, puns, or jokes. Thus, the derisive type of laughter in the ridicule of other persons preceded the more humane and genial laughter more characteristic in modern times. According to *Rapp's theory*, in earliest times when a person saw for the first time some other individual who was crippled, ugly, or malformed in some way, the more "normal" person - for some inexplicable reason - burst out into laughter. It is speculated that the laughter of ridicule may be based on a perception of superiority in oneself, or it may derive from the observation of a mistake or deformity that is not productive of pain or harm to others. Concerning the notion of "release" in *Rapp's theory*, it is hypothesized, further, that the ideas of "relaxation" and "liberty" may be at the foundation of the first laugh of primitive humans. In terms of interpersonal relations, according to *Rapp's theory*, laughter is a means of *communication* among the earliest/primitive humans. *Rapp's theory of the origins of laughter/humor* contains the following logical sequence: the first laugh of primitive humans was like the triumphant beast's victory roar over another beast in a competitive battle, then the "sudden glory" at the perception of one's superiority over an antagonist, next in the sequence is the triumph over social restraint and, finally, via jokes and riddles, the more civilized triumph in an artificial contest deliberately staged for its accompanying relaxation. See also EASTMAN'S THEORY OF LAUGHTER; HOBBES' THEORY OF HUMOR/LAUGHTER; HUMOR, THEORIES OF; SOCIAL COMMUNICATION THEORY OF LAUGHTER; THERAPEUTIC THEORY OF LAUGHTER/HUMOR.

REFERENCES

Rapp, A. (1947). Toward an eclectic and multilateral theory of laughter and humor. *Journal of General Psychology, 36*, 207-219.

Rapp, A. (1949). A phylogenetic theory of wit and humor. *Journal of Social Psychology, 30*, 81-96.

Rapp, A. (1951). *The origins of wit and humor*. New York: Dutton.

RASCH SCALE. See CLASSICAL TEST/MEASUREMENT THEORY.

RATE-DEPENDENCY EFFECT. See REDINTEGRATION, PRINCIPLE/LAWS OF.

RATE LAW. See NEURON/NEURAL/NERVE THEORY.

RATIONAL-ECONOMIC MAN THEORY. See ORGANIZATIONAL/INDUSTRIAL/SYSTEMS THEORY.

RATIONAL-EMOTIVE BEHAVIOR THERAPY (REBT) THEORY. See ABC THEORY/MODEL.

RATIONAL-EMOTIVE THERAPY (RET) THEORY. See ABC THEORY/MODEL.

RATIONALISM/RATIONALIST, DOCTRINE OF. See LEARNING THEORIES/LAWS.

RATIONAL PRINCIPLE. See MIND/MENTAL SET, LAW OF.

RAVEN'S PROGRESSIVE MATRICES THEORY. See INTELLIGENCE, THEORIES/LAWS OF.

RAYLEIGH EQUATION. See VISION/SIGHT, THEORIES OF.

REACTANCE THEORY. A common tendency in human behavior is to react against any attempted restrictions imposed on the individual. The term *psychological reactance* is defined as the motivational state aroused when a person perceives that a specific behavioral freedom is threatened with elimination or is actually eliminated. *Reactance theory* (via Jack W. Brehm and Sharon S. Brehm) holds that under such conditions of threats to personal freedom, oppositional behaviors may be understood as manifestations of a single motivational state and includes the assumption that when reactance motivation is aroused, the person makes attempts to restore the threatened or eliminated freedom. *Reactance theory* makes two predictions: because the desirability of an object or event is assumed to be related to the opportunity to choose it, the more the person perceives that others are attempting to limit one's opportunities, the more attractive the object or event becomes; and when a person perceives that strong pressure is being exerted to force a particular decision, the person will tend to become contrary and resist the pressure by selecting an opposing perspective. *Reactance theory* maintains that individuals possess a finite number of specific behavioral freedoms (i.e., certain behaviors - including emotions, attitudes, beliefs, and overt acts - are "free" if the person is currently engaging in them, or expects to engage in them in the future). The theory does not assume any need or desire for freedom per se but allows for a wide variation in individual differences concerning "free" behaviors. In general, the more important the freedom is to the person, the greater the magnitude of the threat; and the greater the number of freedoms threatened, the greater will be the reactance aroused. An example of a reactance situation is the desire of a girl to marry a boyfriend in spite of parental opposition (cf., the *Romeo and Juliet effect* - named after the main characters in William Shakespeare's tragedy "Romeo and Juliet" produced between 1591 and 1596 - re-fers to a tendency, when restrictions by others such as parents are placed on a couple or set of people such as young lovers, to increase ones' desires to be together). In this example, according to *reactance theory*, the girl will attempt to restore the threatened freedom (of marrying the person whom she chooses). In such cases, two "counterforces" serve to influence restorative action: as the magnitude of pressure to comply increases, both reactance arousal and the motive to comply (by relinquishing the freedom) will increase, and if the costs of direct restora-

tive action are sufficiently high, direct opposition may be prevented. Thus, *compliance motives* counteract or influence *reactance arousal* to determine the resulting behavioral tendency. How much one desires to restore freedom, as well as how strongly the individual actually attempts to do so, reflects the interplay between *compliance* and *reactance* forces. Costs of direct opposition, on the other hand, should act mainly as a suppressor of overt action and, given a chance to restore freedom without incurring unreasonably high costs, the person is predicted to act accordingly. Research on *reactance theory* shows considerable empirical support for the theory, which has been applied to a wide variety of psychological issues, problems, and situations. See also ATTITUDE/ATTITUDE CHANGE, THEORIES OF; ATTRIBUTION THEORY; BOOMERANG EFFECT; COMPLIANCE EFFECTS/TECHNIQUES.

REFERENCES

Brehm, J. W. (1966). *A theory of psychological reactance*. New York: Academic Press.

Brehm, S. S., & Brehm, J. W. (1981). *Psychological reactance: A theory of freedom and control*. New York: Academic Press.

REACTION-TIME PARADIGMS/MODELS. The phenomenon of *reaction-time* (RT) originated in the discipline of astronomy in the late 18th century by way of the concept of the *personal equation*; i.e., individual differences were observed in the ability of astronomers to note the precise time at which a star crossed the transit point when observed through a telescope. Such individual observer differences were called the *personal equation* and stimulated studies of RT in the field of experimental psychology. Such discrepancies were significant, also, in the later development of "mental chronometry" - the measurement of the time required to carry out different mental processes/activities. In the context of experimental psychology, RT is defined as the minimum time between the presentation of a stimulus and the participant's response to it. RT is one of experimental psychology's oldest paradigms or dependent variables, and several types of RT have been studied: *simple* RT is the minimum time-lag between a single stimulus and the participant's making of a single simple response; *choice* RT is an extension of *simple* RT in which the person is presented with two, or more, stimuli and two, or more, corresponding responses; *discrimination* RT is a variation of *choice* RT in which there are two distinctive stimuli and the person is asked to respond to but one of them and refrain from making a response to the other; *complex* (or *compound*) RT is any RT where two, or more, stimuli and/or two, or more, responses are employed (i.e., all possible variations other than the *simple* RT); and *disjunctive* RT refers to an umbrella term that includes the *choice*, *complex*, and *discrimination* RT paradigms. Other usages of RT are: *associative* RT (the time in word association tests/experiments between the presentation of the stimulus word and the person's verbal response); *cognitive* RT (the interval between stimulus recognition and response); *motor preparation* RT (the readiness of the participant to *make* a particular movement as a response in a RT experiment); *sensory preparation* RT (the readiness of the person to *receive* a particular stimulus in a RT experiment); *motor reaction type* (persons whose behavior is characterized by a *set to respond* as quickly as possible with attention to the movement); and *sensory reaction type* (persons whose behavior is characterized by a *set to apprehend* the incoming stimuli). See also HICK'S LAW; PERSONAL EQUATION PHENOMENON; PIERON'S LAW; SIMON EFFECT; TIME, THEORIES OF.

REFERENCES

Woodworth, R. S. (1938). *Experimental psychology*. New York: Holt.

Boring, E. G. (1957). *A history of experimental psychology*. New York: Appleton-Century-Crofts.

REACTIVATION OF MEMORY HYPOTHESIS. See FORGETTING/MEMORY, THEORIES OF.

REACTIVE INHIBITION, PRINCIPLE OF. See INHIBITION, LAWS OF.

READINESS, LAW OF. This law is one of the accessory principles to *Thorndike's law of*

effect. The *law of readiness* states that when a stimulus-response unit is ready to conduct, it yields a satisfying effect as long as nothing interferes with its conducting action. When E. L. Thorndike proposed his *law of readiness* in 1913, it was little more than a guess that was stated in terms of "conduction units" as to the physiological conditions underlying its operation in the acquisition of behavior. Today, the *law of readiness*, and its correlate the *law of unreadiness* - where satisfaction is not forthcoming if the conducting unit is not ready, are important only as historical curiosities in the areas of conditioning and learning. See also EFFECT, LAW OF; EXERCISE, LAW OF; REINFORCEMENT, THORNDIKE'S THEORY OF.

REFERENCE

Thorndike, E. L. (1913). *Educational psychology*. Vol. 2. *The psychology of learning*. New York: Teachers College, Columbia University.

READINESS POTENTIAL EFFECT. See ATTENTION, LAWS/PRINCIPLES/THEORIES OF.

READING, THEORY OF. See DUAL-ROUTE THEORY OF READING.

REAFFERENCE THEORY/PRINCIPLE. The term *reafference*, coined by the German physiologists E. von Holst and H. Mittelstaedt in 1950, refers to a distinction between "active" sensory input that is the result of some movement of the animal, and "passive" input that occurs independently of the organism. The *principle of reafference* has come to be a cover term for those sensory events that are produced by voluntary movements of a sense organ (e.g., events resulting from the movement of an image across the retina that accompany voluntary movements of the eye). This is contrasted with the concept of *exafference* that refers to those sensory events produced by changes in the stimulus itself (e.g., events resulting from movement of an image across the retina that accompany real displacements of the physical object). The seminal studies by von Holst and Mittelstaedt examined the *optokinetic reflex* in the fly - this is a reflex movement of the fly in response to movement of the visual world and compensates for external movement. As a result of the *optokinetic reflex*, the fly's eye is able to look at the same part of the environment successively, an event that is similar to nystagmus in the human eye where rapid movement of the eyes in one direction is followed by a slow drift in the opposite direction. During operation of this reflex system, an *efference/effector copy* is left, theoretically, at some place in the nervous system, and the effector that is activated by the efferent message has some influence on new stimulation that enters the receptor. The *afferent/sensory* message is compared to the *efference/effector copy* and, according to the theory, if they match, the copy is nullified. If the *afference* matches the *efference copy*, it is called *reafference*. However, afferent stimulation that does not match an *efference copy* is called *exafference*. *Reafference theory* is example of the application of control and feedback systems to behavior analysis. In control systems, the mismatch between the *afference* and the motor copy results in an error signal that, in the normal fly, is corrected by *negative feedback*. When the fly's head is rotated, the error signal becomes *positive feedback*. An example of *reafference/feedback* in human behavior may be seen in the classical perception studies by the American psychologist George Malcolm Stratton (1865-1957) who reported that any movement made while wearing inverting lenses causes the participants' world to swing and whirl about them (cf., Kohler, 1962); the left-right reversal of the customary relation of image displacement to body movement causes the field to appear to move in the direction of the person's movement, only faster. As with the fly, there is a *positive* rather than a *negative feedback loop* involving the *efference copy*. Humans have the capability to cope and adapt with such inverted-image-lens conditions (as in Stratton's studies) so that the world eventually appears stationary during the participant's head movements. The fly, however, does not have such an adaptive capability and, as a consequence, circles to exhaustion. See also CONTROL/SYSTEMS THEORY.

REFERENCES

Stratton, G. M. (1896). Some preliminary experiments on vision without inversion of the retinal image. *Psychological Review, 3*, 611-617.

Stratton, G. M. (1897). Vision without inversion of the retinal image. *Psychological Review, 4*, 341-360.

von Holst, E., & Mittelstaedt, H. (1950). Das reafferenz-prinzip. *Die Naturwissenschaften, 20*, 464-467.

Kohler, I. (1962). Experiments with goggles. *Scientific American, 206*, 62-72.

REALISM, DOCTRINE OF. The philosophical *doctrine of realism*, advanced initially by the Greek philosopher Plato (c. 427-347 B.C.), states that abstract concepts have a real and coherent existence and contain a greater genuine reality than the physical objects to which they refer and, thus, are open to empirical investigation (cf., the *doctrine of nominalism*, which states that abstract ideas/concepts have no objective reality and, therefore, are not legitimate entities for scientific study; *nominalists* argue that reality consists only of objective entities, and constructs such as "society," "mind," and "personality" are lacking in scientific validity). The *doctrine of realism* may be contrasted with the *doctrine of idealism*; i.e., the notion that the ultimate reality is mental and such mental representation forms the basis of all knowledge and experience (thus, *idealism* makes it meaningless to refer to the existence of things independent of their perception and experiencing by a conscious observer). The *doctrine of realism* posits, also, that the physical world has a reality separate from perception and mind. In the history of psychology and philosophy, the *doctrine of realism* is associated, often, with the writings of the Scottish philosopher Thomas Reid (1710-1790) and the German philosopher Immanuel Kant (1724-1804), as was used in either of two ways: abstract concepts have a real existence, and the physical world has a reality separate from that of the mind. Due to its comparison with many other theoretical positions, the *doctrine of realism* is defined mainly by "contrast" and, as with many such philosophical and psychological terms, *realism* may apply only to some aspects of a viewpoint and may be understood by its juxtaposition to various other contrasting terms (e.g, nominalism, conceptualism, idealism, phenomenalism, and anti-realism). More recently, the Swiss psychologist Jean Piaget (1896-1980) used the term *realism* in some of his works to describe a young child's belief that his/her perceptual perspective is shared by other individuals. Thus the *doctrine of realism* is a psychological concept, as well as a philosophical point of view, and refers to cognitive processes, arguing that perception makes direct contact with objects in the world, as opposed to representational theories that argue that perception is of mental copies of objects, and not the objects themselves. See also CONCEPT LEARNING AND CONCEPT FORMATION, THEORIES OF; IMAGERY/MENTAL IMAGERY, THEORIES OF; LEARNING THEORIES/LAWS; PERCEPTION (II. COMPARATIVE APPRAISAL), THEORIES OF; PIAGET'S THEORY OF DEVELOPMENTAL STAGES.

REFERENCES

Piaget, J. (1954). *The construction of reality in the child*. New York: Basic Books.

Veatch, H. (1954). *Realism and nominalism revisited*. New York: Basic Books.

REALISTIC CONFLICT THEORY. See CONFLICT, THEORIES OF; PREJUDICE, THEORIES OF.

REALITY MONITORING HYPOTHESIS. See SHORT-TERM AND LONG-TERM MEMORY, THEORIES OF.

REALITY PRINCIPLE. See FREUD'S THEORY OF PERSONALITY.

REAL-SIMULATOR MODEL. See HYPNOSIS/HYPNOTISM, THEORIES OF.

REASONED ACTION AND PLANNED BEHAVIOR THEORIES. This speculation, formulated by the American psychologist Martin Fishbein (1936-) and the Polish-born American psychologist Icek Ajzen (1942-), concerns the relationship between attitudes and behavior, and states that a target behavior is determined by "behavioral intentions" that, in turn, are determined both by "attitudes to behavior" and "subjective norms." The *theory of reasoned action* is a variant of *expectancy-value theory* in which behavior is influenced by the values of the possible outcomes weighted by the estimated probabilities of those outcomes, and first studied by the German-born American psychologist Kurt Lewin (1890-1947) in the 1940s. In *reasoned action theory*, an "attitude to behavior" is the individual's evaluation of the goodness or badness of performing the target action (that is, "attitudes to behavior" are determined by the person's beliefs about the consequences of the behavior multiplied by the evaluation of each consequence, and then summed); and a "subjective norm" is the person's perceived social pressure that is derived from perception of the degree to which "significant others" would prefer the person to perform the target action. The two components of "attitude to behavior" and "subjective social norm" are empirically determined, weighted values, and reflect the relative influence on *behavioral intention* of those variables. Even though the *reasoned action theory* is supported by empirical evidence, it is limited somewhat in that it applies only to behavior that is voluntary. However, an extended version of *reasoned action theory*, called *planned behavior theory*, attempts to correct this shortcoming. This latter theory incorporates a new construct called "perceived behavioral control" into the *reasoned action theory* equation, thus allowing predictions of actions to be made that are under incomplete voluntary or volitional control. *Planned behavior theory* proposes that perceived "behavioral control" is a function of the person's beliefs as to how likely it is that one has the opportunities and resources needed to perform the behavior (cf., *buck fever effect* - refers to a type of "nonbehavior" that happens to individuals in certain social situations when personal prior intentions and expectations of behavior do not occur after meeting an imagined situation in reality; the name *buck fever* derives from the hunting scenario where a novice hunter suddenly sees a deer/buck but makes no movements to shoot the animal). Thus, these two theories, *reasoned action* and *planned behavior*, jointly assert that the conscious intention to behave in a particular way depends on the person's attitude toward the behavior (i.e., the desire to act in that way or not), the subjective social norm (i.e., the beliefs about what others would think about the action), and one's perceived behavioral control (i.e., sensing one's ability to carry out the action). Ultimately, according to these theoretical perspectives, people may perceive barriers to behaving based on several of their own attitudes and cognitions. See also ATTITUDE/ATTITUDE CHANGE, THEORIES OF; EXPECTANCY-VALUE THEORY; INFORMATION INTEGRATION THEORY; LEWIN'S FIELD THEORY; PERSUASION/INFLUENCE THEORIES.

REFERENCES

Fishbein, M., & Ajzen, I. (1975). *Belief, attitude, intention, and behavior: An introduction to theory and research.* Reading, MA: Addison-Wesley.

Ajzen, I., & Fishbein, M. (1977). Attitude-behavior relations: A theoretical analysis and review of empirical research. *Psychological Bulletin, 84,* 888-918.

Ajzen, I. (1985). *From intentions to actions: A theory of planned behavior.* Englewood Cliffs, NJ: Prentice-Hall.

Ajzen, I. (1991). The theory of planned behavior. *Organizational Behavior and Human Decision Processes, 50,* 179-211.

Madden, T. J., Ellen, P. S., & Ajzen, I. (1992). A comparison of the theory of planned behavior and the theory of reasoned action. *Personality and Social Psychology Bulletin, 18,* 3-9.

REBER'S LAW. This is a self-styled, self-proclaimed principle by the American psychologist and lexicographer Arthur Samuel Reber (1940-), stating that the closer anything is examined, the more complex it is seen to be (cf., *Anderson's law* - any system or program, however complicated, if looked at in exactly the right way, will become even more complicated; Brockman, 2004). For other semihumorous "laws," see *Murphy's law(s)* (e.g., anything that can possibly go wrong will go wrong). *Reber's law* is a self-conscious and self-reflective outcome of his work on his

dictionary of psychology and stands at the extreme "personalistic" end of the *personalistic* versus *naturalistic* continuum concerning the development of *lawful* concepts in science. Enunciation of this "law" indicates, perhaps, that *laws* in psychology may be created suddenly - in the immediate present - by individuals and not necessarily developed through painstaking assessment, distillation, and refinement processes involving the "checks and balances" of other investigators' inputs over a relatively long period of time. See also MURPHY'S LAW(S); NATURALISTIC THEORY OF HISTORY; ROECKELEIN'S LAW.

REFERENCES

Reber, A. S. (1995). *The Penguin dictionary of psychology.* New York: Penguin Books.

Roeckelein, J. E. (1996). Citation of *laws* and *theories* in textbooks across 112 years of psychology. *Psychological Reports, 79,* 979-998.

Brockman, J. (2004). What's your law? *World Question Center.* (Internet). http: www.edge.org/q2004; also, http: www.giga-usa.com/quotes/authors/law_of_life_and_nature.

[Website]. Murphy's laws. http.//sh.udm.ru/humor/e_canonic.html.

REBOUND EFFECT. See SLEEP, THEORIES OF.

REBOUND ILLUSION. See APPENDIX A.

RECAPITULATION THEORY/LAW. = biogenetic recapitulation theory = recapitultionism = palingenesis. This theory, developed and taught by the American psychologist Granville Stanley Hall (1844-1924), and often referred to as both a *principle* and a *doctrine,* states that the development of an individual organism is a microcosmic reenactment of the evolution of its species and emphasizes the predetermined progression in development. Hall's *recapitulation theory* was the direct outcome of the impact of *Darwin's evolutionary theory* on Hall's attempts to understand mental development. Hall argued that evolution, rather than physics, should form the basis for science, and he saw in evolution a noteworthy organizing principle that unites the *phylogenetic* emergence of the species with the *ontogenetic* development of a single individual. Hence, the well-known phrase "Ontogeny recapitulates phylogeny" - originally called the *biogenetic law* by the German naturalist Ernst H. P. Haeckel (1834-1919) - captures the essence of the *theory of recapitulation*. Thus, the *phylogenetic principle* states that individuals ("ontogeny") from embryo to adulthood repeat the stages of human evolution ("phylogeny") (cf., *pubertal sexual recapitulation theory* - suggests that the beginning of adult sexuality development at puberty involves a recapitulation of the infantile sexuality stages, and assumes that sexuality at puberty first regresses toward the infantile state to recapitulate). Hall's *evolutionary recapitulation theory* was extended as *development theory* into educational contexts and assumed that every child from the moment of conception to maturity re-creates every stage of development through which the human race from its lowest animal beginnings has passed [cf., *differential k theory* - relates to the two scales of reproductive strategy of different human races ("r") or species: the "r-strategy" has high rates of population increases as compared to the "k-strategy;" whereas "r-selected" individuals reproduce at an early age, the "k-strategy" individuals produce fewer children and nurture them more carefully than the "r-selected" individuals; it is alleged that cold or harsh climates are associated with the "k-strategy," whereas warmer climates are related to the "r-strategy"]. The *theory of recapitulation* has had heuristic manifestations in two main areas: evolutionary biology/embryology, and developmental psychology (including perception and cognition). In the discipline of embryology, *Baer's/von Baer's law* is confused, often, with the *theory of recapitulation/biogenetic law*. *Baer's biogenetic law* - formulated by the Estonian-born German naturalist Karl E. R. von Baer (1792-1876) - is the doctrine that the embryos of different kinds of organisms are at first similar and develop for a time along similar lines, those organisms least closely related diverging first, the others diverging at later periods in proportion to the closeness of relationship. The *recapitulation theory* has been applied also, unsuccessfully, to anthropological contexts (and

renamed the *culture-epoch theory*) where all cultures are assumed to evolve through a series of *epochs* or stages (such as hunting, pastoral, agricultural, industrial), and where each person in a culture is assumed to pass through the same steps as demonstrated in the cultural sequence. The *culture-epoch theory* is known, also, as the *monotypic evolution theory* and the *unilineal/unilinear theory of cultural evolution* [cf., *cultural absolutism theory* - states that a psychological theory developed in one culture has equal validity in a different cultural setting; and the German-American anthropologist Franz Boas' (1858-1942) *theories of cultural determinism* - holds that human behavior is shaped and controlled primarily by social and cultural factors, and *cultural relativism* - states that all cultures are equally good and have their own values and ways of understanding the world]. Hall's notion that the ontogenetic history of individuals represents a *recapitulation*, or repeating, of the species' phylogenetic history is discount-ed, largely, today. See also DEVELOPMENTAL THEORY; PLAY, THEORIES OF.

REFERENCES

Hall, G. S. (1904). *Adolescence: Its psychology and its relations to physiology, anthropology, sociology, sex, crime, religion, and education*. Vol. 1. Englewood Cliffs, NJ: Prentice-Hall.

Hall, G. S. (1923). *Life and confessions of a psychologist*. New York: Appleton.

Diehl, L. (1986). The paradox of G. Stanley Hall. *American Psychologist, 4*, 868-878.

RECENCY EFFECT/LAW. See ASSOCIATION, LAWS/PRINCIPLES OF; IMPRESSION FORMATION, THEORIES OF; SERIAL-POSITION EFFECT.

RECENCY-PRIMACY EFFECTS. See IMPRESSION FORMATION, THEORIES OF; SERIAL-POSITION EFFECT.

RECIPROCAL BLOW EFFECT. See LASHLEY'S THEORY.

RECIPROCAL INHIBITION TECHNIQUE/THEORY. See INHIBITION,

LAWS OF; WOLPE'S THEORY/TECH-
NIQUE OF RECIPROCAL INHIBITION.

RECIPROCITY LAW. See BUNSEN-
ROSCOE LAW; LOVE, THEORIES OF.

RECIPROCITY OF LIKING EFFECT.
The *principle of reciprocity* is a basic, common-sense generalization concerning relationships and interpersonal encounters suggesting
that we often treat other people as they have
treated us [cf., the curious phenomena of the
passing stranger/stranger on a train effect -
also known as the *ancient mariner effect* after
Samuel Taylor Coleridge's (1772-1834) poem
"The Rime of the Ancient Mariner" in which
an old sailor tells his story over and over again
to strangers - refers to cases where persons
divulge the most private information about
themselves to perfect strangers; and the *hard-
to-get effect* - cases where one is selective in
one's social choices in order to appear as more
desirable than those who are more readily
accessible or available]. In the context of the
Austrian-American psychologist Fritz Heider's (1896-1988) *balance theory*, the notion
of *reciprocity* is the principle that social attraction is mutual: if I know you like me, it
increases the likelihood that I will like you. In
the context of *interpersonal attraction theory*,
an important determinant of attraction is *reciprocity* and the nature of others' feelings
toward us. Many studies indicate that the more
others like us, the greater is our liking toward
them. The *reciprocity of liking effect* seems to
be so strong that it occurs even when it is
suspected that the positive sentiment one hears
are merely attempts at flattery. In the area of
helping/prosocial behavior, the *principle of reciprocity* becomes the *norm of reciprocity*,
which posits that we should help those who
help us, that a larger favor is reciprocated
more often than a smaller one, and that returning a favor is more likely when the original
help is perceived to be given intentionally and
voluntarily. In the context of aggressive motivation, the *principle of reciprocity* may be
experienced when dealing with others, especially difficult people. When others engage in
direct provocation toward us, we tend to treat
them much as they have treated us. Thus,
according to the *reciprocity principle*, when

verbally or physically provoked by others, we
tend to respond in kind, often with the unfortunate result that aggression spirals upward, as
sarcastic comments give way to direct insults
that, in turn, often lead to physical confrontation and violence. Related to the psychologist's *principle of reciprocity* are the theologian's *golden rule* (i.e., one should behave
toward others as one would want others to
behave toward oneself; Matthew 7:12; Luke
6:31) and, somewhat, the philosopher's *categorical imperative* [i.e., the doctrine advanced
by the German philosopher Immanuel Kant
(1724-1804) that one's behavior should be
governed by principles which one would have
govern the behavior of all people]. See also
AGGRESSION, THEORIES OF; ATTRIBU-
TION THEORY; BYSTANDER INTER-
VENTION EFFECT; HEIDER'S BALANCE
THEORY; INTERPERSONAL ATTRAC-
TION THEORIES; LOVE, THEORIES OF.
REFERENCES
Heider, F. (1946). Attitudes and cognitive
    organization. *Journal of Psychol-
    ogy, 21*, 107-112.
Latane, B., & Nida, S. (1981). Ten years of
    research on group size and helping.
    Psychological Bulletin, 89, 308-324.
Condon, J., & Crano, W. (1988). Inferred
    evaluation and the relation between
    attitude similarity and interpersonal
    attraction. *Journal of Personality
    and Social Psychology, 54*, 789-797.

RECITATION THEORY. See SHORT-
TERM AND LONG-TERM MEMORY,
THEORIES OF.

**RECOGNITION BY COMPONENTS
THEORY.** See BIEDERMAN'S RECOGNI-
TION BY COMPONENTS THEORY.

**RECONPOSRE THEORY OF DEPRES-
SION.** See DEPRESSION, THEORIES OF.

RECONSTRUCTION THEORY. See
FORGETTING/MEMORY, THEORIES OF.

**REDINTEGRATION, PRINCIPLE/LAWS
OF.** The Scottish philosopher Sir William
Hamilton (1788-1856) first proposed the *prin-
ciple of redintegration*, which refers to an

impression one has that tends to bring back into consciousness the whole situation of which it was a part at one time (cf., *law of piecemeal activity* - E. L. Thorndike's principle that a learned response may still be given when only part of the original stimulus situation is presented). *Hamilton's theory* concerning the nature of memory and association was able to identify a continuing weakness in the *associationistic doctrine*: it presupposed the existence of individual parts of the mind, each of which sets off another part of the mind without any unifying principle to make the parts hold together. Hamilton critiqued the *associationists*, who considered a sequence of mental events as a "remembering mind" that contains only one single idea at a time. Hamilton taught, on the other hand, that the process of perception is such that any one of the elements simultaneously experienced is capable, when presented later, of bringing back the total experience. The person *redintegrates* in memory the original situation where one recalls not only a series of elements but a pattern of elements as well. Thus, Hamilton's *principle of redintegration* suggests that any given mental event is only a part of a much larger whole. Perhaps, Hamilton expected too much of his *redintegration hypothesis* concerning memory, and he failed to explain the process of forgetting. Also, Hamilton apparently neglected the facts of serial association and the occasional explanatory ineffectiveness of the *redintegration principle*. The American psychologist Harry L. Hollingworth (1880-1956) used the term *redintegration* to describe the "functional" process, rather than the "recall" process, in which the part acts for the whole context; he also described the *law of redintegration* as the capability of one aspect of a situation to bring it back in its entirety or the reestablishment of a whole situation or experience by bringing together its several parts ("reintegration"). Al-though the terms *redintegration* and *reintegration* are synonymous, essentially - and even though the shorter form (reintegration) is more euphoric - historical usage from William Hamilton on down favors the spelling "redintegration." The *law/principle of redintegration* was adopted and used by the Scottish psychologist Alexander Bain (1818-1903) as well as by the

American philosopher/psy- chologist William James (1842-1910). Since its inception, the concept of *redintegration* has undergone various logical, contextual, and terminological changes, and it has served as the starting point for much discussion of the psychology of learning [e.g., *state-dependent memory* or *state-dependent learning*, which are defined, currently, as the tendency for information learned in a particular mental or physical state/condition to be most easily remembered in a similar state/condition in the future; cf., *drug-dependent memory* in rats, studied by the American psychologist Donald A. Overton (1935-); and the *initial value(s) law* - in psychopharmacology, the principle that the effect of a drug on a measurable variable may depend on the level of that variable at the time of administration or that the "dose-response" curve of a drug may depend on the starting level of the effect variable; in its relationship to behavior, this law is called the *rate-dependency effect*]. See also ASSOCIATION, LAWS/PRINCIPLES OF; FORGETTING/MEMORY, THEORIES OF; GESTALT THEORY/LAWS; INITIAL VALUE(S), LAW OF; LEARNING THEORIES/LAWS.

REFERENCES

Hamilton, W. (1859/1860). *Lectures on metaphysics and logic*. London: Blackwood.

Hollingworth, H. L. (1926). *The psychology of thought*. New York: Appleton.

Overton, D. A. (1964). State dependent or "dissociated" learning produced by pentobarbital. *Journal of Comparative and Physiological Psychology*, 57, 3-12.

RED QUEEN HYPOTHESIS. See DARWIN'S EVOLUTION THEORY.

REDSHIFT EFFECT. See DOPPLER EFFECT/PRINCIPLE/SHIFT.

REDUCED CUE HYPOTHESIS. See LEARNING THEORIES/LAWS.

REDUCTIONIST THEORY. See ALLPORT'S THEORY OF PERSONALITY.

REDUNDANCY PRINCIPLE. See HABIT/ HABIT FORMATION, LAWS/PRINCIPLES OF.

REFERENCE-GROUP THEORY. See PREJUDICE, THEORIES OF.

REFERENCE MAN/WOMAN MODEL. See DEVELOPMENTAL THEORY.

REFLECTION EFFECT. See ORGANI-ZATIONAL/INDUSTRIAL/SYSTEMS THE-ORY.

REFLEX ACT HYPOTHESIS. See RE-FLEX ARC THEORY/CONCEPT.

REFLEX ACTION, PRINCIPLE OF. See PAVLOVIAN CONDITIONING, PRINCI-PLES/LAWS/THEORIES.

REFLEX ARC THEORY/CONCEPT. The French philosopher Rene Descartes (1596-1690), who also conducted physiological studies, was among the first writers to give a statement of the *reflex theory of action*: animals (and humans) are considered to be mere machines and explained in *mechanistic* terms, where much of the organism's motor behavior is *reflexive* and not dependent on "mind." However, it was the American philosopher and educator John Dewey (1859-1952) who formally adapted the physiologist's *model of the reflex arc* to the study of psychological action (cf., *reflex act hypothesis* - states that psychological acts follow the same general pattern as neurological reflexes, beginning with an external or internal source of stimulation, proceeding to a central regulatory system, and discharging through efferent channels; and *spinal conditioning hypothesis* - the unsubstantiated notion that conditioned reflexes may be established via circuitry in the spinal cord that lack interconnections to central nervous system structures above the spinal cord). The *reflex arc* was the hypothesized neural unit that represented the functioning of a reflex where the abstract arc is schematically indicated by a *sensory* (afferent) neuron stimulated by physical energy, and a *motor* (efferent) neuron to which the impulse is transmitted via an intermediary neuron. The

reflex arc is called, also, the *reflex circuit*. In his theoretical approach, Dewey attacked the psychological molecularism, elementism, and reductionism of the *reflex arc* concept with its distinction between *stimulus* and *response*. Dewey argued that the behavior involved in a reflex response may not be reduced meaningfully to its basic sensory-motor elements anymore than consciousness can be analyzed meaningfully into its elementary components. He maintained that behavior should be treated not as an artificial scientific construct, but rather in terms of its functional significance to the organism in adapting to the environment. This theoretical position by J. Dewey, J. R. Angell, and W. James is called *functionalism theory* and views behavior in terms of active adaptation to the environment, emphasizing the causes and consequences of human behavior, the union of the physiological with the psychological, the objective testing of theories, and the solution of practical problems (cf., *structuralism/structuralist theory*; also, the *theory of utilitarianism* - a social/economic postulate that suggests that the practical usefulness of any plan, object, or event is the proper criterion against which to judge its ultimate value). Dewey was concerned, also, about the contemporaneous cleavage/duality of the organism into a *body* and a *mind*. In his paper on the *reflex arc*, Dewey struggled to rid psychology of the ancient *mind-body dualism* and suggested that behavior should be viewed as being so integrated that it is impossible to split it up into disparate parts. Dewey's *reflex arc theory* was an attempt to show how behavior and psychological events need to be viewed as whole entities, and his approach was a significant protest against the artificial fragmentation of behavior imbedded in the *reflex arc paradigm* of his day. See also HOLISTIC THEORY; MECHANISTIC THEORY; MIND-BODY THEORIES; NEURON/NEURAL/NERVE THEORY; REFLEXOLOGY THEORY; STRUCTURALISM/STRUCTURALIST THEORY.

REFERENCES

Descartes, R. (1661). *L'Homme*. Paris: Le Gras.

Dewey, J. (1896). The reflex arc concept in psychology. *Psychological Review, 3*, 357-370.

Hull, C. L. (1929). A functional interpretation of the conditioned reflex. *Psychological Review, 36*, 498-511.

REFLEX FATIGUE, LAW OF. See SKINNER'S DESCRIPTIVE BEHAVIOR/OPERANT CONDITIONING THEORY.

REFLEXOLOGY THEORY. This theoretical approach refers to a system of psychological thought developed chiefly by the Russian physician Vladimir Mikhailovich Bekhterev (1857-1927) - who initially named his work *objective psychology* and then, later, *reflexology* - and other Russian psychologists that attempts to explain human behavior on the basis of the *reflex* as the fundamental "unit" of behavior, and involves explanations for various processes, including higher mental operations generated from these "units" (cf., *reflex-sensitization principle* - states that after a specified response has been elicited repeatedly by a particular stimulus, it may be elicited, also, by a "neutral" stimulus that previously was not an adequate stimulus for eliciting that specific response). *Reflexology theory* emphasizes the involuntary automatic responses to stimuli, in particular as they influence the behavior of both animals and humans. The theory rests, also, on the early work of the English physiologist Sir Charles Scott Sherrington (1857-1952) and the Russian physiologist Ivan Petrovich Pavlov (1849-1936) who suggested that psychological processes can be explained by the biologically-based associations among sensorimotor interactions. Later, *reflexology* was employed as the basis of a controversial and unconventional method of mental and physical therapy/treatment that was implemented, in one case, by pressing various regions of the soles of the feet, supposedly corresponding to certain areas of the body (e.g., the region along the inner side of the foot allegedly is linked to early memories in the individual's experience). See also PAVLOVIAN CONDITIONING PRINCIPLES/LAWS/THEORIES; PSEUDOSCIENTIFIC/UNCONVENTIONAL THEORIES; REFLEX ARC THEORY/CONCEPT; SKIN-NER'S DESCRIPTIVE BEHAVIOR/OPERANT CONDITIONING THEORY.

REFERENCES

Bekhterev, V. M. (1928/1932). *General principles of human reflexology: An introduction to the objective study of personality*. New York: International Publishers.

Pavlov, I. P. (1928). *Lectures on conditioned reflexes*. New York: International Publishers.

Sherrington, C. S. (1906). *The integrative action of the nervous system*. New York: Cambridge University Press.

REFLEX RESERVE, PRINCIPLE OF. See SKINNER'S DESCRIPTIVE BEHAVIOR/OPERANT CONDITIONING THEORY.

REFLEX-SENSITIZATION PRINCIPLE. See REFLEXOLOGY THEORY.

REFLEX THEORY OF ACTION. See REFLEX ARC THEORY/CONCEPT.

REFRACTORY LAW. See ALL-OR-NONE LAW/PRINCIPLE.

REFRACTORY PHASE, LAW OF. See SKINNER'S DESCRIPTIVE BEHAVIOR/OPERANT CONDITIONING THEORY.

REFRIGERATOR PARENTS THEORY. See SCHIZOPHRENIA, THEORIES OF.

REGIONAL-LOCALIZATION THEORY. See MIND/MENTAL STATES, THEORIES OF.

REGRESSION FALLACY. See PROBABILITY THEORY/LAWS.

REICHENBACH PHENOMENON. See REICH'S ORGONE/ORGONOMY THEORY.

REICHER-WHEELER EFFECT. See TOP-DOWN PROCESSING THEORIES.

REICH'S ORGONE/ORGONOMY THEORY. The Austrian-born American psychoanalyst Wilhelm Reich (1897-1957) formulated a "dissident" *psychoanalytic theory* call-ed the *orgone theory*, which is based on the assumption that a specific form of energy call-ed *orgone energy* fills all space and accounts for all life (cf., *bioenergetics theory* - deals with the energy relationships in living organ-isms, and is a psychotherapeutic technique developed by the American psychiatrist Alex-ander Lowen (1910-); and *Reichenbach phe-nomenon* - named after the German chemist Baron Karl Ludwig von Reichenbach (1788-1869) - refers to a force or emanation, called the "od," "odic," or "odylic" force that a "sen-sitive" person can, allegedly, see coming out of all matter; this and "N-rays" and "auras" proved to be cases of self-deception). Reich argued that not only are patients' symptoms evidence of neurosis but their character struc-ture itself may be neurotic. Reich called his therapeutic approach *character analysis* and he often elicited intense emotions from pa-tients with the result that changes occurred in their bodily attitudes, tonus, and posture. Reich attacked the problems of neurosis by attacking the somatic muscular "armor" of his patients. An individual's emotions, according to Reich, came to mean the manifestations of a tangible biological energy called *orgone* (from the terms *organism* and *orgasm*), and the function of the physiological act of the orgasm is to regulate the organism's energy. One of the problems with a concept such as *orgone*, and a theory of "being" such as *or-gone theory*, is the precise identification of the *orgone*. In order to demonstrate the existence of something (like *orgone*), one must be able to determine where it is not, so as to know, in turn, where it is. That is, if something exists uniformly everywhere, it might as well be no-where. The issue of *orgone* identity led Reich to construct a device he called the *orgone accumulator* - a box composed of layers of different metals that collect *orgones* and con-centrates them, allegedly, on the person sitting inside the box, much to the benefit of their sex lives; the box eventually led to some serious legal problems with the U. S. Food and Drug Administration. The term *orgonomy* refers to *Reich's personality theory* and his associated therapeutic practices that involved elaborate physical massage programs involving manipu-lations, proddings, and probings, and encour-

agements to the patient/client to try to experi-ence the ultimate *orgastic release* that Reich believed to be the evidence of therapeutic breakthrough. The current consensus of scien-tific opinion is that *Reich's orgone theory* is basically a psychoanalytic system gone awry and is an approach that represents some-thing most ludicrous and totally dismissible. See also PERSONALITY THEORIES.

REFERENCES

Reich, W. (1933). *Charakter analyse*, Leipzig: Sexpol Verlag.

Reich, W. (1942). *The function of the orgasm*. New York: Farrar, Straus.

Reich, W. (1945). The masochistic character. In W. Reich (Ed.), *Character an-alysis*. New York: Orgone Institute Press.

REID'S MOVEMENT ILLUSION. See APPENDIX A.

REIK'S THIRD EAR HYPOTHESIS. See THIRD EAR HYPOTHESIS.

REINFORCEMENT RETROACTIVE PARADOX/HYPOTHESIS. See EFFECT, LAW OF.

REINFORCEMENT THEORY. The term *reinforcement* contains a considerable amount of diversity of usage in psychology where most of the definitional variations stem from theoretical issues in *learning theory* concern-ing what reinforcement is and how it functions [cf., Warren (1919) who describes the *law of reinforcement*]. Common to most approaches, however, is the tautological reference to an operation of strengthening, supporting, or solidifying something (e.g. a learned response or some stimulus-response connection) or the event that so strengthens or supports it. In the empirical context of *Pavlovian classical con-ditioning*, *reinforcement* is defined as the un-conditioned stimulus as it is related to, or is paired with, the neutral or conditioned stimu-lus. In the context of *instrumental or operant conditioning*, *reinforcement* is defined as the events [usually stimuli, but see Premack (1962) regarding responses] that are conse-quences of a voluntary response or behavior where such behavior subsequently increases in frequency of occurrence (cf., the *pairing hypothesis* - holds that the mere presence of a stimulus, when some response is reinforced, is sufficient for that stimulus to achieve control over the behavior). A related term, reward, is used by some psychologists as synonymous with reinforcement [cf., *Schafer-Murphy effect* - named after the American psychologists R. Schafer and G. Murphy, refers to a tendency for a person rewarded in some way for making a particular choice/interpretation of a *reversible/ambiguous figure* (i.e., a drawing that initially yields one impression but upon further viewing yields another entirely different impression; typically occurs in a *figure-ground* stimulus via the person's perceptual switching of a previously viewed *figure* into the *background* surface and vice-versa) to make the same interpretation of that *reversible/ambiguous figure* in the future]. However, when writers do not equate the two terms, *reward* and *reinforcement*, the distinction usually centers around the ascribed *subjective* "satisfying" or "pleasurable" aspects of events ("rewards") versus the *objectively* measured influences that events have on behaviors ("reinforcers"). Psychologists distinguish, also, between *intrinsic* versus *extrinsic* rewards, where the former are activities that are interesting and fun to perform in themselves, even though they produce no external benefits (e.g., playing, painting, writing poetry), and the latter refer to response outcomes that are satisfying independent of the events that produce them (e.g., money, food, public recognition). S. Kassin and M. Lepper, and others, suggest that external reward for performing a task may produce an *overjustification effect* (or *oversufficient justification effect*) that refers to providing an external reward for a behavior when there previously was none (or where the task was performed for its own sake without reward) and causes a person to question the justification for responding in the first place; often, in such cases, the result is a reduction in the person's liking for the task associated with the behavior. *Intrinsic* and *extrinsic* rewards may be thought of as part of the *incentive theory of motivation*, which maintains that external stimuli motivate responding by "pulling" the behavior from the individual and is contrasted with the biological, drive-

reduction, and arousal theories of motivation, which assert that behavior is "pushed" by events inside the organism. In other distinctions, the term *reinforcement* refers to the *procedure* of presenting/removing a stimulus event, and *reinforcer* refers to the actual consequent stimulus *event* itself. Historically, E. L. Thorndike preferred the terms *reward* and *punishment* to the older, more philosophically-based terms *pleasure* and *pain*, but he also substituted the terms *satisfiers* and *annoyers* for *rewards* and *punishments*, respectively, because this allowed more range for possible kinds of behavioral aftereffects. By the late 1930s, both C. L. Hull and B. F. Skinner followed up on Thorndike's theory, but they changed his terminology where *satisfiers* now became *reinforcements*. In Hull's *drive-reduction theory*, reinforcement was defined in terms of decreasing degrees of drive stimulation where *rewards* or *satisfiers* now became *drive-reducers*, and learning could take place only when drives were diminished. In Skinner's *descriptive-behavioral* approach, however, the term *drive* was considered to be too vague and subjective so the term *deprivation* was used in its place. Thus, for Skinner, as for Thorndike, a *reinforcer* was defined as anything that would result in a stronger/faster rate of performance of some activity that previously would occur only by chance (cf., the *transituationality principle* - the false generalization that a reinforcer that is effective in one situation will be as effective in all situations). In the period when Hull and Skinner were arguing for the importance of rewards/reinforcers for learning, other theoretical positions were formulated also. For example, E. Guthrie asserted that one learns what one happened to be doing just before the stimulus that leads to the response is removed. According to Guthrie's *associative/contiguity theory*, one learns what one did *last*, and rewards are just a convenient way of making the stimuli disappear, and what one learns is to make both adaptive and nonadaptive responses where rewards per se are irrelevant. In another case, E. Tolman's *purposive/cognitive theory* holds that learning is a matter of frequency of association between stimuli and responses where rewards are related only to the level of motivation. Another *theory of reinforcement*, D.

Premack's *prepotent response theory*, is stated entirely in terms of responses and their probabilities: of any two responses, the more probable response will reinforce the less probable one where the "prepotent" response is designated as the *reinforcer*. A critical test for *Premack's theory* lies in its verification of the *indifference principle* (i.e., the contentions that the reinforcing power of a response depends solely on its probability, and it makes no difference how response probability was determined). A refinement in Premack's approach is called the *disequilibrium principle*, which proposes that the key to reinforcement is not just how much time one spends on a given activity, but whether the individual spends as much time on it as she or he would like. Other *theories of reinforcement* include H. Harlow's, R. Butler's, and K. Montgomery's notions about *sensory reinforcement* and *stimulus-centered drives* as determinants of behavior; and J. Brown's recognition that the stimulus-centered theorists' work in *exploratory* and *curiosity* behavior offered a *drive-increase theory of reinforcement* in opposition to the *drive-reduction theory of reinforcement* (such as Hull's approach). The *theory of stimulus-centered drive* by Harlow, Butler, and Montgomery also relates well to the *physiological arousal theory of drive* and the discovery of the functioning of the "ascending reticular activating system" of the brain. In defense of the *arousal theorists'* approach to defining *reinforcement* (as against the *drive-reduction theorists'* criticisms), the *inverted-U hypothesis* offers a way to show how a theory can explain the reinforcing effects of *both* drive *decrease* and drive *increase*: when the organism is *below* the optimum point of arousal, an *increase* in drive is *rewarding*, but when one is *above* the optimum point, the drive level is aversive, and a *decrease* in drive is *rewarding*. Thus, *arousal theory* has been useful as an attempt to integrate externally- and internally-based drives and serves as a link with contemporary findings in brain physiology, but it is not yet a fully functioning *theory of reinforcement*. Accessory concepts to *reinforcement theory* are the terms *primary reinforcers*, *secondary reinforcers*, *positive reinforcement*, *negative reinforcement*, *partial reinforcement paradox/effect*, and *schedules of reinforcement* - including *continuous*, *fixed ratio*, *variable ratio*, *fixed interval*, and *variable interval* schedules. The concept of *reinforcement* provides overlapping, and sometimes even contradictory, definitions to psychologists who find themselves often trapped lexicographically into the use of the term where part of the difficulty results from attempts to treat the concept as if it represented a single fundamental principle that operates in all circumstances. The ambiguities in the definitions of *reinforcer* and *reinforcement* are likely to remain unresolved for some time, but the worth of the concepts has already been demonstrated in numerous studies and applications. See also CAPALDI'S THEORY; GUTHRIE'S THEORY OF BEHAVIOR; HULL'S LEARNING THEORY; INVERTED-U HYPOTHESIS; LEARNING THEORIES/LAWS; MAXIMIZATION THEORY; MOTIVATION, THEORIES OF; PAVLOVIAN CONDITIONING PRINCIPLES/LAWS/THEORIES; PREMACK'S PRINCIPLE/LAW; PUNISHMENT, THEORIES OF; REINFORCEMENT, THORNDIKE'S THEORY OF; REVERSIBLE/AMBIGUOUS/OSCILLATING FIGURES; SKINNER'S DESCRIPTIVE BEHAVIOR/OPERANT CONDITIONING THEORY; TOLMAN'S THEORY.

REFERENCES

Warren, H. C. (1919). *Human psychology.* Boston: Houghton Mifflin.

Tolman, E. C. (1932). *Purposive behavior in animals and men.* New York: Appleton-Century-Crofts.

Guthrie, E. R. (1935). *The psychology of learning.* New York: Harper & Row.

Skinner, B. F. (1938). *The behavior of organisms: An experimental analysis.* New York: Appleton-Century-Crofts.

Hull, C. L. (1943). *The principles of behavior.* New York: Appleton-Century-Crofts.

Harlow, H. (1950). Learning and satiation of response in intrinsically motivated complex puzzle performance in monkeys. *Journal of Comparative and Physiological Psychology, 43,* 289-294.

Brown, J. (1953). Comments on Professor Harlow's paper, In *Current theory and research in motivation: A symposium*. Lincoln: University of Nebraska Press.

Butler, R. (1953). Discrimination learning by Rhesus monkeys to visual-exploration motivation. *Journal of Comparative and Physiological Psychology, 46*, 95-98.

Montgomery, K. (1954). The role of the exploratory drive in learning. *Journal of Comparative and Physiological Psychology, 47*, 60-64.

Premack, D. (1962).Reversibility of the reinforcement relation. *Science, 136*, 255-257.

Capaldi, E. J. (1966). Partial reinforcement: An hypothesis of sequential effects. *Psychological Review, 73*, 459-477.

Schoenfeld, W. (Ed.) (1970). *The theory of reinforcement schedules*. New York: Appleton-Century-Crofts.

Kassin, S., & Lepper, M. (1984). Oversufficient and insufficient justification effects: Cognitive and behavioral development. *Advances in Motivation and Achievement, 3*, 73-106.

Timberlake, W., & Farmer-Dougan, V. (1991). Reinforcement in applied settings: Figuring out ahead of time what will work. *Psychological Bulletin, 110*, 379-391.

REINFORCEMENT, THORNDIKE'S THEORY OF. = spread of effect = Thorndike's learning theory. The American psychologist Edward Lee Thorndike (1874-1949) anticipated the modern *theory of reinforcement* in his *law of effect*, where he considered the consequences of a response to be essential to the strengthening of the associative bond between stimulus and response. Thus, according to *Thorndike's theory of reinforcement*, the "satisfying consequences" (e.g., re-wards or escape from punishment) strengthen a stimulus-response connection, whereas "annoying consequences" (e.g., punishers/punishment) weaken the connection. In other terms, *Thorndike's spread of effect hypothesis* refers to satisfaction or dissatisfaction associated with a response that spreads to other features of the situation; or refers to the effect of "satisfiers" or "annoyers," to other stimuli present at the time of the response, or to stimuli similar in nature to the originally reinforced stimulus ("stimulus generalization"). Thorndike argued that psychology's main goal should be to study behavior (i.e., stimulus-response units; or the *S-R learning model/theory* that holds that learning is primarily a trial-and-error process in which associative connections between stimuli and responses are established), and not conscious experience or mental elements. His *instrumental conditioning* approach was to develop the notion of *connectionism* and the *laws of connection*; that is, the connections between stimuli/situations and responses, rather than the associations between *ideas* that were formulated by earlier psychologists and philosophers. *Pavlov's law of reinforcement* - that was reported four years after Thorndike's *law of effect* first appeared - resembles *Thorndike's theory of reinforcement*. Many psychologists consider Thorndike to be the "father" of American learning psychology, and his classical *instrumental conditioning* experiments, involving animals in "puzzle-boxes" (where the animal learns to get out of a cage-like box, and its behavior is instrumental in receiving food as a consequence), emphasize the "trial-and-error" aspects of learning (also called the *irradiation theory*), as well as the stimulus-response "connections" that occur by chance and serve to strengthen certain functional behaviors. The term *satisfier* that Thorndike used in his theory (i.e., a stimulus-response bond or connection is strengthened when the response is followed by a "satisfier") was synonymous with the term *reward* until later psychologists (e.g., C. L. Hull and B. F. Skinner) advanced arguments for using the term *reinforcement* over the terms *satisfier* and *reward*. Terminology was, and continues to be, an important issue in the area of *learning theory* development. Thus, although Thorndike's terms *satisfier* and *annoyer* may be outdated by the terminology in more current learning theories, it was an empirical advance over the much earlier rational philosophical approach, such as the Aristotelian terms *pleasure* and *pain*. Thorn-dike's two-part *reinforcement theory* - that is, that one learns (retains) whatever responses are followed by *satisfiers* and does not learn (eliminates) responses that are followed by *annoyers* - and his *laws of learning* (i.e., *exe-cise, readiness, effect, belongingness, associative shifting*) served for many years at the beginning of the 20th century in this country as the basis for educational programs and learning systems. See also ASSOCIATIVE SHIFTING, LAW OF; BELONGINGNESS, PRINCIPLE OF; CONNECTIONISM, THEORY OF; EFFECT, LAW OF; EXERCISE, LAW OF; GENERALIZATION, PRINCIPLES OF; HULL'S LEARNING THEORY; PLEASURE-PAIN, DOCTRINE/THEORY/LAW OF; READINESS, LAW OF; SKINNER'S DESCRIPTIVE BEHAVIOR/OPERANT CONDITIONING THEORY.

REFERENCES

Thorndike, E. L. (1898). Animal intelligence: An experimental study of the associative processes in animals. *Psychological Review Monograph Supplement, 2,* 1-109.

Thorndike, E. L. (1907). *The elements of psychology.* New York: Seiler.

Thorndike, E. L. (1932). *The fundamentals of learning.* New York: Teachers College Press.

Thorndike, E. L. (1933). A theory of the action of the after-effects of a connection upon it. *Psychological Review, 40,* 434-439.

Skinner, B. F. (1938). *The behavior of organisms.* New York: Appleton-Century-Crofts.

Hull, C. L. (1943). *Principles of behavior.* New York: Appleton-Century-Crofts.

Bugelski, B. R. (1994). Thorndike's laws of learning. In R. J. Corsini (Ed.), *Encyclopedia of psychology.* New York: Wiley.

REJECTION-THEN-RETREAT TECHNIQUE. See COMPLIANCE EFFECTS/ TECHNIQUES.

RELATIONAL THEORY. See SPENCE'S THEORY.

RELATION OF MOVEMENTS TO IMAGES, PRINCIPLE OF. See WUNDT'S THEORIES/DOCTRINES/PRINCIPLES.

RELATIVE DEPRIVATION EFFECT. See EQUITY THEORY.

RELATIVITY LAW. See WEBER'S LAW.

RELATIVITY/RELATIVE EFFECT, LAW OF. See HERRNSTEIN'S MATCHING LAW.

RELAXATION PRINCIPLE. See CATASTROPHE THEORY/MODEL.

RELEASE THEORY OF HUMOR. See RELIEF/TENSION-RELEASE THEORIES OF HUMOR/LAUGHTER.

RELIABILITY/VALIDITY THEORY. See MEASUREMENT THEORY; NOMOLOGICAL NETWORK THEORY.

RELIEF/TENSION-RELEASE THEORIES OF HUMOR/LAUGHTER. The *relief/tension-release* class of humor theories places great weight on the relief from stress and on relaxation that derives from the sudden removal of a threat or discomfiture (cf., *release theory of humor* - states that humor tends first to raise one's level of anxiety and then, subsequently, to lower the individual's anxiety-level). For example, the French philosopher Rene Descartes (1596-1650) maintained that laughter results from the joy that comes when an indignation at some evil or malice has been mitigated by the realization that it does not cause personal harm; the British associationist/philosopher David Hartley (1705-1757) asserted that laughter is an expression of pleasure at the elimination of something alarming or painful; and the English psychologist James Sully (1842-1923) indicated that laughter may be produced by relief from strain or by the sudden induction of a playful mood. Other features of the *relief/tension-release theories of humor* are that the humorous process involves a disruption of orderly thought processes due to a sudden triumph of good or pleasurable values centering on a release from the tension produced by controlled thought; and the concept of *relief/ tension-release* is the most common/prevalent factor - among many other potential aspects - leading to the occasion of laughter. See also DESCARTES' THEORY OF HUMOR/ LAUGHTER; FREUD'S THEORY OF WIT/HUMOR; HARTLEY'S THEORY OF HUMOR/LAUGHTER; HUMOR, THEORIES OF; SPENCER'S THEORY OF LAUGHTER/HUMOR; SULLY'S THEORY OF LAUGHTER/HUMOR.

REFERENCE

Roeckelein, J. E. (2002). *The psychology of humor*. Westport, CT: Greenwood Press.

RELIGION, THEORIES OF. See CONDUCT, LAWS OF; KOHLBERG'S THEORY OF MORALITY.

RELIGIOUS INSTINCT HYPOTHESIS. See KOHLBERG'S THEORY OF MORALITY.

REMINISCENCE THEORY OF KNOWLEDGE. See LEARNING THEORIES/ LAWS.

REM SLEEP, THEORY OF. See SLEEP, THEORIES OF.

REORGANIZATION PRINCIPLE AND THEORY. See PERCEPTION (I. GENERAL), THEORIES OF.

REPAIR/RESTORATION/RECUPERATIVE THEORY. See SLEEP, THEORIES OF.

REPEATED REPRODUCTION METHOD. See FORGETTING/MEMORY, THEORIES OF.

REPETITION/FREQUENCY, LAW OF. See ASSOCIATION, LAWS/PRINCIPLES OF; FREQUENCY, LAW OF; SKINNER'S DESCRIPTIVE BEHAVIOR/OPERANT CONDITIONING THEORY.

REPETITION LAW/EFFECT. See FREQUENCY, LAW OF; HEDONISM, THEORY/LAW OF; INHIBITION, LAWS OF.

REPRODUCTION OF THE SIMILAR, LAW OF. See CONDUCT, LAWS OF.

REPRODUCTION THEORY OF IMAGERY. See IMAGERY/MENTAL IMAGERY, THEORIES OF.

REPRODUCTIVE PHASES THEORY. See DEVELOPMENTAL THEORY.

REQUISITE VARIETY, LAW OF. See INFORMATION AND INFORMATION-PROCESSING THEORY.

RESCORLA-WAGNER THEORY/MODEL. See ASSOCIATIVE LEARNING IN ANIMALS, THEORIES OF; BLOCKING, PHENOMENON/EFFECT OF; PAVLOVIAN CONDITIONING PRINCIPLES/LAWS/ THEORIES.

RESEARCH HYPOTHESIS. See NULL HYPOTHESIS.

RESEMBLANCE/SIMILARITY, LAW OF. See ASSOCIATION, LAWS/PRINCIPLES OF; GESTALT THEORY/LAWS.

RESIDUAL DEVIANCE HYPOTHESIS. See LABELING/DEVIANCE THEORY.

RESIDUES, LAW OF. See PARSIMONY, LAW/PRINCIPLE OF.

RESISTANCE, LAW OF. See GESTALT THEORY/LAWS.

RESOLUTION LAW. See WOLPE'S THEORY/TECHNIQUE OF RECIPROCAL INHIBITION.

RESOLUTION, LAW OF. See SKINNER'S DESCRIPTIVE BEHAVIOR/OPERANT CONDITIONING THEORY.

RESONANCE, RESONANCE/PLACE, RESONANCE/VOLLEY THEORIES. See AUDITION/HEARING, THEORIES OF.

RESONANCE THEORY OF LEARNING. See MIND/MENTAL SET, LAW OF.

RESOURCE-ALLOCATION MODEL OF TIME ESTIMATION. See PSYCHOLOGICAL TIME, MODELS OF.

RESOURCE DEPLETION THEORY. See INTELLIGENCE, THEORIES/LAWS OF.

RESOURCE DILEMMA MODEL/PARADIGM. = resource management dilemma = resource conservation dilemma = take-some game. This is a useful and practical model of familiar social dilemmas in which conservation of natural resources is a major goal. In general, *social dilemma models* involve interactive decisions in which personal interests are at odds with collective interests where the pursuit of individual self-interest by every decision-maker leaves everyone else concerned worse off than if each person had acted cooperatively. *Social dilemma models* are presented, usually, in one of three general forms (N-person prisoner's dilemmas, public goods dilemmas, and resource dilemmas), and have been used, in particular, to study problems such as inflation vis-a-vis voluntary wage restraint, conservation of scarce natural resources, environmental pollution, arms races/ multilateral disarmament, crowd behavior, and other social issues involving trust and cooperation. In the *resource dilemma model/paradigm*, players harvest resources (typically in the form of tokens that represent money/currency) from a common resource pool of known size, and after each trial/session, the pool is replenished at a predetermined rate. In this model/game, each player is free to choose how much to take from the pool, and it is in each person's self-interest to take as much as possible; however, if everyone behaves in a greedy manner, then the pool becomes exhausted and depleted, and every player suffers as a consequence. In the *commons dilemma* - a version of *resource dilemma* [named after a reference made by the English economist William Forster Lloyd (1795-1852) in an essay on population growth, where the parable of the "tragedy of the commons" was the *overgrazing* of the commons in 14th-century England, and led to the construction of fences and enclosures, resulting in the disappearance of many of the "commons" areas in England] - the issue of *overgrazing* on a common pasture provides the scenario for cooperation-competition among a group of hypothetical farmers, each requiring grazing space for their cattle. See also CONFLICT, THEORIES OF; DECISION-MAKING, THEORIES OF; HAWK-DOVE AND CHICKEN GAME EFFECTS.

REFERENCES

Lloyd, W. F. (1833). *Two lectures on the checks to population*. Oxford, UK: University of Oxford Press.

Hardin, G. R. (1968). The tragedy of the commons. *Science, 162*, 1243-1248.

Liebrand, W., Messick, D. M., & Wilke, H. (Eds.) (1992). *Social dilemmas: Theoretical issues and research findings*. Oxford, UK: Pergamon.

Komorita, S. S., & Parks, C. D. (1995). Interpersonal relations: Mixed-motive interaction. *Annual Review of Psychology, 46*, 183-207.

Av, W. T., & Ngai, M. Y. (2003). Effects of group size uncertainty and protocol of play in a common pool resource dilemma. *Group Processes and Intergroup Relations, 6*, 265-283.

RESPONSE-BY-ANALOGY PRINCIPLE. See TRANSFER OF TRAINING, THORNDIKE'S THEORY OF.

RESPONSE-DEPRIVATION THEORY. See PREMACK'S PRINCIPLE/LAW.

RESPONSE GENERALIZATION, PRINCIPLE OF. See GENERALIZATION, PRINCIPLES OF.

RESPONSE MAGNITUDE, LAW OF. See SKINNER'S DESCRIPTIVE BEHAVIOR/ OPERANT CONDITIONING THEORY.

RESPONSE-RESPONSE (R-R) LAWS. See SKINNER'S DESCRIPTIVE BEHAVIOR/ OPERANT CONDITIONING THEORY.

RESPONSE-UNIT HYPOTHESIS. See CAPALDI'S THEORY.

RESTORFF EFFECT/PHENOMENON. See von RESTORFF EFFECT.

RESTRAINED-EATING HYPOTHESIS. See HUNGER, THEORIES OF.

RESTRICTED CHOICE, PRINCIPLE OF. See THREE-DOOR GAME SHOW PROBLEM/EFFECT.

RESTRICTED CODE THEORY. The English sociologist Basil Bernstein (1924-2000) formulated *restricted code theory* to account for an informal use of language that is related to immediate/context-bound situations and that involves the use of a reduced semantic and syntactic range. The employment of such restricted language is hypothesized to be indicative of lower-working-class individuals - as compared to middle-class persons/speakers who demonstrate *both* a *restricted* and an *elaborated code* (i.e., a comparatively complex and formal use of language that is not restricted to immediate situations, and is context-free containing a wide semantic and syntactic range). The *restricted code theory* is reduced often - in an unwarranted or specious manner - to the proposition (based on differences in linguistic resources that are available) that middle-class individuals are capable of abstract reasoning, whereas lower-working-class people are not capable of such reasoning. See also LANGUAGE ACQUISITION THEORY; LANGUAGE ORIGINS, THEORIES OF.

REFERENCES

Bernstein, B. (1960). Language and social class. *British Journal of Sociology, 11,* 271-276.

Bernstein, B. (1964). Elaborated and restricted codes: Their social origins and some consequences. *American Anthropologist, 66,* 55-69.

Huspek, M. (1994). Oppositional codes and social class relations. *British Journal of Sociology, 45,* 79-108.

RETICULARIST THEORY. See NEURON/NEURAL/NERVE THEORY.

RETICULAR THEORY. See LIFE, THEORIES OF.

RETINAL PAINTING HYPOTHESIS. The German physiologist/psychologist Hermann L. F. von Helmholtz (1821-1894) advanced the *retinal painting hypothesis* in which *anorthoscopic perception* is explained by a conjectured process whereby the extended image of a figure viewed through a moving slit is spread gradually over the retina and imprinted onto it bit by bit, resulting in a retinal imprint of the whole figure whose form, subsequently, is perceived. Typically, *anorthoscopic* viewing refers to perception of a figure that is revealed one section at a time via a narrow slit behind which the target figure moves. If images - such as simple geometric shapes or letters of the alphabet - are presented in such a fashion, *form perception* occurs and the shapes of the images are perceived clearly in spite of the absence of any retinal image of the corresponding shapes. Another illustration of *form perception* without a corresponding retinal image resides in the *Kanizsa triangle visual illusion* (see Appendix A). The *retinal paining hypothesis* was discredited, eventually, by studies of *eye movements* that occur during *anorthoscopic perception* and that served, largely, to discount Helmholtz's conjectured process. See also APPARENT MOVEMENT, PRINCIPLES AND THEORIES OF; CONSTRUCTIVIST THEORY OF PERCEPTION; EYE MOVEMENT THEORY; PATTERN/OBJECT RECOGNITION THEORY; PERCEPTION (I. GENERAL), THEORIES OF.

REFERENCES

Helmholtz, H. L. F. von (1856). *Handbuch der physiologischen optik.* Leipzig: Voss.

Rock, I. (1981). Anorthoscopic perception. *Scientific American, 244,* 145-153.

Fujita, N. (1991). Slit viewing of 3-D objects and non-rigid body: Criticism of the retinal painting theory and the computational theory, and "perception" of unseen parts. *Japanese Psychological Review, 34,* 61-92.

RETINEX THEORY. See COLOR VISION, THEORIES/LAWS OF.

RETREAT FROM REALITY HYPOTHESIS. See PSYCHOPATHOLOGY, THEORIES OF.

RETRIEVAL FAILURE THEORY. See FORGETTING/MEMORY, THEORIES OF.

RETROACTIVE INHIBITION, LAW OF. See FORGETTING/MEMORY, THEORIES OF; INTERFERENCE THEORIES OF FORGETTING.

RETROSPECTIVE TIME ESTIMATION. See TIME, THEORIES OF.

REVERBERATING CIRCUIT THEORY. See PERCEPTION (II. COMPARATIVE APPRAISAL), THEORIES OF.

REVERSAL THEORY. See APTER'S REVERSAL THEORY OF HUMOR.

REVERSE HALO EFFECT. See HALO EFFECT.

REVERSIBLE/AMBIGUOUS/OSCILLATING FIGURES. See APPENDIX A (NECKER CUBE/ILLUSION, RUBIN FIGURE/ILLUSION, SCHRODER STAIRCASE ILLUSION); GESTALT THEORY/LAWS; REINFORCEMENT THEORY.

REVERSION, LAW OF. See GALTON'S LAWS.

REWARD THEORY OF INTERPERSONAL ATTRACTION. See INTERPERSONAL ATTRACTION THEORIES.

RHYTHM PERCEPTION, THEORY OF. In this theory, P. Desain (1992) proposes a formalized, mathematical *expectancy theory/ model of complex temporal patterns* applicable to such diverse topics as clock/meter inducement, categorical rhythm perception, rhythmicity, and the similarity of temporal sequences. Desain's *(de)composable theory of rhythm perception* accounts for expectancy projected into the future, as well as projections into the past, and generates reinforcement of past events by new data. See also TIME, THEORIES OF.

REFERENCE

Desain, P. (1992). A (de)composable theory of rhythm perception. *Music Perception, 9*, 439-454.

RHYTHM, TIME AND ACCENT THEORIES OF. Concerning the controversy between so-called *time* and *accent theories of rhythm* (cf., Brown, 1911), J. Wallin asserts that absolutely periodic or regular occurrences are not essential to the appreciation of the phenomenon of *rhythm*, although absolute regularity improves the quality of the rhythmic impression. Wallin's studies show that it is slightly easier for one to differentiate between grades of rhythmical qualities than to notice differences in time, and he points to the fact that time and rhythm do not rest upon the same basis precisely. Rhythm is viewed as less a matter of judgment than of feeling or a "rhythm sense." Wallin notes that to define a genuine rhythmical reaction, a movement in time must arouse those sensory processes and motor responses or physiological reactions that lie at the foundation of the feeling of rhythm. Without an active functioning of the physiological or neural substrate, the "rhythmical consciousness" would consist of only a certain awareness of a quasi-rhythmical movement in time. Wallin maintains, also, that the thresholds for rhythm are amenable to the *Weber-Fechner psychophysical law*, having a mathematical constant of one-third. See also FECHNER'S LAW; TIME, THEORIES OF.

REFERENCES

Brown, W. (1911). Temporal and accentual rhythm. *Psychological Review, 18*, 336-346.

Wallin, J. (1911/1912). Experimental studies of rhythm and time. *Psychological Review, 18*, 100-131, 202-222; *19*, 271-298.

Ross, R. (1914). The measurement of time-sense as an element in the sense of rhythm. *Psychological Monographs, 16*, 166-172.

RIBOT'S LAW. The French psychologist Theodule Armand Ribot (1839-1916) formulated this principle concerning *amnesia*, which states that retrograde memory-loss affects events that occurred closer in time to the onset of amnesia, and these events are remembered less well than those events that occurred further back in time. Thus, according to *Ribot's law*, in a traumatic *retrograde amnesia* situation, memories for events occurring immediately before the accident are the ones most likely to be lost. In cases of recovery from *aphasia*, or loss of language, the first language to be recalled is the first one that the person learned originally. See also FORGETTING/ MEMORY, THEORIES OF; JACKSON'S LAW.

REFERENCES

Ribot, T. A. (1881). *Les maladies de la memoire*. Paris: Alcan.

Ribot, T. A. (1885). *Les maladies de la personalite*. Paris: Alcan.

RICCO'S/PIPER'S LAWS. The first generalized principle in the area of visual (and cutaneous-thermal) thresholds was developed by the Italian astronomer Annibale Ricco (1844-1919), and states that when considering very small areas of the retina, such as less than 10-degrees of arc, the absolute threshold is inversely proportional to the area that is stimulated. *Ricco's law* holds well for both fovea and periphery areas of the retina where it states that the product of area stimulated times the luminance is a constant for threshold, but for larger areas the law does not apply well. A principle related to *Ricco's law*, called *Piper's law* - named in honor of the German physiologist Hans Edmund Piper (1877-1915), states that for uniform and moderately sized areas of the retina the absolute threshold is inversely proportional to the square root of the area that is stimulated. Thus, the two related laws of visual threshold and retinal area effects may be compared where *Ricco's law* states that $L \times A = C$, and *Piper's law* states that $L \times$ square root of $A = C$ (where $L =$ luminance or extant "brightness," $A =$ amount of retinal area stimulated, and $C = $ a constant for absolute threshold). Neither of these two laws, however, holds over the full range of stimulus areas. Also, *Ricco's law* deals with "spatial" summation in the visual system, whereas another related law, the *Bunsen-Roscoe law*, deals with "temporal" summation and states that $IT = C$ (where $I =$ threshold intensity or "brightness," $T =$ light flash duration up to .1 second, and $C = $ a constant). See also BUNSEN-ROSCOE LAW; VISION/ SIGHT, THEORIES OF.

REFERENCES

Ricco, A. (1877). Relazione fra il minimo angolo visuale e l'intensita luminosa. *Memorie della Regia Accademia di Scienze, Lettre/Arti in Modena, 17*, 47-160.

Piper, H. E. (1911). Uber die netzhautstrome. *Archiv der Anatomisch und Physiologie, Leipzig, 5*, 85-132.

RIGHT-SHIFT THEORY. In the research area of handedness (cf., Corballis, 1997) and brain function, Marian Annett (2002) proposes her *right-shift theory* (*R-ST*) that attempts to explain the relationship between left- and right-handedness, and left- and right-brain specialization. Statistically, approximately 90 percent of people in the general population demonstrate *right-handedness*, i.e., *left-hemisphere dominance* for motor control. *R-ST* suggests that handedness in humans and non-human primates depends on chance but that it is weighted/biased towards right-handedness in most individuals due to a variable called "right-hemisphere disadvantage." *R-ST* argues for the existence of a single *gene* that accounts for a "right-shift" tendency that evolved in humans for the purpose of facilitating the growth of *speech* in the *left hemisphere* of the brain. Thus, *R-ST* describes a *right-shift* factor for *left-cerebral dominance*. *R-ST* has implications for a wide diversity of issues concerning human abilities and disabilities, including both verbal and nonverbal intelligence, spatial reasoning, dyslexia and educational progress, mental illness, and performance and skills in sports activities. In another line of reasoning concerning *handedness*, Corballis (2003) observes that the strong predominance of right-handedness appears to be a uniquely human characteristic, whereas the left-cerebral dominance for vocalization occurs in many species, including birds, frogs, and mammals. It is speculated that right-handedness may have emerged because of an association between manual gestures and vocalization in the evolution of language; Corballis argues that language evolved from manual gestures, which gradually incorporated vocal elements. Such a transition presumably arrived via changes in the function of *Broca's area* in the brain [i.e., the cerebral area, named after the French physician Paul Broca (1824-1880), that is involved in the *production* of speech] where in monkeys its homologue has nothing to do with vocal control, but contains the so-called *mirror neurons* that embody the production of manual-reaching movements as well as the perception of the same movements performed by others. The *mirror neurons* system is bilateral in monkeys, but mainly left-hemispheric in humans where it is involved both with vocalizations and manual actions. Based on evidence that *Broca's area* is enlarged on the left side in *Homo habilis*, it is suggested that a link between gesture/action and vocalization may go back about two million years, even though other evidence indicates that speech may not have become fully functional or autonomous until *Homo sapiens* appeared on the scene about 170,000 years ago. See also DARWIN'S EVOLUTION THEORY; GALTON'S LAWS; GENETICS, LAWS OF; LANGUAGE ACQUISITION THEORY; LANGUAGE ORIGINS, THEORIES OF; LATERALITY THEORIES; MENDEL'S LAWS/PRINCIPLES; MIRROR NEURONS THEORY; SPEECH THEORIES.

REFERENCES

Corballis, M. C. (1997). The genetics and evolution of handedness. *Psychological Review, 104*, 714-727.

Annett, M. (2002). *Handedness and brain asymmetry: the right-shift theory.* Philadelphia, PA: Psychology Press.

Corballis, M. C. (2003). From mouth to hand: Gesture, speech, and the evolution of right-handedness. *The Behavioral and Brain Sciences, 26*, 199-260.

RINGELMANN EFFECT. See SOCIAL LOAFING EFFECT.

RISK AVERSION EFFECT. See DECISION-MAKING THEORIES.

RISKY-SHIFT/CHOICE SHIFT EFFECT. See DECISION-MAKING THEORIES.

ROECKELEIN'S LAW. In the spirit and tradition of *Maier's law* and *Reber's law*, among others (i.e., where psychologists frivolously and satirically formulate and enunciate some principle, identifying it with their *own*

names), I, similarly, thrust myself into the "eponymic milieu," and offer the present psychological law or principle that applies to the joint areas of perception and psychopathology. *Roeckelein's law* invokes the verb form of the word *pathology* by coining the term *pathologizing*; and *Roeckelein's law* refers to a social-cognitive tendency for individuals to perceive - by either *overpathologizing* (i.e., augmenting) or *underpathologizing* (i.e., discounting) - mental disorders in *other* persons (cf., *medical student syndrome* - the tendency for medical students to perceive new illnesses/symptoms in *themselves* as they study new diseases). Thus, in assessing, regarding, or evaluating another person (as we often do in our "mental mini-experiments" and covert hypotheses-testing activities when interacting with others), we may either *underpathologize* the target person in terms of her/his actual mental health (thereby exhibiting a "discount-ing process" in our perceptions) or we may *overpathologize* the target individual concern-ing his/her actual mental health (thereby exhibit-ing an "augmenting process" in our percep-tions). *Roeckelein's law* is consistent with other traditional psychological principles in which our social, perceptual, and cognitive evaluations of other individuals are influenced by "causative" and "explanatory" variables, such as mental set, predispositions, balance theory, cognitive dissonance theory, stereotypes, prejudices, figure-ground relationships, contextual setting, prior experiences and expectations, simultaneous contrast, and available veridical and background information concerning the target individual. *Roeckelein's law* may be observed, readily, in situations where two (or more) psychologists attempt to communicate with each other. See also ATTRIBUTION THEORY; EXPECTANCY THEORY; COGNITIVE DISSONANCE THEORY; FIGURE-GROUND RELATIONSHIPS, PRINCIPLE OF; GESTALT THEORY/LAWS; IMPRESSION FORMATION, THEORIES OF; KELLY'S PERSONAL CONSTRUCT THEORY; MAIER'S LAW; MIND/MENTAL SET, LAW OF; MURPHY'S LAW(S); PREJUDICE, THEORIES OF; REBER'S LAW; TOLMAN'S THEORY.

REFERENCE

Roeckelein, J. E. (2002). A demonstration of undergraduate students' first impressions and their ratings of pathology. *Psychological Reports, 90,* 613-618.

ROELOFS EFFECT. See APPENDIX A.

ROGERS' THEORY OF PERSONALITY.
The American psychologist/psychotherapist Carl Rogers (1902-1987) developed a *humanistic theory of personality* that essentially is phenomenological in nature and falls between the *psychoanalytic* approach and the *behavioristic* orientation. The *humanistic* outlook (called the *third force* in psychology) toward personality is one of "optimism" where it is argued that individuals contain within themselves the potentialities for healthy and creative growth if they accept the responsibility for their own lives. This orientation differs from the "pessimism" of the *psychoanalytic* approach and the "mechanization" of the *behavioristic* approach. The phenomenological aspect of *Rogers' theory* refers to an emphasis on the person's "inner life" where experiences, values, beliefs, perceptions, and feelings are examined. Rogers' notions of personality and personality-change grew out of his clinical experience and therapeutic relationships, which also led to his development of a method of psychotherapy called *nondirective,* or *client-centered,* therapy. In *client-centered* therapy, the individual comes to perceive the therapist as providing "unconditional positive regard" as well as gaining an understanding of one's internal frame of reference. The goal in this approach is to help a person's *self-concept* become more congruent with her or his total experience and to become a fully functioning individual. Rogers offers a relatively simple theory of how people can change their attitudes and behavior within a permissive climate with an empathic therapist. He presents, also, a more sophisticated 19-proposition *theory of self* that is highlighted by postulates such as: reality for the person is the field as perceived; perceptions may be ignored when they are inconsistent with the concept of *self;* and when the *self-concept* is safe from threat, it can examine contradictory perceptions and incorporate them into a revised concept of self. Rogers' *theory of self* was later expanded and published as a more formal theory. The dynamics of *Rogers' personality theory* focuses on the selective tendencies of the organism to grow, actualize, enhance, and maintain its experiences where the major motivating force is the *self-actualizing* drive, and the main goal of life is to become a "whole" (i.e., "self-actualized") person (cf., the *growth principle* - Rogers' view that in an atmosphere free of coercion and distortion, one's creative and integrative energies lead the individual to optimal self-esteem, fuller insight and adaptation, and realization of one's potential). Rogers' motivational theory of personality emphasizes the two learned needs of "positive regard" and "self-regard." Rogers' *client-centered therapy* is an established and widely used method of treatment, and his *person-centered theory* has become a significant stimulus for research in personality psychology. On the other hand, criticisms of *Rogers' theory* include the observation that his approach is based on a naïve type of phenomenology where data from unreliable self-reports are used; and the assertion by psychoanalytically oriented psychologists that Rogers ignores the influence of the unconscious in determining behavior. See also BEHAVIORIST THEORY; FREUD'S THEORY OF PERSONALITY; MASLOW'S THEORY OF PERSONALITY; PERSONALITY THEORIES; SELF-CONCEPT THEORY; SKINNER'S DESCRIPTIVE BEHAVIOR/OPERANT CONDITIONING THEORY.

REFERENCES

Rogers, C. (1942). *Counseling and psychotherapy: Newer concepts in practice.* Boston: Houghton Mifflin.

Rogers, C. (1947). Some observations on the organization of personality. *American Psychologist, 2,* 358-368.

Smith, M. (1950). The phenomenological approach in personality theory: Some critical remarks. *Journal of Abnormal and Social Psychology, 45,* 516-522.

Rogers, C. (1951). *Client-centered therapy: Its current practice, implications, and theory.* Boston: Houghton Mifflin.

Rogers, C., & Skinner, B. F. (1956). Some issues concerning the control of human behavior: A symposium. *Science, 124*, 1057-1066.

Rogers, C. (1959). A theory of therapy, personality, and interpersonal relationships, as developed in the client-centered framework. In S. Koch (Ed.), *Psychology: A study of a science*. Vol. 3. New York: McGraw-Hill.

Rogers, C. (1961). *On becoming a person*. Boston: Houghton Mifflin.

Krause, M. (1964). An analysis of Carl R. Rogers' theory of personality. *Genetic Psychology Monographs, 69*, 49-99.

Epstein, S. (1973). The self-concept revisited or a theory of a theory. *American Psychologist, 28*, 404-416.

Raimy, V. (1975). *Misunderstandings of the self: Cognitive psychotherapy and the misconception hypothesis*. San Francisco: Jossey-Bass.

Rogers, C. (1980). *A way of being*. Boston: Houghton Mifflin.

ROLE-CONFUSION HYPOTHESIS. See ERIKSON'S THEORY OF PERSONALITY.

ROLE-CONSTRUCT THEORY. See KELLY'S PERSONAL CONSTRUCT THEORY.

ROLE-ENACTMENT THEORY. See HYPNOSIS/HYPNOTISM, THEORIES OF.

ROLE-EXPECTATIONS HYPOTHESIS. See WORK/CAREER/OCCUPATION, THEORIES OF.

ROLE-ROLE THEORY. See SELF-CONCEPT THEORY.

ROLE THEORY OF PERSONALITY. See PERSONALITY THEORIES.

ROLFING THEORY/THERAPY. The *rolfing theory/therapy* refers to a massage treatment or technique of psychotherapy - also known formally as *structural integration theory* - that was developed originally in the 1930s, and popularized in the 1960s and 1970s, by the American physical therapist Ida Pauline Rolf (1896-1979), and consists of deep penetration/massage via the fingers, knuckles, elbows, and hands into the client's muscles in order to correct postural deficits and to "realign" the body vertically and symmetrically with the gravity field. The theory postulates that the body assumes particular characteristic postures due to learned muscle arrangements, and that if one's muscle arrangements are changed, then corresponding personality changes will occur, also, in the client. For example, if the person walks with a shuffle or hesitant gait, then teaching him or her - via postural/muscular changes - to walk briskly, upright, and purposively will influence that individual's personality in positive ways as well. See also ALEXANDER MODEL/TECHNIQUE; PSEUDOSCIENTIFIC/UNCONVENTIONAL THEORIES.

REFERENCE

Rolf, I. P. (1977). *Rolfing: The integration of human structures*. Santa Monica, CA: Dennis-Landman.

ROMEO AND JULIET EFFECT. See REACTANCE THEORY.

ROSENTHAL EFFECT. See EXPERIMENTER EFFECTS.

ROTATING HEAD/PORTRAIT ILLUSION. See APPENDIX A.

ROTTER'S SOCIAL LEARNING THEORY. = internal-external control of reinforcement. The American psychologist Julian Bernard Rotter (1916-) formulated a *social learning theory* that combines the Hullian concept of *reinforcement* with the Tolmanian concept of *cognition* to describe situations where the individual has a number of behavioral options (*behavioral potential theory*). In Rotter's approach, each potential behavior of the person is related to an outcome that has a particular *reinforcement value* associated with it, as well as an *expectancy* concerning the likelihood of the reinforcers following each behavior. Thus, *Rotter's theory* may be characterized as an *expectancy-value model* where the likelihood of a behavior's occurrence is a function of both the *value* of the reinforcer associated with it and the *probability* of the reinforcer occurring. In *Rotter's model*, the value and probability of various reinforcers are unique to the person, and it is the person's internal value and expectancy calculations that are important rather than some objective measure of value and probability. Rotter proposes that situations may be assessed, also, in terms of the outcomes (i.e., expectancy and value of reinforcers) associated with specific behaviors, as well as suggesting that individuals develop expectations that hold across many situations (called *generalized expectancies*). Among Rotter's *generalized expectancies* are *interpersonal trust* (i.e., the degree to which one can rely on the word of others), and *internal* versus *external locus of control of reinforcement* (also called, simply, *locus of control*), which has received a great deal of research attention in psychology. According to Rotter's approach, persons who score high on measures of *internal locus of control* expect that outcomes or reinforcers depend mostly on their *own* efforts, whereas persons scoring high on *external locus of control* have an expectancy that outcomes depend largely on external forces such as *others*, including the factors of luck, chance, and fate. Theoretically, *external locus of control* types of individuals typically feel relatively helpless in relation to events. Rotter developed the "Internal-External (I-E) Scale" to measure individual differences in *generalized expectancies* concerning the extent to which punishments and rewards are under *external* or *internal* control. Variations of the I-E Scale have appeared, also, in research in the areas of health and children's behavior. Although *Rotter's theory* had a large impact on research in personality and social learning psychology for about a decade (his 1966 monograph on *generalized expectancies* was the most frequently cited single article in the social sciences since 1969), its influence has declined recently - perhaps due to the fact that the *locus of control* scale has been found to be more complex than was expected originally. See also BANDURA'S THEORY; EXPECTANCY THEORY; HULL'S LEARNING THEORY; REINFORCEMENT THEORY; TOLMAN'S THEORY.

REFERENCES

Rotter, J. B. (1954). *Social learning and clinical psychology*. Englewood Cliffs, NJ: Prentice-Hall.

Phares, E. (1957). Expectancy changes in skill and chance situations. *Journal of Abnormal and Social Psychology*, 54, 339-342.

Lefcourt, H. (1966). Internal versus external control of reinforcement: A review. *Psychological Bulletin*, 65, 206-220.

Rotter, J. B. (1966). Generalized expectancies for internal versus external control of reinforcement. *Psychological Mono-graphs*, 80, No. 609.

Rotter, J. B. (1971). Generalized expectancies for interpersonal trust. *American Psychologist*, 26, 443-452.

Rotter, J. B. (1975). Some problems and misconceptions related to the construct of internal versus external control of reinforcement. *Journal of Consulting and Clinical Psychology*, 43, 56-67.

Rotter, J. B. (1981). The psychological situation in social learning theory. In D. Magnusson (Ed.), *Toward a psychology of situations*. Hillsdale, NJ: Erlbaum.

Feather, N. (Ed.) (1982). *Expectancies and actions: Expectancy-value models in psychology*. Hillsdale, NJ: Erlbaum.

Lefcourt, H. (Ed.) (1984). *Research with the locus of control construct*. Orlando, FL: Academic Press.

Rotter, J. B. (1990). Internal versus external controls of reinforcement. *American Psychologist*, 45, 489-493.

ROUGH-AND-READY THEORY. See ATTITUDE/ATTITUDE CHANGE, THEORIES OF.

RUBIN FIGURE/ILLUSION. See APPENDIX A.

RULE LEARNING AND COMPLEXITY. See CONCEPT LEARNING/CONCEPT FORMATION, THEORIES OF.

RUMOR INTENSITY FORMULA. See RUMOR TRANSMISSION THEORY.

RUMOR TRANSMISSION THEORY. A *rumor* may be defined as an unconfirmed message passed from one person to another in face-to-face interaction (cf., children's game of "Gossip" or "Chinese Whispers") that refers to an object, person, or situation rather than to an idea or theory. Thus, the notions of "gossip," "grapevine," "hearsay," "tattle-tale," and "scuttlebutt" (along with the *snowball effect* - the increased magnification of material upon the retelling of it) are included in *rumor transmission*. The American sociologist H. Taylor Buckner (1965) notes that whether a rumor is truthful or untruthful is unimportant in studying *rumor transmission*. The essential features of a rumor are that it is unconfirmed at the time of transmission, and that it is passed from one person to another. Buckner's theoretical framework for *rumor transmission* is that the individual is in one of three orientations, situations, or "sets" vis-à-vis a rumor: a *critical set*, an *uncritical set*, or a *transmission set*. If the person takes a *critical set*, he/she is capable of using "critical ability" to separate the true from the false in rumors. If an *uncritical set* is adopted, the person is unable to use "critical ability" to test the truth of the rumor. In the *transmission set* - usually found in laboratory experiments - the individual's "critical ability" is considered to be irrelevant. Thus, in *Buckner's theory of rumor transmission*, whether rumors become more or less accurate as they are passed on depends on the individual's "set" and on the structure of the situation in which the rumor originates and spreads subsequently. In the *rumor intensity formula* - a theoretical proposition advanced by the American psychologists Gordon Willard Allport (1897-1967) and Leo Joseph Postman (1918-) - the suggestion is made that the *strength* of a rumor depends on its importance multiplied by the difficulty of falsifying it. In general, rumors seem to be propagated and governed by the same processes that underlie the phenomena of *assimilation* (i.e., the distortion of a memory via attempts to make it similar to other already-existing memories), *sharpening* (i.e., the exaggeration/magnification of certain prominent details in memory/perception), and *leveling* (i.e., the tendency to perceive/remember material as "good gestalts" where unimportant and incongruous details disappear gradually over time). The technique of *serial reproduction* - a procedure for studying memory in a social context - has been used, also, as a laboratory model of *rumor transmission*. This approach - developed, described, and popularized by the American psychologist Ernest N. Henderson (1869-1967) and the English psychologist Sir Frederic C. Bartlett (1886-1969) - involves a person reading a short story and then telling it from memory to a second person who, in turn, tells it from memory to a third person, etc., in a "round-robin" procedure that is similar to the child's game of "Gossip." When this method is employed, the phenomena of *leveling, sharpening,* and *assimilation* typically are exhibited after about only eight separate transmissions. In a variation of the *serial reproduction* technique, an original stimulus that is different from the short-story stimulus/material - such as a drawing that is reproduced serially from memory by each of the members of the group - may be used to achieve the same results. See also GESTALT THEORY/LAWS; INFECTION THEORY/EFFECT; PERCEPTION (I. GENERAL), THEORIES OF.

REFERENCES

Henderson, E. N. (1903). Introductory: Education and experimental psychology. *Psychological Monographs, 5,* 1-94.

Bartlett, F. C. (1932). *Remembering: A study in experimental and social psychology.* Cambridge, UK: Cambridge University Press.

Allport, G. W., & Postman, L. J. (1947). *The psychology of rumor.* New York: Holt, Rinehart, and Winston.

Charus, A. (1953). The basic law of rumor. *Journal of Abnormal and Social Psychology, 48,* 313-314.

Buckner, H. T. (1965). A theory of rumor transmission. *Public Opinion Quarterly, 29,* 54-70.

Rosnow, R. L. (1980). Psychology of rumor reconsidered. *Psychological Bulletin, 87,* 578-591.

RUMPELSTILTSKIN EFFECT/PHENOMENON. See APPENDIX A.

RUTHERFORD'S FREQUENCY THEO-RY. See AUDITION/HEARING, THEORIES OF.

S

SALIENCE HYPOTHESIS. See DREAM THEORY.

SAME-DIFFERENT THEORY. See SELF-CONCEPT THEORY.

SAMPLE SIZE FALLACY. See PROBABILITY THEORY/LAWS.

SANDER/LUCKIESH PARALLELO-GRAM ILLUSION. See APPENDIX A.

SANTAYANA'S THEORY OF HUMOR. The Spanish-born American philosopher and poet George Santayana (1863-1952) challenged both the *incongruity* and *superiority theories of humor*. *Santayana's theory of humor* indicates that amusement (i.e., the feeling that prompts laughter) is more directly a physical thing than *incongruity* and *superiority theories* claim - it depends on a certain amount of nervous excitement (e.g., a person may be amused merely by being tickled or by hearing or seeing other people who laugh). Although he does critique both the *incongruity and superiority humor theories*, Santayana does not totally reject those theories; for instance, he agrees that people often laugh in situations involving incongruity or degradation. Thus, according to Santayana, when we react to a comic incongruity or degradation, it is never those things in themselves that give pleasure but, rather, it is the excitement and stimulation caused by the person's perception of those things. Santayana insists that it is impossible to enjoy the incongruity itself - as some versions of *incongruity theory* provide - because, as rational animals, humans are averse constitutionally or innately to absurdity, incongruity, or nonsense in any form. Santayana, like Plato before him, maintains that amusement is a pleasure that is mixed with pain, and that is why people prefer to get their mental stimulation - including humor - *without* incongruity. The essence of humor, according to Santayana, is that amusing

weakness should be combined with an "amicable humanity." See also HUMOR, THEORIES OF; INCONGRUITY/ INCONSISTENCY THEORIES OF HUMOR; PLATO'S THEORY OF HUMOR; SUPERIORITY THEORIES OF HUMOR.

REFERENCE

Santayana, G. (1896/1904). *The sense of beauty.* New York: Scribner's.

SATIATION/DISGUST, LAW OF. See CONDUCT, LAWS OF.

SATISFICING HYPOTHESIS. See EXPECTED UTILITY THEORY.

SAUCE BEARNAISE EFFECT. See GARCIA EFFECT.

SAW-TOOTHED THEORY. See LEADERSHIP, THEORIES OF.

SAYRE'S LAW. See MURPHY'S LAW(S).

SCALAR TIMING THEORY. = scalar expectancy theory. *Scalar timing theory* is the most completely developed general quantitative model of animal timing today. It attempts to achieve the following four goals of timing/temporal search: to account for data from human timing experiments as well as for animal timing experiments; to account for data from perceptual experiments ("time estimation"); to account for timing behavior not only in the range of seconds to minutes, but also for shorter and longer durations; and to account for inter-event distributions as well as to fixed time from some event until reinforcement. Three versions of *timing theories*, along with their hypothetical constructs, include: *scalar timing theory* (pulses from an "oscillator" are summed in an "accumulator" and stored in a distribution device); *behavioral theory of timing* (pulses from an "oscillator" advance behavioral states, each of which has some strength); and *multiple oscillator model* (half-phases from "multiple oscillators" are stored in an "autoassociation matrix"). *Scalar timing theory* has been categorized, also, into *information-processing theories* and *connectionist theories*. The notion of an "internal clock" of timing behavior is considered by many researchers to be an *information processing system/model* that contains a number of components such as a "pacemaker," a switch that may connect the pacemaker to an "accumulator," a working (short-term) memory, and a reference (long-term) memory. According to this view, the rate of the pacemaker is not tied to the rate of reinforcement (as it is in the *behavioral theory of timing*), although it may vary randomly between intervals that are being timed. The *connectionist theories of timing* were developed to determine whether an *associationist theory of timing* could account for the data that were explained by *scalar timing theory*. In terms of their "psychological modularity," the three timing theories may be considered to be quite similar; that is, they all have information-processing stages of perception, memory, and decisions; however, their "representations" of each of these stages are different. For instance, J. Crystal reports that a *connectionist theory of time* (based on data from rats' judgments of time intervals in a choice procedure) with "multiple oscillators" is preferred over the *linear timing hypothesis* of *scalar timing theory*. The unique strength of *scalar timing theory* is that it has explicit solutions for several experimental procedures, and has provided precise fits to mean functions and to correlation patterns between indexes of behavior. The notable strength of the *behavioral theory of timing*, on the other hand, is that it provides a parsimonious account of data with emphasis on observed behavior. The outstanding feature of the *multiple oscillator model* is that it provides qualitative fits to some aspects (such as "periodicities" and "systematic residuals") of timing behavior. It may be speculated (e.g., Church, 1997) that the next generation of *timing theories* will include the following features: standards for description and quantitative evaluation; integration of neurobiological evidence into the timing theories; modification of current theories and development of a new theory that deals more efficiently with the combined accounts of the perceptual representation of time, the nature of temporal memory, and decision processes. In another case (Weardon, 1999), it is suggested that the future tripartite division of *scalar timing theory* into "clock," "memory," and "decision processes" is a use-ful general framework for studying timing, including issues related to its neurobiological basis. See also ASSOCIATIVE LEARNING IN ANIMALS, THEORIES OF; BEHAVIORAL THEORY OF TIMING; INFORMATION/INFORMATION-PROCESSING THEORIES; PSYCHOLOGICAL TIME, MODELS OF; TIME, THEORIES OF.

REFERENCES

Gibbon, J. (1977). Scalar expectancy theory and Weber's law in animal timing. *Psychological Review, 84,* 279-325.

Church, R. M., & Broadbent, H. (1991). A connectionist model of timing. In M. Commons & S. Grossberg (Eds.), *Neural network models of conditioning and action.* Hillsdale, NJ: Erlbaum.

Gibbon, J. (1991). Origins of scalar timing. *Learning and Motivation, 22,* 3-38.

Gibbon, J., & Church, R. M. (1992). Comparison of variance and covariance patterns in parallel and serial theories of timing. *Journal of the Experimental Analysis of Behavior, 57,* 393-406.

Church, R. M. (1997). Timing and temporal search. In C. M. Bradshaw & E. Szabadi (Eds.), *Time and behavior: Psychological and neurobehavioral analyses.* Amsterdam, Netherlands: North-Holland.

Crystal, J. (1999). Systematic nonlinearities in the perception of temporal intervals. *Journal of Experimental Psychology: Animal Behavior Processes, 25,* 3-17.

Weardon, J. H. (1999). Exploring and developing scalar timing theory. *Behavioral Processes* (Special issue. Interval timing: Is there a clock?), *45,* 3-21.

Church, R. M. (2003). A concise introduction to scalar timing theory. In W. H. Meck (Ed.), *Functional and neural mechanisms of internal timing.* Boca Raton, FL: CRC Press.

SCALE ATTENUATION EFFECT. See MEASUREMENT THEORY.

SCANNING HYPOTHESIS/MODEL. See DREAM THEORY; ESTES' STIMULUS SAMPLING THEORY.

SCAPEGOAT THEORY. See PREJUDICE, THEORIES OF.

SCHACHTER-SINGER'S THEORY OF EMOTION. The American psychologists Stanley Schachter (1922-) and Jerome Singer (1929-) proposed a *theory of emotions* (called the *cognitive-appraisal/evaluation theory*) in the 1960s that challenged certain aspects of both the *cognitive theory of emotions* and the earlier *James-Lange theory*. Where these other theories assumed that each emotion is associated with a specific physiological state or condition (cf., Funkenstein, 1955), Schachter and Singer argued that individuals who are in a state of physiological arousal for which they have no explanation will *label* that state as an emotion that is appropriate to the situation in which they find themselves (e.g., the arousal will be labeled as "happy" if the person is at a party, but the *same* arousal state will be labeled as "angry" if the person is confronting another person in an argument). The experiments of Schachter and his associates point out the fact that emotions seem to depend on two components (*Schachter-Singer's theory* is sometimes also called a *two-factor theory*: (1) some kind of objective physiological arousal and (2) a subjective cognitive or mental process and appraisal whereby persons interpret and label their bodily changes. People who have no reasonable or objective explanation for their internal, emotional, or aroused state may interpret their mood in subjective terms according to their perception of the present existing environment. The *Schachter-Singer theory*, also, has been referred to as the *jukebox theory of emotions* because one's physiology is aroused by some stimulus, where the arousing stimulus is compared to the coin placed in a jukebox. The stimulus sets off patterns of brain activity, especially in the hypothalamus that, in turn, activates the autonomic nervous system and the endocrine glands, causing a state of general physiological arousal. The body's sensory receptors report these physiological changes to the brain. However, the sensations are vague and can be labeled in many different ways, just as a jukebox activated by a coin can be made to play any one of a number of different songs, depending on which button is pushed. Although the experiments of Schachter and his associates seem to support a *cognitive theory of emotions*, they may actually come closer to the *James-Lange theory* because *Schachter-Singer's theory* implies that the physiological arousal state comes about first, and the cognitive label that defines the emotion comes afterward. Some theorists [e.g., the American psychologist Magda B. Arnold (1903-2002)] argue that Schachter's experiments are interesting but not relevant for a theory of emotion inasmuch as people do not normally look for a label to identify their emotions. The alternative view is that emotions are felt without attending to the physiological changes that accompany them, and people react to the object or event and not to a physiological state within themselves. On the other hand, although some recent studies of emotion have not always agreed with Schachter and Singer's viewpoint, many investigators do offer support for the contention that people often interpret their emotions in terms of external cues. The *Schachter-Singer theory* has been fruitful, also, in suggesting the important research question of the origin or source of one's physiological arousal. For example, one source of arousal that has been explored in recent years is the discrepancy between *actual* and *expected* events. According to the Austrian-born American American psychologist George Mandler's (1924-) *discrepancy-evaluation/constructivity theory*, the greater the gap between what a person *expects* and what *actually* happens in a given situation, the greater the resulting arousal. Such arousal is interpreted, then, cognitively to yield subjective experiences of emotion. The *discrepancy-evaluation/constructivity theory* suggests, further, that arousal level determines the intensity of the emotional experience, whereas cognitive evaluation determines its specific identity or quality. Thus, the *discrepancy-evaluation/constructivity theory* extends the *Schachter-Singer theory* by identifying a major cause of the arousal that people interpret - in terms of external cues - as one emotion or another. See also ARNOLD'S THEORY OF

EMOTIONS; ATTRIBUTION THEORY; COGNITIVE THEORIES OF EMOTIONS; EMOTIONS, THEORIES/LAWS OF; JAMES-LANGE/ LANGE-JAMES THEORY OF EMOTIONS.

REFERENCES

Funkenstein, D. (1955). The physiology of fear and anger. *Scientific American, 192*, 74-80.

Schachter, S., & Singer, J. (1962). Cognitive, social, and physiological determinants of emotional state. *Psychological Review, 69*, 379-399.

Mandler, G. (1990). A constructivity theory of emotion. In N. Stein, B. Leventhal, & T. Tragbasso (Eds.), *Psychological and biological approaches to emotion.* Hillsdale, NJ: Erlbaum.

Sinclair, R., Hoffman, C., Mark, M., Martin, L., & Pickering, T. (1994). Construct accessibility and the misattribution of arousal: Schachter and Singer revisited. *Psychological Science, 5*, 15-19.

SCHAFER-MURPHY EFFECT. See GESTALT THEORY/LAWS.

SCHANZ'S COLOR VISION THEORY. See COLOR VISION, THEORIES/LAWS OF.

SCHEMA THEORY OF MEMORY. See BARTLETT'S SCHEMATA THEORY.

SCHIZOPHRENIA, THEORIES OF. The term *schizophrenia* is a general label for a number of psychotic disorders with various behavioral, emotional, and cognitive features. The term was originated by the Swiss psychiatrist Eugen Bleuler (1857-1939) in 1911, who offered it as a replacement for the term *dementia praecox* (i.e., "precocious madness/ deterioration/insanity"). In its literal meaning, *schizophrenia* is a "splitting of the mind," a connotation reflecting a dissociation or separation between the functions of feeling/emotion, on one hand, and those of cognition/ thinking on the other hand. The "split" in schizophrenia implies a horizontal direction, rather than a vertical direction (as indicated in the disorder called *multiple personality*, which is confused, often, by laypeople with *schizophrenia*). In the simplest terms, *multiple personality* is a "split *within* self," whereas *schizophrenia* is a "split *between* self and others." Various categories, descriptions, and subtypes of schizophrenia have been developed (e.g., acute, borderline, catatonic, childhood or infantile autism, chronic, disorganized, hebephrenic, latent, paranoid/paraphrenic, process, reactive, residual, schizoaffective, simple, and undifferentiated), but there are certain common aspects to all types: (1) deterioration from previous levels of social, cognitive, and vocational functioning; (2) onset before midlife (i.e., about 45-50 years of age); (3) a duration of at least six months; and (4) a pattern of psychotic features including thought disturbances, bizarre delusions, hallucinations, disturbed sense of self, and a loss of reality testing. The *progressive teleological-regression hypothesis* (Arieti, 1974) is a theory of schizophrenia that maintains that the disorder results from a process of active concretization, that is, a purposeful returning to lower levels of psychodynamic and behavioral adaptation that - although momentarily effective in reducing anxiety - tends ultimately toward repetitive behaviors and results in a failure to maintain integration [cf., *deviant filter theory* - holds that patients diagnosed with schizophrenia are unable to ignore unimportant features and stimuli and, therefore, cannot attend to stimuli of greater importance in the environment; and the *von Domarus principle* - named after the Dutch psychiatrist Eilhardt von Domarus (dates unknown) - states that persons with schizophrenia perceive two things as identical simply because they have identical properties or predicates, and that whereas the normal person interprets events on the basis of their objective features, the schizophrenic individual interprets events in idiosyncratic and unrealistic ways; the principle is what logicians have known for over 2,000 years as the "fallacy of the undistributed middle," and is not necessarily restricted to the reasoning abilities in schizophrenics]. In general, current *theories of schizophrenia* focus on biochemical abnormalities, with some cases of schizophrenia appearing to be of genetic origin, perhaps triggered by environmental stresses (cf., *neurodevelopmental hypothesis* - holds that schizophrenia is due largely to abnormalities in the prenatal or neonatal development of the individual's nervous system, leading to deficits in brain anatomy and behavior; *viral hypothesis of schizophrenia* - postulates that schizophrenia may be caused, or precipitated, by a viral infection in the person; *brain-spot hypothesis* - refers to theories that emphasize organic factors in the etiology of mental disease; the *mind-twist hypothesis* - emphasizes a functional, rather than a structural, basis of mental disorders; and *Sutton's law* - named after the notorious Willie Sutton (1902-1980) who robbed banks because "that's where the money is," and is the principle - when applied to clinical diagnosis - that one should look for a disorder where, or in whom, it is most likely to be found and emphasizes the predisposing factors in all diseases and disorders). The major theoretical models of the etiology of schizophrenia are the *specific gene theory* - assumes that the disorder is caused by one or more faulty genes that produce metabolic disturbances (cf., the *founder effect* - relates to population genetics and the high rate of schizophrenia in residents of Sweden above the Artic Circle); *psychoanalytic theory* - gives primacy to aggressive impulses, and suggests that the threats of the intense *id* impulses may provoke schizophrenia depending on the strength of the *ego*; however, few data are available on the psychoanalytic position, and there is no evidence that *ego* impairments cause schizophrenia; *labeling theory* - assumes that the crucial factor in schizophrenia is the act of assigning a diagnostic label to the person where the label then influences the way in which the person continues to behave and, also, determines the reactions of other people to the individual's behavior; that is, the social role *is* the disorder, and it is determined by the labeling process; *experiential/familial theory* - assumes that one's family is a key factor in producing schizophrenic behavior in the person where - in a process called "mystification" - the parent systematically strips the child's feeling and perceptions about himself or herself and the world of all validity so that the child comes to doubt his/her hold on reality (e.g., R. Laing's *theory of schizophrenia* refers to a "double-bind, no-win situation;" cf., *expressed emotions effect* - holds that

there is a high relapse rate in schizophrenia that is to be associated with critical emotions expressed toward mental patients by their families, and indicates that schizophrenia may be a somewhat "protective" device to escape from an undesirable social situation); *biochemical/neurological theories* - at this time, no single biochemical or neurological theory has unequivocal support [cf., *Fiamberti hypothesis* - named after the Italian psychosurgeon Amarro M. Fiamberti (dates unknown), is an outdated theory positing that schizophrenia results from a nervous-tissue deficiency of acetylcholine that may be secondary to an infectious/toxic condition; and the *glutamate hypothesis* - suggests that schizophrenia is caused by an activity deficit at the glutamate synapses]. However, there are promising, but incomplete, findings concerning areas both of brain pathology and of excess activity of the neurotransmitter *dopamine* regarding the incidence of schizophrenia. Other theories include: *social class theory* - emphasizes the consistent correlations found between lowest socioeconomic class and the diagnosis of *schizophrenia*; in this category, the *sociogenic hypothesis* states that simply being in a low social class may in itself cause schizophrenia, and the *social drift theory* (also called the *downward drift hypothesis* and *social selection theory of pathology*) suggests that during the course of their developing psychosis, schizophrenics may "drift" into the poverty-ridden areas of the city, or may drift downwardly to lower levels and standards of socialization and end up in pitiful circumstances; the *environmental stress/family theories* - view schizophrenia as a reaction to a stressful environment, or family, that presents overwhelming and anxiety-producing conditions; the *diathesis-stress hypothesis* - refers to a predisposition to develop a particular disorder: in this case, schizophrenia, as a result of interaction between stressful demands and personal traits; the term *schizophrenogenic parent/mother hypothesis* was coined [by the German-American physician Frieda Fromm-Reichmann (1889-1957)] to refer to the cold, rejecting, distant, aloof, dominant, and conflict-inducing parent who is said to produce schizophrenia in one's offspring (cf., *refrigerator parents theory* - an obsolete theory of autism that characterizes the autistic child's parents as cold, unloving, intellectual, and relatively uninterested in their children). Early researchers studying schizophrenia looked for, and found, pathology in one or both parents of psychotic children; however, more current research suggests that there is no valid scientific evidence confirming the speculation that parental disorders precede and/or precipitate their children's disturbances. Another prominent early viewpoint, the *double-bind theory* (that is lacking, also, in empirical support) emphasizes the situation faced by a person who receives contradictory or "mixed" messages from a powerful person (usually the parent) who has difficulty with close affectionate relationships but cannot admit to such feelings. In the *double-bind* scenario, the parent communicates withdrawal and coldness when the child approaches but, then, reaches out toward the child with simulated love when the child pulls back from the coldness; in this way, the child is caught in a *double bind*: no course of action can possibly prove satisfactory, and all assumptions about what she or he is supposed to do will be disconfirmed. The *constitutional-predisposition theory* combines the *genetic* and the *environmental theories* and argues that a variety of disparate dispositions are inherited but that the emergence of a diagnosable schizophrenic disorder is dependent on the degree of these dispositions and the extent to which they are encouraged by particular types of environmental conditions; this point of view has the largest number of adherents among specialists (cf., the largely discredited *seasonality effect/hypothesis* - states that there is a greater prevalence of schizophrenia in persons who are born in the late winter or early spring). The *two-syndrome hypothesis/theory* suggests that schizophrenia is composed of two separate syndromes: Type 1 that is related to *dopamine sensitivity* and produces symptoms such as delusions and hallucinations, and Type 2 that is related to *genetics* and *brain abnormalities* and produces symptoms such as flat effect and social withdrawal. See also LABELING AND DEVIANCE THEORY; PSYCHOPATHOLOGY, THEORIES OF.

REFERENCES

Bleuler, E. (1911/1950). *Dementia praecox: Or the group of schizophrenias*. New York: International Universities Press.

Von Domarus, E. (1944). The specific laws of logic in schizophrenia. In J. S. Kasanin (Ed.), *Language and thought in schizophrenia*. Berkeley, CA: University of California Press.

Fiamberti, A. M. (1950). Acetylcholine in the physio-pathogenesis and therapy of schizophrenia. *Congres International de Psychiatrie, Paris, 4*, 59-84.

Hollingshead, A., & Redlich, F. (1958). *Social class and mental illness: A community study*. New York: Wiley.

Meehl, P. E. (1962). Schizotaxia, schizotypy, schizophrenia. *American Psychologist, 17*, 827-838.

Scheff, T. (1966). *Being mentally ill: A sociological theory*. Chicago: Aldine.

Kohn, M. (1968). Social class and schizophrenia: A critical review. In D. Rosenthal & S. Kety (Eds.), *The transmission of schizophrenia*. Elmsford, NY: Pergamon.

Laing, R. (1969). *The divided self: A study of sanity and madness*. New York: Pantheon.

Rosenthal, D. (1971). *Genetics of psychopathology*. New York: McGraw-Hill.

Gottesman, I., & Shields, J. (1972). *Schizophrenia and genetics: A twin study vantage point*. New York: Academic Press.

Rosenhan, D. (1973). On being sane in insane places. *Science, 197*, 250-258.

Arieti, S. (1974). *Interpretations of schizophrenia*. New York: Basic Books.

Kety, S. (1976). Genetic aspects of schizophrenia. *Psychiatric Annals, 6*, 11-32.

Murphy, J. (1976). Psychiatric labeling in cross-cultural perspective. *Science, 191*, 1019-1028.

Crow, T. (1985). The two syndrome concept: Origins and current status. *Schizophrenia Bulletin, 11*, 471-486.

Gottesman, I. (1991). *Schizophrenia genesis: The origins of madness*. New York: Freeman.

Fowles, D. (1992). Schizophrenia: Diathesis-stress revisited. *Annual Review of Psychology, 43*, 303-336.

Taubes, G. (1994). Will new dopamine receptors offer a key to schizophren-ia? *Science, 265*, 1034-1035.

Walker, E., Kestler, L., Bollini, A., & Hochman, K. M. (2004). Schizophrenia: Etiology and course. *Annual Review of Psychology, 55*, 401-430.

SCHIZOPHRENOGENIC PARENT/ MOTHER HYPOTHESIS. See SCHIZOPHRENIA, THEORIES OF.

SCHOPENHAUER'S THEORY OF HUMOR. The German philosopher Arthur Schopenhauer (1788-1860) proposed - much like Immanuel Kant earlier - an *incongruity theory of humor*. Whereas Kant located the essence of humor in the "evaporation of an expectation," Schopenhauer located it in a "mismatch" between one's sensory knowledge and one's abstract knowledge of things. According to Schopenhauer, what one perceives through the senses are individual aspects with many characteristics, but when the person organizes his/her sense perceptions under abstract concepts the focus is only on a few characteristics of any individual aspect/thing. This practice allows one to lump very different things under the same concept, and to refer to very different things by the same word. *Schopenhauer's theory of humor* suggests that humor arises when one is struck by some clash between a concept and a perception that are "supposed" to be of the same thing. It may be noted, also, that *Schopenhauer's theory of humor* is a "sudden contrast theory of laughter" (cf., Hobbes' *sudden glory theory*) - in addition to being an *incongruity theory* - in which the cause of laughter in every case is simply the *sudden* perception of the incongruity between a concept and the real objects that have been thought through in some relation, and laughter itself is just the expression of such an incongruity. Additionally, Schopenhauer divides the notion of the ludicrous into two species: wit and folly. Wit is viewed as the case in which one has previously known two or more very different real objects (ideas of sense-percep-tion) and has identified them intentionally through the identity of a concept that comprehends them both. On the other hand, folly is seen as the case in which one starts with a concept under which two objects are subsumed, and the difference between them that the person perceives suddenly. Thus, according to Schopenhauer, every ludicrous thing is either a flash of wit or a foolish action, based on whether the sequence goes from the discrepancy of the objects to the identity of the concept, or vice-versa. Schopenhauer asserts that the reason for one's enjoyment of the ludicrous lies in the primacy of the "will," or as he suggests epigrammatically, "No will: no idea, no world." Essentially, in Schopenhauer's view, one's pleasure at the ludicrous arises from the "victory" of knowledge of perception over that of thought. See also HOBBES' THEORY OF HUMOR/LAUGHTER; HUMOR, THEORIES OF; INCONGRUITY/ INCONSISTENCY THEORIES OF HUMOR; KANT'S THEORY OF HUMOR/ LAUGHTER.

REFERENCE

Schopenhauer, A. (1819/1906). *The world as will and idea*. London: Routledge & Kegan Paul.

SCIENTIST-PRACTITIONER/BOULDER MODEL. See PARADIGM SHIFT DOCTRINE.

SCRIPT THEORY. See BERNE'S SCRIPT THEORY.

SCRIPTURE'S BLOCKS. See APPENDIX A, SCHRODER STAIRCASE ILLUSION.

SCHRODER STAIRCASE ILLUSION. See APPENDIX A.

SEASONALITY EFFECT/HYPOTHESIS. See SCHIZOPHRENIA, THEORIES OF.

SECONDARY LAWS OF ASSOCIATION. See ASSOCIATION, LAWS/PRINCIPLES OF.

SECONDARY MEMORY. See SHORT-TERM AND LONG-TERM MEMORY, THEORIES OF.

SECONDARY REINFORCEMENT, PRINCIPLE OF. See REINFORCEMENT THEORY; SKINNER'S DESCRIPTIVE BEHAVIOR/OPERANT CONDITIONING THEORY.

SECULAR HUMANIST DOCTRINE. See KOHLBERG'S THEORY OF MORALITY.

SECURE-BASE PHENOMENON. See DEVELOPMENTAL THEORY.

SEDUCTION THEORY. The Austrian neurologist/psychoanalyst Sigmund Freud (1856-1939) proposed a *seduction theory* in 1895 (but abandoned it after a few years), in which the cause of neuroses was thought to be traceable to repressed memories of sexual seduction having occurred in one's childhood. After 1897, however, Freud dropped the notion that the "seductions" were based in reality and advanced, instead, a *theory of psychical reality* (i.e., the idea that anything that is interpreted by a person as real should be attended to, including fantasies that are experienced as memories of occurrences - such as sexual seduction during childhood - whether or not they are based on real events) to account for the problems of neuroses. The related Freudian term *primal fantasy/phantasy* refers to a primitive fantasy (imagination or mental imagery), including the following: the primal scene (the vision/observation of sexual intercourse between one's parents), one's castration, one's seduction, or some such similar personal imagined experiences, and which were posited by Freudian analysts to be universal in occurrence and to be transmitted by genetic inheritance (Freud's *genetic theory*) originating from supposed common practices in pre-recorded history. See also DODO HYPOTHESIS; FREUD'S THEORY OF PERSONALITY.

REFERENCES.

Freud, S. (1914). On the history of the psycho-analytic movement. In *The standard edition of the complete psychological works of Sigmund Freud*. London: Hogarth Press.

Freud, S. (1915). A case of paranoia running counter to the psycho-analytic theory of the disease. In *The standard edition of the complete psychological works of Sigmund Freud*. London: Hogarth Press.

Freud, S. (1916). Introductory lectures on psycho-analysis. In *The standard edition of the complete psychological works of Sigmund Freud*. London: Hogarth Press.

SEGMENTAL THEORY. See NEURON/NEURAL/NERVE THEORY.

SEGREGATION, LAW OF. See MENDEL'S LAWS/PRINCIPLES.

SELECTION, LAW OF. See EFFECT, LAW OF; VIGILANCE, THEORIES OF.

SELECTIVE ATTENTION THEORIES. See BLOCKING PHENOMENON/EFFECT; ESTES' STIMULUS SAMPLING THEORY.

SELECTIVE SOCIAL INTERACTION THEORY. See AGING, THEORIES OF.

SELF-ACTUALIZING MAN THEORY. See MASLOW'S THEORY OF PERSONALITY; ORGANIZATIONAL/INDUSTRIAL/SYSTEMS THEORY.

SELF-ATTENTION THEORY. See SELF-CONSISTENCY AND SELF-ENHANCEMENT THEORIES.

SELF-CATEGORIZATION THEORY. See PREJUDICE, THEORIES OF.

SELF-CONCEPT THEORY. = self-psychology theory. Based on *self-consistency theory*, each individual is guided by his/her own *theory of reality* that, in turn, consists of a *self-theory* and a *world-theory* [cf., *heliocentric theory* and its influence on personal self-esteem or self-importance; the theory is the Polish astronomer Nicolas Copernicus' (1473-1543) view of the solar system in which the universe is no longer seen to revolve around humans on Earth, but the Earth is only one planet rotating on its axis and revolving around a medium-sized star, the Sun, in a small corner of the entire universe; such a view deprecates the importance of humans].

The construct of *self-concept* is a *self-theory*, and suggests that without their theories of reality and self, people would experience the world as chaotic; the *self-concept* is the individual's fundamental frame of reference (cf., *congruence-of-images theory* - the notion that in any social system people have images of themselves and others, and all people interact in ways so as to confirm these images). Information that is inconsistent with the *self-theory* or *self-concept theory* is viewed as a threat, and when the organization of a *self-theory* is under stress, the person defends the existing organization and attempts to assimilate new information. According to *self-concept theory*, two self-view stabilizing processes are called "cognitive restructuring" (e.g., the person misperceives another person's behavior in order to achieve congruency), and "selective interaction" (e.g., people choose to interact with others who confirm their self-concept). The theory asserts that the importance of a stable self-concept becomes apparent in its absence; also, a changing and uncertain self-concept can be damaging, theoretically, to one's physical health as well as to one's psychological well-being (cf., *negative self-verification theory* - posits that people who hold negative self-views find it uncomfortable to be with people who see them in a positive way and, therefore, have a tendency to affiliate with people who confirm their negative self-concept, self-image, or self-perception). Both *self-consistency* and *self-enhancement theories* suggest that the self-concept has a powerful influence on how people perceive events; the former theory proposes that people perceive events in ways that are consistent with their self-views; and the latter theory proposes that people perceive events in ways that enhance their self-esteem [cf., *virtual self* - a notion in self-psychology referring to a parent's image of the newborn/neonate's self; the *cognitive self* versus the *psychoanalytic self* (Westen, 1992); and the *fashioning effect* - the influence that a self-determined social role has on one's own self-perception and behavior]. According to the *good-enough mother hypothesis* - formulated by the English psychoanalyst Donald W. Winnicott (1896-1971) - the mother is viewed as one who initially behaves toward a totally dependent infant in a way that is determined exclusively by the infant; the mother allows the infant to feel omnipotent and contributes to the infant's fantasy that the mother is part of the infant itself; later, the mother allows the child to abandon such a fantasy and separate from her in an orderly process. The *good-enough mother hypothesis* suggests that a mother who is "too good" interferes with the regular process of the child's separation, as well as with the normal developmental process of "selfhood." On the other hand, a mother who is too distant, or is not "good enough," generates anxiety in the child. In either scenario, the failure to provide "good-enough" mothering may disrupt the development of a healthy *self-concept* in the child, as well as cause disruption in adulthood of the ability to establish meaningful and healthy relationships with others [cf., *Michelangelo phenomenon* - named after the Italian sculptor Michelangelo Buonarroti (1475-1564), and studied by the American psychologist Stephen M. Drigotas (1966-) and his colleagues - refers to a pattern of interpersonal/relational interdependence in which close partners influence each other's behaviors, values, and dispositions in such a way as to bring them closer to their "ideal selves"]. According to the Austrian-born American psychoanalyst Heinz Kohut (1913-1981), the "grandiose self" is a self-image that a child develops when its natural narcissism is stunted or frustrated by the mother's occasional failure to respond adequately; the "grandiose self" normally becomes more moderate as the child grows older and its parents' responses change toward the child. However, the "grandiose self" (also called the "grandiose-exhibitionist self") may remain unchanged if the child's normal developmental sequence is disrupted (e.g., the mother may never respond adequately, or she responds unrealistically or unpredictably); under such conditions, the child may develop "narcissistic personality disorder" in adulthood. In his *self-psychology theory*, Kohut also identifies the constituent elements of the self as the "pole of goals/ambitions," the "pole of ideals/standards," and the "arc of tension" (between the two poles seeking to activate one's basic skills and talents); he also makes distinctions between the "virtual self" (an image of the infant's self in the parent's mind), the "nuclear self" (the first organization of the self that is revealed at about two years of age), the "cohesive self" (a consistent structure that represents the normally functioning individual), and the "grandiose self" (the normally exhibitionistic and self-centered persona of the infant). In his *self-presentation theory*, also called *role-role theory* (in which roles are used to explain and account for the patterns and regularities of social interactive behavior), the Canadian-born American sociologist Erving Goffman (1922-1982) asserts that individuals exercise conscious and/or unconscious control of the impression that they create in social interactions and situations. *Self-presentation* is a significant form of *impression management* (i.e., the control and regulation of information in order to affect the attitudes/opinions of target persons). Whereas *impression management* may focus on shaping other people's impressions of an individual - such as oneself, an enemy, or a friend/acquaintance - or of an event, *self-presentation theory* focuses exclusively on controlling impressions of oneself. In general, *impression formation* refers to the rapid assessment or perception/understanding of the personality of another individual on the basis of a wide range of characteristics. The form of *self-presentation* called *ingratiation* is the attempt of a person to win the good opinion of a target person via methods such as "other-enhancement" - the ingratiator compliments, flatters, or gives favors to the target person; "opinion conformity" - the ingratiator pretends to share the same attitudes/opinions as the target person; and "biased self-presentation" - ingratiators of both genders emphasize their most attractive features or qualities and minimize their weak characteristics (the *self-verification hypothesis* suggests that each person has a self-concept that he/she wishes would be validated and accepted by others and, thereby, confirms what one already knows about oneself). In the self-monitoring activities that accompany self-presentation, the individual closely observes and controls his/her expressive behaviors (such as facial expression, emotions, dress styles, handwriting, etc.), and may often be highly responsive to social and interpersonal cues to behaviors that are appropriate ("politically correct") to the situation. The *same-different theory* holds that all individuals undergo a developmental self-analysis of how they compare with their peers and, from such an assessment, they come to view themselves as belonging to certain categories and not others; for example, in regard to sexual development, this approach leads one to view oneself as male, female, intersex, androphilic, gynecophilic, ambiphil-ic, transsexual, etc. (cf., Diamond & Karlen, 1980); the *ego-alter theory* posits that social interaction is controlled by the person's self-perception in relation to others (called "alters"); the optimal self-esteem theory is characterized by qualities associated with genuine, true, stable, and congruent high self-esteem, and the concept of *authenticity* serves to delineate the adaptive features of optimal self-esteem (cf., Kernis, 2003); and the *self-discrepancy theory* indicates how different types of discrepancies between self-state representations are related to different kinds of emotional vulnerabilities (cf., Higgins, 1987), where one *domain* of the self (actual; ideal; ought) and one *view* on the self (own; significant other) constitute each type of self-state representation. In *personality disintegration*, the individual's *self-concept* and social behavior is fragmented to the degree that the person no longer presents a unified and predictable set of attitudes, beliefs, behavioral responses, or traits, with the most extreme cases being found in schizophrenics. Detractors of *self-concept theory* (e.g., the behaviorists, radical empiricists, and logical positivists) suggest that the notion of "self" (and even "personality") is a pseudo-concept that is superfluous and meaningless in the scientific analysis of human behavior. The American psychologist B. F. Skinner (1904-1990) notes that "origination" is at the heart of the issue of a "self" or a "sense of self": one begins as an organism and becomes a "person" or a "self" only as he or she acquires a repertoire of behavior, and all "selves" are merely the products of genetic and environmental histories. Skinner asserts that there is no place in the scientific enterprise for the hypothetical notion of "self" as a true originator or initiator of action. See also FESTINGER'S COGNITIVE DISSONANCE

THEORY; OBJECT-RELA-TIONS THE-
ORY; PSYCHOPATHOLOGY, THEORIES
OF; ROGERS' THEORY OF PERSONAL-
ITY; SELF-CONSISTENCY AND SELF-
ENHANCEMENT THEORIES; WORK,
CAREER, AND OCCUPATION, THEORIES
OF.

REFERENCES

Winnicott, D. W. (1957). *Mother and child: A primer of first relationships.* New York: Basic Books.

Goffman, E. (1959). *The presentation of self in everyday life.* New York: Doubleday.

Epstein, S. (1973). The self-concept revisited: Or a theory of a theory. *American Psychologist, 28,* 404-416.

Skinner, B. F. (1974). *About behaviorism.* New York: Knopf.

Shavelson, R. J., Hubner, J. J., & Stanton, G. C. (1976). Self-concept validation of construct interpretations. *Review of Educational Research, 46,* 407-441.

Kohut, H. (1977). *The restoration of the self.* New York: International Universities Press.

Diamond, M., & Karlen, A. (1980). *Sexual decisions.* Boston: Little, Brown.

Epstein, S. (1980). The self-concept: A review and the proposal of an integrated theory of personality. In E. Straub (Ed.), *Personality: Basic aspects and current research.* Englewood Cliffs, NJ: Prentice-Hall.

Lee, B., & Smith, K. (1982). *Psychosocial theories of the self.* New York: Plenum.

Snyder, M., & Gangestad, S. (1982). Choosing social situations: Two investigations of self-monitoring processes. *Journal of Personality and Social Psychology, 43,* 123-135.

Stern, R. (1986). *Theories of the unconscious and theories of the self.* Hillsdale, NJ: Analytic Press.

Higgins, E. T. (1987). Self-discrepancy: A theory relating self and affect. *Psychological Review, 94,* 319-340.

Bacal, H. A., & Newman, K. M. (1990). *Theories of object relations: Bridges to self psychology.* New York: Columbia University Press.

Levin, J. D. (1992). *Theories of the self.* Washington, D.C.: Hemisphere.

Westen, D. (1992). The cognitive self and the psychoanalytic self: Can we put ourselves together? *Psychological Inquiry, 3,* 1-13.

Gross, S. E., & Madson, L. (1997). Models of the self: Self-construals and gender. *Psychological Bulletin, 122,* 5-37.

Drigotas, S. M., Rusbult, C., Wieselquist, J., & Whitton, S. (1999). Close partner as sculptor of the ideal self: Behavioral affirmation and the Michelangelo phenomenon. *Journal of Personality and Social Psychology, 77,* 293-323.

Dweck, C. S. (1999). *Self-theories: Their role in motivation, personality, and development.* New York: Psychology Press.

Ellemers, N., Spears, R., & Doosje, B. (2002). Self and social identity. *Annual Review of Psychology, 53,* 161-186.

Kernis, M. H. (2003). Toward a conceptualization of optimal self-esteem. *Psychological Inquiry, 14,* 1-26.

SELF-CONSISTENCY AND SELF-EN-HANCEMENT THEORIES. According to *self-consistency theory* (e.g., Lecky, 1945/1969), people interpret information and act in ways that are consistent with, and will perpetuate, their "self-views." In contrast, *self-enhancement theory* (e.g., Rogers, 1961) contends that people are striving constantly to feel better about themselves and will, therefore, act and assimilate information in such a way as to achieve this goal (cf., *self-attention theory* - a group dynamics model stating that one's self-awareness increases as the number of people in the majority increases and as the individual's subgroup becomes smaller; and *self-evaluation maintenance model* - a group dynamics model positing that a person seeks group membership on the conditions that the other members in the group excel in areas that are not central to the person's self-concept, and that the person feels superior to other members in other groups in areas that are central to the person's self-concept). Both theories predict that people with *high* esteem, for example, will respond favorably to positive feedback either because it is consistent with their present self-views (*self-consistency theory*) or because it enhances their self-views (*self-enhancement theory*). However, for persons with *low* self-esteem, the two theories make contradictory predictions. *Self-consistency theory* predicts that positive feedback may be rejected by *low* self-esteem persons because it is inconsistent with their self-schema. In contrast, *self-enhancement theory* predicts that positive feedback will be accepted by *low* self-esteem individuals because the feedback functions to bolster their self-image. In general, neither theory has received unambiguous support in the psychological literature: some studies support *self-enhancement theory* and others support *self-consistency theory*. Attempts to reconcile the *self-enhancement/self-consistency* debate or controversy (e.g. Shrauger, 1975) suggest that studies assessing *cognitive* responses to feedback, for example, tend to produce *consistency* effects, whereas studies measuring *affective* responses to feedback tend to produce *enhancement* effects. See also ATTITUDE/ATTITUDE CHANGE, THEORIES OF; FESTINGER'S COGNITIVE DISSONANCE THEORY; ROGERS' THEORY OF PERSONALITY; SELF-CONCEPT THEORY.

REFERENCES

Lecky, P. (1945/1969). *Self-consistency: A theory of personality*. New York: Island Press/Doubleday.

Rogers, C. (1961). *On becoming a person: A therapist's view of psychotherapy*. Boston: Houghton Mifflin.

Jones, S. C. (1973). Self and interpersonal evaluations: Esteem theories versus consistency theories. *Psychological Bulletin, 79*, 185-199.

Shrauger, J. S. (1975). Responses to evaluation as a function of initial self-perceptions. *Psychological Bulletin, 82*, 581-596.

Swann, W. B., Griffin, J. J., Predmore, S. C., & Gaines, B. (1987). The cognitive-affective crossfire: When self-consistency confronts self-enhancement. *Journal of Personality and Social Psychology, 52*, 881-889.

SELF-DEFEATING PROPHECY. See PYGMALION EFFECT.

SELF-DISCREPANCY THEORY. See SELF-CONCEPT THEORY.

SELF-EVALUATION MAINTENANCE MODEL. See SELF-CONSISTENCY AND SELF-ENHANCEMENT THEORIES.

SELF-FULFILLING PROPHECY. See EXPERIMENTER EFFECTS; PYGMALION EFFECT.

SELFISH GENE HYPOTHESIS. See MENDEL'S LAWS/PRINCIPLES.

SELF-MONITORING THEORY/METHOD. In the area of education/learning, the procedure of *self-monitoring* (*S-M*) refers to the process of discriminating target behaviors - paying deliberate attention to some aspect of one's behavior - and related events, and is an important component of *self-regulated* (i.e., independent, self-motivated) thinking and learning. The social psychological construct of *S-M* (i.e., observation and control of expressive behavior and self-presentation) was introduced into psychology in 1974 by the American-based Canadian social psychologist Mark Snyder (1947-), who found that *high* self-monitors regulate their expressive self-presentation and are highly responsive to social and interpersonal cues to situationally appropriate behavior, whereas *low* self-monitoring individuals lack such abilities or motivations. *S-M* requires the person to attend selectively to specific actions or cognitive processes, to distinguish them from other actions/processes, and to discriminate their outcomes. Although there is good agreement among theorists regarding the overt features of *S-M*, psychologists differ in their descriptions of various covert psychological dimensions. Thus, for example, *information-processing* theorists view *S-M* within a cybernetic system consisting of several stages: sensory environmental input (perception), comparison with a standard/corrective behavior, and behavioral outcome. In contrast to this approach concerning covert decision-making, *cognitive-behavioral* theorists emphasize the need for

546

overt forms of *S-M*, such as self-recording, as tools for adapting both covert cognitions and overt behaviors to environmental conditions [cf., the *Coué method/theory* - named after the French pharmacist and proponent of "auto-suggestion" Emile Coué (1857-1926) - that aims at self-improvement, as well as attempting to cure physical diseases, by regularly repeating words over and over to oneself, such as "Every day in every way, I am getting better and better"]. *Metacognitive* theorists conceive of *S-M* in terms of meta-awareness and meta-control of knowledge and of cognitive experiences and strategies; and *social-cognitive* theorists stress the importance and inter-dependence of all three major forms of *S-M*: cognitive, behavioral, and environmental. See also COGNITIVE THERAPY, THEORIES OF; INFORMA-TION/INFORMATION-PRO-CESSING THEORY; SELF-CONCEPT THEORY; SO-CIAL LEARNING/COGNIT-ION THEO-RIES.

REFERENCES

Snyder, M. (1974). Self-monitoring of expressive behavior. *Journal of Personality and Social Psychology, 30*, 526-537.

Snyder, M. (1987). *Public appearances, private realities: The psychology of self-monitoring.* New York: Holt.

Zimmerman, B., & Schunk, D. (1989). *Self-regulated learning and academic achievement: Theory, research, and practice.* New York: Springer-Verlag.

Zimmerman, B., & Paulsen, A. (1995). Self-monitoring during collegiate studying: An invaluable tool for academic self-regulation. *New Directions for Teaching and Learning, 63*, 13-27.

SELF-PERCEPTION THEORY. See AT-TRIBUTION THEORY; DEVELOPMEN-TAL THEORY.

SELF-PRESENTATION THEORY. See SELF-CONCEPT THEORY; SELF-MON-ITORING THEORY/METHOD.

SELF-PSYCHOLOGY THEORY. See SELF-CONCEPT THEORY.

SELF-SELECTION/SELECTIVE SAMP-LING BIAS/EFFECT. See EXPERIMEN-TER EFFECTS.

SELF-SERVING BIAS HYPOTHESIS. See ATTRIBUTION THEORY.

SELF-VERIFICATION HYPOTHESIS. See SELF-CONCEPT THEORY.

SELYE'S THEORY/MODEL OF STRESS. The Austrian-born Canadian endocrinologist and psychologist Hans Selye (1907-1982) was one of the first modern psychologists to examine systematically the construct of *stress* and its effects on the organism, although medical and theoretical interest in *stress* goes back to the Greek physician Hippocrates (460-377 B.C.). In the 1920s, the American physiologist Walter B. Cannon (1871-1945) verified for *stress theory* that the "stress response" is part of a unified mind-body system, where a variety of stressors (such as lack of oxygen, extreme cold, emotional states) trigger the flow of adrenaline and noradrenaline that, in turn, enter the bloodstream from sympathetic nerve endings in the inner portion of the adrenal glands. Such physiological events help to prepare and adapt the body for what Cannon called the "flight or fight" syndrome, or what is known today as *Cannon's emergency syndrome*. Hans Selye spent 40 years of research on *stress* and expanded Cannon's findings to the extent that today *stress* is a major concept in both medicine and psychology. Based on his study of hormone-action in rats, and after many disappointments with his experiments, Selye discovered that many stressors such as surgical trauma, heat, cold, electric shock, and immobilizing restraint all have similar physiological effects on the organism. The body's adaptive response to stress seemed so general to Selye that he called it the *general adaptation syndrome* (*GAS*), which is defined as the pattern of nonspecific bodily mechanisms activated in response to a continuing threat by almost any severe stressor (cf., *levee effect* - a reaction to disaster/stress, or the threat of disaster, by the individual's acquisition of psychic devices used to protect the person or the group, much like a levee that may not provide full protection from flooding, but it does serve to give one a sense of security). According to *Selye's theory*, the *GAS* is divided into three stages: (1) *alarm reaction* - initially, the stressor results in a state of alarm ("shock" and "countershock" phases) and mobilization in which the body's resistance drops below its normal level; (2) *resistance* - this stage develops where the adrenal cortex secretes protective corticosteroids, and where the body becomes highly susceptible to additional and unrelated stresses; and (3) *exhaustion* - this stage occurs if the danger from stress is prolonged, and the individual may become seriously ill and die. The *GAS* has been observed in cases of prolonged exposure to psychological (e.g., maternal separation), environmental (e.g., cold), and physiological (e.g. poison) types of stressors. However, newer research indicates that there are subtle differences in the body's reactions to different stressors, and one weakness of *Selye's model* is that it fails to account for cognitive processes in determining how individuals interpret a specific event to be stressful or not (cf., *closed-loop model of stress* - holds that stress occurs in the context of a *systems model/theory*, which suggests that dynamic feedback patterns control a variety of behaviors and indicate the organism's capacity for stability and order; the *closed-loop model* is in contrast to *Selye's open-loop model* that views stress as a static system where stressors act cumulatively on a passive organism; *environmental-load theory* posits that humans have a limited capacity to handle environmental stress factors, where capacity is determined by the amount of information inputs that can be processed by the person's central nervous system; when the load exceeds the person's processing capacity, the central nervous system responds by ignoring some inputs; in contrast to the *load theory*, the *environmental-stress theory* holds that autonomic and cognitive/perceptual factors combine to form an individual's appraisal of an environmental stress situation as either threatening or nonthreatening; cf., the concept of *eustress* that denotes a type of stress that has a positive, beneficial, or stimulating effect; for instance, the stress involved in getting a job promotion; and *social-stress theory* - holds that effects of certain glandular reactions are altered in some animals as the sizes of the groups increase beyond an optimal number, and social competition may lead to adrenal/glandular stresses that may produce behavioral and physiological deficits). Nevertheless, most medical experts agree with Selye's basic point that prolonged stress can produce physical deterioration (cf., the relatively recent field of *behavioral medicine* and its perspectives on stress). Extending from Selye's work on stress, also, is the development of the new field of study in psychology called *psychoneuroimmunology* (and *health psychology*) that seeks to examine how stress, emotions, and upsetting thoughts affect the body's immune system to make the individual more susceptible to disease. See also ACCOMMODATION, LAW/PRINCIPLE OF; CANNON/CANNON-BARD THEORY; CONFLICT, THEORIES OF; HABITUATION, PRINCIPLE/LAW OF; LAZARUS' THEORY OF EMOTIONS; PSYCHOSOMATICS THEORY; SYSTEMS THEORY.

REFERENCES

Cannon, W. B. (1929). *Bodily changes in pain, hunger, fear, and rage.* New York: Branford.

Selye, H. (1936). A syndrome produced by diverse nocuous agents. *Nature, 138,* 32.

Selye, H. (1950). *Stress.* Montreal: Acta.

Selye, H. (1956). *The stress of life.* New York: McGraw-Hill.

Selye, H. (1976). *Stress in health and disease.* Toronto: Butterworth.

Pomerleau, O., & Brady, J. (Eds.) (1979). *Behavioral medicine: Theory and practice.* Baltimore: Williams & Wilkins.

Selye, H. (1980). *Selye's guide to stress research.* New York: Van Nostrand.

Breznitz, S., & Goldberger, L. (1983). *Handbook of stress.* New York: Free Press.

O'Leary, A. (1990). Stress, emotion, and human immune function. *Psychological Bulletin, 108,* 363-382.

Taylor, S. (1990). Health psychology. *American Psychologist, 45,* 40-50.

SEMANTIC-FEATURE HYPOTHESIS. See CHOMSKY'S PSYCHOLINGUISTIC THEORY.

SEMANTIC SCRIPT THEORY OF HU-MOR. See GENERAL THEORY OF VERBAL HUMOR.

SEMANTIC MEMORY. See FORGETTING/MEMORY, THEORIES OF; SHORT-TERM AND LONG-TERM MEMORY, THEORIES OF.

SEMIOTIC THEORY. See CHOMSKY'S PSYCHOLINGUISTIC THEORY.

SENSATIONALISM/SENSATIONISM, DOCTRINE OF. See EMPIRICAL/EMPIRICISM, DOCTRINE OF.

SENSITIVE DEPENDENCE PHENOMENON. See ORGANIZATIONAL/INDUSTRIAL/SYSTEMS THEORIES.

SENSITIZATION, PRINCIPLE OF. See HABITUATION, PRINCIPLE/LAW OF.

SENSITIZATION THEORY. See NEURON/NEURAL/NERVE THEORY.

SENSORY CONFLICT THEORY. See PERCEPTION (II. COMPARATIVE APPRAISAL), THEORIES OF.

SENSORY DEPRIVATION EFFECTS. See BRAIN-WASHING TECHNIQUES/THEORY.

SENSORY DISCRIMINATION, CLASSICAL THEORY OF. See NEURAL QUANTUM THEORY.

SENSORY HOMUNCULUS HYPOTHESIS. See HOMUNCULUS/SENSORY HOMUNCULUS HYPOTHESIS.

SENSORY MEMORY, THEORY OF. See SHORT-TERM AND LONG-TERM MEMORY, THEORIES OF.

SENSORY SALTATION ILLUSION. See APPENDIX A.

SENSORY-TONIC FIELD THEORY. See PERCEPTION (II. COMPARATIVE APPRAISAL), THEORIES OF.

SEQUENCE EFFECTS. See EXPERIMENTER EFFECTS.

SEQUENTIAL DECISION THEORY. See INFORMATION/INFORMATION-PROCESSING THEORY.

SEQUENTIAL PATTERNING THEORY. See CAPALDI'S THEORY.

SEQUENTIAL PROCESSING THEORY. See INFORMATION/INFORMATION-PROCESSING THEORY.

SERIAL-POSITION EFFECT. = serial position curve = edge effect = end effect. The *serial-position effect* is the generalization that in a free-recall experiment the chance of an individual item from a list being recalled is a function of the location of that item in the serial presentation of the list during learning. The items that are toward the beginning of the list and those toward the end are more likely to be correctly recalled than those in the middle of the list. When the results of a *serial-position learning task* are graphed, with correct recall of items plotted against the serial position of the item during presentation, the curve characteristically is bow-shaped with high probabilities of recall for the first few (called the *primacy effect/law*) and for the last few (called the *recency effect/law*) items. The *serial-position curve* is the same in form for meaningful material as well as for *nonsense syllables* [the German psychologist Hermann von Ebbinghaus (1850-1909) devised over 2,000 consonant-vowel-consonant combinations, called *nonsense syllables*, in order to control for meaning and associations in verbal-test materials; cf., *Hunter-McCrary law*; McCrary & Hunter, 1953). An early theory of the *serial-position effect/curve* was given by W. Lepley, and C. L. Hull, and made great use of the *doctrine of remote associations* (developed initially by H. von Ebbinghaus) and the notion of the acquisition of inhibitory connections to suppress the observed remote errors: such inhibitory factors were assumed to "pile up" most in suppressing responses in the middle of the list and, as a result, most errors should occur at the middle positions. The major premises of the *Lepley-Hull hypothesis* concerning remote associations, however, have been discredited largely, along with the theory that was constructed on that basis. Another *theory of the serial-position effect/curve* was proposed independently by A. Jensen, and by E. Feigenbaum and H. Simon. In Jensen's view, the items on a list that are learned first, or best, are the ones to which the learner first attends (i.e., the first item or two in the list), and these first-learned items then serve as an "anchor point" for learning the rest of the list. Jensen's theory, however, has been criticized because of its vagueness concerning the basic learning mechanism and the implausibility of the argument concerning the attachment of the items to "expanding" anchor points. Feigenbaum and Simon point out that there are ways of distorting the characteristic shape of the *serial-position curve*. For instance, if one item is made clearly distinct from other items (the *von Restorff effect*), it will be learned much faster, or if half the list is colored red and the other half black the curve shows a large decrease in errors on the last item of the red half of the list and the first item of the black half. Feigenbaum and Simon developed an *information-processing theory of serial learning* where "anchor points" and a "macro-processing system" describe the *serial-position* results. Feigenbaum and Simon's theory - in addition to other response-learning and guessing factors - gives a good account of most facts known about the *serial-learning curve*. See also FORGETTING/MEMORY, THEORIES OF; INFORMA-TION/INFORMA-TION PROCESSING THEORY; von RESTORFF EFFECT.

REFERENCES

Ebbinghaus, H. von (1885). *Uber der ge-dacht-nis*. Leipzig:; Duncker.

Lepley, W. (1934). Serial reactions considered as conditioned reactions. *Psychological Monographs, 46*, No. 205.

Hull, C. L. (1935). The conflicting psychologies of learning - a way out. *Psychological Review, 42*, 491-516.

McCrary, J., & Hunter, W. (1953). Serial position curves in verbal learning. *Science, 117*, 131-134.

Feigenbaum, E., & Simon, H. (1962). A theory of the serial position effect. *Brit-ish Journal of Psychology, 53*, 307-320.

Jensen, A. (1962). An empirical theory of the serial-position effect. *Journal of Psychology, 53*, 127-142.

Slamecka, N. (1964). An inquiry into the doctrine of remote associations. *Psychological Review, 71*, 61-76.

Jensen, A., & Rohwer, W. (1965). What is learned in serial learning? *Journal of Verbal Learning and Verbal Behavior, 4*, 62-72.

SERIAL PROCESSING THEORY. See INFORMATION/INFORMATION-PROCESSING THEORY.

SERIAL REPRODUCTION TECHNIQUE. See RUMOR TRANSMISSION THEORY.

SET, LAW OF. See MIND/MENTAL SET, LAW OF.

SET/MOTOR ADJUSTMENTS THEORY. See PERCEPTION (II. COMPARATIVE APPRAISAL), THEORIES OF; WUNDT'S THEORIES/DOCTRINES/PRINCIPLES.

SET-POINT THEORY. See HUNGER, THEORIES OF.

SET SIZE EFFECTS. See IMPRESSION FORMATION, THEORIES OF.

SET-THEORETICAL MODEL. See MIND/MENTAL SET, LAW OF.

SET THEORY. The Russian-born German mathematician Georg Cantor (1845-1918) developed *set theory* as a result of his examination of the circumstances in which a mathematical function is represented by a unique Fourier series (i.e., a generalization that any complex periodic pattern may be viewed as a particular sum of a number of sine waves). Whereas previous investigators had provided results for functions that are continuous on a given interval, Cantor considered set of points at which functions behave in a way that makes their Fourier series inappropriate. Cantor found that he could repeat this

550

construction and obtain from one such set another set, sometimes indefinitely (cf., *extension theorem of semantic entailment* - in logic, a theorem in propositional calculus stating that if a set of premises *p* entails a conclusion *q*, then the addition of further premises from a larger set *s* that includes *p* cannot affect the truth of the conclusion *q*; this theorem is at the basis of the notion of *monotonicity* in logic, stating that a valid argument cannot be made invalid, nor an invalid argument made valid, by adding new premises). Cantor's approach led to a highly original arithmetic of the infinite, extending the concept of cardinal and ordinal numbers to infinite sets. Basic to Cantor's *set theory* is the idea that infinite sets have the same size, or cardinality, if and only if there is a one-to-one relationship between their members. Cantor demonstrated that the set of real numbers is "uncountable" (i.e., it cannot be formed in a one-to-one relationship with the set of integers), and that the set of subsets of a set is always larger than the original set. Cantor proposed - but could not solve - the problem of characterizing the cardinality of the continuum; such a problem is considered to be unsolvable in a more precise form. Other features of Cantor's *theory of sets* have become essential in the areas of topology and modern analysis in mathematics and statistics in psychology. Around 1900, Cantor and his friend Julius W. R. Dedekind (1831-1916) simultaneously developed a naïve *theory of sets* to serve as a foundation for mathematics. Sets, or collections of objects, are represented typically by an upper-case letter or by a pair of brackets enclosing all of its members; for example, the set of "natural numbers" is: $N =$ [1,2,3 ...], and the set of "black American presidents" is: $F = \emptyset$ (this latter set is called a "null set" or "empty set"). *Set theory* inherently contains an interesting logical inconsistency called *Russell's paradox* [named after its enunciation in 1901 by the Welsh philosopher Bertrand Russell (1872-1970)] that centers on the idea that some sets are members of themselves and others are not. The so-called *barber's paradox* points out the paradox or inconsistency via an example: suppose there is a town barber who shaves all and only those men who do not shave themselves - from this it follows logically that if this barber shaves

himself, then he does not, and if he does not, then he does (!) See also BOOLEAN SET THEORY; FOURIER'S LAW/SERIES/ANALYSIS; FUZZY SET THEORY; MIND/MENTAL SET, LAW OF; NEURAL NETWORK MODELS OF INFORMATION PROCESSING.

REFERENCES

Cantor, G. (1897/1915). *Contributions to the founding of the theory of transfinite numbers*. Chicago: Open Court/New York: Dover.

Muir, H. (Ed.) (1994). *Larousse dictionary of scientists*. New York: Larousse.

SEXUAL ORIENTATION THEORIES = homoeroticism = homosexuality theories. The concept of *sexual orientation* refers to the focus and direction of an individual's sexual interest. *Heterosexual* orientation is sexual attraction to members of the opposite sex/gender; *homosexual* orientation is sexual attraction to members of one's own sex/gender; and *bisexual* orientation is sexual attraction to both sexes/genders. Historically, the German physician, sex researcher, and homosexual Magnus Hirschfeld (1868-1935) supported some *hormonal theories of homosexuality* that led others to attempt unsuccessfully to "cure" homosexuality with hormone injections; he also endorsed the *Urnings theory* (i.e., a theory dealing with the issue of men who are sexually attracted to other men) of the German jurist Karl Heinrich Ulrichs (1825-1895) who argued in 1864 that "Urnings" are "hermaphrodites of the mind." Whereas Ulrichs asserted that the "Urning disposition" is natural and inborn, later authorities - such as the German physician Richard von Krafft-Ebing (1840-1902) - labeled "Urningism" a mental illness, and others called it a "sexual inversion." In 1886, Krafft-Ebing combined *Urning theory* with the French physician Benedict A. Morel's (1809-1873) *theory of disease* and concluded that most homosexuals have a mental disorder caused by "degenerate heredity" (called the *degeneracy theory*). Krafft-Ebing's *degeneracy theory* was influential until the beginning of the 20th century when Sigmund Freud's psychoanalytical orientation became popular as a potential explanation of sexual orientation (cf., Friedman & Downey, 2002; Garnets & Kimmel, 2003; Mondimore, 1996; Phillips, 2003). A noteworthy event regarding the social view of homosexuality occurred in 1973 when the American Psychiatric Association (APA) deleted "homosexuality" as a psychiatric disorder from their *Diagnostic and Statistical Manual of Mental Disorders* (APA's "bible of nosology"). Surveys conducted in the late 1940s and early 1950s reported that about ten percent of the general American population was homosexual; more recent surveys in the 1990s, however, of American, English, and French populations indicate that only about three percent of men and one-and-one-half percent of women have a homosexual orientation. The theoretical issue of why people display different sexual orientations has been argued for decades, usually along the lines of the classical *nature versus nurture* debate. Proponents of the *nature*, or biological, side of the issue hold that sexual orientation has its roots in biology and physiology and is influenced primarily by genetics; those on the *nurture*, or environmental and learning, side hold that sexual orientation is a learned behavior primarily and is influenced primarily by early experience and largely under the individual's voluntary control. Advocates of the *nature* position argue that homosexual men and women generally know before puberty that they are "different" and often re-main "in the closet" regarding their sexual orientation for fear of personal and social recrimination; the *nature* proponents cite evidence from family and twin studies that shows a higher incidence of male homosexuality in families having other gay men, as well as a higher rate of homosexuality among men with a homosexual twin, even when the twins are raised in separate environments; they also cite studies indicating that the sizes of specific brain structures may differ between homosexual and heterosexual men (cf., Allen & Gorski, 1992; LeVay, 1991, 1993; LeVay & Ham-er, 1994; Swaab & Hoffman, 1995). Advocates of the *nurture* position of sexual orientation argue that the research supporting the *nature* position basically is flawed methodologically and sometimes confuses the issue of what *causes* homosexuality with what *results* from it; these advocates assert, also, that early sexual experiences and socialization (including gender nonconformity and rejection or attachment-avoidance by parents and peers) determines sexual orientation, and cite evidence showing that the frequency of different sexual orientations differs significantly from one culture to another [cf., the roles played in this debate by speculations such as *performativity theory* (i.e., deconstruction of foundational ideas of gender/sexual identity, or "gender as performance;" Butler, 1991; Hegarty, 1997); *feminist theory* (i.e., the theory suggesting that gender is a major social, historical, and political concept that influences women's choices in all communities and cultures; Belenky, Clinchy, Goldberger, & Tarule, 1997; Squier & Littlefield, 2004; Stewart & McDermott, 2004); *deviance theory* (i.e., the focus on cognitive stereotypes, and perceptions of threats to society, Plasek, 1984); *psychotherapeutic theory* (i.e., the methods employed by therapists in treating gays, lesbians, and bisexuals; Ritter & Terndrup, 2002); the *fraternal birth order effect* (i.e., the probability that a man being homosexual is related positively to his number of older brothers, but not older sisters when the brothers are accounted for; James, 2004); *anthropometric/ steroid theory* (i.e., bone morphology, as a marker of childhood sex steroid exposure, suggests that there are physical differences in heterosexuals and homosexuals, where persons with a sexual preference for men have less long bone growth in the arms, legs, and hands than those with a sexual preference for women; Martin & Nguyen, 2004); *differential risk theory* (i.e., a theory subsumed under *social exchange* and *equity theories* where, in this case, numerous gender differences involved in long-term relationships require members of such close relationships to assume greater interpersonal and social risks and costs as those compared to same-gender relationships; Schumm, 2004); *evolutionary theory* (i.e., the evolutionary value of human homosexuality via the strengthening of social bonds; DeBlock & Adriaens, 2004; Schuiling, 2004); and the *tend and befriend theory of stress and coping* (i.e., the speculation that men and women are hardwired biologically to cope with stress differently, based on differing evolutionary paths; Taylor, 2002)]. Thus, homosexuality is viewed as a complex and multi-factorial issue where its etiology ranges from the biological and evolutionary to the psychological and social, and from the essential and materialist to the constructionist. Currently, it appears that neither the *nature* view nor the *nurture* view can explain exclusively or completely the origin of sexual orientation and, as is the case with most complex psychological behaviors, it is likely that *both* nature and nurture play significant roles in one's sexual orientation. See also DARWIN'S EVOLUTION THEORY; EQUITY THEORY; FREUD'S THEORY OF PERSONALITY; LABELING/DEVIANCE THE-ORY; NATURE VERSUS NURTURE THE-ORIES; SOCIAL EXCHANGE THEORY.

REFERENCES

Krafft-Ebing, R. von (1887/1924). *Psychopathia sexualis*. Stuttgart: Enke.

Plasek, J. W. (1984). Misconceptions of homophobia. *Journal of Homosexuality, 10,* 23-37.

Deaux, K., & Major, B. (1987). Putting gender into context: An interactive model of gender-related behavior. *Psychological Review, 94,* 369-389.

Butler, J. (1991). Imitation and gender insubordination. In D. Fuss (Ed.), *Inside/outside-Lesbian theories, gay theories*. London: Routledge.

LeVay, S. (1991). A difference in hypothalamic structure between heterosexual and homosexual men. *Science, 253,* 1034-1038.

Allen, L. S., & Gorski, R. A. (1992). Sexual orientation and size of the anterior commissure in the human brain. *Proceedings of the National Academy of Sciences, 89,* 7199-7202.

LeVay, S. (1993). *The sexual brain*. Cambridge, MA: M.I.T. Press.

LeVay, S., & Hamer, D. H. (1994). Evidence for a biological influence in male homosexuality. *Scientific American* (May), 44-49.

Swaab, D. F., & Hoffman, M. A. (1995). Sexual differentiation of the human hypothalamus in relation to gender and sexual orientation. *Trends in neuroscience, 18,* 264-270.

Mondimore, F. M. (1996). *A natural history of homosexuality*. Baltimore: Johns Hopkins University Press.

Belenky, M., Clinchy, B., Goldberger, N., & Tarule, J. (1997). *Women's ways of knowing: The development of self, voice, and mind*. New York: Basic Books.

Hegarty, P. (1997). Materializing the hypothalamus: A performative account of the "gay brain." *Feminism & Psychology, 7,* 355-372.

Friedman, R. C., & Downey, J. I. (2002). *Sexual orientation and psychoanalysis: Sexual science and clinical practice*. New York: Columbia University Press.

Ritter, K. Y., & Terndrup, A. I. (2002). *Handbook of affirmative psychotherapy with lesbians and gay men*. New York: Guilford Press.

Taylor, S. E. (2002). *The tending instinct: How nurturing is essential to who we are and how we live*. New York: Holt.

Garnets, L. D., & Kimmel, D. C. (Eds.) (2003). *Psychological perspectives on lesbian, gay, and bisexual experiences*. New York: Columbia University Press.

Phillips, S. H. (2003). Homosexuality: Coming out of the confusion. *International Journal of Psychoanalysis, 84,* 1431-1450.

DeBlock, A., & Adriaens, P. (2004). Darwinizing sexual ambivalence: A new evolutionary hypothesis of male homosexuality. *Philosophical Psychology, 17,* 59-76.

James, W. H. (2004). The cause(s) of the fraternal birth order effect in male homosexuality. *Journal of Biosocial Science, 36,* 51-62.

Martin, J. T., & Nguyen, D. H. (2004). Anthropometric analysis of homosexuals and heterosexuals: Implications for early hormone exposure. *Hormones & Behavior, 45,* 31-39.

Schuiling, G. A. (2004). Death in Venice: The homosexuality enigma. *Journal of Psychosomatic Obstetrics and Gynaecology, 25,* 67-76.

Schumm, W. R. (2004). Differential risk theory as a subset of social exchange theory: Implications for making gay marriage culturally normative and for understanding stigma against homosexuals. *Psychological Reports*, *94*, 208-210.

Squier, S., & Littlefield, M. (Eds.) (2004). Feminist theory and/or science. *Feminist Theory (Special Issue)*, *5*, 123-126.

Stewart, A. J., & McDermott, C. (2004). Gender in psychology. *Annual Review of Psychology*, *55*, 519-544.

SHAPE-SLANT INVARIANCE HYPOTHESIS. See EMMERT'S LAW.

SHARED AUTISM THEORY. See DEINDIVIDUATION THEORY.

SHARED MANIFOLD HYPOTHESIS. See EMPATHY THEORY.

SHEEP-GOAT EFFECT. See PARANORMAL PHENOMENA/THEORY.

SHELDON'S TYPE THEORY. = somatotype theory = typology theory. The American psychologist/physician William Herbert Sheldon (1899-1977) formulated a *constitutional theory of personality* that emphasizes the importance of the physical structure of the body and biological-hereditary factors ("constitutional" variables) as major determinants of behavior. The term *constitution* refers to those aspects of the person that are relatively fixed and unchanging (such as morphology, physiology, genes, endocrine functioning) and is contrasted with those aspects that are relatively more labile and susceptible to modification by environmental pressures (such as education, habits, and attitudes). The *constitutional psychologist* looks to the biological substratum of the person for factors that are important to the explanation of human behavior. *Constitutional psychology* assumes the role of a facilitator or bridge connecting the biological with the behavioral domains. In Sheldon's approach, a hypothetical biological structure (*morphogenotype*) underlies the external, observable physique (*phenotype*) that determines physical development and molds behavior. In order to measure physique, Sheldon devised a photographic technique using pictures of the individual's front, side, and rear in standard poses. This procedure is called the *somatotype performance test*. After examining and judging about 4,000 of these photographs, Sheldon and his associates concluded that there are three *primary* dimensions or components concerning the measurement and assessment of the physical structure of the human body: *endomorphy* - a body that appears to be soft and spherical; *mesomorphy* - a body that appears to be hard, rectangular, and muscular; and *ectomorphy* - a body that appears to be linear, thin, and fragile. All participants in Sheldon's photographs could be assigned a score of from one to seven for each of the three components and, with further anthropometric measurements, a complete description of the *somatotyping* process of individuals was possible. According to Sheldon, the idea of *somatotype* is an abstraction from the complexity of any specific physique, and he developed various *secondary* components by way of accounting for the great variation across individuals. *Secondary* components include: *dysplasia* - an inconsistent or uneven mixture of the three *primary* components in different parts of the body; *gynandromorphy* - called the "g index" and refers to the degree that one's physique possesses characteristics ordinarily associated with the opposite sex; and *textural aspect* - a highly subjective physical aspect reflecting "aesthetic pleasingness." Sheldon also developed three primary components of *temperament* along with their associative *traits*: *viscerotonia* (this is paired with *endomorphy*) - is characterized by enjoyment of food, people, and affection; *somatotonia* (this is paired with *mesomorphy*) - refers to love of physical adventure and risk-taking; and *cerebrotonia* (this is paired with *ectomorphy*) - is characterized by a desire for isolation, solitude, and concealment. The three *temperament* dimensions, in conjunction with a list of 20 defining *traits* for each dimension, constitutes Sheldon's *scale for temperament*. Sheldon's research led to the strong confirmation of the *constitutional psychologist's* expectation that there is a noteworthy continuity between the structural/physical aspects of the person and his/her functional/behavioral qualities. Although Sheldon was successful in isolating and measuring dimensions for describing physique and temperament, he cautioned that the dimensions should not be examined in isolation one by one but, rather, the *pattern* of relations between the variables should be studied. Perhaps the most frequent criticism of *Sheldon's constitutional theory* is that it is no theory at all but simply consists of one general assumption: the continuity between structure and behavior, and a set of descriptive concepts for scaling physique and behavior. Other criticisms focus on procedural/methodological flaws in Sheldon's research, and on the fact that his notion of *somatotype* is not invariant in the presence of nutrition, age, cosmetic surgery, and other environmental changes. See also GALEN'S DOCTRINE OF THE FOUR TEMPERAMENTS; KRETSCHMER'S THEORY OF PERSONALITY; PERSONALITY THEORIES; TRAIT THEORIES OF PERSONALITY.

REFERENCES

Sheldon, W. H. (1940). *The varieties of human physique: An introduction to constitutional psychology.* New York: Harper.

Sheldon, W. H. (1942). *The varieties of temperament: A psychology of constitutional differences.* New York: Harper.

Sheldon, W. H. (1949). *Varieties of delinquent youth: An introduction to constitutional psychiatry.* New York: Harper.

Sheldon, W. H. (1954). *Atlas of men: A guide for somatotyping the adult male at all ages.* New York: Harper.

Humphreys, L. (1957). Characteristics of type concepts with special reference to Sheldon's typology. *Psychological Bulletin, 54,* 218-228.

Sheldon, W. H. (1971). The New York study of physical constitution and psychotic pattern. *Journal of the History of the Behavioral Sciences, 7,* 115-126.

SHIFTING, LAW OF. See VIGILANCE, THEORIES OF.

SHIFT OF LEVEL PRINCIPLE. See GESTALT THEORY/LAWS.

SHORT-CIRCUITING LAW. See PERCEPTION (II. COMPARATIVE APPRAISAL), THEORIES OF.

SHORT-CIRCUIT THEORY. See GESTALT THEORY/LAWS.

SHORT-TERM AND LONG-TERM MEMORY, THEORIES OF. The *dual-memory theory* holds that memory, generally, is a two-stage process: *short-term memory* (STM) that allows for the retention of certain information for very brief periods of time, and *long-term memory* (LTM) that permits information retention for longer periods of time (cf., the *storage-and-transfer model of memory* - is a "multistore" model of memory that states that there are *three* types of memory: sensory, short-term, and long-term). STM or "immediate memory" is a hypothesized memory system having a limited amount of information capacity, and capable of holding the information for a maximum of 20-30 seconds [cf., *primary memory hypothesis* - in 1890, the American psychologist/philosopher William James (1842-1910) suggested that a "primary" memory system is closely related to consciousness and differs from memory for general knowledge; later, in 1969, this memory system came to be known as "short-term" or "working" memory; *iconic memory/store* - refers to a theoretical sensory register, or "sensory information store," allowing a *visual* image to persist for about half a second to two seconds after its stimulus has terminated; this type of memory/image/storage was studied initially by the Hungarian physicist Johann Andreas von Segner (1704-1777) in the mid-1700s, and most currently by the American psychologists George Sperling (1933?-) and Ulrich Neisser (1928-); cf., also, *echoic memory/store theory* - one of the hypothesized "sensory registers" allowing an *auditory* image to persist for up to two seconds after its stimulus has terminated, making speech intelligible and allowing one to localize sounds via binaural time differences between the arrival of sound at the two ears; *precategorical acoustic memory/store theory* - an echoic memory/store that is posited as holding auditory information for brief durations before it has been modified by information processing; for instance, in serial digit recall tasks, the final two items in a list of digits are recalled better when the list is *heard* than when it is *read*, but the effect is lessened if the auditory list is followed by a verbal suffix that does not need to be recalled; such an *auditory suffix effect* indicates the existence of an "auditory memory trace" that decays rapidly and may be suppressed by other verbal information; *post-categorical acoustic memory/store theory* - is a hypothesized memory store for verbal information that has been modified by a degree of information processing, in particular, syntactical analysis/processing; *distributed memory storage/theory* - holds that mental activity is due to the integrated activity and functioning of several brain components, where memory is distributed widely, and only different aspects of memory are stored in different locations in the brain; and is compared with *localized memory storage/theory*, which asserts that specialized memory structures in the brain - such as "Broca's area" for speech production - are involved in particular mental activities; cf., *limited-capacity retrieval hypothesis* - posits that STM is of finite capacity and can store only a few facts at one time, and its limited capacity appears to restrict the number of feelings, ideas, and cognitions that can be considered, or carried out, at any given time; Miller, 1956; *recitation theory* - holds that memory may be optimized when material is rehearsed; *reality monitoring hypothesis* - is the hypothesized process/act of discriminating between *genuine* memories that are gained through perception from external reality and the *apparent* memories that are achieved internally via imagination; such discriminations tend to break down in the course of many mental disorders such as schizophrenia and delusional disorder; the hypothesis refers, also, to the idea that most people are constantly observing themselves, their social and physical environments, and their alertness to making decisions about goals; *adjacency effect* - refers to a memory paradigm where a number of disconnected words/syllables that exceeds one's memory span are presented one at a time at short intervals (e.g., every two

seconds), in a different random order on each of two or more trials; after each presentation, participants are asked to recall as many of the words/syllables as possible; the probability of recalling any given word is related to that word's "adjacency," that is, whether it follows, precedes, or is in-between words recalled on the previous trial; *alternation-of response theory* - suggests that proper division/parsing of a stream of stimuli is an important control device in STM tasks (e.g., lengthening the time interval between right-left alternation-task pairings reduces the error rate); and the *Brown-Peterson paradigm/technique* (Brown, 1958; Peterson & Peterson, 1959) - in memory research, refers to a procedure in which participants are asked initially to memorize some material, then they are distracted in some manner (e.g., "count backwards from some number by threes"), and fin-ally are asked to recall the originally memorized items]. One psychologist, the American cognitive scientist George A. Miller (1920-), sets the STM capacity of humans to be about *seven* pieces, bits, chunks, or items of information in any given instance; and another theorist, the American cognitive scientist Herbert A. Simon (1916-2001), estimates the capacity of STM to be about *five* chunks of information. The chief utility of STM is connected with language/sentence comprehension: in order to understand a simple sentence one must be able to remember its beginning at least up to the time of its end. Theoretically, STM may be said to occupy a place on a temporal continuum between the two phenomena/concepts of "sensory/iconic memory" and "long-term memory." That is, "sensory memory" (a "sensory register" that involves an "iconic store" for vision and an "echoic store" for audition) is a very short-time store of information that is activated when information is being processed by one's sensory organs ("sensory store") and has a duration of a few seconds; on the other hand, LTM is a long-term memory store of information that has a temporal capacity of periods ranging from about 30 seconds upwards to many years, even decades [cf., *logogen theory* - is a model for word recognition, formulated by the English cognitive psychologist John Morton (1933-), and refers to a representation of a word or *verbal* unit in LTM, activated by speech sounds, writing, or an object/event to which it refers; *imagen theory* - refers to a representation of a *visual* image in LTM; and *modality effect* - refers to any result of the presentation of information through different sensory modalities; for example, the poorer *immediate* recall of *simple* verbal information presented to the visual modality as compared to the auditory modality, or the poorer *long-term* recall of *complex* verbal information presented to the auditory modality as compared to the visual modality]. LTM, or *secondary memory*, includes several categories of memory, such as: *episodic memory* (personal experience information is stored with mental tags about when, where, and how the information was acquired); *semantic memory* (factual information about the world, and the "meanings" of things, words, objects, etc.); *perceptual memory* (memory for visual, auditory, and other perceptual information, such as memory for people's faces and voices); *declarative memory* (conscious memory that may be communicated to others); *procedural memory* (memory for procedures, or complex activities, occurring without conscious awareness or thought of the process); and *working memory* (the hypothesized system that holds the input while one formulates an interpretation of it). An alternative to the conventional model of three separate memory stores (sensory, STM, and LTM) is the *levels of processing theory* formulated, primarily, by the Canadian-based Scottish psychologist Fergus I. M. Craik (1935-), the Canadian-based Australian psychologist Robert S. Lockhart (1939-), and the Estonian-born Canadian psychologist Endel Tulving (1927-). The notion of *levels of processing* refers to the depth with which incoming information is analyzed and encoded, and ranges from superficial processing of sensory features to semantic and conceptual processing where deeper levels of processing result in longer-lasting memories (cf., *screen/cover memory* - in psychoanalysis, refers to a non-threatening memory of a childhood experience that is salient for its sharpness relative to the insignificance of its content, and indicates an unconscious memory of something that is important and/or threatening to the individual; and blocking memory - a

memory that intrudes into consciousness and obstructs the retrieval of a different, though related, memory). According to *levels of processing theory*, in the processing and sequencing of information, the early sensory analyses are relatively automatic and effortless, whereas the later deeper analyses require more attention and effort. In support of this theory, research on memory for words/verbal materials indicates that recall is *poor* for words that are processed according to their *visual* appearance, a little *better* for words processed according to their *sound*, and *best* of words processed according to their *meaning*. Related to this theoretical approach is the *domains of processing theory*, which proposes that the more elaboration that is involved in the information processing of material at a given level of processing, the better the material will be remembered (cf., *mnemon* - a theoretical basic unit of memory referring to the minimum physical change in the nervous system that encodes a memory; and *engram theory*, or "memory trace" or "neurogram," is a hypothesized physical representation of a memory in the brain). See also FORGETTING/MEMORY, THEORIES OF; INFORMATION/INFORMATION-PROCESSING THEORY; WORKING MEMORY, THEORY OF.

REFERENCES

Lashley, K. S. (1950). In search of the engram. *Symposium of the Society of Experimental Biology, 4,* 454-482.

Miller, G. A. (1956). The magical number seven, plus or minus two: Some limits on our capacity for processing information. *Psychological Review, 63,* 81-97; *101,* 343-352.

Brown, J. (1958). Some tests of the decay theory of immediate memory. *Quarterly Journal of Experimental Psychology, 10,* 12-21.

Peterson, L. R., & Peterson, M. J. (1959). Short-term retention of individual verbal items. *Journal of Experimental Psychology. 58,* 193-198.

Sperling, G. (1960). The information available in brief visual presentation. *Psychological Monographs, 74,* 1-29.

Neisser, U. (1967). *Cognitive psychology.* New York: Appleton-Century.

Morton, J. (1969). Interaction of information in word recognition. *Psychological Review, 76,* 165-178.

Craik, F. I. M., & Lockhart, R. S. (1972). Levels of processing: A framework for memory research. *Journal of Verbal Learning and Verbal Behavior, 21,* 671-684.

Tulving, E., & Donaldson, W. (1972). *Organization of memory.* New York: Academic Press.

Simon, H. A. (1974). How big is a chunk? *Science, 183,* 482-488.

Craik, F. I. M., & Tulving, E. (1975). Depth of processing and the retention of words in episodic memory. *Journal of Experimental Psychology: General, 104,* 268-294.

SHORT-TERM HABITUATION. See HABITUATION, PRINCIPLE/LAW OF.

SHORT TIME-HORIZON HYPOTHESIS. This theoretical proposition states that psychopathic individuals possess an abnormally constricted *temporal/time horizon* where they show a foreshortened sense of the future. Normally, one's time perspective or horizon becomes broader and more complex with increased age and unique living experiences. However, the *short time-horizon hypothesis* - as regards many mentally disordered persons - indicates the opposite is true. See also TIME, THEORIES OF.
REFERENCE
Lilienfeld, S., Hess, T., & Rowland, C. (1996). Psychopathic personality traits and temporal experience: A test of the short time-horizon hypothesis. *Journal of Psychopathology and Behavioral Assessment, 18,* 285-314.

SIDIS' LAW OF LAUGHTER. The Ukrainian-born American psychologist Boris Sidis (1867-1923) presented his informal, or loosely-suggested, *law of laughter* in the following terms: all unrestrained and spontaneous activities of normal functions give rise to the emotion of joy with its expression of smiles and laughter. Sidis asserted that *play* is essentially the manifestation of "spontaneous, unrestrained activity" and, therefore, constitutes the beginning phase in the ultimate understanding of the nature of laughter. According to Sidis, laughter, smiling, and grinning are the external manifestations of the "play instinct." Sidis considers *humor* to be resident in the higher forms of ridicule where the malicious aspect is not only eliminated but the phenomenon of sympathy seems to emerge. Thus, according to Sidis' analysis, it is possible to love and sympathize with persons whom we may have regarded initially as ludicrous. See also HUMOR, THEORIES OF; McDOUGALL'S THEORY OF HUMOR/ LAUGHTER; SULLY'S THEORY OF LAUGHTER/HUMOR.
REFERENCE
Sidis, B. (1913). *The psychology of laughter.* New York: Appleton.

SIGNAL DETECTION, THEORY OF. = sensory decision theory = detection theory = statistical decision theory. The *theory of signal detection* (TSD) - developed by the American psychologist John A. Swets (1928-) and his colleagues - is a mathematical theory of the detection of physical signals that measures not only an observer's ability to detect a stimulus when it is present but also one's guessing behavior as reflected in a "yes" response when, in fact, no signal is present; in this sense, TSD is a *statistical decision theory* where the decision-making process is studied and decision rules are established. TSD is based on the assumption that sensitivity to a signal is not merely a result of its intensity (as *classical psychophysical theory* asserts), but is dependent, also, on the amount of "noise" present, the motivation of the participant, and the criterion that the individual sets up for responding. TSD represents an innovation in thinking about the way in which information is processed in psychophysical experiments and constitutes *the* major theoretical development in psychophysics since Gustav Fechner's pioneering work of over a century ago. Other models of psychophysical discrimination, such as the *phi-gamma* and *neural quantum* positions, may be viewed as *two-state theories* of perceptual processing. *Two-state theories* imply that in any detection experiment, the perceptual system can signify only two possible states on a given trial: a detection state in which a stimulus is present and a nondetection state in which a stimulus is not present. TSD, on the other hand, is a *multistate theory* that assumes that every trial contains some degree of interference or "noise" that emanates from several possible sources, such as spontaneous firing in the nervous system, changes inherent in the environment or in the equipment used for generating stimuli, and factors deliberately introduced by the experimenter. Such noise always results in a greater-than-zero level of sensation, and the stimulus to be detected always occurs against a background of noise. A major assumption of TSD is that the amount of neural stimulation is normally distributed, and the individual's decision to respond "yes" (i.e., "I detected a signal") is given by whether the total stimulation contributed either by noise alone or by noise *plus* signal exceeds the set-response criterion. The proportion of *hits* (i.e., cases in which the person responds "yes" where a signal is actually present) to *false alarms* (i.e., cases in which the person responds "yes," but where there is no physical signal present) can be varied by manipulating the participant's criterion. A method of representing the data from a TSD experiment is called the *receiver-operating characteristic* (ROC) curve that shows a plot of the number of *hits* and *false alarms* depending on the number of *catch trials* (i.e., the trials where there is no signal present). The result of ROC curve-plotting is a sensitive measure of the participant's true sensory sensitivity. Performance indices of TSD are the response criterion - called *beta*, which is a nonperceptual measure that reflects bias in responding, and a perceptual index - called *d-prime*, which specifies the sensitivity of a given observer and, as such, reflects the observer's ability to discriminate signal from noise. The value of *d-prime* is defined as the separation between the means/averages of the noise and the signal-plus-noise distributions expressed in terms of their standard deviation. The larger the value of *d-prime*, the more detectable the signal and/or the greater the sensory capability of the observer. Although all aspects of TSD have not received unanimous and unqualified support, enough favorable evidence has accumulated so that it has gained general acceptance among researchers concerned with perceptual processes. The principal advantage of TSD is that it permits the inherent detectability of the signal to be separated from attitudinal and motivational variables that influence the observer's criteria for judgment, and TSD becomes useful when it is of interest to learn whether an experimental outcome is attributable to a change in the perceptual system, to variations in response bias, or to both. A. Wright developed a theoretical framework that attempts to bring together TSD, the *phi-gamma hypothesis*, and the *neural quantum theory*, and indicates that the two major variants of *classical threshold theory* and the contemporary TSD may not be as far apart as they might seem. Eventually, it may be possible to integrate these approaches under a single theoretical model. See also ELICITED OBSERVING RATE HYPOTHESIS; NEURAL QUANTUM THEORY; PHI-GAMMA HYPOTHESIS; PSYCHOPHYSICAL LAWS/THEORY.

REFERENCES

Tanner, W., & Swets, J. (1954). A decision-making theory of visual detection. *Psychological Review, 61*, 401-409.

Swets, J. (1961). Is there a sensory threshold? *Science, 134*, 168-177.

Swets, J., Tanner, W., & Birdsall, T. (1961). Decision processes in perception. *Psychological Review, 68*, 301-340.

Atkinson, R. (1963). A variable sensitivity theory of signal detection. *Psychological Review, 70*, 91-106.

Hohe, R. (1965). Detection of a visual signal with low background noise: An experimental comparison of two theories. *Journal of Experimental Psychology, 70*, 459-463.

Green, D., & Swets, J. (1966). *Signal detection and psychophysics*. New York: Wiley.

Krantz, D. (1969). Threshold theories of signal detection. *Psychological Review, 76*, 308-324.

Parducci, A., & Sandusky, A. (1970). Limits on the applicability of signal detection theory. *Perception and Psychophysics, 7*, 63-64.

Swets, J. (1973). The relative operating characteristic in psychology. *Science*, *182*, 990-1000.

Wright, A. (1974). Psychometric and psychophysical theory within a framework of response bias. *Psychological Review*, *81*, 322-347.

Egan, J. (1975). *Signal detection theory and ROC-analysis*. New York: Academic Press.

SIGN-GESTALT THEORY. See TOLMAN'S THEORY.

SIMILARITY-ATTRACTION HYPOTHESIS. See LOVE, THEORIES OF.

SIMILARITY PARADOX. See SKAGGS-ROBINSON HYPOTHESIS.

SIMILARITY/RESEMBLANCE, LAW OF. See ASSOCIATION, LAWS/PRINCIPLES OF; GESTALT THEORY/LAWS.

SIMON EFFECT. This proposition states that the spatial relations between stimuli and responses influence participants' behavior in reaction-time experiments even when spatial position is not the relevant stimulus dimension. The effect of such "task-irrelevant spatial correspondence" between stimulus and response was first described by J. R. Simon and A. P. Rudell (1967) in the *auditory* modality and by J. L. Craft and J. R. Simon (1970) in the *visual* modality. The phenomenon eventually became known as the *Simon effect* (cf., Lu & Proctor, 1995), and is generally based on the assumption that it arises from a conflict between the "spatial code" of the stimulus and that of the response (cf., the *Stroop effect*; and for a "computation model" of the *Simon effect*, see Zorzi & Umilta, 1995). A typical *Simon-effect* task involves a testing paradigm in which the participant is presented with two stimuli (e.g., two geometrical shapes) and is instructed to press a left-hand key in response to one of them (e.g., a circle), and to press the right-hand key in response to the other (e.g., a square). The stimuli are presented randomly to the left or right side of a fixation point on a screen. In such a situation, the stimulus *position* is not "task

relevant," meaning that the coding of stimulus position is not necessary for selection of the correct response. However, even though participants are instructed to ignore stimulus location, their reaction-times are *faster* when the position of the stimulus corresponds to that of the response (i.e., left-left, or right-right) and *slower* when it does not correspond (i.e., left-right, or right-left). The *Simon effect* has been explained variously by psychologists in terms of a coding hypothesis, an attentional hypothesis, an orienting reaction, and an integrated model of attention-orienting as a basic process in generating the spatial code. See also STROOP EFFECT/INTER-FERENCE EFFECT/STROOP TEST; REACTION-TIME PARADIGMS/MODELS.

REFERENCES

Simon, J. R., & Rudell, A. P. (1967). Auditory S-R compatibility: The effect of an irrelevant cue on information processing. *Journal of Applied Psychology, 51*, 300-304.

Craft, J. L., & Simon, J. R. (1970). Effects of an irrelevant auditory stimulus on visual choice reaction time. *Journal of Experimental Psychology, 86*, 272-274.

Lu, C.-H., & Proctor, R. W. (1995). The influence of irrelevant location information on performance: A review of the Simon and spatial Stroop effects. *Psychonomic Bulletin and Review, 2*, 174-207.

Zorzi, M., & Umilta, C. (1995). A computational model of the Simon effect. *Psychological Research, 58*, 193-205.

SIMPLEST PATH, LAW OF. See LEAST EFFORT, PRINCIPLE OF.

SIMPLICITY, LAW OF. See GESTALT THEORY/LAWS; PARSIMONY, LAW/PRINCIPLE OF.

SIMPSON'S PARADOX. See NULL HYPOTHESIS.

SINGLE CHANNEL MODEL. See INFORMATION/INFORMATION-PROCESSING THEORY.

SINGLE-RECEPTOR THEORY. See FOVEAL CONE HYPOTHESIS.

SITUATED IDENTITIES, THEORY OF. See CONSTRUCTIVISM, THEORIES OF.

SITUATED KNOWLEDGE, DOCTRINE OF. See CONSTRUCTIVISM, THEORIES OF.

SITUATIONAL ATTRIBUTION EFFECT. See ATTRIBUTION THEORY.

SITUATIONAL EFFECT. See EXPERIMENTER EFFECTS.

SITUATIONALISM, DOCTRINE OF. See EXPERIMENTER EFFECTS.

SITUATIONAL THEORY OF LEADERSHIP. See LEADERSHIP, THEORIES OF.

SIZE-DISTANCE ILLUSION. See APPENDIX A, CORRIDOR ILLUSION.

SIZE-DISTANCE INVARIANCE HYPOTHESIS. See EMMERT'S LAW.

SIZE-WEIGHT ILLUSION. See APPENDIX A.

SKAGGS-ROBINSON HYPOTHESIS. This hypothesis, credited to the American psychologists Ernest Burton Skaggs (1893-1970) and Edward Stevens Robinson (1893-1937), is derived from the *similarity paradox* in the area of serial and transfer phenomena in human verbal learning (cf., the *acoustic similarity effect* - the tendency for lists of similar-sounding words to be more difficult to learn than lists of dissimilar-sounding words). The classical statement, formulated in 1925-1927, of the relationship between similarity of learned material and interference in human learning is that "the greater the similarity, the greater the interference" (Osgood, 1953); cf., *Kjerstad-Robinson law* - named after the American psychologists Conrad Kjerstad (1883-1967) and E. S. Robinson, and formulated in 1919, states that in verbal learning the amount of material learned during equal portions of the learning time is the same for different lengths of the material to be learned; and the *Muller-Schumann law* (also known as the *associative inhibition paradigm*) - named after the German psychologists Georg Elias Muller (1850-1934) and Friedrich Schumann (1863-1940), and formulated in 1893, states that once an association has been formed between two items, it becomes more difficult to establish an association between either one of these items and a third one. This lawful statement is connected to the work of J. McGeoch and others, but when it is carried to its logical conclusion, it leads to an impossible state of affairs. That is, a stimulus situation can never be precisely identical from case to case, nor can the response, but they may be maximally similar, which is when the greatest facilitation, or ordinary learning, takes place. As Osgood (1953, p. 530) states the *similarity paradox*: "ordinary learning is at once the *theoretical* condition for maximal *interference*, but obviously the *practical* condition for maximal *facilitation*." A distinction was made earlier by H. Wylie between stimulus and response activities where the transfer effect in a learning task is *positive* when an "old" response is associated with a "new" stimulus but *negative* when an "old" stimulus must be associated with a "new" response. This principle has been shown to be valid only within broad limits of materials, but it fails to account for degrees of either stimulus or response similarity. E. S. Robinson was one of the first psychologists to clearly conceive of the *similarity paradox*, and he proposed (via J. McGeoch's "christening") what is known as the *Skaggs-Robinson hypothesis* as a resolution. The experimental aspects of this hypothesis show a "high peak-low valley-medium peak" curve when the relationship is graphed between the variables of "degree of stimulus similarity on a descending scale" on the abscissa/horizontal axis and "efficiency of recall of material" on the ordinate/vertical axis. Thus, the hypothesis states that facilitation of learning is greatest when successively practiced materials are identical ("high peak") and least (with greatest interference) when similarity of materials is moderate ("low valley"). Facilitation of learning increases again as materials become least similar ("medium peak") but never attains the level of the "high peak" condition. Several experiments give limited validation to the poorly defined *Skaggs-Robinson hypothesis*. Later, in the 1940s, many other studies on serial and transfer learning were conducted to examine the *Skaggs-Robinson hypothesis* and attempt to explain the fundamental *similarity paradox* (i.e., that responses can never truly be identical, yet ordinary learning takes place). Osgood (1949) attempts a resolution of the paradox by proposing a model called the *transfer and retroaction surface*, and that represents an important systematic effort to integrate a large range of transfer and retroaction phenomena, but it proved to be inadequate for a number of reasons (e.g., although the verbal learning data give evidence of differences in transfer between identical, similar, and unrelated stimuli, or responses, they have not demonstrated a "continuous gradient" of effects when similarity is varied over the intermediate range). The demise of the *Skaggs-Robinson hypothesis* was aided by its nonanalytic formulation and its lack of specification of the locus of intertask similarity. The hypothesis lapsed into disuse as the analysis of similarity relations in retroaction shifted to the investigation of stimulus and response functions. See also ASSIMILATION, LAW OF; INTERFERENCE THEORIES OF FORGETTING; TRANSFER OF TRAINING; THORN-DIKE'S THEORY OF.

REFERENCES

Muller, G. E., & Schumann, F. (1893). [Muller-Schumann law]. *Zeitschrift fur Psychologie und Physiologie der Sinnesorgane, 6*, 81-190, 257-339.

Wylie, H. (1919). An experimental study of transfer of response in the white rat. *Behavior Monographs, 3*, No. 16.

Robinson, E. S. (1920). Some factors determining the degree of retroactive inhibition. *Psychological Monographs, 28*, No. 128.

Skaggs, E. (1925). Further studies in retroactive inhibition. *Psychological Monographs, 34*, No. 161.

Robinson, E. S. (1927). The similarity factor in retroaction. *American Journal of Psychology, 39*, 297-312.

McGeoch, J., & McGeoch, G. (1937). Studies in retroactive inhibition: X. The influence of similarity of meaning between lists of paired associates. *Journal of Experimental Psychology, 21*, 320-329.

Osgood, C. (1949). The similarity paradox in human learning: A resolution. *Psychological Review, 56*, 132-143.

Osgood, C. (1953). *Method and theory in experimental psychology.* New York: Oxford University Press.

Postman, L. (1971). Transfer, interference, and forgetting. In J. Kling & L. Riggs (Eds.), *Woodworth and Schlosberg's experimental psychology.* New York: Holt, Rinehart, & Winston.

SKILL THEORY. See PIAGET'S THEORY OF DEVELOPMENTAL STAGES.

SKINNER'S DESCRIPTIVE BEHAVIOR/ OPERANT CONDITIONING THEORY. The American psychologist Burrhus Frederic Skinner (1904-1990) developed a distinctive approach to understanding human and animal learning and behavior called *operant reinforcement/conditioning*. In examining Skinner's approach, it is noteworthy that he rejected the use of formal theory in learning and psychology, especially the postulate-theorem, hypothetico-deductive (deductive reasoning) type of approach to theorizing. It may be said that Skinner's general approach follows the *Baconian method* [named after the English philosopher Francis Bacon (1561-1626)] of scientific investigation based on systematic experimentation and inductive logic/reasoning (as contrasted to deductive logic/reasoning), whereby inferences and general principles are derived from particular observations and cases (cf., Thilly, 1902). Skinner's specific position is characterized by a heavy emphasis on the study of "emitted" responses (operants) that are strongly influenced by the consequences (reinforcement) of the responses rather than on "stimulus-elicited" (respondent) responses (cf., *response-response*, or *R-R, laws* - these are principles that are concerned with the associations between responses, in contrast to *stimulus-response*, or *S-R, laws* that are concerned with associations between stimuli and responses). Skinner focused, also, on individual participants/organisms where behavioral laws and equations are expected to apply, rather than on groups of individuals yielding generalized or statistical results. According to Skinner, the employment of a *functional analysis of behavior* (i.e., behavior described in terms of cause-and-effect relationships) allows one to achieve maximum control of behavior. In such an analysis, there would be no need to make inferences or to discuss the mechanisms operating *within* the organism (such as "self," "feelings," or "personality"). Skinner developed, essentially, a program for a *descriptive* science where understanding of behavior and its environmental consequences - with no concern for intervening events - leads to laws and universal principles of behavior (cf., *theory of behavioral power functions* - with both operant conditioning and psychophysical data, this approach attempts to explain converging sets of power functions to solve dimensional problems with the standard power function, and to account for the relation between various types of psychophysical scales; Staddon, 1978). Skinner assumed that behavior is orderly and modifiable, and the behavioral scientists' goal should be to understand, predict, and control behavior. A key concept in Skinner's program (*operant reinforcement theory*) of behavioral change is the *principle of positive reinforcement* that refers to a stimulus or environmental event following a behavior and causing an *increase* in the frequency of that behavior (cf., B. Wolman who cites 10 variants on this same principle). Other important concepts in Skinner's approach are: positive and negative punishment, negative reinforcement, extinction, shaping, differential reinforcement, schedules of reinforcement (including fixed interval, fixed ratio, variable interval, and variable ratio schedules), superstitious behavior, conditioned/secondary reinforcer, generalized reinforcer, stimulus generalization, stimulus discrimination, and chaining (cf., *associative-chain theory* of the early behaviorists concerning complex behavior - holds that each of the several components in serial action is linked associatively to the preceding component with the result that the total act is "chained off" in a smooth sequence of elementary acts). In his early work, Skinner (1938) described various *static laws of the reflex* [cf., the physiological

reflex laws of the English physiologist Sir Charles Scott Sherrington (1861-1952)], including: *law of the threshold* - the intensity of the stimulus must reach or exceed a certain critical value, called the *threshold*, in order to elicit a response; the *law of latency*; *law of response magnitude*; *law of afterdischarge*; and the *law of temporal summation*. Skinner described, also, the *dynamic laws of reflex strength*, *law of the refractory phase*, *law of reflex fatigue*, *law of facilitation*, *law of inhibition* (cf., *law of conflicting associations* - principle of mental association where a thought similar to the desired association tends to inhibit that association), *law of conditioning of Type S*, *law of extinction of Type S*, *law of conditioning of Type R* [cf., the *law of resolution* - formulated by the American biologist Herbert Spencer Jennings (1868-1947), states that the resolution of one physiological state into another becomes easier and more rapid after it has taken place a number of times], and the *law of extinction of Type R*. Skinner's concept of *reflex reserve* employs two measures of responses within extinction: rate of responding and total number of responses before responding returns to its normal rate prior to conditioning. The total number of responses during extinction, often described as "resistance to extinction," was formerly called the *reflex reserve* by Skinner (using a figure of speech to describe a kind of reservoir of responses ready to be emitted during extinction), but he later, apparently, rejected the concept because of his subsequent interpretation of appropriate scientific concepts rather than because of any change in the factual relationships described. Skinner (1938) also provides a number of *laws of the interaction of the reflexes*: *law of compatibility*, *law of prepotency*, *law of algebraic summation*, *law of blending*, *law of spatial summation* (cf., *summation effect* - a tendency for the same stimulus simultaneously striking two different receptors to produce a single sensory quality), *law of chaining*, and the *law of induction*. Other principles in the plethora of laws cited by Skinner (1938) in his early work are: the *law of the extinction of chained reflexes*, *law of stimulus discrimination in Type S*, *law of stimulus discrimination in Type R*, and the *law of the operant reserve*. In general, except for slight differences in terminology, Skinner's views of learning are quite similar to those of E. L. Thorndike's work after 1930. Except for the way each researcher measured the dependent variables, Thorndike's *instrumental conditioning* and Skinner's *operant conditioning* may be considered to be the same set of procedures. Skinner's principles have been applied successfully to teaching and learning settings, to understanding various social problems, to behavior modification and therapy in the clinical setting, to psychopharmacology, to threshold and laboratory studies, and to warfare contexts. The experimental results reported by Skinner, his associates, and his students employing the *idiographic*, or single-subject/participant, design present a degree of lawfulness and precise regularity in behavior analysis and control that is virtually unparalleled among psychologists. Perhaps the criticism most widely leveled at Skinner is that his theory is no theory at all where he has little appreciation for the role of theory and mediating processes in building the science of psychology [cf., the term *hyphen psychologist*, which is a half-humorous sobriquet applied by "pure" behaviorists to theorists who invoke mediational processes, mental constructs, and hypothesized entities occurring between presentation of a stimulus and the organism's response; and the *empty organism theory* - holds that only stimuli and responses (*S-R model*) are needed in behavioral analysis where conscious thought, feelings, and internal drives of the organism may be neglected; this approach has been replaced by the *S-O-R model* where the O represents the "organism," and its contributions to behavioral events and outcomes]. Other criticisms of Skinner's approach include the argument that it is too simplistic and elemental to represent the full complexity of human behavior, especially language behavior. This assessment typically is-sues from humanistic, holistic, and cognitive psychologists and theorists. Skinner's proponents and followers are viewed, also, as being insular and demonstrating no responsibility for the task of coordinating their work closely with that of others who study learning. However, Skinner's position has served to highlight the fundamental opposition between scientists who believe that progress is to be made only by rigorous examination of actual behavior resulting in the discovery of a few generalizations versus those who believe that behavioral observations are interesting only to the degree that they disclose underlying laws of the mind that are only partially revealed in behavior. See also BEHAVIORIST THEORY; CHOMSKY'S PSYCHOLINGUISTIC THEORY; HULL'S LEARNING THEORY; INFECTION THEORY/EFFECT; INHIBITION, LAWS OF; LEARNING THEORIES/LAWS; SKINNER'S DESTRUCTURED LEARNING THEORY; THORNDIKE'S LAW OF EFFECT.

REFERENCES

Bacon, F. (1620/1960). Novum organum. In F. H. Anderson (Ed.), *The new organon and related writings*. New York: Liberal Arts Press.

Thilly, F. (1902). The theory of induction. *Psychological Review, 9*, 136-137.

Sherrington, C. S. (1906). *The integrative action of the nervous system*. New York: Cambridge University Press.

Skinner, B. F. (1935). The generic nature of the concepts of stimulus and response, *Journal of Genetic Psychology, 12*, 40-65.

Skinner, B. F. (1938). *The behavior of organisms: An experimental analysis*. New York: Appleton-Century-Crofts.

Skinner, B. F. (1950). Are theories of learning necessary? *Psychological Review, 57*, 193-216.

Skinner, B. F. (1953). *Science and human behavior*. New York: Macmillan.

Skinner, B. F. (1956). A case history in scientific method. *American Psychologist, 11*, 221-233.

Ferster, C., & Skinner, B. F. (1957). *Schedules of reinforcement*. New York: Appleton-Century-Crofts.

Skinner, B. F. (1957). *Verbal behavior*. New York: Appleton-Century-Crofts.

Skinner, B. F. (1958). Teaching machines. *Science, 128*, 969-977.

Skinner, B. F. (1960). Pigeons in a Pelican. *American Psychologist, 15*, 28-37.

Skinner, B. F. (1961). *Cumulative record*. New York: Appleton-Century-Crofts.

Skinner, B. F. (1963). Behaviorism at fifty. *Science*, *140*, 951-958.

Skinner, B. F. (1968). *The technology of teaching*. New York: Appleton-Century-Crofts.

Skinner, B. F. (1969). *Contingencies of reinforcement: A theoretical analysis*. New York: Appleton-Century-Crofts.

Chomsky, N. (1971). The case against B. F. Skinner. *New York Review of Books*, December 30, 18-24.

Skinner, B. F. (1971). *Beyond freedom and dignity*. New York: Knopf.

Wolman, B. (Ed.) (1973). *Handbook of general psychology*. Englewood Cliffs, NJ: Prentice-Hall.

Skinner, B. F. (1974). *About behaviorism*. New York: Knopf.

Skinner, B. F. (1976). *Particulars of my life*. New York: Knopf.

Staddon, J. E. R. (1978). Theory of behavioral power functions. *Psychological Review*, *85*, 305-320.

Skinner, B. F. (1984). *The shaping of a behaviorist*; and *A matter of consequences*. Washington Square, NY: New York University Press.

Staddon, J. E. R., & Cerutti, D. T. (2003). Operant conditioning. *Annual Review of Psychology*, *54*, 115-144.

SKINNER'S DESTRUCTURED LEARNING THEORY. In a magnificent and courageous exposition (Skinner, 1950), the American psychologist Burrhus Frederic Skinner (1904-1990) questions whether *theories of learning* are necessary at all in a science of behavior (!) Skinner asserts that behavioral science must eventually deal with behavior in its relation to certain manipulable variables, and *theories* - whether neural, mental, or conceptual - refer to intervening steps, involving extra-dimensional systems, in such relationships. However, according to Skinner, instead of prompting one to search for, and explore, relevant variables, *theories* frequently have the opposite effect. That is, when one attributes behavior to a neural or mental event, real or conceptual, one is likely to forget the remaining and essential task of accounting for that neural or mental event. The temptation in

the use of *theories* is to give *theoretical* answers in place of the *empirical* answers that might be found through further study of a phenomenon. Skinner observes that the principal function of *learning theory* is not to suggest appropriate research, but to create a false sense of security or an unwarranted satisfaction with the status quo. Moreover, according to Skinner, research designed with respect to *theory* is likely, also, to be wasteful. Skinner asks the question: "How much research and scientific activity can be done *without* theory?" and suggests that it is possible that the most rapid progress toward an understanding of learning may be made by research that is *not* designed to test *theories* that include various extra-dimensional systems. Apparently, Skinner attempts to "destructure" the traditional strategy that is used in theory-driven research. That is, psychological textbooks on conducting research take their cue from the *logician* rather than from the *empiricist* where the former employ the orderly and rational procedure of developing hypotheses, making deductions, conducting experimental tests, and drawing conclusions and confirmations. Skinner - as a practical *empiricist* and "destructured theorist" - argues that most scientists do *not* actually work in such a logical, formal, sequential, predictable, and theory-structured fashion. Skinner recommends that an acceptable scientific program in the area of learning is to collect *empirical* data and relate them to manipulable variables with the goal of establishing *functional relationships* among relevant variables. See also LEARNING THEORIES/LAWS; SKINNER'S DESCRIPTIVE BEHAVIOR/ OPERANT CONDITIONING THEORY.

REFERENCES

Skinner, B. F. (1950). Are theories of learning necessary? *Psychological Review*, *57*, 193-216.

Skinner, B. F. (1969). *Contingencies of reinforcement: A theoretical analysis*. New York: Appleton-Century.

Richelle, M. (1987). Variation and selection: The evolutionary analogy in Skinner's theory. In S. Modgil & C. Modgil (Eds.), *B. F. Skinner: Consensus and controversy*. New York: Falmer.

SLEEPER EFFECT. See ATTITUDE/AT-
TITUDE CHANGE, THEORIES OF; PER-
SUASION/INFLUENCE THEORIES.

SLEEP, THEORIES OF. The experience of
sleep is characterized by a particular loss of
consciousness accompanied by a variety of
behavioral and neurophysiological effects (cf.,
hyphic-jolts effect/phenomenon - consists of a
sudden single jerk of the body that occurs
typically when one is just about to fall asleep;
apparently, its cause, as well as its cure, is
unknown, and remains a mystery as to its
occurrence). In modern psychology, sleep and
various stages of sleep are defined and characterized typically by particular physiological
events, specifically by distinctive brain-wave
patterns as recorded by an electroencephalograph, metabolic processes, muscle tone (cf.,
Isakower phenomenon - named after the Austrian psychoanalyst Otto Isakower (1899-
1972), refers to strange hallucinations usually
felt in the mouth, hands, or skin; they include
the feelings of an object pulsating or ap-
proaching/receding, and they occur mainly
when falling asleep), heart and respiration
rates, and the presence/absence of rapid eye
movements (REMs). Periods of REM sleep
(cf., *REM sleep theories*; Atkinson, Atkinson,
Smith, & Hilgard, 1987) are evident by its
primary defining feature, the rapid eye movements, and several less detectable factors,
including a lack of *delta waves* (slow, large-
amplitude brain waves), flaccid musculature,
fluctuating heartbeat, erratic respiration, genital changes, and dreaming (80-85 percent
reliability of dreaming during REM sleep).
Non-REM (NREM) sleep, on the other hand,
is usually divided into four separate stages
based on the proportion of *delta waves* observed: stage 1 is 0 percent of total brain activity, stage 2 is up to 20 percent *delta waves*;
stage 3 is between 20-50 percent *delta waves*;
and stage 4 is over 50 percent *delta waves*.
Stages 3 and 4 often are referred to collectively as *slow-wave sleep*. In all the stages
there is a progressively deeper and deeper
sleep and all are characterized by a lack of
REM, a regular heartbeat, rhythmic respiration, low levels of metabolic activity, and
moderate-to-high muscle tone. In terms of
arousal theory, the current conception of sleep

is that it must be considered as a condition
that is qualitatively different, as well as quantitatively different, from the state of wakefulness (cf., *dual-arousal model* - refers to the
physiological relationship between sleep and
wakefulness where the arousal function involves two nerve pathways: the diffuse thalamic system and the reticular activating system; the model indicates that the two systems
permit the brain to operate in a dual manner,
one for stimulus-processing and the other for
executing responses). There are active mechanisms controlling sleep just as there are active
mechanisms controlling arousal during wakefulness. Sleep should be considered not as one
collection but as two separate ones where
quiet sleep (or NREM sleep) and *active sleep*
(or REM sleep) constitute the *duality of sleep*.
Estimates suggest that people spend nearly a
third of their lives sleeping. Laboratory studies indicate that most individuals find it difficult to stay awake for more than 60 hours,
even though some "marathoners" have remained awake for close to 19 days. With sleep
deprivation, most people get cranky and have
difficulty concentrating, especially on boring
tasks (cf., *rebound effect* - a pattern of results,
opposite to those elicited by a drug or some
other special treatment, that occurs when the
drug/treatment is suddenly withdrawn, such as
"rebound insomnia" following abrupt withdrawal from a hypnotic drug, or "REM rebound" following the cessation of a period of
REM deprivation). Among the major theories
that have been formulated to explain the function and purpose of sleep is the *repair/restor-
ative/recuperative theory* that suggests that
sleep serves an important recuperative function, allowing one to recover not only from
physical fatigue, but also from emotional and
intellectual demands (cf., *extensions of waking
life theory*; Plotnik, 1993); however, the *re-
pair/restorative theory* has been criticized on
the basis that sleep, especially REM sleep, is
characterized by high levels of physiological
arousal and, thus, uses substantial amounts of
energy. Another theory, called the *adaptive
nonresponding theory* or the *evolutionary/cir-
cadian theory*, argues that sleep is a part of
circadian rhythms and evolved as a means of
conserving energy (cf., *energy conservation
theory*; McGee & Wilson, 1984), protecting

individuals from predators, and keeping early humans out of harm's way during the night. The *evolutionary/circadian theory* helps explain differences in sleep patterns across species where animals that sleep the longest (e.g., opposums and cats) are least threatened by the environment and can easily find food and shelter, whereas animals that sleep very little (e.g., horses and sheep) have diets that require constant foraging for food, and their only defense against predators is vigilance and running away. A *common/popular theory* is that people sleep in order to dream, and assumes that dreaming is an important activity for good health. Recently, W. Webb (1988) proposed a theory of sleep that combines some of the best explanatory features of both the *restorative* and *adaptive nonresponding theories*. This new theory considers sleep to be a function of *sleep demand* (based on the time of wakefulness preceding sleep), *circadian tendencies* (i.e., bodily rhythms whose cycle corresponds to approximately 24 hours and that include endocrine activity, metabolic function, and body temperature), *behaviors* or events that facilitate or inhibit sleep (such as body position, noise, or worrying), and several other variables such as species differences and developmental stages. See also AROUSAL THEORY; DREAM THEORY.

REFERENCES

Dement, W. (1960). The effect of sleep deprivation. *Science, 131,* 1705-1707.

Kleitman, N. (1963). *Sleep and wakefulness.* Chicago: University of Chicago Press.

Oswald, I. (1966). *Sleep.* Harmondsworth, Middlesex, UK: Penguin.

Roffwarg, H., Munzio, J., & Dement, W. (1966). Ontogenic development of the human sleep-dream cycle. *Science, 152,* 604-619.

Vogel, G. (1975). A review of REM sleep deprivation. *Archives of General Psychiatry, 32,* 749-761.

Cohen, D. (1979). *Sleep and dreaming: Origin, nature, and functions.* New York: Pergamon.

Webb, W. (1981). Some theories about sleep and their clinical implications. *Psychiatric Annals, 11,* 415-422.

Shapiro, C. (1982). Energy expenditure and restorative sleep. *Biological Psychology, 15,* 229-239.

Campbell, S., & Tobler, I. (1984). Animal sleep: A review of sleep duration across phylogeny. *Neuroscience and Biobehavioral Reviews, 8,* 269-300.

McGee, M., & Wilson, D. (1984). *Psychology: Science and application.* New York: West.

Horne, J. (1985). Sleep function, with particular reference to sleep deprivation. *Annals of Clinical Research, 17,* 199-208.

Atkinson, R. L., Atkinson, R. C., Smith, E., & Hilgard, E. R. (1987). *Introduction to psychology.* Harcourt Brace Jovanovich.

Webb, W. (1988). An objective behavioral model of sleep. *Sleep, 11,* 488-496.

Hobson, J. (1989). *Sleep.* New York: Freeman.

Plotnik, R. (1993). *Introduction to psychology.* Pacific Grove, CA: Brooks/Cole.

Espie, C. A. (2002). Insomnia. *Annual Review of Psychology, 53,* 215-243.

SMELL, LAWS/THEORIES OF. See OLFACTION/SMELL, THEORIES OF.

SNOWBALL EFFECT. See INFECTION THEORY/EFFECT; RUMOR TRANSMISSION THEORY.

SOAR THEORY/SYSTEM/PROGRAM. See PROBLEM-SOLVING AND CREATIVITY STAGE THEORIES.

SOCIAL CLASS THEORIES OF SCHIZOPHRENIA. See SCHIZOPHRENIA, THEORIES OF.

SOCIAL COGNITION THEORY. See BANDURA'S THEORY.

SOCIAL/COMMUNICATION MODEL OF HUMOR. See MARTINEAU'S MODEL OF HUMOR.

SOCIAL/COMMUNICATION THEORY OF LAUGHTER. This proposition states that laughter was a primary means of communication for primitive humans. According to the *social/communication theory of laughter*, laughter was originally a vocal signal to other members of the group/tribe that they might relax with safety. Other tenets of this theory are that laughter fulfills a social function as communication between parent and offspring, that laughter is a "social corrective" mechanism, that laughter is a means of communicating "joy," that humor and laughter are "social conflict-resolution" mechanisms, and that laughter is expressive of unity in group opinion. The observations by social scientists that laughter appears early in life, even before language occurs - and, also, that laughter and humor are universal phenomena - seem to indicate that the human laughter and humor responses have survived since earliest times for some utilitarian, social-communication, or adaptive-behavior purpose. See also DUPREEL'S SOCIOLOGICAL HUMOR/ LAUGHTER THEORY; HUMOR, THEORIES OF; MARTINEAU'S SOCIAL-COMMUNICATION MODEL OF HUMOR; RAPP'S THEORY OF THE ORIGINS OF LAUGHTER/HUMOR.

REFERENCES

Wallis, W. D. (1922). Why do we laugh? *Scientific Monthly, 15*, 343-347.

McComas, H. C. (1923). The origin of laughter. *Psychological Review, 30*, 45-55.

Hayworth, D. (1928). The social origin and function of laughter. *Psychological Review, 35*, 367-384.

SOCIAL COMPARISON EFFECT. See DECISION-MAKING THEORIES.

SOCIAL COMPARISON/EVALUATION THEORY. See FESTINGER'S COGNITIVE DISSONANCE THEORY.

SOCIAL COMPLIANCE. See COMPLIANCE EFFECTS/TECHNIQUES.

SOCIAL CONSTRUCTIVISM THEORY. See CONSTRUCTIVISM, THEORIES OF; PARADIGM SHIFT DOCTRINE.

SOCIAL DARWINISM THEORY. See CONSTRUCTIVISM, THEORIES OF.

SOCIAL DETERMINISM, DOCTRINE OF. See NATURALISTIC THEORY OF HISTORY.

SOCIAL DILEMMA MODELS. See RESOURCE DILEMMA MODEL/PARADIGM.

SOCIAL DRIFT THEORY. See SCHIZOPHRENIA, THEORIES OF.

SOCIAL EXCHANGE THEORY. See CONSTRUCTIVISM, THEORIES OF; EXCHANGE/SOCIAL EXCHANGE THEORY.

SOCIAL FACILITATION THEORY. See ZAJONC'S AROUSAL AND CONFLUENCE THEORIES.

SOCIAL IDENTITY THEORY. See CONSTRUCTIVISM, THEORIES OF.

SOCIAL IMPACT, LAW OF. The American social psychologist Bibb Latane (1937-) formulated the *law of social impact* that is designed to explain various *social influence effects*, including the phenomena of conformity, compliance, obedience, and persuasion. The law may be expressed, simply, by the equation: $M = f(SIN)$, where M is the magnitude of the impact, f indicates a function, S is the strength (e.g., credibility) of the influence source(s), I is the immediacy (e.g., "face-to-face" versus "distant") of the influence source(s), and N is the number of influence sources. Thus, in formal terms, the *law of social impact* is characterized as a "multiplicative model" where if any of the variables (S, I, or N) has a zero value/number, the resultant magnitude of the impact becomes zero [cf., *minority social influence* - studied by the Romanian-born French social psychologist Serge Moscovici (1920-), refers to situations in which the deviant/minority subgroup rejects the established majority group norm, and persuades the majority to go over to the minority attitudes/opinions/beliefs or behaviors and, thereby, changes the existing norm; in this approach, the conflict caused by minorities is believed to be a force for innovation and suggests that minorities are most effective when they are consistent, and in concordance, with the group's underlying values]. In the social-influence phenomenon of *obedience* [cf., the "shock" and "prison" experiments, respectively, by the American social psychologists Stanley Milgram (1933-1984) and Philip G. Zimbardo (1933-)], the individual yields to explicit instructions/orders from some perceived authority figure [cf., *Eichmann ef-fect* - named after the evil/notorious Nazi extermination camp chief Otto Adolf Eichmann (1906-1962), who slavishly followed Adolph Hitler's orders during World War II; this *concept/effect*, when applied to laboratory studies, emphasizes the fact that even in normal or peaceful times, an ordinary person may be willing to commit atrocities (one would not normally commit) when one sees oneself merely as an "instrument," not the "source," of some higher authority; cf., also, the Lt. William Calley court-martial case regarding the My Lai massacre of innocent civilians on March 16, 1968 during the Vietnam War, where Calley was merely "following orders;" and the Abu Ghraib prison-abuse scandal, involving the abuse of war prisoners by American soldiers/guards, in Iraq in 2004]. See also ALLPORT'S CONFORMITY HYPOTHESIS; ASCH'S CONFORMITY EFFECT; ATTITUDE/ATTITUDE CHANGE, THEORIES OF; BYSTANDER INTERVENTION EFFECT; COMPLIANCE EFFECTS/TECHNIQUES; DEINDIVIDUATION THEORY; PERSUASION/INFLUENCE THEORIES.

REFERENCES

Milgram, S. (1963). Behavioral study of obedience. *Journal of Abnormal and Social Psychology, 67*, 371-378.

Arendt, H. (1964). *Eichmann in Jerusalem: A report on the banality of evil.* New York: McGraw-Hill.

Zimbardo, P. G., Haney, C., & Banks, C. (1972). A study of prisoners and guards in a simulated prison. *Naval Research Reviews, 9*, 1-17.

Milgram, S. (1974). *Obedience to authority: An experimental view.* New York: Harper & Row.

Zimbardo, P. G. (1974). The psychology of imprisonment: Privation, power, and pathology. In Z. Rubin (Ed.), *Doing unto others: Explorations in social behavior.* Englewood Cliffs, NJ: Prentice-Hall.

Moscovici, S. (1976). *Social influence and social change.* London: Academic Press.

Latane, B. (1981). The psychology of social impact. *American Psychologist, 36*, 343-356.

Latane, B., & Wolf, S. (1981). The social impact of majorities and minorities. *Psychological Review, 88*, 738-753.

Nowak, A., Szamrej, J., & Latane, B. (1990). From private attitude to public opinion: A dynamic theory of social impact. *Psychological Review, 97*, 362-376.

SOCIAL IMPACT THEORY. See INFECTION THEORY/EFFECT; SOCIAL IMPACT, LAW OF.

SOCIAL INFLUENCE EFFECTS. See SOCIAL IMPACT, LAW OF.

SOCIAL INTELLIGENCE. See EMOTIONAL INTELLIGENCE, THEORY OF.

SOCIAL JUDGMENT THEORY. See PERSUASION/INFLUENCE THEORIES.

SOCIAL LEARNING/COGNITION THEORIES. See BANDURA'S THEORY; BEHAVIOR THERAPY/COGNITIVE THERAPY, THEORIES OF; ROTTER'S SOCIAL LEARNING THEORY.

SOCIAL LOAFING EFFECT. See BYSTANDER INTERVENTION EFFECT.

SOCIAL MAN THEORY. See ORGANIZATIONAL/INDUSTRIAL/SYSTEMS THEORY.

SOCIAL MOTION, LAW OF. See MURPHY'S LAW(S).

SOCIAL PENETRATION THEORY. See EXCHANGE/SOCIAL EXCHANGE THEORY.

SOCIAL PSYCHOLOGICAL DUAL-PROCESS MODELS. The basic implicit assumption underlying the early *dual-process models* in social-perception and cognition was a concern over whether certain biases in personal judgment, choices, and decision-making were the result of "bounded rationality," that is, whether human cognitive capacities and decision-making choices are strictly rational or not. Such a general *theoretical duality* (rationality versus non-rationality in decision-makers) was productive in its generation of empirical research in social psychology beginning in the 1930s and 1940s. See also ALLPORT'S CONFORMITY HYPOTHESIS; ASCH CONFORMITY EFFECT; BOUNDED RATIONALITY PRINCIPLE; BYSTANDER INTERVENTION EFFECT; DECISION-MAKING THEORIES; DEINDIVIDUATION THEORY; DUAL-PROCESS MODELS.
REFERENCES
Deutsch, M., & Krauss, R. M. (1965). *Theories in social psychology*. New York: Basic Books.
Liberman, A. M. (2001). Exploring the boundaries of rationality: A functional perspective on dual-process models in social psychology. In G. B. Moskowitz (Ed.), *Cognitive social psychology: The Princeton Symposium on the legacy and future of social cognition*. Mahwah, NJ: Erlbaum.

SOCIAL SCIENCES, LAW OF THE. See MURPHY'S LAW(S).

SOCIAL SELECTION THEORY OF PATHOLOGY. See SCHIZOPHRENIA, THEORIES OF.

SOCIAL SMILE THEORY. See FACIAL FEEDBACK HYPOTHESIS.

SOCIAL STRESS THEORIES OF PATHOLOGY. See PSYCHOPATHOLOGY, THEORIES OF.

SOCIAL-STRESS THEORY. See SELYE'S THEORY/MODEL OF STRESS.

SOCIETAL PROGRESS THEORY. See COMMUNICATION THEORY.

SOCIETAL-REACTION THEORY. See LABELING/DEVIANCE THEORY.

SOCIODRAMA/PSYCHODRAMA. See MORENO'S SOCIAL GROUP TECHNIQUES/THEORY.

SOCIOGENIC HYPOTHESIS. See PSYCHOPATHOLOGY, THEORIES OF.

SOCIOGRAM/SOCIOMETRY. See MORENO'S SOCIAL GROUP TECHNIQUES/THEORY.

SOCIOLOGICAL THEORY OF COMMUNICATION. See COMMUNICATION THEORY.

SOFT/HARD DETERMINISM, DOCTRINE OF. See DETERMINISM, DOCTRINE/THEORY OF.

SOLIPSISTIC DOCTRINE. See MIND/MENTAL STATES, THEORIES OF.

SOLOMON'S OPPONENT-PROCESS THEORY OF EMOTIONS/FEELINGS/MOTIVATION. The American psychologist Richard Lester Solomon (1918-1995) formulated a theory that applies a *homeostatic* (i.e., a state of physiological equilibrium, balance, or stability) *model* to the experience of emotion where it is assumed that emotions have *hedonic* value. That is, they vary in their ability to be unpleasant or pleasant. Solomon's *opponent-process theory* states that an emotional response will be followed in a short time by its *hedonic opposite*. For instance, if one currently feels anger, it will give way to a feeling of calm shortly; if one feels fear, it will give way to relief; and if one feels depression, it will give way to euphoria. It is a major test of Solomon's *opponent-process theory* that the brain automatically activates opposing, or opponent, processes in order to protect itself from emotional extremes and, further, to restore a state of equilibrium to the individual. In most cases, the states of emotional opposites are of roughly the same intensity so that they balance out each other. *Solomon's theory* proposes, however, that when the same stimulus or event repeatedly elicits the same emotion, the first reaction will gradually weaken in intensity, with the overall result of the opponent reaction's gaining in strength. The *opponent-process theory* suggests that the eventual dominance achieved by the opponent emotional states can explain why some individuals may engage in risky and thrill-seeking behaviors such as high-stakes gambling, running dangerous river rapids, or skydiving. See also EMOTIONS, THEORIES/LAWS OF; HEDONISM, THEORY/LAW OF; MOTIVATION, THEORIES OF; OPPONENT-PROCESS COLOR VISION THEORY.

REFERENCES

Solomon, R. L., & Corbit, J. (1974). An opponent-process theory of motivation. I. Temporal dynamics of affect. *Psychological Review, 81*, 119-145.

Solomon, R. L. (1980). The opponent-process theory of acquired motivation: The costs of pleasure and benefits of pain. *American Psychologist, 35*, 691-712.

SOMATOPSYCHICS THEORY. See ORTHOMOLECULAR THEORY.

SOMATOTYPE THEORY. See KRETSCHMER'S THEORY OF PERSONALITY; SHELDON'S TYPE THEORY.

SOMESTHESIS, THEORIES OF. Three basic *theories of somesthesis* (i.e., the bodily sensations including the cutaneous senses, proprioception, and kinaesthesis) that have been proposed since the late 1800s are *von Frey's* "classical" or *four-element theory*, *Head's theory of dual sensibilities*, and *Nafe's pattern theory of feeling*. Following enunciation of the *doctrine of specific nerve energies* by Johannes Muller in 1838, Magnus Blix (in 1882-1883) and Alfred Goldscheider (in 1884-1885) discovered separate sensitive skin spots for *warmth/cold*, and *pressure*, respectively. The German physiologist Max von Frey (1852-1932) added sensitive *pain* spots

to this list and proposed that the four elements of *warmth, cold, pressure,* and *pain* are the necessary aspects in describing tactile sensations. For many researchers, however, von *Frey's classical theory* falls short of explaining common tactile experience, such as active versus passive touch, movement, sensations of impact, and complex qualities of pressure on the skin. At the beginning of the 20th century, the English neurologist Henry Read (1861-1940) proposed his *theory of dual cutaneous sensibilities* based on his observations - follow the peripheral sectioning of cutaneous nerves - that tactile sensitivity occurs in two phases. First, a primitive sensitivity appears (called "protopathic sensibility") regarding heavy pressures and extremes of temperature and pain. Second, as fine discriminations of intensity and good spatial acuity appeared (called "epicritic sensibility"), the sensations of light touch, pressure, and moderate temperature returned. Head also postulated the existence of a subcutaneous "deep sensibility" that remains intact after section of cutaneous nerves. *Head's theory* never gained clear acceptance or rejection and lost utility as a working hypothesis, although it raised important questions, such as the finding that *protopathic* temperature sensibility seems to be punctiform (i.e., capable of being marked by points on the skin), whereas *epicritic* temperature sensibility does not seem to have that feature. In the late 1920s, John Paul Nafe introduced a *quantitative*, or *pattern*, *theory of feeling* that proposes that "specialized receptors" have no factual bases but, rather, particular experiences (such as wet, cold, or pressure) depend on the "pattern" or "arrangement" of neural discharges (cf., *tickling paradox/effect* - a "tickle" is a sensory experience that results from a complex of contact sensations, such as being touched on the soles of the feet or on one's underarms, that is marked by convulsive movements or behaviors of laughter and escape; tickling presumably involves the same sensory receptors as those involved in pain and itch, and it is only the method of stimulation that accounts for the difference between the sensations of tickle and pain; the *tickling paradox/effect* refers to the mysterious phenomenon that persons *cannot* experience the effect of being tickled by tickling themselves!). Nafe's "patterns" comprise variations in the frequency of impulses, the length of time the impulses continue, the area of skin over which the impulses arise, and the relative number of fibers activated. Nafe's theory contrasts, generally, with *von Frey's classical theory*: where *classical theory* is specific and atomistic, *Nafe's theory* is holistic and molecular. Following Nafe's original statement regarding a *pattern theory of feeling*, other researchers refined *pattern theory* and suggested plausible neurophysiological mechanisms for its operation. See also CODING THEORIES; NAFE'S VASCULAR THEORY OF CUTANEOUS SENSITIVITY.

REFERENCES

von Frey, M. (1895). Beitrage zur sinnesphysiologie der haut. *Akademie der Wissenschaften Leipzig. Mathematisch-Naturwissenschaftlich Klasse Berichte, 47*, 166-184.

Head, H. (1920). *Studies in neurology*. London: Oxford Medical Publications.

Nafe, J. P. (1929). A quantitative theory of feeling. *Journal of General Psychology, 2*, 199-211.

Walshe, F. (1942). The anatomy and physiology of cutaneous sensibility: A critical review. *Brain, 65*, 48-112.

Stevens, J. C., & Green, B. G. (1996). History of research on touch. In L. Kruger (Ed.), *Pain and touch*. San Diego, CA: Academic Press.

S-O-R THEORY/MODEL. See LEARNING THEORIES/LAWS.

SOUL THEORY. See MIND-BODY THEORIES.

SOUND-PATTERN/WAVE-PATTERN THEORY. See AUDITION/HEARING, THEORIES OF.

SPACE PERCEPTION THEORY. See BERKELEY'S THEORY OF VISUAL SPACE PERCEPTION.

SPAN, LAW OF. See MIND-BODY THEORIES.

SPATIAL SUMMATION, LAW OF. See SKINNER'S DESCRIPTIVE BEHAVIOR/OPERANT CONDITIONING THEORY.

SPEARMAN'S TWO-FACTOR THEORY. See INTELLIGENCE, THEORIES/LAWS OF.

SPECIAL PROCESS HYPOTHESIS. See HYPNOSIS/HYPNOTISM, THEORIES OF.

SPECIFICATION EQUATION. See CATTELL'S THEORY OF INTELLIGENCE.

SPECIFIC-ATTITUDES THEORY. See PSYCHOSOMATICS THEORY.

SPECIFIC GENE THEORY. See SCHIZOPHRENIA, THEORIES OF.

SPECIFICITY/NONSPECIFICITY THEORIES. See PSYCHOSOMATICS THEORY.

SPECIFIC NERVE ENERGIES, LAW OF. See MULLER'S DOCTRINE OF SPECIFIC NERVE ENERGIES.

SPECIFIC-REACTION THEORY. See PSYCHOSOMATICS THEORY.

SPECIFIC RECEPTOR THEORY. See NAFE'S THEORY OF CUTANEOUS SENSITIVITY.

SPECIFIC TERMINAL/SPECIFIC TISSUE HYPOTHESIS. See NAFE'S THEORY OF CUTANEOUS SENSITIVITY.

SPECIOUS PRESENT. See TIME, THEORIES OF.

SPECTATOR EFFECT. See ZAJONC'S AROUSAL AND CONFLUENCE THEORIES.

SPEECH PERCEPTION, MOTOR THEORY OF. See SPEECH THEORIES.

SPEECH THEORIES. A major research issue behind *speech theories* is the question of why speech is so much easier to acquire than reading and writing skills. One answer is that speech is easy because humans have evolved specialized neural mechanisms (affording a biological advantage) for perceiving and producing it. The heart of this argument is that speakers are endowed with a brain module specialized for controlling the production of speech gestures - the intricate patterns of movement of the vocal tract allowing one to produce the sounds of one's language. A more controversial corollary of this view is that the perception of speech depends, also, on specialized neural structures that automatically transcode speech that one hears into a code for the gestures that were responsible for articulating it. According to this view, the process of gaining access to the small segments of speech (called "phonemes") is difficult because phonemes are only abstractions from a more fundamental *motor* code. Thus, a child may learn to speak adequately without access to the nature of the *motor* code underlying the perception and production of speech. On the other hand, in learning to read, the child is required to develop an *explicit* understanding of phonemes that may be considered to be a difficult or "unnatural" task. The American speech/reading scientist and psycholinguist Alvin Meyer Liberman (1917-2000) was instrumental in the development and research of the modern *motor theory of speech perception*. The early *motor theory of speech perception* (the conventional theory or "horizontal view") states that - in perceiving language - one recovers in the acoustic information how the sound was produced during articulation [cf., *Tadoma method/effect* (a portmanteau word named after two deaf-blind children Tad Chapman and Oma Simpson who were the first to use the method in the early 1960s in the United States, even though the effect was known in the 1890s in Nor-way) - allows an individual who is both deaf and blind to receive/interpret speech by placing his/her thumb lightly in contact with the speaker's lips and the fingers of the same hand on the speaker's jaw and neck; in this way, the deaf-blind individual may detect via touch the pattern of airflow from the speaker's nose and mouth, as well as the articulatory movements in vibrations from the speaker's vocal tract

(cf., *phonatory theory* - concerns speech and voice production where the movements and the vocal cords, caused by the breath pressure, determine the intensity, pitch, and quality of the voice); the *Tadoma method* is similar, in principle, to the *teletactor* - a device for *deaf* individuals that converts sound waves into vibrations that may be sensed tactually on the skin, and the *optacon/optohapt* - an electronic device for *blind* persons that transforms a pattern of light-intensity differences into a pattern of vibrations that is felt by one's fingertips, or a device that converts printed text into vibrations that are transmitted to various parts of the body and, thereby, allows the person to "read"]. Liberman's approach is based on the notion that there are no acoustic invariants that are tied directly to the perception of the sound (the relevant information concerning the articulation may be in a neighboring sound, as well as being dependent on the context in which the sound occurs). The more modern, or revised, *motor theory of speech perception* (the "vertical view") adds the fiat that there is a specific cognitive "module" for speech perception that is separate from other auditory perception mechanisms. In one associative hypothesis, the specific-module is in a "serial architecture" with the general-module, with the speech-module preceding the general-model, and where the processing in the speech-module is not passed on to the general-module. The "module" in *Liberman's model* is comparable to other modules in nature, such as that which enables an animal to localize sound. Peculiar to the phonetic-module is the relation between perception and production, and the fact that it must compete with other modules for the same stimulus variations. Another view - the *constructivist hypothesis for speech production* - claims that each child must work out the speech gestures and their relation to acoustic patterns anew, and is based on feedback from the child's own production practice ("babbling") as well as the perception of the speech of others (cf., *telegraphic speech* - the normal speech of children at about the age of two to three years in which the majority of utterances are only three or four words in length, such as "mommy cook eggs" and where functional words - such as articles, pronouns, and conjunctions - are omitted typically). In the earliest recorded psychological experiment (the "Psammetichus experiment"), as reported by the Greek historian Herodotus (c. 485-c. 425 B.C.) in about 429 B.C., the issue of human *speech production* was investigated. The experiment, performed by the Egyptian pharaoh Psammetichus (664-610 B.C.), attempted to determine whether humans have an innate capacity for speech and, if so, what specific language is innate. The pharaoh ordered that two infants be raised in a remote location by a shepherd who was forbidden to speak in the presence of the infants. After a period of two years, the children began to speak and, in particular, to use the Phrygian word for "bread" over and over again. Based on such results, the pharaoh concluded that the capacity for speech production is innate, and that the "natural language" of humans is Phrygian. See also CHOMSKY'S PSYCHO-LINGUISTIC THEORY; CONSTRUCTIV-ISM, THEO-RIES OF; EMPIRICIST VERSUS NATIVIST THEORIES; KASPAR HAUSER EFFECT/ EXPERIMENT; LANGUAGE ACQUISITION THEORY; McGURK EFFECT/ILLU-SION; NATURE VERSUS NURTURE THE-ORIES; WHORF-SAPIR HYPOTHESIS/ THEORY.

REFERENCES

Liberman, A. M., & Mattingly, I. G. (1985). The motor theory of speech perception revised. *Cognition, 21*, 1-36.

Mattingly, I. G., & Studdert-Kennedy, M. (Eds.) (1991). *Modularity and the motor theory of speech perception.* Hillsdale, NJ: Erlbaum.

Liberman, A. M. (1996). *Speech: A special code.* Cambridge, MA: M.I.T. Press.

Liberman, A. M. (1998). Why is speech so much easier than reading? In C. Hulme & R. M. Joshi (Eds.), *Reading and spelling: Development and disorders.* Mahwah, NJ: Erlbaum.

Diehl, R. L., Lotto, A. J., & Holt, L. L. (2004). Speech perception, *Annual Review of Psychology, 55*, 149-179.

SPENCER'S THEORY OF LAUGHTER/ HUMOR. The English philosopher Herbert Spencer (1820-1903) attempted (like the 16th-century French physician Laurent Joubert) to explain laughter on the basis of physiology and cerebral mechanisms. *Spencer's theory of laughter* (also called the *overflow of nervous energy theory*) states that laughter is analogous to the operation of a siphon or pump: it is an overflow (along the most available and ready channels) of "nervous energy" from a reservoir that has been filled up too much. According to this mechanical, energy-release, or *hydraulic theory*, laughter occurs when we have prepared our minds for something large and meaningful, but what follows actually is something small and insignificant. Thus, Spencer advanced the notion that laughter is similar to nervous energy that is active within any part of the nervous system and that must escape through one or more "channels" that lead to other nerves not connected directly with motor nerves, motor nerves leading to muscular activity, or efferent nerves leading to the viscera. During laughter, the nervous energy escapes via habitual channels: the speech apparatus and the respiratory mechanism. If these channels do not suffice to carry off the amount of energy present, the entire body convulses. Also, according to *Spencer's theory*, the incongruity involved in the ludicrous or humorous situation must be of a "descending" nature or else the state aroused by the inconsistency would be able to relieve the attendant nervous tension. In the case of an "ascending" type of incongruity, the reaction that is produced (e.g., muscle relaxation) is reciprocally inhibitory or prohibitive to the production of convulsions of laughter. Therefore, according to Spencer's analysis, the ludicrous or humorous must present a situation in which we expect (that is, we are "keyed up") for something *great*, but in actuality we are confronted/presented with something *small*. See also DESCARTES' THEORY OF HU-MOR/LAUGHTER; FREUD'S THEORY OF PERSONALITY; HUMOR, THEORIES OF; HYDRAULIC THEORY; INCONGRUITY/ INCONSISTENCY THEORIES OF HU-MOR; JOUBERT'S THEORY OF LAUGH-TER/HUMOR.

REFERENCE

Spencer, H. (1860/1891). The physiology of laughter. In H. Spencer, *Essays: Scientific, political, and speculative.* London: Watts.

SPENCE'S THEORY. The American psychologist and neo-Hullian theorist Kenneth W. Spence (1907-1967) formulated a *theory of discrimination learning*, known as *continuity theory*, that was developed against an elaborate theoretical foundation established by Clark L. Hull (1884-1952). The interconnection of *Spence's theory* with Hull's framework led some writers to label *Spence's theory* the *Hull-Spence theory of discrimination*. In the typical discrimination paradigm, the participant is reinforced positively for responding in the presence of one stimulus ("positive" stimulus) and not reinforced in the presence of another stimulus ("negative" stimulus). With differential training, the individual comes to respond promptly to the positive stimulus, but not to the negative stimulus (cf., *overlearning reversal effect* - refers to an experimental result in a discrimination-learning task situation where organisms who had learned that a primary cue was to be avoided found it easier to shift to a new primary cue than it was for those organisms/participants who had not experienced the former conditioning sessions). Spence provided the classical/traditional *continuity* approach to discrimination learning where the only concepts needed to explain discrimination were simple conditioning, extinction, and stimulus generalization. Spence assumed that the cumulative effects from reinforced responding to the positive stimulus build up a strong "excitatory tendency," whereas "conditioned inhibition" accumulates with the negative stimulus due to the frustration that is consequent on nonreinforced responses made in the presence of the negative stimulus. It was assumed, also, that the excitatory and inhibitory tendencies generalize to similar stimuli with amount of generalization decreasing with decreasing similarity. The overall tendency to respond to any stimulus was given by the generalized excitation minus generalized inhibition to that particular stimulus. Spence's relatively simple theory has shown itself to be very serviceable in giving good accounts concerning discrimination learning. However, over the years, some of the theory's incompleteness and inadequacies also have been noted. For example, the phenomenon of *behavioral contrast* indicates a process of "negative induction" rather than Spence's classical theory prediction of "positive induction," and the phenomenon of *errorless discrimination learning* runs counter to the classical theory explanation of discrimination. Another issue that faced Spence's theorizing was to specify what it is exactly that an individual learns in discrimination training. Against Spence's *absolute stimulus theory* (where a participant learns specific stimulus-response connections) are the opposing viewpoints provided by the *relational theory* (e.g., Kohler, 1925), which holds that the individual learns "relations" between stimuli (such as instructions to a person to "choose the *larger* one of the two stimuli"). Thus, the *relational theory* suggests that the relation between stimuli that an individual learns is one that transcends the specific ("absolute") stimulus pair used to exemplify the relation, and indicates that participants "transpose" the relation along a particular dimension. Such *relational theory* studies are called *transposition* experiments (cf., *generalized oddity problem* - a form of serial learning situation where the participant must generalize a principle established in a series of earlier discrimination problems with different sets of stimuli). Despite the parsimony of *Spence's theory* and the supporting evidence for it, other results suggest that the "absolute" stimulus aspect is either inadequate or incomplete in many ways. Subsequently, a more comprehensive *theory of transposition* was proposed (i.e., *Zeiler's theory*; Zeiler, 1963) that assumes that the person perceives each stimulus in relation to an internal norm or *adaptation level* (cf., Helson, 1964). Spence's *theory of discrimination* learning places great emphasis on the gradual accumulation of "habit strength" and on the algebraic summation of gradients of generalization based on reinforcement and extinction. In general, this *continuity theory* has been contrasted with one that emphasizes the problem-solving behavior of organisms in discrimination learning. The opposing theory, called *noncontinuity theory*, implies that learning a discrimination is not a continuous accumulation of positive and negative habit strength or some similar process but, rather, an organism "tries out" hypotheses about the discrimination problem he or she is faced with by testing one hypothesis and then another (*hypothesis-testing theory*) until the correct solution is found [cf., *discontinuity theory* - a learning theory proposed by the American physiological psychologist Karl Spencer Lashley (1890-1958), which states that an organism does not learn gradually about stimuli that it encounters, but forms "hypotheses" and learns about a stimulus only in relation to its current hypotheses; thus, the learning process may include "sudden jumps" as one hypothesis is replaced by another hypothesis]. Apparently, both the *continuity* and *noncontinuity theories* have something worthwhile to say, and it is a credit to Spence's theorizing that his classic formulation and experimental argumentation was prominent for so many years in the analysis of discrimination learning. Few miniature theories in psychology have proven to be so viable and robust against subsequent research. See also BEHAVIORAL CONTRAST EFFECT/PHENOMENON; BEHAVIORIST THEORY; GENERALIZATION, PRINCIPLES OF; HELSON'S ADAPTATION-LEVEL THEORY; HULL'S LEARNING THEORY; HYPOTHESIS-TESTING THEORY; SERIAL-POSITION EFFECT.

REFERENCES

Kohler, W. (1925). *The mentality of apes.* New York: Harcourt Brace Jovanovich.

Krechevsky, I. (1932). "Hypotheses" in rats. *Psychological Review, 38*, 516-532.

Spence, K. W. (1936). The nature of discrimination learning in animals. *Psychological Review, 43*, 427-449.

Spence, K. W. (1937). The differential response in animals to stimuli varying within a single dimension. *Psychological Review, 44*, 430-444.

Spence, K. W. (1940). Continuous versus non-continuous interpretations of discrimination learning. *Psychological Review, 47*, 271-288.

Lashley, K. S. (1942). An examination of the "continuity theory" as applied to discrimination learning. *Journal of General Psychology, 26*, 241-265.

Hull, C. L. (1943). *Principles of behavior.* New York: Appleton-Century.

Spence, K. W. (1945). An experimental test of the continuity and non-continuity theories of discrimination learning. *Journal of Experimental Psychology, 35*, 253-266.

Hull, C. L. (1952). *A behavior system: An introduction to behavior theory concerning the individual organism.* New Haven, CT: Yale University Press.

Spence, K. W. (1956). *Behavior theory and conditioning.* New Haven, CT: Yale University Press.

Terrace, H. (1963). Discrimination learning with and without errors. *Journal of the Experimental Analysis of Behavior, 6*, 1-27.

Zeiler, M. (1963). The ratio theory of intermediate size discrimination. *Psychological Review, 70*, 516-533.

Helson, H. (1964). *Adaptation-level theory.* New York: Harper & Row.

Hebert, J., & Krantz, D. (1965). Transposition: A reevaluation. *Psychological Bulletin, 63*, 244-257.

SPILLMAN-REDIES EFFECT. See APPENDIX A, SPILLMAN ILLUSION. PERCEPTION (I. GENERAL), THEORIES OF.

SPILLMAN'S ILLUSION. See APPENDIX A.

SPINAL CONDITIONING HYPOTHESIS. See REFLEX ARC THEORY/CONCEPT.

SPIRITUAL THEORIES OF REFLEX ATTENTION. See ATTENTION LAWS.

SPONTANEOUS GENERATION, THEORY OF. See LIFE, THEORIES OF.

SPOT THEORY OF TOUCH/TEMPERATURE SENSES. See ALRUTZ'S THEORY.

SPREADING-ACTIVATION MODEL OF MEMORY. See FORGETTING/MEMORY, THEORIES OF.

SPREAD OF EFFECT HYPOTHESIS. See REINFORCEMENT, THORNDIKE'S THEORY OF.

SQUARE ROOT LAW. See FULLERTON-CATTELL LAW.

S-R LEARNING MODEL/THEORY. See REINFORCEMENT, THORNDIKE'S THEORY OF; SKINNER'S OPERANT CONDITIONING THEORY.

S-S LEARNING MODEL/THEORY. See ESTES' STIMULUS SAMPLING THEORY.

STAGES OF CHANGE THEORY. See WOLPE'S THEORY/TECHNIQUE OF RECIPROCAL INHIBITION.

STAGES OF DYING THEORY. See LIFE, THEORIES OF.

STAGE THEORY OF COGNITIVE DEVELOPMENT. See PIAGET'S THEORY OF DEVELOPMENTAL STAGES; PLAY, THEORIES OF.

STAGE THEORY OF MATE SELECTION. See INTERPERSONAL ATTRACTION THEORIES.

STAGE/ZONE COLOR VISION THEORIES. See COLOR VISION, THEORIES OF; ZONE/STAGE THEORIES OF COLOR VISION.

STAIRCASE/PENROSE STAIRCASE ILLUSION. See APPENDIX A, SCHRODER STAIRCASE ILLUSION.

STAIRCASE PHENOMENON. See WOLPE'S THEORY/TECHNIQUE OF RECIPROCAL INHIBITION.

STAR ILLUSION. See APPENDIX A.

STATE-DEPENDENT MEMORY AND LEARNING EFFECTS. See REDINTEGRATION, PRINCIPLE/LAWS OF.

STATE THEORIES OF HYPNOSIS. See HYPNOSIS/HYPNOTISM, THEORIES OF.

STATIC LAWS OF THE REFLEX. See SKINNER'S DESCRIPTIVE BEHAVIOR/OPERANT CONDITIONING THEORY.

STATISTICAL DECISION THEORY. See SIGNAL DETECTION, THEORY OF.

STATISTICAL HYPOTHESIS. See NULL HYPOTHESIS.

STATISTICAL LEARNING THEORY. See CAPALDI'S THEORY; ESTES' STIMULUS SAMPLING THEORY.

STATUE OF CONDILLAC. See CONDILLAC'S THEORY OF ATTENTION.

ST. AUGUSTINE'S TIME THEORY AND PARADOX. In his *paradox of time*, the African-born philosopher and theologian St. Augustine (A.D. 354-430) questioned – concerning the proposition that things in time change in time - whether things *actually* change in time or do they merely *appear* to change because we *move* in time, and suggested that if we *move* in time, then we *change* in time. In grappling with the *concept of time*, the novelty of St. Augustine's perspective consists in the transference of the reference of time from the "world-soul" to the "human-soul" - even as he continued to regard time as an objective, divinely-created fact. Although St. Augustine considered time as being in the soul or mind, he maintained that time is inconceivable apart from the universe. According to St. Augustine, *time* implies a universe containing *motion* and *change*, and a soul/mind that exists in its own right. Although St. Augustine failed to explain how the mind is an accurate chronometer for the *external* order of physical events, he is credited as being the great pioneer of the study of *internal* time. By a process of agonizing introspection (e.g., when asked what is time, St. Augustine replied that he knows what it is, but confesses that no sooner is the question asked than the answer escapes him), St. Augustine arrived at the idea that time, by its very nature, is subjective. See also ARISTOTLE'S TIME THEORY AND PARADOX; PLOTINUS' THEORY OF TIME; TIME, THEORIES OF.

REFERENCES

Cohen, J. (1971). Time in psychology. In J. Zeman (Ed.), *Time in science and philosophy: An international study of some current problems*. New York: Elsevier.

Whitrow, G. J. (1980). *The natural philosophy of time*. Oxford, UK: Clarendon.

Meagher, R. (1994). Augustine (354-430). In S. Macey (Ed.), *Encyclopedia of time*. New York: Garland.

STEADY-STATE THEORIES. See TIME, THEORIES OF.

STEINZOR EFFECT. This effect from the area of *group dynamics*, named after the American therapist and social/cognitive psychologist Bernard Steinzor (dates unknown), states that in a group setting there is a tendency for group members to comment immediately following the comments of the person sitting opposite them. According to the *Steinzor effect*, in groups consisting of *minimal* leadership, members of a discussion group address most remarks to colleagues sitting *across* a conference table, whereas with a *strong* leader no spatial effect is observed. The *Steinzor effect* also reveals a link between eye contact and dominance. Thus, one may find it difficult to gaze directly at, or even to cross lines of sight with, a dominant individual seated nearby at the same discussion table. In *task* discussions, people direct more comments to those seated across from them in a circle or at a table, whereas in *social* discussions, they are most likely to talk to the person seated next to them. In a small group seated in a *circle*, the greater the seating distance between two people, the greater the chance that they will follow one another verbally. Thus, according to the *Steinzor effect*, location and seating arrangements appear to play a key role in group dynamics and personal interactions. See also INTERPERSONAL ATTRACTION THEORIES; PERSONAL SPACE THEORY; PROXEMICS.

REFERENCES

Steinzor, B. (1950). The spatial factor in face to face discussion groups. *Journal of Abnormal and Social Psychology*, 45, 552-555.

Sommer, R. (1959). Studies in personal space. *Sociometry, 22*, 247-260.

Sommer, R. (1962). The distance for comfortable conversation: A further study. *Sociometry, 25*, 111-116.

STEPWISE PHENOMENON. See GESTALT THEORY/LAWS.

STEREOCHEMICAL THEORY. See OLFACTION/SMELL, THEORIES OF.

STEREOTYPE THEORIES. See PREJUDICE, THEORIES OF.

STERIC THEORY OF ODOR. See OLFACTION/SMELL, THEORIES OF.

STERNBERG-LUBART'S INVESTMENT THEORY OF CREATIVITY. See INTELLIGENCE, THEORIES OF.

STERNBERG'S TRIANGULAR THEORY OF LOVE. See LOVE, THEORIES OF.

STERNBERG'S TRIARCHIC THEORY OF INTELLIGENCE. See INTELLIGENCE, THEORIES/LAWS OF.

STEROID/ANTHROPOMETRIC THEORY. See SEXUAL ORIENTATION THEORIES.

STEVENS' POWER LAW. = Stevens' law = Stevens' power function = power law. The American psychologist/psychophysicist Stanley Smith Stevens (1906-1973) proposed this generalization, which states that the psychophysical relationship between a physical stimulus and the psychological experience or perceived magnitude of that stimulus is given by the equation: $P = k S^n$, where perceived magnitude (P) equals a constant (k) times the stimulus intensity (S) raised to a power, n. On the basis of the stability of his data, Stevens proposed that the psychophysical law is best represented as a power relation rather than a logarithmic relation as described by *Fechner's law*. S. S. Stevens and E. Galanter distinguish between two kinds of perceptual continua, *prothetic* and *metathetic*. *Prothetic* continua are concerned with "how much" and represent dimensions on which discriminations involve an *additive* process on the physiological level (e.g., loudness, brightness, heaviness, and duration), and *metathetic* continua are concerned with "what kind" or "where" and represent dimensions on which discriminations involve a *substitutive* process at the physiological level (e.g., pitch and apparent inclination). Stevens points out that although Fechner's assumption (*Fechner's law*) of the equality of "just noticeable differences" (JNDs) may hold for *metathetic* dimensions, it definitely does *not* hold for *prothetic* dimensions. Using the "magnitude methods" (magnitude estimation; magnitude production), Stevens found that psychophysical magnitude does not increase as a *logarithmic* function of stimulus magnitude, as Fechner had maintained but, rather, as a *power* function in accord with the Belgian physicist Joseph Plateau's (1801-1883) earlier prediction in 1872. That is, perceived magnitude is proportional to physical magnitude raised to some power (*Stevens' power law*). The consistency of Stevens' power function obtained in magnitude estimation experiments led some researchers to assert that it is one of the most firmly established quantitative statements in psychology (cf., R. Warren's *physical correlate theory*). The magnitude-judgment techniques of Stevens led to the development of what has been called the "new psychophysics" in which perceived magnitude is measured directly rather than indirectly as in the classical approach developed by Gustav Fechner. Because a number of challenges may be made to *Stevens' power law*, it may be premature to speak of *the* psychophysical law; the newer investigations hold the promise of generating a broader approach to psychophysical measurement and, perhaps, of generating more general psychological laws, of which the *psychophysical law* may represent only a special case. See also FECHNER'S LAW; OPERATIONISM, DOCTRINE OF; WEBER'S LAW.

REFERENCES

Fechner, G. (1860). *Elemente der psychophysik*, Leipzig: Breitkopf & Hartel.

Plateau, J. (1872). Sur la mesure des sensations physiques, et sur la loi quilie l'intensite de ces sensations a l'intensite de la cause excitante. *Bulletin, Royal Academie/Sciences/Lettres/Beaux-Arts/Belgium*, *33*, 376-388.

Stevens, S. S. (1957). On the psychophysical law. *Psychological Review, 64*, 153-181.

Stevens, S. S., & Galanter, E. (1957). Ratio scales and category scales for a dozen perceptual continua. *Journal of Experimental Psychology, 54*, 377-409.

Stevens, S. S. (1958). Problems and methods of psychophysics. *Psychological Bulletin, 55*, 177-196.

Stevens, S. S. (1960). The psychophysics of sensory function. *American Scientist, 48*, 226-254.

Stevens, S. S. (1961). To honor Fechner and repeal his law. *Science, 133*, 80-86.

Stevens, S. S. (1962). The surprising simplicity of sensory metrics. *American Psychologist, 17*, 29-39.

Stevens, S. S. (1968). Mathematics, statistics, and the schemapiric view. *Science, 161*, 849-856.

Warren, R. (1969). Visual intensity judgments: An empirical rule and a theory. *Psychological Review, 76*, 16-30.

Stevens, S. S. (1971). Issues in psychophysical measurement. *Psychological Review, 78*, 428-450.

Marks, L. (1974). *Sensory processes: The new psychophysics*. New York: Academic Press.

Stevens, S. S. (1975). *Psychophysics: Introduction to its perceptual, neural, and social prospects*. New York: Wiley.

STIGLER'S LAW OF EPONYMY. *Stigler's law of eponymy* - a semi-cynical, self-proclaimed law proposed by the American science historian S. M. Stigler (1999) - states that no scientific discovery is actually named after its original discoverer. This "law" is derived from the observation that many laws (and theories) in science are eponymous and many times there are "priority disputes" concerning naming/eponymy in science. For example, S. S. Stevens' *power law* is claimed (cf., Laming & Laming, 1996) to have been anticipated by the Belgian physicist Joseph A. F. Plateau (1801-1883); and E. Hering's *law of equal innervation* is claimed (cf., Howard, 1996) to have been antedated by the Islamic scholar Alhazen (A.D. 965-1039). See also EMINENCE, THEORIES/MEASURES OF;

HERING'S LAW OF EQUAL INNERVA-
TION; NATURALISTIC THEORY OF HIS-
TORY; STEVENS' POWER LAW.

REFERENCES

Howard, I. P. (1996). Alhazen's neglected discoveries of visual phenomena. *Perception, 25*, 1203-1217.

Laming, J., & Laming, D. (1996). J. Plateau: On the measurement of physical sensations and on the law which links the intensity of these sensations to the intensity of the source. *Psychological Research, 59*, 134-144.

Stigler, S. M. (1999). *Statistics on the table: The history of statistical concepts and methods*. Cambridge, MA: Harvard University Press.

STILES' COLOR VISION THEORY. In 1946, Walter Stanley Stiles (1901-1985) formulated his version of the *line-element theory* of trichromatic visual processes, which he revised and elaborated subsequently. The *line-element* type of theory is concerned with an isomorphic relation between visual data and a mathematical space, without necessarily making inferences regarding intervening processes such as specific physiological factors/events. *Stiles' theory* is regarded as an improvement over H. von Helmholtz's earlier *line-element theory*, and consists of quantitative extensions of Helmholtz's data, such as substitution of a two-color technique for Helmholtz's double-peaked fundamental curves and changes in Fechnerian relationships of two-color thresholds. According to other formulations by Stiles, luminances of differently colored (but equally bright) lights are not additive and, thereby, do not concur with *Abney's law* concerning the mixture of heterochromatic luminances. Stiles' updated theory indicates the usefulness of a *five-* or *seven-receptor theory* where the attempt is to reconcile his *line-element theory* with the older Fechner fractions for visual hue (especially "blue") mechanisms. See also ABNEY'S LAW; COLOR MIXTURE, LAWS/THEORY OF; COLOR VISION, THEORIES/LAWS OF; GRASSMAN'S LAWS; STILES-CRAWFORD EFFECT; YOUNG-HELMHOLTZ COLOR VISION THEORY.

REFERENCES

Helmholtz, H. von (1856-1866). *Handbuch der physiologischen optik*. Leipzig: Voss.

Stiles, W. S. (1946). A modified Helmholtz line-element in brightness-colour space. *Proceedings of the Physics Society of London, 58*, 41-65.

Stiles, W. S. (1959). Color vision: The approach through increment-threshold sensitivity. *Proceedings of the National Academy of Sciences, 45*, 100-114.

STILES-CRAWFORD EFFECT. In 1933, the English physicist Walter Stanley Stiles (1901-1985) and the English physiologist Brian Hewson Crawford (1908-1963) showed that light falling on different parts of the pupil of the eye is not equally effective in producing a sensory result, even though the light may reach the same point on the retina. In particular, the *Stiles-Crawford effect* is a demonstration that light rays passing through the edge of the pupil stimulate the retina less than those rays passing through the center of the pupil because edge rays and center rays do not meet the same conditions along their paths going to a given point on the retina. The majority of the *Stiles-Crawford effect* is due to the properties of the retina itself and is related to foveal cone vision in the light-adapted eye. The effect is found, also, in any part of the retina when deep red illumination is used as the light source, indicating again that the phenomenon is obtained predominantly as a response of the cones in the retina. The exact origin of the *Stiles-Crawford effect* is not certain, but best guesses ascribe it either to the shape of the cones or to the direction in which they point, and where the total internal reflection within the conical point of the cones may be responsible for a concentration of the light in the peripheral areas. The fact that the *Stiles-Crawford effect* is absent in pure rod vision may indicate that the phenomenon is due to differences between rods and cones in shape, in refractive index, and in the distribution of the photoreceptive pigments. The quantitative characteristics of the *Stiles-Crawford effect* have been calculated in detail by P. Moon and

D. Spencer. See also ABNEY'S LAW; STILES' COLOR VISION THEORY.

REFERENCES

Stiles, W. S., & Crawford, B. H. (1933). The luminous efficiency of rays entering the eye pupil at different points. *Proceedings of the Royal Society of London, 112B*, 428-450.

Stiles, W. S., & Crawford, B. H. (1934). The liminal brightness increment for white light for different conditions of the foveal and parafoveal retina. *Proceedings of the Royal Society of London, 116B*, 55-102.

Moon, P., & Spencer, D. (1944). On the Stiles-Crawford effect. *Journal of the Optical Society of America, 34*, 319-329.

O'Brien, B. (1946). Theory of the Stiles-Crawford effect. *Journal of the Optical Society of America, 36*, 506-509.

STIMULATION EFFECTS/NEURONS. See NEURON/NEURAL/NERVE THEORY.

STIMULUS AFTEREFFECTS HYPOTHESIS. See CAPALDI'S THEORY.

STIMULUS ASSOCIATION, PRINCIPLE OF. See ASSOCIATIVE SHIFTING, LAW OF.

STIMULUS-CENTERED THEORY. See REINFORCEMENT THEORY.

STIMULUS COMPLEXITY, THEORY OF. See DEMBER-EARL THEORY OF CHOICE/PREFERENCE.

STIMULUS DISCRIMINATION IN TYPE R, LAW OF. See SKINNER'S DESCRIPTIVE BEHAVIOR/OPERANT CONDITIONING THEORY.

STIMULUS DISCRIMINATION IN TYPE S, LAW OF. See SKINNER'S DESCRIPTIVE BEHAVIOR/OPERANT CONDITIONING THEORY.

STIMULUS GENERALIZATION, PRINCIPLE OF. See GENERALIZATION, PRINCIPLES OF.

STIMULUS-ORGANISM-RESPONSE MODEL. See SKINNER'S DESCRIPTIVE BEHAVIOR/OPERANT CONDITIONING THEORY.

STIMULUS PREEXPOSURE EFFECT. See INHIBITION, LAWS OF.

STIMULUS-RESPONSE MODEL/THEORY/LAWS. See CONCEPT LEARNING/CONCEPT FORMATION, THEORIES OF; LOGAN'S MICROMOLAR THEORY; MOTIVATION, THEORIES OF; SKINNER'S DESCRIPTIVE BEHAVIOR/OPERANT CONDITIONING THEORY; TOLMAN'S THEORY.

STIMULUS-RESPONSE/OPERANT CONDITIONING THEORY OF WORK. See WORK/CAREER/OCCUPATION, THEORIES OF.

STIMULUS SAMPLING THEORY. See ESTES' STIMULUS SAMPLING THEORY.

STOCHASTIC/COMPUTER MODEL THEORY. See LEARNING THEORIES/LAWS.

STOCHASTIC LEARNING THEORY. See ESTES' STIMULUS SAMPLING THEORY.

STOCKHOLM SYNDROME/EFFECT. See BRAIN-WASHING TECHNIQUES/THEORY.

STOMACH-CONTRACTION THEORY. See HUNGER, THEORIES OF.

STORAGE-AND-TRANSFER MODEL OF MEMORY. See FORGETTING/MEMORY, THEORIES OF.

STRESS-DECOMPENSATION MODEL. See PSYCHOPATHOLOGY, THEORIES OF.

STRESS THEORY. See SELYE'S THEORY/MODEL OF STRESS.

STRING/SUPERSTRING THEORIES. See FINAL THEORY.

STROBOSCOPIC MOVEMENT EFFECT/ILLUSION. See APPARENT MOVEMENT, PRINCIPLES/THEORIES OF; APPENDIX A.

STRONG LAW OF EFFECT. See EFFECT, LAW OF.

STROOP EFFECT/INTERFERENCE EFFECT/STROOP TEST. This phenomenon is named in honor of the American psychologist John Ridley Stroop (1897-1973) who designed a test in 1935 that measures an individual's degree of cognitive control. The original test consisted of a series of colored cards on which *names* of colors - rather than the color of the cards - was printed. The participant was asked to name the *color* of the *card* rather than to read the name written (cf., Ligon, 1932; DuBois, 1939). The degree to which individuals are subject to the interference of the printed words is the measure of cognitive control. In another version of testing materials, the *Stroop effect* is the process by which a printed color word (such as the word *red*) interferes with a person's ability to name the color of ink in which the word is printed if the ink color is not the color named by the word. Psychologists studying attention processes are interested in highly practiced cognitive and motor tasks such as reading, typing, or riding a bicycle. Learning such tasks initially requires a great deal of concentrated effort, but with practice, performance of the tasks becomes automatic [cf., *Humphrey's law* - named after the English psychologist George Humphrey (1889-1966) - states that once performance of a task becomes automatized, conscious thought about the task (while performing it) impairs performance (cf., *centipede effect/hyper-reflection effect* - refers to over-consciousness of one's own behavior to the degree that it interferes with skilled performance, social interaction, or sexual performance)]. The term *automaticity* refers to one or more of the following conditions: performance becomes increasingly effortless; performance can be carried out without any conscious attention; and other tasks can be performed at the same time without interference. The *Stroop test* is a good illustration of *automaticity* in reading where the person must name the *ink color* of a word without reading the word itself. This task satisfies two out of three criteria for *automaticity* - it is carried out without attention, and it appears to be effortless. However, the third criterion is violated: it does interfere with naming the ink color. The *Stroop test* is a reminder not to take *automaticity* for granted: tasks may seem automatic in many ways, yet they still make considerable demands on the person's attention. In the *Stroop test*, most people cannot completely ignore the words and simply name the colors. The tendency to think of the words and pronounce them is difficult to resist. The *Stroop test* indicates that even when one tries to suppress a well-practiced memory, it tends to be retrieved *automatically* when the appropriate stimulus occurs (cf., *proof-reader's illusion/effect* - the failure of a proof-reader to notice gross errors in the meaning of the text being checked because different or incompatible levels of processing are required when checking for *meaning* versus *orthography*). Studies on the *Stroop phenomenon* lead to the conclusion that *response competition* is an important contributing factor to *Stroop interference*. See also ATTENTION, LAWS/PRINCIPLES/THEORIES OF; LEVELS OF PROCESSING THEORY; SIMON EFFECT.

REFERENCES

Ligon, E. M. (1932). A genetic study of color naming and word reading. *American Journal of Psychology, 44*, 103-122.

Stroop, J. R. (1935). Studies of interference in serial verbal reactions. *Journal of Experimental Psychology, 18*, 643-662.

Du Bois, P. H. (1939). The sex difference on the color-naming test. *American Journal of Psychology, 52*, 380-382.

Dyer, F. (1973). The Stroop phenomenon and its use in the study of perceptual, cognitive, and response processes. *Memory and Cognition, 1*, 106-120.

Shiffrin, R., & Schneider, W. (1977). Controlled and automatic human information processing. II. Perceptual learning, automatic attending, and a general theory. *Psychological Review, 84,* 127-190.

Logan, G. (1980). Attention and automaticity in Stroop and priming tasks: Theory and data. *Cognitive Psychology, 12,* 523-553.

MacLeod, C. M. (1991). Half a century of research on the Stroop effect: An integrative review. *Psychological Bulletin, 109,* 163-203.

STRUCTURAL HYPOTHESIS/MODEL/ THEORY. See FREUD'S THEORY OF PERSONALITY; MIND/MENTAL STATES, THEORIES OF.

STRUCTURAL INTEGRATION THEORY. See ROLFING THEORY/THERAPY.

STRUCTURALISM/STRUCTURALIST THEORY. See WUNDT'S THEORIES/ DOCTRINES/PRINCIPLES.

STRUCTURED LEARNING THEORY. See MOTIVATION, THEORIES OF.

STRUCTURE-OF-INTELLECT MODEL/ THEORY. See INTELLIGENCE, THEORIES/LAWS OF.

STUDENT RETENTION/ATTRITION MODEL. This *model of student retention* in higher education (cf., Spady, 1970) attempts to account for the factors that contribute to students' remaining in the academic setting until specified educational goals have been achieved. According to W. Spady's *sociological model* - that includes the constructs of *social support* and *college satisfaction* as mediating variables - *social support* has a direct and positive influence on *college satisfaction.* This hypothesis is supported by other educational psychological studies that suggest that high frequency of contact with faculty, as well as support from family members and friends, are significant predictors of college satisfaction and good indicators of student retention. See also BUFFERING MODEL/HYPOTHESIS OF SOCIAL SUPPORT; FIT THEORY OF COLLEGE SATISFACTION; SELF-

CONSISTENCY AND SELF-ENHANCEMENT THEORIES.
REFERENCES
Spady, W. (1970). Dropouts from higher education: An interdisciplinary review and synthesis. *Interchange, 1,* 64-85.

Noel, L., Levitz, R., & Saluri, D. (Eds.) (1985). *Increasing student retention.* San Francisco: Jossey-Bass.

STUMPF'S THEORY OF MUSICAL CONSONANCE AND DISSONANCE. The German philosopher, psychologist, and musician Carl (Karl) Stumpf (1848-1936) proposed a *theory of consonance and dissonance* in music, which states that tonal combinations judged most consonant are those that tend to fuse together. The greater the degree of fusion (as in an octave), the greater is the consonance. Likewise, in dissonance, when tones are played together, the degree to which they separate out and can be heard as single tones, the greater is the dissonance. The phenomenon of *combination tones,* also called *resultant tones,* is the occurrence of an additional tone that is perceived when two separate tones are sounded simultaneously. According to the *combinational tone theory,* there are two types of combination tones: the *difference tone,* sometimes called the *grave harmonic,* whose frequency is the difference in the frequencies of the generating tones, and the *summation tone,* whose frequency is the sum of the frequencies of the generating tones. *Stumpf's theory* emphasizes the fact that tones an octave apart seem to "fuse" into one psychical unity, and such fusion involves musical consonance. But, when one tone is sounded together with another tone a semitone higher, the hearer is keenly aware of the distinctness of the two tones and, at the same time, finds the combination highly discordant. Stumpf regarded the degree of fusion between tones as the basis for musical consonance. The fact that the increasing complexity of vibration ratios, in general, is accompanied by decreasing consonance fits well with *Stumpf's theory.* Stumpf's emphasis on "fusion" makes it distinctly *not* a *physical* but a *psychological* theory. See also AUDITION/HEARING, THEORIES OF; FESTINGER'S COGNITIVE DIS-

SONANCE THEORY; WUNDT'S THEORIES/DOCTRINES/PRINCIPLES.

REFERENCES

Stumpf, K. (1883-1890). *Tonpsychologie.* Leipzig: Hirzel.

Stumpf, K. (1898-1924). *Beitrage zur akustik und musik wissenschaft.* Leipzig: Barth.

SUBJECT EFFECTS. See EXPERIMENTER EFFECTS.

SUBJECTIVE DOMINANCE, LAW OF. See CONDUCT, LAWS OF.

SUBJECTIVE EXPECTED UTILITY THEORY. See DECISION-MAKING THEORIES; EXPECTED UTILITY THEORY.

SUBJECTIVE TIME. See TIME, THEORIES OF.

SUBLIMINAL PERCEPTION EFFECTS/ PHENOMENA. The status of *consciousness* in the information-processing of sensory data traditionally has been a thorny issue, based partly on the definitions of fuzzy, often circular, terms such as *preconscious* (mental contents that are not currently in consciousness but are accessible to it by focusing attention on them), *perception-consciousness system* (a subsystem of the mental apparatus characterized by consciousness, and getting input from the external world by sensory receptors and the preconscious via the activation of memories), *subconscious* (operating/existing outside of consciousness), *conscious/consciousness* (relating to the function of the mind through which one is aware of mental experiences such as thoughts, emotions, perceptions, and wishes; the normal mental condition of the waking state of humans), *unconscious/unconsciousness* (lacking consciousness/awareness of mental experiences such as emotions, perceptions, and thoughts), *subliminal perception/subception* (preconscious processing of stimuli below the intensity/level of one's absolute threshold and not eliciting conscious perception), and *discrimination behavior without awareness* (a state that is distinguished from perception - which implies awareness - and possesses some emotional or cognitive reaction that can be recorded by electronic testing but not observable to the person being tested). Another problem concerning the role of unconscious information processing, such as that of *subliminal perception*, lies in the difficulty of determining accurate sensory thresholds and baselines for individuals (cf., Eriksen, 1960; Merikle, 1982). There is empirical evidence for the existence of subliminal perception in all the sensory modalities through the presentation of stimuli of very low intensity or short duration so as to be "subthreshold," as well as the results from "masking" studies (i.e., the suppression/blocking of the perception of a stimulus by the presentation of another stimulus). On the other hand, experiments have indicated that subliminal messages flashed briefly to persons have only limited power to influence their behavior (e.g., listening to subliminal auditory tapes as one sleeps - in order to boost intelligence scores, give up smoking, or lose weight - do *not* appear to be effective). The studies of other related topics, such as *perceptual defense* (i.e., the process by which stimuli - usually only briefly presented/exposed - that are potentially threatening, unpleasant, or offensive to the person are either distorted, show a heightened threshold, or not perceived at all), and *sensitization/vigilance* (i.e., certain demonstrations showing an abnormally lowered threshold for the perception of particular stimuli/ material) have yielded equivocal results (cf., McGinnies, 1949; Howes & Solomon, 1950). In the light of much experimental evidence, many psychologists subscribe to the belief that unconscious processing of information (even though that information may not necessarily drive one to action, as is presupposed in *subliminal perception*) is a real and genuine phenomenon that should be taken into consideration when accounting completely for mental functioning (cf., the promising, and recent, research on "subliminal learning," "subliminal perceptual learning," "passive perceptual learning," "perceptual learning without perception," and "subliminal neural plasticity;" Watanabe, Nanez, & Sasaki, 2001; Watanabe, Nanez, Koyama, Mukai, Liederman, & Sasaki, 2002; Seitz & Watanabe, 2003; Seitz, Nanez, Holloway, & Watanabe, 2005). See also ATTENTION, LAWS/PRINCIPLES/

THEORIES OF; CONSCIOUSNESS, PHE-NOMENON OF; INFORMATION/INFOR-MATION-PROCESSING THEORY; PER-CEPTION (I. GENERAL), THEORIES OF.

REFERENCES

McGinnies, E. (1949). Emotionality and perceptual defense. *Psychological Review, 56*, 244-251.

Howes, D. H., & Solomon, R. (1950). A note on McGinnies' "Emotionality and perceptual defense." *Psychological Review, 57*, 229-240.

Packard, V. (1957). *The hidden persuaders.* New York: McKay.

Eriksen, C. W. (1960). Discrimination and learning without awareness: A methodological survey and evaluation. *Psychological Review, 67*, 279-300.

Dixon, N. F. (1971). *Subliminal perception: The nature of a controversy.* London: McGraw-Hill.

Erdelyi, M. H. (1974). A new look at the new look: Perceptual defense and vigilance. *Psychological Review, 81*, 1-25.

Dixon, N. F. (1981). *Preconscious processing.* Chichester, UK: Wiley.

Merikle, P. M. (1982). Unconscious perception revisited. *Perception and Psychophysics, 31*, 298-301.

Marcel, A. J. (1983). Conscious and unconscious perception: Experiments on visual masking and word recognition. *Cognitive Psychology, 15*, 197-237.

Watanabe, T., Nanez, J. E., Sasaki, Y. (2001). Perceptual learning without perception. *Nature, 413*, 844-848.

Watanabe, T., Nanez, J. E., Koyama, S., Mukai, I., Liederman, J., & Sasaki, Y. (2002). Greater plasticity in lower-level than higher-level visual motion processing in a passive perceptual learning task. *Nature Neuroscience, 5*, 1003-1009.

Seitz, A. R., & Watanabe, T. (2003). Is subliminal learning really passive? *Nature, 422*, 36.

Seitz, A. R., Nanez, J. E., Holloway, S. R., & Watanabe, T. (2005). Visual experience can substantially alter critical flicker fusion thresholds. *Human Psychopharmacology and Clinical Experiments, 20*, 55-60.

SUBSTITUTION, LAW OF. See CONDUCT, LAWS OF.

SUBTRACTIVE COLOR MIXTURE, PRINCIPLE OF. See COLOR MIXTURE, LAWS/THEORY OF.

SUCCESSIVE CONTRAST EFFECT. See GESTALT THEORY/LAWS.

SUCCESSIVE REPRODUCTION TECHNIQUE. See FORGETTING/MEMORY, THEORIES OF.

SUDDEN GLORY THEORY OF HUMOR. See HOBBES' THEORY OF HUMOR/LAUGHTER.

SUFFICIENT REASON, LAW OF. See MIND-BODY THEORIES.

SUFFIX EFFECT. See FORGETTING/MEMORY, THEORIES OF.

SUGGESTION, LAWS OF. See FREQUENCY, LAW OF.

SUICIDE, THEORIES OF. In his study of *suicide* (the act of killing oneself deliberately), the French sociologist Emile Durkheim (1858-1917) suggests that *egoistic suicide* - deriving from feelings of depression, failure, and self-reproach - results from a lack of personal-social cohesion and is more common among single persons than among married people. Another theoretical approach, called *altruistic suicide*, proposes that suicide is carried out for the benefit of other people and derives from one's sense of failure to one's society (e.g., many suicides in Japan are based on this notion). A third theoretical orientation, called *anomic suicide*, derives from one's sense that life is meaningless and is the result of the perceived absence of social norms and rules and occurs, often, after an unfavorable change in financial or social situations, causing despair bout maintaining a former lifestyle. Thus, according to Durkheim, the cause of suicide - whether it be egoistic, altruistic, or anomic - is based entirely on *social* issues. In the *psychological* domain, the *hopelessness theory of suicidality* emphasizes the developmental, emotional, and cognitive aspects of personal hopelessness, stress, depression, and vulnerability, as well as the psychosocial processes culminating in the suicidal act [cf., *major events effect* - refers to the finding that in the case of personal disasters and emergencies, such as suicides, the rate of the occurrence of such behaviors is *reduced prior* to major events (such as important elections or sporting contests), and that the rate of occurrences of such behaviors (as suicide) *increases following* major catastrophes (such as earthquakes and floods)]. Statistically, in the context of *psychopathology*, it is estimated that about 15 percent of individuals with major depression or bipolar disorder commit suicide each year. See also ANOMIE THEORY; DEPRESSION, THEORIES OF; PSYCHOPATHOLOGY, THEORIES OF.

REFERENCES

Durkheim, E. (1897/1966). *Suicide: A study in sociology*. Glencoe, IL: Free Press.

Lester, D. (1989). A depression paradox theory of suicide. *Personality and Individual Differences, 10*, 1103-1104.

Lester, D. (1997). *Making sense of suicide: An in-depth look at why people kill themselves*. Philadelphia: Charles.

Robbins, P. R. (1998). *Adolescent suicide*. Jefferson, NC: McFarland.

Szasz, T. (1999). *Fatal freedom: the ethics and politics of suicide*. Westport, CT: Praeger.

Abramson, L. Y., Alloy, L. B., Hogan, M., Whitehouse, W., Gibb, B., Hankin, B., & Cornette, M. (2000). The hopelessness theory of suicidality. In T. E. Joiner, Jr. & M. D. Rudd (Eds.), *Suicide science: Expanding the boundaries*. New York: Kluwer.

Lester, D. (2000). *Why people kill themselves: A 2000 summary of research on suicide*. Springfield, IL: Thomas.

Joiner, T. E., Jr., Brown, J. S., & Wingate, L. R. (2005). The psychology and neurobiology of suicidal behavior. *Annual Review of Psychology, 56*, 287-314.

SULLIVAN'S THEORY OF PERSONALITY. = interpersonal theory. The American psychiatrist Harry Stack Sullivan (1892-1949) developed the *interpersonal theory of psychiatry* that defines the hypothetical entity of *personality* as the relatively enduring pattern of recurrent interpersonal situations that characterize a human life, and views the individual's basic existence in terms of one's relationships with other people (cf., Sullivan's term *significant other* - refers to the most influential person, usually the mother, in a child's environment/life; later usage by others gave a more colloquial meaning to the term, denoting an individual with whom someone is romantically or sexually involved). *Sullivan's theory of personality* favors concepts and variables from the fields of social psychology and *field theory* (e.g., Lewin, 1951). According to Sullivan's approach, the essential unit in personality study is the interpersonal situation, not the individual, where the structure and organization of personality consist of *intersocial* events rather than *intrapsychic* events. Primary concepts in *Sullivan's theory* are: *dynamisms* - habits or enduring patterns of energy transformations such as overt talking or covert thinking that are directed toward one or more persons and serve to satisfy one's basic needs; *personifications* - an image one has of oneself or others consisting of feelings, attitudes, and experiences concerning need-satisfaction and anxiety (personifications that are shared by a number of other people are called *stereotypes*); and *cognitive processes* - include *prototaxic* experience (i.e., the discrete series of sensations, images, feelings, and states of the organism), *parataxic* experience (i.e., perceiving causal relationships between events that may include *superstitious* thinking), and *syntaxic* experience (i.e., consensually validated symbol activity such as using words and numbers that give logical order to human communication). Sullivan's account of the *dynamics of personality* emphasizes the concept of *tension-reduction* - tension may arise from anxiety or from the needs of the individual where unsatisfied needs may lead to apathy behavior or to other dynamisms (such as "somnolent detachment," or falling asleep, in infants as a result of inescapable anxiety). Sullivan rejected the notion of *instincts* as a primary source of human motivation, and dismissed Sigmund Freud's concept of *libido*. According to Sullivan, personality development occurs in six distinctive stages (cf., *stage theories* of S. Freud and E. Erikson): infancy, childhood, juvenile era, preadolescence, early adolescence, and late adolescence. Sullivan asserts that personality is not set at an early age but, rather, it may change with variations in interpersonal situations and new learning experiences. If regressions in personality - due to failure, anxiety, or pain - occur in a person's life, the help of a therapist acting as a *participant observer* in the *psychiatric interview* setting is advised. Although *Sullivan's interpersonal theory* is a "down-to-earth" formulation that invites and encourages empirical testing, critics of his theory argue that he (as well as various other social-psychological personality theorists) has cut the personality off from its vital biological and evolutionary heritage and fails to specify the precise learning mechanisms by which a society molds and shapes the individual. See also FREUD'S THEORY OF PERSONALITY; LEWIN'S FIELD THEORY; LIBIDO THEORY; PERSONALITY THEORIES.

REFERENCES

Sullivan, H. S. (1940). *Conceptions of modern psychiatry*. New York: Norton.

Lewin, K. (1951). *Field theory in social science: Selected theoretical papers*. D. Cartwright (Ed.). New York: Harper & Row.

Sullivan, H. S. (1953). *The interpersonal theory of psychiatry*. New York: Norton.

Sullivan, H. S. (1954). *The psychiatric interview*. New York: Norton.

Sullivan, H. S. (1964). *The fusion of psychiatry and social science*. New York: Norton.

Mullahy, P. (1973). *The beginnings of modern American psychiatry: The ideas of Harry Stack Sullivan*. Boston: Houghton Mifflin.

SULLY'S THEORY OF LAUGHTER/HUMOR. In his theory of laughter/humor, the English psychologist James Sully (1842-1923) provides "situations" or "content descriptions" that give rise to laughter. Among these descriptions are the following 12 behavioral classes of laughter-provoking situations: novelties, physical deformities, moral deformities/vices, disorderliness, small misfortune, indecencies, pretenses, desire for knowledge/skill, the incongruous and the absurd, word play, the expression of a merry mood, and the outwitting/getting-the-better-of another person. *Sully's laughter/humor theory* may be called the *play-mood theory of laughter* in that he assumes the enjoyment of the laughable is rooted in a sudden arousal of the behavior of "play-mood" that involves a refusal to take the current situation seriously (one of the key features of the activity of "play"). Sully also indicates the *corrective social function* of laughter in such psychological "play-mood" situations. The notion of "play-mood," according to Sully, refers both to overt/externally expressive playful behavior, and to covert/mental, intellectual, or cognitive manipulations (such as observed in "word-play"). Thus, essentially, Sully's orientation toward laughter/humor is that laughter is an *overt* expression of an already-present *covert* pleasurable state. Critics of Sully's approach question *how* the "play-mood" is achieved or *where* it comes from; also, criticism focuses on the point that children seem to take their play *seriously* more often than not - a fact not discussed by Sully. See also BEHAVIORAL THEORIES OF HUMOR/LAUGHTER; DARWIN'S THEORY OF LAUGHTER/HUMOR; HUMOR, THEORIES OF; SPENCER'S THEORY OF LAUGHTER/HUMOR.

REFERENCE

Sully, J. (1902). *Essay on laughter*. New York: Longmans Green.

SUMMATION EFFECT. See SKINNER'S DESCRIPTIVE BEHAVIOR/OPERANT CONDITIONING THEORY.

SUNK COST FALLACY. See CONCORDE FALLACY/EFFECT.

SUPERIORITY THEORIES OF HUMOR. The *superiority theories of humor* are characterized, generally, by one's cognitive/perceptual comparison of self against others on the bases of intelligence, beauty, strength, wealth, etc., and on a subsequent personally-experienced elation, triumph, superiority, or victory as the result of such "self-others" comparisons. According to the *principle of superiority* in this context, one's laughter, mockery, and ridicule - at the expense of others - is central to the humor experience. See also ARISTOTLE'S THEORY OF HUMOR; BAIN'S THEORY OF HUMOR; BERGSON'S THEORY OF HUMOR; HOBBES' THEORY OF HUMOR/LAUGHTER; HÖFFDING'S THEORY OF HUMOR/LAUGHTER; HUMOR, THEORIES OF; MOTIVATIONAL THEORIES OF HUMOR; PLATO'S THEORY OF HUMOR; RAPP'S THEORY OF THE ORIGINS OF LAUGHTER/HUMOR.

REFERENCE

Roeckelein, J. E. (2002). *The psychology of humor*. Westport, CT: Greenwood Press.

SUPERPOSITION HYPOTHESIS. See VISION/SIGHT, THEORIES OF.

SUPERSTITIONS AND SUPERSTITIOUS EFFECTS. The American psychologist Burrhus Frederic Skinner (1904-1990) explored the phenomena of *superstitious behavior*, *superstitious control*, and *superstitious reinforcement*. In the *superstition effect*, which is the result of "accidental" conditioning, a response from the individual or organism just happens to occur immediately prior to a reinforcement that is really contingent on a fixed period of time elapsing or some other noncontingent or unrelated-to-response factor; the rate of that response in such "accidental" conditioning, however, increases in the future for that given stimulus situation or environment. Also, in other terms, "adventitious" or "accidental" reinforcement may occur where conditioning of an organism's operant response takes place *without* the response being specified by the researcher. Thus, in this context, *superstitious reinforcement* refers to the presence of reinforcing stimuli that follow a response only by *happenstance*, but seems to the individual to be the natural consequences of his/her response or behavior. In human behavior, *superstitious control* may be observed wherein one has the mistaken notion of influencing environmental outcomes - via various "faith-healing," "magical-thinking," or "animistic" practices and behaviors (such as genuflecting, saying prayers, or singing chants) that are designed to protect the self or others, and to alter the environment in some optimal fashion (e.g., it is possible that the "rain dances" and other "magical" practices of certain American Indian tribes originated in this way: a dance was performed initially at some random time and it just *happened* to rain after/during the dance; there was no functional relationship between the two events, but "accidental contingencies" were established that served to maintain the behavior in the future). In defense of *superstitious control* behavior, some psychologists maintain that it serves a positive psychological function in that it may limit or eliminate the development of "learned helplessness" and its debilitating effects. See also LEARNED HELPLESSNESS EFFECT; SKINNER'S DESCRIPTIVE BEHAVIOR/ OPERANT CONDITIONING THEORY.

REFERENCES

Skinner, B. F. (1948). "Superstition" in the pigeon. *Journal of Experimental Psychology, 38*, 168-172.

Skinner, B. F., & Morse, W. A. (1957). A second type of superstition in the pigeon. *American Journal of Psychology, 70*, 308-311.

Jahoda, G. (1969). *The psychology of superstition*. London: Lane.

SUPERSYMMETRY PRINCIPLE. See FINAL THEORY.

SUPPORT THEORY. The Israeli-born American cognitive psychologist Amos Tversky (1937-1996) and his colleagues (e.g., Derek J. Koehler, Lyle A. Brenner, and Yuval Rottenstreich) formulated a *theory of subjective probability*, called *support theory*, according to which different descriptions of the same event can give rise to different judgments. Experimental data confirms the major predictions of the theory: judged probability *increases* by "unpacking" the *focal* hypothesis and *decreases* by "unpacking" the *alternative* hypothesis; judged probabilities are complementary in the binary case and subadditive in the general case (contrary to both classical and revisionist *models of belief*); and subadditivity is more pronounced for probability judgments than for frequency judgments and is enhanced (*enhancement effect*) by compatible evidence. The background rationale of *support theory* is that the study of intuitive probability judgment shows that people often do *not* follow the extensional logic of *probability theory* (e.g., the suggestion that 1,000 people will die in an *earthquake* may appear to be more likely than a more inclusive event, such as 1,000 people will die in a *natural disaster*). The nonextensional *support theory of belief* attaches subjective probability *not* to events (as in other models), but to descriptions of events, called *hypotheses*. According to *support theory*, each hypothesis (A) has a "support value" [s(A)], corresponding to the strength of the evidence for this hypothesis. The judged probability [p(A,B)] that hypothesis A rather than B holds, assuming that one and only one of them obtains, is given by: p(A,B)=s(A)/s(A)+s(B). Thus, judged probability is interpreted in terms of the "support" of the focal hypothesis A relative to the alternative hypothesis B. The key assumption of *support theory* is that "unpacking" a description of an event (e.g., a plane crash, C) into disjoint components (e.g., an *accidental* plane crash, Ca, caused by human error or mechanical failure, or a *nonaccidental* plane crash, Cn, caused by sabotage or terrorism) generally increases its support. Thus, the "support" of the explicit disjunction Ca ∨ Cn is equal to, or greater than, the support of the implicit disjunction C that does not mention any causes. The two premises for this rationale are: "unpacking" an implicit hypothesis may remind people of possibilities they might have overlooked; and the explicit mention of a possibility tends to increase its salience and, thereby, its perceived "support" (cf., *theory of belief* - proposes that uncertainty has two dimensions with various interpretations; for instance, "probability" versus "definiteness;" Narens, 2003). See also DECISION-MAKING THEORIES.

REFERENCES

Tversky, A., & Koehler, D. J. (1994). Support theory: A nonextensional representation of subjective probability. *Psychological Review*, *101*, 547-567.

Koehler, D. J., Brenner, L. A., & Tversky, A. (1997). The enhancement effect in probability judgment. *Journal of Behavioral Decision Making*, *10*, 293-313.

Rottenstreich, Y., & Tversky, A. (1997). Unpacking, repacking, and anchoring: Advances in support theory. *Psychological Review*, *104*, 406-415.

Narens, L. (2003). A theory of belief. Journal of *Mathematical Psychology*, *47*, 1-31.

SURE-THING PRINCIPLE. See DECISION-MAKING THEORIES.

SURPLUS ENERGY THEORY OF PLAY. See PLAY, THEORIES OF.

SURPRISE THEORIES OF HUMOR. The surprise theories of humor are characterized, generally, by unexpectedness/surprise, shock, or suddenness in cognitions or perceptions where such elements are considered by many humor theorists to be *necessary* (though not necessarily *sufficient*) conditions for the humor experience. The concepts of "surprise" and "incongruity" overlap, often, in which there is an instantaneous breaking up of the normal routine course of ideation, thought, or action. See also ARISTOTLE'S THEORY OF HUMOR; DESCARTES' THEORY OF HUMOR/LAUGHTER; HARTLEY'S THEORY OF HUMOR/LAUGHTER; HOBBES' THEORY OF HUMOR/LAUGHTER; HUMOR, THEORIES OF; INCONGRUITY/INCONSISTENCY THEORIES OF HUMOR.

REFERENCE

Roeckelein, J. E. (2002). *The psychology of humor*. Westport, CT: Greenwood Press.

SURROUNDEDNESS, LAW OF. See GESTALT THEORY/LAWS.

SUSTAINED ATTENTIION THEORIES. See VIGILANCE, THEORIES OF.

SUTTON'S LAW. See SCHIZOPHRENIA, THEORIES OF.

SWINDLE'S GHOST. See APPENDIX A.

SYMBOLIC DISTANCE EFFECT. See HICK'S LAW.

SYMBOLIC INTERACTIONISM THE-ORY. See COMMUNICATION THEORY.

SYMMETRY LAW. See GESTALT THEO-RY/LAWS.

SYMPTOM SUBSTITUTION HYPO-THESIS. See WOLPE'S THEORY/TECH-NIQUE OF RECIPROCAL INHIBITION.

SYNAPTIC DEPRESSION MODEL. See HABITUATION, PRINCIPLE/LAW OF.

SYNAPTIC/SYNAPSE THEORY. See HEBB'S CELL ASSEMBLY THEORY; NEURON/NEURAL/NERVE THEORY; PERCEPTION (II. COMPARATIVE AP-PRAISAL), THEORIES OF.

SYNCHRONICITY PRINCIPLE. See JUNG'S THEORY OF PERSONALITY.

SYNECTICS MODEL. See MONTESSORI METHOD/THEORY.

SYNERGY THEORY. See MIND-BODY THEORIES; WUNDT'S THEORIES/DOC-TRINES/PRINCIPLES.

SYNESTHESIA EFFECT. See GALTON'S LAWS.

SYNTHETIC EFFECT/APPROACH. See COGNITIVE STYLE MODELS.

SYNTHETIC HEAT PHENOMENON. See ALRUTZ'S THEORY.

SYSTEMATIC DESENSITIZATION TECHNIQUE. See BEHAVIOR THER-APY/COGNITIVE THERAPY, THEORIES OF; WOLPE'S THEORY/TECHNIQUE OF RECIPROCAL INHIBITION.

SYSTEMIC COUNSELING THEORY. See PREJUDICE, THEORIES OF.

SYSTEMS THEORY. See CONTROL/SYS-TEMS THEORY; GENERAL SYSTEMS THEORY; ORGANIZATIONAL/INDUST-RIAL/SYSTEMS THEORY.

SYZYGY THEORY. See JUNG'S THEORY OF PERSONALITY.

T

TABULA RASA DOCTRINE. See EM-PIRICAL/EMPIRICISM, DOCTRINE OF; LEARNING THEORIES/LAWS.

TADOMA METHOD/EFFECT. See SPEECH THEORIES.

TALBOT-PLATEAU LAW. = Talbot's law. Named in honor of the English physicist William Henry Fox Talbot (1800-1877) and the Belgian physicist Joseph Antoine Ferdinand Plateau (1801-1883), this generalized principle states that when a periodic visual stimulus is repeated - at a rate that is adequately high so that to an observer it appears to be fused - it will match in brightness a steady light that has the same time-average luminance. For instance, if the flickering light consists of equally long "on" and "off" periods, the steady state will have one-half the brightness (called *Talbot brightness*) of the "on" phase. The *Talbot-Plateau law* is demonstrated by use of the *Talbot-Plateau disk* that is a white disk with concentric bands, each band showing black and white alternately, but with the same quantity of black and white, divided differently in each band (1/1, 2/2, 4/4, etc.) [cf., *Maxwell disk/color-mixing wheel* - named after the Scottish physicist James Clerk Maxwell (1831-1879) - is a rotating disk onto which radially slit, overlapping disks of paper/plastic may be mounted to divide the total surface with sections of differing amounts of colors for studying color-mixing effects]. When rotated, the *Talbot-Plateau disk* extinguishes the flicker sensations and shows a uniform gray color. Thus, an intermittent stimulus may be seen as continuous. The effect may be demonstrated, also, by interrupting a beam of light with a rotating disk. The disk, in this case, has segments cut out of it so that part of the time the light may pass through. Under conditions where the light passes only 50-percent of the time, and the disk is rotated slowly so the light is interrupted only two or three times a second, the observer sees the light as interrupted (i.e., seen as alternations of light and dark). However, as the rotation speed of the disk slowly increases, a point is reached at which the light appears as continuous, and the brilliance of the continuous light will be the same as if the total amount of light had been distributed uniformly over a whole revolution of the disk. The *Talbot-Plateau law* was challenged by A. Fick and O. Grunbaum, who noted that it may not hold under special circumstances such as high intensity and conditions where fusion of a peripheral field occurs when the eye is fixated. However, the law's validity is now generally accepted under most conditions. The validity of the *Talbot-Plateau law* has an interesting implication for the functional nature of the visual system: it suggests that the response of this system is proportional to stimulus luminance in those regions that precede the location where fusion occurs. See also FERRY-PORTER LAW; VISION/SIGHT, THEORIES OF.

REFERENCES

Talbot, W. H. F. (1834). Experiments on light. *Philosophical Transactions of the Royal Society of London, 3,* 298.

Plateau, J. A. F. (1835). Sur un principe de photometrie. *Bulletins de l'Academie Royale des Sciences de Bruxelles, 2,* 52-59.

Fick, A. (1863). Uber den zeitlichen verlauf der erregung in der netzhaut. *Archiv fur Anatomie und Physiologie, 22,* 739-764.

Plateau, J. A. F. (1872). Sur la mesure des sensations physiques, et sur la loi qui lie l'intensite de ces sensations a l'intensite de la cause excitante. *Bulletin, Royal Academie/Sciences/Lettres/Beaux-Arts/Belgium, 33,* 376-388.

Grunbaum, O. (1898). On the intermittent stimulation of the retina. *Journal of Physiology, 22,* 433-450.

Arnold, W. (1934). On the theoretical significance of Talbot's law. *Journal of General Physiology, 17,* 97-101.

TALBOT-PLATEAU SPIRAL. See APPENDIX A.

TALION LAW/PRINCIPLE. See FREUD'S THEORY OF PERSONALITY.

TARCHANOFF EFFECT/PHENOMEN-ON. See ELECTRODERMAL ACTIVITY/PHENOMENON.

TASK CYCLE THEORY. See TOLMAN'S THEORY.

TASTE AVERSION EFFECT. See GARCIA EFFECT.

TASTE, THEORIES OF. See GUSTATION/TASTE, THEORIES OF.

TA-TA/SING-SONG THEORIES. See LANGUAGE ORIGINS, THEORIES OF.

TAU- AND KAPPA-EFFECTS. The *tau-effect* was first discovered in *tactile* experiments where a participant makes a comparative judgment of two spatial intervals when the corresponding temporal intervals vary. For instance, if three points are marked off on the participant's skin such that the interval of *time* between stimulating the second and third points exceeds the interval between stimulating the first and second points, the person reports that the *distance* between the second and third points is greater than that between the first and second points. A similar effect of a relation between perceived *space* and *time* is shown when visual or auditory signals replace the tactile. For example, with vision, by flashing three equidistant lights X, Y, and Z successively in the dark with a shorter *time* interval between X and Y than between Y and Z, the space-time *tau-effect/illusion* is created that X and Y are closer together in *space* than is Y and Z. The converse *kappa-effect* holds, as well. For instance, when auditory signals are used, a *shorter duration* is assigned by the participant to the *higher* of two tones when he/she is required to adjust them so that they seem to be temporally equal. The *kappa-effect/illusion* may be observed, also, with the visual modality. For example, if three light sources, X, Y, and Z, are placed at different *positions*, with X and Y closer together than Y and Z, and the lights are flashed successively in the dark - with *equal time* intervals between the three flashes - the space-time *kappa-effect/illusion* is created such that the *time* interval between the X and Y lights is perceived to be *shorter* than that between the Y and Z lights. See also APPARENT MOVEMENT, PRINCIPLES AND THEORIES OF; TIME, THEORIES OF.

REFERENCES

Helson, H. (1930). The tau-effect: An example of psychological relativity. *Science, 71*, 536-537.

Cohen, J., Hansel, C., & Sylvester, J. (1955). Interdependence in judgments of space, time, and movement. *Acta Psychologica, 11*, 360-372.

Jones, B., & Huang, Y. (1982). Space-time dependencies in psychophysical judgment of extent and duration: Algebraic models of the tau and kappa effects. *Psychological Bulletin, 91*, 128-142.

TAXICAB PROBLEM/EFFECT. The Israeli-American cognitive psychologists Amos Tversky (1937-1996) and Daniel Kahneman (1934-) identify the so-called *base-rate fallacy* (i.e., the failure to take account of the "prior probability/base-rate" of an event when subjectively judging its "conditional probability") in the *taxicab problem/effect* of probability judgment. The problem states that a city taxicab was involved in a hit-and-run accident at night. Only the "Blue Cab" and "Green Cab" companies (where 15-percent are Blue Cabs and 85-percent are Green Cabs) operate in the city. An eyewitness to the accident claimed that the cab in question was blue (also, the witness was tested and gave an 80-percent correct judgment of blue and green cabs). The *taxicab problem* poses the question, "What is the *probability* that the cab involved was *blue*?" The participants' median and modal judgment was 80-percent - that agrees with the reliability of the tested witness - but ignores the "relative frequency" or "base-rate" of cabs (i.e., 85-percent Green Cabs and 15-percent Blue Cabs). Tversky and Kahneman state that the correct answer to the question - worked out using *Bayes' theorem* - is 41-percent probability, which is actually closer to the *base-rate* of cabs than to the 80-percent reliability estimates of the eyewitness.

See also BAYES' THEOREM; DECISION-MAKING THEORIES; EXPECTED UTILITY THEORY; PROBABILITY THEORY/LAWS; WELLS EFFECT.

REFERENCES

Kahneman, D., & Tversky, A. (1973). On the psychology of prediction. *Psychological Review, 80*, 237-251.

Tversky, A., & Kahneman, D. (1974). Judgments under uncertainty: Heuristics and biases. *Science, 185*, 1124-1131.

Tversky, A., & Kahneman, D. (1981). The framing of decisions and the psychology of choice. *Science, 211*, 453-458.

Kahneman, D., & Tversky, A. (1988). Prospect theory: An analysis of decision under risk. In P. Gaerderfors & N.-E. Sahlin (Eds.), *Decision, probability, and utility: Selected read-ings.* New York: Cambridge Univer-sity Press.

TAYLOR SYSTEM/THEORY. See ORGANIZATIONAL/INDUSTRIAL/SYSTEMS THEORY.

TAYLOR-WOODHOUSE ILLUSION. See APPENDIX A, MUNSTERBERG ILLUSION.

TECTONICS THEORY. See MIND/MENTAL STATES, THEORIES OF.

TEETER-TOTTER EFFECT. See DEVELOPMENTAL THEORY.

TELEGRAPHIC SPEECH. See SPEECH THEORIES.

TELEOLOGY, DOCTRINE OF. See TOLMAN'S THEORY.

TELEONOMY, DOCTRINE OF. See TOLMAN'S THEORY.

TELEPHONE THEORY OF HEARING. See AUDITION/HEARING, THEORIES OF.

TEMPERATURE ILLUSION. See APPENDIX A.

TEMPLATE MATCHING THEORY. See PATTERN/OBJECT RECOGNITION THEORY.

TEMPORAL-LOBE ILLUSIONS/HALLUCINATIONS. See APPENDIX A.

TEMPORAL SUMMATION, LAW OF. See SKINNER'S DESCRIPTIVE BEHAVIOR/OPERANT CONDITIONING THEORY.

TEND AND BEFRIEND THEORY OF STRESS/COPING. See SEXUAL ORIENTATION THEORIES.

TENDENCY, LAW OF. See VIGILANCE, THEORIES OF.

TENDENTIOUS HUMOR. See CONNECTIONIST MODEL OF HUMOR.

TENSION, LAW OF. See WEBER'S LAW.

TENSION-REDUCTION THEORIES. See MOTIVATION, THEORIES OF.

TERNUS PHENOMENON. See PERCEPTION (I. GENERAL), THEORIES.

TESTING EFFECT. See LEARNING THEORIES/LAWS; MEASUREMENT THEORY.

TETRACHROMATIC THEORY. See HERING-HURVICH-JAMESON COLOR VISION THEORY.

TEXTON HYPOTHESIS. See PATTERN/OBJECT RECOGNITION THEORY.

THALAMIC THEORY OF EMOTION. See CANNON/CANNON-BARD THEORY.

THEORY-BEGGING FALLACY. See PARADIGM SHIFT DOCTRINE.

THEORY OF BEHAVIORAL POWER FUNCTIONS. See SKINNER'S DESCRIPTIVE BEHAVIOR/OPERANT CONDITIONING THEORY.

THEORY-THEORY. See PIAGET'S THE-ORY OF DEVEOPLMENTAL STAGES.

THEORY X. See LEADERSHIP, THEO-RIES OF; ORGANIZATIONAL/INDUST-RIAL/SYSTEMS THEORY.

THEORY Y. See LEADERSHIP, THEO-RIES OF.

THEORY Z. See LEADERSHIP, THEO-RIES OF.

THE QUESTION METHOD/PHENOM-ENON. See PSYCHOPATHOLOGY, THEORIES OF.

THERAPEUTIC THEORY OF LAUGH-TER/HUMOR. The *therapeutic theory of laughter/humor* is based on the premise that laughter and humor are "good" or "healthy" for the body - in a physiological sense - because they restore biological homeostasis, oxygenate the blood, stabilize blood pressure, stimulate circulation, massage the vital organs, aid digestion, and relax the person's entire system; also, they produce psychological feelings of "well-being." According to this theory, ancient or primitive humans initially engaged in activities involving laughter and humor for various biological, instinctual, psychological, and evolutionary purposes. See also HUMOR, THEORIES OF.

REFERENCES
Keith-Spiegel, P. (1972). Early conceptions of humor: Varieties and issues. In J. H. Goldstein & P. E. McGhee (Eds.), *The psychology of humor: Theoretical perspectives and empirical issues.* New York: Academic Press.
Fry, W., & Salameh, W. (Eds.) (1987). *Handbook of humor and psychotherapy: Advances in the clinical use of humor.* Sarasota, FL: P.R.E.

THERMAL SENSITIVITY THEORIES. See NAFE'S VASCULAR THEORY OF CUTANEOUS SENSITIVITY.

THERMODYNAMICS, LAWS OF. These laws, originating in the physical sciences but often invoked in explaining psychological phenomena, refer to the study of principles governing the interrelationships between heat, mechanical work, and other forms of energy and their influence on the behavior of systems. The *first law of thermodynamics*, also called the *law of the conservation of energy* when referring to situations in which heat transfer takes place, is an extension of the result obtained by the English physicist James Prescott Joule (1818-1889), which asserts that when the state of an otherwise isolated closed system is changed by the performance of work, the amount of work needed depends only on the change effected and not on the means by which the work is done nor on the stages through which the system passes. In other terms, the *first law of thermodynamics* states that when a system changes from one state to another, energy is converted to a different form but the total amount of energy remains unchanged, that is, it is "conserved" [cf., *phlogiston theory* - an early chemical theory - proposed by the German chemist/physician Georg Ernst Stahl (1660-1734) in his elaboration of an earlier theory of combustion by the German chemist/physician Johann Joachim Becher (1635-1682) - that posits that when something is burned, a material or substance called *phlogiston* is lost. In a series of meticulous experiments, the French chemist Antoine Laurent Lavoisier (1743-1794), among others, displaced the *phlogiston theory* in the 1770s by demonstrating that such was not the case during combustion, but discussed the true role of *oxygen* in combustion, and indicated that matter can neither be created nor destroyed, but only changed]. The *second law of thermodynamics* is a generalization of experience that may be stated in a number of equivalent ways: as an axiomatic statement formulated by the German mathematician Constantin Caratheodory (1873-1950) that allows for the existence of an integrating factor for the heat transfer in an infinitesimal reversible process for a physical system of any number of degrees of freedom; as a principle by the British natural philosopher/physical theorist Lord William Kelvin (1824-1907) stating that it is impossible to devise a machine that, working in a cycle, produces no effect other than the extraction of a certain quantity from its surroundings and the performance of an equal amount of work on its surroundings; and as a principle by the German physicist Rudolf J. E. Clausius (1822-1888) suggesting that when two systems are placed in thermal contact, the direction of energy transfer in the form of heat is always from the system at the higher temperature to the system at the lower temperature. In other terms, the *second law of thermodynamics* states that in any closed system (i.e., a system that exchanges energy but not matter with the exterior), *entropy* (i.e., the degree of disorder of a closed system) may only increase or, in an idealized condition, remain unchanged [cf., *Maxwell's demon* - named after the Scottish physicist James Clerk Maxwell (1831-1879), refers to the conceptualization of the molecules on either side of a semi-permeable membrane/barrier as tiny "human-like agents" in an effort to try to disprove the *second law of thermodynamics* by governing or regulating the movement of the molecules]. The *third law of thermodynamics*, also called the *Nernst heat theorem* - named after the German phys-ical chemist Walther Nermann Nernst (1864-1941), who formulated it in 1906, and given a modern reformulation by the German physicist Sir Francis Eugen Simon (1893-1956) in 1927 - states that the contribution to the *entropy* of a system by each aspect that is in internal thermodynamic equilibrium tends to zero as the temperature tends to zero. One consequence of the *third law of thermodynamics* is that it is impossible to reduce the temperature of any system, or part of a system, to absolute zero in a finite number of operations. In other terms, the *third law of thermodynamics* refers to the conclusion that as a homogeneous system approaches a temperature of absolute zero, its *entropy* tends toward zero. Occasionally, the science of psychology borrows the concepts and laws/principles from other sciences (cf., Roeckelein, 1997), such as physics. In the present case, the physical *laws of thermodynamics* (including the notions of *entropy* and *conservation of energy*) find service in psychological discussions of topics and issues such as *general systems theory, information-processing theory*, and *Jung's theory of personality*. See also CONSERVATION OF ENERGY, LAW/ PRINCIPLE OF; CONSTANCY, PRINCIPLE OF; ENTROPY

PRINCIPLE; GENERAL SYSTEMS THEORY; HISTORICAL MODELS OF EXPERIMENTAL PSYCHOLOGY; INFORMATION/INFORMA-TION-PROCESSING THEORY; JUNG'S THEORY OF PERSONALITY.

REFERENCES

Muir, H. (Ed.) (1994). *Larousse dictionary of scientists*. New York: Larousse.

Roeckelein, J. E. (1997). Hierarchy of the sciences and terminological sharing of laws among the sciences. *Psychological Reports, 81*, 739-746.

THERMOSTATIC THEORY. See HUNGER, THEORIES OF.

THIBAUT AND KELLEY'S EXCHANGE THEORY. See EXCHANGE/SOCIAL EXCHANGE THEORY.

THINKING/THOUGHT, THEORIES OF. See WHORF-SAPIR HYPOTHESIS/THEORY.

THIRD EAR HYPOTHESIS. This theoretical notion was developed and advanced by the Austrian-born American psychoanalyst Theodor Reik (1888-1969) to denote an experienced analyst's interpretation faculty/ability whereby he/she "hears" things (figuratively speaking) in the patient's/client's words that may not be apparent to an untrained listener. The phrase *listening with the third ear* refers to empathetic capability whereby a therapist acquires a special sensitivity to the unspoken thoughts and feelings behind the patient's spoken words. The term was used originally in the 1800s by the German philosopher Friedrich Nietzsche (1844-1900), but was elaborated more fully in the psychoanalytic milieu by Reik in 1948. Thus, with the trained/intuitive *third ear*, the analyst may interpret the deeper meanings of the utterances of the patient. For example, the patient's overtly spoken words, "My father was a good man," may be interpreted by the therapist to actually mean "Though I feel my father was a moral individual, I never really loved him, but only respected him" (cf., the psychoanalytic/Freudian concept of *transference* - a form of psychic displacement, or defense mechanism, involving the rechanneling of attitudes and emotions from their original source/object onto a substitute, such as may occur when the patient displays childlike/dependent reactions, including both aggressive and sexual behaviors, toward the therapist/analyst; such *transference* behavior, theoretically, is a carryover from the patient's earlier relationships, in particular regarding the relationship between the patient and his or her parents/guardians). See also FREUD'S THEORY OF PERSONALITY.

REFERENCES

Freud, S. (1914). Remembering, repeating, and working-through. In *The standard edition of the complete psychological works of Sigmund Freud.* London: Hogarth Press.

Reik, T. (1948). *Listening with the third ear: The inner experience of a psychoanalyst.* New York: Farrar, Straus.

Reik, T. (1964). *Voices from the inaudible: The patients speak.* New York: Farrar, Straus.

THIRD-FORCE THEORY/THERAPY/ PSYCHOLOGY. See MASLOW'S THEORY OF PERSONALITY; PARADIGM SHIFT DOCTRINE; ROGERS' THEORY OF PERSONALITY.

THIRST, THEORIES OF. The term *thirst* may be defined operationally as the internal, physiological state that results from water deprivation for a given period of time and is usually characterized by dryness in the mouth, throat, and mucous membranes of the pharynx. In terms of *motivation*, the concept of *thirst* is a need/drive state resulting from liquid deprivation that produces a desire for fluids, specifically water, and motivates water-seeking behavior. An early *peripheral theory of thirst*, called the *dry-mouth theory* - proposed by the American physiologist Walter Bradford Cannon (1871-1945) - emphasizes the relationship of salivary-gland function and moisture receptors in the mouth. The common notion that drinking results simply when the mouth is dry has a long history going back to Hippocrates (c. 460-377 B.C.). The *dry-mouth theory of thirst* was revived later in the 18th century by the Swiss physiologist Albrecht von Haller (1708-1777) and continued to enjoy great popularity because of its intuitive appeal. Cannon's *dry-mouth theory*, or *local theory of thirst*, however, has not survived the test of time and experimentation. For example, the removal of the salivary glands in dogs does not disrupt the regulation of water intake in terms of the amount of liquid consumed, nor does the administration of drugs that induce excessive salivation. Severing the nerves associated with the mouth and throat appears, also, to be ineffective in amount of liquid consumed. The organism's need for water is metered by brain mechanisms that give rise to the sensation of thirst when the body's water stores become depleted. The brain seems to be sensitive to at least two different signals: (1) short periods of water deprivation result primarily in a loss of water from the general circulation system producing a state of low volume (called *hypovolemia*) and low blood pressure; and (2) with long periods of deprivation, water is drawn out of the cells to compensate for the critically low volume in the circulatory system, where prolonged deprivation and cellular dehydration accounts for 65-70 percent of the body's water loss with vascular *hypovolemia* accounting for the remaining 30-35 percent of the loss (cf., *hemorrhage and thirst hypothesis* - posits that loss of blood increases thirst; however, experiments with animals yields inconclusive and equivo-cal results regarding this theory). A *multifactor theory of thirst* (cf., Adolph, Barker, & Hoy, 1954) takes such cellular dehydration effects into account. Based on the distinction between intracellular and extracellular fluids, two kinds of thirst may be considered: *cellular dehydration thirst* and *hypovolemic thirst*. A current view of water regulation, called the *double-depletion hypothesis of thirst* (cf., Epstein, 1973), is that although *cellular dehydration thirst* and *hypovolemic thirst* are often present together, they are independent regulatory activities with independent neural systems in control. However, the neural systems for *cellular dehydration* and *hypovolemic thirst* are both disrupted after extensive lesions of the lateral hypothalamus. Also, the relative contributions of peripheral factors, cellular dehydration factors, and hypovolemic factors appear to vary according to the species being studied. See also HUNGER, THEORIES OF.

REFERENCES

Haller, A. (1757-1766). *Elementa physiologiae corporis humani.* Paris: Guillyn.

Cannon, W. (1934). Hunger and thirst. In C. Murchison (Ed.), *Handbook of general experimental psychology.* Worcester, MA: Clark University Press.

Adolph, E., Barker, J., & Hoy, P. (1954). Multiple factors in thirst. *American Journal of Physiology, 178,* 538-562.

Adolph, E. (1964). Regulation of body water content through water injection. In M. Wayner (Ed.), *Thirst.* New York: Macmillan.

Epstein, A. (1973). Epilogue: Retrospect and prognosis. In A. Epstein, H. Kissileff, & E. Stellar (Eds.), *The neuropsychology of thirst: New findings and advances in concepts.* Washington, D.C.: Hemisphere.

Grossman, S. (1975). Role of the hypothalamus in the regulation of food and water intake. *Psychological Review, 82,* 200-224.

Stricker, E. (1990). *Handbook of behavioral neurobiology.* Vol. 10. *Neurobiology of food and fluid intake.* New York: Plenum Press.

THORNDIKE'S LAW OF EFFECT. See EFFECT, LAW OF.

THOUGHT, LAWS OF. The three logical principles of *identity, contradiction,* and *excluded middle/excluded third* constitute the so-called three *laws of thought* (cf., Baldwin, 1901-1905). The *principle of identity* states that "*A* is *A*;" the *principle of contradiction* states that "*A* is not not-*A*;" and the *principle of excluded middle/excluded third* asserts that "everything is either *A* or not-*A*." In terms of formal logic, the first two propositions/principles are "categorical" and the third one is "disjunctive." Thus, the type of formal proposition called "conditional" is missing in these basic laws. According to J. M. Baldwin, ideally the *laws of thought* are all the rules of logic, but of such laws there is one that is the

great *law of thought* and everything else is of minor importance in comparison with it; namely, "if *A* is *B* and *B* is *C*, it may be concluded that *A* is *C.*" See also EXCLUDED MIDDLE, LAW/PRINCIPLE OF; EXCLUSION, LAW OF; WHORF-SAPIR HYPOTHESIS/THEORY.

REFERENCE

Baldwin, J. M. (Ed.) (1901-1905). *Dictionary of philosophy and psychology.* New York: Macmillan.

THOUGHT, MOTOR THEORY OF. See GALTON'S LAWS; WHORF-SAPIR HYPOTHESIS/THEORY.

THOULES RATIO. See CONSTANCY HYPOTHESIS.

THREE-DOOR GAME SHOW PROBLEM/EFFECT. The controversy that surrounds the "correct answer" to the so-called *three-door game show problem,* also known as the *Monty Hall problem/dilemma,* is a noteworthy psychological phenomenon/effect in reasoning/decision-making (i.e., not all individuals can agree as to the "correct answer" to the problem even after simulating or reproducing the game for oneself). The probabilistic aspects underlying the *three-door problem* go back to *Bertrand's box paradox,* first described by the French mathematician Joseph L. F. Bertrand (1822-1900) in 1889, and later by the English-born American bridge expert Alan F. Truscott (1925-) and the English author John Terrence Reese (1913-1996), according to which if a certain action could have been taken *either* because there was no alternative *or* as a result of a choice between two alternatives, then the first possibility is twice as likely as the second, other things being equal (also called the *principle of restricted choice*). In the most recent version of the *three-door problem* (cf., vos Savant, 1990), you are to imagine that you are on a game show, and you've been given a choice of three doors. Behind one door is a new car; behind each of the other two doors is a goat. You pick a door, say door No. 1, and the host - who knows what's behind the doors - opens another door, say door No. 3, which has a goat. The host then says to you, "Do you want to switch your choice and pick door No. 2?" The question/problem is the following: Is it to your advantage to *switch* your choice? (Remember, you have not yet seen what is behind door No. 1, your initial choice). The "correct answer" is "*Yes, you should switch.*" The first door had a one-third chance of winning, but the second door now has a two-thirds chance. The following is offered as a good way to visualize the probabilistic dynamics involved in the *three-door problem*: Suppose (instead of just three doors) there are one-million doors, and you pick door No. 1. Then, the host (who knows what's behind the doors - and will always *avoid* the one with the prize) opens *all* the doors *except* door No. 333,333. Chances are, under these conditions, you would *switch* to that door without much hesitation. The "correct answer" to the *three-door problem* defines certain conditions, the most significant of which is that *the host will always open a losing door on purpose* (there's no way he can always open a losing door by *chance*). Anything else, theoretically, is a different question. In summary, for the *three-door problem*, when you first choose door No.1 from among the three doors, there is a one-third chance that the prize (new car) is behind that one and a two-thirds chance that it's behind the other doors. But, then, the host steps in and gives you a clue. If the prize is actually behind door No. 2, the host shows you door No. 3; and if the prize is actually behind door No. 3, the host shows you door No. 2. So, when you *switch*, you win if the prize is behind door No. 2 *or* door No. 3. You win either way. However, if you *don't* switch, you win only if the prize is behind door No. 1. See also PROBABILITY THEORY/LAWS.

REFERENCES

Bertrand, J. L. F. (1889). *Calcul des probabilities*. Paris: Bossard.

Reese, J. T. (1958/1973). *The expert game*. New York: R. Hale.

vos Savant, M. (1990). Three-door game show problem. *Parade Magazine*, December 2. (In Marilyn vos Savant's weekly column, "Ask Marilyn").

THREE-ELEMENT/TRI-RECEPTOR/ TRICHROMATIC COLOR VISION THE- ORY. See YOUNG-HELMHOLTZ COLOR VISION THEORY.

THREE-PHASE DEVELOPMENTAL THEORY. See MURPHY'S BIOSOCIAL THEORY.

THREE-PRIMARIES LAW. See COLOR MIXTURE, LAWS/THEORY OF.

THREE-SEVEN EFFECT/PHENOMEN-ON. This effect is based on the notion of *population stereotype* (i.e., in a situation involving an apparent arbitrary choice, a particular option may be chosen by a large proportion of a given population, and refers to a manner of thinking/perceiving/behaving that is statistically significant within the population), and is used frequently by performers and conjurers pretending to project their thoughts telepathically onto individuals in an audience. In this case, the performer says that he will think of a two-digit number between 1 and 50, and the number will have both digits odd but not the same. Then, the performer says, as an example, that "15" would be allright but "11" would not because the two odd digits are the same. Subsequently, when asked which members of the audience got "37," it's likely that more than one-third of them thought of the number "37." This is due to the following reasons: the digits "3" and "7" are *population stereotypes*; and the performer's instructions leaves only seven possible two-digit numbers, apart from "15" that is likely to be eliminated by the audience because it was used in the example given by the performer. Another example of *population stereotype* is the result that occurs when people are asked to draw two geometric figures one inside the other; in this case, typically, more than one-third of the respondents draw a circle and a triangle. The *three-seven effect/phenomenon* is employed, often, in bogus demonstrations of the paranormal/parapsychological phenomenon of *telepathy* ("extra-sensory" perception of another person's mental processes). See also ASTROLOGY, THEORY OF; BARNUM EFFECT; PARANORMAL PHENOMENA/THEORY.

REFERENCES

Rigby, K. (1989). Belief in ESP and the mystical number seven: The role of a population stereotype. *Australian Psychologist, 24*, 411-416.

French, C. C. (1992). Population stereotypes and belief in the paranormal: Is there a relationship? *Australian Psychologist, 27*, 57-58.

THREE-STAGE/PROCESS THEORY OF MEMORY. See FORGETTING/MEMORY, THEORIES OF.

THREE-SYSTEMS THEORY OF MOTION PERCEPTION. The experimental study of human visual motion perception was inaugurated in the 19th century by the Austrian physiologist Sigmund Exner (1846-1926), and since then researchers in this area have maintained that motion perception is a "primary sensation" in its own right. More recently, the American cognitive psychologists Zhong-Lin Lu and George Sperling (1995, 2001) propose that human visual motion perception is served by three separate motion systems in their *three-systems theory of motion perception*: a first-order system that responds to moving luminance patterns; a second-order system that responds to moving modulations of feature types (stimuli in which the expected luminance is the same everywhere but an area of higher contrast or of flicker moves); and a third-order system that computes the notion of marked locations in a "salience map" (i.e., a neural representation of visual space in which the locations of important visual features, or "figure," are marked, and "ground" is unmarked). Feature tracking in the system operates interocularly as well as monocularly, and includes both *bottom-up* (e.g., it computes motion from luminance-, feature-, contrast-, depth-, motion-, and flicker-modulation) and *top-down* (e.g., attentional instructions may determine perceived motion direction) *processing*. The *three-systems theory of motion perception* has gained some confirmatory evidence. For example, different gain-control mechanisms for first- and second-order motion, selective impairment of first- versus second- and/or third-order motion by different brain injuries, and new third-order motions (i.e., isoluminant chromatic motion) have been found and classified. Although some contradictions to the *three-systems theory* have been suggested, a newly-resolved *three-systems theory of human visual motion perception* apparently survives in a strengthened theoretical format. See also APPARENT MOVEMENT, PRINCIPLES/THEORIES OF; BOTTOM-UP PROCESSING THEORIES; PERCEPTION (I. GENERAL), THEORIES OF; TOP-DOWN PROCESSING THEORIES.

REFERENCES

Exner, S. (1875). Experimentelle untersuchung der einfachsten psychishen processe. *Archiv fur die Gesamte Physiologie des Menschen und der Tiere, 11*, 403-432.

Lu, Z.-L., & Sperling, G. (1995). The functional architecture of human visual motion perception. *Vision Research, 35*, 2697-2722.

Lu, Z.-L., & Sperling, G. (2001). Three-systems theory of human visual motion perception: Review and update. *Journal of the Optical Society of America, 18*, 2331-2370.

THRESHOLD, LAW/THEORY OF. See CONFLICT, THEORIES OF; NEURAL QUANTUM THEORY; SKINNER'S DESCRIPTIVE BEHAVIOR/OPERANT CONDITIONING THEORY.

THURSTONE'S LAW OF COMPARATIVE JUDGMENT. The American psychologist and psychometrician Louis Leon Thurstone (1887-1955) formulated a mathematical model, called the *law of comparative judgment*, based on the scaling principle used by the German psychologist Gustav Fechner (1803-1887), which states that regardless of the physical values involved, stimulus differences that are detected equally-often are subjectively equal. The *law of comparative judgment* refers to a participant's perception of how two or more stimuli compare on a particular dimension and applies to the scaling of attributes (such as "beauty") for which there are no specifiable physical correlates or physically specifiable attributes. The law employs the psychophysical method of "paired comparisons" that was first introduced in 1894 by J. Cohn in his study of color preferences and then developed further by Thurstone. The paired-comparisons method is regarded as the most appropriate way of obtaining subjective/ value judgments. In the traditional method of paired-comparisons, every object in a set is presented for judgment in a pairwise fashion with every other object in the set (e.g., comparing tones according to "loudness," paintings according to "beauty," odors according to "pleasantness," and faces according to "similarity"). The power in the approach derives from the application of multidimensional and factor-analytic techniques to the data to reveal the underlying dimensions along which the judgments were made. Thurstone's *law of comparative judgment* makes it possible to obtain perceptual scale values associated with a single stimulus by starting quantitatively with individual difference measures. His law of the psychological distance between stimuli is cast in an equation involving a standard (z) score, variances, standard deviations, and a correlation coefficient. However, because experimental data on the values in the equation are not available usually, *Thurstone's law of comparative judgment* equation cannot be tested directly. The American psychometrician Warren S. Torgerson (1924-1999) showed how the theoretical principles of Thurstone's *law of comparative judgment* are applicable to the special case of psychometric rating scales and data (cf., Galton, 1879-1880), and proposed a *law of categorical judgment*, which holds that an individual's psychological continuum can be divided into a specified number of ordered categories or steps. Torgersons's *law of categorical judgment* ideally should provide a scale with equal intervals for psychological measurement. Unfortunately, it is very difficult to obtain stable, useful, and valid ratings at even an ordinal scale level due to various biases in the observers and variability in the objects or persons rated. It is almost always necessary to provide the raters with a common anchor or reference point in order to obtain reliable data in such rating situations. See also DECISION-MAKING THEORIES; MEASUREMENT THEORY; PSYCHOPHYSICAL LAWS/ THEORY.

REFERENCES

Galton, F. (1879-1880). Psychometric experiments. *Brain, 2*, 149-162.

Cohn, J. (1894). Experimentelle untersuchungen uber die gefuhlsbetonung der farben, helligkeiten, und ihrer combinagtionen. *Philosophische Studien, 10*, 562-603.

Thurstone, L. L. (1927). A law of comparative judgment. *Psychological Review, 34*, 273-286.

Torgerson, W. S. (1958). *Theory and method of scaling*. New York: Wiley.

Thurstone, L. L. (1959). *The measurement of values*. Chicago: University of Chicago Press.

THURSTONE'S PRIMARY MENTAL ABILITIES MODEL/THEORY. See INTELLIGENCE, THEORIES/LAWS OF.

TICKLING PARADOX/EFFECT. See SOMESTHESIS, THEORIES OF.

TIME ESTIMATION, THEORIES OF. See TIME, THEORIES OF.

TIMELESS MOMENT PHENOMENON. See TIME, THEORIES OF.

TIME ORIENTATION. See TIME, THEORIES OF.

TIME PERCEPTION, THEORIES/LAWS OF. See TIME, THEORIES OF.

TIME PERSPECTIVE. See TIME, THEORIES OF.

TIME SENSE. See TIME, THEORIES OF.

TIME, THEORIES OF. To the psychologist, the concept of *time* refers to a dimension of consciousness by which one gives order to experiences. However, to the physicist, *time* is one of the three basic quantities (the other two are *distance* and *mass*) by which the universe is described in physical terms; and, to the philosopher, *time* is a diversity of many other concepts, abstractions, and entities. In the area of cosmology (the science that seeks to achieve a comprehensive theory of the creation, evolution, and present structure of the physical universe), a number of cosmological theories attempt to explain the origins and genesis of time. For example, the *big-bang hypothesis/theory* states that at the "beginning" of time, all of the matter and energy in the universe was concentrated in a very small volume that exploded (about eight to thirteen billion years ago), and the resultant expansion continues today. On the other hand, according to the *steady-state theories*, the universe is thought to expand but new matter is continuously created at all points in space left by receding galaxies. The impact of such cosmological theories on the concept of *time* is that they imply the universe has always expanded - with no "beginning" or "end" - at a uniform rate and that it always will expand and maintain a constant density. Regarding the *psychological* aspects of *time*, in "civilized" societies the use of calendars, clocks, and other measurement devices helps to define *time* in terms of a "linear" progression, order, or succession of experienced events. Additionally, to manage and understand the concept of *time*, psychologists employ such terms as *psychological time* (experienced, sensed, or subjective time where the experience of duration is independent of external markers such as clocks, calendars, and day/night cycles, and where time appreciation is dependent on internal or endogenous events such as "chemical clocks," "biological clocks," "circadian rhythms," and "cognitive/mental markers"); *time perception* (the awareness of duration and the experience of the passage of time; subjective time; the perception of when an event occurred relative to other events); *subjective time* (the subjective feeling of duration with its absolute-given present; also called "experiential time" or "private time"); *objective time* (time that is an objectively determinable order in which durations are measured and an absolute present is indifferent; also called "public time"); *psychological moment* (a very short period of time within which successive stimuli are integrated and perceived as a whole; the instant of "now;" the period of time of immediate awareness; the meeting point between past and future); *specious present* (implies the concept of "nowness" and the psychological sense of the "present"); *time sense* (the apprehension of duration, change, order of occur-

rence, and the duration aspect of the attributes of experience); *time perspective* (the improved perspective that comes when events are viewed from a certain distance in time; the terms "temporal horizon" and "time orientation" are synonymous terms here); *temporal/time orientation* (the use of molar temporal units, such as days, weeks, months, or years, in reflecting on, and assessing, time passage); *time estimation* (implies a kind of temporal quantification and assessment that is not necessarily included in "time perception"); *sense of duration* (depends on the number of stimuli that are perceived and stored in the mind: if an interval has many divisions, it tends to appear longer than an equal interval - of objective or clock-time - that has fewer divisions); and *timeless moment/phenomenon* (refers to an absolute instance of time that is not measurable because it is infinitesimally small; in this phenomenon, there is no present, only past and future because - like the "specious present" - the instant one attempts to reflect on such a moment, it is past). Other psychological-theoretical features of time include the following: the notion of change; time as both continuous and discrete; rhythm; reaction-time, the notion of duration [cf., the *duration estimation paradox* - based on the distinction between *prospective time estimation* (i.e., judging how much time will elapse before some *coming* event happens) and *retrospective time estimation* (i.e., judging how much time elapsed during a *past* event), this paradox refers to a tendency for individuals to make more accurate *prospective time estimations* than *retrospective time estimations*)]; the notions of past and future; the notion of "temporal atomicity;" subjective versus objective passage of time; linear versus cyclical time; lack of an absolute "time-unit;" successive or indivisible "nows;" the relationship and representation of time to motion, distance, and space (cf., *jet lag effect* - a bodily/cognitive condition of fatigue and disorientation occasioned by traveling across several time zones in a short period, in particular when traveling in an aircraft in an eastward direction, and caused by a discrepancy between "exogenous" temporal cues and "endogenous" physiological and biological mechanisms such as circadian rhythms and sleep-wake cycles); and "social" time. The question whether the spatial representation of time reveals time's essential character (or is merely an artifact of humans' cerebral and perceptual mechanisms) is at the heart of the psychology and physics of time. Among the pre-modern and modern views, ideas, and *theories of time* in philosophy, physics, and psychology are the following notions (with proponents in parentheses): distinctions may be made between *time* and *duration* (Scholastics of the Middle Ages, 500-1500); the duration of things that are moved is not different from the duration of things that are not moved (Rene Descartes, 1596-1650); time is a "phantasm" produced by a body in motion, and time stands for the fact of succession, or "before" and "after" in motion (Thomas Hobbes, 1588-1679); time is an imaginary representation wholly without ontological significance (Baruch Spinoza, 1632-1677); time is based on the notion of succession that is empirically derived as a result of reflecting on several ideas that are presented successively to consciousness (John Locke, 1632-1704); time may be viewed independently of experience (Ernst Mach, 1838-1916); "absolute" time is distinguished from "popular/subjective" time where absolute time is the only "true" time (Isaac Newton, 1642-1727); time appears short when the period has lively conversation or cheerful music (Thomas Reid, 1710-1796); time - not duration - exists only as events are occurring and is the relation of their succession, and time is purely relative and ideal (Gottfried Wilhelm Leibniz, 1646-1716); time perception is an act of reason rather than of sense, and time is nothing (George Berkeley, 1685-1753); time perception and memory are fundamental acts of mind (David Hartley, 1705-1757); time is not infinitely divisible, but is made up of discrete moments each with the duration of a single idea (David Hume, 1711-1776); time is the a priori form of inner sensible intuitions that have no existence independently of the mind and are a subjective mode in which phenomena appear (Immanuel Kant, 1724-1804); succession is the whole nature of time (Arthur Schopenhauer, 1788-1860); time is a river flowing inescapably into its own current (Heraclitus, c. 535-475 B.C., and Friedrich Wilhelm Nietzsche, 1844-1900); time is one

of the earliest notions of the infant (Thomas Brown, 1778-1820); time has no reality apart from space, or space apart from time and, as separate concepts, both are abstractions from the four-dimensional reality (Samuel Alexander, 1859-1938); chronological time is merely a symbol of space and is, therefore, distinct from the immeasurable flow of duration which is not less than the essence of life itself (Henri Bergson, 1859-1941); the distinction between past, present, and future is only an illusion, however persistent (Albert Einstein, 1879-1955). The bulk of the recent evidence in the *experimental psychology of time* has centered on the study of subjective "micro-time," i.e., with the precision of temporal estimates made of short intervals of clock time, such time estimates being made in the following ways: in numbers or words; by reproduction of a standard interval; or by production of an interval stated by the experimenter. In particular, such investigations have attempted to establish the following: the magnitude of that interval of time; the effects on a supposed optimal interval have been determined by delimiting the interval by signals varying in modality or intensity; "empty" intervals have been compared with intervals "filled" with sensory stimulation; thresholds for the separation of signals have been measured, as well as thresholds for the order of two signals presented in rapid succession; attempts have been made to devise psychophysical scales for psychological time extending to about 20 seconds; and the time taken to make a binary decision has been studied as a measure of subjective probability. A new chapter in the study of *subjective time* has begun recently wherein psychological judgments of duration are combined with judgments of physical distance and speed (e.g., the *tau- and kappa-effects* are included now in studies on the psychology of time). Another relatively recent ("new look") area of psychological time research emphasizes the relationship between temporal experience and other personality correlates both normal and abnormal. Finally, the study of *timing* and *time perception* has a dual history involving both human and animal study. Thus, in addition to *human timing* dealing with the production and organization of temporal patterns, the following topics have been studied in *animal timing*: temporal differentiation; trace conditioning; time discrimination; counting behavior; contingency in classical conditioning; cross-species competence; reinforcement integration; timing in animal learning; theories of timing behavior; pigeons' timing behavior and internal clock models; and human versus animal time. See also ARISTOTLE'S TIME THEORY AND PARADOX; BERGSON'S THEORY OF TIME; EARLY GREEK AND LATER PHILOSOPHICAL THEORIES OF TIME; FRAISSE'S THEORY OF TIME; GUYAU'S THEORY OF TIME; JAMES' TIME THEORY; KALAM THEORY OF ATOMIC TIME; MICHON'S MODEL OF TIME; ORNSTEIN'S THEORY OF TIME; PLOTINUS' THEORY OF TIME; PSYCHOLOGICAL TIME, MODELS OF; SCALAR TIMING THEORY; ST. AUGUSTINE'S TIME THEORY AND PARADOX; TAU- AND KAPPA-EFFECTS; VIERORDT'S LAWS.

REFERENCES

Hawking, S. (1988). *A brief history of time.* New York: Bantam Books.

Roeckelein, J. E. (2000). *The concept of time in psychology.* Westport, CT: Greenwood Press.

TIMING-OF-EVENTS MODEL. See DEVELOPMENTAL THEORY.

TIP-OF-THE-TONGUE PHENOMENON. See FORGETTING/MEMORY, THEORIES OF.

TITCHENER'S CONTEXT THEORY OF MEANING. See MEANING, THEORIES/ ASSESSMENT OF.

TOLMAN'S THEORY. The American psychologist Edward Chace Tolman (1886-1959) formulated a "purposive" *behavioristic learning theory* - also called the *sign-gestalt theory* and *expectancy theory* - that emphasizes the cognitive nature of learning (cf., the *stimulus-response learning theories* of E. L. Thorndike, E. R. Guthrie, B. F. Skinner, and C. L. Hull). In his theory, Tolman is concerned with concepts such as *knowledge, thinking, planning, intention, inference,* and *purpose* (cf., the *doctrine of teleology* - posits that the existence

of everything in the universe may be explained in terms of purpose, and states that behavior may be explained best in terms of ends, purposes, the organisms' goals, and orientation to the future, rather than in terms of instincts and childhood experiences; and the *doctrine of teleonomy* - states that life has purpose where the organisms' behaviors, structures, and functions have evolutionary survival value, and studies behavior patterns having a concealed purpose). Tolman describes animals' behavior in terms of their motives, cognitions ("bits of knowledge"), expectations, and purposes much as if animals possess human characteristics of thought (it has been said that whereas C. L. Hull attempted to "make *men* into *rats*" with his *stimulus-response* approach to learning, Tolman attempted to "make *rats* into *men*" with his *cognitive-purposive* approach to learning). The main tenets of *Tolman's theory* are that behavior should be analyzed in terms of actions (large-scale basis or "molar" aspect) rather than of movements (small-scale basis or "molecular" aspect), that behavior is goal-directed ("purposive"), and that behavior in seeking a particular goal varies according to environmental circumstances (cf., *task cycle theory* - is based on Tolman's cognitive-learning approach; this conjecture refers to the area of organizational/group dynamics and the presence of a sequence of skills that - when indicated by a leader - gives signs and meaning to the group members concerning the task that is set for their completion). Among Tolman's learning constructs are: *expectancy* - a three-term associative unit involving a stimulus, a response to it, and another stimulus that follows the response; and *cognitive/conceptual map* - a mental map of the environment that indicates routes, paths, and environmental relationships that determine what responses the organism will make. One of the basic assumptions of *Tolman's theory* is that knowledge is acquired as a simple result of exposure and attention to environmental events; no reward is necessary, just contiguity of experienced events where expectancies are strengthened every time objective events occur in sequence. Tolman views the concept of *extinction* as a weakening/loss of a specific expectancy, and the concept of *inference* as the process by which new positive events at a goal-location could work their way back to affect any subsequent response selection. Tolman asserts that organisms have internal representations that allow them to demonstrate "goal learning" and discriminations. Evidence for this position comes from experiments on *reward expectancy, place learning, latent learning/latent extinction, partial reinforcement extinction effect/discrimination hypothesis, provisional expectancies/hypotheses theory,* and *vicarious trial-and-error learning.* Tolman's *latent/incidental learning theory* states that learning may occur in the absence of a foreseen goal or reward; such learning is not observable directly but becomes apparent with the later introduction of a goal; the theory is open to criticism on the grounds that it is always possible to identify goals in retrospect, but not prospectively. *Tolman's theory* anticipated many of the later significant developments in learning theory. For example, the current topics of "decision processes," "subjective probability," and "subjective utility" involve concepts that are similar to Tolman's *expectancy value* and *object valence.* J. B. Rotter's *behavioral potential theory* and *expectancy-reinforcement theory* are close to Tolman's *means-ends readiness* and *valence*; J. Deutsch's *structural model* contains aspects similar to Tolman's *insightful behavior of rats*; and F. Logan's *hybrid theory of classical conditioning* and *incentive learning* centers on Tolman's *sensory-sensory contiguity principle of association.* However, Tolman's approach has been criticized as containing too many superfluous/surplus meanings, and as being too anthropomorphic, unparsimonious, teleological, and vitalistic. Tolman's system does not seem to be tight enough to endure, and there is no "Tolman's law" to give him immortality. On the other hand, the *latent learning experiment* is probably as uniquely Tolman's as the *nonsense syllable* is uniquely Hermann von Ebbinghaus'. Perhaps, in the final analysis, Tolman's contribution to learning theory may lie in his emphasis on the *cognitive* aspects of behavior, giving challenges to rigid *behaviorism.* See also AMSEL'S HYPOTHESIS/THEORY; BEHAVIORIST THEORY; CAPALDI'S THEORY; GUTHRIE'S BEHAVIOR THEORY; HULL'S LEARNING THEORY; LEARNING THEORIES/LAWS; LOGAN'S MICROMOLAR THEORY; ROTTER'S SOCIAL LEARNING THEORY; SKINNER'S DESCRIPTIVE BEHAVIOR AND OPERANT CONDITIONING THEORY.

REFERENCES

Krechevsky, I. (1932). "Hypotheses" in rats. *Psychological Review, 39,* 516-532.

Thorndike, E. L. (1932). *The fundamentals of learning.* New York: Teachers College, Columbia University.

Tolman, E. C. (1932). *Purposive behavior in animals and men.* New York: Appleton-Century-Crofts.

Guthrie, E. R. (1935). *The psychology of learning.* New York: Harper and Row.

Skinner, B. F. (1938). *The behavior of organisms: An experimental analysis.* New York: A-C-C.

Hull, C. L. (1943). *Principles of behavior.* New York: A-C-C.

Tolman, E. C., Ritchie, B., & Kalish, D. (1946). Studies in spatial learning. II. Place learning versus response learning. *Journal of Experimental Psychology, 36,* 221-229.

Rotter, J. B. (1954). *Social learning and clinical psychology.* Englewood Cliffs, NJ: Prentice-Hall.

Tolman, E. C. (1959). Principles of purposive behavior. In S. Koch (Ed.), *Psychology: A study of a science.* Vol. 2. New York: McGraw-Hill.

Deutsch, J. (1960). *The structural basis of behavior.* Chicago: University of Chicago Press.

Logan, F. (1979). Hybrid theory of operant conditioning. *Psychological Review, 86,* 507-541.

TOMATO EFFECT. See EXPERIMENTER EFFECTS.

TONES/COMBINATIONAL, THEORY OF. See STUMPF'S THEORY OF MUSICAL CONSONANCE AND DISSONANCE.

TOP-DOWN PROCESSING THEORIES. *Top-down processing* is a generic term referring to the flow of information or data in any given aspect of *cognitive* or *perceptual theory*. The term, also known as *conceptually-driven processing*, was introduced by the American psychologists Donald A. Norman (1935-) and David E. Rumelhart (1942-), and refers to information processing that originates from information that is already stored in memory, in particular, general assumptions about the material being processed, such as the case where the person forms a hypothesis on the basis of existing "schemata" and previous experience concerning what an object might be, and then uses sensory data either to disconfirm or to affirm the hypothesis. For example, when one takes "meaning" or "familiarity" of stimuli into account when perceiving the world, it is called *top-down processing* because processing is based on "higher-level" information such as the meaningful context in which a stimulus is observed (cf., *bottom-up processing*), as well as other information that causes the observer to expect that another stimulus will be presented. The *word-superiority effect* (*WSE*) [i.e., the finding, first reported by the American psychologist James McKeen Cattell (1860-1944) in 1885, that a letter can be identified at a lower threshold and responded to more rapidly when it is part of a familiar word than if it is presented in isolation and, thus, presents a serious challenge to researchers who assert that letters must be recognized first in order to identify words] is a good example of *top-down processing*. The *WSE* is called, also, the *Reicher-Wheeler effect* - named after the American psychologists Gerald M. Reicher (1939-) and Daniel D. Wheeler (1942-). Thus, processes that originate in the *brain* and influence the selection, organization, or interpretation of sensory data are called "conceptually-driven," "hypothesis-driven," or *top-down processing*. Abstract thoughts, prior knowledge, beliefs, values, past experience, expectations, memory, motivations, cultural background, and language all influence and direct *top-down processing*. Another typical example of *top-down processing* is the phenomenon of *reversal* in so-called "ambiguous figures," where the figure seems involuntarily to oscillate between different percepts or interpretations (cf., the *Rubin figure/illusion* or *face-goblet/face-vase illusion*, Appendix A). Usually,

both *top-down* and *bottom-up processing* interact as one attempts to perceive the environment in some comprehensive, organized, and cohesive fashion. For example, in *analysis-by-synthesis theory* (i.e., recognition process where hypotheses are formed and compared with input data until one of the hypotheses produces a match), both *top-down* and *bottom-up processing* are implicated. See also BOTTOM-UP PROCESSING/THEORIES; GESTALT THEORY/LAWS; INFORMATION/INFORMATION-PROCESSING THEORY; PATTERN/OBJECT RECOGNITION THEORY; PERCEPTION (I. GENERAL), THEORIES OF; PERCEPTION (II. COMPARATIVE APPRAISAL), THEORIES OF; THREE-SYSTEMS THEORY OF MOTION PERCEPTION.

REFERENCES

Cattell, J. McK. (1885). Uber die zeit der erkennung und benennung von schriftzeichen, bildern, und farben. *Philosophische Studien, 2*, 635-650.

Norman, D. A., & Rumelhart, D. E. (1975). *Explorations in cognition*. San Francisco: Freeman.

TOPOGRAPHIC HYPOTHESIS/MODEL OF THE MIND. See MIND/MENTAL STATES, THEORIES OF.

TOPOLOGICAL FIELD THEORY. See LEWIN'S FIELD THEORY; PERCEPTION (II. COMPARATIVE APPRAISAL), THEORIES OF.

TOPOLOGICAL PSYCHOLOGY. See LEWIN'S FIELD THEORY.

TORGERSON'S LAW OF CATEGORICAL JUDGMENT. See THURSTONE'S LAW OF COMPARATIVE JUDGMENT.

TOTAL QUALITY MANAGEMENT THEORY/APPROACH. See ORGANIZATIONAL/INDUSTRIAL/SYSTEMS THEORY.

TOTAL TIME HYPOTHESIS/LAW. The American psychologist B. Richard Bugelski (1913-1995) explored the *total time hypothesis* in a learning context, suggesting that total time (number of trials multiplied by trial time) to learn material in paired-associate learning tasks equals a constant. This *hypothesis* has occasionally been elevated to the status of a *law*. The *total time law* is the notion that the amount of learning that will occur in a given time interval is relatively constant no matter how that time is spent in rehearsing the material to be learned (cf., *deJong's law* - the principle that the time taken to perform a task is an exponential function of the time spent practicing it; the *power law of practice* - the time taken to perform a mental task decreases as a fractional power of the number of trials; and the *law of fixation* - the principle that with repeated practice learned material becomes more or less permanently fixed in the mind). Bugelski's studies support the *total time law* where he found that the total time required to learn a list of nonsense syllables (presented in pairs as "paired associates" in which participants were asked to anticipate and say aloud the second syllable of each pair when shown the first syllable) was unaffected by the rate at which items were presented within that total time. Subsequent to Bugelski's work, many other researchers have elaborated upon, and supported, the *total time hypothesis/law* (cf., the *lag effect* as an exception to the *total time hypothesis*; Baddeley, 1976). The *total time law* has potential value for educators and teachers because it suggests that the patterns of rehearsal that a person uses when learning materials is relatively unimportant, and that an essential aspect in learning is that the individual keeps on working. Thus, it takes a certain amount of time to learn some-thing, regardless of the length of the practice period. See also LEARNING THEORIES/ LAWS.

REFERENCES

Bugelski, B. R. (1962). Presentation time, total time, and mediation in paired-associate learning. *Journal of Experimental Psychology*, *63*, 409-412.

Cooper, E., & Pantle, A. (1967). The total-time hypothesis in verbal learning. *Psychological Bulletin*, *68*, 221-234.

Bugelski, B. R. (1970). Presentation time and the total-time hypothesis: A methodological amendment. *Journal of Experimental Psychology*, *84*, 529-530.

Baddeley, A. (1976). *The psychology of memory*. New York: Basic Books.

Bugelski, B. R. (1979). *The principles of learning and memory*. New York: Praeger.

deJong, R., Liang, C.-C., & Lauber, E. (1994). Conditional and unconditional automaticity: A dual-process model of effects of spatial stimulus-response correspondence. *Journal of Experimental Psychology: Human Perception and Performance*, *20*, 731-750.

TOTE MODEL/HYPOTHESIS. The American psychologists George A. Miller (1920-), and Eugene H. Galanter (1924-), and the Austrian-born American psychologist Karl H. Pribram (1919-) describe the *TOTE model/ hypothesis* (an acronym for the sequence: Test-Operate-Test-Exit) that is a postulated basic unit of planned, sensorimotor behavior. This hypothetical mechanism reacts to a stimulus by testing it for incongruity, by operating to remove any incongruity, and then testing it again, and so on indefinitely until the incongruity is eliminated and then, at that time, exiting from the feedback loop. The *TOTE* is intended to be a conceptual alternative to the historical *reflex arc* notion (cf., Dewey, 1896), and to *stimulus-response associationism*, whereby the feedback loop of *TOTE* is the basic element of behavior rather than the *reflex arc* itself; in this alternative, the *reflex arc* is considered to be only one of the many possible manifestations or particularities of the larger *TOTE* pattern. The feedback loop of the *TOTE model* allows energy to flow through the system as well as information/control that may be realized at the cognitive level. A simple example of *TOTE* is the setting of a thermostat to control the temperature of a room, where setting it initially too high ("test") leads to a room that feels too warm, then setting it lower ("operate") and finding the room to feel comfortable ("test"), and then leaving the thermostat at that setting ("exit"). TOTE was advanced as a model of behavior in which actions to be taken are based on plans modified by feedback regarding actions already taken, which is a fundamental aspect borrowed from the field of *cybernetics* (meaning "steersman") - developed largely by the American mathematician Norbert Wiener (1894-1964) - where control mechanisms and their associated communications systems are studied and applied, in particular those systems involving feedback of information to mechanisms concerning its activities. See also ASSOCIATION, LAWS/PRIN-CIPLES OF; CONTROL/SYSTEMS THEORY; CYBERNETIC THEORY; INFORMATION/INFORMATION-PROCESSING THEORY; REFLEX ARC THEORY/CONCEPT.

REFERENCES

Dewey, J. (1896). The reflex arc concept in psychology. *Psychological Review, 3*, 357-370.

Wiener, N. (1948). *Cybernetics: Control and communication in the animal and the machine.* Cambridge, MA: M.I.T. Press.

Miller, G. A., Galanter, E. H., & Pribram, K. H. (1960). *Plans for the structure of behavior.* New York: Holt, Rinehart, & Winston.

TOXICOSIS EFFECT. See GARCIA EFFECT.

TRACE DECAY THEORY/DOCTRINE. See BARTLETT'S SCHEMATA THEORY; FORGETTING/MEMORY, THEORIES OF; GESTALT THEORY/LAWS; von RESTORFF EFFECT.

TRACE MODEL OF DISTRIBUTED MEMORY AND SPEECH PERCEPTION. The American cognitive psychologist James Lloyd McClelland (1948-) and his colleagues describe the *TRACE model of distributed memory and speech perception* that is based on the principles of interactive/reciprocal activation within the domain of *distributed models of information processing.* The model consists of a large number of simple processing elements that transmit excitatory and inhibitory signals to each other via modifiable connections. The *memory trace* of a processing event is the incremental change in the strengths of the interconnections that results from the processing event. The *traces* of separate events are superimposed on each other via the values of the connection strengths that result from the entire set of *traces* in the memory store. Thus, the *TRACE model* consists of a network of units formed by dynamic processing. A modified version - that is called *TRACE II* - simulates a large number of empirical findings on the perception of phonemes and words, and on their interactions. Also, *TRACE II* employs lexical information to segment a stream of speech into a sequence of words, and to discover word beginnings and endings. The *TRACE model* demonstrates how the functional equivalent of abstract representations (prototypes, logogens, rules) may emerge - under the appropriate conditions - from the superimposition of *traces* from specific experiences. See also ENGRAM THEORY; FORGETTING/MEMORY, THEORIES OF; INFORMATION/INFORMATION-PROCESSING THEORY; INTERACTIVE ACTIVATION MODEL OF LETTER PERCEPTION; PARALLEL DISTRIBUTED PROCESSING MODEL; PROTOTYPE THEORY; TRACE THEORY/DOCTRINE; von RESTORFF EFFECT.

REFERENCES

McClelland, J. L., & Rumelhart, D. E. (1985). Distributed memory and the representation of general and specific information. *Journal of Experimental Psychology: General, 114*, 159-188.

McClelland, J. L., & Elman, J. L. (1986). The TRACE model of speech perception. *Cognitive Psychology, 18*, 1-86.

TRAIT CENTRALITY PHENOMENON. See IMPRESSION FORMATION, THEORIES OF.

TRAIT NEGATIVITY BIAS. See MERE EXPOSURE EFFECT.

TRAIT THEORIES OF PERSONALITY. See PERSONALITY THEORIES.

TRAIT THEORY OF LEADERSHIP. See LEADERSHIP, THEORIES OF.

TRANSACTIONAL ANALYSIS TECHNIQUE. See BERNE'S SCRIPT THEORY.

TRANSACTIONAL THEORIES OF LEADERSHIP. See LEADERSHIP, THEORIES OF.

TRANSACTIONAL/TRANSACTIONAL FUNCTIONALISM THEORY. See BERNE'S SCRIPT THEORY; PERCEPTION (II. COMPARATIVE APPRAISAL), THEORIES OF.

TRANSFERENCE PRINCIPLE. See THIRD EAR HYPOTHESIS.

TRANSFER OF TRAINING, THORNDIKE'S THEORY OF. = identical elements/components theory. In general, the topic of *transfer of training* refers to the situation where something learned in one task (e.g., learning to fly a helicopter) may be carried over ("transferred") to another task (e.g., learning to fly a jet aircraft) and where the transfer may either facilitate of inhibit the learning of the second task. Transfer of training is attributed, often, to the existence of "identical elements or components" in the two functions/situations or to the process of generalization (cf., *instance/episode/exemplar theory*, which holds that memory and knowledge systems are built up directly on the basis of specific instances or episodes in one's experience; this theory is contrasted, typically, with *abstraction/prototype theory*, which argues that memory/knowledge is built up by processes of abstract information that is extracted from specific episodes that one experiences; the *identifiability principle* is the conjecture that it is easier to learn to make responses to events when the elements contained in one event or situation are easily identified and distinguished from the other elements; and the *response-by-analogy principle* states that any animal or human - who is in a new or unfamiliar setting and must respond to the demands of the new environment - will respond in a way that is similar to the way it had responded previously in a familiar or similar situation). Early accounts of the operation of transfer of training emphasized the *faculty* (i.e., a power or agency of the mind such as feeling, will, intellect) that was involved in the learning situation. The historic school/system of psy-

chology called *faculty psychology*, and *mental-faculty theory*, approached the study of the human mind by attempting to account for mental processes in terms of a fixed number of such "faculties." A *faculty* was defined in such a broad manner as to cover all the operations of memory and observation and was supposed to be strengthened by exercise on any sort of material. In an *educational theory* context, the *theory of faculty training* holds that training to learn one set of materials (e.g., learning Latin) prepares one to excel on another set of materials (e.g., learning English). Although largely discredited today, *faculty psychology* has recently been revived under the *modularity hypothesis/theory* where the existence of cognitive and perceptual modules (e.g., a language module; a numerical module) are hypothesized. The American psychologist Edward Lee Thorndike's (1874-1949) pioneer experimental work in 1903 was in opposition to the postulates of the traditional *faculty theory*. Thorndike proposed that transfer of material was possible only so far as *identical elements or components* of behavior could be carried over from one learning task to another one. Thorndike and R. S. Woodworth (1901) conducted transfer experiments that attacked a correlate of the *faculty theory* called the *doctrine of formal discipline* (i.e., the educational approach that suggests that some courses should be studied - independently of the content that they might have - because they serve generally to "train the mind"). The transfer effects that Thorndike and Woodworth found were due to specific methods, habits, and ideas that were carried over from the practice tasks that were given previously. Their conclusions were that improvements in performance were due to definite *factors* (rather than general tendencies), and these definite *factors* comprised "common" or "identical" elements. Thorndike consistently held that a change in one function alters any other function only insofar as the two functions have identical elements as *factors*. In more recent times, psychologists seem to prefer the term *common factors* over the term *identical elements*, but Thorndike's *identical elements/components* approach to transfer of training still serves as a useful prescription that points toward features and factors that are definite and concrete vis-à-vis the cause of any observed transfer effect. See also EFFECT, LAW OF; FORMAL DISCIPLINE/TRAINING, THEORY AND DOCTRINE OF; GENERALIZATION, PRINCIPLES OF; MIND/MENTAL STATES, THEORIES OF; OSGOOD'S TRANSFER SURFACE AND MODEL; REINFORCEMENT, THORNDIKE'S THEORY OF; SKAGGS-ROBINSON HYPOTHESIS.

REFERENCES

Thorndike, E. L., & Woodworth, R. S. (1901). The influence of improvement in one mental function upon the efficiency of other functions. *Psychological Review, 8*, 247-261, 384-395, 553-564.

Thorndike, E. L. (1903). *Educational psychology*. New York: Lemcke & Buechner.

Orata, P. (1928). *The theory of identical elements, being a critique of Thorndike's theory of identical elements and a reinterpretation of the problem of transfer of training*. Columbus: Ohio State University Press.

Bruce, R. (1933). Conditions of transfer of training. *Journal of Experimental Psychology, 16*, 343-361.

Gibson, E. (1953). Improvement in perceptual judgments. *Psychological Bulletin, 50*, 401-431.

Osgood, C. E. (1953). *Method and theory in experimental psychology*. New York: Oxford University Press.

TRANSFORMATIONAL THEORY OF LANGUAGE. See CHOMSKY'S PSYCHO-LINGUISTIC THEORY.

TRANSFORMATION THEORY. See DARWIN'S EVOLUTION THEORY.

TRANSGENERATIONAL HYPOTHESIS. See LABELING/DEVIANCE THEORY.

TRANSMETHYLATION HYPOTHESIS. See MENDEL'S LAWS/PRINCIPLES.

TRANSMIGRATION THEORY. See LIFE, THEORIES OF.

TRANSPOSITION, THEORY OF. See DELAYED-REACTION MODEL/PARADIGM; SPENCE'S THEORY.

TRANSSITUATIONALITY PRINCIPLE. See REINFORCEMENT THEORY.

TRAPEZOIDAL/AMES WINDOW. See APPENDIX A.

TRAVELING WAVE THEORY. See AUDITION/HEARING, THEORIES OF.

TREISMAN'S FEATURE INTEGRATION THEORY. See PATTERN/OBJECT RECOGNITION THEORY.

TRIAL AND ERROR, LAW OF. See CONDUCT, LAWS OF.

TRIAL AND ERROR THEORY OF LEARNING. See LEARNING, THEORIES OF.

TRICHROMATIC THEORY. See COLOR VISION, THEORIES/LAWS OF; YOUNG-HELMHOLTZ COLOR VISION THEORY.

TRICOMPONENT MODEL OF ATTITUDE. See ATTITUDE AND ATTITUDE CHANGE, THEORIES OF.

TRIDIMENSIONAL THEORY OF FEELING. See WUNDT'S THEORIES/DOCTRINES/PRINCIPLES.

TRIPARTITE PERSONALITY THEORY. See BERNE'S SCRIPT THEORY; FREUD'S THEORY OF PERSONALITY.

TRIPLE-CODE MODEL. See MOTOR LEARNING/PROCESS THEORIES; NEW STRUCTURALISM THEORY/PARADIGM.

TRIPLE-RECEPTOR THEORY. See FOVEAL CONE HYPOTHESIS.

TROPISM THEORY. See LOEB'S TROPISTIC THEORY.

TROXLER EFFECT. See VISION/SIGHT, THEORIES OF.

TULVING-WISEMAN LAW. This psychological law - named after the Estonia-born Canadian cognitive/experimental psychologist Endel Tulving (1927-   ) and his colleague Sandor Wiseman - describes the functional relationship between recognition memory and recall in experiments in which the same participants are given two memory tests successively on the same verbal items. When the "recognition-failure" data from many such experiments are graphed in a particular way, the dependency between recognition and recall appears to be largely invariant over studies in that the data points can be approximated closely by a simple equation. This result is called the *Tulving-Wiseman law*, and the law or function may be expressed as follows: $P(RN|RL) = P(RN) + c[P(RN)-P(RN)^2]$, where $P(RN|RL)$ is the probability of recognition given recall, and $P(RN)$ is the unconditional probability of recognition. In a typical successive-testing, recognition memory/recall experiment, participants study a list of A-B word pairs and then are tested twice, first for recognition of the B targets and then for recall of B when cued with A items. Subsequently, data are analyzed where each participant-item combination is tallied in a 2×2 contingency table according to success or failure on the recall test; finally, data are plotted on a scatter diagram and characteristically demonstrate an invariant relation between recognition and recall as predicted by the *Tulving-Wiseman law*. See also ENCODING SPECIFICITY HYPOTHESIS/PRINCIPLE; FORGETTING/ MEMORY, THEORIES OF.

REFERENCES

Tulving, E., & Wiseman, S. (1975). Relation between recognition and recognition failure of recallable words. *Bulletin of the Psychonomic Society, 6*, 79-82.

Hintzman, D. L. (1992). Mathematical constraints and the Tulving-Wiseman law. *Psychological Review, 99*, 536-542.

Tulving, E., & Flexser, A. J. (1992). On the nature of the Tulving-Wiseman function. *Psychological Review, 99*, 543-546.

Flexser, A. J., & Tulving, E. (1993). Recognition-failure constraints and the average maximum. *Psychological Review, 100*, 149-153.

Sikstrom, S. P., & Gardiner, J. M. (1997). Remembering, knowing, and the Tulving-Wiseman law. *European Journal of Cognitive Psychology, 9*, 167-185.

TURING'S TEST/MACHINE. See CELLULAR AUTOMATON MODEL.

TWO-FACTOR LEARNING THEORY. See MOWRER'S THEORY.

TWO-FACTOR THEORY OF EMOTIONS. See SCHACHTER-SINGER'S THEORY OF EMOTIONS.

TWO-FACTOR THEORY OF WORK. See WORK/CAREER/OCCUPATION, THEORIES OF.

TWO-STAGE PROCESS THEORY. See PUNISHMENT, THEORIES OF.

TWO-STEP THEORY OF COMMUNICATION. See COMMUNICATION THEORY.

TWO-SYNDROME HYPOTHESIS. See SCHIZOPHRENIA, THEORIES OF.

TWO-THIRDS POWER LAW. See MOTOR LEARNING/PROCESS THEORIES.

TYCHISM, THEORY OF. See ACCIDENTALISM, THEORY OF; PROBABILITY THEORY/LAWS.

TYCHO ILLUSION. See APPENDIX A.

TYPE THEORIES OF PERSONALITY. See PERSONALITY THEORIES.

TYPOLOGY THEORY. See GALEN'S DOCTRINE OF THE FOUR TEMPERAMENTS; JUNG'S THEORY OF PERSONALITY; KRETSCHMER'S THEORY OF PERSONALITY; SHELDON'S TYPE THEORY.

U

UGLY SISTER EFFECT. See FORGET-TING/MEMORY, THEORIES OF.

UNACCOMPLISHED ACTION EFFECT. See ZEIGARNIK EFFECT/PHENOMENON.

UNCERTAINTY PRINCIPLE. See HEISENBERG'S PRINCIPLE OF UNCERTAIN-TY/INDETERMINACY.

UNCONSCIOUS INFERENCE, DOCTRINE OF. The German physiologist/psychologist Hermann Ludwig Ferdinand Helmholtz (1821-1894) developed the *doctrine of unconscious inference* (in German, "unbewusster Schluss"), which refers to a judgment one makes on the basis of a limited amount of data or evidence and is made without conscious awareness (cf., Sigmund Freud's depth psychology *theory of unconscious memory* and *unconsciousness* makes reference to the memory of prior events, emotions, and feelings that may, or may not, be available for conscious retrieval; *psychodynamic/depth theory* indicates that unconscious memories are materials that have been "denied" or "repressed" due to psychic-energy conflicts and mechanisms; on the other hand, *information theory* suggests that failure to access stored information may be accounted for in terms of "information retrieval failure" and due to lexical features or difficulties of the information itself; the term *unconscious cognitive process* refers to the workings of the "unconscious mind" where humans learn, remember, think, and have ideas, desires, and feelings that remain in a "hidden state," but which may emerge suddenly and completely without any prior awareness). The notion of *unconscious inference* was offered by Helmholtz as an explanation for many perceptual phenomena (cf., the *likelihood principle* - Helmholtz's idea that people interpret sensations in such a way as to perceive what is most likely to have given rise to those sensations). For example, concerning the perceptual *principle of inter-*

position: when two objects (A and B) are arranged before an observer such that A is partially blocking B, the observer makes an unconscious inference and concludes that object A must be closer to her than object B. Historically, the *doctrine of unconscious inference* was a very important part of *Helmholtz's theory of perception* and was a corollary of the *empiricist* position - the viewpoint that knowledge results from experience, induction, and learning, and where - in its once extreme form - it asserted that mind at birth was a "blank slate" or *tabula rasa* upon which experience writes its messages. The *empiricist* position competed with the viewpoints of *nativism* - the doctrine that the capacity to perceive time and space is inborn, genetic, or inherited; *rationalism* - the perspective that truth is received through the use of rational thought and deductive reasoning; and *a priorism* - the doctrine that the mind comes equipped with innate ideas where genuine knowledge is possible independent of experience. *Unconscious inference* may be viewed, also, in connection with *Helmholtz's theory of color contrast* (a speculation that never gained general acceptance): red and verdigris are color complimentaries and contrast with each other; a gray-colored stimulus figure appears on a red ground; it contrasts with the red and, by *unconscious inference*, the ob-server sees it as the opposite ("greenish") color. Helmholtz argued that perception may contain many experiential data that are not immediately represented in the stimulus and are, in a sense, additions that accrue to the perception in accordance with its development in past experience. Helmholtz decided to call these unconsciously determined phenomena *inferences* and, in an attempt both to affirm and to deny their inferential nature, he used the paradoxical phrase *unconscious inference*. Helmholtz made three positive statements concerning *unconscious inferences*: they are normally "irresistible" (i.e., they are immediate, unconscious, and not correctible by conscious reasoning); they are formed by experience (i.e., they develop by "association" and "repetition" into unconscious inferences); and they are - in their results - like *conscious* inferences from analogy and are, thus, *inductive* (i.e., the brain makes generalizations quickly and automatically in perception). See also CARPEN-TERED-WORLD HYPOTHESIS; CON-SCIOUSNESS, PHENOMENON OF; CON-STRUCTIVIST THEORY OF PERCEP-TION; EMPIRICIST VERSUS NATIVIST THEORIES; PERCEPTION (I. GENERAL), THEORIES OF; PERCEPTION (II. COM-PARATIVE APPRAISAL), THEORIES OF.

REFERENCES

Helmholtz, H. von (1856-1866). *Physiological optics*. Leipzig: Voss.

Wundt, W. (1862). *Beitrage zur theorie der sinneswahrnehmung*. Leipzig: Wunter'sck.

Freud, S. (1915). The unconscious. In *The standard edition of the complete psychological works of Sigmund Freud*. London: Hogarth Press.

Hochberg, J. (1994). Unconscious inference. In R. J. Corsini (Ed.), *Encyclopedia of psychology*. New York: Wiley.

Chalmers, D. (1996). *The conscious mind: In search of a fundamental theory*. New York: Oxford University Press.

UNCONSCIOUS MEMORY/UNCON-SCIOUSNESS THEORY. See FORGET-TING/MEMORY, THEORIES OF; FREUD'S THEORY OF PERSONALITY; UNCON-SCIOUS INFERENCE, DOCTRINE OF.

UNDERSTIMULATION THEORY. See PSYCHOPATHOLGY, THEORIES OF.

UNDULATORY THEORY. See VISION/ SIGHT, THEORIES OF.

UNIFIED THEORY OF COGNITION. See PROBLEM-SOLVING AND CREATIVITY STAGE THEORIES.

UNIFIED THEORY OF SOCIAL PSY-CHOLOGY. See INFORMATION INTE-GRATION THEORY.

UNIFORMITY OF NATURE THEORY. See FINAL THEORY.

UNIFYING THEORY OF DEVELOP-MENT. See DEVELOPMENTAL THEORY.

UNILINEAL/UNILINEAR THEORY. See RECAPITULATION THEORY/LAW.

UNIT HYPOTHESIS. See GENERALIZA-TION, PRINCIPLES OF.

UNIVERSALISM, DOCTRINE OF. See MIND/MENTAL STATES, THEORIES OF.

UNIVERSALISTIC THEORIES. See WORK/CAREER/OCCUPATION, THEO-RIES OF.

UNIVERSAL LAW OF GENERALIZA-TION. The American psychologist/cognitive scientist Roger N. Shepard (1929-) proposed a *universal law of generalization* for psycho-logical science that attempts to advance a principle in psychology that is comparable in generality to the English physicist and mathematician Sir Isaac Newton's (1642-1727) *universal law of gravitation* in physics. The new law is based on the assumption that because any object or situation experienced by an individual is unlikely to recur in exactly the same form and context, psychology's first general law should be a *law of generalization*. Historically, learning theorists supposed that a *principle of conditioning* (via the mechanisms of reinforcement and/or contiguity) could be the *primary* principle, and where what is learned then generalizes to new situations (left open for later formulation) could be a *secon-dary* principle. Over 2,000 years ago, the Greek philosopher Aristotle (384-322 B.C.) recognized - via his *principle of association by resemblance* - that similarity is fundamen-tal to mental processes, but it was not until the beginning and middle of the 20th century that experimental investigations were conducted on the issue of *generalization/similarity* of stimuli - first by Ivan Pavlov in the 1920s; then by Norman Guttman, H. I. Kalish, and Roger N. Shepard in the 1950s; cf., Mostofsky (1965). Shepard suggests that humans general-ize from one situation to another *not* because they cannot tell the difference between the two situations, but because they judge that the situations are likely to belong to a set of situa-tions having the same consequences. *Gener-alization* - that arises from uncertainty about the distribution of consequential stimuli in "psychological space" - is to be distinguished from failure of *discrimination* - that arises from uncertainty about the relative locations of individual stimuli in that space. Accordingly, in his *universal law of generalization* for psychological science, Shepard posits the notion of a "psychological space" for any set of stimuli by determining metric distances between the stimuli such that the probability that a response learned to any stimulus will generalize to any other is an invariant monotonic function of the distance between them. This probability of generalization, to a good approximation, decays exponentially with this distance, and does so in accordance with one of two metrics, depending on the relation between the dimensions along which the stimuli vary. Shepard asserts that these empirical regularities are mathematically derivable from universal principles of natural phenomena and probabilistic geometry that may – via evolutionary internalization - tend to govern the behaviors of all sentient organisms. Shepard suggests that psychological science undoubtedly has lagged behind physical science by at least 300 years and, just as likely, predictions of behavior may never attain the precision for animate bodies/entities that it has for celestial bodies. However, psychology inherently may not be limited merely to the descriptive characterization of the behaviors of particular terrestrial species, but possibly - behind the diverse behaviors of humans and animals, as behind the various motions of planets and stars - one may eventually discern the operation of universal laws. See also ASSOCIATION, LAWS/PRINCIPLES OF; GENERALIZATION, PRINCIPLES OF.

REFERENCES

Newton, I. (1687). *Philosophiae naturalis principia mathematica*. London: Royal Society.

Mostofsky, D. I. (Ed.) (1965). *Stimulus generalization*. Stanford, CA: Stanford University Press.

Shepard, R. N. (1987). Toward a universal law of generalization for psychological science. *Science, 237*, 1317-1323.

UNIVERSAL LAW OF GRAVITATION. See UNIVERSAL LAW OF GENERALIZATION.

UNIVERSAL MODEL OF HUMAN EMOTIONS. The American neurologist/physician Antonio R. Damasio (1994) developed a *universal model of human emotions* that is based on a rejection of the Cartesian *mind-body dualism*, and is founded on neuropsychological studies and experiments. The model begins with the assumption that human knowledge consists of dispositional representations stored in the brain (where "thought" is the process by which such representations are ordered and manipulated). One of the representations is of the body as a whole and is based on information from the endocrine and peripheral nervous systems. In his model, Damasio defines *emotion* as the combination of a mental evaluative process (simple or complex) with dispositional responses to that process, resulting in an emotional body state - but also toward the brain itself (e.g., via neurotransmitter nuclei in the brain stem). In distinguishing "emotions" from "feelings," Damasio states that the brain is continually monitoring changes in the body, and suggests that people "feel" an emotion when they experience such changes in juxtaposition to the mental images that initiated the cycle. The model distinguishes, also, between "primary emotions" (innate) and "secondary emotions" (feelings allowing one to form systematic connections between categories of objects and situations). Damasio suggests that the neurological mechanisms of emotion and feeling evolved in humans in order to create strong biases to situationally-appropriate behaviors that do not require conscious thought; he argues that the time-consuming process of rational thought may decrease one's chances of survival in situations that require instant decisions. See also EMOTIONS, THEORIES/LAWS OF; MIND-BODY THEORIES.

REFERENCE

Damasio, A. R. (1994). *Descartes' error: Emotion, reason, and the human brain*. New York: Putnam.

UNLEARNING HYPOTHESIS. See IN-TERFERENCE THEORIES.

UNREADINESS, LAW OF. See READI-NESS, LAW OF.

UNREALISTIC OPTIMISM EFFECT. This phenomenon, and its related aspects, studied by the American psychologists Frederick Hansen Lund (1894-1965), Albert Hadley Cantril (1906-1969), and Neil David Weinstein (1945-), among others, refers to a judgmental bias in humans that tends to influence their subjective estimates of the likelihood of certain future events in their own lives as compared to others, especially their peers. For example, the *unrealistic optimism effect* demonstrates that people *overestimate* the likelihood in their lives of *positive/desirable* events (e.g., the possibility of their living to be older than 80 years of age), and *underestimate* the likelihood in their lives of *negative/undesirable* events (e.g., the possibility of having a heart attack before they are 50 years old). Studies on this issue indicate that cognitive, motivational, and social factors such as degree of desirability, perceived probability, personal experience, ego-centrism, perceived controllability, and stereotype salience all tend to affect the amount of optimistic bias evoked by different possible events in people's lives. See also DECISION-MAKING THEORIES; OVERCONFIDENCE EFFECT.

REFERENCES

Lund, F. H. (1925). The psychology of belief. *Journal of Abnormal and Social Psychology, 20,* 63-81, 174-195.

Cantril, A. H. (1938). The predicton of social events. *Journal of Abnormal and Social Psychology, 33,* 364-389.

Weinstein, N. D. (1980). Unrealistic optimism about future life events. *Journal of Personality and Social Psychology, 39,* 806-820.

UPWARD PYGMALION EFFECT. See PYGMALION EFFECT.

URNING THEORY. See SEXUAL ORIENTATION THEORIES.

USE-DISUSE PRINCIPLE. See LA-MARCK'S THEORY.

USE, LAW OF. This principle is one of the corollaries of the American psychologist Edward Lee Thorndike's (1874-1949) *law of exercise,* which states that behaviors, stimulus-response connections, and functions that are exercised, rehearsed, or practiced are strengthened as compared to those behaviors, bonds, or functions that are not used. Some early writers held that the repeated use of a stimulus-response connection unit (neurons) bring about certain synaptic changes that made the passage of the nerve impulse more rapid in the future. For example, in 1926 A. Gates called this native capacity of nervous structure modifiability the *law of modification by exercise* or, more simply, the *law of use* [cf., the *use/disuse, use-inheritance theory* advanced by the French naturalist/evolutionist Jean-Baptiste Pierre Antoine de Monet Lamarck (1744-1829), which holds that the structural or functional changes in organs brought about by their *use* or *disuse* are passed onto the progeny). The notion of a physiological change in nervous structure during the practice (use) of stimulus-response connections anticipated the Canadian psychologist Donald Olding Hebb's (1904-1985) later conceptualizations in perception and learning of *cell assembly* and *phase sequence,* where groups of neurons are functionally interrelated and organized into a complex "closed circuit" created by repeated stimulation of those units. See also DISUSE, LAW/THEORY OF; EFFECT, LAW OF; EXERCISE, LAW OF; FREQUENCY, LAW OF; HEBB'S THEORY OF PERCEPTUAL LEARNING; LA-MARCK'S THEORY.

REFERENCES

Thorndike, E. L. (1898). *Animal intelligence.* New York: Macmillan.

Gates, A. (1926). *Elementary psychology.* New York: Macmillan.

Trowbridge, M., & Cason, H. (1932). An experimental study of Thorndike's theory of learning. *Journal of General Psychology, 7,* 245-258.

Hebb, D. O. (1947). *Organization of behavior.* New York: Wiley.

Hebb, D. O. (1972). *Textbook of psychology*. Philadelphia, PA: Saunders.

US-VERSUS-THEM EFFECT. See IN-GROUP BIAS THEORIES; PREJUDICE, THEORIES OF.

UTERINE THEORY. See PSYCHOPATHOLOGY, THEORIES OF.

UTILITARIANISM, THEORY OF. See REFLEX ARC THEORY/CONCEPT.

UTILITY THEORY. See DECISION-MAKING THEORIES; ELICITED OBSERVING RATE HYPOTHESIS; EXPECTED UTILITY THEORY; HEDONISM, THEORY/LAW OF; LOGAN'S MICROMOLAR THEORY.

UZNADZE/DELBOEUF ILLUSIONS. See APPENDIX A.

V

VALENCE-EXPECTANCY THEORY. See WORK/CAREER/OCCUPATION, THEORIES OF.

VALENCE-INSTRUMENTALITY-EXPECTANCY THEORY. See WORK/CAREER/OCCUPATION, THEORIES OF.

VALIDITY/RELIABILITY. See NOMOLOGICAL NETWORK THEORY.

VALUE THEORY. See DECISION-MAKING THEORIES; MEINONG'S THEORIES.

VANDENBERGH EFFECT. See OLFACTION/SMELL, THEORIES OF.

VASCULAR THEORY. See NAFE'S THEORY OF CUTANEOUS SENSITIVITY.

VEATCH'S THEORY OF HUMOR. This humor theory, proposed by Thomas C. Veatch (1998), states that humor is characterized fully by certain conditions that individually are necessary, and are jointly sufficient, for the humor experience to occur. The conditions of *Veatch's theory of humor* involve a subjective state of apparent emotional absurdity where the perceived situation is viewed as normal and where, simultaneously, some affective commitment of the perceiver (to the way something in the situation *ought* to be) is validated. Thus, according to this approach, humor occurs when one views a situation simultaneously as being normal, as well as constituting a violation of the "subjective moral order" where such an order is defined as the set of principles to which the person both has an affective commitment and a belief that he or she *ought* to hold those principles. Veatch explores the logical properties and empirical consequences of his theory, reviews the widely-recognized aspects and features of humor (e.g., incongruity, surprise, aggression, emotional transformation), suggests practical applications of his theory, and accounts for a wide variety of biological, social-communicational, and other categories/classes of humor-related phenomena. See also HUMOR, THEORIES OF; INCONGRUITY/INCONSISTENCY THEORIES OF HUMOR; SURPRISE THEORIES OF HUMOR.

REFERENCE

Veatch, T. C. (1998). A theory of humor. *Humor: International Journal of Humor Research, 11,* 161-215.

VENABLE'S COLOR VISION THEORY. See COLOR VISION, THEORIES/LAWS OF.

VENTRILOQUISM EFFECT. See APPENDIX A.

VERBAL CONTEXT EFFECT. See COMMUNICATION THEORY.

VERBAL DEPRIVATION HYPOTHESIS. See CHOMSKY'S PSYCHOLINGUISTIC THEORY.

VERBAL LOOP HYPOTHESIS. See CHOMSKY'S PSYCHOLINGUISTIC THEORY.

VERBAL TRANSFORMATION EFFECT. See APPENDIX A.

VIBRATION/VIBRATIONAL THEORY. See OLFACTION/SMELL, THEORIES OF.

VIBRATORY THEORY OF INHERITANCE. See MENDEL'S LAWS/PRINCIPLES.

VICARIOUS BRAIN PROCESS HYPOTHESIS. See LASHLEY'S THEORY.

VICTIM PRECIPITATION HYPOTHESIS. See LOMBROSIAN THEORY.

VIERORDT'S LAW OF TIME ESTIMATION. See VIERORDT'S LAWS.

VIERORDT'S LAWS. There are two separate usages or versions subsumed under the same eponymic principle called *Vierordt's law*, both of which are attributable to the

German physiologist Karl von Vierordt (1818-1884). One usage is related to the study of *sensory thresholds*, and the other usage refers to the area of *time perception*. In the first case, *Vierordt's law* is the proposition that the more moveable a part of the body is, the lower is the two-point threshold of the skin over it. Thus, the two-point threshold decreases (i.e., increased tactile acuity) as one goes from the acromion/shoulder blade to the tips of the fingers. In other terms, *Vierordt's law of outward mobility* in the area of sensory psychology states that tactile acuity increases with increased mobility of body members. However, although *Vierordt's outward mobility law* appears to be true, generally, for the upper extremity, it is not as clearly applicable to various other body areas (cf., Greenspan & Bolanowski, 1996). In the second case, *Vierordt's law of time estimation* is the principle that *short* temporal intervals tend to be *overestimated* and *long* temporal intervals tend to be *underestimated*. Also, in this context of time perception/estimation, the concept of the *in-difference interval* is defined as the intermediate length of time that is neither underestimated nor overestimated. Based on this early *general law of time estimation* by Vierordt in the late 1800s, subsequent research in the area of the *psychology of time* has determined that the overestimation of short durations and the underestimation of long ones is as valid for "filled" durations/intervals as for "empty" durations/intervals. Thus, in turn, and ground-ed in *Vierordt's law of time estimation*, psychologists today study the effect of the different forms of "filling" a temporal interval (ranging from the use of short, discrete auditory tones to long, more continuous and meaningful narratives/events/materials) on one's perceived duration and estimation of time. See also FRAISSE'S THEORY OF TIME; GUYAU'S THEORY OF TIME; SOMESTHESIS, THEORIES OF; TIME, THEORIES OF.

REFERENCES

Vierordt, K. von (1868). *Der zeitsinn nach versuchen*. Tubingen, Germany: H. Laupp.

Vierordt, K. von (1870). Abhangigkeit der ausbildung des raumsinnes der haut von den beweglichkeit der korpert-heile. *Zeitschrift fur Biologie, 6*, 53-72.

Greenspan, J. D., & Bolanowski, S. J. (1996). The psychophysics of tactile perception and its peripheral physiological basis. In L. Kruger (Ed.), *Pain and touch*. San Diego, CA: Academic Press.

VIGILANCE, THEORIES OF. = sustained attention theories. In general, *theories of vigilance* refer to the systematic accounts of how observers maintain their focus of *attention* (i.e., the selective aspects of perception that function to help an organism focus on certain features of the environment to the exclusion of other features) and remain alert to stimuli over prolonged periods of time [i.e., *sustained attention*; cf., the *law of prior entry* - the principle that if a participant is attending to one of two possible stimuli and, if they occur simultaneously, the one to which he/she is attending tends to be perceived as having occurred *before* the other; in social/personality psychology, this is called the *prior entry effect* where the first impression(s) one has of another person tend to be the dominate one(s) and are not easily changed by further acquaintance; cf., also, *laws of attention* (Woodworth, 1921): *selection* - of two or more inconsistent responses to the same situation, only one is made at the same time; *advantage* - one of the alternative responses has an initial advantage over the others due to such factors as intensity and change in the stimulus, or to habits of reaction; *shifting* - the response that has the initial advantage loses its advantage shortly and an alternative response is made, provided the situation remains the same (cf., the *law of shifting*, proposed by the American psychologist Edward Lee Thorndike, which states that it is relatively easy to elicit a response that an organism is capable of performing in any situation - and to which it is sensitive - and, thereby, form an association between the response and the features of that situation); *tendency* - a predisposition when aroused to activity facilitates responses that are in its line and inhibits others; and *combination* - a single response may be made to two or more stimuli, and two or more stimuli may arouse a single joint response]. The various specific *theories* and *models of vigilance* attempt to deal with certain common questions in an observer's behavior during a vigilance task: How is background information stored? How are decisions made during observation? and How do neural attention units function? A sampling of the *vigilance theories* and some of their major tenets are: *expectancy theory* - observers act as "temporal averaging instruments" who form expectancies as to the approximate time course of critical signal appearances on the basis of samples of signal input; readiness to detect a signal is assumed to be positively related to level of expectancy; *elicited observing rate hypothesis* - the observer constantly makes sequential decisions about whether or not to emit observing responses toward the display that is monitored; detection failures occur when the participant does not emit the observing responses due to fatigue or low motivation or does so in an imperfect fashion; *signal detection theory* - the decrement function typically found in a vigilance task reflects a shift to a more conservative response criterion and decision process, rather than a decline in alertness or perceptual sensitivity to signals; *activation/arousal theory* - instead of a "cognitive" appraisal of vigilance, this approach emphasizes a neurophysiological explanation whereby sensory input has two general functions: to convey information about the environment and to "tone up" the brain with a background of diffuse activity that helps cortical transmission via increased alertness; this orientation suggests that the monotonous aspects of vigilance tasks reduce the level of nonspecific activity that is necessary to maintain continued alertness and, consequently, lead to a decline in the efficiency of signal detection; and *habituation theory* - habituation is a lessening of neural responsiveness due to repeated stimulation and is an "active process of inhibition;" this approach argues that the degree of neural habituation in a given task is directly related to the frequency of stimulus presentation so that with the development of habituation the observer's ability to discriminate critical signals is degraded, attention to the task becomes increasingly more difficult, and performance declines over a period of time; this theory holds that habituation accumulates more rapidly at fast,

than at slow, rates and results in a decline in performance at fast stimulus/event rates. The current status of *vigilance theories* is that each model focuses on a somewhat different aspect of the sustained attention situation, even though many theories can account for similar data. To date, the task remains of synthesizing the various theoretical positions of vigilance into a unified framework where stronger "lawful" cause-effect statements may be provided. See also ACTIVATION/AROUSAL THEORY; ATTENTION, LAWS/PRINCIPLES OF; ELICITED OBSERVING RATE HYPOTHESIS; HABITUATION, PRINCIPLE/ LAW OF; IMPRESSION FORMATION, THEORIES OF; REINFORCEMENT, THORNDIKE'S THEORY OF; SIGNAL DETECTION THEORY.

REFERENCES

Woodworth, R. S. (1921). *Psychology: A study of mental life*. New York: Holt.

Deese, J. (1955). Some problems in the theory of vigilance. *Psychological Review, 62*, 359-368.

Baker, C. (1963). Further toward a theory of vigilance. In D. Buckner & J. McGrath (Eds.), *Vigilance: A symposium*. New York: McGraw-Hill.

Davies, D., & Tune, G. (1969). *Human vigilance performance*. New York: American Elsevier.

Mackworth, J. (1969). *Vigilance and habituation*. Baltimore: Penguin Books.

Stroh, C. (1971). *Vigilance: The problem of sustained attention*. New York: Pergamon.

Mackie, R. (Ed.) (1977). *Vigilance: Theory, operational performance, and physiological correlates*. New York: Plenum.

Parasuraman, R., & Davies, D. (1989). *Varieties of attention*. Orlando, FL: Academic Press.

VIRAL HYPOTHESIS OF SCHIZOPHRENIA. See SCHIZOPHRENIA, THEORIES OF.

VIRTUAL SELF. See SELF-CONCEPT THEORY.

VISION/SIGHT, THEORIES OF. One of the earliest theories that attempted to describe a mechanism for human vision was proposed by the Greek mathematician/mystic Pythagoras (c. 582-507 B.C.). He asserted that rays of light sprang from the eyes themselves, much like twin spotlights; somehow, the light striking objects in front of the observer triggered a reaction in the eye, and vision was the result. However, by the 15th century, *Pythagoras' theory* was reversed, where the eyes were considered the receivers, not senders, of light. By that time, some of the greatest scientists of the say began to investigate the question of light's influence on the eye. For example, Leonardo da Vinci (1452-1519) made detailed drawings of the eye's anatomy; Johannes Kepler (1571-1630) formulated the basic *laws of light refraction*, which explained how light rays can be bent as they travel from one medium to another; and Rene Descartes (1596-1650) conducted studies concerning the application of these *refraction laws* to the structural features of the eye, which led to a basic understanding of how the eye focused incoming light [cf., *Maxwellian view* - named after the Scottish physicist James Clerk Maxwell (1831-1879), refers to the elimination of light fluctuations entering the eye due to pupil size fluctuations by concentrating light coming off an object by the use of a spherical, or "fisheye," lens to focus light in the pupil's plane]. By 1666, Sir Isaac Newton's (1642-1727) experiments on the composition of light itself was the formal beginning of inquiries into the physical nature of light as well as inquiries into the way the eye interprets color phenomena [cf., the *inverse square law* - the principle that the intensity of a stimulus that reaches the receptor from a distant source varies inversely as the square of the distance of the source from the receptor (Note: In the context of inferential statistics, the *inverse square law* is the principle that the sampling error tends to be inversely proportional to the square root of the sample size); the *law of illumination* - the principle that the illumination upon a surface varies directly as the luminous intensity of the light source, inversely as the square of its distance, and directly as the cosine of the angle made by the light rays with the perpendicular to the surface; and the *Arago phe-* nomenon - named after the French astronomer and physicist Francois Arago (1786-1853), is the relative insensitivity to light of the very center of the visual field at very low levels of illumination]. According to modern *vision theory*, the stimulus for the sensory modality of vision/sight is electromagnetic radiation (light) between approximately 380 and 740 nanometers (*nm*, where 1 *nm* = 1 billionth of a meter), and where the initial processing of visual information is the receptor system consisting of photosensitive cells (*rods* and *cones*) in the retina of the eye. Vision is the process of transforming ("transducing") physical light energy into biological neural impulses that can then be interpreted by the brain. The electromagnetic radiation can vary in *intensity* (perceived as a difference in *brightness* level) and *wavelength* (perceived as a difference in *hue* or "color"). The *quantum theory of vision* maintains that light energy travels to the eye in the form of discrete or discontinuous changes in energy where wavelength frequencies correspond to definite energies of the light quanta called *photons*. The Dutch physicist Christiaan Huygens (1629-1693) first proposed the *undulatory theory*, which forms a part of the *wave theory of light* that supplanted the earlier *corpuscular/particle theory*. The *wave theory* offers a ready explanation of interference, diffraction, and polarization of light but fails to explain the interaction of light with matter, the emission and absorption of light, photoelectricity, and other phenomena. These can be explained only by a *quasi-corpuscular theory* involving packets of energy - light *quanta* or *photons*. The *quantum theory* was introduced by the German physicist Max Planck (1858-1947) in 1900. Ultimately, it appears that two models are required to explain the phenomenon of light. According to the *complementarity principle* of the Danish physicist Niels Bohr (1885-1962), a system such as an electron can be described either in terms of *particles* or in terms of *wave motion*. *Theories of vision* are systematic attempts to account for the various phenomena of visual perception in relation to the known structure and functions of the visual organs. Included by extension is the study of photoreceptors; the action of nerves and nerve endings [cf., *Hering's law of equal innervation -*

named after the German physiologist Karl Ewald Hering (1834-1918), states that the muscles of each eye always operate in synchrony because they receive the same innervation; the study of responses to light in lower organisms; the higher psychological implications of light, color, form, and their temporal and spatial relations (cf., *Harvey's principle* - when a grating is viewed, the number of vertical stripes per unit of total breath is overestimated and the number of horizontal stripes is underestimated; *Leonardo's paradox* - named after the Italian artist/scientist Leonardo da Vinci (1452-1519), refers to da Vinci's assertion that it is not possible to reproduce via a painting what a person sees binocularly, because in binocular vision, each eye sees something that the other eye does not see; *Hering's law of identical visual direction* - in binocular vision, any pair of corresponding lines of direction in objective space are represented by a single line of direction in visual space; and the *superposition hypothesis* - the binocular vision of newborn infants blends together the monocular visual responses of the two eyes, even when the visual stimulus evokes binocular rivalry in adults, and suggests that such blending is replaced by binocular rivalry after the development/emergence of stereopsis at about age 8-12 weeks old (cf., Brown & Miracle, 2003). In his *computational theory of vision*, the English psychologist David C. Marr (1945-1980) makes a formal analysis of perception that is based on a theory of vision that attempts to explain how the pattern of light falling on the retinas of the eyes is transformed into an internal representation of the colors, shapes, and movements of what is observed; three stages are involved in the process: the "primal sketch," the "two-and-one-half dimensional sketch," and the "three-dimensional model" description. The anatomical and physiological basis for vision may be hypothesized much as is the case for the *theories of color vision*; for example, the three-component *Young-Helmholtz theory*; the *antagonistic/opponent-process theory of Hering*; the *Ladd-Franklin genetic theory*; and the *von Kries duplicity theory*. The *cone* cells ("daylight vision") in the retina are responsible for chromatic/color vision and visual acuity [cf., *Charpentier's law* - named after the

French physician Augustin Charpentier (1852-1916), states that in the retinal fovea, the product of the area of a stimulus and its intensity is constant for stimuli at threshold intensities; *Charpentier bands* - illusory black spokes that may be seen when a black disk with a white sector is rotated slowly; the *blue-arc phenomenon* - an effect produced by a stimulus at the center of the visual field against a dark background; it consists of a pair of bluish, luminous arcs seen as connecting the stimulus with the locus of the blind spot; the *Troxler fading/effect* - named after the Swiss-German physician/philosopher Ignaz P. V. Troxler (1780-1866), is the fading of visual objects in the periphery of the visual field when a point in its center is steadily fixated; this is due to the organization of the peripheral retina, which requires larger eye movements than are needed in the fovea, to break the adaptation brought about by steady fixation; the *Ditchburn-Riggs effect* - named after the English physicist Robert William Ditchburn (1903-1987) and the American psychologist Lorin A. Riggs (1912-), is the phenomenon of the rapid cessation of the vision of contours when the image of the contours undergoes prolonged stabilization with respect to the retina; and the *Rayleigh equation* - named after the English physicist Lord J. W. S. Rayleigh (1842-1919), is an index of one's color vision given by the proportion of light from the red and green portions of the visible spectrum that need to be mixed to make a standard yellow]. The *rod* cells ("night-time vision") are sensitive to minute amounts of light but are not sensitive to colors (cf., Kaneko's *photochemical theory of vision*). Because of the anatomical features of the visual system, the *left* visual field is represented in the *right* occipital lobe of the brain, and the *right* visual field is represented in the *left* occipital lobe. It is much easier to trace anatomically the visual pathway from the retina to the occipital lobes than it is to explain and understand how the eyes and the brain interact to produce the perception of vision (cf., *mind's eye theory* - proposes an as-yet-unidentified neurological structure located in the brain where visual information obtained from the two eyes or from long-term memory is stored temporarily while being processed as a visual image, allowing one to reason from visual images; the *Cheshire cat effect* - relies on the phenomenon of binocular rivalry, where each eye has a different input from the same part of the visual field, and where motion in the field of one eye can cause either the entire image to disappear or parts of the image to be erased; the movement captures the brain's attention momentarily; this effect is named after the Cheshire cat in Lewis Carroll's "Alice's Adventures in Wonderland" where the cat vanishes slowly, beginning with the end of its tail and ending with its grin that remained some time after the rest of the cat had disappeared). More is known about how photochemical processes and mechanisms operate in the *rod* cells than about the *cone* cells. In addition to responding directly to light, the receptor cells are affected, also, by the surrounding receptor cells. Studies have shown that there are both inhibitory and excitatory effects when neighboring receptor cells fire simultaneously. Other studies indicate that various cells in the visual cortex are maximally activated by objects in the visual field with specific shapes, of particular orientations, and moving in particular directions. For instance, D. Hubel and T. Wiesel hypothesize the existence of four general types of hierarchically organized cells (simple, complex, lower-order hypercomplex, and upper-order hypercomplex), and this notion has found anatomical support from other research, but the theory that those cells are arranged hierarchically is not yet supported. Over 100 years ago, the German physican and psychologist Hermann Aubert (1826-1892) provided a number of theoretical and lawful propositions concerning *visual acuity* and *perception*; cf., *Listing's law of visual accommodation* - named after the German physicist Johann Benedict Listing (1808-1882), refers to the case where, if the eye moves from a primary position to any other position, the torsional rotation of the eyeball in the new position is the same as it would be if the eye had turned about a fixed axis, and lies at right angles to the initial and final directions of the line of regard; and *Alexander's law* - named after the Austrian otologist Gustav Alexander (1873-1932), refers to nystagmus, produced either by rotation or thermally, that can be accentuated voluntarily by moving the eyes in the direction of the jerky component of the nystagmus. Among Aubert's eponymous referents are the following: the *Aubert-Fleischl paradox/phenomenon* - named after Aubert and the Austrian physiologist Marxow Ernst Fleischl (1846-1891), is a perceptual effect whereby a moving stimulus seems to move more slowly when the observer fixates on the stimulus than when she or he fixates on the background; the *Aubert-Forster phenomenon* - named after Aubert and the Polish-born German ophthalmologist Carl F. R. Forster (1825-1902), refers to the situation where two objects of different physical sizes are placed at different distances from the observer such that both subtend the same number of degrees of visual arc, the physically closer one can be recognized over a greater area of the retina than the physically more distant one; the *Aubert phenomenon* - refers to the case where a single vertical straight-line stimulus is presented to an observer, and the line is displaced perceptually as the observer tilts his/her head (cf., the *Muller effect* - named after the German psychologist Georg Elias Muller (1850-1934), refers to the case where an observer views a luminous vertical rod in the dark, and it appears to be tilted out of vertical in the same direction as the head; this effect occurs only with small tilts of the head); and the *Aubert-Forster law* - a generalization regarding visual acuity based on the *Aubert-Forster phenomenon* that states that objectively small objects can be distinguished as two at greater distances from the fovea than objectively larger objects subtending the same visual angle (cf., the *Alice in Wonderland effect* - is a visual defect where one sees things as smaller than they are in actuality; in a clinical context, the *Alice in Wonderland syndrome* refers to depersonalization and "Lilliputian hallucinations," that is, hallucinations involving objects that appear to be extremely small, derived from Jonathan Swift's (1726) novel, *Gulliver's Travels* in which the imaginary country of Lilliput has inhabitants who are only six inches tall; and *associative/ geometric illusion* - a visual misperception in which one part of an object or image is viewed erroneously due to the effect of another object/image; Appendix A provides a listing of various *visual illusions/effects*). See also ADAPTATION,

PRINCIPLES/LAWS OF; ATTENTION, LAWS/PRINCIPLES/ THEORIES OF; COLOR VISION, THEORIES/LAWS OF; DOPPLER EFFECT/PRIN-CIPLE/SHIFT; IMAGERY/MENTAL IMAGERY, THEORIES OF; NORMAL DISTRIBUTION THEORY; PERCEPTION (I. GENERAL), THEORIES OF; PERSONAL EQUATION PHENOMENON; PURKINJE EFFECT/PHENOMENON/SHIFT.

REFERENCES

Aubert, H. (1865). *Physiologie der netzhant.* Breslau: Morgenstern.

Aubert, H. (1866). Die bewegungsempfindung. *Archiv fur die Gesamte Physiologie, 39*, 347-370.

Stratton, G. M. (1897). Vision without inversion of the retinal image. *Psychological Review, 4*, 341-360.

Luckiesh, M. (1922/1965). *Visual illusions: Their causes, characteristics, and applications.* New York: Van Nostrand/Dover.

Sharp, W. L. (1928). The floating-finger illusion. *Psychological Review, 35*, 171-173.

Hartline, H., & Ratliff, F. (1957). Inhibitory interaction of receptor units in the eye of *limulus. Journal of General Physiology, 40*, 357-376.

Hubel, D., & Wiesel, T. (1965). Receptive fields and functional architecture in two nonstriate visual areas (18 and 19) of the cat. *Journal of Neurophysiology, 28*, 229-289.

Kelly, J., & VanEssen, D. (1974). Cell structure and function in the visual cortex of the cat. *Journal of Physiology, 238*, 515-547.

Gregory, R. (1978). *Eye and brain: The psychology of seeing.* New York: McGraw-Hill.

Kaneko, A. (1979). Physiology of the retina. *Annual Review of Neuroscience, 2*, 169-191.

Marr, D. C. (1982). *Vision.* San Francisco: W. H. Freeman.

Bundesen, C. (1991). A theory of visual attention. *Psychological Review, 97*, 523-547.

Harris, M., & Humphreys, G. (1994). Computational theories of vision. In A. Colman (Ed.), *Companion encyclopedia of psychology.* London: Routledge.

Crick, F., & Koch, C. (1997). The problem of consciousness. In *Scientific American* (Special Issue), *Mysteries of the mind.* Vol. 7. No. 1.

Brown, A., & Miracle, J. (2003). Early binocular vision in human infants: Limitations on the generality of the superposition hypothesis. *Vision Research, 43*, 1563-1574.

VISUAL CLIFF PHENOMENON/APPARATUS/TEST. See NATURE VERSUS NURTURE THEORIES.

VISUAL-ORIENTATION HYPOTHESIS. See ATTRIBUTION THEORY.

VISUOSPATIAL SKETCHPAD OR SCRATCHPAD MODEL. See WORKING MEMORY, THEORY OF.

VITAL FLUIDS THEORY. See LIFE, THEORIES OF.

VITALISM THEORY. See HOBBES' PSYCHOLOGICAL THEORY; LIFE, THEORIES OF; LOEB'S TROPISTIC THEORY; MECHANISTIC THEORY.

VITAMIN MODEL OF EMPLOYEE SATISFACTION. See WORK/CAREER/OCCUPATION, THEORIES OF.

VIVIDNESS/CLEARNESS, LAW OF. See ASSOCIATION, LAWS/PRINCIPLES OF.

VOLLEY/PERIODICITY THEORY AND VOLLEY PRINCIPLE. See AUDITION/HEARING, THEORIES OF.

von DOMARUS PRINCIPLE. See SCHIZOPHRENIA, THEORIES OF.

von FREY'S FOUR-ELEMENT THEORY. See SOMESTHESIS, THEORIES OF.

von KRIES' COEFFICIENT LAW. In the context of the phenomenon of *chromatic adaptation* (i.e., conditions where a colored stimulus is viewed following adaptation to another color and differs in appearance from the same stimulus seen without pre-exposure and, conversely, where numerous pairs of colors that ordinarily differ may look alike when they are viewed by eyes that have been previously adapted to different kinds of light), the *von Kries coefficient law* - named after the German physiologist Johannes von Kries (1853-1928) - states that the tri-stimulus values of all colors for one condition of adaptation bear fixed ratios to the corresponding tri-stimulus value for the visually equivalent colors observed under another condition of adaptation. However, in one case, D. L. Mac-Adam notes that his own experimental hypotheses - based on *von Kries' law* - were not supported. Consequently, MacAdam hypothesizes the existence of different receptors whose responses are merged onto three channels in the nervous system: the so-called "trichromatic mechanism." See also ADAPTATION, PRINCIPLES/LAWS OF; COLOR VISION, THEORIES/LAWS OF; von KRIES' COLOR VISION THEORY; ZONE/STAGE THEORIES OF COLOR VISION.

REFERENCES

Kries, J. von (1905). Die gesichtsempfindungen. In W. Nagel (Ed.), *Handbuch der physiologisches menchens*. Braunschweig: Vieweg.

MacAdam, D. L. (1956). Chromatic adaptation. *Journal of the Optical Society of America, 46*, 500-513.

von KRIES' COLOR VISION THEORY. = duplicity/duplexity theory. The *duplicity/duplexity theory of vision* was first proposed by Max Schultz in 1866, and later by H. Parinaud and the German physiologist Johannes von Kries (1853-1928). The theory states that vision is mediated by two ("duplex") classes of retinal receptors, the *cones* that are "chromatic" and sensitive to color wavelengths and used in *high* illumination ("photopic vision"), and the *rods* that are "achromatic" and used in *low* illumination ("scotopic vision"). Because the two classes of receptors manifest different wavelength relationships, the shape of a specific function that relates brightness to color may be used to indicate whether rod or cone vision is predominant in a given situation [cf.,

the Anglo-American psychologist William McDougall's (1871-1938) early *color vision theory* that states that there are two distinct receptor mechanisms for light in the retina: rods for dim light and cones for normal and intense light; the theory holds, also, that all colors are reducible to the three basic colors of blues, greens, and reds]. There are anatomical differences between the *rods* and *cones*, even though these two types of receptors are very similar: (1) the rods are smaller and seem to be less highly developed than the cones; (2) there are no rods (only closely packed cones) in the foveal area of the retina; (3) the cones have a better ("one-to-one") supply of nerves; (4) the substance rhodopsin ("visual purple") is present in the rods but not in the cones; and (5) nocturnal animals possess mostly rods and very few cones. Today, the *von Kries duplicity theory of vision* is so well established that it counts as a strong statement of fact. See also COLOR VISION, THEORIES/LAWS OF; FOVEAL CONE HYPOTHESIS; von KRIES' COEFFICIENT LAW.

REFERENCES

Schultze, M. (1866). Zur anatomie und physiologie der retina. *Archiv der Mikroskopische Anatomisch, 2*, 175-286.

Kries, J. von (1895). Uber die natur gewisser mit den psychischen vorgangen verknupfter gehirnzustande. *Zeitschrift fur Psychologie, 8*, 1-33.

Parinaud, H. (1898). *La vision*. Paris: Octave Doin.

von KRIES' DUPLICITY THEORY. See VISION/SIGHT, THEORIES OF; von KRIES' COLOR VISION THEORY.

von KRIES-SCHRODINGER ZONE THEORY. See COLOR VISION, THEORIES/LAWS OF.

von RESTORFF EFFECT. = Restorff phenomenon/effect. The German psychologist and physician Hedwig von Restorff (1906- ?) developed the generalization that if in a given series of stimuli to be learned (such as a list of words), one of them is made physically distinctive in some way (e.g., printed in large type or in a different color from the others), it will be easier to learn and recall. This phenomenon, called the *von Restorff effect*, and also known as the *isolation effect* and the *Kohler-Restorff phenomenon* - named after the German psychologist Wolfgang Kohler (1887-1967) and H. von Restorff, refers to the tendency to remember unusual items better than the more common items. The experiments by H. von Restorff (1933) and W. Kohler and H. von Restorff (1935) provided a *trace theory* basis for the Gestalt psychologists to explain the forgetting of material. A trace regarding learned materials may become distorted through its interactions with a mass of related traces similar to it. Thus, "associative interference" in forgetting experiments is related to the material to be remembered. Von Restorff showed that part of the difficulty of learning a list of syllables stems from their homogeneity: they are all undistinguishable and equally confusable with one another. However, if one item is perceptually distinguishable, then that unique item will be remembered better than the other items. Kohler and von Restorff conceived of the unique item as standing out like a figure against a ground/ background of all the homogeneous items. Being thus distinguished, the trace laid down for the unique item would be isolated from the traces of the rest of the items and, therefore, would not be distorted by interactions with those traces. Accounts of the *von Restorff effect* by stimulus-response associationists have proceeded along similar lines, using principles both of *stimulus generalization* and *associative interference*. See also ASSOCIATION, LAWS/PRINCIPLES OF; ASSOCIATIVE FACILITATION AND INTERFERENCE EFFECTS; GENERALIZATION, PRINCIPLES OF; GESTALT THEORY/LAWS; INTERFERENCE THEORIES OF FORGETTING; TOP-DOWN PROCESSING/ THEORIES; TRACE THEORY/DOCTRINE.

REFERENCES

Restorff, H. von (1933). Analyse von vorgangen im spurenfled. I. Uber die wirkung von bereichsbildungen im spurenfeld. *Psychologische Forschung*, *18*, 299-342.

Kohler, W., & Restorff, H. von (1935). Analyse von vorgangen im spurenfeld. II. Zur theorie der reproduction. *Psychologische Forschung*, *21*, 56-112.

Jensen, A. (1962). The von Restorff isolation effect with minimal response learning. *Journal of Experimental Psychology*, *64*, 123-125.

W

WALLER'S LAW. See NEURON/NEUR-AL/NERVE THEORY.

WANDERING WOMB THEORY. See PSYCHOPATHOLOGY, THEORIES OF.

WARM/COLD EFFECT. See IMPRESS-ION FORMATION, THEORIES OF.

WARM-UP EFFECT. See PERCEPTION (II. COMPARATIVE APPRAISAL), THEO-RIES OF; WOLPE'S THEORY/TECHNI-QUE OF RECIPROCAL INHIBITION.

WATERFALL ILLUSION/EFFECT. See APPENDIX A.

WATSON'S THEORY. See BEHAVIOR-IST THEORY.

WAVE THEORY OF LIGHT. See VISION/ SIGHT, THEORIES OF.

WEAK LAW OF EFFECT. See EFFECT, LAW OF.

WEAR-AND-TEAR THEORIES OF AG-ING. See AGING, THEORIES OF.

WEBER-FECHNER   LAW.   See FECHNER'S LAW.

WEBER'S LAW. = relativity law = Weber's fraction = Weber's function = Weber's ratio. The German physiologist/psychophysicist Ernst Heinrich Weber (1795-1878) formulated this psychophysical generalization that states that the *just-noticeable differences* (or *JNDs*), i.e., the differences between two stimuli that are detected as often as they are undetected, in stimuli are proportional to the magnitude of the original stimulus. Weber described the relationship between existing stimulation and changes in that stimulation in what historians of psychology have called the *first quantitative law of psychology*; cf., the *quotient hy-pothesis* that is an interpretation of *Weber's law* according to which the quotients/ratios of any two successive *JNDs* in a given sensory series are always equal; and *Breton's law*, which is a formula proposed by P. Breton as a substitute for *Weber's law*, that posits a para-bolic relation between stimulus and *JND*. In formal terms, *Weber's law* states that $\Delta I / I = k$, where I is the intensity of the comparison stimulus, ΔI is the increment in intensity just detectable, and k is a constant. The law holds reasonably well for the mid-range of most stimulus dimensions but tends to break down when very low- or very high-intensity stimuli are used. For instance, for very-low intensity tones the *Weber fraction* is somewhat larger than it is for moderately loud tones. Represen-tative values of the *Weber ratio* for the inter-mediate range of some sensory dimensions are: brightness = .02 to .05; visual wave-length = .002 to .006; loudness = .1 to .2; auditory frequency = .002 to .035; taste (salt) = .15 to .25; smell = .2 to .4; cutaneous pres-sure = .14 to .16; and deep pressure = .01 to .03. The *law of progression* refers to a formu-lation devised by the Belgian psychophysicist J. L. R. Delboeuf (1831-1896) as a partial substitute for *Weber's law* and states that suc-cessive sensation increments increase by ar-ithmetical progression when the correspond-ing stimulus-increments increase by geometric progression. Delboeuf's *law of degradation*, another partial substitute for *Weber's law*, states that a sensation is always strongest as it enters consciousness and from then on be-comes less intense; and Delboeuf's *law of tension* states that any change in external stimuli produces a condition of disequilib-rium/tension in the organism that constitutes the excitation whose conscious accompani-ment is the "sensation." An indication of the enduring significance of *Weber's law* is pro-vided by Roeckelein (1996): in a random sample of 136 introductory psychology text-books published from 1885 through 1996, *Weber's law* is cited and described in over 60-percent of the books (an extremely high per-centage for all the laws found in this study), suggesting that it is one of the most popular and frequently cited laws in the psychological literature. E. B. Titchener mentions *Weber's law* in more than 18 different contexts (e.g.,

Weber's law for affection, for auditory sensations, for cutaneous sensations, for organic sensations, etc.) in his textbook. *Weber's law* has even been applied successfully to plants' response systems (cf., Fuller, 1934). S. Smith and E. R. Guthrie mention only one law in their textbook: *Weber's law.* See also FECHNER'S LAW; FULLERTON-CATTELL LAW; WUNDT'S THEORIES/ DOCTRINES/PRINCIPLES.

REFERENCES

Weber, E. H. (1834). *De pulsu, resorptione, auditu et tactu.* Leipzig: Koehler.

Delboeuf, J. R. L. (1883). *Elements de psychophysique.* Liege: (Publisher unknown).

Gamble, E. (1898). The applicability of Weber's law to smell. *American Journal of Psychology, 10,* 82-142.

Titchener, E. B. (1907). *An outline of psychology.* New York: Macmillan.

Smith, S., & Guthrie, E. R. (1924). *General psychology in terms of behavior.* New York: Appleton.

Yoshioka, J. (1929). Weber's law in the discrimination of maze distance by the white rat. *University of California Publications in Psychology, 4,* 155-184.

Fuller, H. (1934). Plant behavior. *Journal of General Psychology, 11,* 379-394.

Roeckelein, J. E. (1996). Citation of *laws* and *theories* in textbooks across 112 years of psychology. *Psychological Reports, 79,* 979-998.

WEDENSKY INHIBITION/EFFECT. See SKINNER'S DESCRIPTIVE BEHAVIOR/ OPERANT CONDITIONING THEORY.

WEISFELD'S ADAPTIVE/EVOLUTION-ARY/ETHOLOGICAL HUMOR THE-ORY. Classical *evolutionary theory* from the discipline areas of anthropology, sociobiology, and ethology is applied by G. E. Weisfeld (1993) to the issue of the adaptive value of humor. Weisfeld's *evolutionary humor theory* proposes that humor evolved to induce the individual to seek out informative social stimulation and to reward others for providing such information. His approach distinguishes the derivative effects of humor (such as group solidarity, competition, courtship, and relaxation) from the fundamental adaptive value of humor. *Weisfeld's theory* does not rest on the traditional assumptions of humor theory concerning tension-reduction/release or pleasure-seeking; his theory avoids group-selection reasoning and it addresses the fitness benefits of the humorist as well as the laugher. The theory accounts for the fact that laughter is a means of social influence, and it applies to chimpanzees as well as humans. Thus, *Weisfeld's humor theory* recognizes both the motivational and affective properties of humor, and not just its cognitive characteristics. Weisfeld's approach helps to explain why aggressive, sexual, and competitive content is particularly funny, why a "playful mood" is necessary for humor appreciation, why intelligent and socially-competent children and adults tend to make good humorists, and why the condition of incongruity is humorous. *Weisfeld's adaptive theory of humor* contains elements that are consistent with existing biological explanations for various "aesthetic" emotions (such as olfaction, music appreciation, and visual art appreciation), and is similar, also, to leading evolutionary explanations for the behavior of "interest." See also DARWIN'S EVOLUTION THEORY; HUMOR, THEORIES OF; INCONGRUITY/INCONSISTENCY THEORIES OF HUMOR; PIDDINGTON'S COMPENSATORY HUMOR THEORY; SOCIAL/COMMUNICATION THEORY OF LAUGHTER; SULLY'S THEORY OF LAUGHTER/HUMOR.

REFERENCE

Weisfeld, G. E. (1993). The adaptive value of humor and laughter. *Ethology and Sociobiology, 14,* 141-169.

WEISMANN'S THEORY. = Weismannism. The German biologist August Friedrich Leopold Weismann (1834-1914) formulated a *theory of genetics* that negates the principle that acquired characteristics are inherited, and postulated a *continuity of germ plasm* through generations. Weismann was a strong supporter of Charles Darwin's (1809-1882) *theory of evolution.* In an attempt to disprove the idea of acquired characteristics proposed by Jean-Baptiste Lamarck (1744-1829), Weismann amputated the tails from mice during five successive generations and found that there was no reduction in the propensity to grow tails. Weismann's early work on the sex cells and development of the Hydrozoa (invertebrate sea animals such as jellyfish, sea anemones, hydroids) led him to develop his *germ plasm/continuity theory*, which postulates that the information required for the development and final form of an organism must be contained within the germ cells, the egg and sperm (he located the germ plasm in what are called today the *chromosomes*), and be transmitted unchanged from generation to generation (cf., *epigenetic theory* - a universally accepted notion that the development of an embryo consists of the gradual differentiation of the fertilized ovum and the separate production/organization of structures and organs; this approach contrasts with the *theory of preformationism*, or *preformation*, that is a discredited theory stating that an embryo is fully differentiated in the ovum or spermatozoon and merely increases in size during development; in a broader context, *epigenetic theory* implies, also, that mind and consciousness developed unpredictably from living matter and reached a high level of complexity in the course of evolution; the theory also includes the notion that new characteristics not determined by the original fertilized egg may emerge in the process of embryonic development, such as a pregnant woman listening to classical music in order to influence her new child's intellectual level; cf., *homunculus/sensory homunculus hypothesis* - a "homunculus" is a completely formed "minute/miniature human figure" considered by some 16th- and 17th-century theorists to exist in the spermatozoon and to expand in size in the transitions from zygote to embryo to infant to adult; this notion is an example of *preformism* and opposes the *epigenetic principle of cumulative development* and *successive differentiation*; the *homunculus hypothesis* was advanced, also, by the early Egyptians who held that a little person resides inside each person's skull and where the homunculus - after looking out through the person's eyes and listening via the person's ears - reacts to the environment by pulling strings to operate the person's muscles; in the *sensory homunculus hypothesis*, it

is suggested that the behavior of an organism is controlled and regulated by a cognitive agent called the "homunculus" that is located within the individual's brain and whose behavior is just as complex as is the individual's behavior that is being explained; in more recent times, the *homunculus* is portrayed as a "tiny, grotesque-looking man" whose distorted body parts indicate the relative sizes of their sensory projection areas in the somatosensory cortex; for example, the head, the hands – especially the thumbs, and feet of the *homunculus* are grossly exaggerated in size to signify their relative importance and representations in the somatosensory cortical regions). In Weismann's view, germ plasms give the *continuity* from parent to offspring; all other cells are merely a vehicle to convey the germ plasm, and it alone is, in a sense, immortal; other cells are destined to die. Weismann also notes that some form of reduction division - that is now known to occur during meiosis - must occur if the genetic material is *not* to double on each generation (cf., *central dogma principle* - the proposition that states that genetic information is transferred from DNA to the proteins that it encodes, and not from protein to DNA; that is, although genes can influence the form of an organism's body or its behavior, the form of the organism's body or its behavior cannot influence its genes; and *genetic memory/storage theory* - posits that information from learning or experience may be stored in a DNA or RNA molecule which, in turn, may be inherited as part of a chromosome). Weismann's ideas are only broadly correct, but it is surprising that he was able in the 1880s to get so near the modern view. He was wrong in his belief that the germ plasm is unalterable and immune to environmental effects, as others were to demonstrate later. Weismann's theories appeared originally in a series of essays, translated as "Essays Upon Heredity and Kindred Biological Problems" (1889-1892), and his "Vortrage Uber Descendenztheorie" (1902) was an important contribution to *evolutionary theory*. See also DARWIN'S EVOLUTION THEORY; GALTON'S LAWS; HARDY-WEINBERG LAW; LAMARCK'S THEORY; MENDEL'S LAWS/PRINCIPLES.

REFERENCES

Darwin, C. R. (1859). *The origin of species.* London: Murray.

Darwin, C. R. (1871). *The descent of man.* London: Murray.

Millar, D., Millar, I., Millar, J., & Millar, M. (1996). *The Cambridge dictionary of scientists.* New York: Cambridge University Press.

WELLS EFFECT. The American psychologist Gary Leroy Wells (1950-) suggests in the *Wells effect* that individuals have a reluctance to make judgments of legal liability solely on the basis of "naked" statistical evidence. For example, evidence that is highly *reliable* (say 80-percent) is sufficient to persuade most people, or to influence their decisions, but "naked" *statistical* evidence (e.g., evidence having an 80-percent *probability*) is *not* sufficient to persuade most people - even though the actual mathematical probability is the same in both instances (i.e., *reliable* evidence versus *statistical* evidence). See also DECISION-MAKING THEORIES; EXPECTED UTILITY THEORY; TAXICAB PROBLEM/EFFECT.

REFERENCES

Wells, G. L. (1978). Applied eyewitness testimony research: system variables and estimator variables. *Journal of Personality and Social Psychology, 36,* 1546-1557.

Wells, G. L. (1984). How adequate is human intuition for judging eyewitness testimony? In G. L. Wells & E. F. Loftus (Eds.), *Eyewitness testimony: Psychological perspectives.* New York: Cambridge University Press.

Wells, G. L. (1993). What do we know about eyewitness identification? *American Psychologist, 48,* 553-571.

Wells, G. L., & Olson, E. A. (2003). Eyewitness testimony. *Annual Review of Psychology, 54,* 277-295.

WERNICKE-GESCHWIND THEORY. See MIND/MENTAL STATES, THEORIES OF.

WERTHEIMER'S PERCEPTUAL THEORY. See GESTALT THEORY/LAWS.

WEVER-BRAY EFFECT. See AUDITION/HEARING, THEORIES OF.

WHEATSTONE-PANUM LIMITING CASE. See PANUM PHENOMENON/EFFECT.

WHITTEN EFFECT. See OLFACTION/SMELL, THEORIES OF.

WHORF-SAPIR HYPOTHESIS/THEORY. = Whorfian hypothesis = Whorf's hypothesis = linguistic relativity hypothesis = Sapir-Whorf hypothesis. The American linguists and anthropologists Benjamin Lee Whorf (1897-1941) and Edward Sapir (1884-1939) formulated the *Whorf-Sapir linguistic hypothesis,* which states that one's *language* influences the nature of one's *perceptions and thoughts,* and was first suggested by the German ethnologist Wilhelm von Humboldt (1767-1835). There are two forms of the *linguistic relativity hypothesis*: a "weak" form (which argues that only perceptions are so influenced; e.g., an Eskimo's perception of *snow* is distinguishable from a non-Eskimo's because the former has many different words in his/her vocabulary/language for different variations in types of *snow*), and a "strong" form (which asserts that abstract conceptual processes are so affected; e.g., the Hopi Indian language handles *time* in a relativistic manner as compared with the English language breakdown of *time* into "past," "present," and "future"). Unfortunately, very little convincing evidence supports completely the *Whorf-Sapir hypothesis.* An early view of the relationship between *language* and *thought* was J. B. Watson's (1878-1958) *behaviorist* approach that asserted that one learns to talk in much the same way that other muscular skills (such as riding a bicycle) are learned, and when one subsequently makes the same muscular movements in a more hidden form (i.e., to oneself covertly rather than aloud or overtly), it is called *thought* [cf., the *motor theory of thinking/consciousness* of E. Jacobson (1932) and L. W. Max (1935), which posits that mental images are accompanied by changes in the corresponding muscular area - such as the arm and eye regions of the body - for motor and visual images, respectively; *Flourens' theory -*

named after the French physician Marie-Pierre Jean Flourens (1794-1867), states that *thinking* depends on the functioning of the cerebrum as a whole; the *laws of thought* - refer to the three logical principles of identity, contradiction, and excluded middle, and are considered to be the basic principles of all reasoning; and the *law of participation* - is a principle of human *primitive thinking*, which asserts that things that are similar are considered to be identical]. According to Watson, what psychologists call *thought* is nothing but talking to oneself (cf., the *motor theory of speech perception* propounded by A. M. Liberman, which holds that speech is assumed to be perceived by an implicit, covert system that "maps" the acoustic properties of the input against a set of deep motor representations of idealized articulation). However, Watson's extreme *behaviorist* view that thinking or thought depends only on the implicit muscle movements of speech has proven to be inadequate [cf., *central theory of thinking* - is the proposition that the center of mentation is a cerebral process located in the *brain* (however, curiously, Aristotle suggested that the *locus* of *thinking/thought* is in the *heart*)]. *Kinney's law* - named after the American educator Richard Kinney (1924-1979), relates to temporal factors and behavioral/quantitative aspects of speech deficiency in postnatally developing *deafness* where the length of time over which changes in speech develop is directly proportional to the length of time during which normal speech has been present; and the *phonemic restoration phantom/effect* - refers to the generalization that a dramatically altered acoustic element in speech is extremely difficult to detect, and where replacing various speech sounds with others still sounds like proper speech. Other competing theories concerning the relationship between *language* and *thought* are: J. Piaget's *cognitive stage development theory*, which emphasizes the idea that language is a result/by-product of a child's advances in cognitive abilities, particularly the ability to symbolize that develops at the end of infancy; and the Russian developmental psychologist Lev S. Vygotsky's (1896-1934) and the Russian neuropsychologist Aleksandr R. Luria's (1902-1977) *linguistic theory* that portrays *language* and *thought*

as developing together and aiding each other in the process (cf., concept of *pure meaning* - Vygotsky's notion maintaining that "pure meaning" is the final union of *language* and *thought* in adult reasoning; *language* and *thought* begin as independent processes, but join together around the age of two years, and lead to the development of egocentric speech, inner speech, verbal thought, concept formation and, ultimately, "pure meaning"). It is suggested that the notion of *linguistic relativity* (like most "large" theories in psychology) is not the kind of theory that will ever be proven completely right or completely wrong; most likely, in the final analysis, it may be proper to say that *language* differences influence people's *thoughts and perceptions* in some ways, as well as, conversely, *thoughts/ cognitions and perceptions* influence one's *language* in other ways (cf., *cloak theory of language* - holds that the structure of a language is a dependent function of the patterns of thought embedded in the particular culture). See also BEHAVIORIST THEORY; CHOMSKY'S PSYCHOLINGUISTIC THEORY; CONCEPT LEARNING/CONCEPT FORMATION, THEORIES OF; LANGUAGE ACQUISITION THEORY; LANGUAGE ORIGINS, THEORIES OF; PIAGET'S DEVELOPMENTAL STAGES THEORY; SPEECH THEORIES; THOUGHT, LAWS OF.

REFERENCES

Watson, J. B. (1924). *Behaviorism*. Chicago: University of Chicago Press.

Vygotsky, L. S., & Luria, A. R. (1930). *Studies in the history of behaviour*. Cambridge, MA: M.I.T. Press.

Jacobson, E. (1932). Electrophysiology of mental activities. *American Journal of Psychology, 44*, 677-694.

Vygotsky, L. S. (1934/1962). *Thought and language*. Cambridge, MA: M.I.T. Press.

Max, L. W. (1935). An experimental study of the motor theory of consciousness. *Journal of Comparative Psychology, 19*, 469-486.

Piaget, J. (1954). *The construction of reality in the child*. New York: Basic Books.

Whorf, B. (1956). *Language, thought, and reality*. New York: Wiley.

Luria, A. R. (1968). *The mind of a mnemonist.* New York: Basic Books.

Kay, P., & Kempton, W. (1984). What is the Sapir-Whorf hypothesis? *American Anthropologist, 86,* 65-79.

Hunt, E., & Agnoli, F. (1991). The Whorfian hypothesis: A cognitive psychology perspective. *Psychological Review, 98,* 377-389.

WIFE/MISTRESS FIGURE. See APPENDIX A, RUBIN FIGURE/ILLUSION.

WILD CHILD PHENOMENON. See KASPAR HAUSER EFFECT/EXPERIMENT.

WILDER'S LAW OF INITIAL VALUE(S). See INITIAL VALUE(S), LAW OF.

WILLMER'S COLOR THEORY. The British physiologist E. N. Willmer (dates unknown) proposed a *theory of color vision* that postulates three mechanisms in the retina: cones, dark-adapting rods, and non-dark-adapting rods. *Willmer's color theory* asserts that color vision may be explained by the relative ratio of rods and cones at various wavelengths, and indicates that when a curve is plotted to show the summation of rod and cone responses at various wavelengths of the visible spectrum, the curve has some affinity to the well-known *color triangle.* Thus, *Willmer's color theory* was developed via analyses of sensitivity to wavelengths and relates to empirically-derived hue/color charts; the theory also attempts to account for the relationship of hue to intensity and with the white-black phenomena in color vision. Willmer (1943) presents his theory, examines the physiology of color vision, and discusses the deficiencies in color-vision theory in the journal *Nature (London)* and, in the same issue of the journal - in response to his article, K. J. W. Craik, H. Hartridge, and A. H. S. Holbourn raise several objections to *Willmer's theory.* Craik describes an experiment that demonstrates that a hue match with yellow or green is impossible when red and blue are used within the photopic/scotopic ratios covering the regions stated in *Willmer's theory,* and Craik also criticizes the theory concerning the production of the "white sensation." Hartridge

describes an experiment that fails to corroborate certain assumptions of *Willmer's theory,* namely, that strong stimulation of the rods and cones simultaneously would cause an appreciation of green, yellow, or orange, whereas weak stimulation of those receptors should result in the perception of violet, mauve, or crimson. Holbourn offers a criticism of *Willmer's theory* by pointing out that any workable color theory must have *three* independent variables, but *Willmer's theory* only has *two* independent variables. See also COLOR VISION, THEORIES/LAWS OF.

REFERENCES

Willmer, E. N. (1943). Physiology of colour vision. *Nature (London), 151-152,* 191, 213-215, 632-635.

Willmer, E. N. (1946). *Retinal structure and colour vision: A restatement and an hypothesis.* Cambridge, UK: Cambridge University Press.

Willmer, E. N. (1950). Some aspects of colour-blindness. *British Medical Journal, 2,* 1141-1145.

Giles, G. H. (1950). Colour vision: Some recent trends in practice. *British Journal of Physiological Optics, 7,* 90-95.

Willmer, E. N. (1955). The physiology of vision. *Annual Review of Physiology, 17,* 339-366.

WINNER'S CURSE EFFECT. See DECISION-MAKING THEORIES.

WITKIN'S PERCEPTION/PERSONALITY/COGNITIVE STYLE THEORY. The American psychologist Herman A. Witkin (1916-1979) conducted research on *cognitive styles* in the 1940s, in particular on individual differences in the perception of the upright in space. An earlier approach toward understanding visual space perception, especially one related to the perception of rotation/movement in space, was provided by the Austrian physicist/philosopher Ernst Mach (1838-1916) in his *theory of bodily rotation* (also called the *Mach-Breuer-Brown theory of labyrinthine functioning),* where he suggested that the sense organs for this experience are to be found in the semicircular canals of the inner ear. *Mach's theory,* with some modification, is still prevalent today. In Witkin's theoretical approach, when stationary *visual* and *bodily* cues are placed in opposition, and one has to judge whether an object is upright, some persons are influenced more by the *visual cues* (such individuals are called *field-dependent*), whereas others depend more on *bodily cues* (these persons are called *field-independent*). The factors of *field dependence* and *field independence* represent a dimension along which one's perceptions may be placed concerning dependence on (or independence from) cues in the environment (called the *field*). In the first and simplest test (called the *rod and frame test* or *RFT*) used to study this dimension, a participant has to align a stimulus (such as a rod) so that it is "truly" vertical when a second stimulus (such as a frame around the rod) is varied with respect to the true vertical. Persons who can set the rod relatively accurately - independently of the orientation of the frame - are called *field-independent* because they rely on *bodily* sensation cues rather than on *visual* cues in the field. The more the tilt in the field controls the person's setting of the rod, the more *field-dependent* the individual. Another test of the *field independent-dependent* dimension is the *embedded-figures test* [described by the German Gestalt psychologist Kurt Gottschaldt (1902-1991) in 1926] in which the participant attempts to locate simple geometric shapes that are hidden in more complex diagrams/drawings; *field-independent* persons perform *better* on this test than do *field-dependent* persons. Later, Witkin and others conducted more elaborate studies using chairs and entire rooms that could be tilted (in the *tilting-room test* or *body-adjustment* test). The study of the trait *field dependence* began in the area of perception, but the large individual differences that were found in tests such as *RFT, embedded-figures*, and the *tilting-room* encouraged research in other areas such as personality, emotions, cognitive style, neuropsychological processes, development, and psychopathology. Witkin argued that individuals move, in general, from *field-dependence* toward *field-independence* as they mature. However, those who become most *field-independent* are those individuals who are raised in ways that foster personal autonomy and a secure sense of self.

Witkin's research led to a variety of studies including dreaming, cultural differences in socialization, intellectual processes, interpersonal relations (e.g., between teachers and students, therapists and patients/clients, and parents and children), brain laterality, and chromosomal aberrations. See also BERKELEY'S THEORY OF VISUAL SPACE PERCEPTION; COGNITIVE STYLE MODELS; GESTALT THEORY/LAWS; LATERALITY THEORIES; PERCEPTION (II. COMPARATIVE APPRAISAL), THEORIES OF; PERSONALITY, THEORIES OF; SELF-CONCEPT THEORY.

REFERENCES

Mach, E. (1886/1959). *The analysis of sensations and the relation of the physical to the psychical*. New York: Dover.

Mach, E. (1902). *The analysis of experience*. Jena, East Germany: Fisher.

Witkin, H. A. (1950). Individual differences in ease of perception of embedded figures. *Journal of Personality, 19*, 1-15.

Witkin, H. A., & Goodenough, D. (1977). Field dependence and interpersonal behavior. *Psychological Bulletin, 84*, 661-689.

Witkin, H. A., & Goodenough, D. (1981). *Cognitive styles: Essence and origins - Field dependence and filed independence*. New York: International Universities Press.

WIT, THEORIES OF. See HUMOR, THEORIES OF.

WOLPE'S THEORY/TECHNIQUE OF RECIPROCAL INHIBITION. The South African-born American psychiatrist Joseph Wolpe (1915-1997) conducted experimental studies early in his career on the production and cure of neuroses in animals which demonstrated that the neuroses could be produced in learning and, also, could be reversible by learning. Later, based on such research, Wolpe derived psychotherapeutic techniques for treating neuroses in humans. *Wolpe's theory* and *technique* constituted one of the many varieties of *behavior modification* (or *behavior therapy*, which is a procedure of direct intervention to alter a person's behaviors to situations that are deemed - by oneself or by others - to be worthy of change; cf., Ahsen, 1989). Wolpe's approach, called *reciprocal inhibition*, is a form of *behavior therapy* that is based on the neurological concept of *reciprocal innervation*, that is, the inhibition of the action of one neural pathway by the activity of another (cf., *staircase phenomenon* or *warm-up effect* - refers to a graduated sequence of increasingly stronger muscle contractions that occur when a corresponding sequence of identical stimuli is applied to a rested muscle; cf., *Bowditch's law*). As a general theory of *behavior modification*, Wolpe's *reciprocal inhibition* refers to the inhibition of one response (e.g., yelling) by the occurrence of another *mutually incompatible* response (e.g., talking softly). The specific method used in *reciprocal inhibition* is called *desensitization* or *systematic desensitization* [cf., *progressive relaxation* - a form of psychotherapy used for treating anxiety disorders whereby skeletal muscles throughout the body are first tensed and then relaxed deeply; it was first described in 1929 by the American physician Edmund Jacobson (1888-1983) and is used, often, as an adjunct to *systematic desensitization*]. In a clinical context, especially in the treatment of *phobias* ("irrational fears"), the procedure of *systematic desensitization* is designed to produce a decrease in anxiety (i.e., "de-sensitize") toward some feared situation of object (e.g., snakes). This is accomplished by exposing the client to a series of approximations to the anxiety-producing stimulus under relaxed conditions until, eventually, the anxiety reaction becomes extinguished. The procedure of *systematic desensitization* has come under heavy criticism from psychoanalytically oriented therapists and theorists over the issue of the *symptom substitution hypothesis* (i.e., the idea that if only the surface or superficial behavioral manifestations of a neurosis are treated in psychotherapy, the presumed unresolved underlying conflict will "erupt" elsewhere, and new symptoms will emerge). The notion of *symptom substitution* derives from the assumption (not accepted by all psychologists) that psychological disturbances are analogous to medical disturbances (as in the *medical/disease model of illness*) in that they can be treated only by removal of the root cause of the disorder (cf., *resolution law* - attempts to find a partial explanation of behavioral modification whereby the changing of one physiological state into another one becomes easier and quicker after it has taken place a number of times; and *stages of change theory* – suggests the following steps be used to gain the self-control required to change an undesirable behavior: pre-contemplation of the advantages and consequences of the change, contemplation of benefits, preparation and action, and maintenance of the change). Wolpe indicates that variables such as food, expression of aggression, and sexual feeling might work, also, to reciprocally inhibit avoidance behavior or anxiety feelings. Wolpe's work on the direct re-education of *sexual behavior* foreshadowed W. Masters and V. Johnson's widely publicized sexual-response studies, and his emphasis on expression of feeling anticipated the procedure of *assertiveness training*. See also ALL-OR-NONE LAW/PRINCIPLE; BEHAVIOR THERAPY/COGNITIVE THERAPY, THEORIES OF; BOWDITCH'S LAW; IMAGERY/MENTAL IMAGERY, THEORIES OF.

REFERENCES

Jacobson, E. (1929). *Progressive relaxation.* Chicago: University of Chicago Press.

Wolpe, J. (1952). Experimental neurosis as learned behavior. *British Journal of Psychology, 43*, 243-268.

Wolpe, J. (1954). Reciprocal inhibition as the main basis of psychotherapeutic effects. *Archives of Neurological Psychiatry, 72*, 205-226.

Wolpe, J. (1958). *Psychotherapy by reciprocal inhibition.* Stanford, CA: Stanford University Press.

Masters, W., & Johnson, V. (1966). *Human sexual response.* Boston: Little, Brown.

Ahsen, A. (1989). Scientific misconduct in behaviorist circles. *Journal of Mental Imagery, 13*, 1-20.

WORD-LENGTH EFFECT. See FORGETTING/MEMORY, THEORIES OF.

WORD-SUPERIORITY EFFECT. See TOP-DOWN PROCESSING/THEORIES.

WORK ADJUSTMENT, THEORY OF.
See WORK/CAREER/OCCUPATION, THE-
ORIES OF.

**WORK/CAREER/OCCUPATION, THE-
ORIES OF.** The psychological study of work,
career, and occupational factors ranges from
theories of decision-making in career development to ergonomic/ergopsychometry/anth-
ropometry, human engineering/human factors,
work fatigue/efficiency, applications research,
and *work motivation theories. Theories of
career development* fall into one of several
classes: trait-oriented, systems-oriented, per-
sonality-oriented, or developmental. Although
no single approach seems to dominate the
field, each has its own particular utility for
career/work/occupation counselors. Once a
person makes a career decision, potential
problems exist in terms of worker productivity, adjustment to the stress/strain of the
workplace, and level of job satisfaction. *Theories in vocational psychology* may be divided
into four main categories: matching approaches (involves theories and methods
based on studies in the area of *differential
psychology* and on *situational theories*); phenomenological approaches (involves *self-
concept theory* and *congruence theory*; cf.,
consistency theory of work behavior - holds
that work behavior is based on two allied
premises: a *balance* concept and a *self-image*
standard; the theory predicts that workers will
engage in satisfying behaviors that maximize
their sense of cognitive *balance* and will be
motivated to perform in a way that is consistent with their *self-image*); developmental
approaches (includes *role theory* and *life-stage
theory*), and decision-making approaches.
Theories of work/job efficiency attempt to
account for effective work performance and
how stress, strain, boredom, fatigue, and other
negative consequences of work affect one's
health and well-being. The *theories of work
motivation* may be grouped into two broad
areas: *universalistic theories* - posit widespread applicability to the work environment,
and *contingency theories* - focus on individual
differences that influence motivation levels.
Among the *universalistic theories* are A.
Maslow's *hierarchy of needs theory* - proposes that human behavior is a result of at-

tempts to satisfy currently unsatisfied needs
where the needs are arranged in a hierarchical
order such that the satisfaction of a prior level
of need leads to a need for satisfaction at a
succeeding level [cf., *existence, relatedness,
and growth theory*, or *ERG theory*, is a variation of Mas-low's *hierarchy of needs theory* as
applied to occupational/industrial settings,
where need categories include *existence* needs
(relative to the person's physical needs such as
food, clothing, and shelter), *relatedness* needs
(relating to interpersonal relations with others,
both on and off the job), and *growth* needs]; F.
Herzberg's *two-factor theory* - asserts that job
satisfaction and dissatisfaction are caused by
different work-related factors such as
achievement, recognition, advancement,
growth, and responsibility as *satisfiers*, and
lack of company policy, administration, technical support/ supervision, salary, job security,
fringe benefits, and status as *dissatisfiers*; and
D. McClelland's *achievement motivation theory* - focuses on the needs of power, affiliation, and achievement as prominent work-
related factors. Among the *contingency theories* are B. F. Skinner's *stimulus-response and
operant conditioning theory* - argues that human behavior is not motivated by needs *within*
an individual but by the *external* environment
and the rewards and punishments that it provides; J. S. Adams' *equity theory* - assumes
that persons are motivated by a desire to be
treated equitably on their jobs; and V. H.
Vroom's *force model* in occupational choice
and *expectancy theory* (also called *valence-
expectancy theory* and *valence-
instrumentality-expectancy theory*) - asserts
that a person's motivation to perform is a
function of both perceived desirability and
attainability of outcomes, and suggests the
behavior is affected by degree of cer-
tainty/uncertainty that some outcome will
follow the behavior, and how much that outcome is valued by the worker (cf., *instrumentality theory* - a cognitive approach to work
motivation that states that a person's attitude
about an event/work depends on the perception of the event's/work's function as an instrument in obtaining the desirable, or undesirable, consequences; and *role-expectations
hypothesis* - posits that confirmation of employees' prior expectations about the nature of

their jobs results in lower job turn-over and higher degrees of organizational commitment and job satisfaction). Closely related to work motivation is the issue of occupational adjustment, which is also a major source of personal identity and role definition. One well-formulated *theory of work adjustment* (cf., Lofquist & Dawis, 1969) maintains that occupational environments provide different patterns of reinforcement that interact with a person's needs and abilities, and where harmony between an individual and the work environment results in satisfaction and, as a consequence, greater level of work stability (cf., *job-characteristics model* - holds that particular needs of employees, such as autonomy, feedback, identity, significance, and task variety, influence job adjustment, satisfaction, and other employee outcomes; *range-of-affect hypothesis* - in the prediction of job satisfaction, this conjecture attempts to explain how the discrepancies between what one already has, and what one wants, determine the potential range of satisfaction yielded by a given job aspect/facet; and *vitamin model of employee satisfaction* - states that different aspects of work, much like taking daily dosages of vitamins, need to be present, at least minimally, in order to produce a satisfied employee). The *theories of motivation and adjustment* have practical implications for work-related activities in organizations and contribute to the maximization of job satisfaction and worker morale. See also BALANCE, PRINCIPLES/THEORY OF; DECISION-MAKING THEORIES; DEVELOPMENTAL THEORY; LEADERSHIP, THEORIES OF; MASLOW'S THEORY OF PERSONALITY; MOTIVATION, THEORIES OF; ORGANIZATIONAL/INDUSTRIAL/SYSTEMS THEORY; PERSONALITY THEORIES; ROLE-THEORY OF PERSONALITY; SELF-CONCEPT THEORY; SITUATIONAL THEORY OF LEADERSHIP.

REFERENCES

Taylor, F. (1903). *Shop management*. New York: Harper.

Gilbreth, F. (1911). *Motion study, a method for increasing efficiency*. New York: Van Nostrand.

Maslow, A. (1943). A theory of human motivation. *Psychological Review, 50,* 370-396.

McClelland, D., Atkinson, J., Clark, R., & Lowell, E. (1953). *The achievement motive.* New York: A-C-C.

Herzberg, F., Mausner, B., & Snyderman, B. (1959). *The motivation to work.* New York: Wiley.

Adams, J. S. (1963). Toward an understanding of inequity. *Journal of Abnormal and Social Psychology, 67,* 422-436.

Vroom, V. H. (1964). *Work and motivation.* New York: Wiley.

Osipow, S. (1968/1983). *Theories of career development.* Englewood Cliffs, NJ: Prentice-Hall.

Lofquist, L., & Dawis, R. (1969). *Adjustment to work.* New York: A-C-C.

Skinner, B. F. (1971). *Beyond freedom and dignity.* New York: Bantam Books.

Super, D. (1994). Career development. In R. J. Corsini (Ed.), *Encyclopedia of psychology.* New York: Wiley.

Latham, G. P., & Pinder, C. C. (2005). Work motivation theory and research at the dawn of the twenty-first century. *Annual Review of Psychology, 56,* 485-516.

WORKING MEMORY, THEORY OF. In memory/learning psychology, as advanced by the English psychologists Alan D. Baddeley (1934-) and Graham J. Hitch (1946-), the *theory of working memory* refers to the temporary storage system that retains currently-received information items while an interpretation process is activated to sort out this input. This *working memory* system allows for manipulation of the information and its passage in, and out of, *short-term memory*. Theoretically, regarding verbal materials, such as sentences, the words in a sentence are held in their literal and original form or state while a more abstract process works to shape and determine the meaning of the sentence. Moreover, the storage system is thought to involve a "central executive" component (language comprehension processor) and two "buffer" components (temporary memory storage also known as "blackboard memory" components) called the *phonological loop model* (an inner-speech, verbal, or mental rehearsal tactic-device, lasting up to two seconds) and the *visuospatial sketchpad/scratch-pad model* (a visual-coding mechanism, assumed to be responsible for establishing and manipulating visuo-spatial images). Concerning its location, it is speculated that the associative processes of *working memory* are carried out mostly in the brain's prefrontal cortex. *Working memory* has been studied by psychologists in diverse human and non-human organisms via techniques such as "object permanence" and "delayed-reaction" tests. See also CHOMSKY'S PSYCHOLINGUISTIC THEORY; DELAYED-REACTION PARADIGM; OBJECT PERMANENCE PARADIGM; SHORT-TERM AND LONG-TERM MEMORY, THEORIES OF.

REFERENCE

Baddeley, A. D., & Hitch, G. J. (1974). Working memory. In G. Bower (Ed.), *Recent advances in learning and motivation*. Vol. 8. New York: Academic Press.

WUNDT ILLUSION. See APPENDIX A.

WUNDT'S THEORIES/DOCTRINES/ PRINCIPLES. The German physiologist, psychologist, philosopher, and founder of experimental psychology Wilhelm Max Wundt (1832-1920) created and developed the first school of psychological thought, called *structuralism/structuralist school*, whose basic ten-et was that *sensations* are the proper subject matter of psychology (the historical psychological *school/theory of functionalism* emphasized the *activity/adaptive* dimension of psychological events, whereas Wundt's *theory/ school of structuralism* emphasized the *contents* of psychological events). Using the method of *introspection* (i.e., looking within one's own experience and reporting on it), Wundt and his students investigated participants' immediate experience through exacting attention to sensations and feelings. The goals of *structuralism* were to analyze conscious processes into basic elements, to determine how these elements are connected, and to establish the laws of these connections (cf., Ahsen, 1986). Wundt proposed a *tridimen-*

sional theory of feeling in which an equilibrium between pleasure-displeasure, tension-relaxation, and excitement-calm/depression occupy three independent and distinct dimensions of feeling. Wundt held that emotions are complex compounds of the elementary feelings and that each of the feelings may effectively be described by defining its position on each of the three dimensions (cf., Wundt's formulation of three *principles of emotional expression* as a reformulation of Darwin's principles: the *principles of innervation, association of analogous sensations,* and *relation of movements to images*). Wundt's *theory of feeling* stimulated a great deal of research in his own, and rival, laboratories but it has not withstood the test of time. Wundt postulated his *doctrine of apperception* to explain how the various elements of conscious experience are combined to form unified conscious experiences. He used the term *apperception* in a fashion similar to that of the German philosopher/psychologist Johann Herbart (1776-1841) to refer to the active mental process of selecting and structuring internal experience. The term *apperception* is rarely used today in experimental psychology, but the concepts underlying it are important, especially to many cognitively oriented psychologists. Wundt designated the active process of combining the various elements into a unity as his *law of psychic resultants* (also called the *principle of creative synthesis/resultants*), which states that the combination of elements creates new properties where every psychic compound has characteristics that are more than the sum of the characteristics of the elements when taken singly (cf., Mill, 1874). In a sense, Wundt's *principle of creative synthesis* (via J. S. Mill) and his *law of psychic resultants* anticipated the Gestalt theorists' viewpoint that in perception the "whole is more than the sum of its parts," where something new is created out of the synthesis of the elemental parts of experience [cf., *synergy theory* - developed by the American functionalist/dynamic psychologist Robert Sessions Woodworth (1869-1962), and emphasizes the idea that mental synthesis is a unitary perceptual or motor response that is generated by the aggregate of sensory elements, and is viewed as stimuli converging on a single response mechanism; and *dynamic*

theory - a general approach employed by both Sigmund Freud and Wilhelm Wundt that is concerned with motivational processes and the unconscious; the term *dynamism* is used to refer to a stable manner of behaving, the purpose of which is to fulfill motives and drives and to protect the individual from debilitating stress]. At the turn of the 20th century, Wundt was involved in an academic controversy called the *imageless thought* debate. The controversy about the *nature of thinking* was between the *structuralist school* of Wundt and E. B. Titchener on the one hand, and the members of the *Wurzburg school* in Germany on the other hand. Wundt postulated that consciousness is made up of only three elements: sensations, images, and feelings; Titchener placed major emphasis on *images* as the vehicles of thought. The Wurzburg psychologists hypothesized that participants' responses are due to *determining tendencies* or *sets* without the use of imagery (i.e., they argued in favor of "image*less* thought"). The topic of *images/imagery* waned with the advent of *behaviorism* in the early 1900s, but then in the 1960s and 1970s, it was revived with the development of the *cognitive* approach in psychology, and *imagery* began to play a significant theoretical role in the areas of learning, perception, thinking, and meaning. Wundt's wide-ranging laboratory investigations of psychological phenomena included the psychology and physiology of seeing, hearing, the "lower" senses, optics, reaction-time experiments, word associations, folk psychology, and psychophysics. Wundt adopted a purely psychological interpretation of *Weber's law*, which he considered to be an example of the *psychological law of relativity* (cf., Muller, 1878). Although there were signs reflecting the theoretical narrowness of Wundt's new experimental psychology, it was through Wundt's vision, largely, that the conception of an independent and inductive psychology became a reality. See also ACH'S LAWS/PRINCIPLES/THEORY; BEHAVIORIST THEORY; DARWIN'S EVOLUTION THEORY; DARWIN'S THEORY OF EMOTIONS; DETERMINING TENDENCY; DONDERS' LAW; DYNAMIC THEORY; FUNCTIONALISM THEORY; GESTALT THEORY/LAWS; HERBART'S DOCTRINE OF APPERCEPTION; IMAGERY/MENTAL IMAGERY, THEORIES OF; MILL'S CANONS; MOTIVATION, THEORIES OF; SET, LAW OF; WEBER'S LAW.

REFERENCES

Wundt, W. M. (1862). *Beitrage zur theorie der sinneswahrnehmung.* Leipzig: Engelmann.

Wundt, W. M. (1873). *Grundzuege der physiologischen psychologie.* Leipzig: Engelmann.

Mill, J. S. (1874). *A system of logic.* New York: Harper.

Muller, G. (1878). *Zur grundlegung der psychophysik.* Berlin: Gruben.

Wundt, W. M. (1896). *Grundriss der psychologie.* Leipzig: Engelmann.

Wundt, W. M. (1897). *Principles of psychology.* Leipzig: Engelmann.

Ahsen, A. (1986). The New Structuralism: Images in dramatic interlock. *Journal of Mental Imagery, 10,* 1-92.

WYER AND COLLINS' THEORY OF HUMOR ELICITATION. This theory of humor (that borrows heavily from several aspects of M. J. Apter's *reversal theory*) specifies the conditions in which humor is experienced both in social and non-social situations. The *theory of humor elicitation* (Wyer & Collins, 1992) emphasizes the following aspects: the interpretation of a stimulus-event that is necessary to evoke humor; the problems of identifying the humor-eliciting characteristics of the stimulus-event interpretation; and the cognitive elaboration of the various implications of the stimulus-event. Moreover, the *theory of humor elicitation* assesses the persons' information-processing objectives at the time a stimulus-event occurs; and, in particular, the theory has been used to conceptualize the humor evoked by witticisms, jokes, and social events that are neither intended nor expected to be humorous. In their *comprehension-elaboration theory of humor,* Wyer and Collins propose a series of eight postulates (memory, encoding, prior and later stimulus-events, incongruity resolution, pragmatic meaning, humor elicitation, comprehension difficulty, cognitive elaboration) concerning the comprehension of semantic and epi-

sodic information, the conditions of humor elicitation, and the elaboration of stimulus-events. Thus, this *theory of humor elicitation* is based on the assumption that situational and individual-differences variables that affect the perception of humor may be viewed in terms of their mediating influence on certain social-information processes involving previously acquired concepts and general knowledge. Overall, the theory focuses on the cognitive foundations of one's responses to ethnic humor and to humor that is directed toward one-self. See also APTER'S REVERSAL THEORY OF HUMOR; HUMOR, THEORIES OF; MOTIVATIONAL THEORIES OF HUMOR.

REFERENCES

Apter, M. J. (1982). *The experience of motivation: The theory of psychological reversals*. London: Academic Press.

Wyer, R. S., & Collins, J. E. (1992). A theory of humor elicitation. *Psychological Review, 99*, 663-688.

X

X, THEORY. See LEADERSHIP, THEORIES OF; ORGANIZATIONAL/INDUSTRIAL/SYSTEMS THEORY.

Y

YAVIS-HOUND PHENOMENA/ SYN-DROMES. The American psychotherapist William Schofield (1921-) suggests that the acronym *YAVIS* embodies the personal qualities that therapists, counselors, and the American general public find *most* appealing in patients, clients, associates, and other individuals. *YAVIS* refers to the attributes of young, attractive, verbal, intelligent, and successful. On the other hand, the acronym HOUND embodies personality characteristics that therapists, counselors, and the American general public find *least* appealing in patients, clients, associates, and other individuals. *HOUND* refers to the qualities of humble, old, unattractive, nonverbal, and dumb. See also PERSONALITY THEORIES.

REFERENCE

Schofield, W. (1964/1986). *Psychotherapy: The purchase of friendship.* Englewood Cliffs, NJ: Prentice-Hall/ New Brunswick, NJ: Transaction.

YERKES-DODSON LAW. This principle is a statement of the relationship between arousal level and quality of performance formulated in 1908 by the American comparative psychologists Robert Means Yerkes (1876-1956) and John Dillingham Dodson (dates unknown). The *Yerkes-Dodson law*, also called the *inverted-U hypothesis*, indicates that there is an optimal level of arousal (e.g., motivation, anxiety) for tasks where moderate levels of arousal facilitate problem solving, but if stress or anxiety is too high (or too low), the person does not process the important and relevant cues (or ignores them), and optimal learning and performance fail to occur. Thus, the *Yerkes-Dodson law* states that increased drive will improve performance up to a point, beyond which there is deterioration of performance. However, the law may need to be qualified by various factors, one of which is task "complexity." That is, the complexity of the task to be performed may need to be ex-

amined and controlled wherein the optimal level of motivation should be higher for a simple task than it is for a complex task. For example, solving difficult mathematical problems within a time limit (a complex task) may be best accomplished by only a slight level of arousal instead of being highly aroused or excited. On the other hand, sorting and re-shelving library books all day (a simple task) may best be done by creating a high level of motivation in the person. On the whole, the *Yerkes-Dodson law* seems reasonable and useful, but it has received only mixed support from psychologists. See also ACTIVATION/ AROUSAL THEORY; INVERTED-U HYPOTHESIS.

REFERENCES

Yerkes, R. M., & Dodson, J. D. (1908). The relation of strength of stimulus to rapidity of habit formation. *Journal of Comparative Neurology and Psychology, 18,* 459-482.

Brown, W. P. (1965). The Yerkes-Dodson law repealed. *Psychological Reports, 67,* 663-666.

Anderson, K., Revelle, W., & Lynch, M. (1989). Caffeine, impulsivity, and memory scanning: A comparison of two explanations for the Yerkes-Dodson effect. *Motivation and Emotion, 13,* 1-20.

Anderson, K. (1994). Impulsivity, caffeine, and task difficulty: A within-subjects test of the Yerkes-Dodson law. *Personality and Individual Differences, 16,* 813-819.

Teigen, K. (1994). Yerkes-Dodson: A law for all seasons. *Theory & Psychology, 4,* 525-547.

YO-HE-HO THEORY. See LANGUAGE ORIGINS, THEORIES OF.

YO-YO EFFECT. See HUNGER, THEORIES OF.

YOUNG-HELMHOLTZ COLOR VISION THEORY. = Helmholtz's color vision theory = Young's color vision theory = three-element/tri-receptor/triple receptor/trichromatic color vision theory. In 1801, the English physician/physicist Thomas Young (1773-1829)

proposed that color vision is due to three different kinds of *visual fibers*. Young's original theory was based on Sir Isaac Newton's (1642-1727) earlier demonstration in physics of the existence of three primary colors (red, green, and blue). Because Young found it difficult to conceive of each sensitive point in the retina as containing an infinite number of particles to be capable of vibrating in perfect unison with every possible undulation of light energy, he suggested that there are only three kinds of *fibers* corresponding to three primary colors (red, green, and blue). Young expanded his theory somewhat in 1807, but it remained unrecognized, essentially, as it sat in the Philosophical Transactions of the Royal Society of London until 1852 when the German physiologist/psychologist Hermann von Helmholtz (1821-1894) rediscovered and popularized it [the Scottish physicist James Clerk Maxwell (1831-1879) is reputed, also, to have "rediscovered" Young's early work at about the same time as did Helmholtz]. Helmholtz wrote his quantitative *line-element* treatment of color vision and color discrimination short-ly before his death [cf., Helmholtz's *theory of accommodation* - states that the shape of the lens of the eye becomes convex as the ciliary muscle relaxes, and flattens as the ciliary muscle contracts; even though the concept of the lens changing shape originated with the French philosopher Rene Descartes (1596-1650), it was Helmholtz who elaborated the physiological mechanism involved in the pro-cess]. As he developed his quantitative theory, Helmholtz studied whether or not hue could be discriminated on the basis of gradations in the intensity of three fundamental processes (red, green, blue) that are evoked whenever the retinal cones are stimulated by light energy. Today, this theory is known as the *Young-Helmholtz theory*, and it postulates three types of cones (red, green, blue), each containing a different chemical substance where each is sensitive maximally to a different region of the electromagnetic spectrum. Consistent with the *law of specific nerve energies*, the red cones (if stimulated in isolation) would give a "red" sensation, green cones would give a "green" sensation, and blue cones would give a "blue" sensation. Also, according to the theory, the rate of firing

("excitability") of each cone type depends on the wavelength of the stimulating light. Thus, the phenomenal or subjective experience of *hue* (i.e., "color") depends on the relative frequencies of impulses set up in the three types of fibers, *brightness* (i.e., "intensity") depends on the total frequency of impulses in all three fibers, and *saturation* (i.e., "purity") depends on the amount of white produced in any quantifiable fusion of the fibers. All the other hues (including yellow, purple, and white or gray) are due to various combinations of the three component activities. The *Young-Helmholtz color vision theory* contains widely accepted ideas by psychologists today and has the advantages of accounting for the *laws of color mixing* and of *parsimony* over other theories that advance the involvement of more than three receptor processes in the visual experience. However, the *Young-Helmholtz theory* does have a number of difficulties associated with it: accounting fully for the experiences of *color-blind* individuals [cf., *Daltonism*, which is red-green color blindness, and is named after the English chemist John Dalton (1766-1844) who had it and first described it]; accounting for the *brightness* functions of both normal and color-blind persons; and accounting for contrary evidence that shows that the *blue component* in color vision has different properties than either the red or green components. See also ACCOMMODATION, LAW/PRINCIPLE OF; COLOR MIXTURE, LAWS/THEORY OF; COLOR VISION, THEORIES/LAWS OF; SPECIFIC NERVE ENERGIES, LAW OF.

REFERENCES

Young, T. (1801). On the mechanism of the eye. *Philosophical Transactions of the Royal Society of London, 91*, 23-88.

Young, T. (1807). On the theory of light and colours. In W. Savage (Ed.), *Lectures in natural philosophy*. Vol. 2. London: Joseph Johnson, St. Paul's Church Yard.

Helmholtz, H. von (1852). On the theory of compound colours. *Philosophy Magazine, 4*, 519-534.

Helmholtz, H. von (1892). Versuch das psychophysische gesetz auf die farben unterschiede trichromatischer augen anzuwenden. *Zeitschrift fur Psychologie und Physiologie Sinnesorgange, 3*, 1-20.

YOUNG'S COLOR VISION THEORY.
See YOUNG-HELMHOLTZ COLOR VISION THEORY.

Y, THEORY. See LEADERSHIP, THEORIES OF.

Z

ZAJONC'S AROUSAL AND CONFLU-ENCE THEORIES. The Polish-born social psychologist Robert B. Zajonc (1923-) proposed the following generalization concerning *social facilitation* (i.e., the tendency to perform a task better in the presence of others than when alone) and *social interference* (i.e., a decline in performance when observers are present): the presence of others *facilitates* performance of *dominant* (i.e., simple, habitual, or instinctive) responses and *interferes* with performance of *nondominant* (i.e., complex, nonhabitual, or unnatural) responses (cf., *audience effect* or *spectator effect* - the influence of passive onlookers/spectators on a person's task performance; *next-in-line effect* - refers to a decrement in recall for an event immediately preceding an anticipated public performance; and *coaction effect* - is the influence on a person's task performance of the presence of other people engaging in the same activity). In the *drive theory of social facilitation*, Zajonc explains both *facilitation* and *interference effects* by linking them to the more general phenomenon of the effect of high *arousal* (drive) on performance. That is, high arousal typically improves performance of simple or well-learned tasks and worsens performance of complex or poorly-learned tasks (cf., Yerkes & Dodson, 1908). According to *Zajonc's theory*, the main effect of the presence of others is to increase *arousal* after which easy responses are easier, and difficult responses become more difficult (cf., *compresence effect* - is an arousal effect generated by other people being present where, depending on conditions, performance is influenced either positively or negatively). Studies of the influence of others' presence and the effects of being observed on one's performance go back to the late 1800s (cf., Triplett, 1898) and the early 1900s (cf., Allport, 1920), and report *social facilitation* in some experiments but *social interference* in other studies. *Zajonc's theory* is able to explain both types of outcome, suggesting that the mere presence of

others who are members of one's own species may enhance *arousal* innately. *Social facilitation* has been observed in athletes, children, chickens, and even cockroaches (that learn a maze faster if watched by other roaches). Other theorists, however, explain such *arousal* in somewhat different terms; for instance, in terms such as *evaluation anxiety* (cf., Geen, 1991), *self-perception* of one's skill at the task (cf., Sanna, 1992), and *self-consciousness* (cf., Baumeister & Showers, 1986). Zajonc's explanation for *social facilitation* is based in the context of a broader *theory of emotion*, in which a person may have an emotional reaction to a stimulus without any corresponding cognitive reaction; this theoretical approach differs from the *two-factor theory of emotion* that posits a two-step self-perception process where one first experiences physiological arousal and seeks an explanation for it, and then it is the labeling of the arousal that is experienced as the emotion. Zajonc has theorized, also concerning the influence of environmental factors on human intelligence, in particular the relationship between birth order and intelligence (cf., *birth order effect* – conjecture that first-born children, and only-children, tend to be high achievers; also, the larger the family size, the lower the average IQ of the children). In attempting to answer the finding of several studies that first-borns tend to have higher IQs than second-borns, who tend to have higher IQs than third-borns, and so on, *Zajonc's confluence theory* suggests that each individual's intellectual growth depends to an important degree on the intellectual environment in which the child develops. Zajonc's *confluence theory* and his interpretation of the correlation between birth order and intelligence, however, are not universally accepted, and have been the source of heated debate. See also ACTIVATION/ AROUSAL THEORY; COGNITIVE THEORIES OF EMOTIONS; MERE EXPOSURE EFFECT; SCHACHTER-SINGER'S THEORY OF EMOTIONS; YERKES-DODSON LAW.

REFERENCES

Triplett, N. (1898). The dynamogenic factors in peacemaking and competition. *American Journal of Psychology, 9,* 507-533.

642

Yerkes, R. M., & Dodson, J. D. (1908). The relation of strength of stimulus to rapidity of habit formation. *Journal of Comparative Neurology and Psychology, 18*, 459-482.

Allport, F. (1920). The influence of group upon association and thought. *Journal of Experimental Psychology, 3*, 159-182.

Rasmussen, E. (1939). Social facilitation. *Acta Psychologica, 4*, 275-294.

Zajonc, R. B. (1965). Social facilitation. *Science, 149*, 269-274.

Quarter, J., & Marcus, A. (1971). Drive level and the audience effect: A test of Zajonc's theory. *Journal of Social Psychology, 83*, 99-105.

Zajonc, R. B., & Markus, G. (1975). Birth order and intellectual development. *Psychological Review, 82*, 74-88.

Zajonc, R. B. (1976). Family configuration and intelligence: Variations in scholastic aptitude scores parallel trends in family size and the spacing of children. *Science, 192*, 226-236.

Zajonc, R. B. (1983). Validating the confluence model. *Psychological Bulletin, 93*, 457-480.

Zajonc, R. B. (1985). Emotion and facial efference: A theory reclaimed. *Science, 228*, 15-21.

Baumeister, R., & Showers, C. (1986). A review of paradoxical performance effects: Choking under pressure in sports and mental tests. *European Journal of Social Psychology, 16*, 361-383.

Geen, R. (1991). Social motivation. *Annual Review of Psychology, 42*, 377-399.

Sanna, L. (1992). Self-efficacy theory: Implications for social facilitation and social loafing. *Journal of Personality and Social Psychology, 62*, 774-786.

ZANFORLIN ILLUSION. See APPENDIX A.

ZEIGARNIK EFFECT/PHENOMENON. = unaccomplished action effect = resumption of interrupted action effect. This phenomenon is the seemingly paradoxical assertion by the Russian female psychologist Blyuma V. Zei-garnik (1900-1988) that the recall of interrupted/unfinished tasks is superior to the recall of completed tasks. Zeigarnik is noted for her doctoral dissertation that was the first formal test of Kurt Lewin's *Gestalt theory* concerning the idea that attainment of a goal relieves tension. In a typical experimental procedure for the *Zeigarnik effect*, participants are asked to perform 15-22 different tasks; some tasks are manual (e.g., stringing beads), and some are mental (e.g., solving puzzles). On half of the activities, participants are allowed to continue until completion, but on the other half of the tasks they are asked to stop and move on to a new activity. Following this phase, the task materials are removed, and the participants are asked to recall some of the activities that they had just experienced. Results of this simple procedure typically show that the number of incomplete or unfinished tasks (called "I") that are recalled is higher than the number of completed tasks (called "C"). A calculated ratio, using "I/C," was always greater than 1.0 in Zeigarnik's experiments. In some cases, the I/C ratio was related, subsequently, to a person's "ambition" level. Among the possible alternative explanations that may account for the *Zeigarnik effect* are that participants may implicitly assume that the interrupted tasks will be completed at a later time; task interruption may set up a new motive involving resentment toward the interrupter, which causes better memory; the interruption of a task emphasizes that task; the participant may attempt to achieve "closure" concerning the incompleted tasks; participants' personal histories in being rewarded for attending to unsolved problems may lead to better memory; and fulfillment and completion may be defined differently by different persons in terms of their own sense of satisfaction. Studies show that the *Zeigarnik effect* is less likely to occur if the participant is ego-involved in the task, and is most likely to occur if the individual has a genuine level of aspiration in the interrupted task (i.e., the task is possible of being achieved ultimately). Other studies indicate that the differential effect between the I and C tasks seems to be quite temporary (typically being lost over a period of 24 hours), and does not occur with all types of tasks. See also

GESTALT THEORY/LAWS; LEWIN'S FIELD THEORY.

REFERENCES

Zeigarnik, B. (1927). Untersuchungen zur handlungsund affekpsychologie. Herausgegeben von K. Lewin, 3. Das behalten erledigter und unereledigter handlung. *Psychologische Forschung*, *9*, 1-85.

Freeman, G. (1930). Changes in tonus during completed and interrupted mental work. *Journal of General Psychology*, *4*, 309-333.

Pachauri, A. (1936). A study of Gestalt problems in completed and interrupted tasks. *British Journal of Psychology*, *27*, 170-180.

Prentice, W. (1944). The interruption of tasks. *Psychological Review*, *51*, 329-340.

Glixman, A. (1949). Recall of completed and incompleted activities under varying degrees of stress. *Journal of Experimental Psychology*, *39*, 281-295.

Reeve, J., Cole, S., & Olson, B. (1986). The Zeigarnik effect and intrinsic motivation: Are they the same? *Motivation and Emotion*, *10*, 233-245.

ZEILER'S THEORY. See SPENCE'S THEORY.

ZEISING'S PRINCIPLE.

This generalization refers to a term - *golden section* - that was used by the German mathematician Adolph Zeising (1810-1876), and called attention to the aesthetic value of the geometric relationships inherent in a rectangle. That is, the *golden section* is the division of a line or area into two parts, or the relations of the sides of a rectangle, in such a manner that the ratio of the smaller to the larger equals the ratio of the larger to the whole. This *principle of proportion* was investigated experimentally by the German physicist/mathematician/philosopher Gustav Fechner (1801-1887) in the area called *experimental aesthetics*. Fechner's seminal research on preferences for shapes gave experimental aesthetics its "reductionistic" quality (i.e., examining aesthetics from "below" from a structural point of view). Investigations have been made by researchers for an *aesthetic formula* (cf., Birkhoff, 1933). In one case, the aesthetic measure (M) of balance or unity (represented by the number 1) is defined as the ratio of order (O) to complexity (C): in the resulting formula, $M = O/C$, the various components of an artwork can be physically specified, measured, and evaluated where the closer it is to 1, the more "harmonious" the object. *Zeising's principle* attempts to answer the persistent question in aesthetics concerning the dimensions of preferred shapes such as encompassed in the concept of the *golden section*. See also EYE PLACEMENT PRINCIPLE; FECHNER'S LAW; GESTALT THEORY/LAWS; WEBER'S LAW.

REFERENCES

Zeising, A. (1855). *Aesthetische forschungen*. Frankfort, Germany: Breitkopf & Haertel.

Zeising, A. (1884). *Der goldene schnitt*. Leipzig: Breitkopf & Haertel.

Fechner, G. (1897). *Vorschule der aesthetik*. Leipzig: Breitkopf & Haertel.

Archibald, R. C. (1920). Notes on the logarithmic spiral, golden section, and the Fibonacci series. In J. Hambridge (Ed.), *Dynamic symmetry*. New Haven, CT: Yale University Press.

Birkhoff, G. (1933). *Aesthetic measure*. Cambridge, MA: Harvard University Press.

Valentine, C. (1962). *The experimental psychology of beauty*. London: Methuen.

Zusne, L. (1970). *Visual perception of form*. New York: Academic Press.

Hintz, J. M., & Nelson, T. M. (1976). Golden section: Reassessment of the perimetric hypothesis. *American Journal of Psychology*, *83*, 126-129.

Child, I. (1978). Aesthetic theories. In E. Carterette & M. Friedman (Eds.), *Handbook of perception*. Vol. 10. New York: Academic Press.

Plug, C. (1980). The golden section hypothesis. *American Journal of Psychology*, *93*, 367-387.

McWhinnie, H. J. (1987). A review of selected research on the golden section hypothesis. *Visual Arts Research*, *13*, 73-84.

Davis, S. T., & Jahnke, J. C. (1991). Unity and the golden section: Rules for aesthetic choice? *American Journal of Psychology, 104*, 257-277.

ZEITGEIST THEORY. See NATURALISTIC THEORY OF HISTORY.

ZEN BUDDHISM. See BUDDHISM/ZEN BUDDHISM, DOCTRINE OF.

ZENO, ACHILLES ARGUMENT OF. The Greek philosopher Zeno of Elea (early 5th century B.C.) was the author/originator of the *sophism* (i.e., a clever and plausible but fallacious argument or form of reasoning) called the *Achilles argument* to prove, theoretically, that motion is impossible. According to the argument, Achilles (who was the fastest possible runner) could never overtake the tortoise (who was the slowest moving animal) if the tortoise had ever so short a start. The reasoning behind the argument is that because the distance between them consists of an infinite series of parts, and when Achilles, by traversing one of these parts, comes to where the tortoise was, the latter will always have gone further. A variation on Zeno's famous "Achilles-tortoise" philosophical *paradox* or scenario is the equally-paradoxical or specious argument that an arrow shot from a bow will never truly reach its target because, theoretically, it will always have gone only half the existing distance to the target at any given moment. See also PROBLEM-SOLVING AND CREATIVITY STAGE THEORIES.
REFERENCE
Baldwin, J. M. (Ed.) (1901-1905). *Dictionary of philosophy and psychology*. New York: Macmillan.

ZIPF'S LAW. This proposition was developed by the American philologist George Kingsley Zipf (1902-1950), and states that an equilibrium exists between *uniformity* and *diversity* in examining various psychological phenomena. In general, *Zipf's law* describes the relationship between the frequency with which a certain event occurs (e.g., the frequency of usage of a word in a language) and the number of events that occur with that frequency. In particular, *Zipf's law* states that

when examining certain aspects of language, it is predicted that there are a very large number of very *short* words (e.g., "auto") that occur with high frequency and progressively fewer *longer* words (e.g., "automobile") that occur with lower frequency. Zipf hypothesized that such uniformities or "tendencies" in language usage are the result of a biological *principle of least effort*. Although this latter notion has not been validated by other researchers (these uniformities are now known to be merely the necessary result of particular stochastic processes), Zipf's *linguistic hypothesis* that frequency of word usage and word length are inversely related seems to be a pervasive phenomenon of language usage, especially in the present age of computers and the perceived need for rapid communication. See also LEAST EFFORT, PRINCIPLE OF.
REFERENCES
Zipf, G. K. (1935). *The psycho-biology of language*. Boston: Houghton Mifflin.
Zipf, G. K. (1945). The repetition of words, time-perspective, and semantic balance. *Journal of General Psychology, 32*, 127-148; *33*, 251-256.

ZOLLNER/POGGENDORFF ILLUSION. See APPENDIX A.

ZOMBIISM THEORY. The phenomenon of *zombiism* (i.e., a corpse-like/robot-like human being believed to belong to the "living dead," who is buried alive and resurrected by witchdoctors in order to carry out their directives, existing in particular in the voodoo cult of Haiti and various West African religions) has been studied by the Irish-Canadian ethnobiologist E. Wade Davis (1953-). In his *zombiism theory*, Davis suggests that in the secret cult activities the ingestion by the victim of a barely sub-lethal dosage of a poison/magic powder (consisting of such substances as pufferfish and other ingredients containing the neurotoxin tetrodotoxin) results in a deep coma resembling death. The witchcraft ceremonies also typically involve a live burial where, along with the poison, extensive neurological damage usually occurs in the victim. Later, when the victim is exhumed/revived, he or she typically has few intact memories or mental capacities, shows no coherent speech, demonstrates a shuffling gait, and has a blank facial expression stereotypical of a "zombie" who is now ready to carry out the biddings of the sorcerer/priest/witchdoctor in charge of the social group or community. Scientific observers of behaviors in primitive cultures, of course, are quick to point out that some apparently zombie-like individuals are simply unfortunate persons with severe/profound mental retardation, and not necessarily victims of a cultish ceremony conducted to create zombies. See also CULTURE-BOUND PHENOMENA/EFFECTS; LABELING/DEVIANCE THEORY; PSYCHOPATHOLOGY, THEORIES OF.

REFERENCE

Davis, E. W. (1985/1997). *The serpent and the rainbow*. New York: Simon & Schuster.

ZONE/STAGE THEORIES OF COLOR VISION. *Zone-* or *stage-theories of color vision* include several theories that give separate accounts of the processes at various stages or levels of the visual mechanism, such as receptor-, retina-, and optic nerve fiber-levels. Examples of the *zone/stage theories of color vision* include propositions by J. von Kries, E. Schrodinger, G. E. Muller, E. Q. Adams, and D. B. Judd. All of these complex *stage theories* employ the German physiologist Ewald Hering's (1834-1918) original notion of *opposing components* in the description of the final stage. See also COLOR VISION, THEORIES/LAWS; HERING-HURVICH-JAMESON COLOR VISION THEORY.

REFERENCES

Hering, E. (1872-1874). *Zur lehre vom lichtsinne*. Vienna: Gerolds.

Kries, J. von (1905). Die gesichtsempfindungen. In W. Nagel (Ed.), *Handbuch des physiologisches menschens*. Vol. 3. Braunschweig: Vieweg.

Schrodinger, E. (1920). Grundlinien einer theorie der farbenmetrik im tagessehen. *Annales de Physiks*, *63*, 397-456, 481-520.

Adams, E. Q. (1923). A theory of color vision. *Psychological Review*, *30*, 56-76.

Muller, G. E. (1930). Uber die farbenempfingungen. *Zeitschrift fur Psychologie und Physiologie Sinnesorgange*, *17*, 1-430; *18*, 435-647.

Judd, D. B. (1951). Basic correlates of the visual stimulus. In S. S. Stevens (Ed.), *Handbook of experimental psychology*. New York: Wiley.

Z, THEORY. See LEADERSHIP, THEORIES OF.

ZWAARDEMAKER SMELL SYSTEM. See OLFACTION/SMELL, THEORIES OF.

ZYZ. The term *zyz* is a trigram or *nonsense syllable* (of the form "consonant-vowel-consonant," or CVC) representative of the experimentally-controlled meaningless "nonwords" and verbal material originally used by the German psychologist Hermann von Ebbinghaus (1850-1909) in his classical memory studies around 1878. *Nonsense syllables* (still used today in psychological laboratories) were constructed, initially, in order to provide materials to participants in memory experiments that are relatively homogeneous, evoke very few mental associations or little prior learning, and are easily partitioned into objectively equal units amenable to quantitative research methodology. Just as Horace B. English and Ava C. English, and Raymond J. Corsini, chose this particular bogus *nonsense syllable* of *zyz* as a suitable *final entry* in their respective dictionaries, it seems appropriate that I do likewise (!). See also FORGETTING/MEM-ORY, THEORIES OF;

REFERENCES

Ebbinghaus, H. von (1885/1964). *Uber das gedachtnis*. Leipzig: Duncker/New York: Dover.

English, H. B., & English, A. C. (1958/1976). *A comprehensive dictionary of psychological and psychoanalytical terms*. New York: David McKay.

Corsini, R. J. (2002). *The dictionary of psychology*. New York: Brunner-Routledge.

Appendix A – Auditory, Cognitive, Tactile, and Visual Illusions/Effects

This appendix provides a listing, along with brief definitions, of various auditory, cognitive, tactile, and visual illusions/effects. Among the *illusions/effects* (i.e., the irresistible or unavoidable misperception of a stimulus object, image, experience, or event) in the *auditory* sense modality are the following:

Audiogravic and *audiogyral illusions/effects* [these were described and studied by the German-born American psychologist Hans Wallach (1904-1998)] - *audiogravic* refers to errors made in attempting to localize the source of a sound when the individual is deprived of visual cues and the body is tilted out of the upright position; *audiogyral* refers to an error in sound localization experienced by a blindfolded individual after he/she is rotated rapidly.

Auditory flutter fusion and *auditory flicker-fusion effect* - the lowest sound interruption frequency that causes a listener to stop hearing "auditory flutter" (i.e., the sensation of hearing an intermittent sound) and starts hearing a continuous sound; this is the *auditory* counterpart of the "critical flicker frequency/critical fusion frequency/flicker fusion frequency effect" in the *visual* sense modality where, in the latter, lights (instead of sounds) are used to determine threshold rates at which light from an intermittent/fluctuating source begins to be seen as continuous/fused rather than as intermittent.

Auditory fusion/binaural fusion - the sensation of hearing two or more sounds as a single sound, using either one ear or both ears (cf., the *precedence effect* - the sensation of hearing only the first of two sounds when the second sound is similar to the first one and follows it within 50 milliseconds).

Auditory masking effect - occurs when one sound obscures another sound, causing the absolute threshold of the first sound to increase and/or its perceived loudness to decrease; cf., *visual masking effect* [first described by the French psychologist Henri Pieron (1881-1964)] - a reduction/elimination of the detectability of a brief visual stimulus by the presentation of a second visual stimulus.

Auditory staircase illusion and *illusion of circular pitch* [first described by the American psychologist Roger N. Shepard (1924-)] - a misperception of musical tones where, in a sequence of tones moving up or down through the 12 tones of an octave that is played repeatedly, the listener hears a single sequence rising or descending endlessly instead of hearing a sequence of 12 tones being repeated.

Auditory suffix effect - a decrement in memory for a list of words that is caused by presenting (at the end of the list, during the learning process) extra words or speech sounds that were not required to be memorized by the learner.

Binaural shift effect - the sensation that occurs when two low-pitched tones having frequencies close to each other are presented separately to one's ears, giving one the perception of a single sound source whose location seems to swing periodically from one side to the other.

Delayed auditory feedback effect - a laboratory procedure where a person speaks into a microphone connected to a tape recorder, and the speech is played back to the speaker via headphones after a brief delay of about one-fifth of a second; the effect on most speakers is a severe disruption of speech accompanied by slurring, stuttering, and an inability to produce intelligible words, especially if the speaker is "field dependent" (i.e., individuals with a weak propensity to differentiate perceptions/experiences from their contexts or backgrounds, and who rely on external, airborne feedback for modulating their speech rather than on internal, bones-in-the-head vibrations for speech modulation, the latter constituting "field independent" speakers).

Equal-loudness contour effect - a procedure described by the American acoustical scientist Harvey Fletcher (1884-1981) and the American engineer Wilden A. Munson (1902-1982), also called the *Fletcher-Munson contour* or the *isophonic contour*, where a plot of the loudness matching of tones (varying in frequency across the audible range) is made with intensity levels (decibel sound pressure level), causing them to sound equally as loud to a listener as a standard comparison tone.

Melodic/semitone/tritone paradox effects - sensory phenomena in the perception of musical tones where ambiguous octave notes (lacking cues to determine pitch) may be perceived as converging/diverging and/or rising/falling, depending upon the particular stimulus tones, chords, and musical intervals employed.

Missing fundamental illusion - a misperception of pitch that occurs when a set of overtones/harmonics associated with a particular fundamental frequency (pure tone with the lowest frequency forming a component of a complex tone) are presented to a person (without the actual fundamental frequency), where the listener hears the sound as having the pitch of the fundamental even though the fundamental frequency was not present in the stimulus-sound.

Phonemic restoration/phantom phoneme effect [this effect was first described by the American psychologist Richard M. Warren (1925-)] - an auditory misperception that occurs when a basic speech sound or single phoneme (or even a whole syllable) is deleted from a tape-recorded sentence and is replaced by a cough or some other intrusive sound; when the "treated" recording is played, listeners perceive the missing phoneme (or syllable) as clearly as if it had actually been present.

Ventriloquism effect - sound is misperceived as emanating from a source that moves appropriately (as in a puppet or dummy), but that actually comes from a different invisible source (as via a ventriloquist who speaks without moving his/her lips).

Verbal transformation effect [this effect was first described by the American psychologist Richard M. Warren (1925-) and the English psychologist Richard L. Gregory (1923-)] - this phenomenon is produced when an auditory stimulus such as a word or phrase is repeated many times (say, 360 times in three minutes) on a loop of audiotape; in this case, the person typically experiences distortions and hears about 30 changes/alterations involving about six different word forms; the effect appears to be age-related with the most distortions experienced by young adult listeners.

Many of the powerful, "irresistible," and "unavoidable" *illusions/effects* in the *visual* and *tactual* sense modalities are eponymous, based on the individual(s)/researcher(s) who first described or published them. Among the eponymous *visual/geometric*, *motion*, and *tactual illusions/effects* are the following:

Aristotle illusion/experiment [named after the Greek philosopher Aristotle (384-322 B.C.) who first described it over 2,000 years ago] - a tactile illusion that is produced when one closes one's eyes and, with two fingers of one hand crossed, a small object such as a pencil is pressed into the cleft between the tips of the crossed fingers, one has the sensation of touching two objects rather than one; the current explanation for this illusion is that when the fingers are crossed, the outsides of two fingers are touched simultaneously and, based on normal conditions and prior experience, such stimulation requires the presence of two separate objects.

Baldwin illusion [named after the American psychologist James M. Baldwin (1861-1934)] - a misperception of linear length that occurs when a line spanning the distance between two very large squares appears to be shorter than a line of equal length spanning the distance between two very smaller squares.

Bourdon illusion [named after the French sensory/perceptual psychologist Benjamin B. Bourdon (1869-1943)] - is a visual/angular misperception that results when two triangles, *abd* and *bce* (having angles of 90-degrees at *a* and *c*, and 10-degrees at *b*) are placed in a way that they touch at point *b* (where the sides *ab* and *bc* are collinear, and where the line *abc* tilts 10-degrees), the line *abc* appears to bend inward in the direction of *e* and *d*; this effect is an example of the generic *contrast illusion* in which the angle, curve, distance, or some other characteristic of a visual stimulus is altered by the juxtaposition of some adjacent angle, curve, distance, etc., and where the illusion is created via the contrasting effect of size, position, direction, etc., of the adjacent figure.

Coriolis illusion [named after the French physicist Gustave Gaspard Coriolis (1792-1843)] - is a motion illusion of rolling (also known as *cross-coupling effect*), causing pilot disorientation or dizziness; occurs during a prolonged turn where the pilot's head is tilted in a plane/line other than the aircraft's angle.

Craik-O'Brien effect [named after the Scottish philosopher/psychologist Kenneth J. W. Craik (1914-1945) and the American physicist Vivian O'Brien (1924-)] - a visual illusion produced by separating two identical grey-colored areas with a blurred contour consisting of a narrow light strip merging into a narrow dark strip, and resulting in the whole grey area adjacent to the light strip to appear as much lighter than the grey area adjacent to the dark strip; also called the *Cornsweet illusion* - named after the American cognitive researcher Tom Norman Cornsweet (1929-) who investigated it extensively; cf., *Mach band(s)* [named after the Austrian physicist/philosopher/psychologist Ernst Mach (1838-1916)] - is an illusory light or dark strip along the edge of a blurred contour between light and dark areas of an image and, thus, is a phenomenon of brightness contrast produced when a dimly illuminated area merges into a more brightly illuminated area, and where the perceived change in brightness is much sharper than the actual change in light intensity and two bands of dark and light are perceived on either side of the gradation.

Delboeuf illusion [named after the Belgian physicist/psychologist Joseph Jean Delboeuf (1831-1896)] - a concentric-circles/relative-size misperception of the apparent change of size in one of two identical circles if a larger circle surrounds it; cf., a similar illusion, *Uznadze illusion* [named after the Georgian psychologist Dmitrii Uznadze (1886-1933)] - consists of a printed figure of two identical, adjacent circles, one enclosed in a larger concentric circle; when looking at the smaller circles alternately with the larger circle, the enclosed circle appears to be smaller than the other small circle.

Duncker's distance paradox/effect [named after the German psychologist Karl Duncker (1903-1940) - results if a dot is in a rectangle, and if the rectangle is moved, one gains the false impression that both the dot and the rectangle move to a greater distance, when summed, than is the actual movement that takes place.

Ebbinghaus/Titchener illusion [named after the German psychologist Hermann von Ebbinghaus (1850-1909) and the English psychologist Edward B. Titchener (1867-1927)]-a figure-ground, comparative-circles/relative-size misperception,

Ehrenstein brightness and square illusions [named after the German psychologist Walter Ehrenstein (1899-1961)]-are two visual illusions where, in one (brightness), a lattice of black lines with their intersection regions erased appears to have white disks with illusory contours at the intersections; and, in the other (square), a square superimposed on a fan-like pattern of diverging lines appears to be distorted into a trapezoid shape.

Franklin effect/experiment [named after the American statesman/scientist Benjamin Franklin (1706-1790) - in 1765, Franklin showed that the afterimage is *positive* on the dark field of the closed eyes, but *negative* on a light field (of white paper) when the eyes are open.

Fraser spiral/twisted-cord illusion [named after the Scottish psychologist and physician James Fraser (1863-1936)]- a twisted-cord/concentric circles misperception occurring against a checkered background; in this illusion, what appears compellingly and mysteriously to be a spiral is actually a series of concentric circles that have been placed on a checkerboard-patterned background.

Gatti illusion [named after the Italian psychologist Alessandro Gatti (?-1938)] - when a display is presented in which a number of equally spaced, concentric equilateral triangles have a square superimposed on them, one gets the false visual perception that the side of the square facing one of the apexes of the triangle appears to be longer than the side of the square that is parallel with one of the triangle's sides.

Helmholtz chessboard illusion [named after the German physiologist, physicist, and psychologist Hermann Ludwig Ferdinand von Helmholtz (1821-1894)] - is a hyperbolic chessboard figure used to demonstrate the curving of ocular direction lines in the visual globe; a misperception of depth results from viewing the chessboard when it is placed in a circle, with the black and white quadrangles shown progressively larger toward the periphery to compensate for the distortion cast upon the retina's periphery, and viewed as if in perspective. The *Helmholtz illusion/irradiation illusion* - a figure-ground misperception of size when comparing a light square on a dark background with a dark square on a light background; or cases where the light areas of an image tend to appear larger than dark areas.

Hering illusion [named after the German physiologist and psychologist Ewald Hering (1834-1918)] - a misperception of a pair of parallel straight lines when superimposed on the center of a series of straight lines arranged in a manner similar to the radiating spokes of a wheel.

Hermann grid illusion [named after the German physiologist Ludimar Hermann (1838-1914)] - a misperception caused by a block pattern of ten-by-ten small black squares separated by narrow white channels where "illusory grey spots" are perceived at the channel's intersections.

Jastrow illusion [named after the Polish-born American psychologist Joseph Jastrow (1863-1944)] - a misperception of size involving the juxtaposition of two identical tapering annular/ring segments.

Kanizsa triangle illusion [named after the Trieste-born Italian psychologist Gaetano Kanizsa (1913-1993)] - a visual illusion of a triangle but without a corresponding retinal image of an actual triangle, which is produced by three dark "Pac-Man" type icons that are situated so that they perceptually form the corners of an imaginary triangle and are oriented to give the sensation that they are disks with segments occluded by the vertices of the triangle.

Landolt circles/rings [named after the Swiss-born German physical chemist Hans H. Landolt (1831-1910)] - a visual acuity test containing circles with a tiny part of each circle's circumference missing, and easily perceived as complete circles in spite of them not being truly closed figures/circles; these figures illustrate the "closure" grouping law, and the phenomenon of "pragnanz," in Gestalt perception psychology.

Lipps' illusion [named after the German philosopher/psychologist Theodor Lipps (1851-1914)] - is a visual misperception under conditions where given a figure consisting of a circle - with the apexes/tips of short-sided right angles tangent to the circle at 12, 3, 6, and 9 o'clock positions - at those certain points on the circle, the circle mistakenly appears to be flattened.

Margaret Thatcher illusion [devised by the British psychologist Peter G. Thompson (1950-) who used a stimulus-photograph of the United Kingdom Prime Minister Margaret Thatcher] - the misperception of a photographed face as natural when it is turned upside down (and the eyes and mouth of the face are manipulated to be inverted, also, relative to the face) and, when turned right-side up, the face appears grotesque or unnatural; this phenomenon is related indirectly to the *differential inversion effect* [described by the American psychologist Robert Yin (1931-)] - is the relatively greater *decrease* in recognizability of human faces (as compared to images of other objects) when the face/photo is inverted.

Morinaga misalignment illusion [named after the Japanese psychologist Shiro Morinaga (1908-1964)] - a misperception of alignment involving three or more arrow-heads (some pointing right, and some pointing left) that are actually aligned with their apexes/tips in vertical straight lines.

Muller-Lyer illusion [named after the German sociologist/psychiatrist Franz C. Muller-Lyer (1857-1916)] - a famous misperception of comparative linear size due to arrowheads that are pointing inward versus outward on the ends of two objectively equal-sized lines.

Munsterberg illusion [named after the German-born American psychologist Hugo Munsterberg (1863-1916)] - an "eccentric chessboard figure" misperception involving a pattern of alternating columns of staggered light and dark rectangles whose rows are actually horizontally aligned but appear to be non-horizontal and non-parallel; related to the *Munsterberg illusion* are the more recent variants called the *café-wall illusion* (1972), the *hollow squares illusion* (1980) - also called the *Taylor-Woodhouse illusion* [named after the English optometrists Stephen P. Taylor (1951-) and J. Margaret Woodhouse (1948-)], and the *lavatory-wall illusion* (1987), all of which involve, also, a misperception of alignment due to alternating, or specially treated, tiles/squares.

Necker cube illusion [named after the Swiss mineralogist Louis-Albert Necker (1786-1861) who observed reversals in line drawings depicting crystals] - this is a two-dimensional representation of a three-dimensional skeletal cube, or a simple line drawing of a transparent box/cube that appears to alternate between different spatial orientations when viewed continuously, and is classified as an "ambiguous/oscillating/reversible" figure (i.e., an image or figure that appears to oscillate or flip involuntarily between several possible alternative), where one interpretation/perception excludes the other(s) while it persists, and where the figure and ground of the image appear to switch or reverse positions; cf., "impossible figures" which are drawings or other representations of objects that could not exist in actual three-dimensional space, such as the figures painted by the Dutch artist Maurits C. Escher (1898-1970) and the Swedish artist Oscar Reutersvard (1915-), or figures demonstrating "perspective reversal" (i.e., a perceptual change that occurs in the apparent spatial orientation of a depicted object).

Orbison illusion [named after the American psychologist William D. Orbison (1912-1952)] - a misperception of shape when a simple geometric figure such as a square or circle is overlaid on a pattern of concentric circles or radiating lines (all having a common center point); the sides of the square or circle mistakenly appear to be concave.

Ouchi illusion (named after the Japanese graphic artist Hajime Ouchi) - a misperception of relative motion that occurs when a checkered pattern of small black and white rectangles (containing a circular area in which the rectangles are positioned at right angles relative to those in the rest of the figure) is moved by turning the head/eyes or the page on which the figure is printed.

Plateau spiral/Talbot-Plateau spiral [named after the Belgian physicist Joseph A. F. Plateau (1801-1883) and the English physicist William H. F. Talbot (1800-1877)] - a spiral figure that is attached to a circular disk and, when rotated, gives the illusion of expanding continuously from its center, or contracting towards its center, depending on the direction of rotation; if one observes the rotating spiral for several seconds, then looks at a blank surface, it produces an opposite motion aftereffect called the "spiral aftereffect."

Poggendorff/Zollner illusion [named after the German physicist Johann C. Poggendorff (1796-1877) and the German astronomer Friedrich Zollner (1834-1882)] - a misperception of linear continuity when a diagonal straight line is interrupted by a rectangle that occludes the middle part of the line, and appears to be displaced from its straight-line path (Poggendorff); and a visual misperception (also called the *herringbone illusion*) where parallel straight lines appear to diverge and converge, alternately, when the parallel lines are intersected by a "herringbone" pattern of oblique stripes (Zollner).

Ponzo illusion [named after the Italian psychologist Mario Ponzo (1882-1960)] - a misperception of linear size when two parallel lines of equal length are placed between a pair of converging lines (also called the *railway* or *railroad illusion* due to the similarity of the stimulus-lines configuration to perceptually converging railroad tracks).

Roelofs effect (named after the results of a study conducted in 1935 by the German vision researcher C. Roelofs) - is a visual-direction illusion in which if a large rectangular frame is viewed offset from the straight-ahead direction, and a small target is presented simultaneously, it is seen as being mislocalized in the opposite direction. Research indicates that there may also be a similar *Roelofs effect/illusion* in the auditory modality; however, audition apparently possesses only one representation of space, in contrast to the two (cognitive and sensorimotor) of the visual modality, and the auditory representation seems to correspond most closely to the cognitive system in vision.

Rubin figure/illusion [named after the Danish psychologist Edgar Rubin (1886-1951), also known as the *face-goblet illusion*, the *face-vase figure*, and the *reversible goblet*] - this is an *ambiguous figure* demonstrating a classical *figure-ground reversal* wherein one's perception of the figure alternates automatically between a goblet/vase and a pair of facial profiles in silhouette [cf., the *old woman/young girl figure*, also called the *wife/mistress figure*, a popular ambiguous figure that does not depend on figure-ground reversal, and which one may perceive *either* as a picture of an old woman/wife *or* as a young/mistress; the creation of this figure is often erroneously attributed to the American psychologist Edwin G. Boring (1886-1968) who published it in 1930, but it originally appeared on an anonymous German postcard in 1888].

Sander/Luckiesh parallelogram illusion [named after the German psychologist Friedrich Sander (1889-1971) and the American lighting engineer/psychologist Matthew Luckiesh (1883-1967)] - a misperception of linear length of two diagonal lines when a large parallelogram is specially constructed so that two long diagonals of *equal* length are positioned in two smaller *unequally* sized parallelograms that are formed within the larger overall parallelogram.

Schroder staircase illusion [named after the German bacteriologist/psychologist Heinrich G. F. Schroder (1810-1885)] - an *ambiguous figure/drawing* showing a staircase that may be perceived either from an "above perspective" or from a "below perspective" [cf., the *staircase illusion/Penrose staircase*, an *impossible figure* devised by the English psychologist/geneticist Lionel S. Penrose (1898-1972) and his physicist/mathematician son Roger Penrose (1931-) - is a depiction of a staircase or flight of stairs in the form of a continuous loop that perceptually rises endlessly; and *Scripture's blocks*, named after the American-born German/English psychologist Edward W. Scripture (1864-1945) - is an *ambiguous figure/drawing* depicting a stack of blocks/cubes that may be perceived either as three cubes or as five cubes depending on how one interprets the available perspective cues, and by inverting the figure/drawing].

Spillman's illusion [named after the German psychologist Lothar A. D. Spillman (1938-)] - is a visual misperception variant of the *Hermann grid illusion* in which a grid is expanded to include both white squares and dark alleys and black squares and light alleys; additionally, there is a gradient of lightness in the alleys from top to bottom of the grid and from left to right. As a consequence, light regions in the grid are seen in the intersections of dark alleys on light background and dark regions at the intersections of light alleys on dark background when the alleys subtend a visual angle of 16-18 minutes at the observer's eye. In the *Spillman-Redies effect*, there is a tendency for the *Ehrenstein illusion* - when placed on a background of random dots (instead of brightness enhancement in the illusory areas) - to result in a misperception where the dots appear to be less densely packed, and the seemingly circular illusory areas appear to be positioned in front of the background.

Swindle's ghost [named after the American psychologist Percy Ford Swindle (1889- ?)] - refers to a positive afterimage that appears after a period of delay. The "ghost" appears under the following conditions: first, a primary stimulus is presented to the participant; then, his/her eye is illuminated for 40 minutes and is followed then by a period of 10 minutes in the dark. The "ghost" or afterimage appears when the eye subsequently is briefly illuminated through the closed lid.

Trapezoidal/Ames window [named after the American painter/psychologist Adelbert Ames, Jr. (1880-1955)] - this is a geometric/visual and movement illusion produced by viewing (frontally from a distance) a distorted window in the shape of a trapezoid (i.e., a quadrilateral having two parallel sides of unequal length); the display looks like a familiar rectangular window turned at an angle, and when it is rotated slowly on its vertical axis (and viewed with one eye at about ten feet, or with two eyes at about twenty feet), it appears mysteriously as a normal rectangular window that oscillates back and forth; one explanation for the oscillating trapezoid window is that we are familiar with rectangular windows in our everyday life and when such a rectangle is turned slowly on its axis we attempt perceptually to keep the longer side of the rectangle closer to us (so as not to violate what we know about rectangles) and this expectation/assumption causes perceptual oscillation in the window (i.e., on the rotating window, when the longer side of the trapezoid starts to recede, we involuntarily and automatically reverse, perceptually, the direction of the turning window so as to keep the shorter side always further away from us, and the longer side always closer to us); in the *Ames distorted room*, one discovers an experimental room so elaborately constructed that sizes and shapes seem to be distorted even though the room itself appears to be rectilinear when viewed with one eye (in a typical display, two people of equal size placed in different locations in the distorted room appear to be of unequal size).

Wundt illusion [named after the German psychologist Wilhelm M. Wundt (1832-1920)] - a misperception, similar to the *Hering illusion*, in which a pair of straight lines seems to be bowed inwards when overlayed on a pattern of lines converging to points on either side of them; Wundt also first described the *horizontal-vertical illusion*, a misperception of linear length that occurs when an inverted T (whose horizontal and vertical lines are actually equal in length) is viewed and the length of the vertical line is compared perceptually with the length of the horizontal line (in such a case, the vertical distance/length seems to be *greater* than an equal horizontal distance/length).

Zanforlin illusion [named after the Italian psychologist Mario Zanforlin (1934 -)] - a misperception of linear size/length (similar in conception to both the *Baldwin illusion* and the *Muller-Lyer illusion*) that occurs when comparing two equal-length straight lines, one of which has two small equally-sized circles at the extreme ends/outside the tips of the line, and the other has two small equally-sized circles just inside the ends, toward center, of that line.

Among the non-eponymous *visual*, *kinesthetic*, and *tactile illusions/effects* are the following:

Assimilative illusion - a visual misperception due to the influence of the surrounding environment on one's interpretation of stimuli; for example, the figure of an animal viewed in a dark alley may be perceived as larger and more ferocious than if the same animal were viewed in a well-lighted environment.

Associative/geometric illusion - a visual misperception in which one part of an object or image is viewed erroneously due to the effect of another object or image.

Contingent aftereffect - a visual anomaly resulting when a person looks at two objects of different colors (until adaptation occurs), and then looks at two neutral/gray objects, the individual tends to see the complementary color of the original colors if the original objects differed in form and if the gray objects were of the same form as the colored objects.

Corridor illusion - a visual, geometric, distorted-size perception that occurs when viewing two or more identical figures (such as equally-sized cylinders or equally-sized full-figures of a person) positioned along a continuum (such as sets of converging lines representing a long corridor and giving one the perception of depth) in such a way that the closer the figures (which are superimposed over the converging lines) seem to be to the point of origin of the corridor, the larger they appear (cf., *Ponzo illusion*); the *corridor illusion* is also called the *size-distance illusion*.

Filling-in illusion - a visual illusion of "filling-in" (i.e., the behavior of the visual system, or other sensory systems, when reacting to a stimulus having gaps where the missing stimulus information is guessed at, it is assumed that the missing data is the same as the information presented and generates a whole perceptual experience *without* the gaps - such as the "blind spot" in the retina where we "fill in" the information that is missing due to a lack of visual receptors at that site) consisting of a central black dot surrounded by a dark region that fades gradually into a lighter background; if one fixates with one eye on the dot, the dark region appears to vanish after a few seconds by a "filling-in" process, but the effect is eliminated if the dark region in the stimulus display is surrounded by a clearly defined ring or boundary.

Floating-finger illusion - the American psychologist Winford L. Sharp (1890-1975) described this illusion in 1928, which may be demonstrated by holding the forefingers of each hand horizontally about nine inches in front of the eyes, with the fingertips touching and the gaze focusing on a point in the distance, and then the fingertips are drawn apart about one-half an inch; the result is a "disembodied" finger having two tips, and seems to float in mid-air; the illusion may be shortened or lengthened by varying the distance between the fingertips.

Haunted swing illusion - a tactile/kinesthetic misperception that occurs when one is placed in a swing that seemingly oscillates/swings in the normal fashion but, in reality, the swing is motionless and the person is situated in a special room where the room itself, with its entire contents, is in motion. A similar effect may be experienced in the "haunted-mansion elevator" at Disneyland/Disneyworld where one misperceives movement upward and downward as if in a normal elevator but, in reality, the elevator is motionless and the surrounding four walls are in motion.

Hole-in-the-hand illusion - first described in 1871 by the American physician and geologist Joseph LeConte (1823-1901), this illusion is produced by holding a cardboard tube to the right (or left) eye, placing the edge of the left (or right) hand against the far end of the tube, and looking at a distant object or surface with both eyes open, with the result that the left (or right) hand appears to have a circular hole through it.

Inverted images effect/illusion - the American psychologist George M. Stratton (1865-1957) developed this approach in which special eyeglasses or goggles (that contain prisms that have the effect of inverting the images projected on the retinas and the visual images experienced by the wearer of the eyeglasses) initially have a disturbing effect on the wearer (turning the world "upside-down"), but then over a few days of adaptation in wearing the goggles, the wearer, once again, experiences the visual world in the normal way (i.e., the visual world automatically reverses/inverts itself and appears to be "right-side up" again).

Kinesthetic aftereffect illusion/hallucination - a misperception (analogous to a visual figural aftereffect) involving the muscle sense in which apparent weight/width is influenced by shifting from an accustomed weight/width to a heavier/wider one, resulting in the experience of comparative lightness/narrowness in the previously-held object; a *kinesthetic hallucination* is a false perception of one' body movement, occasionally observed in schizophrenics who sense that their heads are enlarging, or in amputees who feel movement in a missing, or "phantom," limb.

Kinetic aftereffect illusion/kinetic depth effect - in the former type of misperception, an illusion of motion is experienced in the reverse direction after stopping a prolonged motion; and in the latter type of illusion, there is a tendency for a two-dimensional visual pattern to appear to be three-dimensional when the viewer is in motion.

Oculogravic illusion - a misperception of movement that may be experienced in two situations: when being twirled around or tilted (as on a carnival ride), it is the feeling of being pulled away from the center of the movement; and when a vehicle's forward movement is suddenly increased (or decreased), the acceleration force combines with the gravity force to give the person the sensation of being pitched forward (or downward), accompanied by the individual's eyes rolling up (or down).

Oculogyral illusion - a motion/visual illusion that occurs when a person's body rotates in darkness along with the rotation of a small light at the same velocity as the body; the experience is created of the light moving horizontally with regard to the body whereby adaptation of the person's vestibular (balance/orientation/movement) system in the inner ear causes the individual to underestimate the velocity of the body's rotation; also, it is the person's experience of apparent movement of a faint light due to the individual's slight body movements, and nystagmus, that make it seem that the light has moved.

Point-light display illusion - the Swedish psychologist Gunnar Johansson (1911-) introduced this effect (also called "biological/biomechanical motion") whereby a moving image is created by attaching small light sources to the main joints of a person's body (shoulders, elbows, hips, wrists, ankles, and knees) and filming the individual as he or she moves about in a *darkened* room; the resultant image is irresistibly interpreted as a human body in motion, and affords easy recognition of gender differences in moving persons, as well as of the identification of familiar persons as indicated by their characteristic walks or gaits.

Pseudoscope/pseudophone effects - the English physicist/inventor Charles Wheatstone (1802-1875) - who invented the chronoscope (a device used to measure reaction time in psychological research), the stereoscope (a device that presents two slightly disparate pictures of the same scene to one's eyes, resulting in the experience of a binocular, three-dimensional image), and the Wheatstone bridge (the electrical circuit used for equating resistance, employed in measures such as galvanic skin response and other measurements involving electrical resistance) - designed an optical instrument to create visual illusions by transposing images between the right and left eyes and inverting distance-relations with the result that solid objects appear to be hollow and hollow objects seem to be solid. An analogous device for the auditory sense called the *pseudophone*, developed by the American psychologist Paul T. Young (1892-1978) and his associates, is used to study sound localization, and creates misperceptions in hearing via a "rams-horn type" of device that diverts to the right ear those sounds that would normally enter the left ear, and vice versa; for instance, one shouts something into the participant's right ear/right side of the head and, instead of turning to the right to identify the source of the sound, he erroneously turns to the left side to look for the sound source.

Rebound illusion - refers to the misperception one experiences when watching a moving object that stops suddenly, accompanied by the false impression that the object bounced back.

Rotating head/portrait illusion - a misperception in which a two-dimensional painting/photograph of a head appears to rotate in the same direction as the viewer who moves in front of it from one side to the other; this illusion is based on the experiential factor or assumption that if the head were actually three-dimensional, then the viewer moving from side to side would see it first from one side, then from the front, and finally from the other side, as if the head were rotating in the opposite direction, and the head, under such normal conditions, would appear to be stationary; however, with a two-dimensional painting/photograph of a head, the absence of any apparent contrary rotation seems to make the head rotate in the same direction as the viewer, with the result that the portrait's "stare" appears to the viewer to follow him or her.

Sensory saltation illusion - this tactile misperception (concerning *saltation* or the manner in which a nerve impulse is propagated along a nerve fiber), reported by the American sensory psychologist Frank A. Geldard (1906-1984), is produced when the forearm or other area of the body is given a light tap, and then a second and a third tap follow in rapid succession, where the second tap is given in the same spot as the first, and the third tap is given a few centimeters away; this illusion consists of the second tap as being felt clearly at a point somewhere between the first and the third taps; evidence shows that this tactile illusion arises at a higher level of the sensory system and not at the level of the skin.

Star illusion - a type of *irradiation illusion* (i.e., figures in which light areas of an image appear to be larger than dark areas) where a central dark six-pointed star is surrounded by six dark diamonds, the spaces between the star and each of the diamonds being equal to the diameter of the star and the longest diameter of a diamond, but the spaces appear to a viewer to be much larger.

Stroboscopic movement illusion/effect - is a misperception of movement, making a moving object (such as rotating wheels on a stagecoach in a movie) appear motionless, or even appear to move in reverse, by illuminating it with a series of intermittent light flashes (such as a light in a movie projector); also, a misperception of movement in which separate objects that are slightly different (such as a series of photographs of the same person, or a series of line drawings in different positions on the pages) appear to move continuously when viewed in rapid succession (as in single frames of motion picture film when they are shown rapidly).

Vertical-horizontal illusion - is a misperception of length, devised by the German physiologist/physicist/psychologist Hermann L. F. von Helmholtz (1821-1894), in which there is a tendency to view parallel lines of equal length that are placed in a *vertical* position as being longer/taller than the same parallel lines of equal length that are placed in a *horizontal* position.

Waterfall illusion/effect - a combined visual/apparent movement illusion, first discussed (in terms of rivers rather than waterfalls) by the Greek philosopher Aristotle (384-322 B.C.), that is produced by staring at a fixed point in a waterfall (or some other object in motion, such as a river) for a period of time, and then quickly looking away to a stationary object which, as a result, appears to move in an upwards direction (or, in the case of a rapidly-flowing river, after viewing the river, then looking at things that are really at rest but they seem now to be moving).

Among the types of *cognitive illusions* (i.e., misperceptions due to cognitive processing errors) are the following:

Capgras illusion/syndrome [named after the French physician Jean Marie J. Capgras (1873-1950) - is a clinically-based misidentification/misperception of people in one's environment, seen most frequently in patients diagnosed with paranoid schizophrenia; the individual asserts that one or more of the people around him/her are friends or relatives (the *illusion of a positive double*), or the individual may claim that one or more nearby persons have altered their appearance so that they are not to be recognized (the *illusion of a negative double*); this illusion/syndrome is known, also, as *Fregoli's phenomenon* [where the patient believes that a familiar person, who is believed often to be the patient's persecutor, has taken on different appearances; the name *Fregoli* derives from an Italian actor, mimic, impersonator, film-maker, and magician, Leopoldo Fregoli (1867-1936), who had an amazing skill in changing his facial appearance in a split second], and the Capgras illusion/syndrome itself is known, also, as *illusion of doubles*, or *illusion of false recognition*.

Experimentally-induced false memories - this refers to an experimental procedure which causes people to believe that they can remember experiences that did not occur in actuality.

Eyewitness misinformation effect - a cognitive illusion whereby misleading post-event information or data distorts an eyewitness's recall of an event.

Filled-duration illusion - a misperception of time whereby one experiences a specified period of time to seem to be longer when many events occur during it than when the duration/period is relatively empty of items or events.

Illusory correlations - a misperception based upon an apparent correlation that does not actually exist in a set of data or information being judged.

Memory illusion - refers to the situation where one person describes another person's experiences as personal to oneself, and involves the belief in the first person that events actually occurred, containing very precise detailed recollections of the event or experiences; "verbal overshadowing," or verbal labeling effects, may be present as well as reality monitoring, memory misattribution, and extra-memory effects.

Reid's movement illusion [named after the Scottish clergyman/philosopher Thomas Reid (1710-1796)] - is a combined cognitive/distance-estimation misperception that occurs when a person is instructed to move an object *horizontally* a certain distance, and then is asked to move the same object *vertically* the same distance; the individual typically moves the object (when comparing the two situations) with the result that the horizontal distance is *less* than the vertical distance.

Rumpelstiltskin effect/phenomenon - named after the fairy-tale character of the dwarf "Rumpelstiltskin" who had an influence over a miller's daughter until she gained power over him by learning his name; this effect refers to the tendency for one to have the erroneous impression of understanding something merely by the naming of it, and applies often - in the areas of psychiatry and psychopathology - to the naming of mental disorders.

Size-weight illusion - this is a combined cognitive and tactile illusion, also known as *Charpentier's illusion* (additionally, *Charpentier's illusion* refers to an *apparent movement illusion* called the *autokinetic effect* or *optokinetic effect* in which one perceives a stationary, small, low-intensity light - placed in a darkened room - to be moving; the sense of movement experienced in this illusion is caused by the person's own eye-movements and not by the light-stimulus) named after the French physician Augustin Charpentier (1852-1916) and studied, also, by the German psychologists Georg Elias Muller (1850-1934) and Friedrich Schumann (1863-1940); this illusion may be experienced by placing pieces of lead (or some other heavy substance) into two *different-sized* containers and packing sand around the pieces to prevent them from moving around in the containers, making sure that the actual *total weight* of each container is the *same*; the perceiver typically judges the smaller of the two containers to be heavier than the larger container; thus, the *size-weight illusion*, is an error in perception whereby a smaller object is judged to be heavier than another object of the same actual *weight* but having a much larger *size*, when the two objects are lifted by hand and compared.

Temperature illusion - a misperception of temperature that is demonstrated by the person's overestimation of the temperature of a warm environment when the body (or some part of the body) has been stimulated previously/recently by a less warm environment; the illusion occurs, as well, when dealing with a cold environment.

Temporal-lobe illusions/hallucinations - refers to misperceptions, and distorted perceptions, associated with temporal-lobe epileptic seizures; such illusions include distortions of the sizes or shapes of objects, periodic dreamlike thoughts, feelings of "déjà vu," the sound of "threatening" voices, and sensations/illusions of the head separating from the body.

Tycho illusion [named after the Danish astronomer Tycho Brahe (1546-1601)] - this is a cognitive illusion/misperception whereby Tycho's cosmological system appeared to be physically impossible to his assistant, the German astronomer Johannes Kepler (1571-1630); that is, in Tycho's cosmology (which avoided the then-heresy of displacing the Earth as the center of the universe), it was assumed that the planets revolve around the Sun but, also, that the Sun along with its orbiting planets revolves around a stationary Earth; when such a system is shown in diagram form, the orbits of Mars and the Sun intersect, causing the impression or illusion that these celestial bodies would actually collide which, of course, they do not.

Appendix B – Theories of Humor

This appendix gives a brief survey, arranged alphabetically, of a few dozen *humor theories* expressed epigrammatically with general, slogan-like, or descriptive labels; and indicates, as well, the major proponent(s) of each theory (cf., Bergler, 1956; Roeckelein, 2002).

Anti-annoyance theory or "laughter is nature's antidote for sympathy" theory of William McDougall (1871-1938).
Appendix to the separation-theory theory of Joseph Addison (1672-1719).
Bull-wit theory of laughter reflected by Sydney Smith (1771-1845).
Combined oscillation and contrast theory of Wilhelm Wundt (1832-1920).
Communicating joy theory of laughter by H. C. McComas (c. 1923).
Contrast/contradiction between two ideas theory of Theodor Vischer (1807-1887).
Correction of human follies theory of Ben Jonson (1572-1637) and John Dryden (1631-1700).
Degradation theory of Alexander Bain (1818-1903).
Deliverance from the constraint of rationality theory of Charles Renouvier (1815-1903).
Division theory (separating derision from laughter) of Baruch Spinoza (1632-1677).
Double affirmation theory of A. W. Bohtz (c. 1844).
Double-feature theory of "wise and foolish" laughter of Oliver Goldsmith (c. 1730-1774), John Ray (c. 1705), Wyndham Lewis (1886-1957), and Lord Chesterfield (1694-1773).
Duality theory of Charles Leveque (c. 1863).
Economy of psychic expenditure/saving of psychic energy theory of wit by Sigmund Freud (1856-1939).
Elevation theory of Christian W. Weisse (c. 1830).
Esthetic dead-end theory of laughter by Jean Paul Richter (1763-1825).
Expectation theory of Theodor Lipps (1851-1914).
Extension theory of laughter by C. W. Kimmins (c. 1928).
Five Italian Renaissance theories of laughter by Trissino (1478-1550), Maggi (c. 1560), Muzio (c. 1551), Minturno (c. 1564), and Scaliger (1484-1558).
For-each-otherness theory of R. Hermann Lotze (1817-1881).
Fountain of sound sense theory of George Meredith (1828-1909).
Goodness of the environment theory of laughter of Horace M. Kallen (c. 1909).
Good-old-times theory of laughter of Stephen Leacock (1869-1944).
Gymnastic exercise theory of laughter of G. W. Crile (1864-1943).
Hobbes plus theory of Harald Hoeffding (1843-1931).
I'm ashamed of my ancestors theory of laughter of George Eliot (1819-1880).
Insolence theory of La Rochefoucauld (1612-1680).
Instinctive enjoyment theory of laughter of Max Eastman (1883-1969).
Interrupted love reaction theory of J. Y. T. Greig (c. 1923).
Lack of fundamentality in contradictions theory of laughter of Camille Melinaud (c. 1895).
Lack of self-knowledge theory of Plato (427-348 B.C.).
Liberty theory of Lord Shaftesbury (1671-1713) and A. Penjon (c. 1893).
Mechanization theory of Henri Bergson (1859-1941).
Meeting of extremes theory by Leigh Hunt (1784-1859).
Midwife theory of laughter by Alexander Pope (1688-1744).

Minimal-touch theory of G. Stanley Hall (1844-1924) and Arthur Allin (c.
 1896).
Moral contrast theory of Johann Wolfgang von Goethe (1749-1832).
Nascent cry theory of laughter of David Hartley (1705-1757).
Nascent cry-echoed theory by Pierre-Augustine Beaumarchais (1732-1799).
Not too tragic defect theory of Aristotle (384-322 B.C.).
Nothing theory of Immanuel Kant (1724-1804).
Occult resemblance theory of Samuel Johnson (1709-1784) and Mme. de Stael (1766-1817).
Oscillation theory of laughter by Ewald Hecker (c. 1873).
Overflow of nervous energy theory of Herbert Spencer (1820-1903).
Perception of unreality theory of laughter of Herbert Barry (c. 1928).
Perfection-imperfection theory of Moses Mendelssohn (1729-1786) and G. E. Lessing (1729-1781).
Physio-psychological blend theory of Rene Descartes (1596-1650).
Playful judgment theory of wit by K. Fischer (c. 1889).
Play-mood theory of laughter by James Sully (1842-1923).
Primeval fall from grace theory of laughter of Charles Baudelaire (1821-1867).
Pure sociology theory of laughter by E. Dupreel (c. 1928).
Rationalization theory of laughter of E. F. Carritt (c. 1923).
Reason theory of laughter by Marie-Joseph Blaise Chenier (1764-1811).
Relax in safety theory of laughter of Donald Hayworth (c. 1928).
Relief theory of laughter by J. C. Gregory (c. 1924).
Restfulness theory of K. W. F. Solger (c. 1829).
Roar-of-triumph in an ancient jungle duel theory of laughter by Albert Rapp (c. 1951).
Separation theory of John Locke (1632-1704).
Show-teeth theory of laughter by A. M. Ludovici (c. 1933).
Sin theory of laughter reflected by St. John Chrysostom (c. 345-407).
Split-second before adaptation theory of laughter by William Hazlitt (1778-1830).
Sudden contrast theory of laughter advanced by Arthur Schopenhauer (1788-1860).
Sudden glory theory of Thomas Hobbes (1588-1679).
Sudden relaxation of strain theory endorsed by John Dewey (1859-1952).
Sympathy theory of Voltaire (1694-1778) and Thomas Carlyle (1795-1881).
Tragic contradiction theory of J. Bahnsen (c. 1877).
Trio of philosophical authorities substituting for a theory theory of wit imagined by Poinsinet de Sivry
 (c. 1778), who cites Destouches (laughter originated in a "reasoned joy), Fontanelle ("the
 principle of laughter is folly"), and Montesquieu (laughter is "the expression of pride") as
 the "authorities."
Two Charlie Chaplin theories on laughter reported by Max Eastman (1883-1969).
Two contradictory propositions theory of Leon Dumont (1837-1876).
Two contradictory social situations theory of laughter elaborated by Ralph
 Piddington (c. 1933).
Two nihilistic theories of laughter by Cicero (106-43 B.C.) and Quintilian (c.
 35-c. 95).
Two-types-of-laughter theory of George Dumas (1886-1946).
Unexpected intellectual contrast theory of Emil Kraepelin (1856-1926).
Unification theory of James Beattie (1735-1803).
We don't know theory of Charles Darwin (1809-1882).
Will-to-laugh theory by E. F. Allen (c. 1941)

Appendix C – Imagery Theories

This appendix provides a chronologically-ordered (based on publication date) listing, along with major proponents and brief definitions, of various prominent *theories of imagery*.

Donald O. Hebb's (1968) *imagery theory* - asserts that an image is formed when some of the brain's same neurological structures that are activated during perception are activated in the absence of the appropriate sensory input; this approach suggests that groups of neurons in "cell assemblies" and "phase sequences" operate in a hierarchical manner to produce both generic as well as sharp or detailed images.

Mardi J. Horowitz's (1970/1978) *cognitive model of image formation* - based in clinical observations, this approach attempts to complement data from experimental studies of the use of images in perception, information-processing, and memory; the modeling process in this theory is analogous to formulating the program by which a computer operates in its particular information-processing tasks.

Allan Paivio's (1971, 1982) *dual-coding model* (see main dictionary entry under "Imagery/Mental Imagery, Theories of").

Gordon H. Bower's (1972) *dual-code theory* - emphasizes the distinction between *how* something looks and *what* it looks like (in the former, there is a quasi-pictorial representation, and in the latter, there is something akin to a verbal or propositional representation); in this approach, memory images provide a type of direct contact with the appearance of a thing by re-creating the experience of seeing it; the verbal or propositional representations do not induce a percept-like experience but, rather, convey information only about the properties of the thing; in this theory, the two types of information are stored in two different kinds of codes.

Ulric Neisser's (1972) *percept analogy/analogue theory* - argues that the processes of imagery are related closely to those of perception, where both imagery and perception are instances of *active* construction, rather than *passive* registration and recall; this theory supports the view that the mnemonic effectiveness of an image depends *only* on spatial layout that it represents and *not* on the pictorial quality of that layout; also, the theory suggests that the "inner world" of imagery is constructed in much the same way as the real world is perceived with complexity and dimensionality.

Thomas P. Moran's (1973) *propositional model* - suggests that all mental representations, including those underlying images, are "symbolic" where there are no special image conditions, and where memory consists of a collection of "productions" that contain two parts: the "condition" which states that what information must be in active memory or coming from the senses, and the "action" that is produced.

Zenon W. Pylyshyn's (1973, 1981) *descriptionalist theory* or *tacit knowledge theory* - argues that the only real issue dividing the "images versus propositions" positions is whether certain aspects of cognition that are associated with imagery ought to be viewed as governed by "tacit knowledge;" that is, whether they should be explained in terms of processes that operate on symbolic encodings of rules and other representations (such as beliefs and goals) or whether they should be seen as intrinsic aspects of certain representational media or of certain mechanisms that are not changeable in arbitrary ways by tacit knowledge; the *descriptionalist* approach likens mental images to linguistic descriptions, as compared to the *pictorialist* approach which likens mental images to pictures; a *tacit knowledge* account of image-processing is advanced here over an analog account because the former approach has more generality and, also, because certain empirical results indicate that both mental rotation and mental scanning transformations, in particular, may be influenced by varying instructions given to participants as well as the precise form of the task that is employed.

Arnold Trehub's (1977, 1991) *neural networks model* - this model of pattern recognition and visual imagery is similar to the *array theory*, but includes the features of "mosaic cells" that act as contour extractors, "filter cells" that act to depict certain shapes, "neural axons" that act to generate a visual image of a pattern from memory, "command cell synapses" whose activation corresponds to a mental rotation or size scaling operation on the array pattern, and "concentric subsets" of mosaic cells whose activation corresponds to focal attention.

Roger N. Shepard's (1978, 1981) *psychophysical complementarity theory* - this "general theory" integrates data from experiments on mental transformations, shape recognition, and apparent motion, and uses findings to develop preliminary hypotheses (often invoking *evolutionary theory*) about the mental structures and processes involved in imagined transformations; this approach cuts across the areas of imagery, pattern recognition, and spatial reasoning; Shepard's original work (with J. A. Metzler) on *mental rotation* studied the imagined turning of a form/shape from one orientation in space to another, hypothesizing the involvement of the mental image as passing through all intermediate positions.

Geoffrey E. Hinton's (1979) *structural descriptions theory* - this is a variant of the propositional theory of visual representation in which scenes are represented as graph structures whose nodes correspond to objects and their parts, and whose edges are labeled with the spatial relationship that is true of pairs of parts; this theory addresses the "viewer-centeredness" of images, the incremental nature of image transformation, and the relative ease of examining and transforming different image sub-patterns.

Stephen M. Kosslyn's, et al (1979, 1980) *pictorial/computer-simulation/array theory* - asserts that active-memory representations underlie one's experience of imagery, and such quasi-pictorial properties that people report during the imagery experience arise from the structural properties of the underlying representation; long-term memory stores not only quantitative information, but also displays the facts in a symbolic or propositional format which affords the imagining of parts of objects and, thus, creates detailed images of objects or scenes.

Ronald A. Finke's (1980) *levels of equivalence model* - considers the visual system to be composed of a hierarchy of processing levels, involving the principles of perceptual equivalence, spatial equivalence, transformational equivalence, and structural equivalence; this approach emphasizes the notion that imagery does actually resemble perception in very fundamental ways, and ties mental images to visual processing stages that may be identified in neural terms.

Nigel J. T. Thomas' (1999) *perceptual activity theory* - this philosophical approach attempts to show how the issues of imagery and imagination are related, and maintains that imagination is used often to identify the faculty of "image production;" this orientation emphasizes that neither the "quasi-pictorial" theory nor the "descriptionalist" theory is able to serve as the basis for a general theory of imagination and its role in creative thought; the *perceptual activity theory* views imagery as nondiscursive and relates it to the concept of "seeing as;" also, the theory rejects the traditional symbolic computational view of imagery as merely mental contents, and is compatible with more current approaches to imagery such as the "situated cognition" approach of "active vision" often employed in the field of robotics.

Selected Bibliography - Psychological Theories

Abnormal

Davidson, R. J., Pizzagalli, D., Nitschke, J. B., & Putnam, K. (2002). Depression: Perspectives from affective neuroscience. *Annual Review of Psychology, 53*, 545-574.

Foa, E. B., Zinbarg, R., & Rothbaum, B. O. (1992). Uncontrollability and unpredictability in post-traumatic stress disorder: An animal model. *Psychological Bulletin, 112*, 218-238.

Gleaves, D. H. (1996). The sociocognitive model of dissociative identity disorder: A reexamination of the evidence. *Psychological Bulletin, 120*, 42-59.

Helmes, E., & Reddon, J. R. (1993). A perspective on developments in assessing psychopathology: A critical review of the MMPI and MMPI-2. *Psychological Bulletin, 113*, 453-471.

Hollingworth, H. L. (1930). *Abnormal psychology: Its concepts and theories*. New York: Ronald Press.

Johnson, S. L., & Roberts, J. E. (1995). Life events and bipolar disorder: Implications from biological theories. *Psychological Bulletin, 117*, 434-449.

Lubow, R. E., & Gewirtz, J. C. (1995). Latent inhibition in humans: Data, theory, and implications for schizophrenia. *Psychological Bulletin, 117*, 87-103.

Millon, T. (1983). *Theories of personality and psychopathology*. New York: Holt, Rinehart, and Winston.

Plomin, R., & McGuffin, P. (2003). Psychopathology in the postgenomic era. *Annual Review of Psychology, 54*, 205-228.

Walker, E. F., & Diforio, D. (1997). Schizophrenia: A neural diathesis-stress model. *Psychological Review, 104*, 667-685.

Williams, J., Whiten, A., Suddendorf, T., & Perrett, D. (2001). Imitation, mirror neurons, and autism. *Neuroscience & Biobehavioral Reviews, 25*, 287-295.

Aggression

Anderson, C. A., & DeNeve, K. M. (1992). Temperature, aggression, and the negative affect escape model. *Psychological Bulletin, 111*, 347-351.

Ellis, L. (1989). *Theories of rape: Inquiries into the causes of sexual aggression*. New York: Hemisphere.

Frank, M. G., & Gilovich, T. (1988). The dark side of self- and social-perception: Black uniforms and aggression in professional sports. *Journal of Personality and Social Psychology, 54*, 74-85.

Geen, R. G., & Donnerstein, E. I. (1998). *Human aggression: Theories, research, and implications for social policy*. San Diego, CA: Academic Press.

Milner, J. S. (1991). *Neuropsychology of aggression*. Boston: Kluwer Academic.

Aging and Health
Birren, J. E. (1985). *The handbooks of aging.* 3 vols. New York: Van Nostrand Reinhold.Lowe, M. R. (1993). The effects of dieting on eating behavior: A three-factor model. *Psychological Bulletin, 114,* 100-121.
Murray, M., & Chamberlain, K. (1999). *Qualitative health psychology: Theories and methods.* Thousand Oaks, CA: Sage.
Myerson, J., Hale, S., Wagstaff, D., Poon, L. W., & Smith, G. A. (1990). The information-loss model: A mathematical theory of age-related cognitive slowing. *Psychological Review, 97,* 475-487.
Novy, D. M., Nelson, D. V., Francis, D. J., & Turk, D. C. (1995). Perspectives of chronic pain: An evaluative comparison of restrictive and comprehensive models. *Psychological Bulletin, 118,* 238-247.
Sayette, M. A. (1993). An appraisal-disruption model of alcohol's effects on stress responses in social drinkers. *Psychological Bulletin, 114,* 459-476.
Stone, G. C., Adler, N. E., & Cohen, F. (1979). *Health psychology: A handbook.* San Francisco: Jossey-Bass.
West, R. L. (1996). An application of prefrontal cortex function theory to cognitive aging. *Psychological Bulletin, 120,* 272-292.

Attention
Pashler, H. (1994). Dual-task interference in simple tasks: Data and theory. *Psychological Bulletin, 116,* 220-244.
Sperling, G., & Weichselgartner, E. (1995). Episodic theory of the dynamics of spatial attention. *Psychological Review, 102,* 503-532.

Behavioral Change
Bandura, A. (1971). *Psychological modeling: Conflicting theories.* Chicago: Aldine, Atherton.
Friedman, M. I., & Lackey, G. H., Jr. (1991). *The psychology of human control: A general theory of purposeful behavior.* New York: Praeger.

Biographical Reference
Jones, E. A. (1953-1957). *The life and work of Sigmund Freud.* 3 vols. New York: Basic Books.
Strachey, J. (Ed.) (1953-1964). *The standard edition of the complete psychological works of Sigmund Freud.* 24 vols. London: Hogarth Press.
Zusne, L. (1984). *Biographical dictionary of psychology.* Westport, CT: Greenwood Press.
Zusne, L. (1987). *Eponyms in psychology.* Westport, CT: Greenwood Press.

Child and Developmental

Baldwin, A. L. (1967). *Theories of child development.* New York: Wiley.

Bretherton, I., & Beeghly, M. (1982). Talking about internal states: The acquisition of an explicit theory of mind. *Developmental Psychology, 18,* 906-921.

Cain, K. M., & Dweck, C. S. (1989). The development of children's conceptions of intelligence: A theoretical framework. In R. J. Sternberg (Ed.), *Advances in the psychology of human intelligence.* Vol. 5. Hillsdale, NJ: Erlbaum.

Cirillo, L., & Wapner, S. (1986). *Value presuppositions in theories of human development.* Hillsdale, NJ: Erlbaum.

Crain, W. C. (1985/2000). *Theories of development: Concepts and applications.* Upper Saddle River, NJ: Prentice Hall.

Darling, N., & Steinberg, L. (1993). Parenting style as context: An integrative model. *Psychological Bulletin, 113,* 487-496.

Geert, P. van (1986). *Theory building in developmental psychology.* Amsterdam: North-Holland.

Gopnik, A., & Wellman, H. (1992). Why the child's theory of mind really is a theory. *Mind and Language, 7,* 145-172.

Green, M. (1989). *Theories of human development: A comparative approach.* Englewood Cliffs, NJ: Prentice Hall.

Hala, S., Chandler, M., & Fritz, A. S. (1991). Fledgling theories of mind: Deception as a marker of three-year-olds' understanding of false belief. *Child Development, 62,* 83-97.

Heckhausen, J., & Schulz, R. (1995). A life-span theory of control. *Psychological Review, 102,* 284-304.

Kazdin, A. E. (2003). Psychotherapy for children and adolescents. *Annual Review of Psychology, 54,* 253-276.

Lachman, M. E. (2004). Development in midlife. *Annual Review of Psychology, 55,* 305-331.

Langer, J. (1969). *Theories of development.* New York: Holt, Rinehart, and Winston.

Lerner, R. M. (1986/2002). *Concepts and theories of human development.* New York: Random House/Mahwah, NJ: Erlbaum.

Morton, J., & Johnson, M. H. (1991). CONSPEC and CONLERN: A two-process theory of infant face recognition. *Psychological Review, 98,* 164-181.

Muuss, R. E. H. (1962/1988/1996). *Theories of adolescence.* New York: Random House/New York: McGraw-Hill. (1996 edition with E. Velder & H. Porton).

Parke, R. D. (2004). Development in the family. *Annual Review of Psychology, 55,* 365-399.

Petraitis, J., Flay, B. R., & Miller, T. Q. (1995). Reviewing theories of adolescent substance use: Organizing pieces in the puzzle. *Psychological Bulletin, 117,* 67-86.

Previc, F. H. (1991). A general theory concerning the prenatal origins of cerebral lateralization in humans. *Psychological Review, 98,* 299-334.

Riley, D. (1983). *War in the nursery: Theories of the child and mother.* London: Virago.

Ritblatt, S. N. (2000). Children's level of participation in a false-belief task, age, and theory of mind. *The Journal of Genetic Psychology, 16,* 53-64.

Salkind, N. J. (1981/1985). *Theories of human development.* New York: Van Nostrand/New York: Wiley.

Saxe, R., Carey, S., & Kanwisher, N. (2004). Understanding other minds: Linking developmental psychology and functional neuroimaging. *Annual Review of Psychology, 55,* 87-124.

Slee, P. T., & Shute, R. H. (2003). *Child development: Thinking about theories.* New York: Arnold/Oxford University Press.

Spaccarelli, S. (1994). Stress, appraisal, and coping in child sexual abuse: A theoretical and empirical review. *Psychological Bulletin, 116,* 340-362.

Suddendorf, T., Fletcher-Flinn, C., & Johnston, L. (1999). Pantomime and theory of mind. *The Journal of Genetic Psychology, 160,* 31-45.

Sugarman, L. (1986). *Life-span development: Concepts, theories, and interventions*. London: Methuen.

Thomas, R. M. (2001). *Recent theories of human development*. Thousand Oaks, CA: Sage.

Cognition

Braine, M. D. S., & O'Brien, D. P. (1991). A theory of "if": A lexical entry, reasoning program, and pragmatic principles. *Psychological Review, 98*, 182-203.

Cheng, P. W. (1997). From covariation to causation: A causal power theory. *Psychological Review, 104*, 367-405.

Dell, G. S., Burger, L. K., & Svec, W. R. (1997). Language production and serial order: A functional analysis and a model. *Psychological Review, 104*, 123-147.

Fazio, R. H., & Olson, M. A. (2003). Implicit measures in social cognition research: Their meaning and use. *Annual Review of Psychology, 54*, 297-327.

Feldman, J. A., & Ballard, F. H. (1982). Connectionist models and their properties. *Cognitive Science, 6*, 205-254.

Galanter, E., & Gerstenhaber, M. (1956). On thought: The extrinsic theory. *Psychological Review, 63*, 218-227.

Garbarini, F., & Adenzato, M. (2004). At the root of embodied cognition: Cognitive science meets neurophysiology. *Brain & Cognition, 56*, 100-106.

Geert, P. van (1991). A dynamic systems model of cognitive and language growth. *Psychological Review, 98*, 3-53.

Gigerenzer, G. (1991). From tools to theories: A heuristic of discovery in cognitive psychology. *Psychological Review, 98*, 254-267.

Gigerenzer, G., Hoffrage, U., & Kleinbolting, H. (1991). Probabilistic mental models: A Brunswikian theory of confidence. *Psychological Review, 98*, 506-528.

Hummel, J. E., & Holyoak, K. J. (1997). Distributed representations of structure: A theory of analogical access and mapping. *Psychological Review, 104*, 427-466.

Irwin, F. W. (1971). *Intentional behavior and motivation: A cognitive theory*. Philadelphia: Lippincott.

Juslin, P., & Olsson, H. (1997). Thurstonian and Brunswikian origins of uncertainty in judgment: A sampling model of confidence in sensory discrimination. *Psychological Review, 104*, 344-366.

Karniol, R. (1995). Stuttering, language, and cognition: A review and a model of stuttering as suprasegmental sentence plan alignment (SPA). *Psychological Bulletin, 117*, 104-124.

Koriat, A. (1993). How do we know that we know? The accessibility model of the feeling of knowing. *Psychological Review, 100*, 609-639.

Langer, E. J., & Piper, A. I. (1987). The prevention of mindlessness. *Journal of Personality and Social Psychology, 53*, 280-287.

Levin, J. R., & Allen, V. L. (1976). *Cognitive learning in children: Theories and strategies*. New York: Academic Press.

Lewontin, R. C. (1990). The evolution of cognition. In D. N. Osherson & E. E. Smith (Eds.), *An invitation to cognitive science: Thinking*. Vol. 3. Cambridge, MA: M. I. T. Press.

Maas, H. L. J. van der, & Molenaar, P. C. M. (1992). Stagewise cognitive development: An application of catastrophe theory. *Psychological Review, 99*, 395-417.

Meyer, D. E., & Kieras, D. E. (1997). A computational theory of executive cognitive processes and multiple-task performance: Part 1. Basic mechanisms. *Psychological Review, 104*, 3-65; Part 2. Accounts of psychological refractory-period phenomena. *Psychological Review, 104*, 749-791.

Neisser, U. (1985). Toward an ecologically oriented cognitive science. In T. M. Shlechter & M. P. Toglia (Eds.), *New directions in cognitive science*. Norwood, NJ: Ablex.

Rodenhausen, H. (1992). Mathematical aspects of Kintsch's model of discourse comprehension. *Psychological Review, 99*, 547-549.

Spelke, E. S., Breinlinger, K., Macomber, J., & Jacobson, K. (1992). Origins of knowledge. *Psychological Review, 99*, 605-632.

Nosofsky, R. M., & Palmeri, T. J. (1997). An exemplar-based random walk model of speeded classification. *Psychological Review, 104*, 266-300.

Trehub, A. (1991). *The cognitive brain.* Cambridge, MA: M.I.T. Press.

Wallsten, T. S., & Gonzalez-Vallejo, C. (1994). Statement verification: A stochastic model of judgment and response. *Psychological Review, 101*, 490-504.

Wiles, J., & Dartnall, T. (1999). *Perspectives on cognitive science: Theories, experiments, and foundations.* Stamford, CT: Ablex.

Community Psychology

Shinn, M., & Toohey, S. M. (2003). Community contexts of human welfare. *Annual Review of Psychology, 54*, 427-459.

Tolan, P. H. (1990). *Researching community psychology: Issues of theory and methods.* Washington, D. C.: American Psychological Association.

Criticism

Natoli, J. P., & Rusch, F. L. (1984). *Psychocriticism: An annotated bibliography.* Westport, CT: Greenwood Press.

Roese, N. J., & Jamieson, D. W. (1993). Twenty years of bogus pipeline research: A critical review and meta-analysis. *Psychological Bulletin, 114*, 363-375,

Cultural

Cosmides, L., & Tooby, J. (1989). Evolutionary psychology and the generation of culture. Part II. Case study: A computational theory of social exchange. *Ethology and Sociobiology, 10*, 51-97.

Greenfield, P. M., Keller, H., Fuligni, A., & Maynard, A. (2003). Cultural pathways through universal development. *Annual Review of Psychology, 54*, 461-490.

LaFromboise, T., Coleman, H. L. K., & Gerton, J. (1993). Psychological impact of biculturalism: Evidence and theory. *Psychological Bulletin, 114*, 395-412.

Lehman, D. R., Chiu, C., & Schaller, M. (2004). Psychology and culture. *Annual Review of Psychology, 55*, 689-714.

Morrison, I. (2002). Mirror neurons and cultural transmission. In M. Stamenov & V. Gallese (Eds.), *Mirror neurons and the evolution of brain and language.* Amsterdam, Netherlands: J. Benjamins.

Triandis, H. C., & Suh, E. M. (2002). Cultural influences on personality. *Annual Review of Psychology, 53*, 133-160.

Zhang, L., & Sachs, J. (1997). Assessing thinking styles in the theory of mental self-government: A Hong Kong validity study. *Psychological Reports, 81*, 915-928.

Decision-Making

Arkes, H. R., Christensen, C., Lai, C., & Blumer, C. (1987). Two methods of reducing overconfidence. *Organizational Behavior and Human Decision Processes, 39*, 133-144.

Busemeyer, J. R., & Townsend, J. T. (1993). Decision field theory: A dynamic-cognitive approach to decision making in an uncertain environment. *Psychological Review, 100*, 432-459.

Garling, T. (1989). The role of cognitive maps in spatial decisions. *Journal of Environmental Psychology, 9*, 269-278.

Glimcher, P. W. (2003). The neurobiology of visual-saccadic decision making. *Annual Review of Neuroscience, 26*, 133-179.

Kerr, N. L., & Tindale, R. S. (2004). Group performance and decision making. *Annual Review of Psychology, 55*, 623-655.

Larrick, R. P. (1993). Motivational factors in decision theories: The role of self-protection. *Psychological Bulletin, 113*, 440-450.

Luce, R. D., & Raiffa, H. (1957). *Games and decisions*. New York: Wiley.

Tversky, A., & Kahneman, D. (1974). Judgments under uncertainty: Heuristics and biases. *Science, 185*, 1124-1131.

Tversky, A., & Kahneman, D. (1981). The framing of decisions and the psychology of choice. *Science, 211*, 453-458.

Education

Arnold, D. H., & Doctoroff, G. L. (2003). The early education of socioeconomically disadvantaged children. *Annual Review of Psychology, 54*, 517-545.

Bertrand, Y. (1990). *Contemporary theories and practice in education*. Madison, WI: Magna.

Bigge, M. L. (1971). *Learning theories for teachers*. New York: Harper & Row.

Donovan, M. P. (1998). Hypotheses, theories, and laws - a look at textbooks' treatment of an issue from the CASE standards. *Journal of College Science Teaching, 28*, 137-138.

Legge, G. E., Klitz, T. S., & Tjan, B. S. (1997). Mr. Chips: An ideal-observer model of reading. *Psychological Review, 104*, 524-553.

Marsh, H. W. (1987). The big-fish-little-pond effect on academic self-concept. *Journal of Educational Psychology, 79*, 280-295.

Mayer, R. E. (2004). Teaching of subject matter. *Annual Review of Psychology, 55*, 715-744.

Menges, R. J., & Svinicki, M. D. (1991). *College teaching, from theory to practice*. San Francisco: Jossey-Bass.

Thorpe, L. P., & Schmuller, A. M. (1954). *Contemporary theories of learning with applications to education and psychology*. New York: Ronald Press.

Gender and Sex

Bjorklund, D. F., & Kipp, K. (1996). Parental investment theory and gender differences in the evolution of inhibition mechanisms. *Psychological Bulletin, 120*, 163-188.

Buss, D. M., & Schmitt, D. P. (1993). Sexual strategies theory: An evolutionary perspective on human mating. *Psychological Review, 100*, 204-232.

Denmark, F., & Paludi, M. A. (1993). *Psychology of women: A handbook of issues and theories*. Westport, CT: Greenwood Press.

Fausto-Sterling, A. (1985). *Myths of gender: Biological theories about women and men*. New York: Basic Books.

Feingold, A. (1992). Gender differences in mate selection preferences: A test of the parental investment model. *Psychological Bulletin, 112*, 125-139.

Geer, J., & O'Donohue, W. T. (1987). *Theories of human sexuality*. New York: Plenum Press.

Hartung, C. M., & Widiger, T. A. (1998). Gender differences in the diagnosis of mental disorders: Conclusions and controversies of the DSM-IV. *Psychological Bulletin, 123*, 260-278.

Latane, B., & Bidwell, L. D. (1977). Sex and affiliation in college cafeterias. *Personality and Social Psychology Bulletin, 3*, 571-574.

Skowronski, J. J., & Thompson, C. P. (1990). Reconstructing the dates of personal events; Gender differences in accuracy. *Applied Cognitive Psychology, 4*, 371-381.

Stewart, A. J., & McDermott, C. (2004). Gender in psychology. *Annual Review of Psychology, 55*, 519-544.

General References

Bothamley, J. (1993). *Dictionary of theories*. London: Gale Research International.

Colman, A. M. (2001). *A dictionary of psychology*. New York: Oxford University Press.

Corsini, R. J. (Ed.) (1984/1994). *Encyclopedia of psychology*. 4 vols. New York: Wiley.

Corsini, R. J. (2002). *The dictionary of psychology*. New York: Brunner-Routledge.

668

Craighead, W. E., & Nemeroff, C. B. (Eds.) (2001). *The Corsini encyclopedia of psychology and behavioral science.* 3rd ed. 4 vols. New York: Wiley.

Ellis, W. (Ed.) (1938). *A sourcebook of Gestalt psychology.* London: Paul, Trench, Trubner.

English, H., & English, A. (1958/1976). *A comprehensive dictionary of psychological and psychoanalytical terms.* New York: McKay.

Furnham, A. (1988). *Lay theories: Everyday understanding of problems in the social sciences.* New York: Pergamon Press.

Gilgen, A. R., & Gilgen, C. K. (Eds.) (1987). *International handbook of psychology.* Westport, CT: Greenwood Press.

Glymore, C. (1980). *Theory and evidence.* Princeton, NJ: Princeton University Press.

Harre, R., & Lamb, R. (Eds.) (1983). *The encyclopedic dictionary of psychology.* Cambridge, MA: M.I.T. Press.

Harriman, P. (1966). *Handbook of psychological terms.* Totowa, NJ: Littlefield, Adams.

Hinsie, L. E., & Campbell, R. J. (1970). *Psychiatric dictionary.* 4th ed. New York: Oxford University Press.

James, W. (1890). *The principles of psychology.* 2 vols. New York: Holt.

Kazdin, A. E. (Ed.) (2000). *Encyclopedia of psychology.* 5 vols. New York: Oxford University Press/Washington, D. C.: American Psychological Association.

Kling, J., & Riggs, L. (Eds.) (1971). *Woodworth and Schlosberg's experimental psychology.* New York: Holt, Rinehart, and Winston.

Koch, S. (Ed.) (1959-1963). *Psychology: A study of a science.* 6 vols. New York: McGraw-Hill.

Marx, M. (Ed.) (1963). *Theories in contemporary psychology.* New York: Macmillan.

Marx, M., & Goodson, F. (Eds.) (1976). *Theories in contemporary psychology.* New York: Macmillan.

Neel, A. (1969). *Theories of psychology: A handbook.* London: University of London Press/Cambridge, MA: Schenkman.

Osgood, C. E. (1953). *Method and theory in experimental psychology.* New York: Oxford University Press.

Owens, D. A., & Wagner, M. (Eds.) (1992). *Progress in modern psychology: The legacy of American functionalism.* New York: Praeger Publishers.

Paranjpe, A. C. (1984). *Theoretical psychology: The meeting of East and West.* New York: Plenum Press.

Pashler, H., Yantis, S., Medin, D., Gallistel, R., & Wixted, J. (Eds.) (2002). *Stevens' Handbook of experimental psychology.* 3rd ed. 4 vols. New York: Wiley.

Pfeiffer, J. W., & Ballew, A. C. (1991). *Theories and models in applied behavioral science.* San Diego, CA: Pfeiffer.

Reber, A. S. (1995). *The Penguin dictionary of psychology.* New York: Penguin Books.

Roeckelein, J. E. (1998). *Dictionary of theories, laws, and concepts in psychology.* Westport, CT: Greenwood Press.

Skinner, B. F. (1938). *The behavior of organisms: An experimental analysis.* New York: Appleton-Century-Crofts.

Skinner, B F. (1953). *Science and human behavior.* New York: Macmillan.

Stevens, S. S. (1951). *Handbook of experimental psychology.* New York: Wiley.

Underwood, B. J. (1966). *Experimental psychology.* New York: Appleton-Century-Crofts.

Warren, H. C. (Ed.) (1934). *Dictionary of psychology.* Cambridge, MA: Houghton Mifflin.

Westmeyer, H. (1989). *Psychological theories from a structuralist point of view.* New York: Springer-Verlag.

Wolman, B. B. (1960/1981). *Contemporary theories and systems in psychology.* New York: Harper/New York: Plenum Press.

Wolman, B. B. (Ed.) (1973/1989). *Dictionary of behavioral science.* New York: Van Nostrand Reinhold/San Diego: Academic Press.

Wolman, B. B. (Ed.) (1996). *The encyclopedia of psychiatry, psychology, and psychoanalysis.* New York: Holt.

Woodworth, R. S. (1938). *Experimental psychology.* New York: Holt.

Woodworth, R. S., & Schlosberg, H. (1965). *Experimental psychology.* Rev. ed. New York: Holt, Rinehart, and Winston.

History

Boring, E. G. (1954). The nature and history of experimental control. *American Journal of Psychology, 76,* 573-589.

Boring, E. G. (1957). *A history of experimental psychology.* New York: Appleton-Century-Crofts.

Chaplin, J. P., & Krawiec, T. S. (1960/1968). *Systems and theories of psychology.* New York: Holt, Rinehart, and Winston.

Henle, M. (1986). *1879 and all that: Essays in the theory and history of psychology.* New York: Columbia University Press.

Hilgard, E. R. (1987). *Psychology in America: A historical survey.* New York: Harcourt Brace Jovanovich.

Hillner, K. P. (1984). *History and systems of modern psychology: A conceptual approach.* New York: Gardner Press.

Jones, D., & Elcock, J. (2001). *History and theories of psychology: A critical perspective.* New York: Arnold.

Jones, F. P. (1964). Experimental method in antiquity. *American Psychologist, 19,* 419-420.

Kantor, J. R. (1963/1969). *The scientific evolution of psychology.* 2 vols. Chicago: Principia Press.

Leahey, T. H. (1987). *A history of psychology: Main currents in psychological thought.* Englewood Cliffs, NJ: Prentice-Hall.

Lundin, R. W. (1979/1985/1991/1996). *Theories and systems of psychology.* Lexington, MA: Heath.

Marx, M., & Hillix, W. (1979). *Systems and theories in psychology.* New York: McGraw-Hill.

Murphy, G., & Kovach, J. (1972). *Historical introduction to modern psychology.* New York: Harcourt Brace Jovanovich.

Psychological Review (1994), *101,* 195-360. Special Issue: The centennial issue of the *Psychological Review.* Includes reprints of important, classical, and original articles (along with comments) of the following: The physical basis of emotion - William James; Psychology and history - Hugo Munsterberg; Psychology as the behaviorist views it - John B. Watson; A law of comparative judgment - L. L. Thurstone; Toward a statistical theory of learning - William K. Estes; The physiology of motivation - Eliot Stellar; The visual perception of objective motion and subjective movement - James J. Gibson; The magical number seven, plus or minus two: Some limits on our capacity for processing information - George A. Miller.

Rieber, R. W., & Salzinger, K. (1980). *Psychology: Theoretical-historical perspectives.* New York: Academic Press.

Roccatagliata, G. (1986). *A history of ancient psychiatry.* Westport, CT: Greenwood Press.

Schultz, D. (1981). *A history of modern psychology.* New York: Academic Press.

Schultz, D., & Schultz, S. E. (1992). *A history of modern psychology.* New York: Harcourt Brace Jovanovich.

Simonton, D. K. (2002). *Great psychologists and their times: Scientific insights into psychology's history.* Washington, D. C.: American Psychological Association.

Simonton, D. K. (2003). Qualitative and quantitative analyses of historical data. *Annual Review of Psychology, 54,* 617-640.

Stagner, R. (1988). Theories, theorizing, and theorists. Chapter 1. In R. Stagner, *A history of psychological theories.* New York: Macmillan.

670

Humor

Bergler, E. (1956). *Laughter and the sense of humor*. New York: International Medical Book Corporation.

Feibleman, J. K. (1962). *In praise of comedy: A study in its theory and practice*. New York: Russell & Russell.

Friedman, H. H. (2000). Humor in the Hebrew Bible. *Humor: International Journal of Humor Research, 13*, 257-285.

Friedman, H. H. (2002). Is there humor in the Hebrew Bible? A rejoinder. *Humor: International Journal of Humor Research, 15*, 215-222.

Morreall, J. (2001). Sarcasm, irony, wordplay, and humor in the Hebrew Bible: A response to Hershey Friedman. *Humor: International Journal of Humor Research, 14*, 293-301.

Roeckelein, J. E. (2002). *The psychology of humor*. Westport, CT: Greenwood Press.

Imagery

Bower, G. H. (1972). Mental imagery and associative learning. In L. Gregg (Ed.), *Cognition in learning and memory*. New York: Wiley.

Bugelski, B. R. (1970). Words and things and images. *American Psychologist, 25*, 1002-1012.

Dadds, M. R., Bovbjerg, D. H., Redd, W. H., & Cutmore, T. R. H. (1997). Imagery in human classical conditioning. *Psychological Bulletin, 122*, 89-103.

Finke, R. A. (1980). Levels of equivalence in imagery and perception. *Psychological Review, 87*, 113-132.

Galton, F. (1880). Statistics of mental imagery. *Mind, 5*, 301-318.

Hebb, D. O. (1968). Concerning imagery. *Psychological Review, 75*, 466-477.

Hinton, G. E. (1979). Some demonstrations of the effects of structural descriptions in mental imagery. *Cognitive Science, 3*, 231-250.

Horowitz, M. J. (1970/1978). *Image formation and cognition*. New York: Appleton-Century-Crofts.

Kosslyn, S. M. (1980). *Image and mind*. Cambridge, MA: Harvard University Press.

Kosslyn, S. M. (1987). Seeing and imagining in the cerebral hemispheres: A computational approach. *Psychological Review, 94*, 148-175.

Kosslyn, S. M., Pinker, S., Smith, G. E., & Shwartz, S. P. (1979). On the demystification of mental imagery. *The Behavioral and Brain Sciences, 2*, 535-581.

McMahon, C. (1973). Images as motives and motivators: A historical perspective. *American Journal of Psychology, 86*, 465-490.

Moran, T. P. (1973). The symbolic imagery hypothesis: A production system model. Unpublished doctoral dissertation, Carnegie-Mellon University.

Neisser, U. (1972). Changing conceptions of imagery. In P. W. Sheehan (Ed.), *The function and nature of imagery*. New York: Academic Press.

Paivio, A. (1969). Mental imagery in associative learning and memory. *Psychological Review, 76*, 241-263.

Pylyshyn, Z. W. (1973). What the mind's eye tells the mind's brain: A critique of mental imagery. *Psychological Bulletin, 80*, 1-24.

Pylyshyn, Z. W. (1981). The imagery debate: Analog media versus tacit knowledge. In N. Block (Ed.), *Imagery*. Cambridge, MA: M.I.T. Press.

Roeckelein, J. E. (2004). *Imagery in psychology*. Westport, CT: Praeger.

Sheikh, A., & Panagiotou, N. (1975). Use of mental imagery in psychotherapy: A critical review. *Perceptual and Motor Skills, 41*, 555-585.

Shepard, R. N. (1978). The mental image. *American Psychologist, 33*, 125-137.

Shepard, R. N. (1981). Psychophysical complementarity. In M. Kubovy & J. R. Pomerantz (Eds.), *Perceptual organization*. Hillsdale, NJ: Erlbaum.

Shepard, R. N., & Cooper, L. A. (1982). *Mental images and their transformations*. Cambridge, MA: M.I.T. Press.

Shepard, R. N., & Metzler, J. A. (1971). Mental rotation of three-dimensional objects. *Science*, *171*, 701-703.

Thomas, N. J. T. (1999). Are theories of imagery theories of imagination? *Cognitive Science*, *23*, 207-245.

Tippett, L. J. (1992). The generation of visual images: A review of neuropsychological research and theory. *Psychological Bulletin*, *112*, 415-432.

Yuille, J., & Marschark, M. (1983). Imagery effects on memory: Theoretical interpretations. In A. Sheikh (Ed.), *Imagery: Current theory, research, and application*. New York: Wiley.

Learning and Memory

Anderson, J. R., & Matessa, M. (1997). A production system theory of serial memory. *Psychological Review*, *104*, 728-748.

Barnes, J. M., & Underwood, B. J. (1959). "Fate" of first-list associations in transfer theory. *Journal of Experimental Psychology*, *58*, 97-105.

Bower, G. H., & Hilgard, E. R. (1981). *Theories of learning*. Englewood Cliffs, NJ: Prentice-Hall.

Brandimonte, M., Einstein, G. O., & McDaniel, M. A. (Eds.) (1996). *Prospective memory: Theory and applications*. Mahwah, NJ: Erlbaum.

Colonius, H. (1995). The instance theory of automaticity: Why the Weibull? *Psychological Review*, *102*, 744-750.

Dudai, Y. (2004). The neurobiology of consolidations, or, how stable is the engram? *Annual Review of Psychology*, *55*, 51-86.

Gazda, G. M., & Corsini, R. J. (1980). *Theories of learning: A comparative approach*. Itasca, IL: Peacock.

Gredler, M. E. (1986/1997). *Learning and instruction: Theory into practice*. New York: Macmillan/Upper Saddle River, NJ: Merrill.

Hergenhahn, B. R. (1988). *An introduction to theories of learning*. Englewood Cliffs, NJ: Prentice Hall.

Hergenhahn, B. R., & Olson, M. H. (1993/2001). *An introduction to theories of learning*. Englewood Cliffs, NJ: Prentice Hall/Upper Saddle River, NJ: Prentice Hall.

Hilgard, E. R. (1948/1956). *Theories of learning*. New York: Appleton-Century-Crofts.

Hilgard, E. R., & Bower, G. H. (1966/1975). *Theories of learning*. New York: Appleton-Century-Crofts/Englewood Cliffs, NJ: Prentice-Hall.

Johnson, G. J. (1991). A distinctiveness model of serial learning. *Psychological Review*, *98*, 204-217.

Kjerstad, C. L. (1919). [Kjerstad-Robinson law]. *Psychological Monographs*, *26*, No. 5.

Klein, S. B., & Mowrer, R. R. (1989a). *Contemporary learning theories. Instrumental conditioning theory and the impact of biological constraints on learning*. Hillsdale, NJ: Erlbaum.

Klein, S. B., & Mowrer, R. R. (1989b). *Contemporary learning theories. Pavlovian conditioning and the status of traditional learning theory*. Hillsdale, NJ: Erlbaum.

Kluger, A. N., & DeNisi, A. (1996). The effects of feedback interventions on performance: A historical review, a meta-analysis, and a preliminary feedback intervention theory. *Psychological Bulletin*, *119*, 254-284.

Landauer, T. K., & Dumais, S. T. (1997). A solution to Plato's problem: The latent semantic analysis theory of acquisition, induction, and representation of knowledge. *Psychological Review*, *104*, 211-240.

Lefrancois, G. R. (1982). *Psychological theories and human learning*. Monterey, CA: Brooks/Cole.

Levine, M. (1966). Hypothesis behavior by humans during discrimination learning. *Journal of Experimental Psychology*, *71*, 331-338.

Logan, G. D. (1995). The Weibull distribution, the power law, and the instance theory of automaticity. *Psychological Review*, *102*, 751-756.

Malone, J. C. (1990). *Theories of learning: A historical approach*. Belmont, CA: Wadsworth.

Mewhort, D. J. K., Popham, D., & James, G. (1994). On serial recall: A critique of chaining in the theory of distributed associative memory. *Psychological Review, 101*, 534-538.

Murdock, B. B. (1997). Context and mediators in a theory of distributed associative memory (TODAM2). *Psychological Review, 104*, 839-862.

Murnane, K., Phelps, M. P., & Malmberg, K. (1999). Context-dependent recognition memory: The ICE theory. *Journal of Experimental Psychology: General, 128*, 403-415.

Pearce, J. M. (1994). Similarity and discrimination: A selective review and a connectionist model. *Psychological Review, 101*, 587-607.

Purdy, J. E., Harriman, A., & Molitorisz, J. (1993). Possible relations between theories of evolution and animal learning. *Psychological Reports, 73*, 211-223.

Ratcliff, R. (1990). Connectionist models of recognition memory: Constraints imposed by learning and forgetting function. *Psychological Review, 97*, 285-308.

Ratcliff, R., & McKoon, G. (1994). Retrieving information from memory: Spreading-activation theories versus compound-cue theories. *Psychological Review, 101*, 177-184.

Ratcliff, R., & McKoon, G. (1997). A counter model for implicit priming in perceptual word identification. *Psychological Review, 104*, 319-343.

Robinson, E. S., & Darrow, C. W. (1924). [Kjerstad-Robinson law]. *American Journal of Psychology, 35*, 235-243.

Robinson, E. S., & Heron, T. (1922). [Kjerstad-Robinson law]. *Journal of Experimental Psychology, 5*, 428-448.

Sahakian, W. S. (1970). *Psychology of learning: Systems, models, and theories*. Chicago: Markham.

Sahakian, W. S. (1976). *Learning: Systems, models, and theories*. Chicago: Rand McNally.

Skinner, B. F. (1950). Are theories of learning necessary? *Psychological Review, 57*, 193-216.

Staddon, J. E. R., Davis, D. G. S., Machado, A., & Palmer, R. G. (1994). Cumulative effects model: A response to Williams (1994). *Psychological Review, 101*, 708-710.

Swenson, L. C. (1980). *Theories of learning: Traditional perspectives and contemporary developments*. Belmont, CA: Wadsworth.

Thompson, R. F. (2005). In search of memory traces. *Annual Review of Psychology, 56*, 1-23.

Tolman, E. C. (1938). The determiners of behavior at a choice point. *Psychological Review, 45*, 1-41.

Verhave, T. (1963). Towards an empirical calculus of reinforcement value. *Journal of the Experimental Analysis of Behavior, 6*, 525-536.

Zwaan, R. A., & Radvansky, G. A. (1998). Situation models in language comprehension and memory. *Psychological Bulletin, 123*, 162-185.

Legal Issues

Dalby, J. T., & Clavner, E. L. (1997). *Applications of psychology in the law practice: A guide to relevant issues, practices, and theories*. Chicago: American Bar Association.

Faigman, D. L., & Monahan, J. (2005). Psychological evidence at the dawn of the law's scientific age. *Annual Review of Psychology, 56*, 631-659.

Wiener, R. L., & Hurt, L. E. (2000). How do people evaluate social sexual conduct at work? A psycholegal model. *Journal of Applied Psychology, 85*, 75-85.

Marriage

Karney, B. R., & Bradbury, T. N. (1995). The longitudinal course of marital quality and stability: A review of theory, method, and research. *Psychological Bulletin, 118*, 3-34.

Vormbrock, J. K. (1993). Attachment theory as applied to wartime and job-related marital separation. *Psychological Bulletin, 114*, 122-144.

Measurement and Statistics

Chan, K-Y., Drasgow, F., & Sawin, L. L. (1999). What is the shelf life of a test? The effect of time on the psychometrics of a cognitive ability test battery. *Journal of Applied Psychology, 84*, 610-619.

Donovan, J. J., & Radosevich, D. J. (1999). A meta-analytic review of the distribution of practice effect: Now you see it, now you don't. *Journal of Applied Psychology, 84*, 795-805.

Schmidt, F. L., & Hunter, J. E. (1999). Comparison of three meta-analysis methods revisited: An analysis of Johnson, Mullen, and Salas (1995). *Journal of Applied Psychology, 84*, 144-148.

Motivation and Emotion

Arkes, H. R., & Garske, J. P. (1977/1982). *Psychological theories of motivation.* Monterey, CA: Brooks/Cole.

Forgas, J. P. (1995). Mood and judgment: The affect infusion model (AIM). *Psychological Bulletin, 117*, 39-66.

Izard, C. E. (1992). Basic emotions, relations among emotions, and emotion-cognitive relations. *Psychological Review, 99*, 561-565.

Madsen, K. B. (1968). *Theories of motivation: A comparative study of modern theories of motivation.* Kent, OH: Kent State University Press/.

Madsen, K. B. (1973). Theories of motivation. In B. B. Wolman (Ed.), *Handbook of general psychology.* Englewood Cliffs, NJ: Prentice-Hall.

Madsen, K. B. (1974). *Modern theories of motivation: A comparative metascientific study.* New York: Wiley.

Nettlebeck, T., Henderson, C., & Willson, R. (1989). Communicating emotion through sound: An evaluation of Clynes' theory of sentics. *Australian Journal of Psych-ology, 41*, 25-36.

Panksepp, J. (1992). A critical role for "affective neuroscience" in resolving what is basic about basic emotions. *Psychological Review, 99*, 554-560.

Santas, G. X. (1988). *Plato and Freud: Two theories of love.* Oxford, UK: Blackwell.

Strongman, K. T. (1996). *The psychology of emotion: Theories of emotion in perspective.* New York: Wiley.

Turner, T. J., & Ortony, A. (1992). Basic emotions: Can conflicting criteria converge? *Psychological Review, 99*, 566-571.

Valle, F. P. (1975). *Motivation: Theories and issues.* Monterey, CA: Brooks/Cole.

Wagner, A. (1966). Frustration and punishment. In R. Haber (Ed.), *Research on motivation.* New York: Holt, Rinehart, and Winston.

Weiner, B. (1972). *Theories of motivation: From mechanism to cognition.* Chicago: Markham.

Weiner, B. (1992). *Human motivation: Metaphors, theories, and research.* Newbury Park, CA: Sage.

Parapsychology

Bem, D. J., & Honorton, C. (1994). Does psi exist? Replicable evidence for an anomalous process of information transfer. *Psychological Bulletin, 115*, 4-18.

Wolman, B. B. (Ed.) (1977). *Handbook of parapsychology.* New York: Van Nostrand Reinhold.

Personality

Backman, L., & Dixon, R. A. (1992). Psychological compensation: A theoretical framework. *Psychological Bulletin, 112*, 259-283.

Bergen, R. S., & Dweck, C. S. (1989). The functions of personality theories. In R. S. Wyer & Srull, T. K. (Eds.), *Social intelligence and cognitive assessments of personality.* Hillsdale, NJ: Erlbaum.

Block, J. (1995). A contrarian view of the five-factor approach to personality description. *Psychological Bulletin, 117*, 187-215; 216-229.

674

Blum, G. S. (1953). *Psychoanalytic theories of personality*. New York: McGraw-Hill.

Cattell, R. B. (1983). *Structured personality-learning theory*. New York: Praeger.

Chiu, C., Hong, Y., & Dweck, C. S. (1997). Lay dispositionism and implicit theories of personality. *Journal of Personality and Social Psychology, 73*, 19-30.

Chiu, C., Dweck, C. S., Tong, J. Y., & Fu, J. H. (1997). Implicit theories and conceptions of morality. *Journal of Personality and Social Psychology, 73*, 923-940.

Corsini, R. J. (1978). *Readings in current personality theories*. Itasca, IL: Peacock.

Dweck, C. S., Chiu, C., & Hong, Y. (1995). Implicit theories: Elaboration and extension of the model. *Psychological Inquiry, 6*, 322-333.

Eysenck, H. J., & Wilson, G. D. (1973). *The experimental study of Freudian theories*. London: Methuen.

Falk, J. L. (1956). Issues distinguishing idiographic from nomothetic approaches to personality theory. *Psychological Review, 63*, 53-62.

Galbreath, P. (1991). Self-actualization as a contemporary Christological title. *Journal of Psychology & Christianity, 10*, 237-248.

Hall, C., & Lindzey, G. (1978). *Theories of personality*. New York: Wiley.

Hong, Y., Chiu, C., Dweck, C. S., Lin, D., & Wan, W. (1999). Implicit theories, attributions, and coping: A meaning system approach. *Journal of Personality and Social Psychology, 77*, 588-599.

Kopelman, R. E., & Minkin, B. L. (1991). Toward a psychology of parimutuel behavior: Test of Gluck's laws. *Psychological Reports, 68*, 701-702.

Lindzey, G., Hall, C. S., & Manosevitz, M. (Eds.) (1973). *Theories of personality: Primary sources and research*. New York: Wiley.

Loevinger, J., & Blasi, A. (1976). *Ego development: Conceptions and theories*. San Francisco: Jossey-Bass.

Mehrabian, A. (1968). *An analysis of personality theories*. Englewood Cliffs, NJ: Prentice-Hall.

Mischel, W. (2004). Toward an integrative science of the person. *Annual Review of Psychology, 55*, 1-22.

Mischel, W., & Shoda, Y. (1995). A cognitive-affective system theory of personality: Reconceptualizing situations, dispositions, dynamics, and invariance in personality structure. *Psychological Review, 102*, 246-268.

Ryckman, R. M. (1978). *Theories of personality*. New York: Van Nostrand.

Shackleton, V. J., & Fletcher, C. (1984). *Individual differences: Theories, and applications*. London: Methuen.

Philosophy of Science

Abra, J. (1998). *Should psychology be a science? Pros and cons*. Westport, CT: Praeger.

Barrow, J. (1991). Platonic relationships in the universe? Theories on the laws of nature. *New Scientist, 130*, 40-43.

Boring, E. G. (1953). The role of theory in experimental psychology. *American Journal of Psychology, 66*, 169-184.

Churchland, P. S. (1986). *Neurophilosophy: Toward a unified science of the mind-brain*. Cambridge, MA: M. I. T. Press.

Conant, J. B. (1947). *On understanding science*. New Haven, CT: Yale University Press.

Cooper, G. (1996). Theoretical modeling and biological laws. *Philosophy of Science, 63*, 28-35.

Crawford, C. B. (1989). The theory of evolution: Of what value to psychology? *Journal of Comparative Psychology, 103*, 4-22.

Cummins, R. (2000). "How does it work?" versus "What are the laws?" Two conceptions of psychological science. In F. C. Keil & R. A. Wilson (Eds.), *Explanation and cognition*. Cambridge, MA: M.I.T. Press.

Eliasmith, C. (1998). The metaphysics of science: An account of modern science in terms of principles, laws, and theories. *Dialogue: Canadian Philosophical Review, 37*, 656-658.

Etzioni, A. (1975). Effects of small computers on scientists. *Science, 189,* 347.

Foley, J. P. (1936). Psychological ultimates: A note on psychological "fact" versus psychological "law." *Journal of General Psychology, 15,* 455-458.

Freud, S. (1963/1997). *General psychological theory: Papers on metapsychology.* New York: Touchstone.

Glimcher, P. W. (2005). Indeterminacy in brain and behavior. *Annual Review of Psychology, 56,* 25-56.

Hebb, D. O. (1958). Alice in Wonderland or psychology among the biological sciences. In H. F. Harlow & C. N. Woolsey (Eds.), *Biological and biochemical bases of behavior.* Madison: University of Wisconsin.

Hempel, C. G., & Oppenheim, P. (1948). The logic of explanation. *Philosophy of Science, 15,* 135-175.

Israel, H. E., & Goldstein, B. (1944). Operationism in psychology. *Psychological Review, 51,* 177-188.

Johnson, W., & Wilson, J. T. (1947). Extensional agreement in the terms "hypothesis," "theory," and "law." *Etc., 5,* 49-53.

Little, J. D. C. (1992). Tautologies, models, and theories: Can we find "laws" of manufacturing? *IIE Transactions, 24,* 7-13.

McGartland, M., & Polgar, S. (1994). Paradigm collapse in psychology: The necessity for a "two-methods" approach. *Australian Psychologist, 29,* 21-28.

McGuigan, F. J. (1956). Confirmation of theories in psychology. *Psychological Review, 63,* 98-104.

Mewhort, D. J. K. (1990). Alice in Wonderland, or psychology among the information sciences. *Psychological Research, 52,* 158-162.

Miller, J. G. (1939). Symbolic technique in psychological theory. *Psychological Review, 46,* 464-479.

Morgan, D. L. (1998). Selectionist thought and methodological orthodoxy in psychological science. *The Psychological Record, 48,* 439-456.

Pratt, C. C. (1939). *The logic of modern psychology.* New York: Macmillan.

Radner, M., & Winokur, S. (1970). *Analyses of theories and methods of physics and psychology.* Minneapolis, MN: University of Minnesota Press.

Roeckelein, J. E. (1997a). Hierarchy of the sciences and terminological sharing of laws among the sciences. *Psychological Reports, 81,* 739-746.

Roeckelein, J. E. (1997b). Psychology among the sciences: Comparisons of numbers of theories and laws cited in textbooks. *Psychological Reports, 80,* 131-141.

Rosenblueth, A., & Wiener, N. (1945). The role of models in science. *Philosophy of Science, 12,* 316-321.

Simonton, D. K. (1995). Behavioral laws in histories of psychology: Psychological science, metascience, and the psychology of science. *Psychological Inquiry, 6,* 89-114.

Simonton, D. K. (2004). Psychology's status as a scientific discipline: Its empirical placement within an implicit hierarchy of the sciences. *Review of General Psychology, 8,* 59-67.

Sohn, D. (1993). Psychology of the scientist: LXVI. The idiot savants have taken over the psychology labs or Why in science using the rejection of the null hypothesis as the basis for affirming the research hypothesis is unwarranted. *Psychological Reports, 73,* 1167-1175.

Sorensen, R. A. (1992). Thought experiments and the epistemology of laws. *Canadian Journal of Philosophy, 22,* 15-44.

Staats, A. W. (1981). Paradigmatic behaviorism, unified theory, unified theory construction, and the zeitgeist of separatism. *American Psychologist, 36,* 239-256.

Staats, A. W. (1991). Unified positivism and unification psychology. *American Psychologist, 46,* 899-912.

Staats, A. W., & Mos, L. P. (Eds.), *Annals of theoretical psychology.* Vol. 5. New York: Plenum.

Teigen, K. H. (2002). One hundred years of laws in psychology. *American Journal of Psychology, 115*, 103-118.

Thouless, R. H. (1949). Some problems of terminology in psychological theory. *British Journal of Psychology, 40*, 41-46.

Turner, W. S. (1961). A re-examination of the two kinds of scientific conjecture. *Psychological Record, 11*, 279-298.

Physiology and Biology

Crabbe, J. C. (2002). Genetic contributions to addiction. *Annual Review of Psychology, 53*, 133-160.

Friston, K. J. (2005). Models of brain function in neuroimaging. *Annual Review of Psychology, 56*, 57-87.

Grabowska, A., & Nowicka, A. (1996). Visual-spatial-frequency model of cerebral asymmetry: A critical survey of behavioral and electrophysiological studies. *Psychological Bulletin, 120*, 434-449.

Grossberg, S., Mingolla, E., & Ross, W. D. (1994). A neural theory of attentive visual search: Interactions of boundary, surface, spatial, and object representations. *Psychological Review, 101*, 470-489.

Marshall, P. S. (1993). Allergy and depression: A neurochemical threshold model of the relation between the illnesses. *Psychological Bulletin, 113*, 23-43.

Poulos, C. X., & Cappell, H. (1991). Homeostatic theory of drug tolerance: A general model of physiological adaptation. *Psychological Review, 98*, 390-408.

Trehub, A. (1977). Neuronal models for cognitive processes: Networks for learning, perception and imagination. *Journal of Theoretical Biology, 65*, 141-169.

Psychophysics

Galanter, E. (1992). Intentionalism - An expressive theory. In D. Algom (Ed.), *Psychophysical approaches to cognition*. Amsterdam: North-Holland.

Krueger, L. (1989). Reconciling Fechner and Stevens: Toward a unified psychophysical law. *The Behavioral and Brain Sciences, 12*, 251-320.

Luce, R. D. (1990). "On the possible psychophysical laws" revisited: Remarks on cross-modal matching. *Psychological Review, 97*, 66-77.

Sensation and Perception

Ames, A. (1951). Visual perception and the rotating trapezoidal window. *Psychological Monographs, 65*, No. 324.

Ames, A. (1955). *An interpretive manual for the demonstrations in the Psychological Research Center, Princeton University*. Princeton, NJ: Princeton University Press.

Anderson, B. L., & Nakayama, K. (1994). Toward a general theory of stereopsis: Binocular matching, occluding contours, and fusion. *Psychological Review, 101*, 414-445.

Boring, E. G. (1942). *Sensation and perception in the history of experimental psychology*. New York: New York: Appleton-Century-Crofts.

Bridgeman, B., Aiken, W., Allen, J., & Maresh, T. C. (1997). Influence of acoustic context on sound localization: An auditory Roelofs effect. *Psychological Research, 60*, 238-243.

Craig, G. L., Stelmach, L. B., & Tam, W. J. (1999). Control of reflexive and voluntary saccades in the gap effect. *Perception & Psychophysics, 61*, 935-942.

Crowther, C. S., Batchelder, W. H., & Hu, X. (1995). A measurement-theoretic analysis of the fuzzy logic model of perception. *Psychological Review, 102*, 396-408.

Dassonville, P., & Bala, J. K. (2004). Perception, action, and Roelofs effect: A mere illusion of dissociation. *Public Library of Science (PloS), Biology, 2*, 1936-1945 (e364).

Di Lollo, V., & Bischof, W. F. (1995). Inverse-intensity effect in duration of visible persistence. *Psychological Bulletin, 118*, 223-237.

Feinberg, T., Eaton, L., & Roane, D. (1999). Multiple Fregoli delusions after brain injury. *Cortex*, *35*, 373-387.

Fiske, H. E. (1996). *Selected theories of music perception*. Lewiston, NY: Mellen Press.

Gatti, A. (1926). The perception of the relations of space in visual complexes. *Pubblicazioni dell'Universita Cattolica del Sacro Cuore*, *11*, 81-191.

Geldard, F. A. (1975). *Sensory saltation*. Hillsdale, NJ: Erlbaum.

Graham, C. (Ed.) (1965). *Vision and visual perception*. New York: Wiley.

Haase, S. J., Theios, J., & Jenison, R. (1999). A signal detection theory analysis of an unconscious perception effect. *Perception & Psychophysics*, *61*, 986-992.

Hatfield, G. C. (1990). *Theories of spatial perception from Kant to Helmholtz*. Cambridge, MA: M.I.T. Press.

Higashiyama, A. (1996). Horizontal and vertical distance perception: The discorded-orientation theory. *Perception & Psychophysics*, *58*, 259-270.

Johansson, G. (1973). Visual perception of biological motion and a model for its analysis. *Perception and Psychophysics*, *14*, 201-211.

Jordan, J. S. (1998). *Systems theories and a priori aspects of perception*. New York: Elsevier.

Jussim, L. (1991). Social perception and social reality: A reflection-construction model. *Psychological Review*, *98*, 54-73.

Kenny, D. A. (1991). A general model of consensus and accuracy in interpersonal perception. *Psychological Review*, *98*, 155-163.

Kersten, D., Mamassian, P., & Yuille, A. (2004). Object perception as Bayesian inference. *Annual Review of Psychology*, *55*, 271-304.

Kirschmann, A. (1891). [Law of contrast]. *Philosophische Studien*, *6*, 417-492.

Krumhansl, C. L., & Jusczyk, P. W. (1990). Infants' perception of phrase structure in music. *Psychological Science*, *1*, 70-73.

Landolt, E. (1889). [Landolt circles]. *Societe Francaise d'Ophthalmologie; Bulletin et Memoires*, *1*, 385.

Liebmann, S. E. (1927). Uber das verhalten farbiger formen bei helligkeitsgleichheit von figur und grund. *Psychologische Forschung*, *9*, 300-353.

Mojtabai, R. (1994). Fregoli syndrome. *Australian & New Zealand Journal of Psychiatry*, *28*, 458-462.

Necker, L.-A. (1832). [Necker cube]. *Philosophisches Magazin*, *1*, 329-337.

Orbison, W. D. (1939). [Orbison's illusion]. *American Journal of Psychology*, *52*, 31-45.

Pearce, H. J. (1904). The law of attraction in relation to some visual and tactual illusions. *Psychological Review*, *11*, 143-178.

Roelofs, C. (1935). Optische localization. *Archiv fur Augenheilkunde*, *109*, 395-415.

Spillman, L. A. D., & Levine, J. (1971). [Spillman's illusion]. *Experimental Brain Research*, *13*, 547-559.

Spillman, L. A. D., & Redies, C. (1981). [Spillman-Redies effect]. *Perception*, *10*, 411-415; 417-420.

Treisman, M. (1999). There are two types of psychometric function: A theory of cue combination in the processing of complex stimuli with implications for categorical perception. *Journal of Experimental Psychology: General*, *128*, 517-546.

Wade, N. J. (1987). On the late invention of the stereoscope. *Perception*, *16*, 785-818.

West, M., Spillman, L., Cavanagh, P., Mollen, J., & Hamlin, S. (1996). Susanne Liebmann in the critical zone. *Perception*, *25*, 1451-1495.

Zollner, F. (1860). [Zollner illusion]. *Annalen der Physik und Chemie*, *186*, 500-520.

Social Psychology

Aronson, E., & Gerard, E. (1966). Beyond Parkinson's law: The effect of excess time on subsequent performance. *Journal of Personality and Social Psychology*, *3*, 336-339.

Aronson, E., & Landy, D. (1967). Further steps beyond Parkinson's law: A replication and extension of the excess time effect. *Journal of Experimental Social Psychology, 3,* 274-285.

Chadwick-Jones, J. K. (1976). *Social exchange theory: Its structure and influence in social psychology.* New York: Academic Press.

Feldman, R. S. (1985). *Social psychology: Theories, research, and applications.* New York: McGraw-Hill.

Fiske, A. P. (1992). The four elementary forms of sociality: Framework for a unified theory of social relations. *Psychological Review, 99,* 689-723.

Forsterling, F. (2001). *Attribution: An introduction to theories, research, and applications.* Hove, East Sussex, UK: Psychology Press.

Fox, S., & Thornton, G. C. III. (1993). Implicit distribution theory: The influence of cognitive representation of differentiation on actual ratings. *Perceptual and Motor Skills, 76,* 259-276.

Hong, Y., Chiu, C., Dweck, C. S., & Sacks, R. (1997). Implicit theories and evaluative processes in person cognition. *Journal of Experimental Social Psychology, 33,* 296-323.

Kenny, D. A., & DePaulo, B. M. (1993). Do people know how others view them? An empirical and theoretical account. *Psychological Bulletin, 114,* 145-161.

Krueger, J., & Clement, R. W. (1994). Memory-based judgments about multiple categories: A revision and extension of Tajfel's accentuation theory. *Journal of Personality and Social Psychology, 67,* 35-47.

Levy, S. R., Plaks, J. E., & Dweck, C. S. (1999). Modes of social thought: Implicit theories and social understanding. In S. Chaiken, & Y. Trope (Eds.), *Dual-process theories in social psychology.* New York: Guilford Press.

Lewin, K. (1943). Defining the "field at a given time." *Psychological Review, 50,* 292-310.

Mullen, B., & Goethals, G. R. (1987). *Theories of group behavior.* New York: Springer-Verlag.

Murstein, B. I. (1997). On exchange theory, androcentrism, and sex stereotypy. *Psychological Reports, 81,* 1151-1162,

Olweus, D., & Block, J. (1986). *Development of antisocial and prosocial behavior: Research, theories, and issues.* Orlando, FL: Academic Press.

Schlenker, B. R., Britt, T. W., Pennington, J., Murphy, R., & Doherty, K. (1994). The triangle model of responsibility. *Psychological Review, 101,* 632-652.

Shaw, M. E., & Costanzo, P. R. (1970/1982). *Theories of social psychology.* New York: McGraw-Hill.

Weiner, B. (1998). Discovering general laws of social motivation. In J. G. Adair, D. Belanger, & K. I. Dion (Eds.), *Advances in psychological science.* Vol. 1. Hove, East Sussex, UK: Psychology Press.

West, S. G., & Wicklund, R. A. (1980). *A primer of social psychological theories.* Monterey, CA: Brooks/Cole.

Systems and Organizational Theories

Geyer, R. F. (1980). *Alienation theories: A general systems approach.* New York: Pergamon Press.

Robbins, S. P. (1990). *Organization theory: Structure, design, and applications.* Engle-wood Cliffs, NJ: Prentice-Hall.

Time and Timing

Church, R. M. (1997). Timing and temporal search. In C. M. Bradshaw & E. Szabadi (Eds.), *Time and behaviour: Psychological and neurobehavioural analyses.* Amsterdam, Netherlands: North-Holland.

Farnsworth, P. R. (1926). A modification of the Lipps-Meyer law. *Journal of Experimental Psychology, 9,* 253-258.

Fraisse, P. (1963). *Psychology of time*. New York: Harper & Row.

Fraisse, P. (1984). Perception and estimation of time. *Annual Review of Psychology*, *35*, 1-36.

Fraser, J. T. (Ed.) (1989). *Time and mind: Interdisciplinary issues. The study of time VI*. Madison, CT: International Universities Press.

Goudsmit, S., & Claiborne, R. (1980). *Time*. Alexandria, VA: Time-Life Books.

Lennings, C. J. (1999). Motivation and future temporal orientation: A test of the self-handicapping hypothesis. *Psychological Reports*, *84*, 1070-1072.

Macey, S. (Ed.) (1994). *Encyclopedia of time*. New York: Garland.

Nichols, H. (1891). The psychology of time. *American Journal of Psychology*, *3*, 453-529.

Roeckelein, J. E. (2000). *The concept of time in psychology*. Westport, CT: Greenwood Press.

Ulrich, R., & Wing, A. M. (1991). A recruitment theory of force-time relations in the production of brief force pulses: The parallel force unit model. *Psychological Review*, *98*, 268-294.

Whitrow, G. J. (1972). *The nature of time*. New York: Holt, Rinehart, and Winston.